TRADE UNIONS OF THE WORLD

Other current affairs reference titles from John Harper Publishing include:

Border and Territorial Disputes of the World
The Council of the European Union
Directory of European Union Political Parties
The European Commission
The European Constitution
The European Courts
The European Parliament
Political Parties of the World
Revolutionary and Dissident Movements of the World
Treaties and Alliances of the World

www.johnharperpublishing.co.uk

TRADE UNIONS OF THE WORLD
6th edition

JOHN HARPER PUBLISHING

Trade Unions of the World, 6th edition

Published by John Harper Publishing
www.johnharperpublishing.co.uk
Editorial enquiries: John Harper Publishing, 27 Palace Gates Road, London N22 7BW, UK. Email: jhpublish@aol.com
Sales enquiries: Extenza-Turpin, Stratton Business Park, Pegasus Drive, Biggleswade, SG18 8QB, UK. Email: books@extenza-turpin.com
United States and Canada: Gale Group Inc., 27500 Drake Rd., Farmington Hills, Michigan 48331, USA

1st edition (1987), Longman Group UK Ltd
2nd edition (1989), Longman Group UK Ltd
3rd edition (1991), Longman Group UK Ltd
4th edition (1996), Cartermill International Ltd
5th edition (2001), John Harper Publishing
This edition first published 2005

© John Harper Publishing 2005
ISBN 0-9543811-5-7

All rights reserved. No part of this publication may be reproduced, stored in a retrieval system, or transmitted in any form by any means, electronic, mechanical, photocopying, recording or otherwise, without either the prior written permission of the Publishers or a licence permitting restricted copying issued by the Copyright Licensing Agency Ltd., 90 Tottenham Court Rd., London W1P 9HE, UK

Printed in Great Britain by the Cromwell Press

TABLE OF CONTENTS

About the Contributors	vii
About ICTUR	viii
Preface	viii
Afghanistan	1
Albania	1
Algeria	3
Andorra	6
Angola	6
Antigua and Barbuda	7
Argentina	8
Armenia	10
Australia	11
Austria	17
Azerbaijan	21
Bahamas	22
Bahrain	23
Bangladesh	23
Barbados	26
Belarus	27
Belgium	29
Belize	34
Benin	35
Bhutan	36
Bolivia	36
Bosnia and Herzegovina	38
Botswana	40
Brazil	43
Brunei Darussalam	46
Bulgaria	46
Burkina Faso	50
Burma, see Myanmar	
Burundi	51
Cambodia	52
Cameroon	54
Canada	55
Cape Verde	61
Central African Republic	62
Chad	63
Chile	64
China	66
Hong Kong	70
Macau	72
Colombia	72
Comoros	75
Congo, Democratic Republic of	75
Congo, Republic of	77
Costa Rica	78
Côte d'Ivoire	80
Croatia	81
Cuba	84
Cyprus	85
Czech Republic	86
Denmark	89
Djibouti	93
Dominica	94
Dominican Republic	95
East Timor	97
Ecuador	98
Egypt	99
El Salvador	102
Equatorial Guinea	103
Eritrea	104
Estonia	105
Ethiopia	106
Fiji	107
Finland	109
France	112
Gabon	123
Gambia	124
Georgia	125
Germany	126
Ghana	135
Greece	136
Grenada	140
Guatemala	140
Guinea	142
Guinea Bissau	143
Guyana	144
Haiti	146
Honduras	147
Hungary	148
Iceland	151
India	152
Indonesia	156
Iran	159
Iraq	160
Ireland	162
Israel	165
Italy	167
Ivory Coast, see Côte d'Ivoire	
Jamaica	175
Japan	176
Jordan	183
Kazakhstan	185
Kenya	187
Kiribati	188
Korea, North	189
Korea, South	189
Kuwait	193
Kyrgyzstan	194
Laos	195
Latvia	195
Lebanon	196
Lesotho	198
Liberia	200
Libya	201
Liechtenstein	201
Lithuania	202
Luxembourg	203
Macedonia	205
Madagascar	206
Malawi	207
Malaysia	208
Maldives	211
Mali	212
Malta	213
Marshall Islands	214
Mauritania	214
Mauritius	216
Mexico	218
Micronesia, Federated States of	220

Moldova	220
Monaco	222
Mongolia	222
Morocco	223
Western Sahara	227
Mozambique	227
Myanmar	228
Namibia	230
Nauru	231
Nepal	231
Netherlands	234
Aruba	239
Netherlands Antilles	239
New Zealand	239
Nicaragua	245
Niger	247
Nigeria	248
Norway	250
Oman	256
Pakistan	256
Palau	259
Palestinian Entity	260
Panama	261
Papua New Guinea	262
Paraguay	263
Peru	264
Philippines	265
Poland	268
Portugal	276
Qatar	279
Romania	280
Russian Federation	283
Rwanda	288
St Christopher and Nevis	289
St Lucia	290
St Vincent and the Grenadines	291
Samoa	292
San Marino	292
Sao Tomé and Príncipe	293
Saudi Arabia	294
Senegal	294
Serbia and Montenegro	295
Serbia	296
Montenegro	298
Kosovo	298
Seychelles	299
Sierra Leone	299
Singapore	301

Slovakia	303
Slovenia	305
Solomon Islands	307
Somalia	308
South Africa	308
Spain	315
Sri Lanka	319
Sudan	322
Suriname	323
Swaziland	324
Sweden	325
Switzerland	334
Syria	338
Taiwan	339
Tajikistan	340
Tanzania	341
Thailand	342
Togo	344
Tonga	345
Trinidad and Tobago	345
Tunisia	347
Turkey	349
Turkmenistan	355
Tuvalu	355
Uganda	355
Ukraine	356
United Arab Emirates	358
United Kingdom	359
Bermuda	371
United States of America	372
Puerto Rico	388
Uruguay	388
Uzbekistan	390
Vanuatu	390
Vatican City (Holy See)	391
Venezuela	391
Vietnam	393
Yemen	395
Zambia	396
Zimbabwe	398
Appendix: International and Regional Organizations	400
Index	417

CONTRIBUTORS

Many of the entries for this edition were compiled by ICTUR and its network of specialists in trade union affairs (see following page). Other contributors were as follows:

Duncan Brown (Bulgaria) is a PhD candidate at Keele University, UK, completing a thesis on the development of the Union of Democratic Forces in Bulgaria.

Peter Calvert (Bolivia, Paraguay, Uruguay) is Emeritus Professor of Comparative and International Politics, University of Southampton.

Roman Chytilek (Slovakia, with Lubomir Kopecek) is a Lecturer at the School of Social Studies, Masaryk University, Brno. His areas of research include political parties, interest groups and Canadian studies.

Brandon County (Mali and Niger) is a graduate student studying 20th century African history at Columbia University. His research focuses on labour, nationalism and rhetorics of modernity in Mali and francophone West Africa.

F. J. Harper (various), the compiler of the first edition of *Trade Unions of the World* published in 1987, is a writer and publisher on world affairs and politics.

Olexander Hryb (Ukraine) is a BBC World Service radio producer. Born in Lviv (Ukraine), he completed his doctoral studies at the Graduate School for Social Research (Polish Academy of Science) and the University of Sussex. He has published on Eastern European nationalism, Cossack revival, and media in Ukraine.

Lawrence Joffe (various Middle East & Arab world) is a writer on Middle Eastern affairs, contributing to a range of newspapers and magazines. His publications include *Keesing's Guide to the Middle East Peace Process* (1997).

Lawrence Kefitilwe (Botswana, with Marc Meinardus) is Programme Coordinator Friedrich Ebert Foundation in Gaborone, Botswana.

Lubomir Kopecek (Slovakia, with Roman Chytilek) is Assistant Professor of Political Science in the Faculty of Social Studies, Masaryk University, Brno, Czech Republic. His main fields of research and publication are comparative politics and parties and party systems in post-communist countries and he is managing editor of the electronic journal *Central European Political Studies Review* (www.iips.cz/seps).

José M. Magone (Portugal) is Senior Lecturer in European Politics in the Department of Politics and International Studies at the University of Hull (UK). His publications include *Iberian Trade Unionism* (2001).

David Scott Mathieson (Myanmar) is a doctoral student at the Australian National University. He has written on Burmese political economy and the civil war and his current research is on the economics of conflict in modern Burma.

Marc Meinardus (Botswana, with Lawrence Kefitilwe) is the Resident Representative of the Friedrich Ebert Foundation in Gaborone, Botswana.

Nadia Milanova (Armenia, Azerbaijan, Georgia) is Programme Director for the non-governmental organization Human Rights Without Frontiers International and a former head of the Prague office of the OSCE Secretariat.

Frank Mols (Suriname) is currently working towards his PhD at the Centre for European Studies, University of Exeter (UK). His research interests include nationalism, stateless nations, separatism and international cooperation and integration.

Alvaro Nobrega (Guinea-Bissau) is Lecturer at the Instituto Superior de Ciências Sociais e Politicas of the Universidade Técnica de Lisboa, Portugal and the author of *The Struggle for power in Guinea Bissau*.

Charlie Pericleous (Cyprus) is a doctoral candidate in International Relations at the University of Southampton.

D. J. Sagar (various African) is a writer on international affairs and a former Deputy Editor of *Keesing's Record of World Events*.

Seraphim Seferiades (Greece) is a Senior Lecturer in the Faculty of Politics and History at the Panteion University of Social and Political Science, Athens. Formerly a Fellow in Politics and European History at the University of Cambridge, he has also held posts at Princeton University and the European University Institute, Florence.

Nthakeng Pheello Selinynane (Lesotho) is a Doctoral Fellow with the Centre for Civil Society, University of KwaZulu-Natal, Durban, South Africa. He was founding president of the Lesotho Union of Public Employees, banned in 1995; founding general secretary of the Congress of Lesotho Trade Unions; and two-time general secretary of the Lesotho University Teachers' and Researchers' Union.

ABOUT ICTUR

The **International Centre for Trade Union Rights (ICTUR)** is an organizing and campaigning body with the fundamental purpose of defending and improving the rights of trade unions and trade unionists throughout the world. In 1993 ICTUR was recognized as an important international organization and granted accredited status with both the United Nations and the International Labour Organization.

Active Globally

ICTUR was established in 1987. It aims:
- To defend and extend the rights of trade unions and trade unionists throughout the world.
- To collect information and increase awareness of trade union rights and their violations.
- To carry out its activities in the spirit of the United Nations Charter, the Universal Declaration of Human Rights, the International Labour Organization Conventions and appropriate international treaties.

International Union Rights

Since its launch in 1992, the quarterly journal of the International Centre for Trade Union Rights has won a worldwide reputation for coverage of the key issues affecting trade union rights and labour law around the world.

Featuring expert "on the spot" contributors and tackling issues at a national, regional and international level, *International Union Rights* (IUR) examines contemporary labour issues from an international perspective.

IUR's subscribers include activists, organizers, union leaders, researchers, labour lawyers, academics and human rights organizations.

To join ICTUR or subscribe to International Union Rights, please visit www.ictur.org

Contact:
Daniel Blackburn, ICTUR,
177 Abbeville Road, London, SW4 9RL, UK
Tel: +44 (0)20 7498 4700, fax: +44 (0)20 7498 0611
Web: www.ictur.org, email: ictur@ictur.org

PREFACE

This new edition of *Trade Unions of the World* is the sixth in a sequence stretching back to 1987. The objectives and design of the book have remained fundamentally unchanged since that time. The text is organized by country in A-Z order. Entries for each country begin with a section giving a brief account of the political and economic context. There then follows an overview of the history, development and status of trade unions and the state of labour law and practice. A third section provides data on trade union centres and (where relevant) a fourth section covers significant trade unions not under the umbrella of any of the trade union centres. A final part of the book provides data on international and regional trade union bodies. For the first time, the book is published in association with the International Centre for Trade Union Rights (ICTUR), details of which are given above.

The sources used in the compilation of the current edition are too numerous to be mentioned in detail, but several works of general relevance to more than one country should be mentioned. To ensure consistency, data on GDP and populations have been taken from the *CIA World Factbook*. The ICFTU's *Annual Survey of Trade Union Rights*, which covers close to two-thirds of countries, again proved a most useful source, as did the the *Country Reports on Human Rights Practices* published by the Bureau of Democracy, Human Rights and Labor of the US State Department. The *European Industrial Relations Oberservatory* (EIRO) online database of the European Foundation for the Improvement of Living and Working Conditions is a rich resource for the countries it covers (primarily the EU member states). And, as ever, thanks are due to the many trade union officers and others who took the trouble to respond to our enquiries.

Afghanistan

Capital: Kabul
Population: 28.5 m. (2004 est.)

1 Political and Economic Background

The (communist) People's Democratic Party of Afghanistan (PDPA) took power in 1978 as the sole political party. The Soviet Union intervened militarily in December 1979 to sustain the faltering regime and remained for ten years in the face of escalating resistance from the mujaheddin ("holy warriors"). President Najibullah outlasted the Soviet withdrawal until 1992, when he was deposed, the mujaheddin entered Kabul and the Islamic State of Afghanistan was proclaimed. The various mujaheddin factions agreed to revolve the presidency among them, but the first holder of the office, President Burhannuddin Rabbani, clung onto power and was ultimately overthrown by the Taliban militia in 1996. The Taliban thereafter controlled most of the country, though with persistent conflict with the Northern Alliance and with the Rabbani government retaining international recognition, until their overthrow by US forces in late 2001 and the creation of a transitional administration headed by Hamid Karzai. The situation has since stabilized although the writ of the internationally-backed central government does not extend to all parts of the country. There have been no general elections since 1988 and parliamentary elections planned for 2004 were postponed; however, presidential elections were held in October 2004, resulting in the election of Karzai.

Agriculture, based mainly on livestock rearing and herding and on the growing of cotton and fruits, is the dominant activity of the Afghan economy. There is some small-scale industry. Unrelenting civil war for two decades and the fundamentalist rule of the Taliban contributed to a substantial decline in GDP and Afghanistan remains one of the world's poorest countries.

GDP (purchasing power parity) $20bn. (2003 est.); GDP per capita (purchasing power parity) $700 (2003 est.).

2 Trade Unionism

Afghanistan has ratified neither ILO Convention No. 87 (Freedom of Association and Protection of the Right to Organize, 1948) nor Convention No. 98 (Right to Organize and Collective Bargaining, 1949).

Afghanistan's first unions were reportedly formed in 1967. Following the 1978 revolution, when the (communist) People's Democratic Party of Afghanistan took power, the new regime established the Central Council of Afghan Trade Unions (CCATU) which began to organize a trade union structure. In December 1979 the Soviet Union intervened in Afghanistan and the CCATU was purged and restructured. There were no trade unions outside the CCATU.

The CCATU defined its main policies as: (i) providing leadership for the nation's trade union movement; (ii) improving the working and living conditions of wage earners; (iii) strengthening the state sector and the national economy; and (iv) "defending the gains made by the Sowr (i.e. 1978) Revolution". After the Soviet withdrawal, at a 1990 congress (the first for nine years) it transformed itself into the National Workers' Union of Afghanistan (NUWA) though under a mostly unchanged leadership. Following the capture of Kabul by the mujaheddin in 1992, and the declaration of an Islamic Republic, this structure ceased to exist.

Following the intervention by US-led forces and the ousting of the Taliban regime there has been no indication of trade union activity, and there are no labour courts or collective bargaining mechanisms. There are no reports of strikes or other forms of organized industrial activity.

Albania

Capital: Tirana
Population: 3.54 m. (2004 est.)

1 Political and Economic Background

From the end of World War II until 1990, Albania was a one-party state under the (communist) Albanian Party of Labour (APL) of Enver Hoxha. Albania was a closed society, sealed off from both Eastern and Western Europe, with a rigid Stalinist ideology combined with tribal social structures. However, the reform movement consuming the communist world also found expression in Albania. In March 1991 multi-party elections were won by the reformed APL (subsequently known as the Socialist Party of Albania, PSS), though the results were disputed by the new opposition Democratic Party (DP) which campaigned with union support for new elections; industrial agitation culminated in a general strike. In June the government resigned and was replaced by a succession of temporary administrations.

New elections in March 1992 brought victory to the DP and its leader Sali Berisha became President. The DP again won elections in 1996. In early 1997, however, the collapse of financial pyramid selling schemes precipitated social chaos, resulting in 1,500 deaths and the virtual disintegration of the country, with an armed rebellion in the South, wholesale destruction of businesses and public buildings, pursuit of blood feuds, and looting by criminal gangs. Berisha resigned and a new PSS-led coalition government took office following elections in June–July 1997. The government struggled thereafter to restore central control to parts of the country. The Democratic Party sustained a boycott of Parliament for long periods after losing power in 1997, and accused the government of assassinating some of its members. The PSS retained power at elections in June–July 2001, though the DP remained the dominant party in the north of the country and the DP again boycotted the political process for periods thereafter. The DP and PSS agree on the desirability of achieving membership of the European Union, but this remains a distant goal.

The PSS-led government that took power in June 1991 took the first steps away from the command economy of the communist era, under which Albania had been Europe's most backward economy. It legalized foreign investment, liberalized prices and introduced private home ownership. A Privatization Act of August 1991 envisaged the sale of some 25,000 state enterprises. Subsidies were virtually eliminated. The abolition of collective farms (begun with a law of May 1991) paved the way for redistribution of the land in small plots to the (majority) rural population.

The collapse of the state planned system brought a steep decline in GDP, estimated at some 35% in the period 1989–92. From 1993 this was followed by a recovery, but further crisis resulted from the pyramid selling debacle of 1997. Albania remains a poor, technologically backward country, with high unemployment (officially 15% in 2003 but with high under-employment), considerable legal and illegal economic migration, and dependence on foreign aid and remittances from workers abroad. Modern development is frustrated by rampant corruption and widespread crime encouraged by lack of enforcement of laws. The mainstays of the Albanian economy are agriculture and mining, with agriculture providing a living (much of it at little more than subsistence level) for over half the population; tobacco and cotton are grown as well as food crops. Industry includes the processing of agricultural and mineral raw materials, chemicals and fertilizers. The non-agricultural public sector employs a larger proportion of the workforce than does the private sector.

GDP (purchasing power parity) $16.13bn. (2003 est.); GDP per capita (purchasing power parity) $4,500 (2003 est.).

2 Trade Unionism

Albania ratified both ILO Convention No. 87 (Freedom of Association and Protection of the Right to Organize, 1948) and No. 98 (Right to Organize and Collective Bargaining, 1949) in 1957. It withdrew from the ILO in 1967 but returned in 1991.

The Albanian trade union movement was organized after 1945 on the communist model, with unions coordinated by the Central Council of Albanian Trade Unions (TUA). Independent unions in Albania made their presence felt from the beginning of 1991. They started in the mines, where strikes had already taken place, recruiting 7,000 miners in 200 enterprises. The formation of the United Independent Albanian Trade Unions (BSPSh) was announced soon after. On April 4 it raised a call for a general strike to protest against post-election violence. On May 15 a general strike was launched, led by the miners – now organized in the Independent United Mineworkers' Union (SBPM) – to press demands, (matching those of the DP), for fresh elections. The independent unions were prominent in the demonstrations in Tirana, Shkoder and other cities that forced replacement of the APL government by an "administration of national salvation".

A new labour code was adopted in 1993. Under this and other legislation all workers, except police and security forces and some officers in the judicial system, may join unions, bargain collectively and strike. However, high unemployment and the parlous state of enterprises make meaningful bargaining and enforcement of contracts impossible in much of the economy and in the public sector pay is set administratively. Political strikes are not lawful. Major private sector areas of employment in Albania are agriculture, small shops and craft enterprises and restaurants, but unions are not significant in those areas.

The Albanian labour movement reflected the unstable national political, social and economic environment of the 1990s. The WCL noted that the situation was "confused", although it wished to "encourage the setting up of democratic structures in a country where this seems particularly difficult". Two centres exist, the BSPSh and KSSh (Confederation of Trade Unions, also sometimes called the KS). They have reportedly agreed in some areas not to work against each other. According to the US State Department Human Rights Report for 2003, the BSPSh has 85,000 members, and the Confederation of Trade Unions has 100,000, representing a sharp fall from levels in the mid-1990s. Some unions are not affiliated to either. While the centres are not politically affiliated, they have been embroiled in the complex and conspiratorial world of Albanian politics.

A key issue for unions since 1997 has been the recovery of public order and stability and the lack of social protection in the face of extreme levels of unemployment, exacerbated by wholesale destruction of enterprises in the 1997 disorder. However, the unions have complained of a lack of access to government and tripartism does not function.

3 Trade Union Centres

United Independent Albanian Trade Unions (BSPSh)
Address. Bulevardi 'Zogu i Pare', Pallati 'Ali Kelmendi, Tirana.
Phone. +355 4 232157
Fax. +355 4 232157
E-mail. bspsh@albmail.com
Membership. 85,000 (estimated)
History and character. The BSPSh (variously referred to in English as the United Independent Albanian Trade Unions, the Union of Independent Trade Unions and the Independent Confederation of Trade Unions of Albania) emerged in 1991 in opposition to the official trade unions established in the communist period. Under the leadership of Valer Xheka it became the leading voice of independent trade unionism, with the mineworkers its most important affiliate. It held its first national conference in February 1992.

The BSPSh became riven by factionalism. An emergency congress in Durres in November 1996 elected Democratic Party legislator Azem Hajdari as president and Fatmir Musaku, a former BSPSh deputy leader, as general secretary. Hajdari, the head of the parliamentary control commission for the secret service, claimed that BSPSh leader Valer Xheka was corrupt and had spied for the secret service in the communist era. The BSPSh steering council said that the Durres congress had no legitimacy and opponents said it represented a political takeover, while President Berisha gave his support to Valer Xheka, even though Hajdari was a former close ally in the creation of the Democratic Party. In September 1997 Hajdari was shot four times by a Socialist Party MP inside the parliament building, but survived.

On Oct. 26, 1997, Astrit Balluku, the chairman of the Teachers' Federation in Tirana and a member of the BSPSh executive committee, was shot dead at BSPSh hedquarters. On Nov. 18, 1997, the Court of Appeal recognized Fatmir Musaku as BSPSh general secretary. On Dec. 8, 1997, police occupied BSPSh headquarters to expel the leadership under Xhevdet Lubani. In June 1998, however, the Supreme Court confirmed Lubani as the legitimate leader.

Hajdari was shot dead on Sept. 12, 1998, triggering anti-government riots in Tirana. Sali Berisha accused the Socialist Party of being behind the assassination.

Confederation of Trade Unions (KSSh)
Address. Bulevardi 'Zogu i I', Pallati 'Ali Kelmendi, K3, Tirana.
Phone. +355 42 29169
Fax. +355 42 22956
Leadership. Kastriot Muco (president)
Membership. 100,000 (estimated)
History and character. The KSSh (sometimes referred to as KS) has recruited members in the school, food, petroleum, postal and telecommunications, and railroad sectors.

Algeria

Capital: Algiers
Population: 32.82 m. (2003 est.)

1 Political and Economic Background

Algeria achieved independence from France in 1962 following a lengthy armed struggle spearheaded by the Front de Libération Nationale (FLN). Until 1989, the FLN was the sole permitted political party, but riots and severe unrest precipitated constitutional changes that foresaw a market economy and a more liberal and pluralist society.

In the first round of National Assembly elections in December 1991, the fundamentalist Islamic Salvation Front (FIS) took 47.5% of the vote, compared with 23.5% for the FLN. In consequence, in January 1992 the FLN government canceled the second round of voting and declared a state of emergency. Thereafter fighting between government forces and FIS rebels led to the loss of an estimated 100,000 lives in a conflict notable for the barbarism of the atrocities committed by the rebels and the thousands of "disappearances" blamed on security forces. As a result of elections to the National Assembly in 1997, the National Democratic Rally (RND) became the largest party; both it and the FLN supported the candidacy of Abdelaziz Bouteflika in 1999 presidential elections, which Bouteflika won after all his opponents withdrew, claiming electoral fraud. In September 1999 a national referendum resulted in a massive majority for a peace plan that included an amnesty for rebels who laid down their arms; the FIS's armed wing was subsequently dissolved but not all its members immediately abandoned conflict.

National Assembly elections held on May 30, 2002, saw a substantial victory of the FLN over the RND, which took second place. Ali Benflis of the FLN had been appointed prime minister in August 2000; after the elections he led a new cabinet, reflecting the FLN's greater power. However, considerable conflict arose between the presidency and Benflis. In May 2003 Bouteflika replaced him as prime minister with Ahmed Ouyahia, leader of the RND. Bouteflika won the presidential election of April 8, 2004.

Despite criticism from trade unionists and leftist groups, the Ouyahia government cautiously pressed ahead with privatization, extending its campaign into the important cement industry in 2004. Finance Minister Abdelatif Benachenhou described cement privatization as "a bridgehead to liberalization of the Algerian economy". He added that unions had been pleasantly surprised that the earlier privatization of the steel sector had increased production and salaries; and he promised that the state would "remedy [any] negative social consequences" that privatization might engender in the future.

Despite some moves to a market-oriented system, the state continues to control key sectors of the economy, including the oil and gas sector, which generates one-quarter of national income and 96% of exports. Most of the industrial sector is state-controlled and considered inefficient. Unemployment is reported as high as 30% and a housing shortage is reaching chronic proportions. Such problems may yet increase as the Algerian population is predicted to grow to 42 million by 2025, with some 30 million living in cities. Moreover, the Algerian economy is still labouring under the burden of a public debt estimated at 41.5% of GDP in 2004. Conversely, optimists hope that, given liberalized immigration rules and no major increase in "imported terrorism" from the North African region, the EU may welcome younger Maghrebi workers to fill gaps in their own labour force.

GDP (purchasing power parity) $196bn. (2004 est.); GDP per capita (purchasing power parity) $6,000 (2004 est.).

2 Trade Unionism

Prior to independence the French trade union centres maintained regional organizations in Algeria and there were also independent federations. Following independence, however, the Union Générale des Travailleurs Algériens (UGTA), which was linked with the FLN, became the sole centre. It remained the sole legal (non-peasant) labour organization until the constitutional changes of 1989. Three laws of 1990 laid down a new framework for industrial relations and the rights of trade unions.

Despite the loss of its status as the sole legal centre, the UGTA has in practice remained the only trade union centre, with only a few unions not affiliated. Under 1990 legislation the Labour Ministry must approve the registration of any union. An Independent Trade Union Confederation (CSA) has been in development since 1996, but has yet to receive approval by the Labour Ministry. In addition the FIS's labour front, the Islamic Union of Workers (SIT), was banned in 1992 along with the FIS. The UGTA itself has established a role as a politically autonomous trade union organization focused on the economic interests of its members. Pre-emergency legislation bans unions from associating with political parties or receiving funds from abroad.

Under the 1990 Law on Industrial Relations, strikes are legal provided mandatory conciliation, mediation, and arbitration procedures are followed. Where arbitration fails, workers may strike legally subject to a secret ballot and the maintenance of basic public services in the case of public sector strikes. However, under the state of emergency, in force from 1992, the government took powers to force workers to stay at their jobs in the event of an unauthorized or illegal strike. There have been frequent strikes in recent years over issues such as job losses, inadequate redundancy payments, pay arrears and failure by the government to consult the unions.

The trade union movement has been caught in the crossfire of the conflict between the government and FIS fundamentalist rebels, and many members have been slain. One prominent trade unionist who was attacked by assailants in 1994, but survived, was Al Hashemi Cherif; in 1999 he created the MDS (Democratic Socialist Movement) out of the former *Ettahadi* party and Communists. The UGTA general secretary was killed in 1997, apparently by a member of FIS, although in Algeria the attribution of killings is often uncertain. To FIS extremists the secular, civil character of trade unions makes them anathema. However, it is never clear whether union members have died because of their union activities, or because they were engaged in activities intolerable to the fundamentalists (e.g. women teachers), or simply because they were random victims of indiscriminate violence.

The ICTFU has identified a number of cases of violations of Algerian trade union rights, in a survey released in 2004. The foremost example concerned the National Autonomous Union of Public Administration Staff (SNAPAP), whose applications to form a national confederation have been twice rejected by the government. Allegedly there have been threats and dismissals of potential SNAPAP organisers in various sectors, including harassment of the SNAPAP general secretary in Oran. The government has moreover blocked all attempts to establish branch unions, notably in hospitals.

In October 2003 two new but unregistered teachers' unions, CNAPEST and CLA, went on strike for the right to retire and 100% salary increases. (The ICTFU reported that a teacher with ten years' experience receives a salary which is about the same as the guaranteed national minimum wage.) The teachers' action was declared illegal, and some 300 teachers were suspended as a result. The unions rejected the government's 40% pay rise offer, and 16 union leaders were taken to court. The strike eventually ended on Dec. 9, when the authorities agreed to drop all sanctions against striking teachers, and agreed to register CNAPEST. Smaller independent unions invariably cannot get registered, as they usually do not repreent more than 20% of workers in an enterprise.

Increasingly the UGTA has been contesting privatization; while accepting it in principle, they opposed the inefficient and damaging way it was being implemented, and lack of transparency. As a result, their former support for Bouteflika began to atrophy; a massive two-day strike organized by the UGTA in February 2003 reminded the Algerian authorities that the confederation still maintained considerable power. Ultimately, however, Bouteflika was re-elected in April 2004 with general backing from the UGTA. As of mid-2004, the small yet influential Workers' Party, led by Louisa Hanoun, was collecting 500,000 signatures for a petition to be presented to Prime Minister Ouyahia; it proposed that the government abandon privatization and reconsider its desire to join the World Trade Organization. By December 2004 there was grumbling from unions as airline and telephone liberalization loomed.

Algeria ratified both ILO Convention No. 87 (Freedom of Association and Protection of the Right to Organize, 1948) and No. 98 (Right to Organize and Collective Bargaining, 1949) in 1962.

3 Trade Union Centre

Union Générale des Travailleurs Algériens (UGTA)
General Union of Algerian Workers
Address. Maison du Peuple, Place du 1er Mai, Algiers
Phone. +213 2 67 21 67
Fax. +213 2 66 61 63
Leadership. Abdelmadjid Sidi-Saïd (secretary general)
Membership. 1 million
History and character. The UGTA was created in 1956 as part of the FLN. Its co-founder was the veteran nationalist, Ali Yahia Abdenour. In 1960 Abdenour took over the UGTA secretariat in Tunis, then seat of the FLN provisional government. Abdenour became the first UGTA secretary general after independence in 1962, but left the office in 1963 to pursue his political career, founding LADDH, Algeria's first human rights organization, in 1985.

After independence the UGTA replaced all existing union federations. By the same token, the effective takeover by the FLN of the UGTA undermined its aspiration to remain independent. Legislation adopted in 1971 named the UGTA as the sole recognized labour organization and provided that it should set up a trade union section in any work unit with more than nine workers. A 1975 ordinance made the UGTA the sole bargaining agent, and a provision of the 1976 Constitution placed all mass organizations under the protection and control of the party. This provision was rescinded by the country's 1989 Constitutional amendments. During most of the 1970s and 1980s the UGTA tended to agree with the government and opposed mass strikes, especially in strategic industrial sectors.

UGTA member unions were integrated federations

spanning several industries. But increased independent activity by workers led to the breaking down of these federations into smaller workers' assemblies, a trend which strengthened the managerial control of the UGTA. Following the 1989 Constitutional amendments, the period to January 1992 saw increased trade union activity with strikes running at 250 per month in 1989 (four times the previous year's rate). There were splits within the UGTA, and challenges from newer, smaller unofficial unions, as the labour movement responded to increased political excitement in the wake of the promise of multi-party democracy.

At the 8th (June 1990) congress new statutes and regulations were adopted and a new leadership elected, headed by Abdelhak Benhamouda. The UGTA successfully campaigned for better pay for the low paid, called a widely observed general strike in March 1991, and in November 1991 led the union side in Algeria's first tripartite consultations. In 1993, the UGTA was given responsibility in the administration of social security assets.

The UGTA secretary general, Abdelhak Benhamouda, was assassinated on Jan. 28, 1997, outside UGTA headquarters in Algiers. He was regarded as strongly opposed to the Islamic fundamentalists. To the chagrin of many rank and file UGTA members, he had asked the government to suspend the democratic process in late 1991, after the first round of general elections returned a huge tally of seats for the FIS. A member of the FIS made a televised confession to the murder, but he was found dead in prison before a trial. At the time of his death, Benhamouda was planning the creation of the later successful pro-government party, the RND; it was officially launched in March 1997.

The UGTA urged members to vote "yes" in the September 1999 referendum on the President's peace plan (which was overwhelmingly endorsed by the electorate). New tripartite talks between government, employers and the UGTA were held in September 2000. However, in subsequent years the UGTA began to distance itself from the Bouteflika presidency. It objected to privatization, a policy strongly backed by the European Union, World Bank and IMF. In particular the UGTA opposed the drastic strategy announced in April 2002 by Participation and Promotion of Investment Minister (also known as Privatization and Reform Minister) Nourredine Boukrouh, a Bouteflika appointee. This resulted in a wave of UGTA-backed strikes. In the wake of general elections on May 31, 2002, Abdel Hamid Temmar replaced Boukrouh as Privatization Minister (having previously held this post until 2001).

However, labour unrest continued: for instance, the UGTA-affiliated National Federation of Workers (FNTS) ordered auxillary medical staff and health administrators to go on strike for better treatment by managers, on Oct. 22-23, 2002. Public health specialists had already been striking for 20 days.

The UGTA called massive strikes in Algeria's ten commercial ports, on Feb. 16, 2003, citing fears that privatization in ports would lead to job losses (a charge that the government denied). Unrest culminated in a 48-hour general strike starting on Feb. 25, in protest at privatization and price hikes. Some 95% of workers participated, claimed a union representative. Airports, banks, offices and printing presses of newspapers were forced to close; some factories reportedly went out of business.

Certain leftist critics suggested that the UGTA should have added calls for greater democracy to their demands. They also noted that the strike avoided the oil and gas sector, which generates most of Algeria's foreign earnings, so as to "protect Algeria's image abroad"; and that the UGTA refrained from organizing any marches during the two-day strike. Though the UGTA mainly campaigned against privatization, it did raise issues related to Algeria's more than 30% unemployment, poor social security and pensions apparatuses, and the erosion of worker' incomes which have reportedly driven families into poverty.

Temmar was replaced by Abdelatif Benachenhou in the new government of Prime Minister Ahmed Ouyahia in May 2003. Ouyahia quickly opened the traditional tripartite talks between the government, employers and the UGTA, represented by secretary-general Sidi-Saïd. This move appeared to herald a new mood of friendlier relations and the promise of long-awaited public sector wage rises. In June 2004 talks began over raising the minimum national salary from AD15,000 to AD17,000. *Algeria Focus* opined that the government owed Sidi-Saïd a favour over wages, given the latter's role in delivering so many trade unionist votes for the successful re-election of President Bouteflika that April.

The UGTA spoke favourably of Ouyahia, formerly considered a bitter enemy. Increasingly members of the ruling RND party were represented in the confederation's leadership. The UGTA welcomed the promise of labour law reforms, including the right to strike, but feared changes to the status of public employees, which they felt might end the custom of "jobs for life". The phenomenon of renewable six-monthly contracts in the private sector has made union organization more difficult in recent years, argue UGTA officials. Significantly, the largest circulation private newspaper in Algeria, *Le Matin*, vocally supported the UGTA's resistance to liberalizing government economic measures, including a new hydrocarbons law, steered by Energy Minister Chakib Khelil. Bouteflika responded to this and other attacks on his policy by charging the paper with libel and, in July 2004, getting a major printing house to stop its publication.

Under pressure from the ruling FLN, the UGTA had disaffiliated from the ICFTU in 1963. In 1991 it resumed contacts and re-affiliated in 1994. A prominent female member of the UGTA, also a medical doctor and university lecturer, Cherifa Aït Benamar, was in October 2001 re-elected to the ICFTU Women's Committee. In an interview with ICFTU she praised the role of women unionists as "a major social force" in the struggle for democracy in Algeria. She warned, however, of residual male chauvinism within unions; and said that there was a disparity between the existence of legal rights, and the fear of workers to assert them, or the willingness of firms to accept them.

The UGTA is also a member of USTMA, an umbrella body represensing major trade union centres in North African countries. In July 2001, UGTA secretary general Abdelmadjid Sidi-Saïd was re-elected

president of this body.
International affiliation. ICFTU; USTMA

Andorra

Capital: Andorra la Vella
Population: 67,000 (2000 est.)

1 Political and Economic Background

Under its constitution of May 1993, Andorra is a sovereign parliamentary co-principality with the President of France and Bishop of Urgel (Spain) as joint heads of state. Elections to its legislature (the General Council of the Valleys) in March 2001 resulted in the Liberal Party remaining in power. The newly formed Social Democratic Party also emerged as a significant factor, taking 30% of the vote and 6 of the 28 legislative seats. 80% of GDP is derived from tourism and employment is consequently primarily in services.

GDP (purchasing power parity) $1.3bn. (2000 est.); GDP per capita (purchasing power parity) $19,000 (2000 est.).

2 Trade Unionism

The first trade union, the Andorran Workers' Union was formed in 1990, claiming several hundred members but only a police association is currently reported to exist. The 1993 Constitution recognizes the right to form and join trade unions, although there is no legal protection against anti-union discrimination. The right to strike is not specifically recognized or denied. Andorra is not a member of the ILO.

Angola

Capital: Luanda
Population: 10.98 m. (2004 est.)

1 Political and Economic Background

The former Portuguese province of Angola became independent in 1975 and was ruled as a Marxist state for 15 years by the Popular Movement for the Liberation of Angola (MPLA), with large-scale Cuban military support. Parts of the country continued to be controlled by the National Union for the Total Independence of Angola (UNITA), which received South African support across the border from Namibia and engaged the MPLA in a protracted military struggle.

The MPLA decided at its 1990 congress to adopt a new ideology of "democratic socialism". After the last Cubans left in 1991, a series of attempts to make peace between the MPLA and UNITA was undertaken. However, a peace agreement was only reached after the leader of UNITA, Jonas Savimbi, was killed by government forces in February 2002. Shortly afterwards UNITA embarked on a genuine process of disarmament and demobilization. Some 1.5 million lives may have been lost in the past quarter century of conflict. There have been no elections since 1992 for either the president (nominally elected for 5 years) or the National Assembly (nominally elected for four years). In early 2004 the government indicated that national elections were likely to be held in 2006.

During the 1990s the MPLA moved away from the policies that led in the post-independence era to the expropriation of foreign-owned enterprises and a command economy, but its economic stability has been undermined by almost three decades of civil war aggravated by mismanagement and corruption. Other than a small elite, mainly in Luanda, most of the population lives in poverty. Subsistence agriculture is the main livelihood of 85% of the population with coffee and sugar as export commodities. Oil production and the supporting activities are vital to the economy, contributing about 45% to GDP and more than half of exports.

GDP (purchasing power parity $20.42 billion (2003 est.); GDP per capita (purchasing power parity) $1,900 (2003 est.).

2 Trade Unionism

Under Portuguese rule to 1975 there existed "occupational syndicates"; these organizations functioned mainly to provide welfare services, and free collective bargaining and strikes were banned. Members of these syndicates were predominantly Europeans and *assimilados*, and independent African trade unionism was illegal. However, several underground or exiled unions gave their support to the independence struggle, these becoming identified with the rival factions among the independence forces. Following the winning of power by the MPLA, the União Nacional de Trabalhadores Angolanos (UNTA) became and remained the sole trade union centre although there is now an independent centre, affiliated to the ICFTU, the Central Geral de Sindicatos Independentes e Livres de Angola. Trade Union organization is limited by the small scale of the formal economy, in which there is also massive unemployment. Collective bargaining and the right to strike are formally guaranteed by the Constitution, although collective bargaining is restricted in practice. The government is the country's biggest employer and through the Ministry of Public Administration, Employment and Social Security sets wages and benefits on an annual basis. This involves consultation with the unions, but no negotiation. Despite the restrictions, there are frequent work stoppages. During 2003, a number of public service workers, including teachers, nurses and doctors went on strike or threatened strike action.

Angola ratified ILO Convention No. 98 (Right to Organize and Collective Bargaining, 1949) in 1976 and No. 87 (Freedom of Association and Protection of the Right to Organize, 1948) in 2001. Other conventions it has ratified include No.29 (Forced Labour, 1930), No.100 (Equal Remuneration, 1951), No.105 (Abolition of Forced Labour, 1957), No.111 (Discrimination (Employment and Occupation), 1958), No.138 (Minimum Age, 1973) and No. 182 (Worst Forms of Child Labour, 1999).

3 Trade Union Centres

Central Geral de Sindicatos Independentes e Livres de Angola (CGSILA)
General Centre of Independent and Free Unions of Angola
Address. CP 469, Luanda
Phone. +244 39 55 39
Fax. +244 33 83 31
E-mail. Cgsiladis@netangola.com
Leadership. Ana da Conceição Pedro Garcia (general secretary)
Membership. 50,000
History and character. The CGSILA is the most prominent of the country's independent union centres. In 2003, CGSILA claimed to have remodelled its structure and was operating in 15 of the country's 18 provinces. CGSILA claims to be independent and free of links with all political parties.
International affiliation. ICFTU

União Nacional de Trabalhadores Angolanos (UNTA)
National Union of Angolan Workers
Leadership. Manuel Viage (general secretary)
History and character. The UNTA was first organized in the late 1950s in the Belgian Congo to assist Angolan refugees and exiled MPLA members in their efforts to maintain social contacts and find jobs. After independence in 1975 the UNTA headquarters was transferred to Luanda, where the shortage of skilled workers and personnel for management and training programmes became immediately evident. During the early 1980s, Cuban advisers were assigned to bring industrial workers into the MPLA. With their Angolan counterparts in the UNTA, Cuban shop stewards and union officials undertook educational programmes in technical and management training, labour discipline and productivity, and socialist economics.

Whilst the government-dominated UNTA continues to be closely linked with the ruling MPLA, it has organized industrial action. In early 2001 UNTA organized a three-day national strike in protest at the government's offer of a minimum wage. The strike closed down ministries and health services across the country, but did not affect the country's lucrative offshore oil industry, or the state oil company Sonangol, whose employees do not belong to UNTA.
International affiliation. WFTU

4 Other Trade Union Organizations

Sindicato Independente dos Marítimos de Angola (SIMA)
Independent Union of Maritime and Related Workers
History and character. SIMA is a prominent, but small, independent union. Whilst the law requires that the government recognize labour unions, SIMA has encountered difficulty with provincial government authorities in registering branch associations and organizing dock and rig workers.
International affiliation. ITF

Antigua and Barbuda

Capital: St. John's
Population: 68,000 (2004 est.)

1 Political and Economic Background

Antigua and Barbuda, formerly a West Indian Associated State, became independent in 1981 as a full member of the Commonwealth, with the British sovereign as head of state. The Antigua Labour Party (ALP), and previously the Antigua Trades and Labour Union (ATLU) to which it is linked, has been the dominant political force for most of the period since the 1940s. However, elections in March 2004 resulted in victory for the United Progressive Party (UPP), ending 28 consecutive years of ALP government. The UPP campaigned in 2004 on a programme called "Agenda for Change", advocating a range of social and poverty relief programmes as well as judicial and constitutional reform.

Antigua's economy is heavily dependent on (mainly United States) tourism, which accounts for more than half of GDP. Agriculture is based mainly on locally consumed crops; there is a little light industry.

GDP (purchasing power parity) $750m. (2002 est.); GDP per capita (purchasing power parity) $11,000 (2002 est.).

2 Trade Unionism

Provision for the registration of trade unions was first made in 1939, and the Antigua Trades and Labour Union (ATLU) dates from that year. Unions are well established, representing a majority of the workforce, and operate freely and engage in collective bargaining. Approximately 75% of the workforce are in membership of a trade union. As an independent country Antigua and Barbuda ratified both ILO Convention No.87 (Freedom of Association and Protection of the Right to Organize, 1948) and No. 98 (Right to Organize and Collective Bargaining, 1949) in 1983. The two rival centres are politically aligned, the ATLU with the ALP and the AWU with the UPP. Vere Bird, Prime Minister until 1992 was co-founder and president of ATLU. Baldwin Spencer, the leader of the UPP (and since March 2004 Prime Minister) is also first vice-president and assistant general secretary of AWU.

The ATLU is affiliated to the WCL, while the ICFTU affiliates are the AWU and the Antigua and Barbuda Public Service Association (ABPSA).

The Labour Code recognizes the right to strike, but the Industrial Relations Court may limit this right in a given dispute. A wide range of industries are categorised as "essential services". In these industries disputes may become subject to court mediation on referral by one party, banning strikes under penalty of imprisonment. The ILO's Committee of Experts has requested the government to amend the 1976 Industrial Courts Act in order to address this situation.

3 Trade Union Centres

Antigua Trades and Labour Union (ATLU)
Address. Emancipation House, PO Box 3, 46 North Street, St John's
Phone. +1-268 46 200 90
Fax. +1-268 46 240 56
E-mail. atandlu@candw.ag
Leadership. Wigley George (president); Nathalie Payne (general secretary)
Membership. 7,000
History and character. The ATLU was founded in 1939 and functioned for many years as both a trade union and a political party. It founded and remains close to the ALP. The ATLU represents most non-established workers in the civil service and in statutory bodies but also has membership in the private sector.
International affiliatons. WCL; CTUC

Antigua Workers' Union (AWU)
Address. Freedom Hall, PO Box 940, Newgate Street, St John's
Phone. +1-268 462 0442
Fax. +1-268 462 5220
E-mail. awu@candw.ag
Leadership. Keithlyn Smith (general secretary)
History and character. Originated from a split in the ATLU in 1967 and founded the Progressive Labour Movement (now the UPP) in 1970. The AWU is strongest in the highly unionized tourist industry.
International affiliatons. ICFTU; CTUC

4 Other Trade Union Organizations

Antigua and Barbuda Public Service Association (ABPSA)
Address. PO Box 1285, St. John's
Phone. +1-268 461 5821
Fax. +1-268 461 5821
E-mail. abpsa@candw.ag
History and character. Gained recognition as bargaining agent for civil servants in the 1980s but is rivalled in the public service sector by other unions. It now bargains for some 1,500 civil servants though its membership is little more than one-fifth of this.
International affiliation. ICFTU

Argentina

Capital: Buenos Aires
Population: 39.14 m. (2004 est.)

1 Political and Economic Background

From the overthrow of President María Estela (Isabelita) Perón in 1976 to 1983 Argentina was under military rule. In 1983 the military handed power to a civilian administration under Raúl Alfonsín. The Peronist Carlos Menem who succeeded him in 1989 remained in office until standing down after elections in October 1999 in which Fernando de la Rúa became president as the leader of a coalition of centre-left forces, although lacking a majority in either house of the bi-cameral legislature (Congress). The October 1999 election represented the first occasion on which the Peronists had handed over power other than in the event of a military coup and was seen as an indication of the increasing stability of the Argentine state and society. Peronists continued to govern the major provinces, however, and in the 2001 mid-term elections the Peronist party – the Justicialist Party (PJ) – regained its leading position in the legislature. The 2003 presidential election was won by Néstor Carlos Kirchner, of the Front for Victory faction of the Justicialist Party, after Menem withdrew his candidacy immediately prior to a run-off election, and the Peronists also consolidated their dominant position in the legislature.

Under Menem the Peronists had largely turned their backs on their corporatist, populist past (in which they had been closely linked with the CGT labour confederation) in favour of more conventional centre-right free market policies. The Menem government sought to reverse years of economic decline in which Argentina had experienced hyper-inflation, an escalating burden of foreign debt and a progressive erosion of the position it had enjoyed in the 1930s as one of the leading economies of the western hemisphere. Menem's programme of "major surgery without anaesthetic" included trade liberalization, austerity packages and privatization, with major cutbacks in the public sector. In the three years 1997–99 prices rose by less than 1 per cent and the real GDP growth rate reached 9 per cent in 1997. However, the economy contracted by up to 4 per cent in 1999, affected by the fall in prices of export commodities and a major January 1999 devaluation in Brazil. In the poorer provinces public sector workers went unpaid for periods leading to strikes and other action in 1999. In December 2000 an aid package of $40bn. from the IMF and other donors was unveiled, aimed at assisting recovery and averting default on the foreign debt. Argentina's financial situation remained perilous and forced the floating of the peso (hitherto pegged to the dollar) in early 2002; this triggered a surge of inflation but also fostered an export-led recovery which resulted in strong growth and falling unemployment in 2003-04 albeit with continuing inflationary pressures and a remaining $100 bn of defaulted debt.

GDP (purchasing power parity) $435.5bn. (2003 est.); GDP per capita (purchasing power parity) $11,200 (2003 est.).

2 Trade Unionism

Argentina ratified ILO Convention No. 87 (Freedom of Association and Protection of the Right to Organize, 1948) in 1960 and No. 98 (Right to Organize and Collective Bargaining, 1949) in 1956.

In the twentieth century successive attempts to form a national centre culminated in 1930 in the formation of the CGT. Since the 1940s it has been a major force in Argentine politics. Although trade unionism was suppressed by the military after 1976 it resurfaced strongly through demonstrations and general strikes in the transitional phase preceding the restoration of full civilian rule at the end of 1983. The formal right to belong to a trade union was restored in 1982 and the right to strike in 1983 (although the government retained powers to ban individual strikes). Unions were brought into tripartite discussions with government and business on questions relating to the transition to democracy and the economic crisis. An Act of March 23, 1988 recognized the right of workers to form or be (or not to be) members of a union of their choice and for trade unions to become members of their preferred federations and confederations, and to affiliate to international union organizations. Unions were allowed to set up mutual benefit societies and cooperatives and were allowed to retain their controversial role of administering social welfare (a vast system of health provision, education, tourism, sports facilities).

In a review presented to the World Trade Organization in January 1999, the ICFTU concluded that the situation in respect of trade union rights had "improved immeasurably" since the 1970s and 1980s, although some measures intended to increase labour market flexibility had weakened union rights. All workers except military personnel have the legal right to form and join trade unions and about 40 per cent of the formal workforce are unionized. There is no state interference in the internal affairs of unions. However, there are restrictions on granting legal recognition to enterprise-level unions where another union is already established.

Workers enjoy the right to strike and are in law protected from recriminations by employers. A 1990 report found that two-thirds of disputes between 1986 and 1989 occurred in the public sector. In 1990 Menem restricted the right to strike in "essential industries", namely public health, transport, water supply, gas, oil, phones, education and the judiciary. In 1991 the decree was tested by a major rail strike; when the government proposed to privatize the steel firm SOMISA and impose mass dismissals, a general strike threat was issued by the metalworkers' union UOM. The outcome was that compulsory redundancies were replaced by more generous voluntary severance terms. Legal challenges and union action have since limited the impact of restrictions in the public sector.

While strikes are legal, unauthorized demonstrations and assemblies have led to violent clashes with police on occasions in recent years. Death threats and intimidation have been reported in some disputes.

Argentina's relatively inflexible labour market has been seen as a factor in persistent high unemployment. In the early 1990s the government passed a series of decrees that sought to limit pay increases to those justified by productivity. In August 1996 Menem proposed wide-ranging labour law reforms that broadly aimed to restrict collective bargaining to the enterprise level and encourage flexibility of labour contracts. The unions forcefully opposed the reforms, and there were two general strikes organized by the CGT in September and December 1996. Faced with opposition in Congress, Menem attempted to introduce elements of the reforms by decree, but the decrees were overturned in the courts in 1997. After extended discussions with employers and the CGT a further package of measures was adopted in September 1998. This package confirmed the status of industry-wide collective bargaining and banned future temporary contracts under which workers had no social benefits. Collective agreements that extended beyond the enterprise level required approval by the Ministry of Labour. The role of industry-wide collective agreements has declined, however, and by 1998 64 per cent of workers in the private sector were either employed on individual employment contracts without social security coverage or were not registered at all. A reforming labour law (law 25877), introduced in March 2004, was heralded as a breakthrough and is expected to bring labour rights closer to international obligations under the ILO conventions. Labour commentators say the right to strike must now be respected in law.

3 Trade Union Centre

Confederación General del Trabajo de la Républica Argentina (CGT)
General Confederation of Labour
Address. Azopardo 802, CP 1107, Buenos Aires
Phone. +54 11 4343 1883
Fax. +54 11 4343 1883
E-mail. secgral@cgtra.org.ar
Website. www.cgtra.org.ar (Spanish only)
Leadership. Rodolfo Daer (secretary general)
History and character. The CGT was founded in 1930, but its position was challenged by competing syndicalist, anarchist and socialist federations for a further decade. After becoming Minister of Labour and Social Welfare in a 1943 coup, Col. Juan Domingo Perón nurtured his relationship with it as part of a new politics of charismatic, authoritarian populism. Perón was dismissed in October 1945, but a CGT strike forced his release and paved the way for his election as President in 1946. From then, until Perón's fall and exile in 1955, the CGT leadership consolidated its position in Argentinian society in concert with the Peronist movement. His overthrow was resisted by the unions, and several hundred workers were killed in an abortive Peronist uprising of June 1956.

Government-appointed officials now administered the unions; the CGT was officially disbanded, though continuing clandestinely. This period saw internal differences over the question of its relationship to successive civilian and military governments and even to the exiled Perón. In 1961 union control was restored and two years later the CGT held its first open congress since Perón's fall. Under Augusto Vandor, its secretary general, who advocated "Peronism without Perón", the CGT reached an accommodation with the military regime of 1966. But bitterly disputed union elections of 1968 shattered its unity with the dissidents forming the "CGT of the Argentines".

Perón himself returned to power in September 1973, and was succeeded by his widow, María Estela (Isabelita), on his death in July 1974. Relations were undermined by worsening economic conditions and wage restraint which in 1975 provoked the first CGT-led strikes against a Peronist government and the resignation and flight from the country of the Minister of Social Welfare. Following the March 1976 coup in which Isabelita Perón was deposed, government officials again seized the CGT, and it was officially dissolved in 1979.

As before, however, the organization continued in being. At first underground but later increasingly openly, the CGT was already leading protests and strikes by 1982, even before the 1983 restoration of the right to strike and restoration of civilian government. The CGT found itself in conflict with the new administration of President Raúl Alfonsín, who had repeatedly criticized the close links between the CGT leadership and hard-line members of the previous military government. The CGT's legal status was restored in 1986 but only after ILO mediation.

After the Peronist Carlos Menem came into office in 1989, his free market policies provoked a crisis in Peronism and in the CGT. By November 1989 it had split into two factions, for and against the austerity programme, opposition to which was led by CGT general secretary Saul Ubaldini. The Ubaldini faction fiercely resisted government calls for a voluntary two-year strike ban and was displaced by a "Menemista" group at the head of the official CGT apparatus. For two-and-a-half years the main trade union centre was organizationally split into the (Menemista) CGT–San Martín and the CGT–Azarpado, which was not officially recognized. When reunification occurred in 1992 it was largely on the CGT–San Martín's terms.

The CGT split again in March 2000. A congress staged by the "combative" unions elected Hugo Moyano as secretary general. The "official" CGT remained under the leadership of Rodolfo Daer. Both the dissident and official factions joined strike action in June 2000 to protest against IMF-backed austerity measures introduced against a background of economic stagnation and unemployment rising to 16%.
International affiliation. ICFTU

4 Other Trade Union Centres

Central de Trabajadores Argentinos
Address. Av. Independencia, 766, Buenos Aires
E-mail. Secgeneral@cta.org.ar
Leadership. Victor de Gennaro (secretary-general)

Confederación General del Trabajo-Moyano (CGT–Moyano)
Address. San José 1781, Buenos Aires
Leadership. Hugo Moyano (secretary-general)

Consejo Coordinador Argentino Sindical (CCAS)
Address. Combate de Los Pozos 235, CP 1080 Buenos Aires
Phone. +54 11 4952 77 88
Fax. +54 11 4952 77 94
E-mail. inforcas@ntdate.com.ar
Leadership. Victor R. Huerta (secretary-general)
History and character. Also referred to as the Congreso or Central de Trabajadores Argentinos (CTA) it became prominent in mid-1990s protests against anti-union policies of the Menem government.
International affiliation. WCL

Armenia

Capital: Yerevan
Population: 2.99m. (2004 est.)

1 Political and Economic Background

The Soviet Republic of Armenia declared its independence in August 1990. President Levon Ter-Petrossian, who had led Armenia to independence, was forced from office in February 1998 and was succeeded by Robert Kocharian. The incumbent Kocharian, standing as a non-party candidate, won the second round of a presidential election in March 2003. In legislative elections in May 2003 the Republican Party of Armenia (HHK), which had supported Kocharian in the presidential election, emerged as the leading faction, though with fewer than one-third of the seats in the National Assembly.

Armenia experienced a severe economic contraction following the loss of its Soviet-era markets and the collapse of its central command economy, this being exacerbated by military conflict with neighbouring Azerbaijan over the Armenian-populated enclave of Nagorno–Karabakh, prior to a cease fire in May 1994. The economy has since expanded although the country remains heavily dependent on that of Russia. Most small and medium sized enterprises are now in private control, but much of the inherited Soviet heavy industry is closed. Unemployment is high, though estimates vary widely, and foreign assistance and remittances from workers abroad are important sources of economic support.

GDP (purchasing power parity) $11.79bn. (2003 est.); GDP per capita (purchasing power parity) $3,500 (2003 est.).

2 Trade Unionism

The 1995 Constitution accords the right to form unions but the collapsed state of major enterprises and high unemployment has resulted in a low level of organization and activity. Armenia ratified ILO Convention No. 98 (Right to Organize and Collective Bargaining, 1949) in 2003 but has not ratified Convention No. 87 (Freedom of Association and Protection of the Right to Organize, 1948). A new law on trade unions was adopted in 2000. The Soviet era unions reformed as the Confederation of Trade Unions of Armenia, its sectoral branches benefiting from the continuing check-off of dues in the state enterprises. The Confederation affiliates to the General Confederation of Trade Unions, which associates trade union centres of former Soviet republics. There is little practice of collective bargaining. There is a constitutional right to strike and an Arbitration Commission. Strikes in the private sector, however, are quite rare due to the lack of protection guarantees against arbitrary dismissals.

3 Trade Union Centre

Confederation of Trade Unions of Armenia
Address. Vazgen Sargsyan St. 26, Yerevan 375010
Phone. +374 1 543 385

Fax. +374 1 543 382
E-mail. xachik@xar.am
Website. www.spyur.am/ctua
Leadership. Martin K. Harutyunyan (chairman)

4 Other Trade Union Organization

Miabanutiun ("Unity") Trade Union
Address. Republic Square, House of Trade Unions, 2nd Floor, Suite 43, Yerevan
E-mail. trade_unions@yahoo.com

Australia

Capital: Canberra
Population: 19.94 m. (2004 est.)

1 Political and Economic Background

The Commonwealth of Australia dates from 1901 and comprises six states and two territories. From 1949 to 1972 and again from 1975 to 1983 the federal government was formed by the Liberal/National (Country) Party coalition. The Australian Labor Party (ALP), led by Bob Hawke, a former Australian Council of Trade Unions (ACTU) president, came to power in 1983. In 1993, now led by Paul Keating, the ALP won an historic fifth consecutive term of office. In March 1996, however, the ALP was defeated in a general election and a Liberal–National Party coalition government came into office under Liberal leader John Howard. The Howard government was re-elected in 1998, 2001 and again in October 2004, although the ALP holds power in every state and territory.

The Australian economy was built on the surpluses generated by commodity exports, such as meat, wool, minerals and metals, allowing the growth of tariff-protected industries and a high-wage economy. By the 1980s, however, most commodity prices were on a downward path and Australia faced pressures arising from the need to modernize its economy. In 1992 unemployment reached a record 11 per cent. There has been a shift to the services sector and the government emphasizes the need for Australian industries to remain competitive in world markets. However, commodities still constitute a major component of exports. The latter half of the 1990s saw improved economic performance and this has continued with real GDP growth of 3% in 2003, inflation below 3% and unemployment at 6%.

GDP (purchasing power parity) $571.4.bn. (2003 est.); GDP per capita (purchasing power parity) $29,000 (2003 est.).

2 Trade Unionism

Australia ratified both ILO Convention No. 87 (Freedom of Association and Protection of the Right to Organize, 1948) and No. 98 (Right to Organize and Collective Bargaining, 1949) in 1973.

Trade unionism developed strongly among the nineteenth century British settlers, and there were some 200 unions operating by 1890. The Australian Council of Trade Unions (ACTU), the national centre, dates from 1927. The pattern was traditionally one of craft unionism. As recently as 1988 there were still 308 unions, and nearly half of these had fewer than 1,000 members. The pressure to amalgamate increased after the 1988 Industrial Relations Act extended legal standing only to unions with 1,000 or more members. The number of ACTU affiliates (146 in 1989) fell to 119 in 1991 and to 45 by 2004.

Blue-collar unions have lost much of their earlier pre-eminence in the face of the rise of white-collar and public sector unionism. Indeed, union density in the public sector is now 47% compared with only 18% in the private sector. The overall position has been one of decline, although the last three years has seen a small increase. Factors have been the shift from public to private sector employment; the decline of highly unionized "old economy" industries in the face of the growth of services, where unionization rates are generally lower; the increase in part-time working (29.7% of the workforce now being part-time, with only 17% of part-timers in unions, compared with 26% of full-timers); and the shift from large to small-scale enterprises. In 1976 union density stood as high as 51 per cent, but it has fallen steadily since then and by 2003 was 23 per cent.

The major focus of concern for unions since the 1990s has been the development of enterprise bargaining and the encouragement of greater labour flexibility at the expense of industry-wide collective bargaining. From the establishment of the federal system of conciliation and arbitration in 1904, Australian industrial relations were dominated by its unique highly structured collective bargaining and quasi-judicial conciliation and settlement systems. These resulted in legally enforceable federal and state "awards" defining pay and conditions in detail for each industry and helped the unions, as negotiators, build a strong position. Enterprise bargaining, although not unknown previously, was generally strongly opposed by the unions, which supported the practice of negotiating industry-wide agreements regardless of the varying circumstances of individual employers.

The consensus in favour of this system began to break down in the 1980s as increasing numbers of employers sought the right to manage their own business costs and as free market sentiment increased. By the 1990s the political consensus had fundamentally shifted and the traditionally pro-union ALP had largely adopted policies which accepted the need for greater market liberalization and labour flexibility if Australia was to remain competitive in world markets. The Howard government since 1996 has continued to aggressively press policy objectives that are widely seen as aimed at reducing the power of the unions and ending rigid bargaining and award structures.

Under Labor, the industry-wide system was first modified by the Industrial Relations Act of 1988. While maintaining the (constitutionally prescribed) involvement of the state at each level it empowered the Industrial Relations Commission (IRC) (under Section

115) to certify enterprise agreements which were unique and thus inconsistent with broader awards. This was a very important consideration in Australia, where the pay of some 85% of employees traditionally was regulated by state or federal awards. The really revolutionary step was taken in 1991, when the IRC ruled that direct collective bargaining should be permitted between companies and their employees.

Section 115 had proved important in opening up the path for enterprise agreements. Section 118 facilitated the right of unions to cover a wide range of workers at a single plant. Another section precipitated radical structural change among Australia's unions by effectively requiring them to have membership of at least 10,000 by 1991.

In 1993 the government unveiled a second major industrial relations package, adopted in 1994. It included new national minimum standards of employment, a legal right to strike (not previously formally enshrined in law, although in practice recognized), and – if unions broke laws forbidding secondary boycotts – a conciliation period of up to 72 hours during which an employer must refrain from legal action. The employers' organization, the Australian Chamber of Commerce and Industry (ACCI), claimed that it was "95 per cent an ACTU agenda, 5 per cent a government agenda and zero per cent an employer agenda".

However, the measures also contained provisions for non-union workers to strike "enterprise deals" through the use of agreements (called Enterprise Flexibility Agreements), although unions would have the right to scrutinize such deals. This provision was seen as opening up the possibility of non-union "enterprise bargaining" as potentially a rival channel of wage settlement to that offered by the unions; already some 11 per cent of the workforce was thought to be covered by enterprise deals. The ACTU failed to obtain the agreement of the Industrial Relations minister Laurie Brereton that enterprise bargaining should only take place via a union vehicle. In November 1994 the Industrial Relations Commission ruled that the transport union had forfeited its immunity from civil action by pursuing an industry-wide pay claim for aircraft refuellers and oil tanker drivers – in effect that it had avoided enterprise bargaining. By the end of 1994, the number of enterprise agreements in force numbered 2,700, covering one-fifth of the workforce.

Following the election of the centre-right government in March 1996, the 1996 Workplace Relations Act gave strong backing to enterprise bargaining and gave enterprise-level "Australian Workplace Agreements" (AWAs) primacy over federal and state awards on statutory minimum pay and over certified collective agreements once these had passed their expiry date The Act directed the Industrial Relations Commission to encourage enterprise-level agreements and put union and non-union collective agreements on the same basis.

AWAs are in effect individual contracts, although employers must offer comparable terms to comparable employees. No current employee can be forced to sign an AWA, or be sacked or discriminated against for refusing to do so, and their existing terms and conditions must be respected. AWAs have to be approved by the Office of the Employment Advocate (set up under the Act), and may be referred to the Australian Industrial Relations Commission if their terms are detrimental. The unions have objected to AWAs as weakening collective bargaining and a way of eroding terms and conditions, although some have sought to position themselves as acting as a bargaining agent for employees signing AWAs. Some major employers have preferred to remain with the system of collective bargaining.

Since 1999 the government has repeatedly introduced legislation seeking to reduce award wages and conditions and restrict the role of unions in collective bargaining, including the right to strike. Little of this legislation has been passed as the government has not (prior to the October 2004 elections) had a majority in the Senate.

While the 1996 Workplace Relations Act left intact protections against anti-union discrimination and rights to take industrial action, it weakened union power, curtailing closed shops and narrowing the scope of legal strikes. Under the Act strikes are only legally protected during the period of bargaining and fines may be imposed where action takes place during the term of a collective agreement. In the view of the ICFTU, "the operation of the law effectively denies the right to strike in the negotiation of multi-employer, industry-wide or national level agreements". The Act likewise banned strikes triggered by demarcation disputes and in effect banned sympathy strikes, secondary boycotts and strikes threatening to cause "significant damage" to the economy.

In March 2000 and subsequent years the ILO called on the government to amend the Workplace Relations Act to ensure that AWAs do not undermine collective bargaining, and to amend the Trade Practices Act to allow workers to take sympathy action in support of a legal strike. ACTU secretary Greg Combet stated in response: "the Workplace Relations Act has been found in breach of so many international conventions that there will surely be a day of reckoning".

While the unions have complained bitterly about the 1996 Act, its impact has been blunted by several factors. Unions have won a series of injunctions and court cases frustrating its implementation, and snap strikes and secondary boycotts do in practice occur. Most employers have tended to avoid recourse to legal remedies in trying to reach settlements with unions. While opposing the shift to workplace level bargaining in principle, in practice unions have also shifted resources and expertise into dealing with the changed bargaining context as they try to carve out a clear position for themselves in the changing industrial relations context.

3 Trade Union Centre

Australian Council of Trade Unions (ACTU)
Address. Level 2, 393 Swanston Street, Melbourne, VIC 3000
Phone. +61 3 9663 5266
Fax. +61 3 9663 4051 or +61 3 9663 8220
E-mail. mailbox@actu.asn.au
Website. www.actu.asn.au
Leadership. Sharan Burrow (president); Greg Combet (general secretary)

Membership. 2 million

History and character. The ACTU was founded in 1927 and is the only trade union centre in Australia.

While the ACTU has no formal political affiliation, it has traditionally enjoyed a close and at one time dominating relationship with the ALP, as seen in the period of Labor government from 1983–96. Bob Hawke, Prime Minister 1983–91, was a former ACTU president. His successor as Prime Minister, Paul Keating (1991–96), began his working life as a research officer of the Municipal Employees' Union, now the Australian Services Union (ASU), while his Employment Minister, Simon Crean, was a former ACTU president. After a period as Opposition Leader, Crean is now Shadow Treasurer and his two successors as ACTU president – Martin Ferguson and Jennie George – are Labor members of parliament. In the ALP unions appoint 50% of state conference delegates (from whom federal conference delegates are chosen), although the unions do not vote or participate as a bloc.

Through the period of Labor Party government from 1983-96, the ACTU was party to eight accords between the unions and the government. Each accord had at its heart a commitment to wage restraint in return for certain welfare or desired fiscal measures. Achievement of the accords was widely seen as strengthening the position of the ALP and the ACTU and the relationship between them.

Into the 1980s, the ACTU was at least nominally committed to a programme of sweeping socialization but this has been abandoned as it focuses on defending its members from the erosion of union power. It has strongly supported the campaign for a republic, but in November 1999 a national referendum narrowly decided not to replace the Queen by a President as Head of State.

Even under Labor, the ACTU was apprehensive about the impact of enterprise bargaining and sought to persuade Labor to give it a veto over the recognition process for bargaining units, a quest in which it was only partially successful. Since passage of the 1996 Workplace Relations Act, the ACTU has claimed the Howard government is determined to break the unions. However, it is also aware that the unions face deep-seated challenges arising from underlying structural changes in the economy that go beyond the policies of individual governments. During 1985–95, a period of Labor government, union membership fell faster than in any comparable country except New Zealand (where special factors applied), including countries such as the USA and Britain with conservative governments committed to curbing union power. The ACTU is looking to increase its support in weakly-organized growth sectors such as services and part-time working, and among women, who have a lower unionization rate than do men, and general secretary Greg Combet has said that the service industries must be the union base for the future. It is also encouraging the shift of resources to workplace level to reflect the reality of workplace level agreements.

ACTU's policy has been for many years to encourage amalgamation of existing member unions, in part to reduce disruptive demarcation disputes and in part to assist in the development of powerful, professionally managed and institutionally sophisticated unions able to deal with modern companies on a more equivalent footing. Industry-wide unions are also seen as better fitted to cope with the problems posed for narrowly recruited skill-based craft unions by new technology. Although resisted to some degree by the smaller unions, this process has resulted in the number of affiliated unions falling from 170 in the mid-1980s to 45 by early 2004.

The ACTU and its affiliates operate a wide range of member services and discount schemes. The ACTU also has a training body, Trade Union Training Australia (TUTA Ltd.).

The supreme policy-making body of the ACTU is the biennial congress. Following a policy adopted in 1989 the mandatory proportion of women on the executive has been increased in stages and in October 2000 the target of 50% was reached with an expanded 64-member executive (59 in 2004) There are ACTU state branches (known as trades and labour councils) for each of the six states of Australia, which have wide discretion in dealing with intrastate industrial and political issues.

The ACTU has a strong international dimension to its work. APHEDA (Australian People for Health Education and Development Abroad) is its overseas humanitarian agency, running 60 projects at any one time. The ACTU is the major trade union centre in the South-East Asia and Pacific region and has taken a leading role in recent campaigns for human and trade union rights in East Timor, Burma and Fiji. It participates in the ILO and has accused the Howard government of seeking to downgrade Australia's commitment to the ILO.

International affiliatons. ICFTU; TUAC; CTUC

Affiliates.

1. Association of Professional Engineers, Scientists and Managers, Australia (APESMA)
Address. GPO Box 1272L, Melbourne, VIC 3001
Phone. +61 3 9695 8800
Fax. +61 3 9696 9312
E-mail. info@apesma.asn.au
Website. www.apesma.asn.au
Leadership. Barry Tonkin (national president)
Membership. 21,205

2. Australasian Meat Industry Employees' Union (AMIEU)
Address. Level 1, 39 Lytton Road, East Brisbane, Qld 4169
Phone. +61 7 3217 3766
Fax. +61 7 3217 4462
E-mail. admin@amieuqld.asn.au
Website. www.amieu.asn.au

3. Australian Education Union (AEU)
Address. Ground Floor, 120 Clarendon Street, Southbank, VIC 3006
Phone. +61 3 9693 1800
Fax. +61 3 9693 1805
E-mail. aeu@aeufederal.org.au

4. Australian Institute of Marine and Power Engineers (AIMPE)
Address. 52 Buckingham Street, Surry Hills 2010
Phone. +61 2 9698 3999
Fax. +61 2 9319 7505
E-mail. aimpe@ozemail.com.au

5. Australian Licensed Aircraft Engineers' Association (ALAEA)
Address. 25 Stoney Creek Road, Bexley 2207
Phone. +61 2 9554 9399
Fax. +61 9554 9644
E-mail. alaea@alaea.asn.au
Website. www.alaea.asn.au
Leadership. Michael O'Rance (federal president); David Kemp (federal secretary)
Membership. 3,884

6. Australian Manufacturing Workers' Union (AMWU)
Address. PO Box 160, Granville, NSW 2142
Phone. +61 2 9897 9133
Fax. +61 2 9897 9274
E-mail. amwu2@amwu.asn.au
Website. www.amwu.asn.au
Leadership. Doug Cameron (national secretary)
Membership. 144,176
History and character. Formed by the amalgamation of unions with widespread coverage in metals and engineering, manufacturing, vehicle building, food and printing industries. It also includes some trade, technical and supervisory employees in government agencies.

The union says that average enterprise bargaining wage increases obtained by AMWU members are significantly higher than those obtained by direct negotiation between employees and employers. It has an Education Department that runs courses around the country to help members keep up-to-date with industrial relations developments and develop negotiating skills, and an active Research Department. Members can develop workplace skills through MISTAS, the Manufacturing Industry Skills Training and Assessment Service.

AMWU has a militant tradition. Its national secretary Doug Cameron has been sharply critical of what is seen as the adoption by the Australian Labour Party of free market economic policies, and has called on the ALP to re-discover its working class base. The union continues to call for "fair trade" not "free trade" with a focus on core labour standards. Internationally it is affiliated to the ITF, IUF and UNI (Graphical Sector)

7. Australian Maritime Officers' Union (AMOU)
Address. PO Box 407, Haymarket, NSW 1240
Phone. +61 2 9264 2388
Fax. +61 2 9267 4766
E-mail. amou@amou.com.au

8. Australian Nursing Federation (ANF)
Address. PO Box 4239, Kingston, ACT 2604
Phone +61 2 6232 6533
Fax. +61 2 6232 6610
E-mail. anfcanberra@anf.org.au
Website. www.anf.org.au
Membership. 73,878
Leadership. Coral Levett (federal president); Jill Iliffe (federal secretary)

9. Australian Professional Footballers' Association (PFA)
Address. Suite 46, 54 Victoria St, Carlton South, VIC 3053
Phone. +61 3 9659 3520
Fax. +61 3 9659 3521
E-mail. into@pft.net.au
Website. www.pfa.net.au

10. Australian Salaried Medical Officers' Federation (ASMOF)
Address. Locked Mail Bag No. 13, Glebe, NSW 2037
Phone. +61 2 9212 6900
Fax. +61 2 9212 6911
E-mail. peters@asmof.org.au

11. Australian Services Union (ASU)
Address. 116–124 Queensberry St, Carlton South, VIC 3053
Phone. +61 3 9342 1400
Fax. +61 3 9342 1499
E-mail. asunatm@asu.asn.au
Website. www.asu.asn.au
Leadership. Michael O'Sullivan (national executive president); Paul Slape (national secretary)
Membership. 96,489
History and character. The ASU was formed by the amalgamation in July 1993 of the Federated Clerks Union of Australia, the Federated Municipal and Shire Council Employees' Union of Australia, and the Australian Services Union, and established a unitary organization in 1995. Its 96,000 members work in local government, energy, water, public transport, airlines, shipping, travel, ports, social and community services, information technology and private sector clerical and administrative employment.

12. Australian Workers' Union (AWU)
Address. 685 Spencer Street, West Melbourne, VIC 3003
Phone. +61 3 8327 0800
Fax. +61 2 3 9327 0899
E-mail. members@awu.net.au
Website. www.awu.net.au
Leadership. Bill Ludwig (hon. national president); Bill Shorten (national secretary)
Membership. 136,790
History and character. The AWU was founded in 1886 as the Amalgamated Shearers' Union, based in the wool shearing industry. Its Pastoral Industry Award, still in existence, was the first federal award achieved by a union under the Commonwealth conciliation and arbitration system set up at the start of the 20th Century and set the precedent for Australian industrial relations practice for most of the century. The AWU is committed to defending this system against the encroachment of AWAs and the reduction of awards to basic provisions.

In 1993 the AWU amalgamated with the Federation of Industrial, Manufacturing and Engineering Employees (FIMEE). The AWU, once the "union of the bush", is now a general union and has recently recruited successfully in such diverse areas as horse racing and aviation. It is affiliated internationally to IUF, IMF and ICEM.

13. Australian Writers' Guild (AWG)
Address. 8/50 Reservoir Street, Surry Hills, NSW 2010
Phone. +61 2 9281 1554
Fax. +61 2 9281 4321

E-mail. admin@awg.com.au
Website. www.awg.com.au
Leadership. Simon Hopkinson (president)

14. Blind Workers' Union of Victoria (BWU)
Address. 201 High Street, Prahan VIC 3181
Phone. +61 3 9521 3050
Fax. +61 3 9521 3050

15. Breweries and Bottleyards Employees' Industrial Union of Workers WA (BBEIUW (WA))
Address. PO Box 1455 Canning Vale, WA 6970
Phone. +61 8 9455 4633
Fax. +61 8 9455 4733

16. Civil Air Operations Officers Association of Australia (CAOOAA)
Address. PO Box 394, Port Melbourne, VIC 33207
Phone. +61 3 9646 9277
Fax. +61 3 9646 6799
E-mail. civilair@civilair.asn.au

17. Club Managers' Association Australia (CMAA)
Address. PO Box 845, Auburn, NSW 1835
Phone. +61 2 9643 2300
Fax. +61 2 9643 2400
E-mail. cmaa@cmaa.asn.au

18. Communications, Electrical and Plumbing Union of Australia (CEPU)
Address. Suite 701, Level 7, 1 Rosebery Avenue, Roseberry, NSW 2018
Phone. +61 2 9663 3699
Fax. +61 2 9663 5599
E-mail. edno@nat.cepu.asn.au
Website. www.cepu.asn.au
Electrical Division:
Address. Suite 701, Level 7, 1 Rosebery Avenue, Roseberry, NSW 2018
Phone. +61 2 9663 3699
Fax. +61 2 9663 5599
Website. www.cepu-electrical.asn.au
Plumbing Division:
Address. 52 Victoria Street, Carlton South, VIC 3053
Phone. +61 3 9662 1400
Fax. +61 3 9663 7516

19. Community and Public Sector Union (CPSU)
Address. 191–199 Thomas Street, Haymarket, Sydney, NSW 2000
Phone. +61 2 9334 9200
Fax. +61 2 9334 9250
E-mail. members@cpsu.org
Website. www.cpsu.org.au
Leadership. Mark Gepp (national president); Adrian O'Connell (national secretary)
Membership. 157,682

20. Construction, Forestry, Mining and Engineering Union (CFMEU)
Address. Box Q1641, Queen Victoria Bld, Post Office, Sydney, NSW 1230
Phone. +61 2 9267 3393
Fax. +61 2 9267 2460
Website. www.cfmeu.asn.au
Leadership. Trevor Smith (national president); John Maitland (national secretary)

21. Finance Sector Union of Australia (FSU)
Address. GPO Box 9893, Melbourne, VIC 3001
Phone. +61 3 9261 5300
Fax. +61 3 9670 2950
E-mail. fsuinfo@fsunion.org.au
Website. www.fsunion.org.au
Leadership. Paul Schroder (national secretary)
Membership. 60,803
History and character. The FSU was amalgamated in July 1991 with the Australian Bank Employees Union, the Australian Insurance Employees Union, the AMP Society Staff Association, the Trustee Companies Officers Association, and the Wool Brokers Staffs Association, and increased its strength further by amalgamating with the Commonwealth Bank Officers Association in March 1994. Affiliated internationally to UNI.

22. Flight Attendants' Association of Australia (FAAA) – International Division
Address. 388–390 Sussex Street, Sydney, NSW 2000
Phone. +61 2 9267 2533
Fax. +61 2 9267 9663
E-mail. info@faaa.net
Leadership. Michael Mijatov (divisional secretary)

23. Flight Attendants' Association of Australia (FAAA) – Domestic Division
Address. Unit 18, 538 Gardiners Rd, Alexandria, NSW 2015
Phone. +61 2 9669 5366
Fax. +61 2 9669 5388
E-mail. info@faaadomestic.org.au
Website. www.faaadomestic.org.au
Leadership. Darryl Watkins (divisional secretary)

24. Funeral and Allied Industries Union of New South Wales (F&AI)
Address. PO Box K701, Haymarket, NSW 1240
Phone. +61 2 9283 3277
Fax. +61 2 9283 3279
Leadership. Aiden Nye (secretary)

25. Health Services Union (HSU)
Address. Level 2, 106-108 Victoria Street, Carlton South, VIC 3053
Phone. +61 3 9341 3328
Fax. +61 3 9341 3329
E-mail. hsu@hsu.net.au
Website. www.hsu.net.au
Leadership. Michael Williamson (national president); Craig Thomson (national secretary)

26. Independent Education Union of Australia (IEU)
Address. PO Box 1301, South Melbourne, VIC 3205
Phone. +61 3 9254 1830
Fax. +61 3 9254 1835
E-mail. ieu@ieu.org.au
Website. www.ieu.org.au
Membership. 45,000

Leadership. Richard Shearman (president), Lynne Rolley (general secretary)

27. Liquor, Hospitality and Miscellaneous Workers' Union (LHMU)
Address. Locked Bag 9, Haymarket, NSW 1240
Phone. +61 2 8204 7200
Fax. +61 2 9281 4480
E-mail. lhmu@lhmu.org.au
Website. www.lhmu.org.au
Leadership. Jeff Lawrence (national secretary)
Membership. 135,000. The diverse membership is in four areas: (1) hospitality and leisure (e.g. hotels, motels, restaurants, clubs, casinos, theme parks); (2) contracting and property services (e.g. cleaning, security, contract catering, parking attendants, gardeners); (3) mining and manufacturing (e.g. paints, plastics, chemicals, tanneries, and mining in the Northern Territories); (4) community and health workers (e.g. children's services, hospital workers, aged care, aboriginal health workers).

28. Maritime Union of Australia (MUA)
Address. Level 2, 365–375 Sussex Street, Sydney, NSW 2000
Phone. +61 2 9267 9134
Fax. +61 2 9261 3481
E-mail. muano@mua.asn.au
Website. www.mua.net.au
Leadership. Padraig Crumlin (national secretary)
Membership. 9,500 dock workers and seafarers. Formed by the amalgamation of the Waterside Workers' Federation of Australia (WWF) and the Seamen's Union of Australia on July 1, 1993

29. Media, Entertainment and Arts Alliance (MEAA)
Address. PO Box 723, Strawberry Hills, NSW 2012
Phone. +61 2 9333 0999
Fax. +61 2 9333 0933
E-mail. mail@alliance.org.au
Website. www.alliance.org.au
Leadership. Patricia Amphlett (federal president); Christopher Warren (federal secretary)
Membership. 12,100

30. Medical Scientists' Association of Victoria (MSAV)
Address. Mail Box 98 Trades Hall, 54 Victoria Street, Carlton South, VIC 3053
Phone. +61 3 9663 8122
Fax. +61 3 9663 8109
E-mail. enquiry@msav.org.au
Website. www.msav.org.au
Leadership. Andrew Wootton (president)

31. National Tertiary Education Union (NTEU)
Address. PO Box 1323, South Melbourne, VIC 3205
Phone. +61 3 9254 1910
Fax. +61 3 9254 1915
E-mail. nteunat@nteu.org.au
Website. www.nteu.org.au
Leadership. Carolyn Allport (president); Grahame McCulloch (general secretary)
Membership. 25,200

32. National Union of Workers (NUW)
Address. 552 Victoria Street, North Melbourne, VIC 3051
Phone. +61 3 9287 1850
Fax. +61 9287 1818
E-mail. nuwnat@nuw.org.au
Website. www.nuw.org.au
Leadership. Charlie Donnelly (general secretary)

33. New South Wales Nurses' Association (NSWNA)
Address. 43 Australia Street, Camperdown, NSW 2050
Fax. +61 2 9550 3667
E-mail. gensec@nswnurses.asn.au
Website. www.nswnurses.asn.au
Leadership. Brett Holmes (general secretary)

34. Police Federation of Australia (PFA)
Address. Level 1, 21 Murray Crescent, Griffith, ACT 2603
Phone. +61 2 6239 8900
Fax. +61 2 6239 8999
E-mail. pfa@pfa.org.au
Leadership. Peter Alexander (president); Mark Burgess (chief executive officer)

35. Rail, Tram and Bus Union (RTBU)
Address. 83–89 Renwick Street, Redfern, NSW 2016
Phone. +61 2 9310 3966
Fax. +61 2 9319 2096
E-mail. rtbu@magna.com.au
Website. www.rtbu-nat.asn.au
Leadership. Roger Jowett (national secretary)

36. Rugby League Professionals Association (RLPA)
Address. PO Box 5106, Kahibah, NSW 2290
Fax. +61 2 4944 8806
E-mail. buttos@hunterlink.net.au
Leadership. Tony Butterfield (president)

37. Salaried Pharmacists' Association of Western Australia (SPA of WA)
Address. PO Box 8204 Perth Business Centre, Perth, WA 6000
Phone. +61 8 9328 5155
Fax. +61 8 9328 9107
E-mail. hsoa@hsoa.asn.au
Website. www.hsoa.asn.au
Leadership. Dan Hill (acting secretary)

38. Shop, Distributive and Allied Employees' Association (SDA)
Address. 5th Floor, 53 Queen Street, Melbourne, VIC 2000
Phone. +61 3 9629 2299
Fax. +61 9629 2646
E-mail. sdanat@c031.aone.net.au
Website. www.sda.org.au
Leadership. Don Farrell (national president); Joe de Bruyn (national secretary)

39. Textile, Clothing and Footwear Union of Australia (TCFUA)
Address. Ground Floor, 28 Anglo Road, Campsie 2194
Phone. +61 2 9789 4188
Fax. +61 2 9789 6510
E-mail. tcfua@tcfua.org.au
Leadership. Barry Tubner (president); Tony Woolgar (national secretary)

40. Transport Workers' Union of Australia (TWU)
Address. 52-56 Rouse Street, Port Melbourne, VIC 3207
Phone. +61 3 8645 3333
Fax. +61 3 9676 2669
E-mail. twu@twu.com.au
Website. www.twu.com.au
Leadership. John Allan (federal secretary)
Membership. 80,000. Members are in road transport, airlines, oil and gas distribution, armoured vehicles, distribution facilities, air/express freight etc. Affiliated internationally to ITF.

41. Union of Christmas Island Workers (UCIW)
Address. PO Box 84, Christmas Island, Indian Ocean, WA 6798
Phone. +61 8 9164 8471
Fax. +61 8 9164 8470
E-mail. uciw@pulau.cx
History and character. Christmas Island is an Australian territory with a population of under 3,000. The UCIW represents most of the work force.

42. United Firefighters' Union of Australia (UFU of A)
Address. 410 Brunswick Street, Fitzroy, VIC 3065
Phone. +61 9 419 8811
Fax. +61 9419 9258
E-mail. national@ufuvic.asn.au

43. Victorian Psychologists Association (VPA)
Address. 3rd Floor, Rear Building, Trades Hall, 54 Victoria Street, Carlton South, VIC 3053
Phone. +61 3 9663 8144
Fax. +61 3 9663 8109
Email. enquiry@vicpsych.org.au
Website. www.vicpsych.org.au

44. Western Australian Prison Officers' Union of Workers (WAPOUW)
Address. 63 Railway Parade, Mt. Lawley 6050
Phone. +61 8 9272 3222
Fax. +61 8 9271 2666
Email. wapou@wapou .asn.au
Website. www.wapou.asn.au

45. Woolclassers' Association of Australia
Address. "Kashmir", RMB 123, Culcairn, NSW 2660
Phone. +61 2 6029 7356
Fax. +61 2 6029 7112
E-mail. woolclasserassoc@netconnect.com.au

Austria

Capital: Vienna
Population: 8.17 m. (2004 est.)

1 Political and Economic Background

Austria's republican Constitution was restored in 1945 immediately following the defeat of German forces in World War II, although the country remained under Allied occupation until 1955. Since 1945 the major political parties have been the Social Democrats (SPÖ) and the conservative Austrian People's Party (ÖVP) and they have at times governed in coalition with each other. However, the SPÖ until recently has normally been the larger party, providing the Chancellor (head of government) continuously from 1970 until 1999. In elections in October 1999, the SPÖ won the largest number of seats (65) in the Nationalrat but a coalition government was subsequently formed in February 2000 by the ÖVP and the right-wing Freedom Party (FPÖ) of Jörg Haider, which had won 52 seats each, with Wolfgang Schüssel of the ÖVP becoming Chancellor. Opposition to the xenophobic Freedom Party's participation in government led all other EU member states to suspend bilateral relations with Austria, which had joined the EU in 1995, for a period of several months in 2000 before the other EU states backed down. Elections in November 2002 resulted in the ÖVP strengthening its position by winning 79 seats in the Nationalrat compared with 69 for the SPÖ, while the FPÖ declined to 18 seats – this was the first time the ÖVP had won more seats than the SPÖ since 1966 and the fragmenting FPÖ was reduced to a very minor role in the governing coalition. The decline of the FPÖ was confirmed by the June 2004 elections to the European Parliament when its share of the vote slumped from the 23.4% it had taken in the 1999 elections to only 6.4%, costing it 4 of its 5 seats.

Austria has a developed modern market economy and a high standard of living. Most of the workforce is employed in industry and services. It has low inflation (typically around 1% per annum in recent years) and at 4.4% unemployment in 2003 was well below the EU average. However, growth is sluggish, averaging about 1% per annum since the turn of the century. The state sector has been reduced with the privatization of large manufacturing enterprises, but key basic services remain in state hands. Austria joined the single European currency in 1999.

GDP (purchasing power parity) $245.3bn. (2003 est.); GDP per capita (purchasing power parity) $30,000 (2003 est.).

2 Trade Unionism

Austria ratified ILO Convention No. 87 (Freedom of Association and Protection of the Right to Organize, 1948) in 1950 and No. 98 (Right to Organize and Collective Bargaining, 1949) in 1951.

Organized trade union activity in Austria developed in the second half of the nineteenth century, with legal protection for the formation of trade unions being extended in 1870. The first federation of trade unions (the Provisional Committee of the Austrian Trade Unions) was established in 1893. While many unions were closely associated with the Social Democratic Party, the Christian Social Party from around 1900 also contributed to the development of Christian trade unions. After the civil war of February 1934, the Social Democratic Party and its allied trade unions were dissolved and a United Trade Union was founded, controlled by the Christian groups. This organization was itself dissolved following the Anschluss

(German annexation) in 1938, and workers and employers were brought into the German Labour Front. Only three weeks after the capture of Vienna by Soviet troops on April 13, 1945, the Österreichischer Gewerkschaftsbund (ÖGB, the Austrian Federation of Trade Unions) was formed, uniting former members of Christian, Socialist and Communist unions.

The pattern of trade unionism established after 1945 was one of industrial unionism, whereby all manual workers in a plant belong to one union regardless of job demarcation lines. However, blue-collar and white-collar workers are traditionally organized in separate unions, and there are residual formal differences between the two categories of workers embedded in law. There are 13 national trade unions, all of which are affiliated to the ÖGB. Union density has declined somewhat since the early 1980s. It now stands at around 30% of the economically active workforce. Many large enterprises were formerly in state ownership, and are highly unionized. The unions are less strong in small and medium-sized enterprises and in private sector services.

The reputation of Austrian trade unions since 1945 has been one of a moderate and disciplined reformism, with the ÖGB cooperating with government in the pursuit of policies of balanced growth. Austria's social partnership system sets the context for management-union relations. The social partnership is a phrase used to depict the informal consensus of employers, unions, agriculture and government surrounding the formulation of economic and social policy.

As part of the system of social partnership a parallel structure of Chambers of Labour exists alongside the unions. The Chambers of Labour (AK), the Chambers of Economy (WK – the equivalent of the Chambers of Labour on the employers' side), the Federation of Austrian Industry, and the ÖGB constitute the main social partners in the Austrian system. Chambers of Labour are established by law and funded by compulsory contributions from the wages and salaries of employees. There is a Chamber of Labour in each of the nine Austrian provinces and an umbrella Federal Chamber of Labour (Bundesarbeiterkammer, BAK). The Chambers of Labour are involved in practically every aspect of Austrian daily life, and their main role is to serve the interests of employees at both provincial and federal level. The Chambers carry out a wide range of functions including advice on employment, legislation, housing, urban policies, education, transport, health, and the provision of training, cultural activities, statistical and technical information, health and safety, etc. They provide assistance in legal proceedings, dealing with 10,000 cases per annum. All proposals for legislation at local, provincial and federal level must be submitted to the Chambers of Labour for expert appraisal before being considered by the appropriate legislature. In addition, the Chambers of Labour play an important role in nominating representatives on to a wide range of public bodies. While the Chambers' existence is predicated on representing the interests of the whole working population of Austria, they work very closely with the trade unions. The relationship is broadly complementary, with the Chambers structured regionally while the unions are organized sectorally and the Federal Chamber of Labour acts as a "think tank" for the ÖGB. The unions have sole responsibility for collective bargaining. However, as the Chambers provide many member services performed by unions in other countries, this has limited that element of the unions' value to members. The role of the Chambers has been questioned on the political right, and the ÖVP/FPÖ coalition government has proposed reducing the dues payable to the Chambers, in an effort to reduce their activities.

Elections to the general assemblies of the Chambers of Labour are held every five years and are contested by the political factions. The leadership and administration of the BAK and provincial Chambers of Labour are traditionally dominated by supporters of the Social Democrats (SPÖ). In the Spring of 2000, the faction linked to the SPÖ won 57.5% of the vote, while that linked to the conservative ÖVP got 26.2% (but the majority in the western provinces of Vorarlberg and Tirol). The faction allied to the FPÖ got under 10% of the vote. In contrast, in parallel elections to the employers' representative bodies, the Chambers of Economy, the ÖVP remained the leading force, with two-thirds of the vote, while the FPÖ affiliate took 19.6% and the SPÖ under 10%.

More than 95% of private sector employees are covered by collective agreements, which are nearly always negotiated at national sectoral level, between the appropriate ÖGB affiliate and its opposite number employer association. Traditionally the agreements for blue-collar and white-collar workers in the metalworking sector set the pattern for industry as a whole and are the first to be negotiated in each pay round. There are some 400 collective agreements, many of them applying to a narrow occupational field. Collective bargaining agreements are signed by the ÖGB with the employer organizations and are governed by law. When a wage agreement is negotiated between unions and employers it is applied to the whole industry whether the workers are organized or not. By law the right to engage in collective bargaining is reserved to the unions, but in companies with well established works councils agreements may in practice be supplemented by informal secondary negotiations at the company level. In the public sector the unions negotiate with government officials and settlements are legislated for by Parliament.

A paradox of Austrian legislation is that there is no law that explicitly permits strikes, although the right to strike is assumed. In practice strikes are most uncommon, and for two consecutive years in 1998–99 there were no strikes at all. "Staff meetings" are employed as a way of temporarily withdrawing labour as a warning, but industrial peace is prevalent. The last really serious strike wave was in 1965.

Following their major victory in the elections of November 2002, the centre-right ÖVP formed a coalition with the aggressively anti-union party, the FPÖ. Chancellor Wolfgang Schüssel announced extremely wide-ranging plans to dismantle large parts of the existing welfare state, and to privatize sizeable elements of the economy. This occurred on top of major changes in working practices initiated by employers. Trade union "rigidities" have been widely criticized by employers. Austria has long been a "laboratory" for multi-national employers seeking to introduce new working practices. From the late 1990s, the number employed on reduced hours contracts, and the number of self-employed, have increased dramatically. The trade unions have suffered membership losses for the last ten years, and this process has continued recently at a rate of about 3% per year. Account has to be taken of the high proportion of trade union membership who are retired. These are a vociferous section of the trade union membership, and are particularly threatened by Schüssel's reforms, since pensions are strongly affected. The pension age is to be raised by three years and large cuts in actual payments are to be made. The ÖGB was not consulted and the result in May/June 2003 was the biggest outbreak of demonstrations and industrial action since the war. On June 3, around 18,000 workplaces experienced strikes and on June 17, the ÖGB was able to organize demonstrations involving around one million people. The government responded by organizing a "round table" with employers and unions to attempt to reach a compromise. However, the compromise involved only minor changes to employees' benefit and the situation remains one of tension. Many regard this as a real test for the unions.

Behind these more dramatic events, the unions have continued their tradition of broad political action and extension of services. They have built alliances with anti-globalization groups in holding meetings and demonstrations opposing GATS for example, probably having more success in this direction than many other union movements. Meanwhile, they have built their services, offering advice to workers pushed into flexible forms of work. These include services to non-members as well as members. However, this combination of broad international politics and strong day-to-day advice provision appears not be halting the membership decline. The acid test remains their confrontation with a hostile government intent on ending the old "cosy" relationship that prevailed in the long period of SPÖ-led government.

3 Trade Union Centre

Österreichischer Gewerkschaftsbund (ÖGB)
Austrian Federation of Trade Unions
Address. Postfach 155, Hohenstaufengasse 10–12, 1010 Vienna
Phone. +43 1 53 444 222
Fax. +43 1 534 44 349
E-mail. oegb@oegb.at
Website. www.oegb.at (German only)
Leadership. Friedrich (Fritz) Verzetnitsch (president)
Membership. 1,465,164
History and character. The ÖGB was formed in Vienna in 1945 as a federation of 16 occupational unions, eight regional organizations and three fractions (socialist, communist and Popular Party, the last becoming the Christian fraction in 1951). It played an active role in the post-war emergence of Austria as a democratic, neutral nation. It has emphasized policies of cooperation with government to achieve orderly growth. In the 1930s Austria experienced civil war as a result of the conflict between communism, socialism and fascism and the ÖGB has adopted a non-partisan position. However, the major political forces (Christian Democrats, Social Democrats and, formerly, the Communists) have been given a formal position as "fractions" within its structure and are represented on the National Board (Bundesvorstand), as are members of other minority groups. Fractions similarly exist within the member unions. While the ÖGB as a whole is affiliated to the ICFTU the minority Christian fraction has a parallel affiliation to the WCL. The Social Democrats have traditionally been the predominant voice within the ÖGB and many union officials have sat in Parliament for the Social Democrats. However, the pluralist nature of the federation was reflected in its cautious approach to the inclusion of Haider's Freedom Party in government in February 2000, recognizing that Haider's populist platform had some supporters within the unions. The ÖGB was critical of the diplomatic boycott mounted against Austria in 2000 by other EU member states.

ÖGB opposed the policies of the coalition at the domestic level, on issues such as pension and welfare reform. On June 28, 2000, it organized a "day of action" against government plans on these issues and there were brief work stoppages on the railways. Since 1999 unions have been under increased pressure to concede more deregulation of working practices. Other issues for the ÖGB include the call (opposed by the employers) for harmonization of the legal status of blue-collar and white-collar employees (residual differences lying in the areas of rules concerning dismissal and sick leave payment). It is campaigning for the 35-hour week (which it prefers to see won through collective bargaining rather than by law); average normal working hours under collective agreements are 38.5. The enlargement of the EU by admitting states from former Eastern Europe is a sensitive issue in Austria and the ÖGB argues that the creation of European wide norms to prevent "social dumping" by countries with lower wage and social costs must be an essential element of such enlargement. It wishes to see the development of European wide collective bargaining.

Total ÖGB membership peaked at 1.67 million in 1981 and declined only slowly in the subsequent two decades, to the 1999 level of 1.46 million. The membership is 68% male, a proportion that has remained little changed for the last two decades. Although not affected by the sharp declines that have affected trade unions in some other countries, the ÖGB is seeking to build union membership in under-represented sectors, such as part-time and "non-standard" working and in services.

The highest forum is the quadrennial national congress the delegates to which are elected by the members of the national unions affiliated to the federation in accordance with their membership strength. Between congresses the highest policy-making body is the Bundesvorstand, comprising the presidium, delegates of the unions and representatives of minority groups. Day-to-day work is done by the presidium, led by the president. There is also an audit commission elected by the national congress to monitor the financial activities of the ÖGB and adherence to congress resolutions. There are provincial and district offices throughout the country.

As a voluntary occupational association the ÖGB is financed primarily by its membership. It concludes collective bargaining agreements (its affiliated unions being empowered only to negotiate such agreements), represents the interests of its membership in the legislative sphere, and offers welfare and social insurance programmes and occupational training.

The 1995 congress decided on a plan to reduce the Austrian unions to three super-unions, for manufacturing, services and the public sector. However, little has resulted from this. Following the merger of the Metal, Miners and Energy Workers' union with the Textile, Garment and Leather Workers' union, to form Gewerkschaft Metall-Textil (Austria's biggest blue-collar union) in June 2000, there are 13 member unions. Metall-Textil and the Commercial, Clerical and Technical Employees, with about 300,000 members each, are the largest unions. The structure in practice has been fairly stable, with the last previous merger being in 1992, when the Agriculture and Forestry Workers merged with the Food, Beverage and Tobacco Workers.
International affiliatons. ICFTU, ETUC, TUAC

Christian Democratic Fraction (FCG- ÖGB)
Address. Hohenstaufengasse 10–12, Vienna 1010
Phone. +43 1 53444 210
E-mail. j.kastner@fcg.at (press office)
Website. www.fcg.at (German only)
Leadership. Fritz Neugebauer (president)
History and character. The Christian fraction of the ÖGB was formed in 1951, replacing the Popular Party fraction, which had been formed in 1945. It has fractions within each of the member unions. It is non-confessional and independent of political parties, although many officials have links with the Christian Democratic ÖVP. It is separately affiliated to the WCL.

The ÖGB Affiliated unions.

1. Gewerkschaft Bau-Holz (Construction and Woodworkers)
Address. Ebendorferstrasse 7, 1010 Vienna
Phone. +43 1 401 47 0
Fax. +43 1 401 47 258
E-mail. bau.holz@gbh.oegb.or.at
Website. www.bau-holz.at/ (German only)
Leadership. Johann Driemer (president)
Membership. 161,812

2. Gewerkschaft der Chemiearbeiter (Chemical Workers)
Address. Stumpergasse 60, 1060 Vienna
Phone. +43 1 577 15 01
Fax. +43 1 597 21 01 23
Website. www.oegb.or.at/chemie (German only)
Leadership. Wilhelm Beck (president)

3. Gewerkschaft Druck und Papier (DUP, Printing and Paper Trade Workers)
Address. Seidengasse 15–17, 1072 Vienna
Phone. +43 1 523 82 31
Fax. +43 523 82 31 28
Website. www.dup.or.at (German only)
E-mail. Djp@drupa.oegba.or.at

4. Gewerkschaft der Eisenbahner (GDE, Railway Workers)
Address. Margaretenstrasse 166, 1050 Vienna
Phone. +43 1 546 41 511
Fax. +43 1 546 41 513
E-mail. gde@eisenbahner.at
Website. www.eisenbahner.at/ (German only)
Leadership. Wilhelm Haberzettl (president)

5. Gewerkschaft der Gemeindebediensteten (GDG, Municipal Employees)
Address. Maria-Theresien Strasse 11, 1090 Vienna
Phone. +43 1 313 16 8300
E-mail. gdg@gdg.oegb.or.at
Website. www.gdg.at (German only)
Leadership. Günter Weninger (president)

6. Gewerkschaft Handel, Transport, Verkehr (HTV, Workers in Commerce and Transport)
Address. Teinfaltstrasse 7, 1010 Vienna
Phone. +43 1 534 54 -0
Fax. +43 1 534 54 325
E-mail. htv@htv.oegb.or.at
Website. www.htv.or.at (German only)
Leadership. Peter Schneider

7. Gewerkschaft Hotel, Gastgewerbe, Personlicher Dienst (HGPD, Hotel, Restaurant and Personal Services)
Address. Hohenstaufengasse 10, 1013 Vienna
Phone. +43 1 534 44 501
Fax. +43 1 534 44 505
E-mail. hgpd@hgpd.oegb.or.at
Website. www.oegb.or.at/gewerkschaften/hgpd (German only)
Leadership. Rudolf Kaske (president)
Membership. 52,280

8. Gewerkschaft Kunst, Medien, Freie Berufe (KMFB, Artists, Media and Freelance Workers)
Address. Maria Theresien-Strasse 11, A-1090 Vienna
Phone. +43 1 31316 83800
Fax. +43 1 313 16 7700
E-mail. sekretariat@kmsfb.at
Website. www.kmsfb.at/ (German only)
Leadership. Peter Paul Skrepek (president)
Membership. 16,000

9. Gewerkschaft Agrar, Nahrung, Genuss (ANG, Agricultural, Food, Beverage and Tobacco Workers)
Address. Plösslgasse 15, 1040 Vienna
Phone. +43 1 501 46
E-mail. and@ang.at
Website. www.ang.at (German only)
Leadership. Rainer Wimmer (president)

10. Gewerkschaft Metall-Textil (Metalworkers and Textiles)
Address. Plösslgasse 15, 1040 Vienna
Phone. +43 1 501 46 0

Fax. +43 1 50146 13300
Email. metaller@metaller.at
Website. www.oegb.or.at.gmbe (German only)
Leadership. Rudolf Nürnberger (president)
Membership. 300,000
History and character. Metall-Textil was formed in June 2000 by the merger of Metall-Bergbau-Energie (Metalworkers, Mining and Energy) with Textil-Bekleidung-Leder (Textiles, Garment and Leather-workers).

11. Gewerkschaft Öffentlicher Dienst (GÖD, Public Employees)

Address. Teinfaltstrasse 7, 1010 Vienna
Phone. +43 1 53454 0
E-mail. goed@goed.at
Website. www.goed.at (German only)
Leadership. Fritz Neugebauer (president)
Membership. 230,000

12. Gewerkschaft der Post und Fernmeldebedien-steten (Postal and Telegraph Workers)

Address. Biberstrasse 5, PF 343, 1010 Vienna
Leadership. Hans-Georg Dörfler (president), Rudolf Randus (national secretary)
Membership. 78,436

13. Gewerkschaft der Privatangestellten (GPA, Commercial, Clerical and Technical Employees)

Address. Deutschmeisterplatz 2, A-1013 Vienna.
Phone. +43 1 313 930
Fax. +43 1 313 93 566
E-mail. gpa@gpa.at
Website. www.gpa.at (German only)
Leadership. Hans Sallmutter (president)
Membership. 300,000
History and character. This is Austria's biggest white-collar union, covering all private sector white-collar employees.

Azerbaijan

Capital: Baku
Population: 7.87 m. (2004 est.)

1 Political and Economic Background

The Azerbaijan Republic declared independence from the USSR in 1991. Heydar Aliyev, a former KGB general, assumed power amid civil strife in 1993. His re-election in 1998 was marked by ballot-rigging. In August 2003 President Aliyev's son, Ilham Aliyev, was named Prime Minister by presidential decree. Two weeks before the presidential elections of October 2003 President Aliyev withdrew his candidacy in favour of his son, and Ilham Aliyev went on to win the election, being credited with 76.84% of the vote. Six hundred people, including numerous prominent opposition figures, were detained after protests against the conduct of the election. Aliyev's New Azerbaijan Party (YAP) dominates the legislature. Azerbaijan's political progress since independence has been held back by a still unresolved territorial conflict with Armenia over the Armenian-populated enclave of Nagorno-Karabakh (although a cease fire since 1994 has generally held) and bitter political factionalism.

Azerbaijan is a producer of oil, cotton and natural gas, with oil and gas providing 90% of export revenues. It has major oil reserves which remain to be properly exploited although production has been increasing steadily since the mid-1990s after a downturn in the immediate post-Soviet period. The private sector comprises mainly small-scale enterprises, and most employees in the formal sector work for larger enterprises, which remain in state hands. However, as a condition of further IMF credits, plans to begin privatization of large enterprises were announced in August 2000. In 2003, 32.3% of the total employment was in the state sector, compared to 67.5% in 1991 and 46.2% in 1998. Output remains far below Soviet levels and corruption and patronage are considered major obstacles to economic progress. Unemployment is officially negligible but is estimated at 15-20%.

GDP (purchasing power parity) $26.5bn. (2003 est.); GDP per capita (purchasing power parity) $3,400 (2003 est.).

2 Trade Unionism

The 1994 Trade Union Act provides for the right to form unions and for these to bargain collectively. Azerbaijan ratified ILO Conventions No. 87 (Freedom of Association and Protection of the Right to Organize, 1948) and No. 98 (Right to Organize and Collective Bargaining, 1949) in 1992. However, trade unions have remained closely controlled by the government. The main unions are constructed on the Soviet system and affiliated to the Azerbaijan Trade Unions Confederation. In the critical energy sector, membership of the Union of Oil and Gas Industry Workers' Union is mandatory for the 60,000 employees of the state oil company; meanwhile foreign-owned oil companies have prevented union organizing activities, the government being able to grant exemptions from national labour laws to multinationals. Police and military personnel may not join unions. Unions are prohibited from engaging in political activity.

Although a 1996 law provides for collective bargaining in state enterprises this has not developed. The labour code imposes restrictions on the right to strike in broadly defined essential services and the criminal code imposes penalties in case of disruption by strike action of transport.

3 Trade Union Centre

Azerbaijan Trade Unions Confederation (ATUC)
Address. 3 Giandjlar Square, Baku
Phone. +994 12 92 66 59
Fax. +994 12 92 72 68
E-mail. ahik@azern.com
Leadership. Sattar S. Mehbaliyev (chairman)
Membership. 1,338,000 in 25 industrial trade unions.
History and character. The ATUC organizes nearly all employees in the formal economy, where the state continues to own most large enterprises, and its sectoral

branch unions benefit from automatic check-off of dues (although these are reportedly not always transferred to the unions). In November 2000 the ICFTU announced it had accepted the Confederation into affiliation. However, the US State Department Human Rights Report for 2003 noted the ATUC's continuing "close alignment" with the government and that the "overwhelming majority of labour unions still operate as they did under the Soviet system and remain tightly linked to the government". The ATUC has supported the ruling New Azerbaijan Party in parliamentary elections and ATUC chairman Sattar S. Mehbaliyev is a deputy in the National Assembly. The ATUC participates with the employers' association and government in the negotiation of a tripartite general collective agreement covering labour market, employment and economic and other policy issues; the current agreement was concluded in June 2004.

International affiliation. ICFTU. In November 2004 the ATUC also affiliated to the Moscow-based General Confederation of Trade Unions (GCTU), a grouping of centres from the successor states to the Soviet Union.

4 Other Trade Union Organization

Committee for Oil Industry Workers' Rights Protection (COIWRP)
Address. 36 Shamsi Badalbeyli str., Baku
Phone. +994 12 943 376
Fax. + 944 12 941 458
History and character. Established in 1996 to defend the rights of oil workers in all of the companies operating in Azerbaijan. In 1997, the State Oil Company (SOCAR) established the Trade Union of Oil and Gas Workers (ATU), which lacked independence.

Bahamas

Capital: Nassau
Population: 300,000 (2004 est.)

1 Political and Economic Background

The Bahamas became independent from the United Kingdom in 1973. From 1967 until 1992, Sir Lynden Pindling's populist Progressive Liberal Party (PLP) formed the government, deriving its main support from the black community. The 1992 general election ended the PLP's run of five consecutive victories and put in power the conservative Free National Movement (FNM) with Hubert Ingraham as Prime Minister. The FNM was re-elected in 1997 but the PLP, now led by Perry Christie, returned to power at the general election in May 2002.

Tourism is the mainstay of the economy, employing half the workforce and generating 60 per cent of GDP. There is also offshore banking and finance. Industry is relatively undeveloped. Despite some unemployment (around 7 per cent) and slow recent economic growth, the general standard of living remains one of the highest in the Caribbean. There is now relatively little difference in economic approach between the FNM and PLP, the PLP having largely abandoned its one-time hostility to foreign investors and advocacy of Bahamian self-reliance, while retaining its view that the government should have an active role in economic development.

GDP (purchasing power parity) $5.05bn. (2003 est.); GDP per capita (purchasing power parity) $16,700 (2003 est.).

2 Trade Unionism

Trade unions developed after World War II. The first union centre was the Bahamas Federation of Labour, founded in 1942, but this ceased to function as a federation in 1969. The principal trade union centre is now known as the Commonwealth of the Bahamas Trade Union Congress. The Bahamas ratified ILO Convention No.98 (Right to Organize and Collective Bargaining, 1949) in 1976 and Convention No.87 (Freedom of Association and Protection of the Right to Organize, 1948) in 2001. Under domestic law all private sector and most public sector workers (with the exception of police, defence, fire brigade and prison officers) may join unions. About one-quarter of the work force is unionized and the hotel sector is highly organized.

Collective bargaining is widely practiced. Strikes must be approved by a majority vote of the work force, supervised by the Department of Labour. In 1996, with union support, the Industrial Relations Act was amended to set up an Industrial Tribunal. Disputes may be referred to this for a binding decision.

3 Trade Union Centres

Commonwealth of the Bahamas Trade Union Congress (CBTUC)
Address. 3 Warwick Street, PO Box CB 10992, Nassau, New Providence
Phone. +1 242 394 7400
Fax. +1 242 394 7401
E-mail. tuc@bahamas.net.bs
Leadership. Obie Ferguson Jr. (president); Borris Delancy (secretary general)
History and character. The Commonwealth of the Bahamas Trade Union Congress was established in its present form in 1976. In 1996 it played a leading role in discussions leading to adoption of the Industrial Relations (Amendment) Act and the creation of the Industrial Tribunal. In 1998 it was awarded a medal struck by the government for service to the community.
International affiliations. ICFTU; CTUC

National Congress of Trade Unions
Address. PO Box GT 2887, Nassau
Phone. +1 242 356 7459
Fax. +1 242 356 7457
Leadership. Kingsley Black (general secretary)
International affiliation. CTUC

Bahrain

Capital: Manama
Population: 678,000 (2004 est., includes 235,000 non-nationals)

1 Political and Economic Background

Bahrain became fully independent in 1971 having previously been a British protected state. It is an hereditary emirate, in which the al-Khalifa family has ruled since the 18th Century. The National Assembly was dissolved in 1975, but following the accession of Sheikh Hamad in 1999 a new National Charter was adopted by referendum in February 2001 proposing the creating of a bicameral parliament with an elective lower house (including female suffrage) and creation of a constitutional monarchy. Numerous political prisoners were released and legislative elections in October 2002 resulted in the election of a legislature dominated by independents and moderate Sunni Islamists. However, the polls were boycotted by many Shias (the majority population), believing the legislature had no real power to limit the Sunni ruling family and dominant elite. There was unrest in 1994–96 among the Shia population. Political parties remain prohibited though "societies" carry out some of the functions of parties.

Bahrain was the first Arab oil producer but its wells are small. Despite efforts at diversification into light manufacturing and services, its economy still largely depends upon petroleum production and processing, which account for 60% of government revenues and 30% of GDP. The oil sector is government-controlled. A large number of multi-national firms with business in the Gulf have Bahrain as a base. Two-thirds of the workforce is foreign (mainly manual labourers from the Indian subcontinent), though foreigners comprise only a third of the total population. Government policy is to displace as many foreigners as possible with nationals, but this has had little impact in view of the welfare system for nationals and the generally lower wages paid to non-nationals.

GDP (purchasing power parity) $11.29bn. (2003 est.); GDP per capita (purchasing power parity) $16,900 (2003 est.).

2 Trade Unionism

Bahrain has ratified neither ILO Convention No. 87 (Freedom of Association and Protection of the Right to Organize, 1948) nor Convention No. 98 (Right to Organize and Collective Bargaining, 1949).

Until recently independent trade unionism was not permitted in Bahrain. A system of Joint Labour-Management Committees (JLCs), established by ministerial decree, provided a form of employee representation in larger enterprises. By 2002 some 20 JLCs had been set up in large companies. The Ministry of Interior was empowered to exclude worker candidates considered a threat to national security. The worker representatives on the JLCs elected the 11 members of the General Committee of Bahrain Workers (GCBW), set up in 1983, which had a coordinating role. The Labour Ministry closely supervised its work. The system covered approximately 70% of the indigenous work force, but a lesser proportion of foreign workers.

On Sept. 24, 2002, the King promulgated a new trade union law that grants workers for the first time the right to form and join unions. The Workers' Trade Union Law established a union federation, the General Federation of Workers' Trade Unions in Bahrain (GFWTUB), that has replaced the GCBW. The new law also recognises the right to strike (with significant restrictions for a number of services deemed "essential"). Although the new law on trade unions falls short of ILO standards in a number of important respects it is nonetheless widely regarded as a genuinely progressive step. The first union formed under the new law appeared on October 8 in the petrochemicals sector.

While the prior system of JLCs provided a forum for the discussion of pay and conditions, there was no system of collective bargaining. The government generally set public sector rates administratively and these provided benchmarks for the private sector. There was no formal prohibition on the right to strike, although acts considered detrimental to employee-employer relationships or the economic condition of the country were banned by the 1974 Security Act. There were no major strikes in recent years, but occasional walkouts and other protests did occur.

The WFTU records the Syrian-based Bahrain Workers' Union (BWU) as their affiliate, but this does not appear to have any real presence in Bahrain. The GFWTUB has as yet no international affiliation.

A variety of abuses of foreign workers are reported. Many are present illegally, no longer working for their sponsoring employers, and are vulnerable to late or non-payment of wages and in some cases continue to pay fees to their original sponsor. In 1998, 38,000 illegal workers participated in a government amnesty whereby they could legalize their status or leave the country without punishment. Domestic servants are not protected by the labour laws.

3 Trade Union Centres

General Federation of Workers Trade Unions in Bahrain (GFWTUB),
International affiliations. None

Bahrain Workers' Union
Address. PO Box 12660, Damascus, Syria
Phone. +963 11 459544
International affiliations. WFTU.

Bangladesh

Capital: Dhaka
Population: 141.3 m. (2004 est.)

1 Political and Economic Background

Bangladesh (formerly East Pakistan) broke away from Pakistan in 1971, with the assistance of the Indian

Army, under the leadership of Sheikh Mujibur Rahman and his Awami (People's) League. Bangladesh's history since then has been characterized by the inability of successive governments to build a democratic consensus, military interventions in government, and periods of virtual paralysis when opposition parties have made effective administration of the country impossible.

At elections in June 1996 the Awami League returned to power for the first time since the assassination of its leader, Sheikh Mujib, in a military coup in 1975. However, the government of the League's leader, Prime Minister Sheikh Hasina Wazed, then faced a sustained campaign of strikes and demonstrations led by the major opposition party, the Bangladesh Nationalist Party (BNP), which from mid-1999 boycotted parliament. The BNP had itself previously faced a similar campaign of protests, strikes and boycotts by the Awami League and its allies when in office 1990–96, and this pattern was repeated when the BNP regained power in the October 2001 elections. Sheikh Hasina is the daughter of Sheikh Mujib, while the leader of the BNP (and currently Prime Minister of Bangladesh) is Begum Khaleda Zia Rahman, the widow of Gen. Ziaur Rahman, who had come to power as a result of the overthrow and death of Sheikh Mujib.

Bangladesh's economy is primarily based on subsistence agriculture, with the cultivation of rice the most important activity. Bangladesh is routinely subject to catastrophic cyclones and floods. The country is densely populated and struggles to generate jobs for a population expanding by 3 million per annum: there is high unemployment and under-employment. Some 65 per cent of the workforce are engaged in agriculture and only 10 per cent in manufacturing and industry, with the jute industry as the largest single industrial source of employment. State-owned enterprises are considered highly inefficient but governments have commonly backed down from implementing reforms in the face of entrenched and highly politicized resistance. There is a heavy reliance on international aid.

GDP (purchasing power parity) $259bn. (2003 est.); GDP per capita (purchasing power parity) $1,900 (2003 est.).

2 Trade Unionism

Pakistan ratified ILO Convention No. 87 (Freedom of Association and Protection of the Right to Organize, 1948) in 1951 and Convention No. 98 (Right to Organize and Collective Bargaining, 1949) in 1952; Bangladesh in turn ratified both Conventions in June 1972. The rights embodied in these conventions have been almost continuously threatened or weakened by contradictory national legislation, and periodic martial law. However, in practice a degree of union activity has persisted throughout the last 50 years regardless of the edicts of military and other governments, often serving as a vehicle for political dissent.

Trade union activity in Bangladesh has a long and at times bloody history, dating back to a revolt by tea plantation workers in 1920 (when the country was part of British-ruled India) and the formation in that year of the All-India Trade Union Congress. The East Pakistan Trade Union Federation was formed following the creation of Pakistan in 1947, and split into five factions shortly before the achievement of independence by Bangladesh in 1971.

There is no accepted national trade union centre, and there has been considerable fluidity and confusion in respect of the status of trade union confederations. The ICFTU-APRO Committee on Affiliation Questions found in April 1987 that there were at that time "17 or more trade union centres, and also 10 labour fronts" linked to political parties, and that trade union leaders often seemed to "shift their loyalties for various considerations". This situation has not changed and there is a proliferation of centres whose status is doubtful. The ICFTU itself says it has no less than five affiliates in Bangladesh: the Bangladesh Jatio Sramik League (BJSL), the Bangladesh Jatiyatabadi Sramik Dal (BJSD), the Jatiya Sramik Party (JSP), the Bangladesh Free Trade Union Congress (BFTUC) and the Jatio Sramik League (JSL). The ICFTU reported in February 2000 that these would henceforth function as one organization, the Bangladesh Confederation of Trade Unions (BCTU), with 900,000 members, although they appear to have retained separate identities. The WCL records one affiliate, the Bangladesh Sanjunkta Sramik Federation (BSSF). The WFTU claims to have six affiliates. Some of the confederations associate for campaigning purposes in the umbrella SKOP.

Union density in Bangladesh is low relative to the size of the total labour force, although unions are strongly entrenched in some parts of the formal economy, especially state-owned enterprises. In 1989 there were 3,905 unions with a total membership of 1,175,878 putting unionization at only 3 per cent. This low rate was not improved by government repression: in 1988–89 the registration of no less than 80 unions was cancelled for violations of the Industrial Relations Ordinance. Ten years later, the ICFTU reported that about 1.8 million of the country's 5 million workers in the formal sector belonged to unions, out of a total work force of approximately 58 million. The ICFTU noted, however, that "many so-called 'unions' are not controlled by workers but are directed by political factions or criminal elements, a situation that has been tolerated by successive governments". Partly as a result, there are nowadays a total of 25 registered national trade union centres in Bangladesh and approximately 5,450 trade unions. There are also a number of unregistered national centres. Only 15% of unions are in any case affiliated to one of the 25 registered centres.

Unions are highly politicized. Virtually all federations are associated with political parties, and it is normal for a party to have a union wing. Political relationships can advance or retard a federation's cause. The relationship between the various unions is often hostile and there are frequently violent clashes between supporters of different unions.

General strikes are not uncommon, and are usually called on political rather than industrial grounds.

Strikes indeed were a major component of the opposition parties' resistance to the rule of Khaleda Zia, who was Prime Minister after the overthrow of Ershad in 1990 until elections in 1996. This pattern continued in the period of Awami League government from 1996. A strike called by Khaleda Zia's Bangladesh Nationalist Party (BNP) and its allies in mid-February 2000 was the 55th national stoppage since 1996 in a campaign aimed at toppling the government of Prime Minister Sheikh Hasina. Strikes have continued to be a feature of opposition since the change of government in 2001.

There are many restrictions on union activities. Thirty per cent of workers in any workplace must belong to a union before it can be registered, and a union can be wound up if membership falls below this level. Registration of a union is mandatory, but the government may refuse registration on a variety of grounds and such refusals do occur. Unions cannot be registered on a nationwide basis. The ICFTU says that: "would-be unionists are forbidden to engage in many activities prior to registration, and legally are not protected from employer retaliation during this period. Employers usually discourage registration or any union activity, sometimes with violence or working in collaboration with local police. Requests for registration frequently result in the names of union members being given to the employers concerned, who immediately dismiss them. In consequence, trade unions are rare and there is little collective bargaining." A particular problem is reported in the garment sector, where the ICFTU believes, the government has actively worked with employers to prevent unions from being set up.

In the public sector, only those employed on the railways and in posts and telecommunications may legally form unions. Teachers, nurses, supervisory staff, and workers in export processing zones may not form unions, and although unregistered unions exist they cannot legally bargain collectively. The Registrar of Trade Unions has wide powers to investigate the internal affairs of unions and cancel registrations.

Under the 1980 Bangladesh Export Processing Zones Authority Act, workers in the zones, where 90,000 are employed (90% of them women), have not had the protection of the labour laws and trade unions have not been permitted to exist. The Act suspended labour laws in the EPZs as a strategy to attract foreign investment. The government in 1992 said it would end restrictions on the formation of unions in the zones by 1997, and apply the labour law in full by 2000, but this did not happen. However, under pressure from US trade negotiators, the government accepted the creation of Workers' Welfare Committees in 2001. It further pledged to introduce full freedom of association in the EPZs from January 2004, following a threat to cancel US GSP trade preferences, but by mid-2004 this pledge had not been honoured and the international textile union ITGLWF had lodged a complaint with the ILO.

The support of 75% of the workforce is needed to make a strike legal. Workers in broadly defined essential services are prohibited from striking. Strikes lasting more than 30 days may be banned by the government and referred to the labour court for adjudication. Special Powers legislation enables the authorities to detain union activists without charge and under a Public Safety Act effective Feb. 15, 2000, jail terms of up to 14 years' hard labour may be imposed for crimes including obstruction and damaging property during strike action. In 2003 police fired on a workers' demonstration in the garment sector, killing one person. The previous day their advocate/leader had been arrested on his way to join negotiations.

In the public sector, wages and conditions are generally set by government-appointed commissions. In the private sector organized collective bargaining is uncommon. There is a Labour Court but according to the ICFTU it has a backlog of cases and "there are indications that many of its decisions have been the result of corrupt intervention by employers". Bangladesh has been regularly criticized by the ILO for non-observance of the conventions. In February 1998 the government and the union umbrella SKOP signed an agreement that included a commitment to implementation of the conventions.

3 Trade Union Centres

Bangladesh Free Trade Union Congress (BFTUC)
Address. Section 6, Block A, Lane 1, House 19, Mirpur, Dhaka-1216
Phone. +880 2 801 7001
Fax. +880 2 801 5919
E-mail. bftuc@dhaka.agni.com
Leadership. M.S. Alom Mendu Mia (president); Mamunur Rashid Chowdhury (general secretary); A.R. Chowdhury Repon (international secretary)
Membership. 175,000
History and character. The BFTUC was established in 1983 by national unions and industrial federations that believed in the concept of free, independent, non-partisan and democratic trade unionism. It continues to emphasize those values. The BFTUC has 35 affiliated national industrial federations and unions.

The BFTUC describes its objectives as including providing support to the formation of unions among unorganized workers, advancing women's equality, providing education, training and welfare programmes, and offering self-employment training and income generating and cooperative activities for unemployed workers and BFTUC members.

The BFTUC has been campaigning to organize women in the informal sector and has 55,000 women members. Its Workers' Cooperative programme and self-employment training programme, started in 1998, provide an opportunity for unemployed members and women to be self-reliant with BFTUC assistance. The BFTUC child labour elimination programme gives the opportunity to 200 children per year working in hazardous occupations to receive non-formal education and training instead of working.
International affiliation. ICFTU

Bangladesh Ganotantrik Sramik Federation
Address. 3rd floor, 31 F, Topkhana Road, Dhaka
International affiliation. WFTU

Bangladesh Jatio Sramik League (BJSL)
Address. GPO Box 2730, Dhaka
Phone. +880 2-9554499
History and character. The Bangladesh Jatio Sramik League was founded in 1969, its first conference being opened by Sheikh Mujibur Rahman. It played an active role in the 1971 war for independence, training 40,000 Sramik League fighters. In 1974 the government declared a state of emergency, banning strikes and restricting trade union activities. In 1975 the rival centres – Bangladesh Trade Union Kendra (BTUK) and the Bangladesh Sanjukta Sramik Federation (BSSF) – were dissolved by the government of Sheikh Mujibur. The BJSL became the only recognized trade union centre in the country (and the Bangladesh Krishak Sramik Awami League became the only legal political party); many thousands of trade unionists belonging to anti-government groups were imprisoned. In 1975 a new government dissolved all national trade union centres, although grass-roots trade unionism continued. After 1978, a breakaway group from the BJSL formed an organization affiliated to the WFTU, but the main body affirms its belief in a free and democratic trade union movement.

In 1999, ten BJSL members, including its president Nashu Miah, were arrested in connection with a dispute over nonpayment of wages at a jute mill. They remained in prison for four months until the courts ordered their release.
International affiliation. ICFTU

Bangladesh Jatyatabadi Sramik Dal
Address. 28/1 Naya Paltan 4th Floor, Vip Road, Dhaka 1000
Phone. +880 2418214
Fax. +880 2 869723
E-mail. bils@agni.com
International affiliation. ICFTU

Bangladesh Jatyo Sramik Jote
Address. 35-36 Banga Bandhu Avenue, Dhaka 1000
Fax. +880 2 8622 719
International affiliation. WFTU

Bangladesh Labour Federation
Address. 24-25, Dilkusha Commercial Area, floor 5, Sadharan Bima Sadan - G.P.O. Box 2514, Dhaka 1000
Phone. +880 2 9560104
Fax. +880 2 7171335
E-mail. mdhk@bijoy.net
International affiliation. ICFTU

Bangladesh Mukto Sramik Federation
Address. G.P.O Box No. 2730, Dhaka
Phone. +880 2 9135648
Fax. +880 2 8111650
E-mail. mojiburbhuiyan@hotmail.com
International affiliation. ICFTU

Bangladesh Sanjunkta Sramic Federation (BSSF)
Address. 23/2 Topkhana Road (Ground Floor), Dhaka 1000
Phone. +880 2 9554657
Fax. +880 2 81 6152
E-mail. bssf@citechno.net
Leadership. Mukhlesur Rahman (president)
International affiliation. WCL

Bangladesh Trade Union Kendra
Address. 23/2 Topkhana Road, 3rd floor, Dhaka 1000
Fax. +880 2 837464
International affiliation. WFTU

Jatio Sramik Federation
Address. 3rd floor, 31 F, Topkhana Road, Dhaka
Fax. +880 2 955 7975
International affiliation. WFTU

Jatyo Sramik League
Address. 23 Road, Banga Bandhu Av, 3rd floor, Dhaka
International affiliation. WFTU

Socialist Labour Front
Address. 23/2 Topkhana Road, Dhaka
Fax. +880 2 95 94 772
International affiliation. WFTU

Barbados

Capital: Bridgetown
Population: 278,000 (2004 est.)

1 Political and Economic Background

Barbados gained independence from the United Kingdom in 1966. The country is politically stable with a two-party system. The Barbados Labour Party defeated the governing Democratic Labour Party (DLP) in elections in 1994, and was re-elected in January 1999 and May 2003. Owen Arthur has been Prime Minister since 1994.

75% of the labour force are in the services sector, including tourism and offshore finance. There is also some light manufacturing and the agricultural sector is traditionally based on sugar cane cultivation, although agriculture only employs 10% of the workforce and generates 6% of GDP. Under rigorous IMF-backed austerity measures unemployment rose to one-quarter of the workforce in the early 1990s but fell to 12% by 1998 and by 2003 was just under 11%. The government has carried out a programme of privatizing state-owned enterprises.

GDP (purchasing power parity) $4.36bn. (2003 est.); GDP per capita (purchasing power parity) $15,700 (2003 est.).

2 Trade Unionism

Following riots in 1937, the British government in 1939 passed legislation, the Trades Disputes (Arbitration and Equity) Act, legalizing the formation of trade unions.

Barbados ratified ILO Convention No. 87 (Freedom of Association and Protection of the Right to Organize, 1948) and Convention No. 98 (Right to Organize and Collective Bargaining, 1949) in 1967.

About 30 per cent of the work force are organized. The Barbados Workers' Union (BWU) includes in membership a majority of the country's trade unionists. A significant union outside the BWU is the National Union of Public Workers (NUPW), the largest public service union.

While there is no law on recognition for collective bargaining purposes, custom and practice has been for employers to give recognition when 50 per cent of employees are in a union. In the late 1990s, however, the BWU reported that some foreign-owned companies were breaking this custom. This led to strikes in 1998 against six foreign-owned companies; in five cases the companies ultimately said they would recognize the union, while in a sixth, the company said it would relocate to Trinidad and Tobago. In general trade union rights are widely respected, and the multinationals' efforts to resist unions were rejected by even the employers' organizations. Although legislation does contain potentially anti-union provisions that have been criticized by the ILO, these have never been invoked.

The government meets the social partners in the National Economic Council and other tripartite bodies.

The influence of trade unions is reflected in the fact that in a 1997 poll for Barbados's "10 national heroes", five came from the trade union movement. These included Grantley Adams, first president of the BWU and later Prime Minister, Sir Hugh Springer, first BWU general secretary and later Governor, and Sir Frank Walcott, general secretary of the BWU from 1948-91.

3 Trade Union Centre

Barbados Workers' Union (BWU)
Address. Solidarity House, Harmony Hall, PO Box 172, St. Michael, Bridgetown
Phone. +1246 426 3492
Fax. +1246 436 6496
E-mail. bwu@caribsurf.com
Website. www.bwu-bb.org
Leadership. David Giles (president general); LeRoy Trotman (general secretary).
Membership. 25,000
History and character. The BWU, a general union, was registered in October 1941, and was a direct descendant of the Barbados Progressive League formed after the 1937 disturbances. In its early years it recruited mainly from among ships' carpenters, foundry and port workers and sugar factory employees, but it absorbed a clerks' union in the 1950s and thereafter developed a significant white-collar element. Frank L. Walcott became general secretary in 1948 and held this post until 1991.

The BWU from the first participated actively in politics, its first president being Grantley Adams, the founder of the Barbados Labour Party (in 1938) and Prime Minister of Barbados from 1954–58 and of the short-lived West Indies Federation from 1958–62, while the first BWU general secretary was Sir Hugh Springer, later the Governor General of Barbados.

A split developed in the early 1960s when the union leadership broke with the Barbados Labour Party and transferred support to the more left-wing Democratic Labour Party, led by Errol Barrow (which took power in 1961 and held it continuously until 1976). Grantley Adams led a breakaway group called the Barbados Progressive Union of Workers in 1963 (although this soon folded). The BWU was recognized as the bargaining agent for a wide range of occupations in 1966.

The BWU runs a labour college (opened in 1974), which receives a government subsidy and provides training in industrial relations and union affairs, and there is also an associated BWU Cooperative Credit Union.

There are no affiliated unions. The BWU recruits members in all occupational fields, and negotiates directly with companies on behalf of the different sectors of its membership. A principal issue for the BWU currently is that of contract work, where workers who are in effect employees are put on individual contracts.

LeRoy Trotman, general secretary since 1991, is a former president of the ICFTU.
International affiliations. ICFTU; CCL;CTUC.

4 Other Trade Union Organization

National Union of Public Workers (NUPW)
Address. PO Box 174, Dalkeith House, Dalkeith Road, St. Michael, Bridgetown
Phone. +1246 426 1764
Fax. +1246 436 1795
E-mail. nupwbarbados@sunbeach.net
Leadership. Joseph E. Goddard (general secretary)
Membership. 8,000. The NUPW recruits predominantly in the public sector.
History and character. Founded in January 1944 and registered as a Trade Union in 1964; name changed in 1971 from Barbados Civil Service Association (BACSA) to National Union of Public Workers. Its political orientation is broadly social democratic. The union's objective is to ensure the complete organization of all persons employed by the government of Barbados and to bargain effectively on their behalf. The NUPW negotiates collective agreements, represents members in grievance cases, provides certain health benefits and a group medical insurance scheme, and has an educational arm (the Public Workers' Academy). It is affiliated to the CTUC, the Caribbean Congress of Labour and the global union federations UNI and PSI.

Belarus

Capital: Minsk
Population: 10.31 m. (2004 est.)

1 Political and Economic Background

Belarus is a former Soviet republic that declared its independence in August 1991. Although an integrated component of the Soviet Union prior to that time it had held a seat at the United Nations since 1945. Since July 1994, when he won the country's first presidential election campaigning on an anti-corruption and anti-privatization ticket, Alexander Lukashenko has presided over an authoritarian regime in which he has consolidated power in his own hands and a number of political opponents have disappeared. He remained in power after July 20, 1999, the date of expiry of his presidential term, under the authority of a constitutional referendum in 1996 whose legality was widely disputed. He then won the September 2001 presidential election officially with 75.62% of the vote, second place (with 15.39%) being taken by Vladimir Goncharik (Uladzimir Hancharyk), the chairman of the Federation of Trade Unions of Belarus (FPB) – although Goncharik claimed he had actually won 40% of the vote. The US and EU member states boycotted Lukashenko's inauguration on the grounds that the elections had not been free and fair.

On 17 October 2004 a further referendum was staged, and won, by Lukashenko ending the constitutional limit of two presidential terms. Elections to the House of Representatives the same day resulted in a legislature dominated by nominally independent pro-Lukashenko deputies. Only 12 of the 110 deputies were members of political parties, 8 of the 12 being from the Belarusan Communist Party (KPB), and none was from an opposition party. The conduct of the elections attracted general international condemnation. However, almost alone in former Eastern Europe, Belarus has turned its back on aspiring to join the EU and Lukashenko has been indifferent to external criticism.

During the early 1990s Belarus experienced industrial collapse, shortages of consumer goods, and hyper-inflation, and the privatization programme was beset by allegations of corruption. Lukashenko has in response largely reverted to the old command type economy, re-imposing state controls over prices (leading to shortages) and increased state regulation of the private sector, while subsidizing indebted state enterprises. The majority of workers are employed in the state industrial and agricultural sectors, with the state sector generating 75% of output. Belarus has remained close to Russia, which takes 50% of its exports, including low-quality industrial goods which would fail to find a market in the West, and supplies Belarus with energy at favourable prices. Although living standards are low and underemployment common, the economy reports solid growth (estimated by the IMF at 4.8% in 2003 and by the government at 6.8%) and there are social safety nets.

GDP (purchasing power parity) $62.56bn. (2003 est.); GDP per capita (purchasing power parity) $6,100 (2003 est.).

2 Trade Unionism

Belarus (as the Belarusian Soviet Socialist Republic) ratified ILO Conventions No. 87 (Freedom of Association and Protection of the Right to Organize, 1948) and No. 98 (Right to Organize and Collective Bargaining, 1949) in 1956.

Independent trade unionism emerged in the Belarus Free Trade Union or Free Trade Union of Belarus (SPB, sometimes referred to as the SFB), which was founded in 1991. The Belarus branch of the former Soviet All-Union Central Council of Trade Unions, the official trade union structure, was re-constituted as the Federation of Trade Unions of Belarus (FPB). According to the FPB it represents 4.4 million members (including pensioners) and 92% of the work force is organized. The official unions retained a strong position through their control of areas of social welfare, such as pensions, and dominated centralized bargaining. As with other re-organized Soviet unions it generally accommodated to the new regime, but the decline of living standards led to increasing tensions. In October 1999 the Ministry of Justice refused to register the Belarusian Independent Association of Industrial Trade Unions (BIAITU), comprising three official unions with 340,000 members, that had taken positions critical of the government. The Minsk city authorities subsequently refused to allow a demonstration against the Justice Ministry's ruling.

Under the Constitution all workers, except security and military personnel, may join and form unions of their own choosing, engage in collective bargaining and strike. However, the membership of independent unions is small and activists are subject to considerable harassment and intimidation. Union members have been arrested for activities including distributing literature and holding unauthorized meetings, refused permission to enter work places and forced out of their jobs. Enterprises have refused to recognize and negotiate with the independent unions.

Strikes are prohibited in areas where work stoppages endanger "life and health". An order by the Cabinet of Ministers of March 28, 1995, defined these areas to include transport, radio and television, telecommunications, the petroleum and chemical industries and the food industry. A strike on the Minsk metro in August 1995 led to police raids on the offices of the SPB and the associated Belarusian Congress of Democratic Trade Unions (BKDP). Registration of the SPB (as also the local organization of Minsk metro workers) was suspended by a presidential decree (No. 336) of Aug. 21, 1995 preventing it from functioning; its offices in enterprises were closed, its bank account frozen and payroll deductions to pay union dues ended. The FPB was given the task of participating in drawing up new trade union legislation. In September 1995, SPB officials were reportedly prevented from leaving the country to meet with representatives of the Polish union Solidarity.

Under a decree signed by Lukashenko in January 1999 all trade unions, as well as organizations such as political parties, were subject to compulsory re-registration, with the threat of dissolution for those organizations not approved. In July 1999 Lukashenko signed a decree which sought to move workers to individual rather than collective contacts. The FPB and independent unions joined in staging a demonstration against this decree and falling living standards on Sept. 30, 1999. In 2000 there was extensive interference by the government in the affairs of the unions, including elections.

FPB leader Vladimir Goncharik stepped down in

2001, the union having been subjected to government pressure after Goncharik said he would run in the September 2001 presidential elections. Former vice-president of the union Frantz Vitko was elected leader of the FPB in late 2001. In 2001 the authorities froze the bank accounts of the FPB and banned the established check-off system of deducting union contributions from salaries. When Vitko resigned under the financial pressures that ensued Leonid Kozik, a former official of the office of President Lukashenko, was elected in his place. With a pro-government union leader installed the check-off ban was promptly withdrawn.

The FPB elections have been widely criticised and formed the substance of a complaint by FPB member unions and the ICFTU to the ILO Freedom of Association Committee in 2003. In June 2003 these and various other allegations were presented before the Standards Committee of the International Labour Conference, resulting in the issuing of a "special paragraph" on Belarus. In November the Belarusian authorities informed the ILO that the ILO's technical assistance programmes in Belarus would not be permitted to continue. Later that month the Governing Body of the ILO took the rare measure of approving a Commission of Inquiry on Belarus to investigate the ongoing pattern of serious violations of freedom of association in the country; it has since reported.

3 Trade Union Centres

Belarusian Congress of Democratic Trade Unions
Address Partizansky prospect, Building 12A, room 7, BY - 220070 Minsk
Phone. +375 2-493179
Fax. +375 2-493179
E-mail kanakh@mail.ru
Membership. 15,000 in 4 affiliates
International affiliation. ICFTU

Belarus Free Trade Union (SPB)
Address. 24 Zakharova Street, Minsk 220030
Phone. +375 17 284 31 82
Fax. +375 17 284 59 94
E-mail. spb@user.unibel.by
Leadership. Gennady Bykov (president)
History and character. Founded in 1991, but its registration was suspended by presidential decree in August 1995 for two years. It has faced continuing harassment and interference by the government since that time including efforts to install pro-government officials in leadership positions in its affiliates.

Federation of Trade Unions of Belarus (FPB/FTUB)
Fax. + 375 17 210 43 37
Leadership. Leonid Kozik (president)
History and Character. The descendant of the Soviet era official unions, the FPB has come into increasing conflict with the Lukashenko government over falling living standards and interference in union affairs. In January 2001 the Justice Ministry warned the FPB that it was not allowed to put forward its leader, V. Goncharik, as a candidate in the national presidential elections due in 2001. He went on to take an official 15.39% of the vote, and claimed he had actually won 40%, sufficient to have forced a run-off election. The current leader, Leonid Kozik, installed in July 2002, previously worked closely with the authorities, in the office of President Lukashenko.
International affiliation. WFTU; GCTU

Belgium

Capital: Brussels
Population: 10.35 m. (2004 est.)

1 Political and Economic Background

Belgium is a constitutional monarchy and a member of the European Union. A division exists between the majority Flemish (Dutch)-speaking population of the north (Flanders) and the (generally poorer) French-speaking south (Wallonia), with Brussels a bilingual island within Flanders; there is a small German-speaking community in the east.

A process of regionalization that started in 1970 and was marked by considerable tension culminated in the adoption of a new federal structure in 1993. Under this Belgium became a federation of three regions, Flanders, Wallonia and Brussels, each with its own government and legislature, and three communities (Flemish, French and German) for educational and cultural purposes. The regions have considerable powers in the social and economic fields.

At federal level the national divisions are reflected in the composition of the legislature with the Flemish and Walloon communities having their separate parties for each ideological stream. The (Flemish) Christian People's Party (CVP) has generally been the strongest single party in recent decades, providing the Prime Minister in coalition governments which have included coalitions with the Liberals in 1981–88, the Socialists and the People's Union (VU) in 1988–91 and the Socialists in 1992–99. Following elections in June 1999, however, the CVP went into opposition for the first time since 1958, with a coalition government being formed comprising the Flemish and Walloon Socialist, Liberal and Green parties, with the Prime Minister, Guy Verhofstadt, coming from the Flemish Liberals (VLD). Following elections in May 2003 Verhofstadt arranged a further coalition between the Socialist and Liberal parties, this time without the Greens. At regional level, the 2004 elections resulted in the Christian Democrats regaining their position as the leading party in the Flemish region, going on to form a coalition government that excluded the far-right Flemish Bloc, which had emerged as the second strongest group in the Flemish parliament. In Wallonia the Socialists came first and head the coalition.

Belgium has a generally prosperous economy based on services and a wide range of industries, and Brussels is the leading administrative centre for the institutions of the European Union. However, linguistic division is exacerbated by the fact that the north in general is more prosperous and has a more modern entrepreneurial and technology-based economy. During the 1980s, the old industrial sectors such as coal mining and iron and steel, which were heavily concentrated in Wallonia, suffered a severe decline and this contributed to the atmosphere of crisis that led to the constitutional re-basing of the country as a looser federation. Unemployment is a continuing problem (over 8% in 2003) and Belgium also has a lower rate of participation in the work force than neighbours such as the Netherlands and Germany, let alone the US and Japan. This reflects factors such as early retirement and Belgium's regime of high taxes and generous social provision; the incoming Liberal-led government in 1999 introduced measures to reduce employers' social contributions to try to assist job creation.

GDP (purchasing power parity) $299.1bn. (2003 est.); GDP per capita (purchasing power parity) $29,100 (2003 est.).

2 Trade Unionism

Belgium ratified ILO Convention No. 87 (Freedom of Association and Protection of the Right to Organize, 1948) in 1951 and Convention No. 98 (Right to Organize and Collective Bargaining, 1949) in 1953.

Trade unions in Belgium have a long history, with origins in the guilds of craftsmen that survived through the industrial revolution and provided a basis for the development of nineteenth-century craft unionism. They have traditionally been divided on linguistic, political and religious grounds. The two principal centres (as they have been since the end of World War II) are the Confederation of Christian Unions (CSC/ACV) and the (socialist) General Federation of Belgian Labour (FGTB/ABVV). Reflecting the balance of forces in political life, in Belgium it is the Christian rather than the socialist centre that has traditionally been the larger and the CSC/ACV, which has about 1.6 million members, has long been the WCL's leading affiliate in western Europe. The FGTB/ABVV has a membership of something over one million. For many years these two trade union centres (accounting for about 90 per cent of union members) kept apart, a habit reinforced by their political links (the CSC/ACV with the Christian Democrats, the FGTB with the Socialists) and poor personal relations between their leaders, but relations have improved since the late 1980s. The third significant centre is the General Confederation of Liberal Trade Unions of Belgium (CGSLB/ACLVB), which has 220,000 members.

The relative strength of the main centres has not greatly changed in recent times. A measure of comparative strength is provided by the social elections that took place in enterprises in May 2000 for works councils (conseils d'enterprise, CE), which remain valid for four years. The CSC took 52% of the votes, the FGTB took 33% and the CGSLB 10%, with the balance being made up by the small Confédération Nationale des Cadres (CNC), with 2%, and by independents. Union density has fallen since the early 1980s as a result of a shedding of jobs in heavy industry where the unions were strong, but union density is the highest in any developed country outside Scandinavia (in the private sector 54% of workers are union members).

The unions' strength is reflected in their role in the process of "concertation" or social and economic partnership, a partnership that in turn reinforces the position of the unions. The foundations of the state-backed system of social partnership were laid during reconstruction after World War II and despite periods of difficulty this has remained well entrenched. The social partners meet in the bilateral National Labour Council (Conseil National du Travail, CNT/Nationaler Arbeitsraad, NA), established in 1952, which has been described by the government as a "social Parliament". The CNT provides advice and recommendations to the government and Parliament on social and employment-related issues. The CNT also provides the central representative organizations of employers and unions with a forum for negotiation of a two-yearly private sector framework bargaining agreement that gives the context for sectoral and plant-level negotiations. Likewise only unions affiliated to trade union centres represented on the CNT can participate in the public sector general bargaining committees.

The ILO Committee of Experts on the Application of Conventions and Recommendations has for many years criticized the preferential status the CNT gives those centres considered "most representative" by the government, to the detriment of independent unions. The criteria used by the government are not formally defined but include representative status (numerical strength and nationwide organization), organizational stability, and the ability to ensure respect for the agreements signed by members. The government also takes into account the fact that as the CNT works on the basis of unanimity it needs to be constructed on a basis that encourages consensus. It remains the case that only the Christian, socialist, and liberal trade union confederations are permitted to participate in the CNT. Representation is not strictly proportional to membership strength: there are 12 seats reserved on the CNT for the unions (the same number as for the employers' organizations), with 6 representatives from the FGTB, five from the CSC, and one from the CGSLB. It cannot be doubted, however, that the present system in use in Belgium has proved satisfactory to the great majority of Belgian trade unions. The unions are generally resistant to concepts of "de-regulating" Belgian society by reducing centralized bargaining and allowing more flexibility relating to specific circumstances.

The unions also participate in other state-sponsored institutions, including (at trade union centre level) the tripartite Central Economic Council (Conseil Central de l'Economie, CCE/CRB), set up in 1948, which has a consultative role on issues relating to the state of the economy as a whole, and the High Council on Preventive Measures and Protection at Work, which deals with health and safety. The unions carry out the role of paying unemployment benefits on behalf of the state.

Belgium has a bi-annual collective bargaining round, during which lengthy negotiations between the social partners build-up to the declaration of a new national intersectoral agreement. The following year witnesses the negotiation of sectoral agreements, with company level agreements generally following in the second year, before the cycle begins again. The intersectoral agreement ratified in January 2003 set a pay norm of 5.4% for 2003 and 2004. The pay norm is a guide to subsequent sectoral and company level negotiations.

Strikes are permitted, including in essential services, other than in the case of seamen, the armed forces and magistrates. In 1993 the main centres united to call the first general strike for 58 years in opposition to a government austerity package. Although it did not prevent introduction of the measures, its impact was considerable, especially in Wallonia. The practice is not to prosecute strikers who fail to observe pre-strike procedures in collective bargaining agreements. Employers have sought to use the civil courts to obtain back-to-work orders but the legal position is ambiguous and courts sometimes say that labour conflicts are not within their jurisdiction. In 2002 a so-called "gentlemen's agreement" reached under the aegis of the federal Ministry of Employment between the unions and employers' organizations put an end to this practice, at least in theory. The social partners are, under the terms of the agreement, now resolved to find solutions to industrial disputes through social dialogue.

3 Trade Union Centres

Centrale Générale des Syndicats Libéraux de Belgique (CGSLB)
Algemene Centrale der Liberale Vakbonden (ACLVB)
General Confederation of Liberal Trade Unions of Belgium
Address. Koning Albertlaan 95, B-9000 Gent
Phone. +32 9 222 5751
Fax. +32 9 221 0474
E-mail. aclvb@aclvb.be *or* cgslb@cgslb.be
Website. www.aclvb.be (French/Dutch)
Leadership. Guy Haaze (national president)
Membership. 220,000
History and Character. The CGSLB, the smallest of the three Belgian centres, traces its origins back to the nineteenth century and adopted its present name in 1939. Its structure has changed little since that time other than adapting to national decentralization by creating regional organizations in 1989. It has links with the Belgian liberal parties although without political affiliation. It affiliates local and regional unions directly without occupationally based union structure.

The CGSLB is represented on the CNT and CCE. It argues for more flexibility than is provided by the system of two-yearly collective agreements and greater worker participation in the negotiating process.

The CGSLB complains that it has been denied affiliation to ETUC, which has a monopoly in representing union views in some EU bodies, in an "arbitrary fashion". It is instead affiliated to the European Confederation of Independent Trade Unions (CESI).
International affiliations. TUAC; CESI

Confédération des Syndicats Chrétiens (CSC)
Algemeen Christelijk Vakverbond (ACV)
Confederation of Christian Trade Unions
Address. Chaussée de Haacht 579, 1031 Brussels
Phone. +32 2 246 3111
Fax. +32 2 246 3010
E-mail. acv@acv-csc.be
Website. www.acv-csc.be
Membership. 1.5m.
Leadership. Luc Cortebeek (president); Josly Piette (secretary general)
History and character. The CSC/ACV is the larger of the two main Belgian centres. It is particularly strong in (Dutch-speaking) Flanders where its one million members outnumber those of the FGTB 2:1, whereas the FGTB and CSC have a similar level of support in Wallonia. The CSC is the leading European affiliate of the WCL and Willy Peirens, the CSC's former president (until 1999) was WCL president 1989–97.

The CSC has a long history. In 1886 the Christian Weavers of Ghent established the Ligue Antisocialiste des Ouvriers du Coton, the germ from which the CSC grew, in opposition to the first International developed from 1864 by Karl Marx. Thereafter Christian trade unions grew in a somewhat haphazard way, often in connection with the development of cooperatives, mutual savings banks and workers' improvement and self-help bodies. In Flanders, the model for Christian syndicalism was taken from the Medieval craft guilds. By 1901 there were 62 Christian associations with 11,000 members.

In 1904 the Sécretariat Général des Unions Professionelles Chrétiens de Belgique was formed, and between 1904 and 1908 professional "federations", with nearly 40,000 members, were created covering a wide range of trades and industries. In 1909 the Confédération Nationale des Syndicats Chrétiens et Libres was formed, with separate organizations for Dutch-speaking Flanders and French-speaking Wallonia, as part of the Ligue Démocratique Belge. In 1912 the organizations for Flanders and Wallonia were fused, and the confederation held its first convention autonomously from the Ligue Démocratique Belge. In 1923 the present name was adopted. All normal trade union activity ended after the German occupation of Belgium in 1940, but the CSC office resumed its work on the day Brussels was liberated (Sept. 4, 1944). During the 1970s a greater regional devolution of powers was carried out by the CSC, in parallel with the broader political process whereby increasing regional autonomy was granted to the three regions of Brussels, Flanders and Wallonia. The CSC established regional executives in 1974, and in 1978 special committees for the three regions were established at national headquarters.

The CSC/ACV is built on two pillars, the regional structure of 22 regional federations with 150 local secretariats, and its 16 "centrales professionnelles" (sectoral unions).

During the recession of the early 1980s the CSC called for work-sharing programmes to be adopted, but the employers proved unwilling to follow this lead in any significant way. The unions also faced challenges to the right to strike and exercise union powers, and to social security benefits. In the late 1980s, under the leadership of Willy Peirens, the CSC developed a much closer relationship with the socialist centre, the FGTB.

The CSC has no formal organizational ties to any political party, and since 1945 CSC officials have not taken political office, other than at the minor local level. Officially, the Christian Workers' Movements (MOC/ACW) give political expression to CSC policies; however, the MOC (in Wallonia and Brussels) has since 1972 been a pluralistic movement (with elected candidates belonging to different political parties). On the Flemish side, the ACW looks to the Christian Democratic Christelijke Volkspartij (CVP) for the implementation of its policies. A number of politicians have emerged through the CSC route, among them former CVP prime ministers Wilfred Martens, in office most of the period 1979–92, and his successor Jean-Luc Dehaene (1992–99).

In the late 1990s the main priorities of the CSC/ACV included defending jobs and social security and campaigning for a fairer tax system. In 2002 the confederation carried out a thorough reorganization in an attempt to break with the traditional separation of blue collar workers from white collar and professional/managerial staff. The CSC/ACV now groups these workers together under the responsibility of the relevant sectoral federations.

CSC/ACV has an associated International Institute of Workers' Education.

International affiliations. WCL; ETUC; TUAC

Affiliated unions.

1. Bâtiment et Industrie (Building and Industry)
Address. rue de Trèves 31, 1040 Brussels
Phone. +32 2 285 02 11
Fax. +32 2 230 74 43
E-mail. Batiment_industrie@acv-csc.be
Website. www.acvbi.be
Leadership. Jacquy Jackers (president); Raymond Jongen (secretary general)
Membership. 285,000.
History and character. Formed in 1998 from the merger of the former Wood and Building Workers' Union with the union for miscellaneous industries.

2. Métal (Métal-CSC) (Metalworkers)
Address. rue de Heembeeck 127, 1120 Brussels
Phone. +32 2 244 99 11
Fax. +32 2 241 99 00
E-mail. ccmb@cav-csc.be
Website. www.csc-metal.be
Leadership. Tony Janssen (president); Marc de Wilde (secretary general)
Membership. 220,000

3. Centrale Chrétienne des Mines, de l'Energie, de la Chimie et du Cuir (CCMECC-CSC) (Mines, Energy, Chemicals and Leather)
Address. Avenue d'Auderghem 26-32, 1040 Brussels
Phone. +32 2 238 73 32
Fax. +32 2 280 03 97
Leadership. Alfons Van Genechten (president); Michel André (secretary general)
Membership. 60,000

4. CSC Textura (Textiles and Clothing)
Address. Koning Albertlaan 27, 9000 Gent
Phone. +32 9 222 57 01
Fax. +32 9 220 45 59
E-mail. acv.csc.textura@acv-csc.be
Leadership. Dirk Uyttenhove (president), Rein De Tremerie and Jan Callaert (joint general secretaries)
Membership. 90,595

5. Centrale Chrétienne de l'Alimentation et des Services (CCAS, Food and Services)
Address. Rue des Chartreux 70, 1000 Brussels
Phone. +32 2 500 28 99
E-mail. ccvd-ccas@acv-csc.be
Website. www.acv-voeding-diensten.be
Leadership. Eric Delecluyse (president)
Membership. 192,000

6. Centrale Nationale des Employés et Cadres (CNE)
Address. Rue du Page 69-75, 1050 Brussels
Phone. +32 2 538 91 44
Website. www.cne-gnc.be
Membership. 135,000. Organizes French- and German-speaking salaried staff and managers in the private sector.
Leadership. Raymond Coumont

7. Landelijke Bedienden Centrale–Nationaal Verbond Kaderpersonneel (LBC/NVK)
Address. Sudermanstraat 5, 2000 Antwerpen
Phone. +32 3 220 8711
Fax. +32 3 231 6664
E-mail. vakbond@lbc-nvk.be
Website. www.lbc-nvk.be
Membership. 255,000

8. Sports (Sporta-as)
Address. Rue des Chartreux 70, 1000 Bruxelles
Phone. +32 2 500 28 30
Fax. +32 2 500 28 39
E-mail. sporta@acv-csc.be

9. Centrale Chrétienne des Communications et de la Culture (SCCC) (Posts, Telecommunications, Railways, Shipping, Radio and TV etc.)
Address. Galerie Agora, rue Marché aux Herbes 105, BP 38/40, 1000 Brussels
Phone. +32 2 549 08 00
Fax. +32 2 512 85 91
E-mail. sccc@acv-csc.be
Leadership. Michel Bovy (president)
Membership. 53,000

10. Centrale Chrétienne des Services Publics (CSC-CCSP) (Public Services)
Address. rue de Trèves 31, bte 2, 1040 Brussels
Phone. +32 2 238 72 11
Fax. +32 2 230 45 62
E-mail. ccsp@acv-csc.be
Website. www.ccsp.be/
Leadership. Luc Hamelinck (president)
Membership. 127,000

11. Centrale Chrétienne du personnel de l'Enseignement technique (CCPET-CSC) (Technical Education)
Address. Rue de la Victoire 16, 1060 Brussels
Phone. +32 2 542 09 00
Fax. +32 2 542 09 08
E-mail. ccpet-uceo@acv-csc.be
Leadership. Prosper Boulangé (secretary general)
Membership. 8,500

12. Centrale Chrétienne des Professeurs de l'Enseignement moyen et normal libre (CEMNL) (Teachers in Secondary Education and Teacher Training)
Address. Rue de la Victoire 16, 1060 Brussels
Phone. +32 2 238 73 23
Fax. +32 2 238 73 23
E-mail. cemnl@acv-csc.be
Website. www.cemnl.be
Leadership. Charles Malisoux (secretary general), Willem Miler (president)
Membership. 9,000

13. Fédération des Instituteurs Chrétiens (FIC)
Address. Rue de la Victoire 16, 1060 Brussels
Phone. +32 2 539 00 01
Fax. +32 2 534 13 36
Website. www.fic.be
Leadership. Régis Dohogne (secretary general); Jacqueline Pirard (president)
Membership. 16,000

14. Union Chrétienne des membres du Personnel de l'Enseignement officiel (UCEO-CSC)
Address. Rue de la Victoire 16, 1060 Brussels
Phone. +32 2 542 09 00
Fax. +32 2 542 09 08
E-mail. ccpet-uceo@acv-csc.be
Leadership. Prosper Boulangé (secretary general)
Membership. 3,500. Represents French and German speakers.

15. Christelijke Onderwijs Centrale (COC)
Address. Oudergemselaan 26, 1040 Brussels
Phone. +32 2 238 72 68
Fax. +32 2 230 38 83
E-mail. coc@acv-csc.be
Leadership. Hubert Buys (president)
Membership. 40,000

16. Christelijk Onderwijzers Verbond (COV) (Teachers' Union)
Address. Koningstraat 203, 1210 Brussels
Phone. +32 2 227 41 11
Fax. +32 2 219 47 61
E-mail. cov@acv-csc.be
Leadership. Guy Bourdeaud'hui (general president)
Membership. 39,000

Fédération Générale du Travail de Belgique (FGTB)
Algemeen Belgisch Vakverbond (ABVV)
General Federation of Belgian Labour
Address. Rue Haute 42, 1000 Brussels
Phone. +32 2 506 8211
Fax. +32 2 506 8229
E-mail. paul.gruseling@fgtb.be
Website. www.abvv.be (Dutch, French, English, German)
Leadership. Michel Nollet (president); Mia De Vits (secretary general)
Membership. 1,186,638
History and character. The FGTB traces its history back to a Trade Union Committee established by the Belgian Workers' Party (POB) in 1898. It became the Belgian Trade Union Confederation in 1937, and in 1945 took its present name, uniting a number of trade union federations on the basis of a statement of principle declaring its political independence.

Following an Extraordinary Congress of May 1978, the FGTB statutes provided for three inter-regional organizations covering Flanders, Brussels and Wallonia which correspond to the country's regional authorities. The FGTB's core strength is in the French-speaking heavy-industry region of Wallonia, where it has comparable support to the CSC, whereas it is much weaker than the CSC in Dutch-speaking Flanders. It has 18 regional organizations and interregional offices for Flanders, Brussels and Wallonia.

The FGTB emphasizes that it continues to adhere to socialist principles. In practical terms its current concerns include combating unemployment (its top priority); enhancing social dialogue; developing quality employment; lowering working hours; protecting public services and advancing social equality. It is also concerned at the "democratic deficit" in the EU, which it sees as leading to a gulf between people and politicians reflected in the rise of right-wing populist parties. It participates in the National Labour Council (CNT) and the Central Economic Council (CCE). The FGTB complains of efforts to undermine social partnership embodied in the CNT and CCE and that the CCE increasingly focuses on competitiveness to the exclusion of other issues.

There is a wide range of associated research, training, educational and social organizations attached to the FGTB.
International affiliations. ICFTU; ETUC; TUAC
Affiliated unions. There are seven sectoral affiliates as follows:

1. Centrale Générale
Address. Rue Haute 26–28, 1000 Brussels
Phone. +32 2 549 0549
Fax. +32 2 514 1691
E-mail. accg.nat@unicall.be
Membership. 299,232.
History and character. Represents blue-collar workers in a wide variety of sectors including construction, mining, chemicals, forestry, security, cleaning companies and agriculture. Absorbed the mineworkers' union in 1994.

2. La Centrale du Métal
Address. Rue Jacques Jordaens 17, 1000 Brussels
Phone. +32 2 627 7411
Fax. +32 2 627 7490
E-mail. cmb.nat@village.uunet.be
Website. www.abvvmetaal.be (Flemish and French only)
Membership. 180,232. Blue-collar workers in metal, electricity, steel making and similar.

3. La Centrale du Textile, Vêtement, Diamant (Textiles, Clothing, Diamonds)
Address. Opvoedingsstraat 143, 9000 Gent
Phone. +32 9 242 86 86
Fax. +32 9 242 86 96
E-mail. abwtkd.fgtbtvd@glo.be
Leadership. Donald Wittevrongel (president)
Membership. 55,000

4. Union Belge des Ouvriers du Transport (UBOT) (Transport)
Address. Paardenmarkt 66, 2000 Antwerp
Phone. +32 3 224 31 11
Fax. +32 3 234 01 49
Membership. 26,796

5. La Centrale de l'Alimentation-Horeca-Services (Food, Hotels, Restaurants, Catering)
Address. rue des Alexiens 18, 1000 Brussels
Phone. +32 2 512 97 00
Fax. +32 2 512 53 68
Email. horval@horval.be
Website. www.horval.be (Flemish and French only)
Membership. 78,745

6. Syndicat des Employés, Techniciens et Cadres de Belgique (SETCa) (White-collar, Technical and Management Staffs)
Address. Rue Haute 42, 1000 Brussels
Phone. +32 2 512 5250
Fax. +32 2 511 0508
E-mail. national@setca-fgtb.be
Website. www.setca.fgtb.be
Leadership. Christian Roland (president)
Membership. 250,000. Members are white-collar workers, technical staff and managers in the private sector. SETCa has also absorbed the former small Syndicat du Livre, representing white and blue-collar employees in the printing business, press and media.

7. Centrale Générale des Services Publics (Public Services)
Address. Place Fontainas 9–11, 1000 Brussels
Phone. +32 2 508 58 11
Fax. +32 2 508 59 02
Membership. 279,759. Represents all public servants and workers in public enterprises including central, state and local government, public education, cultural institutions, posts and telecoms and public transport.

Belize

Capital: Belmopan
Population: 273,000 (2004 est.)

1 Political and Economic Background

Belize (known until 1973 as British Honduras) became independent in 1981 as a full member of the Commonwealth. In the most recent elections, in March 2003, the left-of-centre People's United Party (PUP) government was re-elected, having won power from the conservative United Democratic Party in 1998.

Belize's main economic activities are agriculture, fisheries and forestry, with sugar, citrus products, fisheries products and bananas being major sources of export revenue. However, agricultural output is liable to severe disruption through disease, drought, flooding and hurricanes and its value is subject to commodity price fluctuations. Clothing (mainly for export) is also an expanding industry, as is tourism. The PUP government followed an expansionary economic policy after coming to office in 1998, resulting in rapid growth for two or three years.

GDP (purchasing power parity) $1.28 bn (2002 est.); GDP per capita (purchasing power parity) $4,900 (2002 est.).

2 Trade Unionism

Following labour unrest in the 1930s the British authorities legalized trade unionism in 1941, the first registered union being the British Honduras Trade Union (1943) and the unions were a force in the period of anti-colonial agitation. Belize ratified ILO Conventions No. 87 (Freedom of Association and Protection of the Right to Organize, 1948) and No. 98 (Right to Organize and Collective Bargaining, 1949) in 1983. About 11% of the workforce, including most civil service employees, are in some eight unions, under the umbrella of the National Trade Union Congress of Belize (NTUCB). A new Trade Union and Employers' Recognition Act 2000 also came into force in December 2000. Union activities are generally free from administrative interference by the government. The 2000 Act included provision for trade union recognition by employers; however, unions have in practice not been recognized in some sectors, notably the banana industry and the export processing zones.

Under the new Act, employers are now required to recognize unions for collective bargaining purposes, once 51% of workers so express their desire. Disputes may be referred to the Labour Commissioner for (non-binding, but usually accepted) guidance.

3 Trade Union Centre

National Trade Union Congress of Belize (NTUCB)
Address. PO Box 2359, Belize City Centre, Belize City
Phone. +501 227 1596
Fax. +501 227 2864
E-mail. ntucb@btl.net
Leadership. Horris Patten (president); George Frazer (general secretary)
Membership. The NTUCB is the national centre and affiliates the Belize Workers' Union, the Belize National Teachers' Union, the Belize Energy Workers' Union, the Belize Water Services Workers' Union, the Belize Communications Workers' Union, the Association of Public Service Senior Managers, the Public Service Union and the Christan Workers' Union.
International affiliations. ICFTU; CTUC; CCL

4 Other Trade Union Organization

Christian Workers' Union (CWU)
Address. PO Box 533, Belize City
Phone. +501 227 2150
Leadership. Antonio González (president); James McFoy (secretary general)
History and character. This organization was founded in 1963 and is a small general workers' union.
International affiliations. WCL

Benin

Capital: Porto Novo
Population: 7.25 m. (2004 est.)

1 Political and Economic Background

Benin (named Dahomey until 1975) became a self-governing republic within the French Community in 1958 and gained full independence in 1960. The current President, Mathieu Kérékou, originally came to power in a military coup in 1972, proclaiming the creation of a socialist society with Marxism-Leninism as its revolutionary philosophy and the Benin People's Revolutionary Party (PRPB) as sole legal party. Following intense social conflict, with students and civil servants prominent, the PRPB renounced Marxism-Leninism in 1989 and Benin ceased to be a People's Republic. In 1991 multi-party elections were held which resulted in Kérékou being replaced by Nicephore Soglo. With increasing unrest, in 1994 Soglo began to rule by decree, but the 1995 legislative elections returned a majority for parties opposed to him. In 1996 Kérékou was elected president, in elections generally considered fair, but March 1999 legislative elections resulted in a majority for opposition groups led by Soglo's Benin Renaissance Party. Kérékou was re-elected in 2001 and legislative elections held in 2003 were won by a coalition of parties supporting the President.

The economy of Benin remains underdeveloped and dependent on subsistence agriculture, cotton production, and regional trade. The nationalization-driven economic policies of the 1970s were dismantled from the middle of the 1980s and state owned enterprises such as oil, cement, telecommunications, water and electricity have been privatized. Fewer than 100,000 of the population are categorized as employed (nearly half of these being engaged in the community, social and personal services).

GDP (purchasing power parity) $7.74 billion (2003 est.); GDP per capita (purchasing power parity) $1,100 (2003 est.).

2 Trade Unionism

Benin ratified ILO Convention No. 87 (Freedom of Association and Protection of the Right to Organize, 1948) in 1960 and Convention No. 98 (Right to Organize and Collective Bargaining, 1949) in 1968.

Several trade union centres, with different international affiliations, existed after independence but in 1974 Kérékou established a single centre, the Union Nationale des Syndicats des Travailleurs du Bénin (UNSTB). The UNSTB survived under political pluralism but is now rivaled by its fellow ICFTU affiliate the Central des Syndicats Autonomes du Bénin (CSA) which is about half its size. 1993 merger talks proved unfruitful but relations between the two centres are generally good. The WCL has an affiliate centre, the Confédération Générale des Travaillaurs du Bénin (CGTB).

Up to 75% of employees in the small formal sector are in unions, with public sector occupations most organized. In practice, unions generally operate freely, although on a small scale. The law prohibits anti-union discrimination and provides for private sector collective bargaining, although pay is set administratively in the public sector. Since the 1990s, there have been a number of strikes by civil servants and other groups affected by IMF-backed structural adjustment programmes.

An ICFTU report on core labour standards in Benin published in June 2004 highlighted frequent violations of basic workers' rights such as the right to organize and the right to collective bargaining. The report found that legal restrictions exist on the right to strike, and civil servants are exposed to serious limitations on their right to strike, including restrictions on the notice period required before strikes can take place. The report also found that child labour is prevalent in Benin, and enforcement of legislation is often limited to the formal wage economy. Most children work in the informal economy, mainly in agriculture (on family farms and plantations) and also as vendors and domestic servants. Although Benin has ratified the core ILO Conventions on Forced Labour, the practice does exist. Many women and children are trafficked for forced prostitution, forced labour on plantations and domestic work. Moreover, many children are sold to neighbouring countries (like Togo and Côte d'Ivoire) and forced to work on plantations or in domestic work under harsh and dangerous conditions while receiving very low pay, if any at all.

3 Trade Union Centres

Central des Syndicats Autonomes du Bénin (CSA)
Autonomous Trade Unions Centre
Address. 1 blvd. St. Michel, Bourse du Travail, 04 BP 1115, Cotonou
Phone. +229 300 182
Fax. +229 300 448
E-mail. csabenin@intnet.bj
Leadership. Sanni Bonaventure (president)
Membership. 20,000
History and character. The origins of the CSA lay in concern that the former state-sponsored UNSTB would be unable to establish itself as genuinely independent of political parties. After the establishment of political parties there were merger talks between the UNSTB and the CSA and they continue to cooperate over industrial matters. The CSA membership opposed a merger, recalling the role of the UNSTB as sole officially sanctioned centre in the 1970s and 1980s.

International affiliation. ICFTU

Confédération Générale des Travaillaurs du Bénin (CGTB)
General Confederation of the Workers of Benin
Address. BP 06-2449 PK 3, Route de Porto-Novo, Cotonou
Phone. +229 33 50 07
Fax. +229 30 44 63
E-mail. Cgtbpdd@bow.intnet.bj
Membership. Pascal Todjinou (secretary general)
International affiliation. WCL

Union Nationale des Syndicats des Travailleurs du Bénin (UNSTB)
National Union of the Unions of the Workers of Benin
Address. Bourse du Travail, BP 69, Cotonou
Phone. +229 30 36 13
Fax. +229 30 36 13
E-mail. UNSTB@intnet.bj
Leadership. Nicodème Julian Codjo Assogba
Membership. About 40,000
History and character. All pre-existing unions and federations were absorbed into this organization in 1974. The UNSTB became a designated mass organization of the PRPB, the then sole legal party, and there were no unions outside it. Several federations threatened to secede in 1989 following its failure to back industrial action, notably by civil servants. The following year it declared its intention to become independent of the party and a special assembly dismissed Romain Vilon Ouezo (the general secretary since its inception, a member of the PRPB politburo and vice-president of the Permanent Committee of the National Assembly).
International affiliation. ICFTU. The UNSTB left the WFTU in 1990.

Bhutan

Capital: Thimphu
Population: 2.19 m. (2004 est.)

1 Political and Economic Background

Bhutan is a monarchy, in which power is shared between the hereditary King, a partly elected National Assembly (whose role was increased in 1998), a Council of Ministers, a Royal Advisory Council, and the Buddhist priesthood. There are no political parties. Some 110,000 ethnic (Hindu) Nepalis are in UNHCR camps in Nepal having fled Bhutan in the face of the "one nation, one people" policy adopted in the late 1980s.

Bhutan's economy is almost entirely dependent upon agriculture (mostly at subsistence level) and forestry, which account for 92 per cent of the active workforce. To complement traditional handicrafts and carpet weaving, a number of industrial estates have been established to encourage small-scale enterprises, but there has been little inward investment. Foreign nationals, especially from Nepal and India, carry out much non-agricultural work, and there is little indigenous skilled labour.

GDP (purchasing power parity) $2.7bn. (2002 est.); GDP per capita (purchasing power parity) $1,300 (2002 est.).

2 Trade Unionism

Bhutan is not a member of the ILO. Trade unionism is not permitted and does not appear to exist inside the country although a Federation of Bhutanese Trade Unions exists in exile in Nepal. There is no collective bargaining.

3 Exile Organization

Federation of Bhutanese Trade Unions (FOBTU)
Address. GPO Box 8975, EPC 1834, Kathmandu, Nepal
Phone. +977 23 580219
Website. www.freewebs.com/fobtu
Leadership. Nandi K.S. Neopaney (president); Chet Nath Timsina (general secretary)
History and character. Founded on May 1, 2000, as an exile organization in Nepal; reports some 14 affiliated sectoral unions and works with Nepalese trade unions and international groups but does not appear to have a presence inside Bhutan.

Bolivia

Capitals: La Paz (administrative) Sucre (legal)
Population: 8.72 m. (2004 est.)

1 Political and Economic Background

Bolivia claimed independence from both Spain and Peru in 1825 but then experienced almost continuous political instability, with a long series of military coups. Since 1982, however, there has been an elected civilian government although the society remains very unstable. At elections in June 2002, former President Gonzalo Sánchez de Lozada of the Nationalist Revolutionary Movement (MNR) was chosen, and his party obtained a majority in both houses of Congress. However, he was forced to resign in October 2003 in the face of widespread popular unrest, and was succeeded by Vice President Carlos Meza

Until the 1980s the mainstay of the Bolivian economy was tin mining, but the majority of the workforce is engaged in subsistence agriculture and the country is one of the least developed and poorest in Latin America. In the 1980s Bolivia experienced hyperinflation, with inflation in 1985 at 23,000 per cent. A stabilization plan introduced in 1985 returned the economy to relative normality but failed to alleviate poverty. The workforce suffered successive pay freezes under an IMF/World Bank programme intended to cut the enormous national debt; major enterprises closed down and unemployment reached 25 per cent of the workforce. During the 1990s successive governments sought to liberalize the economy and many state enterprises have been privatized. Overall living standards remain low, with a poorly diversified economy and widespread under-employment.

GDP (purchasing power parity) $21.01bn. (2003 est.); GDP per capita (purchasing power parity) $2,400 (2003 est.).

2 Trade Unionism

Significant labour organization began early in the twentieth century. The (1921) first congress of Bolivian workers saw violent conflicts between anarchist and Marxist factions. Thereafter the key central was the Bolivian Workers' Central (Central Obrera Boliviana – COB), strongly influenced by its most powerful industrial affiliate, the mineworkers' union Federación de Sindicatos de Trabajadores Mineros de Bolivia (FSTMB). The FSTMB was founded in 1944, and in the April 1952 MNR revolution that overthrew military rule, the tin miners served as an armed militia. After this the FSTMB led in building the COB, with Juan Lechín Oquendo (the FSTMB executive secretary from its foundation until 1986) becoming COB executive secretary. Lechín became Minister of Mines in the Estenssoro government, presiding over the nationalization of the tin mining industry as Comibol. After this the FSTMB and the COB played a major part in sustaining MNR rule and in 1960 Lechín was elected Vice-President of Bolivia.

In 1964, however, Lechín was expelled from the MNR for opposing government plans to rationalize the loss-making Comibol by removing the union veto over management decisions, cutting the workforce, and expelling Communists from the FSTMB leadership. The resultant unrest split the MNR, destabilized the government, and opened the way to the 1964 coup. Juan Lechín was deported, precipitating a general strike and several days of heavy fighting between miners and industrial workers and the armed forces in which there were numerous casualties. Further serious disorders occurred in mining areas later the same year, with at least 30 deaths officially reported. In 1967 tin miners in Oruro, Huanini and Siglo Veinte, in sympathy with guerrillas led by Ernesto (Che) Guevara (who was captured and killed in October 1967), proclaimed the region "a free territory" and 21 miners were killed during the suppression of the insurrection. From 1969 successive civilian and military governments failed to achieve political stability, and militant and at times insurrectionist tactics remained a feature of the COB and the FSTMB, despite the extended periods of exile imposed upon Lechín and other union leaders.

After 1974 individual unions were suppressed and the COB was likewise officially suspended from 1971 to 1978. A new military coup in 1979 was followed by a COB general strike and 200 deaths. After widespread resistance in La Paz and the mining areas to a new coup in 1980, the new regime again banned the COB and all trade union activity. Lechín and Simon Reyes, another leader of the FSTMB, were arrested and exiled.

The COB ban was lifted on the 1982 restoration of civilian rule but the organization rejected an invitation to participate in the government, and vigorously opposed its austerity measures. In 1983 the government granted majority representation on the Comibol board to the FSTMB, but rejected the COB programme. New austerity measures led to a COB general strike; from now on a pattern became established whereby the increasingly enfeebled government announced various austerity measures and then withdrew or sharply modified them in the face of strikes called by the COB.

New austerity measures approved by the IMF and the collapse of the International Tin Agreement led to an estimated 27,000 miners losing their jobs between 1985 and 1988. In protest the COB organized a series of general strikes, to which the government responded with declarations of states of siege and temporary detention or internal exile. In August 1986, some 5,000 miners marched on La Paz in a vain bid to prevent the government closing seven of the 24-state-owned mines and selling nine to miners' cooperatives. It was branded as insurrectionist and broken up by the army 60 km. from the capital.

A mass COB hunger strike of 1988 was estimated to have involved 4,000 workers, especially redundant miners, in protest against government social and economic policies. The President agreed to provide alternative stop-gap employment for unemployed miners.

Through the 1990s the COB sustained continual protests and industrial activity against privatization and other government policies, while in the mines, the FSTMB continued to oppose privatization or the introduction of joint ventures. In March 1996 the COB called an indefinite general strike which was met by the declaration of a state of siege by the government; the two sides reached agreement to end the strikes at the end of April but the state of siege was not lifted until October 1996.

On May 5, 1997, six COB leaders, including the executive secretary Edgar Ramírez, began a hunger strike saying the government refused to negotiate with them over demands for a living wage, and opposition to privatization and private pension funds. The hunger strike was timed to coincide with the run-up to national elections on June 1 and 70 other union leaders joined the hunger strike during May. It was finally called off on May 27 after agreement was reached with the government to set up working parties to examine the COB's demands.

Violence has continued to be a feature of industrial relations. In 1998, amid a general strike called by the COB, deaths were reported in particular from the coca-growing region of Chapare, where tensions were exacerbated by government threats to eradicate the coca crop. Imprisonment and internal exile remain punishments meted out to strikers. The rise of the indigenist movement in the region has strengthened the COB in resisting US-sponsored attempts to eradicate coca production and impose free market ideas, and both played an important role in the unrest of 2002-03.

Bolivia ratified ILO Convention No. 87 (Freedom of Association and Protection of the Right to Organize,

1948) in 1965 and Convention No. 98 (Right to Organize and Collective Bargaining, 1949) in 1973, but has been held by the ILO to be substantially in breach of its obligations. Following an ILO visit in 1997 Bolivia said it would make substantial changes to protect workers against anti-union discrimination and end the authorities' powers to dissolve unions, but action was not forthcoming.

The labour code requires government permission to establish a union and that there may be only one union per enterprise. The authorities have extensive powers to supervise unions, which they may dissolve by administrative order. National Labour Court procedures for dealing with discrimination by employers against workers engaged in trade union activities are long drawn-out. Nonetheless, perhaps 30 percent of workers in the formal economy belong to trade unions.

Under the Labour Code, public employees (other than in health, education and petroleum) are in theory not permitted to join trade unions, but in practice nearly all civilian government workers are organized.

Strikes are formally banned in the public sector. In the private sector workers may strike if 75% of the workforce vote in favour, although compulsory arbitration can be imposed. General and solidarity strikes are illegal. Nonetheless, as seen above, strikes on a large scale are common, and often heavily involve the public sector.

3 Trade Union Centre

Central Obrera Boliviana (COB)
Bolivian Workers' Central (Confederation)
Address. Edif. COB, Calle Pisagua 618, CP6552, La Paz
Phone. + 591 2 228-3220
Fax. +591 2 228-0420
Leadership. Alberto Camacho Pardo (executive secretary); Oscar Salas Moya (secretary general)
History and character. The COB is the only Bolivian trade union central. The history of the COB, as that of its principal affiliate, the Federación de Sindicatos de Trabajadores Mineros de Bolivia (FSTMB), is one in which insurrectionism, violent repression and considerable influence on the history of Bolivia, are intertwined (see above).

The COB remains highly politicized and it and its affiliates engage in constant opposition, strikes and demonstrations against various aspects of the government's efforts to implement "neo-liberal" policies. In recent years its affiliated teachers' and coca growers' unions have shown particular militancy. The government declared the objective of making Bolivia, one of the major producers of coca and cocaine products, a "zero coca" producer by 2002, but the COB has demanded an end to coca eradication programmes. Overall its influence declined with the privatization in the 1990s of state enterprises in which it was strongly represented, but in recent years it has been able successfully to resist further privatizations. In the private sector, including privatized state industries, employers try to deal directly with their work force when bargaining occurs but are not always successful.

The 1996 Agrarian Reform Law extended national labour law protections to employed rural workers, but enforcement is problematic in this sector. This affects particularly the indigenous people who make up over 50 per cent of the population. The strength of the COB, almost unique in Latin America, stems largely from the fact that it represents both urban and rural workers, through its affiliate, the Confederación Sindical Unica de los Trabajadores Campesinos de Bolivia (CSUTCB),

The COB appointed a new leadership in December 1997 after a crisis triggered by the report of an independent commission accusing COB leaders of corruption, leading to the resignation of secretary general Edgar Ramírez.

The COB joined the WFTU in 1988.
International affiliations. WFTU

4 Other Trade Union Organizations

Confederación Sindical de los Trabajores Campesinos de Bolivia
Address. Calle Sucre, esq. Yanacocha, La Paz
Phone. +591 2 236-9433
Leadership. Felipe Quispe (executive secretary)
History and character. Founded 1979 to represent rural workers; affiliated to the COB.

Corriente de Renovación Independiente y Solidaridad Laboral (CRISOL)
Address. Calle Batallón Colorados No. 104-A (Final), Casilla 7492, La Paz
Phone. +591 2 244-1483
Fax. +591 244-2798
E-mail. crisolbol@yahoo.com
Website. geocities.com/crisol_bol
Leadership. Luis Antezana (executive secretary); Francisco Figueroa (secretary general)
International affiliation. WCL, CLAT

Bosnia and Herzegovina

Capital: Sarajevo
Population: 4.0m. (2004 est.)

1 Political and Economic Background

The former Yugoslav republic of Bosnia-Herzegovina declared its independence in March 1992 following a referendum which had been boycotted by most of its Serbian minority, who feared separation from Serbia proper. Although Bosnia-Herzegovina (with a then 44% Muslim, or "Bosniak", population) quickly received international recognition as an independent state, a Bosnian Serb Republic was declared within its territory by ethnic Serbs (31% of the population). The general war that followed also involved a separate conflict with the Croat population (17% of the whole). "Ethnic cleansing", primarily of Muslims, transformed the demographic balance of whole areas, and hundreds of thousands fled abroad or to neighbouring former

Yugoslav republics in the worst European conflict since World War II. In 1995 intensive military intervention by NATO against Serb forces provided the context for negotiations leading to the Dayton Agreement of November 1995. Under this the integrity of a unified Bosnia-Herzegovina was maintained but the country for many purposes broke into two entities, one controlled by the Serbs (Republika Srpska) and the other by a Muslim–Croat federation (the Federation of Bosnia and Herzegovina), of similar geographical size but with the Federation having the larger population. Stability is underpinned by the presence of an international peacekeeping force and a UN-appointed High Representative has responsibility for the civil implementation of the Agreement. Nationalist parties have been dominant in the two entities. At the union level the main nationalist parties – the Party of Democratic Action (SDA, Muslim), the Croatian Democratic Union (HDZ) and the Serb Democratic Party (SDS) – temporarily lost their ascendancy to a coalition of moderate parties in 2001, but regained their dominant position in elections in October 2002. The parliamentary and governmental structure is complex and designed to ensure a degree of representation for each of the three constituent peoples in both the Federation and Serb Republic as well as at the union level. In addition the High Representative retains considerable powers of intervention, which he exercises, and the country has limited sovereignty.

Bosnia's economic infrastructure was severely damaged by the 1992–95 war and reconstruction continues. Several hundred thousand refugees have returned to the country. However, large-scale industrial enterprises have been damaged by the loss of the former Yugoslav market and in most cases are unable to compete effectively in international markets. A period of rapid economic growth after 1995 has been followed by slower progress since the turn of the century. Privatization and development of significant legitimate private sector employment has been slow and unemployment, under-employment, inter-enterprise debt and non-payment of wages remain major problems. There is a heavy dependence on international aid and remittances from refugees abroad, and a substantial informal sector.

GDP (purchasing power parity) $24.31bn. (2003 est.); GDP per capita (purchasing power parity) $6,100 (2003 est.).

2 Trade Unionism

Bosnia and Herzegovina ratified ILO Conventions No. 87 (Freedom of Association and Protection of the Right to Organize, 1948) and No. 98 (Right to Organize and Collective Bargaining, 1949) in 1993.

Prior to the collapse of Yugoslavia in 1991–92, Bosnian trade unions were integrated into the overall Yugoslav trade union system and performed a wide range of social and economic functions. Trade union structures collapsed during the 1992–95 war. Since the 1995 Dayton Agreement trade unions have organized separately in the Serbian and Muslim–Croat entities. In the Federation the Confederation of Independent Trade Unions of Bosnia and Herzegovina (SSSBiH) is the centre and in the Serb Republic this role is performed by the Confederation of Trade Unions of the Republika Srpska (SSRS). Although the trade union centres of the two entities are separate and in reality divided by their different national compositions, they have a dialogue to develop co-operation, assisted by the ICFTU. In September 2003 the two centres agreed to form an umbrella organization at the state (union) level as part of this process, although the Bosnian law on associations does not provide for the registration of trade unions at the union level. The SSSBiH is affiliated to the ICFTU and the SSRS hopes to achieve affiliation. Croats have some independent organization in areas of the Federation where they are the majority, although they are generally represented by the Federation unions. A series of four corresponding labour laws were introduced recently, at union level and for each of the entities and the Brcko district (which is subject to a separate post-Dayton agreement), which provide a legal basis for freedom of association. There is still no law governing trade union recognition or collective bargaining, but a law on strikes in both entities theoretically protects strikers against retaliation. Many workers remain reluctant to participate in industrial action, however, for fear of dismissals and other reprisals.

Trade union activity is constrained by a range of factors. These include widespread unemployment (reported to affect 42% of the work force) and the collapsed state of industry. A 1999 ICFTU report noted that many owners of enterprises held their positions thanks to the ruling party and "woe betide those who protest". There is little collective bargaining. Strikes have occurred infrequently and are mostly local in character, although 2003 saw a considerable increase in the number of actions. When strikes did occur they were mostly concerned with non-payment of wages. In practice many workers continue working for long periods without pay for lack of any alternative to the jobs they have.

3 Trade Union Centres

Confederation of Independent Trade Unions of Bosnia and Herzegovina
Savez Samostalnih Sindikata Bosne i Hercegovine (SSSBiH)
Address. Obala Kulina bana 1, 71000 Sarajevo
Phone. +387 33 202029
Fax. +387 33 664872
E-mail. sinbih@bih.net.ba
Leadership. Edhem Biber (president)
History and character. Claims descent from a union established in 1905 and inherited the Yugoslav era trade union structures on the declaration of Bosnian independence in 1992. It has 22 branch trade unions and claims a membership of 270,000, although other sources suggest 200,000. Many workers in the state-owned sector are members of the SSSBiH affiliates but its influence is weakened by continuing privatization, high unemployement and the poor financial condition of state enterprises. It represents workers in the

Federation's tripartite Economic and Social Council.

The SSSBiH is preoccupied primarily with the consequences of privatization and the high rate of unemployment and problems such as wage arrears. The first post-war trade union demonstration since the war took place on Oct. 25, 1999, attended by a crowd variously estimated as 8,000 and 30,000. It was called by the SSSBiH and demands included payment of wage arrears, signing of collective agreements, and new labour legislation.Shop stewards have reported cases of harassment by criminal gangs. Following his strident criticism of corruption in the privatization process, Edhem Biber, the president of SSSBiH, received a series of threats throughout May and June 2003, during which time he was reportedly followed on several occasions.

International affiliation. ICFTU

Confederation of Trade Unions of the Republika Srpska
Savez Sindikata Republike Srpske (SSRS)

Address. Ulica Srpska 32, 78000 Banja Luka
Phone. +387 51 310 711
Fax. +387 51 304 241
Leadership. Cedo Volas (president)
History and character. Founded in August 1992 on the territory of the Republika Srpska. It reports a membership of 190,000.

Botswana

Capital. Gaborone
Population. 1.56 m. (2004 est.)

1 Political and Economic Background

Botswana achieved independence from the UK as a republic in 1966. Following independence, Botswana developed into a true multi-party democracy with a comparatively tolerant political culture that allowed for the existence of political parties of all shades, although every election since independence has been won by the Botswana Democratic Party (BDP).

The practice of liberal democracy during the period when many African countries were opting for one-party systems and military regimes was a very powerful weapon that Botswana employed successfully to win the sympathy of foreign governments and donor agencies, at least up to the early 1990s. Economically Botswana won praise as a successful model of capitalist development in Africa. Its post-independence economic success is based on diamond discoveries of the 1970s. The opening of the diamond mines at Orapa, Letlhakane and Jwaneng, and the coal mine at Morupule, brought vast amounts of revenue to the government. The way in which the government managed and utilized these proceeds was to create a basis for stability which the country has enjoyed for over thirty years. However, Botswana's economic success has been coupled with growing disparities in income and economic opportunities. Economic growth has proceeded side by side with growing poverty, especially in remote rural areas, increasing unemployment and problems related to urbanization. The Botswana economy continues to depend heavily on the exploitation and export of diamonds. Diamonds account on average for 71% of export earnings, followed by copper nickel.

The labour market is characterized by a passive policy that puts emphasis on growth to deal with the problem of unemployment and underemployment. Unemployment stands today at around 22% in official figures. Real unemployment and underemployment is estimated to reach as high as 40% amongst youth, according to unofficial sources. In addition, there is no national social security scheme covering all workers and existing social safety nets are inadequate. Employment growth in the private sector has been slow, with the burden of employment creation falling on central and local government. While employment in central government grew by almost 30% during the period 1996-2000, private sector employment increased by only 9%.

GDP (purchasing power parity) $14.2bn. (2004 est.); GDP per capita (purchasing power parity) $9,000 (2004 est.).

2 Trade Unionism

Botswana ratified ILO Conventions No. 87 (Freedom of Association and Protection of the Right to Organize, 1948) and No. 98 (Right to Organize and Collective Bargaining, 1949) in 1997. All private sector workers and all public sector employees except those involved in national security may join unions.

The first union to be formed was the Francistown African Employees' Union (FAEU) in 1948 under the leadership of G. M. K. Mmusi. This was based only in Francistown because of restrictions imposed by the District Commissioner on the formation of trade unions. The union was recognized by the colonial government in 1964 but collapsed six years later. The late development of trade unions can be put down to under-development of the economy during colonial rule when unemployment was high. In 1959, the Bechuanaland Protectorate Union was formed in Serowe under the presidency of Lenyeletse Seretse. It was formed at the instigation of Tshekedi Khama. In 1962, the Bechuanaland Trade Union Congress was formed under the leadership of Klaas K. Motshidisi as its first general secretary. It was closely allied with the Bechuanaland People's Party and collapsed in 1965. After independence the local unions, financially supported by the ICFTU, formed the Bechuanaland Federation of Labour with G. M. K. Mmusi as general secretary.

The labour movement in Botswana developed in the early 1970s with the establishment of the Botswana Trade Union and Education Centre, comprising a handful of trade unions. In April 1977 the Botswana Federation of Trade Unions (BFTU) was founded and it replaced the Botswana Trade Union and Education Centre. All the major trade unions are currently affiliated to the BFTU and it is the only trade union federation in Botswana. The BFTU, which is not connected with any political party, participates in tripartite and other structures but, having only an advisory role, its influence has been limited. The BFTU has been particularly vocal on the adoption of international labour standards contained in the ILO Conventions and on the issue of privatization of state owned enterprises (parastatal corporations) and its effects on job security of employees.

The trade union movement has generally been politically neutral in that it has not formed any alliances with any particular political party, including the ruling party. There was, however, a public perception, especially in the mid-1990s, that the leaderships of the Botswana Mine Workers' Union and the Manual Workers' Union were aligned with the Botswana National Front, at that time the main opposition party and a strong contender in the 1994 general elections, although there was never a public declaration of the alliance.

The trade union movement does not have any significant negotiating power especially since the extent of its negotiating role is not prescribed by law. The law merely recognizes the right of trade unions to negotiate with employers on matters that have a bearing on the terms and conditions of employment of their members. As to what the exact extent of the negotiation process is, the law is silent. This has often resulted in confusion between employers and trade unions on the scope of negotiable as opposed to consultative matters.

The prevalent type of trade union is the in-house union. The Botswana Manual Workers' Union is considered the most important trade union in the country, notwithstanding the fact that its rate of unionization is not known with any measure of precision. Owing to the inability of trade unions to employ full-time, competent personnel to run their affairs, the organization and administration of individual unions is relatively poor, with day to day activities carried out by persons who have full-time jobs elsewhere. Very few trade unions are either industrial or sectoral. As far as in-house trade unions are concerned, the rate of unionization is relatively high, with some unions being able to achieve closed shops in some of their branches. The converse is true for industrial unions. Workers mainly regard trade unions as a means to negotiate better pay packages and/or represent them when they have a grievance or have been charged with misconduct. They are consequently inclined to the view that an in-house union is likely to represent their interests better since its officials will be their colleagues, who experience similar problems as them first hand.

Due to the lack of resources of both trade unions and the BFTU, there are no statistics to show the rate of unionization in the different workplaces, industries and sectors. What is agreed, however, is the fact that the rate of unionization among women is very low across the different age groups, compared with that of their male counterparts.

Relations between government and trade unions are limited to participation in tripartite structures such as the Labour Advisory Board, the Minimum Wages Advisory Board and other such structures set up by government where the labour movement is deemed to be a stake holder. The participation of trade unions is, however, not very significant in terms of their ability to influence government and participation in or contribution to government policies has been limited to matters relating to labour and employment. The government does not provide funding to trade unions or the BFTU and does not interfere in trade union elections. It has likewise not sought to give preference to some unions over others.

3 Trade Union Centre

Botswana Federation of Trade Unions (BFTU)
Address. P. O. Box 440, Gaborone
Phone/Fax. +267 3163261
E-mail. bot.ftu@info.bw
Leadership. Ronald Baipidi (president); Henry Teboho Makhale (general secretary)
History and character. The Botswana Federation of Trade Unions was founded in 1977. The main unions forming the BFTU were the Botswana Mining Workers' Union, the Botswana Bank Employees' Union, the Botswana Commercial and General Workers' Union, the Botswana Construction Workers' Union, and the Botswana Railways Workers' Union. The BFTU is the only national federation and its affiliates include well over 90% of the existing trade unions, including all the major unions.

Membership of the BFTU is open to all registered trade unions irrespective of their political or ideological orientation. The BFTU relies on subscriptions from its affiliates to run its activities. The BFTU has established a Women's Council to encourage women's participation in the labour movement, and the Executive Officers of the Women's Council are ex-officio members of the Executive Board but without the right to vote. However, all the decision making or governing structures of the BFTU are dominated by men. Former infighting and divisions within the BFTU have been resolved and independent unions which together have about 40,000 paid-up members have re-affiliated to the BFTU. This has brought unity within the organization.

There has recently been a deliberate move towards merging the different in-house trade unions belonging to the same or related industries into single and bigger sectoral unions. This move will see the BFTU affiliation reduced from the current 25 affiliates to 13. This is consistent with the BFTU's attempt to encourage bigger and more influential trade unions, compared with the current smaller and consequently extremely incapacitated trade unions. The re-affiliation of two major unions, the Manual Workers' Union and Commercial Workers' Union, has been seen as a major achievement.
International affiliations. SATUCC, OATUU, ICFTU, ICFTU/AFRO

Affiliate Members (ranking by size).

1. National Amalgamated Local and Central Government & Parastatal Manual Workers' Union
Address. P. O. Box 374, Gaborone
Phone. +267 3952790
Fax. +267 3957790
Leadership. Simon Kgaoganang (general secretary)

2. Botswana Mining Workers' Union
Address. P. O. Box 14, Selibe Phikwe
Phone. +267 2610693
Fax. +267 2614104
Leadership. Baagi Lebotse (general secretary)

3. Botswana Commercial & General Workers' Union
Address. P. O. Box 62, Gaborone
Phone/Fax. +267 3951111 / 71557419 c/o Mr. Phia Nyadoro
Leadership. Goitsimang Lebekwa (general secretary)

4. Botswana Manufacturing & Packaging Workers' Union
Address. P. O. Box 2906, Gaborone
Phone. +267 71715760
Leadership. Keitumetse Sebudi (executive secretary)

5. Botswana Wholesale, Furniture & Retail Workers' Union
Address. Private Bag 440, Gaborone
Phone. +267 5330030
Fax. +267 5330031
Leadership. Mbusewa Kenalemang (general secretary)

6. Botswana Beverages & Allied Workers' Union
Address. P. O. Box 502671, Gaborone
Phone. +267 71707331
Leadership. Juku B. Ratsatsi (administrative secretary)

7. Botswana Bank Employees' Union
Address. P. O. Box 111, Gaborone
Phone/Fax. +267 3905893
Leadership. Edith Molefhi (general secretary)

8. Botswana Railways Amalgamated Workers' Union
Address. P. O. Box 181, Gaborone
Phone. +267 3951405
Fax. +267 3919187
Leadership. Cristopher Phikane (general secretary)

9. Botswana Construction Wood Workers' Union
Address. P. O. Box 1508, Gaborone
Phone. +267 71504783 / 71876280
Leadership. Candy Keabile (general secretary)

10. Botswana Postal Services Workers' Union
Address. P. O. Box 87, Gaborone
Phone. +267 3901116
Fax. +267 3901079
Leadership. Modise Moopi (general secretary)

11. Botswana Vaccine Institute Staff Union
Address. P. O. Box 0031, Gaborone
Phone. +267 3912711
Fax. +267 3956798
Leadership. Elliot Modise (general secretary)

12. Central Bank Union
Address. P. O. Box 712, Gaborone
Phone. +267 3606565
Fax. +267 3913862
Leadership. Esan Motlaleng (general secretary)

13. Botswana Agricultural Marketing Board Workers' Union
Address. Private Bag 0053, Gaborone
Phone. +267 3951341
Fax. +267 3952926
Leadership. Edwin Molatlhegi (general secretary)

14. Botswana Housing Corporation Staff Union
Address. P. O. Box 502477, Gaborone
Phone/Fax. +267 3909911
Leadership. Felistus Keleeme (general secretary)

15. Botswana Telecommunication Employees' Union
Address. P. O. Box 502485, Gaborone
Phone. +267 3161617
Fax. +267 3161618
Leadership. Ethopha Mokeresete (general secretary)

16. University of Botswana Non-Academic Staff Union
Address. Private Bag 0022, Gaborone
Phone. +267 3555251
Fax. +267 3185096
Leadership. Gadzani Mhotsha (general secretary)

17. National Development Bank Staff Union
Address. P. O. Box 225, Gaborone
Phone. +267 3952801
Fax. +267 3974446
Leadership. Nelly Molefe (general secretary)

18. Botswana Power Corporation Workers' Union
Address. Private Bag 59, Palapye
Phone. +267 4920418
Fax. +267 4922844
Leadership. Emanuel Tseleng (general secretary)

19. Botswana Meat Industry Workers' Union
Address. P. O. Box 181, Lobatse
Phone. +267 5334034
Fax. +267 5334035
Leadership. Preston Tlhase (general secretary)

20. Botswana Diamond Sorters & Valuators' Union
Address. P. O. Box 1186, Gaborone
Phone. +267 3669651
Fax. +267 3951150
Leadership. Edward Keloneilwe (general secretary)

21. Botswana Private Medical & Health Services Workers' Union
Address. P. O. Box 440, Gaborone
Phone. +267 3901999
Fax. +267 3904717
Leadership. Leaname Keagakwa (general secretary)

22. Institute of Development Management Workers' Union
Address. P. O. Box 1352, Gaborone
Phone. +267 3952371
Fax. +267 3913296
Leadership. Bontle Keitumetsi (general secretary)

23. Botswana Hotel Travel & Tourism Workers' Union
Address. P. O. Box 254, Selibe Phikwe
Phone. +267 4920915
Fax. +267 4921889
Leadership. Kebabone Kgositlou (chairperson)

24. Botswana Saving Bank Employees' Union
Address. P. O. Box 1150, Gaborone
Phone. +267 3912555
Fax. +267 3906948
Leadership. Samon Moraloki (general secretary)

25. Air Botswana Employees' Union
Address. P. O. Box 92, Gaborone
Phone. +267 3952812
Fax. +267 3974802
Leadership. Violet Chebani (general secretary)

Brazil

Capital: Brasilia
Population: 184.1 m. (2004 est.)

1 Political and Economic Background

Brazil is a federal republic. It was under military rule from 1964 to 1985, when a civilian government was formed under President José Sarney, although a process of liberalization had set in earlier in the decade with the staging of multi-party elections in 1982. In 1990 Sarney was succeeded by Fernando Collor de Mello of the National Reconstruction Party, the first Brazilian president to be elected by universal suffrage for 29 years. He had narrowly defeated the candidate of the Workers' Party (PT) Luís Inácio da Silva ("Lula") a leading figure in the trade union movement. Collor was impeached on corruption charges by the Chamber of Deputies in 1992, stripped of office, and replaced by Itamar Franco as interim president. The 1994 elections were comfortably won by Fernando Henrique Cardoso, founder of the Brazilian Social Democrats (PSDB), with 54.3% of the vote; Lula was again runner-up, with 27%. Cardoso was re-elected in October 1998 but the 2002 presidential elections resulted in victory for Lula, who was supported by a broad coalition, reflected in the formation of a heterogeneous coalition government including parties that had originally opposed his candidacy.

Brazil has a diversified industrial, agricultural and service economy. After rapid expansion in 1964–74 the economy was rocked by the oil price rises of the 1970s. Heavy external borrowing and IMF assistance became necessary, and by the mid-1980s external debt amounted to about US$100bn. Inflation was rampant and reached an annualized rate of 16,000 per cent. Following several crises, a 1988 agreement rescheduled the country's debt. Since that time Brazil has undergone successive national rescue plans aimed at controlling inflation while encouraging growth and privatizing state enterprises, which once accounted for about half industrial output. Most rescue plans have faced intense domestic opposition at the impact on living standards. While inflation fell from its worst levels, by 1993 it was back to close to 2,500 per cent annually. In mid-1994 the Plano Real was introduced and under it inflation dropped to 2% by 1998, and 4.9% in 1999. However, Brazil was severely affected by the knock-on effects of the Asian economic crisis; there was a flight of capital from the country from August 1998, necessitating a $41.5bn. IMF support programme in November 1998. In January 1999 Brazil devalued its currency and declared it free floating, a move which had an adverse impact on its Mercosur trading partners. GDP growth was depressed to under 1% in 1999, although rising again in 2000.

The country is undergoing a process of technological catch-up, driven by forces such as the growth in services and rising consumer expectations, and there is a gradual opening of its closed, authoritarian and paternalistic government and business structures. Brazil nonetheless remains characterized by extremely unequal distribution of wealth, with extreme affluence contrasting with problems of shanty town development, violent drug-related crime, and street children in the cities and a large class of landless peasants in the countryside. Social spending is reduced by heavy budget commitments to high public sector pensions and debt repayments.

Lula toned down much of his former left-wing rhetoric prior to the 2002 elections, conceding the need for fiscal responsibility. His government has followed an orthodox economic policy, emphasizing sustainable economic growth and price stability: the immediate impact of his austerity policies was a contraction of GDP of 0.2% in 2003, with resultant discontent, but the economy performed strongly in 2004, with growth expected to be about 4.3%, reflected in strong job creation, while inflation at 7% was modest compared with historical levels. In August 2004 Lula announced: "After much work and sacrifice… we are finally beginning a new cycle of recovery and growth".

GDP (purchasing power parity) $1,375 billion (2003 est.); GDP per capita (purchasing power parity) $7,600 (2003 est.).

2 Trade Unionism

Brazil ratified ILO Convention No. 98 (Right to Organize and Collective Bargaining, 1949) in 1952, but has not ratified Convention No. 87 (Freedom of Association and Protection of the Right to Organize, 1948).

Labour organization in Brazil began in the first decade of the twentieth century. Two general confederations, the Confederación Nacional de Trabajo (CNT) and the communist-led Confederación General del Trabajo (CGT), were formed in the 1920s. Under the government of Getúlio Vargas (1930–45) unions were restructured on corporatist lines, with Mussolini's example in Italy as a model; strikes were prohibited, union structures absorbed into the state, and agricultural workers forbidden to organize. After 1946 greater freedom was allowed and the CGT reorganized, but attempts to create a unified national trade union centre were unsuccessful. Tight government control resumed after the 1964 military coup, with union affairs dominated by pro-government officials exercising authoritarian control. During the 1970s, although nominal rights to free collective bargaining and to strike existed, they were in practice largely negated by active government intervention in union affairs, and most strikes were declared illegal under the national security laws.

National reorganization of the labour movement began in 1981 with the first National Workers' Congress (CONCLAT). This brought together urban and rural workers and all ideological tendencies and reached agreement on the need for a unified national centre. After an initial failure there was success in August 1983 when a CONCLAT attended by 5,000 delegates set up Brazil's first national trade union centre, the CUT. Conservative and communist-led unions, including the main occupational federations, boycotted its formation, objecting to an arrangement whereby workers could organize to elect their own delegates if their unions refused to participate. These critics claimed that the CONCLAT would over-represent the liberal professions. The "combatives" however, the main force behind the formation of the CUT, believed they had made sufficient concessions in acceding to participation by unrepresentative existing occupational federations and confederations, and decided to proceed.

The non-participants at the August congress staged their own in November, there creating a rival semi-permanent organization which took the name of the National Coordination of the Working Classes (Coordenação Nacional des Classes Trabalhadores, also known as CONCLAT). This body was officially not described as a trade union centre, but as a deliberative and executive body to prepare the way for the formation of such a centre. In the view of the CUT, this CONCLAT was dominated by accommodationist conservatives (pelegos) and communist machine bosses. Technically both the CUT and the CONCLAT were illegal, Brazilian labour law not permitting the formation of collective organizations of unions representing workers in different occupations, but the government tacitly acquiesced.

Following the return of civilian government prohibitions on national and regional inter-trade organizations were lifted, and in 1985, the CUT and the CONCLAT cooperated for the first time in a general strike. In 1986 CONCLAT was reformed as a permanent organization to be called the Central Geral dos Trabalhadores (CGT). Thereafter the CUT, and to a lesser extent the CGT, adopted a generally confrontational attitude towards successive governments, rejecting efforts to secure a social pact, and staging a succession of general strikes and other protests, which received declining support from their members. In 1991 a third centre, Força Sindical (FS) was created under the leadership of Luis Antônio Medeiros, who called for a "trade unionism that gets results" rather than what was seen as the sterile confrontational policies of the existing centres. The CUT, CGT and FS are today the leading Brazilian centres, and all are now affiliated to the ICFTU.

In the period of military rule there was high profile union resistance to the regime, and heavy handed suppression of their organizations by the state. Restoration of civilian rule was followed by numerous strikes, exacerbated by wage controls and other measures to deal with economic difficulties, which placed the repeal of authoritarian employment legislation in doubt. However, the 1988 constitution provided for the freedom of all workers to form autonomous trade unions and to strike. Labour laws adopted that year were regarded as the most fundamental reform for 40 years, providing for a broad right to strike, indemnity for workers dismissed without justification, the right of workers (including public servants) to form unions, and an end to control of unions by the Ministry of Labour. Since the late 1980s there has been a process of bedding in of new institutions and a general decline of authoritarian and populist tendencies. This has also been reflected in the positions taken by many unions.

Unions are funded by the "imposto sindical" (union tax), a compulsory levy equivalent to a day's pay, payable to the Ministry of Labour. The proceeds are divided between local, provincial and national unions according to their membership, with 20 per cent retained by the Labour Ministry (in theory to provide for unemployment benefits). Under the "unicidade" system only one union is in theory permitted for each occupational category in a given geographical area (although this is widely disregarded in practice). The unicidade is opposed by the unions as a relic of previous state control. In November 1998 the government proposed the abolition of the unicidade and the union tax, but this was not approved by Congress. About 16% of the work force is organized, with the unions main strength being in the Sao Paulo "ABC" industrial zone (the largest industrial area in the Southern hemisphere) and in public service areas. All workers may join unions except those in the police, armed forces and fire services.

The government may cancel collective agreements that are not consistent with its wage policy (although this power is not currently applied), and there are restrictions on collective bargaining for public servants. While all workers have a general right to strike (other than military, police and firemen), abuse of the right to strike is unlawful; such abuse includes not maintaining basic essential services or ignoring a labour court decision to end a strike. The courts have in recent years been less inclined to rule strikes "abusive", although they continue to show a willingness to intervene in labour disputes.

Unions have complained about the circulation of union "blacklists" which list the names of all workers who have taken a case to an industrial tribunal. As many as two million labour cases are currently believed to be tied up in the industrial tribunals system.

Hundreds of landless rural workers and activists of the landless peasants' movement, the MST, have been killed during land disputes. The most celebrated victim of the gunmen was the leader of the CUT-affiliated Rubbertappers' Union and ecologist Chico Mendes. Chico Mendes had received a United Nations prize for making "an outstanding contribution to the life of our planet" for his work to protect the Amazonian forests from landowner depredation. He was shot dead in December 1988, and his convicted killers subsequently escaped. Occupations of unused land by the MST, and frequently violent evictions by landowners and police, are a continual feature of the Brazilian countryside. Rural workers have continued to report serious incidents of harassment and persecution, but in May 2003 the courts finally called those responsible for one high profile murder to account. Two landowners were sentenced to just under 20 years in prison for ordering the killing of rural workers' union leader João Canuto de Oliveira in 1985.

On Oct. 19, 2003, the leader of the São Paulo bus drivers' union was shot dead, the tenth killing of a transport workers' leader in three years.

Forced labour and debt bondage still persist in certain regions of Brazil. An ILO report published in October 2003 estimated that at least 40,000 people were working in conditions of slavery. The Lula government has launched a National Plan to eradicate slave labour. The government points to the difficulty of detecting such violations and enforcing labour laws in remote regions. The 1988 Brazilian Constitution categorically forbade the normal employment of any citizen under 14 but child labour remains a problem.

In July 2003 the government launched the tripartite National Labour Forum to study and extend reforms to the labour laws. 400 representatives of government, employers and unions participated in working groups and up to 10,000 are reported to have attended a series of conferences that were organized across the country. In mid-2004 a draft labour Bill was presented to congress proposing: (i) legal recognition of the central union federations, (ii) strengthening of union role in collective negotiations, (iii) replacing the government imposed union tax with a dues structure over the course of three years, and (iv) extending bargaining rights from municipal to state and national level. The government has also announced its intention to ratify ILO Convention No. 87 as a priority.

3 Trade Union Centres

Confederação Geral dos Trabalhadores (CGT)
General Confederation of Workers
Address. Rua Thomaz Gonzaga 50, 2° andar, Liberdade, Sao Paulo CEP 01506-020
Phone. +55 11 279 6577
Fax. +55 11 279 6452
E-mail. cgt@cgt.org.br
Website. www.cgt.org.br (Portuguese only)
History and character. The CGT was founded on March 23, 1986, at the second national congress of the Clase de Trabajadora de Brasil (CTB), convened by the CONCLAT (see above). The CGT was created to give permanent form to the work of the CONCLAT, and was described as the successor to the previous CGT banned by the military government in 1964. In establishing the new organization, the congress rejected ILO Convention No. 87 – adopted by President Dutra in 1948 but never ratified by the Brazilian Senate – which provides for full freedom and autonomy for trade unions, on the ground that "this divides the Brazilian trade union movement", a decision reflecting the basis of the new CGT in machine unionism of both the "yellow" and communist type.

It was resolved at the founding congress that the CGT would be independent and maintain fraternal relations with all three international organizations (i.e. ICFTU, WFTU and WCL). However, reflecting the changed shape of the international trade union movement in the wake of the collapse of Communism, it joined the ICFTU in 1991.
International affiliations. ICFTU

Central Única dos Trabalhadores (CUT)
Unitary Workers' Centre
Address. Rua Caetano Pinto 575, Sao Paulo, SP 03041-000
Phone. +55 11-21089200
Fax. +55 11-21089310
Website. www.cut.org.br (Portuguese only)
Leadership. João Antonio Felício (secretary general); Luiz Marinho (president)
Membership. Approximately 7 million, but represents up to 22 million in collective bargaining
History and character. The CUT was created at a national workers' congress (CONCLAT) held in August 1983 (i.e. after the return of civilian rule). The congress was boycotted by major conservative and communist-led unions, which subsequently formed their own organization (ultimately becoming the CGT).

Luís Inácio da Silva (Lula) was the leading figure in the creation of the CUT. He had emerged from within the Sao Paulo autêntico independent trade union movement in the late 1970s and gone on to found in 1980 the Workers' Party (Partido dos Trabalhadores, PT) in 1980 as the political voice of the "combative" wing of the labour movement. The PT and CUT developed in alliance in the late 1980s, the PT winning control of some city administrations and Lula running in successive national presidential elections with CUT support in 1990, 1994, and 1998. Lula went on to win the presidency in 2002, to take office in January 2003.

The CUT is the most militant of the three centres, reflecting its membership base. The CUT's membership is reportedly split slightly less than one-third manufacturing workers, more than one-third public servants, and one-third farm workers. Its agenda is influenced by the struggle over privatization of public services and the prominence in Brazil of land issues.
International affiliations. ICFTU

Força Sindical (FS)
Address. Palácio do Trabalhador, Rue Galvão Bueno 780, 13°andar, Sao Paulo SP 01506-000
Phone. +55 11 277 5877
Fax. +55 11 277 5877
E-mail. secgeral@fsindical.org.br
Leadership. João Carlos Gonçalves (interim president)
Membership. 2.1 million
History and character. The FS was created in 1991 under the leadership of Luis Antônio Medeiros, formerly a leader within the CGT. Its slogan was "a trade unionism that gets results" and it advocated a new culture of dialogue as a way of moving on from the con-

frontational policies of the centres (CGT, CUT) created in the aftermath of the return to civilian rule. Two-thirds of its membership are in manufacturing industry. The FS favours a more open market economy, free from Brazil's traditional state corruption and paternalism, and more equal distribution of wealth. It generally supported the efforts of the Cardoso government from 1994 to get to grips with Brazil's underlying economic problems, but criticized the government for lacking a social dimension to its economic reforms. The FS favours worker participation and co-determination. In October 2000 the FS initiated a "40 day march" from Sao Paulo to Brasilia to demand an increase in the minimum wage. The FS has grown quickly over the past decade. It supported political parties that have formed part of the Lula coalition.
International affiliation. ICFTU

4 Other Trade Union Organizations

Central Autónoma de Trabalhadores (CAT)
Address. Rua Jandaia, 218 – Bela Vista, CEP 01316-100, Sao Paulo
Phone. +55 11 3101 0429
Fax. +55 11 3101 0429
E-mail. cat@uol.com.br
Leadership. Laerte Teixeira Da Costa (president); Luis Eduardo Gauterio Gallo (secretary general)
International affiliations. WCL

Confederação Brasileira de Trabalhadores Cristâos (CBTC)
Address. Res. Areas Especiales, Lote 09, Caixa Postal 07925, CEP 70 649 970, Cruzeiro Velho, Brasilia D.F.
Phone. +55 61 233 0669
Fax. +55 61 361 8203
E-mail. cbtcnacional@bol.com.bz
Leadership. Walter De Souza Matos Filho (president)
International affiliations. WCL (extraordinary member)

Brunei

Capital: Bandar Seri Begawan
Population: 365,000 (2004 est.)

1 Political and Economic Background

The Sultanate of Brunei, having been a British protectorate since 1888, was largely self-governing from 1959, and became fully independent in 1984. Since 1962, following an unsuccessful left-wing rebellion, the Sultan has ruled by decree. Major responsibilities within the Cabinet are held by the Sultan, Hassanal Bolkiah (as Prime Minister), and by other members of the royal family. A non-elective Legislative Council was abolished shortly after independence; however, in September 2004 it re-convened for the first time in two decades and the Sultan signed a new constitution providing for the restoration of limited elections. No date was set for elections, however, and a majority on the Legislative Council would be appointed by the Sultan.

The Brunei economy is largely dependent on the production of petroleum and gas, and on oil refining and gas liquefaction. Together, these account for almost all of Brunei's exports and half of gross domestic product; the state has participation in most oil and gas activities. Brunei has enjoyed a high standard of living owing to oil and gas revenues and the government has been able to subsidize food and housing and there is a well-developed system of welfare services and other social benefits. Most employment is for the government or relates to government contracts, while 40% of the workforce are foreigners coming in as temporary residents. Brunei's Economic Council believes that the current structure is unsustainable long-term and that Brunei must develop an independent and competitive private sector.

GDP (purchasing power parity) $6.5bn. (2002 est.); GDP per capita (purchasing power parity) $18,600 (2002 est.).

2 Trade Unionism

According to the law all workers except the military and police may join unions. Registered unions have legal status, and the government has not prevented registration of unions, but they are little developed. The US State Department reports that "there is little interest on the part of workers in forming trade unions", reflecting good wages and benefits and a cultural tradition that favours consensus. It says that of the three registered unions (all of them in the oil sector), one is "passive" and the other two "generally inactive". They represent less than 5% of the petroleum sector workforce. Unions may not affiliate with international federations. Collective bargaining is not generally practiced. Strikes are thought to be lawful under existing legislation but in practice do not occur. Brunei is not a member of the ILO.

Bulgaria

Capital: Sofia
Population: 7.52 m. (2004 est.)

1 Political and Economic Background

The Bulgarian Communist Party (BCP) came to power after World War II and then ruled according to the Soviet model until the disintegration of the regime in 1989-90. From the adoption of a multi-party system in 1990 until 2001, the leading parties were the Bulgarian Socialist Party (BSP), the successor to the Communist Party, and the Union of Democratic Forces (UDF), formed in 1989 as an umbrella organization of anti-communist groups and parties but in 1997 transformed into a Christian democrat political party. Until 1997, Bulgaria was governed by a series of short-lived governments from both parties, twice formed by the BSP and once by the UDF, and three interim caretaker governments. In 1997, following an economic crisis, the UDF won a pre-term general election and became the first post-1989 government to complete its full term in office.

In elections in June 2001, however, the UDF lost office to a new political movement formed three months previously by the country's former king, the National Movement Simeon the Second (NMSS). Currently NMSS, despite defections, governs in coalition with a party representing the country's Turkish minority, the Movement for Rights and Freedoms. Following a further fragmentation of the UDF into separate parties, the BSP is the second largest formation in parliament followed by a UDF offshoot led by former UDF Prime Minister, Ivan Kostov, The Union of Strong Democrats, and then by the rump UDF led by a former Foreign Minister, Nadezhda Mihailova. The office of the President was occupied successively by two UDF representatives after the first presidential elections in 1991, Zheliu Zhelev (1991-96) and Petar Stoyanov, (1996– 2001) but, in another upset, was taken by a former leader of the BSP, Georgi Purvanov, in the 2001 presidential elections.

Bulgaria has a significant base of industries in areas such as food processing, chemicals, metal and energy. Privatization proceeded slowly for much of the early 1990s, hindered by political instability, opposition to privatization within the BSP and, in part, union opposition. Corruption within the privatization process contributed to an economic crisis in 1996-1997 which saw a collapse of the Bulgarian currency, the leva, and hyperinflation, leading to a drop in the real value of wages of about a third. Economic stability was restored with the introduction of a currency board in 1997. The UDF government of 1997-2201 committed itself, with IMF support, to the introduction of structural reforms including liberalization of agricultural polices, reform of social insurance, enhanced enforcement of laws, and an accelerated privatization program. While GDP growth averaged just under 4% p.a. in their term of office and some 73% of privatizable state assets had been transferred to the private sector by 2001, a lack of transparency and accusations of corruption in the privatization process, along with incomplete social insurance reforms, contributed to popular disenchantment witth the UDF government. A major part of the incoming NMSS government's programme in 2001 was a promise to restore economic prosperity within 800 days of assuming office, a pledge whose economic basis rested to a large extent on the privatization of two of Bulgaria's largest remaining state-owned companies, the Bulgarian Telecommunications Company and Bulgartabac, the country's tobacco-producing company. Both of these faced significant problems, including court challenges to the decisions of the Privatization Agency (particularly over the rights of workers in the privatized companies). Currently the Privatization Agency states that 2,878 of the 2,973 companies marked for privatization have been sold, amounting to 87% of the total value of state-owned assets. GDP growth since 2001 has been maintained at about 4% p.a. and inflation in the single-digit range; however unemployment at 17% of the workforce remains high and incomes remain well below the EU average.

GDP (purchasing power parity) $57.13bn. (2004 est.); GDP per capita (purchasing power parity) $7,600 (2004 est.).

2 Trade Unionism

Bulgarian trade unions first appeared in the 1880s, and the General Workers' Trade Union Association was formed in 1904. After the Communist Party consolidated its ruling position from 1944, unions were incorporated into the structure of the state and organized through the Central Council of Trade Unions (CCTU). Bulgaria ratified ILO Convention No. 87 (Freedom of Association and Protection of the Right to Organize, 1948) and Convention No. 98 (Right to Organize and Collective Bargaining, 1949) in 1959, although a single state-controlled trade union structure was in place at that time. While the CCTU was officially subordinate to the party, in practice it exercised a degree of autonomy in its affairs and some influence on the formulation of national labour relations strategy. This tradition would influence the post-1989 trade unions' perception of their function and role within the emerging democratic structures.

The 1991 Constitution, adopted after Bulgaria embraced multi-party democracy, guarantees the right of all workers to form or join trade unions of their own choosing. However, the unionized proportion of the work force (estimated at between 22 and 25%) has fallen with the decline of large state enterprises and the development of small and medium-sized enterprises in the private sector. The 2003 government census estimated that trade union membership had fallen from 2,191,101 in 1993 to 514, 957 in 2003.

There are two main trade union centres, the Confederation of Independent Trade Unions of Bulgaria (KNSB, or CITUB) and the Confederation of Labour "Podkrepa", both affiliates of the ICFTU, accounting between them for about half a milion members. A number of smaller trade unions, not considered representative by the government, are estimated to have between them up to 5,000 members.

In December 1989, faced with de facto trade union pluralism, the CCTU emulated the Communist Party, dismissed its leadership and changed its name to the Confederation of Independent Trade Unions of Bulgaria. In February 1990 the old CCTU statutes were completely overhauled, and later in the year the KNSB withdrew from the WFTU. After its reincarnation KNSB adhered firmly to a nonpartisan stance, insisting that industrial and not political priorities should determine its actions.

Podkrepa (Support) was formed by intellectuals in February 1989 as a trade union for the scientific, technical and cultural professions. Its president, Konstantin Trenchev, was imprisoned with several other activists in June, but its statutes and programme were published in September, and it was involved in widespread strikes in 1989–90 which contributed to the disintegration of the Communist regime. It was a full founder member of the UDF. In the first multi-party elections in June 1990 (narrowly won by the BSP), Podkrepa sponsored UDF candidates while KNSB stayed neutral. Strike action by Podkrepa members contributed to the resignation of the BSP government in January 1991, replaced by a non-party caretaker government led by a Sofia lawyer, Dimitur Popov. The BSP government had instigated an Agreement on Social Peace with the unions and employers' bodies which gave the unions a substantial role in formulating economic policies which affected their members. One of the first actions of the Popov government was to formalise this agreement into a tripartite National Commission, involving KNSB, Podkrepa, the National Union of Private Producers (Vuzrazhdane – "Regeneration"), the Union for Economic Incentive, the Union of Production Cooperatives, the Central Cooperative Union, and Bulgarian Economic Chamber, which gave the unions a mandatory role in the formulation of the national economic strategy. In July 1991, the UDF fragmented into three parties, UDF-Centre, UDF-Liberal and a rump UDF. Podkrepa gave active support to the rump UDF and, during the election campaign preceding the general election of September 1991, the union's branch network became in effect the UDF's regional structures. The UDF, led by Philip Dimitrov, narrowly won the election but in office, Prime Minister Dimitrov proved less than sympathetic to union participation in government and dissolved the National Commission, in part due to antipathy to cooperation with KNSB, in his eyes a former Communist structure, and in part due to his government's commitment to orthodox economic monetarism. During a period of economic crisis in May 1992 a successor, a National Council for Social Partnership, was briefly revived but abandoned by the unions, which judged that the government had failed to act on its recommendations.

The effect on the unions of the government's actions was twofold: on Podkrepa's perception of its role and on cooperation between the unions. On the former, the Law on Political Parties, agreed between the UDF and the BSP in early 1990 and enacted into law in April 1990, and subsequently the 1991 Constitution, had placed restrictions on the involvement of trade unions in political activity and appeared to separate trade unions from the political process. Podkrepa, in particular, had effectively side-stepped this requirement by actively campaigning, and providing support, for the UDF. With the election of a UDF government in 1991, though, Trenchev announced that Podkrepa's political aims had been achieved and reduced the organization's role in the UDF from full membership to that of observer. However, in response to Dimitrov's dissolution of the National Council, Trenchev later announced that Podkrepa was withdrawing completely from the UDF and would henceforth concentrate on the role of improving conditions for its members. On the latter, while Podkrepa and KNSB had cooperated in the past on the various tripartite bodies, the relationship between the two was uneasy. Podkrepa shared some of Dimitrov's reservations about the origins of KNSB within the Commmunist Party and its links with the BSP and moved in 1991 to persuade the UDF to divest it of its property. However the changed political climate after September 1991 brought the two unions closer together in a recognition of mutual interests. Both unions issued joint memoranda to the government in 1992 and cooperated on a series of strikes.

The Dimitrov government fell after a lost vote of confidence in October 1992 and was succeeded by a non-party "government of experts" led by Liuben Berov, a former economics adviser to President Zhelev. Berov, in office from 1992 to 1994, reinstituted tripartism through the creation of a National Council for Tripartite Co-operation (NCTC) and a wide network of branch commissions for negotiations at national and industry levels. The NCTC from 1992 became a forum for national incomes policy, and in 1993 broadened its responsibility to consideration of legal drafts across a wide range of social and employment related matters. In 1997 the incoming UDF government, inheriting a position of economic recession and hyper-inflation, effectively excluded the unions from discussion of adoption of an IMF structural adjustment programme, although tripartism resumed thereafter. The ICFTU Annual Survey of Trade Union Rights for 1999 noted that for several years there had been problems with the co-option of unrepresentative unions, often linked to political parties, onto the NCTC. In March 1998 the government initiated a census of trade union members that showed that only the KNSB and Podkrepa satisfied the criteria for being nationally representative and were thus qualified to participate in national-level tripartite bodies. A similar census in 2003 repeated the results of 1998.

Both the KNSB and Podkrepa are affiliated to the ICFTU. In February 1999 a WCL delegation visited two organizations wishing to affiliate to the WCL, the Association of Democratic Syndicates (ADS) and the National Trade Union "Promyana", an offshoot of Podkrepa. Both had been excluded from the NCTC. In October 1999 Promyana was affiliated to the WCL.

The 1992 labour code provides for collective bargaining. According to the unions, while collective bargaining is practiced it is undermined by employers not honouring agreements and by the lack of means of enforcing agreements. The labour code also provides a right to strike, but strikes are not allowed in electricity, communications and health, and "political" strikes are unlawful. Under 1990 legislation a majority of workers in an enterprise must vote for strike action for it to be lawful. Public sector workers prevented from striking have used go-slows as an alternative. Strike action to oppose government policies in areas such as privatization and tax increases were a feature of post-1989 Bulgaria. Strikes, go-slows, and demonstrations generally take place without government interference. Protests by blocking roads to protest against wage arrears were reported in 1999. In November 1997 the KNSB and Podkrepa said they had a list of 246, mainly foreign-owned, enterprises that were taking advantage of Bulgaria's economic difficulties to violate the labour code. Violations were said to be most common in regions of high unemployment. This was compounded by long delays in remedying grievances through the labour courts.

A working group on revision of the labour code to bring it into conformity with international standards began work in May 1999. It comprised government officials, representatives of the Bulgarian Business Chamber, Podkrepa, and the KNSB, with representatives of the Bulgarian Investors' Business Association (foreign investors) participating as non-members. In a statement issued on May 10, 2000 Podkrepa criticized the apparent wish of the government to distance itself from enforcement of labour legislation and leave matters to employers in the absence of representative employers' associations able to bind their members. The current government honoured a pledge to re-establish effective tripartism by founding an Economic and Social Council (ESC) in 2001 involving both KNSB and Podkrepa, representatives of employers' organizations and NGOs. The role of the ESC is to express the views of the social partners and other representatives of civil society on Bulgaria's main economic and social problems. While the unions viewed the ESC as a step forward, the slowness with which it was established (administrative problems and difficulties in choosing representatives of NGOs meant that it did not hold its first meeting until 2004) led both trade union centres to complain of a lack of government dialogue with the trade unions. Union disaffection with the Government's economic policies., which they considered transferred a large part of the tax burden from businesses to the low-paid, first became apparent in 2003 when KNSB organized a series of protests. These protests ended when KNSB reached agreement with the government and employers' organizations to resolve some of its concerns. However, when it became apparent that these changes were not reflected in the 2004 state budget, both centres cooperated in a campaign charging that the government's economic policies violated the European Social Charter.

3 Trade Union Centres

Confederation of Independent Trade Unions of Bulgaria (KNSB/CITUB)
Address. 1 Macedonia Square, 1040 Sofia
Phone. +359 2 987 70 65
Fax. +359 2 988 59 69
E-mail. jhristov@knsb-bg.org
Website. www.knsb-bg.org
Leadership. Dr. Jeliazko Hristov (president)
History and character. The KNSB's origins lie in the Central Council of Trade Unions (CCTU), which was established following the 1944 coup which led to the consolidation of power by the Bulgarian Communist Party. Until the 1980s no unions were permitted outside the CCTU structure and it was closely controlled by the ruling party. Since the end of the Communist regime it has sought to transform itself from an official single trade union structure to a new independent organization in a pluralist context.

The 5th (November 1989) extended CCTU plenum repudiated the "conciliatory and yielding" posture of the official unions and acknowledged a widespread view that the confidence of working people could be regained only if the unions became uncompromising defenders of their interests. In a founding resolution the Bulgarian trade unions were now proclaimed independent of political organizations, and a month later the 6th extended plenum removed the entire collective leadership headed by Petur Dyulgerov and installed a new team led by Krastyo Petkov.

During January 1990, a consultative CCTU ballot revealed substantial support for diversity of forms of property, opposition to the participation of political parties, and support for the newly independent unions entering the forthcoming elections in their own right. Petkov's position was legitimized at the 11th extraordinary congress of Feb. 17–18, 1990, which elected him unopposed as chairman and launched the Confederation of Independent Trade Unions of Bulgaria (KNSB). The extraordinary congress then became the constituent congress of KNSB and invited federations and unions to affiliate or leave it in freedom. Contacts were opened with the ETUC; WFTU affiliation lapsed. KNSB developed a critical view of the BSP (the reformed Communist Party) and stayed officially neutral during the June 1990 elections. At its third congress, KNSB approved a compromise resolution on the property and assets of the former state unions, currently in government hands, that amounted to renouncing its claims on the bulk of them.

"The transition to a market economy", the KNSB concluded in 1993, had so far "proved to be beneficial only for a thin layer of old and new profiteers". It called for faster structural reform including privatization, but insisted that this should proceed by agreement. With some variations, and with the exception of brief periods when the Kostov government took office in 1997 and Simeon's government in 2001, this has been a constant theme of KNSB's view of the reform process. In 2003, KNSB claimed 19 constituent unions and had 390,000 members
International affiliations. ICFTU; ETUC

Confederation of Labour "Podkrepa" (Support)
Address. 2 Angel Kantchef Street, 1000 Sofia
Phone. +359 2 980 7766
Fax. +359 2 981 2928
E-mail. president@podkrepa.org
Website. www.podkrepa.org
Leadership. Dr. Konstantin Trenchev (president)
History and character. Founded by a group of intellectuals in February 1989, it immediately applied to the regime for official registration, declaring its aims to be the defence of members' interests and opposition to arbitrariness and encroachments by unscrupulous firms and state enterprises. Despite the imprisonment of several leaders, Podkrepa published its statutes and programme in September. At its first (March 1990) congress it claimed 70,000 members and half a million two years later.

Podkrepa was a founder member of the coalition of opposition forces known as Sayuz na Demokratichni Sili (Union of Democratic Forces, UDF), its largest adherent and a powerful advocate of free market policies. It sponsored several candidates of the UDF in the first multi-party elections in June 1990. These were narrowly won by the (former communists) of the BSP. Podkrepa remained involved in industrial unrest through a prolonged period of political chaos when formation of a stable government became impossible. The UDF itself became involved in government for the first time in December 1990, although the government fragmented as did its relationship with Podkrepa.

Podkrepa's subsequent evolution showed a deteriorating relationship with the UDF government. In August 1992 Konstantin Trenchev was arrested and charged with incitement to destroy public property in connection with an attack on the Sofia headquarters of the Bulgarian Communist Party. The Podkrepa secretary Svilen Marinov was arrested one day after Trenchev. Podkrepa also faced internal difficulties as in January 1993 some Podkrepa branches broke away, a number of them becoming prominent founders of a new Community of Free Trade Union Organizations. Podkrepa's rival KNSB was also rebuilding itself and despite a partial rapprochement with KNSB, Podkrepa continued to regard its rival as a "communist trade union" that had not changed its totalitarian character. It declined an invitation to participate in the October 1993 KNSB Congress. While Podkrepa broke formal ties with the UDF in 1991, it nevertheless maintained a close ideological association with the UDF, different factions within Podkrepa reflecting the split in the UDF between those who favoured working with the former communist party for the sake of establishing a stable democracy and those who advocated decommunization before democratization.

While, unlike the UDF, Podkrepa managed to maintain its unity, the strains engendered by this ideological divide resulted in the formation of two breakaway trade unions seeking a more political role, a short-lived Podkrepa within the UDF in 1995 and in 1997, Promyana. This ideological closeness and Podkrepa's roots as a dissident organization have given Podkrepa, and in particular its founder president, Konstantin Trenchev, some influence over the UDF, notably in 1999 when accusations by Trenchev of corruption within the UDF government brought about a cabinet reshuffle. With the recent fragmentation of the UDF this relationship has loosened but still retains some potency. Podkrepa has 25 member organizations and 4 associated member organizations, and, according to the government census of 2003, 109,000 members .
International affiliations. ICFTU (since 1991); ETUC

4 Other Trade Union Organization

National Trade Union "Promyana" (NTU Promyana)
Address. Graf Ignatiev str. 10A, 1000 Sofia
Phone. +359 2 986 3209
Fax. +359 2 986 6605
Leadership. Pancho Mutafchiev (president)
International affiliation. WCL

Burkina Faso

Capital: Ouagadougou
Population: 13.57 m. (2004 est.)

1 Political and Economic Background

Burkina Faso (named Upper Volta until 1984) became a self-governing republic within the French Community in 1958 and gained full independence in 1960. A 1966 military coup was followed by alternating periods of military and civilian rule. Blaise Compaoré took power as leader of a "Popular Front" in a military coup in 1987 and then went on to be elected president at the end of military rule in 1991 and against in 1998. During the 1990s the legislature was dominated by Compaoré's Congress for Democracy and Progress (CDP). Elections in May 2002 resulted in another victory for the CDP, but with barely a majority.

One of the poorest countries in the world, land-locked Burkina has a backward economy, in which about 90% of the population is engaged in (mainly subsistence) agriculture. The West African area within which Burkina Faso lies has been subject to long periods of drought, and this, together with widespread disease, has sharply reduced agricultural output. Cotton is the key crop. There are limited mineral resources, while manufacturing (mainly textiles and the processing of tobacco and food products) accounts for only about 10% of total GDP. Burkina Faso has a large trade deficit and is heavily dependent on multilateral and bilateral sources of finance. In 1991 it initiated an austere IMF structural adjustment plan, and like 13 of the 14 countries in the African franc zone Burkina participated in the 1994 devaluation of the CFA franc. A large proportion of the male workforce has seasonal employment in neighbouring countries. The internal crisis in neighbouring Côte d'Ivoire continues to hurt trade and industrial prospects and deepens the need for international assistance.

GDP (purchasing power parity) $14.55 billion (2003 est.); GDP per capita (purchasing power parity) $1,100 (2003 est.)

2 Trade Unionism

Burkina Faso (as Upper Volta) ratified ILO Convention No. 87 (Freedom of Association and Protection of the Right to Organize, 1948) in 1960 and Convention No. 98 (Right to Organize and Collective Bargaining, 1949) in 1962.

Unions in Burkina Faso (then Upper Volta) date from 1947, when the Union Syndicale des Travailleurs Voltaïques (USTV) was established; by 1978 six centres were in existence. Although having only a few thousand members, the unions were significantly involved in Burkina Faso's turbulent politics. In 1966 the Yameogo regime was brought down by army intervention following a general strike. President Lamizana was likewise deposed in a 1980 coup after several weeks of strikes and protests led by teachers and supported by the four main federations. The successor regime of Colonel Zerbo banned the right to strike in 1981, describing it as "a luxury which our economy cannot allow in the difficult world situation". There were further coups in November 1982 and August 1983, following which the National Revolutionary Council (NRC) government eased restrictions on unions and militants dismissed under Zerbo were permitted to apply for their former jobs.

Relations between the NRC regime and the unions deteriorated following the 1985 arrest and detention of some 20 union leaders who had signed a declaration protesting against the introduction of economic austerity measures. Union discontent – particularly among the teachers – contributed to the 1987 coup in which NRC leader Thomas Sankara was overthrown, killed and replaced by his erstwhile friend and colleague Capt. (now President) Blaise Compaoré. Relations with the unions improved thereafter, pay and conditions were reviewed and more than 1,000 dismissed teachers were reinstated.

Most workers, including those in the public sector, are permitted to join unions, although their scale is limited by the small size of the formal economy. The unions operate without major restrictions. There are several confederations, including two (the CSB and ONSL) affiliated to the ICFTU and one (the CNTB) affiliated to the WCL.

The right to strike is recognized. However, the government has the right to requisition all civil servants in the event of a strike. Some civil servants are banned from striking, notably labour inspectors and uniformed personnel. In October 2001, the Minister of Justice announced that, under a major reform of the justice system, magistrates would no longer be allowed to go on strike. This followed a strike by magistrates in April 2001.

Collective bargaining exists in the small formal economy and is backed up by labour tribunals. The right to strike is frequently exercised and generally respected by the government. Strikes are staged for both economic and political causes and sometimes have considerable political impact. In May 2003, the major trade unions called a general strike to protest the privatization of parastatal organizations and the government's decision to grant interest-free loans to cabinet members. Unions also demanded salary and pensions' increases and lower taxes. The government refused to negotiate and none of the unions' demands were met.

In practice trade unionists are often subjected to intimidation. In the early 2000s, some union leaders were transferred away from their membership base and trade union meetings were raided. There have been reports that the authorities have sought to undermine or weaken trade unions, especially during strike action.

Child labour is prevalent in Burkina Faso. Statistics from the Ministry of Labour estimated that, in the year 2000, 50% of children were employed in some form of activity. Although Burkina has ratified the core ILO Conventions on Forced Labour, the practice does exist.

3 Trade Union centres

Confédération Nationale des Travailleurs du Burkina (CNTB)
National Confederation of Workers of Burkina
Address. BP 445, Ouagadougou
Phone. +226 31 23 95
Fax. +226 31 08 50
Leadership. Laurent Ouedraogo (secretary general)
International affiliation. WCL

Confédération Syndicale Burkinabe (CSB)
Trade Union Confederation of Burkina
Address. Bourse du Travail 01, BP 1469, Ouagadougou
Phone. +226 50 31 83 98
Fax. +226 50318398; +226 50 33 71 71
E-mail. cosyby2000@yahoo.fr
Leadership. Jean-Mathias Liliou (secretary general)
International affiliations. ICFTU

Organisation Nationale des Syndicats Libres (ONSL)
National Organisations of Free Trade Unions
Address. BP 99, Ouagadougou
Phone. +226 50 34 34 69
Fax. +226 50 34 35 69
Leadership. Abdoulaye Yra (secretary general)
Membership. 6,000
History and character. ONSL was founded in 1960 and formerly known as the Organisation Voltaïque des Syndicats Libres (OVSL). In the 1990s it increased its influence through agitation against the social impact of structural adjustment.
International affiliations. ICFTU

Burundi

Capital: Bujumbura
Population: 6.23 m. (2004 est.)

1 Political and Economic Background

Burundi was granted independence as a monarchy in 1962, having previously been administered by Belgium since the termination of German rule during World War I, first under a League of Nations mandate and from 1946 as a UN trusteeship. The monarchy was overthrown in 1966 and the Republic of Burundi declared. Tribal antagonism between the Tutsi and the majority Hutu led to serious internal unrest between 1969 and 1972 and confirmation of Tutsi dominance. The Tutsi-dominated Party of the Union for National Progress (UPRONA, originally created in 1958) was formally recognized as sole political party in the 1974 Constitution and retained this position after a 1987 coup which brought the Military Committee of National Salvation (MCNS), headed by Maj. Pierre Buyoya, to power.

In the early 1990s Burundi, as many other countries in Africa, sought to move from a one-party state to a measure of pluralism and UPRONA also moved a number of Hutus into leadership positions. In 1993, presidential elections resulted in the defeat of UPRONA's candidate, Buyoya, by the candidate of the Burundi Front for Democracy (FRODEBU), Melchior Ndadaye, a Hutu, who however appointed a number of UPRONA members to his government in an attempt to maintain stability. In October 1993 Ndadaye was killed in an unsuccessful coup attempt by dissident Hutu army officers, and this precipitated a period of inter-ethnic violence and political confusion. In July 1996 Buyoya returned to power in a coup and in 1998 signed a new constitution embracing power-sharing between Hutus and Tutsis, under which he also became president. However, violence continued.

Peace talks facilitated by former South African President Nelson Mandela resulted in the signing in July 2001 of the Arusha power-sharing agreement designed to end the civil war. Under the terms of the agreement, a new transitional government was formed in November 2001, composed of Tutsis and Hutus. It was agreed that President Buyoya would hold the presidency for a term limited to only 18-months at the start of a three-year transitional period. The transition was relatively orderly and in April 2003 Domitien Ndayizeye, leader of the FRODEBU, replaced Buyoya as President. However, Hutu rebel opposition to the Arusha peace process – and in particular to Tutsi control of the armed forces – continued, led by the Forces for National Liberation (FNL).

The Burundi economy is based almost exclusively on agriculture (largely subsistence), which accounts for 90% of the labour force, and is also conditioned by the country's landlocked position, its high density of population and its paucity of natural resources. The principal cash crop is coffee (which accounts for some 90% of foreign exchange earnings but whose international markets and prices are subject to wide fluctuations). The Tutsi minority, 14% of the population, dominates the coffee trade at the expense of the Hutu majority, 85% of the population. The small manufacturing sector is based mainly on the processing of agricultural products. Since 1993 the fragile economy has been further damaged by ethnic violence, which has led to the death or displacement of more than 1 million people.

GDP (purchasing power parity) $3.78 billion (2003 est.); GDP per capita (purchasing power parity) $600 (2003 est.).

2 Trade Unionism

Burundi ratified ILO Conventions No. 87 (Freedom of Association and Protection of the Right to Organize, 1948) and No. 98 (Right to Organize and Collective Bargaining, 1949) in 1993 and 1997 respectively.

The small scale of the formal economy and interethnic violence have limited the development of trade unionism. Most union workers are urban civil servants. The right to organize and the right to strike in the civil service are regulated by a law of November 2002. The Labour Code allows workers to form unions, except those in the army and gendarmerie, while section 14 of the Labour Code excludes state employees and magistrates from the scope of the code.

All previously existing unions were absorbed into the (Tutsi-dominated) Union des Travailleurs du Burundi (UTB) in 1967, this being closely linked to UPRONA. Another organization, the Fédération des Syndicats Chrétiens Ouvriers et Paysans du Burundi (FSCOPB), founded in 1958 and associated with the Belgian Confédération des Syndicats Chrétiens (CSC), had been closely linked with the Hutu tribe, and many of its members were killed in conflicts with the Tutsi. Subsequently, the Confederation of Free Unions of Burundi (CSB) was formed, but it maintained close links with the government. Since gaining independence from the government in 1992, the CSB has been dependent financially on a system of check-offs, or voluntary contributions, as are local unions. In 1995 a rival trade union, the Confederation of Burundi Unions (COSYBU), was founded.

3 Trade Union Centres

Confédération des Syndicats du Burundi (COSYBU)
Confederation of Burundi Unions
Address. Avenue du 18 Septembre, Ex. Hôtel Central 8, BP 220, Bujumbura
Phone. +257 24 81 90
Fax. +257 24 81 90
E-mail. cosybu@yahoo.fr
Leadership. Pierre-Claver Hajayandi (president)
History and character. COSYBU was founded in 1995 and is affiliated to the ICFTU. In September 2004 the COSYBU president, Pierre-Claver Hajayandi, and treasurer, Célestin Nsavyimana, were detained by the authorities for several days after addressing a workers' meeting in which they reportedly criticised government plans to submit a new draft constitution to a national referendum.
International affiliation. ICFTU

Cambodia

Capital: Phnom Penh
Population: 13.36 m. (2004 est.)

1 Political and Economic Background

The Kingdom of Cambodia became independent from France in 1953. In the 1960s it became affected by spill-over from the war in Vietnam. Prince Sihanouk was deposed by a pro-US regime in 1970. In 1975 the Chinese-backed Khmers Rouges under Pol Pot, preaching a form of virulently anti-Vietnamese communist agrarian fundamentalism, gained control of the country after a civil war and established Democratic Kampuchea (DK). Sihanouk was head of state until April 1976 before being removed. Under the Khmers Rouges millions were forced out of the cities and in one of the worst examples of state terror of the century perhaps two million died. In 1979, the Pol Pot regime was driven out of Phnom Penh by Vietnamese-backed communist rebels, who went on to establish single party rule in a renamed People's Republic of Kampuchea (PRK). Fighting continued throughout the 1980s, with Russia and Vietnam backing the PRK government and China arming the Khmers Rouges, which also allied with Prince Sihanouk. In 1989 the country was renamed Cambodia as Vietnamese forces began to withdraw. Under the 1991 Paris Accords, Prince Sihanouk returned as head of state in 1993 and a coalition government was formed, with two joint Prime Ministers. One of these, Hun Sen, subsequently consolidated power in his own hands in a July 1997 palace coup, becoming sole Prime Minister the following year. Following elections in July 1998, a coalition government was formed between the Cambodia People's Party (CPP, Hun Sen's party) and the United National Front for an Independent, Neutral, Peaceful and Cooperative Cambodia (FUNCINPEC). The 2003 elections ultimately resulted in a continuation of the coalition, with Hun Sen of the dominant CPP remaining Prime Minister.

Pol Pot refused to participate in the 1993 settlement and continued to fight in the jungle. However, the Chinese cut off aid in 1996, Pol Pot died in April 1998, the military leader Ta Mok was captured in March 1999, and in 1998-99 most remaining Khmers Rouges forces surrendered, were captured or dispersed. 1999 was considered the first peaceful year in Cambodia for three decades.

The country's infrastructure, industrial sector and financial institutions were destroyed in the 1970s. The PRK government directed an economy of three sectors: state, cooperative and family (private), and inaugurated Cambodia's first five-year plan in 1985, with "export and thrift" as the primary economic guidelines. But Cambodia was heavily dependent on aid from the Soviet Union and Vietnam, and in 1991 Soviet aid was cut by 80 per cent. As some kind of normalization was established, IMF credits were granted to Cambodia in 1994. The IMF again suspended its Cambodia programme after the 1997 coup, but resumed loans in October 1999. In recent years Cambodia has shown progress in rebuilding the economy; growth averaged 5% per annum in 2001-03 with tourism and textiles among growth sectors. However, the infrastructure is poor, and virtually non-existent in rural areas, and the government has identified problems of bureaucratic restrictions and corruption. 80 per cent of the labour force is engaged in agriculture. The garment sector is the principal source of export earnings and in October 2004 Cambodia became only the second least developed country to join the World Trade Organization.

GDP (purchasing power parity) $25.02bn. (2003); GDP per capita (purchasing power parity) $1,900 (2003).

2 Trade Unionism

Cambodia became a member state of the ILO in 1969 and has ratified all of the fundamental conventions except for Convention No. 182, the Worst Forms of Child Labour convention.

Under the Vietnamese-backed People's Republic of Kampuchea (PRK) government, the Kampuchean Federation of Trade Unions (KFTU) was established in 1979. This was chaired by a member of the politburo of the ruling KPRP party and was the sole union centre. It was active in the 1980s and (as the Cambodian Federation of Trade Unions) is still recorded as a WFTU affiliate although no longer in existence.

In 1997 a comprehensive labour code was adopted that guaranteed the right to workers in the private sector to form unions and bargain collectively. Public workers do not have the right to bargain collectively. Most urban workers are employed in small-scale enterprises, or are self-employed skilled workers or unskilled day labourers. Most unions have therefore been formed in the fast growing, mainly foreign-owned garment industry. In 2003 it was estimated that 25 to 30% of the approximately 200,000 workers in the garment sector were union members. In November 2003, the first genuine collective bargaining agreement was signed in the industry. In September 2003, nine individual tourism and service industry unions joined the Cambodia Tourism and Service Workers' Federation, representing over 3,500 hotel, casino, and airport workers. Despite the ban on public sector organizing, one public sector union was formed as an "association" called the Cambodia Independent Teachers' Association.

By 2003 the Ministry of Labour (MOSALVY) had registered 511 factory unions and 14 national labour federations. This represents a dramatic increase of union density in the garment industry since the labour code was passed in 1997. It also reflects a greater willingness on the part of MOSALVY to register unions in contrast to its earlier years in which it placed significant obstacles for unions, particularly independent ones, to register.

Nevertheless, violations of basic labour rights remain pervasive. The ICFTU in its 2003 report on trade union violations noted that violations of freedom of association are commonplace. However, there is some evidence that conditions are improving since the institution of an ILO factory-monitoring programme linked to a trade agreement with the United States.

Most of the labour federations have close ties to the Cambodia People's Party (CPP) government or to individuals within it. The most prominent pro-government union is the Cambodian Union Federation (CUF). The prominent opposition union, the Free Trade Union of Workers of the Kingdom of Cambodia (FTUWKC), is linked with the Sam Rainsy party. Its leader, Chea Vichea, was murdered in January 2004 in what some believe was a political related killing. There are two unions in the garment sector that are considered to be politically independent: the National Independent Federation of Textile Unions of Cambodia (NIFTUC) and the Coalition of Cambodia Apparel Workers' Development Union (CWCADU).

3 Trade Union Centres

Free Trade Union of Workers of the Kingdom of Cambodia (FTUWKC)

History and character. The FTUWKC was organized in December 1996 and registration was conceded by the government in December 1998. The FTUKWC has recruited in garment factories and in February 1998 led a demonstration outside the US Embassy calling for the ending of Cambodia's trading privileges until labour conditions in the garment trade were improved. Later that year, the government said that it would monitor conditions in the garment sector and cancel licenses of employers in violation. Its second congress was held in March 1999, the majority of delegates being women workers in the garment industry. It received a WCL visit in September 1999. The FTUWKC president Chea Vichea was murdered in January 2004.

Cameroon

Capital: Yaoundé
Population: 16.06 m. (2004 est.)

1 Political and Economic Background

The Republic of Cameroon acquired its present name in 1984 and comprises the former territories of the Federal Republic of Cameroon, created in 1961 from the trusteeship of French Cameroon (independent since 1960) and the British trusteeship of Southern Cameroons. Until 1990 the sole legal party (holding all the seats in the unicameral National Assembly) was the Rassemblement Démocratique du Peuple Camérounais (RDPC), established in 1985 to replace the Union Nationale Camérounaise. The RDPC won disputed multi-party elections in 1992 and again in 1997 and 2002. The elected President, Paul Biya, has held the position since 1982.

Agriculture represents the major sector of the economy, accounting for more than 40% of gross domestic product and 70% of the workforce, but the industrial sector accounts for a further quarter of GDP. Industries include petroleum production and refining and food processing. During the 1990s the government followed IMF and World Bank programmes intended to encourage investment and increase efficiency, but with mixed success and uncertain commitment, with problems of bureaucratic inertia and corruption. State industries have been progressively privatized.

GDP (purchasing power parity) $27.75bn. (2004 est.); GDP per capita (purchasing power parity) $1,800 (2004 est.).

2 Trade Unionism

Cameroon ratified ILO Convention No. 87 (Freedom of Association and Protection of the Right to Organize, 1948) in 1960 and Convention No. 98 (Right to Organize and Collective Bargaining, 1949) in 1962.

Unions developed on the French model, with divisions along political lines, and at the beginning of the 1960s there were about 100 unions and several competing centres. The number of unions fell rapidly during the 1960s and in 1971 four survivors dissolved into a sole centre (Syndicat Central Unique), later known as the National Union of Cameroon Workers (Union Nationale des Travailleurs du Caméroun, UNTC), and thereafter as the Organization of Cameroon Workers' Unions (Organisation des Syndicats des Travailleurs Camérounais, OSTC). Before 1991 workers were restricted to joining unions affiliated to the sole trade union centre.

At a 1991 congress the OSTC resolved on complete restructuring and a further change of name to the Confederation of Cameroon Trade Unions (CSTC). In 1992 a new labour code provided for workers to have freedom to form and join unions of their own choosing. During 1993 the government introduced cuts in public sector salaries; in the case of teachers and doctors the reduction was almost half. The CSTC responded with strikes. This marked the beginning of a deteriorating relationship between it and the ruling party. Since 1993 there has been continual interference in the affairs of the CSTC by the government and the government also backed the creation of a rival organization, the USLC.

Trade unions must be registered and in recent years, the government has refused registration to some public sector unions, particularly those of teachers. Collective bargaining is provided for under the 1992 labour code but no collective bargaining negotiations have taken place in recent years. There is a right to strike (but not for civil servants) and strikes and strike threats are not uncommon. Some provisions of the labour code do not apply in export processing zones (EPZs) and the unions say that they are denied access to EPZ enterprises. The government is currently reviewing the labour code.

3 Trade Union Centres

Confédération Syndical des Travailleurs du Cameroun (CSTC)
Confederation of Cameroon Trade Unions (CCTU)
Address. BP 998, Yaoundé
Phone. +237 225454/704029
Fax. +237 225456/315029
Leadership. Andre Jule Mousseni (president)
History and character. The CSTC, under different names, functioned as the trade union arm of the ruling RDPC until the relative liberalization of the early 1990s when it declared its independence of political parties. Thereafter relations with the RDPC deteriorated. In 1994 and early 1995 the CSTC suffered extreme forms of government interference in its internal affairs. The freedom of movement of its general secretary Louis Sombes was restricted and a new leadership imposed. Ministry supervision of CSTC affairs was instituted. Only in January 1995 were Sombes supporters able to force an extraordinary congress and secure his re-election. According to the ICFTU, the government was behind the formation of a rival centre, the USLC, in 1995 and engineered a split in the CSTC itself in 1997, when the Minister of Labour ruled that neither faction could be recognized. In April 1998 a congress held under ILO auspices resulted in the election of a reform slate led by Benoît Essiga, but the government refused to recognize the new leadership. In 2003 Essiga formed a new federation, the CGTLC. In January 2003, and again in April, Benoît Essiga, who is also president of the rail workers' union, was arrested following a dispute on the railway. ICFTU described this as evidence of clear collusion between the Camrail company and the authorities.
International affiliation. ICFTU; CTUC; OATUU

General Confederation of Free Workers of Cameroon (CGTLC)
Leadership. Benoît Essiga
History and character. CGTLC was launched in March 2003 by the former CSTC president Benoît Essiga.
International affiliation. None

Union des Syndicats Libres du Cameroun (USLC)
Union of Free Trade Unions of Cameroon
Address. BP 13.306, Yaoundé
Phone. +237 211266
Fax. +237 9829317
E-mail. USLC@iccnet.cm
Leadership. Flaubert Moussole (president); M'Bom Mefe (secretary general)
History and character. The USLC was created as a rival national centre to the ICFTU-affiliated CSTC in 1995, according to the ICFTU with government encouragement. Its secretary general, André Jules Mousseni, was a former deputy secretary general of the CSTC who took over as CSTC secretary general in 1994 when Louis Sombes was deposed by the government, before Sombes was restored by the membership in January 1995.
International affiliation. WCL; OATUU

Canada

Capital: Ottawa
Population: 32.51 m. (2004 est.)

1 Political and Economic Background

Canada comprises ten provinces and three territories. At the federal level in the period from the 1960s to the early 1990s there were two main national parties, the Liberals (who held office for nearly all the period from 1963-84) and the Progressive Conservatives, who were in government from 1984–93. The third (minority) party at federal level was the social democratic New Democratic Party (NDP). Since then, however, while the Liberals have won four national elections in succession (in 1993, 1997, 2000 and 2004, in the last case without an overall majority) under Prime Ministers Jean Chrétien and Paul Martin, the conservative vote has fragmented, the NDP has subsided to a marginal position nationally, and voting patterns have polarized very sharply on a regional basis.

In the most recent general elections, in June 2004, the Liberals won 135 of the seats in the 308-member House of Commons. The Conservative Party of Canada, a merger between the moderate traditionalist Progressive Conservatives and the recently formed and more radical right-wing Canadian Alliance (based mainly in the western provinces) won 99 seats. The results underscored the deep divisions between the different regions of Canada, showing fault-lines between east and west and between (mainly French-speaking) Quebec and the rest of the country. The Conservative Party, campaigning on a platform of opposition to "big government" in Ottawa, won 68 of the 92 seats in the four western provinces of Manitoba, Saskatchewan, Alberta and British Columbia; the Liberals maintained their dominant role in the traditional industrial heartland of Ontario; and the separatist Bloc Québécois came first in Quebec. Quebec voters in a 1995 referendum only narrowly rejected a call for outright independence. The New Democratic Party recovered ground somewhat compared with the 2000 general elections, taking 19 seats with 15.7% of the vote (compared with 13 seats and 8.5% in 2000); however, its vote is comparatively scattered (other than it having virtually no presence in Quebec), which is a weakness given Canada's use of the first-past-the-post electoral system and also the intensified regional basis of political allegiances. Patterns of control of legislatures at provincial level do not always exactly mirror those in national elections – in Manitoba and Saskatchewan, for example, where the Conservatives have been the main force in national politics, the New Democratic Party won the most seats in the 2003 provincial elections.

Canada is one of the Group of Seven (G-7) leading industrialized countries. Its economy is closely integrated with that of the United States, its major trading partner, and this relationship has intensified further as a result of the 1989 US–Canada Fair Trade Agreement (FTA) and the North American Free Trade Agreement (NAFTA) of 1994. Since 1980 most jobs created in Canada have been in the service sector: 75% of the labour force is now in services, 15% is in manufacturing, 5% construction and only 3% in the agricultural sector. Real growth rates averaged 3% per annum after 1993, following a severe recession in the period 1990-92, but there was a brief downturn in 2001 followed by recovery. In November 2004 the Finance Minister raised the official growth estimate for 2004 from 2.7% to 3%. Unemployment declined to 7.6% by 1999 from 11.2% in 1993 and was 7.8% in 2004. The Liberal government since taking office in 1993 has sought to reduce subsidies, control government spending and carry out privatization. In 2004 Canada ran a budget surplus for the eighth year in succession, and Canada was the only major industrial country running both budget and current account surpluses.

GDP (purchasing power parity) $958.7bn. (2004 est.); GDP per capita (purchasing power parity) $29,800 (2004 est.).

2 Trade Unionism

Although the legal model of freedom of association and collective bargaining in Canada was heavily influenced by the American Wagner Act model of the 1930s, Canadian unions have historically and to this day been more influenced by the social unionism models of the labour movements in the UK and Continental Europe than has the American labour movement. The Canadian labour movement was instrumental in the formation and development of the New Democratic Party, a political party that is active at both the federal and the provincial levels and which continues to attract the support of a large part of the labour movement.

Jurisdiction over labour relations resides primarily with the provinces under Canada's Constitution (only approximately 10% of Canadian workers are governed by federal labour legislation). This creates the possibility for vast discrepancies in the scope and form of labour legislation across jurisdictions. However, between the 1940s and the 1990s, the provinces and the federal government adopted very similar labour legislation models of freedom of association and collective bargaining. The "Canadian model" is characterized by mandatory union recognition by employers if a specified majority of "bargaining unit" employees indicate their support for collective bargaining. Once certified, a union becomes the "exclusive bargaining agent" for all employees in the bargaining unit; minority unions are not generally recognized in Canadian labour law. Strikes and lock-outs are prohibited during the term of a collective agreement and all disputes about the meaning or application of collective agreements are channelled into private labour arbitration.

More recently, Canadian labour laws in various provinces led by right-of-centre, neo-liberal governments have been reformed in a manner designed to impede union organizing and collective bargaining. For example, governments in Ontario, British Columbia, Alberta, Nova Scotia, and Newfoundland & Labrador have replaced the traditional "card-check" model of verifying employee support for collective bargaining with mandatory recognition ballots similar to the US model (although in Canada the ballots are usually held within 5-10 days of the date the union files its application for certification). Mandatory ballots have ensured employers an opportunity to campaign against the union prior to the ballot. Thus, changes in administration can have, and recently have had, a marked effect on the scope and form of labour legislation.

All jurisdictions have introduced legislative protection against "unfair labour practices". These laws usually appear in the form of a prohibition of employer interference, by threat, intimidation, coercion, or promise, in the selection, formation, and administration of unions. The scope and form of remedies available for breach of these provisions varies across jurisdictions. Canada ratified ILO Convention No. 87 (Freedom of Association and Protection of the Right to Organize, 1948) in 1972, but has not ratified Convention No. 98 (Right to Organize and Collective Bargaining, 1949). Canadian governments have been found in violation of the ILO's Conventions on numerous occasions, including most recently in regards to Ontario's exclusion of agricultural workers from the right to engage in collective bargaining. In 1992 the ILO reprimanded the federal government and those of Manitoba, New Brunswick, Newfoundland and Nova Scotia for restricting Convention No. 98 by imposing a wage freeze on public sector employees.

A main feature of Canada's industrial relations system is its decentralization. Nearly all agreements are concluded between a single employer and a single union. Thus collective bargaining in the private sector is most often a localized process based on a single establishment of a single firm. Negotiations are rarely conducted across provincial boundaries or on an industry-wide basis. In the early 1990s, for example, only about 15% of unionized workers in Canada were covered by multi-employer bargaining arrangements. One effect of decentralization is a proliferation of arrangements: as many as 10,000 collective agreements may be concluded in a single year, with an overwhelming majority of them being made between a single employer and a single union.

The Canadian Charter of Rights and Freedoms (1982) protects "freedom of association". The Supreme Court of Canada ruled in 2001 that this freedom includes a right to organize and to join unions and may include a requirement for the state to enforce unfair labour practices legislation to ensure that these rights are not interfered with (*Dunmore v. Ontario*). However, in other respects, Canadian courts have interpreted the Charter's protection of freedom of association narrowly. For example, the Supreme Court ruled in a series of cases in the late 1980s that freedom of association does not include a right to strike or a right to engage in collective bargaining.

The "right to strike" is generally protected, subject to a variety of restrictive temporal and procedural preconditions. Strikers are generally protected from retaliation by employers. However, employers are in most cases entitled to hire replacement workers during a strike and to continue to operate the business, and the striking employees' employment is often protected only for a limited period of time after the strike begins (for example, in Ontario, an employer is not required to reinstate a striking worker after six months have passed from the start of the strike). The number of strikes tended to fall through the 1990s but remained at a higher level than in the UK and a much higher level than the USA. The right to strike in Canada has limitations. There has been persistent controversy at the federal level and in most provinces over the denial of the right to strike to workers in "essential services" and the definition of what are essential services, and "back-to-work" legislation is a common tactic used by governments to terminate public sector strikes. In Alberta, the right to strike is denied to hospital employees such as kitchen staff, porters and gardeners and the ILO has disputed that these are essential services. It has likewise criticized the prohibition of strikes in non-essential sectors such as agriculture and horticulture, as in Ontario, and railways and ports, by the federal government. In March 1993 a grain-handlers' strike was ended by a federal back-to-work order, but the the ILO Committee on Freedom of Association concluded that grain handling was not an essential service and recommended that the government refrain in future from using such powers where the service in question is not essential.

Union density has stabilized in the 30–33 percent range for the last 25 years and Canada avoided the sharp decline in density experienced in most western industrialized countries in the 1980s; in 2002, overall union density in Canada was approximately 32.2%. This figure, however, somewhat masks the fact that private sector unionization has fallen over the past several decades while the overall density rate has been sustained by continued strong union coverage in the public sector. For example, between 1997 and 2002, private sector union density in Canada fell from 21.5% to 19.6% while public sector density remained at approximately 75.8%. It is noteworthy also that, while union density decreased between 1997 and 2000, the total number of workers covered by collective agreements actually increased by over 350,000 to approximately 4.2 million. There are regional differences in density, with the highest levels in the provinces of Newfoundland (39.1%) and Quebec (40.4%) and the lowest in the western province of Alberta (24.5%) and central province of Ontario (28.1%).

The national centre is the ICFTU-affiliated Canadian Labour Congress (CLC), formed in 1956, which has a membership of 2.5 million. There are no other nationwide centres. The Confederation of Canadian Unions (CCU), which says it is rank-and-file based, has less than 7,000 members. There are, however, alternative centres based on French-speaking Quebec, the largest of which, the Confédération des Syndicats Nationaux (CSN), has some 232,000 members. There are also important unions in areas such as teaching, construction, and the health service without affiliation either to a Canadian or American centre.

There has been a continuing process of merger and rationalization of craft-based unions. The two largest unions are both in the public sector. The Canadian Union of Public Employees (CUPE) has slightly over 500,000 members and the National Union of Public and General Employees (NUPGE) has approximately 337,000. Both increased their membership during the 1990s, especially CUPE, which increased its membership by over 50,000 members between 1997 and 2001. The largest private sector union is the Canadian Auto Workers' (CAW), with approximately 260,000 members, followed by the United Food and Commercial Workers with 230,000 members. All four are affiliated to the CLC. An important independent union not linked to the CLC or other trade union centre is the 245,000-strong Canadian Teachers' Federation.

The Canadian economy is highly integrated with the American economy and relies heavily on US based inward investment, often in the form of branch plants of US-based multinational corporations. The close integration between the economies has historically facilitated an unusually close relationship between the labour movements of the two countries. Although the majority of Canadian union members today belong to national (i.e. Canadian-based) unions, many unions continue to be constituted as Canadian branches of international (i.e. US-based) unions. In 2001, for example, approximately 29.5% of union members belonged to so-called "international" unions. However, at the organizational level, there has been a contrary trend, towards greater Canadian autonomy, encouraged by the deep problems US unions faced with falling memberships in the 1980s, when the Canadian unions were generally sustaining their position far better. In a dramatic moment, the CAW left the US-based United Auto Workers in 1985 after 50 years' affiliation, following years of disagreement over the Canadians' demand for full national control of wage bargaining, strike authorization and staff appointments. The schism followed breakaways from the United Paperworkers' International Union in 1974, and the Oil, Chemical and Atomic Workers' Union in 1980 as well as ruptures in international links between woodworkers and food workers. The Teamsters' Union, expelled from the CLC in 1960 for "poaching" union members, was readmitted to the CLC in 1992 on a basis that emphasized the autonomy of the Canadian branch, which had been re-named Teamsters Canada.

Canadian unions have filed cases under the North American Agreement on Labour Cooperation (NAALC), a side agreement to the NAFTA, which commits governments to uphold existing labour legislation in areas such as freedom of association, collective bargaining and the right to strike. However, early cases pursued against Mexican authorities with the assistance of Canadian unions for failing to enforce Mexican labour laws during organizing campaigns and for failure to ensure safe working conditions were generally perceived by the labour movements of the three NAFTA countries to be non-effectual. As a result, the Canadian labour movement's enthusiasm (to the extent that it ever existed) for the NAALC appears to have waned in recent years.

3 Trade Union Centre

Canadian Labour Congress (CLC)
Congrès du Travail du Canada (CTC)
Address. 2841 Riverside Drive, Ottawa K1V 8X7
Phone. +1 613 521 3400
Fax. +1 613 521 8949
E-mail. communications@clc-ctc.ca
Website. www.clc-ctc.ca
Leadership. Kenneth V. Georgetti (president); Hasan Yousef (secretary-treasurer)
Membership. 2.5 million
History and character. The CLC was formed in 1956 by merger of the Trades and Labour Congress (TLC) with the Canadian Congress of Labour (CCL). The TLC represented mainly craft unions and the CCL mainly industrial unions, in both cases with their affiliates having international headquarters predominantly in the United States.

The CLC is the only national trade union centre. However in Quebec there are three significant provincial centres outside the CLC, and overall the CLC includes only some 53% of the unionized work force. It has members in all areas of the economy, but its two largest unions, the Canadian Union of Public Employees (CUPE) and National Union of Public and General Employees (NUPGE) are both based in the public sector. The overall shape of CLC membership has shifted over the last two decades, with the decline of manufacturing jobs and a great increase in women members in the public sector, with little net effect on total CLC membership, which was 2.2 million in the mid-1980s. The largest private sector affiliate is the Canadian Auto Workers' (CAW), which recruits in a wide range of sectors. During 2000, however, the CAW was accused of "raiding" the membership of another CLC affiliate, the Service Employees' International Union (SEIU), and faced disciplinary sanctions. Those sanctions were subsequently lifted.

The CLC supports the New Democratic Party (NDP), which it helped to found in 1961, and its policies tend to correspond closely to the social democratic outlook of that organization. This alliance has been similar in some respects to that between the trade union centres and the social democratic parties in countries such as the UK (TUC and Labour Party) and Germany (DGB and SPD), or that in the USA between the AFL-CIO and the Democrats. However, whereas in these other countries the alliance has been with one of the two leading parties of government, the CLC's alliance with the NDP has been more peripheral in impact. Since its foundation the NDP has not succeeded in displacing the Liberal Party of Canada as the principal anti-conservative party at the federal level, and it took only 13 seats in the 2000 elections to the House of Commons and 19 in 2004. It has never seriously challenged to become the party of national government. It has, however, had somewhat more success at the provincial level, holding power in the most populous province of Ontario from 1990–95, as well as being in government for periods in several other provinces. At provincial level, periods of NDP government have been marked by enactment of pro-union legislation, which is often then reversed (as in Ontario in 1995, Manitoba in 1997, and British Columbia in 2001) when power was lost to a right-of-centre party.

The CLC has little direct involvement in collective bargaining, which is highly decentralized. It organizes boycotts of "unfair" employers, sometimes in association with US unions. At national level it has a strong focus on political lobbying. The CLC's current concerns include pension rights, defending public services, fairness in taxation, achieving full collective bargaining, organizing the growing services sector, and combating inequality and discrimination in the workplace and society. It also reflects the general Canadian interest in global and developing world issues. In 1999 the CLC led a labour delegation protesting at the World Trade Organization conference in Seattle, calling for mechanisms to ensure workers' rights and labour standards to be brought into the world trade system.

The ruling body is the national convention, held every three years. Between conventions the ruling body is the 42-member executive council. Its structure includes 12 provincial and territorial federations and 125 district labour councils. The CLC is predominantly English-speaking, but the Francophone minority in Canada is recognized by the simultaneous publication of all documents in both languages. A Women's Bureau was established in 1972.

International affiliations. ICFTU, TUAC, CTUC

Affiliated Unions. CLC affiliates include provincial federations of labour, Canadian branches of US-based international unions, and Canadian occupationally based unions. The following list provides details on some of the more prominent affiliates. Further information on international unions based in the US can be found in the US country section.

1. Canadian Auto Workers (CAW)
Address. 205 Placer Court, North York, Ontario, M2H 3H9
Phone. +1 416 497 4110
Fax. +1 416 495 6559
E-mail. caw@caw.ca
Website. www.caw.ca
Leadership. Basil "Buzz" Hargrove (national president); Jim O'Neill (national secretary-treasurer)
Membership. 230,000
History and character. The CAW is the largest private sector union in Canada. Its membership is diverse (only 90,000 members are employed in the auto sector) and it is the leading Canadian union in fisheries, aerospace, electronics, auto and auto parts, speciality vehicles and shipbuilding. In 2000 it was put under sanctions by the CLC after charges of raiding the membership of another CLC union, but those sanctions were subsequently lifted.

2. Canadian Federation of Nurses' Unions (CFNU)
Address. 2841 Prom. Riverside Drive, Ottawa, Ontario K1V 8X7
Phone. +1 613 526 4661
Fax. +1 613 526 1023
E-mail. cfnu@nursesunions.ca
Website. www.nursesunions.ca
Leadership. Linda Silas (secretary) Paula Worsford (treasurer)
History and character. Founded in 1981 and reorganized in 1999 as the national affiliating body for nurses to the CLC.

3. Canadian Union of Postal Workers (CUPW)
Address. 377 Bank Street, Ottawa, Ontario K2P 1Y3
Phone. +1 613 236 7238
Fax. +1 613 563 7861
E-mail. bpausche@cupw-sttp.org
Website. www.cupw-sttp.org
Leadership. Dale Clark (national president); Lynn Bue (1st vice-president)
Membership. 45,000

4. Canadian Union of Public Employees (CUPE)
Address. 21 Florence Street, Ottawa, Ontario K2P OW6
Phone. +1 613 237 1590
Fax. +1 613 237 5508
E-mail. cupemail@cupe.ca
Website. www.cupe.ca
Leadership. Paul Moist (national president); Claude Genereux (national secretary-treasurer)
Membership. Over 500,000 in approximately 2,156 locals
History and character. CUPE is Canada's largest and fastest-growing union, active in health care, education, local government, social services, libraries, utilities, transport and emergency services. More than half its members are women and about 25 per cent work part-time. A particular focus for the union is opposition to the privatization of public services.

5. Communications, Energy and Paperworkers' Union of Canada (CEP)
Address. 350 Albert Street, Suite 1900, Ottawa, Ontario K1R 1A4
E-mail. info@cep.ca
Website. www.cep.ca
Leadership. Brian Payne (national president); André Foucault (national secretary-treasurer)
Membership. 150,000
History and character. Formed in 1992 by the amalgamation of the Canadian Paperworkers' Union, the Communications and Electrical Workers' of Canada, and the Energy and Chemical Workers' Union. It has members in a wide range of sectors including pulp and paper, telephone companies, oil, gas, chemicals, mining, media, printing, hotel workers and

computer programmers. Internationally it is affiliated to the ICEM, UNI and IMF international trade secretariats.

6. International Association of Machinists and Aerospace Workers (IAMAW)
Canadian office:
Address. 15 Gervais Drive, Suite 707, North York, Ontario M3C 1Y8
Phone. +1 416 386 1789
Fax. +1 416 386 0210
E-mail. info@iamaw.ca
Website. www.iamaw.ca
Leadership. Dave Ritchie (general vice-president for Canada)
Membership. 50,000 (Canada)

7. Industrial, Wood and Allied Workers of Canada (IWA)
Address. 500-1285 West Pender Street, Vancouver, British Columbia, V63 4B2
Phone. +1 604 683 1117
Fax. +1 604 688 6416
E-mail. national@iwa.ca
Website. www.iwa.ca
Leadership. Dave Haggard (national president); Neil Menard (1st vice-president)
Membership. 55,000

8. National Union of Public and General Employees (NUPGE)
Address. 15 Auriga Drive, Nepean, Ontario K2E 1B7
Phone. +1 613 228 9800
Fax. +1 613 228 9801
E-mail. national@nupge.ca
Website. www.nupge.ca
Leadership. James Clancy (national president); Larry Brown (national secretary-treasurer)
Membership. 337,000
History and character. NUPGE, Canada's second largest union (after the Canadian Union of Public Employees, CUPE), is itself a federation of 14 independent member unions, these being mainly unions of public employees at the provincial level. Its membership includes 30,000 private sector members. Internationally it is affiliated to PSI.

9. Public Service Alliance of Canada (PSAC)
Address. 233 Gilmour Street, Ottawa, Ontario K2P 0P1
Phone. +1 613 560 4200
Fax. +1 613 236 1654
E-mail. org@psac.org
Website. www.psac.com
Leadership. Nycole Turmel (national president); John Gordon (national executive vice-president)
Membership. 137,000

10. Service Employees' International Union (SEIU)
For general entry for the international union, see under USA
Canadian office:
Address. 810–75 The Donway West, Toronto, M3C 2E9
Phone. +1 416 447 2311
Fax. +1 416 447 2428
Website. www.seiu.ca
Leadership. Sharleen Stewart (international vice-president, Canada)

11. Teamsters Canada
Address. 2540 Daniel Johnson Boulevard, Laval, Quebec, H7T 2S3
Phone. +1 450 682 5521
Fax. +1 450 681 2244
Website. www.teamsters-canada.org
Leadership. Robert Bouvier (president)
Membership. 110,000
History and character. This is the Canadian affiliate of the US-based International Brotherhood of Teamsters (IBT). Expelled from the CLC in 1960 following disputes about demarcation boundaries with other affiliates, the Teamsters continued to organize in Canada. In 1976 the Canadian Conference of Teamsters was established within the IBT. In 1992 greater autonomy was granted to the Canadian branch, which was re-named Teamsters Canada, and in 1993 re-affiliation to the CLC was agreed.

Members cover a wide variety of occupations beyond transport workers, with 17 trade divisions including aeronautics, bakeries and laundries, construction and building materials, port side industry and warehousing.

12. United Food and Commercial Workers International Union (UFCW)
See also entry for the International Union under the United States
Canadian office:
Address. 300–61 International Boulevard, Rexdale, Ontario, M9W 6K4
Phone. +1 416 675 1104
Fax. +1 416 675 6919
E-mail. info@ufcw.ca
Website. www.ufcw.ca
Leadership. Michael J. Fraser (Canadian director)
Membership. 230,000 (Canada)

Provincial federations of labour.

These affiliate directly to the CCL. The leading federations are:

1. Alberta Federation of Labour
Address. 350, 10451–170 Street, Edmonton, Alberta T5P 4T2
Phone. +1 780 483 3021
Fax. +1 780 484 5928
E-mail. afl@telusplanet.net
Website. www.afl.org
Leadership. Les Steel (president)
Membership. 120,000

2. British Columbia Federation of Labour
Address. 200–5118 Joyce Street, Vancouver, BC V5G 1H1
Phone. +1 604 430 1421
Fax. +1 604 430 5917
E-mail. bcfed@bcfed.com
Website. www.bcfed.com
Leadership. Jim Sinclair (president); Angela Schirer (secretary-treasurer)
Membership: 470,000

3. Manitoba Federation of Labour
Address. 101-275 Broadway, Winnipeg, Manitoba R3C 4M6
Phone. +1 204 947 1400

E-mail. mbfedlab@mfl.mb.ca
Website. www.mfl.mb.ca
Leadership. Rob Hillard (president); Peter Olfert (treasurer)
Membership: 90,000

4. Ontario Federation of Labour
Address. 15 Gervais Drive, Suite 202, Toronto, Ontario M3C 1Y8
Phone. +1 416 441 2731
Fax. +1 416 441 1893
E-mail. info@ofl-fto.on.ca
Website. www.ofl-fto.on.ca
Leadership. Irene Harris (executive vice-president); Ethel LaValley (secretary-treasurer)
Membership. 650,000

5. New Brunswick Federation of Labour
Address. 96 Norwood Avenue, Moncton, New Brunswick, E1C 6L9
Phone. +1 506 857 2125
Fax. +1 506 383 1597
E-mail. fttnbfl@nbnet.nb.ca
Website. www.intellis.net/fttnbfl
Leadership. Blair Doucet (president); Maurice Clavette (secretary-treasurer)
Membership. 32,000

6. Newfoundland and Labrador Federation of Labour
Address. 330 Portugal Cove Place, 2nd Floor, NAPE Building, St. John's, NF, A1B 3P2
Phone. +1 709 754 1660
Fax. +1 709 754 1220
E-mail. fed@nlfl.nf.ca
Leadership. Reg Anstey (president)
Membership. 55,000

7. Quebec Federation of Labour
Address. Fédération des travailleurs et travailleuses du Québec, 565 boulevard Crémazie Est, bureau 12100, Montréal (Québec), H2M 2W3
Phone. +1 514 383 8000
Fax. +1 514 383 8001
Website. ftq@ftq.qc.ca
Leadership. Henri Masse (president)

8. Saskatchewan Federation of Labour
Address. 220-2445 13th Avenue, Regina, Saskatchewan, S4P 0W1
Phone. +1 306 525 0197
Fax. +1 306 525 8960
E-mail. info@sfl.sk.ca
Website. www.sfl.sk.ca
Leadership. Larry Hubich (president)
Membership. 85,000

4 Other Trade Union Organizations

Canadian Teachers' Federation (CTF)
Address. 110 Argyle Avenue, Ottawa, Ontario K2P 1B4
Phone. +1 613 232 1886
E-mail. info@ctf-fce.ca
Website. www.ctf-fce.ca
Leadership. Marilies Rettig (president); David Eaton (secretary general)
Membership. 245,000 in 14 provincial/territorial member organizations

Centrale des Syndicats Démocratiques (CSD)
Address. 801, 4e rue, Quebec City, Quebec G1J 2T7
Phone. +1 418 529 2956
Fax. +1 418 529 6323
E-mail. csdmtl@globetrotter.qc.ca
Leadership. François Vaudreuil (president)
Membership. 60,000
History and character. The CSD was founded in 1972 following a rift in the Confédération des Syndicats Nationaux (see below) over organizational and ideological issues. CSD is non-partisan and practices direct democracy. It affiliated to the WCL in 2000.
International affiliation. WCL

Centrale des syndicats du Québec (CSQ)
Address. 9405 rue Sherbrooke Est, Montreal, Quebec H1L 6P3
Phone. +1 514 356 8888
Fax. +1 514 356 999
Website. www.csq.qc.net (French only)
Leadership. Monique Richard (president)
Membership. 140,000 members in 14 unions and federations. Members are primarily in public sector areas such as health and education.

Christian Labour Association of Canada (CLAC)
Address. 5920 Mississauga Drive, Mississauga, Ontario L4W 1N6
Phone. +1 905 670 7383
Fax. +1 905 670 8416
E-mail. headoffice@clac.ca
Leadership. Ed Grootenboer (executive director)
History and character. CLAC is a confederation that represents workers in more than 500 enterprises across English-speaking Canada and has expanded its membership in the 1990s. Its main strengths are in wood and building, health care, services and transport.
International affiliation. WCL

Confédération des Syndicats Nationaux (CSN)
Address. 1601 ave De Lorimier, Montreal, Quebec H2K 4M5
Phone. +1 514 598 2098
Fax. +1 514 598 2052
E-mail. intcsn@csn.qc.ca
Website. www.csn.qc.ca (French only)
Leadership. Marc Laviolette (president); Lise Poulin (secretary-general)
Membership. 232,000
History and character. The CSN originated in 1921 as the Confédération des Travailleurs Catholiques du Canada (CTCC, Confederation of Catholic Workers of Canada). The two main influences in the subsequent development of the CTCC were the efforts of the Catholic clergy to create confessional unions, and the nationalist resistance within the union movement to the attempt of the American Federation of Labour to control Canadian trade unionism. Membership in the

organization – which was at that time concentrated mostly in the textile, clothing, pulp and paper, and metalworking industries, and the retail trades – had reached 94,000 by 1960, when the CTCC became officially secular and changed its name to the CSN. The CSN's membership more than doubled from 1960 to 1970 with the unionization of the public sector in Quebec. There was a split in 1972, with more conservative unions opposing the confrontation between the CSN and the Quebec government, and breaking away to form the CSD (see above). Membership fell to 160,000 in 1976, but then grew to reach 250,000 by 1990 and is now reported at 232,000.

Although the CSN has a Canada-wide charter, the vast majority of members in its 2,174 affiliated unions (syndicats) are in the (mainly French-speaking) province of Quebec. There are also some unions in Ontario and New Brunswick. The CSN membership constitutes one-quarter of the unionized workforce of Quebec. About 80% of the women members of CSN are in public services, while 80% of the men are in the private sector. The local unions are affiliated to regional councils and industrial federations. The CSN has 29 regional offices in Quebec and 650 employees.

The CSN is independent of political parties and in its relationships with other sectors of the Canadian labour movement, although it has worked with other unions on common campaigns. Since 1990 it has campaigned for the independence of Quebec from Canada and opposed trade liberalization within NAFTA, which exposes Quebec's industrial base to lower-cost competition. Its international relations are primarily with francophone countries and Latin America. It was affiliated to the WCL from 1946–86, but is now affiliated to the ICFTU.

International affiliation. ICFTU

Cape Verde

Capital: Cidade de Praia
Population: 415,300 (2004 est.)

1 Political and Economic Background

Cape Verde achieved independence from Portugal in 1975 and had a one-party system under what became the African Party for the Independence of Cape Verde (PAICV) until moving to a multi-party system after 1990. In 1991 the newly formed Movement for Democracy (MPD), which had been set up by exiles in Lisbon calling for a multi-party democracy and a free enterprise economy, defeated the PAICV in elections to the National Assembly and the MPD's presidential candidate Antonio Mascarenhas Monteiro was also elected. Monteiro was re-elected in 1996. In early 2001 the PAICV were returned to power after a ten-year absence – in legislative elections in January, the PAICV gained 40 of the 72 seats, while in February the party recaptured the presidency when Pedro Pires, a veteran of the liberation struggle, narrowly defeated the MPD candidate.

Cape Verde has few natural resources. Some three-quarters of the population are dependent upon subsistence agriculture, but prolonged periods of drought have necessitated the import of over 80% of food requirements, a large proportion of it under aid programmes. Much of the rural workforce is underemployed. The formal economy is service-oriented, with commerce, transport, tourism, and public services accounting for over 70% of GDP. Together with foreign aid, a major contribution to the economy is made from remittances from nationals working or residing abroad (who are estimated to number nearly 1 million). Fish processing and canning provide a limited amount of employment. Economic reforms are aimed at developing the private sector and attracting foreign investment to diversify the economy.

GDP (purchasing power parity) $600 million (2003 est.); GDP per capita (purchasing power parity) $1,400 (2003 est.).

2 Trade Unionism

There appears to have been no organized trade union activity before independence from Portugal. The UNTC-CS was created as the trade union arm of the ruling PAICV in the 1970s, but its legal monopoly was broken by the 1991 PAICV electoral defeat. The 1992 Constitution provides that workers shall have the right to join unions free of government control and a 1991 legislative decree provides protection against discrimination on the grounds of union activity. The UNTC-CS accepted pluralism and is now a member of the ICFTU. It is the main centre and is composed of 14 unions with about 20,000 members. A second centre, the CCSL, is also composed of 14 unions, with about 18,000 members.

Cape Verde ratified ILO Convention No. 87 (freedom of Association and Protection of the Right to Organize, 1948) in 1999. It ratified Convention No. 98 (Right to Organize and Collective Bargaining, 1949) in 1979, but little collective bargaining takes place. The ILO has cited the government for its inability to provide examples of signed collective bargaining agreements. There is a constitutional right to strike, which the government generally respects, but the government has on occasion made use of requisition orders to force strikers back to work, as in the case of disputes in the late 1990s involving workers at the ENACLO petrol company and seafarers opposed to the proposed privatization of the national maritime company CNN.

3 Trade Union Centres

Conferência Cabo-Verdiana de Sindicatos Livres (CCSL)
Council of Free Labour Unions
Address. Rua Dr. Julio de Abreu, CP 155, Praia
Phone. +238 2616 319
Fax. +238 2616 319
E-mail. ccsl@cvtelecom.cv
Leadership. Jose Manuel Vaz (president)
Membership. 18,000

Uniao Nacional dos Trabalhadores de Cabo verde–Central Sindical (UNTC-CS)
Trade Unions of Cape Verde Unity Centre
Address. CP 123, Praia
Phone. +238 2600 820; +238 2613 155
Fax. +238 2613 629
E-mail. untc@cytelecom.cv
Website. www.untc-cs.org
Leadership. Júlio Ascensão Silva
Membership. 20,000
History and character. In 1976 the organizing Commission of Cape Verde Unions was formed as a complement to the Guinea-Bissau National Union of Workers (UNTG). Two years later he UNTC-CS was established as the arm of the ruling PAICV. It is no longer controlled by the PAICV.

In 1991 the government confiscated the 1st May social centre which had been built for the UNTC-CS by international trade union donors. The government handed over the property to a breakaway faction. In 1998, however, the courts ruled the building belonged to the UNTC-CS as internationally recognized.
International affiliation. ICFTU.

Central African Republic

Capital: Bangui
Population: 3.74 m. (2004 est.)

1 Political and Economic Background

The French territory of Ubangui-Shari became a self-governing republic within the French Community in 1958 as the Central African Republic and gained full independence in 1960. Col. Jean-Bedel Bokassa took power in 1966 (under him the country being renamed the Central African Empire from 1977 until his overthrow in 1979). Gen. André Kolingba came to power in 1981, and from 1986 there was a semi-civilian government with power exercised through Kolingba's Rassemblement Démocratique Centrafricain as the sole legal party. In April 1991, Kolingba, in line with many other African states at that time, announced a move to multi-party democracy but efforts to involve other parties in constitutional change repeatedly failed. In 1992 Bangui was hit by strikes supporting a sovereign national conference to set the country's constitution. When elections were finally held in 1993, the winner was Ange-Félix Patassé (a one-time Prime Minister under Bokassa, who had denounced Bokassa after being exiled by him) and the Central African People's Liberation Party (MLPC). In December 1994 a referendum approved constitutional changes increasing the powers of President Patassé. There were army mutinies in 1996 and 1997 aimed at overthrowing Patassé; the instability led to intervention by French troops and deployment of a United Nations peacekeeping force, which oversaw presidential elections in September 1999 in which Patassé was re-elected. In March 2003, however, Patassé was deposed in a coup led by Gen. François Bozize, who dissolved the National Assembly, subsequently establishing an unelected National Transition Council.

The economy is based on subsistence agriculture, although the diamond industry accounts for more than half of exports. This is a poor landlocked country with little infrastructure and few workers with modern skills, while the economy has also suffered disruption from military rebellions and unrest. The economy was forecast to contract in 2004 and purchasing power parity per capita GDP has shrunk since the 1990s.

GDP (purchasing power parity) $4.18bn. (2004 est.); GDP per capita (purchasing power parity) $1,100 (2004 est.).

2 Trade Unionism

Several labour federations were in existence at the time of independence in 1960, and the Central African Republic ratified ILO Convention No. 87 (Freedom of Association and Protection of the Right to Organize, 1948) in 1960 and Convention No. 98 (Right to Organize and Collective Bargaining, 1949) in 1964.

In the 1970s the ICFTU-affiliated General Union of Workers of Central Africa (Union Générale des Travailleurs de Centrafrique, UGTC), with its affiliated occupational federations, was the sole permitted organization. In 1973, and again in 1977, UGTC general secretaries were dismissed for participating in anti-government activities. President Dacko suspended the right to strike in 1980 and in 1981 dissolved the UGTC after it attempted to break the ban. He announced the formation of a new body, the National Confederation of Central African Workers (CNTC) but all union activities were suspended after a military coup that September. The CNTC resumed functioning but suffered harassment by the state. The last days of the Kolingba regime were marked by further repression, and in 1993 CNTC headquarters were surrounded by troops at the start of a planned civil service strike.

The 1995 Constitution provides for trade union pluralism and freedom of association. Several union federations have been formed, but the small scale of the formal economy has limited trade unionism, and most union members are public servants. The principal organization is the ICFTU-affiliated Union Syndicale des Travailleurs de Centrafrique (USTC), which has about 15,000 members. It has difficult relations with the government, with salary arrears having been a source of tension. Trade unions are banned from holding meetings of a political nature and union officials must be employed full-time in the industry the union represents. Collective bargaining is not specifically authorized by the labour code and where bargaining occurs the government generally becomes involved. There is a right to strike in both private and public sectors, subject to conciliation and arbitration procedures, and teachers have staged lengthy strikes over the issue of pay arrears. From 2000 there were several strikes by civil servants over unpaid salaries, contributing to the atmosphere of anti-government unrest and demonstrations. Strikes occurred in the health and education sectors in 2002 for similar reasons.

3 Trade Union Centre

Union Syndicale des Travailleurs de Centrafrique (USTC)
Union of Central African Workers
Address. BP 1390, Bangui
Phone. +236 61 60 15
Fax. +236 61 60 15
Leadership. Théophile Sonny-Colé (secretary-general)
Membership. 15,000
History and character. In the late 1990s relations between the USTC and the government were strained by factors including pay arrears for civil servants and the government's refusal to negotiate a social pact, and there were frequent strikes. Security forces ransacked the USTC headquarters and telephone lines were cut off. Following December 1998 legislative elections the USTC called for the formation of a representative government and organized protests against the defections in the National Assembly which had allowed the MLPC to form a government. Following these protests, in January 1999 USTC general secretary, Théophile Sonny-Colé, was detained and beaten, apparently by members of the presidential guard, before being released after international pressure.
International affiliation. ICFTU

4 Other Trade Union Organizations

Confédération Nationale des Travailleurs de Centrafrique (CNTC)
National Confederation of Central African Workers
Address. BP 2141, Bangui
Phone. +236 04 60 91
Fax. +236 61 35 61
E-mail. cntc@intnet.cf
Leadership. Jean-Richard Sandos Oualanga (secretary general)
International affiliation. WCL

Confédération Syndicale des Travailleurs de Centrafrique (CSTC)
Address. BP 386 KM 5, Bangui
Phone. +236 61 38 69
Fax. +236 61 40 21
E-mail. sabinkpokolo@yahoo.fr
Leadership. Kpokol Sabin (secretary general)
International affiliation. WCL

Chad

Capital: N'Djaména
Population: 9.54 m. (2004 est.)

1 Political and Economic Background

The Republic of Chad achieved independence from France in 1960 and became a one-party state in 1962 under N'Garta Tombalbaye's Chadian Progressive Party. Tombalbaye's overthrow in 1975 ushered in a lengthy north-south civil war and a series of shortlived regimes, leading in late 1990 to the seizure of power by the Patriotic Salvation Movement (MPS) led by Col Idriss Déby. In 1992 the new regime agreed to legitimize political parties, but assassinations and union repression continued. The pluralist momentum then slowed fostering fears that Déby was seeking to install an authoritarian regime. In 1993 a Sovereign National Conference – organized by a tripartite commission – met and inaugurated an intended 12-month transition to democracy, but clashes continued. Finally in April 1995 a transitional government took office entrusted with overseeing preparations for elections. Déby was elected President in 1996 and the MPS became the dominant force in the legislature, following elections to a new National Assembly in 1997; both sets of elections were reportedly marked by ballot rigging. Déby managed to renew his mandate by (once more allegedly rigged) electoral victories in May 2001 and April 2002.

The economy of Chad has been disrupted by civil conflict for decades, its difficulties compounded by both drought and torrential rains. Chad's primarily agricultural economy is expected to be boosted by major oilfield and pipeline projects that began in 2000. Oil reserves in the south of the country are estimated at some 1bn barrels. Over 80% of Chad's population relies on subsistence farming and stock raising for its livelihood. Cotton, cattle, and gum arabic provide the bulk of Chad's export earnings, but the country began to export oil in 2004. The country remains heavily dependent on external aid and assistance from international donors. Structural adjustment programmes since the 1990s have involved privatization and public sector wage cuts, which have on occasion provoked industrial action.

GDP (purchasing power parity) $10.67bn. (2003 est.); GDP per capita (purchasing power parity) $1,200 (2003 est.).

2 Trade Unionism

Chad ratified ILO Convention No. 87 (Freedom of Association and Protection of the Right to Organize, 1948) in 1960 and Convention No. 98 (Right to Organize and Collective Bargaining, 1949) in 1961.

French unions maintained branches in Chad until independence in 1960. Between then and 1988 there were two trade union centres, the Trade Union Confederation of Chad (CST) and the National Union of Workers of Chad (UNATRAT) which reflected tribal and geographical cleavages. A great deal of their energy was absorbed by rivalry and eventually a decision was taken to establish a national negotiating team to achieve unity. In 1988 the National Union of Chadian Trade Unions (UNST) was launched under a new general secretary, but it was dissolved two years later when Déby took power. Under the new regime the trade union movement split: UNST dissidents formed a new centre, the WCL-affiliated Free Confederation of Chadian Workers (CLTT) while loyalists staged a 1991 general strike to force reinstatement of their organization. The authorities agreed provided there was a change of name and the Union of Trade Unions of Chad (UST) was born. It is Chad's ICFTU affiliate and the main trade union organization in the country. There are today several other federations and unions in existence, including the CLTT, and some unions are reported to have close ties to government officials. However, as Chad's economy is based on subsistence agriculture, with a small formal economy, the unions operate on a modest scale. The private sector is small scale and much of it informal and unions mostly represent employees in the state sector.

Strikes were illegal after 1975 and public employees barred from union membership after 1976. Unions were also prohibited from engaging in political activity and, while collective bargaining was permitted, collective agreements required government approval. In 1996 a new labour law substantially liberalized restrictions on trade union activities. It ended the 1975 ban on strikes and a 1976 ban on public servants forming or joining trade unions. It also ended the prohibition on trade unions engaging in political activity. The requirement for government approval of collective bargaining agreements was also ended, although the Ministry of Labour retained the right to comment on agreements and ask for re-negotiation. The requirement remained that authorization for the formation of associations is required from the Ministry of the Interior. This provision has been used on occasions in respect of trade unions.

3 Trade Union Centres

Confédération Libre des Travailleurs du Tchad (CLTT)
Free Confederation of Chadian Workers
Address. BP 553, Avenue Charles de Gaulle, N'Djaména
Phone. +235 51 76 11
Fax. +253 52 44 56
Leadership. Brahim Bakass (president)
History and character. The CLTT was founded early in 1991 by dissidents from the defunct national centre UNST, and became for the government an alternative rallying point to the reformed UST.
International affiliation. WCL

Union des Syndicats du Tchad (UST)
Union of Trade Unions of Chad
Address. BP 1143, N'Djaména
Phone. +235 51 42 75
Fax. +235 52 29 05
E-mail. ustchad@yahoo.fr
Leadership. Djibrine Assali Hamdallah (secretary-general); Boukinebe Garka (chairman)
Membership. 25,000
History and character. The UST's origins lie in the National Unions of Chadian Workers (UNST) formed by a 1988 merger of the tribally and geographically divided CST and UNATRAT. Its chief objectives included the building of a trade union culture in Chad and the extension of membership into a large part of the public sector. The UNST was dissolved in 1990 but its adherents re-established it ten months later under its present name.

The UST was legally recognized in 1992. That year it led a series of battles with the government over its economic adjustment programme; the security forces occupied its headquarters and ICFTU officials were denied visas to enter the country. In October all UST activities were temporarily suspended on the grounds that they were political. Despite this its influence was sufficiently great for it to have a place in the machinery overseeing the introduction of democracy. Secretary-general Djibrine Assali Hamdallah was made second vice-president of the Sovereign National Conference and elected to its supervisory council. In 1993 and 1994 the UST was to the fore in organizing industrial agitation against non-payment of wages and for the maintenance of living standards. This brought it into further conflict with the government. In 1995 the UST warned of the possibility of electoral fraud during the period of transition to democracy and it was suspended for a period following its call for a boycott of the presidential elections in 1996. Its largest affiliate, the teachers' union, was reported to have broken away in 1998. In May 2001 secretary-general Djibrine Assali Hamdallah and chairman Boukinebe Garka were detained by the authorities on the grounds that they had been involved with opposition political parties in an attempt to organize meetings following the contested presidential poll of that month.
International affiliation. ICFTU

Chile

Capital: Santiago
Population: 15.82 m. (2004 est.)

1 Political and Economic Background

Chile was ruled by a military junta led by General Augusto Pinochet from the time of his violent overthrow of the Allende government in 1973 until 1981. In that year Pinochet became President for an eight-year term under a new constitution. Among other provisions this constitution formally prohibited Marxist and totalitarian groups. The 1980s brought growing opposition which eventually forced a relaxation of control; political parties were in 1984 partially freed and in 1987 allowed to register. In a 1988 plebiscite a majority voted against Pinochet remaining in office for a further eight years upon the expiry of his term in 1990. Elections in December 1989 resulted in the election as president of the Christian Democrat Patricio Aylwin Azócar at the head of a coalition of centre-left parties, the Coalition of Parties for Democracy (Concertación de los Partidos por la Democracia, CPD). Aylwin presided over municipal elections, the first for 21 years, in 1992, and inaugurated constitutional amendments to reassert the primacy of the presidency over the armed forces and to correct a right-wing bias in the electoral system. Pinochet remained Commander-in-Chief of the Armed Forces, but both Aylwin and Eduardo Frei (another Christian Democrat, who succeeded him as president in 1993, also as the candidate of the CPD) took incremental steps to subordinate the military to the civil power.

In January 2000 Ricardo Lagos (a Socialist, and former ally of Allende), became the third CPD candidate in succession to be elected President (for a six-year term), in a narrow victory over the right-winger Joaquín Lavin. The Christian Democrats remained the largest single group in the new Lagos cabinet and the incoming government's programme was seen as broadly consistent with that of the previous administration. In congressional elections in December 2001 the CPD parties won 62 of the 120 seats in the Chamber of Deputies. Pinochet was arrested in London in October 1998 pending possible extradition to Spain, but was allowed to return to Chile in 2000.

The military after 1973 reversed the socialist policies of the preceding administration, including the return to private ownership of many of the enterprises nationalized under Allende, the encouragement of foreign investment, the dismantling of import barriers and the adoption of a fully free market economic system. In the 1990s civilian governments continued to pursue free market policies while trying to shift the emphasis of government intervention to social spending. Real growth averaged more than 7% per annum in the period 1991–97. Like other South American countries, however, Chile was affected by the 1997–98 financial crisis originating in Asia and in 1999 the economy contracted by 1 per cent; since then there has been recovery but with growth at a more modest 2 or 3 per cent per annum. Inflation has been under control in recent years and was expected to be below 3% in 2004. There is a traditional dependence on relatively few economic sectors, such as copper mining, fishing and forestry.

GDP (purchasing power parity) $154.7bn. (2004 est.); GDP per capita (purchasing power parity) $9,900 (2004 est.).

2 Trade Unionism

Chile ratified both ILO Convention No. 87 (Freedom of Association and Protection of the Right to Organize, 1948) and No. 98 (Right to Organize and Collective Bargaining, 1949) in 1999.

The first Chilean union centre, the Federation of Chilean Workers (Federación Obrera de Chile, FOCH) was formed in 1909. Legalized trade unionism and collective bargaining developed in the 1930s under the Popular Front government, and in 1936 the Confederación de Trabajadores de Chile (CTCH) was created; this, however, broke into socialist and communist factions during the 1940s. A reunified centre, the Central Unica de Trabajadores de Chile (Central Union of Workers, CUT), was created in 1953, its membership including Christian democrats, socialists and communists.

In 1970 the CUT strongly backed Allende's election and several CUT leaders became ministers. However, industrial unrest in the copper mines and strikes by lorry owners and other small businessmen destabilized the Allende government, paving the way for the 1973 coup, following which the CUT was banned. Strikes were declared illegal, collective bargaining suspended and some unions disbanded. Numerous trade unionists were executed, imprisoned or exiled, and the government intervened actively in the surviving unions by controlling their assets or appointing their officers.

The 1980 Pinochet labour code made trade union affiliation and the payment of union dues voluntary; allowed collective bargaining but restricted the bargaining arena to the individual workplace; stipulated that a strike could be called only if approved by a secret ballot and after compulsory arbitration; and limited strikes to a maximum period of 60 days, the employer having the right to declare a lock-out and hire other labour after 30 days. Strikes were prohibited in any sector connected with national security, public services, "the normal supply of the market" or the "public interest". The essential elements of these decrees were entrenched in the 1981 constitution.

Union resistance to the Pinochet regime was more open from 1981. In 1982 Tuscapel Jimenez, leader of the public employees' union, was found murdered shortly after announcing plans to establish a broad-based trade union front to oppose the government's economic policies. In 1983 the copper workers' union, the CTC, led a day of national protest, which led to widespread arrests of trade unionists and others. After this 60 CTC and other union leaders formed a coalition of labour groups opposed to the regime known as the National Workers' Command (CNT) to campaign for the reestablishment of democracy and the "free exercise of labour rights". This immediately initiated a long series of days of protest, leading to violence and mass arrests. The CNT embraced both left-wing and Christian Democratic elements, and although officially illegal established itself as the effective trade union voice in the country.

After disturbances during two days of CNT protest in 1985 union leaders were arrested and charged with violations of the national security law. Rodolfo Seguel (the copper workers' leader) and CNT general secretary Arturo Marínez were imprisoned but later released after further CNT protests in which four people died, and a hunger strike.

A CNT attempt in 1986 to hold its first national convention was prevented by the government, but thereafter, in an effort to improve the effectiveness of trade union opposition, the CNT worked towards the creation of a pluralistic single trade union confederation. Its efforts bore some fruit with the formation of the CUT in 1988. By 1990 there were three (technically illegal) national union centres in Chile, CUT – the largest with about 450,000 members, the Democratic Workers' Centre (CDT) and the Chilean Workers' Central (CTCh). The CTCh was led by figures closely associated with Pinochet.

Under President Aylwin (who took office in March 1990) the Pinochet labour code was amended in 1991 to permit the formation (without official approval), of central union organizations, enabling the CUT to achieve legal status in April 1992. The legislation also allowed trade union centres to affiliate to international trade union organizations, and the CUT went on to affiliate to the ICFTU. The new government also brought a resumption of tripartite dialogue.

Unions now operate independently of the state, although there are ties with political parties. There are legal prohibitions against discrimination by employers against union members, but enforcement is only by a requirement to pay compensation. Union density is estimated at about 10%.

In December 2001 a major reform of the Labour Code brought some improvements to the protection of trade union rights by permitting unions to be structured on geographic as well as industrial lines and by lowering the number of workers required to form a trade union. Limits were also placed on the ability of the government to interfere in trade unions' internal affairs. Unions had hoped that the new law would bring in national level bargaining, and would require employers to participate, but the actual reforms guaranteed only company level bargaining rights and provided for "voluntary" national bargaining.

In the private sector there is a right to strike, but workers at 30 companies providing essential services such as water and electricity may not go on strike and are subject to compulsory arbitration. Employee associations in the public sector do not have collective bargaining rights, and strikes are also not permitted in the public sector, although in practice groups such as teachers and health workers have gone on strike.

On Aug. 14, 2003, the CUT called a one-day general strike in protest at neo-liberal policies and wage reductions and to demand greater respect for workers' rights. This was the first general strike since 1990. It was met with tear gas and water cannons and 200 protesters were arrested.

In 2002 high-ranking military officers were tried and convicted of the murder of public sector union leader Tucapel Jimenez in 1982.

3 Trade Union Centres

Central Autónoma de Trabajadores (CAT)
Phone. +56 2 698 7318
Fax. +56 2 695 3388
Address. Calle Sazie 1761, Santiago 6510480
E-mail. catchile@entelchile.net
Leadership. Osvaldo Herbach Alvarez (president); Pedro Robles (secretary general)
International affiliation. WCL

Central Unitaria de Trabajadores (CUT)
Unified Workers' Centre
Address. Av. Libertador Bernardo O'Higgins 1346, Santiago
Phone. + 56 36194336
Fax. + 56 23619452
E-mail. intercut-chile@123.cl
History and character. The modern CUT was formed in 1988 by disparate worker organizations in an effort to create a unified centre. The CUT backed Aylwin's candidature in 1989. It is Chile's largest centre with more than half of the country's trade unionists. It affiliated to the ICFTU in 1994.

Manuel Bustos, who was president of the CUT from its foundation until 1996, died on Sept. 26, 1999. He had suffered prolonged detention by the authorities for union activities in the 1980s but on his death the Chilean government called three days of mourning and gave a state funeral. He had been elected to the national legislature for the Christian Democrats in 1990.
International affiliation. ICFTU

China

Capital: Beijing
Population: 1.30bn. (2004 est.)

1 Political and Economic Background

The People's Republic of China was formally established in 1949 with the final defeat on the mainland of the Nationalist forces of Chiang Kai-shek by the Communist forces led by Mao Zedong. Under the 1982 constitution (still in force) China is defined as "a socialist state under the people's democratic dictatorship led by the working class and based on the alliance of the workers and peasants". The sole and ruling political party is the Communist Party of China (CPC).

Under Mao, China pursued a series of initiatives including the "Great Leap Forward" of the late 1950s and the "Cultural Revolution" of the mid-1960s which provided the context for wholesale political purges allied with the implementation of fundamentalist communist economic policies that brought widespread famine and destitution. These campaigns alternated with periods when more pragmatic policies were followed. In the final years before Mao's death in 1976 a power struggle set in between radicals, who became known as the "gang of four", and moderates including Deng Xiaoping (purged during the Cultural Revolution and again in 1976 as a "capitalist roader"). By the beginning of the 1980s Deng had established control, denounced the excesses of the Great Leap Forward and the Cultural Revolution and set China on a course which emphasized the progressive loosening of centralized command economy policies while retaining the tight grip on power of the CPC. During the 1980s the commune system was ended, free markets for farm products were developed, and state businesses began to pay orthodox taxes instead of transferring their entire profits to the government. Central product allocation was reduced and (within limits) private businesses permitted. Certain coastal regions (the Special Export Zones – SEZs) were allowed economic autonomy and to develop cautious trading relations with neighbouring capitalist states. Finally, trade in privately-owned land was legalized. An important development during this period was the creation of a labour market to replace administrative allocation of labour. Labour contracts similar to those found in capitalist countries were introduced. It also became easier to terminate the employment of workers.

During the 1990s, in the wake of the collapse of communist regimes in most of the rest of the world and the crushing of the democracy movement in Tiananmen Square in June 1989, the CPC retained power through a continuation and development of this broad policy, first under Deng and then his successor Jiang Zemin. The process of reforming state enterprises and encouraging the private sector intensified over the decade.

China is now committed to what it calls a "socialist market economy" or "socialism with Chinese characteristics". In this the state retains control of a number of large state-owned enterprises (SOEs) in key industries.

However, most SOEs are being, or have been, privatized, although there is official hesitation at the rate at which this is to be done. Foreign investment in SOEs is encouraged, with some restrictions. Inefficient SOEs are being closed. By 2002 the number of SOEs had fallen to 159,000, down from twice that number in the mid-1990s. While the economic reforms have been highly successful in stimulating growth, the privatization policy has created tension because of rising unemployment and accusations of favouritism and corruption in privatization. It has had serious implications for the system of social welfare, which was enterprise-based. The policy of winding up inefficient enterprises has been moderated by the impact on employment and social stability, and the central government is also unable to ensure uniform implementation of its policies in all areas of the country.

China has a labour force of around 750 million. The percentage of workers employed in agriculture has now fallen below 50% and employment in the industry and service sectors has expanded rapidly, led by private investment. However, China has a massive underemployment problem. There are between 80 and 120 million surplus workers, including rural labourers and laid-off workers from SOEs. Large numbers of rural labourers have moved to the industrialized areas along the coastal strip and in the south-east of the country, where demand for labour is high. Many of these are young women, who have been employed, often under very poor conditions, in the burgeoning manufacturing industries exporting around the world. These factories are usually owned and managed by investors from Taiwan, Hong Kong and Korea. They are connected through complex supply chains to major Western merchandisers and retailers. Temporary labour shortages were reported in 2004 in the manufacturing centre of Guangdong province, in part because of an increase of agricultural incomes which had reduced the outflow of labour from the farms.

While precise division between public and private is impossible because of the diversity of forms of ownership in China, about two-thirds of China's GDP is generated in the non-state sector. In 2001 the rules of the Communist Party were changed to allow membership to "entrepreneurs" for the first time. While per capita incomes are still low, output has quadrupled in the past two decades and the size of China's population is such that total GDP is now second only to that of the USA. Annual growth in GDP in 2003 was 9.1%, the highest rate for seven years. China's emergence as a major economic power was underlined when, in October 2004, it was invited to participate in a special session of G-7 finance ministers and central bank governors – the first time it had participated in G-7 deliberations. China also joined the World Trade Organization in December 2001.

GDP (purchasing power parity) $6.45 trillion (2004 est.); GDP per capita (purchasing power parity) $5,000 (2004 est.).

2 Trade Unionism

China has a single trade union system organized through the All-China Federation of Trade Unions (ACFTU).

Trade unions developed in the first quarter of the twentieth century in harness with the nationalist and revolutionary politics of the Kuomintang (KMT). The first All-China Labour Congress was held in 1922, and the All-China General Labour Federation was founded at the second such conference held in 1925 (the ACFTU officially dates its origin to May 1, 1925). By 1927 the All-China General Labour Federation claimed 3 million members. Following the establishment in 1927 of KMT rule under Chiang Kai-shek in Shanghai, however, many trade unionists were executed, and thenceforth the unions were restricted, with national and general federations prohibited, and government-sponsored "yellow" unions installed. The Red Army under Mao Zedong, which took power in 1949, was peasant-based, but in 1948 the Communist Party (CPC) organized the ACFTU which functioned for 18 years as sole trade union centre. The ACFTU held its first congress since 1957. Until 1966 it and its associated unions were active at workplace level, principally in the areas of education, labour safety, welfare and propaganda. In 1966, however, Mao launched the Cultural Revolution to eliminate those accused of "bourgeois tendencies". Trade unions were replaced by workplace revolutionary committees and the ACFTU was itself dissolved in December 1966. Trade unions were denounced as counter-revolutionary in purpose and methods. Following the death of Mao in 1976, however, the "gang of four" radicals were arrested and many of the policies adopted in the late 1960s reversed.

In October 1978, the ACFTU held its first congress since 1957 and its newspaper, *The Workers' Daily* (*Gongren Ribao*), which had been suppressed in 1966, resumed publication in the same month. In a statement to the congress, ACFTU chairman Ni Zhifu recalled that: "In December 1966 the office building (of the ACFTU) was occupied by force and *The Workers' Daily* was closed and sealed, at the personal instigation of Jiang Qing (Mao's widow and one of the gang of four). Many trade unions at the provincial, municipal and autonomous regional levels, as well as basic-level trade unions, were battered and crushed. Their office buildings were occupied by force, properties divided and files lost". The first union to resume its activities, after 12 years' suspension, was the All-China Federation of Railway Workers' Unions, which began its national congress at the end of October 1978.

China has not ratified ILO Convention No. 87 (Freedom of Association and Protection of the Right to Organize, 1948). It resumed participation in the work of the ILO in 1983, and the ACFTU says that "since 1983, the Chinese trade unions have actively urged the Chinese government and departments concerned to draw up plans for ratification and application of international labour conventions".

In recent years, trade unionism in China has been regulated by the Trade Union Law. It was passed by the National People's Congress in 1992 and extensively revised in 2001. The law contains a number of internal tensions. On the one hand, it gives official trade unions wide-ranging powers and responsibilities, and ensures that they are adequately resourced. On the other hand it ensures that trade unions are subordinate to the Communist Party, and attenuates their capacity to advocate for employees by requiring them to "mobilize… employees …to complete production duties and working duties with great efforts" (Article 7). Unions operating under the law are thus torn between representing employees and implementing party-state policy, which seeks to maintain labour discipline.

One source of these tensions is that for much of the period under Communist rule, Chinese trade unions operated almost entirely in state-owned and collective enterprises. These enterprise were "mini welfare states", which provided benefits that in a developed country would be delivered through the social security system. A major role of the unions in these enterprises was to influence the distribution of these benefits. They tended not to adopt an oppositional or countervailing role to the employer, as the employer was the state, of which workers were supposed to be the masters. The law still reflects this legacy. However, now that China's private sector is increasingly important, and the public sector is operating on more of a private sector model, the legacy of this earlier style of unionism inhibits the evolution of the law towards a system suited to a market economy. As the party-state opposes the development of an independent activist union movement, the tensions within the law are likely to remain.

It is well known that China does not comply with ILO Convention No. 87 or Convention No. 98 (Right to Organize and Collective Bargaining). It has not ratified those Conventions. This is because, although the Trade Union Law creates a right to form trade unions (Article 3), and provides a significant degree of union security (see, e.g. Articles 3, 11, 17, 18, 50-55), it does not enable independent unions to be formed. The 2001 revisions confirm that all unions must be subordinate to the ACFTU (Article 2) according to the principle of democratic centralism. This means that "trade union organizations at a lower level shall be under the leadership of trade unions organizations at a higher level".

A further problem with these provisions is that they do not explicitly prevent senior managers being union members, or even from holding executive positions in unions. Thus, especially in state-owned enterprises, many directors have held union office. Some unions thus simply legitimate management plans. One attempt to limit the conflict of interest here is the new Article 9, although this stops short of banning management participation in unions outright.

The 2001 law makes new provision for collective bargaining, although the legal framework as set out in the law, as well as in the 1994 Labour Law, is incomplete. Neither the Trade Union Law, nor the Labour Law, deals extensively with unfair labour practices or other aspects of the collective bargaining process, although an employer cannot refuse to negotiate without a "tenable reason" (Article 53). A new Collective Contract Law has been mooted and is urgently needed. Despite the absence of a comprehensive collective bargaining framework, collective agreements are being concluded in increasing numbers of workplaces. By the end of 2001, some 270,000 collective contracts had been concluded. However, it is unclear if many of these involved genuine bargaining.

A further shortcoming in relation to collective bargaining is that there is no clear right to strike in China. Nevertheless, strikes are not expressly prohibited. Recent years have seen large numbers of worker protests in China. These are usually associated with claims for arrears rather than for improvements in working conditions. The ACFTU does not usually organize these strikes; indeed, it often attempts to prevent them (see further below). This is because, while unions have a role in representing workers where a work stoppage occurs (Article 27), they are also required to "assist the enterprise to … resume production and working order as soon as possible".

The Trade Union Law contains many provisions requiring unions to safeguard workers' rights to "democratic management" (e.g. Articles 5, 6, 19, 23, 35-38). This concept has been implemented in the public sector in a relatively straightforward way through workers' congresses (which are similar in some ways to European Works Councils). The law says that the trade union committee of an enterprise is the "working body" of the "workers' congress", tasked with the implementation of its decisions. According to the ACFTU, the workers' congress system has been set up in almost all state-owned enterprises in large and medium-sized cities. The events of 1989 had the effect of extending the role of the workers' congresses, but the trend of economic reform has been to emphasize the right of managers to make decisions and overcome obstacles to radical restructuring. In many enterprises the workers' congress is effectively moribund. How democratic management is to be realized in the private sector is not entirely clear, although unions have a right to be consulted on significant issues of operation and management, including the design of new facilities and processes and in the implementation of safety systems.

One area where trade unions potentially have clout is in the enforcement of labour standards. Notoriously, very many Chinese firms breach the Labour Law and the 2002 Law on Work Safety, especially those firms which are smaller and/or located in the private sector. Both the Trade Union Law and the Work Safety Law give extensive powers to unions to ensure that standards are met (Trade Union Law Articles 21-26, Labour Safety Law Article 52). These provisions typically give unions the power to complain of a violation, and require the employer to investigate the complaint and make amends if a violation has occurred. If an employer refuses to do so, the union can refer the matter to local authorities. Unions have legal capacity and can sue in their own right. It remains to be seen to what extent unions will exercise these powers.

A puzzling feature of the Labour Law (Articles 80 and 81) is that unions have an ambiguous role in the mediation and arbitration of labour disputes. Thus, dispute resolution within the enterprises consists of a tripartite committee with employer and employee representatives and a trade union chair but where the dispute is taken beyond the enterprise, the labour dispute arbitration committee (LDAC) is constituted by employer representatives, the trade union and a chair from the local labour bureau. Thus, it is unclear whether a trade union is an employee representative or an impartial mediator. By the end of 2001, China had, according to the *People's Daily*, established some 3,192 LDACs.

The law provides unions with funding through a levy on employers amounting to 2% of the total wage bill. Moreover, the wages of full-time trade union committee members must be paid by the enterprise. Other committee members are entitled to three paid working days per month of union leave. It would seem, however, that many firms do not comply with this requirement.

3 Trade Union Centre

All-China Federation of Trade Unions (ACFTU)
Address. 10 Fuxingmenwai Street, Beijing 100865
Phone. +86 10 685 92730
Fax. +86 10 685 62031
E-mail. acftuild@public3.bta.net.cn
Website. www.acftu.org.cn
Leadership. Wang Zhaoguo (chairman) (elected 2003); Zhang Junjiu (first secretary of secretariat) (elected 2003).
Membership. 134 million
Publications. The Workers' Daily: www.ggrb.com.cn.
History and character. The ACFTU is the largest national trade union organization in the world, reporting 1,713,000 primary trade union organizations and 134 million members. There are no legal trade unions outside the ACFTU. It is constituted in accordance with the Trade Union Law as a "mass organization of the working class formed voluntarily by the Chinese workers and staff members". The overwhelming majority of workers in state enterprises are in unions, but significant numbers of workers in the private sector and foreign-owned or joint venture enterprises are not organized.

The ACFTU is governed by a its National Congress, which convenes every five years. Between meetings of the Congress, the ACFTU is managed by an Executive Committee, composed of 267 members. The Executive Committee in turn elects the members of the Presidium, which exercises decision-making power when the Executive Committee is not in session. The routine work of the ACFTU is handled by its Secretariat. There are 31 trade union federations for the provinces, autonomous regions and municipalities. In parallel are 10 national industrial unions. The ACFTU is organized on the Soviet model on the principle of democratic centralism, i.e. that lower level bodies must be guided by higher levels.

The ACFTU was affected by the reform movement of the late 1980s that culminated in the crushing of the occupation of Tiananmen Square in June 1989. In 1988 Zhu Hou Ze was appointed as ACFTU 1st secretary. Zhu had been dismissed as head of the party propaganda department in February 1987 because he was associated with the policies of the then party leader Hu Yaobang, who had failed to stop student demonstrations. As ACFTU 1st secretary Zhu probably encouraged moves to invigorate workers' congresses and to make unions more responsive to the welfare concerns of workers. He also appears not to have prevented members from participating in the reform and democracy movements of 1989. In December of that year he was replaced by Yu Hon-Gen, former president of the National Coal Corporation.

The 1992 Trade Union Law confirmed the ACFTU's role as the sole national organization of trade unions and defined the role of the unions as an instrument of official policy. This role was re-emphasized in the ACFTU's revised constitution of 1993. ACFTU chairman Wang Zhaoguo is a member of the CPC Politburo and there is a close mesh between union and party at all levels.

The 14th (five-yearly) National Congress of the ACFTU was held in September 2003. At that meeting a new ACFTU Charter was promulgated. The new Charter maintains the democratic centralist structure of the ACFTU. The Charter imposes obligations on ACFTU member unions that are not always consistent with representing the interests of employees. In private firms, for example, unions are to, "construct consultation systems, implement democratic participation, represent workers' political rights and material interests, protect the national and social interest, respect the lawful rights and interests of investors and work together [with them] to develop the enterprise" (Article 29). The congress also reaffirmed the Chinese Communist Party's leading role and adopted the "Three Represents" ideology of former CCP Chairman Jiang Zemin (i.e. that the party should represent the advanced forces of production, the forward direction of advanced culture and the fundamental interests of the majority of the Chinese people). It endorsed the development of further strategies to form trade unions in private firms, promoting the direct election of local ACFTU union chairpersons, and extending membership to migrant rural workers (who are likely to suffer the most severe labour abuses).

The ACFTU has also shown awareness of the problems of social dislocation caused by economic reforms, unemployment, widespread non-payment of benefits and dissatisfaction as privatization is seen to make well-connected individuals wealthy at the expense of those who had built up the enterprises through their labour. The ACFTU is emphasizing its role in assisting workers to find new jobs, in providing re-training and organizing consumer cooperatives, and in organizing social benefits. The ACFTU has a consultative role in drafting and revising laws, at national and local level, affecting labour and social welfare.

Where industrial action occurs in China, it tends to consist of essentially individualistic acts by isolated dissidents and has not represented a challenge to the existing trade union structure. However, the restructuring of the economy has led to the development of wider forms of industrial unrest, focused on living standards and working conditions, rather than broader political aspirations. Traditionally, workers have depended on the enterprise for a wide range of benefits, such as health care and housing. As many SOEs are effectively bankrupt, there are many cases of workers going unpaid for extended periods, with laid-off workers not getting subsistence allowances and pensioners not receiving their pensions. Enterprises have reportedly covered losses by diverting money from pension funds and embezzlement by senior managers is said to be not uncommon. While the enterprise-based system has broken down, an adequate state back-up system has not yet been constructed in its place. Laid-off workers, and workers owed back pay, have in some places laid virtual siege to government offices or blocked roads and railroads until dispersed by the police.

The approach adopted in dealing with such unrest has varied by locality. In some instances, the authorities have sought to find solutions to grievances; in others, demonstrations have been broken up by riot police or the army and leaders detained. There are reports that some activists have been subjected to administrative detention merely for taking up causes before labour disputes and arbitration committees. According to the ICFTU: "in some large plants, work committees, comprising officials from local ACFTU branches, the local labour bureau authorities and the Public Security Bureau (PSB), have been set up to monitor and pre-empt worker action. Many medium and large enterprises have detention facilities and security officials can detain and sentence protesting workers to three years in a labour camp".

In general branch unions have avoided giving support to any form of militancy such as work stoppages or go-slows and normally work to prevent such actions developing. However, according to the *China Labour Bulletin*, at "local plant level branch chairpersons are being laid off along with other workers, and more often than not it is the local party secretary who takes up the vacant union position". The history of past purges of union officials who fell out of step with official policy is a deterrent to local unions adopting positions unacceptable to higher bodies.

The official unions have been seeking to define a role that is in alignment with official policy while also helping to mitigate the impact of restructuring. The unions have opened employment agencies and set up vocational training organizations where workers have been re-trained. They also have set up service businesses and market places and run a "warmth" programme to assist needy families. The unions are involved in efforts to reform the social security, employment, housing and medical insurance systems.

The ACFTU participates in the Workers' Group of the ILO and in various UN fora. However, it is not a member of the ICFTU, the major international union confederation. The ICFTU's present policy towards the ACFTU was adopted in November 2002. It states that "the ICFTU, noting that the ACFTU is not an independent trade union organisation and, therefore, cannot be regarded as an authentic voice of Chinese workers, reaffirms its request to all affiliates and Global Union Federations having contacts with the Chinese authorities, including the ACFTU, to engage in critical dialogue." Some ICFTU members refuse to maintain contact with the ACFTU.

International affiliation. None

4 Other Trade Union Organizations

Efforts to create independent trade unions featured in the brief reform movement of 1989. The Workers' Autonomous Federations (WAFs) were founded in May, and represented the first major attempt to set up autonomous unions since 1949. The WAFs seem to have had particular success in Shanghai; there and elsewhere they focused on income discrepancies, poor working conditions, the lack of democracy at the workplace, the lack of involvement in policy-making, and the deterioration of living standards.

On June 2, 1989, the ACFTU called for the crushing of the independent unions. On June 4 troops put down demonstrations in Tiananmen Square. However the first secretary and vice-president of the ACFTU, Zhu Hou Ze, was regarded as having favoured the reform movement and this led to his dismissal in December 1989; he was replaced by Yu Hon-Gen, former president of the National Coal Corporation. The leader of the Beijing Federation, Gou Hai Feng, expressed similar views and was arrested in August, charged with having set fire to a bus. On June 14, the Public Security Bureau declared WAFs illegal. A number of their members were posted on wanted lists and some are believed to have been sentenced to death. On June 16 delegates to the UN Special Session on Prevention of Discrimination and Protection of Minorities heard of 13 workers executed for "counter-revolutionary crimes" and 67 arrested for their involvement in WAFs.

Around the time of the first anniversary of the Tiananmen Square events the authorities released several hundred prisoners incarcerated since June 1989. It was thought, however, that none of the WAF leaders was among them and also that the official position that only 45 of these were still held might be an underestimate. In 1999 the ICFTU reported that many activists involved with the WAFs were still in prison, psychiatric hospitals run by the Public Security Bureau, or forced labour camps. Others involved with the movement had been deported.

In 1992 an underground Free Labour Union of China was formed but its leaders were quickly arrested and imprisoned for "organizing and leading a counter-revolutionary group". They became known as the "Beijing 16". Since that time there have been recurrent efforts by individuals or small groups of dissidents to organize unions, or circulate petitions calling for free unions. Those involved have generally been imprisoned on criminal charges or subjected to "re-education through labour", a form of administrative detention which dispenses with the need for a trial. The treatment of those subjected to "re-education through labour" is said to be commonly worse than in the criminal justice system, with torture used.

SPECIAL ADMINISTRATIVE REGIONS OF CHINA

HONG KONG

Population: 6.86 m. (2004 est.)

1 Political and Economic Background

Hong Kong reverted from British to Chinese rule, as a Special Administrative Region (HKSAR), on July 1, 1997. China's policy towards Hong Kong has been defined by the term "one country, two systems", indicating that it would not attempt to bring Hong Kong into conformity with mainland

China but would seek to exercise sovereignty within the context of Hong Kong's different political, economic and judicial framework. The period since 1997 has largely been characterized by continuity from the period of British rule. The administration is headed by a chief executive, appointed by the Chinese government.

After a transitional period following the handover to China, in which there was a Provisional Legislative Council, the first elections to the Legislative Council under Chinese rule were held on May 24, 1998. Candidates of the opposition Democratic Party and allies won 13 of the 20 directly-elected seats, while the pro-Beijing Democratic Alliance for the Betterment of Hong Kong (DABHK) won only five. However, the legislature as a whole, where the majority of the 60 seats were reserved for specific groups, remained controlled by forces allied to Beijing or business groups favouring stable relations with Beijing. There were mass demonstrations in 2003 against a proposed new security law, leading the government to withdraw the measure and to a swing against pro-Beijing parties in district council elections in November 2003. However, the DABHK emerged as the largest party from Legislative Council elections in September 2004, with 25 of the 60 seats, including 8 of the 30 directly elected geographical constituencies.

Hong Kong is a key Asian manufacturing, financial and trading centre, with a buoyant free market economy. It represents a major economic asset and stepping-stone to international markets for China, which since 1997 has not sought to impose economic models and policies prevailing elsewhere in the country. Hong Kong enjoyed high growth rates throughout the 1980s and 1990s, but was badly hit by the Asian economic crisis of 1997–98, with unemployment at over 8% in 1999 at its highest for 25 years. Rapid recovery from 1999 was followed by a further downturn in 2001-02 but with a resumption of economic growth in 2003-04.

GDP (purchasing power parity) $213bn. (2004 est.); GDP per capita (purchasing power parity) $28,800 (2004 est.).

2 Trade Unionism

Trade unionism first appeared early in the twentieth century, although unions did not achieve legal status until 1948. For many years Hong Kong trade unionism was clearly divided between the ICFTU-affiliated Hong Kong and Kowloon Trade Union Council (HKTUC) and the Hong Kong Federation of Trade Unions (HKFTU), each founded in the aftermath of legalization. The HKTUC was allied to the (Taiwanese) Chinese Federation of Labour. The larger HKFTU was oriented to Beijing. In addition many small unions operated independently of these centres. Both the HKTUC and the HKFTU continue in the aftermath of the reversion to Chinese rule in 1997. The HKTUC, however, has progressively declined as the relevance of its pro-Taiwanese orientation has disappeared, while the HKFTU is seen as closely aligned to the wishes of the Hong Kong authorities.

The final years of British rule also saw the emergence of a third centre, the Confederation of Trade Unions of Hong Kong (HKCTU), an ICFTU affiliate, and this has become the main focus of trade unionism independent of the HKFTU. The HKCTU sought to expand the rights available to free trade unions in the last years of British colonial rule in preparation for the handover to China.

Under British rule Hong Kong was not a member of the ILO in its own right and the UK made declarations on its behalf concerning the various conventions, including ILO conventions No. 87 (Freedom of Association and Protection of the Right to Organize, 1948) and No. 98 (Right to Organize and Collective Bargaining, 1949). Under the terms of agreement for the transfer of Hong Kong from British to Chinese rule, China was to continue to apply these conventions.

Under the Basic Law of the SAR (in effect, Hong Kong's constitution), the right to join unions is protected. However, as under British rule, there are no rights in respect of union recognition and collective bargaining, or institutional framework for these. Employers generally refuse to recognize unions and in practice less than one per cent of workers are covered by collective agreements. While there is a right to strike, the right is not protected in law, and employers can dismiss striking employees for breach of their contracts without compensation. In 2001 legislation was introduced that gave workers who were dismissed for participating in strike action the right to sue for compensation for unfair dismissal.

In the last days of British rule, Lee Cheuk-yan, the general secretary of the HKCTU, who was also a member of the Legislative Council, introduced a private member's bill which incorporated three ordinances designed to bring Hong Kong into compliance with ILO standards. The measure provided for unions to have rights to be recognized for collective bargaining or consultation, for workers dismissed for trade union activities to be reinstated, and to end the ban on the use of union funds for political purposes. The ordinances were passed at the last sitting of the Council under British rule in June 1997, but immediately suspended when the Chinese took control the following month. In October 1997 the new Provisional Legislative Council overturned the main provisions of the new legislation, effectively returning the situation to what it had been in the period before June 1997. In November 1998 the ILO Committee on Freedom of Association supported a complaint filed by the HKCTU against the government and called on the Hong Kong authorities to strengthen protections for trade unions and regretted the repeal of the collective bargaining legislation. The government indicated that it did not feel further action was necessary, and the HKFTU likewise declined to support the HKCTU on this issue.

In 1999 Lee Cheuk-yan again sought to introduce collective bargaining legislation in the Legislative Council, to which he had been elected in the first elections in May 1998. However, in July 1999 the president of the Legislative Council ruled the move inadmissible on the ground that bills relating to public expenditure, political structure and government operation could not be introduced as private members' bills unless approved by the chief executive. The government said that the measures proposed by Lee would add HK$40 million to its budget.

Since 1997 there has been some tightening of restrictions on freedom of association and right of assembly, but trade unionists have remained able to strike and stage demonstrations. In May 1999, in the face of government moves to restructure the civil service, civil servants staged a one-day "sick-out" and a protest rally organized by the Hong Kong Federation of Civil Service Unions and the HKCTU attracted 20,000. Strikes are not common, however, there being only one small strike in 2003, and most individual employment contracts make striking a breach of contract that can lead to dismissal. There has been no interference with the international affiliation of the HKCTU to the ICFTU.

In 2002 a draft security law was proposed that many criticized as a threat to freedom of association. Demonstrations including a protest by 500,000 people in July 2003 and an international campaign against the law resulted in the proposals being withdrawn.

An estimated 22% of employees are in unions, with large numbers of small unions. The trade unions are represented in the Legislative Council.

3 Trade Union Centres

Hong Kong Confederation of Trade Unions (HKCTU)
Address. 19th Floor, Wing Wong Commercial Building, 557–559 Nathan Road, Kowloon
Phone. +852 2770 8668
Fax. +852 2770 7388
E-mail. hkctu@hkctu.org.hk
Website. www.hkctu.org.hk
Leadership. Lee Cheuk-yan (general secretary)
Membership. 140,000
History and character. Established in response to the Tiananmen Square events of 1989 and the approach of transfer of sovereignty to China. In 1990 the HKCTU set itself the target of overtaking the pro-Beijing HKFTU and establishing a strong base before transfer to China. Despite steady growth, it did not reach that goal and attributes the continued success of the HKFTU in retaining members to the range of services the HKFTU is able to provide members.

The HKCTU describes its foundation as being the struggle for the rights of workers to organize independent and democratic trade unions and engage in collective bargaining with employers. The federation's slogan is "solidarity, rice bowl, justice, democracy". Its general secretary, Lee Cheuk-yan as a member of the SAR's Legislative Council, has promoted legislation to this end (see above).

The HKCTU identifies with opposition politics but not with one group. In the first elections to the new Legislative Council, in May 1998, general secretary Lee Cheuk-yan was elected on the Frontier platform, while chair Lau Chin-shek was elected on the Democratic Party platform.
International affiliation. ICFTU

Hong Kong Federation of Trade Unions (HKFTU)
Website. www.hkftu.com.hk (not in English)
Leadership. Cheng Yiu Tong (chairman)
Membership. 257,000
History and character. The HKFTU was founded in 1948 and in the British colonial period was oriented to Beijing. Following the handover of the territory to China in 1997 the HKFTU affirmed its support for the new HKSAR government and its policy of "one country, two systems". It opposed the rival HKCTU's submission of a complaint to the ILO as an attempt to "internationalize the internal affairs" of the HKSAR. The rival HKCTU characterizes the HKFTU as an in instrument of the alliance between the authorities and the business oligarchies, but concedes that it has retained the affiliation of more workers, which is attributed to the HKFTU's substantial resources which allow it to run supermarkets, travel agencies, discount stores and health clinics at below-market rates.

Hong Kong and Kowloon Trades Union Council (HKTUC)
Address. 12 F Kam Shek Commercial Bldg., 17 Waterloo Road, Kowloon.
Phone. +852 2384 5150
Fax. +852 2770 5396
Leadership. Tong Woon Fai (president); Liew Nan Kiem (general secretary)
Membership. 30,000
History and character. Historically aligned with the Taiwanese Chinese Federation of Labour. It has declined in the face of the growth of the HKCTU in the 1990s.
International affiliation. ICFTU

4 Other Trade Union Organization

Joint Organization of Unions – Hong Kong
Address. Flat B, 5/F, Harvard House, 105-III, Thomson Road, Wanchai.
Phone. +852 575 5544
Fax. +852 25914636
E-mail. jou_hk@yahoo.com
Leadership. Butt Yil Cheung (president)
International affiliation. WCL

MACAU

Population: 445,000 (2004 est.)

1 Political and Economic Background

Macau, comprising a small peninsula in the south of the People's Republic of China and three neighbouring islands, was under Portuguese administration from the sixteenth century. It reverted to China as a Special Administrative Region in 1999. Under Portuguese rule it did not develop as a major commercial centre in the manner of Hong Kong, and its economy is based on tourism, including gambling (which represents an estimated 40% of GDP), and textiles.

GDP (purchasing power parity) $9.1bn. (2003 est.); GDP per capita (purchasing power parity) $19,400 (2003 est.).

2 Trade Unionism

Under the Portuguese constitution basic trade union rights were extended to Macau. However, there has been relatively little development and most unions are politically allied to Beijing and concentrate on welfare, social and cultural activities. Under the Basic Law, as with Hong Kong, China guaranteed that international labour conventions previously applied under Portuguese rule would remain in force. There has been little development of collective bargaining. There is a legal right to strike but protections against retribution are lacking.

Colombia

Capital: Bogota
Population: 42.31 m. (2004 est.)

1 Political and Economic Background

Since the end of the Rojas dictatorship in 1957, the presidency of Colombia has tended to alternate between the Liberal (PLC) and Conservative (PSC) parties, with the Cabinet being effectively bipartisan. President Barco Vargas (1986–90) formed a single-party government, but his PLC successors Gaviria Barco and Ernesto Samper Pizano returned the country to coalition rule; Samper was re-elected in 1994. Elections in 1998 resulted in the election of Andres Pastrana Arango, an independent conservative, as President, while the 2002 presidential election was won by Alvaro Uribe Velez of the conservative Colombia First coalition, who enjoyed the backing of the PSC and again formed a Cabinet including both the PSC and PLC.

Drug trafficking and guerrilla warfare have for years scarred the political and economic life of Colombia, which has also suffered a series of assassinations of political and trade union figures. Left-wing insurgents, notably the Colombia Revolutionary Armed Forces (FARC) and National Liberation Army (ELN), as well as right-wing death squads, are still active despite repeated attempts at national reconciliation by successive governments.

The economy has been adversely affected by the lack of stability and low investor confidence and the government has been forced to implement austerity measures while depending on foreign aid. The economy is also vulnerable to price fluctuations of coffee, oil and other export commodities. However, economic growth was forecast to be close to 4% in 2004. In July 2004 the government announced plans for a wide-ranging privatization programme, starting with electricity distribution operations, to raise funds for social and infrastructure programmes at a time when debt interest represented some 20 per cent of total spending.

GDP (purchasing power parity) $263.2bn. (2004 est.); GDP per capita (purchasing power parity) $6,300 (2004 est.).

2 Trade Unionism

Trade union organization appeared in the first decade of the twentieth century and unions were first legalized by the Liberal government in 1930. Colombia ratified ILO conventions No. 87 (Freedom of Association and Protection of the Right to Organize, 1948) and No. 98 (Right to Organize and Collective Bargaining, 1949), in 1976, and in 1977 unions became independent legal bodies, formally ending their direct political ties. About 6–7% of the workforce is unionized, with 89% of union members working in the public sector. In the private sector most union members belong to single enterprise unions but the unions are generally weak and little collective bargaining takes place.

There have been constant splits and re-organizations of Colombian trade union centres over the decades. There are now three main centres, which between them have the affiliation of most of the 2,500 registered unions. The longest established centre, although itself affected by breakaways at different times, is the Confederación de Trabajadores de Colombia (CTC), which dates from the 1930s, is affiliated to the ICFTU, and traditionally is close to the Liberal Party. The Confederación General de Trabajadores Democráticos (CGTD), is politically independent and affiliated to the WCL. It was formed in 1992. The centre-left Central Unitaria de Trabajadores (CUT) was founded in 1986 and is the largest centre, with 45–50% of all unions affiliated to it.

Colombia is probably the most dangerous country in the world for trade unionists; it is certainly the most dangerous of those countries in which free trade unionism is protected by law. This bleak reality undercuts all formal legal protections.

The history of violence is a long one. A 1928 strike at the US-owned United Fruit company resulted in "the massacre of the banana workers" when several hundred were killed by the army. In 1977 the then four leading confederations joined in a general strike in which about 18 people were killed in clashes with the security forces. By the 1980s "disappearances" and assassinations of political and union leaders by paramilitary groups were endemic. Violence continued throughout the 1990s. Large numbers of trade unionists fell victim to gun squads in the run-up to the 1990 presidential elections. In May the vice-president of the CTC was killed and the toll approached 1,000 for the three-year period to end-1990. After initial promise, the term of office of President Gaviria saw a large number of murders. The ICFTU *Survey of Violations of Trade Union Rights* found that 46 Colombian trade unionists had been murdered in 1993 and another 33 forced into hiding. The head office of the oil workers' union USO was bombed in February 1993. While some of the killings were linked to drug barons and landowners, unions charged the security forces of complicity in some instances.

The ICFTU further estimated that there were 253 trade unionists murdered in 1996 and 156 in 1997. The teachers' union FECODE said that 61 teachers were killed in 1997 while four had disappeared. Many hundreds of trade unionists had left their homes because of death threats. Many of the murders were linked to industrial disputes, and were reportedly rarely investigated. Most of these deaths were attributed to paramilitaries with fewer reports of attacks by the security forces and guerrilla groups. Army and intelligence sources have sought in some instances to link union activists to guerrilla groups and lists of activists, effectively death lists, are reported to circulate.

In March 2000 the ICFTU reported that between 2,500 and 3,200 trade unionists had been killed since 1987, by paramilitary forces (sometimes with the complicity of the regular army), drug traffickers or far-left guerrillas. Among those killed in 1998–99 were CUT 1st vice-president Jorge Ortega Garcia (Oct. 20, 1998) and César Herrera Torreglosa, general secretary of the agricultural workers' union SINTRAINAGRO (Dec. 13, 1999). Rank-and-file union members particularly affected in this period were members of teachers' unions, agricultural workers and miners, while another centre of violence had been the oil-refining town of Barrancabermeja, the base of the oil workers' union, the USO. Arrests or convictions of those responsible for such murders are virtually unknown. Between 1986 and 2002 there were just five convictions resulting from the assassination of more than 4,000 trade unionists over the course of six years. However, on Dec. 19, 2002, sentences were handed down in the case of the attempted assassination of Wilson Borja, formerly the president of the state workers' union FENALTRASE. The two principal accused, former army officers, were each sentenced to 18 years in prison. A former army lieutenant was also sentenced to 42 months in prison for his part in the attempted assassination.

In May 1998 the ILO, documenting more than 300 killings of trade unionists since 1995, criticized the government for having failed to provide evidence of arrests or convictions in a single case. In November 1999 the government undertook to cooperate with the unions to end acts of anti-union terror, and the Labour Minister agreed to call on the ILO to despatch a "direct contacts mission" to evaluate how violence could be curbed. The CUT, CTC and CGTD have taken a number of joint initiatives in favour of peace and reconciliation. In 2002, however, the levels of violence recorded against trade union members again reached appalling levels, with some 184 trade unionists assassinated according to ILO figures.

Colombia's employment standards are laid down in the 1991 Constitution and the labour code, the latter regulating the right of association, organization of unions, federations and confederations, collective bargaining agreements, the right to strike and other union rights.

The ICFTU has noted the following restrictions on trade union activity: the labour code prohibits more than one union in any workplace; officers of unions must belong to the relevant trade or occupation; the authorities may supervise and intervene in the internal affairs of unions; industrial and branch unions must have 50% of workers in membership to bargain collectively; federations and confederations may not conduct collective bargaining; some public employees may not bargain collectively; the right to strike is restricted in many public services; and confederations and federations may not call strikes. Trade unions complain that legal measures brought in to combat terrorism, such as the introduction of witnesses with hidden identities, have also been used against trade union activists. In the period from 1996 the government made proposals to amend the labour laws to reduce the restrictions on trade unions but these measures were not acted on by Congress.

The centres cooperate with each other. In February 1997 they organized a public sector strike after the government declared a state of economic emergency. The oil workers' union the USO also threatened to shut down the state-run oil industry to oppose what it saw as a proposed creeping privatization. After a week, the government agreed wage increases and to set up a joint commission with the unions to study privatization plans, to review the criminal penalties being applied against trade union activists, and to set up a Commission for the Protection of Workers' Human Rights. The government also said it would promote a bill on collective bargaining in the public sector. In March, the constitutional court ruled that the economic state of emergency was unjustified.

The centres staged a general strike in September 1998 to protest against the impact of structural adjustment programmes on wages and jobs. They also staged a strike, mainly in the public sector, on Aug. 31–Sept. 1, 1999, in support of a 41-point economic and social recovery programme. The government agreed to hold discussions and not to penalize civil servants who had taken part in the strike.

3 Trade Union Centres

Confederación General de Trabajadores Democráticos (CGTD)
General Confederation of Democratic Workers
Address. Calle 39 A, n° 14–48, Apartado Aéreo 5415, Santafe de Bogota
Phone. +57 1 288 1560
Fax. +57 1 573 4026
E-mail. cgtd@col1.telecom.com.co
Leadership. Mario de J. Valderrama (president); Julio Roberto Gomez Esguerra (secretary general)
History and character. The CGTD was created in 1992 by fusion of the former WCL affiliate, the CGT, and the CTDC. The latter had itself been established in 1988 by the merger of the former leftist Trade Union Confederation of Colombian Workers (CSTC) and the Union of Workers of Colombia (UTC) together with a faction of the CTC. The CGTD is described as having a mix of Maoist and social Christian influences, reflecting the forces brought together at its creation. About 30% of Colombian unions are affiliated to it.

The WCL reported in 1998 that in the previous eight years, 27 leaders of the CGTD had been assassinated.
International affiliation. WCL

Confederación de Trabajadores de Colombia (CTC)
Confederation of Workers of Colombia
Address. Calle 39, No. 26A–23, Barrio de la Soledad, Bogota
Phone. +57 1 268 2084
Fax. +57 1 268 8576
E-mail. ctc@colnodo.apc.org
History and character. The CTC dates back to the 1930s and is traditionally allied to the moderate free-enterprise Liberal Party. A former president, José Raquel Mercado, was assassinated by the revolutionary leftist M-19 movement in 1976. The CTC affiliates about 12–15% of Colombian unions.
International affiliation. ICFTU

Central Unitaria de Trabajadores (CUT)
Central Union of Workers
Leadership. Carlos Rodriguez (president); Boris Houtes de Oca (secretary general)
Address. Calle 35, No. 7-25, Piso 9, Bogotá
Phone. +57 1 3237 550/60
Fax. . +57 1 3237 550
E-mail. cut@cut.org.co
Website. www.cut.org.co (in Spanish only)
History and character. The centre-left CUT, created in 1986 by affiliates of pre-existing centres, is the leading union centre in Colombia, representing some 45–50% of Colombia's unions. The CUT has been a regular target for terrorist attack: nearly 800 of its members were murdered between 1987 and 1992 alone. Its 1st Vice-President, Jorge Ortega Garcia was

shot dead at home on Oct. 20, 1998, during a national strike called over privatization and austerity measures. He had fled abroad for periods on several occasions during the previous few years because of death threats. The recent CUT president Luis Eduardo Garzon was the winner of the 2000 AFL–CIO human rights award in recognition of his and the CUT's continuing role in the search for peace and reconciliation in Colombia.

Comoros

Capital: Moroni
Population: 651,900 (2004 est.)

1 Political and Economic Background

The Comoros comprise Grande Comore (Njazidja), Anjouan (Nzwani) and Mohéli (Mwali). The predominantly Muslim islands achieved independence from France in 1975, although neighbouring Mayotte (largely Christian) chose to remain under French administration. Politically, the Comoros have been very unstable, enduring over 20 coups or attempted coups since independence, instigated mainly by groups based abroad, particularly in France. Increasing political instability and violence arose from 1997 as the islands of Anjouan and Mohéli sought to secede from the Comoros. In April 1999, the military seized power in a bloodless coup led by army chief of staff Col. Azali Assoumani, who became head of state.

Col Assoumani sought to resolve the secessionist crisis through a confederal arrangement. Consequently, in February 2001 the Fomboni accord on national reconciliation was signed by representatives of the military government and the three islands. A new constitution approved in a national referendum in December 2001 provided for greater autonomy, under which each island would have its own president and legislative assembly while respecting the unity and territorial integrity of the Comoros state. There would also be a rotating union president (initially from Grande Comore) and a union legislature comprising appointed and directly elected members.

Presidential elections for the autonomous islands of Grande Comore, Anjouan and Mohéli were held in the first half of 2002. Col Assoumani won the election for the union presidency held in March and April 2002. Elections were held in March 2004 for assemblies on each of the three islands. Candidates supporting Col Assoumani suffered a serious defeat.

Agriculture occupies more than 80% of the workforce, although there is high unemployment and rural under-employment and Comoros is not self-sufficient in food. Most of this activity is on a subsistence basis with production seriously affected by erosion and drought, and markets for the few agricultural and agriculture-based exports are liable to wide fluctuations. The Comoros' economy has been severely disrupted by domestic upheavals and natural disasters and the country depends heavily on assistance from France and from Arab states in the Gulf area, and on agreements with the EU. Unemployment is estimated at 20%. A major contribution to the economy is made from remittances from nationals working abroad (who are estimated to number around 150,000).

GDP (purchasing power parity) $441 million (2003 est.); GDP per capita (purchasing power parity) $700 (2003 est.)

2 Trade unionism

The Comoros ratified ILO Conventions No. 87 (Freedom of Association and Protection of the Right to Organize, 1948) and No. 98 (Right to Organize and Collective Bargaining, 1949) in 1978. The economy is based on subsistence agriculture and fishing and very small-scale commerce and there are only some 7,000 employees in the formal economy, the majority of them working for the government. Unions of teachers, civil servants and dock workers exist. There are two national centres: the Union des Travailleur des Comores (UTC), an affiliate of the Organization of African Trade Union Unity (OATUU), and the Union Syndicate.

There are no restrictions on workers joining unions and unions joining federations or affiliating with international bodies. The law protects workers from employer interference in their right to organize and administer their unions. Unions have the right to bargain collectively; however, employers set wages in the small private sector, and the government, especially the Ministries of Finance and Labour, set them in the relatively larger public sector. Strikes and worker demonstrations have occurred in response to political crises, economic restructuring mandated by international financial organizations, and the failure of the government – occasionally for months at a time – to pay civil servants.

Democratic Republic of Congo

Capital: Kinshasa
Population: 58.32 m. (2004 est.)

1 Political and Economic Background

Following a military coup in 1965, Congo became a one-party state ruled by President Marshal Mobutu Sese Seko, leader of the Mouvement Populaire de la Révolution (MPR). It was renamed as Zaire in 1971 in accordance with Mobutu's Africanization programme. From 1990 other political parties were allowed. A transitional administration, the High Council of the Republic (HCR) was elected in 1992 but came into conflict with Mobutu. After a lengthy period of confusion with at one point two rival cabinets coexisting, an election date of July 1995 was set. In May 1995 however, the elections were indefinitely postponed.

Mobutu was overthrown in May 1997 by the forces of Laurent Kabila, leader of the Alliance of Democratic

Forces for the Liberation of Congo–Zaire, and died later that year in Morocco. On taking power Kabila announced that he would become President and that the country would be renamed as the Democratic Republic of Congo (DRC). Widespread massacres of ethnic Tutsis were reported. All political party activity and demonstrations were banned, but presidential and legislative elections were promised for April 1999. No elections were held, however and Kabila himself faced serious military rebellion with the forces of several African countries fighting on different sides. He was assassinated in January 2001, his son, Joseph Kabila, then becoming President. The new President eased restrictions on party political activity and sought to implement a peace process. This culminated in April 2003 with the signing of a peace agreement which provided for a two-year transitional period during which President Kabila would be supported by four Vice Presidents – one from Kabila's government, one from the unarmed civilian opposition and two from the principal rebel groups.

The DRC's weak economy has deteriorated since the 1980s and despite considerable natural resources it is one of the world's poorest countries. It has been affected by huge influxes of refugees from several African states (including, in 1994, perhaps one million fleeing from Rwanda and Burundi), and in the late 1990s military conflict (exacerbated by foreign intervention) within its own borders. Foreign-owned businesses have scaled back their activity. Lack of infrastructure, corruption and the absence of a reliable legal and policy framework for business, are factors that have discouraged investment.

GDP (purchasing power parity) $40.05bn. (2004 est.); GDP per capita (purchasing power parity) $700 (2004 est.).

2 Trade Unionism

The DRC ratified ILO Convention No. 98 (Right to Organize and Collective Bargaining, 1949) in 1969, and Convention No. 87 (Freedom of Association and Protection of the Right to Organize, 1948) in 2001.

The trade unions were consolidated into the Union Nationale des Travailleurs du Zaire (UNTZa) in 1967 under the auspices of the ruling party. Thereafter it operated as the sole union centre. It was able to adopt more independence from the ruling party by the late 1980s. Following Mobutu's 1990 decision to allow freedom of association, as part of a move to political liberalization, some 80 new union organizations were founded: in the view of the ICFTU, only four were representative.

The ICFTU reported that by 1997 there were at least 199 trade unions although this was "largely because the authorities, politicians, employers and others were behind the creation and registration of a number of in-house unions and other unrepresentative and phantom unions, particularly in the public sector and state enterprises".

Following the seizure of power by Kabila in 1997, UNTZa was renamed as the Union Nationale des Travailleurs du Congo (UNTC). This remains the leading federation. However, the position of the trade unions has been undermined by the collapse of large parts of the formal economy and the shortage of regularly paid jobs. Collective bargaining scarcely exists in practice. Unions mainly represent public sector employees. Legal strikes can only be called following a lengthy arbitration and appeal process, and are not common. There have been strikes by civil servants, university administrators, health workers and other public sector workers over unpaid wages, with government action varying between giving concessions and arresting and imprisoning union leaders.

In 2003 two union leaders from the telecoms sector were sacked for calling a strike, and the police and military attacked a railway workers' protest camp. The ICFTU reported that in 2003 the provincial leader of a nurses' union was found drowned just before a union protest.

3 Trade Union Centres

Confédération Démocratique du Travail (CDT)
Address. 5ème Rue n.211 Limette, BP 10897, Kinshasa 1
Phone. +243 880 4573
Email. cdtcongo@yahoo.fr
History and character. Emerged as third largest union centre under pluralism, with 139 seats gained in the 1994 trade union elections. Affiliated to the ICFTU in 1994.
International affiliation. ICFTU

Confédération Générale du Travail du Congo
Address. A/1, Rue Lokolama No.A/1, B.P. 8416, Kinshasa, 1 Kalamu
International affiliation. WFTU

Confédération Syndicale du Congo (CSC)
Address. BP 3107, Kinshasa
Phone. +243 1398372
Fax. +243 1398126
E-mail. c.s.c.congo@ic.cd
Leadership. Symphorien Dunia (president)
History and character. This is the second largest confederation in the DRC. Its president, Fernand Kikongi, was elected president of the WCL in December 1997. Kikongi told the 2nd CSC congress, held in Kinshasa in July 1999, that the trade unions had to find ways to assist in national reconstruction in the face of economic collapse, instability, closure of enterprises and malnutrition.
International affiliation. WCL

Union Nationale des Travailleurs du Congo (UNTC)
National Union of Congolese Workers
Address. Zone de la Gombe, BP 8814, Avenue Mutombo, Katshi 5, Kinshasa 1
Phone. +243 12 22 148
Website. www.untc.org
History and character. Founded 1967. Formerly known as Union Nationale des Travailleurs du Zaire (UNTZa), once the single union centre of Zaire. It launched a contributory national health insurance scheme (UPM) in 1986, and thereafter a number of education, health, rural cooperative, agricultural, banking and other projects. It

began to move away from the regime in the late 1980s with protests against the steady decline in the purchasing power of Zairean workers, which it attributed to "currency depreciation and abuse perpetrated under the guise of economic liberalism". In 1990 UNTZa was able to break away from the ruling party and expelled its general secretary Kombo Ntonga Booke, who was a member of the party central committee.

Of the three centres it remained closest to the regime, and in Zaire's first free pluralist trade union elections since 1967, it comfortably held first place with 1,126 seats. The UNTZa affiliated to the ICFTU in 1994; it remained the strongest trade union centre, comfortably winning the second (1994) "social" trade union elections by securing 1,324 seats, ahead of the 1,196 gained by its nearest rival the WCL-affiliated Confédération Syndicale du Zaire (CSZa). In 1997, after the fall of Mobutu and renaming of the country, UNTZa was renamed the UNTC.

International affiliation. OATUU, ICFTU

Congo

Capital: Brazzaville
Population: 2.99 m. (2004 est.)

1 Political and Economic Background

The Republic of Congo became a self-governing republic within the French Community in 1958 and achieved full independence in 1960. After some years of disturbed political conditions, a military coup took place in 1968, and in the following year a nominally Marxist regime was established under the Parti Congolais du Travail (PCT) as the sole political party. The country was renamed the People's Republic of the Congo in 1970 but reverted to its original name in 1991 after the PCT abandoned Marxism–Leninism.

A 1992 referendum approved a new multi-party constitution, and the country's first democratic elections followed the same year. Pascal Lissouba, leader of the Pan-African Union for Social Democracy (UPADS) was elected President, defeating the incumbent Denis Sassou-Nguesso of the PCT, who had been President since 1979. Further presidential elections scheduled for July 1997 were postponed because of internal unrest.

In October 1997, after four months' fighting, "Cobra" militias backing Sassou-Nguesso (who was also supported militarily by the government of Angola) overthrew Lissouba, who went into exile in France. Sassou-Nguesso was declared the winner, with close to 90% of the vote, in presidential elections staged in March 2002, while legislative elections later that year also resulted in victory for the President's party, the PCT, and its allies.

Agriculture, much of it at subsistence level but also including cash crops such as coffee, cocoa, sugar and palm oil, provides a livelihood for much of the population. However, the country is also an oil producer and the development of this sector in the 1970s and 1980s funded development as oil became the main contributor to government revenues. From the late 1960s the main sectors of the economy were progressively nationalized. As the country moved away from one-party rule, however, it embraced market principles and received external support for restructuring, although this has been disrupted by civil war and instability.

GDP (purchasing power parity) $2.15bn. (2004 est.); GDP per capita (purchasing power parity) $700 (2004 est.).

2 Trade Unionism

Congo ratified ILO Convention No. 87 (Freedom of Association and Protection of the Right to Organize, 1948) in 1960, but did not ratify Convention No. 98 (Right to Organize and Collective Bargaining, 1949) until 1999.

Trade unionism developed under the French but under one-party rule was coordinated by the Confédération Syndicale Congolaise (CSC). The CSC was designated by name in a decree as the sole trade union and benefited from compulsory check-off from the pay of all workers, which was introduced in 1973. However, the move to pluralism in the early 1990s was reflected in the CSC assuming independence from the ruling party and the emergence of alternative centres.

The current labour code provides for the free formation of trade unions and is generally close to compliance with ILO standards, although enforcement of the code is lacking. The formal waged sector is small but most employees in it are in unions. Collective bargaining is practised, though not widely, and there is a legal right to strike, subject to giving a period of notice and non-binding arbitration procedures. A leading recent cause of strikes has been salary arrears for public servants.

In addition to the CSC, there are now two ICFTU affiliates: the Confédération des Syndicats Libres Autonomes du Congo (COSYLAC), and the Confédération Syndicale des Travailleurs du Congo (CSTC). There is also a WCL affiliate, the Confédération Africaine des Travailleurs Croyants (CATC).

3 Trade Union Centres

Confédération Africaine des Travailleurs Croyants (CATC)
Address. BP 624, 23 avenue Monseigneur Augouard – Quartier du Méridien, Brazzaville
Phone. +242 81 19 20
Fax. +242 81 18 28
Leadership. M'Villa-Biyaoula Fulgence (president); Mafoua Alain-David (permanent secretary)
International affiliation. WCL

Confédération Syndicale Congolaise (CSC)
Congolese Trade Union Confederation
History and character. The CSC was formed in 1964. CSC secretary-general Bokamba Yangouma was a member of the PCT political bureau under one-party rule. However, a strong independence movement gathered in CSC, leading to threats of secession on the part of some federations. The CSC responded with a gener-

al strike for its independence from the PCT in September 1990, and this marked the opening of a period of greater freedom of political action.
International affiliation. WFTU

Confédération Syndicale des Travailleurs du Congo (CSTC)
Address. BP 14743, Brazzaville
Telephone. +242 364 394
Fax. +242 364 394
Email. cstcorg@yahoo.fr
Leadership. Michel Souza (president)
History and character. In 2003 the CSTC changed its leadership following an extraordinary congress, which the ICFTU reports was attended only by a dissident group (which the ICFTU believes was funded by the Ministry of Labour). ICFTU reports that another "wing" of the union continues to exist under the leadership of Louis Gondou, but has been banned from operating.
International affiliation. ICFTU

Confédération des Syndicats Libres Autonomes du Congo (COSYLAC)
Address. BP 14861, Brazzaville
Phone. +242 83 42 70
Fax. +242 82 42 65
E-mail. b.oba@congonet.cg
International affiliation. ICFTU

Costa Rica

Capital: San José
Population: 3.96 m. (2004 est.)

1 Political and Economic Background

Following a brief but bitter civil war in 1948 the dominant party, normally forming the government, was the social democratic National Liberation Party (PLN). In its earlier periods of office the PLN undertook a major programme of reform, including the dissolution of the army, a programme of nationalization (especially of the banks) and the establishment of a developed system of social security. In 1990, the PNL administration of President Arias was succeeded by a conservative government led by the Social Christian Unity Party (PUSC) of Rafael Caldéron. Four years later the PLN returned to power under President José María Figueres but elections in February 1998 resulted in the election as President of the PUSC candidate Miguel Angel Rodríguez, the PUSC also winning the largest number of seats in the Legislative Assembly. The PUSC retained the presidency in 2002 – the first time the party had won the presidency for successive terms – with the election of Abel Pacheco de la Espriella. The country has in recent decades developed a reputation for political stability and a tradition of consensus politics.

Costa Rica has a mixed economy including tourism, electronics and commercial agriculture (with the main export crops being coffee and bananas). Prices and levels of demand for coffee and bananas are liable to severe fluctuations in the international markets. Moreover, requirements for labour on the coffee estates vary seasonally so that there is frequent widespread rural under-employment.

The PUSC administration from 1990 pursued drastic IMF-backed "shock measures" but these met considerable opposition from public sector trade unions. Through the 1990s successive governments sought to strengthen the private sector economy while retaining social measures, but this policy was undermined by continuing government deficits and generally high inflation. In 1998 PUSC presidential candidate Rodríguez won a narrow victory on a platform that promised to deliver 6% per annum growth, attract foreign capital and privatize state companies. Political resistance subsequently slowed his programme. His successor, Pacheco, has likewise faced difficulties in implementing economic reforms, in part because the PUSC lacks an overall majority in the legislature. In 2003 privatization plans triggered strike action in the energy and telecommunications sectors. Growth in real GDP was forecast at 5.6% for 2004 but with inflation remaining over 9%.

GDP (purchasing power parity) $35.34bn. (2004 est.); GDP per capita (purchasing power parity) $9,100 (2004 est.).

2 Trade Unionism

The first artisans' union was recorded in 1905, and the growth of trade unionism (including the appearance of the first trade union centres) was fostered by favourable labour legislation introduced by the 1940–43 government of President Rafael Calderon Guardia. The 1949 Constitution guaranteed basic workers' rights, including a minimum wage and limitations on hours of work, and the rights to lock out and to strike (except in public services) were guaranteed. Costa Rica ratified ILO Conventions No. 87 (Freedom of Association and Protection of the Right to Organize, 1948) and No. 98 (Right to Organize and Collective Bargaining, 1949) in 1960.

Three of the then six national union centres – the Democratic Workers' Union (CATD), the Costa Rican Confederation of Democratic Workers (CCTD) and the National Confederation of Workers (CNT), all of social democratic persuasion – confederated in August 1991 to form the 90,000-member Rerum Novarum (CTRN) with ICFTU affiliation. This is the largest centre. The WCL's affiliate is the CMTC and the WFTU also claims a number of affiliates. There are also independent unions not affiliated to any of the centres.

For years the unions faced a powerful rival in the Catholic-inspired Solidarismo movement, which by 1990 claimed members in some 1,200 associations, apparently ahead of the unions. The associations were affiliated either to the Solidarista Union (SURSUM) or to the Pope John XXIII School and sought harmonious relations between employers and employees. Members also gained practical benefits such as credit unions in return for renouncing the right to strike, and in 1990 established their own bank, financed by the US agency USAID.

Article 273 of the former (1943) labour code required only five people to form a Solidarismo association whereas the figure for unions was 20. The Solidarist Act of 1984 granted the associations special legal status. The six national union centres were vehemently opposed to Solidarismo, arguing that employer preference was intended to eliminate independent unionism, as had actually occurred in the banana plantations. In 1989 Solidarismo employees at Tres Rios textiles did hold a brief and successful strike to gain greater control over their association, and there were other manifestations of discontent, but their associations continued to be the subject of repeated ICFTU complaints.

Business interests prevented modernization of the 1943 labour code in the 1980s, but in 1989 President Arias's Minister of Labour announced an agreement with the unions on new draft regulations which would promote union development by giving activists protection against dismissal. Its introduction into law was however blocked by fierce opposition from employers and Solidarismo. The same year the ICFTU submitted a complaint to the ILO about government efforts to promote Solidarismo, which it saw as a barrier to an independent trade union movement.

Finally in October 1993 the legislature unanimously adopted a new labour code, much of which addressed problems identified by the ILO Committee of Experts. Among these was a reduction in the threshold membership of unions to 12 (a provision which removed the advantage enjoyed by Solidarismo); the banning of Solidarismo from collective bargaining; a series of protections against unfair dismissal, especially of union activists; and an end to workplace offences punishable by fine.

In its 1999 *Annual Survey of Trade Union Rights*, however, the ICFTU said that in the view of the unions the 1993 changes to the labour code had proved a "dead letter". Specific grievances included that:

1. Although the legal advantages of Solidarismo associations have been removed, employers still continue to set up such associations and the Labour Ministry to register them. In 1996, for example, only ten collective agreements were signed with trade unions while 45 agreements were reached with solidarist associations.

2. In the private sector it was "virtually impossible" to form trade unions because of hostility by employers and the reluctance of the government to enforce labour legislation. This was especially a problem in the nine export processing zones (EPZs) and on the banana plantations where trade unionists were dismissed and blacklisted. The ICFTU said the Labour Ministry takes 2–3 years to hear complaints, and in the case of the plantations and EPZs invariably found against the unions.

The trade unions have found it easier to organize in the public sector, where protections have been greater. Although 12% of the work force overall is unionized, most union members are in the public sector. Few private sector workers are in unions. There are restrictions on the right to strike in the public sector, although such strikes have occurred, usually of short duration. In February 1998 the Supreme Court ruled that public sector workers, except those in essential positions, had the right to strike, and in practice the government had not enforced penalties against public sector strikers. The position of the unions in the public sector has been eroded to some degree during the 1990s by the impact of privatization, a process during which many public sector union leaders also lost their jobs. In September 2000 the ICFTU complained that the courts were now undermining long-standing collective bargaining agreements in state industries such as the oil industry. A constitutional court ruling of May 2000 declared collective agreements in public universities, schools, the highways department and others to be unconstitutional. Workers in these industries have been deprived of the right to bargain.

Strikes are banned not only in "essential services", but also in the transport sector and by port workers, although this is an improvement on the earlier ban that extended to all public sector strikes. Legal strikes are possible only if a union can obtain 60% support of all workers in the enterprise (a requirement criticized by the ILO Committee of Experts). Only two strikes were legal out of a total of 398 during the period 1996–97. As many as 15 leaders and members of the port workers' unions were arrested in September 2003 during a strike demanding implementation of the collective agreement.

Particular controversy has surrounded conditions in the banana sector, where unions have been particularly opposed by employers, and where there have been allegations of unsafe use of pesticides. In 1997 revelations about the conditions in the plantations by the SITRAP banana workers' union received international notice and led to threats by government ministers to prosecute the union for treason. In December 1997, after international pressure, Del Monte signed an agreement allowing the SITRAP banana workers the right to organize in the industry. In April 1999 the ICFTU filed a complaint with the ILO alleging violations of trade union rights by the banana exporting company Cobasur against the SITRASUR banana workers' union. The Latin American banana workers' coordinating council, COLSIBA, is based in Costa Rica.

3 Trade Union Centres

Central de Trabajadores de Costa Rica
Address. Pintarenas, Aptdo 185, 150 Santa Teresita, San José
Fax. +506 661 1160
International affiliation. WFTU

Central del Movimiento de Trabajadores Costarricenses (CMTC)
Address. Apartado Postal No. 4137–1000, Calle 20, Av. 3–5, Casa No. 321, 'Continguo a la Iglesia La Medalla Milagrosa', San José
Phone. +506 221 7701
Fax. +506 222 6519
Leadership. Dennys Cabezas (president); José Angel Obando (secretary-general)
History and character. The Central de Trabajadores Costarricenses (CTC) was created by the regional organization of Christian unions, CLASC, as the

Federation of Christian Workers and Peasants of Costa Rica (FOCC) in 1964, becoming the CTC in 1972 and the CMTC in the 1990s.
International affiliations. WCL

Confederación Costarricense de Trabajadores (Rerum Novarum) (CTRN)
Costa Rican Confederation of Workers
Address. Apdo Postal 7 – 1100, 1000 San José
Phone. +506 283 2647
Fax. +506 283 4244
E-mail. ctrnovan@sol.racsa.co.cr
History and character. The CTRN was formed in 1991, with 90,000 members, by the merger of three pre-existing broadly social democratic centres.
International affiliation. ICFTU

Confederación Unitaria de Trabajadores
Address. Apdo postal 186-1009, Av.12, Calle 1-3, casa No.42, 1009 San José
Fax. +506 221 4709
International affiliation. WFTU

Confederación de Trabajadores de Costa Rica
Address. Casa Sindical Carlos Luis Falla, 50 metros norte Iglesia St.Teresita, Bo Aranjues, San José
Fax. +506 661 2078
International affiliation. WFTU

Côte d'Ivoire

Capital: Yamoussoukro
Population: 17.33 m. (2004 est.)

1 Political and Economic Background

Côte d'Ivoire (Ivory Coast) became a self-governing republic within the French Community in 1958 and gained full independence in 1960. From independence power was held by the Parti Démocratique de la Côte d'Ivoire (PDCI) led by Félix Houphouët-Boigny, the only legal political party. The PDCI's aim was to consolidate the country's independence on the basis of a free-enterprise economy, in cooperation with other West African states, and the maintenance of good relations with France. Until recent times it has been relatively stable politically by African standards.

Reflecting developments in many African states at that time Houphouët-Boigny in May 1990 endorsed a change to multi-partyism. The PDCI won multi-party elections later that year but the move to multi-partyism exposed ethnic divisions, particularly between the mainly Muslim North and the Christian South. Houphouët-Boigny died in 1993 and was succeeded by the president of the Assembly Henri Konan-Bédié (a southerner), who successfully resisted (with French backing) an attempted northern-led coup. The PDCI easily won further (disputed) elections in 1995. Konan-Bédié was overthrown in a bloodless coup on Dec. 24, 1999, and replaced by a military junta led by Gen. Robert Guëi, who said he would end corruption and hold elections by October 2000. Presidential elections were held as promised, with Laurent Gbagbo of the Ivoirian Popular Front (PFI) party apparently winning, after other leading contenders had been barred from standing. However, on Oct. 24 Guëi declared himself the winner after he dissolved the National Electoral Commission and arrested its members. This resulted in widespread demonstrations, joined by troops, forcing the collapse of the Guëi regime, and Laurent Gbagbo assumed the presidency.

Côte d'Ivoire has remained highly unsettled. An attempted coup in September 2002 failed to depose Gbagbo but left the northern half of the country in the hands of rebels. Gbagbo reluctantly accepted a proposed settlement, the Marcoussis Accord, signed in January 2003 under French auspices and backed by leading African heads of state. Under the terms of the accord a government was established representative of the political parties and rebel factions; however, neither the rebels, who still control the north, nor the forces loyal to Gbagbo, laid down their arms. In early November 2004 Gbagbo's forces bombed rebel areas, killing nine French peacekeepers, in retaliation for which the French destroyed the Ivoirian air force. The UN Security Council on Nov. 15, 2004, imposed an embargo on arms supplies to both government and rebels.

Côte d'Ivoire's economy, one of the largest in Africa, is based on agriculture, with cocoa (of which it is the world's largest producer) and coffee being major cash crops. There is a large immigrant agricultural work force from neighbouring Burkina Faso, which has become the target for political attacks, and Burkina has been seen as aiding the northern rebels. There is also a manufacturing sector. In the 1980s, as revenues from export commodities declined, corrective public expenditure cuts provoked outbreaks of civil and industrial unrest. The state divested itself of many commercial enterprises in which it had a stake and increased the role of the private sector as part of a structural adjustment programme. Nevertheless, by 1992 Côte d'Ivoire was one of the most heavily indebted countries in Africa and under new pressure to introduce unpopular measures including the imposition of substantial pay cuts. That year's IMF-approved restructuring plan proposed to cut back the number of civil servants from 105,000 to 85,000. 1994 brought a 50% devaluation of the CFA franc and a boost for exports which contributed to the first year of growth in the 1990s. From 1996–99 growth averaged 5% per annum, but since 2000 GDP has declined with commodity prices generally depressed and with continuing political instability and military clashes. The country remains heavily indebted and international donor programmes have been limited or ended because of corruption.

GDP (purchasing power parity) $24.51bn. (2004 est.); GDP per capita (purchasing power parity) $1,400 (2004 est.)

2 Trade Unionism

Trade unions developed under French rule and at independence in 1960 there were three national trade union centres. Côte d'Ivoire ratified ILO Convention No. 87

(Freedom of Association and Protection of the Right to Organize, 1948) in 1960 and Convention No. 98 (Right to Organize and Collective Bargaining, 1949) in 1961. In 1962, however, a single union system was organized through the Union Générale des Travailleurs de Côte d' Ivoire (UGTCI) under the leadership of the ruling PDCI. There was industrial unrest in the 1980s, mainly involving white-collar public sector employees such as teachers, as the country sought to deal with its high debt. The government response included dismissals, fines, conscription and threats of imprisonment. In 1990 the UGTCI recorded its intention to protect itself against "rebellious affiliates which had aligned themselves with the protesters and strikers". In 1991, however, several UGTCI affiliates broke away and a greater degree of pluralism was established, in line with the broader political changes in the country (as much of Africa) at that time. The UGTCI remained close to the government and other unions said they faced discriminatory treatment.

About 15% of the workforce is in the formal sector and all employees except the armed forces and police are legally entitled to join unions, although only a minority of workers are unionized. Collective bargaining agreements exist in bigger enterprises and parts of the civil service. There is a right to strike although lengthy negotiation procedures mean strikes are often illegal. The UGCTI has rarely called strikes. Strikes typically occur among white-collar employees in the public sector over issues such as pay arrears. The effective functioning of trade unions has recently been seriously affected by the general state of political turmoil and economic decline.

3 Trade Union Centres

Centrale des Syndicats Libres de Côte d'Ivoire (Dignité)
Address. Adjamé Blvd Nangui Abrogoua, BP 2031, Abidjan 03
Phone. +225 2037 74 89
Fax. +225 2037 85 01
E-mail. dignite@aviso.ci
Leadership. Basile Mahan Gahé (secretary-general)
History and character. Dignité emerged in the early 1990s. Members at the state agro-industrial company Ihro La Mé were sacked in 1993 for organizing union elections. A major dispute erupted at the plant which cost 15 lives in the months to come and culminated in the arrests of four Dignité leaders including the secretary-general in 1994. In June 1995, 618 Ihro La Mé workers and their families were reported living in the jungle after eviction from their houses by the army. Dignité members at the port of Abidjan also experienced repression: they were dismissed and replaced by new employees. After a protest march in February 1998, police reportedly damaged the Dignité headquarters and surrounded it for a week. In February 1999 police occupied Dignité headquarters to prevent a protest march called following the dismissal of trade unionists. In 2002 it was reported to have 186 affiliated trade unions and 20 professional groups.
International affiliation. WCL

Federation of Autonomous Trade Unions of Côte d'Ivoire
Fedération des Syndicats Autonomes de Côte d'Ivoire (FESACI)
Leadership. Marcel Ette (secretary-general)
History and character. Founded in 1992 on the initiative of the National University Researchers' and Teachers' Union (SYNARES), which was associated with political currents opposed to the ruling PDCI. In 2002 it had 30 affiliated trade unions in both government employment and the private sector.

Union Générale des Travailleurs de Côte d' Ivoire (UGTCI)
Address. Bourse du Travail Avenue 1, Rue Barrée à Treichville 05, BP 1203, Abidjan 05
Phone. +225 24 16 95
Fax. +225 24 08 83
Leadership. Adiko Niamkey (secretary general)
History and character. The UGTCI was formed in 1962 by merger of the four existing trade union centres and for many years, as the close ally of the ruling PDCI, was the sole centre. UGTCI remains the largest centre and in 2002 was reported as comprising 231 affiliated trade unions, nine regional unions, 30 local unions, and nine trade union federations, with secretary-general Niamkey serving on the political bureau of the PDCI.
International affiliations. ICFTU; OATUU

Croatia

Capital: Zagreb
Population: 4.50 m. (2004 est.)

1 Political and Economic Background

Croatia was formerly a constituent republic of Yugoslavia. In May 1990, Franjo Tudjman became president after multi-party elections as the leader of the nationalist Croatian Democratic Union (HDZ). In May 1991 the HDZ government won a 94% referendum majority in favour of independence and declared secession from Yugoslavia in June. Military conflict broke out with Yugoslavia, primarily in areas of Croatia with a large ethnic Serb population, and this did not finally cease until 1995, although the government achieved control over most of the country, as well as international recognition, within the first few months. Tudjman remained in office until his death on Dec. 10, 1999, with the HDZ exercising a dominant and in respects authoritarian role in political life. However, elections in January 2000 resulted in victory for an opposition coalition led by the Social Democratic Party (SDP) and the Croatian Social Liberal Party, while Stipe Mesic of the Croatian People's Party became President. Under constitutional amendments approved in November 2000 Croatia moved from a presidential system of government to a parliamentary system with a Prime Minister as head of government, although the President retained substantial powers in the foreign and security policy areas and continued to be directly elected for a five-year term. The most recent legislative elections, held in November 2003, saw the re-emergence of the HDZ as the largest party in parliament, with 66 of the 152 seats, and it went on to form a minority coalition government with the support of small parties; the SDP, which won 36 seats, leads the opposition. Mesic was re-elected as President in January 2005 while the government is headed by Prime Minister Ivo Sanader, the leader of the HDZ.

Croatia was among the most prosperous republics of former Yugoslavia with a diverse economic base. Its progress to a market economy after independence proved fitful, with a significant private sector established but many major enterprises still in state hands or with the state having a stake. The process of privatization in the 1990s was also criticized as benefiting allies of the ruling HDZ. As in other former Yugoslav republics, there were major problems of inter-enterprise debt, wage arrears, unemployment and under-employment. Since the turn of the century growth has averaged 4% per annum and unemployment has fallen to about 14% but there are high budget deficits and continuing resistance to sweeping market reforms. Croatia aspires to join the EU, a fact which is likely increasingly to shape social and economic policy, but the HDZ embodies a strong strain of nationalist protectionism.

GDP (purchasing power parity) $47.05bn. (2003 est.); GDP per capita (purchasing power parity) $10,600 (2003 est.).

2 Trade Unionism

Croatia ratified ratified ILO Conventions No. 87 (Freedom of Association and Protection of the Right to Organize, 1948) and No. 98 (Right to Organize and Collective Bargaining, 1949) in 1991, following its declaration of independence.

Under communism the Union of Trade Unions of Croatia was affiliated to the Yugoslav national centre. The first completely independent union was the Trade Union of Railroad Engineers of Croatia, founded in November 1989, which was quickly followed by several others. These and other dissident unions participated in the eighth congress of the former official body on May 11, 1990, and the inaugural congress of the Union of Autonomous Trade Unions of Croatia (SSSH) was held on the two following days.

This congress was dominated by conflict between communists and HDZ supporters. Although a reformed constitution and autonomous orientation were adopted, a communist president, Josip Klisovic, was elected. In reaction to this a congress of the Independent Trade Unions of Croatia (NHS) was held in June by unions defecting from SSSH and some of the new unions which had stayed aloof. A number of unions opposed to the SSSH leadership had stayed within its ranks and at an extraordinary session of the national council replaced the president with a working council pending the holding of elections. When these were held at a January 1991 meeting of the council Dragutin Lesar was elected president. Meanwhile, in December 1990 the Croatian Association of Trade Unions (HUS) had been formed under the sponsorship of the ruling HDZ.

All workers are entitled to form or join unions of their own choosing and an estimated 64% of the formally employed work force is unionized. However, the use of short-term contracts has become more frequent, with such workers reluctant to join unions, and the unions are weak in the small and medium-sized private business sector as well as foreign-owned enterprises. There are now one major (SSSH) and four minor confederations (including NHS and HUS) designated as representative under the 1999 Act on Trade Union Representativity as well as a number of independent unions. The SSSH represents about two-thirds of the organized workforce.

In May 1993 an agreement, brokered by the European Trade Union Confederation (ETUC), united the (then three) contending national centres over the principles that should govern the distribution of the assets of the former state unions. Demands were laid on the Croatian government to restore these assets. In January 1998 the government announced it would take title to the assets until an agreement could be reached and approved by Parliament. In response to a request by the ILO, the government then gave the confederations more time and in July 1999 the five confederations signed an agreement on the division. The unions believed the government might be planning to confiscate assets permanently.

Conventional industrial relations began to emerge even before the war, beginning in June 1991, that established the country's independence, and throughout 1991 sectoral agreements were signed, principally by one union centre, the SSSH. The agreements were however frequently vulnerable to government intervention. At the height of the war emergency the three leading centres, SSSH, HUS and NHS, signed an agreement with the government about cooperation and activity in circumstances of war (the War Agreement), although they later withdrew in protest against government employment policy. Threats of combined industrial action by those three national centres succeeded in October1992 in forcing withdrawal of a government decree suspending the application of collective agreements and imposing wage controls. Although the trade union movement remains fragmented, the different trade union organizations do collaborate on issues of common concern and a trade union general assembly, with delegates from the different organizations, was convened for the first time in February 2003. The centres participate in the national tripartite structures, with all five of the trade union centres participating in the tripartite Office for Social Partnership.

The labour code provides a framework for collective bargaining contracts and protection of the right to strike. Collective bargaining is practiced, although implementation has been undermined by high unemployment (19% in 1999 but 14% by 2003) and the poor finances of some enterprises, with employers sometimes withdrawing from agreements because of the precarious state of the enterprise. There is no adequate mechanism for enforcement of collective contracts where employers ignore their provisions. There is no system of labour courts and there is a huge backlog of employment-related cases in the civil courts – a problem endemic to the Croatian judicial system where there was a backlog of 1.4 million cases in 2003. A new labour law adopted in 2003 aimed at liberalizing employment contracts, as part of efforts to prepare the economy for ultimate EU accession, provoked union opposition, although as passed included some provisions welcome to the unions.

The right to strike is embodied in the constitution and retaliation against workers engaged in legal strikes is unlawful. However, there are significant formal restrictions on the right to strike. Strikes are legal only after mediation has failed, the government providing a mediation service through the Office for Social Partnership; arbitration can be used only where both parties consent. Workers may also only strike at the end of a contract period unless provided otherwise in the contract. In 1996 the Supreme Court ruled that strikes over wage arrears are unlawful, yet this has been a major cause of discontent, with an estimated 10% of the working population experiencing wage arrears in 1999. The issue has declined but disputes over wage arrears still occur. The right to strike is restricted in the public sector and state sector employers have according to the unions used coercion and intimidation to discourage strikes in some instances. In practice these various restrictions are commonly disregarded by the authorities.

In August 1993 the first meeting of a tripartite Economic and Social Council (GSV) was held. Under the 1995 labour code works council elections were to be held to determine which unions have "most representative" status for purposes of involvement on the GSV. Such elections were held for the first time in 1996, with the SSSH winning the great majority of seats, but there was controversy about the criteria for establishing representative status and the work of the GSV lapsed. It resumed in July 1999 after the Act on Trade Union Representativity defined the basis for representation. Kresimir Sever, the president of the NHS, is current president of the Economic and Social Council.

3 Trade Union Centre

Savez Samostalnih Sindikata Hrvatske (SSSH)
Union of Autonomous Trade Unions of Croatia (UATUC)
Address. Trg Kralja Petra Kresimira IV br 2, 10000 Zagreb
Phone. +385 1 465 5026 (international dept)
Fax. +385 1 465 5011 (international dept)
E-mail. sssh@sssh.hr
Website. www.sssh.hr (Croatian)
Leadership. Vesna Dejanovic (president)
Membership. 350,000
History and character. The SSSH was formed in May 1990 by dissident independent unions founded under communism in the former Yugoslavia as well as former official unions. It suffered almost immediate defections from unions unprepared to accept its initial communist leadership but subsequently established its position as the leading Croatian trade union centre. It represents about 66% of the organized workforce and affiliates 22 branch trade unions for specific industrial sectors. It has been accepted internationally as the principal voice of Croatian trade unionism; it affiliated to the ICFTU in 1996 and has had observer status with ETUC since 1998.

The SSSH supported the opposition coalition in the election campaign that led to the defeat of the ruling HDZ in elections in January 2000 (but the HDZ then returning to power in 2003). It favours Croatia's candidacy for EU membership, and in a declaration in November 2000 called on the government to involve the trade unions in the accession process, to ratify the European Convention on Human Rights and European Social Charter, and to implement the European works council directive in multinational firms.

The SSSH has established an Industrial Democracy Centre to undertake trade union education activities. It has sections for women and the unemployed and is trying to organize the informal sector, which according to the SSSH absorbs 40% of the workforce (the official figure is 20%), in areas such as tourism and catering.
International affiliation. ICFTU; ETUC.

4 Other Trade Union Organizations

Association of Croatian Public Sector Unions
Matica Nezavisnih Sindikata Javnih Djelatnika
Address. Ilica 51, 10000 Zagreb
Phone. +385 1 484 7337
Fax. +385 1 484 7338
Leadership. Vilim Ribic (president)

Croatian Association of Trade Unions
Hrvatska Udruga Sindikata (HUS)
Address. Trg Kralja Petra Kresimira IV br 2, 10000 Zagreb
Phone. +385 1 465 9688
Fax. +381 465 5009
E-mail. hus@zg.hinet.hr
Leadership. Zdenko Mucnjak (president)

Independent Trade Unions of Croatia
Nezavisni Hrvatski Sindikati (NHS)
Address. Vodovodna 11, 10000 Zagreb
Phone. +385 1 377 9338
Fax. +385 1 377 2936
E-mail. nhs@zg.tel.hr
Leadership. Kresimir Sever (president)
Membership. 40,000
History and character. Founded in 1992 and with its membership particualrly in the public sector.

Workers' Trade Union Association of Croatia (WTUAC)
Udruga Radnickih Sindikata Hrvatske (URSH)
Address. Kralja Drzislava 4/1, 10000 Zagreb
Phone. +385 1 461 7791
Fax. +385 1 461 2896
E-mail. ursh@inet.hr
Website. www.ursh.hr
Leadership. Boris Kunst (president)
History and character. The WTUAC was established in

1994 and was originally known as the Trade Union Association of Public Sector Employees, its goal being to provide a unified voice for public sector workers in place of the politically divided representation of the existing centres. It subsequently broadened its representation to other sectors of the economy and emphasizes the independence of its 34 member unions from government and political parties. In 1995 it joined EUROFEDOP.

Cuba

Capital: Havana
Population: 11.31 m. (2004 est.)

1 Political and Economic Background

Revolutionary forces led by Fidel Castro overthrew the Batista regime at the beginning of 1959. A Marxist–Leninist programme was proclaimed in 1961, and four years later the existing leading political organization became the Communist Party of Cuba. This remains the sole legal political party and politically the Cuban system remains substantially unreconstructed in the wake of the collapse of Communism in Europe. However, despite continuing US sanctions, Cuba was successful in reducing its diplomatic isolation in the late 1990s.

For decades, the Soviet Union heavily subsidized Cuba for geopolitical reasons. The 1990 withdrawal of subsidies worth $4bn–$6bn. per annum had serious implications for Cuba, which had in effect relied on subsidies to offset the failure of its domestic state-directed economy. The Cuban government announced in 1995 that GDP had declined by 35% between 1989–93. In 1994 agricultural markets were liberalized to some degree and the state has also sought to reduce subsidies to unprofitable enterprises. Cuba has reported growth since 1994 but living standards are still considered depressed relative to the 1980s. An estimated 78% of the workforce remain employed in the state sector. The leading exports are sugar and tobacco and there has been an increase in tourism.

GDP (purchasing power parity) $32.13bn. (2004 est.); GDP per capita (purchasing power parity) $2,900 (2004 est.).

2 Trade Unionism

Trade unions first appeared in Cuba in 1865 in the tobacco and printing industries. The first workers' congress was held in 1898. The Confederation of Workers of Cuba (Confederación de Trabajadores de Cuba, CTC) was formed in 1939. The CTC (now the Central de Trabajadores de Cuba) has been the sole trade union centre since the 1959 revolution. Every workplace is organized and a collective agreement is in place between management and the CTC union.

Cuba ratified ILO Conventions No. 87 (Freedom of Association and Protection of the Right to Organize, 1948) and No. 98 (Right to Organize and Collective Bargaining, 1949) in 1952.

There were some attempts to set up independent trade unions in the 1990s but these have not met with success and have been in effect small dissident groups. Activists associated with these groups have lodged complaints with international organizations claiming that their attempts to register as trade unions have been denied. The Cuban authorities deny that any such registration process is required under Cuban law and claim that the independent trade unionists are free to participate in elections at their workplace.

In April 2003 Cuba's compliance, or lack of, with international labour standards was brought sharply into focus when a major government crackdown on dissidents led to the arrest and sentencing to lengthy prison terms of seventy-six people, among whom were six labour activists. The ICFTU and WCL have led international outcry against the arrests. The incident was further criticised by the Workers' Group of the ILO and many national trade union federations.

The ICFTU has sought to press the cause of independent trade unions within Cuba. The WCL affiliates an organization in exile (Solidaridad de Trabajadores Cubanos), based in Venezuela. A WCL delegation was refused entry to the country in January 1999.

3 Trade Union Centre

Central de Trabajadores de Cuba (CTC)
Workers' Central Union of Cuba
Address. Calle San Carolos y Peñalver, Municipio Centro-Habana, Prov. Ciudad Habana
Membership. The CTC reports that 98% of Cuba's 4 million workers are members.
History and character. The CTC traces its origins to the Confederación de Trabajadores de Cuba of 1939, an organization that became Cuba's only centre of consequence but whose history was marked by violent internal feuds. Important CTC elements sought accommodation with the Batista regime, and several, including the secretary-general Eusebio Mujal, followed him into exile. Under Castro, the CTC disaffiliated from the ICFTU to become the principal supporter of the World Federation of Trade Unions (WFTU) in the Americas. In 1960 the secretary-general, David Salvador, was deposed and imprisoned, and at the next national congress only one list of candidates was presented. The CTC and its 19 member unions today take on what they describe as a 'dual role' within Cuban society – (i) to further the economic, political and social interests of the country as a whole; and (ii) to protect the rights and interests and advance the standard of living of Cuban workers. The CTC has retained its monopoly status within Cuba.
International affiliation. WFTU

4 Other Trade Union Organization

Organization in exile

Solidaridad de Trabajadores Cubanos (STC)
Cuban Workers' Solidarity
Address. Apartado 50, Zona Postal 1204, San Antonio de los Altos, Estado Miranda, Caracas, Venezuela

Phone. +58 2 235 77 09
Fax. +58 2 237 71 71
E-mail. stc@webstc.com
Leadership. Heriberto Fernández (secretary-general)
International affiliation. WCL

Cyprus

Capital: Nicosia
Population: 775,100 (2004 est.)

1 Political and Economic Background

Cyprus achieved independence from the UK in 1960 under a constitution based on power-sharing between the majority Greek and minority Turkish communities. A period of inter-communal conflict was followed by Turkish military intervention in 1974 that confirmed the de facto partition of the island. In 1983 the Turkish-controlled part of the island was proclaimed the Turkish Republic of Northern Cyprus (TRNC), although this has not been internationally recognized other than by Turkey. After many unsuccessful attempts to reconcile the two communities, UN Secretary General Kofi Annan submitted a settlement plan in November 2002. After much negotiation, the settlement plan was put to simultaneous referenda on April 24, 2004, a week before Cyprus' accession to the European Union (EU) on May. 1. The Greek Cypriot community overwhelmingly rejected the settlement plan, with 75.8% voting against, whilst 64.9% of the Turkish Cypriot community voted in favour of the plan to reunite the island. This failure to agree on a settlement plan resulted in only the Greek-controlled south of Cyprus joining the EU on May 1, 2004.

In (Greek Cypriot-controlled) Cyprus, an alliance between the Progressive Party of the Working People (AKEL), which won the majority of seats in the House of Representatives in May 2001 and the centre-right Democratic Party (DIKO), resulted in Tassos Papadopoulos (DIKO) becoming the fifth President of the Republic of Cyprus in February 2003. In the TRNC, the government is a coalition led by the Republican Turkish Party (CTP), which remained the largest party in elections in February 2005.

The Greek Cypriot portion of the island is relatively prosperous with a service-based economy including tourism. In the northern Turkish enclave, which has about one-fifth of the total population, the economy has tended to stagnate since partition and per capita GDP is only one-third that of the Greek area. Foreign investment in the TRNC has been restricted by its lack of international recognition and it depends mainly on agriculture, government jobs and aid from Turkey.

Greek Cypriot area: GDP (purchasing power parity) $14.82bn. (2003 est.); GDP per capita (purchasing power parity) $19,200 (2003 est.).

Turkish Cypriot area: GDP (purchasing power parity) $1.217bn (2003 est.); GDP per capita (purchasing power parity) $5,600 (2003 est.).

2 Trade Unionism

Cyprus ratified ILO Conventions No. 87 (Freedom of Association and Protection of the Right to Organize, 1948) and No. 98 (Right to Organize and Collective Bargaining, 1949) in 1966.

The British colonial authorities repressed the underground trade union movement in the 1930s, primarily because of its associations with nationalist and communist politics; however, unions not considered to be a security risk were permitted in 1937 and there was rapid growth thereafter.

Different trade unions operate in the Turkish and Greek parts of the island. Cyprus is highly unionized. All workers, other than those in the police and military, may join unions and in the Greek area the police may join associations with collective bargaining rights. In the Greek area there are 179,000 union members and some 70% of the work force are in unions. In the Turkish sector an estimated 50–60% of private sector workers, and all public sector workers, are unionized. Unions in the TRNC say that some employers have set up company unions and that the authorities have sponsored public sector unions in opposition to the independent unions.

The trade union movement is fragmented with many small unions and no dominant centre. The principal Greek centres are the Pancyprian Federation of Labour (PEO), affiliated to the WFTU, and the Cyprus Workers' Confederation (SEK), affiliated to the ICFTU. In the Turkish sector, the principal centre is the ICFTU-affiliated Cyprus Turkish Trade Unions Federation (Turk-Sen). The WFTU also records an affiliate, Dev-Is (Revolutionary Trade Unions Federation).

In 1985, SEK and Turk-Sen reached an agreement under ICFTU auspices providing for reciprocal visits and closer cooperation on union issues. During the 1990s the unions from both the Greek and Turkish sides issued a number of common statements endorsing the principle of the reunification of the island as a federal republic based on UN resolutions, with unitary employment and social standards.

Collective bargaining is widely practiced. All workers have the right to strike, other than in essential services, although in the Turkish portion employers have the right to recruit replacement labour during strikes. In the Greek sector, the government's Industrial Relations Service mediates some 280 cases annually, more than 90% of which are resolved without strike action. In the Turkish sector, because of high inflation, a tripartite commission reviews wages several times a year and makes cost of living adjustments.

3 Trade Union Centres

Greek Cypriot area

Demokratiki Ergatiki Omospondia Kyprou (DEOK)
Democratic Labour Federation of Cyprus
Address. 40 Byron Av., 1096 Nicosia
Phone. +357 267 6506

Fax. +357 267 0494
E-mail. deok@cytanet.com.cy
Website. www.deok.org.cy
Leadership. Diomides Diomidous (general secretary)
Membership. 7,500 in four affiliated unions
History and character. Founded in 1962 after a split in the SEK. Was recognized by the government in November 1998 as a social partner in consultative and tripartite national bodies and boards.
International affiliation. WCL; CTUC

Pankypria Ergatiki Omospondia (PEO)
Pancyprian Federation of Labour
Address. PO Box 1885, 31–35 Archermos Street, 1514 Nicosia
Phone. +357 22 866400
Fax. +357 22 349382
E-mail. peo@cytanet.com.cy
Website. www.peo.org.cy
Leadership. Pambis Kyritsis (general secretary)
Membership. 68,100
History and character. The PEO was founded in 1941. There are 9 affiliated occupational unions. It is, with SEK, one of the two main Greek Cypriot centres. The PEO has favoured reconciliation of the two communities in a non-aligned demilitarized federal state.
International affiliation. WFTU; CTUC

Synomospondia Ergaton Kyprou (SEK)
Cyprus Workers' Confederation
Address, 11 Strovolos Avenue, 1687 Strovolos, SEK Building Nicosia
Phone. +357 2 84 9849
Fax. +357 2 84 9850
E-mail. sek@sek.org.cy.net
Website. www.sek.org.cy
Leadership. Demetris Kittenis (general secretary)
Membership. 66,300
History and character. Founded in October 1944. In its early years the SEK faced bitter opposition both from the communist-controlled unions and, because of its support for self-determination for Greek Cypriots, from the colonial government. In 1949 SEK delegates took part in the founding conference of the ICFTU. Many of its leaders were arrested, imprisoned or killed during the struggle for independence in the late 1950s, seriously weakening the organization, but recovery took place in the 1960s. The SEK's political orientation is social democratic, but it supports no political party. It comprises seven federations organizing workers on the basis of occupation.
International affiliations. ICFTU; ETUC; CTUC

Turkish Cypriot area

Cyprus Turkish Trade Unions Federation (TURK-SEN)
Address. 7–7A Sht Mehmet R. Huseyin Sokak, PO Box 829, Lefkosa–KKTC, Mersin 10, Turkey
Phone. +357 392 22 72444
Fax +357 392 22 87831
Leadership. Onder Konuloglu (president); Arslan Bicakli (Chairman); Nihad Elmas (international secretary)

Membership. 12,000
History. This federation was founded in 1954 and registered in 1955. It consists of 15 unions
International affiliations. ICFTU; ETUC, CTUC, and Confederation of Trade Unions of Turkey

Revolutionary Trade Unions Federation (DEV-IS)
Address. 7, Serabioglu Sok. Nicosia, Mersin 10, Turkey
Phone. +357 392 22 72640
Leadership. Bayram Celik (President and General-Secretary)
Membership. 4,500
History. Founded in 1976, the federation is composed of two unions.
International affiliation. WFTU

4 Other Trade Union Organizations

Cyprus Union of Bank Employees (ETYK)
Address. 8 Prevezis Str. PO Box 21235 Nicosia
Phone. +357 22 672000
Website. www.etyk.org.cy
E-mail. etyk@etyk.org.cy
Leadership. Loizos Hadjicostis (chairman)
Membership. 9,700
History and Character. The Cyprus Union of Bank Employees was established in 1955. Members of the union are all bank employees as well as the employees of the insurance companies owned by banks.
International affiliation. UNI

Pancyprian Public Servants' Trade Union (PASY-DY)
Address. Dem. Severis Ave. 3, Nicosia 1066
Phone. +357 2 662 337
Fax. +357 2 665 199
E-mail. pasydy@spidernet.co.cy
Website. www.pasydy.org
Leadership. Glafkos Hadjipetrou (general secretary)
Membership. 16,400, representing 90% of white-collar central government employees.

Czech Republic

Capital: Prague
Population: 10.25 m. (2004 est.)

1 Political and Economic Background

The Communist Party became the dominant, and by 1948, the sole, political force in Czechoslovakia after the Red Army took control of the country in the latter stages of World War II. A brief liberalization of the regime under Alexander Dubcek in the "Prague Spring" of 1968 was crushed by military force by the Soviet Union and its allies and the Communist Party leadership purged. An underground dissident movement continued and, following the fall of the Berlin Wall in 1989, mass protest led by the Civic Forum alliance led to the rapid collapse of the regime in the so-called "velvet revolution". In December 1989, dissident leader Vaclav Havel became President and the Communist Party issued an apology for its past actions.

In June 1992 elections resulted in victory for the neo-liberal Civic Democratic Party (ODS) in the Czech lands and for the nationalist Movement for a Democratic Slovakia (HZDS) in Slovakia. Two months later they concluded a dissolution agreement and on Jan. 1, 1993, two separate and independent states were peacefully established. In the Czech Republic the government has been led by the left-of-centre Czech Social Democratic Party (CSSD) since elections in June 1998 and the break-up of the former centre-right coalition; the CSSD remained the largest party in parliament as a result of elections in June 2002 and provides the Prime Minister. The Communist Party (now known as the Communist Party of Bohemia and Moravia, KSCM) remains a significant force, taking 18.5% of the vote and 41 seats in the 2002 elections and with the CSSD, which lacks a majority in its own right, often looking to it for support in parliament. The Czech Republic joined the European Union on May 1, 2004.

The Czech Republic made one of the most successful transitions of a Communist state to a free market economy. After 1989 successive governments steered towards economic liberalization. By November 1991 some 10% of the country's small enterprises had been sold to private bidders in a programme of "little privatization". The sale of 4,000 large enterprises began in 1992, despite difficulties caused by maladministration of sale vouchers, and by the end of 1993 the private sector was responsible for more than half of GDP. The separation of Slovakia in 1993 in general left the Czech Republic with the more dynamic sectors of the economy whereas decaying heavy industries were concentrated in Slovakia. In 1997, however, the country faced a financial crisis that resulted in austerity measures and in 1998–99 experienced recession with unemployment rising to 9% (from 3% in the mid-1990s) as restructuring of inefficient enterprises continued. A modest recovery was under way by 2000 and although growth lagged behind that in some of the other new EU accession states, the central bank expected growth of 4% in 2004, driven by investment and exports, with industrial production having increased 10% year-on-year in the first eight months of 2004. Foreign-owned companies now account for half of industrial output and 70% of exports and have capitalized on the strong skills base and central location in the enlarged EU. In September 2004 the unemployment rate stood at 9.1%, with unemployment concentrated in the geographically relatively isolated regions of northern Bohemia and northern Moravia.

GDP (purchasing power parity) $161.1bn. (2004 est.); GDP per capita (purchasing power parity) $15,700 (2004 est.).

2 Trade Unionism

A highly developed but fragmented pattern of trade unionism existed in Czechoslovakia before World War II. Unions were dissolved during the war, but competing Christian, social democratic and communist unions were re-established in 1944. Once the Communist Party finally consolidated its complete authority in 1948 the Central Council of Trade Unions (URO) became the sole trade union centre, organizing the Revolutionary Trade Union Movement (ROH). In the 1968 "Prague Spring", the Dubcek government radically reorganized the unions, allowing them to assert their independence and acknowledging an ultimate right to strike. As late as March 1969 the URO congress showed defiance of the Soviet-led occupation of August 1968 and reaffirmed these reforms but dissent was suppressed soon after.

Thereafter the unions corresponded to the conventional Soviet bloc model for almost 20 years. Where disputes occurred they were generally settled by trade union branch arbitration commissions which were convened with considerable frequency: in 1987 almost 5,000 commissions dealt with some 36,000 disputes. In the last days of communism the URO helped draft a new labour code, described by chairman Miroslav Zavadil as a "legal document guaranteeing the social certainties of the working people and contributing to the intensification of discipline and to the more flexible deployment of the labour force". Structural amendments to the URO statutes were approved at a special national conference in September 1988.

Yet when, a year later, change came, the involvement of the unions was tardy. Industrial dissidents formed "Strike Readiness Committees" which spread rapidly across the country. By December 1989 they were thought to have mobilized more than 5 million workers and an Association of Committees (ASC) was formed. Faced with this competition the URO crumbled despite an attempt to build a new identity. Zavadil resigned on Nov. 26 and his successor Karel Henes offered the ASC negotiations. He announced that the URO had severed its connections with the Communist Party and its plant-based party cells dissolved. It was re-launched as the Action Committee on Dec. 11, but in practice its fate had been determined by defections to the ASC. Negotiations were broken off and the Action Committee was never in a position to re-establish itself.

Although opposed in principle to the URO, the ASC firmly opposed fragmentation. Its approach decisively ensured trade union unity despite the emergence of some small independent centres. Early in 1990 each enterprise in Czechoslovakia organized elections (many under ASC supervision) and sent delegates to a national congress at which the Confederation of Czechoslovakian Trade Unions (CSKOS) was founded.

On its establishment, CSKOS declined to affiliate to the WFTU and quickly demonstrated its independence with the threat of a general strike to force the government to consult it on new union rights and social security regulations. CSKOS had 5.5 million members on the eve of foundation of the Czech Republic. This represented an apparent loss of more than one quarter from the URO, but the earlier figure reflected the involuntary membership of the URO.

The new structure of trade unionism evolved in step with nationalism and was thus fated not to last. CSKOS rested on two subordinate national bodies. Growing Czech and Slovak nationalism forced a rule change just three months into the life of the new organization (see below) and in May 1991 the Slovak Confederation threatened a general strike against the dismissal of the Slovak prime minister and his replacement by a Christian Democrat.

CSKOS doubted the advantages to either nation of splitting into two separate states. A memorandum it submitted to the government in the summer of 1992 forecast economic hardship and an explosion of the black market and disputed the assumption that the Czech part of the country could expect easy expansion once economically separate from Slovakia. The September 1992 general council blamed the impending division of Czechoslovakia on mistakes committed by the old regime. In speeches to the ICFTU and the ETUC on Oct. 9 its president Richard Falbr expressed the determination of CSKOS to stay united, but within a month the Czech–Moravian Chamber of Trade Unions (CMKOS) had to be founded in acknowledgement of the new national realities with Falbr himself as president.

Under the reformed Czechoslovak state the point of origin for the constitutional status of trade unions and employers bodies was the Charter of Fundamental Rights and Liberties in the constitutional law of Jan. 9, 1991. It lists trade union rights and freedoms to be protected by the constitutional court (a new court was established by the Czech Republic in June 1993). The basic legal document specifically shaping employment practice is the labour code. International pacts on human rights and basic freedoms that have been ratified by the Republics take precedence over the law. These include ILO Conventions No. 87 (Freedom of Association and Protection of the Right to Organize, 1948) and No. 98 (Right to Organize and Collective Bargaining, 1949), ratified in 1993. In March 1992, Czechoslovakia became the first East European country to sign the European Convention on Human Rights.

Most workers remain in unions affiliated to CMKOS, although total union membership has been falling, and currently stands at around 25% of the workforce, partly reflecting restructuring of older industries. CMKOS is politically independent.

In October 1990 the social partners in Czechoslovakia established a Council of Economic and Social Accord. This tripartite body had the responsibility of discussing all drafted legislative regulations, bills and legal standards prior to their submission to the government and to Parliament. In the Czech Republic a tripartite Economic and Social Council continued in being. However, tripartism, under which the country was largely strike free from the revolution to 1994, fell into abeyance in the mid-1990s as the centre-right government of Vaclav Klaus ignored the unions. In 1997, there was considerable industrial unrest as the government introduced austerity measures to combat a financial crisis involving bank closures and currency devaluation. Average real wages had only just returned to pre-1989 levels in 1996 and there was widespread disenchantment at the economic crisis. This culminated in a demonstration, described as the largest since 1989, in Prague on Nov. 8, 1997, at which CMKOS leader Richard Falbr said the problem was not economic liberalization but the way it had been implemented, and called for the resignation of the government. Later that month Klaus was forced out of office in connection with a past privatization scandal, paving the way for the election of a Social Democratic-led government in June 1998.

Employers and government have opposed industry-wide bargaining and in the private sector collective bargaining typically occurs at the enterprise level. In the state sector wages and conditions are regulated by law. According to CMKOS the number of workers covered by collective agreements is falling. Strikes are lawful only after mediation efforts have failed. In 1999 there were demonstrations in Prague against the problem of wage arrears in some manufacturing enterprises.

The ICFTU reports "frequent" violations of trade union rights, such as direct and indirect pressure on employees who seek to join unions. Employees have been encouraged to resign their union memberships with promises of improved conditions, or have simply been threatened with dismissal. Employers also barred unions from access to premises and refused to process "check-off" payments. Recently CMKOS reported that employers were using tactics to prevent collective agreements from being recognized as valid.

While ICFTU-affiliated CMKOS is overwhelmingly dominant, the WFTU claims a Czech affiliate, the Trade Union Congress of Bohemia, Moravia and Silesia (OSCMS) while the Christian Labour Confederation (KOK) is affiliated to the WCL. Minority unions have the right to engage fully in collective bargaining and KOK successfully opposed moves by CMKOS to persuade Parliament to change this.

3 Trade Union Centre

Czech–Moravian Confederation of Trade Unions (CMKOS)
Address. Winstona Churchilla 2, 113 59 Prague 3
Phone. +420 2 2446 1111
Fax. +420 2 2422 6163
E-mail. mocmkos@mbox.vol.cz
Website. www.cmkos.cz (Czech and English)
Leadership. Milan Stich (president)
Membership. 772,000
History and character. The Czechoslovak Confederation of Trade Unions (CSKOS) was founded in March 1990, in the aftermath of the "velvet revolution" of late 1989, at a national congress whose delegates were chosen at nationwide enterprise elections. It inherited the assets of the former communist trade union structure, the Central Council of Trade Unions (URO). In April 1990 a Confederation of Trade Unions was established for each nation, the Czech–Moravian Chamber (CMK-CSKOS) and the Confederation of Trade Unions of the Slovak Republic (KOZ SR), and in June the name of the organization was changed to the Czech and Slovak Confederation of Trade Unions. From this point on, as separatist tendencies grew, the new organization sought to avoid a split along nationalist lines. As late as July 1992 a comprehensive CSKOS memorandum foretold dire economic and political consequences should the separation of the Czech and Slovak lands be carried through; within a few weeks however, trade unionists on both sides were forced to start preparations for the inevitable. CMKOS was formed in November 1992 in advance of the foun-

dation of the Czech Republic. In May 1998, at the second congress, the name was changed from the Czech–Moravian Chamber of Trade Unions to the Czech–Moravian Confederation of Trade Unions (both CMKOS).

CMKOS is similar in orientation to CSKOS, which defined itself as an independent voluntary grouping of republic and other associations of individual unions and of self-standing unions. Its prime objectives were to achieve unity through trade union solidarity and common interests; to defend the rights and legitimate interests of affiliates; and to represent them in international non-sectoral organizations and in tripartite and collective bargaining activities. In the run-up to joining the EU it was particularly concerned with representing its members and workers generally in the national process of preparation for accession.

The CMKOS is not affiliated with any political party.

CMKOS affiliated 40 unions at the time of formation of the Czech Republic; this total has now fallen to 35 with the merger of smaller unions.

International affiliations. ICFTU; ETUC; TUAC

4 Other Trade Union Organization

Krestanska Odborova Koalice (KOK)
Christian Labour Confederation
Address. Karlovo nam. 5, 12000 Prague 2.
Phone. +420 2 2491 1829
Fax. +420 2 2491 1829
E-mail. kokanton@seznam.cz
Leadership. Anton Alois (president)
International affiliation. WCL

Denmark

Capital: Copenhagen
Population: 5.41 m. (2004 est.)

1 Political and Economic Background

Denmark is a constitutional monarchy and a member state of the European Union. Other than the period of Nazi occupation in World War II, the Social Democratic Party (SD) was the most significant force in Danish politics from the 1930s (when it laid the foundations of the welfare state) until the early 1980s, usually forming the government in coalition with other parties. From 1982–93 Prime Minister Poul Schlüter of the Conservative People's Party (KFP) led centre-right coalition governments. From January 1993 the SD again led a series of coalition governments, with its leader Poul Nyrup Rasmussen as Prime Minister. In a general election in November 2001, however, the SD lost its status as the largest party in parliament, a position it had held in every national election since 1924, and a new centre-right government was formed, led by the Liberal Party (Venstre) and including the Conservative Party. The government was re-elected in February 2005.

Denmark has a developed economy, with modern industrial, service and commercial agricultural sectors. Denmark lacks major global corporations, in contrast to neighbouring Sweden, but has a reputation for efficiency in its predominantly small and medium-sized enterprises. It has a large public sector workforce, an extensive welfare system and high taxation. Unemployment levels fell from over 12% in 1993 to 5.5% by the end of the decade, partly as a result of stricter job availability criteria but also reflecting a period of sustained growth; in 2004 unemployment was just over 6%, but in 2003-04 the economy showed virtually nil growth. Denmark did not adopt the common European currency (euro) at its launch in January 1999 and a referendum on its adoption on Sept. 28, 2000 resulted in a vote to stay outside the eurozone (although the currency is peggd to the euro).

GDP (purchasing power parity) $167.2bn. (2004 est.); GDP per capita (purchasing power parity) $31,100 (2004 est.).

2 Trade Unionism

Denmark ratified ILO Convention No. 87 (Freedom of Association and Protection of the Right to Organize, 1948) in 1951 and Convention No. 98 (Right to Organize and Collective Bargaining, 1949) in 1955.

Unions developed in the nineteenth century, and the Landsorganisationen i Danmark (LO, the Danish Confederation of Trade Unions) was founded in 1898. In 1899 – following a major dispute – the LO and the Confederation of Danish Employers (DA) reached a basic agreement on the right to organize and industrial partnership which formed the bedrock for subsequent trade union growth and industrial relations. The unions also administer unemployment insurance schemes directly on behalf of the government.

Overall union density has declined somewhat in recent years but is still very high by international standards at around 80% (compared with 84% in the mid-1990s). There are three centres representing employees. Unlike in many countries, these are not the result of political fragmentation, but are rather (as in other Scandinavian countries) based on the level of educational qualifications of their members, and professional sections of the workforce are highly unionized. In broad terms, the largest centre, the LO, with 1.38 million members, represents skilled and unskilled workers, in all areas of the economy. The second-largest centre, the Salaried Employees' and Civil Servants' Confederation (FTF), with 450,000 members, represents those with an intermediate level of qualifications (particularly primary teachers, nurses and bank workers), while the smallest, the Danish Confederation of Professional Associations (AC), with 253,000 members, represents graduates. All three are affiliated to the ICFTU. Reflecting the momentum in the economy to a more highly skilled workforce, the LO is gradually losing membership while the AC and FTF (and especially the former) are continuing to grow – a pattern similar to that, for example, in Sweden. Relations between these centres are generally good, but it is the LO that is the dominant voice of Danish trade unionism. The unions retained a strong organizational base through the 1980s and 1990s, a period when unions in many other countries lost ground in the face of the decline of traditional industries and deregulation, and in some sectors 95% or more of workers are unionized. There are still many small unions – a survey published in 2001 found that one-third of the then total of 169 unions had fewer than 1,000 members – and demarcation disputes and competition for members have been features of the trade union landscape.

A factor in the enduring strength of the unions has been the Danish system of industrial relations. Under this unions and employers have taken primary responsibility for negotiating stable agreements which have underpinned the development of a free market economy in alliance with a secure system of employment rights and social provision. The Danish system is characterized by reliance on agreement rather than on legislation and this is a continuing preference of both employers and unions; the unions have been suspicious of the possibility that deeper integration of the EU might lead to a model in which labour relations are put in a legislative framework defined in Brussels. The political system, in which governments are commonly formed by weak or minority coalitions and legislation adopted by consensus, and the centrist orientation of much of the electorate, has also meant that the national consensus in favour of the welfare state, high taxation (among the highest in the world) and the value of responsible trade unionism has survived the worldwide movement to neoliberalism relatively unscathed. Historically governments have avoided direct intervention in negotiations between employers and unions.

Wage indexation, long a feature of collective agreements, was suspended during 1983–87. The 1987 Central Wage Agreement that followed suspension lasted four years, but clamour for a return to decentralized bargaining grew. The 1989 establishment of sectoral negotiating groups in most manual and some white-collar trades (on a pattern already established in engineering) was a partial response and set a pattern into the 1990s for more decentralized bargaining. The current pattern in the private sector is that negotiation of collective agreements takes place at sectoral level (with unions forming cartels for negotiating purposes) and is then subject to an overall settlement between the LO and DA with the aid of the Public Conciliation Service (Forlingsinstitutionen). Thus in March 2004 the LO and DA accepted an overall compromise settlement drawn up by the Forlingsinstitutionen to bring a conclusion to sectoral negotiations covering most of the private sector, the LO membership as a whole then voting to accept the settlement (although the leaders and memberships of some LO affiliates were not in favour, all were then bound to the compromise). The settlement covered a three-year period and focused on issues such as pensions and work benefits rather than pay increases. In the public sector, negotiations continue to begin at the centre followed by decentralized negotiations in individual sectors. Most public sector unions reached three-year agreements in 2002 (with separate framework agreements for the central and local government areas, and lower-level agreements negoriated within those frameworks), with local and central government contracts due for re-negotiation in 2005. In the public sector there is considerable union resistance to the "new wage" system, introduced in 1998, which is intended to give employers more flexibility within a decentralized system in recompensing the special qualifications or contribution of individual employees. The FTF-affiliated teachers' and nurses' unions have called for abolition of the "new wage" system. In specific areas, such as health, unions form bargaining cartels that comprise unions from different confederations. In general the employers' side in both the public and private sectors is pressing for more flexibility in agreements to adjust to conditions at enterprise or local level, and in respect of individual employees, while most unions have tended to a more collectivist approach. However, developments in decentralization have been comparatively modest and the centre-right government elected in 2001 has proved reluctant to push radical reform of Denmark's labour market.

The DA/LO basic agreement lays down principles of cooperation between the two sides at sectoral and enterprise level. Under it there are no strikes or lock-outs while an agreement is in force. With some 80% of Danish workers in unions and about half of all employers members of an employers' association, agreements are strong, although unofficial disputes do occur. The agreement also provides for lawful notice of industrial action by either side, for rules governing unfair dismissals and for regulations governing shop steward representation. If the parties cannot agree, the Conciliator intervenes, with power to postpone industrial action. Where a dispute occurs nonetheless, arbitration may occur under rules of 1908 governing the conduct of disputes: these provide for renewed efforts by the DA and the LO and then for arbitration, and finally for reference to the Industrial Court. The number of working days lost each year through strike action is typically low. In 2003 there were 681 disputes but these resulted in only 55,100 lost working days - the lowest since 1989.

In 2003 there was widespread disruption of life in the Danish dependency of the Faroes Islands caused by strikes over a pay claim led by the Association of Faroese Trade Unions, representing five unions of manual workers with 12,000 members.

3 Trade Union Centres

Akademikernes Centralorganisation (AC)
Danish Confederation of Professional Associations
Address. Nørre Voldgade 29, Postboks 2192, DK-1017 Copenhagen K
Phone. +45 3369 4040
Fax. +45 3393 8540
E-mail. ac@ac.dk
Website. www.ac.dk (Danish; English section)
Leadership. Sine Sunesen (president)
Membership. 253,000 (2004, includes self-employed and students)
History and character. The AC was founded in 1972 and has 22 affiliated organizations representing graduates. The AC has no party political affiliations. Its main purpose is to safeguard the salary and employment terms of its members and it engages in collective bargaining in both the public and private sectors on behalf of its member organizations. Reflecting the increasing profession-

alization of the workforce, the AC is continuing to grow. As a social partner it is engaged in councils and committees across a range of social and economic issues. It cooperates with the LO and FTF in dealings at European and international levels and represents both the LO and FTF as the Danish member of the steering committee of EUROCADRES (the Council of European Professional and Managerial Staff).
International affiliations. ICFTU; TUAC; ETUC; NFS; EUROCADRES
Affiliates. The following are among the larger affiliates:

1. Danish Medical Association
Address. Trondhjemsgade 9, DK-2100 Copenhagen Ø
Phone. +45 35 44 82 23
E-mail. sho@dadl.dk (international secretary)
Website. www.dadl.dk
Leadership. Jesper Poulsen (president)
Membership. 21,860

2. Association of Danish Lawyers and Economists
Address. Gothersgade 133, PO Box 2126, DK-1015 Copenhagen K
Phone. +45 33 95 97 00
E-mail. djoef@djoef.dk
Website. www.djoef.dk
Membership. 45,000

3. Danish Association of Masters and PhDs
Address. Nimbusparken, Peter Bangs Vej 32, 2000 Frederiksberg
Phone. +45 38 15 66 00
E-mail. dm@magister.dk
Website. www.magister.dk
Membership. 20,000, plus 12,000 students

Funktionærernes og Tjenestemændenes Fællesråd (FTF)
Salaried Employees' and Civil Servants' Confederation
Address. Niels Hemmingsens Gade 12, Postbox 1169, 1010 Copenhagen K
Phone. +45 33 36 88 00
Fax. +45 33 36 88 80
E-mail. ftf@ftf.dk
Website. www.ftf.dk
Leadership. Bente Sorgenfrey (president)
Membership. 450,000
History and character. The FTF was founded in 1952 by 11 non-LO white-collar organizations. Among their concerns were the failure of staff salaries to keep pace with wage increases awarded to manual workers, and a desire for politically neutral leadership (i.e. unlike that of the socialist-inclined LO). The LO and FTF achieved a working relationship by 1973, after the LO had earlier regarded the new organization with some hostility. The FTF is independent of any political party.

The FTF now affiliates some 100 independent unions, the largest of which are the teachers' union, the nurses' union, the pre-school teachers' union and the financial services union. More than 95% of Danish nurses, teachers and bank employees are unionized. 75% of FTF members are in the public sector, with most members in the private sector being in banks and insurance companies.

The FTF has representation on more than 150 committees and councils dealing with health, safety, professional education, consumer issues and social problems. With the LO it administers the Danish Trade Union Council for International Development Cooperation.
International affiliations. ETUC; TUAC; ICFTU; NFS
Affiliated unions. The following are the largest of the FTF's 100 affiliated unions.

1. Danish Pre-School Teachers' Union (BUPL)
Address. Blegdamsvej 124, 2100 Copenhagen
Phone. +45 35 46 50 00
E-mail. bupl@bupl.dk
Website. www.bupl.dk (Danish only)
Membership. 58,000

2. Danish Union of Teachers (DLF)
Address. Vandkunsten 12, 1467 Copenhagen K
Phone. +45 33 69 63 00
Fax. +45 33 69 63 33
E-mail. dlf@dlf.org
Website. www.dlf.org (Danish; English section)
Leadership. Anders Bondo Christensen (president)
Membership. 85,000 (65,000 active teachers)
History and character. The DLF is the only union organizing primary and lower secondary education and 97% of teachers in this category are DLF members. Internationally it is affiliated to Education International and the European Trade Union Committee for Education.

3. Danish Nurses' Union (DSR)
Address. Vimmelskaftet 38, Postbox 1084, 1008 Copenhagen K
Phone. +45 33 15 15 55
Fax. +45 33 15 24 55
E-mail. dsr@dsr.dk
Website. www.dsr.dk (Danish; English section)
Leadership. Connie Kruckow (president)
Membership. 73,000 (95% of Danish nurses)

4. Danish Financial Services Union (FINANSFORBUNDET)
Address. Langebrogade 5, Postboks 1960, 1411 Copenhagen K
Phone. +45 32 96 46 00
Fax. +45 32 96 12 25
E-mail. post@finansforbundet.dk
Website. www.finansforbundet.dk
Membership. 50,000, constituting 90% of employees in this sector.

Landsorganisationen i Danmark (LO)
Danish Confederation of Trade Unions
Address. Islands Brygge 32D, 2300 Copenhagen S
Phone. +45 35 24 60 00
Fax. +45 35 24 63 00
E-mail. lo@lo.dk
Website. www.lo.dk (Danish; English summary)
Leadership. Hans Jensen (president)
Membership. 1,385,775 (end 2003)
History and character. The LO was founded in 1898 in

an attempt to coordinate the nascent Danish labour organizations. The following year it reached the first collective agreement with the Danish employers, this forming the basis for the future development of the Danish industrial relations system which emphasizes direct agreement between highly organized union and employer groups. It is also historically linked to the Social Democratic Party, the leading Danish party for much of the period from the 1930s. However in 1995 the old organic relationship, whereby LO members sat on the party's governing bodies, and vice versa, was ended. Then in February 2003 an extraordinary congress of the LO, aimed at the creation of a "new LO", decided to end direct financial support for the party. Although this move was made with considerable reluctance by some of the LO's affiliates, it was seen as necessary to broadening the appeal of the LO and also to facilitating union mergers with affiliates of the FTF and potentially for an ultimate merger of all the Danish centres.

The LO is Denmark's main trade union centre, representing in particular unskilled and semi-skilled workers and industrial crafts. Within traditional areas of employment it dominates, with density sometimes as high as 95 per cent. Approximately one-third of its membership is in the public sector, one-third is in companies affiliated to the Danish Employers' Confederation, and one-third is in other private companies. Membership is almost exactly equally divided between men and women. However, reflecting changes in the composition of the workforce, the LO represents an ever declining proportion of the unionized workforce, as the AC and FTF gain ground. This has resulted in a gradual absolute decline of LO membership in recent years, with a fall of 7% from 1990-2003.

Rationalization of the union structure along industrial lines has been discussed for many years but has faced considerable resistance from unions based on traditional crafts or distinctive occupational categories. The number of affiliated unions is now 20, compared with 26 in 1993, 30 in 1989 and 65 in 1966, but many of the remaining unions are still quite small. To help coordination the LO has set up seven cartels uniting unions for different industrial sectors (building, construction and wood; industrial; trade; transport and services; municipal employees; state employees; graphical industry and media). These cartels have varying relationships with their member unions. In 2003 the 12,000-member telecommunications workers' union (Telekommunikationsforbundet) merged with the Metalworkers but retained a separate identity as an independent section of the union. Then, in 2004, the Danish General Workers' Union (SID) merged with the National Union of Women Workers to form the Fagligt Faelles Forbund (3F). The new union, representing mainly unskilled workers, has 374,000 members and is one of the two largest LO affiliates. The restaurant workers' union RBF also indicated that it wished to merge with 3F although the Danish Timber Industry and Construction Workers' Union (TIB) had pulled out of talks leading to the formation of 3F. Against a background of pressure on union memberships, demarcation disputes have occurred between various LO unions. The LO has a demarcation committee which seeks to resolve disputes, but the ultimate sanction of expulsion from the LO has never been used. Outsourcing of jobs formerly in the public sector to private contractors has been a particular source of demarcation disputes.

The LO constitution guarantees the sovereignty of member unions. The role of the LO is to provide coordination to union activities, develop and advocate policies at the national level and propose and coordinate guidelines for collective bargaining. While collective bargaining remains a pivotal aspect for the LO, increasingly it is focusing on legislative policy in areas such as taxation, social conditions and employment. In February 2003 an extraordinary LO congress adopted a new platform of values giving more weight to the individual within the collective system. In the 2004 private sector bargaining round, negotiations took place at sectoral level and were then subject to an overall compromise agreement between the LO and the DA achieved with the aid of the Conciliation Service.

The LO is active at the EU level (and has a Brussels office). Like most business organizations and political leaders it urged a vote in favour of Danish adoption of the common European currency in a national referendum on Sept. 28, 2000. However, divisions in the union movement were reflected in a tied vote on the issue on the executive of the LO's third biggest affiliate, the public employees' union, following opinion polls showing a majority of public sector workers opposed adoption of the common currency. In the event the referendum resulted in a decision not to adopt the currency. Notwithstanding its support for the euro, reflecting the strength of Euroscepticism in Denmark, the LO is opposed to any development of a "United States of Europe". It is resistant to implementation of EU standards through legislation by Brussels rather than by local agreement on the Danish model. In that respect it shares a common position with the DA.

The LO runs three labour colleges and its unions are actively involved in the Workers' Educational Association (AOF). The training system (FIU), aimed mainly at shop stewards, involves 40,000 annually. Internationally it runs the Danish Trade Union Council for International Development Cooperation, in association with the FTF, and has a particular interest in the Baltic region and central and eastern Europe.

International affiliations. ICFTU; ETUC; TUAC; NFS

Affiliated unions. The largest afffiliates are listed below. Other affiliates include the Danish Artistes' Union (Artist Forbund); the National Union of Plumbers and Allied Workers (Blik- og Rørarbejderforbundet i Danmark); the Danish Union of Electricians (Dansk El-Forbund); the Danish Hairdressers' and Beauticians' Union (Dansk Frisør og Kosmetiker Forbund); Union of Enlisted Privates and Corporals in the Army (Haerens Konstabel- og Korporal Forening, HKKF); Danish Union of Railwaymen (Dansk Jernbaneforbund); Danish Painters' Union (Malerforbundet i Danmark); National Union of Nursery and Childcare Assistants (Paedagogisk Medhjaelper Forbund); Restaurant Trade Union (RestaurationsBranchens Forbund); and National Federation of Social Educators (Socialpaedagogernes Landsforbund).

1. Fagligt Faelles Forbund (3F)
Address. 3F Kampmannsgade 4, 1790 Copenhagen V
Telephone. +45 70 300 300
Fax. +45 70 300 301
E-mail. 3f@3f.dk
Website. www.3f.dk
Leadership. Poul Erik Skov Christensen (president)
Membership. 374,000
History and character. 3F held its inaugural congress in September 2004. It was formed by the merger of the Kvindeligt Arbejderforbund i Danmark (National Union of Women Workers, KAD) and the Specialarbejderforbundet i Danmark (SID, Danish General Workers' Union). The merger had received overwhelming approval in membership ballots of the two unions earlier in the year. The SID provided the majority (303,000) of the members of the new union and SID president Poul Erik Skov Christensen became leader of 3F. The two unions' 300 local offices were to be cut back to 72.

The KAD was founded in 1885 and was a rare example of a union exclusively for women. Its members were mainly unskilled, divided equally between industry and the services sector. In industry, half the members worked in iron and metal and one-quarter in food and catering. In services they were mainly employed as cleaners, but other occupations included care workers and laundry workers. The union primarily functioned as a conventional trade union on the lines of other LO affiliates but it also had a specific involvement in campaigning on women's issues. However, its membership had fallen by 25% since 1990. The SID was the second largest LO affiliate, but its membership was eroding as the proportion of unskilled jobs in the economy declined. About 50,000 of the combined union's membership are in the public sector.

2. Forbundet af Offentligt Ansatte (Danish Union of Public Employees)
Address. Staunings Plads 1–3, 1790 Copenhagen V
Phone. +45 46 97 26 26
E-mail. foa@foa.dk
Website. www.foa.dk (Danish; English section)
Leadership. Dennis Kristensen (president)
Membership. 198,000. This is the third largest Danish union with members in four sections covering child care services; mechanical engineering, maintenance and miscellaneous; social and health care services; and catering and cleaning.

3. Handels- og Kontorfunktionaerernes Forbund i Danmark (HK, National Union of Commercial and Clerical Employees)
Address. Weidekampsgade 8, PO Box 470, 0900 Copenhagen C
Phone. +45 33 30 4343
E-mail. hk@hk.dk
Website. www.hk.dk (Danish; English summary)
Leadership. John Dahl (president)
Membership. 377,000
History and character. The HK was founded in 1900 and joined the LO in 1932. It is (with the newly formed 3F) one of the two largest LO affiliates. More than 75% of its members, who have clerical, administrative and technical jobs in both the private and public sectors, are women. The majority of its members are covered by collective agreements. The HK has 41 regional branches, is divided into four sectors, and employs 1,000 staff.

4. Dansk Metalarbejderforbund (Danish Union of Metalworkers)
Address. Nyropsgade 38, 1780 Copenhagen V
Phone. +45 3363 2000
Fax. +45 3363 2100
E-mail. metal@danskmetal.dk
Website. www.danskmetal.dk (Danish only)
Leadership. Thorkild Jensen (president)
Membership. 142,000

5. Naerings- og Nydelsesmiddelarbejder Forbundet (Danish Food and Allied Workers' Union, NNF)
Address. C.F. Richs Vej 103, PO Box 79, DK-2000 Frederiksberg
Phone. +45 3818 7272
Fax. +45 3818 7200
E-mail. nnf@nnf.dk
Website. www.nnf.dk (Danish; English section)
Membership. 40,000

6. Teknisk Landsforbund (Danish Union of Professional Technicians)
Address. Nørre Voldgade 12, 1358 Copenhagen K
Phone. +45 33 43 65 00
E-mail. tl@tl.dk
Website. www.tl.dk
Leadership. Ole Skals Pedersen (president)
Membership. 32,000

7. Forbundet Trae- Industri-Byg I Danmark (TID, Danish Timber Industry and Construction Workers' Union)
Address. Mimersgade 41, 2200 Copenhagen N
Phone. +45 3531 9599
Fax. +45 3531 9450
E-mail. tib@tib.dk
Membership. 68,000

Djibouti

Capital: Djibouti
Population: 466,900 (2004 est.)

1 Political and Economic Background

Djibouti, formerly the French Territory of the Afars and Issas, became independent in 1977 following a referendum and was ruled by President Hassan Gouled Aptidon from independence until succeeded by his nephew, Ismael Omar Guelleh, who was elected in April 1999. Tension between the majority Issas (of Somali ethnic origin) and the Afars (of Ethiopian ethnic origin) resulted in an armed insurgency by the Afars, organized as the Front for the Restoration of Unity and Democracy (FRUD). The government signed peace accords with the two main FRUD factions in 1994 and 2001, allowing for increased Afar representation in government. Djibouti's first multi-party legislative elections took place in January 2003. A bloc of four pro-government parties won about 62% of the vote, against 37% for an opposition alliance led by the former leader of the FRUD armed wing, Ahmed Dini Ahmed.

Djibouti has few natural resources, little arable land and hardly any industry. Unusually for an African country, some four-fifths of the population lives in urban areas. The country is heavily dependent on foreign assistance to help support its balance of payments and to finance development projects. A free trade zone has been created to encourage the establishment of new industries and there is an entrepot trade based on the strategic position of the seaport, the airport and the railway link to the Ethiopian capital of Addis Ababa. Unemployment is estimated as high as 50% and per capita consumption dropped an estimated 35% over the seven years through to 2003 because of recession, civil war, and a high population growth rate (including immigrants and refugees).

GDP (purchasing power parity) $619 million (2002 est.); GDP per capita (purchasing power parity) $1,300 (2002 est.).

2 Trade Unionism

Djibouti ratified ILO Conventions No. 87 (Freedom of Association and Protection of the Right to Organize, 1948) and No. 98 (Right to Organize and Collective Bargaining, 1949) in 1978.

Trade unions developed under French rule. Following independence until 1992 control by the government over individual unions was exercised through the single state-organized peak association, the General Union of Djibouti Workers (UGTD). However, a new national centre, the ICFTU-affiliated Union of Djibouti Workers (UDT), was formed in 1992 in the face of official discouragement. Since 1995 the UGTD and UDT have formed a confederation.

In 1995 the UGTD and UDT joined in protests against austerity measures introduced as part of an IMF/World Bank structural adjustment programme. This led to the dismissal of the leadership of both centres and a series of actions against the unions. In 1995 the government sponsored the creation of a "Djibouti Labour Congress" (CODJITRA), led by Ministry of Labour officials, and in May 1996 security forces closed the UGTD-UDT headquarters, which was not restored to the UGTD-UDT until 1998. Since the 1995 protests, the ICFTU has claimed that the government has repeatedly promised that the situation would improve, and that it would allow the UDT and UGTD to hold congresses but nothing has materialised. Furthermore, union leaders have been repeatedly harassed, by being dismissed from their posts, and protest demonstrations have been met with police violence.

Despite the continuing attacks, the UDT and UGTD are reported to have increased their support in recent years and to represent some 70% of workers in the formal economy. There is a formal right to collective bargaining but this scarcely exists in practice.

3 Trade Union Centres

Union Djiboutienne du Travail (UDT)
Union of Djibouti Workers
Address. BP 2767, Djibouti
Phone. +253 355 084; +253 340 678
Fax. +253 355 084; +253 340 678
E-mail. Udt_djibouti@yahoo.fr
Leadership. Ahmed Djama Egueh (president); Aden Mohamed Abdou (general secretary)
History and character. Founded in 1992, the UDT achieved government recognition in 1993 and since 1995 has acted in confederation with the UGTD in the face of continual government harassment. It joined the ICFTU in 1994.
International affiliations. ICFTU

Union Générale des Travailleurs de Djibouti (UGTD)
General Union of Djibouti Workers
Leadership. Kamil Diraneth Hared (general secretary)
History and character. Functioned as the official union arm of the ruling party, but has been in serious conflict with the government from 1995, since when it has acted in confederation with the UDT, sharing its headquarters.

Dominica

Capital: Roseau
Population: 69,000 (2004 est.)

1 Political and Economic Background

Dominica, formerly a West Indies Associated State, became a fully independent member of the Commonwealth in 1978 as a republic. The three major political parties are the conservative Dominica Freedom Party (DFP), and two centre-left parties, the United Workers' Party (UWP) and the Dominica Labour Party (DLP). The most recent elections, in January 2000, resulted in the UWP losing power and the formation of a coalition government of the DFP and DLP, with Roosevelt (Rosie) Douglas of the DLP becoming Prime Minister. Douglas and his successor as Prime Minister, Pierre Charles, both died in office, with the DLP's Roosevelt Skerrit succeeding Charles in January 2004.

Agriculture, primarily banana production, employs 40 per cent of the workforce and the government has sought to diversify the economy in view of the vulnerability of banana exports (typically representing half of all exports) to price fluctuations and natural disasters such as hurricanes. The economy contracted 1% in 2003, in part because of a downturn in the banana sector, and the government has initiated an unpopular austerity programme including ending price controls.

GDP (purchasing power parity) $380m. (2003 est.); GDP per capita (purchasing power parity) $5,400 (2003 est.).

2 Trade Unionism

Dominica ratified ILO Conventions No. 87 (Freedom of Association and Protection of the Right to Organize, 1948) and No. 98 (Right to Organize and Collective Bargaining, 1949) in 1983. All workers have the right to form unions, collective bargaining is practiced in non-agricultural sectors (including the public sector), there is a right to strike and there is also recourse to mediation and arbitration by government. However, unions are very small in scale and represent less than 10% of the workforce.

There is no trade union centre: the Dominica Trade Union fulfilled this role in the 1950s, but was subsequently weakened by the defection of some of its members to non-affiliated organizations. There are two ICFTU affiliates. Relations between the various organizations were poor during the 1960s and early 1970s, but have since improved. The unions now operate under a loose umbrella, the Joint Unions Steering Committee.

3 Trade Union Centre

There is no trade union centre.

4 Other Trade Union Organizations

Dominica Amalgamated Workers' Union (DAWU)
Address. PO Box 137, 40 Kennedy Avenue, Roseau
Phone. +1767 448 2343
Fax. +1767 448 0086
E-mail. dawu@hotmail.com
Leadership. Elias Leah Shillingford (acting general secretary)
International affiliations. CTUC; WCL

Dominica Public Service Union
Address. Valley Road/Windsor Lane, PO Box 182, Roseau
Phone. +1767 448 2101
Fax. +1767 448 8060
E-mail. dcs@cwdom.dm
Leadership. Thomas Letang (general secretary)
History and character. This is the successor to the Dominica Civil Service Association (DCSA), which was originally founded as a staff association in 1938 and became a trade union in 1961. It is the major public service union in Dominica.
International affiliations. CTUC

Dominica Trade Union (DTU)
Address. 70–71 Independence Street, Roseau
Phone. +1767 449 8139
Fax. +1767 449 9060
E-mail. domtradun@hotmail.com
Leadership. Harold Sealy (general secretary)
History and character. Founded in 1945, the DTU was at its peak in its earliest years, having over 8,000 members from a wide occupational spectrum in the 1945-50 period. Until the 1960s it remained the only union in Dominica, but the labour movement fragmented thereafter and the DTU declined and had only a few hundred members by the 1990s. Its one-time political influence (when successive First Ministers were DTU members) has ended.
International affiliations. CTUC; ICFTU

National Workers' Union
Address. 69 Independence Street, PO Box 387, Roseau
Phone. + 1767 448 465
Fax. +1767 448 1934
Leadership. Rawlings Jemmott (president)
International affiliations. WCL

Waterfront and Allied Workers' Union (WAWU)
Address. 43 Hillsborough Street, PO Box 181, Roseau
Phone. +1767 448 2343
Fax. +1767 448 0086
E-mail. wawuunion@hotmail.com
Leadership. Kertist Augustus (president); Catherine Valerie-Solomon (secretary/treasurer)
Membership. Over 1,000
International affiliations. ICFTU; CTUC

Dominican Republic

Capital: Santo Domingo
Population: 8.83 m. (2004 est.)

1 Political and Economic Background

Thirty years of authoritarian rule by Generalissimo Rafael Trujillo ended in 1961 with his assassination, which was followed by some years of confusion, civil war, and United States military intervention in 1965. Joaquín Balaguer of the anti-Marxist Social Christian Reform Party (PRSC), or Reformist Party, was elected President in 1966 (having previously held that office under Trujillo) and then held that office until 1978 and then again from 1986 until 1996, when Leonel Fernández of the centrist Dominican Liberation Party (PLD) was elected. He was succeeded as President following elections in May 2000 by Hipólito Mejía Domínguez, whose left-of-centre Dominican Revolutionary Party (PRD) had previously won a majority in both houses of the National Congress in 1998 elections. The 2002 legislative elections left the PRD as the largest party, but it lost its majority in the Chamber of Deputies (the lower house) and in May 2004 it also lost the presidency, with Leonel Fernández returning to power.

The economy of the Dominican Republic has historically been based on agriculture, although a majority of the labour force is now employed in services. Although sugar has traditionally been the principal crop, output varies because of climatic and international market factors. Manufacturing industry mainly centres on processing of agricultural products, while tourism is a major and growing earner of foreign exchange. There has been extensive development of export processing zones.

In January 1995 President Balaguer announced the termination of subsidies to 33 state-owned companies, but declined to privatize them. After his election in 1996, Fernández launched a major programme of economic measures, including devaluation, raised sales taxes, income tax cuts, and privatization, although some measures were stalled in the legislature. The economy grew by more than 7% in 1998 and 8% in 1999. Despite this, the PRD won the presidential election in 2000, its candidate Hipólito Mejía Domínguez promising wide-ranging reform, including large-scale investment in infrastructure and social programmes. The lack of improvement in social and economic conditions under Mejía resulted in periodic outbreaks of civil unrest and in 2003 there was a sharp decline in the dollar value of the peso, triggering inflation. In November 2003 and January 2004 there was loss of life in clashes between protesters and security forces and this unrest provided the context for Mejía's defeat in the May 2004 presidential election. High inflation and unemployment persisted in 2004, after a 0.7% decline in GDP in 2003.

GDP (purchasing power parity) $52.71bn (2004 est.); GDP per capita (purchasing power parity) $6,000 (2004 est.).

2 Trade Unionism

Workers' organizations developed in the 1920s and a Dominican Confederation of Workers (Confederación Dominicana de Trabajadores, CDT) was formed in 1930. Trujillo's assumption of power later that year, however, led to the dissolution of the CDT; some unions nevertheless continued to exist, and Trujillo also sponsored his own trade union centre, the CTD. This expired after his assassination in 1961 and was replaced by independent rival centres, including affiliates of the regional organizations of the three world centres. The trade union movement has traditionally been divided along ideological lines. The three largest centres are the ICFTU-affiliated CNTD and CTU, and the WCL affiliate the CASC. The WFTU also reports an affiliate and some unions are unaffiliated to any centre. The 1992 labour code permits workers to form trade unions with as few as 20 members: they may be enterprise unions, or sectoral unions and they have the right to federate or confederate. The various trade union centres tend to be unstable with frequent breakaways and ruptures. Overall, although all employees except police and military are legally free to form unions, less than 10% of the workforce is in unions and collective bargaining is not widely practiced. Strikes are legal subject to the support of an absolute majority of the workforce and a number of pre-strike procedures. Recent strikes have involved nurses, doctors, professors and teachers.

Although the Dominican Republic ratified ILO Conventions No. 87 (Freedom of Association and Protection of the Right to Organize, 1948) in 1956 and No. 98 (Right to Organize and Collective Bargaining, 1949) in 1953, the 1951 Trujillo labour code remained in force until 1992. International pressure over reported violations of human and civil rights culminated in a United States decision to remove the Dominican Republic from its Generalized System of Preferences effective from June 1992. In response a new labour code was adopted that relaxed restrictions on unions. The code established permissive procedures for the registration of unions and banned employers from dismissing employees for union activities. It gave public employees in non-essential industries the right to strike; withdrew the previous prohibition against general strikes; and ended the 48-hour maximum duration limit on strikes. Under the code collective agreements could be concluded at the enterprise or sector level. In January 1993 new labour courts established by the code began to function. Ostensibly the code applied to all workers in the private sector, even those in the export processing zones, despite the opposition of ADOZONAS, their employers' association.

In its 2003 *Annual Survey of Trade Union Rights* the ICFTU said that enforcement of labour legislation was inadequate, and that significant problems remained. In the 40 export processing zones (EPZs), where 190,000 were employed (mainly women garment workers), employers commonly ignored the labour laws and the government had been unable or unwilling to apply them. Conditions in the EPZs are poor and pay is low. ICFTU and the Global Union Federations recorded serious violations in 2003, including the circulation of blacklists of union organizers and physical violence against union leaders. A union must represent 50% of the workers in an enterprise before it can be recognized for collective bargaining purposes, and employers commonly got rid of activists before this figure is achieved. Union activity in the sugar plantations has been curtailed. Haitian migrant workers employed there are often in the Dominican Republic illegally and cannot join unions.

3 Trade Union Centres

Central General de Trabajadores (CGT)
Address. Calle Juan Erazo No. 14, 5ta Edif. CNUS, Villa Juana, Santo Domingo, D.N.
Phone. +1809 221 6843
Fax. +1809 686 8755
E-mail. central.gt@codetel.net.do
Leadership. Rafael Abreu (secretary-general)
International affiliation. WCL

Confederación Autónoma Sindical Clasista (CASC)
Address. Juan Erazo 39, Apartado Correos 309, Santo Domingo, D.N.
Phone. +1809 687 8533
Fax. +1809 686 8602
E-mail. cascnactional@codetel.net.do
Leadership. Gabriel Del Río Doñé (secretary-general)
International affiliation. WCL

Confederación Nacional de Trabajadores Dominicanos (CNTD)
Address. C/José de Jesús Ravelo 56, Esquina Juan Erezo, Sector Villa Juana, Santo Domingo, D.N.
Phone. +1809 221 2117
Fax. +1809 682 0195
E-mail. cntd@codetel.net.do

History and character. The CNTD (like the leftist CUT) originated in the United Workers' Front for Autonomous Trade Unions (FOUPSA) founded in 1961; when FOUPSA split the more right-wing faction in 1962 took the name National Confederation of Free Workers (CONATRAL). CONATRAL adopted a neutral position at the time of the US-led intervention in 1965 and received the assistance of the US-backed American Institute for Free Labour Development (AIFLD). The CONATRAL in turn became the CNTD in 1971. In 1988 it absorbed the membership of the Unión General de Trabajadores Dominicanos (UGTD). In 1991–92 the CNTD was a key organizer of the pressure which induced the Balaguer regime to rescind and replace the Trujillo labour code.
International affiliation. ICFTU

Confederación de Trabajadores Unitaria (CTU)
Address. Calle Juan Erazo No. 14 Edif. De law Centrales Sindicales, 3era, Santo Domingo.
Phone. +1809 6889 757
Fax. +1809 6899 889
Leadership. Nelsida Altagracia Marmolejos (president); Jacinto de los Santos (secretary-general)
History and character. Formed by the 1991 merger of four confederations, the CTM, the CTC, the CTI, and the CUT. Claims to be the largest centre in the country and may indeed rival the CNTD.
International affiliation. Many of the constituent unions formerly had affiliations to the WFTU, but the CTU is now ICFTU-affiliated.

Corriente Unitaria de Trabajadores
Address. Jose marti No.161, Apartado Postal 146-E, Santo Domingo
Fax. +1809 682 2684
International affiliation. WFTU

East Timor (Timor-Leste)

Capital: Dili
Population: 1.02 m. (2004 est.)

1 Political and Economic Background

Long ruled from Goa or Macau, Portuguese Timor was established as a separate colony in 1896. In May 1974 the newly installed leftist government in Portugal announced that it would free all of its colonies. Arrangements for East Timor, however, were interrupted by an Indonesian-backed coup in August 1975. In the ensuing conflict, the forces of the Revolutionary Front of Independent East Timor (Fretilin) briefly gained control of the capital, Dili, and declared independence on Nov. 28, before being crushed by a full-scale Indonesian invasion on Dec. 7. Thereafter Indonesia ruled East Timor as its 27th province against a background of continued conflict that led to heavy loss of life. Following the collapse of the Suharto regime in Indonesia in May 1998, the new Indonesian government allowed a referendum in East Timor in August 1999 which resulted in a 78.5% majority in favour of independence. The result precipitated a violent counter-attack by pro-Indonesian militias, with support from within the Indonesian military, followed by the despatch of a UN international intervention force and the creation of a UN interim administration. This paved the way to the election in August 2001 of a Constituent Assembly (in which Fretilin emerged as the leading force) and achievement of independence in May 2002.

About 70% of the population is engaged in subsistence agriculture. East Timor's modern economic infrastructure suffered severe damage in 1999, with widespread damage done by Indonesian militias as they withdrew, and there has since been an international reconstruction programme.

GDP (purchasing power parity) $440m (2001 est.); GDP per capita (purchasing power parity) $500 (2001 est.).

2 Trade Unionism

Section 52 of the Constitution defines the right of every worker to join professional associations or trade unions, which shall be independent of employers and government. However, reflecting the preponderance of subsistence and informal work and the recent creation of the country, there has thus far only been a small-scale development of trade unions, this including the founding of a trade union centre, the Timor Lorosae Trade Union Confederation, in 2001. A rival National Syndicate Union, claiming to have 1,000 members, was launched in March 2003. National labour relations machinery is in only an embryonic state. Collective bargaining is not generally practiced although some agreements are in force. Occasional strikes have been reported since independence and the right to strike is constitutionally guaranteed, subject to the maintenance of essential services. East Timor joined the ILO in August 2003 but by the end of 2004 had yet to ratify any of its conventions.

3 Trade Union Centre

Timor Lorosae Trade Union Confederation (TLTUC)
Konfederasaun Sindicatu Timor Lorosa'e (KSTL)
East Timor Trade Union Confederation
Leadership. Jose Conceicao da Costa (president); Rigoberto Monteiro (acting general secretary)
Membership. Claims 4,700 (2003)
E-mail. secretariat@tltuc.org
History and character. The TLTUC/KSTL was established in February 2001, during the period of UN administration, and has been developing with particular support from Australian trade unions, the ICFTU and ILO in training union officials. It is recognized by the ILO as the peak organization in East Timor. It embraces pre-existing unions for teachers and nurses and is expanding to other sectors – a small maritime and transport union being set up in 2003. It has been active in resolving numerous disputes. It maintains a position of political non-alignment.

Ecuador

Capital: Quito
Population: 13.21 m. (2004 est.)

1 Political and Economic Background

Ecuador has been a separate republic since 1830 and has had prolonged periods of political instability, with the military as a major factor in political life. This pattern continued in the 1990s. Successive governments proved unable to implement programmes backed by international funders involving privatization and structural reforms. In 1996 Abdal Bucaram Ortíz of the Ecuadorean Roldosist Party (PRE) was elected on a populist platform which had as its slogan, "vote for the madman, vote for the clown". In office, however, he attempted to press ahead with the previous government's austerity and privatization measures, leading to massive price rises and widespread protests led by unions and Indian groups (one-third of the country's population, and disproportionately the poorest, being highland Indians), organized as the Patriotic Front. He was also accused of embezzlement of government funds and amid mounting chaos was declared "mentally incapacitated" by Congress and deposed in February 1997. After a brief interlude with multiple claimants to the presidency, Congress voted in its Speaker to serve as President for an interim term of 18 months.

In July 1998 Jamil Mahuad of the centre-right Popular Democracy Party (DP) was elected President but his period in office was marked by a deepening political and economic crisis as he attempted to implement recovery measures while appeasing intense domestic opposition of the sort that had toppled Bucaram. During 1999, Ecuador, which owed $16 billion, defaulted on interest payments to its international creditors, who indicated that they would not provide further bail-outs without structural reform; banks collapsed and accounts were frozen; and hyper-inflation set in as there was run on the national currency, the sucre. There were repeated strikes and protests. On Jan. 6, 2000 Mahuad declared a state of emergency, following a week in which the sucre had lost 35% of its value, and ahead of a general strike planned for Jan. 15. On Jan. 9 he further announced the "dollarization" of the economy, i.e. that the sucre would be replaced by the US dollar as the national currency. On Jan. 18 thousands of Indians mobilized by the Confederation of Indian Nationalities of Ecuador (CONAIE), protesting against poverty, corruption and dollarization, occupied the Congress and other government buildings, and were joined by elements of the Army. On Jan. 21 Mahuad was ousted and replaced by a three-man junta comprising an army colonel, the CONAIE president and a former president of the Supreme Court, before the armed forces commander in turn dissolved the junta and secured the succession to the presidency of the Vice-President, Gustavo Noboa.

Noboa subsequently went ahead with plans for the replacement of the sucre by the dollar, Congress approving this in March. He also announced an increase in the minimum wage to help offset the impact of dollarization, but planned to press ahead with reforms of the labour market and the opening up of the oil, electricity and telecoms sectors to foreign investment. Extensive funding by international agencies was expected to help Ecuador deal with the impact of dollarization and cope with its economic crisis.

Presidential elections in October 2002 resulted in victory for Lucio Gutiérrez, who as an army colonel had played a central role in the ouster of President Mahuad in 2000. During his campaign he made significant promises to the Indian, social and labour movements. His first act as President was, however, to go to Washington to negotiate new austerity measures with the IMF. His promises of progressive labour reform have not yet materialized. After the first few months of his presidency, it became clear that he had formed alliances with the traditional political parties of the right; there was a consequent break with the social and labour movements that had helped bring him to power. Since the crisis of 1999-2000 the economy has stabilized, with inflation under greater control, and the country has benefited from increasing oil prices (oil accounting for 40% of export earnings). However, there are continuing problems of widespread under-employment and poverty with real incomes below 1990s levels.

GDP (purchasing power parity) $45.65bn. (2004 est.); GDP per capita (purchasing power parity) $3,300 (2004 est.).

2 Trade Unionism

Workers' associations developed during the 1920s, with the right to join trade unions recognized in the 1928 Constitution, and the three main trade union centres – CEDOC, CTE and CEOSL – were formed in 1938, 1944 and 1962 respectively. CEOSL is affiliated to the ICFTU, CEDOC to the WCL and the CTE to the WFTU. The centres are politically independent.

Notwithstanding their different international alignments, the different centres have a history of working together and have been a factor in blocking changes sought by successive governments to reduce budget deficits and dependence on foreign loans. In 1971 they set up a loose coordinating organization, the United Workers' Front (Frente Unitario de Trabajadores, FUT). In the 1990s FUT coordinated a series of general strikes to protest against government attempts at economic reform and austerity measures. The unions, in association with Indian groups and other organizations, were actively involved in the strikes and protests that led to the deposing of President Bucaram in February 1997.

The FUT called further strikes and protests through 1997–99. Some of these resulted in violence: five people were reported killed in clashes in a general strike in October 1998. In March and again in July 1999 President Mahuad declared a state of emergency in the face of strikes and protests demanding an end to plans to privatize state-owned telephone and electric companies, a moratorium on repayments on foreign debts, and unfreezing of bank accounts. Mahuad partly capitulated to these protests, but his announcement of plans to abandon the sucre and dollarize the economy led to his fall in a coup staged against the background of popular insurrection in January 2000.

Despite its general instability, Ecuador has not seen widespread death squad-type activity against trade unionists. However, in May 2002 several hundred armed men broke up a peaceful and legal strike at one of the country's largest banana plantations, Los Alamos, owned by the former presidential candidate, Alvaro Noboa.

Ecuador ratified ILO Convention No. 98 (Right to Organize and Collective Bargaining, 1949) in 1959 and No. 87 (Freedom of Association and Protection of the Right to Organize, 1948) in 1967. The labour code guarantees (private sector) workers the right to join trade unions of their own choosing. However, the majority of the workforce works on the land, in the informal economy, or in small enterprises, and only about 12% of workers, mainly in larger enterprises and the public sector, are in unions. While the majority of public servants are formally prohibited from setting up trade unions and from striking, in practice unions of such employees do exist, are dealt with by the government for collective bargaining purposes, and go on strike. The two largest individual unions are reported to be the teachers' union and the union of social security workers, both affiliated to the far-left Democratic Popular Movement (MPD, which won only three seats in the last elections to Congress in 2002). Unions are not legally permitted to participate in the activities of political or religious parties. In addition the right to bargain collectively is reserved exclusively to works' councils, and may not be asserted by federations or confederations.

In April 2002, Human Rights Watch comprehensively documented widespread use of child labour in Ecuador's banana plantations, as well as a range of significant obstacles to the freedom to organize trade unions and bargain collectively. This, together with the failure of the authorities to bring anybody to justice in the Los Alamos case, has led the US Trade Representative to threaten to withdraw trade benefits under the Andean Trade Preferences and Drug Enforcement Act. Labour rights issues have also featured in the early stages of negotiations of a Free Trade Agreement with the United States.

3 Trade Union Centres

Central Ecuatoriana de Organizaciones Clasistas (CEDOC)
Address. Calle Rio de Janeiro 407 y Juan Larrea, CP 3207, Quito
Phone. +593 2 231269
Fax. +593 2 528142
Leadership. Mecia Tatamuez (president); Bolívar Pozo Guerra (secretary-general)
History and character. The CEDOC was established in 1938, with the assistance of the Roman Catholic Church, as the Ecuadorean Confederation of Catholic Workers. It affiliated to the International Federation of Christian Trade Unions (IFCTU, the predecessor of the World Confederation of Labour, WCL) in 1952, and to the regional organization of the WCL, CLAT, on its formation in 1954. In 1972 the organization adopted its current name, reflecting the loosening of earlier ties with the Church. The CEDOC assists members by providing or organizing a range of services, including legal aid, social and cultural clubs, neighbourhood committees, cooperatives, credit unions, and local workers' education institutes. Its orientation is humanistic, and it has no political affiliation.
International affiliation. WCL

Confederación Ecuatoriana de Organizaciones Sindicales Libres (CEOSL)
Ecuador Confederation of Free Trade Union Organizations
Address. Casilla Postal 1373, Quito
Phone. +593 2 522 511
Fax. +593 2 500 836
E-mail. ceosl@hoy.net
Leadership. Jaime Arceniaga Aguirre (president); Guillermo Touma Gonzalez (general secretary)
History and character. CEOSL was founded in 1962 and is the largest centre in Ecuador. It participates in the United Workers' Command (FUT) grouping of national centres and was an active participant in successive strikes and other protests in the late 1990s that contributed to the toppling of two Presidents (see above). CEOSL former leader José Chávez was detained on Jan. 15, 2000, under the State of Emergency declared by President Mahuad, and accused of subversion for his role in the crisis engulfing in the country, but released on Jan. 19. CEOSL was active in resisting attempts to amend labour laws (Trole I, II, III) to the benefit of employers in 2001-2, and in 2003 presented a proposal to reform the law on subcontracted labour.
International affiliation. ICFTU

Confederación de Trabajadores del Ecuador (CTE)
Address. Calle 9 de Octubre 1248 y Marieta de Veintimila, Casilla Postal 17 01 4166 Quito
Fax. 593 2 580 747932
International affiliation. WFTU

Egypt

Capital: Cairo
Population: 76.12 m. (2004 est.)

1 Political and Economic Background

Egypt was declared a republic in 1953 and has since been ruled by a series of presidents with strong executive powers, currently Hosni Mubarak, who was re-elected unopposed to a fourth six-year term in September 1999. Mubarak's National Democratic Party (NDP) has won every election since it was set up in 1978.

The government has faced persistent problems with terrorist activity by Islamic fundamentalists (one faction of which assassinated Mubarak's predecessor as President, Anwar Sadat, in 1981) and emergency legislation in force since 1981 has restricted a range of civil liberties, with phases of mass arrests. There are an estimated 12,000 political detainees. Religious-based political parties are nominally banned but the fundamentalist Muslim Brotherhood is the main source of opposition to the government. Following elections in October 2000, however, 17 members of the Muslim Brotherhood were allowed to take seats in parliament for the first time in a decade, constituting the largest opposition bloc.

Large parts of the economy were nationalized in the 1950s and early 1960s and the public sector still accounted in the early 1980s for about three-quarters of industrial production. Key sectors of the economy remain under state control, and the private sector consists mainly of small employers. There is a large informal sector. In 1991 Egypt agreed a programme of far-reaching economic reforms with the IMF and the World Bank. According to their joint plan, Egypt was to make progress to a market economy, cut subsidies and control its budget deficits. Egypt also benefited from major debt relief, following the 1991 Gulf War, which saw the state's external debts reduced considerably.

Although the pace of structural reforms, including privatization, remained slow, impressive national economic growth in the later 1990s partially mitigated the rising unemployment rates of the early 1990s. The government also successfully brought rampant inflation under control although improved economic conditions, especially for the middle class, resulted in massive increases in imports. This phenomenon harmed prospects for domestic industrialization, as local industry cannot yet compete successfully with imported goods in terms of price or quality. The fundamental problem remains of the labour market absorbing a population that grows by about 1.3m. a year. Between 1980 and 2000, Egypt's population grew by 55%, adding another 24m. to the total figure. The vast majority of Egypt's 76m. people live on less than 6% of the land, around the Nile and its delta. Massive migration to the cities has exacerbated the housing shortage. The Toshka "mega-project" seeks to free up agricultural land in order to ease population density and unemployment in the delta, but needs ten years before it can yield discernible results.

Since 2000 Egypt has been in the grip of a serious recession. The *Middle East Times* reported in May 2004 that 800 factories had closed in the new industrial satellite cities; most workers still live below the poverty line; longed-for investment had dwindled; and the price of basic staples had shot up by between 33% and 109%. Meanwhile, only 10% of manufacturing output is exported. Commentators suggest that the labour force lacks know-how; training is limited, and too little attention is paid to improving product quality or global marketing.

To some extent, labour unions, like other civic institutions, suffer from the restrictions pursuant to Egypt's emergency laws. First instituted in 1967, these laws have been continually re-ratified and never rescinded. Egypt's government is still wary of a repeat of the bread riots of 1977, which at one stage seemed to threaten a revolution. Some trade unionists feel that they, together with human rights activists and liberals, have been caught in a dragnet occasioned by the state's attempt to quash militant Islamists. The extensive and popular though semi-illegal Muslim Brotherhood is said to operate through institutions, including labour unions and professional associations.

In recent years the Egyptian government has begun to address the problem of child labour. In March 1996, Parliament adopted a new "Comprehensive Child Law" drafted by the National Council for Childhood and Motherhood, which raised the minimum employment age from 12 to 14 years. Egypt signed the 1997 Oslo Action Plan, calling for the immediate removal of children from hazardous occupations and the eventual elimination of child labour.

GDP (purchasing power parity) $295.2bn. (2004 est.); GDP per capita (purchasing power parity) $4,000 (2004 est.).

2 Trade Unionism

The first trade union appeared in 1899 and thereafter unions tended to develop in association with contending political factions. Legal recognition was given to trade unions in 1942. After its creation from the merger of various Communist factions in 1947, the Democratic Movement for National Liberation (DMNL, also known as Haditu) was especially active in union affairs. Haditu inspired a wave of strikes in early 1952, but chose to suspend these when nationalists in the Egyptian military overthrew the monarchy in July that year. Egyptian Communists initially backed the new rulers, the so-called Free Officers; as orthodox Stalinists, they accepted that a nationalist revolution should precede a socialist one. However, in January 1953 Egypt's government began smashing Haditu party structures and imprisoning Haditu members, including affiliated unionists.

An Egyptian Trade Union Federation (ETUF) was established under President Gamal Abdul Nasser in 1957 as a centre for all existing unions. Also in 1957 Egypt ratified ILO Convention No. 87 (Freedom of Association and Protection of the Right to Organize 1948), having ratified Convention No. 98 (Right to Organize and Collective Bargaining, 1949) in 1954. In principle, most workers in both the public and private sectors may join unions. However, the main membership of unions is in the public sector. In 1995, nearly 30 percent of the non-agricultural labour force was unionized.

While perhaps the largest trade union centre in the Arab world, ETUF is a legally prescribed monopoly single trade union structure. All unions are required to belong to it – a stipulation that the ILO has warned Egypt infringes on workers' rights to freedom of association – and there is close integration between ETUF and the ruling party. The government has claimed that the single-trade-union structure reflects the historical unity of the Egyptian trade union movement. At the September 2003 conference of the ruling NDP, a package of policies was adopted that was designed to ease restrictions on parties and trade unions, entitled "New Thinking: the Rights of the Citizen".

Collective bargaining is permitted in the private sector, but unions there are weak and the scale of enterprises mostly small. Unions may negotiate collective bargaining contracts in the public enterprises, but there is no obligation on the employers' side to negotiate and in practice wages and conditions are generally set administratively. Under the system inherited from Nasser, public sector workers have traditionally enjoyed considerable job security. Despite moves towards privatization, the public sector remains Egypt's largest employer.

Strikes are regarded as a form of disorder, not a contractual dispute, and hence have been considered illegal. (At least this was the case until the passage in 2003 of a new labour law – see below). In practice the ETUF prefers to resolve disputes through the courts rather than by industrial action. However during the early 1970s, during the early rule of President Sadat, there were many, often Communist-inspired, wildcat strikes against government economic policy and perceived injustices against workers. More wildcat strikes (usually short-lived and sometimes broken up by the security forces) took place in the late 1990s over issues such as privatization, cuts in wages and benefits at loss-making state enterprises, failure to pay annual bonuses, and compulsory early retirement. In 1999 alone there were 164 separate labour protests. Nearly all these strikes were in the public sector or at privatized state enterprises. The authorities remain wary of labour protests. On May Day 2004, for instance, police broke up a demonstration in Cairo where trade unionists demanded a 40% wage increase.

General economic and social changes have also had a major impact on unions. In recent years privatization and factory liquidations have drastically reduced the number of public business sector workers and, since almost all trade union members belong to the public business sector, this has led to a huge decline in the number of Egyptians registered as union members. According to one 2001 study, 82% of jobs added between 1988 and 1998 in the private non-agricultural sector in Egypt were not protected by a formal employment contract.

In 2003 the government passed a unified labour law after ten years of often arduous negotiation with concerned parties. According to an article in *Al Ahram* in January 2002 on the then-draft legislation, the measure departed from the hitherto existing status quo, of virtually lifelong guaranteed public sector employment combined with a ban on strikes. In its place came a new compromise: now there would be renewable fixed-term contracts (which benefited employers), balanced by a limited right to strike and the creation of a national council for setting minimum wage rates (which benefited workers). However, private sector firms which already employ very few trade unionists have, in practice, long enjoyed "flexibility" in hiring and firing workers (often by tacitly denying employees formal contracts). Such employers also feared an increase in strikes. Non-unionized workers in the private sector equally feared that the new law's guarantees of protection would be hard to enforce. By the same token, ETUF itself objected to aspects of the law. Meanwhile, owners, or potential owners, of newly privatized enterprises (including foreign investors) generally welcomed the legislation as it brought transparency and legal clarity to the labour market. However, commentators noted the law carries the risk of segmenting the labour market into a minority of highly protected workers, and a majority lacking any real (or enforceable) protection.

Increasingly labour activists have called for an open trade union system, and the more independently-minded have charged the ETUF with being a government puppet. In 2004 Kamal Abbas, head of the Centre for Trade Union Workers' Services, criticized the ineffectiveness of a committee headed by the ministry of planning, which is supposed to decide on the minimum wage, strike action and limited time contracts (consequent to the new labour law). Moreover, another committee, which is meant to consider labour complaints and smooth access of workers to the notoriously bureaucratic court system, also seldom meets.

In 2004 the small Nasserist Party, which is opposed to privatization, announced the creation of a Labour Front to ensure that workers press for their rights. However, Nasserists carry little power, given the nature of the party system in Egypt.

Formal sector non-agricultural employment is predominantly male. Women work on the land or in the informal sector. There is use of child labour in agriculture and in areas such as brick-making, carpet-making and textiles.

3 Trade Union Centre

Egyptian Trade Union Federation (ETUF)
Address. 90 El Galaa Street, Cairo
Membership. 2.5 million
Leadership. El-Sayed Rashid (chairman)
History and character. The ETUF (also referred to as the General Federation of Trade Unions – GFTU) was founded in 1957 as the unifying body for 1,300 separate unions (now reduced to 23). It is the sole permitted trade union centre, a position that it favours. It has close links with government and the ruling party. The federation's function is thus similar to that of other state-backed umbrella bodies, the Federation of Chambers of Commerce and the Federation of Egyptian Industries.

Some ETUF officials are members of the legislative People's National Assembly or the Consultative Council (Majlis ash-Shoura) and represent workers' interests in those forums. In November 2001 ETUF chairman El-Sayed Rashid was named deputy to the Speaker of the National Assembly, additional to his ETUF responsibilities. This followed his winning of a seat in Alexandria's Sidi Gaber constituency for the ruling National Democratic Party (NDP) in elections for a tranche of 150 parliamentary seats, held on Oct. 18, 2000. Given such demonstrated closeness between the ETUF and the NDP, it is not surprising that public disagreements between the federation and government are rare.

The ETUF is formally represented on a five-member committee on labour complaints, together with judicial and business representatives, but evidently the committee does not meet regularly.

The federation also participates vigorously in the national debate about privatization. In 1999 the ETUF – under then secretary general, Mohamed Morsi el-Amin – issued a major report on the application of Egypt's privatization programme, in accordance with World Bank and IMF guidelines. The report praised the Egyptian government for ameliorating the programme's impact on workers. It noted in particular the fact that "no worker had been dismissed", although many were offered early retirement and compensation. Evidently 19,000 workers were to be offered the chance to buy shares in 16 companies; and 250,000 workers had already benefited from compensation, thus far totalling LE 1.2 billion. The ETUF was uncomfortable with the idea that Egypt's new labour law (see above) might erode lifelong job security.

The ETUF is an active partner in improving regional labour links, within the Arab world, Mediterranean basin and the broader world. Many thousands of Egyptians work in other Arab countries and send remittances back to their families in Egypt – an important contribution to national GDP. ETUF's role regarding these expatriate workers is not clearcut. However, in February 1998 the federation protested in the strongest terms about the mass sacking and expulsion of Egyptians who worked for the Qatari government (as civil servants, clerks, military officers and teachers). The ETUF brought the case before the Arab Labour Organization and ILO, citing "arbitrary expulsions" and "gross violations of the rights of Egyptian workers".

In November 2001 ETUF chairman Rashid predicted more co-operation between Egypt and African countries over manpower. In June 2004 he called for better links with American labour, and the creation of a single "labour bloc" for energy syndicates in the Mediterranean. The ETUF often takes stances on issues not directly linked to manpower in Egypt. In May 2001 the Federation condemned Israel's "inhumane" bombing of Palestinian lands. In 2002 the ETUF spoke out against terrorism at home and abroad. It also called called for the protection of Palestinian children "against repressive Israeli practices", and highlighted circumstances which aggravate Palestinian unemployment. In October 2003 the ETUF issued a statement to all international organizations and regional trade unions decrying Israel's recent raids on Syrian territory.

Egyptian oil and chemical workers' unions (constituents of the ETUF) condemned "foreign threats" against Iraq, in January 2003. They also refused to normalise relations with the Israeli General Federation of Labour until "the realisation of a just and comprehensive peace in the region".

The ETUF has cordial links with the ILO, and in consonance with one of the ILO's long running campaigns, the federation held a national conference in early 2003 to "devise a national strategy to eliminate child labour in Egypt". The conference was organised under the auspices of the State President's wife, Suzanne Mubarak.

International affiliations. ICATU; OATUU.

El Salvador

Capital: San Salvador
Population: 6.59 m. (2004 est.)

1 Political and Economic Background

El Salvador became fully independent from Spain in 1839. Throughout its history, the military has tended to rule directly or be an important factor in political life. José Napoleón Duarte, the founder of the Christian Democratic Party (PDC), was elected President in 1972 but then forced to flee following a military coup. He returned in 1979, after the collapse of the military regime, and was appointed President by the civilian-military junta. During a prolonged period of unrest marked by violent guerrilla activity led by the Farabundo Martí National Liberation Front (FMLN) and activities by right-wing death squads, the PDC maintained its grip on power until it lost control of the legislature in elections in 1988. In 1989 the right-wing National Republican Alliance (ARENA) candidate Alfredo Cristiani was elected President to the great concern of the unions, which suffered assassinations of leaders and attacks on their premises throughout the year. Cristiani implemented a liberal economic programme and opened talks with the insurgent FMLN guerrillas, which had launched major military offensives in 1990. In January 1992, by which time more than 75,000 people had died, the government and the FMLN signed a peace agreement and the FMLN later than year reorganized itself as a political party. Cristiani was succeeded as President in 1994 by Armando Calderón Sol, and in 1999 by Francisco Flores, also both of ARENA. In March 2000 legislative elections resulted in the FMLN taking more votes than ARENA for the first time, although ARENA retained control of the National Assembly in coalition with other parties. In the March 2003 legislative elections the FMLN took 31 of the 84 seats in the Legislative Assembly, ahead of ARENA with 27. However, the ARENA candidate, Antonio Elías Saca, was victorious in the presidential election of March 2004, defeating by a wide margin the FMLN candidate, a hardline former secretary general of the Salvadorian Communist Party.

El Salvador's dominant economic activity is agriculture and its exports are dominated by coffee and textiles. Its trade deficits are offset by remittances from the large numbers of Salvadorans living abroad and by external aid. It has pursued privatization and lowered tariff barriers and eliminated capital controls. Despite the end of civil war, and 5% per annum average economic growth in the 1990s, the country remains poor, with great inequalities of wealth. It adopted the dollar as its currency at the start of 2001, the third Latin American country to do so, in an effort to build confidence with foreign investors.

GDP (purchasing power parity) $30.99bn. (2004 est.); GDP per capita (purchasing power parity) $4,800 (2004 est.).

2 Trade Unionism

The first trade union federation was formed in 1922 and a degree of trade union activity persisted throughout the period of military rule. Centres affiliated to the ICFTU, WCL and WFTU appeared from 1958–65. The history of El Salvador's unions is bound up with politics, with divisions on ideological lines, fluid structures and transient alliances and reorganizations. Coordinating centres appear from time to time. During the civil conflict of the 1980s there were sharp differences between the unions about government policy. The centres listed below are those affiliated to the ICFTU and WCL; there is now no WFTU affiliate.

El Salvador has ratified neither ILO Convention No. 87 (Freedom of Association and Protection of the Right to Organize, 1948) nor No. 98 (Right to Organize and Collective Bargaining, 1949). The personal security of trade unionists was for many years threatened by the prevalence of terrorism and political assassination. Perhaps 10,000 trade unionists lost their lives during the period of greatest unrest.

Unions and collective bargaining are lawful in the private sector and under the 1994 labour code trade union rights were extended to workers in agriculture. There are legal protections against discrimination based on union activities. Trade unions are nominally banned in most of the public sector, although workers may form associations that do, in practice, carry out collective bargaining and go on strike and public sector associations are among the most powerful unions. There has been a series of public sector strikes over privatization in recent years. There are about 150 unions and public employee associations. Together with campesino organizations these bodies represent around 300,000 workers. The labour code nominally bars political activities by trade unions although this is ignored in practice.

Legislation requires that unions may only call strike action after the collective agreement has expired, and then only in furtherance of the negotiation of a new agreement. Unions are also required to participate in negotiations, mediation and arbitration processes prior to being able to call a legal strike.

Particular concern has attached in recent years to conditions in the export processing zones (EPZs), where 90,000 (mostly young women) are employed. General labour laws in principle apply in the zones. In 1996, following international controversy over conditions, including the imposition of codes of conduct by some US retailers on their suppliers, legislation was adopted applying sanctions, such as loss of tax concessions, against EPZ companies breaking the labour laws. However, employers have ensured that unions have been largely excluded from the zones. There are no collective agreements in the EPZs.

3 Trade Union Centres

Central Autónoma de Trabajadores Salvadoreños (CATS)
Address. Av. Sierra Nevada, casa 830, Colonia Miramonte, San Salvador
Phone. +503 2610 404
Fax. +503 2604 617
E-mail. cats@terra.com.sv
Leadership. William Huezo (secretary general)
History and character. This influential centrist organization was formed in 1966 and was first known as UNOC and later as the Consejo Sindical Salvadoreño (CONSISAL) and then Central de Trabajadores Salvadoreños (CTS). The CTS as a Christian Democrat organization was a supporter of the 1980s government of President Duarte, but by 1988 was criticizing it for its failure to end the civil war and prosecute those responsible for political assassinations, and had joined the opposition alliance, the UNTS.
International affiliation. WCL

Central de Trabajadores Democráticos (CTD)
Address. 1a Avenida Norte y 19 calle Poniente #12, Residencial Viena, San Salvador.
Phone. +503 235 8043
Fax. +503 235 8043
E-mail. comutcd@netcomsa.com
History and character. The CTD was formed in the mid-1980s with the backing of the AFL-CIO in the United States.
International affiliation. ICFTU

Federación Nacional Sindical de Trabajadores Salvadoreños (FENASTRAS)
Address. 10a Ave. Norte, No. 120, San Salvador
Phone. +503 22 0141
Fax. +503 22 2849
Leadership. Juan José Huezo (general secretary)
Membership. 36,000
History and character. FENASTRAS was formed in 1975. It was a particular target for attacks, including killings and torture, during the 1980s civil war and its headquarters was bombed in October 1989. It was a member of the opposition UNTS alliance, founded in 1986, which developed links with the FMLN.
International affiliation. ICFTU

Equatorial Guinea

Capital: Malabo
Population: 523,100 (2004 est.)

1 Political and Economic Background

The former Spanish overseas provinces of Fernando Pó and Río Muni achieved autonomy in 1963 and independence in 1968. The current President, Brig.-Gen. Teodoro Obiang Nguema Mbasogo, seized power from the dictatorial regime of Francisco Macias Nguema (his uncle) in a coup in 1979. Ruling through a Supreme Military Council, the regime banned all political parties until 1987, when Obiang announced the formation of a single "party of government", the Democratic Party of Equatorial Guinea (PDGE). A new constitution, providing for the introduction of multi-party politics, was adopted by referendum in 1991. Obiang was first elected (unopposed) as President in 1989 and subsequently secured re-election in 1996 and 2002. Elections to the legislature held in April 2004 resulted in an overwhelming victory for the PDGE and allied parties.

Subsistence farming is the main livelihood for most workers, and since independence production of the main cash crops of cocoa and coffee has declined drastically because of mismanagement. However, the discovery and exploitation of large oil reserves have contributed to dramatic economic growth in recent years. A number of aid programmes sponsored by the World Bank and the IMF have been cut off since the mid-1990s because of corruption and mismanagement. No longer eligible for concessional financing because of large oil revenues, the government has been unsuccessfully trying to agree on a "shadow" fiscal management programme with the World Bank and IMF. Businesses, for the most part, are owned by government officials and their family members.

GDP (purchasing power parity) $1.27 billion (2002 est.); GDP per capita (purchasing power parity) $2,700 (2002 est.)

2 Trade Unionism

The government ratified several ILO core conventions in 2001, including Conventions No. 87 (Freedom of Association and Protection of the Right to Organize, 1948) and No. 98 (Right to Organize and Collective Bargaining, 1949), but has yet to adapt its legislation accordingly. Whilst the constitution provides for the right to organize unions, in practice union recognition is denied. The authorities have consistently refused to register the Equatorial Guinea Workers' Union (UST) which cannot operate openly. The authorities have also refused to legalize the public sector union, the Sindicato Independiente de Servicios (SIS). The oil industry is the major source of private sector formal employment and international oil companies recruit local workers through a government-controlled agency that screens applicants to prevent opponents of the regime from getting jobs.

Eritrea

Capital: Asmara
Population: 4.45 m. (2004 est.)

1 Political and Economic Background

Eritrea is a former Italian colony that established de facto independence from Ethiopia in 1991 after 30 years of insurgency and, after a referendum, declared independence in May 1993. The ruling People's Front for Democracy and Justice (PFDJ) was established in 1994 on the basis of the Eritrean People's Liberation Front (EPLF) which had led the struggle for independence. There have been no elections to the National Assembly, which is controlled by the PFDJ and elects the President (a post held since independence by Isayas Afewerki).

Eritrea is a poor country with little infrastructure and few skilled workers. Like the economies of many African nations, the economy is largely based on subsistence agriculture, with 80% of the population involved in farming and herding. A border war with Ethiopia in 1999-2000 caused serious damage to Eritrea's economy. Since the war ended, the government has maintained a firm grip on the economy, expanding the use of the military and party-owned businesses to push ahead with Eritrea's development agenda.

GDP (purchasing power parity) $1.27 billion (2002 est.); GDP per capita (purchasing power parity) $2,700 (2002 est.).

2 Trade Unionism

Eritrea ratified ILO Conventions No. 87 (Freedom of Association and Protection of the Right to Organize, 1948) and No. 98 (Right to Organize and Collective Bargaining, 1949) in 2000. Since securing independence, the government has said it favours a free and independent trade union movement and there are no legal restrictions on the formation of unions. However, some government policies restrict the formation of unions, including within the civil service, the military, the police, and other essential services.

Factory based unions were established in Eritrea in 1948. In 1952 the first congress was held of the National Union of Eritrean Workers for Independence (NUEWI) but this was speedily suppressed by the Ethiopian regime, which banned all unions in November 1953. Trade unions had an essentially political character during the struggle for independence, and sent delegates to the first congress of the EPLF in 1977. The founding congress of the National Union of Eritrean Workers (NUEW) was convened in liberated areas in 1979. Because of its integration in the liberation movement, the NUEW (now the National Confederation of Eritrean Workers) gained considerable influence in the ruling party. Many figures in the EPLF leadership were recruited from the ranks of the unions.

Under a new labour code ratified in November 2001, a tripartite board composed of workers, employers, and Ministry of Labour officials is required to resolve differences.

3 Trade Union Centres

National Confederation of Eritrean Workers (NCEW)
Address. PO Box 1188, Asmara
Phone.+291 111 6187
Fax. +291 1126 606
E-mail. ncew@eol.com.er
Membership. 25,000
History and character. The NCEW was founded (as the National Union of Eritrean Workers) in November 1979 in the liberated areas, but traced its origins to the National Union of Eritrean Workers for Independence set up in the 1950s. It held further congresses in 1983 and 1988 but during the war for independence essentially functioned as part of the EPLF. It was active in the Eritrean diaspora. The December 1992 congress – the first after independence – approved a labour code issued by the provisional government but expressed concern

that international financial interests were pushing the country into privatization. The NCEW is now reported to be independent of the government and the PFDJ. It comprises some 250 unions and five federations, the largest being the Textile, Leather, and Shoe Federation.
International affiliation. ICFTU

Estonia

Capital: Tallin
Population: 1.34m (2004 est.)

1 Political and Economic Background

Estonia, absorbed into the USSR in 1940, achieved its independence with the dissolution of the Soviet Union in 1991. Elections in March 2003 resulted in the formation of another centre-right coalition government. There is a multiplicity of small parties. There is a remaining 29% ethnic Russian population, many originally resettled from Russia under Soviet rule, who complain of discrimination. Estonia joined the European Union on May 1, 2004.

The immediate effect of the loss of former Soviet markets after 1991 was severe. In the two years 1991-93 the Russian share of Estonian exports fell from over 90 to 38 per cent, with Finland becoming the major trading partner. In August 1993 privatization began in earnest with the creation of the Privatization Agency and much of the former state sector has now been privatized. During the transition to a market economy many jobs were lost in large-scale industry, notably in textiles, engineering and oil shale processing but the services sector grew in importance. Currently, Estonia is experiencing high growth rates and surging foreign investment. However, on most social indicators Estonia compares poorly with other European countries, including other new Central and East European new member states, and income inequality is the greatest of all the new EU member states.

GDP (purchasing power parity) $17.35bn. (2004 est.); GDP per capita (purchasing power parity) $12,300 (2004 est.).

2 Trade Unionism

Estonian trade union density is currently the lowest of all the Baltic countries. The rate of unionization in Latvia is 25 per cent, and Lithuania claims 15 per cent; Estonian membership figures are perhaps 14 per cent, following a collapse in membership after independence. Membership figures have continued to decline sharply since independence. With 30 per cent of the national economy dependent upon production industries and major unrest in the public sector over wages and conditions, potential exists for union recruitment and activism, particularly following EU accession. However, currently both social dialogue and collective bargaining are weakly developed due to employer hostility, especially among incoming foreign investors, and high unemployment. Industrial relations are described by local experts as "employer dominated".

Trade unions in Estonia are mainly organized on a sectoral basis. The Confederation of Estonian Trade Unions (EAKL) was formed in April 1990 following the creation of a new independent trade union association, and since that time has been involved in bipartite and tripartite activities. It organizes employees in the private sector (industry, transport and services), as well as blue-collar workers in local authorities and health care. In September 1992 trade unions in the cultural, media, health and education spheres split from EAKL to form the Estonian Employees' Unions' Confederation (TALO). An additional small number of employees are organized in independent unions outside the two major confederations.

The 1992 Constitution provided for the right to join unions and Estonia ratified ILO Conventions No. 87 (Freedom of Association and Protection of the Right to Organize, 1948) and No. 98 (Right to Organize and Collective Bargaining, 1949) in 1994. Since June 2004, a Trade Unions Act has guaranteed the right to form trade unions and rights to information and consultation as well as defining relationships with central and local government. The Estonian minimum wage is currently EKR 10.95 (EUR 0.70) an hour. Legal deficiencies exist in equal employment legislation and are a cause of serious concern to the European Commission. A Collective Agreements Act of April 1993 establishes the main basis for bipartite and tripartite agreements. However, such acts as exist are rarely applied in practice.

On Dec. 4, 2003, TALO held a one-day strike to support its demands for pay increases for education and culture workers and to protest at the government's public sector wage policy. This was the first national strike since Estonia gained its independence in 1991, with only a limited number of warning strikes and other protest actions having previously been staged. In 2004 EAKL demanded a 20% wage increase for public sector employees and a lifting of the ban on public sector employees going on strike; EAKL trade unions organized a protest on April 15, 2004. Wages of workers at lower levels of the wage scale such as civil servants in care services, customs, police and prisons are below the national average. In addition, trade unions claim that Estonia is violating international labour standards as, according to Estonian legislation, public sector employees have no right to strike.

In the private sector, Scandinavian multinational media companies with the world's strongest trade unions at home are maintaining their Baltic subsidiaries as union-free zones. In 2004 journalists in Estonia agreed to build a works council in the Norwegian media corporation Schibsted, which has major holdings in Estonian newspapers and broadcasting. Further assistance is being given to Estonian trade unions in the retail service sector and construction industries by Scandinavian trade union organizations.

3 Trade Union Centres

Confederation of Estonian Trade Unions (EAKL)
Address. 4 Ravala Blvd, 10143 Tallinn
Phone. +372 66 12 383

Fax. +372 66 12 542
E-mail. eakl@eakl.ee
Leadership. Kadi Parnits
Membership. 47,500 (2002 est.)
International affiliation. ICFTU; ETUC

Estonian Employees' Unions' Confederation (TALO)
Address. Gonsiori 21, 10147 Tallinn
Phone. +372 64 19 800
E-mail. talo@online.ee
Leadership. Toivo Roosimaa
Membership. 37,000 (2002 est.)
International affiliation. ETUC

Ethiopia

Capital: Addis Ababa
Population: 67.85 m. (2004 est.)

1 Political and Economic Background

Emperor Haile Selassie was deposed in 1974 and Ethiopia became a socialist state under military rule; all major sectors of the economy rapidly entered state ownership, including the land, which hitherto had been held largely on a feudal basis. Under Lt.-Col. Mengistu Haile Mariam, head of state 1977–91, the (Marxist) Workers' Party of Ethiopia (WPE) became the country's sole political party. During the Mengistu era, Ethiopia received considerable economic assistance from the USSR and military help from Cuba in its efforts to combat secessionist movements in Eritrea, Tigre and the Ogaden. By early 1991, large areas were under rebel control and Eritrea had established de facto independence. Mengistu fled and the Ethiopian People's Revolutionary Democratic Front (EPRDF) took power under President Meles Zenawi. The EPRDF and its allies won overwhelming victories in elections in 1995 and 2000 – held amidst reports of widespread intimidation of opponents – with Meles Zenawi remaining Prime Minister.

Ethiopia's economy is largely agricultural and pastoral, and has suffered not only from the internal upheavals of the Eritrean war but also from prolonged periods of almost total drought and widespread famine; both of these factors have led to mass migrations (and also removals of population). International prices for commodity exports have been generally low (including for the crucial coffee crop), and the level of exports has been sharply reduced by climatic conditions, disruption and disease. Some 80% of the workforce is engaged in the agriculture sector. Much of the country's previous modest manufacturing capacity lay in Eritrea, now lost. The poverty of the country has been exacerbated by heavy expenditure on continuing border conflict with Eritrea, which escalated into full-scale war in 1998–2000, when tens of thousands died in the conflict. Real GDP declined in both 2003 and 2004.

GDP (purchasing power parity) $46.81bn. (2004 est.); GDP per capita (purchasing power parity) $700 (2004 est.).

2 Trade Unionism

The first clandestine trade unions were formed after 1947, and the basis of a trade union centre known as the Ethiopian Labour Union (ELU) was formed in 1954. After liberalization in 1962, the ELU was reorganized as the Confederation of Ethiopian Labour Unions (CELU), linked to the ICFTU. Ethiopia ratified ILO Conventions No. 87 (Freedom of Association and Protection of the Right to Organize, 1948) and No. 98 (Right to Organize and Collective Bargaining, 1949) in 1963.

Following the installation of a Marxist military regime, the CELU was abolished in 1975 and reformed in 1977 as the All-Ethiopian Trade Union (AETU) and in 1986 as the Ethiopian Trade Union (ETU). The role and tasks of the ETU were embodied in law. Unions were legally obliged to spread knowledge of the development plans of the government and Marxist–Leninist theories among the workers, and to implement the decisions and directives of the authorities. It affiliated to the communist-oriented WFTU. Following the fall of Mengistu, the seventh (1993) congress of the ETU renamed itself as the Confederation of Ethiopian Trade Unions (CETU) and proclaimed its complete independence. This began a deterioration of relations with the authorities and the government closed CETU down in 1994 and then restructured it in 1997.

There is a constitutional right for most workers to join unions and legal protection against discrimination by employers against union members. However, only a small proportion of the total workforce is employed in the formal waged economy and the total of union members is estimated at about 300,000. Teachers, public officials and medical personnel may not join trade unions (they may only join "associations") and there has been particular conflict in teaching. Unions may also not engage in political activity. The Ethiopian Teachers' Association (ETA) president, Dr. Taye Woldesemayat, was arrested in May 1996 and subsequently accused of conspiracy against government officials and inciting an armed uprising. He was detained and in June 1999 was sentenced to 15 years' imprisonment. Dr Woldesemayat was released on May 10, 2003, after the Supreme Court ruled that he had been charged under the wrong article of the constitution. In May 1997 police shot dead a member of the ETA executive council while seeking to arrest him on terrorism charges. The government has taken control of ETA offices, detained its officials, and transferred its assets to a faction supporting the government. There has also been government interference in the affairs of other unions, with instances of union leaders fleeing the country.

Collective bargaining exists in the small unionized sector. Collective bargaining agreements are conditional on their approval by the Ministry of Labour, which must verify that such agreements conform to the basic policies of the government. There is a legal right to strike, subject to lengthy strike notice and conciliation and arbitration procedures. However, there is reported to be scepticism among unions as to the willingness of the government and courts to respect and enforce the law. Strikes are prohibited in a range of essential services.

In November 2003 Labour Proclamation 42 was amended to permit multiple unions to operate in a single enterprise but, despite the changes to the main industrial law, the laws on industrial action and the ban on unionization in various sectors (such as teaching) continued to restrict freedom of association.

3 Trade Union Centre

Confederation of Ethiopian Trade Unions (CETU)
Membership. Formerly reported as 120,000 but believed to have declined because of government harassment.
History and character. The Confederation of Ethiopian Labour Unions (CELU) was founded in 1963 and developed with the assistance of western unions. Following the fall of Haile Selassie in 1974, the new Marxist military regime first purged the CELU leadership and then after sporadic strikes and disturbances dissolved CELU in November 1975 and in January 1977 set up a new All-Ethiopian Trade Union (AETU). AETU's first leader, Ato Tewodros Bekele, was killed a month later, one of many victims of Ethiopia's power struggles, and his successor Temesgen Madebo shared his fate later the same year.

At its third (1986) congress the AETU changed its name to the Ethiopian Trade Union (ETU). Following the change of regime, and in line with reform trends at that time evident in much of Africa, the seventh (1993) congress (which transformed the organization into the Confederation of Ethiopian Trade Unions) proclaimed the complete independence and autonomy of the trade unions. It adopted positions critical of the government's economic policies.

From this point the CETU began to find itself the subject of hostile state attention. During 1994 it was excluded from its head office, its registration cancelled, and its accounts were frozen. There were raids on its property and its leadership was eventually driven into exile in Kenya. The lock-out continued in defiance of rulings in the CETU's favour by the Court of Appeal.

In April 1997 CETU was restructured, reportedly with government involvement; its registration was restored and headquarters and bank accounts reopened. Its former president Dawi Ibrahim and two executive council members fled the country saying their lives were in danger.
International affiliation. WFTU

4 Other Trade union Organization

Ethiopian Teachers' Association (ETA)
Address. ETA is contactable via Education International (www.ei-ie.org)
History and character. ETA president Dr. Taye Woldesemayat was recently released from prison but the association has been a particular target for repression. The ETA offices in Addis Ababa have been closed by the police and bank accounts have been frozen.
Membership. (estimated) 95,000
Affiliation. Education International

Fiji

Population: 881,000 (2004 est.)
Capital: Suva

1 Political and Economic Background

Fiji became a fully independent member of the Commonwealth on independence from the UK in 1970. Its post-independence politics have been dominated by tensions between the indigenous (Melanesian-Polynesian) Fijian population, comprising 51% of the population, and the Indo–Fijians, 42% of the population. Traditionally, the Indo–Fijians have dominated the private business sector, while the indigenous population have dominated the government and armed forces.

From independence until April 1987, the Alliance Party, representing the indigenous population, was in power. A new government was then formed by parties drawing mainly on support from those of Indian descent. This precipitated military intervention led by the army commander, Sitiveni Rabuka, and power was restored to representatives of the indigenous population. In 1990 a new constitution was framed with the intention of giving indigenous Fijians a built-in majority in the legislature through reservation of seats on an ethnic basis.

Rabuka's Fijian Political Party (FPP) won the 1992 general election, the first since the 1987 coup, and he was re-elected in 1994 despite splits within his coalition. In 1997 a new constitution was adopted, based on the recommendations of the Reeves Commission, which ended the provisions of the 1990 constitution entrenching the legislative dominance of the indigenous population. This allowed Fiji to be re-admitted to the Commonwealth, of which it had ceased to be a member after the 1987 coup. In elections in May 1999, the ethnic Indian Fijian Labour Party (FLP), won 37 of the 71 seats in the House of Representatives, and its leader Mahendra Chaudhry became Prime Minister. On May 19, 2000, George Speight, a businessman, and his supporters seized the Parliament and took the Prime Minister and 30 MPs hostage. Martial law was declared on May 26 but the military showed no inclination to release the legislators, while military decrees were issued to remove Indo-Fijians from the public services. After 55 days Chaudhry and other remaining hostages were released from Parliament, but Chaudhry was deposed as Prime Minister by the military and an interim government appointed, headed by Laisenia Qarase as Prime Minister, that included individuals with links to the coup plotters. General elections in August–September 2001 resulted in formation of a coalition government led by Qarase's party, the National Unity Party, with Qarase continuing as Prime Minister. The new coalition was dominated by indigenous Fijians.

Agriculture dominates the Fijian economy, with sugar as the principal cash and export crop – about 70% of the workforce are engaged in commercial or subsistence agriculture. There is also a small manufacturing sector and a growing tourist industry, although this has been affected by political instability.

GDP (purchasing power parity) $5.01bn. (2004

est.); GDP per capita (purchasing power parity) $5,800 (2004 est.).

2 Trade Unionism

Fiji ratified ILO Convention No. 98 (Right to Organize and Collective Bargaining, 1949) in 1974 but did not ratify Convention No. 87 (Freedom of Association and Protection of the Right to Organize, 1948) until 2002.

Union activity developed following the Industrial Associations Ordinance of 1942, but was affected by racial divisions between Fijians, Indians and Europeans. When racially based unionism declined in the 1960s the Fiji Trades Union Congress (FTUC) emerged as the dominant central organization. Its main base of support remained in the ethnically Indian population, however. Other than for restrictions in the government sector, most workers enjoyed the right to form and join unions of their own choosing.

In 1985 the Fiji Labour Party (FLP) was created as a multi-racial party (although it drew most of its support from the Indian community) with the FTUC as the prime mover. After elections in April 1987 the FLP formed the government in alliance with the National Federation Party (NFP), but this was almost immediately overthrown in a military coup.

After the 1987 coup union rights were severely curtailed provoking international protests from ICFTU affiliates in Australia and New Zealand. The military regime opened negotiations with the ICFTU-affiliated FTUC and gave assurances that rights would soon be restored; Australian and New Zealand unions dropped a threatened air traffic ban, and an ICFTU delegation visited Fiji the following year. But unions continued to suffer legal adversity, detentions of leaders and an arson attack on the FTUC head office. In 1988 the then FTUC national secretary, Mahendra Chaudhry, was arrested and interrogated by police, accused of attempted arms shipments. A further ICFTU visit produced another report critical of the government's failure to recognize the FTUC or to re-establish the country's Tripartite Forum. Continued representations from the FTUC itself for re-establishment of formal industrial relations institutions were made without effect, and the government proceeded towards the establishment of racially based unions.

In 1992 Chaudhry was brought before a Fijian court, charged with holding dual trade union office, an offence against 1991 legislation which also banned industrial associations (formed mainly among indigenous Fijian workers) from participating in disputes and introduced mechanisms to facilitate the formation of employer-sponsored unions. The case against Chaudhry – who held office in two FTUC affiliates as well as his national post – was adjourned on technical grounds.

The 1997 constitution (formally in effect from July 27, 1998) eased restrictions on the unions and reversed legalized discrimination against Indo-Fijians. As a result of elections in May 1999, Chaudhry, as leader of the ethnic Indian Fijian Labour Party (FLP), became Prime Minister. However, Chaudhry was taken hostage in May 2000 and then deposed by the military (see above), and the 1997 constitution was overturned and a constitutional review commission set up dominated by indigenous Fijians.

Historically most workers have been generally free to join unions and an estimated 40%-50% of the formally employed work force is unionized, with heavy organization of the major foreign exchange earning sectors, sugar and tourism, as well as the public sector. There is a legal requirement on employers to recognize a union where it has recruited more than half the workforce. In practice unions are usually successful in preventing discrimination against workers for union activities, although the law does not require that workers dismissed for union activities must be reinstated. However, the unions have made little headway in the newer economic sectors such as the garment industry.

While some unions remain ethnically based, both Indo-Fijians and ethnic Fijians hold leadership roles, and the FTUC has also sought to emphasize its multi-ethnic base. However, unions have also been formed outside the FTUC fold, primarily recruiting the indigenous population. The FTUC has accused the government in office since 2001 of sponsoring breakaway union organizations, with a rival to the FTUC, the Fiji Islands Council of Trade Unions, being created in 2002.

The right to bargain collectively is recognized. Restrictions were imposed in the years after the 1987 coup, but were lifted after 1992. Most collective bargaining takes place at the enterprise level and employers are required to recognize a union if half the workforce are members of it. While national labour laws apply in the export processing zones, the unions have had little success in organizing workers or achieving collective contracts in the zones. Strikes are generally legal, subject to notice and ballot provisons and other than in the case of union recognition disputes, but industrial associations, to which many indigenous Fijians belong, may not strike. In addition, the Labour Minister may declare strikes illegal and in practice most strikes are declared illegal and referred to a Permanent Arbitrator to achieve a settlement while the workers return to work; most disputes are resolved under the auspices of the Permanent Arbitrator.

3 Trade Union Centre

Fiji Trades Union Congress (FTUC)
Address. 32 Des Voeux Road, PO Box 1418, Suva
Phone. +679 3315377
Fax. +679 3300306
E-mail. ftucl@is.com.fj
Leadership. Daniel Urai (president); Felix Anthony (national secretary)
History and character. The FTUC was founded in 1952 as the Fiji Industrial Workers' Congress, with sugar workers' unions its main affiliates. Under its present name from 1966, the FTUC steadily broadened its base among Fijian unions. It is the only Fijian trade union centre.

In 1985 it launched the Fiji Labour Party (FLP) to challenge government policy (the FTUC having previously been politically unaffiliated). Although the FLP was nominally separate, FTUC treasurer Robert

Kumar became FLP treasurer also; Mahendra Chaudhry, then FTUC assistant national secretary, became FLP assistant secretary-general. FTUC vice-president Krishna Dutt became the party's secretary-general and Public Service Association president, Timori Bavadra, its president. The FLP allied with the opposition National Federation Party (NFP), and in 1987 this coalition came to power. Bavadra became Prime Minister and senior FTUC officials also joined the government, but their success was brief for the government was overthrown after a month in a military coup led by Lt.-Gen. Sitiveni Rabuka.

Although civilian government was restored the FTUC operated thereafter for some years under severe constraint. Its offices were burned down and a number of union leaders were imprisoned. The FTUC still continued to function, however, criticizing restrictions on collective bargaining, deregulation, the creation of free trade zones, and the government objective of registering racially based unions.

In 1997 the FTUC warmly greeted the new constitution, which reversed legalized discrimination against Indo-Fijians and eased restrictions on unions. In May 1999, former leader of the FTUC and the then general secretary of the Fiji Public Service Association, Mahendra Chaudhry, became Prime Minister. Following the May 2000 seizure of Chaudhry and other parliamentarians by supporters of George Speight, the FTUC allied itself with the main employers' association, religious, community and other civic groups to try to find a solution that did not result in reversal of the gains of the 1997 constitution. FTUC national secretary Felix Anthony was briefly detained by the military. Following the replacement of Chaudhry as Prime Minister the FTUC called for the return of the 1997 constitution and condemned the establishment of a constitutional review commission dominated by indigenous Fijians and with a minority of Indo-Fijians allegedly motivated by "financial greed".

Since the restoration of civilian government (with Chaudhry now leading the opposition in Parliament) there have been strained relations between the government and the FTUC. The Labour Minister has accused the FTUC of displaying a "militant attitude" while the FTUC has charged the government with sponsoring the breakaway of unions now forming the Fiji Islands Council of Trade Unions.
International affiliations. ICFTU; CTUC

4 Other Trade Union Organization

Fiji Islands Council of Trade Unions (FICTU)
Address. 68 Knolly Street, Suva
Phone. +679 3303186
Leadership. Attar Singh (general secretary)
History and character. Established in August 2002 as a breakaway from and rival to the FTUC, apparently with government support. It attracted nine of the 35 unions in Fiji which were led by opponents of the Labour Party. However, although favoured by the government, it failed to dislodge majority support for the FTUC and the government has been obliged to continue consulting the FTUC on industrial relations matters.

Finland

Capital: Helsinki
Population: 5.21 m. (2004 est.)

1 Political and Economic Background

Finland became independent from Russia in 1917. For a quarter century from 1966 to 1991, the Finnish Social Democratic Party (SDP) led a series of centre-left governments. In 1991 a centre-right coalition came to office, headed by the Centre Party (KESK). In 1995, however, elections restored the SSDP's position and its leader Paavo Lipponenen became Prime Minister of a five-party "rainbow coalition" government also including conservative, liberal, left-wing and green parties. This coalition was confirmed in office as a result of elections in March 1999. In elections in March 2003 KESK regained its position as the largest party, again leading a coalition government. Finland joined the European Union in 1995.

Since World War II Finland's primarily rural economy has diversified into a wide range of industries and services that have greatly raised living standards. Its industries include wood, metal, engineering, telecommunications and electronics and exports contribute one-third of GDP. The collapse of the USSR, Finland's major export market, led to a period of major economic difficulties in the early 1990s. The centre-right government sought to improve Finland's competitiveness by austerity policies but drastic measures including currency devaluation and tough national agreements with the unions did not bring quick success. By the end of 1993, the country's longest-ever recession had seen GDP decline by around 15% and unemployment reached 20% the following year. There has been marked recovery since that point, with unemployment down to 10% by 1999 and 9% in 2004. In October 2004 rankings by the World Economic Forum put Finland in first place, ahead of the US and Sweden, in its annual "current competitiveness" league table which focuses on ability to compete in world markets and general business environment including government policies, infrastructure and skills. Finland was the only Scandinavian country to adopt the European single currency at its launch in January 1999.

GDP (purchasing power parity) $142.2bn. (2004 est.); GDP per capita (purchasing power parity) $27,400 (2004 est.).

2 Trade Unionism

The Congress of Trade Unions in Finland (SAJ) was formed by the SDDP in 1907 with 18 affiliates and 25,000 members. This Marxist-led organization was dissolved by the government in 1930 but reorganized the same year (purged of communist influence) as the Confederation of Finnish Trade Unions (SAK). Thereafter the unions were constrained by world economic depression, right-wing political influences and, finally, war. After 1945 they recovered but in 1959-60 split between the SAK and a new rival Finnish Trade Union Federation (SAJ). A decade later the SAJ and the

SAK reunited as the Central Organization of Finnish Trade Unions (also known as SAK); membership of the united centre rose from 560,000 to over one million by 1980.

Finland is one of the most highly unionized countries in the world, with around 80% of the working population in unions (which also have pensioners in their membership totals). There are three trade union centres, with a correlation between educational qualifications and affiliation to the different centres (as in other Scandinavian countries). SAK, with more than 1,060,000 members, is the largest organization and although its membership its diverse it represents in particular manual and semi-skilled workers and trades. The Finnish Confederation of Salaried Employees (STTK) represents primarily white-collar and technical employees and reports 643,000 members. Its membership doubled in the early 1990s with the collapse of the rival Confederation of Salaried Employees of Finland (TVK). AKAVA, with 436,000 members, is an organization representing mainly graduate professionals and highly educated staff. All three centres have larger memberships than in the 1980s (in the case of SAK, only marginally so) reflecting the continued strength of unions in Finland despite underlying changes such as the shift to services that have weakened unions in many countries. In Finland union membership rose even in the severe recession of the early 1990s.

The three centres have had a cooperation agreement between them since 1978 and all three are affiliated to the ICFTU. The SAK, STTK and AKAVA in particular cooperate in areas such as education, lobbying and solidarity work. Reflecting the importance of the social dimension of the European Union, the three centres have joint representation in Brussels.

Finland ratified ILO Convention No. 87 (Freedom of Association and Protection of the Right to Organize, 1948) in 1950 and Convention No. 98 (Right to Organize and Collective Bargaining, 1949) in 1951. The pattern of industrial relations is influenced by the institutional strength of the unions and a highly developed system of tripartism and national collective agreements. The foundation stone for this system is seen as having been laid at the height of the "winter war" with the Soviet Union in the so-called "January betrothal" of 1940, when as an expression of national unity the Central Organization of Finnish Employers (STK), with government support, accepted SAK as a negotiating partner. Since the 1960s, the union centres and employers' organizations (with government participation) have typically negotiated incomes policy agreements covering a wide range of aspects of working conditions including salaries and benefits, working hours, unemployment benefits, social security provisions, pensions and taxation. Framework agreements negotiated at the centre are mirrored in sectoral and enterprise agreements. Industrial action during the lifetime of these agreements has tended to be uncommon. Employers have recently been calling for a ban on sympathy strikes.

There is a close involvement of the unions in politics. 118 of the 200-member Parliament elected in March 2003 are union members. Of these 70 belong to AKAVA, 36 to SAK and 19 to the STTK. Union members are found in a range of political parties and there is no cross-party union lobby. In terms of representing union issues, those from SAK are typically the most active and those from AKAVA the least. The strongest ties are between SAK and the Social Democrats, although there is also a minority SAK involvement with the Left Alliance. Unions commonly provide financial or other support to political candidates.

3 Trade Union Centres

AKAVA (Confederation of Unions for Academic Professionals in Finland)
Address. Rautatieläisenkatu 6, FI-00520 Helsinki
Phone. +358 150 21
Fax. +358 9 1502 603
E-mail. arja.joivio@akava.fi
Website. www.akava.fi (in Finnish, Swedish and English)
Leadership. Risto Piekka (president)
Membership. 436,000 in 32 affiliates
History and character. AKAVA was founded in 1950 and represents employees with university-level, professional or other high-level training. It represents 80% of employees in the areas it serves. Half of the members work in the public sector, with slightly more than 50% being women. Its seeks to safeguard the economic and professional position of its members and is involved in research, policy negotiations and lobbying. It provides collective bargaining for its members, at national and regional levels, although a few member unions undertake their own collective bargaining.

AKAVA's affiliates function as both trade unions and professional associations, with an emphasis on education and training. AKAVA seeks to ensure that members enjoy a status and income level in keeping with their training, experience and special skills. It supports the preservation of the welfare state while emphasizing the need for taxation policy to provide an incentive to work and provide employment.

AKAVA is active at the international and especially the European level, with a special interest in EURO-CADRES, the European Council of Professional and Managerial Staff.
International affiliations. NFS; ETUC: EURO-CADRES: ICFTU; TUAC
Affiliates. AKAVA has 32 affiliates, the largest of which include:

1. Trade Union of Education in Finland
Address. Rautatieläisenkatu 6, FI-00520 Helsinki
Phone. +358 9 150 271
Fax. +358 9 145 821
Website. www.oaj.fi (Finnish, Swedish, English)
Membership. 113,000

2. Finnish Association of Graduate Engineers
Address. Ratavartijankatu 2, FI-00520 Helsinki
Phone. +358 9 229 121
Fax. +358 9 2291 2922
Website. www.tek.fi (Finnish, Swedish, English)
Membership. 60,000

3. Union of Professional Engineers in Finland
Address. Ratavartijankatu 2, FI-00520 Helsinki
Phone. +358 201 801 801
Fax. +358 201 801 880
Website. www.insinooriliitto.fi (Finnish, English)
Membership. 55,000

4. Finnish Association of Graduates in Economics and Business Administration
Address. Ratavartijankatu 2, FI-00520 Helsinki
Phone. +358 201 299 299
Fax. +358 9 299 299
Website. www.sefe.fi (Finnish, Swedish, English)
Membership. 41,000

Suomen Ammattiliittojen Keskusjärjestö (SAK ry) Central Organization of Finnish Trade Unions (SAK)
Postal address. PO Box 157, FI-00531 Helsinki
Address. Hakaniemenranta 1, Helsinki
Phone. +358 9 77 211
Fax. +358 9 772 1447
E-mail. sak@sak.fi
Website. www.sak.fi (in English, German, French, Spanish, Russian, Estonian, Polish, Swedish and Finnish)
Leadership. Lauri Ihalainen (president)
Membership. 1,062,167
History and character. The SAK traces its history back to 1907 (see above). Under Finland's system of centralized agreements on wages and conditions it has enjoyed substantial economic and political influence.

Although it is politically independent the SAK majority has traditionally been associated with the Social Democrats (SDP), with a minority supporting the Left Alliance. However, a growing number of members define themselves as politically non-aligned and the influence of political groups in local unions has dramatically diminished.

SAK negotiates framework agreements with the employers, these setting the context for sectoral negotiations involving its member unions. It formulates policy and acts as a lobby and advocate for labour to government and (increasingly) at EU level.

SAK has 24 affiliated unions in both private and public sectors. Some of these represent very small constituencies, such as the Finnish Social Democratic Journalists' Union with 340 members. The largest affiliated union is the 205,600-member Municipal Workers' Union. The second largest union was created in 2000 when four private sector service unions merged into Service Unions United. In general there is tendency to create larger unions representing several occupational groups. The Chemical Workers' Union and Textile and Garment Workers' Union were to merge during 2004. Also six public sector unions, including the Trade Union for the Municipal Sector (KTV), have stated their objective to form a joint union, to be launched at the beginning of 2006. The unions involved in the process represent almost a quarter of a million wage earners.

Local SAK organizations – of which there are some 150 – unite all the branches of different affiliates within particular localities, typically at the municipality level.

At international level SAK participates in development work and has a particular interest in the ex-Soviet Baltic states. SAK and the white-collar confederation STTK are members of SASK, the Trade Union Solidarity Centre of Finland, which provides development assistance to Third World countries.
International affiliations. ICFTU; ETUC; TUAC; NFS
Affiliates. The following SAK affiliates each have more than 30,000 members, listed in order of size (as of Jan. 1, 2003).

1. Municipal Workers' Union (KTV)
Address. PO Box 101, FI-00531 Helsinki
Phone. +358 9 77031
Fax. +358 9 770 3397
Website. www.ktv.fi (Finnish, Swedish, English)
Membership. 205,588

2. Service Unions United (PAM)
Address. PO Box 54, FI-00531 Helsinki
Phone. +358 9 77571
Fax. +358 9 701 1119
Website. www.pam.fi (Finnish, Swedish, English)
Membership. 200,690

3. Metalworkers' Union (Metalli)
Address. PO Box 107, FI-00531 Helsinki
Phone. +358 9 77071
Fax. +358 9 770 7277
Website. www.metalliliitto.fi (Finnish, Swedish, English)
Membership. 168,459

4. Construction Trade Union
Address. PO Box 307, FI-00531 Helsinki
Phone. +358 9 77021
Fax. +358 9 770 2241
Website. www.rakennusliitto.fi (Finnish, Swedish, English, Russian)
Membership. 80,870

5. Finnish Transport Workers' Union (AKT)
Address. PO Box 313, FI-00531 Helsinki
Phone. +358 9 613 110
Fax. +358 9 739 287
Website. www.akt.fi (Finnish, English)
Membership. 50,321

6. Paperworkers' Union
Address. PO Box 326, FI-00531 Helsinki
Phone. +358 9 70891
Fax. +358 9 701 2279
Website. www.paperiliitto.fi (in Finnish only)
Membership. 48,534

7. Wood and Allied Workers' Union (PUU)
Address. PO Box 318, FI-00531 Helsinki
Phone. +358 9 615 161
Fax. +358 9 753 2506
Website. www.puuliitto.fi (Finnish, Swedish, English)
Membership. 48,257

8. Finnish Foodstuff Workers' Union (SEL)
Address. PO Box 213, FI-00531 Helsinki

Phone. +358 9 393 881
Fax. +358 9 712 059
Website. www.selry.fi (Finnish, Swedish, English, German, French, Russian)
Membership. 39,735

9. Chemical Workers' Union (KEMIA)
Address. PO Box 324, FI-00531 Helsinki
Phone. +358 9 773 971
Fax. +358 9 7538 040
Website. www.kemianliitto.fi (in Finnish only)
Membership. 34,616

10. Finnish National Union of State Employees and Special Services (VAL)
Address. PO Box 321, FI-00531 Helsinki
Phone. +358 9 701 0120
Fax. +358 9 735 525
Website. www.valry.fi (Finnish, Swedish, English)
Membership. 34,210

11. Finnish Electrical Workers' Union
Address. PO Box 747, FI-33101 Tampere
Phone. +358 3 252 0111
Fax. +358 3 252 0210
Website. www.sahkoliitto.fi (Finnish, Swedish)
Membership. 31,294

STTK (Finnish Confederation of Salaried Employees)
Address. Pohjoisranta 4A, PO Box 248, FI-00171 Helsinki
Phone. +358 9 131 521
Fax. +358 9 652 367
E-mail. webmaster@sttk.fi
Website. www.sttk.fi (in Finnish, Swedish and English)
Membership. 643,000 in 21 affiliated unions
Leadership. Mikko Mäenpää (president)
History and character. The STTK is the second largest centre and the leading voice of salaried employees in Finland. The rival Confederation of Salaried Employees of Finland (TVK), which dated back to 1922 and was considered second in importance to the SAK, collapsed into bankruptcy in the early 1990s, resulting in STTK doubling its membership. Affiliated unions organize employees in a wide range of sectors: industry, private services, local and regional government and the state.

The rate of unionization of salaried employees has been increasing since the 1960s and now stands at 80%. Some 68% of STTK's members are women and the STTK emphasizes the concept of equal pay for work of equal value. STTK negotiates framework collective agreements and its member unions negotiate at sectoral level. STTK favours an activist government role in supporting employment and training and supports experiments with new models of sharing working time. STTK also promotes life long learning and educational issues in general.

In common with other Scandinavian unions, STTK participates in a wide range of international forums and especially at EU-level. STTK is also a member of SASK, the Trade Union Solidarity Centre of Finland.
International affiliations. ETUC; NFC TUAC; ICFTU

Affiliates. Largest affiliated unions include:

1. Union of Health and Social Care Services (TEHY)
Address. PO Box 10, FI-00060
Phone. +358 9 1552 700
Fax. +358 9 148 3038
Website. www.tehy.fi (Finnish; Swedish, English)
Membership. 125,000

2. Union of Salaried Employees (TU)
Address. PO Box 183, FI-00181 Helsinki
Phone. +358 9 172 731
Fax. +358 9 1727 3330
Website. www.toimihenkilounioni.fi (Finnish, Swedish, English)
Membership. 122,000

3. Pardia – Confederation of State Employees' Unions
Address. Pohjoisranta 4 A 24, FI-00170 Helsinki
Phone. +358 9 131 521
Fax. +358 9 1315 2315
Website. www.pardia.fi (Finnish only)
Membership. 80,000

4. Federation of Municipal Officers (KVL)
Address. Asemamiehenkatu 4, FI-00520 Helsinki
Phone. +358 9 155 231
Fax. +358 9 155 2333
Website. www.kvl.fi (Finnish; Swedish, English)
Membership. 71,000

5. Finnish Union of Practical Nurses (SuPer)
Address. Ratamestarinkatu 12, FI-00520 Helsinki
Phone. +358 9 2727 9171
Fax. +358 9 2727 9120
Website. www.superliitto.fi (Finnish; Swedish, English, Estonian)
Membership. 57,000

6. Financial Sector Union SUORA
Address. Ratamestarinkatu 12, FI-00181 Helsinki
Phone. +358 9 229 141
Fax. +358 9 2291 4300
Website. www.ammattiliittosuora.fi (Finnish, Swedish, English, German)
Membership. 35,000

France

Capital: Paris
Population: 60.42 m. (2004 est.)

1 Political and Economic Background

France has a parliamentary system in which the directly elected President, who is elected for a seven-year term (five years with effect from 2002), has considerable executive powers. In 1995, Jacques Chirac, of the conservative Rally for the Republic party, became President, bringing to an end the 14-year presidency of Socialist François Mitterand. In 1997 elections to the

National Assembly (lower House), conversely, the Socialist Party (PS) emerged as the largest single party, and left-leaning parties in an overall majority, ending a four-year period of centre-right governments and bringing a new period of "co-habitation" with a conservative President in office and a Socialist-led government. Among the major initiatives taken by the new Socialist-led government was the introduction of a 35-hour week, legislated for in 1998 and in force in companies of 20 or more employees from Feb. 1, 2000. The Socialist Party has abandoned its former commitment to nationalization and presents its position as bridging the gap between the relatively pro-free market "third way" of the incumbent British Labour government and the "social market orientation" of parties such as the German SPD. In 2002 Chirac was re-elected as President and the Union for a Presidential Majority (UMP), supporting Chirac, won a substantial victory in the elections to the National Assembly, taking 357 of the 577 seats, compared with 140 for the PS.

The economy is diverse and largely market-based. Despite a number of privatizations, the state continues to have majority ownership of companies in a range of key industries such as electricity, gas, aircraft manufacture, railways and telecommunications. There is a large public sector and one-quarter of all salaried employees work for the state. France has sluggish economic growth rates and relatively high structural unemployment, unemployment remaining at close to 10% in recent years after falling from a peak of 12.6% in 1997. A report commissioned by the French government and published in October 2004 noted that France's low growth rate relative to countries such as the UK and USA reflected a "work deficit" arising from under-employment of workers over 50 and unemployment among unskilled young people. France has substantial social provision and taxation (at 43.6% of GDP in 2004) and government spending remain relatively high – France failed in each year from 2002-04 to meet EU criteria that budget deficits should not exceed 3% of GDP. France is a member of the EU and joined the single European currency zone on its creation at the start of 1999.

GDP (purchasing power parity) $1.661 trillion (2004 est.); GDP per capita (purchasing power parity) $27,600 (2004 est.).

2 Trade Unionism

France ratified ILO Conventions No. 87 (Freedom of Association and Protection of the Right to Organize, 1948) and No. 98 (Right to Organize and Collective Bargaining, 1949) in 1951.

Trade union organizations were given legal recognition in 1884 and the oldest confederation still in existence, the Confédération Générale du Travail (CGT), was founded in 1895. The early CGT was strongly influenced by both revolutionary socialist and syndicalist ideas as well as by reformism. In 1919 unions influenced by social Catholicism founded the Confédération Française des Travailleurs Chrétiens (CFTC). The CGT was weakened in the inter-war period by the 1921 creation of the breakaway Confédération Générale du Travail Unitaire (CGTU), in which communists took control; the CGTU rejoined the CGT in 1936 but the majority of its adherents were expelled in 1939 following the Nazi-Soviet pact. Existing union centres were dissolved by the Vichy government under the Nazi occupation in 1940, but in 1943 the underground leaders of the CGT and CGTU agreed to the formation of a united centre. The CFTC, however, refused after the war to accept a merger with the CGT, which in turn was split again in 1947 by the formation of the CGT-Force Ouvrière (FO), which went on to join the anti-communist ICFTU. The CFTC in its turn developed into two distinct federations in 1964, a minority retaining the old name and the overwhelming majority reorganizing as the (secular) Confédération Française Démocratique du Travail (CFDT).

These four centres, together with the Confédération Générale des Cadres (CGC, now known as the CFE-CGC), were officially designated as "nationally representative" in 1966, this designation being favoured by the government as simplifying the process of dealing with the unions in a context where the largest communist-led CGT federation was generally hostile to signing any agreements. Unions affiliated to a recognized centre enjoyed the benefits of being able to conclude national-level collective bargaining agreements or, from 1968, to form an enterprise branch union without having to prove representative status in the workplace or industry concerned. However, this formula also tended to exacerbate the political fragmentation of the labour movement as it conflicted with the idea of locally well-rooted bargaining agents.

These same five centres have been officially regarded as "nationally representative" since the 1960s, although the picture has become more complex from the 1990s with the emergence of four other centres. France has not therefore had a single dominant trade union centre accepted as speaking for the organized labour movement. The two ICFTU affiliates, the CFDT and the CGT-FO, do not together represent a clear majority force in the labour movement in the way that the ICFTU affiliates do in most other Western nations. Also, like in Italy, the main lines of division have been based on ideology and, in some respects, religion, although this factor has declined noticeably since the 1980s. Only in the 1990s, with the collapse of Communism in Europe, has the antagonism between the traditionally orthodox Communist-led CGT and the politically heterogeneous but vehemently anti-Stalinist CGT-FO begun to recede. The CGT has tended to become much more pragmatic and more independent of the Communist Party, whose decline in membership and electoral support accelerated sharply in the 1990s. Looking for a different basis than anti-communism on which to construct its identity, the CGT-FO has turned to a higher level of mobilization in defence of public sector workers' conditions and private sector workers' wages.

The CFDT was closely associated with the Socialists into the mid-1980s, though recently it has taken a more neutral stance, ready to negotiate and sign unpopular agreements with both the French employers' association and with the government in the interests of trade union realism. The CFTC, which affiliates to the WCL, remains essentially religious-based in inspiration. Meanwhile there are now two major teacher union federations (the FEN and FSU) and two new general trade union centres (UNSA and Sud–Group of Ten) affiliating independent unions that do not wish to affiliate to the major five centres. Competition between all these centres is still considerable, and they commonly still take positions and sign agreements in opposition to each other, in fluctuating coalitions. This appearance of union disunity is one of the reasons commonly given for workers not joining the unions, even though strike calls are commonly supported by far wider numbers.

Every five years (most recently in December 2002) all private sector employees (and, separately, all private employers) may take part in the election of more than 14,000 councillors to local industrial tribunals or conciliation boards (conseils de prud'hommes), with the responsibility of adjudicating individual employment disputes. The prud'homme tribunals are organized into a series of sections for industry, commerce, agriculture, miscellaneous and management. The unions compete actively for support in these elections because they are widely interpreted as measuring support for the different confederations and also because they offer an opportunity to raise their profile in areas of union weakness such as small business and service industries.

The 2002 elections confirmed that the CGT, with one-third of the votes, remained the leading force as it had been consistently since 1979 when the industrial tribunal electoral system was established. However, since 1979 the CGT share of the vote had declined from 42.4% to 32.1%, with all the other centres making gains at its expense. The CGT is based especially in traditional industries and in the public sector and is weakest among management. The CFDT had been making considerable gains among managers, and in 1997 beat the specialist management confederation the CFE-CGC into second place in the vote for the management staffs electoral college. However in 2002, following its endorsement of the employers' unemployment insurance reforms, the CFDT's overall share of the vote stagnated (at 25.2%). In that year too, the new trade union centres, UNSA (5.0%) and Sud–G10 (1.5%), established a real presence for the first time, confirming the enduring fragmentation of the French trade union movement. The turnout among employees in industrial tribunal elections has been falling progressively since 1979 (to 32.7% in 2002).

All enterprises of more than 50 employees are legally required to have works councils (comités d'enterprise), with responsibilities predominantly in the welfare, health and safety, and social areas. The CFDT, in contrast to the industrial tribunal elections, now holds a roughly equal share to the CGT in works council elections. Between 1981 and 1991 the CGT's share of the vote in the biennial works council elections fell from 32% to 20.4%, but then stabilized. The results of works council elections also illustrate the significance of representation by workers who stand on non-union affiliated slates; this figure rose to 30.9% in 1991, but through the years of growing social conflict in the 1990s fell back to its mid-1980s level by 2000-2001. Just under two-thirds of those entitled to vote cast their votes for their comités d'entreprise delegates.

Results of the 2000 and 2001 biennial elections to comités d'enterprise (% of votes):

	2000	2001
CFDT	22.9	22.8
CGT	24.4	22.6
CGT-FO	12.4	13.1
CFE-GCC	5.7	6.1
CFTC	5.3	6.0
Other unions	7.4	6.5
Non-unionized	21.9	23.0

Union density, having stood at 24% in 1975, fell to only 9% by the end of the 1990s, the lowest in the European Union. In the private sector only 6% of employees are paid-up union members, and trade unionism has virtually no presence in wide swathes of the economy, especially small and medium sized enterprises and the expanding service sector. Not only are the relatively highly politicized and disunited unions one factor for these low levels, but employer hostility to unions and high levels of victimization of union activitists are another. With their strength concentrated in the public sector and in state-owned enterprises, the unions have been strongly resistant to privatization, and have enjoyed considerable success in this. The precipitous fall in union membership from the late 1970s ended in the early 1990s. However, France's economy is being driven forward by an expansion of "new economy" IT-related innovation, the service sector, and the growth of informal working patterns, none of which are helping the trade unions. The two largest centres, the CFDT and CGT, have a combined membership (1.41 million) which is only half that of the biggest individual German union, IG Metall. Membership slumped across the board from the late 1970s as old economy jobs were lost and unemployment increased and the unions failed to compensate by building their position in newer areas of the economy.

The union movement in France has nonetheless an influence greater than membership statistics alone might suggest. This is because although most workers do not join unions, most nonetheless support them to a greater or lesser extent, as shown in the elections for Comités d'entreprise and other representative bodies. Strike action, although no longer as frequent as in the 1970s, occurs on a wider scale than in most leading industrialized countries and is intensified in its effects by occurring particularly in critical public services such as public transport, education and health care, where the unions are strongest. While the other centres are often characterized as "pragmatic" and "moderate" compared with the CGT, the CGT-FO and CFDT have also involved themselves in strikes and demonstrations with some frequency. Street demonstrations and one-day strikes as means of placing political pressure on politicians are an accepted tactic legitimated by their regular occurrence and their occasional success. In 1995 President Chirac's first right-wing prime minister was thus forced to withdraw his pension reform proposals in the face of a growing transport strike that had the support of two-thirds of French people polled.

The French industrial relations system has tended to buttress the position of the trade union centres. The unions are generally weak at the enterprise level, and indeed the main employers' organization (Mouvement des enterprises de France, MEDEF, until 1998 known as the Conseil National du Patronat Français, CNPF) is campaigning for collective bargaining to be devolved to this level in part for that very reason. The system of devolved bargaining, which many French unions disparage as the "Anglo-Saxon system", depends on strong workplace unionism and to some extent on the willingness of employers to recognize unions as negotiating partners; it also runs independently of direct government intervention. The French system tends to rely on the state to drive forward collective bargaining and the whole process of social partnership.

This pattern is reinforced by the system whereby trade unions are designated as "representative" and therefore empowered to negotiate on behalf of the workers in an industry, without needing in practice to demonstrate representativeness in any objective way. Notionally, representative status is accorded on the basis of criteria including membership, independence from employers, dues paid, experience and stability and even patriotism in World War II. However, the same five centres (CGT, CGT-FO, CFDT, CFTC, CFE-CGC) have been the only ones recognized as nationally representative since the 1960s. While these undoubtedly remain the major centres, their representativeness relative to the workforce as a whole, including those not in unions, is clearly questionable. Unions affiliated to any of these centres are automatically accorded recognition as representative at sectoral or enterprise level, regardless of their real strength, and this gives them a range of benefits including allowing them to negotiate sector-level and enterprise agreements, organize work place elections where their candidates have a monopoly in the first round of voting, and appoint union delegates in companies. The system has the effect of artificially strengthening the hand of the unions, by giving them a role in enterprises even when they have little real membership, while also discriminating against independent unions. In collective bargaining the "single signature" rule means that one or more "representative" union may in principle bind all workers in a particular sector or company to an agreement even if it or they only represents a minority of the workforce. In 2003 despite widespread strike action national union confederations representing a minority of the workforce were thus able to give the force of law to a national pension reform agreed with the employers.

The new right-wing government elected in 2002 has been steadily implementing measures aimed at freeing the employers from many of the labour market restraints they have increasingly complained about. These include repealing the legal extension of the 35-hour week to workers who work in firms with less than 20 employees and requiring public sector workers to work two-and-a half more years to achieve a full pension. It is also testing the water for a possible reform of the representative status of trade unions. The small confederations, UNSA and the Groupe des Dix, which do not enjoy representative status, have called for changes to the rules. The biggest confederations, the CGT and the CFDT, have indicated a willingness to show flexibility on the issue. However, the weaker confederations which do enjoy representative status, the CGT-FO, CFTC and CFE-CGC, have rejected any changes to the rules for the time being.

Although the 1990s saw the increasing presence of trade union delegates in larger firms, in most small and medium-sized companies they do not exist at all. In 1995, the CFDT, CFE-CGC and CFTC (but not the CGT and CGT-FO) reached agreement with MEDEF to introduce a system of "mandating". The agreement was renewed in 1999. Under this (where a sectoral agreement to this effect exists) a union may mandate employees to conclude collective agreements, or elected staff representatives may reach agreements, subject to approval by sectoral union-employer committee. The move was viewed with suspicion by the CGT and FO as eroding the monopoly position of the unions in bargaining, while its adherents saw it as a means of extending collective bargaining mechanisms into a wider range of work places. The pattern of early sectoral agreements was that these were introduced mainly in agriculture and service areas with many small employers, while the CFDT and CFTC were most involved in mandating (although both the CGT and FO, despite not signing the inter-sectoral agreement, participated to some degree). However, actual impact at work place level was modest, partly because of the opposition of many employers. The 1998 legislation on the 35-hour week also made it possible for mandating to take place without a prior sectoral agreement, but only in respect of negotiation of working hours. All the centres, except the small CFTC, require that a candidate for mandating must already be a member of the union. However, as in collective bargaining generally, the application of mandating does not embody any clear criteria of representativeness at the work place level.

The small size of their memberships has also created issues in terms of the financing of unions because membership dues are insufficient to finance operations and the other sources of financing are often not transparent. Among the practices that were the subject of government and newspaper reports and public debate in 1999–2000 were the payment of union officers through the payroll of publicly funded social welfare agencies and pension funds jointly managed by unions and employers. In January 2000 the newspaper *Le Monde*, citing a confidential government watchdog report, said that in 1995-98 the five nationally representative unions received (apparently with the approval of MEDEF) more than 34 million francs in salaries for union officials from the CRI compulsory complementary pension fund, which they jointly administer with the employers. In response to criticism the CGT said that reform of the system was needed but that "the social functions fulfilled by the unions justify the existence of a transparent and fair system of public financial support in parallel to funding through union member dues". All the main union centres acknowledge that they cannot function without funding beyond that provided by union dues, but in public statements have begun to recognize the need for more transparency in this. The CFE-CGC has called for a system of direct state funding based on election results. In contrast, reflecting its historical antagonism to statist involvement in union affairs, the CGT-FO opposes public funding of unions as weakening the independence of the unions in respect of the state. In some rare cases, the unions as part of collective agreements have negotiated forms of additional funding from employers as a contribution to "social dialogue". Thus an agreement in June 2000 between Renault and four of the five centres provided for the company to give funding to all unions achieving at least 5% of the vote in works council elections.

Collective bargaining at the end of the 1990s and into 2000 was dominated by the issue of working hours, job creation and job flexibility, within the context of the 35-hour week legislation. In some sectors, such as banking, resolution of these issues was accompanied by industrial action. Pay restraint characterized much bargaining in the late 1990s, in part influenced by France's relatively high and persistent unemployment, and also by the focus on working hours and job creation engendered by the 35-hour legislation. However, after peaking in 1997, unemployment decreased between then and 2002 and skill shortages developed in some areas, leading to increasing pay demands. Strikes remain a feature of French industrial relations, with huge strike waves in 1995 and 2003 separated by a period of higher conflict than during the 1980s.

France has a range of institutions in which the unions are represented. When after the Second World War the social protection institutions managing social security funds (for health, pensions and family allowances), supplementary pension funds and (in the late 1950s) unemployment insurance were set up, they were to be jointly managed by those who paid into them – the employers and the representative union centres. This largely remains the case today, with the chair of each of the institutions rotating between the employers and the unions. However, lack of agreement between unions and the national employers' associations about the size and division of contributions has led to regular deficits that have been increasingly funded by the state through a generalised social insurance tax. The major employers' association, the MEDEF, who regret the legitimacy union participation endows the very small trade union movement, pulled out of the social insurance system and threatened to pull out of the other systems in 2000 and 2001 to force the unions to make concessions in negotiations for a a "new social constitution" that is intended to update the role of the social partners in an era where the unions are much weaker than they were between 1945 and 1950 when the core system was established. In an attempt to become the privileged partner of the MEDEF and of the new right-wing government from 2002, the CFDT has strongly associated itself with this call and with trying to modernize the whole social policy area. This policy has interrupted what many believed would be a natural convergence between the CFDT and CGT as the latter adapted to a more realistic and pragmatic role in the aftermath of establishing its independence from the Communist Party. In May 2003 the CFDT's agreement to sign up to the government's project harmonizing downwards pension conditions between the public and private sector is generally credited with having led to the defeat of what up till that point had been a united union protest strike movement.

3 Trade Union Centres

Confédération Française Démocratique du Travail (CFDT)
French Democratic Confederation of Labour
Address. 47–49 avenue Simon Bolivar, 75950 Paris Cedex 19
Phone. +33 1 42 03 80 00
Fax. +33 1 42 03 81 44
E-mail. international@cfdt.fr
Website. www.cfdt.fr (French only)
Leadership. François Chérèque (secretary-general)
Membership. 889,160 (includes retired members)
History and character. The CFDT was formed in 1964 by the majority faction of the Confédération Française des Travailleurs Chrétiens (CFTC), the minority retaining the previous name (for origins of the rift, see entry for CFTC). The founders of the CFDT sought to restrict the religious influence within the federation and to reshape it as a democratic socialist centre. It played a significant role in the industrial unrest of 1968, leading to a period of greater politicization. After 1978 however there came a period (under the leadership of Edmond Maire) of "resyndicalization" – i.e. emphasizing closely defined trade union issues – with the emphasis on union adaptation to economic change. The CFDT joined the ICFTU in 1979. Under Jean Kaspar, Maire's successor as secretary-general, the CFDT sought to unite all centres except the CGT. In 1992 Nicole Notat, former national secretary, became the CFDT's first woman leader. She was succeeded by François Chérèque in May 2002.

The CFDT had a membership of close to 1 million in 1980 but then suffered considerable losses of members in the 1980s, as was true of other confederations. However, it says that after 10 years of renewed growth in the 1990s it reached just under 900,000 in the early 2000s, before losing a few tens of thousands in protest against the continuation of its "new realism" policies. It came second to the CGT in industrial tribunal elections in 2003 but has about the same share of the vote in works council elections with a reported membership slightly higher than that of the CGT.

The CFDT emphasizes the importance of participation of its members in the democratic process; favours constructive dialogue with government and employers; seeks to combat social exclusion; and supports a trade unionism based firmly in the workplace. It emphasizes its independence of the state, the churches, and of political parties. The CFDT was closely associated with the Socialist Party until 1988, after which it abandoned a reference to socialism in its statutes, and in the 2002 elections it did not officially endorse any party. Its focus since the end of the 1970s on achieving negotiated compromise settlements made it more attractive to the employers than the traditionally more militant CGT and the protest-oriented CGT-FO.

The CFDT saw a number of the left-wing activists who had joined in the 1960s and 1970s, when the CFDT was viewed as to the left of the CGT, leave in the 1990s. Widespread strike action in public services against proposed social security reforms in December 1995 saw the CFDT divided, with a minority actively supporting the strikes. This minority claimed it was the inheritor of an earlier tradition, prevalent in the 1970s, emphasizing broad political objectives and the achievement of socialism. The minority identified with the social movements that took place in France under the Jospin government of 1997-2002, while the majority did not. Some dissidents joined the independent union Solidaires, Unitaires et Démocratiques (SUD) created by a group of expelled members in 1988. More members quit the CFDT in 2003 after it endorsed the government's proposals to increase the number of years workers would have to work in order to qualify for a full pension.

The CFDT has improved its relations with the CGT, as the latter established its independence of the Communist Party. Thus it supported the affiliation of the CGT to the European Trade Union Confederation. But relations remain difficult as the CGT has benefited from the adhesion of some former CFDT members.

The CFDT, as one of the five confederations designated as nationally representative, benefits from the privileges such status confers, including the right for its affiliated unions to enter into collective bargaining agreements with a presumption that they are representative regardless of their actual membership in a particular sector or enterprise. However, the CFDT has taken the initiative with the CGT (and in so doing attracted the opposition of the other centres) in arguing that reform is needed to improve the legitimacy of the unions in view of their low membership. The CFDT has called for the system to be revised so that "representativeness" would be more objectively determined at work place level by ballots. It also argues that the current system means that employers can usually find a minority union to sign an agreement, however unsatisfactory it is to the majority, and this is then binding on all.

In response to public controversy over the extent of funding of unions from the resources of jointly-managed social funds and other non-union sources, in July 2000 the CFDT disclosed that of its 220 million franc budget in 1999, 159 million came from the CFDT's own resources, of which 104 million was membership dues from its affiliated unions.

The CFDT structure comprises 1,500 unions in the private and public sector; 18 professional federations and confederal unions; and 22 regional unions comprising 95 departmental unions or similar. The professional federations, grouping unions in the same sector of the economy, provide co-ordination to collective bargaining; the inter-professional regional unions serve especially to support solidarity among workers and combat social exclusion.

The Institut Belleville is the CFDT's organ for international trade union cooperation.

International affiliations. ICFTU; ETUC; TUAC. The CFDT left the WCL in 1978 and then joined the ICFTU.

Affiliates. The 18 CFDT professional federations and confederal unions are based at 47–49 avenue Simon Bolivar, 75950 Paris Cedex 19, other than where shown below. Their e-mail and website addresses are as follows:

1. Fédération des banques et sociétés fianciéres
Phone. +33 1 5641 5450
E-mail. banques@cfdt.fr
Website. www.cfdt-banques.fr

2. Fédération chimie énergie (FCE)
Phone. +33 1 5641 5300
E-mail. fce@cfdt.fr
Website. www.fce.cfdt.fr

3. Fédération communication et culture (FTILAC)
Phone. +33 1 5641 5380
E-mail. ftilac@cfdt.fr

4. Fédération des établissements et arsenaux de l'état (FEAE)
Phone. +33 1 5641 5680
E-mail. feae@cfdt.fr

5. Fédération des finances et affaires économiques
Phone. +33 1 5641 5555
E-mail. finances@cfdt.fr
Website. www.digiplace.com/cfdt-finances

6. Fédération formation et enseignement privés (FEP)
Phone. +33 1 5641 5470
E-mail. fep@cfdt.fr

7. Fédération générale agroalimentaire (FGA)
Phone. +33 1 5641 5050
E-mail. fga@cfdt.fr

8. Fédération générale de la métallurgie et des mines (FGMM)
Phone. +33 1 5641 5070
E-mail. fgmm@cfdt.fr

9. Fédération générale des transports-équipements (FGTE)
Phone. +33 1 5641 5600
E-mail. fgte@cfdt.fr

10. Fédération de l'habillement, du cuir et textile (HACUITEX)
Phone. +33 1 5641 5590
E-mail. hacuitex@cfdt.fr

11. Fédération nationale construction bois (FNCB)
Phone. +33 1 5641 5560
E-mail. fncb@cfdt.fr

Website. www.cfdt-construction-bois.fr

12. Fédération nationale INTERCO
Phone. +33 1 5641 5252
E-mail. interco@cfdt.fr
Website. www.interco-cfdt.fr

13. Fédération unifiée des postes et des telecoms (FUPT)
Phone. +33 1 5641 5400
E-mail. fupt@cfdt.fr

14. Fédération protection sociale, travail, emploi (PSTE)
Phone. +33 1 5641 5150
E-mail. pste@cfdt.fr

15. Fédération des services
Address. Tour Essor 14 rue Scandicci, 93508 Pántin Cedex
Phone. +33 1 48 10 65 90
E-mail. services@cfdt.fr

16. Fédération des services de santé et services sociaux
Phone. +33 1 5641 5200
E-mail. santesociaux@cfdt.fr
Website. www.fed-cfdt-sante-sociaux.org

17. Fédération des syndicats généraux de l'éducation nationale (SGEN)
Phone. +33 1 5641 5100
E-mail. sgen@cfdt.fr
Website. www.sgen-cfdt.org

18. CFDT cadres
Phone. +33 1 5641 5500
E-mail. contact@cfdt-cadres.fr

19. Union confédérale des retraités (UCR)
Phone. +33 1 5641 5520
E-mail. union-retraites@cfdt.fr

20. Union des fédérations des fonctions publiques et assimilés (UFFA)
Phone. +33 1 5641 5440
E-mail. uffa@cfdt.fr

Confédération Française des Travailleurs Chrétiens (CFTC)
French Confederation of Christian Workers

Address. 13 rue des Ecluses – Saint Martin, 75483 Paris, Cedex 10
Phone. +33 1 44 52 49 00
Fax. +33 1 44 52 49 18
E-mail. communication@cftc.fr
Website. www.cftc.fr (French only)
Leadership. Jacques Voisin (president); Jacky Dintinger (secretary-general)
Membership. 160,000 (est)
History and character. Unions influenced by social Catholicism developed from the mid-1880s, and the CFTC itself was formed in November 1919 at a constituent congress of 321 unions with nearly 100,000 members. The CFTC participated the same year in the establishment of the International Federation of Christian Trade Unions, the predecessor of the WCL. The CFTC, like the CGT, recruited many new members in 1936 and lost fewer of them in the rest of the decade. The Vichy government dissolved all unions in 1940 and the CFTC thereafter supported the Council of the Resistance. Open activity resumed in August 1944 when the underground leaders of the CFTC and the CGT formed an inter-confederal committee of understanding, but the CFTC rejected CGT proposals for a merger after the war.

In its early period the CFTC was fundamentally Catholic in emphasis, but after World War II a fraction known as the minoritaires, grouped around the journal *Réconstruction,* pressed to release the federation from the religious strait-jacket to permit it to challenge the CGT and the FO. In 1947 the CFTC began the process of weakening its links with the Catholic Church by abolishing a constitutional provision whereby its activities were to be based on the papal encyclical Rerum Novarum. By 1964 the reformers were in the majority, and a special congress voted to change the name of the organization to the Confédération Française Démocratique du Travail (CFDT – see separate entry). A minority, composed largely of miners' and white-collar unions, consequently separated themselves, retaining the previous name as the CFTC.

The CFTC today maintains its social Christian orientation, emphasizing as fundamental the primacy of the individual and the inalienable rights (and duties) of each individual; the defence of the family; the rejection of the class struggle; the development of contractual relations between free and independent organizations; and the rejection of the politicization of trade unions. Nevertheless the organization does not require religious adherence of its members. It takes a particular interest in similarly-oriented unions affiliated to the WCL in the developing world. It regards its commitment to the WCL as having primacy over its membership in ETUC, although that position has been a source of controversy within the CFTC.

The CFTC, although considered "nationally representative" in the French system, is considerably weaker than the main three nationally representative general trade union centres (CGT, CFDT and CGT-FO). However its share of the overall vote in the most recent (2002) industrial tribunal elections, 9.7%, was further ahead of the CFE-CGC, which represents only managerial and professional staff, than in 1997. In work place elections it averages between 5% and 6% of the vote, but it has greater support in some regions, such as Alsace, Lorraine and the Nord-Pas-de-Calais and in sectors such as private education, health, social services and metalworking. It has capitalized on the recent development of mandating in enterprises without union delegates.
International affiliations. WCL; ETUC

Confederation Française de L'Encadrement CGC (CFE-CGC)
French Confederation of Professional and Managerial Staff
Address. 59/63, rue du Rocher, 75008 Paris

Phone. +33 1 55 30 12 12
Fax. +33 1 55 30 13 13
E-mail. presse@cfecgc.fr
Website. www.cfecgc.org (French only)
Leadership. Jean-Luc Cazettes (president); Jean-Louis Walter (secretary-general)
Membership. 140,000
History and character. Founded in 1944 as the Confédération Générale des Cadres (CGC), taking its present name in 1981. The CFE-CGC is one of the five confederations (with the CGT, CGT-FO, CFDT and CFTC) considered "nationally representative", although it is the only one not that does not usually recruit across the whole workforce. Its members are managers and professionally qualified staff (two-thirds) and technicians and supervisors (one third).

The CFE-CGC has traditionally had a pragmatic orientation and has emphasized that its members are the driving force of economic progress and have a unique role in constructing new forms of economic citizenship and in facilitating the partnership of labour and capital. It viewed the decline of trade unions in France, as many other countries, in the latter part of the twentieth century as reflecting a failure of the unions to adapt to changes in the structure and expectations of the workforce. However, the CFE-CGC also experienced this decline, its membership falling from 398,000 in 1976 to 181,000 by 1991 before stabilizing, rising and then falling again to 140,000 by the end of 2002.

In the 1997 industrial tribunal (conseils de prud'hommes) elections the CFE-CGC lost its customary first place in the vote for the managerial and professional staff electoral college, taking only 22% of the vote compared with 31.5% for the CFDT. The CFE-CGC's subsequent plans to intensify and broaden its recruitment efforts, including among self-employed professionals, and to reform its "highly centralized and hierarchical" structures to increase accessibility and grass-roots involvement, appeared incapable of halting the structural decline that was associated with the privatization of nationalized industries, and the shrinkage in total size of the very largest of French firms – where it had traditionally been strongest. However, in the 2002 industrial tribunal elections its overall vote rose by one percentage point to a 7% share.
International affiliation. TUAC

Confédération Générale du Travail (CGT)
General Confederation of Labour
Address. 263 rue de Paris, 93516 Paris, Montreuil Cedex
Phone. +33 1 48 18 80 00
Fax. +33 1 49 18 18 57
E-mail. internat@cgt.fr
Website. www.cgt.fr (French only, some English sections on international issues)
Leadership. Bernard Thibault (secretary-general)
Membership. 650,000 (includes retired members)
History and character. The CGT was founded at Limoges in 1895 and from the beginning was affected by ideological divisions between socialists, syndicalists and others. Before 1914 it campaigned against militarism but during the First World War the CGT secretary, Léon Jouhaux, served as a "commissioner of the nation", mobilizing it behind the war effort. Membership, which had been only 400,000 among a six million industrial workforce grew rapidly after the war to 2.5 million by 1920, but tensions generated by conflicting responses to the example of the Russian Revolution led to expulsions of members of the revolutionary minority, and the formation in 1921 of the Confédération Générale du Travail Unitaire (CGTU). The CGTU, and the French Communist Party (PCF, formed 1920) to which it was linked, subsequently engaged in a bitter ideological struggle with the CGT. In 1936, during the Popular Front era, the CGTU was readmitted to the CGT and the unified organization led a wave of strikes that stimulated a massive surge in membership, major pay rises and to the 40 hour week. By the end of 1936 the CGT was four to five million strong, only to decline to a quarter of this figure by 1939 in increasingly unfavourable political conditions.

Rapid shifts in PCF policy on the eve of World War II led to its adherents being purged from the CGT, and they pursued a policy of sabotaging war production before the fall of France. After the German invasion of the Soviet Union in June 1941, however, the PCF became a major factor in the Resistance. The CGT had been dissolved by the Vichy regime in November 1940 but certain of its leaders were recruited into a new official labour organization by the Pétain government. These included René Bélin, who became Minister of Labour and was responsible for the implementation of a corporatist Labour Charter. In May 1943 the communists were readmitted to the (clandestine) CGT, with three of the eight seats on the executive board.

In September 1945, in step with a surge of post-war support for the PCF (which participated in the post-war De Gaulle government) Benoît Frachon, a communist, was appointed a co-equal CGT secretary-general with Jouhaux, and during 1946–47 the communists achieved control of most of the CGT apparatus. Communist policies stressed the demands of economic recovery, including a wages standstill backed by the CGT, and confrontation between the different wings of the CGT was initially avoided. Membership in 1946 stood at more than 5 million. However, the onset of the Cold War, the removal of PCF ministers from the government and the party's switch to a strategy of industrial confrontation in 1947 precipitated the break-up of the CGT. A minority led by Jouhaux broke away to form the CGT-Force Ouvrière (see separate entry). Many non-communists remained loyal to the CGT however, and it remained the premier union centre throughout the post-War period. Into the 1970s the CGT still claimed 2.25 million members.

Membership of the CGT began to fall steadily from the late 1970s. A CGT official said in 1985 that at least 700,000 members had been lost in the previous seven years. All the main French trade union centres lost membership during this period, but the disproportionately large losses of the CGT were variously attributed to factors such as the decay of heavy industries in which it was strong, unemployment, its image of ideological and bureaucratic inflexibility and adherence to the PCF sometimes at the expense of union issues, and its failure to respond to social and economic modernization and to recognize the importance of organizing white-collar employees in the small business sector.

During the 1990s the position of the CGT stabilized to some degree. It remains the strongest centre in traditional industrial sectors, and in the industrial tribunal elections of 2002 (the most recent) it retained first place, with 32.1% of the votes, an almost identical position to 1992 and 1997. It is relatively weak in the more dynamic sectors of the economy, however, and now has a smaller membership than the CFDT.

The collapse of the Soviet Union and the end of the Cold War had serious repercussions for the CGT. A CGT representative held the post of secretary-general of the (communist-dominated) World Federation of Trade Unions continuously from 1947 until in 1978 the CGT failed to offer a candidate, criticizing the insufficient autonomy of the trade unions of the Soviet bloc countries. The CGT remained within the WFTU, however, as its most prominent affiliate in the western world. It was not until 1994, five years after the general collapse of communism in Eastern Europe, that the CGT officially severed its ties to the WFTU. In 1999, 25 years after it first applied for membership, the CGT was admitted to the European Trade Union Confederation (ETUC), its application endorsed by the CFDT and approved by all member organizations except the CGT-FO.

The CGT under secretary-general Louis Viannet (who was succeeded by his favoured successor, the leader of the 1995 railway workers' strike, Bernard Thibault, in 1999) began to moderate its tradition of militancy in favour of a modernized approach seeking dialogue and negotiation. Viannet termed this a policy of "moving from a trade unionism of protest to a trade unionism of proposals". This shift in emphasis reflects an awareness of a need to change in view of the CGT's dwindling strength and its lack of impact or relevance in wide areas of the economy, especially its more dynamic sectors, as it stood out against virtually every aspect of labour market reform. The CGT nonetheless remains far more inclined to embrace industrial action than most other western European centres: Bernard Thibault was at the centre of calls for strike action against the 2003 Raffarin government pension reforms, although expeditiously declining to call for a general strike which he argued should come from the bottom, rather than from the top. The CGT, through its unemployed committees, was also the centre most involved in supporting and working with the locally-based unemployed associations that were particularly active, and staged many occupations of government offices, in 1997–98.

Traditionally the CGT followed the communist line of opposing the development of what has become the European Union. Only in the latter part of the 1990s did it come to a grudging acceptance of the EU, a factor that assisted its admission to ETUC.

While relations between the different centres and their affiliates tend to fluctuate from one issue to another, and historic frictions still exist between the CGT and the FO, since 1995 the CGT has noticeably improved its relations with both the CGT-FO and the CFDT, which is now much more the CGT's equal. The intense negotiations with employers in all sectors in 1998–2000 on the implementation of the 35-hour week put a premium on the unions finding unity of purpose, although this was not always achieved in practice.

International affiliation. ETUC (since 1999)

Confederation Générale du Travail – Force Ouvrière (CGT-FO)
General Confederation of Labour – Workers' Strength

Address. 141 Avenue du Maine, 75680 Paris, Cedex 14
Phone. +33 1 40 52 82 00
Fax. +33 1 40 52 82 02
Website. www.force-ouvriere.fr (French only)
Leadership. Jean-Claude Mailly (secretary-general)
Membership. 300,000 (est.)

History and character. The CGT–Force Ouvrière was formed in 1948, with the secession from the CGT of a significant number of trade unionists opposed to the communist methods and policies of the CGT. At the time of the breakaway the CGT had an estimated 5 million members. The new group was led by Léon Jouhaux, who had been secretary-general of the CGT from 1909 to 1946 until compelled to accept a division of his authority, as co-secretary, with the communist Benoît Frachon, himself a former official of the communist CGTU. The immediate cause of the secession was a wave of communist-led strikes and violent disturbances in November–December 1947, viewed by the FO as a co-ordinated attempt to threaten the stability of the new post-war French Republic, which was governed by a centre-left alliance of popular republicans and socialists. A further source of division between the CGT and the FO was the issue of US economic aid to Europe: the CGT executive (in accordance with Soviet policy) denounced the Marshall Plan as "a war machine of American imperialists against the liberty and independence of other nations", but the FO favoured acceptance of such aid. Most of the strength of the new FO was in the white-collar and public services sectors.

Perhaps the main reason for the secession of nearly one million CGT members to form the CGT-FO was the belief that the policies of the CGT were controlled not by the members themselves but by the French Communist Party. Indeed, the CGT-FO retains the title CGT in its name because it claims that it remains true to the fundamental democratic principles that characterized the CGT from its original 1906 Charter of Amiens. This ideological tension between the CGT and CGT-FO declined in the 1990s with the end of the Cold War and the re-positioning of the CGT, but a degree of friction remains. In general, relations between the CFDT and CGT are much better than those between the CGT and the FO.

The FO, despite being the sole ICFTU-affiliated centre in France for three decades, failed to achieve the dominant status enjoyed by ICFTU affiliates in most other western industrial countries. This partly reflected the continued (if declining) strength of the CGT, but was also in part a result of the existence of the

CFDT as a major democratic socialist alternative (the CFDT itself also affiliating to the ICFTU in 1979).

The FO emphasizes that it stands independent of any political party or religion and in practice has sought to avoid being associated with any party, in contrast to the one-time close identification of the CGT with the Communists and the CFDT with the Socialists. It has traditionally included diverse political elements and became a target for entryism by far-left groups such as the Trotskyist Workers' Party (Parti des Travailleurs, PT), activity facilitated by the relatively small size of the FO. Internal political conflicts in the 1990s culminated in an unsuccessful challenge to the leadership of Marc Blondel (secretary-general since 1989) at the 1996 congress (the 18th), following which his opponent Jacques Mairé and some other regional and sectoral leaders defected to the Union National des Syndicats Autonomes (UNSA). However, the 19th congress, in March 2000 demonstrated a restoration of unity and Blondel was re-elected with 97% of the vote. In February 2004 Jean-Claude Mailly was elected unopposed as Blondel's successor.

FO's strategy since the fall of the Berlin Wall in 1989 and the end of the direct communist threat in the 1990s and 2000s has sometimes confused its supporters. This has been reflected in continuing membership decline and less support in elections for industrial tribunals and works councils. In 2002 the FO received just 18.3% of the prud'homme tribunals vote, a decline of 2.3 percentage points from 1997, while its share of works council elections hovered around 12-13%.

While the Communist-led CGT opposed the development of the EU, the FO was an enthusiastic advocate of the European project. In the 1990s their positions came closer together, the CGT embracing a grudging acceptance of the EU and the FO's enthusiasm cooling somewhat. While the FO at the industrial level remains less militant than the CGT and more committed to dialogue and negotiation it also regularly backs strike action and protests as part of fluctuating alliances with other centres. In 1995 and 2003 it participated alongside the CGT in protests against welfare reforms proposed by the conservative government of first Alain Juppé and then of Jean-Pierre Raffarin. However, the CGT-FO's key unitary factor is scepticism about and hostility to the "communist" CGT and in late 1998 Blondel said of the CGT's growing rapport with the CFDT that "their close relationship will last no longer than it takes to dance a tango". In 1999 the FO stood alone in opposing the CGT's admission to ETUC, 25 years after it first applied.

The FO has traditionally opposed "corporatism". In the 1980s it declined (unlike the CFDT and CGT) to participate in the socialist government elected in 1981 believing that "it is not possible to be the ruler and the ruled at the same time", and rejected that government's policy of "social compromise". Blondel has emphasized that the union movement should be independent and cannot "be lawmaker, joint lawmaker, manager or joint manager of private or state capitalist interests". FO therefore opposed the socialist government's 35-hour legislation, believing that pay rises should have been prioritised, and that vigorous collective bargaining rather than government legislation held the key to ensuring long-term advances.

International affiliations. ICFTU; ETUC; TUAC

Affiliated unions. The FO structure comprises 27 professional federations, grouping unions in the different sectors of the economy.

1. Action Sociale
Address. 7 Passage Tenaille, 75680 Paris Cedex 14
Phone. +33 1 40 52 85 80
Fax. +33 1 40 52 85 79
Leadership. Michel Pinaud (secretary-general)

2. Administration Générale de l'Etat
Address. 46 rue des Petites Ecuries, 75010 Paris
Phone. +33 1 42 46 40 19
Fax. +33 1 42 46 19 57
Leadership. Francis Lamarque (secretary-general)

3. FGTA Agriculture, Alimentation et Tabacs (agriculture, food and tobacco)
Address. 7 Passage Tenaille, 75680 Paris Cedex 14
Phone. +33 1 40 52 85 10
Fax. +33 1 40 52 85 12
E-mail. rafael.nedzynski@fgta-fo.org
Leadership. Rafael Nedzynski (secretary-general)

4. Bâtiment-Travaux Publics, Bois, Céramique, Papier Carton – Matériaux de Construction (building and allied trades)
Address. 170 Avenue Pannentier, 75010 Paris
Phone. +33 1 42 01 30 00
Fax. +33 1 42 39 50 44
Leadership. Michel Daudigny (secretary-general)

5. Cheminots (railwaymen's federation)
Address. 61 rue de la Chapelle, 75018 Paris
Phone. +33 1 55 26 94 00
Fax. +33 1 55 26 94 01
Leadership. Eric Falempin (secretary-general)

6. Coiffure, Esthetique et Parfumier (hairdressers and beauticians)
Address. 3 rue de la Croix Blanche, 18350 Nerondes
Phone. +33 2 48 78 89 32
Fax. +33 2 48 74 81 26
Leadership. Guy Marin (secretary-general)

7. Cuirs, Textiles-Habillement (leather and textiles)
Address. 7 Passage Tenaille, 75680 Paris Cedex 14
Phone. +33 1 40 52 83 00
Fax. +33 1 40 52 82 99
Leadership. Francis Van de Rosieren (secretary-general)

8. Enseignement, Culture et Formation Professionelle (education, culture, professional development)
Address. 6-8, rue Gaston-Lauriau, 93513 Montreuil Cedex
Phone. +33 1 56 93 22 22
Fax. +33 1 56 93 22 20
Leadership. François Chantron (secretary-general)

9. Employés et Cadres (white collar staff)
Address. 28 rue des Petits Hôtels, 75010 Paris

Phone. +33 1 48 01 91 91
Fax. +33 1 48 01 91 92
Leadership. Rose Boutaric (secretary-general)

10. Energie, Electrique et Gaz (energy, electricity, gas)
Address. 60 rue Vergniaud, 75640 Paris, Cedex 13
Phone. +33 1 44 16 86 20
Fax. +33 1 44 16 86 32
E-mail. federation@fnem-fo.org
Leadership. Max Royer (secretary-general)

11. Finances
Address. 46 rue des Petites Ecuries, 75010 Paris
Phone. +33 1 42 46 75 20
Fax. +33 1 47 70 23 92
Leadership. Michel Monteil (secretary-general)

12. Fonctionnaires (civil servants)
Address. 46 rue des Petites Ecuries
Phone. +33 1 44 83 65 55
Fax. +33 1 42 46 97 80
E-mail. fofonctionnaires@force-ouvriere.fr

13. Fédéchimie CGTFO (chemical industries)
Address. 60 rue Vergniaud, 75640 Paris, Cedex 13
Phone. +33 1 45 80 14 90
Fax. +33 1 45 80 08 03
E-mail. fedechimiecgtfo@wanadoo.fr
Leadership. Michel Decayeux (secretary-general)

14. Livre (publishing/print trades)
Address. 7 Passage Tenaille, 75680 Paris Cedex 14
Phone. +33 1 40 52 85 00
Fax. +33 1 40 52 85 01
Leadership. Patrice Sacquepee (secretary-general)

15. Métaux (metalworkers)
Address. 9 rue Baudoin, 75013 Paris
Phone. +33 1 53 94 54 00
Fax. +33 1 45 83 78 87

16. Mineurs, Miniers et Similaires (miners and related)
Address. 7 Passage Tenaille, 75680 Paris Cedex 14
Phone. +33 1 40 52 85 50
Fax. +33 1 40 52 85 48
Leadership. Bernard Fraysse (secretary-general)

17. Défense, Industries de l'Armement et Secteurs Assimilés (defence)
Address. 46 rue des Petites Ecuries, 75010 Paris
Phone. +33 1 42 46 00 05
Fax. +33 1 45 23 12 89
Leadership. Charles Sistach (secretary-general)

18. Personnel des Services des Départements et des Régions
Address. 46 rue des Petites Ecuries, 75010 Paris
Phone. +33 1 42 46 50 52
Fax. +33 1 47 70 26 06
Leadership. Michèle Simonnin (secretary-general)

19. Pharmacie
Address. 7 Passage Tenaille, 75680 Paris Cedex 14

Phone. +33 1 40 52 85 60
Fax. +33 1 40 52 85 61
Leadership. Gilbert Lebrument (secretary-general)

20. Police
Address. 146-148 rue Picpus, 75013 Paris
Phone. +33 1 53 46 11 00
Fax. +33 1 44 68 07 41
Leadership. Jean-Jacques Penin (secretary-general)

21. PTT (post, telegraphs, telephones)
Address. 60 rue Vergniaud, 75640 Paris, Cedex 13
Phone. +33 1 40 78 31 50
Fax. +33 1 40 78 30 58
Website. www.fo-ptt.com
Leadership. Jacques Lemercier (secretary-general)

22. Services Publics et de Santé (public services and health)
Address. 153–55 rue de Rome, 75017 Paris
Phone. +33 1 44 01 06 00
Fax. +33 1 42 27 21 40
Website. www.fo-sante.com
Leadership. Jean-Marie Bellot(secretary-general)

23. Spectacle-Presse-Audiovisuel (entertainment, press and broadcasting)
Address. 2 rue de la Michodière, 75002 Paris
Phone. +33 1 47 42 35 86
Fax. +33 1 47 42 39 45

24. Transports
Phone. +33 1 40 52 85 45
Fax. +33 1 40 52 85 09
Leadership. Gérard Apruzzese (secretary-general)

25. L'équipement des transports et des services
Address. 46 rue des Petites Ecuries, 75010 Paris
Phone. +33 1 44 83 86 20
Fax. +33 1 48 24 38 32
Leadership. Jean Hedou (secretary-general)

26. Union des cadres et Ingénieurs (managers and technicians)
Address. 2 rue de la Michodière, 75002 Paris
Phone. +33 1 47 42 39 69
Fax. +33 1 47 42 03 53
Leadership. Hubert Bouchet (secretary-general)

27. Voyageurs-Représentants-Placiers (sales representatives)
Address. 6–8 rue Albert-Bayet, 75013 Paris
Phone. +33 1 45 82 28 28
Fax. +33 1 45 70 93 69
Leadership. Loic Louvel (secretary-general)

4 Other Trade Union Organizations

Confédération des Syndicats Libres (CSL)
Confederation of Free Trade Unions
Address. 37 rue Lucien Sampaix, 75010 Paris
Phone. +33 1 55 26 12 12
Fax. +33 1 55 26 12 00

E-mail. csl@ifrance.com
Membership. 50,000 (est.)
History and character. A small conservative-inclined organization, founded in 1959 and formerly known as the Confédération Française du Travail. It describes its orientation as "neither red nor yellow" but as the "colour of the tricolour", patriotic, independent of political and religious affiliations, and opposed to the class struggle. It was in sixth place in the 1997 industrial tribunal elections, with just over 4% of the vote, having strengthened its position over the preceding decade, but was barely able to mount a challenge in the 2002 elections.

Fédération Syndicale Unitaire (FSU)
United Union Federation
Address. 3/5 Rue de Metz, 75010 Paris
Phone. +33 1 44 79 90 30
Fax. +33 1 48 01 02 52
Leadership. Gérard Aschieri (secretary general)
Website. www.fsu.fr (French only)
Membership. 150,000 (est.)
History and character. Founded in 1993 from a split in the previously dominant teacher federation, FEN, this is now the largest union in the central government civil service, reflecting its leadership position among teachers, who represent half of civil servants employed by central government. It has strongly resisted government efforts to reform the education system and played a leading part in the strikes against the pension reforms of 2003. On this basis its 2004 Congress recognised the limited effectiveness of teachers on their own and decided to seek greater unity with all those other unions who are ready to challenge the shift towards neo-liberalism.

Union Nationale des Syndicats Autonomes (UNSA)
National Federation of Independent Unions
Address. 21 rue Jules Ferry, 93177 Bagnolet cedex
Phone. +33 1 48 18 88 57
Fax. +33 1 48 18 88 90
E-mail. sg@unsa.org
Leadership. Alain Olive (secretary general)
Website. www.unsa.org (French only)
Membership. 360,000
History and character. The UNSA was founded in 1993 as an alliance of independent unions, mainly from the civil service sector. Most prominent among these was the National Education Federation (FEN), historically the biggest teaching union, although it has now lost this position to the FSU. It was also joined by dissidents from the FO and by four autonomous unions that had belonged to the Group of Ten. UNSA has yet to achieve official recognition alongside the CGT, FO, CFDT, CFTC and CFE-CGC as nationally representative. By 1995 its 4.8% share of all representative elections across both public and private sectors was already greater than that of the CFTC and CFE-CGC. In the 2002 industrial tribunal elections its share was 5%.

UNSA initially built a close relationship with the CFDT. In May 1999 its admission to membership of the European Trade Union Confederation (ETUC) was approved (with the support of the other French members except the CGT-FO) on the basis of a partnership agreement with the CFDT whereby the two would form one delegation and speak with one voice. UNSA is also strongly in favour of changing the rules on representative status, to prevent affiliates of the big five nationally representative centres having the automatic right to conclude collective agreements in work places where they are a minority. It has welcomed the initiative of the CFDT in proposing reform of this system to require majority approval for agreements and thereby improve the legitimacy of the unions. Its relations with the CFDT were put under considerable strain, however, by the CFDT's decision to support the government's 2003 pension reforms to which UNSA, as an essentially public sector-based trade union centre, was very strongly opposed.
International affiliation. ETUC

Union Syndicale – G10 Solidaires
Solidarity G10 Trade Union
Address. 93 bis rue de Montreuil, 75011 Paris
Phone. +33 1 58 39 30 20
Fax. + 33 1 43 67 62 14
E-mail. contact@solidaires.org
Website. www.g10.ras.eu.org
Membership. 65,000 (est.)
History and character. This new trade union centre is based mainly in the public sector based around the SUD-PTT. The SUD (Solidaires, Unitaires, Démocratiques) group were originally expelled from the CFDT in 1988 and then in 1992 affiliated to the Group of Ten unions (originally established in 1981). Since 1995 and particularly in 2001 and 2003, the SUD tendency expanded far beyond the Post Office and France Telecom (where it is second to the CGT in its share of Board elections). It has attracted both individual union branches and national organizations (such as the Finance Ministry's Tax Staffs union (SNUI). Many of the new recruits were former dissidents from the CFDT, and G10 Solidaires played a prominent role in the ultimately defeated struggle to stop the government's 2003 pension reforms (the Fillon law). From 1998 the G10 registered itself as a Centre of Autonomous Federations and National Unions, and subsequently changed its name to G10 Solidaires. It received just 1.5% of the vote in the 2002 industrial tribunal elections, but in the regions where it put up candidates they received roughly 5%.

Gabon

Capital: Libreville
Population: 1.36 m. (2004 est.)

1 Political and Economic Background

Gabon gained full independence from France in 1960. On the death of President Leon Mba in 1967, Vice-President Omar Bongo became head of state. The following year he declared Gabon a one-party state, under the Gabonese Democratic Party (PDG), which it remained until 1990. Progress towards pluralism was slow and free elections for the presidency were not held until 1993 when Bongo was narrowly returned for his fourth term. Multi-party legislative elections had taken place in 1990, returning the PDG with an overall majority. Facing a divided opposition, President Bongo was re-elected (for an extended seven-year term) in December 1998, with some 67% of the vote. The most recent elections to the National Assembly (in December 2001) again gave the PDG a majority.

Gabon has one of the highest per capita incomes in Africa, with its relative wealth being based largely upon its (depleting) petroleum reserves. Gabon depended on timber and manganese until oil was discovered offshore in the early 1970s. The oil sector now accounts for 50% of GDP. The oil price increases of the 1970s fuelled heavy spending in Gabon and the country became heavily indebted in the 1980s as oil prices fell, pushing it into a series of debt rescheduling arrangements and austerity measures leading to political tensions. There is substantial immigration of workers from poorer west African countries, who work in the informal and service sectors. The state dominates some sectors of the economy, including the key export sectors of oil and timber, although some basic services have been privatized. While Gabon has a significant modern sector, 60% of the labour force work in agriculture, much of it at subsistence level.

GDP (purchasing power parity) $7.301 bn. (2003 est.); GDP per capita (purchasing power parity) $5,500 (2003 est.).

2 Trade Unionism

Under French rule a pluralistic system of trade unionism developed on the French model. As an independent state, Gabon ratified ILO Convention No. 87 (Freedom of Association and Protection of the Right to Organize, 1948) in 1960 and Convention No. 98 (Right to Organize and Collective Bargaining, 1949) in 1961, but a single-trade-union structure was imposed in 1969 under the Gabonese Trade Union Confederation (COSYGA). Under legislation of 1980 employers were required to deduct a mandatory trade union solidarity tax from the pay of all workers for the benefit of COSYGA.

COSYGA remained the sole trade union centre until 1991, when it lost this status in parallel with the development of a measure of political pluralism. In mid-1991 the new independent Gabonese Confederation of Free Trade Unions (CGSL) was formed. The compulsory payroll tax in favour of COSYGA was ended in 1992 and COSYGA itself also adopted a more independent position, joining the CGSL in strikes and protests against aspects of government policy in the mid-1990s.

A revised labour code adopted in 1994 provided increased protection of trade union rights. All workers are legally free to join trade unions and virtually the entire private sector workforce is unionized. Nonetheless, the ICFTU has claimed that trade unionists in both the public and private sectors are often discriminated against. Under the labour code collective bargaining is to take place on an industry-wide rather than enterprise basis. There is a right to strike subject to pre-strike arbitration procedures. In the public sector, the right to strike is limited where there is risk to public safety. In September 2003, the trade unions, government and employers signed a social truce, agreeing to a three-year hiatus on strikes and establishing a 35-member mediation committee to negotiate disputes.

3 Trade Union Centres

Confédération Syndicale Gabonaise (COSYGA)
Gabonese Trade Union Confederation
Address. BP 14017, Libreville
Phone. +241 72 14 98
Fax. +241 70 07 04
Leadership. Martin Allini (secretary-general)
History and character. A single union centre, the Fédération Syndicale Gabonaise (FESUGA), was created in 1969 by the amalgamation of the three main existing centres as an organ of the ruling PDG. It changed its name to COSYGA at its 1978 congress. Its founding statutes affirmed "responsible participation" in economic and social development of the country, and it launched various production and consumer cooperatives, and ventures in workers' education. After 1991, however, COSYGA evolved into a more independent organization. COSYGA affiliated to WCL after being visited by a WCL delegation in September 1994. It is considered to be broadly aligned with the government but critical on issues where it sees the government acting against worker interests.
International affiliation. WCL

Confédération Gabonaise des Syndicats Libres (CGSL)
Gabonese Confederation of Free Trade Unions
Address. BP 8067, Libreville
Phone. +241 77 37 82
Fax. +241 70 46 99 (c/o M. Martin)
E-mail. c.libres@voila.fr
International affiliation. ICFTU

The Gambia

Capital: Banjul
Population: 1.55 m. (2004 est.)

1 Political and Economic Background

Gambia became independent as a full member of the Commonwealth in 1965 and a republic in 1970. In July 1994 Sir Dawda Kairaba Jawara, then President of the Republic and leader of the ruling People's Progressive Party (PPP), was overthrown in a bloodless coup by young army officers led by Capt. Yahya Jammeh, who became head of state. Jammeh, as candidate of the newly formed Alliance for Patriotic Reorientation and Construction (APRC), was elected as President in September 1996; he was re-elected in October 2001.

In January 1997 the APRC won a majority of seats in the first elections to a newly created National Assembly. (The PPP did not contest the election, having been banned.) The APRC increased its majority in the Assembly in elections held in January 2002, winning all but three of the 48 elective seats.

The Gambia has no important mineral or other natural resources and has a limited agricultural base. About 75% of the population depend on crops and livestock for its livelihood. Small-scale manufacturing activity features the processing of peanuts, fish, and hides. A decline in tourism since 2000 has held back economic growth. Unemployment and underemployment rates are extremely high.

GDP (purchasing power parity) $2.56bn. (2003 est.); GDP per capita (purchasing power parity) $1,700 (2003 est.).

2 Trade Unionism

The Gambia ratified ILO Conventions No. 87 (Freedom of Association and Protection of the Right to Organize, 1948) and No. 98 (Right to Organize and Collective Bargaining, 1949) in 2000.

The Gambia Labour Congress had its origins in 1929 and participated in the founding congress of the WFTU in 1945. It was affiliated to the PPP, the former ruling party that was banned after the 1994 coup. The two principal centres now are the Gambian Workers' Confederation (affiliated to the WCL) and the Gambia Workers' Union (affiliated to the ICFTU), both of which are recognized by the government.

Under the 1990 Labour Act all employees except civil servants have a legal right to join unions and bargain collectively. Under it employee contracts may not prohibit union membership. Strikes are lawful subject to notice periods and the courts may ban strikes that are considered politically motivated. More than half the workforce is employed in the informal economy, and strikes rarely occur.

3 Trade Union Centres

Gambian Workers' Confederation (GWC)
Address. Trade Union House, 31 Leman Street, PO Box 698, Banjul
Phone. +220 223 080
Fax. +220 227 214
Leadership. Pa Moudou K.B. Faal (secretary-general)
History and character. The National Investigation Agency arrested Pa Faal in December 1996 and again in April 1997, when he planned to travel abroad.
International affiliation. WCL

Gambia Workers' Union (GWU)
Address. 12 Clarkson Street, PO Box 979, Banjul
Phone. +220 28 17 7
Leadership. Ebrima Garba Cham
International affiliation. ICFTU

Georgia

Capital: Tbilisi
Population: 4.69 m. (2004 est.)

1 Political and Economic Background

Georgia is a former republic of the USSR that became independent in 1991. It has experienced considerable conflict since that time. Its first post-independence leader, Zviad Gamsakhurdia, was deposed in January 1992 in a military coup that resulted in former Soviet Foreign Minister Eduard Shevardnadze coming to power as chairman of the governing military council. Shevardnadze was elected President in 1995 and re-elected in April 2000, and the Citizens' Union of Georgia party he founded in 1993 had a majority in Parliament. The legislative elections of Nov. 2, 2003, triggered a series of events with ramifications for the presidential elections and the whole political spectrum of the country. Irregularities and fraud led to a political crisis, street protests, and the resignation of President Shevardnadze on Nov. 23. Extraordinary presidential elections were held on Jan. 4, 2004. Mikhail Saakashvili, joint candidate of the National Movement and the United Democrats, was elected President with 96.2% of votes. The Citizens' Union of Georgia, the former ruling party, disappeared from the political scene. In the final results of the parliamentary elections announced on April 18, 2004, the newly emerged coalition of the National Movement and the Burdjanadze-Democrats that led the November events, known as the Rose Revolution, got 66.24% of the proportional vote and a total of 153 parliamentary seats (135 proportional and 18 constituency seats) in the 235-seat parliament.

The central government has no control of the breakaway region of Abkhazia, from which both the army and the majority ethnic Georgian population were driven out in 1993, or of much of South Ossetia. In 2004, elections were held in both breakaway regions – parliamentary elections in South Ossetia in May, and presidential elections in Abkhazia in October. There are an estimated 283,000 internally displaced persons.

The Georgian economy was badly damaged by the loss of former Soviet markets followed by civil conflict in 1992–93 surrounding the overthrow of Gamsakhurdia and the Abkhaz revolt. Under Shevardnadze and with backing from the IMF (which it joined in May 1992) it sought to develop a market economy and achieved healthy growth from 1993, although affected by the Russian crisis of 1998. Nonetheless some 50% of the population lives below the poverty line in winter and 40% in summer. Economic activities include commercial agriculture, tourism and mining, with a small industrial sector.

GDP (purchasing power parity) $12.18 bn. (2003 est); GDP per capita (purchasing power parity) $2,500 (2003 est.).

2 Trade Unionism

The right to form and join trade unions is provided by the 1995 Constitution and the 1997 Law on Trade Unions. Georgia ratified ILO Convention No. 87 (Freedom of Association and Protection of the Right to Organize, 1948) in 1999 and No. 98 (Right to Organize and Collective Bargaining, 1949) in 1997. A Law on Collective Bargaining was enacted in 1997. Despite the existing legislative framework, unions face some interference in their activities. Though allowed by law, the practice of collective bargaining was not widespread, according to the 2003 US State Department Report on human rights in Georgia.

The national centre is the Georgian Trade Union Amalgamation (GTUA), founded in 1990, when the Georgian unions seceded from the Soviet AUCCTU. It faced major attacks on its independence in 1991–92, but has since established itself as generally free from government interference. In 2001, however, the ICFTU general secretary expressed deep concern over serious violations of trade union rights and in particular, cases of systematic obstruction through harassment, interference, and interminable court cases against the GTUA, which has been affiliated with the ICFTU since 2000. In 2004, the general secretary of the General Confederation of Trade Unions (GCTU), a grouping of centres from the successor states to the Soviet Union, criticized the Georgian government for taking legal action against the GTUA president, Irakli Tugushi, with regard to its property.

3 Trade Union Centre

Georgian Trade Union Amalgamation (GTUA)
Address. Shartava Street 7, 380122 Tbilisi
Phone. +995 32 934087
E-mail. gtua@geo.net.ge
Leadership. Irakli Tugushi (president)
Membership. Claims 650,000 in 34 sectoral and regional unions, but dues-paying membership believed much lower.
History and character. The GTUA (also referred to as Amalgamated Trade Unions of Georgia, ATUG) is the successor to the Confederation of Independent Trade Unions of Georgia (CITUG), which was founded in 1990, when the Georgian unions seceded from the Soviet AUCCTU.

The CITUG did not fare well under independence. It supported the democratic opposition to the dictatorial rule of former President Gamsakhurdia. In August 1991, it was abolished along with all its branch unions at an extraordinary congress convened on the president's orders and packed with his delegates. The congress established in its place a single trade union centre and most of its property was confiscated by the state. In opposition to this move the CITUG unions in the medical, cooperative, transport and communications sectors began to meet in secret but their efforts were overtaken by the fall of Gamsakhurdia in January 1992.

Following Gamasakhurdia's overthrow it resisted efforts by the Military Council to bring it under control and its present structure was created in 1992 and most property returned. In 1998–99, however, it was still trying to get back union property transferred to the state in 1991–92. Its claim was contested by the CITUG president at that time, who had subsequently set up the Free Trade Union of Georgia, claiming the GTUA was not the legitimate successor to the CITUG.

The US State Department Human Rights report for 2003 said that the GTUA has no affiliation with the government and receives no government funding, except for support to send 200 children each year to summer camp. In 2004, the GTUA president Irakly Tugushi was summmoned to the Prosecutor General's Office for questioning on the trade unions' property. Newly installed Georgian President Mikhail Saakashvili demanded that the GTUA leadership sign over to the state the ownership rights of all property and real estate owned by the trade unions. The GTUA president at first rejected the ultimatum and demanded an international audit of its property. Later, the trade unions yielded to the pressure and gave away their rights to various hotel and other facilities. Radio Free Europe/Radio Liberty reported that they had created, on the basis of real-estate holdings, a fund for development of national culture that the trade unions would administer jointly with the government. The Prosecutor General's Office called for an investigation of the remaining real estate holdings of the trade unions.
International affiliation. Affiliated to the ICFTU in November 2000

Germany

Capital: Berlin
Population: 82.42 m. (2004 est.)

1 Political and Economic Background

Following World War II Germany was partitioned by the Allied forces, the US, British and French zones of occupation becoming the Federal Republic of Germany (FRG, West Germany) and the Russian zone becoming the German Democratic Republic (GDR, East Germany). In 1990, following the collapse of the GDR, the two Germanys were united on the basis of the West German political, social and economic order. Post-unification Germany is a federal republic in which there are 16 states (länder), each of which enjoys substantial powers in the economic and social fields.

From 1949 to 1966 the Christian Democratic Union (CDU) and its Bavarian counterpart, the Christian Social Union (CSU), dominated the federal government in West Germany, although the (liberal) Free Democratic Party (FDP) participated until 1956 and again from 1961; other smaller parties were also within the government until 1960. After 1966 there were successively coalitions of the CDU, CSU and Social Democratic Party (SPD) – the "grand coalition" – from 1966 to 1969; of the SPD and FDP from 1969 to 1982; and of the CDU, CSU and FDP from 1982 to

1998. In elections to the lower house (Bundestag) in September 1998, however, the SPD emerged as the largest party and the SPD's Gerhard Schröder succeeded the CDU's Helmut Kohl as Chancellor, heading a coalition government in which the SPD was joined by the Greens (the so-called "red-green coalition"). The coalition retained power in elections in September 2002, though the SPD won only three more seats in the Bundestag (251) than did the CDU/CSU. A mixed pattern of political control exists at state level but with the CDU as the strongest party overall. The Party of Democratic Socialism (PDS), which is directly descended from the ruling Socialist Unity Party of Germany (SED) that formerly ruled in East Germany, retains a significant following in the east of the country – although it failed to reach the 5% of the vote threshold to achieve party list representation in the 2002 Bundestag elections, it won 6.1% of the national vote and seven seats in the June 2004 elections to the European Parliament.

Germany has the largest economy in Europe and is noted especially for the scale, strength and diversity of its manufacturing sector. It is traditionally the motor economy of the EU but Germany has faced an immense task in privatizing, integrating and modernizing the former East German command economy against a background where East Germans had high expectations of sharing immediately in West German prosperity. The post-unification era has seen a sustained and costly effort to rebuild the east, with transfer payments still averaging $70 bn per annum. Despite this immense transfer of resources (much of which has had the effect of subsidizing uncompetitive enterprises and unemployment), the gap between the former east and west has actually increased in recent years. Growth in real GDP in the east averaged only 1% per annum in 1996-2003, compared with 1.3% in the west, and in August 2004 unemployment in the east stood at 18.3%, more than twice that in the west (8.4%). Almost half the population of the east depends on state benefits. There is a continuing outflow of workers with skills from the east and the population of the east fell from 18.1 million in 1991 to 17.0 million by 2003. The economic difficulties of the east have been reflected in the strong showing in recent elections in that part of the country of both the PDS and the far-right National Democratic Party – the PDS taking 28% and 23.6% of the vote, respectively, in state elections in the eastern länder of Brandenburg and Saxony in September 2004.

The costs of integration have been a major contributor to Germany's persistent deficits, Germany having failed for four successive years to 2004 to meet the requirement of the EU stability and growth pact that the public spending deficit should not exceed 3% of GDP. Germany has been reluctant to reduce its generous social welfare provision or undertake radical deregulation of its economy and labour practices, and in the view of critics this has contributed to a problem of persistent structural unemployment in both west and east. Economic growth has been sluggish in recent years, with real GDP growing well below 1% per annum since 2001. In October 2004 the European Commission forecast that Germany's growth rate in 2005 would be the lowest for any of the EU's 25 member states. This weak economic performance has pushed issues surrounding the ageing population and the implications for Germany's pension provision, the costs of welfare schemes, and inflexibility in the workforce and business methods, to the top of the political agenda. Anxieties about the implications for long-term state provision have been reflected in the steadily increasing proportion since 2000 of German household income converted into savings, a factor that has damped down domestic demand. Efforts to promote labour market reform and move people off benefits into work have provoked opposition particularly in the east. However, a new system, Hartz IV, cutting benefits to the long-term unemployed, while increasing incentives to find work, came into effect in January 2005.

GDP (purchasing power parity) $2.271 trillion (2004 est.); GDP per capita (purchasing power parity) $27,600 (2004 est.).

Trade Unionism

West Germany ratified ILO Convention No. 87 (Freedom of Association and Protection of the Right to Organize, 1948) in 1957 and Convention No. 98 (Right to Organize and Collective Bargaining, 1949) in 1956. These ratifications apply to united Germany.

German trade unionism can be traced back to the period of industrialization in the nineteenth century. Despite attempts by the Imperial German state to limit organization, by 1914 over 2.5 million workers were members of social democratic unions, 340,000 members of Christian unions and 105,000 in liberal or "yellow" Hirsch-Duncker unions. The unions were a significant industrial and political force in the Weimar Republic after World War I, though power was constrained by political and religious divisions. The Nazi seizure of power in 1933 led to the crushing of the labour movement, with unions abolished and workers organised into the German Labour Front (Deutsche Arbeitsfront).

Organized labour in West Germany emerged from World War II in a weak position. The political and economic strength of capital (the US Marshall Plan; the hegemony of German Christian Democracy; and the impact of migration from the east into the labour market) saw the post-war economy re-established as a capitalist market economy, with unions forced to accept the legal separation of collective bargaining from workplace co-determination and strong legal regulation of industrial relations, especially industrial conflict. Nevertheless, as the West German economy underwent rapid rebuilding and economic growth, unions became increasingly important labour market organizations.

Unions belonging to the German Trade Union Federation (DGB) were reorganized on the principle of unitary (neither politically nor religiously affiliated) and industrial trade unionism. These organizational principles sought to overcome pre-war political and religious divisions within the union movement, divisions that persist in other western European states. Although there is a religious-based centre (the

Christian Trade Union Federation, CGB), was formerly a separate white-collar workers' union (the German Salaried Employees' Union, DAG), and is a German Civil Servants' Federation (DBB), which recruits those with the employment status of *Beamte,* the DGB and its affiliates are structured as inclusive of all occupational and educational groups, and have consistently organized over 80% of all trade unionists.

West German trade union organization remained incredibly stable between 1945-90, with workers organized in sixteen or seventeen DGB-affiliated industrial unions for most of the period. Despite the concept of industrial unionism and the small number of DGB unions, there have been notable discrepancies in the size of DGB unions (for example, in 1985 the Metalworkers' union, IG Metall, had over 2.5 million members compared to the 42,196 members of the Gardening, Agriculture and Forestry union, GGFL) and not all unions are strictly industrial unions. Some remain essentially occupational unions such as the teachers' union, GEW, while the former public sector union (ÖTV) organized a vast number of different industries across the public sector.

Considering the central role accorded to trade unions within the German economic system as bargaining partners, union density in West Germany remained relatively low, at least when compared with other west European states which have adopted social partnership. In 1985, membership of DGB unions stood at 7,883,000, representing a density of 29.8%. If the membership levels of the rival confederations and unions are added, density rose to 36%. Union density remained stable, staying within a corridor of 35-40% (for all confederations) throughout the post war period prior to unification. Furthermore, membership levels were higher among workers in the key sectors of manufacturing and the public sector, reaching 50%. These higher rates were reflected in the concentration of union members in IG Metall, the chemical workers' union IG Chemie, and the ÖTV. In 1988 these unions represented 58% of total DGB membership.

West German trade unions developed four main roles. Firstly, and most importantly, trade unions are responsible for collective bargaining under the 1949 Collective Bargaining Act. In most sectors of the economy, multi-employer bargaining sets binding collective agreements for all firms belonging to an employers' association. The DGB is not actively involved in collective bargaining. Instead bargaining is carried out between the relevant trade union(s) and employers' associations within an industry, with negotiations formally taking place between the regional employers' association and the appropriate district organization of the union. This regional process of negotiation should not, however, disguise the central role that both the national union and employers' associations play in controlling the content and pace of negotiations across regions. This centralized control of bargaining provides both unions and employers' associations with a mechanism to ensure that the agreements reached in a region are broadly acceptable to the membership as a whole. The first regional agreement reached usually takes the form of a pilot agreement (Pilotabschluss), whose contents are – for the most part – transferred to other bargaining regions. The regional approach to collective bargaining also means that unions are normally in a position to target specific regions where membership is strong, is located in key industries and has experience of industrial conflict. In this way Baden-Württemberg is often used in the engineering industry to reach a pilot agreement that then becomes a model for the rest of the metalworking sector. In fact, the dominant role played by the metalworking industry within the German economy often means that the agreements reached by IG Metall act as a pace-setter for subsequent bargaining rounds in other industries. With traditionally high levels of employer organization (leading to high collective bargaining coverage) and additional mechanisms to extend collective agreements to firms that are not members of employers' associations, the outcome of collective bargaining has been to establish wide-ranging collective regulation of the employment relationship. Furthermore, the scope of collective agreements is wide with agreements covering pay rates, payment systems and many other conditions of employment, such as working time, holidays and overtime pay. Where necessary unions have taken large-scale industrial action to secure improvements in pay and conditions, notably the 1984 strike in metalworking and printing over the introduction of the 35-hour week. Often industrial action has been unnecessary with employers willing concede high settlements when the economy has been strong. Alternatively, the scale and cost of industrial action at a regional or industry level also means that unions and employers have to use the strike and lockout (respectively) periodically.

Secondly, unions have tried to control workplace industrial relations. The "dual system" of worker representation in Germany separates collective bargaining from workplace co-determination, conducted between an establishment's management and works council. Workplace co-determination is regulated by the Works Constitution Act (1952 amended 1972, 1988, and 2001), which covers the election of works councils; works councillors' information, consultation and co-determination rights; and the legal obligations under which participation rights are guaranteed – to work with the employer "in the spirit of mutual trust" for "the good of the employees and the establishment". The legal rights that trade unions possess under the Works Constitution Act are limited to specific initiative and supervisory rights that allow unions to challenge malpractice, and participation and advisory rights, which include the training of works councillors by the union, promotion of union candidates in elections and participation in works council and works meetings. Nevertheless, trade unions and works councils became, to a large degree, mutually dependent. DGB unions consistently won over three-quarters of all seats in works council elections (a level of representation that has far exceeded membership density) and have provided councillors with expert legal advice and training. In return, works councillors elected on union-slates have worked to build and maintain union membership within the establishment. This relationship is frequently strengthened by the role works councillors play within the union structures. The importance of the works council should be contrasted with the declining influence of union workplace organizations, which consist of elected or appointed union workplace representatives (Vertrauensleute). Significantly, works councillors have tended to accept and follow union policies, ensuring that the collective agreements negotiated by the unions are implemented correctly in the establishment. During periods of economic growth, works councils have also been able to "negotiate" – using their co-determination rights – substantial improvements upon the conditions established in industry-wide agreements.

Thirdly, German unions have been actively involved in the regulation of the labour market as a "social partner". The height of this involvement was during the period of "Concerted Action", during the period of the SPD–FDP federal government in the 1970s. However, while the DGB and affiliated unions can be involved in the tri-partite pacts, binding corporatism (or incomes policies found in other west European states) is limited in Germany by the constitutionally guaranteed freedom of collective bargaining (Tarifautonomie). Nevertheless, unions have played and continue to play an important role as social partner, notably in co-shaping the highly-valued vocational training system. Finally, the DGB and it affiliated unions provide important services to individual members (as well as to works councils), particularly in relation to the highly legalized regulation of the employment relationship.

As a consequence of the environment in which the unions were restructured after World War II, union policies have generally been pragmatic and cautious in character, and intended to assist the rebuilding of the economy while stabilizing the institutions of democracy. Radical and authoritarian political currents have been absent at all levels in the leadership to a marked degree. The unions' status in society and numerical strength benefited from the perception that they had contributed to the re-building of the German economy after World War II, and the anti-union political currents that affected many western countries in the 1980s were not pronounced in Germany. Management generally accepted unions as a co-determining factor in the running of industry, an acceptance institutionalized in labour representation on company boards and in company decision-making. While at any one time a majority of the DGB leadership is likely to be of an SPD orientation, care is always taken to ensure that there are CDU members in the elected leadership as well, an orientation which corresponds to that of a number of individual unions. Both major political parties have maintained support organizations for their union members, the loosely structured AfA for the SPD and the autonomous CDA for the CDU.

To a considerable degree the unions have retained their role and position in unified Germany. However, the cumulative effects of globalization, structural change and unification have created problems for the German economy from the 1990s onwards and have had important repercussions for industrial relations practices and trade unions.

Unification created huge organizational and representational problems for German unions. In the GDR unions affiliated to the Free German Trade Union Confederation (FDGB) were organized on the Soviet model. At its peak the FDGB claimed a membership of 9.6 million unionists, pensioners, students and others, comprising "97.7 per cent of all production workers, office employees, intellectuals and professional people", according to official claims. This figure exceeded union membership in the much larger West German state. The approach of unification stimulated reorganization at the FDGB where a number of leaders rapidly fell into disgrace. It still claimed 8.6 million members at the start of 1990, but an extraordinary congress converted it into a confederation, a step that freed the 16 industrial unions to formulate their own statutes. Despite this they were slow to change, notwithstanding increasing competition from the powerful and proximate DGB as well as newly emerging independent unions. That autumn the presidents of the FDGB's affiliates concluded a separate organization was not viable and the confederation was dissolved at the end of 1990. Most constituent unions soon shared its fate. By April 1991, 3 million former FDGB members had joined a DGB affiliated union and trade unionism in the new länder proceeded thenceforth within the expanding structures of the West German unions.

DGB unions were then faced with the issue of organizational expansion, while the subsequent economic collapse of the former GDR economy and the mass unemployment it created placed enormous strain upon declining union resources. There have also been claims of weaker organizational ties of union members and works councillors in the new Länder, reflecting over-optimistic expectations in DGB unions, which has provided employers with additional opportunities to undermine collective agreements and develop more co-operative relations with works councils, at the expense of union influence in the establishment. Nevertheless, collective bargaining has been established with industry-wide agreements that sought to equalize western and eastern income over time, and IG Metall successfully mobilized the east German membership in 1993 to protect agreements over staged wage equalisation. However, coverage rates do remain lower in the new länder and there is evidence of employers resigning from or refusing to join employers' associations, or illegally undercutting the terms laid down in collective agreements, with the tacit support of works councils.

It is important not to over-estimate the importance of unification as the cause of German economic and industrial relations problems. Globalization, the creation of the single European market and the recent eastwards expansion of the EU, have led employers increasingly to consider extensive rationalization or transferring production overseas to reduce wage costs. This decline in the manufacturing base has been complemented with an increase in services, but the economy has suffered from large-scale unemployment and difficulties in effectively regulating a private services sector which provides gainful employment.

The impact of these developments for unions and industrial relations is threefold. Firstly, a worsening labour market situation has weakened German unions' bargaining power and enabled employers to pursue their demands for greater flexibility through further decentralization of multi-employer collective bargaining. Increasingly unions have been forced to conclude industry-wide collective agreements that contain clauses to allow plant-specific agreements to be reached by works councils and managers in an establishment. These can include deviations below the standards set by the collective agreement. Despite this adaptability, collective bargaining coverage continues to fall – with many firms not joining employers' associations or bargaining directly with unions – and there is evidence of the illegal undercutting of collective agreements by those firms in employers' associations. The trend toward decentralization has been reinforced by the ability of employers to use the threat of relocating production, or more realistically, withholding investment, to force concessions from works councils. The opportunity for employers to play German plants off against each other has also been enhanced where a firm has establishments in both eastern and western Germany. With the total remuneration package in the new länder remaining considerably below western levels, pressure has been placed on west German councils to make concessions.

Secondly, the structure of the German economy and labour markets has changed with the (comparatively late) contraction of the manufacturing base and the expansion of the private services sector. This has had a dramatic impact on trade union membership. While the retention of a large proportion of industrial employment undoubtedly contributed to the resilience of the German unions in the 1980s, the workers hit hardest by de-industrialization are those male blue-collar workers that have been traditionally well-organized and supportive of class-based policies. By contrast, unions continue to experience difficulties in organizing women, younger workers and those with atypical work patterns – workers who constitute a large component of service sector employment. Finally, business restructuring has resulted in a shift towards smaller business units, notably in the new länder where the trend has also been for both newly founded and (re-)privatized firms to employ fewer workers, with establishment size notably smaller than in the west. The reduction in establishment size creates additional problems for unions in representing workers, with union membership levels, and works council and collective bargaining coverage considerably lower in small and medium-sized firms.

The extent of the problems which unions face can be seen in the data on works council and collective bargaining coverage and, of course, union membership. Surveys suggest that the proportion of workers covered by collective bargaining fell between 1995 and 2001 from 83.1% to 70.7% in western Germany and from 73.4% to 56.2% in eastern Germany. Similarly, the proportion of workers represented by works councils had fallen by 2002 to 49.2% in west Germany and 40.0% in east Germany. Finally, union density had fallen from 38.3% in 1980 to 24.9% by 2001, with unions belonging to the main DGB confederation only recruiting one in five workers into membership. In terms of numbers, membership of DGB unions had fallen from 13,749,000 after unification in 1991 to 7,363,147 by 2003.

The problems facing the German economy have also impacted upon union demarcations and structure. Increasingly the traditional distinctions between industries and industrial branches have become blurred as a result of firm restructuring and diversification. This has led some employers to try and move to avoid, or to agree "cheaper" collective agreements, but has also led increasingly to demarcation disputes between unions, especially when trying to break into weakly regulated sectors. This situation has not been helped by a merger process that has seen the number of DGB unions fall from 16 in 1980 to eight. The creation of the united private and public services union Ver.di (which incorporated the former non-DGB white collar workers' union DAG that recruited across all industries) has added to the problem of demarcation disputes. Indeed, German union structure can be classified increasingly as general and occupational unionism rather than the traditional industrial unionism.

Perhaps the clearest indication of the problems facing German unions is the "defeat" of the metalworkers' union, IG Metall, in its attempts to implement the 35-hour working week in eastern Germany in 2003. After a four-week strike in the east German metalworking sector failed to force the employers' associations to concede the reduction of the working week from 38 to 35 hours (the amount nominally worked in the west), IG Metall was obliged to call off the strike and admit defeat. The defeat had important ramifications within the union, where there was an acrimonious debate about the strike and the IG Metall leadership. Significantly, the defeat of IG Metall, traditionally the pace-setting or vanguard DGB union, has also led to wider discussion within the union movement about future policy. It is noticeable that the issue of working time has subsequently come to dominate debate over industrial relations, with employers seeking cost savings through a return to the 40-hour week, and unions where possible making concessions in return for job security, as reflected by agreements at Siemens and Daimler-Chrysler in 2004.

The debates over the development and regulation of the economy and industrial relations are not confined to the unions. Increasingly neo-liberal economists and business leaders have criticized the level of labour market regulation and the legal framework that underpins collective bargaining and workplace representation through works councils. The employers' associations have generally been cautious about calling for a major overhaul of the collective bargaining system. However, in February 2000, the leaders of the four main employers' and business associations (the Confederation of German Employers' Associations, BDA; the Confederation of German Industries, BDI; the German Association of Chambers of Commerce, DIHT; and the Central Association of German Crafts, ZHD) jointly called for changes to the Collective Agreement Act. These criticisms are now being reflected in the policies of the Christian Democratic

(CDU/CSU) and liberal (FDP) opposition parties, which focus upon "modernizing labour law" through amendment of both the Collective bargaining Law (Tarifvertragsgesetz) and the Works Constitution Act (Betriebsverfassungsgesetz) effectively to allow the legal undercutting of terms and conditions established in collective agreements. For the time being the SPD–Green federal government have indicated that such reforms will not be undertaken, though Chancellor Schröder has indicated that such reforms would not be ruled out if (employers and) unions were unable to institute greater flexibility through collective bargaining.

The SPD-led federal government, having largely failed in its attempts to facilitate consensual changes to labour market regulation through the tripartite "Alliance for Jobs" (largely due to differences between unions and employers over "employment-oriented" pay increases), have increasingly attempted, notably through implementing proposals of the Hartz Commission, to push through more radical reforms of the labour market. This has included the removal of laws protecting workers from dismissal in companies with 5-9 employees and restricting the number of unemployed workers entitled to unemployment benefit with the explicit aim of "encouraging" the unemployed into the expanding low-wage sector.

In summary, it is perhaps an overstatement to say that German trade unions are facing a crisis, but membership developments; the decline in collective bargaining coverage; and a more neo-liberal approach to labour market reform from the social democratic government, all provide indications of the considerable problems facing German unions. The pragmatic concession-bargaining agenda that unions have pursued since the 1990s, in order to try and maintain a regulatory framework for industry-wide collective bargaining, is increasingly running counter to the effective cornerstones of union policy – reducing work time to create employment and increasing income levels to boost consumption. With increasing decentralization of decision-making to establishment level, there is also a fear of sectionalism (Betriebsegoismus) and greater tensions between works councils and unions. Nevertheless, German unions remain important political and economic actors and are also at the forefront of attempts to improve co-ordination of union activities at European level.

3 Trade Union Centre

Deutscher Gewerkschaftsbund (DGB)
German Trade Union Federation
Address. Burgstrasse 29-30, D-10178 Berlin
Phone. +49 30 24060 211 (press office)
Fax. +49 30 24060 324 (press office)
E-mail. info@bundesvorstand.deb.de
Website. www.dgb.de (German, with sections in English, French and Spanish)
Leadership. Dieter Schulte (president); Ursula Engelen-Kefer (vice-president)
Membership. 7,363,147 (2003)
History and character. The General German Federation of Trade Unions (ADGB) was founded in 1868 by delegates representing 142,000 workers. Bismarck's Anti-Socialist Law of 1878 sharply curtailed union activity, but when this law expired in 1890 a new and overwhelmingly social democratic confederation, the General Kommission der Gewerkschaften (General Commission of Trade Unions), was formed. After World War I this was in turn succeeded by a reborn ADGB, set up in 1919 and the largest confederation in the Weimar period. The ADGB, in common with other trade union organizations, was abolished after the accession to power of Hitler in 1933, when the unions were co-ordinated into the Labour Front (Deutsche Arbeitsfront).

Following the surrender and Allied occupation of Germany in 1945, trade unions were at first permitted only on a land (state) or zonal basis, and in April 1947 the Deutscher Gewerkschaftsbund (DGB) was set up in the British zone (which included the Ruhr). After initial resistance from the French military government, the three occupying powers agreed to the establishment of a tri-zonal federation. At a 1949 Munich conference a tri-zonal DGB was formed by 101 unions representing over 4.8 million members. Workers in the Soviet zone were by this time organized in an entirely separate body, the FDGB, and the constitution of the DGB provided that only unions operating within the territory of the new West German Federal Republic would be admitted to membership (although it also operated in West Berlin).

Among the principles adopted at the founding convention were: (i) the participation of organized labour in economic planning; (ii) the nationalization of key industries such as mining, iron and steel, large chemical, and power industries and major credit banks; (iii) freedom for unions to engage in collective bargaining with employers. The evolution of federal public policy after 1949 led for some years to strained relations between the (Christian Democratic) coalition government and the DGB, and the ultimate enactment of legislation providing a framework for modified forms of co-determination, while the issue of nationalization waned in significance. Historically, the DGB has been associated with the main outlines of policy of the Social Democratic Party (SPD), although it is politically unaffiliated.

Sixteen industrial federations were created on the industrial union principle, which united all workers at a plant in the same union. These federations are autonomous and bargain separately (the DGB as an umbrella organization neither negotiates nor concludes collective bargaining agreements), but must accept the DGB constitution. They have no direct religious or political affiliations. The DGB's role is to co-ordinate joint demands and broad campaigns for its affiliates and represent the union movement as a whole. It also provides information and advice to unions at company level and to works councils. The form of organization adopted in the 1940s reflected a compromise between those advocating a highly centralized structure, with coordinated industrial sector unions, and those who advocated a central organization on the model of the British TUC, where the individual unions are freely associated bodies with total autonomy. In practice the larger unions, such as IG Metall, enjoy a degree of autonomy, arising from their industrial strength, virtually comparable with that of the major British unions.

The DGB is entitled to equal representation in the executive bodies for the self-regulation of social insurance funds (health, accident and pension funds) as well as the Federal Office of Employment. Its representatives also sit on a range of other public bodies.

The DGB has an executive board (of which the president is a member) elected by a delegate congress every four years. A federal executive committee is formed by the executive board and the presidents of the member unions. However the highest decision-making body between conventions is the federal council, which is composed of the executive committee, the presidents of the regions of the DGB and representatives of the DGB's affiliates.

During the 1980s, while union centres throughout the western world experienced losses in membership, the position of the DGB remained stable. Membership of 7.88 million in 1980 was little changed at 7.94 million in 1990. The DGB faced particular challenges following the unification of Germany, absorbing the unionized workforce in the former East Germany. Most DGB affiliates recorded large membership gains as they absorbed members from the new länder only to lose numbers under the impact of the recession and shake-out in inefficient industries in the east from 1991 onwards. This was exacerbated by losses in west Germany caused by structural changes in the economy. DGB membership surged to 11.8 million in 1991 only to fall back to 8.3 million by 1998. While the loss of members was most extreme in the east, where membership fell by an average 11.7% per annum in the period 1991–98, there was also decline in the west, averaging 2.1% per annum in the same period. The only affiliate not to suffer heavy losses after 1991 was the Police Union (GdP).

One consequence of falling membership was the merger of affiliates. In the late 1990s the number of DGB affiliates was reduced from 16 to 11. In 1996 the horticulture, agriculture and forestry union (Gewerkschaft Gartenbau-, Land- und Forstwirtschaft, GGLF) merged with the building and construction union IG Bau-Steine-Erden (IG BSE) to form IG Bauen-Agrar-Umwelt (IGBAU). In 1997 three affiliates merged to form Industriegewerkschaft Bergbau, Chemie, Energie (IGBCE) (mining, chemicals and energy), while the textile and clothing workers' union Gewerkschaft Textil-Bekleidung and wood and plastics union Gewerkschaft Holz und Kunststoff were absorbed into IG Metall in 1998–99.

The number of affiliates fell to eight during 2001 with the completion of a proposed merger of four DGB unions, together with the independent DAG, to form the DGB-affiliated Ver.di (Vereinigte Dienstleistungsgewerkschaft), larger than IG Metall. The unions involved were the Public Services, Transport and Traffic Union (ÖTV), the Media union (IG Medien), the Commerce, Banking and Insurance union (HBV) and the Postal Workers' union (DPG). Between them these unions had lost in the range between 23% (DPG) and 36% (HBV) of their members in the period 1991–98. The objectives of the merger were to rationalize the unions' cost base in view of declining memberships, avoid demarcation conflicts and create the scale and resources to organize service areas that are currently little unionized. The new organization is decentralized, retaining separate decision-making and collective bargaining for its different sectors. Further rationalization of DGB affiliates is considered likely. An increasing problem is that the historic demarcation lines between DGB affiliates have been confused by the rapid development of new sectors. In telecommunications, IG Metall, IG BCE and Ver.di unions have all signed collective agreements.

In November 1996 an extraordinary reform congress meeting at Dresden agreed a new basic programme (Grundsatzprogramm). The programme was widely interpreted as marking the formal abandonment by the DGB of its historical demand for nationalization of key industries, in favour of a social market economy. Its key themes included:

1. Concern that radical market deregulation would undermine the functioning of the collective bargaining system. The trade unions had a "fundamental interest in the existence of well-functioning employers' associations" which could conclude and enforce collective agreements, and the spread of individual contracts was undermining this.

2. Concern that such "market radicalism" would in turn undermine the consensual nature of the state. "The trade unions will not accept a market economy which dispenses with the social state framework rooted in the constitution."

3. Fears of the impact of globalization on German workers with their relatively high costs: the DGB pressed for cooperation between the ILO and WTO on the implementation of core labour standards to prevent countries with unregulated labour markets from achieving competitive advantage.

4. Awareness of the challenges to the union structure posed by the rise of non-traditional employment: home-working, self-employment, individual contracts, part-time working, temporary agency work, fixed term contracts, and the informal economy. Such forms of labour were difficult to reconcile with the traditional forms of collective bargaining and standard conditions of employment, and those involved in such employment were outside union structures. This was reflected in the membership of the unions. The unions also had to be increasingly aware of the needs of those not in the working economy at all, such as the unemployed, pensioners and the prematurely retired. A "more open" union culture was required, with more attention paid to small workplaces.

5. Emphasis on finding at the European level a coordinated Europe-wide collective bargaining policy, an executive accountable to the European Parliament, and a strengthening of the European Trade Union Confederation (ETUC).

6. The extension of co-determination in the workplace, including expanding the role of works councils to smaller enterprises.

While arguing for the extension of the role of works

councils co-determination, in areas such as work organization and job protection, the DGB has also sought the further involvement of trade unions in steering works council activities. It is concerned at the trend for works councils to reach agreements with employers that modify or undermine collective bargaining agreements reached with unions. The DGB has also called for more regulation of temporary work agencies and measures to ensure temporary workers have the same terms and conditions as regular employees. In 1997 the DGB launched an "Action Programme for Employment and Social Justice". This emphasized job creation and advocated a basket of policies including reducing overtime, encouraging part-retirement, introducing a 35-hour week, increasing vocational training and an active employment policy to assist the long-term employed get back to work.

The DGB was founded on the principle that it should be a unified union, not exclusively representative of any party or political tendency. However, it has a historic majority identification with the SPD, just as the employers' associations have a majority identification with the conservative parties. Between 75 and 85% of DGB officials are estimated to be members of the SPD, and three-quarters of SPD members of the Bundestag are members of DGB-affiliated unions (Chancellor Schröder is himself a member of Ver.di). While the DGB did not officially endorse any party in the 1998 elections, at which the SPD regained power after 16 years, its electoral platform focused on the failures of the CDU–FDP government to stop the rise in unemployment and called in many respects for policies similar to those advocated by the SPD. Walter Riester, the vice-president of IG Metall, went on to become Minister of Labour in the incoming SPD-led government.

At the same time, tensions arose over what some in the DGB saw as the pro-business "new middle" (neue mitte) policies of the new government. While union leaderships have made some moves towards accepting the need for greater flexibility, there is a continuing basic unease about policies that emphasize the primacy of the market and encouragement of entrepreneurship. Within the SPD there has also been a current of opinion seeking more distance (on the model of the Labour Party and the British TUC) between the party and the unions. This is reinforced by the fact that the DGB, with declining membership, and little representation in many dynamic sectors of the economy, can no longer speak with assurance as the voice of labour.

International affiliations. ICFTU; ETUC; TUAC
Affiliated unions. There are now 8 industrially based affiliates.

1. IG Bauen-Agrar-Umwelt (IGBAU) (construction, agriculture and environment)
Address. Olof-Palme-Strasse 19, Frankfurt-am-Main 60439
Phone. +49 69 95737 0
Fax. +49 69 95737 800
E-mail. international@igbau.de
Website. www.igbau.de (German only)
Leadership. Klaus Wiesehuegel (president).
Membership. 461,162

History and character. Formed by the 1996 merger of the horticulture, agriculture and forestry union (Gewerkschaft Gartenbau-, Land- und Forstwirtschaft, GGLF) and the building and construction union IG Bau-Steine-Erden (IG BSE).

2. Industriegewerkschaft Bergbau, Chemie, Energie (IGBCE) (mining, chemicals and energy)
Address. Königsworther Platz 6, Hannover 30167
Phone. +49 511 7631 453
Fax. +49 511 7631 713
E-mail. (European department) abt.europa@igbce.de
Website. www.igbce.de (German, English section)
Leadership. Hubertus Schmoldt (president)
Membership. 800,762

History and character. The IGBCE held its founding congress in October 1997 and was the result of the merger of three previous DGB affiliates, IG Bergbau and Energie (mining and energy), IG Chemie-Papier-Keramik (chemicals, paper and ceramics) and the much smaller Gewerkschaft Leder (leatherworkers). Hubertus Schmoldt, formerly president of IG Chemie, became president of the new union. Internationally it is affiliated to the European Mine, Chemical and Energy Workers Federation (EMCEF) and the International Federation of Chemical, Energy, Mine and General Workers' Unions (ICEM).

3. Gewerkschaft Erziehung und Wissenschaft (GEW) (education and science)
Address. Reifenberger Str. 21, Frankfurt 60489
Phone. +49 69 78973 0
Fax. +49 69 78973 202
E-mail. info@gew.de
Website. www.gew.de (German only)
Leadership. Eva-Maria Stange (president)
Membership. 260,842

History and character. In May 1997, Dieter Wunder became the first president of a DGB affiliate to be voted out of office, being succeeded by Eva-Maria Stange, the first woman to lead the union and the first leader of a DGB affiliate from the former East Germany. She had previously been a member of the East German GUE teachers' union, which was absorbed into the GEW after unification. 44% of the GEW's membership (i.e. a disproportionately large number) were reported to be in east Germany. In October 1997 GEW was one of five DGB affiliates that announced their intention to merge (together with the independent DAG) to form a new super-union, Ver.di. In July 1998, however, GEW withdrew from merger discussions. Concern had developed that the 289,000 members of GEW would lose identity and distinctive representation in a super-union of more than 3 million members.

4. IG Metall (IGM) (metalworkers)
Address. Lyoner Str. 32, Frankfurt 60528
Phone. +49 69 6693 2667 (international dept.)
Fax. +49 69 6693 2843
Website. www.igmetall.de (German; English section)
Leadership. Jürgen Peters (president)
Membership. 2,525,348

History and character. Prior to the creation of Ver.di, IG Metall was the largest union in, and the spearhead of, the DGB. It united workers on the industrial union principle throughout metal manufacturing, metal processing and engineering. The union has traditional acted as the pace-setting union in collective bargaining rounds and has, consequently, been involved in most industrial action. After an initial surge, membership has fallen considerably since unification. This reflects the collapse of the former GDR economy and wider contraction of German manufacturing and the growing diversification of metal industry employers into areas such as telecommunications and IT, eroding IG Metall's organizational area.

In 1998–99 IG Metall absorbed two other DGB unions, Gewerkschaft Textil-Bekleidung (GTB, textile and clothing), which joined with effect from June 1998, and Gewerkschaft Holz und Kunststoff (GHK, wood and plastics), which joined at the end of 1999. The textiles and clothing sector had been severely reduced by cheaper international competition, and of the 300,000 jobs in this sector in eastern Germany before unification only 24,000 were left by the late 1990s. The GTB had lost 43% of its members since 1991. GHK had likewise been badly affected by loss of members, losing 33% in the period 1991–96.

IG Metall has been the leading force on the issue of working hours reduction, successfully winning a determined fight to achieve a 35-hour working week through strike action in 1984, which was finally implemented in 1995. It was also successful in hindering attempts by east German employers to end staged equalization of pay and conditions in the new länder in 1993, again through strike action. However, in 2003 the union was damaged by the failure of its use of the strike weapon in an attempt to introduce the 35-hour week in the new länder, with bitter divisions within the union over the strike and the general political direction of the union. Finally, a compromise was reached whereby IG Metall president Klaus Zwickel stood down, Jürgen Peters was elected president and Berthold Huber vice president by a union congress in 2003. Peters (a leading advocate of the failed strike) has been strongly critical of the direction of SPD policy.

IG Metall is the leading individual member of the International Metalworkers' Federation trade secretariat.

5. Gewerkschaft Nahrung-Genuss-Gaststätten (NGG) (food, beverages, catering)
Address. Haubachstr. 76, Hamburg 22765
Phone. +49 40 38013 0
Fax. +49 40 3892637
E-mail. hauptverwaltung@ngg.net
Website. www.gewerkschaft-ngg.de (German only)
Leadership. Franz-Josef Möllenberg (president)
Membership. 236,507

6. Gewerkschaft der Polizei (GdP) (police)
Address. Stromstr. 4, Berlin 10555
Phone. +49 30 399921 0
Fax. +49 30 399921-211
E-mail. gdp-bund-hilden@gdp-online.de
Website. www.gdp.de (German only)
Leadership. Konrad Freiberg (president)
Membership. 181,100

7. TRANSNET Gewerkschaft GdED
Address. Weilburger Strasse 24, Frankfurt 60326
Phone. +49 69 7536 0
Fax. +49 69 7536 222
E-mail. info@transnet.org
Website. www.transnet.org (German, English, Spanish, French and Turkish sections)
Leadership. Norbert Hansen (president)
Membership. 283,332
History and character. The new name was adopted in May 2000 by the Gewerkschaft der Eisenbahner Deutschlands (railway workers' union, GdED) to reflect better the broadening of its membership to include workers in other transport, services, and telecommunications. In addition to recruiting in the telecoms field GdED is also looking to gain members in passenger transport areas dominated by the ÖTV. Norbert Hansen, GdED president, is also president of the European Transport Workers' Federation (ETF) and the union emphasizes international cooperation between unions in the transport field. It is also a member of the ITF.

8. Vereinte Dienstleistungsgewerkschaft e. V. (ver.di) (united services union)
Address. Paula-Thiede-Ufer 10, 10179 Berlin
Phone. +49 30 6956 0
Fax. +49 30 6956 3141
Website. www.verdi.de (German; English, French, Spanish, Polish Czech and Russian sections)
Leadership. Frank Bsirske (president)
Membership. 2,614,094
History and character. Ver.di came into being in 2001 as the result of a merger between the following unions: the non-DGB white-collar workers' union DAG; the postal workers' union DPG; the retail trade, banking and insurance union HBV; the media union IG Median; and the public sector and transport union ÖTV. Given the size and coverage of the union, it is structured into thirteen sectors. Sectoral coverage includes financial services, utilities and disposal, health, social services, welfare and churches, social insurance, education, science and research, federal government (Bund) and federal states (länder), local authorities, the media, art and culture, printing and paper, industrial services and production, telecommunications, information technology, data processing, postal services, forwarding companies and logistics, transport, commerce, and special services. Despite the hope of using the merger to break into new areas of private services, the union has not been able halt membership losses, leading to increasing pressure being put upon the numerous offices the union has inherited.

4 Other Trade Union Organizations

Christlicher Gewerkschaftsbund Deutschlands (CGB)
German Christian Workers' Federation
Address. Obentrautstraße 57, 10963 Berlin
Phone. +49 30 21 02 17-30
Fax. +49 30 21 02 17-40
E-mail. CGB.Bund@cgb.info
Website. www.cgb.info (German only)
Leadership. Wolfgang Jaeger (president)
Membership. 300,000
History and character. The CGB, which was founded in 1959, is of a social Christian orientation, although the churches have generally not actively supported religious-based unionism since World War II. It is a

general federation of 16 affiliated unions, with members spread across the blue and white-collar sectors and the public service.

The CGB was little affected by unification, gaining only a few thousand new members in former East Germany, giving it 311,000 members in 1991. Conversely, it was also little affected by the general loss of trade union memberships in the east after 1991 and its membership remained little changed through the 1990s. There has been persistent conflict between its metalworkers' affiliate and IG Metall.
International affiliations. CESI

Deutscher Beamtenbund (DBB)
German Civil Servants' Federation
Address. dbb forum Berlin, Friedrichstraße 169/170, 10117 Berlin
Phone. +49 30 4081-40
Fax. +49 30 4081-4999
E-mail. info@dbb-forum-berlin.de
Website. www.dbb.de (German; English and French summaries)
Leadership. Erhard Geyer (president)
Membership. 1,250,000
History and character. The DBB traces its origins back to 1918: it was dissolved by the Nazis in 1933 and recreated in 1950. It represents both white-collar and wage-earning public employees, as well as civil servant status employees (Beamte), and by law must be involved in the formulation of legislation and regulations relating to civil service matters. The DBB undertakes to defend and promote the social, legal and professional interests of its members and those of its affiliated organizations. It is politically independent.

Members include teachers, policemen, employees and civil servants of the armed forces, railway and post office officials, employees in the justice system, and social services staff. They work in the public sector and the privatized services sector. There are 37 member unions and state associations in all 16 of the länder. Unlike most trade union organizations, the DBB did not suffer membership losses in the 1990s.

"Beamte", or career public servants (in 1995 constituting 1.9 million of 5.4 million public sector employees), have traditionally enjoyed guaranteed lifetime employment in exchange for a duty of loyalty, which includes a prohibition on taking strike action. The 1997 Act on Civil Service Law Reform took some steps towards making performance rather than seniority the key to promotion and remuneration and reforming pension schemes. The DBB opposed the reforms saying they were aimed at cutting costs rather than introducing modern management methods. In the summer of 1997 it organized demonstrations (along with DGB public sector affiliates, including the GEW teachers' union, most of whose members are classified as career public servants) against the new law.

Organs of the DBB include the DBB-Tarifunion, which represents employees on wages and salaries issues; the DBB-Frauen, representing the 320,000 women members; and DBB-Jugend (youth). The DBB has permanent contacts with government. It has a legal claim to involvement in the formulation of general legislation and regulations governing public service matters. It provides a social service and has an education programme and college (BISOWE).
International affiliations. CESI; CIF

Ghana

Capital: Accra
Population: 20.76 m. (2004 est.)

1 Political and Economic Background

Ghana became an independent member of the Commonwealth in 1957 and a republic in 1960 under the leadership of the socialist Kwame Nkrumah. Nkrumah was overthrown in 1966 and there was then a succession of mainly military administrations until Flt.-Lt. Jerry Rawlings seized power temporarily in 1979, and then permanently in 1981. A civilian constitution was approved in a referendum in April 1992 and Rawlings was elected President later that year as the candidate of his National Democratic Congress party. He was re-elected four years later and according to the constitution was obliged to stand down as President by the end of 2000. He did so and elections in December 2000 resulted in the election of John Kufuor, of the opposition centre-right New Patriotic Party (NPP), a development seen as indicating greater political stability and the consolidation of pluralism in the country. Kufuor was re-elected in December 2004, with his New Patriotic Party also holding a parliamentary majority.

Ghana's foreign exchange generating resources include gold, timber and cocoa. Under Rawlings from the mid-1980s Ghana moved away from state economic control and encouraged the private sector. During the 1990s Ghana enjoyed annual average GDP growth above 4% and international donors such as the IMF and the World Bank backed the government's economic liberalization programme. However, Ghana remained reliant on international assistance and austerity measures led to periodic outbreaks of discontent. In the four years since Kufuor came into office, inflation has been sharply reduced and growth has run at 5% per annum. Some 60% of the working population are engaged in subsistence agriculture.

GDP (purchasing power parity) $44.44bn. (2004 est.); GDP per capita (purchasing power parity) $2,200 (2004 est.).

2 Trade Unionism

Ghanaian trade unionism has a long history stretching back before World War II, by which time there were a number of well-established unions. Provision for the registration of trade unions was made under British rule in 1941, and the organized labour movement subsequently became linked to the political movement for independence. The TUC was the sole central organization from its creation in 1945 but has been reorganized on a number of occasions in response to political developments. More recently WCL affiliates have formed their own federation.

The foundation statute governing employment relations in Ghana is the Industrial Relations Act 1958. Ghana ratified ILO Convention No. 87 (Freedom of Association and Protection of the Right to Organize, 1948) in 1965 and Convention No. 98 (Right to Organize and Collective Bargaining, 1949) in 1959.

The constitution formally provides for free collective bargaining in both the private sector and in the state-owned enterprises (SOEs). National strikes are rare. Most open disputes are at company level and occasionally they may lead to government intervention. The ICFTU has complained of the wide discretionary powers given the Registrar of Trade Unions to refuse to register unions and of lengthy pre-strike procedures which mean that there has been no legal strike since independence, but strikes in pursuit of improvements to wages and conditions are not uncommon.

In October 2003 a new labour law created a tripartite National Labour Commission that would work to help resolve disputes. The new law removed control of the issuing of bargaining certificates (required by unions seeking to enter into collective bargaining arrangements) from the TUC and into the hands of the Labour Office.

3 Trade Union Centre

Trades Union Congress of Ghana (TUC)
Address. Hall of Trade Unions, PO Box 701, Accra
Phone. +233 21 662 568 / 666803
Fax. +233 21 66 71 61
E-mail. tuc@ighmail.com
Leadership. Kwasi Adu-Amankwah (secretary general)
History and character. The TUC of Ghana was founded in 1945 as the Gold Coast Trades Union Congress. It became closely linked to Nkrumah's Convention People's Party and was reorganized following the Nkrumah's fall in 1966. It was dissolved in 1971 and reorganized again in 1972. Following the 1981 Rawlings' coup the TUC secretary-general Alhaji A. M. Issifu was forced to resign and a radical faction supporting the new regime announced that all senior officials of member unions had been dismissed. The union movement remained in turmoil in 1982–84, as workers' defence committees vied with the radicalized unions for the representation of Ghana's workers. However, following a 1984 reorganization of defence committees, the labour movement was restored to its former structure. The TUC committed itself to the new government's basic goals, but criticized aspects of government policy. The TUC's principal concern was to maintain living standards in the face of price liberalization under the economic recovery programme.

The TUC was actively involved in the move to greater democracy in the early 1990s and had ten members of the Consultative Assembly that wrote the new civilian Ghanaian constitution adopted in a referendum in April 1992. It subsequently opposed government austerity measures and called for "circumspection" in the privatization process. In 2000 the TUC was consulted in the drafting of a proposed new labour code.

In recent years the TUC has continued to actively criticize elements of government policy, including the sudden ending of oil subsidies in 2003, which had an immediate economic impact on workers.

The TUC comprises 17 affiliated national unions. There is an associated Ghana labour college, founded in 1967.
International affiliation. ICFTU

4 Other Trade Union Organization

Ghana Federation of Labour (GFL)
Address. PO Box 209, Accra, Ghana
Phone. +233 22 205369 / 27/552433
Fax. +233 22 20 62 51
Leadership. Abraham Koomson (general secretary)
International affiliations. WCL (affiliated 1999)

Greece

Capital: Athens
Population: 10.65 m. (2004 est.)

1 Political and Economic Background

Greece entered the post-World War II era with a protracted and bloody civil war (1946-49) fought between a government backed by British and American support and the communist-led Democratic Army. The communist forces were defeated, but the parliamentary regime established following the end of the hostilities had a distinctly authoritarian hue. After a brief centrist interlude, the right maintained a firm grip on power between 1952 and 1963 and was none too scrupulous about the means it employed to retain it. Widespread popular disenchantment brought a centre-left government to power in 1963-64, but the king intervened to bring it down in July 1965. On April 21, 1967, middle-ranking officers launched a coup designed to thwart a new centre-left victory in elections planned for May of that year. The military regime lasted for seven years, collapsing in July 1974 amidst severe domestic and foreign crisis. Democratic elections and a referendum held in November 1974 created a parliamentary regime (the Third Hellenic Republic) and abolished the monarchy. Greece joined the European Community in 1981.

Since 1974 the dominant political parties have been the Pan-Hellenic Socialist Movement (PASOK) and the conservative New Democracy party (ND). The ND was in government from 1974 to 1981 and again from 1990 to 1993, while PASOK held power first in 1981–1990 and subsequently between October 1993 and March 2004, when it was defeated by ND in the elections of that month. From the late 1980s onward PASOK has largely abandoned its earlier left-wing rhetoric in favour of a more conventional social democratic identity supportive of Greek membership in the EU and NATO.

Greece has a relatively small industrial base; services, including tourism, shipping, trade, and banking predominate. There is a significant informal economy (up to 30% of GNP) and many small enterprises. In the early 1980s PASOK pursued an expansionary policy, relaxing fiscal and income controls and espousing partial socialization of industry. Mounting economic difficulties gradually forced a reversal, however, and in 1987 PASOK began to liberalize the economy, a policy continued since then. A driving force for economic policy in recent years has been the effort to achieve the qualifying criteria for joining the European Monetary Union. Though Greece failed to meet the criteria required for participation in the single European currency at its launch in 1999, it did succeed in joining in 2001 (although in September 2004 the ND government issued revised statistics indicating that Greece had achieved membership on the basis of inaccurate official statistics). The double-digit inflation of the 1980s and early 1990s was brought under control, and since 1995 Greece has been enjoying growth rates above the EU average, although remaining the poorest EU country (of those that joined before 2004) apart from Portugal. Governments have had less success in tackling the problem of continually high unemployment (9.3% in 2003), and issues pertaining to economic restructuring and privatization, where there is considerable resistance from unions, professional groups and public opinion. The public debt remains high (at 103.8% of GDP in 2004, down from 105% in 1999) while the state sector still accounts for 45% of GDP. EU funding is a significant factor in assisting economic restructuring.

GDP (purchasing power parity) $213.6bn. (2004 est.); GDP per capita (purchasing power parity) $20,000 (2004 est.).

2 Trade Unionism

Because of late industrialization, a labour movement emerged relatively late in Greece, only in the last quarter of the 19th century. However, the Greece business sector's reliance on trade with a concomitant hesitance to invest in industry, and a strong penchant for financial speculation and economic adventurism, produced a fluid labour market and made projects for the strategic incorporation of the labour movement appear both relatively expensive and useless. As early as the 1910s progressive labour legislation was introduced by the governments of Eleftherios Venizelos, but was stalled by acerbic employer resistance. During the inter-war period, the labour movement faced repression. The extremely narrow political-legal space allotted to the labour movement, constant intervention by the state in the internal life of trade unions, and the coercive presence of the police and army in virtually all forms of labour protest precluded the ideological incorporation of the labour movement and produced an intensely conflictive political culture. As a result a vicious circle was set in motion: the more coercive the state became, the more coercion was needed.

These structural features had two important consequences. First, the labour movement was characterized by the strong role that politics and party organizations played in its functioning. Unlike the situation in Western Europe, such organizations had a longer history than trade unions and, as a result, trade union discourse developed not as a forerunner but as a subspecies of political discourse. Even more crucially, by precluding genuine union autonomy, the constrictive political environment made it appear that having a well-defined political goal was a prerequisite for undertaking meaningful trade-union action. Second, the labour movement was characterized by intense segmentation and an almost permanent organizational fluidity. Although trade unions and the outer marks of a generally robust trade union life existed, they had only limited functional content, concealing a constantly low union density, membership instability, and a broad array of organizational irrationalities. This had contradictory consequences regarding the political sociology of trade union leaders. Whilst it was relatively easy for them to rise to the leadership (especially when they were linked to the state), the bureaucratic structures they were erecting were exceedingly weak, unable to control the movement and, much less, ensure its incorporation into channels of vertical communication with the state. This, in turn, precluded the institutionalization of the movement, giving it an informal, unpredictable and intermittently convulsive dynamic. This convulsive dynamic tended to spread to society at large though informal communication networks rather than through the industrial shop floor.

This informal mode of communication between unions and their potential membership rendered labour's mobilizing capacity largely immune to adverse environmental effects, and became particularly evident during the years of the German occupation in the 1940s, when the labour movement played a decisive role in the national resistance movement. The eruption of a wave of political strikes in 1942-43 (more than 100) and the emergence of new participatory institutions despite the coercive presence of the German occupation forces essentially abolished the old state and created hopes for the development of rational organizational structures. These, however, were crushed in the 1946-49 Civil War.

As trade unions were denied all autonomy by the repressive state in the 1950s and 1960s, the problem of trade union under-representation increased. At a time when genuine labour activists were persecuted, a caste of leaders developed, "ironically known as *ergatopateres* (workers' fathers). Sustained by patronage relations with the government, their main task was to control the movement by convening rigged conferences and de-registering troublesome branches. Since their income was received from the government rather than from members' dues, they were under no real pressure to act effectively as workers' representatives" (N. Kritsantonis, 'Greece: From State Authoritarianism to Modernization', in A. Ferner and R. Hyman (eds.), *Industrial Relations in the New Europe*, Oxford: Blackwell, 1992, pp. 613-14). This period further crystallized the Greek labour movement's contentious repertoire. If union autonomy was severely compromised by the actions of a repressive state, then the response would have to be similarly political. The eruption of labour militancy that marked the mid-

1960s developed largely outside union organizational channels and was spearheaded by political, not narrowly economic, developments.

After 1974 there was considerable liberalization and efforts were made for the institutionalization of the labour movement. All workers other than those in the armed forces could now freely join unions whilst discrimination against unions was declared illegal (indeed courts reinstated workers dismissed for organizing unions). Union autonomy remained compromised, however, and union affairs open to government intervention despite the formal guarantees of Article 12 of the 1975 Constitution. As a result, the Greek workers' traditionally low propensity to organize along with their strong penchant for plebiscitarian political action remained, this time in the context of progressively rising unemployment. This helps explain both the outbreak of intermittent strike waves against the background of relatively low union densities and the enormous political factionalism that beset the trade union movement in the late 1970s and 1980s. It also lies at the core of contemporary union dilemmas.

Under legislation introduced in 1982 there is a prescribed three level structure of trade unions: primary (local or enterprise-level); secondary (regional or sectoral); and tertiary (national centres). These form a pyramid, at the apex of which are the General Confederation of Greek Workers (GSEE) representing both private and public sector workers, and the Confederation of Public Servants (ADEDY), representing civil servants. Of the three union forms only the local or enterprise unions (primary level) can recruit workers directly (however, 20 workers are needed to form an enterprise union, and this excludes many of Greece's large number of small and medium-sized enterprises). One major consequence of this organizational structure is the enormous fragmentation ensuing: there exist about 4,000 primary unions, 81 professional federations, and 72 labour centres. As a result there is great overlap of activities, inter-union antagonism (since workers in one and the same enterprise or region are sought by different unions), and generally poor co-ordination. A related problem is the total absence of unionization among workers in the informal sector and the unemployed. At its 31st conference in November 2002, the GSEE sought to address some of these problems, albeit with questionable results. Proposals for the merging of several professional federations and labour centres were tabled in favour of establishing secretariats and coordinating councils at the prefectural and regional levels for the purpose of exploring merger possibilities over the next five-year period (see also below). It seems that the number of union bodies will not diminish before more bodies are created.

In 1998 union density was estimated at about 30% compared with 40% at the start of the 1980s. However, whilst density for the GSEE had been declining (from 42.6% in 1983 to 23.5% in 1998), for the ADEDY it has been steadily rising (from 26.9% in 1983 to 49.4% in 1998). But it merits attention that the GSEE membership downward drift has lately been reversed. At its 32nd conference of March 2004, the GSEE claimed 450,160 members, up from 420, 610 in March 2001.

Most union funding comes not from dues but from a state body, the Workers' Welfare Foundation (literally, the Workers' Hearth, OEE), whose board comprises representatives of employers, government and the unions. The OEE was established in 1931 with the goal of elevating the economic, cultural and intellectual condition of the workers. Its main role, however, has been to fund unions on criteria that were described in a 1998 report by the GSEE's research arm, INE-GSEE, as "neither impartial nor objective". The OEE's funds come mainly from compulsory contributions paid by all employers and employees, irrespective of whether they are union members.

The unions are politicized and politically divided, a condition encouraged by a tradition of political interference: both the GSEE and ADEDY remain arenas for political battles (indeed in the period 1985–89 the GSEE virtually disintegrated over its relations with the PASOK government). PASOK supporters organize in the PASKE faction, New Democracy supporters in the DAKE and the Communists in the DAS.

Greek trade unionism remains heavily male-dominated. Women make up 30% of the (formal) work force but in 1998 constituted only 6% (133 of 2067) of elected members of union administrative boards/executive committees.

The GSEE draws up a framework National General Collective Agreement (most recently in May 2004 covering 2004/2005) with the central employers' organizations. There are no restrictions on private sector collective bargaining but there are restrictions in the civil service (though this has been balanced by the substantially entrenched power of the Civil Servants' Confederation, ADEDY). Before the 1990s Greek industrial relations oscillated between turbulent disputes and compulsory arbitration by the Ministry of Labour. A 1990 law on free collective bargaining, however, marked the withdrawal of the state from regulation of incomes, repealing a statute of 1955 and ending the long-standing system of compulsory arbitration. This law was the first explicit acknowledgment of the principle of voluntary negotiation. While still providing for voluntary arbitration, it now put mediation centre-stage through the services of a National Mediation and Arbitration Service (OMED). The 1990 Act also introduced two new types of agreement to supplement existing national and occupational agreements: sectoral agreements (which, like occupational agreements may be reached at the national, regional or city level), and enterprise agreements. Under the terms of the Act national agreements apply automatically to all employees without further Ministry of Labour intervention while more limited agreements have legal standing provided they improve on the minimum laid down in the national agreements. During the 1990s there was a steady increase in the number of collective bargaining agreements concluded directly between employers and unions and a corresponding decrease in the number of arbitration decisions reached through OMED, but this began to change in 2001-03. Fewer collective agreements and more arbitration agreements were registered for 2003 than in previous years, and the number of collective agreements at sectoral level declined significantly, from 96 in 2002 to 52 in 2003.

In the recent period there has been a marked upsurge in industrial action. A major landmark was the 24-hour national general strike jointly called by GSEE and ADEDY in April 2001 in opposition to government proposals to reform the social insurance system. A follow-up strike in May 2001 eventually forced the government to back down from its initial plans. The number of strikes and working hours lost continued to rise in 2002. Though adequate data are largely missing (due to poor functioning of the local labour inspectorates responsible for collecting the relevant data), it has been reported that in the first half of 2002 there were 23 strikes involving 103,294 strikers and 816,913 working hours lost (up from 15 strikes, 4,411 strikers and 45,618 working hours lost in 1999). Widespread strike activity also occurred during 2003, both in the public and the private sectors. The unions' basic demands related to pay policy reform and higher pay increases. The unions argue that, as Greece's unit labour costs have been low and declining, a solution to Greece's poor competitiveness cannot be found by lowering labour remuneration, but lies in areas such as the quality of training. Important factors in the recent wave of strike activity also included the rapid rise in inflation after the introduction of the euro and the manner of setting pay and pay scales in the public sector. In the private sector industrial action was sparked by the closure of several enterprises and an ensuing cluster of collective redundancies. The courts sometimes declare strikes illegal, for reasons such as lack of sufficient notice, but active enforcement of such rulings is not usual. Skeleton staffing must be maintained in a range of basic services, such as electricity, postal services, transport and banking, during strike action.

3 Trade Union Centres

General Confederation of Greek Labour (GSEE)
Address. 28 Octovriou 69 & Ainianos 4, 10210 Athens
Phone. +30 210 8834 611-15
Fax. +30 210 8202186, 210 8202187
Website. www.gsee.gr
Leadership. C. Polyzogopoulos (president)
Membership. About 450,000
History and character. The GSEE was founded in 1918. Following the 8th congress in 1946 the government deposed the elected executive and imposed one in its favour, and the GSEE thenceforth remained subject to government intervention. Following the downfall of the military dictatorship in 1974 the GSEE retained a semi-official character, and was opposed by a significant proportion of the labour force organized in independent unions which the government neither recognized nor funded. A turning point in GSEE evolution was its 22nd congress held in December 1983, electing a PASOK majority with a large communist minority: though contested, this was a congress broadly representative of existing tendencies within the organized labour movement. In the period 1986–89, however, internal strife broke out between PASOK supporters and practically everybody else. The communists and others boycotted the 23rd (1986) and 24th (1988) congresses accusing the PASOK government of direct interference in the confederation's affairs. The boycotted 1988 congress elected only members of the PASOK faction (PASKE) to the governing body and in 1989 the courts installed a new administration representing all five factions.

Factionalism remains institutionalized within the GSEE. PASOK supporters organized in PASKE remain the leading element but New Democracy (which was unrepresented in the 1980s, when the GSEE was split between PASOK and a strong communist faction) is now a factor. The 32nd congress, held in March 2004, elected a 45-member administrative board (to remain in office for three years) comprising 21 seats for PASKE (which lost its absolute majority), 11 for DAKE (the New Democracy faction), 10 for DAS (the faction of the Communist Party, KKE), 2 for "Autonomous Intervention", the faction supporting the Coalition of the Radical Left (Synaspismos), and 1 for ASKE, another faction also supporting ND.

Though GSEE policy reflects a compromise between these different currents, the confederation is in the process of reviewing its objectives in the face of current challenges and problems, including organizational restructuring and recruiting more young people, women and foreign economic migrants. GSEE officials hope that the objectives, set in accordance with the decisions of the 31st organizational conference of November 2002, will create a new powerful dynamic for the Greek union movement.

The GSEE negotiates a National General Collective Agreement (every two years) with the employers, which serves as a framework for sectoral and enterprise agreements. Attached to the GSEE is the Institute of Labour (INE/GSEE-ADEDI) which was set up in 1990 to carry out research and to plan and implement trade union education and training and vocational training.
International affiliations. ICFTU; ETUC; TUAC

4 Other Trade Union Organization

Civil Servants' Confederation (ADEDY)
Address. 2 Psilla Street and Filellinon St, 10557 Athens
Phone. +30 210 3246109, 3244677
Fax. +30 210 3246165
Website. www.adedy.gr
Leadership. S. Papaspyros (president)
Membership. 280,000 in 60 federations
History and character. ADEDY is the umbrella organization for civil servants. Like the GSEE it is divided into factions allied to political parties. The public service is highly organized, with 90% unionization. In 1999 civil servants for the first time were able to bargain collectively over terms and conditions, excluding pay and pensions. Prior to this, although ADEDY lacked the formal right to engage in collective bargaining, and conditions were set by government, in practice it was consulted informally. Public sector workers outside the civil service are represented by GSEE unions. Although these have had full collective bar-

gaining rights, their weaker bargaining power has meant that agreements reached in consultation with ADEDY have tended to be applied across the board.

ADEDY has regularly led brief strikes in recent years on issues such as pay, taxation and privatization. Indeed the 24-hour general strike it held on Nov. 4, 2003, in opposition to government pay policy was the most widespread action in a wave of strikes that marked late 2003–early 2004.

In May 2004 the Greek government published a draft Presidential Decree (PD) regulating fixed-term contracts in the public sector. The aim is to complete transposition of the 1999 EU Directive on fixed-term work into Greek law, following criticism that earlier implementing legislation failed to comply with the Directive, as it excluded many public sector workers from some of its provisions. ADEDY viewed the decision as a positive development in principle, yet called for several amendments, including the demand that the PD should also cover the private sector.

ADEDY is in favour of the idea of a single third-level organization for all workers. It has joined the GSEE to create a consolidated bipartite National Coordinating Trade Union Council (or "trade union congress") to investigate and take decisions on strategy and tactics for the union movement. Joint secretariats are to be set up in sectors where there is potential for unified action, while there are plans to move towards an eventual GSEE-ADEDY merger within the next five years.
International affiliation. ETUC

Grenada

Capital: St George's
Population: 89,000 (2004 est.)

1 Political and Economic Background

Grenada (a former West Indies associated state) became an independent member of the Commonwealth in 1974. In 1979 Maurice Bishop's left-wing New Jewel Movement staged a coup and formed a People's Revolutionary government. Parliament was dissolved and the Constitution suspended and close diplomatic and economic links were established with Cuba and countries of the Soviet bloc, while relations with the United States deteriorated. Factional conflict within the government led to Bishop's murder in October 1983 and a Commonwealth Caribbean force together with some 2,000 US troops landed on the islands and imposed order, following which an interim advisory council was appointed and the 1974 Constitution restored. 1984 elections to the House of Representatives were won overwhelmingly by the New National Party (NNP) which also accordingly secured a large majority in the nominated Senate. The last foreign military personnel were withdrawn in 1985.

The centrist National Democratic Congress held office from 1990–95, but in 1995 was defeated at the polls by Keith Mitchell's conservative New National Party (NNP). In January 1999 the NNP won a landslide victory in a general election, taking all 15 seats in the House of Representatives; in November 2003 Mitchell won a third general election in succession, though with a reduced majority for the NNP.

Grenada's economy is based on agriculture and services, and there is only a limited manufacturing sector. Tourism is the major foreign exchange earner.

GDP (purchasing power parity) $440 m. (2002 est.); GDP per capita (purchasing power parity) $5,000 (2002 est.).

2 Trade Unionism

Grenada ratified ILO Convention No. 98 (Right to Organize and Collective Bargaining, 1949) in 1979 and Convention No. 87 (Freedom of Association and Protection of the Right to Organize, 1948) in 1994. All workers may join trade unions, which are well established and estimated to represent about 45% of the workforce. Legislation provides protection against anti-union discrimination and employers must recognize a union where it has majority support. There is a right to strike and there are mechanisms for resolving disputes through the Labour Commissioner and arbitration tribunals. Union leaders play a significant part in the political process.

3 Trade Union Centre

Grenada Trades Union Council (GTUC)
Address. PO Box 411, Tanteen, St George's
Phone. +1809 440 3733
Fax. +1809 440 6615
E-mail. gtuc@caribsurf.com
Website. www.grenadatuc.org
Leadership. Ray Roberts (general secretary)
History and character. The GTUC was founded and registered in 1955. It is the island's only centre and has all significant unions in membership. It receives a government subsidy to assist its work.
International affiliations. ICFTU; CTUC

Guatemala

Capital: Guatemala City
Population: 14.28 m. (2004 est.)

1 Political and Economic Background

Guatemala has suffered from persistent military interventions in government, instability and civil strife. In December 1996 thirty years of war between left-wing guerrillas and the Army came to an end with the signing of a peace accord between the government of President Alvaro Arzú of the centre-right National Advancement Party (PAN) and the Guatemalan National Revolutionary Movement (URNG), which subsequently reorganized itself as a political organization. In February 1999 a report by the independent Historical Clarification Commission attributed 90% of crimes in the war, in which up to 200,000 died, to the Army.

The first elections held since the peace accord, in November–December 1999, resulted in the conservative Guatemalan Republican Front (FRG), gaining control of the legislature and the presidency. Elections to the unicameral Congress on Nov. 9, 2003, resulted in a hung parliament, while the December presidential run-off election produced victory for Oscar Berger Perdomo of the Great National Alliance (GANA) – a coalition dominated by the faction of the PAN led by Berger. The former revolutionaries of the URNG won only two seats in the November legislative contest.

Agriculture employs more than half of the workforce (in some cases at subsistence level) and accounts for 2/3 of exports, with coffee, sugar and bananas as the main exports, although there is also a manufacturing sector based largely on the processing of agricultural products and clothing assembly. Successive governments have sought to follow economic liberalization policies. There are great inequalities of wealth, significant problems of corruption, and widespread poverty.

GDP (purchasing power parity) $56.5bn. (2004 est.); GDP per capita (purchasing power parity) $4,100 (2004 est.).

2 Trade Unionism

Trade unionism developed in a period of reformist civilian government prior to a military coup in 1954. In 1952 Guatemala ratified ILO Convention No. 87 (Freedom of Association and Protection of the Right to Organize, 1948) and No. 98 (Right to Organize and Collective Bargaining, 1949). Thereafter the unions were held back by tactics of repression (including the assassination of union leaders by death squads), blacklisting and corruption, as well as more formal legal restrictions.

Under the labour code unions may not participate in party politics, while the right to strike is generally limited. Prior to reforms in 2001 the right to strike could be denied to agricultural workers at harvest time and to workers in essential public services (with heavy penalties prescribed for violators). These constraints have been less significant in practice than the general climate of fear and violence in which industrial and political relations have historically been conducted. The disappearance and assassination of trade unionists have been the subjects of complaints to the ILO by the world centres and several damning reports. Murders, torture and intimidation continued into the 1990s, though not on the scale of the late 1980s when 2,000 trade unionists were thought to have been murdered in one year. The WCL reported in late 1998 that: "the hopes that the (December 1996) peace treaty had brought about have not come true" and that systematic violence continued. Despite the apparent progress on the statute books, the labour law reforms in 2001 had "virtually no real impact on freedom of association", according to the ICFTU's 2003 *Annual Survey of Trade Union Rights*.

Unions currently complain particularly about conditions in the export processing zones (EPZs, or maquiladoras) and the banana plantations. According to the ICFTU, labour rights are simply ignored in the maquiladora sector in complete disregard of a 1996 government initiative (in response to international pressure) which threatened sanctions against employers in the EPZs who flouted labour laws. The ICFTU reported that employers in the EPZs blacklist activists and have largely excluded the unions while the labour inspection system is inefficient and corrupt. There has been considerable anti-union violence in the banana plantations. In 1999 a bitter dispute developed between the SITRABI banana workers' union and a Del Monte subsidiary after 900 workers were dismissed. The dispute flared out of control when 200 armed men raided a union meeting and briefly kidnapped the SITRABI leadership. However, the International Union of Food and Agricultural Workers (IUF) in March 2000 signed an agreement with Del Monte which established a framework for local negotiations. At this point Del Monte agreed to respect minimum labour standards.

The Solidarismo movement of Costa Rica is also present in Guatemala. There are reported to be some 4000 solidarist associations with 170,000 members. Employers have sponsored the formation of such associations as an alternative to trade unions. These membership organizations carry out trade union-like activities but are in fact a "compliant" alternative. They do little to defend workers' rights despite constant attacks.

There are centres affiliated to ICFTU and WCL, while UNSITRAGUA remains unaffiliated, preferring to maintain dialogues with all the international federations. The Union Guatemalteca de Trabajadores (UGT) is a loose coordinating body for the confederations. In September 1997 this called on the people of Guatemala to step up the struggle against "violence, impunity, corruption, insecurity, cost of living, clearance sales of public property, ignoring of peace agreements".

All employees other than members of the armed forces enjoy freedom of association under the constitution and the labour code. In formal terms the labour code provides protection for trade union activities and prohibits anti-union discrimination, and the government also moved in the 1990s to simplify its procedures for registering a union to give it legal status. However, the history of violence and repression, the hostility of employers and the military, the lack of protection through the labour courts, and poverty and widespread unemployment have had the result that, according to the Ministry of Labour, only 2% of the 3.5 million workforce are in unions. The unions have most strength in the public sector, where strikes are also common. The practice of collective bargaining is limited by the general weakness of the unions and employer resistance and most unionized workers are not covered by collective agreements.

3 Trade Union Centres

Confederación de Unidad Sindical de Guatemala (CUSG)
Address. 12 Calle "A", 0-37 Zona 1, Guatemala City
Phone. +502 232 8154

Fax. +502 232 8154
E-mail. cusg@guate.net
History and character. Founded in 1983, with social democratic orientation.
International affiliation. ICFTU

Central General de Trabajadores de Guatemala (CGTG)
Address. 3ra Avda. 12-22, Zona 1, Guatemala City
Phone. +502 232 1010
Fax. +502 251 3212
E-mail. cgtg@guate.net
Leadership. José Pinzón (secretary-general)
History and character. Is descended from the Central Nacional de Trabajadores (CNT), which operated clandestinely after the disappearance of 21 of its leaders arrested on June 21, 1980. Eight CGTG leaders were murdered between 1992–98 and none of the cases has been solved.
International affiliation. WCL

Unión Sindical de Trabajadores de Guatemala (UNSITRAGUA)
Address. 9a, Avenida 1-43 de la Zona 1, Ciudad de Guatemala
Phone. +502 238 2272
Fax. +502 220 4121
E-mail. unsitragua@hotmail.com
Leadership. UNSITRAGUA maintains a 'horizontal' leadership committee. Contact Albi Irene Barrinetos (international relations)
International affiliation. None

Guinea

Capital: Conakry
Population: 9.25 m. (2004 est.)

1 Political and Economic Background

Guinea became fully independent from France in 1958. The first President, Ahmed Sekou Touré, dominated the political stage for the next quarter of a century, pursuing a policy of socialist revolution and internal suppression. After his death in 1984, the armed forces staged a coup, forming a Military Committee for National Recovery (CMRN) under the leadership of Maj.-Gen. Lansana Conté. The 1982 Constitution was suspended after the coup, as was the socialist and nationalist Parti Démocratique de Guinée (PDG), which had been the ruling and sole legal party. A new constitution was approved by referendum in December 1990; in early 1991 the CMRN was dissolved and a mixed military and civilian Transitional Committee of National Recovery was set up as the country's legislative body. In April 1992 legislation providing for the legalization of political parties came into effect.

President Conté was confirmed in office in December 1993 in Guinea's first multi-party elections. In legislative elections in June 1995, the Party of Unity and Progress (PUP), led by Conté, won a majority of seats in the new National Assembly. Conté was subsequently re-elected in December 1998 and December 2003. The PUP also maintained its control of the National Assembly in (delayed) elections held in June 2002.

Guinea has considerable resources (including 30% of world bauxite reserves) and 80% of export earnings come from mining, especially bauxite, gold and diamonds. However, 85% of the population is engaged in subsistence agriculture. Fighting since 2000 along the Sierra Leonean and Liberian borders, as well as refugee movements, have caused major economic disruptions, including a loss in investor confidence. Foreign mining companies have reduced expatriate staff. Guinea is not receiving multilateral aid; the IMF and World Bank cut off most assistance in 2003.

GDP (purchasing power parity) $19.02 billion (2004 est.); GDP per capita (purchasing power parity) $2,100 (2004 est.).

2 Trade Unionism

Following independence in 1958 Guinea ratified ILO Conventions No. 87 (Freedom of Association and Protection of the Right to Organize, 1948) and No. 98 (Right to Organize and Collective Bargaining, 1949) in 1959.

From 1958 Sekou Touré combined the position of President with leadership of the sole union centre, the Confédération Nationale des Travailleurs de Guinée (CNTG). After his death, the new regime announced that free unions would be permitted. The WCL-affiliated CNTG continues to exist, is still the largest centre, and is still considered close to the state. (There also exists another WCL-affiliated centre, the smaller Union Générale des Travailleurs de Guinée, UGTG.) There are now two ICFTU-affiliated rivals, the Organisation Nationale des Syndicats Libres de Guinée (ONSLG) and the Union Syndicale des Travailleurs de Guinée (USTG). The USTG has faced repression, including arrests of leading figures and an attempt on the life of its president. It has agitated against the impact of economic restructuring on employment.

There is a constitutional right to form unions for all workers except members of the armed forces and protection against discrimination based on union membership. However, most of the workforce is engaged in subsistence agriculture and unions mainly represent civil servants, employees of the national utilities and workers in foreign-owned companies. There is a right to strike, subject to a notice period, but binding arbitration can be imposed in essential services, including public transport and communications. Strikes are prohibited in essential services, which, as well as hospitals, police and the army, are broadly defined to include transport, radio and television, and communications. The police and security services have sometimes reacted violently to strikers and their families during strikes.

3 Trade Union Centres

Confédération Nationale des Travailleurs de Guinée (CNTG)
National Confederation of Guinean Workers
Address. Bourse du Travail, Coriche Sud 004, BP 237, Conakry
Phone. +224 41 50 44
Fax. +224 41 50 44
Leadership. Rabiatou Serah Diallo (secretary general)
History and character. Sekou Touré became leader of the Guinea branch of the French Confédération Générale du Travail (CGT) in 1948, by which time he had also founded the PDG, which demanded independence from France. When Touré became the first President of independent Guinea in 1958 his union (renamed as the Confédération Nationale des Travailleurs de Guinée – CNTG – in 1956) became the sole trade union organization and was integrated into the structure of the PDG (the sole legal party).

Following Touré's death in 1984 and the consequent military coup, the CNTG's new leader, Mohamed Samba Kébé, stated that the trade union movement was now "free and had good relations with the Military Committee of National Recovery" and a 1986 ordinance affirmed the legal independence of the organization from the state. In 1993, however, the ILO criticized the government for involving itself in the affairs of the CNTG to block the efforts of reformers and the ICFTU stated in 1999 that the CNTG remains indirectly funded by the state. The CNTG is now affiliated to the WCL. It remains the largest trade union centre in Guinea.
International affiliation. WCL

Organisation Nationale des Syndicats Libres de Guinée (ONSLG)
National Organization of Free Unions of Guinea
Address. BP 4033, Conakry
Phone. +224 41 52 17
Fax. +224 4302 83
Leadership. Yamoudou Toure (secretary general)
E-mail. onslguinee@yahoo.fr
International affiliation. ICFTU

Union Générale des Travailleurs de Guinée (UGTG)
General Union of the Workers of Guinea
Address. BP 5522, Conakry
Phone. +224 45 30 76
Leadership. Mamadou Mara (president)
International affiliation. WCL

Union Syndicale des Travailleurs de Guinée (USTG)
United Trade Union of Guinean Workers
Address. BP 1514, Conakry
Phone. +224 45 60 00
Fax. +224 41 25 65
E-mail. fofi1952@yahoo.fr
Leadership. Ibrahima Fofana (secretary general)
International affiliation. ICFTU

Guinea-Bissau

Capital: Bissau
Population: 1.39 m. (2004 est.)

1 Political and Economic Background

Guinea-Bissau became formally independent of Portugal in 1974 (its independence having been proclaimed unilaterally in 1973). Initially the governments of both Guinea-Bissau and Cape Verde (the latter independent from 1975) were formed by the African Party for the Independence of Guinea and Cape Verde (PAIGC) with a view at that stage to the eventual integration of the two countries. A new constitution, adopted in May 1984, defined Guinea-Bissau as an anti-colonialist and anti-imperialist republic with a policy of national revolutionary democracy. The PAIGC, as the sole and ruling party, was described as the leading political force in society and in the state.

In 1989 João Vieira, the President since 1980, was elected unopposed but pressure mounted for the establishment of democracy. In 1991 the ruling PAIGC approved a plan to introduce a multi-party system but the country's first free elections were not held until July 1994. They brought an overwhelming victory to the PAIGC, while in presidential elections Vieira won a narrow victory over Kumba Ialá of the Social Renewal Party (PRS). In June 1998 Vieira faced a military rebellion led by Ansumane Mané; this led to an agreement introducing various constitutional reforms, but in May 1999 Vieira was removed from power in a coup. In elections to the National People's Assembly in November 1999 the PAIGC lost power for the first time since independence, with the PRS becoming the leading party. In January 2000 PRS leader Kumba Ialá was elected President. He lost support at home and international financial assistance was limited to minimum development aid, reducing the resources available to him to maintain stability in the Armed Forces and Civil Service. On Sept. 14, 2003, the military staged a coup and established a transitional council with Arthur Sanhá, secretary-general of the PRS, as Prime Minister and Henrique Rosa, a Creole close to the Catholic Church, as interim President. Legislative elections were held on March 28, 2004, resulting in the return to power of the PAIGC, with PAIGC leader Carlos Gomes becoming Prime Minister and Rosa remaining as President.

Guinea-Bissau is a poor country with low life expectancy and most of the workforce depends on subsistence farming and fishing. Industry is virtually non-existent and commerce, in which many city dwellers are involved, takes place mostly in the informal markets. The 1998 military revolt caused an exodus of foreign investors and continuous political instability and corruption has kept them away since then. The main employer is the state and the number of public servants exceeds the scale of the Guinean public administration. Tax yields are low and Guinea-Bissau cannot rely on its internal revenues to meet the internal and external debts. There is offshore oil but this has yet to be exploited.

GDP (purchasing power parity) $1.063 billion (2003 est.); GDP per capita (purchasing power parity) $800 (2003 est.).

2 Trade Unionism

After independence, Guinea-Bissau ratified ILO Convention No. 98 (Right to Organize and Collective Bargaining, 1949) in 1977 but it has not ratified Convention No. 87 (Freedom of Association and Protection of the Right to Organize, 1948). Before the 1974 revolution the Portuguese political system was corporatist, not allowing independent trade unions. The sole trade union, the Sindicato dos Empregados do Comércio, Indústria e Agricultura (SNECIA) was created under this system, grouping the workers of commerce, industry and agriculture.

On Aug. 3, 1959, a strike organized by the PAIGC ended in violence causing the death of 50 people. In response the state political police (PIDE) arrested many members of the party founded by Amilcar Cabral. The PAIGC then moved to Guinea Conakry to organize an army to fight for the independence of Portuguese Guinea. The UNTG (União Nacional dos Trabalhadores da Guiné) was therefore born in exile and aimed to obtain the support of the international trade union movement against the Portuguese colonial presence. After independence the PAIGC transferred to Bissau the political and economic structure it had during the colonial period. The SNECIA was extinct and the UNTG inherited its funds and patrimony. As the party had a monopolistic view of the state, no other political force or trade union was allowed to exist in the country until the 1990s political opening.

The democratization process implied important constitutional reforms to allow the workers to form and join unions of their own choice. Association is deeply rooted in African societies. The number of formal and informal associations in the cities and within traditional society is astonishing. However, concerning trade unionism, the possibilities are limited since most of the workforce is engaged in subsistence agriculture and there is only a small formal economy in which unions operate, with most union members working for the government or parastatals. There are reported to be 21 functioning unions, of which 15 are affiliated to the UNTG and 6 to the Confederação Geral dos Sindicatos Independentes. Formal collective bargaining is limited to the very small banking sector. To advise the Prime Minister on employment and wages issues there is a Council, the Conselho Permanente de Concertação Social, in which the employers, the unions and the government itself are represented. There is a legal right to strike, subject to a notice period.

3 Trade Union Centre

União Nacional dos Trabalhadores da Guiné (UNTG)
National Union of Workers of Guinea-Bissau
Address. Caixa Postal 98, Avenida Osvaldo Vieira No. 13, Bissau
Phone. +245 20 10 36
Fax. +245 20 18 50
E-mail. untgcs@hotmail.com
Leadership. Desejado Lima da Costa (secretary-general)
History and character. The UNTG when in exile was affiliated to the ICFTU, but after independence transferred its affiliation to the WFTU. As an arm of the ruling party before 1991, it emphasized the need to mobilize the workers to achieve greater productivity and overcome problems of backwardness. It has now re-affiliated to the ICFTU. After the adoption of a multi-party system in the early 1990s, it retained close relations with the PAIGC with its president, Desejado de Lima, being a PAIGC Member of Parliament. The UNTG has 15 affiliated unions plus a Working Women Commission
International affiliation. ICFTU

4 Other Trade Union Organization

Confederação Geral dos Sindicatos Independentes (CGSI)
General Confederation of Independent Unions
The confederation was created to provide an alternative to UNTG affiliation. It has 6 affiliated unions that operate on a high level of independence. The confederation has no headquarters or a fixed address and it is possible that it might not survive.

Guyana

Capital: Georgetown
Population: 706,000 (2004 est.)

1 Political and Economic Background

Guyana (formerly British Guiana) became a fully independent member of the Commonwealth in 1966 and a republic in 1970.

The principal division in Guyanan politics is racial. The People's Progressive Party (PPP) was founded as a left-wing anti-colonial party by Cheddi Jagan in 1950 but came to be supported almost exclusively by the Indian-descended community (49% of the population). Jagan won elections and held office under colonial rule, but following independence power was held continuously until 1992 by the People's National Congress Party (PNC), with its base in the African-descended community (32% of the population).

The PPP was in its early years heavily communist-influenced, but in October 1992 Jagan was elected president as a democratic socialist. Jagan died in March 1997 and in elections in December 1997 his widow, Janet Jagan, was declared the winner in the face of claims by the PNC that the vote had been rigged (similar claims against the PNC had been a feature of its years in office). The PPP also won a majority in the legislature. Through several months in 1998 there were repeated disturbances and attacks on

Indian-owned businesses which the PPP said were being organized by the opposition (which boycotted the National Assembly for a time) to destabilize the government. Janet Jagan stood down as President in August 1999 on grounds of ill health and was succeeded by Bharrat Jagdeo. The PPP won legislative elections held in March 2001 but this victory was then followed by a further prolonged boycott of parliament by the PNC and there were violent disturbances in July 2002.

In the 1970s the ruling PNC adopted a strongly left-wing position influenced by Marxism–Leninism. The 1980 constitution declared a socialist society and three-quarters of the economy was socialized. From 1987, however, under Desmond Hoyte, the PNC shifted to free market policies and the PPP under Jagan was elected in 1992 on a platform that promised to continue this policy to attract foreign investment. Prior to 1998 Guyana had enjoyed six consecutive years of growth at 5% p.a., but the political unrest contributed to negative growth in 1998. Since then growth has been at a slower rate, with estimated 0.5% real growth in GDP in 2004. Agriculture is the principal productive sector and sugar the main export crop. The bauxite sector is also a major export earner.

GDP (purchasing power parity) $2.797bn. (2004 est.); GDP per capita (purchasing power parity) $4,000 (2004 est.).

2 Trade Unionism

Unions have existed since the establishment of the British Guiana Labour Union (BGLU) by Hubert Critchlow in 1922. The Guyana Trades Union Congress (GTUC or TUC) was founded in 1941. Guyana ratified ILO Convention No. 87 (Freedom of Association and Protection of the Right to Organize, 1948) in 1967 and Convention No. 98 (Right to Organize and Collective Bargaining, 1949) in 1966. The constitution protects trade union rights and legislation passed by the PPP government since 1992 has included the Trade Union Recognition Act, in effect from 1999, which requires employers to recognize a union where it enjoys majority support. The Trade Unions Recognition Board issued 30 certifications and denied four in the first four years of the Act's operation. There is no legislation to specifically prohibit anti-union discrimination. About 32% of the workforce is unionized with most union members working in the public sector and state-owned enterprises.

The unions have been divided in their allegiances between the PNC and the PPP, with the division (as of the two political parties) largely on racial lines. The Guyana Agricultural and General Workers' Union (GAWU), the biggest union in Guyana, is close to the PPP and has had a difficult relationship with the ICFTU-affiliated Guyana Trades Union Congress (GTUC), where the influence of PNC supporters is strong. For many years, the GAWU stood outside the GTUC, calling itself a suspended member, and was the leading member of a Federation of Independent Trade Unions in Guyana (FITUG) set up in opposition to the GTUC in 1988 by unaffiliated or PPP-supporting unions.

The GAWU subsequently rejoined the GTUC. In April–June 1999, however, a nine-week public service pay strike (ultimately referred to arbitration) was led by the Guyana Public Service Union (GPSU), whose president, Patrick Yarde, also headed the GTUC. GTUC support for the strike led the GAWU to suspend its membership in the GTUC. The GAWU argued that the strike was politically inspired by supporters of the opposition PNC and had led to intimidation of workers, attacks on police, denial of medical treatment to Indian patients, attacks on Indian businesses, and lost jobs.

Collective bargaining exists in both in the public and private sectors and under the Trade Union Recognition Act employers must bargain with unions enjoying majority support. The centralized bargaining position formerly allotted to the GTUC under a 1984 Act was ended in 1993 (i.e. after the PNC lost power). The state's involvement in Guyanese industrial relations arose from its position as employer of nearly half the nation's workforce, and was shaped in part by close links between the ruling PNC and the GTUC. Before 1992, when the PPP was in opposition, strikes were often led by the Guyana Agricultural & General Workers' Union (GAWU). Retaliatory measures by employers against strikers are restricted by the Trade Union Recognition Act. In 2001 the government cancelled "check-off" procedures for public servants, an interference in union affairs that the Guyana Public Service Union says has damaged its financial position.

3 Trade Union Centre

Guyana Trades Union Congress (GTUC)
Address. Critchlow Labour College, Woolford Avenue, Non Pareil Park, Georgetown
Phone. +592 2 61493
Fax. +592 2 70254
E-mail. gtuc@guyana.net
Leadership. Lincoln Lewis (general secretary); Carvil Duncan (president)
History and character. The GTUC originated in 1941 as the British Guiana Trades Union Council. While in power the PNC government (while disavowing an intention to control the GTUC) generally retained a dominant influence in it, allegedly in part by the creation of small PNC-controlled unions which made exaggerated membership claims to secure a disproportionate representation at GTUC congresses. There has been persistent conflict between the GTUC and the pro-PPP Guyana Agricultural and General Workers' Union (GAWU), the leading individual union in Guyana. The GAWU suspended its affiliation again in May 1999, GAWU leader Komal Chand stating that "the TUC cannot earn the respect of all the workers when it continues to facilitate paper unions and allows affiliated unions to register with greater numbers of members than they represent at the workplaces".

The GTUC's former role in centralized collective bargaining was ended in 1993. It comprises 22 affiliated unions.
International affiliations. ICFTU; CTUC

4 Other Trade Union Organizations

Guyana Agricultural and General Workers' Union (GAWU)
Address. 104–106 Regent Street, Lacytown, Georgetown
Phone. +592 2 72091
Fax. +592 2 72093
E-mail. gawu@networksgy.com
Membership. 21,000
Leadership. Komal Chand (president); Seepaul Narine (general secretary)
History and character. The GAWU is the biggest union in Guyana. It was founded in 1946 as the Guiana Industrial Workers' Union but lapsed in the 1950s when the country's constitution was suspended by the colonial power. It was resurrected as the Guyana Sugar Workers' Union in 1961, then renamed in 1962 as the Guyana Agricultural Workers' Union and finally took its present name later in the decade. Its membership is predominantly of Asian descent.

The GAWU is affiliated to the PPP and says that from 1964–92, while the PNC was in government and had the support of many of the unions, Guyana declined from being among the most prosperous economies in the Caribbean to the level of Haiti.

Having rejoined the Guyana Trades Union Congress (GTUC), GAWU in May 1999 again suspended its membership after the GTUC executive council recommended its affiliates to take part in a 3-day general strike to support striking public sector workers. The GAWU maintained that grievance procedures had not been exhausted, that the pay demands were unreasonable in view of the difficult economic situation, and that the strike was politically motivated by a section in the GTUC allied to the opposition PNC.
International affiliation. WFTU; IUF

National Workers' Union (NWU)
Address. PO Box 12 12213, Bourda, Georgetown
Phone. +592 2 72091
Fax. +592 2 70322
Leadership. Rohan Jahessar (president)
International affiliation. WCL

Haiti

Capital: Port-au-Prince
Population: 7.66 m. (2004 est.)

1 Political and Economic Background

Haiti was ruled from 1957 to 1986 by the authoritarian and repressive Duvalier family, after which there was civil turmoil and military intervention. Jean-Bertrand Aristide, a reformist priest, was elected President in 1990 but was deposed by the army the following year. He was restored by US intervention in September 1994, but thereafter, although the army was disbanded, and elections were successfully held in 1995, the political situation remained unstable. Aristide handed power to his elected successor, René Préval, in 1996. In 2000 Aristide won the presidential election, while the legislative elections resulted in victory for Aristide's Lavalas Family party. However, there was widespread scepticism about the validity of these elections, international aid was suspended, and opposition forces refused to recognize the Aristide government. A prolonged period of unrest culminated in an armed uprising, beginning in the north-western town of Gonaïves on Feb. 5, 2004, which met little resistance and resulted in the flight of Aristide on Feb. 29. A UN-backed international force was deployed to Haiti to keep order and in March 2004 Haiti's Chief Justice, Alexandre Boniface, was sworn in as acting President and a broad-based transitional government established. Elections were scheduled to be held by the end of 2005.

Haiti is the poorest country in the western hemisphere. Violent repression and rampant corruption during the Duvalier regimes stymied economic development. Since then economic embargoes and ineffective government have left the vast majority of the population in a state of abject poverty. There is massive unemployment and under-employment. Around 70% of the population is dependent on agriculture, which is mainly subsistence farming, and there has been little job creation in the formal economy since 1995. Only around 100,000 workers out of a working population of 4 million are employed in the formal economy. Of those 100,000, some 25,000 are working in the export business, mainly in garment assembly. The main export market is the USA, which accounts for 84% of Haiti's exports.

GDP (purchasing power parity) $12.3bn. (2004 est.); GDP per capita (purchasing power parity) $1,600 (2004 est.).

2 Trade Unionism

Several trade union centres functioned in the period from 1946–57, but following the assumption of power by François "Papa Doc" Duvalier in 1957, unions were either eliminated or brought under government control. Haiti ratified ILO Convention No. 98 (Right to Organize and Collective Bargaining, 1949) in 1957, shortly before Duvalier came to power, and Convention No. 87 (Freedom of Association and Protection of the Right to Organize, 1948) in 1979.

During Aristide's first brief period in office in 1991, the unions enjoyed some assistance from the administration. But after his overthrow, union operations were effectively nullified by repression, and a great number of leading figures were killed or driven into exile. Despite the return to civilian government in 1994, there remained serious restrictions on trade union rights, including freedom of association and the right to strike. Collective bargaining coverage is minimal, and workers and trade union activists face serious intimidation and violence. There is no protection against anti-union discrimination, which occurs on a regular basis.

Approximately 5 per cent of the workforce is

unionized, about half in the industrial sector. Unions are concentrated in the Port-au-Prince area, in state enterprises and the civil service. There are two trade union centres, the Coordination Syndical Haitien, and the new and more militant Intersyndicale Premier Mai – Batay Ouvriye (May 1st – Workers' Fight Federation).

3 Trade Union Centres

Coordination Syndical Haitien
Haitian Trade Union Coordination
This body loosely groups together a large number (14) of the established unions.

Intersyndicale Premier Mai – Batay Ouvriye (May 1st – Workers' Fight Federation)
Address. P.O. Box 13326, Delmas, Port-au-Prince
Email. batay@batayouvriye.org
Website. www.batayouvriye.org (Creole, French, Spanish and English)
History and character. Batay Ouvriye formed in 2001 as a militant union centre. It has a strong presence in and around the second city of Cap-Haitien.

Honduras

Capital: Tegucigalpa
Population: 6.82 m. (2004 est.)

1 Political and Economic Background

Honduras has had a number of military regimes but since 1981 has experienced civilian administration, with the military nonetheless remaining an important factor in politics. In 1993 the centrist Liberal Party of Honduras (PLH) won back power from the conservative National Party of Honduras (PNH), and the PLH secured a further victory in presidential and congressional elections in November 1997. The government has sought to reduce the independent power of the military: in 1997, the (Roman Catholic) Archbishop of Tegucigalpa became head of the national police force on an interim basis during its transition from military to civilian control, while the post of Commander-in-Chief of the Armed Forces was abolished. It was reported that a planned coup by a section of the Army in July 1999 had been thwarted. In elections in November 2001 the PLH lost control of both the presidency and the Congress, with the candidate of the PNH, Ricardo Maduro, being elected President and the PNH also coming first in the legislative elections.

Honduras is a poor and heavily indebted country with great inequalities of income. The economy is largely agricultural, with bananas, coffee, timber and sugar as leading exports. There is vulnerability to hurricane damage and fluctuations in commodity prices. There is also a substantial export processing sector. Both the main parties, the PLH and PNH, campaigned on free market platforms in the 1997 and 2001 elections. President Maduro undertook to implement the structural reforms and fiscal measures necessary to gain debt relief assistance from the IMF, but his economic policies have proved widely unpopular both with the public and some sections of his own party. Maduro signed a debt relief agreement with the IMF in February 2004 which committed his government to pursue its tough economic programme, but doubts were expressed about the ability of the government to deliver on this programme in view of popular hostility to it and the country's reputation for public sector inefficiency and corruption.

GDP (purchasing power parity) $17.55bn. (2004 est.); GDP per capita (purchasing power parity) $2,600 (2004 est.).

2 Trade Unionism

Widespread strikes and unrest in 1954 forced the US-owned United Fruit Company to negotiate with its employees. In 1955 the government extended legal recognition and the right to strike to trade unions, and Honduras ratified ILO Conventions No. 87 (Freedom of Association and Protection of the Right to Organize, 1948) and No. 98 (Right to Organize and Collective Bargaining, 1949) in 1956. Thereafter trade unionism remained alive in Honduras despite the assassination of many union activists (especially in peasant unions), the use of blacklisting, intimidation and corruption by employers, and waves of organized repression. There was a general improvement in the human rights situation in Honduras in the late 1990s.

Unions operate free of government control but represent only an estimated 11% of the workforce. Much of the population works on the land and peasant organizations affiliate to the unions. Attempts have been made by employers to introduce a solidarismo movement in Honduras, on the Costa Rican model, though only with limited success.

While the labour code provides formal protection against victimization by employers for union activities, harassment or dismissal of union organizers nonetheless occurs. The courts may compel employers to re-hire workers dismissed for union activities but such rulings are not common. Collective bargaining exists in companies where unions are established. There has been international criticism of conditions in the export processing zones (EPZs, or maquiladoras), where 125,000 are employed, and US companies imposed controls on suppliers after unfavourable publicity in 1996. South Korean and Taiwanese-owned firms have been particularly criticized. However, a significant minority of plants in the EPZs have agreed to recognize unions after the employers' association adopted a voluntary code in 1997 recognizing the right to organize. Controversy has also surrounded practices in the banana plantations, where the unions allege the indiscriminate use of dangerous pesticides. The unions are highly critical of the labour inspection scheme.

3 Trade Union Centres

Central General de Trabajadores (CGT)
Address. Apartado Postal 1236, Tegucigalpa DC

Phone +504 225 25 09
Fax. +504 225 25 06
History and character. The CGT is traditionally closely linked to the National Party of Honduras (PNH), which was in office from 1989 to 1993 and returned to government in 2001. Its membership, previously reported as 65,000, includes organizations of peasants and shanty dwellers.
International affiliation. WCL

Confederación de Trabajadores de Honduras (CTH)
Honduras Workers' Confederation
Address. Apartado Postal 720, Tegucigalpa
Phone. +504 238 7859
Fax. +504 237 4243
Leadership. Dinora Aceituno (general secretary)
History and character. The CTH is the largest union centre in Honduras and was founded in 1964.
International affiliation. ICFTU

Confederación Unitaria de Trabajadores de Honduras (CUTH)
Address. Barrio Bella Vista, 10 Calle, 8 y 9 Avda, Casa 829, Comayaguela
Phone. +504 220 4732
Fax. +504 220 4733
E-mail. cuth@mayanet.hn
Leadership. Israel Salinas (general secretary)
History and character. Founded in 1992.
International affiliation. None

Federación Unitaria de Trabajadores de Honduras (FUTH)
Address. Boulevard Comunidad Economica Europea, Barrio La Granja, Contiguo al Banco Atlantida, Apdo. 1663, Tegucigalpa
Fax. +504 234 3010
International affiliation. WFTU

Hungary

Capital: Budapest
Population: 10.03 m. (2004 est.)

1 Political and Economic Background

Following World War II Hungary was under communist control for more than four decades until it became one of the first Soviet bloc countries to break free. Political change and liberal economic reforms accelerated from the mid-1980s and in February 1989 the ruling Hungarian Socialist Workers' Party conceded political pluralism. In October 1989 the Hungarian Republic was declared in succession to the former People's Republic. Power has changed hands at successive elections since the introduction of multi-partyism. Elections in May 1990 resulted in the formation of a government by the centre-right Hungarian Democratic Forum (MDF). In May 1994 elections, the reformed former communists of the Hungarian Socialist Party (MSzP) became the largest party and formed a coalition government with the liberal Alliance of Free Democrats (SzDSz). Elections in May 1998 resulted in the MSzP taking second place to the centre-right Federation of Young Democrats–Hungarian Civic Party (FIDESz–MPP), FIDESz–MPP then leading a coalition government, while the elections of April 2002 saw a further change, with the MSzP returning to power, again in alliance with the Free Democrats.

Prior to 1989 the Hungarian economy was predominantly under state ownership. Hungary's post-communist transition has been among the most successful of any country, with continuity between different governments, after overcoming the initial shock that resulted in falling living standards in the early 1990s. It has largely completed its privatization programme and over 80% of GDP is now generated by the private sector. It joined the OECD in 1996 and the European Union on May 1, 2004. In recent years it has enjoyed solid economic growth and a generally stable social and economic environment. However, Hungary faces strict fiscal discipline if it is to meet the government's targets to reduce the budget deficit and inflation rates to allow it to join the eurozone in 2010.

GDP (purchasing power parity) $139.8bn. (2004 est.); GDP per capita (purchasing power parity) $13,900 (2004 est.).

2 Trade Unionism

The first Hungarian unions were founded in the 1860s under the Austro-Hungarian Empire and a Central Trade Union Council (formed by the Social Democratic Party) was put on a permanent basis in 1899. Under the Horthy regime (1920–44) independent unionism was curbed or banned but under communist rule the Council became the Central Council of Hungarian Trade Unions (SZOT). For 40 years SZOT was Hungary's official and inclusive centre, though challenged briefly in 1956 when independent workers' councils emerged to stage a general strike against military intervention by the USSR. Hungary ratified ILO Conventions No. 87 (Freedom of Association and Protection of the Right of Organize, 1948) and No. 98 (Right to Organize and Collective Bargaining, 1949) in 1957, i.e. shortly after the suppression of the independent workers' councils formed outside the single trade union structure. Hungary's pre-1989 constitution did not formally prohibit the formation of other trade unions outside this structure, provided they undertook to protect and construct socialist society.

Organizational change in SZOT – aimed at separating the centre from the state – anticipated the fall of communism by about a year. In March 1990, SZOT was dissolved with two-thirds of its affiliates forming a new centre the Confederation of Hungarian Trade Unions (MSzOSz). Although it quickly lost about half of its members MSzOSz became and remained the principal centre. In 1993 it reported a membership of 1,370,000, of whom almost two-thirds were wage-earners, but active membership is now under 500,000. Initially MSzOSz inherited all the substantial assets of SZOT, estimated at 4.5 billion forints, but under pressure of legislation the centres agreed a division among themselves and MSzOSz retained only 40 per cent. The trade union press was also the subject of an amicable settlement, with the daily *Népszava* (Voice of the People) becoming the joint property of all unions.

MSzOSz is now affiliated to the ICFTU, which also has two other smaller Hungarian affiliates. These are the Autonomous Trade Union Confederation (ASzSz) and the Democratic Confederation of Free Trade Unions (LIGA). The WCL's affiliate is the MOSz (National Federation of Workers' Councils) and there is no WFTU affiliate. Public service unions have also formed the Forum for the Cooperation of Trade Unions (SzEF). Some unions do not affiliate to any of these centres. In general, the different centres have tended to have positive relations with each other.

The 1992 labour code recast the legal framework of trade unions and industrial relations and provided for trade union pluralism and collective bargaining. Among the issues it covered were wages and taxes, union elections, the administration of unemployment benefit, and the distribution of the assets of the former communist unions. It also provided for the establishment of works councils in any enterprise employing more than 50 workers. When elections to works councils were held in 1993, MSzOSz showed a clear lead with 53% of the vote, followed by LIGA with 17% and MOSz with 15%.

Union density overall is about 30% and has not changed greatly following the initial impact of the changes in 1989–90. Some large-scale industrial enterprises, such as chemicals, electricity and the railways are almost completely unionized, but unions are weak in small enterprises and emergent private sector services. Some employers actively discriminate against union organizers and the unions complain of lack of redress because of ambiguities in the law and backlogs of cases in the labour courts. Some foreign-owned companies have set up company unions.

The 1992 labour code provides for collective bargaining at the industry or enterprise level. About 40% of workers are covered by collective agreements, struck mostly at workplace level, but many private sector employers actively resist collective bargaining. Collective bargaining coverage has fallen in recent years, although in some industries (water, energy and sewage) coverage remains close to 100%. The detailed content of collective bargaining agreements has commonly been shrinking in recent years, and often includes little more than the basic terms guaranteed by the labour code. Public servants may negotiate working conditions, but Parliament must approve salary increases. In 1999 the government proposed to give works councils the right to conclude collective bargaining agreements, which was interpreted by the unions as a threat to their position. However, in 2001 union lobbying succeeded in postponing elections to the public sector councils by three years. Unions have argued that the power of the councils should be reduced and workplace-level unions strengthened. Union demands were met in 2002 when the newly elected Socialist government repealed several laws introduced by the previous government. One consequence was that the works councils are no longer able to conclude agreements which have legal effect equivalent to collective agreements. Employees except the military and police officers have the right to strike, though strikes have been fairly uncommon in the post-communist period.

The unions have generally supported the process of political and economic reconstruction, including associated job losses in inefficient industries, under which Hungary has become a market economy and one of the most successful and stable of the post-communist societies. However, the centre-right government elected in 1998 was accused of moving away from tripartism and seeking to weaken the position of the unions. The tripartite Interest Reconciliation Council (IRC), on which the trade union centres were all represented, provided a framework for agreement on the minimum wage, wage recommendations and broader socio-economic issues. However, arguing that it wished to end corporatism, the government in 1999 abolished this and set up alternative structures, such as the National Labour Affairs Council (OMT) which the unions say provide forums for airing opinions but are disregarded by government. One consequence is that there was no tripartite agreement for 2000 on a general wage recommendation, although the unions and employers made a bilateral recommendation. The government has also abolished the Ministry of Labour, which was established in 1990 to monitor employment, wages and wage policy, labour legislation, vocational training, and labour safety regulation and to represent the government in tripartite structures. The functions of the Ministry have been split between the Economics Ministry and newly created Ministry of Social and Family Affairs (the latter being given employment issues and responsibility for drafting labour-related legislation).

The unions' relations with government improved significantly following the election victory in 2002 of the Hungarian Socialist Party. In 2004 the unions were focussing efforts on the consequences of accession to the European Union.

3 Trade Union Centres

Autonóm Szakszervezetek Szövetsége (ASzSz)
Autonomous Trade Union Confederation
Address. Benczúr út. 45, 1046 Budapest
Phone. +36 1 1-4612400
Fax. +36 1-4612464
E-mail. autonom@euroweb.hu
Membership. 120,000
International affiliations. ICFTU; ETUC

Független Szakszervezetek Demokratikus Ligája (LIGA, or FSzDL)
LIGA Democratic Confederation of Free Trade Unions
Address. Benczúr u. 41, H - 1068 Budapest
Phone. +36 1-3215262
Fax. +36 1-3215405
Website. www.liganet.hu (Hungarian, English section)
Leadership. István Gaskó (president)

Membership. 50,000. Leading affiliates represent railway workers, metalworkers, teachers, transport and construction workers.

History and character. LIGA was the first non-communist union confederation in Hungary. It was founded early in 1989 to break communist control and, though it failed to gain majority status after this it emerged as a strong minority and second to MSzOSz in the works councils elections of 1993. It was seen as close to the liberal Alliance of Free Democrats (SzDSz). It is one of the ICFTU's three Hungarian affiliates.

International affiliations. ICFTU, ETUC, TUAC

Magyar Szakszervezetek Országos Szövetsége (MSzOSz)
National Confederation of Hungarian Trade Unions

Address. Magdolna u. 5-7, H - 1086 Budapest
Phone. +36 1-3232656
Fax. +36 1 3232654
E-mail. kgyorgy@mszosz.hu
Website. www.mszoz.hu (Hungarian; English section)
Leadership. Dr. László Sandor (president)
Membership. 465,000 active members and 250,000 pensioners and apprentices, in 43 affiliated unions.

History and character. MSzOSz was formed out of the former official communist centre SZOT, which was the only national centre until 1988. Radical changes in organization, policy and personnel began that year and anticipated the impact of the collapse of the Berlin Wall in 1989. The December 1988 congress ended the dependence of SZOT on the party, redefined its principal objective as safeguarding the interests of the employed, and determined to convene a transformation congress. In March 1990 SZOT was dissolved and MSzOSz founded with the support of about two-thirds of SZOT affiliates.

From that point on MSzOSz focused on advocacy of agreements on behalf of wage-earners in the fairly hostile atmosphere of the early 1990s. The other centres were sharply critical of the way it had inherited SZOT's assets, and a law of July 1991 would have divided these on the basis of electoral support in a special poll. However, MSzOSz reached an agreement with other centres in September 1992 by which it retained 40%. The works council elections of 1993 confirmed and legitimized the premier position of MSzOSz, with it taking over half of all votes. In 1993 its ICFTU affiliation figure was 1,368,500, but membership is now about half this.

MSzOSz, despite being the leading single centre, has not been able to achieve unequivocal national leadership, partly because of its descent from the communist-era SZOT and partly because of its closeness to the reformed communist Hungarian Socialist Party (MSzP).

MSzOSz's orientation is broadly social democratic although it comprises a spectrum of views. It supported Hungary's accession to the EU and called for ratification of the European Social Charter (ratified by Hungary in 1999) and a programme of "social stabilization" alongside financial and economic stabilization to meet EU standards. This would include comprehensive reform in areas such as social security, pensions, health insurance, taxation and health and safety. MSzOSz calls for a 38-hour week and active measures to combat Hungary's problems of unemployment (8.8% in 1999, though this had fallen to 5.8% by 2003) and underemployment, Hungary having a rate of participation in the work force well below the EU average, especially in older age groups most affected by the restructuring of the Hungarian economy. It also wishes to see the European Trade Union Confederation (ETUC) develop as an effective pan-European voice for labour.

MSzOSz says that it has contributed positively as a social partner to the successful restructuring of the Hungarian economy in the 1990s. It was critical of the movement of the centre-right government elected in 1998 away from tripartism and accused it of abandoning social dialogue, as in the 1999 abolition of the Council for Interest Conciliation. MszOSz's relations with the Socialist government elected in 2002 are much improved.

International affiliations. ICFTU; ETUC; TUAC

Munkástanácsok Országos Szövetsége (MOSz)
National Federation of Workers' Councils (NFWC)

Address. Tárogáto út. 2-4, 1021 Budapest
Phone. +36 1 275 1445
Fax. +36 1 394 2802
E-mail. munkastanacsok@pronet.hu
Leadership. Imre Palkovics (president); Jozsef Suhajda (secretary general)

History and character. Workers' Councils emerged in 1989 as they had during the events of 1956. In the context of trade union pluralism MOSz has sought to provide an alternative, sympathetic to Christian democratic values.

International affiliation. WCL; ETUC

Szakszervezetek Együttmüködési Fóruma (SzEF)
Forum for the Cooperation of Trade Unions

Address. Puskin út. 4, 1088 Budapest
Phone. +36 1 338 26 51
Fax. +36 1 318 73 60
E-mail. szef@mail.matavnet.hu
Website. www.szef.hu (Hungarian; English section)
Leadership. Dr. Endre Szabó (president)
Membership. Reports 274,000 active members and 172,000 retired.

History and character. SzEF represents mainly white-collar workers in public education, social services and health care, cultural institutes, state and local government, and the legal system. It was founded in June 1990 by a loose alliance of 30 organizations as a standing consultative forum. In response to deteriorating conditions in the public service it was re-launched as a professional organization at the first SzEF congress in May 1995. It joined the ETUC in 1998 and held its second congress in 1999. It is independent of political parties.

International affiliations. ETUC

Iceland

Capital: Reykjavik
Population: 294,000 (2004 est.)

1 Political and Economic Background

Iceland was a Danish possession until 1944, although with home rule from 1874. Since independence the leading party has usually been the liberal-conservative Independence Party (IP), which has led coalition governments with a range of other parties. This pattern was confirmed at the most recent elections, in May 2003, following which the IP formed another coalition government with the Progressive Party as the junior partner. The IP's David Oddsson was Prime Minister from 1991 until September 2004, when he became Foreign Minister.

Iceland's economy has traditionally had a heavy dependence on fishing and fishing products, which generate the bulk of export earnings although providing only 12% of jobs. Fish stocks in the North Atlantic are in decline and Iceland has ongoing disputes with various nations over fishing rights, while fear of loss of control of fisheries is a leading reason for Iceland not wishing to join the EU. The economy is diversifying into areas including financial services, tourism, software development and biotechnology. There has been a gradual process of privatization since the early 1990s. Iceland has a high standard of living with a developed welfare state, low unemployment (3.4% in 2004), notably even income distribution and a high level of social cohesion.

GDP (purchasing power parity) $8.678bn. (2004 est.); GDP per capita (purchasing power parity) $30,000 (2004 est.).

2 Trade Unionism

Iceland ratified ILO Convention No. 87 (Freedom of Association and Protection of the Right to Organize, 1948) in 1950 and Convention No. 98 (Right to Organize and Collective Bargaining, 1949) in 1952. The labour laws were revised in 1996, with the objective of bringing them into compliance with the European Convention for the Protection of Human Rights and Fundamental Freedoms.

Iceland's workforce of 150,000 is highly organized, with union density estimated at 80%. The law prohibits acts of antiunion discrimination and employers may be required to reinstate workers dismissed for union activities. There are two trade union centres, both affiliated to the ICFTU. The larger is the Icelandic Federation of Labour (ASÍ), to which about 73,000 workers are affiliated including a high proportion of private sector employees. The other centre is the Confederation of State and Municipal Employees of Iceland (BSRB), which has 18,000 members in the public sector. The unions are politically independent.

Prior to 1988 the ASÍ and the Confederation of Icelandic Employers (CIE) usually made a national framework agreement to be followed by federation level bargaining. This pattern broke down and the government intervened with a ban on strikes and a wage freeze, leading the ASÍ to file a complaint with the ILO Committee on Freedom of Association in 1991. In 1995 the Committee asked the government "to refrain in future from having recourse to such measures of legislative intervention". In recent years, the government has played almost no role in private-sector collective bargaining.

Most workers have the right to strike. Public sector workers have had the right to strike since 1986, although with a requirement to maintain services essential to health and safety.

3 Trade Union Centres

Althydusamband Íslands (ASÍ)
Icelandic Federation of Labour
Address. Saetún 1, Reykjavik 105
Phone. +354 53 55 60
Fax. +354 53 55 61
E-mail. asi@asi.is
Website. www.asi.is (Icelandic only)
Leadership. Gretar Thorsteinsson (president); Ari Skulason (general secretary)
Membership. 73,000
History and character. The ASÍ was established on a permanent basis in 1916. The federation was organizationally part of the Social Democratic Party until 1940, when it became (as it remains) an independent trade union federation without political ties. It affiliates close to half the Icelandic work force. Public sector workers are organized separately in the BSRB.

Originally individual trade unions were direct members of the ASI; after about 1950, however, unions in a number of sectors organized their own national federations, and now have indirect membership in the ASÍ through those federations. Only a few unions remain directly affiliated to the ASÍ. The federation is financed mainly by pro rata contributions from the member unions, but receives limited government funding to support some of its cultural, educational and other activities.

The ASÍ established a Workers' Educational Association in 1969, and it also has its own art gallery and travel bureau, and a share in a cooperative trade union bank.
International affiliations. ETUC; ICFTU; TUAC; NFS

Bandalag Starfsmanna Rikis og Baeja (BSRB)
Confederation of State and Municipal Employees of Iceland
Address. Grettisgata 89, 105 Reykjavik
Phone. +354 525 8300
Fax. +354 525 8309
E-mail. bsrb@bsrb.is
Website. www.bsrb.is (Icelandic, summary in English)
Leadership. Ogmundur Jonasson (chairman)
Membership. 18,000
History and character. Founded in 1942, the BSRB represents 28 unions of public service employees. Two-thirds of its members are women.

The BSRB provides support for collective bargaining by its member unions. A particular concern is the privatization of public services. The BSRB says that while it is not categorically opposed to privatization per se, it has opposed "privatization for the sake of privatization", which it says was carried out through the 1990s.

International affiliations. ICFTU, ETUC, NFS, PSI, TUAC

India

Capital: New Delhi
Population: 1.065bn. (2004 est.)

1 Political and Economic Background

India gained independence from the United Kingdom in 1947, when the sub-continent was divided into the new states of India and Pakistan. The Union of India, now comprising 28 self-governing states and seven union territories, is under its constitution (with amendments which came into force in 1977) "a sovereign socialist secular democratic republic". The legislative field is divided between the Union and the states, the former possessing exclusive powers to make laws on foreign affairs, defence, citizenship and trade with other countries. Central legislative power is vested in Parliament, consisting of the President (who appoints a Prime Minister – the head of government – and a Council of Ministers), the indirectly-elected Council of States (Rajya Sabha, the upper house) and the directly elected House of the People (Lok Sabha).

The Indian National Congress–Congress (I) party, which has a broadly socialist and secularist orientation, has been the governing party for most of the period since it led India to independence in 1947, although it has suffered various splits. It first went into opposition after elections in 1977, having tried to rule through widely detested emergency powers from 1975. It regained power in 1980 and then held office until 1996, other than for a period in 1989–91. Successive Congress Prime Ministers, Indira Gandhi and her son Rajiv, were assassinated, in 1984 and 1991 respectively. The 1990s saw the emergence as a major force of the Hindu nationalist Bharatiya Janata Party (BJP), which won the largest number of seats in the Lok Sabha at elections in 1996, 1998 and 1999, and with the BJP's leader, Atal Bihari Vajpayee, serving as Prime Minister in a a series of coalition governments from 1998. Elections in April–May 2004, however, brought the Congress (I) back to power, leading a coalition government for the first time since 1996.

India's population is 80% Hindu and tensions between the majority and the 14% Muslim minority have been a recurrent theme, although the BJP in government largely moderated its earlier Hindu fundamentalism. A 1999 report by Human Rights Watch said that oppression of India's 160 million Dalits ("untouchables") had increased dramatically in the 1990s. There are separatist movements active in some parts of the country, notably Kashmir and various of the north-eastern states.

India has a diversity of industries, ranging from traditional areas such as textiles, chemicals, food processing, steel, cement and machinery, to important new sectors in pharmaceuticals and information technology. The country's manufacturing base is increasingly competitive and, with the expanding services sector, is the main driver of economic growth, GDP expanding by 8.4% in the fiscal year to April 2004. GDP has increased an average of 6% per annum since 1990. However, the dominant economic activity in India is still peasant cultivation, which accounts for two-thirds of the labour force, although agriculture represents only 21% of GDP. The comparatively poor state of this sector and the dissatisfaction of the rural population was a principal factor in the defeat of the BJP government in the 2004 general election, and the incoming Congress government promised that investment in rural infrastructure and agri-business would be a priority. There is a vast informal economy and the population growth rate (adding 15–20 million per year) is a major downward drag on per capita income growth.

India has had some success in attracting inward investment but onerous regulations have been a deterrent and it suffers from poor infrastructure in areas such as power, telecommunications and transport. India has a wide range of public sector enterprises and there has been only an intermittent campaign to privatize these in the face of entrenched opposition. Both the bureaucracy and the unions have strongly resisted privatization. The government continues to run substantial budget deficits. Since the 1990s governments have sought to move away from central planning and introduce free market reforms, but these have been held back by the weakness of successive coalition governments and the entrenched Indian tradition of bureaucratic regulation. India began to open export processing zones (EPZs) in the 1980s but only a handful survived.

GDP (purchasing power parity) $3.033 trillion (2004 est.); GDP per capita (purchasing power parity) $2,900 (2004 est.).

2 Trade Unionism

India has ratified neither ILO Convention No. 87 (Freedom of Association and Protection of the Right to Organize, 1948) nor No. 98 (Right to Organize and Collective Bargaining, 1949). However, freedom of association was formally introduced into national legislation by the Trade Union Act of 1926 and collective bargaining and the right to strike both exist, although these have been increasingly restricted.

Illiteracy, caste and religious animosities inhibited the early development of trade unions. Development was also restricted because unions tended, at least until World War I, almost always to recruit members from a narrow labour aristocracy. The seasonal and migratory nature of much industrial labour, as well as the control of workers through company housing, also contributed to a relatively weak trade union movement. In 1920, however, the All-India Trade Union Congress

(AITUC) was formed; this remained the principal centre until after independence in 1947 when it became the focus of intense conflict between nationalists and communists. This stemmed from differences that had surfaced during World War II when the Communist Party chose, against nationalist opinion, to support Britain's war effort. Having done so, its members were able not only to escape imprisonment, unlike their nationalist colleagues, but also effectively to gain control of the AITUC. The wartime split led the ruling Congress Party in 1947 to favour and sponsor the creation of a rival Indian National Trade Union Congress (INTUC).

There is no one clearly dominant trade union centre. INTUC has generally been considered the largest in recent decades, and still claims to have 6 million members. Its close relationship with the Congress Party was undoubtedly a major factor in its favour for most of the period since independence, and it likewise declined in influence in the 1990s as the Congress's power waned. Conversely, the Bharatiya Mazdoor Sangh (BMS), with links to the BJP, has benefited from the rise of that party and the movement it represents. In 1996 – the year that the BJP first became the largest party in the Lok Sabha – official figures of the "verified memberships" of the different centres indicated that the BMS had overhauled INTUC. While the BMS's rivals challenged the validity of the figures, it is clear that the BMS has emerged as a major player. The third largest centre is the Hind Mazdoor Sabha (HMS) claiming five million members and founded by socialists opposed to government domination of INTUC. It has a strong industrial base and, like INTUC, is affiliated to the ICFTU. The All-India Trades Union Congress (AITUC) was the national centre until independence when Congress inspired the foundation of the INTUC: AITUC is linked to the Communist Party of India (CPI) and has a WFTU affiliation. The Centre of Indian Trade Unions (CITU) is linked to the Communist Party of India–Marxist (CPI(M)), with particular strength in West Bengal and Kerala.

The total number and membership of trade unions is uncertain and contentious and it is common for unions to exaggerate membership figures. Official "verified membership" figures are always disputed, partly because verification has significance for determining representation on public bodies. The high level of politicization, the lack of a sound mass base in many sectors, the looseness of ties between local and central unions, and the lack of adequate financial resources have reduced the organizational cohesion of the unions. Furthermore, there is no institutionalized system for the recognition of a union, which in effect depends on union strength in a given plant and the attitude of the employer. Total union membership is estimated as being approximately of the order of 13–15 million. As a percentage of the entire active workforce of over 400 million, the unionized proportion is very small. However, whereas most Indians work on the land or in the informal economy, most union members are in the much smaller formal sector of the economy, which accounts for only about 30 million jobs. Unions are also concentrated in key industries and service sectors, such as railways, telecommunications, airlines and banks, and so have an influence disproportionate to their numerical strength. This has been amplified by their close alliances with political parties. Other than some traditional strongholds such as the jute industry, the unions are strongest in India's extensive public sector industries, which is reflected in the particular opposition of unions to privatization. Many new private sector enterprises are resistant to recognizing unions, which employers see as difficult to deal with, resistant to change and highly political.

Nearly all agricultural workers (except in tea and other plantations), as well as domestic and casual workers, are unorganized. It is estimated that the range of legal protections of workers' rights are effective or meaningful only in respect of the 30 million workers in the formal industrial sector, compared with a total workforce of some 400 million. The influence of organized labour is further weakened by the high levels of unemployment and under-employment and availability of non-union casual labour.

The plight of rural workers in particular is, however, now being taken up more vigorously not only by well-established organizations like INTUC, but also by bodies like the Confederation of Indian Rural Workers' Unions (Hind Keth Mazdoor Sabha – HKMS) which is affiliated to the HMS. The Confederation has appealed for rural poverty and unemployment to be relieved not so much by aid and food hand-outs, but by the creation of job opportunities for the needy through a programme of extensive public works. Many workers on the land face seasonal unemployment and destitution. Workers' advocacy organizations, such as the Self Employed Women's Association (SEWA), have done much to organize workers in the informal economy and to give these workers a voice and collective identity that is being heard at national and international levels. SEWA, founded in 1972, has some 700,000 members.

While the different centres sometimes have found common ground (notably in resisting, with some success, proposals to amend the labour laws), they are generally divided by political alignments. The INTUC and AITUC both supported the Emergency declared from 1975–77 (despite the suspension of trade union rights and ban on strikes), in line with the position of the political parties with which they were associated, i.e. the Congress Party and the Communist Party of India (CPI). In 1994 the communist centres, AITUC and CITU, together with the socialist HMS and a number of industrial and public service federations, farmers' and agricultural workers' organizations, women's and youth and students' movements, convened the National Platform of Mass Organizations (NPMO). The immediate impetus behind formation of the platform was opposition to the (Congress Party) government's decision to sign the 1994 GATT agreement. This culminated in a general strike, claimed to be the biggest ever in India, on Sept. 29, 1994. The participating organizations claimed the backing of 25 million, with total stoppages in West Bengal, Kerala, Tripura, Tamil Nadu and Bihar, 85% of all coal miners on strike, and a complete shut-down of banking and insurance. Some four million public sector employees also participated. Following the 1998 election of a BJP-led government committed to pushing ahead with reform and privatization of the state sector, including the closure of some particularly unsuccessful enterprises, the NPMO called a one-day national strike on Dec 11, 1998. Organizers claimed the strike was the biggest since independence and it was supported by 56 unions, most of them affiliates of the communist-linked centres, together with most opposition parties (except Congress) and even two of the governing coalition parties. The strike was most successful where it enjoyed the support of state governments, in West Bengal, Kerala and Tripura, all ruled by the Communist-led Left Front, and in Bihar and Tamil Nadu, where regional opposition parties held power. Neither the BMS nor INTUC participated, reflecting their political alignments and the commitment of Congress and BJP to the reform process.

The BJP party (in power in coalition from 1998-2004) has moderated some of its earlier Hindu fundamentalist rhetoric but there are substantial concerns remaining. In March 2000 the BJP-led government, under pressure from Congress-I and also several of the BJP's own coalition partners, reluctantly ordered the government of Gujarat to restore a ban on civil servants being members of the semi-secret fundamentalist organization Rashtriya Swayamsevak Sangh (RSS, Organization of National Volunteers). This has close links to both the BJP and the BMS.

Bonded labour was outlawed in 1976 but there are still widespread reports of its existence, especially on the land. Bonded labourers are bound to work for their creditor until a debt is settled; the effect of a low rate of pay and high interest rates is such that bonded status is commonly life-long or even hereditary. The problem of child labour appears to be equally intractable. Urban child employment tends mostly to be concentrated in hotels and restaurants, building construction sites, automobile workshops, and fireworks and match factories, and children are also widely used as domestic servants. In rural areas children are used in agriculture, herd tending and the hand loom industry. Children are also bonded.

Official and unofficial strikes and demonstrations, often of a highly political nature, are frequent. Many strikes revolve around issues of parity of pay, promotional opportunities and status. There were strikes through the 1990s over austerity measures, threats to public sector jobs and terms and conditions, and planned privatization. General strikes are not uncommon but are often localized in effect and confined to a few sectors. However, union militancy has been one factor in the slow progress in reducing the Indian public sector as governments have tended to back down in the face of labour militancy.

The BJP-led government of Prime Minister A.B. Vajpayee was re-elected in the autumn of 1999 on a platform that included reforming India's highly inefficient state-run sector. In January 2000 it faced concerted strikes by power workers in Uttar Pradesh and by dockers nationwide, seen as challenging government plans for eventual privatization. In the power strike, about 4,000 of the 90,000 strikers were sacked, and the main leaders jailed, although reinstatement was offered as part of the compromise settlement.

Employer-union attitudes are commonly adversarial, and the government frequently acts as mediator, a role encouraged historically by the close association of many unions (notably those of INTUC) with the governing Congress Party. Likewise the ideology of the Congress Party, the dominant party for most of the period since independence, has favoured tripartism, which is embedded in the industrial relations system.

In June 2002 the Second National Commission on Labour presented its proposals for labour law reform. The Commission was boycotted by several unions (BMS and INTUC participating). Its findings have been criticized by the unions for promoting the goal of "flexible" working, placing restrictions on the right to organize strike action, and limiting trade union freedoms. The Commission proposed that the "flexible" law would have broad application to the millions of workers in India's informal economy. Organizations such as SEWA have expressed some support for this principle, but trade unions have strongly criticized this approach, calling for separate legislation for, for example, formal sector workers and agricultural workers.

In recent years India has experienced several nation-wide strikes in protest at government policies, largely sparked by opposition to the impacts experienced by workers of large-scale privatizations and economic adjustments. Unions claim that the general strike of May 21, 2003, was observed by some 30 million workers in opposition to these same policies.

The right to strike has recently been under threat in at least one high profile case. A public sector strike in July 2003 in the state of Tamil Nadu, called in protest at changes to employee pension rights, met with a hard-line response. More than 170,000 public sector workers were dismissed and thousands were arrested. Replacement staff were asked to sign contracts renouncing trade unionism. When the case came before the Supreme Court the judges found against the workers, ruling that government employees have no "legal, moral or equitable right to go on strike". The case is being vigorously challenged by India's trade unions in legal and political forums and in mass demonstrations.

3 Trade Union Centres

All-India Trade Union Congress (AITUC)
Address. 24 Canning Lane, New Delhi 110001
Phone. +91 11 2338 7320
Fax. +91 11 2338 6427
E-mail. aitucong@bol.net.in
Leadership. Gurundas das Gupta (secretary-general)
History and character. The AITUC was founded in 1920 and was the primary trade union centre until independence in 1947 and the formation of the Congress Party-linked INTUC. Since then it has been closely linked to the Communist Party of India (CPI). Its traditional strongholds are Karnataka, Andhra Pradesh, Bihar, Gujarat, Delhi, and Punjab. It partici-

pates in the National Platform of Mass Organizations which has opposed the efforts of the Congress Party and BJP-led governments to reform public sector enterprises and liberalize the economy. Globally it is one of the most prominent members of the WFTU.
International affiliations. WFTU; CTUC

Bharatiya Mazdoor Sangh (BMS)
Address. Ram Naresh Bhavan, Tilak Gali, Paharganj Ganj, New Delhi 110 055
Telephone. +91 11 235 84212
Fax. +91 11 235 82648
E-mail. bms@indiya.com
Leadership. H. G. Dave (president); Harshubaih Dubey (general secretary)
History and character. The BMS was founded in July 1955. BMS goals and objectives are inspired by the basic tenets of a Hindu Nationalist socio-cultural organization, the Rashtriya Swayamsevak Sangh, which is also the mother organization of the BJP political party, in government from 1998-2004. The BMS constitution specifically bars politicians and the BMS itself avoids direct political alignments or affiliations. However, the BMS has grown steadily in influence in association with the BJP following that party's establishment as a breakaway from the Janata party in 1980. Its rise paralleled that of the BJP, which went from obscurity in the early 1980s to being the third largest party at the 1989 elections, to second in 1991 and then first in elections in 1996, 1998 and 1999. By the mid-1990s, according to official figures for "verified memberships" the BMS was the largest centre, and although this was strongly disputed by its rivals, its rise had clearly been remarkable.

The BMS opposed the New Economic Policy launched by the Congress party in 1991 on the grounds that economic self-reliance would be undermined; that economic sovereignty would be jeopardized; that there would be adverse effects upon employment and inflation, and that the changes were being rushed through under dictation from the World Bank and the IMF. As an alternative the BMS suggested patronizing indigenous consumer goods; publication by manufacturers of their production costs; introduction of new technology on a selective basis "where suitable to the Indian condition"; and (ultimately) evolution of an indigenous economic system.

The formation of a BJP-led government at national level in 1998 inevitably influenced the BMS's positions to some degree. The BJP by this point had become strongly committed to achieving the New Economic Policy goals that had largely gone unfulfilled by the Congress party. The BMS, however, criticized the new government for adopting the Congress programme of economic liberalization, while not endorsing the sort of full-scale protests mobilized by some of the other centres. BMS campaigns included opposition to opening up the insurance sector to the market and against the lifting of restrictions on agricultural imports under World Trade Organization rules.
International affiliations. CTUC

Centre of Indian Trade Unions (CITU)
Address. 13 A Rouse Avenue, New Delhi 110002
Phone. +91 11 2322 1288
Fax. +91 11 2332 1284
E-mail. citu@ vsnl.com
Leadership. M. K. Pandhe (general secretary)
Membership. 2.8m. (1997)
History and character. CITU was formed in 1970. CITU reported that many of its members and officials were driven from their homes or killed in attacks by Congress supporters and other factions in the early and mid-1970s. CITU is closely linked to the Communist Party of India (Marxist), whose power base is in West Bengal, Kerala and Tripura, in all of which communist-led Left Front governments held office in the late 1990s. In 1998 there were reports that a large number of CITU members were defecting to the Communist Party of India-affiliated AITUC amid friction between the Communist Party of India and Communist Party of India (Marxist), the main components of the Left Front coalition ruling West Bengal. The CITU participates in the National Platform of Mass Organizations, which opposed the efforts of the Congress Party and BJP-led governments in the 1990s to reform public sector enterprises and liberalize the economy.
International affiliations. CTUC

Hind Mazdoor Sabha (HMS)
Indian Labour Organization
Address. (Delhi office) 120 Babar Road, New Delhi 110001
Phone. +91 11 234 13519
Fax. +91 11 234 11037
E-mail. hms@nde.vsnl.com
Website. http://members.rediff.com/hms (English)
Leadership. Umraomal Purohit (general secretary)
Membership. over 4 million
History and character. The HMS was founded on Dec. 29, 1948, in rejection of the communist domination of the AITUC and the control of the INTUC by the Congress Party. It defines its ideals as "secularism, socialism, democracy, free trade unionism and nationalism". It is independent of government, employers and political parties and says it is the only major centre in India not linked to a political party. It has been, however, seen as close to the socialist Janata Dal party.

Its position was one of extreme difficulty during the Emergency from 1975–77 when the HMS leadership was divided over the issue of acquiescence in the suspension of trade union rights.

The HMS believes in "the overall development of its members", and many of its affiliates run schools, holiday homes, education centres, community halls, and medical and family planning facilities. It has been undertaking a massive workers' education programme and has its own education and research institute, the Maniben Kara Institute, at Bombay, and a Rural Workers' Institute at Talegaon in Maharshtra state. Its Rural Workers' Federation not only organizes rural workers but also assists them in establishing self-employment programmes.

The HMS identifies the New Economic Policy of the 1990s, unemployment, privatization, and the ever increasing mass of unorganized casual and contract workers as among the principal problems facing the Indian trade union movement. It believes the new world trade order will produce joblessness in many domestic industries. It favours an extension of workers' participation in industrial management, a concept that has had little practical result in India despite numerous experiments since 1947.

The HMS has 2,300 affiliated trade unions, organized into 16 industrial federations. Major unions are the railway trade unions throughout India, transport and dock workers' unions in the 10 major ports, Air India employees, plantations, coal, textiles, steel, engineering, forestry, chemicals, seafarers and electricity. About 15% of its membership are women and it is seeking to increase that proportion.
International affiliations. ICFTU; CTUC

Indian National Trade Union Congress (INTUC)
Address. Shramik Kendra, 4 Bhai Veer Singh Marg, New Delhi 110011
Phone. +91 11 2374 7767
Fax. +91 11 2336 4244
E-mail. intuchq@del13.vsnl.net.in
Website. http://members.rediff.com/intuc
Leadership. Rajendra Prasad Singh (general secretary); Sanjeeva Reddy (president)
Membership. 6 million
History and character. INTUC was founded on May 3, 1947, inspired by Gandhian principles, and claims to be the largest trade union centre in India. It is closely linked to the Congress Party and this has allowed it to stay at the centre of trade union affairs and be influential in all industrial relations legislation for most of India's post-independence history.

INTUC says that unlike "the Western trade union movement, whose main concern is the conditions of employment", or the "Eastern trade unions' highly regimented attitude and approach", Gandhi's concept of the movement, on which the INTUC's policies and programmes are based, puts more emphasis on "human considerations". It defines its aim as being to foster a society that is free from hindrances to the development of the human personality and progressively eliminates exploitation and inequality. It defines itself as being "in the vanguard of India's march towards her cherished goal of establishing a secular and socialist democracy" and favours "national ownership and control" of industry.

INTUC is calling for greater protection for the unorganized mass of rural workers, many of them dependent on seasonal employment, and the creation of a system of unemployment benefit.
International affiliations. ICFTU; CTUC

4 Other Trade Union Organization

Confederation of Free Trade Unions of India (CFTUI)
Address. Siddharthnagar - Kurduwadi - Dist. Solapur, PIN 413208 Maharashra State, India
Phone. + 91 2183 223 202
Fax. +91 2183 223 453
E-mail. cftui@hotmail.com
Leadership. T. Ambareesh (president); Rohidas E. More (general secretary)
History and character. The CFTUI is the former BATU India, a WCL affiliate that acted as an organizing centre and promoter of union education in the subcontinent. In 1994 BATU India resolved to transform itself into the CFTUI in order to consolidate its ranks and build up solidarity. It held its first ordinary congress in April 1999 and became a full member of WCL the same year.
International affiliation. WCL

Indonesia

Capital: Jakarta
Population: 238.5 m. (2004 est.)

1 Political and Economic Background

Indonesian independence was recognized by the Netherlands in 1949. Some 88% of the population are Muslims, making it the most populous predominantly Muslim country in the world. From 1966–98, President Suharto ruled through his New Order regime and from 1971 the government-sponsored Golkar ("Joint Secretariat of Functional Groups") held an absolute majority of seats in the legislature.

For much of Suharto's long period of rule, the Indonesian economy grew rapidly, growth exceeding 6% per annum for a quarter of a century. However, the impact of the late 1997 Asian economic crisis on Indonesia was severe. The domestic currency collapsed, GDP contracted by 14% in 1998, and there were massive outflows of capital and rampant inflation. Although Suharto was re-elected in March 1998, widespread unemployment, the return home of laid-off migrant workers from other Asian countries, and cuts on subsidies on prices of fuel, electricity and transport, led to strikes and riots in May 1998 in which 1200 people were killed. Suharto resigned on May 21 and was succeeded by his Vice-President, B.J. Habibie. Mob violence against Chinese-owned businesses at the time of the fall of Suharto is estimated to have led to the withdrawal of $20bn. from the economy by Chinese business interests.

Legislative elections in June 1999 resulted in defeat for Golkar and victory for an alliance of the National Awakening Party (PKB), the Democratic Party for Struggle (PDI-P) and the National Mandate Party (PAN). In October 1999 the People's Consultative Assembly elected Abdurrahman Wahid, leader of the PKB and a liberal Muslim cleric, as President, although the Vice-President, Megawati Sukarnoputri of the PDI-P, emerged as an increasingly dominant force. After an impeachment process in the legislature, Abdurrahman Wahid was dismissed as President and replaced by Megawati through the Assembly's decision in July 2001. The most recent legislative elections, in April 2004, gave 17 parties representation in the legislature, headed by Golkar; the second round of presidential elections in September 2004 resulted in the defeat of Megawati by former general and Security Minister Susilo Bambang Yudhoyono, whose newly formed Democrat Party had come fourth in the earlier legislative contest. The military retains a strong position in Indonesian politics. Although East Timor has now achieved independence after a quarter-century of conflict, there are continuing separatist conflicts in Papua (Irian Jaya) and Aceh.

Some 45% of the labour force are engaged in agriculture (although this generates less than 17% of GDP); however, Indonesia also has a range of industries including petroleum, textiles and mining and exploitation of rubber and wood resources, and 16% of the workforce is in industrial employment, with industry producing 44% of GDP. There are endemic problems of corruption and an uncertain environment for foreign investment. Real GDP was expected to increase 4.1% in 2004 with inflation at 6.6% and unemployment at 8.7%.

GDP (purchasing power parity) $758.8bn. (2004 est.); GDP per capita (purchasing power parity) $3,200 (2004 est.).

2 Trade Unionism

Indonesia is one of the few Asian countries to have ratified all eight fundamental ILO conventions, including ILO Convention No. 98 (Right to Organize and Collective Bargaining, 1949) in 1956 and Convention No. 87 (Freedom of Association and Protection of the Right to Organize, 1948) in 1998.

The first union formed in Indonesia was a teachers' union (in 1897) whose members were all Dutch teachers from public schools. Later, some trade unions were also formed in other government public sector services, such as the post office workers (Postbond, 1905) and plantation workers (Cultuurbond, 1907). However, these unions' memberships were still Dutch only. The first union to recruit indigenous Indonesian workers was the Trade Union of Rail and Tramway Workers (VSTP, 1908), whose members were workers from three private railway companies operating in some big cities across Java. Seven years later, its members were predominantly Indonesian. In 1916, Semaun, a Javanese, was elected as its chairperson.

Later trade unions followed VSTP, such as the pawnshop workers (PPPB, 1914) and the sugar factory workers (PFB, 1917). The PFB was formed by Surjopranoto, a nationalist close to some Islamic leaders. The VSTP and PPPB emerged alongside PFB as the backbone of the trade union movement in Indonesia. By then, the first Indonesian federation, Persatuan Pergerakan Kaum Buruh (United Workers' Movement) was formed in early 1920; Semaun became its leader and Surjopranoto the co-leader, but this federation lasted only for a year due to internal conflict. In 1923, Semaun, the chairperson of VSTP, called for a general strike of workers following a dispute on a wage raise. But the Dutch colonial government easily suppressed the strike by labelling Semaun's call as communist propaganda. However, strikes became a common occurrence because daily wages were so low and could not meet even the minimal living costs.

There were several times attempts to consolidate trade unions into one single centre, especially after a communist rebellion in 1926, but these were unsuccessful. Union activities continued under government surveillance. This situation lasted until World War II, when the Dutch colonial government surrendered to the Japanese. Under the Japanese occupation, trade unions were liquidated and workers were forbidden to form independent unions. After Japan surrendered to the Allies, Indonesia was given back to the Dutch. Soon workers organized themselves and in 1945 formed the Front of Indonesian Workers (BBI) to be part of the nationalist movement to gain the country's independence from the Dutch.

By 1959, there were at least 10 trade union federations with hundreds of local unions, many of them linked to political parties. SOBSI, related to the Communist Party (PKI) was the biggest trade union federation with membership of over 60% of organized labour. After the 1965-6 creeping coup against President Sukarno which brought Suharto to power, the communists were brutally repressed and linked organizations including SOBSI were crushed. Leaders were detained without trial.

The Suharto regime's official ideology was the philosophy of Pancasila, which stressed the objectives of national unity and consensus (and remains the official basis of many parties in the post-Suharto era). Under 1985 legislation Pancasila was "the sole ideological foundation" of all mass organizations: for the union movement, it meant they could have no concept of the strike, because "strike action represents force from one side upon the other". In practice this ideology was used to curb the development of independent trade unionism.

In 1973 the All-Indonesian Labour Federation (FBSI) was created under government auspices as a central coordinating body; the existing trade union centres remained in existence, however. In 1985 the FBSI was reorganized as the All-Indonesia Union of Workers (SPSI) and its affiliated industrial unions brought under tighter central control. In 1990 they were reorganized again, this time into 13 industrial sectors. SPSI, the sole legally registered trade union centre, was unsuccessful in its efforts to gain international recognition and affiliation to the ICFTU and was criticized as an instrument of the government and for the level of involvement of former military officers in its leadership both centrally and locally.

Civil servants were coordinated in a separate association, the Indonesian Corps of Civil Servants (KORPRI), set up by the government in 1971 and chaired by the Minister of Internal Affairs. KORPRI was seen as a mechanism of the ruling Golkar party. Other than the SPSI, the sole recognized trade union was the Indonesian Teachers' Association (PGRI), which was registered in 1990 and claimed 1.3 million members. Although restricted in its activities, this body participated in international teaching organizations.

In April 1994 the ILO governing body censured Indonesia for violations of trade union rights including suppression of independent unions, intimidatory use of the military, and restrictions on collective bargaining and strike action. However, efforts continued to develop trade unions outside government control. The Prosperous Labour Union of Indonesia (SBSI, established in 1992), led by Muchtar Pakpahan, was accused by the government of being the instigator of a 1994 riot in Medan, North Sumatra and Pakpahan was imprisoned. The Centre for Indonesian Workers' Struggle (PPBI) leader, Dita Indah Sari, was also sent to jail after leading a workers' demonstration in Surabaya in 1996.

Collective bargaining was protected in law under Suharto, but many difficulties existed in practice and rules favoured the monopoly position of the SPSI as a bargaining agent. A 1994 decree said that unions independent of the SPSI could be set up and negotiate collective agreements in enterprises where at least half the workforce agreed to the establishment of the union. However, if an independent enterprise union wished to join a federation it could only join one affiliated to the SPSI. Around 1,200 non-SPSI enterprise-level unions had been formed by the end of 1997, according to government figures. Representatives of the Department of Manpower or the army were reported commonly to involve themselves in collective bargaining, and agreements were often ignored by employers or proved unenforceable. Employers enjoyed broad freedom to dismiss workers for trade union activities without redress and employers' representatives themselves took leadership posts in the SPSI at regional and national levels. At enterprise level, employers were sometimes able to control SPSI unions but this was not always the case and the formation of SPSI enterprise unions was sometimes resisted by employers. Normally, however, the agreement of employers was necessary to allow an enterprise-level SPSI union to function.

Although nominally legal in private enterprises not deemed vital to the national interest, legal strikes were difficult to stage, and most industrial action tended to be short-lived unofficial actions that not uncommonly ended in violent clashes with the police or military. Although SPSI enterprise-level unions staged strikes over issues such as non-payment of the minimum wage, such actions were not supported by the SPSI centrally or through its industrial federations. Industrial actions nonetheless increased steadily during the 1990s, with the level of officially recorded strikes rising from 19 in 1989 to 350 by 1996. Under a 1996 decree the army was permitted to intervene "particularly in cases pertaining to strikes, work contracts, dismissals and changes in status or ownership of a company".

After Suharto's fall in 1998, the government of President Habibie announced a series of changes affecting trade unions, including the ratification of ILO Convention No. 87. In September 1998 the government announced postponement of the entry into force of the 1997 labour law, and that it would be amended after consultations as it was not consistent with ILO Convention No. 87. In September 1999 a government decree removed the requirement that unions must have Pancasila as their guiding principle. The SPSI (now the Confederation of All Indonesian Workers' Union, KSPSI) remained dominant in the union-side of many tripartite institutions, although by 2004, at least 86 union federations had registered at the Department of Manpower.

In this new era of freedom of association, many new trade unions have formed as a result of internal conflicts in existing unions. There is no reliable data on membership levels. Most unions claimed membership of workers who do not pay union dues.

Notwithstanding the considerable liberalization in the treatment of trade union activity following Suharto's fall, industrial disputes have continued to escalate into clashes between strikers and the military. The military remains a potent force in Indonesian society not always within the control of the government. In September 2000, the Chief of Police issued an instruction letter which says that security guards are not allowed to join and establish their own independent union. This letter is often used by employers to control the workers and has caused some serious infringement cases.

Many trade unions are concerned by the government-run programme called "Labour Law Reform", which receives much technical assistance from the ILO. The most obvious impact is the abolition of the notion of "protection" from the Indonesian labour law system. One provision restricts the right to initiate sympathy strikes. Another has legalized outsourcing.

3 Trade Union Centres

Konfederasi Serikat Buruh Sejahtera Indonesia (KSBSI)
Confederation of Indonesia Prosperous Labour Union
Address. Jl. Otista III, no 20, Bidara Cina, Jatinegara, Jakarta 13330
Phone. +62 21 7079 0872
Fax. +62 21 8195 676
E-mail. sbsi@pacific.net.id
Leadership. Rekson Siliban (chairman)
Membership. 2,100,000 (claimed)
History and character. The SBSI was founded in 1992 and grew rapidly through a high-profile campaign of enforcing employment legislation. From its inception the SBSI faced severe state repression including arrests and raids. Its national congress of July 1993 was broken up by soldiers only 40 minutes into the proceedings. In the first two years of its life the SBSI suffered the murder of three activists, the arrest of 250 and the dismissal of 2,500 from employment.

The SBSI called successfully for a general strike to achieve employment law enforcement in February 1994; it was blamed for riots in Medan (North Sumatra) in April and June, many local leaders were apprehended, and in September its former leader, Muchtar Pakpahan, was arrested and sentenced to prison. Although the sentence was quashed by the Supreme Court in September 1995, it was re-imposed in October 1996 and he also subsequently faced charges arising out of July 1996 riots.

Failure of the authorities to grant official registration to the SBSI attracted condemnation by the WCL (to which it affiliated in June 1997) and the ICFTU. Repression intensified before presidential elections in March 1998, when Suharto was re-elected. The police closed the SBSI office in Jakarta until after the election.

Following the riots of May 1998 and Suharto's resignation, Muchtar Pakpahan was released from prison on May 26 and granted an amnesty. The SBSI was given official recognition and representatives of the SBSI were included in Indonesia's delegation to the annual ILO conference. Tensions between the SBSI, the government and the military continued however and troops surrounded the SBSI Jakarta office on July 24, 1998, following the threat by the SBSI to stage a demonstration demanding the resignation of President Habibie. In the event only a token march was held.
International affiliation. WCL

Konfederasi Serikat Pekerja Indonesia (KSPI)
Indonesian Trade Union Confederation
Address. Plaza Basmar 2nd Floor, Jl. Mampang Prapatan no. 106, Jakarta 12760
Phone. +62 21 7989 005
Fax. +62 21 7989 005
Leadership. Rustam Aksan (chairman)
Membership. 2,937,662 (claimed)
History and character. Formed in 2003 by merger of a number of ICFTU-affiliated unions.
International affiliation. ICFTU

Konfederasi Serikat Pekerja Seluruh Indonesia (KSPSI)
Confederation of All Indonesian Workers' Union
Address. Jl. Raya Pasar Minggu Km. 17 no 9, Jakarta 12740
Phone. +62 21 797 4359
Fax. +62 21 797 4361
Leadership. Jacob Nuwawea (chair)
Membership. 4,576,440 (claimed)
History and character. The All-Indonesia Union of Workers (SPSI), from which the KSPSI is derived, was the sole legally registered trade union centre under Suharto. The union was criticized as an instrument of the government. SPSI's previous monopoly status ensured that the present day union has inherited an enormous membership and well established structures. The union's new leader Jacob Nuwawea served simultaneously as the Labour Minister.

4 Other Trade Union Organizations

Persutuan Guru Republik Indonesia (PGRI)
Indonesian Teachers' Unity
Address. Jl. Tanah Abang III no. 24, Jakarta 10160
Phone. +62 21 384 1121
Fax. +62 21 3446 504
Leadership. W. F. Rindo Rindo (chairman)
Membership. 1,598,716

Iran

Capital: Tehran
Population: 69.02 m. (2004 est.)

1 Political and Economic Background

The Islamic Republic of Iran was proclaimed in 1979 after the overthrow of Shah Reza Pahlevi and is a theocracy. The Ayatollah Ruhollah Khomeini, the country's "supreme leader" from 1979, died in 1989 and was succeeded by Ayatollah Sayed Ali Khamenei. He has substantial authority over areas such as the military and the judiciary and is the most powerful political figure. The position of supreme leader is held for life after selection by the Assembly of Experts, made up of clerics, who are elected from a list approved by the government. The supreme leader has power of appointment over the Guardians' Council, a body of clerics and jurists which vets legislation for its compatibility with Islamic law and also supervises elections. The President since 1997 has been Mohammad Khatami, who is seen as a mildly reformist force. In elections to the legislature (Majlis) in February 2000 candidates of the informal Islamic Iran Participation Front, supporters of President Khatami, won a majority. However, the Guardians' Council disqualified 44% of prospective candidates for the legislative elections of February 2004 (including 80 incumbent legislators), resulting in a legislature dominated by religious conservatives.

Under the 1979 Constitution all large-scale industry, including oil, minerals, banking, foreign exchange, insurance, power generation, communications, aviation and road and rail transport, were put under public ownership. Oil is the major contributor to foreign exchange earnings and Iran has benefited from rising oil prices in recent years. The private sector comprises mainly small-scale trading and services. Real per capita GDP more than doubled between 1960 and 1976 but then rose only 5% over the next 21 years of war, revolution and clerical rule. However, real GDP was projected to increase by 6.1% in 2004, although with continuing problems of high unemployment.

GDP (purchasing power parity) $478.2bn. (2004 est.); GDP per capita (purchasing power parity) $7,000 (2004 est.).

2 Trade Unionism

Iran has ratified neither ILO Convention No. 87 (Freedom of Association and Protection of the Right to Organize, 1948) nor No. 98 (Right to Organize and Collective Bargaining, 1949).

Trade unions organized vigorously and openly after World War II until the Shah assumed full powers after the overthrow of the government of Dr. Mohammed Mussadeq in 1953. The Shah thereafter suppressed independent trade unions and promoted the government-controlled Workers' Organization of Iran (WOI), although unofficial strikes contributed to the instability of the regime in the late 1970s. After the fall of the

Shah in 1979, independent trade unionism was vigorously suppressed. In the period up to 1983 many thousands of militants were arrested and detained.

After the elimination of independent organizations, the Biet Alomal, "the Workers' House", was founded in 1982. It is headed by the Minister of Labour and is the only permitted national labour organization. The Worker' House provides coordination to the Islamic Labour Councils, whose role and regulations are prescribed by the state. 1985 legislation provided for the establishment of an ILC, made up of representatives of the workers and one representative of management, in every enterprise or industrial, agricultural or services unit of more than 35 employees. The purpose of the councils was: (i) to encourage cooperation between workers to enhance productivity; (ii) to represent the problems of the workers to management and to cooperate with management in devising methods to improve working conditions; and (iii) to cooperate with the unit's Islamic association. In turn each council was to be consulted by management on issues affecting wages, working hours and conditions, and would appoint a (non-voting) delegate to represent it on the enterprise's board of directors. A tripartite body would be set up in every district, composed of representatives of the Islamic councils, enterprises and the Ministry of Labour and Social Affairs; these bodies would have powers to supervise and dissolve the labour councils and to rule on disputes between the councils and management. The councils serve as instruments of government control, although in some cases they have proved able to represent workers in blocking layoffs.

In 1991 Iran adopted a new labour code which formally allows employers and employees to establish guilds or trade unions. In the case of employees the choice open to them is for an Islamic labour council, or a trade or guild union, or workers' representatives. Guild unions in Iran denote regional organizations that issue vocational licences and help members to find jobs. Their membership is open to the self-employed, as well as to the employed. All guilds must register with the Minister of Labour: if their statutes are approved they are entitled to set up provincial trade centres and a Supreme Centre of Trade Societies at national level. The code does not state explicitly whether independent unions will be permitted to function, but allows the authorities to appoint a representative to any union organization and in practice independent unions are not permitted. Efforts to form a national workers' organization in 1997 were broken up.

In June 2003, following lengthy discussions with the ILO, the government indicated that it would move towards the acceptance of independent trade unions. However, the plan appears to have been shelved following a vigorous campaign by the ILCs, which accused the government of breaking the labour law.

Provisions of the labour law do not extend to workers on temporary contracts or workers of workplaces with fewer than ten employees. According to the Secretary of the Labour House in Sistan and Baluchistan, 28,500 enterprises out of 29,000 in the south-eastern province fell outside the coverage of the labour law in 2003.

Under the labour code agreements may be made locally or centrally but in either case they are subject to approval by the Ministry of Labour and Social Affairs. Disputes are to be referred to a local tripartite Board of Inquiry and thereafter to a tripartite National Dispute Board. Following significant industrial unrest in 1991-93, new legislation banning strikes and demonstrations by workers was promulgated by the Majlis in October 1993. Despite this, strikes still occur, and according to one estimate there were 181 protests and strikes by workers in the period from March 1998 to March 1999. A principal cause of strikes was unpaid wages.

In January 2004, just weeks before the parliamentary elections, the military opened fire on workers protesting at the dismissal of 1500 their colleagues from the Copper Smelting Complex in Shahre-Babak, southern Iran. At least four workers were killed and many were injured.

There are no affiliates of the ICFTU or WCL. The WFTU recognizes an exile group.

Iraq

Capital: Baghdad
Population: 25.37 m. (2004 est.)

1 Political and Economic Background

Iraq has been an independent state since 1932. The Republic of Iraq was declared in 1958 following the overthrow of the monarchy. From 1979 power was concentrated in the hands of Saddam Hussein, his family and close associates, controlling an extensive security apparatus. Saddam was President (his presidency being approved by a reported 99.6% of the electorate in a 1995 referendum), Prime Minister, Chairman of the Revolutionary Command Council and leader of the Ba'ath (Renaissance) Arab Socialist Party, the only legal party after the overthrow of a previous military regime in 1968. While Shia Muslims were the majority (60–65%) population, the Sunni Muslims were dominant under Saddam.

Despite engaging in two catastrophic wars, first with Iran (1980–88) and then with a US-led coalition following his 1990 invasion of Kuwait, Saddam retained power through ruthless eradication of rivals and the lack of any democratic alternative. However, after the Gulf War of 1991 Kurdish forces remained in control of parts of the north of the country, under international protection, and Iraq remained subject to UN sanctions, although these were moderated under an oil-for-food scheme introduced in 1996. The government controlled all major industries, including the critical oil sector. The impact of two decades of war and sanctions on the economy was immense.

After a period of mounting tension, US-led forces invaded Iraq in March 2003, quickly overthrowing the Ba'ath regime and ultimately (in December 2003) capturing Saddam himself. A Coalition Provisional Authority (CPA) was established to administer the country and this set up an Iraqi Governing Council (IGC), representative of major political groups, to prepare the way for the return of powers to the Iraqis themselves. In June 2004 a caretaker Iraqi government was appointed under Prime Minister Iyad Allawi in succession to the IGC and sovereignty formally returned to the Iraqi authorities by the CPA, which ceased to exist; however, the occupying forces remained as an essential underpinning to the new government against a background of widespread disorder. Legislative elections were held in January 2005, intended to lead to the adoption of a new constitution and the establishment of a permanent government by the end of 2005.

Much of the infrastructure of the country is in a state of collapse and a vast rebuilding programme underway, this being hampered by attacks by insurgents on foreign workers. Real GDP was expected to contract by a further 21.8% in 2004 and during 2004 negotiations were underway with Iraq's international creditors to secure reduction of the country's $125bn sovereign debt.

GDP (purchasing power parity) $37.92bn. (2004 est.); GDP per capita (purchasing power parity) $1,500 (2004 est.).

2 Trade Unionism

The first trade unions formed in the 1920s were violently suppressed. At the end of World War II 16 unions were formed to cover workers in all sectors except the oil industry, but in the following decade these were broken up or severely curtailed. Following the overthrow of the monarchy in 1958 the first oil workers' union was formed and the General Federation of Trade Unions (GFTU) established. After 1968 all unions were organized in the GFTU and became instruments of the Ba'ath party. The GFTU affiliated to the WFTU.

Repression of opposition trade unionists intensified after 1978, with many imprisoned or forced into exile. In 1979 the general secretary and the president of the GFTU were executed after being accused of conspiring against the security of the state. Conscription of labour occurred following the beginning of the war with Iran in 1980. In 1987 the Iraqi government passed a decree making all workers in the state sector civil servants without rights of association. The GFTU did not protest against the withdrawal of trade union rights and was accused by the ICFTU of having cooperated in the conscription of troops during the war against Iran.

Iraq has not ratified ILO Convention No. 87 (Freedom of Association and Protection of the Rights to Organize, 1948), but it ratified Convention No. 98 (Right to Organize and Collective Bargaining, 1949) in 1962. However, there are no legislative protections for collective bargaining. In the state sector pay levels are set administratively, and in the relatively small formal private sector by the employer or by individual negotiation. The 1987 labour law restricts the right to strike and in practice strikes have not been reported for two decades.

Under the US-led occupation, the status of the 1987 law was initially unclear, although the occupying powers appear to have been willing to rely on the law's restrictive provisions to prevent public sector bargaining and other trade union activities. It was widely reported that a group of lawyers were engaged by the Coalition Provisional Authority to work on the drafting of a new labour code, but national, regional and international trade unions complain that they were not consulted. By mid-2004 the ILO had drafted a provisional labour code, but there was no timetable for implementation.

The trade union situation changed radically in 2003, with underground activists and progressive forces working vigorously to establish new and independent trade unions. In the early stages of 2004 the Iraqi Federation of Trade Unions (IFTU) emerged as a dominant force in the new trade unionism, effectively unionizing dozens of workplaces in a short space of time with no resources. The IFTU was recognized as the "legitimate" trade union centre by the Iraqi Governing Council, a decision that was later adopted by the interim government.

Relations between the IFTU and the GFTU are strained. The IFTU claims that the other federation has done nothing to defend workers' rights during the occupation. The regional International Confederation of Arab Trade Unions still lists GFTU as its national affiliate, and has a strong tradition of recognizing only one centre per country. A third organization, the Federation of Workers' Councils and Unions of Iraq or "union of the unemployed" has also been campaigning for recognition as a national centre and separate structures emerged prior to 2003 in the Kurdish controlled areas.

In December 2003 the IFTU's temporary headquarters, previously empty offices belonging to the GFTU's transport section, were raided by US soldiers, IFTU leaders were temporarily detained and the offices were closed.

3 Trade Union Centres

General Federation of Trade Unions of Iraq (GFTU)
Address. PO Box 3049, Tahrirr Square, Rashid Street, Baghdad
Phone. +964 1 887 0810
Fax. + 964 1 886 3820
Leadership. Jamil Jabbouri (president); Karim Hamzeh (secretary general)
History and character. Founded 1959. The GFTU was closely associated with the Ba'ath Party during the rule of Saddam Hussein. During that time GFTU was the sole permitted trade union organization. It described its objectives at that time as being to build and defend the homeland; to protect the interests of the working masses and to increase production in the interest of national prosperity.
International affiliation. WFTU; ICATU

Iraq Federation of Trade Unions (IFTU)
Address. c/o Mechanics' Union, House No 14, Street No 12, Area 902, Unity District (Al Wahda), Baghdad
E-mail. postmaster@iraqitradeunions.org
Leadership. Rasem Hussien Abdullah (president)
History and character. Founded in 2003. The IFTU's organizing campaign has focused on working quickly to establish democratic channels from the workplace to a national-level federation. The organization has as yet no

or very few fee-paying members, but it can claim a considerable democratic mandate by virtue of a series of workplace ballots that were held in many large workplaces. These ballots elected local level representatives into 12 prototype unions, organized along industrial/sectoral lines. Local level representatives feed into the decision-making process of a 39 member IFTU executive body.
International affiliation. None

4 Other Trade Union Organization

Federation of Workers Councils and Unions in Iraq – Union of the Unemployed of Iraq (FWCUI – UUI)
Address. Bab Al-Sharki, Al Rashid St, Old Labour Union
Phone. +4178 882 5589
E-mail. asojabbar@yahoo.com
Website. www.uuiraq.org
History and character. In May 2003 labour activists founded the Union of the Unemployed in Iraq (UUI), which later claimed a membership of some 150,000 unemployed people. The Federation was founded after its first conference on December 8, 2003.

Ireland

Capital: Dublin
Population: 3.97 m. (2004 est.)

1 Political and Economic Background

Ireland achieved independence from the United Kingdom in 1921. The leading political parties are the conservative-nationalist Fianna Fáil (FF) and the traditionally more liberal Christian Democratic Fine Gael (FG). Following elections in June 1997, FF returned to power under Prime Minister Bertie Ahern, leading a coalition including the small Progressive Democrats party. FF also won the next general election, in May 2002, falling just short of an absolute parliamentary majority and again forming a coalition with the Progressive Democrats. The social democratic Labour Party, originally founded as the political wing of the trade union movement, has only ever had a minority position.

Since it joined the European Union in 1973 Ireland has changed from being one of the poorest of the EU member states, with a rather backward rural economy, to become the second wealthiest in terms of per capita GDP. It enjoyed a sustained economic boom in the 1990s, encouraged by EU funding and inward investment by international companies, many of them capitalizing on its skilled English-speaking workforce. Annual growth rates were the highest in the EU, with GDP increasing an average 8% per annum from 1995-2002, while inflation remained under control. While growth slowed in 2003-04, the economy has remained buoyant by European standards: the budget announced on Dec. 1, 2004, projected that GDP would rise a further 5.1% in 2005. Despite a planned 9.1% increase in public spending, much of it to fund social programmes, the projected public spending deficit of 0.8% of GDP is well under the 3% ceiling mandated by the EU's stability and growth pact, at a time when many of Ireland's EU partners (including France and Germany) are failing to meet this target. Although unemployment was formerly a problem, the unemployment rate by 1999 had fallen to 5.5%, the lowest in 30 years, and is forecast at 4.4% for 2005. Agriculture has declined in importance and industry and services now drive the economy. Ireland joined the single European currency at its launch on Jan. 1, 1999.

GDP (purchasing power parity) $116.2 bn. (2004 est.); GDP per capita (purchasing power parity) $29,600 (2004 est.).

2 Trade Unionism

Ireland ratified ILO Conventions No. 87 (Freedom of Association and Protection of the Right to Organize, 1948) and No. 98 (Right to Organize and Collective Bargaining, 1949) in 1955. The constitution guarantees the right of citizens to form associations and unions, as well as the right not to join unions.

An Irish Trade Union Congress, the predecessor of the present Irish Congress of Trade Unions (ICTU) was founded in 1894, and unions developed strongly under British rule. The ICTU is Ireland's only national trade union centre. Some Irish unions also affiliate to the British Trades Union Congress (TUC); likewise, some unions in the British province of Northern Ireland affiliate to both the TUC and ICTU. The number of ICTU affiliates has gradually reduced through mergers but there are still 57 member unions, some of them quite small. Figures show a decline in union density in recent years, although union membership is actually at an historic peak. The apparent discrepancy is explained by the rapid expansion of employment. About half the work force is unionized.

Ireland faced major economic difficulties in the early to mid-1980s. However, since 1987, it has had a series of three-year tripartite partnership agreements providing a framework for the management of the economy, social change and wage increases. These have been the Programme for National Recovery (1987–90), the Programme for Economic and Social Progress (1990–93), the Programme for Competitiveness and Work (1994–97), Partnership 2000 (1997–2000) and the Programme for Prosperity and Fairness (2000–02). In addition to covering a wide range of social and economic objectives these agreements have provided the framework for detailed collective bargaining. A 1998 public opinion survey undertaken for the ICTU found that 94% of the public believed that the unions' participation in these agreements had been successful, while the agreements are generally considered to have created an environment of economic stability and industrial peace that has encouraged foreign investment. The most recent agreement, called Sustaining Progress, runs from 2003–05.

The right to strike, in both private and public sectors, is protected by immunity from civil suits for trade unions. Police and military personnel may form associations but may not strike. The Industrial Relations Act of 1990 maintained immunities and permitted peaceful picketing, but did introduce a Code of Practice providing for voluntary arbitration in essential public services. The Act also established the Labour Relations Commission (LRC) with overall responsibility for promoting good industrial relations through conciliation and advisory services and the preparation of codes of practice. Disputes that can not be resolved directly between employers and unions are referred to the LRC, whose conciliation service resolves the majority of such cases. In the case of continued dispute, referral may be made to the Labour Court, an independent body with equal numbers nominated by the ICTU and the Irish Business and Employers' Confederation (IBEC). Although the Court's decisions are not binding they are normally respected.

A National Minimum Wage Act came into effect in 2000, providing what the ICTU says is the highest minimum in the EU. Prior to this there was no prescribed minimum wage other than in limited sectors (notably agricultural workers) where rates were set by Joint Labour Committees set up under the Labour Court.

A Code of Practice issued in 2000, supported by reforms under the Industrial Relations Act 2001, introduced "right to bargain" provisions. Union bargaining was thenceforth augmented by arrangements which aimed to secure "voluntary" agreements over representation. The ICTU demanded that this scheme be bolstered, and for the first time called for a statutory recognition scheme to be introduced. A further set of reforms under the Industrial Relations Amendment Act 2003, however, stopped short of introducing such a system.

3 Trade Union Centre

Irish Congress of Trade Unions (ICTU)
Address. 31–32 Parnell Square, Dublin 1
Phone. +353 1 889 7777
Fax. +353 1 887 2012
E-mail. congress@ictu.ie
Website. www.ictu.ie
Leadership. Peter Cassells (general secretary)
Membership. 767,397
Northern Ireland Committee - Irish Congress of Trade Unions: *Address.* 3 Crescent Gardens, Belfast BT7 1NS, Northern Ireland; *Phone.* 247940; *Fax.* 246898; *E-mail.* info@ictuni.org
History and character. The Irish Trade Union Congress was founded in 1894. This body split in two in 1945 with the formation of the breakaway Congress of Irish Unions (which rejected the inclusion of British-based unions), but was reunited under the present name in 1959. The principle of a united Irish trade union centre persisted through the period of British rule to the separation of the North from the rest of Ireland. The ICTU is politically non-aligned.

Reported membership grew slightly during the 1990s, reflecting a broad public acceptance of the positive role of trade unions. The proportion of members who are women rose steadily to 44%. The ICTU has recorded continuing membership growth in recent years despite the disaffiliation of ASTI and the expulsion of Amicus.

The ICTU's role has been strengthened by the development of tripartism in recent years. Since 1987 the ICTU has participated in a series of three-year partnership agreements with employers and government. The programmes have covered a wide range of issues relating to international competitiveness, the distribution of the national wealth, enhancing social inclusion, and building a knowledge-based society. Detailed areas of the programme cover topics such as taxation, pensions, workplace relations and modernizing the public service, as well as providing a framework for wage bargaining.

Reflecting the importance of the EU in Ireland's recent development, in 1994 the ICTU set up a specialist unit, the European Information Service. In 2003 ICTU's global outlook received a boost with the launch of the Global Solidarity website and the expansion of international development education programmes.

International affiliations. ICFTU; ETUC; TUAC
Affiliated unions. There are 57 affiliated unions. The trans-national character of many of these unions reflects the complex historical entanglements of Ireland and the United Kingdom, the close economic relationship between the two countries and the ambiguous status of the British province of Northern Ireland. Just as unions based in Britain (i.e. the United Kingdom excluding Northern Ireland) have members in the Irish Republic, unions based in the Irish Republic have members in Northern Ireland, and there are even unions affiliated to the ICTU which have members only in Northern Ireland.

In recent years the Association of Secondary Teachers, Ireland (ASTI) left the ICTU and Amicus was expelled from membership following an inter-union dispute over recruitment. IMPACT, CPSU and PPSEU held discussions around a possible merger and the creation of a 72,000-member "super union".

The following unions have in excess of 3,000 members in the Irish Republic. These include unions based in Britain with an Irish regional office in the Republic, or with an Irish regional office in Northern Ireland and a district office in the Republic (in which case the address given is that in the Republic), or unions operating only in the Republic.

1. Amalgamated Transport and General Workers' Union
Head office – see entry under United Kingdom
Office in Republic of Ireland.
Address. 55–56 Middle Abbey Street, Dublin 1
Phone. +353 1 873 4577
Leadership. John Bolger (secretary)
Membership in the Republic of Ireland. 18,203
Membership in Northern Ireland. 29,048

2. Building and Allied Trades Union
Address. Arus Hibernia, 13 Blessington Street, Dublin 7
Phone. +353 1 830 1911
Website. www.batu.ie
Leadership. P. O'Shaughnessy (general secretary)
Membership in the Republic of Ireland. 9,030
Membership in Northern Ireland. Nil

3. Civil and Public Service Union
Address. 19/20 Adelaide Road, Dublin 2

Phone. +353 1 676 5394
Website. www.cpsu.ie
Leadership. B. Horan (general secretary)
Membership in the Republic of Ireland. 13,000
Membership in Northern Ireland. Nil

4. Communication Workers' Union
Address. Aras Ghaibreil, 575 North Circular Road, Dublin 1
Phone. +353 1 836 6388
Website. www.cwu.ie
Leadership. C. Scanlon (general secretary)
Membership in the Republic of Ireland. 19,600
Membership in Northern Ireland. Nil

5. Graphical, Paper and Media Union
Head office – see entry under United Kingdom
Office in Republic of Ireland.
Address. The Anchorage, Charlotte Quay, Dublin 4
Phone. +353 1 269 7788
Website. www.gpmu.ie
Membership in the Republic of Ireland. 4,811
Membership in Northern Ireland. 2,652

6. Irish Bank Officials' Association
Address. 93 St. Stephens Green, Dublin 2
Phone. +353 1 475 5908
Fax. +353 1 478 0567
E-mail. iboa@eircom.net
Website. www.iboa.ie
Leadership. Larry Broderick (general secretary)
Membership in the Republic of Ireland. 10,095
Membership in Northern Ireland. 5,540

7. Irish Medical Organisation
Address. 10 Fitzwilliam Place, Dublin 2
Phone. +353 1 676 7273
Website. www.imo.ie
Leadership. G. McNeice (chief executive)
Membership in the Republic of Ireland. 4,252
Membership in Northern Ireland. Nil

8. Irish Municipal, Public and Civil Trade Union (IMPACT)
Address. Nerney's Court, Dublin 1
Phone. +353 1 817 1500
Fax. +353 1 817 1501
E-mail. rnolan@impact.ie
Website. www.impact.ie
Leadership. Peter McLoone (general secretary)
Membership in the Republic of Ireland. 60,000
Membership in Northern Ireland. Nil

9. Irish National Teachers' Organisation
Address. 35 Parnell Square, Dublin 1
Phone. +353 1 872 2533
Website. www.into.ie
Leadership. John Carr (general secretary)
Membership in the Republic of Ireland. 24,017
Membership in Northern Ireland. 6,093

10. Irish Nurses' Organisation
Address. Whitworth Building, Morning Star Avenue, North Brunswick Street, Dublin 7

Phone. +353 1 664 0600
E-mail. ino@ino.ie
Leadership. Liam Doran (general secretary)
Membership in the Republic of Ireland. 28,000
Membership in Northern Ireland. Nil

11. MANDATE
Address. 9 Cavendish Row, Dublin 1
Phone. +353 1 874 6321
Website. www.mandate.ie
Leadership. O. Nulty (general secretary)
Membership in the Republic of Ireland. 37,089
Membership in Northern Ireland. Nil

12. Operative Plasterers and Allied Trades Society of Ireland
Address. 72 Shantalla Road, Beaumont, Dublin 9
Phone. +353 1 862 5185
E-mail. info@plasterersunion.com
Leadership. N. Irwin (general secretary)
Membership in the Republic of Ireland. 3,000
Membership in Northern Ireland. Nil

13. Public Service Executive Union
Address. 30 Merrion Square, Dublin 2
Phone. +353 1 676 7271
Leadership. D. Murphy (general secretary)
Membership in the Republic of Ireland. 8,000
Membership in Northern Ireland. Nil

14. Services Industrial Professional Technical Union
Address. Liberty Hall, Dublin 1
Phone. +353 1 874 9731
Website. www.siptu.ie
E-mail. info@siptu.ie
Leadership. J. McDonnell (general secretary)
Membership in the Republic of Ireland. 200,000
Membership in Northern Ireland. 7,001

15. Teachers' Union of Ireland
Address. 73 Orwell Road, Rathgar, Dublin 6
Phone. +353 1 492 2588
Fax. +353 1 492 2953
E-mail. tui@tui.ie
Website. www.tui.ie
Leadership. James Dorney (general secretary)
Membership in the Republic of Ireland. 10,338
Membership in Northern Ireland. Nil

16. Technical, Engineering and Electrical Union
Address. 5 Cavendish Row, Dublin 1
Phone. +353 1 874 7047
Fax. +353 1 874 7048
E-mail. teeu@teeu.ie
Website. www.teeu.ie
Leadership. Owen Wills (general secretary)
Membership in the Republic of Ireland. 28,628
Membership in Northern Ireland. Nil

17. Union of Construction, Allied Trades and Technicians
Head office – see entry under United Kingdom
Office in Republic of Ireland.
Address. 56 Parnell Square West, Dublin 1

Phone. +353 1 873 1599
Leadership. J. Moore (national secretary)
Membership in the Republic of Ireland. 10,832
Membership in Northern Ireland. 2,840

4 Other Trade Unions

Association of Secondary Teachers, Ireland
Address. ASTI House, Winetavern Street, Dublin 8
Phone. +353 1 671 9144
Fax. +353 1 671 9280
E-mail. info@asti.ie
Leadership. Charlie Lennon (general secretary)
Membership in the Republic of Ireland. 16,510
Membership in Northern Ireland. Nil

Amicus
Head office – see entry under United Kingdom
Office in Republic of Ireland.
Address. 15 Merrion Square, Dublin 2
Phone. +353 1 676 1213
Leadership. J. Tierney (national secretary)
Membership in the Republic of Ireland. 21,000
Membership in Northern Ireland. 10,000

Israel

Capital: Jerusalem
Population: 6.20 m. (2004 est.)
Note: for Israeli-occupied West Bank and Gaza, see under Palestinian Entity

1 Political and Economic Background

The state of Israel declared its independence in 1948, following the end of the British mandate to administer what was then Palestine. It consolidated its position and expanded its territory as a result of a series of wars with its Arab neighbours, in 1948, 1956, 1967 and 1973. In the mid-1990s it conceded a limited form of self-rule for Palestinians in the Gaza Strip and West Bank, territory taken in 1967. Talks on the long-term status of the Palestinian entity broke down under the (right-wing) Likud government of Binyamin Netanyahu, resumed following the election of a Labour government headed by Ehud Barak in May 1999, then were stalled following renewal of violence in the occupied territories in autumn 2000. Against this background Likud leader Ariel Sharon heavily defeated Barak in prime ministerial elections in February 2001, and Sharon has since remained Prime Minister in a series of coalition governments. There is persistent tension in Israeli politics over the degree to which Israel should exchange occupied territory, and allow full Palestinian autonomy, in exchange for the prospect of improved security.

Israel has a diversified modern economy, with important commercial agriculture and a high profile in technology-based innovation. Government has traditionally dominated the economy, although the private sector has become more vigorous and the main trade union centre, Histadrut, has also played a major role in the economy through its ownership of enterprises in sectors including agriculture, transport and construction. Immigrants from the Jewish diaspora built the country, and in the period 1989–98 Israel absorbed a further 750,000 Jewish immigrants from the former Soviet Union. There are significant disparities between the living standards of Jewish and Palestinian workers and a reliance on imported labour in sectors such as construction and agriculture. Economic growth rates have been low since the turn of the century, putting pressure on government spending programmes and with unemployment rising to a record high of over 10%. Notwithstanding heavy annual subventions from the United States the public debt is in excess of annual GDP.

GDP (purchasing power parity) $120.9bn. (2004 est.); GDP per capita (purchasing power parity) $19,800 (2004 est.).

2 Trade Unionism

The Histadrut, the dominant labour organization in Israel, was formed in Palestine in 1920 as an expression of both trade union and Zionist aspirations, and played a major role in building the state of Israel. It served to provide a wide range of health, education and welfare services, and through the Hevrat Ovdim, Histadrut became a major owner of enterprises, generating 20% of GDP.

Histadrut dominates Israeli trade unionism, but there is also a much smaller National Labour Federation, the Zionist Histadrut Haovdim Haleumit. There are also a small number of independent individual unions, representing secondary teachers, doctors and university professors.

Histadrut historically has been close to the Labour Party. Political parties receive funding from the Histadrut budget in proportion to their representation on its elected governing bodies, and from its foundation in 1920 until 1994 Labour always had an absolute majority within the Histadrut. Relations with the Likud government of Binyamin Netanyahu (1996–99) were poor. In 1996–97 Histadrut led a series of nationwide public sector strikes against the Netanyahu government's policies on privatization and public sector pensions. In December 1997 the government agreed to consult with Histadrut on restructuring plans and backed down on the pension issue.

Israel ratified ILO Conventions No. 87 (Freedom of Association and Protection of the Right to Organize, 1948) and No. 98 (Right to Organize and Collective Bargaining, 1949) in 1957. A wide range of labour laws, mostly passed in the 1950s, provides the framework for the regulation of hours, holidays, youth and women's employment, disputes, national insurance, etc. In general workers are free to join unions of their own choosing. However, Palestinians from the occupied territories (now with limited Palestinian self-rule) of the Gaza Strip and West Bank may not join trade unions operating in Israel, and unions based in the Gaza and West Bank may not operate in Israel. Non-resident workers in Israel are covered by collective agreements negotiated by Israeli unions. Prior to the outbreak of the second intifada in late 2000 as many as 150,000 Palestinians were working in Israel, although that figure has now declined to almost none. A continuing source of tension between the Histadrut and the Palestinian PGFTU concerns the wage deductions that Histadrut collected from many migrant PGFTU members in return for the protection of Histadrut-negotiated collective agreements while working in Israel. PGFTU officials claim that Histadrut has not yet passed on an agreed percentage of these deductions.

Strikes are common, and in the late 1990s strikes over the impact of privatization on jobs and benefits were widespread. Where essential services are affected the government may ask the labour courts to impose back-to-work orders while negotiations continue, as happened particularly in the case of major public sector strikes organized by Histadrut in 1997. In 2003 the Likud-led government continued to provoke Histadrut, and recent strike calls have mired both parties in court cases, with the authorities endeavouring to prevent Histadrut actions. Emergency powers legislation permits the authorities to issue "back-to-work" orders to strikers in a widely-defined range of "essential service" industries. In November 2003 the ICFTU reported that threats against the life of Histadrut chairman, Amir Peretz, had been received at the height of trade union struggles.

The Histadrut remains the largest union but there are also large independent unions including the Grade School Teachers' Union, High School Teachers' Union, National Union and Doctors' Union. These non-Histadrut unions have about 250,000 members.

3 Trade Union Centre

Histadrut
General Federation of Labour in Israel
Address. 93 Arlosoroff Street, 62098 Tel-Aviv
Phone. +972 3 692 1513
Fax. +972 3 692 1512
E-mail. histint@netvision.net.il
Website. www.histadrut.co.il
Leadership. Amir Peretz (chairman)
Membership. 650,000. Membership has fallen from a previous height of 1.65 million. Histadrut membership is open to all ethnic groups and three-quarters of Arab and Druze workers in Israel are members.
History and character. The Histadrut was founded in 1920 in Haifa by 4,400 (Jewish) members of different trades, who decided to create a single organization to represent all crafts and professions. As Jewish settlers came in increasing numbers to Palestine, the Histadrut took on a broad role in developing housing, social services, and education and in training workers and building the economy. At the same time it fostered the development of cooperative enterprises and settlements, creating an entire network of enterprises and communities, and as part of its work, oversaw the creation of trade unions. As well as its role as a trade union, Histadrut is the most important economic organization in Israel, involved in a wide range of enterprises directly or in cooperation with private investors, although this role has been declining.

The Histadrut is not a federation of autonomous unions; a worker joins directly, and through this membership becomes a member of the appropriate trade union. The basic unit is the enterprise works committee, and all Histadrut members in each district elect the local Histadrut branch – the labour council. Each individual union is governed by a council elected by the union membership. Judicial control of the elected bodies is exercised by the court of honour, which at present is elected by the Histadrut council. Local courts, elected by local labour councils, hear claims by individual members or institutions relating to the affairs of the organization. However, these courts may not try criminal cases.

The Histadrut's trade union department represents 27 national trade unions. One responsibility of the department is to ensure Histadrut policies are implemented by the individual unions. All Histadrut members automatically have membership in the appropriate trade union. Within the various unions are works committees (at plant level) and local unions (members of the same trade in the same locality); these are linked to other trades through the local labour councils (multi-union local bodies). Each national union has a council, elected by secret ballot on party political lines, as its governing body; the council elects a national secretary, who represents the national union at Histadrut headquarters.

At local and enterprise level, candidates for office stand as individuals, but national elections are based on political slates. Political parties receive funding from the Histadrut budget in proportion to their representation on its elected governing bodies. From 1920–94 Labour always had an absolute majority, but in May 1994 former Labour Health Minister Haim Ramon's "New Life in the Histadrut" slate (backed by Mapam, the CRN and the Shas party) polled 46.2% and Labour only 32.82%. Ramon subsequently put together a coalition administration of Histadrut, with backing from the Labour list. In December 1994, after the assassination of Prime Minister Yitzhak Rabin, Haim Ramon was appointed Minister of the Interior and resigned from his Histadrut post. Amir Peretz, M.K., was elected Histadrut chairman. In 1998 the coalition led by Peretz received 58.6% of the vote. This coalition includes members from a wide spectrum of political parties.

At the national level collective bargaining agreements are negotiated between the Histadrut executive committee and employers, and specific agreements between the national trade unions and employers in their industries. A high degree of wage standardization exists throughout the economy, and the wage policy set by the Histadrut executive committee is binding on the unions, no matter how strong their individual bargaining power.

Up to 1994, Histadrut's health insurance system (Kupat Holim) embraced 75% of the population, but a law effective from 1995 introduced a new health tax payable by all citizens to fund nationwide health care. This had an immediate impact upon Histadrut membership, which declined from about 1,250,000 to 600,000. In effect this step broke the link between membership of the Histadrut and entitlement to health care, as each citizen now has the right to choose his or her preferred health scheme. While this shift coincided with the outlook of the new Histadrut leadership, it does pose a financial problem since health income subsidized some of the organization's other activities.

In conjunction with the Ministry of Labour and the trade unions, Histadrut operates a nationwide network of vocational training schools and apprenticeship classes. Mishlav (the Israel Institute for Education through Correspondence) offers day and evening classes at secondary school level. The Histadrut Department for Higher Education conducts university-level courses in management and the Culture and Education Centre conducts a wide range of activities, reaching the whole community, including the Arab and Druze populations.

The Histadrut pension funds deal with pensions and various other benefits such as holiday and compensation payments. Mish'an, established in 1931, provides loans for a variety of purposes, and operates old age homes and pensioners' clubs, and programmes for children and orphans. Dor le Dor provides financial aid for the elderly, and Lev Zahav offers them nursing services on behalf of the National Insurance Institute.

Every member of the Histadrut is simultaneously a member of Hevrat Ovdim (General Cooperative Association of Labour in Israel), which is in turn open only to members of Histadrut. It is an autonomous establishment acting as a holding company for the Histadrut's assets.

Every woman member of the Histadrut is a member of Na'amat (Working Women's Movement in Israel). It has its own governing bodies, the highest of which is the convention, elected every four years at the same time as the general Histadrut elections. Na'amat operates child care, nursery school, vocational training and adult education programmes. Na'amat also lobbies for legislation of specific interest to women.

Hano'ar Ha'oved Ve'halomed is the youth organization, with its own elective bodies. Its trade union department provides professional direction to youths serving apprenticeships and youths working in holiday jobs, while also supervising their conditions of employment, protecting their wages and protecting them from exploitation.

The Histadrut is represented on all government councils with labour and social welfare responsibilities, and in many cases the Minister of Labour is required to consult the Histadrut on the application of the laws. It is the recognized representative of workers in the labour courts.

In 1958 the Histadrut established the Afro-Asian Institute for Labour Studies to provide courses in trade union, economic and social matters for trade union and community activists from Africa and Asia. A parallel Latin American Centre was founded in 1962. At the end of 1990, the Eastern and Central European Foundation was set up for the purpose of offering labour education facilities to the trade union movements of the former Soviet bloc countries. These institutes were amalgamated in 1994, under the framework of Peoples – The International Institute for Solidarity and Development of the Histadrut.
International affiliations. ICFTU; TUAC

4 Other Trade Union Organization

Histadrut Haovdim Haleumit
National Labour Federation in Eretz-Israel (NLF)
Address. 23 Shprintzak Street, Tel-Aviv 64738
Phone. +972 3 695 8351
Fax. +972 3 696 1953
E-mail. hol@netvision.net.il
Leadership. Abraham Hirschson (chairman)
History and character. The National Labour Federation in Eretz-Israel was founded in Jerusalem in 1934, to unite those workers who believed in solving the country's social and economic problems on the basis of the teachings of Herzl, Nordau and Jabotinsky.

The NLF is committed to the principles of Zionism, and has as its banner the national flag. It believes in the separation of the functions of employers and trade unions, and in this respect stood in opposition to the Histadrut national trade union centre which also developed as a major employer in its own right. Like the Histadrut it was also a major provider of health care services (especially in the occupied territories). Although disclaiming political affiliations, it has been seen as sympathetic to Likud.
International affiliations. None

Italy

Capital: Rome
Population: 58.06 m. (2004 est.)

1 Political and Economic Background

For nearly half a century following the end of World War II, the Italian political system was characterized by the instability of individual administrations set against the overall dominance of the Christian Democratic Party, which was continuously in government until 1992. In the early 1990s, however, the established party system disintegrated amid a torrent of scandals, mostly concerning illegal party financing and other corruption. The party establishments reacted by creating new party names and alliances, thus giving a new façade to Italian politics while maintaining underlining orientations. A bipolarization of the party system has occurred with the emergence of two blocs – the centre-left Olive Tree and the centre-right House of Freedoms. The House of Freedoms won 368 of the 630 seats in the Chamber of Deputies in the most recent general election in May 2001, while the Olive Tree took 242. Silvio Berlusconi, the leader of Forza Italia, the biggest component of the House of Freedoms, became Prime Minister for a second time, forming Italy's 59th government since World War II.

Italy has a diversified mainly private sector economy, with 29% of the workforce employed in manufacturing and 69% in services. The state still has a stake in a range of enterprises, but the reduction of the state's role in the economy was symbolized by the closure of the state holding company, Iri, in June 2000. There is a sharp disparity between living standards in the prosperous north and the backward south, with the south beset by problems of unemployment, corruption, organized crime and dependence on central government support. The contrast has been reflected in the creation of a separatist northern party, the Lega Nord. Italy took action in the 1990s to control its chronic problems of high inflation and public deficits in order to meet EU convergence criteria to join the European currency zone, which it did at its foundation in January 1999. This process was assisted by a series of tripartite social pacts emphasizing wage moderation and increasing labour flexibility. In 2004, however, the European Commission launched an investigation into the reliability of Italy's official figures according to which its annual budget deficits since 1997 had never exceeded the EU growth and stability pact ceiling of 3% of GDP. Italy's public debt, at 106% of GDP, remains second only to that of Greece in Europe and the persistently sluggish rate of economic growth has put increasing pressure on the system of welfare and pension provision.

GDP (purchasing power parity) $1.55 trillion (2004 est.); GDP per capita (purchasing power parity) $26,700 (2004 est.).

2 Trade Unionism

Italy ratified ILO Conventions No. 87 (Freedom of Association and Protection of the Right to Organize, 1948) and No. 98 (Right to Organize and Collective Bargaining, 1949) in 1958. Freedom of association has prevailed since the end of World War II.

The (socialist) Confederazione Generale di Lavora (CGL) and the (Catholic) Confederazione Italiana dei Lavoratori (CIL) were founded in the first decade of the twentieth century; both faced intense opposition from employers, with especially violent conflict in the agrarian sector where the unions recruited many agricultural labourers. During the period of political upheaval and labour unrest following the end of World War I, the claimed membership of the CGL increased to 2 million and that of the CIL to over one million. In 1925, under Mussolini, fascist unions were accorded monopoly representation and by 1927 all other unions had been abolished. In June 1944 (when Italy was effectively divided between German and Allied occupying forces), socialist, communist and Christian democrat trade unionists in the "Pact of Rome" agreed on the formation of a unified national centre, the Italian General Confederation of Labour (Confederazione Generale Italiana del Lavoro – CGIL). Under the Pact, each of the three political tendencies was to have equal representation on the CGIL executive bodies. However, the CGIL progressively disintegrated and by 1950 a tripartite division had developed, with the CGIL led by communists, the Confederazione Italiana dei Sindacata Lavoratori (CISL) led by Christian democrats (but with some socialist influence) and the Unione Italiana del Lavoro (UIL), the smallest of the three, led by social democrats and republicans. These three remain the leading centres. The CGIL, CISL and the UIL are all now ICFTU affiliates, the CGIL having left the WFTU in 1978.

Italy's union centres have tended to be weak and under-funded, reflecting the relatively recent development of trade as opposed to class unionism, and the disunity of the labour movement. Local chambers of labour, linked directly to their respective trade union centres and uniting workers regardless of industry, have often been of more significance than industrially based unions. Competition between the centres has traditionally led to exaggeration of their membership figures (which are not independently certified). Low dues levels have been offset by fees received from the government as contractors providing social welfare assistance through the "patronati" arrangements. In 2003, CGIL claimed more than 5.5 million members, the CISL 4.2 million and the UIL 1.8 million.

The memberships of all the confederations are greatly inflated, however, by the number of pensioners included. This is a vastly greater component of membership than in any other comparable country, reflecting the prevalence of early retirement in Italy. Around half of the members quoted by the unions (though only a quarter of those in UIL) are pensioners. These are organized in separate affiliates. So large are the pensioners' unions within the confederations that each confederation has rules designed to limit the representation of its pensioners' unions in the decision-making bodies.

The pensioners' unions are active in providing a wide range of services to members and each has a non-profit mutual aid organization attached. They are also a substantial political force, the three confederal pensioners' unions adopting an annual common platform for negotiation with central and local government. The pensioners' unions are organized on a local and territorial basis so their organizational structure matches the structure of local government, assisting them in exerting influence. In the period 1993–97 the pensioners' unions reached some 2,000 collective agreements with municipal authorities. These covered issues such as reduced pensioner charges for utilities, local tax reductions, services such as home helps, health care and housing, and local leisure facilities. Pension issues have come to the fore in recent years because of the mounting burden of costs on the state. In 1995 the government adopted legislation aimed at a progressive raising of the retirement age, but retirement ages remain extremely low, giving rise to the phenomenon of the so-called "baby pensioners", especially in the public sector. A schedule adopted with the agreement of the three confederations in 1997 for white-collar workers provided only for the retirement age to be raised to 54 in the private sector by 1998 and in the public sector by 2000. The 1995 legislation also provided for the introduction of private pension funds to reduce the burden falling on the state.

The reported memberships of all three confederations were higher in the late 1990s than they had been in the early 1980s. From 1980–96 the combined membership of the three confederations rose by 1,636,492, or 18.2%, to a new record high of 10,642,287. However, the driver of this growth was the increase in pensioner numbers, pensioners making up 47.6% of members by 1996 compared with only 20% in 1980. The number of active workers in membership of the three confederations actually fell by 25.8% in the same period. Worst affected was CGIL, whose membership of active workers fell by 33.2%, while CISL lost 25.3%, and the UIL 6.4%. Overall, while the three confederations had 49% of the active workforce in membership in 1980, this had fallen to 36.6% by 1996.

The fall in active membership reflected in part the loss of jobs in manufacturing sectors, this especially affecting CGIL, traditionally the biggest force among blue-collar manufacturing workers. It also reflected the lack of success in recruiting in newer service industries and smaller enterprises, and among women, and workers in "irregular" forms of employment. The most unionized sectors are agriculture, public administration and manufacturing industry, in that order, while commerce and services generally are least organized.

Outside the main centres are numerous independent unions. Many of these reflect the interests of narrow occupational or professional groups who have felt neglected by the main confederations. Independent unionism flourished particularly in the 1980s as a result of the extreme compression of wage differentials that took place in the 1970s and into the early 1980s, which led to widespread dissatisfaction with the confederations' strategy of trying to flatten differentials. The proliferation of independent unions is particularly apparent in public sector areas, where there are some 700 trade unions, some of them with only a few dozen members. About 45% of public sector employees are unionized, with about two-thirds of these belonging to unions affiliated to the three main confederations. Leading autonomous unions include the Unione General del Lavoro (UGL), formerly known as CISNAL, and the Confederazione Italiana Sindacati Autonomi Lavoratori (CISAL). While these are weak overall, they have influence in particular sectors. In teaching, the autonomous unions Gilda and Cobas called a national teachers' strike and demonstration on Feb. 17, 2000, against new assessment procedures for performance related pay agreed by the three confederations. The protest was sufficiently well supported to cause the government to back down on implementation. In the loss-making Italian State Railways (FS) successive plans to tackle chronic problems of overmanning and inefficiency have been frustrated in part by minority autonomous unions that have been prepared to engage in disruption of services.

In the north, the Lega Nord, which has advocated the independence of "Padania" (the lands north of the Po), has also tried to set up its own trade union organization, the Sindacato Nazionale Padano (SinPa). According to Lega Nord's leader, Umberto Bossi, the three confederations had "robbed the northern workers". Although a mass organization drive for SinPa in 1997 was a conspicuous failure, it has had some success in plant-level elections, calling for regional level collective bargaining to take account of the higher cost of living in the region.

The 1990s saw important changes in the development of social partnership in Italy. The Italian economy was previously characterized by deficit spending, high inflation, lack of consensual relationships between employers and unions, and direct state involvement in matters that in countries such as Germany were settled by collective bargaining between the two sides of industry. For 18 years from 1975 Italy had a system of wage indexation (the Scala Mobile) that by the 1990s had become a principal target for economic reformers as a driver of inflation not linked to productivity. It was finally abandoned in 1992. Thereafter there have been a series of national agreements extending the scope of social partnership. The process has involved achieving agreement between the social partners and government, with such agreements then embodied (sometimes in amended form) in legislation. In July 1993 a tripartite agreement was reached on incomes and employment policy, the structure of collective bargaining, and worker representation at company level. In September 1996 the social partners entered into a Pact for Employment, this including provision for area (local and regional) pacts in order to promote jobs and investment in areas of high unemployment. These area agreements were to focus on planning for investment in infrastructure, increasing local level bargaining on work flexibility, and reducing bureaucracy. In 1997 legislation was adopted to increase flexibility, including the legalization of temporary work agencies. In December 1998, a new social pact was agreed following the formation of the D'Alema government, this including measures such as further public investment, tax relief for companies, increased training schemes and action against irregular employment in the black economy. In July 2000, on the basis of the 1998 pact, the government said that it would use higher than expected tax receipts to reduce the tax burden on small and medium enterprises and on families, and help the poorest in society.

While negotiation and implementation of these various agreements has been accompanied by periodic threats of withdrawal by the various parties, the general willingness to seek convergence through discussion has represented a change in Italy's social and economic culture in which confrontational posturing has tended to be a tradition. Italy's over-riding need to achieve convergence with its EU partners in target areas such as inflation and size of the public deficit has been one factor. Another has been a growing willingness by the unions to accept that without greater flexibility, unemployment and regional under-development could not be tackled effectively. Most of the 450,000 new jobs created in 1998–99 were in areas such as part-time work, fixed-term contracts and temporary agency work. For the unions, the challenge has become to adapt to changing realities and build new positions. In the area of temporary work, the operation of temporary work agencies was legalized only in 1997, but in 1998 the temporary workers' organizations attached to the three confederations signed a collective agreement with the temporary workers' agencies association, Confiterim. In 1999 the parties reached agreement to extend the activities of agencies to low-skilled workers, agriculture and construction, the unions thereby agreeing to further flexibility but cementing a bargaining role in the process. The regulation of temporary work represented an advance for the unions on a situation in which a vast shadow economy of unregulated irregular work had grown up over which the unions had no influence.

One aspect of increased social partnership is that the trade union centres showed more willingness in the 1990s to work together to find a coherent and unified voice for organized labour. This is not an entirely new process. From the 1960s, as the CGIL accepted the EEC and liberal Catholicism strengthened, relations between the CGIL and CISL improved. In 1972 CGIL, CISL and UIL jointly agreed that to achieve a unitary policy the confederations must be independent of the government and political parties, and they all accepted that union officials could not also be leaders of political parties, members of parliament, senators or town, provincial or regional councillors. A loose CGIL-CISL-UIL federation was then in place from 1972 until falling apart in disputes over the operation of the Scala Mobile in 1984.

Encouraged by the process of social partnership, by 1997, the leaders of all three centres were talking of merging their respective organizations into a unified centre by 2000. The merger project had lapsed by 1999, however, reflecting the fact that while the confederations have found common ground in many areas, they are divided in others, particularly the CGIL and CISL. Notwithstanding the decline of the old polarities in Italian politics, there are residual political differences, with the CISL seen as broadly sympathetic to the Partito Popolare Italiano (PPI), the heir to the Christian Democratic tradition, while the CGIL and UIL leaderships are close to the social democratic Democrats of the Left (Democratici di Sinistra, DS). These differences were reinforced in October 1998 when the PPI left the government to go into opposition, and more so after the victory of the centre-right in 2001.

The leaders of the confederations have also pointed to philosophical differences in that the more centralized CGIL adheres to a view of itself as the leader of a "labour movement", comprising both union and non-union workers, wile CISL sees itself as an association, stressing the role of union members in the individual workplace. CISL strongly favours worker representation on the board of companies, while CGIL opposes arguing that trade unions cannot represent the interests of both workers and employers.

The CGIL and CISL have also differed on the question of how far flexibility should be extended, the CGIL refusing to sign area agreements involving what it saw as too many concessions on this issue. The CISL has taken the view that the problems of areas of high unemployment (especially in the south where unemployment has run at four times the level in the prosperous north of the country) can only be met by local agreements on setting wage levels below those in national agreements, but this view has been opposed by CGIL and the UIL.

Collective bargaining permeates the industrial relations system (often with direct political involvement) and tends to be wide-ranging. For example, the development of occupational pensions since 1997 came mainly though the establishment of sector-level large-scale schemes negotiated through collective bargaining. Under the 1993 tripartite agreement, private sector bargaining takes place at two levels. At national levels sectoral agreements are negotiated that must take into account the planned inflation rates agreed by the social partners and overall national competitiveness and set minimum rates of pay. These agreements may be supplemented by company-level or (particularly in the case of small enterprises) local area agreements that deal with specific local conditions and reflect performance and productivity. Traditionally the local level is the natural locus of Italian trade union activity more than is the enterprise and while sectoral agreements are widespread, only a minority of workplaces (mostly in large companies) are covered by company-level agreements. The principle applied by custom in collective bargaining is that an agreement applies to all workers in a bargaining unit, whether or not they are members of the signatory organizations. In the civil service pay and conditions are established by law, following negotiations with the trade unions, while such employees are immune from dismissal other than for disciplinary reasons. However, following an agreement with the unions in March 1997, nearly 3 million public employees, including state employees such as teachers and postal workers and employees of local authorities such as administrators and health workers, were removed from civil service status. Their bargaining arrangements were brought into line with the private sector, leaving only 800,000 employees (including the police and armed forces) with civil servant status. One consequence is that public sector managers may now be removed for inefficiency.

The 1993 agreement also led to the strengthening of private sector workplace representation by the establishment of a new structure, the unitary trade union representation body (Rappresentanze Sindacali Unitarie, RSU). The RSUs, which were extended to the public sector from 1997, have a dual function in that they not only carry out the role of participation and consultation typically seen in European works councils but also engage in collective bargaining as the representative of the trade unions. RSUs are made up of two-thirds delegates elected by all employees and one-third nominated by the trade unions that have signed the collective agreement in force in the company. The unions have traditionally been weak at the company level in the Italian system and the creation of the RSUs has been seen as consolidating their role and providing a more robust framework for industrial relations at this level. Elections to the RSUs also provide a benchmark for measuring the strength of the various unions. About 80 per cent of the votes have gone to candidates on lists presented by CGIL, CISL and UIL.

While conciliation and arbitration procedures exist, historically the adversarial nature of industrial relations has been such that the parties have tended to have recourse to other means of resolving disputes such as appeals to the courts, intervention by the state or resolution by conflict. Individual labour disputes run at extraordinary levels, with more than one million cases pending in the courts in 2000. There has traditionally been a virtually unrestricted right to strike, and this has been freely exercised. During the 1990s, however, the level of collective industrial disputes fell sharply from the level in the 1980s. Essential public services remained prone to disruption, often as a result of action by minority unions. This was despite 1990 legislation stipulating that providers of essential public services and unions must reach collective agreements on providing a guaranteed minimum service in the event of industrial action. Application of the 1990 law is supervised by an independent Guarantee Authority, but violations have been commonplace.

The general elections of May 2001 have led to major repercussions on the trade union situation, which underwent a rapid change after the victory of the centre-right coalition. Only a few months later, the White Book on the labour market issued by the Berlusconi government provided indications differing from those which had characterized the relationship between the public authorities and special interest organizations up to 2001. This important political document, which represents the political programme of government action, is characterized in particular by sharp criticism of the method of negotiation ("social concerted action") which has provided the basis for relationships with the trade unions since the agreement of July 23, 1993. Instead of "strong" negotiation with the social partners, the government called for a new method of relationship, "social dialogue", based on the European experience. In the social dialogue approach, when the government intends to intervene in social policy, it will consult the social partners, and if the latter request it, will leave the underlying issue to be regulated by the agreement between the social partners themselves. If no agreement is reached, the government will consider itself free to intervene with it own regulatory measures. The basic difference between "concerted action" and "social dialogue" is that the government commits itself to negotiation with the social partners only in the former case. In the "social dialogue" model, on the other hand, the government merely either implements the agreement reached between the parties, or registers the failure to reach an agreement. The new model has not yet actually been applied, but has allowed the government to undertake "separate" agreements, i.e. only with some of the historical trade unions, trying to isolate the largest trade union (CGIL).

The disagreement within the coalition formed by CGIL, CISL and UIL was one of the most difficult episodes of the trade union movement. The signing of the Pact for Italy in July 2002 between CISL and UIL on the one hand and Confindustria (Confederation of Italian Industries) and the government on the other, excluding CGIL, represents a return of the historical problems of a trade union system without rules for verifying the consensus opinion of the workers, thus enhancing conflict between the various union organizations. The request made by CGIL for a workers' referendum on the agreement signed by CISL and UIL was rejected by the latter organizations, going against the established practice by which the general agreements signed by the trade unions have always been subject to consultation of the workers. This contrast reflects differing basic views of trade union democracy. In the view of CISL and UIL, it is the confirmation of the legitimacy of the agreements, since the trade union negotiates on the basis of the mandate conferred by its members, deriving its legitimacy from the associative structure. CGIL, on the other hand, has a different and more extensive view of trade union democracy, calling for a type of legitimacy deriving from all the workers, whether or not they are members of a trade union; they must be guaranteed the right of expressing their consensus or disagreement with the bargaining decisions of the unions.

The Pact for Italy has laid the basis for the reform of the labour market, implemented by the new government majority with Law no. 30 of 2003 (delegation law) and subsequent provision no. 276 of 2003 (delegation legislative decree). Under this legislation, the centre-right majority has encouraged the recourse to flexible and "non-typical" forms of work, abrogated important provisions for the protection of workers (for example, Law no. 1369 of 1962 on contracting), and provided fewer constraints on employers (in case of temporary employment in enterprises providing manpower, company transfers, contracting etc.).

The role of the trade unions has been affected by legislation. There has been particular criticism raised by bilateral bodies (with equal representation of trade unions and employers) as regards the management of the labour market as well as the preliminary certification of flexible employment contracts (with the purpose of reducing court disputes). It has, in fact, been asserted that assigning bilateral bodies with functions of labour market management, i.e. the "encounter" between labour supply and demand, produces in the end a basic transformation of the role of the trade unions, virtually producing a conflict with persons whose interests it should represent.

Before proceeding with the implementation of the law to reform the labour market, in the spring of 2002 the government sought to revise the existing system of protecting workers in case of illegal dismissal. The issue was of major importance; since 1970 Italy has had an extremely effective system for protecting workers in case of unjustified dismissal. The system is based on a double level of protection. Besides payment of damages, in proportion to the wages not paid since the day of dismissal up to re-entry, workers can apply to the judge to issue an order for the return to the previous job and workplace. This "real protection" of the job (introduced by Art. 18 of the Workers' Statute) is limited to companies with over 15 employees, but has an important symbolic value and has provided one of the reasons for the affirmation of a widespread trade union movement in Italy, protecting workers from the risk of reprisals in case of trade union activity and participation in protest movements not approved by the employers.

Attempts by the government to amend this rule led to a widespread social protest, with the participation of all the various trade unions, including those which signed the agreement of July 2002 ("Pact for Italy"). In the face of trade union mobilization and demonstrations held throughout the country (notably a demonstration held on April 16, 2002, which brought two million workers to Rome and is considered to be the largest mobilization in Italy in the post-war period) the centre-right majority and employers' federation Confindustria abandoned the proposed reform, seeking mediation with the more moderate trade unions and resulting in the signature of the Pact for Italy. In a referendum held in June 2003, part of the trade union movement subsequently attempted to extend this provision to all enterprises, without distinguishing the levels of worker protection on the basis of the number of employees. However, the referendum failed to reach the quorum provided for its validity, and the overwhelming vote in favour of the extension of the protection has only implied a symbolic meaning.

The elements of crisis in the organized trade union movement have not irreversibly damaged the relationships between the major confederations. The government initiative for a (new) reform of the pension system, started in 2004, has led to a common position of CIGL, CISL and UIL to counter the plan of the centre-right majority which would tend to reduce pension expenditure. A general strike and actions undertaken in February and March 2004 were jointly promoted, with the result of stopping, at least temporarily, the government's plans.

3 Trade Union Centres

Confederazione Generale Italiana del Lavoro (CGIL)
Italian General Confederation of Labour
Address. Corso d'Italia 25, 00198 Rome
Phone. +39 6 84 761
Fax. +39 6 884 5683
Website. www.cgil.it (Italian only)
Leadership. Guglielmo Epifani (secretary-general)
Membership. 5,458,710 of whom 2,564,094 were active (2003)
History and character. The CGIL was formed by agreement between socialists, communists and Christian democrats in the "Pact of Rome" of June 1944 as a unified trade union centre. The CGIL at first functioned only in southern and central parts of Italy controlled by the Allies, but was accepted as nationally representative at a conference with the chambers of labour from the industrialized north in June 1945 after the surrender of German forces in that area. Under the Pact of Rome, socialists, communists and Christian democrats were to enjoy equal representation on the CGIL executive bodies. However, tensions between the different factions were encouraged after 1945 by the emergence of the Christian Democrats as the major political party and by the intensification of the ideological division of Europe, which was reflected in a campaign of strikes and violent unrest led by communists within the CGIL in 1947–48. By 1950 most socialists and Christian democrats had withdrawn from the CGIL (see CISL and UIL), and the confederation after that time was dominated by supporters of the Communist Party (PCI), although with a socialist minority, with close financial and other ties to the party.

The CGIL was for many years closely associated with the policies of the Soviet Union and its allies, but a modification of its position enabled the formation of the CGIL-CISL-UIL federation in 1972. In 1974, in step with the move to advocacy by the PCI of Eurocommunism, it downgraded its relationship with the WFTU, of which it had previously been the largest Western European affiliate, to that of associate, and withdrew altogether in 1978. In 1987 the CGIL called for union pluralism in Poland. The CGIL mainstream is now seen as broadly sympathetic to the policies of the Democrats of the Left (DS) party. The DS is descended organizationally but not ideologically from the Italian Communist Party (PCI) and is of social democratic orientation; the ideological descendants of the PCI are the Communist Refoundation Party (PRC), which also has support within CGIL. At the first congress of the DS, in February 1997, Massimo D'Alema (the party leader) described CGIL secretary general Cofferati as being "closed and deaf" on the need for a radical overhaul the generous welfare and pension system. He warned that CGIL would be marginalized if it failed to adapt to social change.

CGIL membership rose from an average of 4.57 m. in the early 1980s to around 5.2 m. in the early 1990s, since when it has remained fairly stable. However, the proportion of its membership that are pensioners has escalated, reaching 55% by 1999. In the period 1980–96 the number of CGIL members who were in the active workforce fell by 33%. Traditionally CGIL's strength has been in manufacturing industry – where it has had about the same membership as the CISL and UIL combined – but this sector has declined and CGIL has had much less success in growing service sectors. While all three of the main centres have experienced this problem to some degree, the fall in membership among the actively employed has been most pronounced in the CGIL.

As in the other confederations, the pensioners are organized in their own union, which in the case of CGIL was founded as early as 1949. To offset the dominance of pensioner interests, the CGIL has rules that prevent any affiliate having more than 25% of the vote in decision-making bodies. The only affiliate affected by this is its pensioners' union (Sindacato pensionati italiani, SPI).

Of the three main centres the CGIL was the most reluctant to relinquish the Scala Mobile system of automatic wage indexation. When in July 1992 then secretary-general Bruno Trentin finally agreed to sign the tripartite agreement ending it, the resultant hostility led him to tender his resignation (subsequently rescinded).

During the 1990s relations with the other centres improved in step with the development of social partnership, as reflected in a series of tripartite agreements from 1993. In May 1997 the CGIL executive committee proposed the creation of a unified trade union centre by 2000, and the CISL and UIL also embraced this project. However, conflicts developed (in particular with CISL) over issues such as wage flexibility, where the CGIL proved unwilling to agree local area pacts that visualized lower wages to increase job creation, and over political alignments. CGIL secretary-general Sergio Cofferati told the May 1999 CISL assembly that it was no longer possible to continue with the merger project.

On May 20, 1999, Massimo D'Antona, the head of the juridical council of CGIL and an adviser to the Minister of Labour, was assassinated by the Red Brigades terrorist organization. A Red Brigades statement called him the "political-operational pivot between the government and the confederal unions, the person who developed the political impact of the social pact and of the neo-corporatist strategy".

In May 1998 Sergio Cofferati said that the unions must press for uniform labour legislation across the EU and for European-level collective agreements, although this would take a decade or more to achieve.

In recent years, CGIL has led a protest movement against the government programme of economic liberalization, obtaining a significant consensus among the workers. There have been very important initiatives against plans for the reform of legislation providing guarantees in case of individual dismissals and the support of peace. Starting in 2000-01, under Cofferati's leadership, the confederation has sought a close relationship with the "anti-globalization" and pacifist movements. In this new context, the confederation has implemented a programme based not only on the defence of rights acquired during the 20th century, but also on the capacity to extend the rights of citizenship to the underprivileged, including the areas of social marginalization and instability in the context of the "universal extension of rights".

On Sept. 20, 2002, after the expiry of Sergio Cofferati's mandate, Guglielmo Epifani was elected to lead the confederation. While ensuring continuity, Epifani seems to assign priority to the problem of restoring the unity of the confederations, attempting to overcome the divisions between the unions.

International affiliations. ICFTU; ETUC; TUAC. The CGIL joined the ETUC in 1974 and in 1989 (with CISL and UIL support) became the first formerly communist-oriented West European union to enter the TUAC. The 1991 congress resolved to seek entry into the ICFTU, and it joined the following year, again with the backing of the other two centres.

Confederazione Italiana Sindacati Lavoratori (CISL)
Italian Confederation of Workers' Trade Unions
Address. Via Po 21, 00198 Rome
Phone. +39 6 84731
Fax. +39 6 841 3782
E-mail. cisl@cisl.it
Website. www.cisl.it (Italian with English section)
Leadership. Savino Pezzotta (secretary-general)
Membership. 4,183,128 of whom 1,993,271 were active (2003).
History and character. CISL was founded in 1950 as a primarily Christian democratic split from the CGIL, and in its early years it received direct support from both the Roman Catholic Church and the AFL-CIO. It is one of the three main Italian confederations, all of which are affiliated to the ICFTU.

CISL has a diverse membership. It lags behind CGIL in manufacturing but is traditionally the leading confederation in the public sector. It is also the leading centre in representation of the self-employed. Like CGIL it has become increasingly an organization of pensioners, its pensioners' union (the Federazione nationale dei pensionati, FNP) representing 50% of total membership by 1999. To prevent sectional interests distorting policy, CISL rules limit any affiliate to 25% of the delegates at its congresses. Its membership in the active workforce fell by 25% from 1980–96.

CISL describes itself as non-partisan, non-ideological and non-denominational. Although many of its affiliates have a Catholic orientation, and many members are from the Christian democratic tradition, it also combined with CGIL and the UIL to oppose measures from Christian Democrat governments seen as inimical to its members. CISL was the first main union centre to adopt an incompatibility rule barring elected officers from running for political office. Thus Franco Marini, predecessor of D'Antoni in the office of secretary-general, resigned before taking up the position of Minister of Labour in 1991.

Following the electoral collapse of the Christian Democrats (the dominant party since World War II) amid corruption scandals in 1992–94, the party was re-launched as the Partito Popolare Italiano (PPI) in 1994. Participation by the PPI in the Prodi government of 1996–98 was a factor in encouraging CISL's positive engagement with government at that time. Conversely, after the PPI left the government in October 1998 the CISL had poorer relations with the succeeding coalitions led by the Democrats of the Left (DS). On Nov. 20, 1999, CISL organized an anti-government demonstration without the support of the other centres, criticizing the government on issue such as widening gap in employment between north and south and lack of action to reduce the tax burden on families. The CGIL and UIL are broadly sympathetic to the DS.

In May 1998 CISL secretary-general Sergio D'Antoni backed a strategy of creating a new alliance of Christian-oriented social, economic and political organizations, including the PPI, although CISL deputy secretary-general Raffaele Morese, expressed doubts about this initiative saying CISL should engage only in trade union, and not political, activities.

CISL says it seeks to protect not just the formally employed but those who have an irregular or marginal role in the labour market, including home workers, those in informal or undeclared employment, the unemployed, the disabled, the young and elderly. It advocates a strong regional policy to assist the economically backward southern region of the country. The CISL accepts that there needs to be much greater flexibility in wage policy and market regulation, and a different tax regime, for the south if jobs are to be created there. In contrast to the other centres, CISL sees flexibility as strengthening the unions, through increasing the role of local area and company bargaining.

CISL was the first of the major confederations to back the policy of "concertation", which led to a tripartite basis for economic reform, the defence of wages and jobs while containing inflation. It backed Italy's accession to the single European currency. It favours economic democracy and worker representation on company boards, an area where it disagrees with CGIL.

D'Amato said at the May 1999 CISL assembly that the goal was to cut the number of affiliated sectoral federations from 17 to 10.

The CISL signed the Pact for Italy in July 2002, together with the UIL. However, conflicts arising from the government initiatives regarding protection from dismissal, pensions and the renewal of the public employee contracts, have led the CISL leadership to remark that the phase of dialogue with the government must be considered closed.

The CISL's recent programme has been characterized by the tendency to encourage the decentralization of industrial relations to the local and company level. They have also encouraged the new functions attributed to the social partners in the reform being called for in the welfare system, although the government has thus far postponed this reform.

CISL maintains several institutes and research centres. Prof. Enzo Tarantelli, then director of the CISL Research Institute, was murdered by Red Brigades terrorists in 1985.

International affiliations. ICFTU; ETUC; TUAC

Unione Italiana del Lavoro (UIL)
Italian Labour Union

Address. Via Lucullo 6, 00187 Rome
Phone. +39 647 531
Fax. +39 647 53 208
E-mail. info@uil.it
Website. www.uil.it (Italian with some information in English)
Leadership. Luigi Angeletti (general secretary)
Membership. 1,758,729
History and character. The UIL was founded in 1950 and named after an earlier organization which had split from the USI (Anarcho-Syndicalist Federation) in 1918 and opposed the fascists until banned under Mussolini. The UIL was created with predominantly republican and social democrat leadership, in opposition to the communist domination of the CGIL and the mainly Christian democratic control of CISL, and was expressly non-confessional. In the post-war ideological division of the trade union movement, the UIL was partly funded by the AFL-CIO. Subsequently it evolved to a left-wing reformist position which it still maintains.

The UIL describes itself as socialist, non-confessional and politically independent, and as being an advocate of full internal union democracy rather than adherence to ideological positions influenced by outside forces (i.e. in contrast, it argues, to the CGIL and CISL). It has, however, also called on occasions for unification of the various centres and backed the failed integration project launched in 1997. In recent years it has on occasions acted as a peacemaker between CISL and CGIL.

The UIL is the smallest of the three Italian centres. UIL membership includes a high proportion of pensioners, although at 25% in 1999 this was far less than the proportion of pensioners in the membership totals of the CGIL (55%) and CISL (50%). Similarly the proportion of members who are in the active workforce has declined less than that of the CGIL and CISL, falling 6% in the period 1980–96.

While nominally politically independent, and adhering to the self-imposed rule whereby union and political office cannot be held simultaneously, there are close ties to democratic socialist politics. UIL general secretary Giorgio Benvenuto stood down to become deputy finance minister early in 1992 and was then briefly leader of the Italian Socialist Party (PSI) in 1993. The UIL is now seen as close to the Democrats of the Left (DS), ideologically the successor to the PSI.

Pietro Larizza, who succeeded Benvenuto as UIL general secretary, was appointed president of the National Council for Economic Affairs and Labour (CNEL) in June 2000, and was succeeded by Luigi Angeletti.

UIL is the third-largest trade union centre and like CISL, its political strategy has been based on seeking a discussion with the new government, although this strategy has had disappointing results. Together with CISL, UIL signed the Pact for Italy and has been in agreement with CISL on major issues. In the congress held on March 3-6, 2002, UIL confirmed its position as a trade union with a lay and reformist orientation, as well as its basic approval of the social "concerted action" policy, by re-electing Luigi Angeletti as a leader.

The UIL has created a variety of service organizations for members. These include ITAL (Institute for the Protection and Welfare of Workers; this operates both in Italy and in many countries to which Italians have emigrated); ENFAP (National Vocational Training Agency); UNIAT (National Union of Tenants); CREL (Centre for Economic and Labour Research); Instituto Progretto Sud (to develop cooperation with "the unions of the South", i.e. the Third World); ACPA (Citizens' Association for the Environment), and others.

The basic units are the branch workplace and regional unions. The UIL as a national confederation is formed by national unions of all categories and territorial, regional and provincial unions.

International affiliations. ICFTU; ETUC; TUAC

4 Other Trade Union Organizations

Confederazione del Comitati di Base (Cobas)

Address. Via Manzoni 55 00185 Rome Rome
Phone. +39 6 77591926
Fax. +39 6 77206060
E-mail. internazionale@cobas.it
Website. www.cobas.it (Italian only)
History and character. Cobas originated in the late 1980s as rank-and-file movements dissatisfied with the leadership of the three main confederations. They comprised particularly skilled or professional groups that thought their interests were neglected by the confederations, and who rejected the partisan alignments of the confederations. Their main influence has been in public sector areas such as the state railways, essential services and the educational system. Their strength declined in the 1990s.

The Cobas have pursued a policy of sharp conflict on all fronts, both on the general political level and in the companies. This organization, mainly present in some large corporations (FIAT) and in the civil service, joining together smaller groups, is characterized by firm opposition to any type of social "concerted action". However, the change in policy by CGIL between 2000 and 2001 seemed to have deprived Cobas of some of the political support it had previously. Due to the informal nature of the organization it is hard to determine the number of supporters, and no figures are available.

Confederazione Italiana Sindacati Autonomi Lavoratori (CISAL)
Italian Confederation of Free Workers' Unions
Address. Viale Giulio Cesare 21, 00192 Rome
Phone. +39 6 32 07941
Fax. +39 6 32 12521
E-mail. cisal@cisal.org
Website. www.cisal.org (Italian only)
Leadership. Francesco Cavallaro (general secretary)
History and character. CISAL was founded in 1957 and now associates 50 autonomous trade unions. CISAL has support mainly in schools and public administration. At its congress in November 1999, it resolved to end the practice of signing "pirate agreements" with conditions inferior to those negotiated by the confederal unions, and to begin a process of reconciliation with the confederations, especially CISL.
International affiliations. European Confederation of Independent Trade Unions (CESI)

Unione Generale del Lavoro (UGL)
General Labour Union
Address. Via Margutta 19, 00187 Rome
Phone. +39 6 32 4821
Fax. +39 6 32 4822
Website. www.ugl.it (Italian only)
Leadership. Stefano Cetica (general secretary)
History and character. Founded in 1950, the UGL was known as the Confederazione Italiana dei Sindacati Nazionali dei Lavoratori (CISNAL) until 1996. Its links with right-wing politics made CISNAL's relationships with other trade union centres difficult. UGL says it is a union that emphasizes the centrality of the individual human being. Its structure includes 18 affiliated industrial federations. It affiliated to the WCL in December 1997.
International affiliations. WCL

Jamaica

Capital: Kingston
Population: 2.71 m. (2004 est.)

1 Political and Economic Background

The pro-Western Jamaica Labour Party (JLP) was founded in 1943 as the political wing of the Bustamante Industrial Trade Union. This formed the government from independence from the UK in 1962 to 1972, and again from 1980–89. In 1989 the People's National Party (PNP), previously in power from 1972–80 under Prime Minister Michael Manley, returned to office and has since won successive general elections in 1993, 1997 and 2002. During the 1970s the PNP took a radical left-wing course, opposing US policy and associating with Cuba, but in more recent years has adopted a centrist position. Manley retired in 1992 and was succeeded as Prime Minister by Percival Patterson, who retains that position.

The Jamaican economy is based principally upon sugar, bauxite and tourism, with services now the dominant factor in the economy. Since the 1990s the PNP has applied policies of market liberalization and deregulation, ending most price controls and privatizing state enterprises. Jamaica continues to be affected by sluggish growth, however, and remains less prosperous than most of its neighbours in the English-speaking Caribbean with high unemployment (16% in 2004), inflation over 10%, a heavy burden of government debt, and serious crime problems.

GDP (purchasing power parity) $10.61bn. (2004 est.); GDP per capita (purchasing power parity) $3,900 (2004 est.).

2 Trade Unionism

Jamaica ratified ILO Conventions No. 87 (Freedom of Association and Protection of the Right of Organize, 1948) and No. 98 (Right to Organize and Collective Bargaining, 1949) in 1962, and there has been significant trade union activity since the 1940s.

The development of Jamaican trade unionism proceeded in harness with that of the country's political party system, with the Bustamante Industrial Trade Union (BITU), founded as a general union in 1938 by Alexander Bustamante, providing the basis for the creation of the Jamaica Labour Party in 1943. Similarly the National Workers' Union of Jamaica (NWU) was founded as an affiliate of the People's National Party (PNP) in 1952. Both the BITU and NWU were previously affiliated to the ICFTU, but ICFTU representation is now coordinated in the Jamaica Confederation of Trade Unions (JCTU).

The right to form unions and bargain collectively is regulated by the Labour Relations and Industrial Disputes Act (LRIDA) of 1975 (as amended) which prohibits discrimination against workers for union membership. Unions operate freely and about 15% of the workforce is organized.

Collective bargaining is developed. Where agreement between management and unions cannot be reached issues may be referred for adjudication to the Ministry of Labour, and appeals against Ministry decisions may be made to the independent Industrial Disputes Tribunal (IDT). The IDT deals with some 35–40 cases per year.

The right to strike is prohibited under LRIDA in a range of "essential services" and the Labour Minister is empowered to refer all disputes to compulsory arbitration. "Essential services" has been interpreted widely, incurring criticism from the ILO. Legislation passed in 2002 removed public transport services, telephone workers, banking services and air transport services from the list of excluded industries.

The labour laws apply to the export processing zones (where about 10,000 are employed), but no unions have been established in the zones.

Jamaica has a number of bipartite and tripartite institutions including the Labour Advisory Council and the National Planning Council. Unions are consulted about industrial relations matters and assist in the development of social programmes.

3 Trade Union Centre

Jamaica Confederation of Trade Unions (JCTU)
Address. 1A Hope Boulevard, Kingston 6
Phone. +1876 977 5170
Fax. +1876 977 4575
E-mail. jctu@cwjamaica.com
Website. www.jctu.org
Leadership. Lloyd Goodleigh (general secretary)
Membership. Comprises 11 of Jamaica's major trade unions.
International affiliations. ICFTU; CTUC

4 Other Trade Union Organizations

Bustamante Industrial Trade Union
Address. 98-100 Duke Street, Kingston
Phone. +1876 922 2443/6
Fax. +1876 967 0120
E-mail. bitu@cwjamaica.com
Leadership. George Fyffe (general secretary); Rt. Hon. Hugh Shearer (president general)
International affiliations. IUF

National Workers' Union of Jamaica
Address. 130-132 East Street, P.O. Box 344, Kingston
Phone. +1876 922 1150/4
Fax. +1876 922 6608
E-mail nwyou@toj.com
Leadership. Lloyd Goodleigh (general secretary); Clive Dobson (president)
International affiliations. CTUC

Trades Union Congress
Address. P.O. Box 19, Kingston
Phone. +1876 922 5313/3292
Fax. +1876 922 5468
Leadership. Hopeton Caven (general secretary); Edward Smith (president)

Japan

Capital: Tokyo
Population: 127.33 m. (2004 est.)

1 Political and Economic Background

The Liberal Democratic Party (LDP) was in office continuously from its formation in 1955 until 1993 when, undermined by a series of scandals and splits, it lost control of the lower house for the first time and gave way to a coalition of opposition parties. Since 1994, however, the LDP has been much the largest party in coalition governments of shifting composition; in the most recent elections to the House of Representatives in November 2003 the LDP won 237 of the 480 seats, compared with the 177 won by the opposition Democratic Party. The LDP, as the normal party of government, is deeply enmeshed in the ruling structures of the country. It is traditionally pro-business but is also highly protective of agriculture and contains a number of policy "tribes" (zoku), consisting of LDP parliamentarians able to dominate specific policy making areas in conjunction with government officials and representatives of interest groups. LDP leader Junichiro Koizumi has been Prime Minister (head of government) since April 2001.

Japan suffered catastrophic defeat in World War II. In the following decades it rebuilt its economy on the basis of intensive government-industry cooperation, a strong work ethic and the development of world-class export-oriented companies in sectors such as automobiles and electronics. In the late 1980s the soaring value of the yen led to a phase of speculative investment and an asset price bubble that burst in the early 1990s to be followed by years of sluggish domestic demand, nil or negligible growth, deflation, commercial collapses and rising unemployment. With business investment depressed by low profitability and lack of confidence and consumers not spending, the economy appeared incapable of generating any growth without a series a series of injections of government spending, these producing a mounting burden of public debt. In all from 1992–99 the government announced ten supplementary spending packages with a total value in excess of $1 trillion without producing any sustained growth. Much of this money reportedly went into "pork barrel" public works projects to aid political interests rather than supporting innovation and restructuring. Western interest in the "Japanese model" as a paradigm for success, at its peak in the late 1980s, gave way to the perception of Japan as a country unable to adapt to the transformation of world markets and rise of lower-cost competitors.

The economy was held back in 2000-03 by weakness in Japan's export markets, especially the USA and Europe, with little or negative growth in real GDP each year. Growth in real GDP, as announced in November 2004, was 2% in the fiscal year to March 2004 but there were widespread doubts by late 2004 as to whether Japan had yet begun a period of sustained recovery. Deflation has been a persistent problem since the 1990s, reducing company revenues and increasing the weight of debt, and the Bank of Japan continues to adhere to a loose monetary policy until prices begin to rise – in September 2004 the IMF forecast that deflation would fall back to zero in 2005. One factor in the continuing absence of inflationary pressures despite some economic growth has been the continuing falls in the remuneration of Japanese workers – in 2004 wages fell for the seventh year in succession. There has been a huge and continuing expansion of less well paid temporary, contract and part-time workers, this group increasing from 15% of the workforce in 1997 to between 25 and 30 per cent. There is a persistent budget deficit of about 7% of GDP and the public debt stands at 140% of GDP.

GDP (purchasing power parity) $3.582 trillion (2004 est.); GDP per capita (purchasing power parity) $28,200 (2004 est.).

2 Trade Unionism

In the mid-1930s there were 420,000 trade union members and a Japan Confederation of Labour (Nihon-Rodei-Sodomei). By 1940, this confederation had been dissolved by the government, and until the defeat of Japan in World War II workers were mobilized in Sangyo Hokoku (Service to the State through Industry). Following World War II the Trade Union Law of December 1945 for the first time formally guaranteed workers the right to organize trade unions, and Article 28 of the 1946 Constitution guaranteed workers the right to organize, bargain collectively and to strike. Sodomei was re-established in 1945 but the trade union movement was divided by intense ideological conflict over the following decade against a background of appreciable industrial unrest and underwent a complex process of fragmentation.

As of the mid-1980s, there were two major centres, Sohyo (with 4.36 million members) and Domei (with 2.16 million members), while a third significant centre, Churitsuroren, had 1.56 million members. These three accounted for 65% of organized labour. Domei alone was internationally affiliated (to the ICFTU). Churitsuroren and Domei were based overwhelmingly in the private sector, while 60% of Sohyo members were in the public sector. In the period 1987–89 the mainstream trade union movement underwent unification. In 1987 a new private sector trade union centre, Rengo, was formed by the affiliates of Domei and Churitsuroren and a number of the private sector affiliates from Sohyo. Then, in 1989, private sector Rengo and Sohyo merged to form the Japanese Trade Union Confederation (Rengo), which became the third largest national centre affiliated to the ICFTU.

As of 2002, according to Ministry of Labour figures, there were 10,801,000 union members. Of these 6,945,000 (64%) were in unions affiliated to Rengo (down by 175,000 from the previous year, with the union's own figures for 2004 showing a further fall to 6,800,000). The only alternative trade union centre of any significance is Zenroren (National Confederation of Trade Unions), which had some 1,018,000 members in 2002 (showing a small increase from 2001 Ministry of Labour figures) – Zenroren itself claims a higher membership of 1,390,000. There is also a small third centre, Zenrokyo (National Trade Unions Council), which has only 172,000 members (having fallen sharply from more than 250,000 members in 2001). There are some large independent unions, the biggest of which is Zenkensoren (National Federation of Construction Workers' Unions). In addition, unions federate in some important sectoral bodies, most notably the Japan Council of Metalworkers' Unions (IMF-JC), with 2,480,000 members,

The basic rights of private sector workers – comprising 82% of all organized workers – are guaranteed by the Trade Union Law of 1945 and the Labour Relations Adjustment Law, but public sector employees are covered by separate legislation. In addition Japan ratified ILO Conventions No. 98 (Right to Organize and Collective Bargaining, 1949) in 1953 and No. 87 (Freedom of Association and Protection of the Right to Organize, 1948) in 1965. Managers with direct authority in respect of hiring, firing, promotions and transfers are barred from joining unions under the Trade Union Law. With middle managers (who mostly have only shared or ambiguous involvement in hiring and firing) themselves now significantly affected by de-layering in big companies, and the unions anxious to find new sources of recruitment, the trade unions have pushed through collective bargaining to broaden the areas of supervisory personnel they may recruit. Public sector employees, other than police, fire fighters, prison employees, the Self Defence Forces and the Coast Guard, are permitted to organize and may not be discriminated against for so doing; such organizations may negotiate with the employer within limits but may not take industrial action. For many years controversy has surrounded the position of firefighters, as these are usually allowed to join unions in countries where the military and police are not; in 1995 the government agreed a consultation process with Rengo affiliate Jichiro for the firefighters. The national federations have long pursued the firefighters' case in a complaint to the Freedom of Association Committee of the ILO. Despite the Committee's recommendations the government has not changed its position: firefighters are still barred from joining trade unions.

The basic form of trade union organization in Japan is the single-enterprise union, which is either workplace- or enterprise- based, and which organizes all full time workers regardless of job classification. (A parallel system exists in the public sector, based on individual offices, corporations, etc.). Industrial federations and confederations – which are poorly funded relative to the enterprise unions – have negligible control over their affiliated enterprise unions, and the role of the industrial federations has often been peripheral. Their role is weakened by the fact that as multiple trade union centres existed into the 1980s there are commonly several industrial federations operating in any one sector. Their role has tended to increase somewhat in more recent years, however, as the industrial federations have become involved in such issues as the introduction of new technology and the problems of depressed areas and industries, and increasing job mobility may ultimately weaken the dominance of enterprise unionism.

Although industrial relations were commonly adversarial in the 1940s and 1950s, with a strong ideological element in trade unionism at that time, the character of enterprise unionism has come to reflect and reinforce that of modern Japanese industrial relations. This is characterized by a close relationship between the two sides of industry, involving a high degree of both formal and informal consultation in good faith. To a considerable degree, the view prevails that "the union exists because the company exists". Japan's consistently strong performance after World War II enabled large employers in effect to guarantee a job for life, and individuals entering the workforce typically made career plans involving a commitment to a particular firm rather than to type of occupation. Employers preferred to re-train workers in line with changes in technology and business focus, rather than lay them off and recruit new workers. Furthermore, as salary levels were rigidly tied to seniority, loyalty brought an increasing reward. The enterprise unions became enmeshed in the company to the degree that union chairmen were often given access to highly confidential information about the company's position and strategies. The process of consultation provided for a degree of flexibility in making decisions about working conditions that could reflect the enterprise's underlying condition. A pattern was created of union officers moving on to management positions within the same company, often switching roles on the same day. Large employers have adopted policies that have entrenched the position of the enterprise unions. The majority of large companies operate union shop agreements, with union membership for new workers becoming compulsory within a set period of joining the company. Where closed shops exist, the activism and commitment of members to the union is not tested by voluntary payment of contributions, and apathy is considered widespread with union dues seen as a tax on the job.

While the foundations of this system have been disturbed to some degree by Japan's persistent economic difficulties since the 1990s, and major corporations have initiated lay-offs and begun to link pay more to performance, the changes have not yet been fundamental. Both Rengo and Nippon Keidanran (the employers' body formed in the 2002 merger of the Japan Federation of Employers' Associations and the Japan Federation of Economic Organizations) remain wedded to a view of industrial relations that emphasizes the desirability of jobs for life and payment linked to length of service (basic salaries in large companies rising with age until 50). Surveys at the end of the 1990s indicated that more than half of Japanese corporations would prefer to retain the lifetime employment system if at all possible, regardless of short-term business results. Indeed, some research indicates that average length of service at one place of employment actually increased in the 1990s.

One consequence of the enterprise union system is that it has excluded large sections of the workforce. The typical union member is in full-time work and employed by a major company or in the public sector. In 2003 some 51.9% of employees in private sector companies with more than 1,000 employees were union members. In contrast, a mere 1.2% of employees in companies of fewer than 99 employees were in unions. The enterprise union system is based on the existing major companies; it lacks the flexibility to deal effectively with new companies in emergent industries and with new forms of irregular work. The industrial federations are in most cases poorly resourced to undertake organizational activities and the enterprise unions are by definition more concerned with what happens in their own company rather than in the sector as a whole.

While trade union leadership nationally is aware of this problem and has set goals to broaden organizational work, this aspiration has had little impact. The total number of workers in unions has fallen over the last two decades, standing at 12.47 million in 1981 and 10.5 million in 2003. However, with the expansion of the workforce this means that density has declined from 30.8% in 1981 to 19.6% by 2003. Furthermore, the unions have lost members steadily since the late 1990s. Although density declined every single year 1981–99, union membership actually peaked at 12.7 million in 1994. After that it fell for five straight years thereafter, reflecting job losses in unionized sectors, and in 1999 falling below 12 million for the first time since 1973.

The process of wage bargaining is coordinated in the "shunto" or "Spring Labour Offensive" in which co-ordinated wage demands are presented to all employers each Spring. The agreements reached through the shunto affect wage determination for all workers, including those denied true collective bargaining rights and non-union workers. The shunto – which in effect coordinates what would be the otherwise limited bargaining power of Japanese enterprise unionism – was first employed on a significant scale (under Sohyo leadership) in the 1950s. It was encouraged thereafter by the rapid development of the Japanese economy and labour shortages, with Domei unions (which had initially opposed the practice) joining in the 1960s. Despite the militant format of the shunto, since the 1970s wage increases achieved through this process have generally trailed productivity gains and although most strikes occur around the time of the shunto the level of industrial disputes has been low since the 1970s. Simultaneously with negotiations in the private sector, settlements for labour in public corporations and national enterprises are reached through mediation by the Public Corporation and National Labour Relations Commission and are subsequently embodied in an arbitration award. In practice the Commission normally links public sector awards closely to those in the private sector. The same is true of awards for public service employees reached through the National Personnel Authority and for local public service awards made at municipality level.

Japan's protracted economic difficulties since the 1990s have put strains on the bargaining system. With the economy stagnant, wage increases in absolute terms have fallen to new low levels, in the range 2–3% each year 1995–2000, and falling to a record low of 1.63% for major private employers in 2003 (but against a background of a deflationary economy experiencing almost zero growth). Unemployment rose steadily from 2.9% in 1994 to 5.4% by 2003 and although these levels are not high by international standards, the phenomenon of radical restructuring and downsizing is a new one and has unsettled the unions, as have the growth in part-time and discretionary working. At the same time, employers have shown increasing dissatisfaction with the stranglehold of national norms and have begun to show increasing awareness of the interests of shareholders as opposed to employees. In Spring 2000, the five major companies in the steel sector, facing increasing competition among themselves for market share, for the first time put forward and agreed different basic wage increases rather than acting as a group. The development was seen as significant as this sector customarily sets trends for industry as a whole.

The number of days lost in industrial disputes declined steadily after the high inflation of the mid-1970s, and strikes are now rare. Indeed, there has been a trend for unions to reallocate strike funds to cover shortfalls in general operating costs caused by falling memberships since the mid-1990s. The right to strike is guaranteed in the private sector, but employees in national and local government and the national enterprises (postal service, forestry service, government printing and the mint) are prohibited from striking. The right to strike is also restricted in the electric power and coal mining industries, the merchant marine and in the public utilities generally. Political and sympathetic strikes (which are rare) are generally considered unlawful, as are wildcat strikes, strikes involving sabotage or a threat to safe workplace practices, and strikes violating industrial peace clauses of existing collective bargaining agreements. Unions engaged in legitimate strikes are exempt from civil and criminal liabilities; where strike action is considered illegitimate, employers may seek to dismiss or discipline the strike leaders but rarely seek damages from the union, or to impose sanctions on those who merely followed the strike call. The Labour Relations Adjustment Law provides for conciliation, mediation and arbitration, which may be carried out through the Labour Relations Commission; this body (which is structured at both national and local levels) is tripartite in composition. In practice, however, most disputes are settled directly between employers and unions. A Public Corporation and National Enterprise Labour Relations Commission exists to adjust disputes in the national enterprises (where industrial action is prohibited), and this is supplemented by a Grievance Handling Joint Adjustment Council. Local public enterprises are excepted from certain areas of the Trade Union Law and Labour Relations Adjustment Law, but disputes in this field are adjusted by the Labour Relations Commission.

Japan has an ageing population. In April 2000 Rengo and the employers' association Nikkeiren issued a joint statement calling on companies to make their operations more family friendly, by expanding child care and allowing more flexible working time arrangements. The ageing population is also putting pressure on the pensions system. The qualifying age for the basic state pension is to be raised in stages from 60, one year every three years from 2001, until it reaches 65 by 2013. In response to this, unions are seeking a raising of company retirement ages, which in major companies are currently nearly always set at 60, so that employees do not have to retire before they qualify for a state pension. This was a leading issue in the Spring 2000 shunto. Some companies have also warned that as a result of low interest rates and the ageing workforce, company pension scheme reserves would prove insufficient without further injections of funds.

3 Trade Union Centre

Rengo
Japanese Trade Union Confederation
Address. Sohyo Kaikan bldg., 3-2-11 Kanda Surugadai, Chiyoda-ku, Tokyo 101-0062
Phone. +81 3 5295 0526
Fax. +81 3 5295 0548
E-mail. jtuc-kokusai@mud.biglobe.ne.jp
Website. www.jtuc-rengo.org (Japanese; English)
Leadership. Kiyoshi Sasamori (president)
Membership. 6,800,000
History and character. Rengo was formed as a unified national trade union centre in 1989 by the merger of the former private sector Rengo (itself created in 1987, and based largely on the former Domei) and the public sector Sohyo. As of 1999, 63.3% of the Japanese unionized work force were in Rengo affiliated unions.

Domei and Sohyo had their origins in the complex restructuring and splits that affected the Japanese trade union movement for two decades after World War II. Sohyo originated in 1950 as a breakaway from a communist-dominated All-Japan Congress of Industrial Unions, which existed from 1946–58. Sohyo's initial intent to affiliate to the ICFTU changed in opposition to that organization's stance on the Korean War, the 1951 Japan-US Security Treaty and related issues. In the mid-1950s a faction within the leftist leadership of Sohyo emphasizing economic demands, rather than conflict with the USA, gained the ascendancy, and in 1956 Sohyo and other unions initiated the full shunto. Radical politics and class struggle ideology declined thereafter at Sohyo and by the 1980s it was emphasizing the modernization of industrial relations to take account of the changed realities of Japanese economic and political life. The drive to privatize the National Corporations, particularly the Japan National Railways which was split into a number of private companies in 1987, seems to have convinced most Sohyo public sector affiliates that it was necessary to ally with the more thriving private sector unions. Domei, whose membership was overwhelmingly in the private sector, was formed in the early 1960s and pursued polices based mainly on a contractual approach to industrial relations.

New Rengo had to reconcile the different political traditions of the former Domei and Sohyo. Throughout its history Sohyo was linked to the Japan Socialist Party (JSP, renamed the Social Democratic Party of Japan, SDPJ, in 1991). The JSP, founded in 1945, was briefly involved in a coalition government in 1947–48 but then was in opposition for several decades, providing the principal opposition to the ruling LDP. Its party platform in the 1960s advocated non-alignment and a democratic transition from capitalism to socialism but by the 1980s the party was moving from its more leftist positions to a European socialist model. The party was heavily dependent on Sohyo support, having a much weaker membership base than socialist parties in western European countries. As of 1985, 65 of the 111 Socialist members of the House of Representatives and 29 of the 43 Socialist members of the House of Councillors were former officers of Sohyo or its member unions. Domei in contrast was the most important supporter of the small Democratic Socialist Party (DSP), which had originated as a right-wing breakaway in 1960 from the Socialist Party.

Rengo's founding president Akira Yamagishi was an advocate of building a centre-left challenge to the LDP, which had dominated Japanese politics since World War II, and sought a fusion of the SDPJ and the DSP. At the same time, many of the traditional party alliances of former Domei and Sohyo unions remained intact and relations between the two parties were poor. The absolute dominance of the LDP was indeed broken in elections in July 1993 elections when the LDP, although remaining the largest party, lost power to an opposition coalition which included the DSP and the SDPJ. However, Japanese politics had become highly unstable and fractious, with continuing political realignments and Rengo's own strategy fell victim to this. In April 1994 the SDPJ left the coalition and in June 1994 a new government was formed with Tomiichi Murayama of the SDPJ as Prime Minister but with the LDP as the dominant force and the SDPJ abandoning some of its historic policies. The September 1994 decision of Rengo president Akira Yamagishi to stand down early on grounds of ill health was viewed as influenced by his disappointment at seeing his hopes for a DSP and SDPJ merger dashed by the SDPJ entering government, thus leaving the two parties opposed to each other. In addition, some union leaders believed Rengo was becoming too deeply embroiled in party politics, which would only result in a split, and should re-focus on economic issues. As a result of further political realignments, by the time of the 1998 elections to the House of Councillors (upper house) Rengo was giving its main support to the Democratic Party of Japan (DPJ), formed in 1996, but also supported other candidates opposed to the LDP and the Japan Communist Party. Following elections to the House of Representatives in June 2000 the DPJ remained the largest opposition party, increasing its total of seats from 95 to 127, a position it retained in the 2003 elections, when it won 177 seats.

Organizationally, Rengo is built on a base of unions formed at the enterprise level, but enterprise unions are absent in many small companies, as well as often representing only full-time workers. From Rengo's foundation a goal was to expand the unionized sector beyond full-time employees in big corporations and the public sector so as to reach out to the large number of non-core part-time and irregular workers and to workers in small and medium-sized enterprises where unions rarely exist. In 1996 Rengo launched a project to recruit 1.1 million members over three years, setting up a regional union structure to which individual workers who were not in enterprise unions could affiliate directly. This initiative has also been taken up by some of its key industrial federation affiliates. However, these measures have thus far had little impact on the overall position and Rengo's membership declined from 7.88 million in the late 1980s to 7.48 million by 1998, and further to 6.8 million by 2004.

To some degree this reflects a perception by employees in irregular work and smaller enterprises that trade unionism is irrelevant to their needs. It also reflects the fact that resources are concentrated at the enterprise union level and enterprise unions are concerned with the position in their own companies rather than broader organizational drives. With membership dues falling the trend has been for unions to cut staffing levels, with an impact on scale of operations. Likewise pursuit of a policy of equal opportunities for women has only had modest impact, only 6.5% of officers of Rengo affiliates being women as of 1998. In Japan not only are women responsible for most household duties, there is a strong perception, which affects all areas of society, that this burden precludes them from effectively exercising other responsibilities. Japanese unions, being enterprise based, customarily do not represent the unemployed. However, in September 1999, Rengo affiliate Zensen Domei (the Japanese Federation of Textile, Garment, Chemical, Mercantile, Food and Allied Industries Workers' Unions) said it would set up an organization specifically for the unemployed. Zensen Domei has also increased membership levels with a campaign focussing on recruiting part-time workers and seeking membership from unorganized workplaces (i.e. not only recruiting in organized workplaces or as part of recognition campaigns).

Japan's protracted economic difficulties in the 1990s, the historically unprecedented levels of unemployment, the mounting demands of employers for more labour flexibility, and the declining number of union members, put Rengo on the defensive. General secretary Kiyoshi Sasamori told the 1999 congress that "job security is the life line of labour unions" and Rengo has concentrated on trying to defend established positions in areas such as automatic increases for seniority and jobs for life. It calls for increased government spending to stimulate the economy and increase jobs. Overtime (often unpaid) is widespread in Japan and Rengo has called for reduced overtime working to allow job-sharing and for tighter restrictions on dismissals. A 1996 Rengo survey showed that average annual hours worked per employee were 2,040 and it has campaigned to reduce this to 1,800 (government figures indicated that average hours worked fell from 1,919 in 1996 to 1,840 in 1999).

While there has been no wholesale repudiation of the established system by big corporations, some employers are more aggressively pursuing a policy of restructuring and cutting costs and calling for wages and conditions to more realistically reflect the position of individual companies. Kiyoshi Sasamori said in May 2000 that advocates of such changes "propose a shift to American-style management, which focuses on short-term profits and caters to shareholders – a shift from a far-sighted to a short-sighted system". The vital issues of deregulating markets and reforming the bureaucracy have to some degree divided the unions, however. Unions representing export-oriented sectors such as autos and electronics are not unsympathetic to the view that areas of the economy that are inward-looking with low productivity should be reformed, and there remains a fault line between the private and public sectors.

Rengo has encouraged unification and realignment of its affiliates, but this has been a slow process. There are 61 affiliated industry federations and some of these are very small, with only a few thousand members, lacking resources to organize effectively. Kiyoshi Sasamori has said that he wishes to see the Rengo affiliates at industry level reduced to about 20 in the coming years.

Rengo has an associated think tank, the Research Institute for the Advancement of Living Standards (RIALS). Its Japan International Labour Foundation (JILAF) promotes international cooperation in the labour area. In 1995 Rengo set up the Institute of Labour Education and Culture (ILEC) which runs programmes and workshops.

Rengo participates in the tripartite Industry and Labour Round-Table Conference, set up in 1970. The focus of the Conference series in recent years has been mainly on structural change. It also takes part, as the representative of organized labour, on the Government-Labour-Management Council on Employment Problems, established in September 1998.

International affiliations. ICFTU; TUAC

Affiliates. The following are the major Rengo affiliates, in order of size.

1. Jichiro (All-Japan Prefectural and Municipal Workers' Union)

Address. Jichiro Kaikan Bldg, 1 Rokuban-cho, Chiyoda-ku, Tokyo 102-8464
Phone. +81 3 3263 0263
Fax. +81 3 5210 7422
E-mail. info@jichiro.or.jp
Website. www.jichiro.gr.jp (Japanese; English section)
Membership. 993,788
History and character. Founded in 1954, this is the largest Japanese trade union with more than 3000 local unions and 47 prefectural headquarters. Its members are primarily employees of local government and enterprises established by local authorities, and its main concern is the impact of privatization and downsizing on job security and working conditions. Although 40% of members are women, 90% of elected officials are men and while Jichiro has adopted a programme to rectify the imbalance, this is proving difficult in practice. Jichiro runs a range of mutual aid programmes for members and has also established an Asia Children's Homes project, which has built homes in Vietnam, Laos and Cambodia. It is a member of Public Services International (PSI).

2. UI. Zensen (Japanese Federation of Textile, Garment, Chemical, Mercantile, Food and Allied Industries Workers' Unions)

Address. Zensen Domei Kaikan Bldg, 4-8-16 Kudan-Minami, Chiyoda-ku, Tokyo 102-0074
Phone. +81 3 3288 3549
Fax. +81 3 3288 3728
E-mail. soumu@zensen.or.jp
Website. www.zensen.or.jp (Japanese only)
Membership. 757,548
History and character. Prior to merger with CSG Rengo, Zensen was based in the textile industry but as this sector has declined it has diversified into new areas such as the computer industry. The union achieved international prominence due to strong membership growth in a period during which most Rengo affiliates experienced losses. Zensen's success was attributed to strong campaigns organizing non-union workplaces and reaching out to part-time workers.

3. Jidosha Soren (Confederation of Japan Automobile Workers' Unions, JAW)

Address. c/o U-Life Center, 1-4-26 Kaigan, Minato-ku, Tokyo 105-0022
Phone. +81 3 3434 7641
Fax. +81 3 3434 7428
Website. www.jaw.or.jp (Japanese only)
Membership. 689,936
History and character. Founded in 1972, and previously the largest Rengo private sector affiliate. It comprises 12 federations of enterprise-based unions.

4. Denki Rengo (Japanese Electrical, Electronic and Information Union)

Address. Kaikan Bldg, 1-10-3 Mita, Minato-ku, Tokyo 108-8326
Phone. +81 3 3455 6911
Fax. +81 3 3452 5406
Website. www.jeiu.or.jp (Japanese; English section)
Membership. 678,325

5. Japan Association of Metal, Machinery and Manufacturing Workers (JAM)

Address. Yuai Kaikan Bldg, 2-20-12 Shiba, Minato-ku, Tokyo 105-0014
Phone. +81 3 3451 2141
Fax. +81 3 3452 0239
E-mail. zenkin@union.email.ne.jp
Website. www.jam-union.or.jp (Japanese only)
Membership. 401,000
History and character. JAM was formed in September 1999 by the merger of two Rengo affiliates, Zenkin Rengo (Japanese Federation of Metal Industry Workers' Unions) and the smaller Kinzoku Kikai (National Metal and Machinery Workers' Union of Japan).

6. Nikkyoso (Japan Teachers' Union)

Address. Nihon Kyoiku Kaikan Bldg, 2-6-2 Hitotsubashi, Chiyoda-ku, Tokyo 101-0003
Phone. +81 3 3265 2171
Fax. +81 3 3230 0172
E-mail. international@jtu-net.or.jp
Website. www.jtu-net.or.jp (Japanese; English section)
Membership. 331,279

7. Seiho Roren (National Federation of Life Insurance Workers' Unions)

Address. Tanaka Building, 3-19-5 Yushima, Bunkyo-ku, Tokyo 113-0034
Phone. +81 3 3837 2031

Fax. +81 3 3837 2037
Website. www.liu.or.jp (Japanese only)
Membership. 291,041

8. Kikan Roren (Japan Federation of Basic Industry Workers' Unions)
Address. IS River Side Building, 1-23-4 Shinkawa, Chuo-ku, Tokyo 104-0033
Phone. +81 3 3555 0401
Fax. +81 3 3555 0407
Website. www.kikan-roren.or.jp (Japanese only)
Membership. 252,790

9. Denryoku Soren (Confederation of Electric Power Related Industry Workers' Unions of Japan)
Address. Tds Mita 3F, 2-7-13 Mita, Minato-ku, Tokyo 108-0073
Phone. +81 3 3454 0231
Fax. +81 3 3798 1470
Membership. 235,732

10. Jyoho Roren (Japan Federation of Telecommunications, Electronic Information and Allied Workers)
Address. Zendentsu Rodo Kaikan Bldg, 3-6 Kanda Surugadai, Chiyoda-ku, Tokyo 101-0062
Phone. +81 3 3219 2231
Fax. +81 3 3253 3268
E-mail. info@joho.or.jp
Website. www.joho.or.jp (Japanese only)
Membership. 233,593

11. Service Ryutsu Rengo (Japan Federation of Service and Distributive Workers' Unions)
Address. 2-23-1 Yoyogi, Shibuya-ku, Tokyo 151-0053
Phone. +81 3 3370 4121
Fax. +81 3 3370 1640
Website. www.jsd-union.org (Japanese, English section)
Membership. 175,588

12. JEC Rengo (Japanese Federation of Energy and Chemistry Workers' Unions)
Address. 1-28-10 Hongo, Bunkyo-ku, Tokyo 113-0033
Phone. +81 3 5684 2591
Fax. +81 3 5684 2709
Website. www.jec-u.com (Japanese only)
Membership. 175,588

13. Zentei (Japan Postal Workers' Union)
Address. Zentei Kaikan Bldg, 1-2-7 Koraku, Bunkyo-ku, Tokyo 112-8567
Phone. +81 3 3812 4261
Fax. +81 3 5684 7201
Website. www.zentei.or.jp (Japanese only)
Membership. 140,725

14. Shitetsu Soren (General Federation of Private Railway and Bus Workers' Unions of Japan)
Address. Shitetsu Kaikan, 4-3-5 Takanawa, Minato-ku, Tokyo 108-0074
Phone. +81 3 3473 0166
Fax. +81 3 3447 3927
Membership. 136,225

15. Kokku Rengo (Japan Public Sector Union)
Address. Hosaka Building, 1-10-3 Kanda-ogawamachi, Chiyoda-ku, tokyo 101-0052
Phone. +81 3 5209 6205
Fax. +81 3 5209 6206
Membership. 132,221

16. Unyu Roren (All Japan Federation of Transport Workers' Unions)
Address. Zennittsu Kasumigaseki Bldg, 3-3-3 Kasumigaseki, Chiyoda-ku, Tokyo 100-0013
Phone. +81 3 3503 2171
Fax. +81 3 3503 2176
Website. www.unyuroren.or.jp (Japanese only)
Membership. 126,827

17. Food Rengo (Japan Federation of Food and Tobacco Workers' Unions)
Address. Hiroo Office Bldg 8F, 1-3-18 Hiroo, Shibuya-ku, Tokyo 150-0012
Phone. +81 3 3446 2082
Fax. +81 3 3446 6779
Website. www.ny.airnet.ne.jp/jfu (Japanese only)
Membership. 112,049

18. Zen Yusei (All Japan Postal Labour Union)
Address. Zenyusei Kaikan Bldg, 1-20-6 Sendagaya, Shibuya-ku, Tokyo 151-8502
Phone. +81 3 3478 7101
Fax. +81 3 5474 7085
E-mail. zenyusei@mrj.biglobe.ne.jp
Website. www.zenyusei.or.jp (Japanese, with English section)
Membership. 87,699

19. Kotsu Roren (Japan Federation of Transport Workers' Unions)
Address. Yuai Kaikan Bldg, 2-20-12 Shiba, Minato-ku, Tokyo 105-0014
Phone. +81 3 3451 7243
Fax. +81 3 3454 7393
Membership. 72,525

20. JR-Rengo (Japan Railway Trade Unions Confederation)
Address. Toko Bldg, 1-8-10 Nihonbashi Muro-machi, Chuo-ku, Tokyo 103-0022
Phone. +81 3 3270 4590
Fax. +81 3 3270 4429
Website. http://homepage1.nifty.com/JR-RENGO/ (Japanese only)
Membership. 65,800

21. JR-Soren (Japan Confederation of Railway Workers' Unions)
Address. Meguro Satsuki Kaikan Bldg, 3-2-13 Nishi Gotanda, Shinagawa-ku, Tokyo 141-0031
Phone. +81 3 3491 7191
Fax. +81 3 3491 7192
Website. www.jru7.net/ (English) or www.jr-souren.com/ (Japanese)
Membership. 62,300

22. Sonpo Roren (Federation of Non-Life Insurance workers' Union of Japan)
Address. 4F Kanda Ms Building, 27 Kanda-higashi-matsushitacho, Chiyoda-ku, Tokyo 101-0042
Phone. +81 3 5295 0071
Fax. +81 3 5295 0073
Website. www.fniu.or.jp (Japanese only)
Membership. 58,669

4 Other Trade Union Organizations

Japan Council of Metalworkers' Unions (IMF-JC)
Address. 4F, Takara Meiji Yasuda Building, 2-15-10, Nihon-bashi, Chuo-ku, Tokyo 103-0027
Phone. +813 3274 2288 (International Affairs)
Fax. +813 3274 2476
Email. imf-jc@mxi.mesh.ne.jp
Website. www.imf-jc.or.jp
Membership. 2,483,237
International affiliation. IMF

Zenken Soren
National Federation of Construction Workers' Unions
Address. 2-7-15 Takadanobaba, Shinjuku-ku, Tokyo 169-8650
Phone. +81 3 3200 6221
Fax. +81 3 3209 0558
E-mail. zenkensoren@pop17.odn.ne.jp
Website. www.zenkensoren.org (Japanese only)
Membership. 715,000.
History and character. This is the largest Japanese independent union (i.e. without affiliation to one of the national centres).

Zenrokyo
National Trade Union Council
Address. Kotsu bldg, 5-15-5 Shinbashi, Minato-ku, Tokyo 105-0004
Phone. +81 3 5403 1650
Fax. +81 35403 1653
Membership. 172,000

Zenroren
National Confederation of Trade Unions
Address. Zenroren Kiakan 4F, 4-4, Yushima 2-chome Bunkyo-ku, Tokyo 113-8462
Phone. +81 3 5472 5841
Fax. +81 3 5472 5845
Website. www.zenroren.gr.jp (Japanese and English)
Leadership. Yoji Kobayashi (president); Mitsuo Bannai (general secretary)
Membership. The Japan Institute of Labour reports Zenroren's latest claim as 1,390,000 but the Ministry of Labour has previously reported closer to 1,000,000. Zenroren says the difference is because the government figures "exclude local unions which are not affiliated to any national industrial unions, but to the prefectural federations under Zenroren, as well as pensioners' unions". By either calculation, Zenroren represents some 9-10% of the unionized workforce.
History and character. Zenroren was formed in 1989 as the self-described "national centre of militant trade unions" in opposition to "anti-communism and labour-capital collaboration" by the Rengo trade unions. Zenroren says it is independent of political parties, but it is closely aligned with the Japan Communist Party (whose best electoral performance was in 1979 when it won 39 seats in the lower house of parliament – it is now reduced to nine). Its programme has had a broadly political and anti-US flavour.

Zenroren has accused Rengo of undermining the "Spring struggle" (shunto) and of cooperating in corporate restructuring. Its key issues in recent years have included the struggle against unemployment, in which it has sought to work with other unions and social forces; the demand for improved social security systems; and opposition to US–Japan military cooperation. It has called for large wage increases and cuts in taxes on consumption to revive the economy.

In July 2000 a Zenroren delegation visited the ACFTU Chinese trade union centre and agreed on the establishment of friendly relations. The visit reflected the restoration of relations between the Japan Communist Party and the Communist Party of China.
International affiliations. None

Jordan

Capital: Amman
Population: 5.61 m. (2004 est.)

1 Political and Economic Background

The Hashemite Kingdom of Jordan is a monarchy in which King Hussein ruled from 1952 until his death in February 1999, when he was succeeded by his son, Abdullah ibn al-Hussein. Independents loyal to the King dominate the legislature and the King enjoys a high degree of authority. Political parties have been legal since 1992.

Jordan has few natural resources, though it does have one of the highest adult literacy rates in the Middle East, last estimated at 89.2%. A similarly impressive 65% of women below the age of 30 work. However, Jordan's high population growth rate, limited resources, vulnerability to regional political crises, and young age structure, have led to high unemployment in recent years. Likewise Jordan has in recent years suffered from a high national debt.

The country benefited from substantial Arab aid in the 1970s and early 1980s oil boom but this support then declined. The Gulf War of 1991, in which Jordan sided with Saddam, led to large scale repatriation of its citizens and a surge of unemployment. It also signalled the sudden ending of lucrative remittances from salaries earned in oil-rich economies. However, in the longer term it probably led to some of Jordan's better trained and educated workers – invariably of Palestinian origin – being able to contribute more directly to the domestic economy.

Jordan's peace treaty with Israel, signed in 1994, raised hopes for economic benefit. There were, for instance, ambitious plans to establish joint industrial parks and free trade zones along the Jordan-Israel border, and to co-operate economically and ecologically along the Dead Sea and at the northern tip of the Gulf of Aqaba. The signing of the treaty also coincided with an American agreement to forgive Jordanian debts, and to encourage greater investment in its economy.

However, bilateral trade has been disappointing, and many mooted joint projects have fallen victim to political problems, with the partial exception of Israeli-assisted industrial zones in Irbid and on the Israeli-Jordanian border. Peace with Israel proved generally unpopular, as long as it appeared that Palestinians in the West Bank and Gaza were not receiving their "peace dividend" from Israel. Numerous professional bodies, including trade unions, have tended to ostracise Jordanians who seek closer economic links with Israel, or Israelis. Such feelings intensified with the outbreak of the Al Aqsa intifada across the border in late 2000. The aftermath of the terror attacks on the USA, in September 2001, and the US-led invasion of Iraq, in March 2003, have also exacerbated political tensions within Jordan. On Dec. 23, 2004, unions protested against a new trade deal between Israel and Jordan. Nonetheless, unions participated in the early January 2005 roll-out of ambitious government-led reforms of the public sector, touted as one of the largest such exercises in the Arab world.

Jordan has made efforts to implement IMF structural adjustment programmes, ending subsidies and price controls in some areas, but has continuing problems of low growth, public debt and unemployment, thought to be as high as 25–30%. Particularly worrying is the economy's inability to absorb its better educated labour pool. Jordanians seem reluctant to do certain jobs and there are 300,000 foreign workers. King Abdullah II is seen as sympathetic to liberalizing the economy and encouraging foreign investment. A free trade agreement signed with the USA in October 2002 eliminates all tariffs on two-way trade in goods and services over a 10-year period between the USA and Jordan – a provision Washington has with only three other countries, Canada, Mexico and Israel. Jordan acceded to the World Trade Organization in 2000.

GDP (purchasing power parity) $23.64bn. (2004 est.); GDP per capita (purchasing power parity) $4,300 (2004 est.).

2 Trade Unionism

Jordan ratified ILO Convention No. 98 (Right to Organize and Collective Bargaining, 1949) in 1968, but has not ratified Convention No. 87 (Freedom of Association and Protection of the Right to Organize, 1948). In toto, Jordan has ratified 19 ILO Conventions, including seven core conventions, the most recent being Convention No.182 (Worst Forms of Child Labour). Domestic servants and agricultural workers are not covered by the labour code.

Workers in the private sector and in some state-owned companies (but not otherwise in the public sector) may join unions and an estimated 30% of the workforce are organized into unions, all of which belong to the General Federation of Jordanian Trade Unions (GFJTU). Non-citizens may not join unions. Workers may file complaints of anti-union discrimination with the Labour Ministry, which can order their reinstatement.

Collective bargaining exists in the unionized sectors and there is a framework for mediation and arbitration, including referral to an industrial tribunal, whose decisions are legally binding. Strikes are illegal while these processes are underway, and in practice are rare, although threatened from time to time. Strikes in public sector enterprises are not permitted.

The Jordanian Communist Party played an important role in organizing union activity in the West Bank region during the period 1949-67 (despite the formal banning of the party during this period). The number of unions in the West Bank, then under Jordanian control, grew from 16 in 1961 to more than 40 four years later. Unions played a central role in politicizing and organizing the local population, even though the Hashemite monarchy considered their commitment to democratic institutions as threatening. However, Israel's acquisition of the West Bank as a result of the June 1967 six-day war ultimately severed ties between unionists located there and their comrades east of the Jordan River. This trend was formalized when Jordan voluntarily and unilaterally abrogated its responsibility for the territory in 1988 – a move that unions opposed. Indeed, many Jordanian unions continued operating West Bank branches as if nothing had changed.

With the longstanding absence of political parties (because of the emergency laws that were only relaxed after 1992) many Jordanians used unions as vehicles for political expression. One case of this came in 1970-71, when unions were active in the opposition to King Hussein's counterattack against Palestinian militants (culminating in "Black September"). The king then passed a law that entitled him to dismantle the unions, though he never exercised this right in full.

The collapse of the Soviet Union in 1991 adversely effected Jordan's leftist parties, the traditional sponsors of many trade unions in the country. Also in 1991, the monarchy published a National Charter, which vowed to ensure pluralism and to resolve social, economic and political conflict through negotiation. Nonetheless, smaller strikes escalated during the 1990s, possibly as a means of indirectly expressing political grievances (open political dissent being rare). A Labour Law of 1996 partially met unionist aspirations. During 1999, the Labour Ministry intervened in various disputes to find solutions where there had been a breakdown in discussions, leading to the reinstatement of workers who had struck illegally.

The unions (especially the Engineers' Union, the largest and richest of them all, and Journalists' Union) have been in the forefront of protests about Iraq and the Palestinian situation. Many unions urged their members to blacklist companies which fostered ties with Israeli firms. Recently Ali Abu Sekher, director-general of the Engineers' Union, was detained for two months for his role in a committee against "normalizaion". The Supreme Court had ruled that according to the Trade Unions Law, unions could not organize such a committee. The Law also demanded mandatory membership of unions for professionals, mainly so as to help unions organize pensions and training for their members. However, in practice, the law afforded professional unions with greater political independence, including the right to sack members, which was not its intention. Some government officials have urged the state to amend the law, so as to enforce better democratic procedures within unions. So far the issue of mandatory membership has not been tested in a court of law.

In June 2002 then Prime Minister Ali Abu Ragheb reminded unions of the law prohibiting political action; he advised them to concentrate solely on labour affairs. At the time the Professional Unions Association, led by its acting president, Hashem Gharaybeh, was leading a campaign to boycott American products, in protest at US policy over Israel. The Association groups together 13 professional unions, representing a total of 100,000 members. Six of the 13 are dominated by the Muslim Brotherhood; all of them agreed to place a ban on "normalization" with Israel after Jordan and Israel signed their peace treaty in 1994. Of late the government has begun criticizing unions that take on overtly religious overtones.

In October 2002 Jordan's Minister of State for Political Affairs, Mohammad Adwan, called for the dissolution of committees linked to unions that oppose the normalization of ties with Israel. Adwan stated that such boycotts were illegal, and harmed both the national economy and Jordanian interests. In 2003 unions were also prominent in demonstrations against the US invsion of Iraq.

3 Trade Union Centre

General Federation of Jordanian Trade Unions (GFJTU)
Address. PO Box 1065, Amman 11118
Phone. +962 6 567 5533
Fax. +962 6 568 7911
E-mail. gfjtu@go.com.jo
Membership. 200,000
Leadership. Mazen Al-Maayta
History and character. Established in 1954, the GFJTU (formerly the Jordan Federation of Trade Unions – JFTU) has traditionally avoided political matters, focusing instead on workplace issues. The Government subsidizes and audits the GFJTU's salaries and activities. The federation now has 17 unions affiliated, having lost two following Jordan's withdrawal of administrative responsibility for the West Bank in 1988. Although affiliation is not compulsory, all Jordanian unions belong to it. However, the GFJTU is said to have lost some credibility in latter years, because it was seen by radicals as an appendage of the government.

In August 1999, GFJTU leader Mazen al-Maayta applauded the government's decision to set the national minimum wage at 80 Jordanian dinars a month; however, his vice-president, Fathallah Emrani, and the head of the Public Service Workers' Union, Abud Jada', disagreed, and felt a higher basic wage was needed to keep pace with rising standards of living. The wage, it was pointed out, was less than the 82 dinars given to needy families each month by the National Aid Fund. Some government officials thought that a minimum wage would help working class Jordanians take up jobs currently held by some million low-paid foreign workers; although certain economists argued to the contrary.

The GFTU has a longstanding relationship with the ILO, which has provided the federation with fellowships and study tours, seminars, workshops and research co-operation. On May 29-31, 2004, the GFTU hosted a regional workshop to the which was organized by ICFTU and held in Amman (Jordan). The GFTU also participates in the International Confederation of Arab Trade Unions (ICATU) and co-operates in training programmes in conjunction with the German-based Friedrich Erbert Foundation.
International affiliation. ICFTU

Kazakhstan

Capital: Astana
Population: 15.14 m. (2004 est.)

1 Political and Economic Background

Kazakhstan became an independent state upon the dissolution of the Soviet Union in December 1991. It has been ruled since independence by President Nursultan Nazarbayev, who had also been the chairman of the Supreme Soviet in 1990–91. Nazarbayev has broad powers, which he has extended by decree. He was re-elected in January 1999 for a seven-year term with 80% of the vote, several potential candidates having been barred by decree from standing. Elections to the Majlis, the lower house of parliament, in September–October 2004 resulted in an overwhelming majority for pro-presidential parties, the conduct of the elections being criticized by observers. In November 2004, 22 members of the Majlis from different parties formed a Labour bloc ("Enbek").

Kazakhstan has immense energy fossil fuel reserves and is rich in minerals. However, it has a legacy of traditional heavy industries, many of them redundant or obsolescent, from the Soviet period and the collapse of demand for its products with the end of the Soviet Union imposed severe difficulties. In 1992 Kazakhstan launched an ambitious programme to privatize state industries, but this had limited success; by mid-1994 the private share of the economy was not above 20 per cent. Negative growth rates, hyper-inflation and removal of price controls led to serious unrest in 1994. Privatization picked up pace thereafter. Kazakhstan was badly affected by the effects of the Asian and Russian economic crisis of 1997–98, together with falls in prices for oil, metals and grains, its major exports. However, its economy improved strongly in the period 2000-04, with growth in GDP around 10% per annum, benefiting from price rises for oil and gas, good harvests and inward investment.

GDP (purchasing power parity) $105.5bn. (2004 est.); GDP per capita (purchasing power parity) $6,300 (2004 est.).

2 Trade Unionism

As of 2004 there were reported to be 43 registered trade unions in Kazakhstan, with trade unions most entrenched in the mining, metalworking, chemicals, transport, health and construction sectors. Trade union density is about 8.3%.

There are currently three national trade union centres, although some unions do not affiliate to any of these. The Federation of Trade Unions of the Republic of Kazakhstan (FTUK) coordinates what were the official Soviet-era trade unions. It now has about 1.5 million members. The Confederation of Free Trade Unions of Kazakhstan (CFTUK) was formed in 1991 and struggled to establish itself in the face of the continued dominance of the official trade unions, which benefited from inheriting the assets of the Soviet-era unions, official approval and the use of the check-off system to generate dues in the state sector. The CFTUK membership fluctuated between 50,000 and 250,000 and most workers continued to be members of the official unions. A third centre, the Confederation of Labour of Kazakhstan (CLK) was established in 2004, attracting unions from both the FTUK and the CFTUK. All three centres participated in the Tripartite Commission on Social Partnership in 2004 but the CFTUK was excluded in January 2005.

There was frequent industrial unrest in the years after independence in mining areas. A 32-day strike in the Karaganda coalfields ended in June 1992 with an agreement that 15 per cent of output would be the property of the miners' collectives. Leaders of the strike broke away from the Miners' Union of Kazakhstan (an affiliate of the Federation of Trade Unions of the Republic of Kazakhstan) to form the Independent Miners' Union (IMU). As a result of Kazakhstan's acute economic difficulties in the 1990s, many workers were owed back wages, and in 1999 many enterprises were paying their workers in scrip rather than cash, partly because their customers in the former Soviet Union were not paying cash. Wage arrears were the leading cause of strikes, demonstrations, blockading of railways and even mass hunger strikes in factories. Protests were broken up by police action and those taking part sentenced to prison. In June 1998 a new national security law defined "unsanctioned gatherings, public meetings, marches, demonstrations, illegal picketing, and strikes" as a threat to national security. At the same time some trade union officials were seemingly involved primarily in ensuring their share of the spoils of privatization.

The issue of wage arrears has declined in Kazakhstan's now buoyant economy, although strikes over the issue still occurred in 2003. Harassment of independent unions has declined and such unions now participate in national dialogue on social and economic issues and organize more freely, although the effectiveness of many unions is uncertain. The influence of the unions was in part behind the enactment of a law on social partnership in 2000 and the ratification in recent years of a series of fundamental ILO Conventions, including Convention No. 87 (Freedom of Association and Protection of the Right to Organize, 1948) in 2000 and Convention No. 98 (Right to Organize and Collective Bargaining, 1949) in 2001.

Collective bargaining is not widely practiced. A new labour law came into effect in January 2000. This provides for a system of individual contracts, but with "optional" collective contracts, and ended the requirement that the union should agree to the termination of a worker's contract.

3 Trade Union Centres

Confederation of Free Trade Unions of Kazakhstan (CFTUK/KSPK)
Address. Karaganda, prospekt N.Abdirov # 14, of.10
E-mail. office_kspk@mail.kz
Leadership. Sergei Belkin (chairman)
History and character. The CFTUK (or KSPK) was organized in 1991 under the leadership of Leonid Solomin. The new confederation faced active harassment from the authorities as well as from the leaders of the old monopoly official trade unions. In the post-communist era the new independent unions confronted serious violations of workers' rights and non-payment of wages was endemic; the period was one of strikes, demonstrations, blockades of railways and hunger strikes, and the CFTUK coordinated this activity. The CFTUK led demonstrations in 1996 following which Solomin was in 1997 investigated by the National Security Agency (KNB) on charges including violating a provision of the 1995 constitution that prevents unions from receiving funds from abroad, although the charges were eventually dropped. The independent unions were assisted with training by Western unions and gradually achieved recognition by the authorities, including membership of the National Tripartite Commission on Social Partnership.

In May 2003 an organization committee on the creation of a consolidated trade union centre was established, led by Solomin, who delegated his powers in the CFTUK to his vice-president, Sergei Belkin. Differences culminated in a split in March 2004 when a substantial group of branch and regional trade unions broke away from the CFTUK to form the Confederation of Labour of Kazakhstan, led by Solomin, leaving the CFTUK much diminished in size. In January 2005 the CFTUK lost its place on the Tripartite Commission on Social Partnership.
International affiliations. None

Confederation of Labour of Kazakhstan (CLK)
Address. Astana, prospect Pobedy #63/1, of.26
Phone/fax. +3172 58 03 97
E-mail. knok_astana@mail.ru
Leadership. Serik Abdrakhmanov (president); Leonid Solomin (vice-president); Murat Mashkenov (secretary-general)
Membership. 500,000
History and character. The CLK was founded on March 2, 2004, at the instigation of the former leader of the

Confederation of Free Trade Unions of Kazakhstan, Leonid Solomin. Its goal is to bring all the trade unions in Kazakhstan together in a unified body. The new organization was founded with an initial membership of 400,000 (by January 2005 500,000), these coming from seven branch unions from the old official trade union centre (Federation of Trade Unions of Kazakhstan) as well as unions from the Confederation of Free Trade Unions, the Confederation of Non-Governmental Organizations of Kazakhstan, the International Academy of Information and a number of trade unions which had not previously affiliated to any centre. Its president, Serik Abdrakhmanov, is a deputy in parliament. The Confederation has achieved official recognition and joined the National Tripartite Commission on Social Partnership.

Federation of Trade Unions of the Republic of Kazakhstan (FTUK/FPRK)
Website. www.fprk.kz (Russian only)
Address. Astana, prospekt Abai # 94
Phone. +3172 21 68 14
Fax. +3172 21 68 35
E-mail. fprkastana@nursat.kz
Leadership. Siyazbek Mukashev (chairman)
Department of information and international cooperation
Director – Kairat Sadykov
Fax. + 3172 21 62 13
Phone. + 3172 21 57 42
E-mail. ksadykov@nursat.kz
infofprk@nursat.kz
Membership. 1.5 million
History and character. The FTUK is the successor organization to the communist era official trade unions and inherited their assets. Although it has lost its functions as an arm of the state, it still suffers to some degree from the perception that its affiliated unions are in the pocket of the government. Dissatisfaction with the management of trade union assets has also caused discontent and encouraged the formation of rival centres. The FTUK nonetheless still retains 1.5 million members, in particular employees of public sector organizations, such as doctors, teachers and state officials, as well as students. In the post-independence era the Federation was an organized political force, electing a bloc of deputies to parliament, but this is no longer the case.
International affiliation. GCTU

Kenya

Capital: Nairobi
Population: 30.02 m. (2004 est.)

1 Political and Economic Background

Kenya achieved independence from the United Kingdom in 1963 and became a republic the following year. Daniel Arap Moi, leader of the Kenya African National Union (KANU), became Kenya's second President in 1978, in succession to Jomo Kenyatta, and then held the office for five successive terms, until 2002. KANU was for many years the sole legal party until a multi-party system was conceded in principle in 1991; in practice opposition groupings found it hard to maintain legality. Throughout 1993 and 1994 opponents of the government faced heavy-handed suppression, and at one point one-quarter of the parliamentary opposition was in jail. Political pluralism gathered strength thereafter and in the December 2002 elections Moi's favoured successor and KANU candidate Uhuru Kenyatta (Jomo's son) was defeated by Mwai Kibaki of the National Rainbow Coalition of opposition parties (NARC). KANU also lost the parliamentary elections held at the same time, with the NARC taking 125 of the 210 seats in the National Assembly.

Kenya's economy is primarily based on agriculture, which occupies 75–80% of the workforce. Export crops include tea and coffee. There is a manufacturing sector based on consumer goods and agricultural processing, and tourism. A privatization programme was initiated in 1991 but many key enterprises are still in state hands. International assistance has been restricted for several years because of doubts over government commitment to economic reform and the level of official corruption. In July 2000 the government won a renewal of IMF financial support with a pledge to push ahead with privatization and anti-corruption measures, with the state telecoms, railways and Mombassa container terminal key enterprises scheduled for privatization. IMF lending was again suspended in 2001 because of corruption – Kibaki and the NARC then going on to win the 2002 elections on a platform highlighting "zero tolerance" for corruption. However, official corruption continues to blight relations with international donors, leading to suspensions and shortfalls in international aid. Major problems include persistent inter-ethnic conflict, the HIV/AIDS epidemic, high crime levels, power shortages, long-term GDP growth lagging population growth, widespread unemployment and under-employment, and localized drought and famine. After contracting in 2000, GDP grew 1.2% in both 2001 and 2002 and by 1.8% in 2003. The proportion of the population living below the poverty line rose from 48% in 1990 to 56% in 2001, with highly unequal income distribution.

GDP (purchasing power parity) $33.03bn. (2004 est.); GDP per capita (purchasing power parity) $1,000 (2004 est.).

2 Trade Unionism

Trade unions developed after World War II under British colonial labour legislation, and were closely linked to nationalist politics. The Central Organization of Trade Unions (COTU) was founded in 1965 and since then has been the sole trade union centre. There is one major union outside COTU, the Kenya National Union of Teachers (KNUT), which has about 260,000 members, more than 40% of the organized workforce. Unions must be registered with the government to have legal status.

Kenya ratified ILO Convention No. 98 (Right to

Organize and Collective Bargaining, 1949) in 1964 but has not ratified Convention No. 87 (Freedom of Association and Protection of the Right to Organize, 1948). In practice workers in the formal economy have the right to join unions of their choice although this is circumscribed in some sectors. For many years civil servants and professionals such as university academic staff, doctors and dentists were only allowed to belong to associations with no collective bargaining rights. In 2001 the Union of Kenyan Civil Servants, banned since 1980, was re-registered, and in 2003 the University Academic Staff Union was registered after a 10-year battle. In the export processing zones there is considerable resistance to the formation of unions. An organizing campaign in 2003 led to the Tailors and Textile Union winning the first EPZ collective agreement covering 12,000 workers in the Athi River zone.

Workers in many small firms face dismissal if they join unions. Overall, however, the trade union base in Kenya is relatively broad and established and COTU has affiliates in a wide range of industries, with new unions registered in several sectors in the 1990s. There are now some 42 unions representing about 600,000 workers, comprising up to one-third of all workers in the formal sector. Under the Trade Disputes Act it is illegal to dismiss or discriminate against workers for trade union activities and although long delays occur in hearing cases workers affected have often been reinstated. A tripartite task force is examining labour law reform in an effort to bring the law into compliance with ILO standards. The new law is scheduled for 2005.

Collective bargaining is permitted by labour legislation and collective agreements must be registered with the Industrial Court. Most workers (including in essential services) have a legal right to strike after giving a period of notice. The concept of "essential services" is far in excess of that recognized by the ILO, and in Kenya the term is extended to include education, water, health and air traffic control. Workers in these industries must provide a longer period of notice and the dispute may be subject to binding arbitration. In practice, the government commonly involves itself by instituting mediation and referral to the Industrial Court and by declaring strikes illegal if this process breaks down. A strike by nurses in 1997-98 resulted in the nurses being dismissed and being required to re-apply for their jobs. In 1998 a strike by the teachers' union KNUT was declared illegal and the government arrested teachers' leaders and broke up union meetings, bringing the strike to an end. In 2003 strikes called by EPZ workers seeking to replicate the success of the Athi River organizing campaign were declared illegal and workers were dismissed.

3 Trade Union Centre

Central Organization of Trade Unions (COTU)
Address. Solidarity Building, Digo Road, PO Box 13000, Nairobi
Phone. +254 2 76 13 75
Fax. +254 2 76 26 95
Email. info@cotu-kenya.org
Website. www.cotu-kenya.org
Membership. About 350,000
History and character. COTU was founded in 1965 in succession to the Kenya Federation of Labour and the African Workers' Congress, which were dissolved. The legislation establishing COTU gave the Kenyan President the right to dismiss the three leading officials of the centre.

During the early 1990s, in line with the movement to political liberalization then sweeping much of Africa, COTU sought to establish its independence from the ruling KANU party, criticizing government policies and corruption. This led to a period of tension in which the government in 1993 actively interfered in COTU affairs to secure a more compliant leadership. COTU is now considered to be passive politically although some of its affiliates press for greater independence from the state, political reform and opposition to corruption. In 2001 COTU's constitution was amended, removing the seats that were reserved on its board for government officials.

The COTU affiliates 32 of the 36 registered unions, but does not include in membership the largest and most influential single union, the Kenya National Union of Teachers (KNUT). Some COTU unions are reported to have evolved on an ethnic basis.
International affiliation. ICFTU

Kiribati

Capital: Tarawa
Population: 101,000 (2004 est.)

1 Political and Economic Background

The Republic of Kiribati, formerly the Gilbert Islands, became an independent state within the Commonwealth in 1979. Its politics tend to be fought out between comparatively loose alliances built around individual personalities and there is an elected President (since July 2003, Anote Tong, whose principal rival for the presidency was his brother Harry, an ally of former President Teburoro Tito). Kiribati has few resources and little infrastructure and 90% of the work force is occupied in fishing or subsistence farming. External aid (mainly from the UK and Japan) is a major component of the national income and one-fifth of GDP now comes from tourism.

GDP (purchasing power parity) $79 m. (2001 est.); GDP per capita (purchasing power parity) $800 (2001 est.).

2 Trade Unionism

Kiribati ratified its first four ILO conventions in 2000, among them Conventions No. 87 (Freedom of Association and Protection of the Right to Organize, 1948) and No. 98 (Right to Organize and Collective Bargaining, 1949). Freedom of association is provided for by the (1979) Constitution and in practice the government has not interfered in the formation of trade unions. Despite the very small base of the formal sector economy, unions have developed and in 1982 a national centre was set up, the Kiribati Trade Union Congress (KTUC), which achieved affiliation to the ICFTU. Its 2,500 members are mostly in the public sector.

Collective bargaining is allowed under the Industrial Relations Code. In the public sector pay tends to be set administratively, although there is bargaining in some agencies and state-owned enterprises. Industrial relations are generally harmonious and although there is a legal right to strike, no strikes have been recorded since 1980.

3 Trade Union Centre

Kiribati Trade Union Congress (KTUC)
Address. PO Box 502, Tarawa
Phone. +686 26277
Fax. +686 25257
E-mail. kiosu@tskl.net.ki
Leadership. Tatoa Kaiteie
Membership. 2,500
History and character. Founded in 1982 by the seven registered trade unions in Kiribati. All unions are affiliated to the KTUC. The KTUC has been active in promoting self-help and educational projects, with help from Japanese unions, the ICFTU regional organization APRO and other trade union sources.
International affiliation. ICFTU; CTUC

North Korea

Capital: Pyongyang
Population: 22.70 m. (2004 est.)

1 Political and Economic Background

The Democratic People's Republic of Korea (North Korea) was established in 1948 in what had been the Soviet zone of occupied Korea. Political control is exercised by the communist Korean Workers' Party (KWP), which was led until his death in 1994 by President Kim Il Sung, the "Great Leader". Since 1994 the dominant figure has been his son, Kim Jong Il (the "Dear Leader"), as leader of the party (the position of President being effectively abolished in 1998 when Kim Il Sung was declared "Eternal President").

In 1991 North Korea joined the UN, a move from which it had recoiled previously on the grounds that it would lead to South Korean admission and affirmation of the division of the country. In the event the two countries joined simultaneously.

North Korea has adhered rigidly to Stalinist-type central planning. Industry, like land, is nationalized, with production centred upon steel, cement, chemicals, military equipment and machine building rather than consumer products. North Korea struggled to recover from the 1991 collapse of the Soviet Union, its biggest market and chief source of aid. Famine in the period 1994–98, caused by natural disasters and the failure of collectivized farms, cost hundreds of thousand of lives and North Korea was forced to accept foreign food aid. There was a partial relaxation of state controls on market activities of farmers in 2003.

GDP (purchasing power parity) $29.58bn. (2004 est.); GDP per capita (purchasing power parity) $1,300 (2004 est.)

2 Trade Unionism

A single-trade-union system is in force, coordinated by the General Federation of Trade Unions of Korea (GFTUK), and unions function on the former Soviet model, with responsibility for mobilizing workers behind productivity goals and state targets, and for the provision of health, educational, cultural and welfare facilities. North Korea has remained one of the most closed societies on earth and no form of independent trade unionism has been tolerated. There is no collective bargaining or strikes.

By joining the UN North Korea became eligible to join the ILO but did not move beyond observer status.

3 Trade Union Centre

General Federation of Trade Unions of Korea (GFTUK)
Address. PO Box 333, Pyongyang
Fax. +850 2 381 2100
History and character. Founded on Nov. 30, 1945, the GFTUK is described as a political organization of the working masses. It conducts ideological education to ensure its members fully understand the ideas of Kim Il Sung and to enable them to contribute towards the socialist construction and management of the economy.
International affiliation. WFTU

South Korea

Capital: Seoul
Population: 48.60 m. (2004 est.)

1 Political and Economic Background

The Republic of Korea (South Korea) was established as an independent state in 1948 in what had been the post-World War II US occupied zone. The division of the country stood in the way of UN entry (simultaneously with North Korea) until 1991.

Korea's history post-independence was characterized by mainly authoritarian governments led or dominated by military figures, with episodes of civil unrest. In the mid-1980s a powerful pro-democracy movement gathered pace, leading to the adoption of a new constitution in 1987. Since then South Korea has had civilian rule. Kim Dae-jung was elected President in December 1997, presiding over a coalition government led by his centre-left Millennium Democratic Party (MDP). The MDP won fewer seats than the conservative Grand National Party (GNP) in legislative elections in April 2000. Roh Moo-hyun won the presidency on the MDP ticket in December 2002, campaigning on the basis of reducing the power of the family-owned industrial conglomerates (chaebol) which dominate the South Korean economy and of continuing Kim's "sunshine policy" of engagement with the North. In late 2003, however, Roh split with the MDP, and in April 2004 the newly formed pro-presidential Uri Party won elections to the National Assembly, taking 152 of the 299 seats, and the MDP being reduced to a rump of only nine seats. The result was widely interpreted as marking a further shift away from the right-wing authoritarian policies of the past.

South Korea's economic rise has been one of the prime Asian success stories. It has taken the country from a backward low-income economy at independence to become a leading world player by the 1990s in industries such as automobiles, electronics, chemicals, shipbuilding and steel, with per capita GDP on a purchasing power parity basis now 15 times that in North Korea. The South Korean model was based on close interlocks between government and industry, directed credits, and protectionism with a focus on labour productivity balanced by job security.

The Asian financial crisis of the late 1990s had a particularly severe impact on South Korea, however. The crisis exposed fundamental weaknesses in the financial sector and in Korea's system of closed markets and government intervention. Structural adjustment programmes required by the IMF as a condition of bail-outs began a move to more open markets. The crisis, though severe, proved brief as a 1998 contraction of GDP by 10.7% turned into growth of 10.9% in 1999. Since then growth rates have fluctuated, but with no further recession – in October 2004 the IMF forecast that South Korean GDP would increase 4.6% in 2004, below the governments's 5% target. Unemployment is low, running at 3-4% in 2004. The Uri Party won the 2004 elections on a programme which promised further steps to combat corruption and increase transparency in South Korea's business sector, especially the closely controlled chaebol conglomerates. Corruption, opaque corporate governance and poor labour relations are often identified as problematic aspects of the South Korean economy.

GDP (purchasing power parity) $857.8.7bn. (2004 est.); GDP per capita (purchasing power parity) $17,800 (2004 est.).

2 Trade Unionism

The first Korean trade union was the Song-Jin Dockers' Union organized in May 1898, and unions began to develop after the annexation of Korea by Japan in 1910, becoming a centre of opposition to Japanese rule. Following the end of Japanese rule and the establishment of US military government in the south of Korea, a General Council of Korean Trade Unions was formed under communist control and this led general strikes in 1946 and 1947. In 1946 however the General Federation of Korean Trade Unions was created with US backing; it became a founder member of the ICFTU in 1949. Communist organizations were banned in 1947.

Following a 1961 military coup (which inaugurated the 18-year rule of General Park, assassinated in 1979), all labour organizations were dissolved and replaced by the Federation of Korean Trade Unions (FKTU). After industrial unrest in the late 1960s, trade union rights were restricted by a series of measures brought into force in the early 1970s. The government justified these measures as necessary to create a stable market for foreign investors and in the interest of national security.

Under the Trade Union Law of 1980 only one union was permitted in each enterprise; only enterprise-level unions could negotiate with employers, without any intervention by third parties (i.e. seriously weakening the role of industry-wide federations); and there were restrictions on the dues which unions could collect from their members. Disputes were to be settled directly between union and employer, under the authority of tripartite labour committees representing the interests of employers, workers and the government but whose members were nominated by the government. The immediate effect of this legislation was to reduce total union membership from 1,200,000 to 820,000.

The anti-government political activity of the 1980s was reflected in major strikes, which drew fierce repression by the state. In 1986 the Labour Minister dissolved 14 dissident unions in the Seoul-Inchon area, an anti-reform stance backed by FKTU. 1987 however inaugurated the "Great Workers' Struggle": it was the most disputatious year for a decade with 3,749 separate disputes, mostly for pay but also for the right to engage freely in trade union activities. Labour unrest on this scale challenged employers, government and the FKTU leadership. Despite the technical illegality of the strikes, the authorities tended to tolerate them, and perhaps half gained concessions on pay and conditions. A short-lived Committee for the Democratization of Trade Unions tried to make the FKTU more representative and replace its leadership. Such "democratic unions", which found support among white-collar financial workers, grew to number 300. They were the industrial counterpart of the country's wider dissident movement, in contrast with the majority of the so-called "company unions".

One result of the 1987 upheavals in Korean society was a great increase in trade union membership. The peak of membership was reached in 1989 when 1,932,000 people were in the unions, but the 1990s brought decline, and official figures recorded 1,803,400 organized workers at the end of 1991.

The government only recognized as legitimate unions affiliated to the FKTU or the Korean Federation of Free Clerical and Financial Workers, despite the view of the courts that non-affiliation was not a sufficient reason to deny registration. This factor continued to compromise the FKTU's independent status, but it remained the largest national centre with a claimed membership of 1.44 million out of some 1.8 million organized workers. New unions founded after 1987 which stayed aloof from it formed 14 (later 17) regional councils and a number of industrial councils, but were prevented by law from forming an alternative centre. A total of 602 (with an initial membership approaching 200,000) formed such a centre nonetheless in 1990 under the title Korean Trade Union Congress (KTUC, or Chonnohyup) but it came under heavy repression. Also formed in 1990 was the, mainly white collar, Korea Congress of Independent Industrial Trade Union Federations (KCIIF, or Upjonghweui), which united with the KTUC in the National Workers' Rally.

There was severe repression of the non-FKTU unions in 1990 and 1991. In 18 months 848 trade unionists were arrested, of whom 615 were associated with the KTUC. There were also many raids on union offices. In November 1991 the centre staged a commemorative rally on the anniversary of the death of Chun Tae-Il, a textile worker who burned himself to death in 1970, and turned out the largest dissident labour protest in the country's history.

Korea became a member of the ILO in 1991, and the Ministry of Labour then began a systematic review of employment law in the light of ILO Conventions. It had previously claimed that Korean employment law satisfied 105 of the ILO's 115 Conventions. A Labour Reform Study Committee was set up, involving representatives of the FKTU and the employers' confederation, the KEF. This was supposed to report by 1994 but its report was kept secret amid charges that independent experts and public interest representatives had made recommendations unpalatable to both the KEF and FKTU. Even before ILO entry the KTUC and the KCIIF formed the National Workers' Joint Committee for Ratification of Basic ILO Conventions and Employment Law Reform. In 1992 this Committee lodged a freedom of association complaint against the government over its prohibition of more than one union per enterprise, the prohibition of third party interventions in disputes, and bans on unions for teachers and many public servants. In 1993 the ILO called on Korea to make fundamental reforms, but the government told the ILO that its employment laws had to be judged in the light of the country's "Confucian tradition" whereby family concepts and not adversarialism were the norm. Korea's admission to the OECD in 1996 was made conditional on it undertaking reforms in areas such as freedom of association. However, despite liberalization, Korea has still not ratified the basic ILO conventions on freedom of association and collective bargaining, Nos. 87 and 98.

In 1993 the KTUC, KCIIF and unions based at Hyundai and Daewoo, came together to form the Korean Council of Trade Union Representatives (KCTU, Chonnodae), which in turn in 1995 became the Korean Confederation of Trade Unions (KCTU, Minju Nachong). The KCTU adopted a position critical of the quasi-monopoly position enjoyed by the FKTU and campaigned to achieve recognition for itself and its affiliates. In December 1996–January 1997 it led strikes against government labour legislation. In the period 1997–99 significant improvements were made in the position of the trade unions. In 1997 the previous ban on third parties such as federations giving support to unions in disputes was ended, as was the prohibition against political activities by unions (although funding of political parties by unions remained unlawful). Teachers' unions belonging to the FKTU and KCTU were legalized from July 1999. On Nov. 23, 1999, the Ministry of Labour finally accorded legal recognition to the KCTU, which by this time had also achieved affiliation to the ICFTU alongside the FKTU. It is about half the size of the FKTU.

Despite the progress made since the mid-1980s, and especially in the late 1990s, barriers to free trade unionism remain in Korea. At the workplace level, a ban on trade union pluralism has permitted only one union to operate in each enterprise. The 1997 law introduced changes that were scheduled to authorize trade union pluralism at this level by 2002; however, this has been postponed until 2006. More than one million white-collar government employees may not form trade unions or bargain collectively, although since January 1999 they may form workplace councils with limited rights. The government of President Roh Moo-hyun introduced an early bill that would extend a limited right to organize and collective bargaining to civil servants, but the bill stalled as the promising start for labour relations quickly soured.

Strikes are prohibited in government agencies, state run enterprises and the defence industry and compulsory arbitration may be imposed (although this is not common) in a wide range of industries deemed to be in the "essential public interest", including public transport, utilities, public health, banking and telecommunications. While industrial conflict is not widespread, it not infrequently takes a violent turn with heavy police intervention and with arrest and imprisonment of strikers, often on charges of "obstruction of business". According to the KCTU, in June 1999 there were 61 individuals in prison for various forms of trade union activity, while the ICFTU complained in July 2000 that the government had "once more fully embarked on the path of repression and violence" in dealing with strikes and other trade union actions. The heavy-handed response to union demonstrations continued into 2003, during the year 213 trade unionists being arrested for their participation in strikes or for "disrupting business". In one incident 1,749 railroad workers were arrested and briefly detained when police broke up their rally. At least three trade union leaders committed suicide. The ICFTU believes that the position of trade unionists in Korea in respect of freedom of association is worse than in any other of the OECD group of industrial nations.

Underlying trends in the economy have also proved detrimental to the unions. More than 50% of the work force is said to be in various forms of irregular work, such as subcontracting or in the informal economy and such workers are outside the protection of the Labour Standards Act. The enterprise-based system of unions is a weakness in situations where employers are hostile. Trade union density reached a peak of 19.8% in 1989, in the wake of the political upheaval, but since then has gradually declined, to a level of 11.4% by 2004. Only 5% of women workers are organized.

The history of employer and government antagonism to independent trade unionism has historically gone hand-in-hand with a paternalist and protective employment system, particularly in large enterprises, somewhat akin to the Japanese model. The Asian crisis from 1997 subjected this system to unprecedented strain. The OECD urged Korea to adopt greater labour flexibility, backed up by an improved social welfare safety net, to assist economic reconstruction. Many small enterprises closed; for the first time major employers such as Hyundai, where lifetime employment had been taken for granted, initiated compulsory lay-offs after this was legalized in February 1998. Unemployment rose to 8.7 per cent in 1998 before falling in 1999. Workers were affected by casualization of employment and many workers lost their jobs without redundancy payments and with little or no social security. In 1998 wages fell for the first time since 1975. The crisis led to some increase in industrial militancy, but disputes remained at a relatively low level: only 146,000 workers were involved in industrial disputes in 1998 and efforts by the unions to mount demonstrations in 1998–99 against restructuring programmes were thinly attended. The unions became involved with the government and employers' confederation in the Tripartite Commission, which was set up to try to restore national confidence, but both the FKTU and KCTU withdrew claiming bad faith by the other parties.

One result of the crisis, which was widely attributed to the opaque business practices of Korean financial institutions and conglomerates (chaebols) was that the unions demanded greater transparency in business, including union participation in decision-making. In the years following the crisis Korean unions continued to face the challenges of globalization and restructuring. The state responded to union demonstrations with severe repression, arresting hundreds (in several cases union leaders being sentenced to prison terms). Unions recognized an opportunity for progress when the government of Roh Moo-hyun promised freedom of association to civil servants and an amnesty for trade union prisoners, but companies complained that the new government was "lenient" on workers, who then soon found themselves once more on the receiving end of government crackdowns. Despite the serious divisions the arrests have caused, the unions have proven willing to continue to cooperate with the government as they believe that pro-labour reforms can be obtained. To this end, FKTU has rejoined the Tripartite Commission and the issue is being debated within the KCTU.

3 Trade Union Centres

Federation of Korean Trade Unions (FKTU, Nochong)
Address. FKTU Bldg 168-24, Chungam-Dong, Yongsan-Ku, Seoul 140-050
Phone. +82 2 715 3954
Fax. +82 2 715 7790
E-mail. fktu@fktu.org
Website. www.fktu.org (Korean and English)
Membership. 1.1 million
History and character. The Korean Labour Federation for Independence Promotion (KLFIP) was established in 1946, and after the creation of the Republic of Korea in 1948 was re-named as the General Federation of Korean Trade Unions (GFKTU). This became one of the founding members of the ICFTU the following year. In 1961, following a military coup, all its affiliates were dissolved by military decree, and the FKTU was created in its place under the guidance of the military authorities. Until 1999 the FKTU remained the sole legal trade union centre in South Korea, while also maintaining its affiliation to the ICFTU. The FKTU was severely weakened under 1980 legislation which excluded it from direct involvement in industrial disputes and collective bargaining, leaving it only a generalized role of representing the interests of organized labour to government.

The role of the FKTU in the widespread movement for constitutional reform in 1985–87 is open to various interpretations. In its official publications, the FKTU places itself at the heart of the movement and outlines its support of the reforms gained. However, the federation's close ties to the Chun regime were most vividly demonstrated when it supported the President's 1987 decision to suspend talks on constitutional revisions. A number of "democratic unions" during the widespread labour unrest of 1987 derided what they perceived to be the FKTU's tendency to compromise too quickly. In an attempt to gain legitimacy amongst workers whose democratic aspirations had been raised by the 1988 constitutional reforms, the FKTU pledged to adopt a more political role. It established a political-education committee, called for an end to restraints on the political activities of unions, and decided to support pro-union candidates, whether from opposition parties or from the ruling Democratic Justice Party, in impending legislative elections. At a special convention of 1988 the FKTU elected a new reformist leadership pledged to increase its independence. However, independent trade unions, brought into being in the 1980s unrest, remained outside the FKTU fold and in 1993 created the KCTU, which was hostile to the FKTU's monopoly on legal status.

In 1995 the FKTU jointly created with the Ministry of Labour and employers' organization KEF, the Korea International Labor Foundation (KOILAF) to address the impact of globalization and inward investment on Korea's economy and society.

In the late 1990s crisis the FKTU initially participated in the Tripartite Commission with employers and government, set up to restore confidence and find solutions, but withdrew complaining that employers were arbitrarily laying off workers and that the government was pushing through restructuring programmes without reference to the needs of the workers. The FKTU demanded improved social safety nets for workers affected by unemployment and reduced working. However, FKTU efforts to mobilize workers, as in a general strike call in June 1999, met with a lukewarm response. In 2004 FKTU agreed to rejoin the Tripartite Commission.

The FKTU has 24 affiliated industrial federations; 16 municipal and provincial offices; and 50 local offices. Affiliated bodies include the FKTU Research

Institute and the FKTU Education Centre.
International affiliation. ICFTU

Korean Confederation of Trade Unions (KCTU, Minju Nochong)
Address. 5th floor, Daeyoung Bldg., 139 Youngdeungpo-2-ga, Youngdeungpo-ku, Seoul 150–032
Phone. +82 2 636 0165
Fax. +82 2 635 1134
E-mail. inter@kctu.org
Website. www.kctu.org (Korean and English)
Leadership. Dan Byung-ho (president); Lee Soo-ho (general secretary)
Membership. 573,490 in 1,226 individual unions (July 1999)
History and character. An Association for Korean Workers' Welfare and Benefits (AKWW) was formed in March 1984 by leaders of non-FKTU unions and enjoyed brief success in its campaigns until, in 1985, it was suppressed. This movement re-emerged as the Federation of Korean Democratic Workers (FKDW) at the end of the decade and shortly after became the Korea Trade Union Congress (KTUC, or Chonnohyup).

The KTUC was founded in January 1990 by 602 independent unions formed since 1987 and launched in defiance of legislation forbidding the establishment of an alternative centre. Its chairman was arrested in February 1990 following the detention of 150 other union leaders. Over the next year-and-a-half its activists accounted for three-quarters of those arrested by the state. At the end of this period however the organization had consolidated its position by winning many workplace positions in the 1991 workplace elections, and by calling a highly successful demonstration in Seoul.

The Korean Congress of Independent Industrial Federations (KCIIF, Upjonghweui), also formed in 1990, was a loose coalition of white collar federations in finance, nursing, the media, construction, and the public sector, and also included the banned teachers' federation Chonkyojo. In June 1993 the KTUC and KCIIF, with some other unions, joined forces to create the Korean Council of Trade Union Representatives (KCTU, Chonnodae) as a single focal point for unions outside the FKTU monopoly structure. This in turn in November 1995 became the Korean Confederation of Trade Unions (Minju Nochong), claiming a membership of 862 enterprise unions and 418,000 members. Although trade union involvement in politics was banned, members of the Democratic Party assisted in the formation of the KCTU.

The KCTU's programme announced in March 1996 emphasized the need to end the prohibition of more than one union in an enterprise, which entrenched the monopoly position of the FKTU, an organization which, it said, had "submitted and yielded" to military repression in the 1980s and made "the union structure a supplementary mechanism of labour control". Other elements of the programme included securing trade union rights for 1.5 million public servants and also for teachers; an end to the ban on trade unions engaging in political activities; and an end to state interference in trade union affairs.

On Nov. 22, 1999, the KCTU finally achieved legal recognition. All its affiliated unions are now legalized.

Its policy objectives include: the repeal of repressive legislation such as the National Security Law; worker participation in the management of enterprises; increased involvement of women in the trade union movement, and gender equality; opposition to the extension of subcontracting and irregular employment; improvement in Korea's poor health and safety record; full rights for migrant workers; and opposition to monopolies and ologopolies in Korean economy and society. The KCTU wishes to develop the industrial union system to overcome the limitations of enterprise unionism.
International affiliation. ICFTU

Kuwait

Capital: Kuwait City
Population: 2.26 m. (2004 est. – includes 1.29 m. non-nationals)

1 Political and Economic Background

Kuwait has been ruled by monarchs (Amirs) from the al-Sabah family for more than 200 years, and members of the family hold all the key government posts. Under the 1962 constitution there is a National Assembly, but there are no political parties (although loose tendencies exist) and the Amir has ruled by decree for periods, most recently in 1986–92. Kuwait was invaded and occupied by Iraq in 1990, and its sovereignty restored by US led military action in 1991. Following this the ruling family said that the 1962 Constitution would be respected. The most recent National Assembly elections were held in July 2003, all candidates officially being "non-partisan"; only 136,715 men were entitled to vote out of a local population of 898,000, while women were barred from either voting or standing for election. Of the population of two-and-a-quarter million, more than half are foreigners.

The economy is based on oil, which generates 80% of government revenues and provides a high standard of living for native Kuwaitis. More than 90% of indigenous Kuwaitis work for the state, whereas foreigners constitute 98% of the private sector labour force and 80% of the total labour force.

GDP (purchasing power parity) $41.46bn. (2004 est.); GDP per capita (purchasing power parity) $19,000 (2004 est.).

2 Trade Unionism

Trade unions were first accorded legal recognition under legislation of 1964. By law, employers guilty of anti-union discrimination must reinstate victimized workers. There are 14 unions, with a total of about 60,000 members, affiliated to the national trade union centre, the Kuwait Trade Union Federation (KTUF). The Bank Workers' Union and Kuwait Airways Workers' Union, with a combined membership of

4,500 workers are each independent of the KTUF. Nine of the KTUF's affiliates represent civil and public servants and three represent petrol and chemical sector employees. There are various restrictions on the right to join unions and their free operation, which the ILO has repeatedly found in violation of Convention No. 87 (Freedom of Association and Protection of the Right to Organize, 1948), which Kuwait ratified in 1961. One serious restriction is the requirement that a new union must have at least 100 members, of which at least 15 must be Kuwaiti citizens. This is a serious obstacle to organizing as only 6% of Kuwati citizens work in the private sector, the majority of private sector workers being migrant workers.

There are more than one million foreign workers (constituting 80% of the workforce), who may join a union only after five years' residence. Although this restriction is not always enforced, in practice only a few thousand foreign workers are in unions, representing just 5% of the unionized sector. Furthermore, foreign workers may join unions only as non-voting members and union officials must be citizens. The government involves itself directly in union affairs, contributing up to 90% of most union budgets and retaining extensive powers of oversight. Unions are barred from engaging in political or religious activities and in principle may be dissolved for threatening "public order and morals" although this has not happened in practice. Only one trade union may be formed in any occupational area and the formation of more than one national centre is not permitted.

More than 90% of all working Kuwaitis are to be found in the civil service or elsewhere in the public sector. "Kuwaitization" (the displacement of foreign by indigenous employees) has progressed much further in the state sector than in the private sector, and the pace of change was hastened by the impact of the 1990–91 occupation by Iraq and subsequent Gulf War. Little more than one-third of pre-War foreign nationals on the government payroll were rehired. Despite numerous restrictions, however, Kuwaiti nationals were again in a minority in the population by the end of 1992.

Kuwait has not ratified ILO Convention No. 98 (Right to Organize and Collective Bargaining, 1949). In the government service there is no collective bargaining as such, but the government consults informally with the unions. Collective bargaining is allowed in the private sector, although restricted by the low level of unionization. There is a mechanism for mediation and arbitration. There are no legal protections for strikers and strikes are not common. Disputes are referred to compulsory arbitration.

Domestic servants are not protected by labour legislation and foreign workers may not switch jobs without permission from their original sponsoring employer before they have been in the country for two years. Some foreign workers are in effect indentured servants.

A long-promised new labour law that has been a work in progress for decades was reported to be almost complete in early 2004, but this claim has been made on previous occasions.

3 Trade Union Centre

Kuwait Trade Union Federation (KTUF)
Address. PO Box 5185 Safat, 13052 Kuwait City
Phone. +965 563 6386
Fax. +965 562 7159
Email. ktuf@hotmail.com
History and character. The KTUF was founded in 1968. It has 14 member unions, divided into two sectors (state and oil), with close to 60,000 members. It is the sole legal trade union centre.

In the 1980s it opposed US policy in the Middle East and offered support for the "peace initiatives" of the Soviet Union. Two former presidents of the KTUF, Nasser al Faraq and Mliehan al Harbi, were arrested and tortured by the Iraqi forces during the 1990–91 occupation. Both died within days of their release. Their successor Hayef al Agami escaped from Kuwait shortly after the invasion in August 1990. The KTUF joined with the democratic opposition during the Gulf War to demand restoration of the 1962 Constitution, with guarantees of freedom of expression and women's equality. It also campaigned actively for the return of Kuwaitis detained in Iraq.
International affiliation. WFTU

Kyrgyzstan

Capital: Bishkek
Population: 5.08 m. (2004 est.)

1 Political and Economic Background

Kyrgyzstan declared its independence from the Soviet Union in August 1991. Its President since that time has been Askar Akayev, who was re-elected for a third term in October 2000. The majority of successful candidates in the legislative elections of 2000, which were highly confused and marked by widespread irregularities, were officially non-partisans. Kyrgyzstan is a primarily agricultural country, producing cotton, wool and meat, but with a range of industries. It has introduced market reforms and much of the government's stake in enterprises has been sold off. It suffered sharp economic decline following the break-up of the Soviet Union; it has shown recovery since the mid-1990s, with GDP increasing by 6% per annum and over in 2003-04, but industrial production still remains below Soviet-era levels and there is considerable poverty, unemployment and underemployment. Child labour exists in some sectors, especially seasonal agriculture asnd the informal economy.

GDP (purchasing power parity) $7.81bn. (2004 est.); GDP per capita (purchasing power parity) $1,600 (2004 est.).

2 Trade Unionism

Kyrgyzstan ratified ILO Conventions No. 87 (Freedom of Association and Protection of the Right to Organize, 1948) and No. 98 (Right to Organize and Collective Bargaining, 1949) in 1992. The post-Soviet era labour law of 1992 provided for the right of all workers to belong to trade unions and the 1998 labour code confirmed these rights; the right to join and form trade unions is observed. The majority of trade unions affiliate to the Kyrgyzstan Federation of Trade Unions (also referred to as the Federation of Trade Unions of the Kyrgyz Republic), although there is no requirement to do so and there are a number of small unaffiliated unions. The right of unions to negotiate collectively is recognized by law and collective bargaining is practiced in some industries. The right to strike is not codified, but although infrequent occasional strikes have been reported and these have been tolerated.

3 Trade Union Centre

Kyrgyzstan Federation of Trade Unions (KFTU)
Address. 207 Chuy Ave., 720032 Bishkek
Phone. +10 996 312 21 49 30
Leadership. Sagyn Bozgunbayev (president)
Membership. 980,400 (2001)
History and character. The former Soviet official unions were reconstituted as the Federation of Trade Unions of the Kyrgyz Republic after independence. The Federation reports that 94% of workers are in unions and that most of these unions affiliate to it. The Federation has criticized aspects of government policy, especially privatization, although in general the unions carry out similar functions to those in the Soviet era. It is involved in the enforcement of labour laws. Although the Federation is not internationally affiliated other than to the General Confederation of Trade Unions (GCTU), which affiliates centres from the former Soviet republics, a number of individual unions affiliate to international trade union secretariats.

Laos

Capital: Vientiane
Population: 6.01 m. (2004 est.)

1 Political and Economic Background

The Lao People's Democratic Republic was established in 1975 following the victory of the communist Pathet Lao forces. The country is ruled by the (communist) Lao People's Revolutionary Party (LPRP). All but one of the candidates in the most recent elections to the National Assembly, in February 2002, were members of the LPRP, the exception being an individual with close ties to the party.

Some 80% of the population are engaged in subsistence agriculture, primarily the cultivation of rice. Laos suffers from very limited infrastructure, and outside the principal towns there are few roads and no electricity. Although remaining under firm communist political control, from the mid-1980s Laos encouraged the development of private enterprise and enjoyed steady economic growth, averaging 8% per annum 1988–96, before being hit by spill-over from the Asian financial crisis of 1997–98, which affected Thailand, its main market. It has since recovered (real GDP being forecast to rise by 5.5% in 2004) but living standards remain low and there is a continuing reliance on foreign aid.

GDP (purchasing power parity) $10.32bn. (2004 est.); GDP per capita (purchasing power parity) $1,700 (2004 est.).

2 Trade Unionism

Laos has been a member of the ILO since 1964, but has ratified neither Convention No. 87 (Freedom of Association and Protection of the Right to Organize, 1948) nor Convention No. 98 (Right to Organize and Collective Bargaining, 1949); it has ratified only four conventions in all, and none since 1964 – i.e. the era preceding the communist takeover. A single trade union system prevails, organized through the Lao Federation of Trade Unions (LFTU), which is controlled by the ruling LPRP, although the low level of economic development, with most workers engaged in subsistence or informal activities, means that the unions are comparatively small in scale. There is no development of collective bargaining in the private sector and in the state sector the government sets wages and conditions, although there are forms of consultation with the official unions. Strikes are not illegal but rarely occur and disruptive actions are liable to sanctions under the penal code.

3 Trade Union Centre

Lao Federation of Trade Unions (LFTU)
Address. 87 Lane Xang Avenue, PO Box 780, Vientiane
Leadership. Bosaykham Vongdara (acting president)
History and character. The LFTU is linked to the ruling LPRP and absorbed the few small pre-existing unions after the establishment of the present regime in 1975. The constitution provides for it to have a role in mobilizing and uniting the workers in the task of national construction. No union may be formed outside the LFTU structure and the LFTU officially works under the guidance of the party, with the salaries of its senior officials also paid by the government. The state is the main employer in the formal economy and the LFTU's 77,000 members are reported to be mainly public servants.
International affiliation. WFTU. The LFTU has participated in the work of the ASEAN Trade Union Council since 1999 and in 2002 ICFTU-APRO made its first official visit to the LFTU.

Latvia

Capital: Riga
Population: 2.31m. (2004 est.)

1 Political and Economic Background

Latvia was an independent state from 1920 until annexed by the USSR in 1940. It repudiated Soviet rule in May 1990 and its independence was recognized by the Soviet Union in September 1991. The last Russian troops left in 1994. Since independence there has been a multiplicity of political parties, with no clear dominant party emerging, and each election since 1991 has been won by a party formed less than one year before the poll and with at least half of all parliamentary deputies losing their seats. In the most recent elections, in October 2002, the newly formed New Era party of Einars Repse, the former head of the central bank, came first, Repse subsequently becoming Prime Minister of a coalition government. This collapsed in February 2004, with Indulis Emsis, of the Alliance of the Greens and Farmers' Union, becoming Prime Minister of another centre-right coalition. Latvia joined the European Union on May 1, 2004.

The loss of former Soviet markets led to a decline in the contribution of industry to GDP from 38% to 28% between 1990 and 1997. The immediate impact of the collapse of the former planned economy was a sharp fall in GDP, with further setbacks caused by a banking crisis in 1995 and the 1998 Russian financial crisis. There has since been strong recovery, with 7.4% real growth in GDP forecast for 2004, although per capita GDP remains substantially below the levels of the established EU member states. Services are now the main driver of growth. Most enterprises have now been privatized, though the state retains a substantial interest in some sectors.

GDP (purchasing power parity) $23.9bn. (2004 est.); GDP per capita (purchasing power parity) $10,200 (2004 est.).

2 Trade Unionism

All workers, except uniformed members of the military, may join trade unions. The Free Trade Union Confederation of Latvia (LBAS) is the only centre and is descended from the old Soviet era trade union structure. LBAS did not restructure itself until 1990. In 1991 the level of union density was as high as 77%, reflecting the compulsory nature of trade unionism in the past. The subsequent decline in the proportion of workers in unions has continued in recent years, from 25% in 1998 to 20% in 2002. The most dramatic decline in this latter period was for the under-30 age group, for which the proportion in unions halved – from 15% to 8%. Just as the opening up to the free market of larger enterprises has proceeded relatively slowly in Latvia, the trade union sector appears relatively ossified. The US State Department Human Rights report for 1999 said that, "in general the trade union movement is undeveloped and still in transition from the socialist to the free market model".

Latvia ratified ILO Conventions No. 87 (Freedom of Association and Protection of the Right to Organize, 1948) and No. 98 (Right to Organize and Collective Bargaining, 1949) in 1992. There have been several changes in the law relevant to trade unions since 2000. Completely new laws introduced in 2002-03 include the Labour Protection Law, the State Labour Inspection Law, the Labour Law, the Labour Dispute Law, and the Law on Protection of Employees in the Case of Insolvency of the Employer. Significant amendments have been made to the Law on Strikes. The Law on Trade Unions now states that unions can be registered if they have at least 50 members or one quarter of the workforce in a particular organization.

During 2002 medics of the Latvian Health and Social Workers' Trade Union went on strike three times for more government financing and higher wages. The union claimed seven thousand participated in a street march. The dispute was resolved when the new government increased funding for health care. However, the union continued to protest government policy in 2003. In February 2002 the Latvian Journalists' Union protested against the dismissal of the director-general of Latvian state television, arguing it was politically motivated, and sought assistance from the International Federation of Journalists to lobby the Latvian government.

3 Trade Union Centre

Free Trade Union Confederation of Latvia (LBAS)
Address. Bruninieku 29/31, 1001 Riga
Phone. +371 727 0351
Fax. +371 727 6649
E-mail. lbas@com.latnet.lv
Website. www.lbas.lv (Latvian; Russian; English)
Leadership. Peteris Krigers (president)
Membership. 200,000 in 26 branch unions
History and character. LBAS is the reformed Soviet era trade union structure, reorganized in 1990. It is politically independent but in 2002 LBAS agreed to consult with the Latvian Social Democratic Workers' Party, a democratic socialist party descended from the Soviet-era ruling party which (as the Latvian Social Democratic Union) had won 14 parliamentary seats in 1998, but failed to secure a sufficient percentage of the popular vote to win a seat in the October 2002 elections.
International affiliation. ICFTU; ETUC

Lebanon

Capital: Beirut
Population: 3.78 m. (2004 est.)

1 Political and Economic Background

Lebanon became fully independent from France in 1944. It was formerly a regional commercial and financial centre but the economic infrastructure and political authority progressively decayed following the outbreak of civil war in 1975. The war, fought out by militias largely organized on religious lines, and with intervention by Lebanon's neighbours on the different sides, disrupted the fragile compromise on which the state had been established since the National Covenant of 1943. Under this compromise, the President was conventionally a Maronite Christian, the Prime Minister a Sunni Muslim, and the Speaker of the National Assembly a Shia Muslim.

Since the end of the war in 1991 considerable stability has been restored. Although Israel withdrew its troops from southern Lebanon in 2000, parts of the country are under military control by Syria (including parts of Beirut) or the Shia militants of Hizbollah. The economic infrastructure was progressively rebuilt during the 1990s. There is relatively little industry, with most of the private sector workforce in services. Lebanon has also suffered from the long-term emigration of educated professionals, only a few of whom have returned to participate in the peacetime economy. In April 2004 it was reported that remittances were the main source of foreign exchange earnings for Lebanon.

Once buoyant banking institutions are slowly recovering, as is tourism; but many Lebanese complain that Syria uses their country as a place to "dump" cheap and subsidized produce. Similarly, there is resentment at the influx of up to a million Syrian citizens who are taking jobs that some Lebanese feel should be reserved for local workers. In September 2004 it was announced that a newly founded labour party would take up issues of workers' rights and demands.

GDP (purchasing power parity) $17.82bn. (2003 est.); GDP per capita (purchasing power parity) $4,800 (2003 est.).

2 Trade Unionism

Lebanon ratified ILO Convention No. 98 (Right to Organize and Collective Bargaining, 1949) in 1977 but has not ratified Convention No. 87 (Freedom of Association and Protection of the Right to Organize, 1948).

The first trade unions appeared under French rule. The labour movement tended to remain fractured on craft, religious or political lines as it came under pressure from the same forces that destroyed the country's unity. The unions lost members and in many respects ceased to function during the civil war. The labour movement remains fragmented and this is reflected in the fact that the ICFTU records no less than 13 affiliates for Lebanon, far more than for any other country. The closest to a trade union centre is the General Confederation of Lebanese Workers (CGTL), although this is not itself affiliated to the ICFTU.

There are an estimated 160 unions and associations, with some 375,000 members; about 200,000 workers are reported to be in the 22 organizations affiliated to the CGTL. Palestinian refugees may organize their own unions, but few of them are in unions. Government employees may not form unions or bargain collectively. The government must authorize the formation of unions and approve the results of all trade union elections, and unions may be dissolved administratively.

Unions may not engage in political activities. Governments of Lebanon still warily recall how unions led the mass protests of 1992, which brought down the government of then Prime Minister Omar Karami. There has been regular government interference in union elections and affairs, including those of the CGTL. According to an article by Gary C. Gambill, in the *Middle East Intelligence Bulletin*: "Syria has pushed its client regime in Beirut to effectively eliminate the Lebanese labour movement, leaving unskilled Lebanese workers with little capacity to voice their grievances.

Syrian intelligence was heavily involved in the July 1995 crackdown against widespread demonstrations organized by Lebanon's [CGTL]."

3 Trade Union Centre

Confédération Générale des Travailleurs du Liban (CGTL)
General Confederation of Lebanese Workers
Leadership. Ghassan Ghosn (president)
History and character. Founded in 1958, the CGTL loosely confederates some 22 trade union organizations. In the years following the end of the civil war in 1991, the CGTL called a succession of strikes and protests, notably in July 1995, on issues such as living standards, privatization, corruption and restrictions on civil liberties. These protests attracted hostile attention from the government, assisted, it is alleged, by the Syrian intelligence agency. Elias Abu Rizk, then president of the CGTL, called for a nationwide strike and demonstrations on Nov. 28, 1996, to protest the pending and controversial closure of unlicensed radio stations by then prime minister, Rafiq Hariri.

Abu Rizk was re-elected CGTL president in April 1997, despite a campaign of government intimidation including seizure of CGTL premises. The government then recognized a breakaway faction, under the leadership of Ghoneim Zoghbi, and arrested Abu Rizk. His deputy, Yasser Nehme, was also fired. The regional head of the ILO then visited Lebanon in June, to intercede on Abu Rizk's behalf. In May 1998 the government withdrew its support for Zoghbi's faction, and in July it recognized Elias Abu Rizk's legitimate candidacy. On Sept. 30, 1998, the executive committee of the CGTL overwhelmingly re-elected Abu Rizk to his former post.

Although Abu Rizk has been described as a popular leader, controversy continued in ensuing years. In early 1999 he insisted on the need for urgent dialogue between unions, firms and government, to address the twin scourges of mass emigration of skilled workers, and a national unemployment rate that was unofficially estimated at 25%. In April 2000 Abu Rizk relayed an ILO survey that indicated that 48% of families in Lebanon were living in "ultra poverty". In August-September 2000 general elections, Abu Rizk stood as a candidate for the opposition Democratic Change list.

Elias Abu Rizk was ousted once more as head of the CGTL in March 2001. Two months later a shop belonging to Maroun Abu Rizk, elder brother to Elias, was bombed in Marjayoun, southern Lebanon; allegedly Maroun had collaborated with Israelis, and had levied taxes for the Israeli-allied force, the South Lebanon Army. Elias Abu Rizk himself had often condemned Israeli actions in Lebanon. In June 2003 Lebanon's Criminal Appeals Court was still deliberating the case of Abu Rizk and Nehme. The pair were accused of "spoiling Lebanon's image abroad" by telling the ILO in 1997 that union elections held then had been rigged. Another court accused them of forgery regarding the same suspect elections.

Ghassan Ghosn replaced Abu Rizk as CGTL president, but, to the government's chagrin, continued the CGTL tradition of critical engagement. In January

2003 he blamed Beirut's political class for "abandoning its role to look after society" by pushing the public transport sector towards privatization, at the expense of workers' rights. Ghosn cited the case of the Lebanese Transport Company, which had debarred workers from joining a union.

In September 2003 he accused the finance ministry of breaking promises of better wages and promotions to workers of the Electricité du Liban (EDL) Workers and Employees' Union. These promises were made in August 2001 by a labour ministry arbitrator. Charbel Saleh, head of the EDL workers' union, announced that members would strike from Dec. 29, 2004, over issues of medical coverage and compensation. The union also asked the government to separate the EDL from "internal political conflicts". EDL, a state-owned enterprise, is $3bn. in debt. There was also a persistent dispute between teachers' unions and the authorities during early 2004.

On May 27, 2004, the CGTL called a one-day strike in Beirut to demand that the government repeal a 40% tax on petrol (levied in an effort to reduce the country's massive debt). Police opened fire during the protest when demonstrators stormed the Labour Ministry building. Six died in the conflagration, marking the worst civil unrest in more than a decade. The incident embarrassed the government, as Beirut was preparing to host in June a meeting of the Organization of Petroleum Exporting Countries (OPEC) for the first time since 1972; the summit coincided with soaring oil prices, which were having a devastating effect on ordinary Lebanese workers. On June 30, 2004, the CGTL called off another one-day strike.

In August 2004 new fears arose about political intervention designed to weaken, and possibly even destroy, the CGTL. Confederation pesident Ghosn held a conference that month, which was supported by the Shiite Amal movement and Syrian Social Nationalist Party. At the event Ghosn warned about an imminent Lebanese "economic and social collapse". He called for the doubling of the minimum wage, reduction of "unjust" indirect taxes, and preservation of the threatened National Social Security Fund. In addition Ghosn rejected privatization projects and arbitrary dismissals and demanded the establishment of a fund for unemployment, to be financed by the CGTL, the labour ministry and the Lebanese Industrialists' Association. In January 2005 Ghosn ascribed to CGTL lobbying the decision by Mohammed Karaké, director-general of the National Fund for Social Security, to pay some of the arrears. At the same time, the union centre "deplored the absence of social dialogue" in Lebanon as a whole.

Lesotho

Capital: Maseru
Population: 1.86 m (2004 est.)

Lesotho is a constitutional monarchy which has experienced considerable instability since independence from Britain in the 1960s. The first post-independence election of 1970 was annulled by the ruling Basotho National Party (BNP), to be followed by 16 years of one-party rule, which was terminated by a military coup of January 1986. After seven years the junta was forced by global trends and local pressures to agree to an election and a constitutional order, which was restored in March 1993, with the Basotho Congress Party (BCP) winning elections. The nascent democracy was rocked by intermittent mutinies in the army and police, strikes throughout the working sectors, seditious acts from the former ruling party and two brief coups. After a virtual coup of September 1998 South African military intervention under the auspices of the Southern African Development Community restored order. The local political parties agreed on the modification of the election model to combine elements of the winner-takes-all, first-past-the-post model with the more representative elements of the proportional representation model. This allowed entry of nine other parties into parliament in the May 2002 elections even though the cabinet still consists exclusively of the largest party, the Lesotho Congress for Democracy (LCD), whose formation in parliament and usurpation of ruling party status from the BCP in 1997 was largely responsible for the upheavals of 1998.

The main economic activity for the majority of the population is agriculture, which remains largely subsistence in nature. The primary sector, comprising agriculture, mining and quarrying, is the largest internal employer, absorbing 70 percent of the labour force. Since 2002 the tertiary sector has become the second largest sector, accounting for 41.3 percent of GDP. Until recently the government remained the main source of internal employment, while temporary migration to the mines in neighbouring South Africa is still the main source of employment for rural males. From the late 1980s a vibrant textile and apparel manufacturing industry emerged and grew rapidly, making it possible that for the first time in the country's history private sector employment exceeded that of the civil service at the beginning of this century. This trend was noticeably accelerated by preferential access to the US market under the Africa Growth and Opportunity Act (AGOA). Manufacturing employment, which remains dominated by female workers, leapt from roughly 26,000 in 2000 to approximately 50,000 in 2002. Since 2001 the government has, with the technical support of the ILO, tried to move away from the practice where a statutory minimum wage is established centrally for each job category by a tripartite Wages Advisory Board subject to the veto of the Minister of Employment and Labour. The ultimate goal is to devolve the process to bilateral sector-wide consultations between employers and workers, with the government acting only as a facilitator. Due to the prior practice where the minister had a final say in the determination of the minimum wage, remuneration rates have remained significantly low in comparison with the average worker's needs and the cost of living.

GDP (purchasing power parity) $5.58bn. (2004 est.); GDP per capita (purchasing power parity) $3,000 (2004 est.).

2 Trade Unionism

Lesotho has ratified all the major conventions of the ILO, including ILO Conventions No. 87 (Freedom of Association and Protection of the Right to Organize, 1948) and No. 98 (Right to Organize and Collective Bargaining, 1949), both in 1966. However, implementation continues to be hard to realise in practice for the most part. Labour relations and standards are governed by the Labour Code Order No. 24 of 1992, which was evolved by a tripartite process, and was widely acknowledged as a good basis for a further democratization of labour relations. During the late 1990s the Code was substantially amended with ILO technical support. The process, which involved the three social partners, focused mainly on the creation of an independent, accessible, and effective mechanism for mediation and arbitration of disputes. As a result a putatively highly effective Directorate of Dispute Prevention and Resolution (DDPR) has been in place for about six years, and has earned a positive reputation and growing goodwill. The government, however, has legislated since 1995 to exclude civil servants from all labour laws, thus rendering them vulnerable to workplace mistreatment and leaving them with only the costly avenue of the High Court for redress.

The manufacturing sector, which has formed the hub of unionism over the past ten years, continues to be a lightning rod in the relations between organized labour and the government. In November 2003 at least four women members of the newly-formed Factory Workers' Union (FAWU) were shot dead by the police during a march to present a memorandum of grievances to employers and the national authorities. The union's general secretary and his deputy, together with the national organizer, were charged with contravening conditions of the march and inciting damage to property.

There is no one national trade union centre, the two main centres previously being the Congress of Lesotho Trade Unions (COLETU) and the Lesotho Trade Union Congress (LTUC). There have been recent efforts, cutting across seemingly entrenched rivalries, towards forming a single national centre. As a result, some unions which were under the Lesotho Federation of Democratic Unions (LFDU), whose general secretary was Ts'eliso Ramochela, came together with some affiliates of COLETU to form a new federation – the Lesotho Congress of Democratic Unions – in May 2004. However, some leaders of COLETU and the LTUC, together with some unions therein, felt that the merger was "rushed" and that details like membership and property audits should precede a formal merger. On this count mainly, COLETU and the LTUC remained out of the new merger – which effectively became a merger of one federation with some affiliates from another federation.

The various unions do not affiliate formally to any political party, though the affiliations of individual trade union leaders tend to be well known. The exception is the formation of the Lesotho Workers' Party by the Lesotho Clothing and Allied Workers' Union (LECAWU) in 2001. This won one of the compensatory seats in parliament in the 2002 elections, this being taken by the union's general secretary Macaefa Billy. The law does not allow MPs to be union leaders; Billy stood down as general secretary in favour of Daniel Maraisane but friction between them over control of the union resulted in Billy forming the Factory Workers' Union (FAWU), with Willy Mats'eo as its general secretary, as a splinter from the LECAWU. The LECAWU went on to become a founding member of LECODU while the newly-formed FAWU remained under the COLETU.

3 Trade Union Centres

Congress of Lesotho Trade Unions (COLETU)
Address. PO Box 13282, Maseru 104
Phone. +266 22 322 035
Fax. +266 22 321 951
Leadership. Vuyani Tyhali (general secretary)
Affiliates. Factory Workers' Union; Lesotho Teachers' Trade Union; Lesotho University Teachers and Researchers' Union; Non-Academic Workers' Union; Lesotho Wholesale, Catering and Allied Workers' Union; Lentsoe La Sechaba Workers' Union; Lesotho Transport and Allied Workers' Union; Drivers, Earthmoving Operations and Allied Workers' Union.
International affiliation. CTUC

Lesotho Congress of Democratic Unions (LECODU)
Address. PO Box 15851, Maseru 104
Phone. +266 22 323 559
Fax. +266 22 323 559
Leadership. Ts'eliso Ramochela (general secretary)
History and character. LECODU was formed in May 2004 by a merger of unions in the Lesotho Federation of Democratic Unions (LFDU) with some affiliates of COLETU, the LFDU general secretary Ts'eliso Ramochela becoming general secretary of the new centre.
Affiliates. Lesotho Transport and General Workers' Union; Lesotho Association of Teachers; National Union of Retail and Allied Workers; Lesotho Clothing and Allied Workers' Union; National Union of Hotels, Food and Allied Workers; Construction and Allied Workers' Union of Lesotho; National Union of Textile Workers; Lesotho Commercial, Catering, Food and Allied Workers' Union; Lesotho Security and Allied Workers' Union; Lesotho Industrial and Allied Workers' Union.
International Affiliation. CTUC

Lesotho Trade Union Congress (LTUC)
Address. PO Box 727, Maseru 100
Phone. +266 22 312 768
Fax. +266 22 312 76
Leadership. Simom M. Jonathane (general secretary)
Affiliates. Lesotho Industrial, Commercial and Allied Workers' Union; Lesotho Commercial, Distributive Allied Workers' Union; Lesotho Steel, Metal and Allied Workers' Union; National Union of Publishing, Printing and Allied Workers; Lesotho Brickmaking and Allied Workers' Union.

Liberia

Capital: Monrovia
Population: 3.39 m. (2004 est.)

1 Political and Economic Background

The Republic of Liberia, an independent state from 1847, was founded by freed black slaves from the USA, whose descendants dominated the government until 1980. President (then Master-Sergeant) Samuel K. Doe seized power in a bloody 1980 coup and ruled through the People's Redemption Council. A civil war broke out in 1989 and led to Doe's overthrow and death in 1990. Fighting continued, however, with internationally sponsored peace agreements collapsing until 1996. In 1997 elections were held resulting in a large majority in the legislature for the National Patriotic Front of Liberia and the election of its presidential candidate, Charles Taylor, who had launched the rebellion that led to the overthrow of Doe in 1990.

Fresh fighting erupted in mid-2000 and by 2003 rebel forces of the Liberians United for Democracy (LURD) and the Movement for Democracy in Liberia (MODEL) had closed in on Monrovia. President Taylor – who had been indicted for war crimes by UN prosecutors in Sierra Leone – came under intense international pressure to agree to resign. Taylor stood down as President in August 2003 and took up an offer of refuge in Nigeria. Shortly afterwards, a peace agreement was signed under the terms of which Gyude Bryant, a little known businessman, was installed as chairman of a transitional government of national unity, which was intended to hand power to an elected administration by January 2006.

About 70% of the workforce are engaged in agriculture, largely at subsistence level. The country is also a source of primary commodities, notably iron ore, timber, rubber and diamonds, exploitation of which tends to be in the hands either of the state or of multinationals. However, since 2001 the UN has imposed sanctions on the export of timber and diamonds. Civil war and misgovernment have destroyed much of Liberia's economy, especially the infrastructure in and around Monrovia. Despite the 2003 peace agreement, the country faces massive problems, including a lack of infrastructure, corruption and the continued threat of inter-ethnic violence. The Liberian maritime registry, the "flag of convenience" shipping network that covers around a third of the world's shipping tonnage, has generated annual revenues averaging around $18 m. Much of the money is reported to have been diverted into the accounts of former President Taylor and his cohorts.

GDP (purchasing power parity) $3.261bn. (2004 est.); GDP per capita (purchasing power parity) $1,000 (2004 est.).

2 Trade Unionism

Liberia ratified ILO Conventions No. 87 (Freedom of Association and Protection of the Right to Organize, 1948) and No. 98 (Right to Organize and Collective Bargaining, 1949) in 1962. Trade unions have had legal status since 1963 but there has been only modest development and they have been subject to numerous restrictions.

Before the civil war of 1989-96 the main focus of trade union activity was in the plantations of the Firestone rubber company, then the biggest employer in the country, which saw battles for union recognition. This closed its operations in 1989 as a result of the civil war, resuming operations, on a smaller scale, in 1996.

Civil conflict and economic collapse since the 1990s has seriously undermined the trade union movement, although there are a number of functioning unions. Most of the population is engaged in subsistence agriculture and in the towns there is wholesale unemployment and dependence on informal economic activity. There has been persistent government interference in union affairs, especially in leadership struggles. The main union centre is the Liberian Federation of Labour Unions (LFLU), affiliated to the ICFTU, but WCL affiliates have also traditionally been active in Liberia. Under the constitution unions are barred from taking part in political activity. There is a nominal right of all workers, except civil servants, to engage in collective bargaining but this has little practical application. In November 2004 the National Transitional Government opened round table discussions with the management of Firestone and officials of the General Agricultural Workers' Union (GAWUL), and the Firestone Workers' Union (FAWUL) in an effort to amicably resolve strike action, which began on plantation in October.

3 Trade Union Centres

Liberian Federation of Labour Unions (LFLU)
Address. J.B. McGill Labor Center, Gardnersville Freeway, PO Box 415, Monrovia
Phone. +231 331 389; +231 226 888
Fax. +231 226 132; +231 226 219; +231 226 064
E-mail. 1fluorganization2001@yahoo.com
Leadership. Aloysius S. Kie (president); J. Walker Barnes (vice-president); G. Isaac William (secretary general)
History and character. Formed in 1980 by amalgamation of the United Workers' Congress and the Liberia federation of Trade Unions (the latter formed in 1977 by merger of the former Congress of Industrial Organizations and Labour Congress of Liberia, both of which had been founded in the 1950s). In June 2004 the LFLU inducted into office a leadership to lead the organization during the transitional period.
International affiliation. ICFTU

4 Other Trade Union Organizations

Federation of Organizations Affiliated to ODSTA/WCL
Address. PO Box 4436, Ashmun Street, Monrovia
Leadership. Levelaku B. Stanley (president)
International affiliation. WCL

United Seamen Ports and General Workers' Union of Liberia (USPOGUL)
Mobile. +37747-553439/00231-553439
E-Mail. seafareruspogul@yahoo.com
Leadership. C. Alfred Thomas, Sr. (president)

Libya

Capital: Tripoli
Population: 5.41m. (2003 est.)

1 Political and Economic Background

The monarchy was overthrown in a military coup in 1969 led by Col. Moamer al Kadhafi, who has remained the ruler of the country as the "leader of the revolution" although holding no official position. There is a hierarchy of people's committees, which form an indirect electoral base for the General People's Congress, which functions as the legislature. Kadhafi's Arab Socialist Union is the sole permitted political party and there is no significant organized domestic opposition.

The economy is based on oil, which is government controlled. There has been some effort since 1992 to diversify and encourage the private sector but there is extensive state regulation and the majority of the work force are in the state sector. As of 2002 it was estimated that less than 30% of the population participated in the formal labour market. The native labour force consisted then of 1.2m. workers; much work is performed by some 2m. foreign workers, both skilled and unskilled, from 24 other African countries and the West. In October 2000 there were reports of hundreds of black African migrant workers being killed in "xenophobic" riots in coastal towns. UN sanctions were suspended in 1999 and Libya has been seeking to encourage foreign investment.

GDP (purchasing power parity) $35bn. (2003 est.); GDP per capita (purchasing power parity) $6,400 (2003 est.).

2 Trade Unionism

Under the old Sanussi monarchy the federal government would often rely on provincial authorities to quash militant workers: for instance, after 1959 the governor of Tripolitania used "blackleg" urban unemployed to break a strike called by the Libyan General Labour Union. The state then charged the LGLU general secretary with state security offences; though he was later released, the LGLU was effectively smashed.

Two major union federations survived: the Libyan General Workers' Federation and the Libyan Federation of Labour and Professional Union. In the absence of effective political parties, these two bodies engaged in overt political rivalry, notably in 1960. Labour unrest died down in 1961, and a year later Libya ratified ILO Convention No. 98 (Right to Organize and Collective Bargaining, 1949). During the June 1967 Arab-Israeli war students joined forces with protesting trade unionists; oil and dock workers went on strike, refusing to pump oil or load tankers. The regime called a mass trial in response, which effectively removed militant union leaders by August 1967.

Under the Kadhafi regime, independent trade unions are not permitted and a single-trade-union system is in force, organized by the General Federation of Producers' Trade Unions (GFPTU), created in 1972. This is closely associated with the regime and is affiliated internationally to the WFTU. No strikes have been reported for many years. According to the government, workers may strike but do not need to because they control their enterprises. External sources, however, reject this assessment. Libya has still not ratified ILO Convention No. 87 (Freedom of Association and Protection of the Right to Organize, 1948).

Liechtenstein

Capital: Vaduz
Population: 33,000 (2004 est.)

1 Political and Economic Background

The Principality of Liechtenstein is a constitutional and hereditary monarchy. The government was formed by the Patriotic Union (VU) party from 1997-2001 and the opposition led by the (more conservative) Progressive Citizens' Party (FBPL), the two parties switching roles as a result of elections in February 2001. Prior to 1997 these two parties were in coalition continuously from 1938. In March 2003 the electorate voted in a referendum to approve constitutional revisions which gave the Crown Prince sweeping new powers, including to dissolve parliament and appoint an interim government, rule by emergency decree, dismiss individual members of the government, and veto parliamentary legislation by not signing bills within six months.

Liechtenstein enjoys a high standard of living. Its industrial sector employs a substantial number of resident foreigners together with thousands who come to work daily from neighbouring Switzerland and Austria. The other major sector of the economy is financial services, Liechtenstein being a centre for offshore banking. There is virtually no unemployment.

GDP (purchasing power parity) $825m. (1999 est.); GDP per capita (purchasing power parity) $25,000 (1999 est.).

2 Trade Unionism

All workers, including foreign workers, are free to join unions. There is only one trade union, the Liechtenstein Employees' Association (LANV). Collective bargaining agreements are usually based on agreements reached in Switzerland and the LANV has negotiated agreements covering about 50% of workers. There is a right to strike, other than in essential services, but strikes are rare.

Liechtenstein is not a member of the International Labour Organization.

3 Trade Union Centre

Liechtensteiner Arbeitnehmerverband (LANV)
Liechtenstein Employees' Association
Address. Dorfstrasse 24, 9495 Triesen
Phone. +423 399 38 38
Fax. +423 399 38 39
E-mail. info@lanv.li
Website. www.lanv.li (in German)
Leadership. Sigi Langenbahn (president)
Membership. 1,300
History and character. Founded in 1920, the LANV is the only union in Liechtenstein and represents all sectors, though the majority of workers are not members. Its activities include negotiation of collective bargaining agreements and it also has a role in representing Liechtenstein workers as a whole in tripartite forums. The LANV is politically independent but has a Christian social orientation emphasizing social partnership.
International affiliation. WCL

Lithuania

Capital: Vilnius
Population: 3.61 m. (2004 est.)

1 Political and Economic Background

Lithuania, under Soviet rule from World War II, resumed de facto independence in 1990. Its independence was recognized by the USSR in September 1991. The Lithuanian Reform Movement (Sajudis) led the drive for independence, and won elections in 1990, but in 1992, in the face of economic adversity, the electorate voted the reformed communists of the Lithuanian Democratic Labour Party (LDDP) into office. In 1996 elections resulted in the formation of a coalition government led by the conservative Homeland Union (TS) party, itself the successor to Sajudis. Since the mid-1990s right of centre parties and the Social Democratic Labour Party have each held power and party politics have remained fractious and unstable. In April 2004 the President, Rolandas Paksas, was forced from office after impeachment proceedings for alleged links to Russian organized crime. In legislative elections in October 2004, the newly formed Labour Party, founded the previous year by a Russian-born populist business magnate, Viktor Uspaskich, came first with 28.4% of the vote and 39 of the 141 seats. It subsequently formed a coalition government with the Social Democrats and the Social Liberals.

The early 1990s were marked by deep economic difficulty in the aftermath of independence and the collapse of the Soviet planned economy, and disputes over the pace and nature of privatization. GDP grew strongly thereafter before declining in 1999 in the wake of the financial crisis of August 1998 in Russia, Lithuania's leading trading partner. There has since been recovery but unemployment remains relatively high, at 10.7% in 2003. There is a continuing privatization programme with 80% of enterprises now privatized although a few significant enterprises remain under state control. Foreign direct investment has slumped following the near completion of the privatization process. Lithuania gained accession to the EU on May 1, 2004 along with seven other Central and East European states.

GDP (purchasing power parity) $40.88bn. (2003 est.); GDP per capita (purchasing power parity) $11,400 (2003 est.).

2 Trade Unionism

The 1992 Constitution and the 1991 Law on Trade Unions recognize the right to form and join trade unions. Lithuania ratified ILO Conventions No. 87 (Freedom of Association and Protection of the Right to Organize, 1948) and No. 98 (Right to Organize and Collective Bargaining, 1949) in 1994. The Law on Trade Unions formally extends this right to employees of the police and armed forces, although the Collective Agreements Law of 1991 did not allow collective bargaining by government employees involved in law enforcement and security related work until 2003. However, after the new Labour Code came into force (on Jan. 1, 2003) state employees, including employees of the police and armed forces, gained the right to collective bargaining and to conclude collective agreements. According to the law, unions, in order to be registered, must have at least 30 founding members in large enterprises or have a membership of one-fifth of all employees in small enterprises (not less than three workers). About 14% of the labour force are unionized, with a total of 200,000 union members.

Independent trade unionism began as early as 1988 with the formation of the Lithuanian Workers' Union (LDS), linked to the movement for national independence, Sajudis. The history of the trade union centres since independence has been a complex one of fragmentation and changes of name, with disputes over the assets of the former official unions. The LDS and the Lithuanian Trade Unions Unification (LPSS, primarily descended from the former official unions), affiliated to the ICFTU in 1994. The LDS is now known as Solidarity ("Solidarumas") and the LPSS has become a component of the Lithuanian Trade Union Confederation (LPSK), these two successor organizations retaining the ICFTU affiliation. The third centre is the Lithuanian Federation of Labour (LDF). There are also a number of unions not affiliated to any of these centres, although these in total have only about 4% of the unionized workforce. The LPSK is much the biggest centre, representing 60% of all trade union members.

Collective bargaining is provided for under the Collective Agreements Law, although collective bargaining is not widespread. The government issues wage guidelines for the state sector. There is a legal right to strike; however, there are lengthy pre-strike procedures and a two-thirds majority in favour of action is required in a secret ballot. Strike action in the services of internal affairs and state security, enterprises of centralized electricity energy, supply of heating and gas, and urgent medical support is forbidden. The highest level tripartite body is the Tripartite Council of the Republic of Lithuania (LRTT), on which the LPSK has two representatives and Solidarumas and LDF each have one.

3 Trade Union Centres

Lithuanian Federation of Labour
Lietuvos Darbo Federacija (LDF)
Address. V. Mykolaicio-Putino 5-140, LT-2600 Vilnius
Phone/Fax. +370 5 2 31 20 29
E-mail. janinasv@one.lt
Leadership. Vydas Puskepalis (president)
Membership. 20,000
History and character. In 1919 a Christian trade union – the Lithuanian Labor Federation – was established. It was dissolved during the Soviet occupation, but in 1991 when independence was restored the LDF was recreated. For some time (until 1996) this centre was a part of the former Lithuanian Trade Unions Community. LDF collaborates with the other trade union centres; it is a member of the World Confederation of Labour (WCL) and since 2002 has been a full member of the European Trade Union Confederation (ETUC). It retains a distinctively social Christian dimension.
International affiliation. WCL; ETUC

Lithuanian Trade Union Confederation
Lietuvos Profesiniu Sajungu Konfederacija (LPSK)
Address. J. Jasinskio 9-213, LT-2600 Vilnius
Phone. +370 5 2 496 921
Fax. +370 5 2 498 078
E-mail. lpsk@lpsk.lt
Website. www.lpsk.lt
Leadership. Arturas Cerniauskas (president)
Membership. 124,000
History and character. The LPSK (or LTUC) was established on May 1, 2002, when two Lithuanian national trade union centres – Lithuanian Trade Unions Unification (LPSS) and Lithuanian Trade Unions Centre (LTUC) – united. Currently the LPSK consists of 25 branch trade unions, which unite approximately 124,000 members. This is the largest trade union centre in Lithuania. It became a member of ICFTU (through the LPSS) in 1994 and a member of ETUC in 2002. It also represents Lithuanian workers in the ILO.
International affiliations. ICFTU; ETUC

Lithuanian Trade Union - Solidarity
Lietuvos Profesine Sajunga "Solidarumas"
Address. V. Mykolaicio-Putino g. 5-212, 03106 Vilnius
Phone. +370 5 2 621 743
Fax. +370 5 2 133 295
E-mail. lds@centras.lt
Leadership. Aldona Balsiene (president)
Membership. 52,000
History and character. Solidarumas is the renamed (in June 2002) Lithuanian Workers' Union (LDS), originally formed as a branch of Lithuania's national revival movement 'Sajudis'. It consists of 19 city/region workers' unions and 11 trade federations. The LDS became a member of the ICFTU in 1994 and gained observer status with ETUC in 1998 and is now a full member.
International affiliation. ICFTU; ETUC

Luxembourg

Capital: Luxembourg-Ville
Population: 463,000 (2004 est.)

1 Political and Economic Background

Historically the strongest party has been the (Christian democratic) Christian Social People's Party (CSV). Since 1919 it has formed coalition governments with various other parties and the Prime Minister has almost continuously come from the CSV. From 1984 to 1999 the CSV ruled in coalition with the social democratic Luxembourg Socialist Workers' Party (LSAP). Following elections in June 1999, a new coalition was formed in which the CSV was joined by the liberal Democratic Party (DP). The CSV again came first in the most recent elections, in June 2004, and formed a new coalition with the LSAP, which had won the second largest number of seats, Jean-Claude Juncker continuing as Prime Minister. Luxembourg is a founder member of the EU and a base for a number of its institutions. It joined the single European currency at its launch on Jan. 1, 1999. A large majority of the population is formally Roman Catholic.

The Luxembourg economy was traditionally based on iron and steel, but as that industry declined it has successfully developed a range of other industries and a major financial services sector, in addition to its role as a pivotal centre of the EU. 90% of the workforce are now employed in services and only 8% in industry. Economic growth averaged 5% per annum from the mid-1980s to the end of the century, and although Luxembourg has been affected by the sluggish pace of the European economy in recent years, it retains a high standard of living with the highest per capita income in the EU. More than one-third of the labour force is foreign, coming primarily from other EU countries.

GDP (purchasing power parity) $25.01bn. (2004 est.); GDP per capita (purchasing power parity) $55,100 (2004 est.).

2 Trade Unionism

Luxembourg ratified ILO Conventions No. 87 (Freedom of Association and Protection of the Right to Organize, 1948) and No. 98 (Right to Organize and Collective Bargaining, 1949) in 1958. The workforce is highly organized, with about 57% belonging to unions. There are two major trade union centres, the Luxembourg Confederation of Christian Trade Unions (LCGB) and the Luxembourg Confederation of Independent Trade Unions (OGB-L). The OGB-L also forms the core of the Luxembourg General

Confederation of Labour (CGTL), an umbrella which is the affiliate of the ICFTU. The centres are independent politically, but there are traditional links between the LCGB and the Christian Social People's Party (CSV) and between the OGB-L and the social democratic Luxembourg Socialist Workers' Party (LSAP).

The trade union movement is fragmented and relations between unions can be fractious. Under the Luxembourg system, which is somewhat akin to that in Belgium, the designation of being "nationally representative" confers significant rights and discriminates against unions without this status. These rights include representation on the country's numerous and influential tripartite bodies, such as the National Conciliation Office and the Tripartite Coordination Committee. In addition, only "nationally representative" organizations, or their affiliates, can conclude legally enforceable collective bargaining agreements. The status of being "nationally representative" is ultimately determined by government on criteria that are not explicitly defined but depend on quantitative (number of members) and qualitative (stability) factors. A bill to redefine this issue was presented in 2003.

There are currently only two union organizations considered "nationally representative" for both blue- and white-collar workers, the LCGB and the OGB-L, the two main trade union centres. However, many workers support unions not linked to these two. In 1999 banking union ALEBA and the private sector union UEP announced they had formed a new federation (ALEBA/UEP). ALEBA complained to the ILO Committee of Experts on Freedom of Association after the Minister of Labour refused to register an ALEBA collective agreement that was put forward in the name of the new federation. The ILO Committee was critical of the practice and invited the government to review the criteria for assessment of national representative status. In early 2003 ALEBA/UEP went a step further, joining with two other unions to form a broader private sector federation, ALEBA/UEP-NGL-SNEP.

"Social elections" are held every five years (most recently in November 2003) at which workers vote for members of employee committees/works councils and for the so-called "professional chambers". The chambers are consulted on all legislative matters relating to the interests of those whom they represent. Some 93,000 private sector white-collar workers elect representatives to the Chamber of Private Sector White-Collar Staff (Chambre des Employés Privés) while 101,000 blue-collar workers elect representatives to the Chamber of Labour (Chambre du Travail). Turnout in the 2003 election of representatives to the chambers was low, with 34% of private sector white-collar workers voting, and only 30% of blue-collar workers. In the Chamber of White-Collar Staff, the OGB-L took 15 seats and the LCGB ten, while ALEBA/UEP-NGL-SNEP took seven. In the Chamber of Labour, LCGB won nine seats and OGB-L won 23. In the light of these results it now seems unlikely that ALEBA/UEP-NGL-SNEP will achieve its ambition of national representative status, its successes being confined largely to the banking sector where ALEBA was already strong prior to the creation of the new federation.

Collective bargaining is widely practiced in Luxembourg, and employers are obliged to bargain when asked to do so by a "representative" trade union. In the event of breakdown, there is mandatory conciliation procedure through the tripartite National Conciliation Office (Office National de Conciliation). A strike (or lock-out) may not be called until the chair of the Office says that all attempts at conciliation have failed. There was a public sector general strike in 1998 over the issue of civil service pension reform, but industrial relations are generally characterized by a certain level of restraint and there are few strikes.

3 Trade Union Centres

Confédération Générale du Travail du Luxembourg (CGT-L)
Luxembourg General Confederation of Labour

Address. 60 Boulevard J.F. Kennedy, 4170 Esch/Alzette
Phone. +352 54 05 45
Fax. +352 54 16 20
E-mail. ogb-l@ogb-l.lu
Website. www.ogb-l.lu (French/German)
Leadership. John Castegnaro (president)
Membership. 45,000
History and character. The CGT-L was founded in 1927 by the metal workers' union and the federation of railway workers. In 1978 the trade union Lëtzebuerger Aarbechterverband (the precursor of the present Confederation of Independent Trade Unions, OGB-L) took the initiative to form a united trade union movement based on the Austrian or West German model. The Christian trade unions in Luxembourg organized in the LCGB (see below) refused to become part of this new organization, as did some unions in the CGT-L. The outcome was that both the OGB-L and CGT-L continued in existence, with the CGT-L becoming a loose federation embracing the OGB-L, the National Federation of Railway Workers, Transport Workers and Officers (FNCTTFEL) and the Luxembourg Federation of Publishing and Printing Workers (FLTL).

The OGB-L is the dominant factor in the CGT-L, providing it with offices and services, and is the recognized trade union centre within Luxembourg. The CGT-L is a federal umbrella, which holds the affiliations to ICFTU and ETUC. John Castegarno is president of both the OGB-L and the CGT-L.
International affiliations. ICFTU; ETUC; TUAC

Lëtzeburger Chrëschtleche Gewerkschafts-Bond (LCGB)
Luxembourg Confederation of Christian Trade Unions

Address. 11 rue du Commerce, 1351 Luxembourg
Phone. +352 49 94 24 1
Fax. +352 49 94 24 49
E-mail. lcgb@euromail.lu
Website. www.lcgb.lu (French/German)
Leadership. Robert Weber (president); Marc Spautz (secretary general)
Membership. 38,000

History and character. The LCGB was formally created in 1921, although it traces its origins back to the nineteenth century. Its orientation is social-Christian, and it gives no financial aid to political parties and is not involved in party politics. It provides a range of welfare and similar services and conducts collective bargaining. It comprises nine sectoral unions.
International affiliations. WCL; ETUC; TUAC

Onofhängege Gewerkschaftsbond Lëtzebuerg (OGB-L)
Luxembourg Confederation of Independent Trade Unions
Address. 60 Boulevard J.F. Kennedy, 4170 Esch/Alzette
Phone. +352 54 05 45
Fax. +352 54 16 20
E-mail. ogb-l@ogb-l.lu
Website. www.ogb-l.lu (French/German)
Leadership. John Castegnaro (president); Jean-Claude Reding (secretary general)
History and character. The OGB-L was formed in January 1979 as the successor organization to LAV (Lëtzebuerger Aarbechterverband), founded in 1916. It is, with the Christian-influenced LCGB, one of the two Luxembourg trade union centres considered "nationally representative" for all private sector workers. It is the leading force within the CGT-L, which serves as a loose umbrella and holds the affiliations with the ICFTU and ETUC. The OCB-L comprises 15 occupationally based unions.

Macedonia

Capital: Skopje
Population: 2.07 m. (2004 est.)

1 Political and Economic Background

Macedonia, formerly a Yugoslav republic, became independent with the break-up of Yugoslavia in 1991. Its path to general international recognition was obstructed by Greek objections to the name Macedonia, and in 1993 it was admitted to the UN under the title "Former Yugoslav Republic of Macedonia". However, Macedonian independence was achieved without violent upheaval.

Elections in autumn 1998 resulted in the formation of a coalition government led by the nationalist Internal Macedonian Revolutionary Organization (IMRO), the party that led Macedonia to independence. In 2001 there was a seven-month armed insurrection against the central government among the country's Albanian minority; this was settled by international intervention involving a short-term deployment of NATO troops to supervise disarmament by the insurgents, and the adoption of legislation by the Macedonian parliament enhancing the civil and political rights of the Albanians. Further elections in September 2002 resulted in victory for the "Together for Macedonia" coalition and the formation of a government led by the Social Democratic Union of Macedonia (SDSM, the reformed former ruling League of Communists of Macedonia) and including the Liberal Democratic Party (LDP) and the (Albanian) Democratic Union for Integration (DUI).

Macedonia was the poorest Yugoslav republic and the collapse of the planned economy, loss of former markets as a consequence of the disintegration of Yugoslavia, and an economic blockade by Greece (maintained until 1995), led to several years of plummeting output in which GDP halved. There was then a sustained recovery from 1996 until the country was affected by loss of access to markets in Serbia and elsewhere as a result of the 1999 Kosovo crisis, when refugees for a time inflated the population by one-sixth (most subsequently returning home). This was followed by further dislocation to trade and investment in 2001 as a result of the Albanian insurgency within Macedonia (itself a knock-on effect from the Kosovo crisis), with GDP shrinking 4.5% in 2001. There has since been a modest recovery but there are substanial problems of unemployment and under-employment and a very large black economy.

GDP (purchasing power parity) $13.81bn. (2003 est.); GDP per capita (purchasing power parity) $6,700 (2003 est.).

2 Trade Unionism

Macedonia ratified ILO Conventions No. 87 (Freedom of Association and Protection of the Right to Organize, 1948) and No. 98 (Right to Organize and Collective Bargaining, 1949) in 1991, following independence. The Federation of Trade Unions of Macedonia (SSM) is the trade union centre and is the successor to the former Yugoslav official trade union structure, whose assets it has retained. Independent unions are permitted and in the 1990s an Association of Independent and Autonomous Unions (UIASM) was formed, which gained affiliation to the WCL. There is no ICFTU affiliate. The position of the unions has deteriorated since independence as a result of wholesale privatization and the country's economic dificulties, including widespread unemployment (generally estimated as affecting one-third of the workforce), and the growth of the informal sector and small businesses. It is these changes to the economy, rather than formal protections for trade union rights, that have been to the fore with the trade unions; the leading causes of periodic work stoppages and other protests such as road blockades have been pay arrears, issues relating to privatization, and management changes in the state sector. Collective bargaining with the trade unions takes place in 50% of enterprises, though agreements are not always honoured in view of the parlous state of many enterprises. The unions were affected by the 2001 inter-ethnic tension which threatened for a time to split unions.

3 Trade Union Centre

Federation of Trade Unions of Macedonia (SSM)
Address. 12 Udarna brigada, br. 2 a, Skopje
E-mail. ssm_federation@mt.net.mk

Leadership. Vanco Muratovski (president)
History and character. The SSM is the successor to the former Yugoslav official trade unions. It comprises 17 sectoral branch unions, of which the largest is the Trade Union of Education, Science and Culture (SONK), which has 35,000 members. The SSM represents labour in social dialogue, including on the Social and Economic Council, but complains that such dialogue is intermittent and often ineffective. It has been active in leading protests on issues such as wage arrears, which have been widespread in recent years, and in May 2002 there was a public sector general strike, specifically over demands for an increase in the minimum wage. Although the September 2002 elections brought the victory of the SDSM-led coalition "Together for Macedonia", which the SSM supported, relations with the new government have continued to be at times confrontational, the government being under pressure from the IMF, World Bank and EU to rein in very high public sector deficits. Since the new government came into office there have been continuing strikes over issues such as alleged corrupt privatization of state assets, management corruption, worker benefits, and unpaid wages. In January 2005 it was reported that the SSM newspaper would close down, its journalists not having been paid for several months.
International affiliations. Observer status with ETUC

Madagascar

Capital: Antananarivo
Population: 17.5 m. (2004 est.)

1 Political and Economic Background

The Republic of Madagascar became fully independent from France in 1960. It was under military rule from 1972, with Didier Ratsiraka becoming President in 1975. Until 1990 parties only existed within the National Front for the Defence of the Revolution (FNDR). In 1993 multi-party elections were held which resulted in Ratsiraka losing power, but he was re-elected in 1996. In National Assembly elections in 1998 Ratsiraka's Association for the Rebirth of Madagascar (AREMA) and predominantly pro-Ratsiraka independent candidates won a majority of seats.

Serious unrest erupted in the aftermath of the disputed presidential election of December 2001 which resulted in the opposition candidate, Marc Ravalomanana, coming in first place but short of an outright victory over Ratsiraka. After a series of massive street protests, Ravalomanana, the mayor of Antananarivo and a successful businessman, proclaimed himself President in February 2002 and formed a government. With Ravalomanana in control of Antananarivo, Ratsiraka relocated his own government to his stronghold of Toamasina on the east coast and a low-level civil war ensued which ended in July 2002 when Ratsiraka fled the country and forces loyal to Ravalomanana gained control of the whole island. Whilst the war was underway the High Constitutional Court had in April confirmed Ravalomanana's victory in the presidential poll and he had been officially sworn in as President in May. Elections to the National Assembly held in December 2002 resulted in an overwhelming victory for a coalition of parties supporting Ravalomanana.

Agriculture, including fishing and forestry, is a mainstay of the economy, accounting for more than a quarter of GDP and employing four-fifths of the population. The small manufacturing sector includes textiles and processing of agricultural products. Having discarded past socialist economic policies, Madagascar has since the mid-1990s followed a World Bank and IMF led policy of privatization and liberalization. President Ravalomanana has worked aggressively to revive the economy following the 2002 political crisis, which triggered a 12% drop in GDP that year.

GDP (purchasing power parity) $13.02bn. (2004 est.); GDP per capita (purchasing power parity) $800 (2004 est.).

2 Trade Unionism

Madagascar ratified ILO Convention No. 87 (Freedom of Association and Protection of the Right to Organize, 1948) in 1960 and Convention No. 98 (Right to Organize and Collective Bargaining, 1949) in 1998. Under the Ratsiraka regime from 1975 until the early 1990s independent trade unions were restricted in their activities and preference given to government-controlled bodies. The 1992 Constitution and the 1995 labour code gave workers, except those in essential services, the police and military, the right to form and join unions of their own choosing. However, the formal economy is small and the base of unions is narrow and they have little influence. Unions are strongest in the public sector. There are currently two WCL affiliates in Madagascar (SEKRIMA and USAM) and one centre affiliated to the ICFTU (FMM).

Collective bargaining is lawful but in practice is little used. There is a legal right to strike, with restrictions in essential services and subject to conciliation, mediation and arbitration procedures. In law union rights exist in the export processing zones. However, trade union rights are reported in practice to be denied to the 27,000 workers in the zones who are effectively unable to join unions or go on strike; in these zones, according to the ICFTU, the "authorities are unable, or unwilling, to enforce the labour law". One of the national trade union centres, the FMM, has denounced the deplorable conditions in the zones, where wages are often below the legal minimum, working hours excessively long and sexual harassment is rife

3 Trade Union Centres

Fivondronamben'ny Mpiasa Malagasy (FMM)
Confederation of Malagasy Workers
Address. BP 846, Antananarivo 101
Phone. +261 22 205 20
History and character. Founded 1957 but largely lapsed into inactivity during the period of military rule.
International affiliation. ICFTU

Sendika Kristianina Malagasy (SEKRIMA)
Christian Confederation of Malagasy Trade Unions
Address. BP 1035, Route de Majunta-Soarano, Antananarivo 101
Phone. +261 20 222 74 85
Fax. +261 20 222 74 85
Leadership. Jean Chrysostôme Razafimandimby (confederal secretary)
Membership. 7,000
History and character. Formed in 1938 as a section of the Catholic-inspired CFTC (France), the organization became the CCSM in 1956 and adopted the name SEKRIMA in 1964, From 100,000 members in the mid-1950s, it declined in importance during the 1960s under the first republic. It virtually ceased to exist after 1972, but it revived in the 1980s.
International affiliation. WCL

Union des Syndicats Autonomes de Madagascar (USAM)
United Autonomous Unions of Madagascar
Address. BP 1038, Lot III M 33, Andrefan' Ambohijanahary, Antananarivo 101
Phone. +261 20 222 74 85
Fax. +261 20 222 74 85
E-mail. usam@dts.mg
Leadership. Norbert Rakotomanana (president); Samuel A. Rabemanantsoa (secretary)
International affiliation. WCL

Malawi

Capital: Lilongwe
Population: 11.91 m. (2004 est.)

1 Political and Economic Background

The former British protectorate of Nyasaland, Malawi became a republic within the Commonwealth in 1966, two years after gaining independence from the UK. Dr Hastings Kamuzu Banda, Malawi's first Prime Minister under British rule, became President in 1966 and his conservative and traditionalist Malawi Congress Party (MCP) was henceforth the sole legal party. All Malawi citizens were party members.

Resistance to the Banda regime culminated in the 1992 announcement that the imprisoned union leader Chakufwa Chihana would chair an interim committee of a new opposition group, the Alliance for Democracy (AFORD). In 1993 Malawians voted decisively for a multi-party system; after a turbulent period elections in May 1994 were won by the United Democratic Front (UDF) of Bakili Muluzi, who became President, with Chihana in third place. Chihana and other AFORD leaders joined Muluzi in government in September. In 1995 Banda was tried and acquitted on murder charges. The UDF remained the largest party following legislative elections in June 1999, with Muluzi being re-elected in the presidential contest. In the May 2004 elections the MCP re-emerged as the largest party in the National Assembly, with the UDF in second place. However, the UDF candidate, Bingu Wa Mathurika, an economist and Muluzi's nominated successor, won the presidential contest, and the UDF remained in government as part of a broad coalition with smaller parties and independents, with the MCP leading the parliamentary opposition.

Some 90% of the labour force work on the land and tobacco, tea and sugar generate the bulk of export earnings. Poor in natural resources, Malawi's small-scale industry is largely based on food processing. The country's landlocked position and poor access to potential markets have contributed to its low level of development and there is little inward investment. There is a substantial reliance on international aid.

GDP (purchasing power parity) $6.845bn. (2004 est.); GDP per capita (purchasing power parity) $600 (2004 est.).

2 Trade Unionism

Malawi ratified ILO Convention No. 98 (Right to Organize and Collective Bargaining, 1949) in 1965 but did not ratify Convention No. 87 (Freedom of Association and Protection of the Right to Organize, 1948) until 1999. Most workers, including civil servants (but excluding police and military personnel) may lawfully join unions and there are legal protections requiring reinstatement of employees dismissed for union activities. However, only 12% of formal sector employees are union members, and the formal sector comprises just 10% of the workforce. The unions report that some employers actively prevent union organization. The Malawi Congress of Trade Unions (MCTU) has been the only trade union centre since independence. A Congress of Malawi Trade Unions (COMATU) was also created in the late 1990s.

Under the 1996 Labour Relations Act (LRA) where a union represents 20% of the workforce in an enterprise, or 15% in a sector, it may engage in collective bargaining at that level and agreements are legally binding. The LRA provides for industrial councils to be set up as a forum for negotiation and dispute resolution where collective bargaining does not take place. The ICFTU says there is ambiguity in the interpretation of which strikes are legal; however, as the law requires a secret ballot prior to strike action, most that occur may be illegal. In 1997 a strike by the CSTU public servants' union led to the detention and alleged torture by police of a number of union activists before the resumption of negotiations led to the strike being called off. In 1998 the government responded to a general strike called by the MCTU against price rises by calling on employers to dismiss strikers. Strikes are not lawful in essential services. National labour law applies in the export processing zones but union organizers have difficulty obtaining access to the zones. There are few functioning mechanisms for protecting workers' rights under the legislation. The Industrial Relations Court has a two-year backlog and cannot monitor cases or enforce laws adequately.

3 Trade Union Centre

Malawi Congress of Trade Unions (MCTU)
Address. PO Box 1271, Lilongwe
Phone. +265 1755614
Fax. +265 1752162
E-mail. mctu@malawi.net
Leadership. Austin Kalimanjira (general secretary)
Membership. 45,000 in 19 affiliated unions
History and character. The MCTU was founded on independence in 1964 in succession to the Nyasaland Trades Union Congress. It is also variously referred to as the Trades Union Congress of Malawi (TUCM) and the Malawi Trades Union Congress (MTUC). Its affiliation to the ICFTU was suspended in 1993-94 on the grounds of its compliant attitude to the Banda regime. By the late 1990s the MCTU faced increasing government interference in its affairs, including disruption of its meetings, as it called protests against price rises and working conditions. The government said that opposition politicians were using the MCTU as a vehicle to promote unrest.
International affiliation. ICFTU, CTUC

4 Other Trade Union Organization

Congress of Malawi Trade Unions (COMATU)
Address. PO Box 1443, Lilongwe
Phone. +265 1757230
Fax. +265 1770885
Leadership. Phillmon E. Chimbalu (general secretary)
Membership. Three affiliated unions.
International affiliation. CTUC

Malaysia

Capital: Kuala Lumpur
Population: 23.52 m. (2004 est.)

1 Political and Economic Background

Malaysia gained independence from the United Kingdom in 1957. The major political force is the National Front, a coalition of parties representing the country's major ethnic groups (Malay, Chinese and Indian). The National Front has held power since its formation in 1973, when it superseded the Alliance Party, which had itself held power since independence. The leading party within the National Front is the United Malays National Organization (UMNO), which is based on the numerically dominant Malay population. UMNO's leader Mahathir bin Mohamad was Prime Minister from 1981 until October 2003, when he stood down in favour of his deputy, Abdullah Ahmad Badawi. In the most recent elections, in March 2004, the National Front won 198 of the 219 seats in the House of Representatives.

Malaysia has developed in recent decades from an economy based on primary commodities, with rubber, tin, palm oil and timber as its staples, to a diversified industrial economy. Manufacturing supplanted agriculture as the largest sector of the economy in 1985. In the 1990s growth averaged 8% per annum and the government proclaimed its "Vision 2020" goal of raising Malaysia to the same level as developed western economies by the year 2020. Against that background, the impact of the 1997–98 Asian financial crisis, which led to a 7% contraction in GDP in 1998, had a particularly severe impact on confidence in Malaysia. Mahathir responded with a series of emotive statements claiming that foreigners were using the crisis to try to take over the Malaysian economy. Malaysia imports labour and during the crisis, in January 1998, the government ordered all employers to arrange for the deportation of foreign workers on temporary contracts, although Indonesian workers were exempted.

The 1998 recession, though deep, proved short-lived and since then Malaysia has achieved real GDP growth each year, although growth was virtually nil in 2001 as a result of the global slowdown and slump in the electronics market, the biggest contributor to Malaysia's exports. However, the rate of growth (and inflows of foreign investment) has not returned to the boom levels of the 1990s and new Prime Minister Abdullah Badawi has tended to distance himself from the "Vision 2020" goals of Mahathir, putting more emphasis on smaller-scale rural development projects to help the less high-profile parts of the economy. Particularly buoyant growth was recorded in 2004 and by late year it seemed likely that the government's earlier forecast of GDP growth of 5–5.6% in 2004 would prove an underestimate. The budget deficit rose from 1.8% of GDP in 1998 to 5.6% in 2002 as the government engaged in pump-priming infrastructure and other projects in the wake of the severe 1998 recession; however the budget presented in September 2004 targeted deficit reductions, with the goal of reducing the deficit from 4.5% in 2004 to to 3.8% in 2005.

Following a series of race riots, in 1971 Malaysia introduced the New Economic Policy with the aim of raising the economic status of the Malay majority (bumiputras) to that of the wealthier Chinese minority, an objective which has been the cornerstone of successive National Front governments. In 1991 the NEP (which had raised the bumiputra share of corporate activity to 20 per cent) was replaced by a more moderate National Development Policy (NDP) that was less prescriptive about patriation of assets. In September 2004 Prime Minister Abdullah signalled a further easing of the bumiputra affirmative action policy, warning that ethnic Malays must improve their knowledge and skills to compete in the global economy and that "a continuing reliance on crutches will further enfeeble [Malays]".

GDP (purchasing power parity) $207.8bn. (2004 est.); GDP per capita (purchasing power parity) $9,000 (2004 est.).

2 Trade Unionism

Chinese hongs, or guilds, were predecessors of trade union organizations before World War II, and there was also some organization among immigrant Indian workers, under the influence of trade union developments in the subcontinent. After the War and defeat of Japan the Malayan Communist Party (MCP) formed the General Labour Union (GLU), later the Pan-Malayan Federation of Trade Unions (PMFTU). To counteract this influence the British encouraged the development of "free" trade unions, and British trade unionists came to assist in the education of union officers. Following widespread industrial unrest from 1946–48, a State of Emergency was declared, the MCP was outlawed and the PMFTU was de-registered. The free trade unions formed the Malaysian Trades Union Congress (MTUC) in 1949.

The MTUC is the national trade union centre, reporting 235 affiliates with 507,560 members in 2002. Its centre of gravity shifted with the emergence of the teachers' union as the largest affiliate in place of the plantation workers, though the majority of its members are in the private sector. The Congress of Unions of Employees in the Public and Civil Services (CUEPACS) affiliates unions organizing around 120,000 public sector staff members. For many years there were regular attempts made to merge these two organizations into a United Malaysian Labour Movement (UMLM) and harmonize representation at the ILO, but they were bedeviled by CUEPACS' fears over the loss of its identity and controversy over the leadership of the new organization. However, public sector unions affiliate to both the MTUC and CUEPACS. CUEPACS benefited directly from a 1990 decision of the government to allow quasi-governmental employees' organizations to affiliate to it.

Many trade unionists were arrested in 1987 under the Internal Security Act to "calm rising racial tension", among them Dr. V. David, then MTUC secretary-general and Transport Workers' leader, on his return from a US convention where he had criticized conditions in the free-trade zones and complained of the denial of trade union rights to young women workers in the electronics industry. He and two other union leaders spent a year in a political detention camp for "rehabilitation". David coupled his MTUC leadership with membership of the opposition in the National Assembly. When the AFL-CIO called (unsuccessfully) for Malaysia's preferences under the United States General System of Preferences to be suspended for disrespect of international union rights standards, Mahathir described this as "an imperialist plot by the West to ruin Malaysia's economy".

The oppositionist politics of the MTUC leadership at that time was the major factor leading a number of unions, including the National Union of Bank Employees, the National Union of Commercial Workers, the National Union of Petroleum and Chemical Workers, and several others, to launch a rival Malaysian Labour Organization (MLO) in 1989. The MLO's constitution stipulated that office bearers could not hold a position in any political party. Registered as a trade union in 1990, the MLO had about 135,000 members in 32 unions two years later. It was endorsed by the government as an alternative to the highly political MTUC; the MTUC counter-charged that the MLO was a political arm of the ruling party. The government certainly assisted the MLO (and enraged the MTUC) by naming it as an advisor to its 1992 ILO delegation and inviting it to join the National Labour Advisory Council (NLAC). MLO officials were also appointed to two of the four union places on the Employee Provident Fund, previously a preserve exclusively of the MTUC. After 1992, however, with less anti-government forces in control of the MTUC the rationale for the MLO declined and it merged back into the MTUC in 1996.

In 1995 there were officially recorded 502 unions with 701,334 members. This represented union density of only 8.6%, with density lowest in mining and construction and highest in electricity, gas and water. These figures comprised 364 in-house trade unions with 299,618 members and 138 national trade unions with 401,144 members. By 2003 the number of unionized workers had risen slowly to 803,879, in 581 unions. About 63% of union members are in unions affiliated to the MTUC. Under the 1959 Trade Unions Act unions are not allowed to organize outside their primary occupational area and this has limited the growth of sizable national unions: the teachers' union is the only one of the MTUC's affiliates to have more than 30,000 members.

Malaysia has not ratified ILO Convention No. 87 (Freedom of Association and Protection of the Right to Organize, 1948). The Department of Trade Union Affairs (headed by the Director General of Trade Union Affairs) is set up within the Ministry of Human Resources to enforce the Trade Unions Act, register trade unions and ensure that they "function in a healthy, democratic and responsible manner". The Director General must also give his approval for a union to affiliate internationally.

The right of association is limited by the Societies Act of 1966, under which any association (including trade unions) of seven or more members must register. The Trade Unions Act of 1959 as amended gives the Director General of Trade Union Affairs wide discretionary powers to deny recognition to new unions or to suspend existing unions. Peninsula-based unions may not have members from Sabah and Sarawak, and vice versa. If seven workers petition for a union the Director General has to consider their request; recognition by the employer is mandatory if wanted by a majority of employees. The Trade Unions Act restricts a union to representing workers in a "particular establishment, trade, occupation or industry". This provision has been invoked on a number of occasions to force unions to disaffiliate members. General Electric, Hitachi and Mitsumi Electronics are among companies that have successfully called on the Director General of Trade Union Affairs to bar their employees from remaining as members of the MTUC-affiliated Electrical Industry Workers' Union. It is reported that employees of a furniture manufacturer were not allowed to join the Metal Industry Employees' Union because the company used both metal and wood for its products.

The government has adopted a policy of officially discouraging the formation of a national union in the large electronics sector, the most important sector for exports, and for many years the MTUC seemed to have reluctantly accepted that it was better to have enterprise unions in that sector than none at all (although employers also reportedly have resisted the formation of enterprise unions). In September 2003, however, the MTUC filed a complaint with the ILO pointing to restrictions on the right to form trade unions under the 1959 Act, noting in particular that the Director General of Trade Union Affairs has consistently refused to allow the creation of an industrial union for workers in the electronics industry, allowing only company-based in-house unions. The MTUC also cited a string of recent cases where the Director General had refused recognition and bargaining rights in manufacturing companies. The MTUC argued that the implementation of the Act was the "main cause of the very low level of unionization in the country", and MTUC secretary-general G. Rajasekaran said the decision to file the complaint had been taken after years of failure to achieve a solution, with "no intention to tarnish Malaysia's name". In response the Human Resources Minister stated that the complaint was baseless; that the government "gives total encouragement to formation of unions"; and that union density was 12%, above the international norm, with unions formed in all sectors of the economy. The government statement did not deny, however, that efforts to form a national industrial union in the electronics sector had been blocked.

Employers are barred from penalizing workers for participating in lawful trade union activities. However, according to the ICFTU, many employers "go to extreme lengths to deny union recognition and evade collective bargaining. They often challenge government directives to accord union recognition and refuse to comply with Industrial Court awards to reinstate wrongfully dismissed workers." Some categories of workers are excluded from union membership. These include categories of workers defined as "confidential", "managerial and executive", defence forces and the police. Foreign workers (of whom a majority are in any case probably in the country illegally) are not allowed to join unions. Work permits issued to foreign workers stipulate that they may not join "associations". This is a particular factor in the plantations, where the government estimates that as much as 90% of the workforce in the plantations is foreign. The National Union of Plantation Workers (NUPW), traditionally the largest MTUC affiliate, saw its membership halved after 1980 under the impact of rising numbers of contract and undocumented workers unable to join a union. In 2003 the International Federation of Building and Wood Workers called for the right to unionize to be extended to foreign workers in Malaysia. Unions do exist in the free trade zones, where national labour laws apply.

A range of legislation not specifically aimed at trade unions, such as the Internal Security Act, allowing detention without trial, the Police Act, the Sedition Act, and the Printing Presses and Publications Act, are seen as inhibiting unions' political activities and freedom of expression. This is reinforced by the possibility of dissolution under the Societies Act. Unions are also prohibited from using funds for political purposes, which are defined in detail.

ILO Convention No. 98 (Right to Organize and Collective Bargaining, 1949) was ratified by Peninsula Malaysia in 1961 and by Sabah and Sarawak in 1964. Collective bargaining is widespread where unions are set up. There are restrictions on collective bargaining in the public sector under the Industrial Relations Act of 1967 and amendments, and in so-called "pioneer industries". The parties to a dispute must notify the Ministry of Human Resources and the Ministry's Industrial Relations Department may become involved in conciliation efforts. If these fail, the Ministry is empowered to refer the dispute to the Industrial Court. The tripartite Industrial Court has a record of making findings on the workers' side more often than not, although its procedures are slow.

For a strike to be legal it must first be approved by two-thirds of the workforce in a secret ballot. Unions may not strike over recognition issues. There are additional restrictions on strikes in "essential services". In practice, significant strikes are rare and brief, most being settled by conciliation with the assistance of the Ministry of Labour or in the Industrial Court. The government has powers to impose compulsory arbitration making strikes illegal and punishable by imprisonment.

The unions are represented on a wide range of advisory boards and official bodies, including the Industrial Court, the National Labour Advisory Council. The MTUC has eight representatives on the latter body, CUEPACS five, and the National Union of Plantation Workers, one.

3 Trade Union Centre

Malaysian Trades Union Congress (MTUC)
Address. 10-5 Jalan USJ 9/5T, Subang Jaya, Selangor 47620
Phone. +60 3 8024 2953
Fax. +60 3 8024 3225
E-mail. mtuc@tm.net.my
Website. www.mtuc.org.my
Leadership. Sayed Shahir Syed Mohamud (president); G. Rajasekaran (secretary-general)
Membership. 507,560 in 235 affiliated unions (2002)
History and character. The MTUC, founded in 1949 by the "free" trade unions, was initially known as the Malayan Trades Union Council; in 1958 it became the Malayan Trades Union Congress, and took its present name with the formation of Malaysia.

The former MTUC secretary-general, Dr V. David, was detained by the Malaysian government from October 1987 until his conditional release in June 1988. David symbolized the strongly oppositionist stance of the MTUC at that time and at the 29th (1988) biennial delegates' conference, he and the president were re-elected. However, when the 1992 convention met it proved a triumph for a reform slate headed by G. Rajasekaran of the Metal Industry Employees' Union, which swept all incumbents except the president from their places. David's defeat ended 14 years as MTUC secretary-general. Rajasekaran has since remained MTUC secretary-general and has generally sought to pursue positive relations with the government, though with tensions with authoritarian aspects of Mahathir's administration; the MTUC has viewed Mahathir's successor, Abdullah Badawi, as more likely to adopt a consensual approach to the trade unions.

The MTUC says that its membership is 64% Malay, 16% Chinese, 17% Indian and 3% other; 59% are men and 41% women. In recent years the proportion of its membership in the public sector has declined (from 30% in 1992 to 21% by 2002) while overall membership has increased steadily – by 65% from 1992-2002. As of 2002 the MTUC included 43 public sector unions with 108,996 members and 192 private sector unions with 398,564 members. The largest member union is the National Union of the Teaching Profession, with 76,311 members, but many of its affiliates are small and the MTUC has called for an end to restrictions on unions organizing across trades. Some public sector affiliates (including the National Union of the Teaching Profession) are also affiliated to the public sector Congress of Unions of Employees in the Public and Civil Services (CUEPACS).

The MTUC called for an end to the mass importation of foreign workers of the 1990s, which it said threatened wage levels, and continues to call on the government to end the recruitment of foreign workers by unscrupulous recruiting agents. However, it welcomed the government's announcement in October 2004 of an amnesty for illegal immigrants already in the country. It calls for minimum wage regulations and a 40-hour week; better social provision for workers injured at work; the opportunity to organize freely in the free trade zones; an end to restrictions on collective bargaining in "pioneer" industries; and retraining and re-employment programmes for laid-off workers. It calls for the abolition of laws suppressing dissent, including the Internal Security Act, and for a reformed and independent judiciary, Election Commission and other public bodies. It calls for a revitalization and strengthening of the Industrial Court and Labour Courts. It is opposed to privatization of essential services such as medicine, electrical supply, water, postal service and railways, and says that in Malaysia privatization is used for "political patronage" rather than economic reform. Health and safety issues in Malaysia's workplaces are also at the top of its agenda.

The MTUC is not allied politically.
International affiliations. ICFTU; CTUC

4 Other Trade Union Organizations

Congress of Unions of Employees in the Public and Civil Services (CUEPACS)
Address. No. 34, Jalan Gajah off Jalan Yew, Pudu, 55100 Kuala Lumpur
Phone. +60 3 9285 6110
Fax. +60 3 9285 9457
E-mail. webmaster@cuepacs.org.my
Website. http://cuepacs.redirectme.net
Leadership. Nordin Abdul Hamid (president); Abdul Rahman Manan (executive secretary)
Membership. 120,000 in 140 affiliates
International affiliation. CTUC

National Council of Unions of the Industrial and Lower Income Group of Government Workers
Majlis Kebangsaan Kesatuan Pekerja – Pekerja Kakitangan Rendah, Kerajaan Malaysia (MKTR)
Address. 434 Jalan Hose, 50460 Kuala Lumpur
Phone. +60 3 2144 6161
Fax. +60 3 2142 9763
E-mail. mktr@tm.net.my
Website. www.mktr.org
Leadership. Asran Bin Mamat (president); Ahmad Shah Bin Mohd Zin (secretary-general)
Membership. 45,000 dues paying members in 22 unions.
History and character. The MKTR was founded in 1956. It unites unions of lower-paid workers in the public sector and says it represents 200,000 of the one million public sector workers. It represents its unions either directly to government or via CUEPACS.

Maldives

Capital: Malé
Population: 339,000 (2004 est.)

1 Political and Economic Background

Maldives was a British protectorate until 1965. President Maumoun Abdul Gayoom has been President since 1978, being re-elected five times, most recently in October 2003, when his nomination by the Majlis (parliament) was endorsed by more than 90% of the votes in a referendum. Although not illegal, political parties are discouraged and do not exist, candidates for the Majlis running as individuals. Riots were reported in the capital in both 2003 and 2004, which the government attributed to "criminal elements". The government was accused by Amnesty International in 2003 of systematically suppressing dissent.

Tourism (accounting for 60% of foreign exchange earnings) and fishing are the leading sources of employment, with the majority of workers engaged outside the formal wage economy. The Maldives is made up of numerous very low-lying coral islands which incurred considerable damage from the Indian Ocean tidal wave of December 2004.

GDP (purchasing power parity) $1.25bn. (2002 est.); GDP per capita (purchasing power parity) $3,900 (2002 est.).

2 Trade Unionism

While the formation of unions is not expressly prohibited, neither are there any protections in law for creating and joining unions. In practice, trade unions do not exist and there have been no recent reports of efforts to set up unions. Maldives is not a member of the ILO.

Mali

Population: 11.96 m. (2004 est.)
Capital: Bamako

1 Political and Economic Background

Mali was ruled by France until 1960. An officers' coup led by Lieutenant (later General) Moussa Traoré toppled Modibo Keita's radical government in 1968. Constitutional reforms promulgated in 1979 replaced the ruling military committee with a one-party state. Traoré remained in power as president until widespread demands for political reform led to another military coup in 1991. A transitional government headed by Amadou Toumani Touré ran the country until a new constitution was approved and elections were held in 1992. The Malian Alliance for Democracy (ADEMA) won the legislative elections in March and its leader, Alpha Oumar Konaré, gained the presidency the following month. Konaré was re-elected in 1997 in a poll boycotted by most opposition groups after a disputed first round of balloting. Returning to politics after a decade, Touré was elected president in 2002 with the support of two dozen minor parties. ADEMA retained control in the National Assembly.

Mali is one of the world's poorest and least developed countries. Most of the workforce is engaged in subsistence farming and itinerant livestock herding, both of which are vulnerable to the region's periodic droughts. Cotton is the main cash crop. There is limited small-scale industry based mainly on food processing. Mali is heavily dependent on foreign aid. The country is carrying out an IMF-backed structural adjustment programme and has recorded an average annual growth rate of 5% since 1996.

GDP (purchasing power parity) $10.53.bn (2004 est.); GDP per capita (purchasing power parity) $900 (2004 est.).

2 Trade Unionism

Mali ratified ILO Convention No. 87 (Freedom of Association and Protection of the Right to Organize, 1948) in 1960 and Convention No. 98 (Right to Organize and Collective Bargaining, 1949) in 1964. Branches of the metropolitan French confederations existed before independence in 1960, but trade union activity was subsequently coordinated in a single-trade-union system organized by the Union Nationale des Travailleurs du Mali (UNTM). The UNTM participated prominently in the movement for political reform and multiparty democracy in 1991–92. The UNTM remains the national centre but a breakaway group, the Trade Union Confederation of Mali Workers (CSTM) was formed in 1997.

The 1992 Constitution and the labour code provide for freedom of association, other than for the military and police. The unions are well established in the small formal sector, including teachers, health workers and civil servants, and virtually all salaried employees are reported to be unionized. There is a constitutional right to strike for all workers, but strikes by civil servants and other public sector workers are subject to notice periods and mediation procedures. Bargaining occurs between unions, employers' organizations and the Ministry of Labour. The labour code prohibits retribution against strikers and there is a labour court for resolution of disputes.

The ICFTU reported in 1999 that freedom of association and the right to bargain collectively "were generally respected for several years" after the national constitution was approved in 1992. In June 1996, however, three union general secretaries were among those arrested for involvement in a general strike called by the UNTM in protest at the government's refusal to enter into dialogue with it and the UNTM subsequently came under significant harassment. Such attention testifies to the political power the labour movement gained from the UNTM's pivotal role in the 1991 transition to multiparty democracy.

3 Trade Union Centres

Confédération Syndicale des Travailleurs du Mali (CSTM)
Workers' Trade Union Confederation of Mali
Address. BP E102, Bamako
Phone. +223 220 46 21
Fax. +223 222 50 85
Leadership. Hammadoun Amion Guindo (secretary-general)
Membership. 15,000 (2003 est.)
History and character. The CSTM groups together four trade unions that split from the UNTM in 1997. Despite rumours of government sponsorship, the CSTM has remained autonomous.
International affiliation. ICFTU

Union Nationale des Travailleurs du Mali (UNTM)
National Workers' Union of Mali
Address. Bourse du Travail, Boulevard de l'IndÈpendence, BP 169, Bamako
Phone. +223 222 36 99
Fax. +223 223 59 45
Leadership. Siaka Diakité (secretary-general)
Membership. 122,000 (2003 est.)
History and character. Founded in 1963 with strong representation among civil servants and salaried employees, the UNTM was closely supervised under the Keita and Traoré regimes. The single-party system that developed in the 1970s saw the UNTM as a political intermediary between workers and the state. In the late 1980s the UNTM became involved in numerous protests over rising prices, delays in payment of public sector wages, and political corruption. UNTM industrial action was a major feature of the civil unrest that ousted Traoré in March 1991 and union representatives served in the 1991-92 transitional government.

Relations with the government deteriorated as a result of the 1994 CFA franc devaluation, about which the UNTM had not been consulted. The UNTM called a strike in June 1996 to protest at the lack of dialogue with the government. On April 16, 1997, the UNTM headquarters were surrounded by troops after charges of fraud in national legislative elections had led to demonstrations. The constitutional court declared the elections invalid and the elections were re-run in July (with the ruling ADEMA party retaining power), and again troops surrounded the union headquarters amid further protests about electoral fraud. In August of the same year, the government was reported to have funded the congress of a breakaway rival centre, the CSTM. In October 1997 police occupied the UNTM headquarters and sealed the general secretary's office. The UNTM has, however, succeeded in maintaining its autonomy and continues to challenge programmes to privatize state industries.

International affiliation. ICFTU, OATUU

Malta

Capital: Valletta
Population: 397,000 (2004 est.)

1 Political and Economic Background

Malta gained its independence from the United Kingdom in 1964. The leading parties are the conservative Nationalist Party (NP) and the socialist Malta Labour Party, with the NP winning the elections of 1998 and 2003. Malta joined the European Union on May 1, 2004, in accordance with the positive result of a referendum on the issue in March 2003, although the Malta Labour Party had consistently opposed accession.

The economy is based on the export of manufactured goods, including electronics and textiles, freight trans-shipment and tourism. More than one-third of the workforce are in the public sector and fears of the impact of EU accession on public sector subsidies and economic controls were a factor in the opposition of the Labour Party to the NP government's application for EU membership.

GDP (purchasing power parity) $7.08bn. (2004 est.); GDP per capita (purchasing power parity) $17,700 (2004 est.).

2 Trade Unionism

Malta ratified ILO Conventions No. 87 (Freedom of Association and Protection of the Right to Organize, 1948) and No. 98 (Right to Organize and Collective Bargaining, 1949) in 1965. Before World War II unions acted principally as beneficial guilds, but the General Workers' Union (GWU) was formed in 1943 as a full trade union, with early strength among the white-collar and skilled workers of the British naval dockyards. The Confederation of Malta Trade Unions (CMTU) was founded in 1959. The GWU (which is affiliated to the ICFTU) and the CMTU (a WCL affiliate) are the two trade union organizations recognized under the 1976 Industrial Relations Act as being representative at the national level. Trade union density has increased in the last two decades and by June 2003, according to official figures, there were 86,061 members of 33 trade unions, constituting 62.5% of the workforce, compared with a trade union density of 45.5% in 1983. Trade union density is particularly high in the public and parastatal sectors, where 90% of employees are covered by collective agreements, but lower than average in the private services sector. Members of the police and armed forces are excluded from union membership. Anti-union discrimination by employers was prohibited under the 1976 Industrial Relations Act and trade union rights and immunities were codified in the Employment and Industrial Relations Act of 2002, which provides for a Registrar of Trade Unions.

The GWU is closely linked to the Labour Party, being officially amalgamated with it for 14 years from May 1978. The CMTU does not have direct political links, though as a member of the WCL its orientation is essentially social Christian. From 1983 to 1986 the Labour administration excluded the CMTU from the official Maltese delegation to the ILO, although it continued to send unofficial participants.

Annual tripartite discussions provide a framework for industrial relations and income policy. There is a right to strike for all workers except uniformed military and the police. The responsible minister may under the Industrial Relations Act of 1976 compulsorily refer disputes to the tripartite Industrial Tribunal for binding settlement (i.e. in effect limiting the right to strike). Most disputes in recent years have been in the highly unionized public sector, with private sector disputes rare and usually quickly settled. The Department of Industrial and Employment Relations usually assists in resolving disputes.

The GWU, CMTU and the Malta Workers' Union (UHM) are represented on the influential tripartite Malta Council for Economic and Social Development (MCESD). However, despite recent internationally-fostered efforts to reduce tensions between the two union centres, strong historic divisions remain.

3 Trade Union Centres

Confederation of Malta Trade Unions (CMTU)
Address. 13/3 South Street, PO Box 467, Valletta CMR 01
Phone. +356 237313
Fax. +356 250146
E-mail. cmtu@kemmunet.net.mt
Leadership. Charles Magro (general secretary)
Membership. 36,000 in 10 unions
History and character. The CMTU was founded in 1959. It was known as the Malta Confederation of Trade Unions until 1978 when the Labour government, which had a close association with the rival GWU, prohibited by law the use of the word Malta in the name. After Labour lost power in 1987 the word Malta appeared again in the CMTU name. The CMTU makes no financial contributions to political parties and is politically non-aligned but has been the choice of those who reject the GWU's association with the Labour Party. All the CMTU member unions urged a "yes" vote in the March 2003 referendum on EU accession, thus allying with the Nationalist Party government against the opposition Labour Party and the GWU.

International affiliations. WCL; CTUC; ETUC
Affiliates. The majority of members are in the largest affiliate, the Malta Workers' Union. The largest other affiliates are the Malta Union of Teachers (MUT, with 5,839 members) and the Malta Union of Bank Employees (MUBE, 2,950 members).

Malta Workers' Union
Union Haddiema Maghqudin (UHM)
Address. "Dar Reggie Miller", St Thomas Street, Floriana, VLT 15
Phone. +356 212 20847
Fax. +356 212 46091
E-mail. info@uhm.org.mt
Website. www.uhm.org.mt
Leadership. Gaetano Tanti (president); Gejtu Vella (secretary-general)
Membership. 25,600
History and character. The UHM has its origins in a government clerical employees' union founded in the 1960s, adopting its present name in 1978; it now has members in both public and private sectors, organized in seven sections. It emphasizes its independence of any political party.
International affiliations. INFEDOP; EUROFEDOP

General Workers' Union (GWU)
Address. Workers' Memorial Building, South Street, Valletta VLT 11
Phone. +356 244 451
Fax. +356 242 975
E-mail. info@gwu.org.mt
Website. www.gwu.org.mt
Leadership. Salv Sammut (president); Tony Zarb (secretary general)
Membership. 47,254 (2003)
History and character. The GWU was founded in 1943 and has a membership distributed throughout the major sectors of the economy but with particular strength in the public and parastatal sectors. It comprises eight trade sections which engage in collective bargaining, as well as youth and pensioners' sections, and represents 55% of organized workers. Politically it is identified with the Malta Labour Party, and its president and general secretary have in the past participated in Cabinet meetings. For 14 years from 1978 the two were statutorily fused, and though the fusion was dissolved in 1992 they still share many common goals.

When the Nationalist Party took power in 1987, after 16 years of Labour government, the GWU engaged in a series of actions opposing its plans for management of the important parastatal sector, and especially privatization. Conflict reached a peak in 1988 when dry dock workers blockaded the main port by anchoring a tanker across the mouth of the breakwater, thus preventing a visit by four British warships. Later, arrests of union members for interrogation about the incident led to further demonstrations.

GWU opposition to Nationalist Party government policy extended to Malta's bid for EU membership, launched in 1990. In this the GWU was allied with the Labour Party, and called for a "no" vote in the March 2003 referendum on accession, when the Nationalist Party secured a vote of 53% in favour. The GWU's particular concern was that EU accession would force an end to government subsidies to the dry dock, a GWU stronghold. However, in November 2003 the GWU and the government reached agreement on a restructuring plan for the drydocks that avoided any compulsory redundancies.

The ICFTU claimed that GWU general secretary Tony Zarb and president James Pearsall were "brutally attacked" by police in August 1999 during an industrial dispute at Malta International Airport.

The GWU is a multi-industrial union at the national level and its blue and white-collar membership is grouped in sections organized on an industrial or professional basis. Each section has its own executive committee and is autonomous but must abide by GWU principles.

The GWU owns the company that has a monopoly on freight handling at the country's main cargo facility (generating revenue for the union), but in 2004 the government announced it would open the operation to competitive tendering to achieve lower tariffs and greater efficiency.
International affiliations. ICFTU, ETUC; CTUC.

Marshall Islands

Capital: Dalap-Uliga-Darrit (Majuro)
Population: 58,000 (2004 est.)

1 Political and Economic Background

The Marshall Islands are a group of atolls in the central Pacific, an independent nation in a compact of free association with the United States. There is small-scale farming, a little tourism, and a heavy dependence on US financial support.

GDP (purchasing power parity) $115m. (2001 est.); GDP per capita (purchasing power parity) $1,600 (2001 est.).

2 Trade Unionism

The formal economy is very small. The 1979 Constitution accords a general right of association, but no trade unions have been formed. There is no legislation concerning trade union organization, collective bargaining or strike action.

Mauritania

Capital: Nouakchott
Population: 2.92m. (2003 est.)

1 Political and Economic Background

The Islamic Republic of Mauritania was constituted in 1960, nominally as a parliamentary democracy, in practice as a one party state. From 1978 until 1992 it was ruled by a Military Council of National Salvation, headed from 1984 by the Armed Forces Chief of Staff, Col. Moaouia Ould Sid'Ahmed Taya. In line with developments in much of Africa at that time, the early 1990s brought greater pluralism, reflected in a new Constitution in 1991. However, although other political parties have been legalized, Taya has remained in power and was most recently re-elected as President in 2003 with 67% of the vote amid allegations of electoral fraud by his opponents. His Democratic and Social Republican Party (PRDS) also has a majority in the National Assembly, although its majority was eroded in the most recent elections in 2001.

The majority of the population depends on subsistence level agriculture and herding. Iron ore and fish products account for most export revenues. Recurrent drought and plagues of locusts since the 1970s have led to urbanization of much of the former farming and nomadic population. There is extensive urban unemployment and an estimated half of the population lives below the poverty line. In addition, by late 2004 Mauritania had an external debt burden of $2.5bn., and still relies heavily on foreign assistance. At least a third of Maritania's active population works in the informal sector.

Traditionally, slavery was common among the black or mixed-race descendants of freed slaves (haratin) of the south. In 1980 Mauritania officially abolished slavery and in 1984 the UN recorded that it had virtually disappeared. On May 21, 1999, the government created a Commissariat for Human Rights, Poverty Alleviation and Integration, specifically to address "the vestiges and consequences of slavery".

GDP (purchasing power parity) $5.195bn. (2003 est.); GDP per capita (purchasing power parity) $1,800 (1999 est.).

2 Trade Unionism

Mauritania ratified ILO Convention No. 87 (Freedom of Association and Protection of the Right to Organize, 1948) in 1961. After considerable pressure, in 2001 it ratified Conventions No. 182 (against the worst forms of child labour) and No. 98 (Right to Organize and Collective Bargaining, 1949).

Before political pluralism was established in the early 1990s the Union of Mauritanian Workers (UTM) was the only permitted trade union organization. The UTM had close links with the regime and did not support the 1991 protests against it. However disagreements were increasingly open between the UTM secretary-general and leading affiliated federations such as the miners and fishermen.

The 1991 Constitution provided for trade union pluralism, but the labour code legitimizing pluralism did not come into force until 1993. In practice the UTM's privileged position under law persisted until 1994, when an independent organization, the General Confederation of Mauritanian Workers (CGTM) finally achieved recognition after more than a year of litigation. The UTM is now reported by both the ICFTU and WCL as being an affiliate and the CGTM is affiliated to the ICFTU.

According to the US State Department the UTM is still regarded by many workers as closely allied with the government and ruling PRDS and has lost ground to both the CGTM and a third confederation, the Free Confederation of Mauritanian Workers (CLTM), which achieved recognition in 1998 and affiliated to the WCL in 2000. A ICFTU report for 2001 noted that the government could still dissolve any trade union involved in what it considered to be an "illegal" or "politically motivated" strike.

As of 2004 there were plans afoot to harmonize the positions of the three union centres (CLTM, UTM and CGTM) "in the interests of the workers". CLTM secretary-general Samory Ould Beye expressed the wish that ultimately they might form a single front, "in the light of the new labour code", agreed to since 2001. He said the three centres were united on issues of raising salaries, rest-days on Saturdays, improvements in social security, and the right to form professional associations.

Under the 1991 Constitution all workers except police and armed forces may join unions of their own choosing. Most of the workforce is in the informal sector, but the great majority of workers in the formal waged economy are in unions. Agreements on wages and conditions are often negotiated on a tripartite basis between employers, unions and government. There is a constitutional right to strike but in some cases the authorities have intervened to prevent industrial action and although strikes occur they tend to be infrequent and short lived. There is also provision for binding arbitration to end disputes. The government provides financial assistance to the trade union confederations to assist them in their educational and training activities and the confederations are also represented on labour tribunals and consultative bodies.

During late 2004 labour unions were campaigning for an across-the-board wage rise of 2%. Then on Jan. 18, 2005, Labour Minister Salka Mint Bilal Ould Yamar surprised many by announcing a 386% increase in the Mauritanian minimum wage. According to Middle East Online, this would boost salaries for the private sector to at least 61.5 euros ($80.5) monthly. The wage rise was the first to be announced since 1982.

3 Trade Union Centres

Confédération Générale des Travailleurs de Mauritanie (CGTM)
General Confederation of Mauritanian Workers
Address. BP 6164, Nouakchott
Phone. +222 2 58057
Fax. +222 2 58057
Leadership. Abdallahi Ould Mohamed (secretary-general)
History and character. Independent trade union formed in 1993 but banned until passage of the law on trade union pluralism in July that year. It achieved legal recognition in January 1994 after a lengthy legal process but continued to complain of pressure on members from the authorities to renounce membership. The CGTM is politically independent but tends to be associated with opposition groups.

It has 25,000 members, 15% of whom are women. In April 2002 the CGTM created a national women's

committee. In March 8, 2004, the committee secretary, Mahjouba Mint Salek, a founding member of the GGTM, announced a two-year campaign – endorsed by the ICFTU – aimed at seeing more women enter the formal labour market and join unions. Mint Salek also praised the success of the regional committee in the Trarza region, where unemployed female agricultural workers were helped to find land to rent, and encouraged to set up co-operatives.
International affiliation. ICFTU

Confédération Libre des Travailleurs de Mauritanie (CLTM)
Free Confederation of Mauritanian Workers
Address. BP 6902, Nouakchott
Phone. +222 5 29 4437
Fax. +222 5 252 43276
E-mail. cltm95@yahoo.fr
Leadership. Samory Ould Beye (secretary-general)
History and character. The CLTM has run a long campaign with the ODSTA (regional organization of the WCL) and the FPTI (Confédération Panafricaine des Travailleurs de l'Industrie) to run projects that improve the working conditions of miners. The centre has co-operated on matters of hygiene, health and safety with the state's chief inspector of work, Amar Goufeif. At the same time, the CLTM has struggled to achieve legal recognition from government authorities. The centre sends delegates to regional conference of the ILO, which institution has supported the CLTM's claims.

In 1998 it appeared that the CLTM had won a significant legal victory. Matters came to a head after the Mauritanian government arrested and effectively placed under house arrest five perceived dissidents on Feb. 8, 1998, including CLTM secretary-general Ould Beye and CLTM workers' education director, Sid'Ahmed Ould Salek. The pair were released in May, by which stage pressure from the ILO convinced the Mauritanian public prosecutor that the CLTM was entitled to operate freely, as its constitutional by-laws did indeed conform to the national Labour Code, Book III. The ILO made similar representations on behalf of Mauritania's Transport Workers' Federation. The CLTM affiliated to the WCL in 2000.

Despite the CLTM's formal success, however, there have been numerous cases of tension since between it and the Mauritanian government. Ten CLTM members were wounded in May Day clashes with police in 2000. A CLTM-sponsored march for social justice, on Oct. 16, 2000, was declared illegal (with 40 protesters arrested) as were demonstrations by fishing unions belonging to the CLTM in 2002.

The CLTM is involved in local campaigns to eradicate both child labour and slavery, which are both reported in Mauritania. As of mid-2004 the CLTM was taking a lead role in harmonizing the positions of the three union centres. While praising the new labour code in part, Ould Beye complained that a right to strike was still effectively "non-existent". Anomalies in the law persisted, he added, including many that "flagrantly violated the fundamental conventions of the ILO". Ould Beye highlighted the vulnerability of workers in cases where firms closed; and also the "anarchic" situation in recruitment, engendered by the absence of official labour offices and lack of work inspectors. While welcoming recent meetings held with the Ministry of Public Works, he said trade unionists were still waiting to see what would materialize in practice.
International affiliations. WCL

Union des Travailleurs de Mauritanie (UTM)
Union of Mauritanian Workers
Address. BP 630, Bourse du Travail, Nouakchott
Phone. +222 2 51 681
Fax. +222 2 56 521
Leadership. Mohamed Ely Ould Brahim (secretary-general)
History and character. Founded 1961 and traditionally associated with the ruling PRDS, having been the sole authorized trade union organization prior to the reforms of the early 1990s. It has lost ground to the two confederations (CGTM and CLTM) that have been formed since that time.

In 1969 the UTM had split over suggestions that it formally merge with the then ruling PPM party. Unions that opposed integration with the PPM, like the National Union of Mauritanian Teachers, plus numerous students and miners, broke away to form a "Progressive" UTM. This new body was henceforth shunned by the government. Meanwhile, the mainstream UTM suffered problems, too, when in 1983 then UTM secretary-general Elkory Ould H'metty was jailed for allegedly acting on behalf of "Libyan interests". Released from prison in 1985, Ould H'metty took over again from his former deputy, Beijjel Ould Houmeit. Yet the administration of the UTM was paralyzed by internal conflict, and constituent local unions atrophied, opening the way for future gains at the UTM's expense by the CGTM and CLTM.

Internal conflicts evidently persisted into 2003. In December that year an objection was raised at the 10th African regional meeting of the ILO, in Addis Ababa, regarding the UTM delegate to the gathering, Hamady Touré. It was alleged that he had not been democratically elected by members of his centre, in June 2003, and indeed doubt was cast on the legitimacy of all UTM official elected at the UTM's June congress. As of 2004 it appeared that the UTM had accepted its diminished status, and was willing to harmonize its positions with the rival centres.
International affiliations. ICFTU; also reported by WCL

Mauritius

Capital: Port Louis
Population: 1.22 m. (2004 est.)

1 Political and Economic Background

A former British colony, Mauritius gained independence in 1968 and became a republic within the Commonwealth in March 1992. The head of state is the President, a largely symbolic office, who is elected by the unicameral National Assembly. The head of government in the Prime Minister.

Parliamentary elections in December 1995 ended 13 years of coalition government headed by Sir Aneerood Jugnauth of the Militant Socialist Movement (MSM). In subsequent elections in September 2000 an opposition alliance between the MSM and the Mauritian Militant Movement (MMM) regained power decisively. Jugnauth regained the premiership, but in September 2003 he resigned in favour of MMM leader Paul Berenger. Shortly afterwards Jugnauth was elected as President.

Since independence in 1968, Mauritius has developed from a low-income, agriculturally based economy to a middle-income diversified economy with growing industrial, financial, and tourist sectors. The government's development strategy centres on expanding local financial institutions and building a domestic information telecommunications industry. Mauritius has attracted more than 9,000 offshore entities, many aimed at commerce in India and South Africa, and investment in the banking sector alone has reached over $1bn. The standard of living is one of the highest in Africa.

GDP (purchasing power parity) $13.85bn. (2004 est.); GDP per capita (purchasing power parity) $11,400 (2004 est.).

2 Trade Unionism

Mauritius ratified Convention No. 98 (Right to Organize and Collective Bargaining, 1949) in 1969. It has not ratified Convention No. 87 (Freedom of Association and Protection of the Right to Organize, 1948) but all workers except the police and security forces have the right to form and join trade unions.

The trade union movement is developed but fragmented with many small unions. In total there are close to 350 unions with over 125,000 members, representing some 25% of the workforce. There is a tradition of diversity in labour federations, and there is no unified centre. The Mauritius Labour Congress (MLC) and the Mauritius Trade Union Congress (MTUC) are both affiliated to the ICFTU. The WCL affiliate is the National Trade Unions Confederation.

Workers in the export processing zones (EPZs) make up about 20% of the country's labour force. Labour legislation applies in the EPZs, but there are also specific labour laws that allow longer working hours (45 hours a week plus ten hours' compulsory overtime in the EPZs compared to 35 to 48 hours in non-EPZ sectors). Freedom of association is generally respected in practice, although this is not the case with some employers in the EPZs. As a result, union membership levels are low in the EPZs. Because EPZ workers do not benefit from the more advantageous labour regulations that apply outside the zones, the government has created the Export Processing Zone Welfare Fund to finance social services for EPZ workers and their children. The fund derives its revenues from a tripartite system of monthly payments from the state, employees, and employers.

Collective bargaining is legally recognized, although there is reported to be very little collective bargaining in the EPZs. The right to strike is also recognized under the Industrial Relations Act (IRA), but there are limitations. The IRA imposes a 21 day cooling off period before any strike can begin, and the Labour Ministry can order that the case be taken before the industrial court for binding arbitration. The government also has the right to declare any strike illegal that is likely to cause extensive damage to the economy. The MLC states that the IRA Amendment Act, adopted in June 2003, restricts the right of public service unions to declare a dispute over pay.

3 Trade Union Centres

Federation of Progressive Unions (FPU)
Address. Arcades Rond-Point, Rose-Hill
Phone. +230 464 3392
Fax. +230 464 3625
E-mail. fpumel@intnet.mu
Leadership. Rajesnarain Gutteea (general secretary)
Membership. 35,000
International affiliation. CTUC; WCL

General Workers' Federation (GWF)
International affiliation. OATUU; WFTU

Mauritius Labour Congress (MLC)
Address. 8 Louis Victor de la Faye Street, Port Louis
Phone. +230 212 4343
Fax. +230 208 8945
E-mail. mlcongress@intnet.mu
Leadership. J. Lollbeeharry (general secretary)
Membership. 30,000
History and character. The MLC was formed in 1963 as a result of a merger of the Mauritius Trades Union Congress and the Mauritius Confederation of Free Trade Unions. It is one of the two main trade union centres and includes unions covering all the main sectors of the economy: sugar, tea, transport, docks, aviation, banks, insurance, construction, textiles, public service, parastatals and local authorities.
International affiliation. ICFTU; CTUC; OATUU

Mauritius Trade Union Congress (MTUC)
Address. Emmanuel Anquetil Labour Centre, James Smith Street GRNW, Port Louis
Phone. +230 2108 567
Fax. +230 2108 567
E-mail. mtuc_unions@yahoo.com
Leadership. Radhakrisna Sadien (president)
Membership. 29,000
International affiliations. ICFTU

National Trade Unions Confederation (NTUC)
Address. c/o FCSU, Room 308, 3rd Floor, Jade Court, Jummah Mosque Street, Port Louis
Phone. +230 216 1977
Fax. +230 216 1475
International affiliation. WCL
Affiliates. The NTUC's principal affiliates are:

1. Federation of Civil Service Unions (FCSU/FSCC)

Address. Room 308, 3rd Floor, Jade Court, Jummah Mosque Street, Port Louis
Phone. +230 216 1977
Fax. +230 206 1475
E-mail. fcsu@intnet.mu
Leadership. Soondress Sawmynaden (general secretary)
Membership. 25,000

2. Organization of Artisans' Unity (OAU)

Address. 42 Sir William Newton Street, Port Louis
Phone. +230 212 4557
Fax. +230 208 2438
Leadership. Roy Ramchum (general secretary)
Membership. 2,700
History and character. Traditionally based in the tea and sugar industries in rural areas. It has recently organised textile workers in the export processing zone and hotel and catering workers.

Mexico

Capital: Mexico City
Population: 105.0m. (2004 est.)

1 Political and Economic Background

The Institutional Revolutionary Party (PRI) formed the government continuously from 1929 until 2000. In the 1930s the party developed a huge network for social control and patronage, including labour and peasant unions and professional associations, and this system survived periods of discontent to keep the party in power. The political orientation of the PRI tended to depend largely on the faction represented by the presidential incumbent. In the 1990s, however, the position of the PRI eroded. President Carlos Salinas de Gortari fled into exile in 1995 in view of his unpopularity. In 1997 the PRI lost its overall majority in the federal Chamber of Deputies (the lower house), although remaining the largest party. Then, in elections in July 2000, the PRI lost the presidency to Vicente Fox of the Alliance for Change (dominated by Fox's National Action Party, PAN) and suffered further erosion of its position in the legislature, with PAN narrowly becoming the largest party but no party in overall control. The PRI remained in power in half the 32 states. The mid-term legislative elections in 2003 saw the PRI, in alliance with the small Green Ecologist Party of Mexico (PVEM) recover first position in the Chamber of Deputies, thereby weakening the Fox government.

Parts of Mexico have been affected by relatively low-level guerrilla insurgency, occasionally flaring into full-scale local revolt as in the 1993–94 rebellion led by the Zapatista National Liberation Army (EZLN) in the southern state of Chiapas.

Mexico has a diversified economy at widely varying levels of development including both subsistence peasant cultivation and modern assembly plants for electronic products. Some 58% of the workforce are employed in services, 24% in industry and 18% in agriculture – the last sector generating only 4% of GDP, however. Most Mexican enterprises are small: 97 per cent employ fewer than four people. Privatization has been extensive, with the number of state enterprises reduced from 1,155 in 1982 to less than 200 by the end of the 1990s. The government is trying to further increase competition in the major sectors of the economy but this has been a slow process. There are great disparities of wealth within the country and widespread under-employment. Mexico had recurrent financial crises in the 1980s and 1990s and real wages by the end of the century had still not recovered to the levels of before the last major crisis in 1994. Mexico joined the North American Free Trade Area (NAFTA) in 1994, since then tripling its trade with the US and Canada, and in March 2000 signed a free trade agreement with the European Union, the first Latin American country to do so. Following the NAFTA agreement the maquiladoras – factories engaged in re-assembly of imported parts for export – proliferated in northern Mexico in the 1990s, but between October 2000 and March 2002 some 270,000 jobs, one in five, were lost in this sector, with 300 manufacturing companies seeking lower wage costs relocating to China between 2001 and 2003, while some firms relocated to Central America. There has since been a partial recovery in this sector, with employment in mid-2004 at its highest level since 2001. The economy as a whole has of late shown very modest growth, in part because of slowdowns in export markets, with real GDP increasing by 0.3% in 2001, 0.9% in 2002 and 1.2% in 2003, and forecast at 1.3% for 2004.

GDP (purchasing power parity) $941.2bn. (2004 est.); GDP per capita (purchasing power parity) $9,000 (2004 est.).

2 Trade Unionism

Mexico ratified ILO Convention No. 87 (Freedom of Association and Protection of the Right to Organize, 1948) in 1950 but has not ratified Convention No. 98 (Right to Organize and Collective Bargaining, 1949). The Mexican constitution and federal labour law provide for the right of workers to form and join unions. Most unionized workers are to be found in the formal sector, which employs about 50% of the labour force. The public sector is particularly heavily organized, the unions are strong in industrial areas, and there are also many peasant organizations. There have traditionally been elements of corruption, racketeering and strong-arm methods in the Mexican union movement.

Since the 1930s, the dominant force has been the Confederación de Trabajadores de México (CTM), which is closely allied with the PRI, the party of government continuously from 1929 until the end of the century. Fidel Velásquez, "Don Fidel", as secretary-general of the CTM from 1941 until his death on June 21, 1997, aged 97, was regularly consulted by national Presidents and was seen as able to deliver millions of votes to the PRI. In exchange the government entered into social and economic pacts with the CTM. Its support for successive government policies is probably a major factor explaining the historically low level of union unrest in Mexico. The CTM (along with two other national federations) is affiliated to the ICFTU. The WCL has in the past criticized the CTM's role as a "transmission belt" for the ruling party.

The CTM is the dominant factor in the loose Congress of Labour (Congreso del Trabajo, CT) which provides an umbrella for dozens of federations and independent unions. The CT was founded in 1966 to provide a unifying voice for labour, each organization having one vote, on the principle that only unanimous decisions would be binding. Many unions and federations outside the CTM such as the Revolutionary Confederation of Workers and Peasants (CROC), claimed as an affiliate by the WCL, have also historically been allied to the PRI. Officials of pro-PRI unions have campaigned for and run as PRI candidates for political office and there has always been a strong group of union (and especially CTM) representatives in the PRI delegations in the legislature.

The recent decline of the PRI has encouraged the development of unions not linked to it. In July 1997 elections, the PRI lost its absolute majority in the Chamber of Deputies for the first time in nearly seven decades. The following month, 100 unions, saying they represented one million workers, announced they would unite in a new organization (the UNT) to challenge the CTM and work with the opposition to alter federal labour laws.

While competitive unions have been allowed in the private sector, a legal trade union monopoly has existed in public administration. The single-union rule in the public sector was widely seen as one of the mechanisms by which the PRI had controlled the state apparatus for decades in alliance with the 1.8 million member Federation of Unions of Government Workers (FSTSE). On May 12, 1999, the Supreme Court ruled that under the constitution, municipal, state and federal employees were free to join unions other than those belonging to the FSTSE. However, the Supreme Court had made a similar ruling in 1996 in respect of the states of Jalisco and Oaxaca without this affecting practice.

To have legal status unions must be registered with the Federal Labour Secretariat (Secretaria del Trabajo y Prevision Social, STPS) or the appropriate conciliation and arbitration boards (JLCA). These bodies are reported to have refused registration on occasions to unions hostile to the government or major employers. In addition, as the composition of labour boards is tripartite, there have been cases of registration being refused to organizations hostile to unions represented on the boards. The registration requirement has tended to entrench the position of unions, such as those affiliated to the CTM, allied with the government. Independent unions denied registration cannot bargain or call strikes, and are excluded from tripartite organizations. Collective agreements also often include closed shop and exclusion clauses allowing unions to control hiring and force the sacking of workers expelled by the union. These exclusion clauses were declared to be illegal by the Supreme Court in April 2001, but it is by no means certain that this will bring about an end to the practice.

There is a tradition of tripartite framework agreements and collective bargaining occurs at all levels. There is no official collective bargaining in the public sector though unions have bypassed official structures, transforming "general working conditions" discussions into actual collective bargaining agreements. Notice must be given of strike action. If a conciliation and arbitration board rules a strike illegal, employees must return immediately to work or face dismissal. Conversely, if a strike is ruled legal, the employer must close the plant and may not hire new replacement workers. In practice, although strike notices are common, actual strikes are not, although unofficial stoppages occur more frequently.

A major contributor to economic and employment growth over recent years has been the maquiladora (sub-contract assembly) sector launched in 1966. By its peak in 2000 the sector had grown to provide employment to around 1.3 million workers in some four thousand or so (mainly US-owned) plants close to the US border. The competitive advantage of the maquiladora sector has been low cost labour for exported products. The firms exhibited a much greater growth rate than that shown by the Mexican economy as a whole. US unions expressed growing concern at the use of the maquiladora sector – which began as a zone to give work to migrants denied entry into the United States – to undercut domestic activity and labour standards. The ICFTU says that so-called "protection contracts" are widespread in the maquiladoras. Under these, sham unions are registered with their organizers paid to avert strikes and independent union organizing.

Mexico's record for union corruption and poor democracy was further tarnished in 2002 when a federal magistrate issued indictments following allegations of embezzlement against PEMEX union leaders in relation to a donation worth tens of millions of dollars by the union to the PRI during the 2000 presidential campaign. Similar accusations flared alleging corruption, theft and a lack of transparency and democracy against several unions.

The country's reputation for violence against trade union activists was demonstrated on April 1, 2002, when, in the Labour Board offices, hired thugs assaulted labour lawyers Arturo Alcalde Justiani and Arturo Hernández Calzada who were pleading a case on behalf of the Mexican Pilots' Union (ASPA). Similarly violent attacks are not uncommon against union activists and organizers.

3 Trade Union Centres

Confederación de Trabajadores de México (CTM)
Confederation of Mexican Workers
Address. Vallarta No. 8 Col. Tabacalera CP 06030, Mexico, DF
Phone. +52 5 35 0658
Fax. +52 5 90 50966
E-mail. ctmrelaciones@netservice.com.mx
Leadership. Leonardo Rodríguez Alcaine (secretary-general)

Membership. Reports 5 million
History and character. The CTM is by far the largest and most influential Mexican centre, and has always been closely allied to the PRI. It was formed in 1936, and soon became the dominant force in Mexican trade unionism, its power surviving a series of breakaways by factions critical of the relationship with the PRI. The dominant figure in the CTM for decades was Fidel Velázquez (Don Fidel), who was the secretary-general from 1941 until his death in 1997 and also exercised significant influence over parts of the labour movement outside the CTM. CTM officials have held numerous political offices, including seats in Congress and as state governors for the PRI. The CTM has played a key role in the development of the social security system and federal institutions in the field of social and economic welfare and in creating housing schemes for the low-paid. Its critics maintain that it is bureaucratic and has prevented the development of union democracy and effective plant and industry-level collective bargaining.

In the 1980s and 1990s the CTM entered into a series of tripartite pacts with government and employers aimed at controlling price and wage inflation and controlling public deficits. A series of financial crises triggered by problems including foreign debt, inflation and lack of investor confidence punctuated the agreement of such pacts. The pacts (which have now lapsed) produced episodes of tension between the CTM leadership and rank and file and CTM and government as one consequence was that real wages fell behind.

In the 2000 presidential election campaign (where it supported the defeated PRI candidate Francisco Labastida Ochoa) the CTM called for free collective bargaining without government interference, for pension contributions to be tax free, better protection of the consumer's right to fair prices, expansion of the social welfare system, a more equitable tax system aimed at financing improved public services and greater devolution to the regions.
International affiliation. ICFTU

Confederación Revolucionaria de Obreros y Campesinos
Revolutionary Confederation of Workers and Peasants
Address. Hamburgo 250 Col. Juarez, Mexico DF 06600, Mexico
Phone +52 55-52085444 –49
Fax. +52 55-52085444
E-mail. crocnacional@ifocel.net.mx
Website. www.croc.org.mx
International affiliation. WCL

Union Nacional de Trabajadores (UNT)
National Union of Workers
Address. c/o Sindicato de Telefonistas, Rio Neva nº 16, 1er piso, Col. Cuauhtemoc, 6500 México
Phone. +52 5551 401483
Fax. +52 5551 401483
E-mail. untcioac@hotmail.com
Membership. 1.5 million
History and character. The National Union of Workers (UNT) is a relatively new national federation, founded in November 1997 by an alliance of around one hundred member unions. One of UNT's more vocal member unions is the Frente Auténtico del Trabajo/Authentic Labor Front (FAT). The UNT has built a reputation as an independent movement, representing a firm break with the charges of cronyism and corruption levelled at Mexico's more established federations.

The UNT responded to federal law reforms proposed by President Fox by putting forward its own reform proposals calling for an open registry of unions and contracts, for an end to the corrupt labour boards and for a system of independent labour courts, and the right to strike.
International affiliation. ICFTU

Micronesia, Federated States of

Capital: Palikir (Pohnpei Island)
Population: 108,000 (2004 est.)

1 Political and Economic Background

The UN trusteeship of these islands ended in 1990 and they are now an independent state in a compact of free association with the United States. There is a parliamentary system of government but no formal political parties.

These are remote and scattered islands with little infrastructure. There is subsistence farming and fishing with considerable unemployment and the economy depends on US financial assistance.

GDP (purchasing power parity) $277m. (2002 est.); GDP per capita (purchasing power parity) $2,000 (2002 est.).

2 Trade Unionism

There is a general constitutional right to form associations but no trade unions have been formed. The government is the main formal employer, and sets wages administratively. Micronesia is not a member of the ILO.

Moldova

Capital: Chisinau
Population: 4.45 m. (2004 est.)

1 Political and Economic Background

Moldova declared independence from the Soviet Union in 1991. Its post-independence politics have been somewhat volatile, with numerous small parties periodically allying and fragmenting. The exception has been the Communist Party (PCRM), which has a strong, centralized structure; previously in opposition, it won a landslide victory in the February 2001 parliamentary elections, taking 71 of the 101 seats with 49.9% of the vote and forming the government, with PCRM chairman Vladimir Voronin being elected President by the Assembly and Vasile Tarlev becoming Prime Minister. The PCRM is the only officially communist party to have been elected to power in the independent states created out of the former Soviet Union.

Moldova was established on the basis of the former Moldovan Soviet Socialist Republic and had never previously existed as an independent state. A proportion of its population is unreconciled to rule from Chisinau and Russia has provided backing for a de facto breakaway entity created on the east bank of the Dniester River – the Dniester Moldovan Republic (DMR) – with a mainly Ukrainian and Russian population. Although not enjoying international recognition, the DMR is outside the control of the central government, electing its own parliament and president.

The Moldovan economy has an agricultural base, with 40% of the labour force working in the farm sector. Land privatization has been undertaken and state-owned enterprises privatized through a voucher system. Since 2001 President Voronin has sought to continue with privatization while strengthening social safety nets. Like most former Soviet republics Moldova experienced deep recession in the early 1990s with the loss of its former markets. There was a further recession in 1998–99 as a knock-on from the crisis in Russia, Moldova's major trading partner. There has been positive growth since 2001, with GDP increasing at a rate of 6 or 7 percent per annum in the period 2001-04, although Moldova remains the poorest country in Europe; some 25% of the workforce is employed in other countries.

GDP (purchasing power parity) $7.79bn. (2004 est.); GDP per capita (purchasing power parity) $1,800 (2004 est.).

2 Trade Unionism

Moldova ratified ILO Conventions No. 87 (Freedom of Association and Protection of the Right to Organize, 1948) and No. 98 (Right to Organize and Collective Bargaining, 1949) in 1996. The constitution and other legislation, including the Trade Union Law of 2000 and the Labour Code of 2003, provide for trade union rights and in practice unions are well entrenched and engage in collective bargaining in most sectors. Union officials may not be dismissed by their employers without the consent of a higher-level union body.

National minimum wage levels are set though tripartite negotiations, providing a framework for sectoral and enterprise-level collective bargaining. There is no right to strike for government employees or those in essential services, including public transport, telecommunications and energy. In other sectors, a strike is legal only if approved by two-thirds of the work force in a secret ballot. The leading cause of strikes in recent years has been wage arrears.

The old Soviet-era trade union structure, renamed the General Federation of Trade Unions of Moldova (FGSRM), inherited the assets of the former official trade unions and retained an effective monopoly after independence, with virtually all enterprises unionized. The FGSRM joined the ICFTU in 1996. In late 2000 a bloc of unions broke away to form the "Solidaritate" (Solidarity) union, although 80% of union members have remained within the FGSRM, now renamed the Confederation of Trade Unions of the Republic of Moldova (CSRM). The ICFTU has accused the government of "trying to break the independent union movement and introduce government-controlled unions" by sponsoring the formation of Solidaritate, which is close to the Communist Party, in power since February 2001. According to the ICFTU, government officials in some districts have made efforts, directly or through state enterprise directors, to persuade union branches to disaffiliate from the CSRM. In some cases these efforts have been successful, unions disaffiliating from the CSRM to join Solidaritate including the Federation of Unions of Chemical Industry and Energy Workers. The government has countered that the establishment of two trade union centres increases the freedom of choice for workers and that it treats both centres equally and without discrimination. The government says it accords CSRM and Solidaritate equal representation in negotiation of the national-level collective bargaining agreement and are that they are consulted equally as social partners in areas such as the drafting of labour legislation

3 Trade Union Centre

Confederatia Sindicatelor din Republica Moldova (CSRM)
Confederation of Trade Unions of the Republic of Moldova
Address. 129 August 31 Street, 2012 Chisinau
Phone. +3732 232 789
Fax. +3732 237 698
E-mail. cfsind@cni.md
Website. www.csrm.md
Membership. 543,000
History and character. The CSRM (previously known as the General Federation of Trade Unions of Moldova, FGSRM) is the reformed trade union structure from the Soviet era. It retained the assets of the former structure, such as social and holiday facilities and a continuing role in the administration of the state social insurance system. Until the breakaway of Solidaritate in 2000 it was the only trade union centre in Moldova and still retains about 80% of the organized workforce. Its biggest affiliates are the "Agroindsind" (food and agricultural workers) federation with 178,658 members and the Education and Science Union with 139,681 members.

In the 1990s the FGSRM was active in leading protests over the problem of wage arrears and this has remained a problem, exacerbated by the impact of price inflation on late payment. Since the Communist Party victory in the February 2001 elections, the CSRM has faced persistent challenges from the newly formed Solidaritate, which has benefited from the support of the ruling party. Unions which refused to sign up to a declaration of support for government policy in 2002, such as Agroindsind, have reportedly faced harassment from government officials, such as tax inspectors, and in June 2004 a rival federation of food and agricultural workers to Agroindsind was set up under Solidaritate auspices. The CSRM also says that it has been exluded from certain national-level bodies of various types in favour of Solidaritate, although it has retained its position on the main consultative bodies.

International affiliation. ICFTU; GCTU

Monaco

Capital: Monaco Ville
Population: 32,000 (2004 est.)

1 Political and Economic Background

The Principality of Monaco is a hereditary monarchy in which the Prince appoints the government, with French involvement. There is a popularly elected 24-member National Council.

Economic activities include light manufacturing, tourism and financial services, and Monaco is a leading tax haven. Nationals of Monaco and foreign residents do not pay income tax, and taxation on company profits is low. Only 16% of the population are Monegasques, with a wide range of foreign residents.

GDP (purchasing power parity) $870m. (2000 est.); GDP per capita (purchasing power parity) $27,000 (2000 est.).

2 Trade Unionism

Freedom of association and the right to strike are guaranteed by the 1962 Constitution. Monaco is not a member of the International Labour Organization.

Trade unions, organized as the Union des Syndicats de Monaco, participate in Monaco's consultative Tripartite Economic Council along with the Employers' Federation of Monaco. Anti-union discrimination is prohibited by law but union density is estimated at less than 10%. There is no ICFTU or WCL affiliate. Collective bargaining is practiced. Strikes rarely occur and are prohibited in the case of government employees.

Mongolia

Capital: Ulan Bator
Population: 2.75 m. (2004 est.)

1 Political and Economic Background

From 1924 until 1990 Mongolia was a one-party communist state ruled by the Mongolian People's Revolutionary Party (MPRP). In 1990 political pluralism was introduced, the MPRP retaining power in elections that year and in 1992. In 1996, the MPRP was heavily defeated by a coalition of opposition parties known as the Democratic Union, but the MPRP returned to power in a landslide victory in elections in July 2000. The elections of June 2004 resulted in a hung parliament; after two months of deadlock a coalition of opposition parties and the MPRP agreed to form a "grand coalition government", with the Prime Minister coming from the Democratic Party.

Most of the labour force is engaged in herding and cultivating the land, with mining and processing of minerals the major form of industrial activity. Mongolia was badly affected by the loss of Soviet aid in 1990-91. From 1996, the Democratic Union pushed ahead with a programme to liberalize the economy and attract foreign investment, and although most larger enterprises remained under state control the private sector now generates 75% of GDP. The MPRP government elected in 2000 was seen as divided between traditional communists and those who believed in continuing free market reforms but at a moderate pace. GDP grew at a rate of 4% in 2002 and over 5% in 2003 but substantial unemployment and underemployment and poverty remains, especially in areas such as the shanty towns around Ulan Bator.

GDP (purchasing power parity) $4.88bn. (2004 est.); GDP per capita (purchasing power parity) $1,800 (2004 est.).

2 Trade Unionism

Mongolia ratified ILO Conventions No. 87 (Freedom of Association and Protection of the Right to Organize, 1948) and No. 98 (Right to Organize and Collective Bargaining, 1949) in 1969.

Trade unions were established in the 1920s after the communist Mongolian People's Revolutionary Party (MPRP) came to power, although there was little development until after World War II. Until 1990 the unions functioned in accordance with the Soviet bloc model: there were no organizations outside the single structure of the Central Council of Mongolian Trade Unions (CCMTU) and the Council's constitution named the MPRP as the leader and guide of the working masses.

Following the end of the one-party state, Mongolia adopted a new constitution in 1992. Under this all workers may form or join union or professional organizations of their choosing. The CCMTU transfigured itself into the Confederation of Mongolian Trade Unions (CMTU), now affiliated to the ICFTU, and most union members affiliated to this. A small Association of Free Trades Unions was formed in the 1990s but this has now merged into the the CMTU.

Union membership was reported to have fallen to 430,000 by 1999, representing less than half of the workforce, and is since reported to have stabilized at around 400,000. This reflects the impact of privatization and downsizing of state enterprises and the development of small non-union firms.

Collective bargaining is provided for and there is a Labour Dispute Settlement Commission to assist resolution of conflicts. There is a right to strike, other than in essential services, which include police, utilities, and transportation workers.

3 Trade Union Centre

Confederation of Mongolian Trade Unions (CMTU)
Address. Sukhbaataryn Talbai 3, Ulan Bator 11
Phone. +976 11 321987
Fax. +976 11 322 128
E-mail. cmtu@mongol.net
History and character. The Central Council of Mongolian Trade Unions was formed under communist rule in 1927. At its 13th Congress in 1987 dissatisfaction began to be expressed at the way in which union reform was failing to keep pace with economic change. Delegates strongly criticized the centre for being too bureaucratic and out of touch with the membership. In 1990, reformed as a federation (later a confederation) it held an extraordinary congress and adopted a new action programme and constitution. The following year its long-standing affiliation to the WFTU was suspended, and it later joined the ICFTU. It has eleven affiliated unions.
International affiliations. ICFTU

Morocco

Capital: Rabat
Population: 31.69 m. (2003 est.)

1 Political and Economic Background

The Kingdom of Morocco was established in 1957 (the former French and Spanish protectorates having joined together as an independent sultanate the previous year). Under the 1992 constitution the powers of the monarch were reduced, although direct criticism of the monarchy is still not considered acceptable. King Hassan II was the monarch from 1961 until his death on July 23, 1999, when he was succeeded by his son, Mohammed VI.

Elections to a reformed legislature held in 1997 resulted in no individual party achieving dominance, eleven parties winning between 11 and 42 seats each in the lower house. In February 1998 the King appointed Abderrahmane Youssoufi, the leader of the Socialist Union of Popular Forces (USFP) as prime minister in a coalition government dominated by opposition parties. The change of government was reflected in pledges to investigate the fate of hundreds of government opponents who had "disappeared" in the period from the 1960s to the 1980s. The USFP is traditionally associated with the Confédération Démocratique du Travail (CDT – see below, under trade union centres).

Youssoufi had been sentenced to death in absentia in the 1970s, before receiving a Royal pardon in 1980. As prime minister he partly succeeded in reforming electoral and labour laws, assisted by his finance minister and the head of the USFP parliamentary faction, Fathallah Oualalou. Driss Jetou, a non-party official, replaced him as Morocco's prime minister on Oct. 9, 2002. King Mohammed VI has largely continued the policies of his late father, though he has pledged to achieve greater political openness and economic transparency. Opponents still accuse the regime of being beholden to the *makhzen*, a powerful yet largely anonymous clique of powerbrokers who traditionally advise the monarch.

Following massive terror attacks on Casablanca in 2003, the government wants to accelerate the alleviation of poverty and combat Islamic extremists. The Rabat government also wishes to resolve the long-standing dispute over Western Sahara, and address other pressing concerns, such as the rights and status of Berbers, who constitute almost a third of the population.

Unlike most Arab countries, Morocco is not a major oil producer, and its economy benefited from the slump in oil prices from the mid-1980s. It is the world's leading exporter of raw and refined phosphates. Agriculture (badly affected by drought in recent years) employs 40-50% of the work force and fluctuations in farm output because of drought make overall economic performance erratic. Other sectors include fishing, light manufacturing and tourism. According to estimates in 2003, services account for 40% of the work force, and industry for 15%. Morocco has a mixed economy and launched a privatization programme in 1990. It has continuing problems with the level of its external debt and in attracting foreign investment. However, favourable rainfall helped economic growth reach 6% in 2003.

Morocco ratified ILO Convention No. 138 (Minimum Age Convention, 1973) on Jan. 5, 2000 and Convention 182 (Worst Forms of Child Labour, 1999) on Jan. 26, 2001. In February 1999 it was estimated that Morocco still had around 1.8m. working minors under the age of 15.

GDP (purchasing power parity) $128.3bn. (2003 est.); GDP per capita (purchasing power parity) $4,000 (2003 est.).

2 Trade Unionism

Although Morocco ratified ILO Convention No. 98 (Right to Organize and Collective Bargaining, 1949) in 1957 it has never ratified Convention No. 87 (Freedom of Association and Protection of the Right to Organize, 1948). However, the right to form unions is enshrined in the constitution, which says that any group of eight workers may organize a union. Multiple unions exist within different enterprises. There is no law specifically prohibiting anti-union discrimination and union activists can be dismissed without effective sanctions, while some employers promote company unions.

For many years three major centres dominated the trade union environment in Morocco: the UMT, the UGTM and the CDT. To these have more recently been added the Union Nationale Marocaine du Travail (UNMT) and the Fédération Démocratique du Travail (FDT). Although created only in April 2003, the FDT already appears to have garnered as much influence as the established centres. There are also about a dozen smaller federations in Morocco. Accurate figures for the number of the centres' members are elusive due to double-counting and non-paying adherents, and estimates vary widely, but in total they have several hundred thousand members. Although union density is only about 5.8 per cent, or 600,000 workers out of 9 million (according to the UNDP), organized trade unionism arguably constitutes the strongest independent social force in Morocco.

Under the 1992 constitution the upper house of the legislature, the Chamber of Counsellors, or Majlis al-Mustasharin, has 270 members indirectly elected as representatives of local authorities, professional chambers and trade unions. Twenty-seven seats are reserved for trade unionists and wage-earners (constituting 10% of the total); members hold their seats for nine-year terms. Elections were held on Dec. 5, 1997, when the CDT took 11 seats, the UMT eight seats, and the UGTM took three seats, while five smaller union bodies took one seat each. Further joint elections for union delegates to the Mustasharin were held in September 2003, at which the CDT and FDT took most seats.

The UMT has no political party affiliation, and the UGTM is affiliated to the centrist Independence Party (Istiqlal). Traditionally the CDT was affiliated with the Socialist Union of Popular Forces (USFP) of Abderrahmane Youssoufi, prime minister until 2002. Since then, however, it appears that the USFP-CDT alliance has come asunder. By contrast, the FDT, created in April 2003, is led by a parliamentary legislator for the USFP, which suggests that a significant realignment between the party and unions has occurred.

The unions have been affected by past waves of repression and "disappearances". Scores of trade unionists, many of them members of the UMT, were arrested during 1991. That year also, two of the UMT leaders thought missing since 1972 were discovered to have been in detention since that time. In 1992 the CDT leader, Noubir Amaoui, made statements to the press critical of the monarchy and Morocco's political system, was tried and received a two-year prison sentence. Driss Laghnimi, regional secretary of the UGTM, was jailed soon after for making insulting remarks about King Hassan. They were not released until July 1993.

The change of government after elections in late 1997, and the accession of a young new king, Mohammed VI, after the death of his father, King Hassan II, in July 1999, were seen as improving respect for civil liberties. Indeed, 1999 was the fourth consecutive year without reports of "disappearances". However, the ICFTU reported in 1999 that trade unionists continued to be arrested and imprisoned, and in September that year it lodged a complaint with the ILO. On Oct. 8, 1999, ICFTU general secretary Bill Jordan wrote to Prime Minster Youssoufi complaining of the detention of strikers under the penal code. Jordan observed that the continuation of this practice "is all the more incomprehensible, given that it clearly runs counter to the new, more open political and social climate announced recently".

In November 1999 King Mohammed VI dismissed the hard-line Interior Minister, Driss Basré, who was regarded as having been the driving force behind past abuses by the security forces. Nonetheless, questions remained over the powers allowed to the centres. In December 2003, for instance, the credentials committee of the African regional meeting of the ILO, held in the Ethiopian capital, Addis Ababa, complained that all of the Moroccan delegates sent to the conference appeared to be government appointees.

Collective bargaining exists in many industries, and also in some service and public sector areas, although for most employees collective bargaining does not occur. Disputes over non-implementation of agreements by employers are common. The Ministry of Labour provides conciliation services and unions have made increasing use of the courts in industrial disputes. While the right to strike exists in law and open disputes are not uncommon, government agencies tend to intervene in disputes on an ad hoc basis. In sectors where national security is deemed to be at stake, strikes are outlawed and in some cases union officials have been imprisoned. The year 2004 was marked by numerous strikes, especially in the public health sector, ports and railways.

Labour laws are enforced to some degree in the public sector and large enterprises (although in some cases the authorities lack the resources or the will to enforce laws where employers are resistant). But in small businesses and the informal sector breaches are common and child labour occurs. The custom of families adopting young girls and using them as indentured domestic servants is socially accepted and unregulated.

A new labour law came into force in June 2004, which aimed at improving employee protection and professional relations, promoting transparency and bringing Morocco's legislation closer to European laws. The law's enactment resulted in changes to regulations concerning laying-offs, and the reinforcement of rights to negotiation. A conference held at the Marrakech School of Commerce on Jan. 30, 2005, praised the law for helping to "modernise the business environment". However, some delegates commented that it still failed to cover workers in private houses and "traditional" sectors such as corner shops or garages.

3 Trade Union Centres

Confédération Démocratique du Travail (CDT)
Democratic Confederation of Labour
Address. 64 rue El Mortada, Quartiers Palmiers, 01 Casablanca
Phone. +212 22 994470
Fax. +212 22 994473
E-mail. cdt@mis.net.ma
Leadership. Mohamed Noubir El Amaoui (secretary-general)
History and character. The CDT was founded in November 1978. A general strike called by the CDT in 1981, and attendant demonstrations, resulted in incidents in which dozens died in clashes with the security forces. During the 1980s the CDT built its influence mainly in the public sector. It criticized the government on issues such as corruption, emphasis on short-term prestige projects, lack of respect for trade union

freedoms, the absence of a proper framework for collective bargaining, and dependence on external forces such as the International Monetary Fund. In 1991, the CDT opposed the participation of Moroccan troops in the Gulf War coalition. In 1992–93 secretary-general Amaoui was imprisoned after describing the government as "a bunch of thieves with no future" but was released after widespread international protests.

The CDT took 11 of the 27 seats allocated to trade unionists in elections to the Assembly of Counsellors, on Dec. 5, 1997, thus making it the largest union bloc in the house. The Confederation has historically been allied to the Union Socialiste des Forces Populaires (USFP, National Union of Popular Forces), which is in turn affiliated to the Socialist International.

The USFP was constituted in its current form in 1974. Its leader, Abderrahmane Youssoufi, was appointed Prime Minister on Feb. 4, 1998 but was replaced as premier by a non-party appointee on Oct. 9, 2002, following national parliamentary elections. These 2002 elections also saw the CDT break its allegiance to the USFP. The CDT secretary general, El Amaoui, created his own political party that year and the centre continued to complain of unwarranted interference, filing a case of alleged anti-union discrimination with the ILO committee on freedom of association in December 2002. Tensions within the CDT, meanwhile, led to the creation of a breakaway union centre, the FDT, in 2003 (see below). In sectoral elections to the Chamber of Counsellors held in September 2003, the FDT won 26% of votes from workers in national education, compared to 24% for the CDT.

Fédération Démocratique du Travail (FDT)
Democratic Federation of Labour

Leadership. Tayeb Mounchid (secretary-general)

History and character. The Democratic Federation of Labour (FDT) was founded in April 2003 as a breakaway from the CDT, following general complaints about a "lack of internal democracy" in the latter body. Its secretary general is Tayeb Mounchid, a member of parliament from Rabat for the established socialist political party, the USFP.

Like the CDT, the FDT is particularly strong amongst public sector workers. In September 2003, in sectoral elections to the Chamber of Counsellors, the FDT won 26% of votes from workers in national education, compared to 24% for the CDT; it also took nearly half of the votes cast within the public health sector.

Two FDT members, Bougnine Lahcen and Saili Mohamed, were involved in protests over alleged human rights abuses in Moroccan-administered Western Sahara in October 2003. The FDT national council met in January 2004, and FDT officials held two sessions of a "social dialogue" with Morocco's Prime Minister in June and October that year. The FDT was heavily involved in a growing wave of industrial action by doctors and health workers towards the end of 2004, including a sit-in at the Ministry of Health, via its affiliate health union, the SNSP.

Union Générale des Travailleurs du Maroc (UGTM)
General Union of Moroccan Workers

Address. 9 rue du Rif, Angle Route de Médiouna, Casablanca

Phone. +212 2 28 78 71

Fax. +212 2 28 21 44

E-mail. ugtmaroc@iam.net.ma

Leadership. Abderrazzaq Afilal (secretary-general)

History and character. Founded in 1960, the UGTM is linked to the centrist Independence Party (Istiqlal). The centre won three seats in elections to the upper house, Chamber of Counsellors, in December 1997.

Istiqlal, one of the Koutla bloc of left-nationalist parties, is led by Abbas el-Fassi and was represented in the coalition government formed by Youssoufi in 1998. In elections to the lower house, the Chamber of Representatives, held on Sept. 27, 2002, Istiqlal won 48 seats just behind the 50 seats of its chief rival, the USFP, which came first in the ballot. Istiqlal narrowly squeezed out the USFP to take first place in September 2003 local elections.

While the UGTM has public and private sector members, its traditional core strength is among agricultural workers. In the past it has been less militant than the other federations, but it did participate in the 1990s demands for reform. The UGTM opened a research and training centre in Rabat in 1998. In 2004 the UGTM was involved in strikes in the agricultural sector.

International affiliation. WCL

Union Marocaine du Travail (UMT)
Moroccan Workers' Union

Address. 232 Avenue des Far, Casablanca

Phone. +212 2 30 0118

Fax. +212 2 30 78 54

Leadership. Mahjoub Ben Seddiq (secretary-general)

History and character. The UMT was founded in 1955 and is the oldest of the main Moroccan centres. It has members in both the public and private sectors. In 1960 it suffered the secession of the UGTM and three years later the UMT left the ICFTU after the formation of the All-African Trade Union Federation (the predecessor to the OATUU). The AATUF opposed African centres having affiliations to non-African international organizations.

However in 1990 the UMT re-affiliated to the ICFTU after its secretary-general Mahjoub Ben Seddiq declared that the UMT could not afford to remain isolated from the world. Ben Seddiq is Morocco's best-known trade unionist. He has led the UMT since its inception, and in the late 1950s he worked with Abderrahmane Youssoufi, who later founded the USFP and became prime minister. However, the UMT is proud of its independent status and is not directly affiliated to any political party. According to a US Department of Labour Report on Morocco, dated July 2004, the UMT "dominates the private sector and has negotiated the most collective labour agreements". The report quoted commentators to the effect that the UMT enjoyed close ties to the monarchy.

The UMT won nine seats in December 1997 elections to the upper house, the Chamber of Counsellors, taking second place to the CDT, which took 11 seats. The centre is strong amongst farming communities; it garnered nearly half of all votes cast amongst agricultural sector trade unionists during additional elections to the Chamber in September 2003.

Even so, the centre feels that it has suffered a legacy of discrimination at the hands of the state. In 1991 the UMT discovered that long-missing leaders had been incarcerated in state jails for 20 years. In July 1998, it reported that a total of 1,400 elected officials had been sacked for union activities in recent years, and that many faced criminal charges after calling strikes. In October 1998, a UMT leader, Abdelhaz Rouissi, who had been missing since October 1964, was pronounced officially dead, as part of the process whereby the Consultative Council of Human Rights sought to establish what had happened to those who had disappeared in the 1960s–1980s. In December 2000 the UMT submitted a report to the ICFTU regarding the harrassment of its officials by a militia hired by the multinational company where they were employees. With government support all dismissed officials were reinstated.

The UMT cited the garment, textile, construction, food, public transport, cleaning and agricultural sectors as also having poor sanitary and safety conditions in 2002. On International Women's Day, March 8, 2004, the UMT, in conjunction with ICFTU, launched a two-year campaign to see more women unionized, and to protect female workers from the effects of globalization. According to Amal El-Amri, head of the UMT Women's Committee, the chief target of activities in the first year would be women working in the informal economy and export processing zones. Currently the UMT has 306,000 members, of whom only 12% are women.

The National Federation of Professional Groups affiliated to the UMT in May 2004. In September 2004 the UMT opposed a new "organic law" relating to strikes, despite meetings held in July 2004 with Morocco's prime minister. There was also evidence of internal strife, as witnessed by Ben Seddiq's sacking of his deputy, Mohamed Abderrazak, on April 1, 2004, and the UMT national secretary, Salim Redouane, on March 12. These moves coincided with a scandal involving the centre and Morocco's Caisse Nationale de Sécurité Sociale (National Social Security and Pensions Fund), although the scandal may not have been directly linked to the sackings. In the Moroccan press, Redouane condemned the dismissals as "illegal and ridiculous", justified by "false pretexts", and representative of the "inert state" of UMT officials.
International affiliation. ICFTU

Union Nationale Marocaine du Travail (UNMT)
National Labour Union of Morocco
Address. 352, Bd. Mohammed V - Rabat
Leadership. Abdelslam Maâti (secretary-general)
History and character. The UNMT is affiliated to the Party of Justice and Development (PJD), a moderate Islamist group that did well in elections to the Chamber of Representatives held on Sept. 27, 2002. The UNMT itself was founded in 1973. It tends to represent workers in public education, public health, building trades, textiles and agriculture. In elections in December 1997 to the upper house, the Chamber of Counsellors, the UNMT won two of the seats reserved for the trade unions. In September 2003 the UNMT also gained many votes within the agricultural sector, during additional elections to the Chamber.

The PJD was founded in 1999 but evolved from the former Constitutional and Democratic Popular Movement, which itself was founded in the 1960s. It took third place in the 2002 elections with 43 seats; the longer established USFP and Istiqlal received 50 and 48 seats respectively. However, it fared much worse in the late 2003 municipal elections when, responding to public anger at the Casablanca bombings, it cautiously fielded fewer candidates. The party backs adherence to sharia law and Islamic finance, shunned calls to join the socialist-led government, and is led by Abdelkrim El Khatib.

In November 2000, security forces in Agadir (in the south) forcibly broke up a sit-in demonstration by UNMT unionists, who were striking for better working conditions in a cannery. Allegedly one died and eight were seriously injured. The UNMT participated in May Day demonstrations in 2001, which the Moroccan press noted was a significant assertion of an Islamist desire to enter the mainstream of trade unionism. Less than a month later UNMT-affiliated health sector workers conducted a major sit-in to protest ministerial "indifference to union demands"; protests were prohibited in the province of Rabat-Salé.

The unofficial though popular and widespread Islamist movement Al Adl Wa Al-Ihssane – distinct from the PJD – also applauded the working class on May 1, 2001; denounced the "degradations" affecting it; and called for the creation of a single syndicalist front to protect the proletariat and to evolve more effective trade unionist action. It was thought that Adl favoured the UNMT over other union centres. The newspaper *Maroc-Hebdo* editorialized that the UNMT, by dint of its more assertive posture under Maâti's leadership, seemed to be embarrassing the other established union centres into consulting with it and to be "set on upsetting the political chessboard". While discounting the arrival of an Islamist-unionist "tidal wave", the paper nonetheless concluded that Adl was showing signs of wishing to detach itself from its "strictly religious" image and that this phenomenon – namely, of diversifying into other sectors, including trade unionism – should put the classical syndicate centres on the alert.

Also in 2001, the UNMT reaffirmed its commitment to "social dialogue" with the government. At the same time it launched a campaign to improve working standards in primary and secondary education. As of early January 2005, sections of the UNMT co-operated with the UMT and three health syndicates in organizing strikes after the health minister failed to satisfy their collective demands for a reshuffling of the status of doctors and nurses.

WESTERN SAHARA

Sovereignty over Western Sahara is disputed, with Morocco and the Polisario Front engaging in military conflict from 1975–91 prior to the intervention of a UN peacekeeping force. Moroccan trade unions exist in the Moroccan-controlled area of Western Sahara, which comprises most of the territory and all the population centres. Most union members in Western Sahara itself are employees of the Moroccan government or state-owned organizations.

Polisario has sponsored a labour front, the Sario Federation of Labour (UGTSARIO). In April 1996 the federation encouraged Saharawi phosphate workers and their families to go on strike over bad working conditions and occupy the headquarters of the company "Fos Bucraa" in the capital of Western Sahara, El Ayoune. In recent years UGTSARIO's active presence in Western Sahara has diminished, and it has had to restrict trade union activities to the refugee camps located in western Algeria where the Polisario Front is based. However, the UGTSARIO still enjoys good ties with some European, Arab and African trade union centres.

UGTSARIO has worked hard to keep alive its cause and, if not experiencing a revival, at least it has survived the years. In 2004 the group criticized Moroccan fellow trade unionists for neglecting their plight, and that of Moroccan workers, who, it charged, paid 2.5% of their wages to fund Morocco's "expansionist adventures". The 5th conference of the UGTSARIO, held in a refugee camp in May 2004, called on the world to "dismantle the wall of shame [Moroccan-erected barrier] which tears Sahrawi families ...and which prevents the development of Western Sahara". Delegates denounced the "obstacles" Morocco placed in the way of a long-delayed referendum, pursuant to UN Security Council Resolution 1495. They also condemned abuse of workers, including forced disappearances, torture and arbitrary detention; and called on the ILO to send a team to investigate poor working conditions in the area. Mohamed Cheikh Mohamed Lebib was re-elected secretary general.

Mozambique

Capital: Maputo
Population: 18.81 m. (2004 est.)

1 Political and Economic Background

Mozambique achieved independence from Portugal in 1975 after more than a decade of guerrilla war against Portuguese colonial rule. A people's republic was declared, with Marxism-Leninism as the official ideology, and the Front for the Liberation of Mozambique (Frelimo) became the sole legal party. The regime continued to be opposed militarily by the anti-communist Mozambique National Resistance (Renamo). In 1989 Frelimo abandoned Marxism-Leninism and in 1990 a new constitution was adopted providing for a multi-party electoral system and a free market economy. In October 1992 Frelimo and Renamo signed a peace accord, which was implemented by 1994. The first multi-party elections, in October 1994, resulted in Frelimo taking 129 of the 250 Assembly seats and Renamo 112, while the incumbent President, Joaquim Chissano of Frelimo, was elected. Chissano and Frelimo won again in presidential and legislative elections in December 1999 although Renamo disputed the validity of the results. Frelimo won a solid victory in the next elections held in December 2004. Chissano was replaced as President by Frelimo's Armando Guebuza.

At independence in 1975, Mozambique was one of the world's poorest countries. Frelimo mismanagement of the economy and a brutal civil war from 1977-92 exacerbated the situation. During the 1990s, and with the end of the civil war, Mozambique carried out market-oriented reforms, privatized many state enterprises, and encouraged foreign investment. It enjoyed high economic growth rates, giving it a reputation as one of the most economically successful African states in the period post-democratization. In spite of these gains, Mozambique remains dependent upon foreign assistance for much of its annual budget, and the majority of the population remains below the poverty line. Subsistence agriculture continues to employ the vast majority of the country's workforce.

GDP (purchasing power parity) $21.23bn. (2004 est.); GDP per capita (purchasing power parity) $1,200 (2004 est.).

2 Trade Unionism

Mozambique joined the ILO in 1976 and ratified Conventions No. 87 (Freedom of Association and Protection of the Right to Organize, 1948) and No. 98 (Right to Organize and Collective Bargaining, 1949) in 1996.

Trade union activities were closely circumscribed under Portuguese rule. In 1983 a single-trade-union system, the OTM, was created under the control of the ruling Frelimo party. With the adoption of pluralism, trade union rights were embodied in the 1990 constitution and 1991 labour law. Since then the OTM has remained the national trade union centre while emphasizing its independence from the state. It is now affiliated to the ICFTU. However, a number of independent unions have also established a Confederation of Free and Independent Unions of Mozambique (CONSILMO).

Labour legislation provides for collective bargaining and since 1991 the government has abandoned its former role of setting all wages administratively. The minimum wage is negotiated through the tripartite Consultative Commission on Labour, which includes representatives of both the OTM and CONSILMO. There is a constitutional right to strike other than for civil servants, the police, armed forces and workers engaged in essential services, which are defined to include areas such as health care, water, electricity and posts and telecommunications. The labour law prohibits retribution against strikers. Labour disputes are normally arbitrated through a system of workers' committees, however.

3 Trade Union Centre

Organização dos Trabalhadores de Moçambique (OTM)
Mozambique Workers' Organization
Address. Rua Manuel António de Sousa 36, Maputo
Phone. +258 1 30 8836
Fax. +258 1 32 1671
E-mail. otmdis@teledata.mz
Leadership. Joaquim Fanheiro (secretary general)
Membership. 250,000
History and character. The OTM was created in 1983 following a decision of the ruling Frelimo party to create trade unions on the basis of the pre-existing production councils. The OTM's stated aims were "to develop socialist consciousness among the workers", to mobilize the workers to raise their productivity, to improve working conditions and to help to develop the country and combat famine and poverty. According to its original constitution the OTM was guided and led by Frelimo, but in 1990 the second congress declared its independence of all non-union bodies. This position has since been maintained, although critics in opposition unions say it is still close to Frelimo. In July 2000 the OTM called off a threatened general strike after the government agreed an increase in the minimum wage; had it gone ahead this would have been the first strike ever led by the OTM.

The OTM has 14 affiliate unions: the National Union of Commercial and Insurance Workers (SINECOSSE); the National Union of Public Service Employees (SINAFP); National Union of Dockworkers (SINPEOC); the National Union of Port and Railway Workers (SINPOCAF); the National Union of Civil Aviation, Postal and Communication Workers (SINTAC); the National Union of Agro-Fishery and Forestry Workers (SINTAF); the National Union of Textile and Clothing Workers (SINTEVE); the National Union of Sugar Workers (SINTIA); the National Union of Food and Beverage Workers (SINTIAB); the National Union of Cashew Workers (SINTIC); the National Union of Metal and Energy Workers (SINTIME); the National Union of Chemical, Rubber, Paper and Graphic Workers (SINTIQUIGRA); the National Union of Merchant Marine and Fishery Workers (SINTIMAP); and the National Union of Bank Workers (SNEB).
International affiliations. ICFTU; CTUC

4 Other Trade Union Organization

Confederaçãodos Sindicatos Independentes e Livres de Moçambique (CONSILMO)
Confederation of Free and Independent Unions of Mozambique
Leadership. Jeremias Timane (general secretary)
History and character. CONSILMO has 4 affiliate unions: the National Union of Security Guards of Mozambique (SINTESPGM); the National Union of Civil Construction Workers (SINTICIM); the National Union of Hotel and Tourism Workers (SINTIHOTS) and the National Union of Transport Workers (SINTRAT).

Myanmar (Burma)

Capital: Rangoon
Population: 47.72 m. (2004 est.)

1 Political and Economic Background

Burma achieved independence from the United Kingdom in 1948. In 1962 the constitution was suspended and Gen. Ne Win took power at the head of a Revolutionary Council. In 1964 all political parties were banned except the government-controlled Burma Socialist Programme Party (BSPP). In 1988, amid mounting chaos, a new military regime took power, abolished all state organizations, renamed the country Myanmar and set up a State Law and Order Restoration Council (SLORC) to rule the country. In 1990 elections were held for a new Constituent Assembly, but these resulted in victory for the opposition National League for Democracy. The regime refused to allow the elected legislature to convene, and the country has since remained under military rule. Many of the elected members from 1990 were either imprisoned, or fled into exile where they formed the National Coalition Government of the Union of Burma (NCGUB), which nominally works with the scores of other political parties, insurgent groups and other exiled political groups. In 1997 the SLORC was replaced by the State Peace and Development Council (SPDC). Most political parties inside Myanmar are banned, and the activities of the few legal parties are severely restricted.

Following the Ne Win coup, many of the major sectors of the economy – notably industry, transport, internal and external trade, communications and finance – were brought into public ownership and control. In the 1990s the government aimed to increase private sector activity and foreign investment, although state control remains dominant in key areas such as energy, heavy industry and the rice trade. 65% of the workforce are engaged in agriculture.

GDP (purchasing power parity) $74.53bn. (2004 est.); GDP per capita (purchasing power parity) $1,800 (2004 est.).

2 Trade Unionism

Trade unions first developed in the 1920s in reaction to the then widespread use of immigrant Indian and Chinese labour and union activities subsequently became closely linked to nationalist politics, with many strikes in the 1945–48 period. Following independence in 1948 (which led to the emigration of most non-Burmese workers), trade union rights granted in 1926 under British rule were incorporated in the constitution. In 1955 Burma ratified ILO Convention No. 87 (Freedom of Association and Protection of the Right to Organize, 1948). Unions were active both politically and industrially and although in 1961 the total membership of the 173, mainly one-shop, registered unions then in existence was put at only 64,000 of an urban labour force of one million, there were many unregistered unions.

In 1964, however, Gen. Ne Win abolished all trade unions, under the Law Defining the Fundamental Rights and Responsibilities of the People's Workers. In 1968 Ne Win set up a new system for workers' representation, consisting of local workers' councils at factory and township level, and a central *asiayone* (union) presided over by the Minister of Labour and controlled by Burma Socialist Programme Party (BSPP) officials. The primary task of the workers' councils was to ensure labour discipline and explain government policies and targets.

During August and September 1988 a general strike was in force throughout Rangoon and other areas of Burma in support of demonstrators' demands for the installation of a democratically elected government. The Armed Forces took control of the country on Sept. 18 and ordered a return to work. The new regime dissolved the previous government-controlled union structure and passed a Law on the Formation of Associations and Organizations, effectively banning the formation of any labour organization without official approval. In 1998 the ILO Conference condemned the government for its continuing failure to observe Convention No. 87. In response the Foreign Ministry announced that it would "cease participation in activities connected with Convention 87". In addition to internal controls, the government requires that Burmese seamen working on foreign ships do not participate in any activities of the International Transport Workers' Federation (ITF).

Burma has not ratified Convention No. 98 (Right to Organize and Collective Bargaining, 1949) and collective bargaining is not practiced. The Central Arbitration Board, set up to resolve labour disputes, has not functioned since 1988. In the public sector the government sets wages and in the private sector market forces generally apply.

Burma's human rights violations and use of forced labour have attracted intense criticism from unions and human rights organizations. In 1989 the United States suspended Burma's eligibility for trade concessions under the Generalized System of Preferences (GSP) programme, pending steps to afford its labour force internationally recognized worker rights. In 1997 Burma's trade benefits on its exports to the EU were canceled. In 1998 an ILO Commission of Inquiry found the regime guilty of "widespread and systematic" use of forced labour on a massive scale, including transportation of supplies for the military, and the building of roads, railways and bridges. In June 1999 the ILO Conference agreed to suspend Burma from receiving ILO technical assistance or attending ILO meetings due to its "flagrant and persistent failure to comply" with Convention 29 on forced labour. This move, seen as amounting to the de facto exclusion of Burma from the ILO, was greeted by the ICFTU as "an unprecedented move in the annals of this agency". In response the government said it would "cease participation in activities connected with Convention 29." In May 1999, the SPDC passed Order 1/99, requesting SPDC officials not to exercise their rights to using "voluntary labour" contained in the 1914 Village Act. The regime claimed this ended the use of forced labour. Yet the use of forced labour is believed to have increased in border regions since 1998 when the regime required military commanders to become more self-sufficient logistically. Forced labour (including forced child labour) has also been used for the construction of civilian infrastructure such as roads, the reclamation of land for agriculture, and harvesting. Despite frequent reports by the ILO citing continued forced labour and human rights abuses, the SPDC refuses to cooperate with the international labour movement on workers' rights.

A Federation of Trade Unions of Burma is reported to work underground, but its scale and effectiveness is low level and largely restricted to information gathering for advocacy purposes.

3 Trade Union Centre

There is no trade union centre.

4 Other Trade Union Organization

Federation of Trade Unions of Burma (FTUB)
E-mail. ftub@hotmail.com
Website. www.tradeunions-burma.org
Leadership. Hla Oo (president), Maung Maung (general secretary)
History and character. The FTUB was created in 1991 and its initial membership was made up of workers and students who had participated in the 1988 uprising. Unions affiliated to the FTUB played a major role in the 1988 democracy movement, and its president is an elected MP living in exile. The FTUB now works underground inside Burma "to educate, organize and strengthen Burmese workers and other pro-democracy groups to assert their rights and push the military regime to enter substantive tripartite negotiations with the National League for Democracy and the leaders of Burma's ethnic peoples". It also mobilizes exiled workers in Thailand and campaigns for their rights and conditions, and coordinates strategies with other union organizations throughout the world for political reform in Burma.

Myo Aung Thant, a member of the FTUB executive committee was sentenced in 1998 to life imprisonment for labour organization activities inside Burma. In 2003, three members of the FTUB, U Nai Min Kyi, U Yae Myint and U Naing Yatkha, were sentenced to death for high treason and charged with plotting the assassination of senior SPDC members. The ostensible reasons for their sentences were that they had attended FTUB training on the Thai–Burma border, were relaying information on forced labour to the ILO, and had published an article in a Burmese magazine which uncovered corruption in the national football league. The SPDC accuses the FTUB of "terrorist" incidents inside the country, including a bombing campaign since 1997, but this is unlikely, and probably stems more from the FTUB passing evidence of forced labour onto the ILO. The FTUB maintains offices in Thailand, the United States, Japan and Australia.
International affiliations. ICFTU

Seafarers' Union of Burma (SUB)
Address. PO Box 38, Phat Phong Post Office, Bangkok 10506, Thailand
E-mail. seagull@ksc.th.com
Leadership. Koh Koh Kaing (general secretary)
History and character. The Seafarers' Union of Burma was created in 1994 by the FTUB to represent the rights of Burma's 20-30,000 sailors working in international waters. Many sailors suffer from extortion at the hands of government and shipping company officials. Just to apply for a passport and a seaman's card costs an individual a reported US$1,500 in bribes. Most work on flag of convenience ships (FOC) and suffer from poor working and pay conditions throughout the world. The union is banned in Myanmar, but it is viewed as the legitimate representation of Burmese sailors' rights by other maritime unions. The SPDC forces sailors to join the regime-created Myanmar Overseas Seafarers' Association (MOSA), which has no international legitimacy. The SUB is campaigning for a suspension of all shipping links with Burma.
International affiliation. International Transport Workers' Federation (ITF)

Namibia

Capital: Windhoek
Population: 1.95 m. (2004 est.)

1 Political and Economic Background

Namibia became independent in 1990 following 75 years of South African rule and 23 years of guerrilla war. Under a constitution drawn up by all parties in the Constituent Assembly elected in 1989, Namibia has a liberal constitution with a limited executive presidency. The South West African People's Organization (SWAPO) won 41 of the 72 seats in the Constituent Assembly and its leader, Sam Nujoma, became the country's first President. In elections in December 1999 SWAPO retained control of the legislature and Nujoma was re-elected President after the constitution had been amended to allow him to stand for a third term, but in May 2004 Hifikepunye Pohamba was nominated as SWAPO candidate for the next presidential election.

Extraction and processing of a wide range of minerals are the bedrock of the formal economy, while employing only 3% of the workforce, and give Namibia a high GDP by African standards. However, 50% of the population are engaged in subsistence agriculture and there is widespread under-employment. The economy is closely integrated with that of South Africa.

GDP (purchasing power parity) $13.85bn. (2004 est.); GDP per capita (purchasing power parity) $7,200 (2004 est.).

2 Trade Unionism

The development of trade unionism in Namibia was heavily influenced by developments in South Africa, which was the country's colonial power until independence in 1990. Black workers could only join trade unions from 1978 onwards; previously it had been legal only for white and coloured workers to form and join trade unions. Early attempts to establish trade unions for black workers inside Namibia were supported by South African trade unions but could not succeed due to the repression by the colonial regime. The SWAPO-linked National Union of Namibian Workers (NUNW) essentially had to operate in exile from its inception in 1971 until the mid-1980s. At that time, political prisoners released from Robben Island together with community activists started to build industrial trade unions inside the country. They enjoyed enormous support even beyond the workplace and became the most significant mass movement inside Namibia before independence.

Today, the NUNW has nine affiliated industrial unions covering virtually all sectors of the economy. Their combined membership is 60,000–70,000 and unionization rates are very high in the public sector, the mining and textile industries as well as the wholesale and retail sectors. Affiliated in the pre-independence years to the WFTU, the NUNW has been affiliated to the ICFTU since 1998.

The Namibian labour movement is divided largely along political lines and a rival federation was formed in May 2002 when the Namibia People's Social Movement (NPSM) and the Namibia Federation of Trade Unions (NAFTU) merged to form the Trade Union Congress of Namibia (TUCNA). TUCNA's 13 affiliated trade unions have a combined membership of about 20,000 while the Public Service Union of Namibia (PSUN), with 25,000 members, is currently not affiliated to any union federation. The TUCNA unions and PSUN oppose the NUNW's political link with SWAPO.

Namibia ratified most ILO core conventions, including Conventions No. 87 (Freedom of Association and Protection of the Right to Organize, 1948) and No. 98 (Right to Organize and Collective Bargaining, 1949) in 1995. The 1990 constitution and the 1992 Labour Act provided for freedom of association, including for public servants, farm workers and domestic servants. About 30-50% of workers in the formal economy are members of trade unions. The 1992 Labour Act provided for the office of labour commissioner and a labour inspectorate, for a labour court supplemented by district courts, and for a tripartite advisory body, the Labour Advisory Council. The Act also provided for the establishment of Wages Commissions to set minimum wages in particular sectors. Minimum conditions of employment were laid down in the Act, provision for trade union recognition was made and individual employment rights were established. Provisions were also made for the registration of trade unions.

The 1992 Labour Act recognizes the right to bargain collectively and guarantees basic union rights, including the right to have subscription fees deducted from members' salaries. The Act also guarantees the right to strike, subject to conciliation procedures, other than for workers involved in essential services. Disputes over dismissals must be referred to a labour court for arbitration.

In 1999 the government reached agreement with labour and employers to review the 1992 Labour Act. The NUNW felt that the labour courts were ineffective, had a backlog of cases, failed to enforce rulings and were biased in favour of employers. In early 2004, a new Labour Amendment Bill was tabled in parliament. It is expected to address some of the shortcomings of the Labour Act of 1992.

Trade unions have managed to improve the working conditions through collective bargaining in several sectors where workers are well-organized. The Labour Act compels employers to recognize trade unions representing the majority of workers as the "exclusive bargaining agent". On the other hand, wages and working conditions are still very poor for many workers such as domestic workers, security guards, farm workers and petrol attendants. There is no national minimum wage in Namibia but unions have managed to negotiate minimum wages at sectoral level for workers in agriculture and the construction industry.

3 Trade Union Centre

National Union of Namibian Workers (NUNW)
Address. Private Bag 50034, Bachbrecht, Windhoek
Phone. +264 61 215 037
Fax. +264 61 215 589
E-mail. nunw@mweb.com
Leadership. Peter Naholo (acting general secretary)
Membership. 60,000-70,000
History and character. The NUNW was established by SWAPO on April 24, 1971. It functioned as part of SWAPO and operated from exile in Angola. Influenced by developments in South Africa, the NUNW in the mid-1980s set up industrial affiliates inside Namibia and from 1986 these affiliates began to operate openly although police raids and detentions continued. In 1989 the NUNW held its first consolidation congress in Windhoek, and united the internal and external leadership with John ya Otto, SWAPO Secretary for Labour as general secretary. Several union leaders joined the new SWAPO government after 1989 and it has since then remained close to the party through an "affiliation accord". The NUNW nominates candidates to SWAPO's list of parliamentarians ahead of national elections.
International affiliations. ICFTU; CTUC; OATUU

4 Other Trade Union Federation

Trade Union Congress of Namibia (TUCNA)
Address. c/o NPSM, PO Box 22679, Windhoek
Phone and Fax. +264 6121 2828
Leadership. Aloysius Yon (general secretary)
Membership. 18,000–20,000

Nauru

Capital: government in Yaran District
Population: 13,000 (2004 est.)

1 Political and Economic Background

Nauru is a very small island, which became independent in 1968 as a special-status member of the Commonwealth. The Nauruan economy was at independence almost wholly dependent on the extraction of phosphate rock derived from the country's substantial guano deposits, which supported a relatively high standard of living. This resource is now exhausted, however, and the exploitation of it (in the hands of a government-owned corporation) has rendered 90% of the country a wasteland. The government has instituted drastic public spending cuts, and called on income from phosphate sales put into trust funds, to deal with this situation, but the country is dependent on aid from Australia. There has been political turmoil and constant changes of government in recent years.

GDP (purchasing power parity) $60m. (2001 est.); GDP per capita (purchasing power parity) $5,000 (2001 est.).

2 Trade Unionism

The 1968 constitution provides for a general right of citizens to form and belong to trade unions or other associations. However, no trade unions currently exist and efforts in the past to form unions met with government discouragement. Much of the work force has in any case been transient imported labour. There are virtually no private sector employees and in the public sector pay and working conditions are determined administratively. Nauru is not a member of the ILO.

Nepal

Capital: Kathmandu
Population: 27.07 m. (2004 est.)

1 Political and Economic Background

The Kingdom of Nepal is a monarchy in which the King exercises executive powers. All political parties were banned in 1961 and for the next 30 years Nepal experienced direct rule by the monarchy. The 1962 constitution established a tiered, party-free system of elected village and provincial councils (panchayats). Limited reforms to this system were approved in a 1980 national referendum, which also rejected the restoration of a party system.

After social unrest a new constitution providing for parliamentary government was adopted in 1990, and free elections were held in 1991. Thereafter the two leading parties were the Nepali Congress Party (NCP), which originated in the 1940s as the Nepalese wing of the Indian National Congress, and the United

Communist Party of Nepal. These parties from 1991 ruled separately or in coalition, with a series of unstable administrations, and in the most recent general election, in May 1999, the NCP won 111 of the 205 seats in parliament, allowing it to form the government. In June 2001 King Birendra was assassinated by a member of his own family. Against a background of political turmoil, in May 2002 King Gyanendra dissolved parliament and then in October the government, thereafter ruling through an appointed cabinet. A new coalition government, representing most of the main party factions, was formed in May 2004 but the King remained a powerful force. In February 2005 the King again dismissed the government and assumed emergency powers. Meanwhile Nepal has since the late 1990s faced an increasingly serious Maoist insurgency, spearheaded by the Nepal Communist Party–Maoist (NCP-M). The Maoists now control considerable stretches of rural territory where the writ of the government does not run and also cause sporadic disruption in the capital. There have been peace talks and periods of truce between government and rebels but no durable settlement of the conflict; by August 2004 the conflict had resulted in 10,000 deaths since it began in 1996, with a peak in 2002.

Nepal is a poor and economically undeveloped country in which subsistence agriculture is the occupation of 80% of the workforce. Most industrial activity is concentrated on the processing of agricultural products. Production of textiles and carpets accounts for 80% of foreign exchange earnings. In recent years Nepal has sought to encourage trade and investment and reduce subsidies and many former state-owned enterprises have been privatized since 1992. There is a heavy dependence on foreign development aid and widespread under-employment. Nepal joined the World Trade Organization in April 2004, being the first least-developed country to do so.

GDP (purchasing power parity) $38.29bn. (2004 est.); GDP per capita (purchasing power parity) $1,400 (2004 est.).

2 Trade Unionism

Trade unions can be traced from 1947 at which time there was an All-Nepal Trade Union Congress (ANTUC) and the Biratnagar Labour Union, organized under the influence of the Socialist Party of India. The jute and sugar strikes of that year were the first in the history of Nepal. A split in ANTUC led to the formation of a new organization, Majdur Sabha, under the leadership of G. P. Koirala (later to be NCP Prime Minister from 1991–94), but ANTUC operated underground under communist leadership, including that of Adhikari, later to succeed him. After King Birendra's coup of 1960 all unions disappeared from open activity and only the state-sponsored Nepal Labour Organization (NLO) was allowed to function. This embodied the principles of panchayat democracy; local units of the NLO were permitted to bargain collectively and to elect district committees, from which the King would nominate four representatives to the National Assembly. With the emergence of multi-party democracy in 1990 however, the NLO, which had been increasingly inactive, was disbanded.

Since 1990 there has been a proliferation of trade unions. The majority of the 57 "active" national level trade unions affiliate to one of the three national centres – 17 to the Nepal Trade Union Congress (NTUC), 15 to the General Federation of Nepalese Trade Unions (GEFONT) and 14 to the Democratic Confederation of Nepalese Trade Unions (DECONT) – but 11 are unaffiliated. The Nepal Trade Union Congress is ICFTU-affiliated and close to the Nepali Congress Party, while GEFONT is close to the United Communist Party of Nepal; DECONT was created in 1997 as a breakaway from the NTUC, reflecting factionalism in the Nepali Congress Party. The ICFTU's *Trade Union World* noted in November 1999 that NTUC and GEFONT claimed to have a number of members "that is as impressive (because they started from nothing) as it is impossible to check (since there are no reliable statistics in Nepal)", but are certainly inflated. According to official figures there are about half-a-million trade unionists in Nepal. This is lower than the totals claimed in aggregate by the various national centres, but the centres include as members not just those who are paid-up but those who have indicated support and qualifying criteria are vague. Continual fluctuations in the governing coalitions have also encouraged members to move from one union to another, as there are substantial perceived advantages in being linked to a union whose political party holds power. Both the Congress and Communist parties have been accused of showing favouritism towards their associated trade union centres while in power. When the Communists formed the government in 1994 they were said to have "automatically" registered their own affiliated unions but interfered in the registration of unions associated with the Nepali Congress Party's labour organization.

The different centres have historically tended not to cooperate with each other. However, joint rallies and protests were held in 2002-03 in response to the dissolution of parliament and dismissal of the elected government and there has been some effort to work together in the face of the ongoing national political and economic crisis. The crisis has resulted in an unfavourable environment for the trade union movement and some unions have folded. The All Nepal Federation of Trade Unions is linked to the insurgent Nepal Communist Party–Maoist (NCP-M) and condemned by the trade union centres.

Nepal became a member of the ILO in 1966 and ratified Convention No. 98 (Right to Organize and Collective Bargaining, 1949) in 1996. It has not ratified Convention No. 87 (Freedom of Association and Protection of the Right to Organize, 1948). However, the 1990 constitution provides for the freedom to establish and to join unions and associations. It permits restriction of unions only in cases of subversion, sedition, or similar conditions. The 1993 Trade Union Act prohibits employers from discriminating against trade union members or organizers, and there have been relatively few reports of this. However, according to GEFONT, employers anxious to eliminate activists will denounce them to the police as being Maoist sympathizers.

Trade unionism currently only involves mainly the small minority of the workforce in the formal sector, with construction and transport being particular strongholds of trade unionism. In view of conditions prevailing in parts of the economy, the unions have emphasized the need to tackle issues such as child labour and debt slavery, both of which have been widespread in Nepal. In debt slavery, the condition of servitude may be passed from one generation to another, with one generation of a family working to pay off the debts of the one before. In 2000 the Kamaiya system of bonded labour was made illegal. Thousands of the former labourers are being given land and the system is being dismantled, although progress has been slower than many had hoped.

The 1992 Labour Act provides for collective bargaining, although the organizational structures to implement the Act's provisions have not been established. Collective bargaining agreements cover an estimated 20 percent of wage earners in the organized sector. Virtually all bargaining takes place at the enterprise level.

Strikes are lawful, subject to approval by 60% of the workforce in a secret ballot, other than in essential services. However, the government may order a strike to be ended and suspend a union if it disturbs the peace or adversely affects the national economic interest. In March 1999 the government banned all strikes in the communications, transportation, and security sectors, pending completion of the parliamentary elections in May. This forced the ending of a strike at the state-controlled Royal Nepal Airlines.

Trade union activities in recent years, especially since the breakdown of talks with the Maoists in 2001 triggered an escalation of the conflict and the dismissal of the government in 2002, have taken place against a background of political unrest and violence. The unions have called for a restoration of constitutional government and the end to the increasing militarization of the country while also condemning the insurgency.

3 Trade Union Centres

Democratic Confederation of Nepalese Trade Unions (DECONT)
Address. Baburam Acharya Street, Sinamangal 9, PO Box 13440, Kathmandu
Phone. +977 1 4486987
Fax. +977 1 4488486
E-mail. info@decont.org
Website. www.decont.org
Leadership. Rajendra Bahadur Raut (president); Khila Nath Dahal (general secretary)
Membership. Reports 251,037 members and 18 affiliated unions
History and character. DECONT was formed in 1997 as a breakaway from the Nepal Trade Union Congress and describes itself as "the first independent and democratic trade union that is not affiliated with any political parties". However, it has been linked particularly to two major figures in the Nepali Congress Party, both of whom have served as Prime Minister, Krishna Prasad Bhattarai and Sher Bahadur Deuba. It now has 18 affiliated unions, the largest of which are the construction workers, agricultural workers and carpet workers.
International affiliation. None, but some of its member unions affiliate to the relevant global union federations.

General Federation of Nepalese Trade Unions (GEFONT)
Address. PO Box 10652, Manmohan Labour Building, Putalisadak, Kathmandu
Phone. +977 1 4248072
Fax. +977 1 4248073
E-mail. info@gefont.org
Website. www.gefont.org
Leadership. Mukunda Neupane (chairperson); Binod Shrestha (general secretary)
Membership. Reports 310,575, of whom 52,175 are paid-up members
History and character. GEFONT was founded underground in 1989 and claims to be the country's largest and most active trade union confederation, uniting 15 industrial federations. It is closely associated with the United Communist Party of Nepal (UCPN), one of Nepal's two leading parties. It led a series of strikes against the Nepali Congress Party government in 1993–94, prior to November 1994 elections in which the UCPN became the largest party and formed the government. Several of the UCPN representatives elected to Parliament were GEFONT officials, including GEFONT chairman Mukunda Neupane and vice-chairman Salim Ansari, the latter becoming Minister of State for Forest and Soil Conservation. A number of other GEFONT members were appointed to advisory roles in the government.

GEFONT has formed a "Forum for Liberation from Debt Slavery" and says it has recruited 10,000 victims of debt slavery, who pay a token 1 rupee per year in membership fees. Organization of such victims has to be clandestine. GEFONT says that Nepalese society is still semi-feudal in character and the elimination of feudal production relations is one of its goals. The Federation of Agricultural Workers – Nepal, with 75,000 members, is its biggest affiliate, but of these only 3,000 are paid-up members.

GEFONT has called for an end to human rights violations by both the government and the Maoist rebels, a truce and dialogue between the government and the insurgents, and for the trade unions and the political parties to which they are linked to bury their differences in the interest of uniting constitutional forces.
International affiliations. None; however, two of the GEFONT industrial federations have affiliated to the relevant global union federation.

Nepal Trade Union Congress (NTUC)
Address. Central Office, PO Box 5507, Kupondol, Lalitpur, Kathmandu
Phone. +977 1 527443
Fax. +977 1 527469

E-mail. ntuc@wlink.com.np
Website. www.ntuc.org.np
Leadership. Laxman Bahadur Basnet (president); Achut Raj Pandey (general secretary)
Membership. Reports 192,000
History and character. The NTUC came into being after the establishment of a multi-party system in Nepal in 1990 and is linked to the Nepali Congress Party (NCP), one of the two leading political parties in the country. It is particularly associated with the faction of the party led by former Prime Minister Girija Prasad Koirala, and supporters of other factions of the party have formed the Democratic Confederation of Nepalese Trade Unions.

With the assistance of international donors and the government, the NTUC has set up 132 schools to provide remedial training for child labourers.
International affiliation. ICFTU. Nine of its affiliated industrial unions are affiliated to the relevant global union federation.

4 Other Trade Union Organizations

All Nepal Federation of Trade Unions
Leadership. Shalikram Jamarkattel (president)
History and character. This is the trade union front of the Nepal Communist Party–Maoist (NCP-M), the principal Maoist insurgency group. The NCP-M operates mainly in undeveloped rural areas; by November 2002, when the King dissolved the government, the NCP-M was thought to control about a third of Nepal's 75 districts, especially remote western district. The NCP-M supports itself by extortion from businesses, bank robberies and tax collecting in areas it controls. It has set up its own systems of village administration in areas under its control and in January 2004 announced the establishment of "autonomous provincial regional people's governments". The All Nepal Federation of Trade Unions in August 2004 threatened to close down businesses in Kathmandu it said were pro-government and demanded compensation for the families of those killed in the conflict. A hotel targeted in the campaign was bombed and dozens of businesses closed their doors and their workers stayed away in fear of being attacked. On Sept. 15 the All Nepal Federation of Trade Unions called off its campaign after the government agreed to free two of its leaders and provide information on the whereabouts of 22 others, while employers also agreed to pay workers for time lost while the businesses were closed. Its campaign was condemned by the trade union centres as an attack on the right to work.

Nepal Trade Union Federation (NTUF)
Address. Ga 1/262, Dilli Bazar, P.O.Box No.46, Kathmandu
Phone. +977 1527 443
Fax. +977 1411 642
Leadership. Ganesh Shah (president)
Membership. 20,000
History and character. This small organization held its third national convention in November 2004. It is linked to a Communist faction and criticizes the "monopoly" of worker representation by a few trade unions.
International affiliation. WFTU

Netherlands

Capital: Amsterdam
Population: 16.32 m. (2004 est.)

1 Political and Economic Background

From 1994-2002 Prime Minister Wim Kok led a so-called "purple coalition" government comprising his own Labour Party (PvdA), the liberal People's Party for Freedom and Democracy (VVD) and the Democrats 66 (D66). The opposition was led by the centre-right Christian Democratic Appeal (CDA), which had participated in a series of coalition governments from 1977–94. In elections in May 2002, however, the PvdA declined to only 15.1% of the vote and 23 seats in the Second Chamber (lower house), allowing CDA leader Jan Peter Balkenende to become Prime Minister in a coalition government including the VVD and the List Pim Fortuyn, whose leader, Pim Fortuyn, had been assassinated nine days before the elections. The coalition proved highly unstable and further elections were held in January 2003, following which Balkenende continued as Prime Minister in a new coalition including the VVD and D66 but without the List Pim Fortuyn, which had fragmented and slumped electorally.

The economy is diversified, with leading industries including food processing, chemicals, petroleum refining and electrical machinery. Although agriculture occupies only 4% of the work force, Netherlands is one of the world's largest exporters of food. Growth in GDP was in the range 3–4% per annum in the period 1997–2000 and the Netherlands proved successful in job creation, with labour shortages rather than high unemployment a feature of the late 1990s. However, the economy slowed to a complete standstill in 2001-03, putting pressure on the public finances and leading to tensions between government and unions. There is an underlying concern at the decline of Dutch competitiveness relative to its main competitors and the issue of an aging population. The Netherlands is a member of the EU and joined the single European currency at its launch on Jan. 1, 1999.

GDP (purchasing power parity) $461.4bn. (2004 est.); GDP per capita (purchasing power parity) $28,600 (2004 est.).

2 Trade Unionism

The Netherlands ratified ILO Convention No. 87 (Freedom of Association and Protection of the Right to Organize, 1948) in 1950 and Convention No. 98 (Right to Organize and Collective Bargaining, 1949) in 1993.

Before World War II trade unionism in the Netherlands was divided into three main streams, represented by the general confederation, the Netherlands Federation of Trade Unions (Nederlands Verbond van Vakverenigingen, NVV), and Roman Catholic and Protestant federations. In the post-war period these organizations increasingly cooperated, and from the late 1950s they sought to coordinate their policies through a formal consultative framework. In January 1976, the Netherlands Trade Union Confederation (Federatie Nederlandse Vakbeweging, FNV) was formed by the NVV and the Netherlands Catholic Federation of Labour (Nederlands Katholiek Vakverbond, NKV), the NVV accepting the NKV's condition that special recognition should be accorded to the role of religious inspiration in the new confederation. The (Protestant) Christian National Federation of Trade Unions (Christelijk Nationaal Vakverbond, CNV), however, proved unwilling to surrender its sovereignty, and did not join the federation.

The FNV is the leading trade union centre, with 1.2 million members, while the CNV has about 355,00. Both the FNV and CNV have experienced reorganization in recent years as affiliates have merged or reconfigured and the trade union centres have faced budgetary pressures. There is a traditional general alignment of the FNV with the Labour Party (PvdA) and the CNV with the Christian Democratic CDA, though both are politically independent. The third centre represented in national tripartite discussions is the Federation of Managerial and Profesional Staff Unions, MHP, with 215,000 members. In addition there are numerous mainly small independent unions without affiliation to any of these centres, this being encouraged by the comparatively easy process of setting up a union. Their aggregate membership is about 125,000, mainly clustered in areas of the economy where unions affiliated to the three centres are weak, although in 2003 some 95% of collective agreements were negotiated with unions affiliated to the three centres. All employees, including members of the Armed Forces and the police, may join unions, and unions also affiliate the unemployed and (increasingly) the self-employed. Discrimination against union members is illegal and not prevalent.

Trade union membership in the Netherlands declined sharply during the 1980s, when many industrial jobs were lost, but rose during the 1990s phase of buoyant economic growth. All the trade union centres continued to report increasing memberships in the late 1990s, although this rate of increase was slower than that of the number of jobs. A contributory factor to the growth in union membership was female entry as the Netherlands' traditionally low level of female participation began to rise. However, the more difficult economic conditions since the turn of the century have put pressure on union memberships, with some facing financial difficulties as a result. Union density is now about 27% overall. In sectors such as transport, utilities, metalworking, public administration and education, densities are in the range 40-55%. In contrast, service sectors and new technology industries have below-average densities, and the union membership profile tends to be one of an aging membership, with relatively poor representation in groups such as young people and ethnic minorities. Given that the unions directly represent little more than one-quarter of the workforce but effectively negotiate (via collective bargaining) on behalf of 80%, the issue of the unions' representativeness has surfaced to some degree in Dutch politics, though the centre-right Balkenende government has avoided turning this into a major issue.

Since World War II the Dutch model of industrial relations has been that of the "Social Partnership", emphasizing the search for consensus and stability within the context of bipartite and tripartite institutions. The Social and Economic Council (SER), created in 1950, comprises 15 representatives of the employers, 15 of the unions, and 15 independent experts nominated by government, and is the main advisory board to the government on social and economic issues. The Stichting van de Arbeid (Foundation of Labour, STAR) is a consultative body on which both sides of industry have an equal number of seats; it is a non-binding forum for the discussion of industrial issues. The FNV, CNV and MHP represent the trade union interest on these bodies.

In 1982, in response to the high unemployment of the early 1980s, an agreement on wage restraint (the Wassenaar Agreement) was reached within the Foundation of Labour that then formed the basis for subsequent collective agreements. The unions abandoned index-linked inflationary pay claims in exchange for non-pay benefits such as reductions in working hours, training and education, and day care. The social partnership model continues, and in 2003, against a background of nil economic growth, the unions agreed to a policy of wage restraint in exchange for a scaling down of planned cutbacks in government spending. However, efforts in 2004 to achieve a new social agreement proved the most contentious for years as the Balkenende government pressed for a variety of reforms to improve competitiveness. A new agreement was only reached in November 2004 after months of controversy, in which the unions had abrogated the wage restraint provisions of the 2003 agreement and then staged a series of strikes and demonstrations (involving all three trade union centres), which shook the government's apparent early determination to marginalize the influence of the unions. The new agreement was ultimately signed by all the employers and unions represented in the tripartite institutions and seen as a compromise. The Netherlands has an aging population and issues to do with early retirement were to the fore in the controversy, in addition to unemployment benefits and government proposals to release non-signatory employers from the wages provisions of collective bargaining agreements (on which the government backed down).

Within the centrally agreed Social Partnership framework, unions and employers negotiate detailed sectoral agreements (CAOs) that, once ratified by the Minister of Social Affairs and Employment, are binding on all employers, signatory or not. While this system has come under pressure from employers seeking greater flexibility, and there is a trend to more skeletal framework agreements that are then given detailed definition at enterprise level depending on circumstances, this broad approach still largely applies. The initiative in proposing a change to this system in 2004 came from the government rather than the main employers' organization, the Confederation of Netherlands Industry and Employers (VNO-NCW), and the government ultimately backed down. One result is that while union density is about 27%, some 68% of workers in 2003 were covered by a sector-wide collective agreement (with 80% covered by some form of collective agreement). Unusually, in the Dutch model, employers in some industries contribute to union costs in negotiating such agreements via the "union bargaining subsidy", and this can be a significant slice of income.

At the end of the 1990s, because of labour shortages, employers were commonly paying higher wages than provided for in collective agreements; conversely, as the economy weakened after 2000, pay rises agreed in collective agreements shrank accordingly. The unions have increasingly accepted the introduction of performance-related pay linked to the individual worker's contribution and other forms of flexibility – the majority of collective agreements now include some forms of flexibility, though this remains a matter of some resistance on the union side. According to the Confederation of Netherlands Industry and Employers (VNO-NCW), by 2000 some 84% of employees under collective bargaining agreements had an element of individual performance related pay in their contracts. At the enterprise level, works councils (which must by law be established in all enterprises with more than 50 employees, and in smaller enterprises if requested by the majority of workers – though in practice not all qualifying enterprises have works councils) are active in defining issues such as working hours within the framework of sectoral collective agreements, although the role of works councils provided for in such agreements varies widely. The trade unions formerly were wary about the spread of works councils, but in practice the councils are usually dominated by trade union representatives, and the unions have come to support them as a useful tool.

The Netherlands lacks legislation on strike issues. Indeed, the basic right to strike was ambiguous under Dutch law until the Supreme Court in 1986 ruled that it was guaranteed by application of the European Social Charter, which Netherlands had ratified in 1980. However, it is not uncommon for employers to turn to litigation to challenge individual strikes and the courts have ruled that strikes undertaken without exhausting negotiating procedures, or that adversely affect third parties, may be illegal. Claims against unions for damages rarely succeed, however. The Netherlands normally has one of the lowest rates of days lost per year to strike action of the EU member states, although there are pockets with traditions of militancy, notably the ports of Rotterdam and Amsterdam and the building trade. The civil service is covered by separate legislation and most civil servants do not have the right to strike.

3 Trade Union Centres

Christelijk Nationaal Vakverbond (CNV)
National Federation of Christian Trade Unions
Address. Postbus 2475, 3500 GL Utrecht
Phone. +31 30 2913911
Fax. +31 30 2946544
E-mail. cnv@cnv.nl
Website. www.cnv.nl (Dutch; English section)
Leadership. Doekle Terpstra (president)
Membership. 355,000
History and character. The CNV was founded in June 1909 as an inter-confessional (Christian) organization, but in practice quickly became a Protestant federation. After the formation of the FNV in 1976 some Catholic organizations affiliated. The CNV continues to emphasize its Christian base, stating that "the Christian values of justice, solidarity and stewardship give direction to the solutions for social issues of our time". It is one of the leading affiliates of the WCL. It is independent of any church or political party.

At national level the CNV participates the tripartite Social and Economic Council (SER) and, with the employers, the Foundation of Labour (STAR). Its member unions conduct collective bargaining. During 2000 the CNV underwent reorganization partly as a result of budgetary pressures, which have led to reductions in the numbers of CNV officers. After the January 2003 elections, in which the CDA came first and the Labour Party (PvdA) second, the CNV favoured a coalition between the two, but a centre-right coalition, led by the CDA and excluding the PvdA, was ultimately formed. The CNV has been critical of the social and economic policies of the Balkenende government and cooperated with the FNV in the wave of strikes and demonstrations staged by the unions during bargaining on the 2004 social agreement.

The CNV has a strongly international focus. A current key campaign for the CNV is putting pressure on multinationals and governments not to invest in countries that violate the ILO's core labour standards, and to get the WTO to adopt these standards as binding. The Actie Kom Over is a CNV organization that assists trade union organizations in Africa, Asia, Latin America and eastern and central Europe. The CNV also makes an annual award to trade union leaders worldwide who have distinguished themselves by their commitment in the face of risks.

There is a CNV youth organization, a women's union, and a study institute, and the CNV has its own holiday resorts and travel organization.
International affiliations. WCL; ETUC; TUAC
Affiliated unions. There are 11 affiliated unions, of which the following are the largest:

1. CNV Publieke Zaak
Address. Postbus 84500, 2508 AM Den Haag
Phone. +31 70 4167167
Fax. +31 70 4167100
E-mail. denhaag@cnvpubliekezaak.nl
Website. www.cnvpubliekezaak.nl (Dutch; English section)
Membership. 82,000

History and character. This public services union was known as the CFO until 2002. It was formed by the merger of three unions in 1983, but traces its history back to a union of Christian municipal employees founded in 1903. Represents civil servants and health care workers. Affiliated to EUROFEDOP and European Federation of Public Service Unions (EPSU).

2. CNV Bedrijvenbond
Address. Prins Bernhardweg 69, 3991 DE Houten
E-mail. info@cnv.net
Website. www.cnv.net
Membership. 90,000
History and character. This is a general union, organizing workers in 23 sectors of industry, transport and agriculture.

3. Hout- en Bouwbond CNV (Wood and Construction)
Address. Oude Haven 1, 3984 KT Odijk
Phone. +31 30 6597711
Fax. +31 30 6571101
Website. www.hbbcnv.nl (Dutch only)
Membership. 48,000

4. Onderwijsbond CNV (Teachers' Union)
Address. Postbus 732, Boerhaavelaan 5, 2700 AS Zoetermeer
Phone. +31 79 3202020
Fax. +31 79 3202195
Website. www.ocnv.nl (Dutch only)
Membership. 59,000
History and character. Formed in 1997 by the merger of the Catholic Teachers' Union (KOV) and the Protestant Christian Teachers' Union (PCO).

5. Dienstenbond CNV (Services Union)
Address. Postbus 3135, 2130 KC Hoofddorp
Phone. +31 23 565 1052
Fax. +31 23 565 0150
Website. www.cnvdibo.nl (Dutch only)
Membership. 33,000.
History and character. Has had this name since 1978 but traces its origins back to 1894. It absorbed the CNV Printing Union in 1995.

Federatie Nederlandse Vakbeweging (FNV)
Netherlands Trade Union Confederation
Address. Postbus 8456, 1005 AL Amsterdam
Phone. +31 20 581 6300
Fax. +31 20 684 4541
Website. www.fnv.nl (Dutch; English section)
Leadership. Lodewijk de Waal (president)
Membership. 1.2 million
History and character. The FNV was founded in 1976 by the partial merger of the social democratic NVV and the Roman Catholic NKV. By the end of 1981 all affiliated trade unions of NVV and NKV had merged or federated with their corresponding unions in the other federation and in 1982 the NVV and NKV were formally liquidated and the merger completed. The NVV had historically been an ICFTU affiliate, while the NKV was affiliated to the WCL. The NVV and NKV jointly sought a restructuring of the international trade union movement aimed at a linking of the ICFTU and WCL. This was not forthcoming and the NKV left the WCL in 1981, the year before its merger with the NVV was concluded.

In the early 1980s recession membership of unions declined sharply, and the FNV's share fell as it failed to keep pace with the changing composition of the workforce. FNV 2000 (1987) contained a comprehensive set of recommendations designed to make trade unionism more relevant to members and potential recruits and its findings were integrated into FNV practice pushing membership up by over 100,000 in three years from 1988. While union membership did not keep pace with the increase in jobs in the economy as a whole in the late 1990s, the FNV was nonetheless successful in increasing its membership during this period.

At the beginning of 1998 four FNV affiliates, the Industrial, Services, Transport, and Agriculture and Foodstuffs unions, merged to create the super-union FNV Bondgenoten ("Allied Unions"), which became the largest union in the country with 500,000 members.

The FNV has a broadly social democratic alignment and is associated with the Labour Party (PvdA) although officially politically independent. Wim Kok, the Labour Prime Minister from 1994-2002, is a former FNV president. Reflecting the role of the Catholic federation in its creation, its constitution also recognizes the place of religion as an "inspiration for trade union activities".

At national level the FNV participates in the tripartite Social and Economic Council (SER) and, with the employers, the Foundation of Labour (STAR). The FNV since the early 1980s has participated in annual agreements whereby moderate wage claims have been agreed in return for steady amelioration of working conditions and benefits. Issues of working hours and stress are considered of particular importance in the Netherlands. The FNV also has a strong international focus to its work, working to support unions in developing countries.

The FNV is involved in areas such as policy development with respect to social security, economic development, labour law, international relations, etc. Other activities are research, training and education, publicity, and promotional activities. Services rendered to members include: legal aid and assistance supplied by the FNV's Legal Aid Service, expert advice through the Centre for Works Councils, advice on taxation questions, and cheap holiday opportunities in hotels or holiday parks linked to the trade union movement. Since 1999 it has been offering portfolio planning for its members, 20% of whom participate in company share option schemes.

In May 2002 the centre-left "purple coalition" led by the Labour Party (PvdA) was defeated at a general election after eight years in power. The removal from office of the PvdA coincided with a deteriorating economic position, with the economy at a standstill, and this set the scene for a difficult period for the FNV. In June 2003 the FNV's own problematic financial position (aggravated by a sharp decline in the value of its stock market portfolio) forced it to implement a radical cross-cutting programme, cutting its budget by a quarter, shedding jobs and ending subsidies to smaller union affiliates. In October 2003 the FNV accepted (with the other two trade union centres) a social agreement involving wage restraint, in return for a scaling back of government cost-cutting measures, in view of the national economic situation. It did so with muted enthusiasm, taking the unusual step of putting the issue to a ballot of the membership, which, however, endorsed the agreement.

Relations with the Balkenende government subsequently deteriorated and in October 2004 the FNV led strikes and demonstrations as part of its campaign to strengthen the unions' bargaining position in negotiations on a new social partnership agreement. A compromise agreement was signed in November 2004, with some important concessions achieved by the unions; again, the agreement was put to a membership ballot, and was endorsed by an overwhelming majority of those who voted.

International affiliations. ICFTU; ETUC; TUAC

Affiliated unions: There are 14 affiliated unions. In addition to those large unions for which details are given below, there are unions for military personnel; hotel and restaurant workers; journalists; the police; sport; women; the self-employed; hairdressers and seafarers.

1. AbvaKabo (public sector)
Address. Postbus 3010, 2700 KT Zoetermeer
Phone. +31 79 353 6161
Fax. +31 79 352 1226
E-mail. post@abvakabo.nl
Website. www.fnv.nl/abvakabo (Dutch only)
Leadership. Guus van Huijgevoort (president)
Membership. 360,000. This is the major public sector union in the Netherlands and, as a result of privatization, now also has members in the private sector.

2. Algemene Onderwijsbond (AOB) (Teachers' Union)
Address. Postbus 2875, 3500 GW Utrecht
Phone. +31 30 298 9898
E-mail. info@aob.nl
Website. www.aob.nl (Dutch only)
Leadership. Walter Drescher (president)
Membership. 75,000
History and character. Formed by 1997 merger of teachers' unions ABOP and NGL, this is the largest Dutch education union.

3. FNV Bondgenoten (Allied Unions)
Address. Postbus 9208, 3506 GE Utrecht
Phone. +31 30 273 8222
Fax. +31 30 273 8225
E-mail. info@bg.fnv.nl
Website. www.bondgenoten.fnv.nl (Dutch only)
Leadership. Henk van der Kolk (president)
Membership. 495,000.
History and character. FNV Bondgenoten was formed in 1998 by the merger of four FNV unions, Industriebond (industrial workers), Dienstenbond (Services), Vervoersbond (Transport) and Voedingsbond (Agriculture and Foodstuffs). The objective was to strengthen the bargaining position of the merging unions and to provide better member services. It is the largest union in the country with a diverse membership including sectors such as agriculture, retailing, financial services, information technology and electronics, textiles, chemicals, paper, metal industry, breweries, transport, and call centres. It has a predominantly male membership – only 19% of members are women. The union was structured with local branches representing all its members and in addition 15 industrial groups, including one group specifically for benefit recipients and older people, this group being the largest with 100,000 members. At its formation it had 1,000 employees, although this number was to be reduced substantially in the medium-term. In December 2001, facing a serious financial deficit, in part because of the costs of the merger, Bondgenoten announced a further programme of restructuring and cost-cutting.

In June 1999 a union targeting the self-employed, Zelfstandige Bondgenoten (http://fnvzzp.cms.fnv.nl) was launched under Bondgenoten auspices.

4. FNV Bouw (building and construction workers)
Address. Postbus 520, 3440 AM Woerden
Phone. +31 34 857 5575
E-mail. info@fnvbouw.nl
Website. www.fnvbouw.nl (Dutch only)
Leadership. Dick van Haaster (president)
Membership. 160,000. About half of all building workers are members of Bouw and it also recruits among the self-emploed in the construction trades. Over 97% of its members are male.

5. FNV KIEM (arts, information industry and media)
Address. Postbus 9354, 1006 AJ Amsterdam
E-mail. algemeen@fnv-kiem.nl
Website. www.fnv-kiem.nl (Dutch only)
Leadership. René van Tilborg (president)
Membership. 50,000

Vakcentrale Voor Middengroepen en Hoger Personeel (MHP)
Federation of Managerial and Professional Staff Unions
Address. Postbus 575, 4100 AN Culemborg
Phone. +31 34 585 1900
Fax. +31 34 585 1919
E-mail. info@vc-mhp.nl
Website. www.vakcentralemhp.nl (Dutch only)
Leadership. A.H. Verhoeven (president)
Membership. 215,000
History and character. MHP (or UNIE-MHP) originated in 1966 and was known by the acronym NCHP until 1990 and then as Vakcentrale MHP. Its membership is primarily managerial and technical. It is independent of political parties and religious affiliations. MHP participates in the tripartite Social and Economic Council (SER) and the Foundation of Labour (STAR). It has at times negotiated agreements separately from FNV and CNV, though it joined the other centres in concerted action over the 2004 social agreement.

International affiliations. ETUC; EUROCADRES
Affiliates. The MHP comprises the following organizations:

1. Unie Van Onafhankelijke Vakorganisaties (UOV)

Address. Postbus 400, 4100 AK Culemborg
Phone. +31 34 585 1851
Fax. +31 34 585 1500
E-mail. info@unie.nl
Website. www.uov.nl (Dutch only)
History and character. The UOV is itself a federation of 20 independent union organizations, most of them smaller unions based in individual major companies, but with its major component being the 100,000-member multi-sectoral De Unie – Vakbond voor Industrie en Dienstverlening, the Union for Industry and Services (www.unie.nl).

2. Centrale van Middelbare en Hogere Functionarissen (CMHF)

Address. Postbus 176, 2260 AD Leidschendam
Phone. +31 70 419 1919
Fax. +31 70 419 1940
E-mail. centrale@cmhf.nl
Website. www.cmhf.nl (Dutch only)
History and character. This is a federation of civil service unions.

3. Vereniging van Nederlandse Verkeersvliegers (VNV) Dutch Airline Pilots' Association

Address. Postbus 192, 1170 AD Badhoeverdorp
Phone. +31 20 449 8585
Fax. +31 20 449 8588
E-mail. secr@vnvn-dalpa.nl
Website. www.vnvn-dalpa.nl (Dutch only)

4. Beroepsorganisatie Banken en Verzekeringen (BBV) Banking and Insurance Union

Address. Postbus 1558, 3600 BN Maarsen
Phone. +31 34 655 2552
Fax. +31 34 655 2160
E-mail. bbv@bbv-vkbv.nl
Website. www.bbv-vkbv.nl (Dutch only)

NETHERLANDS DEPENDENCIES

The Kingdom of the Netherlands comprises, in addition to the Netherlands in Europe, the Netherlands Antilles and with separate status, the island of Aruba. The principal island of the Netherlands Antilles is Curaçao.

ARUBA

Federación de Trabajadores Arubanos (FTA) Aruban Workers' Federation
Address. Bernardstraat No. 23, San Nicolas
Phone. +297 58 45 448
Fax. +297 58 45 504
Leadership. José Rodolfo Geerman (president); Juan Giron (secretary-general)
International affiliation. WCL

NETHERLANDS ANTILLES

The pattern of trade unionism is fragmented, with different unions operating on the various islands.

Federación Boneriana di Trabao (FEDEDBON) Bonaire Federation of Labour
Address. Apartado 324, Kaya Korona 85, Kralenendijk, Bonaire
Phone. +597 7 8845
Fax. +597 7 8845
Leadership. Gerald Teodulo Bernabela (president)
International affiliation. WCL

Central General di Trahadonan di Corsow (CGTC)
Address. PO Box 2078, Dr. Martin Luther King Boulevard 95, Otrabanda, Willemstad, Curaçao
Phone. +599 9 462 3995
Fax. +599 9462 7700
Leadership. Kenneth Valpoort (secretary-general)
International affiliation. WCL

Sentral di Sindikatonan di Korsou (SSK) Trade Union Centre of Curaçao
Address. Schouwburgweg 44, PO Box 3036, Willemstad, Curaçao
Phone. +599 9737 0255
Fax. +599 9737 5250
International affiliation. ICFTU

Windward Islands Federation of Labour (WIFOL)
Address. Walter Nisbeth Road, PO Box 1097, Philipsburg, St Maarten, N.A.
Phone. +599 5 4227 97
Fax. +599 5 4266 31
E-mail. wifol@sintmaarten.net
Leadership. Theophilus Thompson (president); Curtis Vanterpool (general secretary)
Membership. 3,500. WIFOL represents the majority of workers on the island of St Maarten, St Eustasius and Saba, most of whom are employed in tourism.
International affiliation. WCL

New Zealand

Capital: Wellington
Population: 3.99 m. (2004 est.)

1 Political and Economic Background

New Zealand, an independent member of the Commonwealth, is a parliamentary democracy in which the social democratic Labour Party and the conservative National Party have alternated in power since the 1930s. In recent years, Labour held office from 1984-90, and the National Party from 1990–99. The Labour Party, led by Prime Minister Helen Clark, returned to government (in coalition with the minority left-wing Alliance Party) following elections on Nov. 27, 1999. The Labour Party entered another trimester in government after elections on July 27, 2002. The Labour Party governs through a network of relationships – with its partner in government, the Progressive Party; with its confidence and supply partner, United Future; and with the Green Party, with which it has a formal working relationship.

Under Prime Minister David Lange (1984–89) Labour began to move away from many of its traditional statist policies, introducing market deregulation, liberalization of foreign exchange controls, the phasing out of many subsidies, privatization, a shift to indirect taxation and reform of industrial relations legislation. These policies were accelerated under the National Party in the 1990s, although the incoming Labour-led government elected in November 1999 criticized previous "excesses" in neo-liberalism and market deregulation.

Historically New Zealand's economy was built on agriculture, with a heavy reliance on the British market. In the last two decades or so, however, it has increasingly diversified its economic base. About 65% of the labour force is now employed in services, 25% in industry (mainly small-scale) and only 10% in agriculture. In the 15 years to 2002 three broad services sector industry groups – Wholesale and Retail Trade, Restaurants and Hotels; Finance, Property and Business Services; and, Community, Social and Personal Services (which includes health, education and government administration) – added more than 90% of new jobs. In contrast Agriculture, Hunting, Forestry and Fishing employed only slightly more people in 2002 than in 1987. Despite a strong recovery in manufacturing during the 1990s there are 11,000 fewer jobs in that sector.

In April 2003 New Zealand's economic growth rate peak of 4.4% was at the top of the OECD league. The Labour government aims to lift the growth trend rate of about three per cent through ongoing transformation of the economy – the core of which is its Growth and Innovation Framework. Complementing the growth rate has been the fall in unemployment, which by November 2003 reached its lowest for 16 years.

GDP (purchasing power parity) $85.34bn. (2004 est.); GDP per capita (purchasing power parity) $21,600 (2004 est.).

2 Trade Unionism

Trade unionism has a long history, although New Zealand has never ratified ILO Convention No. 87 (Freedom of Association and Protection of the Right to Organize, 1948) and only ratified Convention No. 98 (Right to Organize and Collective Bargaining, 1949) in June 2003. The first trade union federation was formed in 1909 and became known as the "Red Federation". Its history was one of industrial turmoil, and in 1913 the United Federation of Labour, which was linked to the newly formed Social Democratic Party, was formed and became the leader of organized labour. This was superseded by the Alliance of Labour in 1919. Following the election of a Labour government for the first time in 1935 the New Zealand Federation of Labour (NZFL) was formed in 1937. On its 50th anniversary the NZFL merged with the public sector group, the Combined State Unions, to form the New Zealand Council of Trade Unions (NZCTU). This is effectively the national centre, with ICFTU affiliation, although there are several dozen unions not in affiliation and some of these were associated with the short-lived small New Zealand Trade Union Federation (NZTUF), set up in 1994. All sectors of workers, except members of the armed forces, may join unions. Police officers may not strike although they may organize and bargain collectively, with disputes referred to compulsory binding arbitration.

There have been considerable fluctuations in the legislation relating to trade unions within the last two decades depending on which government has been in power. For most of the last century registered trade unions enjoyed monopoly bargaining rights and apart from a short period between 1983 and 1984, benefited from compulsory membership. This regime of compulsory unionism was favoured by the New Zealand Federation of Labour, but widely criticized elsewhere as limiting freedom of association and by 1990 had become increasingly politically unacceptable. The system of union registration had also encouraged the formation of many small unions but the requirement in the 1987 Labour Relations Act that unions have a minimum membership of 1,000 ensured that the number of unions dropped dramatically (259 to 112) between 1985 and 1989.

In October 1990, however, the National Party was returned to power in a landslide and this proved a watershed for the unions. The new government's Employment Contracts Act (ECA) of 1991 was considered the most radical reform of New Zealand's labour laws in the 20th Century and remained in force until 2000.

The Act promoted freedom of association by prohibiting any form of compulsory union membership or non-membership. In the field of bargaining, the Act supported individual bargaining and individual contracts rather than collective agreements and did little to encourage union membership or union representation. While strikes remained legally permissible the scope of a lawful strike was severely restricted so that in general a strike was lawful only if those who took part were those employees covered by the collective bargaining and the strike related only to a single employer. Strikes to force an individual employer into becoming a party to a multi-employer agreement were unlawful. The one major positive change for employees was that all employees (not just union members) were given access to the personal grievance procedures which provided remedies for unjustified dismissals and some other employment grievances such as harassment.

Membership in NZCTU-affiliated unions fell from 530,000 in 1988 to 350,000 in 1991 and in 2000 stood at 200,000. The fall has been attributed to the effect of the ECA, exacerbated by privatization and high unemployment. These changes combined with the financial consequences of the abolition of compulsory membership resulted in the demise of several large unions and the amalgamation of others.

The impact of an unregulated environment was quickly apparent in the structure of collective bargaining. National bargaining was terminated in several sectors and the unions, weakened by unemployment, found resistance difficult to organize. By 1993 there had been a 45% fall in the number of workers covered by collective agreements. Many new contracts ended check-off arrangements.

The NZCTU condemned the ECA as a blatant attempt to de-unionize the workforce and individualize the employment relationship although it was strongly welcomed by the New Zealand Employers' Federation (NZEF). In 1994 the NZCTU gained a symbolic victory with an ILO ruling that the ECA breached ILO Conventions 87 and 98 in respect of freedom of association, collective bargaining and the right to strike. The government took no notice of the ILO's position, however, justifying the Act as part of a series of measures to liberalize the economy.

The overall impact of the ECA is disputed and is difficult to isolate from other economic factors and trends. According to the NZCTU it encouraged the growth of "poor quality jobs", with an increase in casual and part-time work and exploitation of vulnerable workers by bad employers. It had also led to a "collapse of trust and good will" in industrial relations as employers issued workers with "take it or leave it" contracts. It also seems that the Act failed to generate the productivity gains its backers expected. The effects on union membership and bargaining were clear. In 1989-90 48% of the work force were covered by collective agreements compared to only 24% by 1998-99. Although days lost to work stoppages had declined to only 12,000 by 1998, compared with 331,000 in 1990, this was a continuation of a downward trend in evidence since the high point of industrial unrest in the late 1970s. The ECA contributed to a decline in union membership to one-quarter of the employed work force by the late 1990s, compared with two-thirds of the workforce in the heyday of compulsory unionism in the late 1980s. As bargaining agents were no longer restricted to unions, some employers encouraged the setting up of non-union employee representative bodies for collective bargaining although unions still remained by far the most important bargaining agent overall – 86% of collective agreements in 1998-99 being negotiated with a union.

One indicator of the overall impact of the Act is a Canadian study, "An Index of Labour Market Wellbeing for OECD countries", released in September 2003. It revealed that between 1980 and 2001 New Zealand workers suffered a 6.5% fall in their real hourly earnings. Of the 16 countries studied New Zealand was the only one that showed a decline in earnings. The index measured income returns, equality and uncertainties due to job loss, injury and inadequate retirement income. However, in the post-ECA period, from the June 2003 quarter to the September 2003 quarter, the Labour Cost Index (LCI) recorded an increase of 0.8% in salary and wage rates (including overtime). This was the largest rise since the series began in the December 1992 quarter.

In elections in November 1999 the Labour Party returned to office on a platform that included a pledge to repeal the ECA and in October 2000 it was replaced by a new Employment Relations Act (ERA). The ERA was strongly supported by the unions, with few reservations, but criticized by many employers as likely to lead to heavy compliance costs and legal disputes and as risking a return to the old days of excessive union power. The ERA did not involve a restoration of what were widely accepted as discredited past practices, such as compulsory union membership, national awards, and fixed relativities. While recognizing the contemporary prevalence of terms and conditions based on individual contracts, it attempted to shift the balance in favour of collective bargaining by giving legislative recognition to trade unions, giving registered unions the exclusive right to negotiate collective agreements and introducing a new legislative concept (based on Canadian models) of good faith negotiations in collective bargaining. There was, however, no provision for compulsory arbitration when negotiations broke down even if an employer had failed to bargain in good faith. The Act further promoted collective representation by giving new employees (for their first 30 days of employment) the right to the same terms as those provided for in the collective contract where one existed and restored unions' rights of access to the workplace. The ERA gave the right to unions to take industrial action to win multi-employer contracts but did not otherwise significantly expand the right to strike (sympathy strikes remaining unlawful) but did significantly inhibit an employer's ability to employ replacement workers during a strike. The Act also set up new institutions to improve mediation and industrial relations.

Although the Act has been portrayed as pro-union by employers, the NZCTU has argued that it was so moderate a change to New Zealand's employment laws as to be "ineffective in achieving its stated objectives" and that many employers had used sophisticated legal strategies to frustrate the Act and weaknesses in law had been exposed. The NZCTU proposed four key objectives to government in the review of the Act: real promotion of collective bargaining; concrete and meaningful good faith provisions; an end to freeloading by non-union members; and protection of vulnerable workers in change of employer situations caused by transfer, sale, or contracting out of a business. Partly as a result of these criticisms an Employment Relations Law Reform Bill was introduced into Parliament on Dec. 11, 2003. This Act proposes only moderate reforms and is unlikely to fully satisfy NZCTU criticisms of the Act.

3 Trade Union Centre

New Zealand Council of Trade Unions (NZCTU)
Address. PO Box 6645, Wellington
Phone. +64 4 3851334
Fax. +64 4 3856051
E-mail. ctu@nzctu.org.nz
Website. www.union.org.nz
Leadership. Ross Wilson (president); Carol Beaumont (secretary)
Membership. 300,000-plus in 34 affiliated unions
History and character. The NZCTU held its founding conference at Wellington in 1987. It was formed out of the merger of the New Zealand Federation of Labour (NZFL), which comprised 150 (mainly private sector) unions, and the public sector Combined State Unions (CSU).

The NZCTU was formed at a point when, under the impact of compulsory unionism legislation introduced in 1984, two-thirds of the workforce was in unions. However, following the election in 1990 of a National Party government, and enactment of the Employment Contracts Act (ECA) of 1991, trade union membership slumped dramatically, with the decline in membership in the decade from 1987 probably greater than for any other union centre in a developed western country. This hastened the process of consolidation of NZCTU affiliates, of which in 2000 there were only 19. In 1993 the Trade Union Federation (TUF) was formed as an alternative body from a core of blue-collar unions. In 2000, it merged with the NZCTU. According to NZCTU president, Ross Wilson, since the return of a Labour government in November 1999 the climate has changed and unions have notified a sharp increase in membership. While dozens of unions are unaffiliated to the NZCTU, many of these are small. At the end of 2002 only 34 of the 174 registered unions were CTU affiliates. However, CTU affiliates comprise 88 percent of total union membership and represent 18 of the 20 largest unions in New Zealand.

In 2000 the NZCTU focused on backing the new Labour government's legislation to repeal the ECA and replace it with the Employment Relations Act (in force from October 2000). The NZCTU backed the government's bill as introduced, other than criticizing its retention of the ban on strikes undertaken for broad social and economic causes, noting the past use of action in opposition to South African sports tours and the docking of ships carrying nuclear weapons. It particularly welcomed the measure's emphasis on restoring the principle of positively endorsing and encouraging collective bargaining and on fostering an atmosphere in which negotiations would be conducted in "good faith". The NZCTU argued that the bill complemented the government's proposals to invest in skills, training and innovation, and that this rather than cutting labour costs is the key to productivity.

In the aftermath of the repeal of the ECA the NZCTU's "Fairness at Work" campaign included working to achieve improvements in workplace health and safety, a fair minimum wage, paid parental leave, more protection for contract workers and better holidays. Paid parental leave of $325 per week for 12 weeks began on July 1, 2002. This increased in line with the average weekly earnings to $334.75 per week from July 1, 2003. However, unions are pushing for a minimum of 14 weeks, with breastfeeding breaks and facilities to allow New Zealand to ratify the ILO Convention on maternity protection. The new Holidays Act passed by Parliament on Dec. 16, 2003, secured a minimum of four weeks annual leave from 2007, bereavement leave and accumulated sick leave. A NZCTU/Accident Compensation Corporation training partnership will see more than 5,000 workplace health and safety representatives trained by May 2004. The NZCTU has also seen more than 6,000 young workers go through the Modern Apprenticeship Scheme since it was introduced in 2001. It has also participated in industry training, and regional and industry development initiatives in sectors such as the wood industry, TCF and health sectors.

At March 2003 334,000 New Zealanders, or 22% of wage and salary earners, belonged to a union. Since the ERA was passed union membership has increased about 31,000. Another development under the ERA, as a result of the low membership threshold for registration being 15, has been a sharp rise in the number of unions – from 82 in December 1999 to 175 in March 2003. Despite the membership of unions with less than 1000 members having risen six-fold since 1991, overwhelmingly membership increases are a result of growth in the large established unions. The majority of new unions are enterprise or workplace based, a new phenomenon for New Zealand unionism. These organizations have extremely limited resources and typically exist to negotiate a collective agreement for members and little beyond.

The public and community services sector (core government, health and education) have shown the biggest membership gains. However, these gains have been almost offset by heavy losses of membership in the finance, manufacturing and energy sectors. Almost 53% of all union members work in the public sector and the private sector has seen a large decline in unionism. Overall, in the eleven years to December 2002, the labour force grew by 28.8% while union membership fell 34.9%. There is scope for further growth in union membership in New Zealand with a recent survey of worker representation finding about 16% of the workforce would be either "very" or "fairly" likely to join a union if there were one available in their workplace. Unions are faced with the challenge of recruiting non-standard workers (e.g. part-time, casual and temporary employees) and in small workplaces or those with high staff turnover. Unions also need to target younger workers who entered the workforce under the more individualised bargaining environment of the ECA.

International affiliations. ICFTU; TUAC; CTUC
Affiliates:

1. Amalgamated Workers' Union (Northern) (AWUNZ)
Address. Private Bag 68-905, Auckland
Phone. +64 9 378 6170
Fax. +64 9 378 6190
E-mail. auckland@awunz.org.nz
Website. www.awunz.org.nz
Leadership. Ray Bianchi (secretary)

2. Association of Salaried Medical Specialists (ASMS)
Address. PO Box 10763, Wellington
Phone. +64 4 499 1271
Fax. +64 4 499 4500
E-mail. asms@asms.org.nz
Website. www.asms.org.nz
Leadership. Ian Powell (executive director)
Membership. 2,208

3. ASTE – Te Hau Takitini O Aotearoa (Association of Staff in Tertiary Education)
Address. PO Box 27-141, Wellington
Phone. +64 4 801 5098
Fax. +64 4 385 8826

E-mail. national.office@aste.ac.nz
Leadership. Sharn Riggs (national secretary)

4. Association of University Staff of New Zealand Inc. (AUS)
Address. PO Box 11-767, Wellington
Phone. +64 4 382 8491
Fax. +64 4 382 8508
E-mail. national.office@aus.ac.nz
Website. www.aus.ac.nz
Leadership. Helen Kelly (general secretary)
Membership. 6,237

5. BTU: New Zealand Building Trades Union
Address. PO Box 11 356, Wellington
Phone. +64 4 385 1178
Fax. +64 4 385 1177
E-mail. national@nzbtu.org.nz
Website. www.nzbtu.org.nz
Leadership. David O'Connell (secretary)
Membership. 1,400

6. CLAW: Clothing, Laundry and Allied Workers Union of Aotearoa
Address. PO Box 50 216, Porirua
Phone. +64237 5062
Fax. +64 237 8157
E-mail. clothing.union@clear.net.nz
Leadership. Maxine Gay (secretary)
Membership. 750

7. CANZ: Corrections Association of New Zealand
Address. PO Box 9844, Wellington
Phone. +64 385 0304
Fax. +64 385 0306
E-mail. canz@xtra.co.nz
Leadership. John Slater
*Membership.*1,957

8. Dairy Workers' Union
Address. PO Box 9046, Hamilton
Phone. +64 7 839 0239
Fax. +64 7 838 0398
E-mail. nzdwu@wave.co.nz
Website. www.nzdwu.org.nz
Leadership. Roy Potroz (secretary)
Membership. 6,200

9. Engineering, Printing and Manufacturing Union (EPMU)
Address. PO Box 31546, Lower Hutt, 38 Bouverie Street, Petone
Phone. +64 4 568 0086
Fax. +64 4 576 1173
E-mail. andrew.little @epmunion.org.nz
Website. www.nzepmu.org.nz
Leadership. Andrew Little (secretary)
Membership. 53,275 (at 1 March 2002)

10. FinSec (Financial Sector Union)
Address. PO Box 27-355, Wellington
Phone. +64 4 385 7723
Fax. +64 4 385 2214
E-mail. union@finsec.org.nz
Website. www.finsec.org.nz
Leadership. Robin Woller (president)
Membership. 8,412, in the finance and information sectors.

11. Flight Attendants and Related Services Association (FARSA)
Address. PO Box 73-083, Auckland Airport, Auckland
Phone. +64 9 256 1821
Fax. +64 9 256 1841
E-mail. union@farsa.co.nz
Website. www.farsa.co.nz
Leadership. Terry Law (executive officer)
Membership. 1,419

12. Furniture, Manufacturing & Associated Workers Union
Address. PO Box 13 035, Christchurch
Phone +64 3 366 0803
Fax +64 3 377 6799
E-mail. unifurn@xtra.co.nz
Leadership. Len Wilson-Parr (secretary)
Membership. 620

13. ISTANZ: Independent Schools Teachers' Association
Address. PO Box 77 048, Mt Albert, Auckland
Phone. +64 9 846 2640
Fax. +64 9 846 7426
E-mail. malcolmw@ihug.co.nz
Website. www.farsa.co.nz
Leadership. Malcolm Walker (national secretary)

14. Meat and Related Trades Workers' Union of Aotearoa
Address. PO Box 17-056, Greenlane, Auckland
Phone. +64 9 520 0034
Fax. +64 9 523 1286
E-mail. meat.union@xtra.co.nz
Website. www.meatunion.org.nz
Leadership. Graham Cooke (secretary)
Membership. 5,064

15. National Distribution Union
Address. Private Bag 92 904, Onehunga, Auckland
Phone. +64 9 622 8355
Fax. +64 9 622 8353
E-mail. ndu@nduunion.org.nz
Website. www.nduunion.org.nz
Leadership. Bill Anderson
Membership. 19,297

16. NZEI Te Riu Roa: NZ Educational Institute
Address. PO Box 466, Wellington
Phone. +64 4 384 9689
Fax. +64 4 385 1772
E-mail. nzei@nzei.org.nz
Website. www.nzei.org.nz
Leadership. Lynne Bruce (national secretary)
Membership. 42,772

17. New Zealand Meatworkers & Related Trades Union, Inc.
Address. PO Box 13-048, Christchurch

Phone. +64 3 366 5105
Fax. +64 3 379 7763
E-mail. nzmeatworkersunion@clear.net.nz
Website. www.nzmeatworkersunion.co.nz
Leadership. Dave Eastlake (secretary)
Membership. 12,415

18. New Zealand Merchant Service Guild IUOW
Address. PO Box 11 878, Wellington
Phone +64 4 382 9131
Fax +64 4 382 9106
E-mail. nzmsg@xtra.co.nz
Website. www.nzmsg.co.nz
Leadership. Helen McAra (general secretary)
Membership. 613

19. New Zealand Nurses' Organization
Address. PO Box 2128, Wellington
Phone. +64 4 385 0847
Fax. +64 4 382 9993
*E-mail.*nzno@nurses.org.nz
Leadership. Geoff Annals (chief executive officer)
Membership. 33,000

20. New Zealand Professional Fire Fighters' Union
Address. PO Box 38 213, Petone, Wellington
Phone. +64 4 568 4583
Fax. +64 4 568 3292
E-mail. nzpfu@ihug.co.nz
Leadership. Derek Best
Membership. 1,638

21. New Zealand Seafarers' Union
Address. PO Box 1103, Wellington
Phone. +64 4 499 3560
Fax. +64 4 499 8872
E-mail. dmorgan@seafarers.org.nz
Leadership. Dave Morgan (national president)
Membership. 790

22. New Zealand Trade Union Federation (NZTUF)
Address. PO Box 11 891 Wellington
Phone. +64 4 384 8963
Fax. +64 4 384 8007
E-mail. tuf@tradeshall.org.nz
Leadership. Maxine Gay (president)

23. ITF New Zealand Inspectorate
Address. PO Box 27004, Wellington
Phone. +64 4 801 7613
Fax. +64 4 384 8766
E-mail. kathy@munz.org.nz
Leadership. Kathy Whelan (co-ordinator)

24. NZWG: New Zealand Writers' Guild
Address. PO Box 47-886, Auckland
Phone. +64 9 360-1408
Fax. +64 9 360-1409
*E-mail.*dominic@nzwritersguild.org.nz
Website. www.nzwritersguild.org.nz
Leadership. Dominic Sheehan (secretary)
Membership. 538

25. PWA: Postal Workers' Association (Auckland) Inc
Address. 117 Hutchinson Ave, New Lynn, Auckland 7
Phone. +64 9 827-4611
*E-mail.*mhunter@ihug.co.nz
Leadership. Michael Hunter (secretary)

26. New Zealand Postal Workers' Union
Address. PO Box 11-123, Wellington
Phone. +64 4 385 8264
Fax. +64 4 384 8007
E-mail. pwu@TradesHall.org.nz
Leadership. Quentin Findlay (secretary)

27. Post Primary Teachers' Association
Address. PO Box 2119, Wellington
Phone. +64 4 384 9964
Fax. +64 4 382 8763
E-mail. gensec@ppta.union.org.nz
Website. www.ppta.org.nz
Leadership. Kevin Bunker (general secretary)
Membership. 14,503

28. Public Service Association (PSA)
Address. PO Box 3817, 11 Aurora Terrace, Wellington 6015
Phone. +64 4 917 033
Fax. +64 4 917 2051
E-mail. enquiries@psa.org.nz
Website. www.psa.org.nz
Leadership. Kathy Higgins (president)
Membership. 40,946

29. Rail and Maritime Transport Union Inc. (RMTU)
Address. PO Box 1103, Wellington 6001
Phone. +64 4 499 2066
Fax. +64 4 471 0896
E-mail. wbutson@rmtunion.org.nz
Website. www.rmtunion.org.nz
Leadership. Wayne Butson (general secretary)
Membership. 3,591

30. Service Workers and Food Union of Aotearoa
Address. Private Bag 68-914, Newton, Auckland
Phone. +64 9 355 1855
Fax. +64 9 355 1854
E-mail. fent@ihug.co.nz
Website. www.sfwu.org
Leadership. Darien Fenton (national secretary)
Membership. 22,534

31. Tertiary Institutes Allied Staff Association (TIASA)
Address. PO Box 1594, Rotorua
Phone. +64 7 346 1989
Fax. +64 7 346 3860
E-mail. tiasa@wave.co.nz
Leadership. Peter Joseph (national secretary)
Membership. 1,587

4 Other Trade Union Organizations

Several dozen, mainly small, specialized or regional, unions are unaffiliated to the NZCTU national trade union centre. The more significant among them include the following:

AMEA: Aviation & Marine Engineers Association
Address. P O Box 3471, Auckland
Phone. +64 9 358-0050
Fax. +64 9 358-0063
E-mail. union@amea.co.nz
Website. www.amea.co.nz
Leadership. George Ryde (national secretary)
Membership. 643 (March 2002)

AWUNZ: Amalgamated Workers Union (Southern) Christchurch Office
Address. PO Box 25075, Christchurch
Phone. +64 3 366-0519
Fax. +64 3 379-7697
E-mail. awunz.chch@xtra.co.nz
Website. www.ubd-online.co.nz/amalgamatedworkers, www.awunz.co.nz
Leadership. Calvin Fisher (secretary)
Membership. 3,525 (March 2002)

Bakers' & Pastrycooks' Union
Address. Private Bag 68-905, Newton, Auckland.
Phone. +64 9 376-1151
Fax. +64 9 376-0141
E-mail. bakersunion@clear.net.nz
Leadership. Ian McGovern (secretary)

Chemical Workers' Union: National Office
Address. PO Box 82-228, Auckland
Phone. +64 9 535-5530
Fax. +64 9 535-5560
E-mail. northernchemicalunion@hotmail.com
Leadership. Pat Brown
Membership. 625 (March 2002)

Manufacturing and Construction Workers' Union
Address. PO Box 11-123, Wellington
Phone. +64 4 3858 264
Fax. +64 4 3848 007
E-mail. m.c.union@tradeshall.org.nz
Leadership. Graeme Clarke (general secretary)
Membership. 3,100

National Distribution Union
Address. Private Bag 92-904, Onehunga, Auckland
Phone. +64 9 622 8355
Fax. +64 9 622 8353
E-mail. everyone@ndunion.org.nz
Website. www.ndunion.org.nz
Leadership. Mike Jackson (national secretary)
Membership. 20,406 (March 2002)

New Zealand Airline Pilots' Association
Address. P O Box 74-347, Market Road, Auckland
Phone. +64 9 523-1191
Fax. +64 9 524-4525
E-mail. office@nzalpa.org.nz
Website. www.nzalpa.org.nz
Leadership. Keith Molloy (president)
Membership. 1,526 (March 2002)

New Zealand Building Trades Union (NZBTU)
Address. PO Box 11 356, Wellington
Phone. +64 4 385 1178
Fax. +64 4 385 1177
E-mail. national@nzbtu.org.nz
Website. www.nzbtu.org.nz
Leadership. David O'Connell (secretary)
Membership. 1,430 (March 2002)

New Zealand Tramways and Public Passenger Transport Union: National Office
Address. Private Bag 68-905, Newton, Auckland
Phone. +64 9 376-5743
Fax. +64 9 376-5728
Website. www.tradeshall.org.nz
Leadership. Gary Froggatt (national secretary)
Membership. 1,115 (March 2002)

NUPE: National Union of Public Employees
Address. 3rd floor, Trade Union Centre, 199 Armagh Street
PO Box 13032, Christchurch.
Phone. +64 3 377-3582
Fax. +64 3 3774385
E-mail. nupe@xtra.co.nz
Leadership. Nadine Marshall
Membership. 1,412 (March 2002)

Southern Local Government Officers' Union
Address. PO Box 13-316, Christchurch
Phone. +64 3 379-8319
Fax. +64 3 366-4755
E-mail. slgou@xtra.co.nz
Leadership. Peter Lawson (secretary)
Membership. 2,328 (March 2002)

Nicaragua

Capital: Managua
Population: 5.36 m. (2004 est.)

1 Political and Economic Background

The Frente Sandinista de Liberación Nacional (FSLN or Sandinistas) came to power in 1979 following the overthrow of the right-wing Somoza regime that had ruled Nicaragua since 1933. In the 1980s the Reagan administration's support for contra guerrillas opposing the Sandinistas, under Daniel Ortega Saavedra, for some years turned Nicaragua into a leading focus of international political attention. By the late 1980s the Sandinistas were brought to the negotiating table and in 1990 elections were held which brought victory to the National Opposition Union (UNO) led by Violeta Barrios de Chamorro, with a peaceable transfer of power. She pursued a policy of national reconciliation that after a time provoked disquiet within her own party. In 1992 charges of collusion between her administration and the Sandinistas briefly interrupted US aid but the flow was resumed. Further elections were held in October 1996, resulting in victory for Arnold Alemán, the candidate of the Liberal Alliance coalition, which also became the largest group in the legislature, taking 44 of the 93 seats. The FSLN, led by

Ortega, remained the main opposition, taking 37 seats. This pattern was repeated in the most recent elections, in 2001, when the Constitutional Liberal Party (PLC, formerly the largest component of the Liberal Alliance) won the presidency and a majority in the Assembly (though with the party subsequently splitting) while the FSLN remained in second place. Under constitutional changes enacted in 2000, the PLC and FSLN agreed to divide control of the Electoral Council, Supreme Court and the audit office between them – a move seen as consolidating the position of the two main parties at the expense of weaker parties. The FSLN continues to be under the leadership of Ortega and now defines itself as a democratic socialist party; in July 2003 Ortega apologized for the revolutionary government's treatment of the Catholic Church.

Since the end of the 1980s military conflict, Nicaragua has experienced relative stability, although there have been tensions over the issue of redistribution of land and other assets seized by the Sandinistas. The Nicaraguan economy, which is based on agriculture, with coffee, cotton, sugar and bananas as the principal crops, was adversely affected by the 1980s civil war but showed recovery in the 1990s. Post-Sandinista governments have sought to liberalize the economy in the face of opposition from the Sandinistas. Under President Chamorro, reforms had the effect of reducing the state sector to 30–40% of GDP. In September 1999 the World Bank approved Nicaragua's application to be included in the Heavily Indebted Poor Countries Initiative (HIPC). Nicaragua remains one of the poorest countries in the Americas, with national GDP growth barely keeping pace with the growth in population, very unequal income distribution, high unemployment and a dependence on international aid and debt relief under HIPC.

GDP (purchasing power parity) $11.6bn. (2004 est.); GDP per capita (purchasing power parity) $2,300 (2004 est.).

2 Trade Unionism

The first national trade union organization – the Organized Labour of Nicaragua (OON) – was formed in 1924, but faltered because of its support for Gen. Sandino (assassinated in 1934), who led opposition to the US military presence in the country. The position of trade unions was difficult under the rule of the Somoza family, although unions independent of the government managed to retain a degree of organizational identity for much of that period. Nicaragua ratified ILO Conventions No. 87 (Freedom of Association and Protection of the Right to Organize, 1948) and No. 98 (Right to Organize and Collective Bargaining, 1949) in 1967.

Substantial anti-government industrial unrest occurred in 1978–79, but the fall of Somoza came as result of military action. In the first three years after the Sandinista revolution, union membership quadrupled, reaching 100,000. During the 1980s civil war the right of free association and to strike was subject to suspension from time to time under emergency powers. However, opposition trade unions did continue to function through the period of Sandinista rule, while the Sandinistas attempted to organize workers and other social groups in "mass organizations".

A new labour code adopted in 1996 reinforced the right of all workers in both private and public sectors, other than the police and armed forces, to form unions and bargain collectively. The ICFTU reported to the WTO in October 1999 that "the industrial relations climate has improved somewhat over recent years. It is now fairly easy to get a union registered and recognized". However, the labour code is not uniformly enforced and in the export processing zones (where about 60,000 are employed) some foreign-owned firms have excluded the unions. The 1996 labour code provides for a right to strike subject to extensive mediation and compulsory arbitration procedures, although there has reportedly not been a legal strike since 1990.

The trade union movement within the country is very fragmented and divided ideologically and in its attitude to the policies of the Sandinistas. Pro-Sandinista unions associate in the National Workers' Front (FNT) and non-Sandinsta unions in the Permanent Congress of Workers (CPT). Both the WCL and ICFTU are represented in the country. Estimates of memberships of unions are generally unreliable.

3 Trade Union Centres

Central Sandinista de Trabajadores (CST)
Sandinista Workers' Centre
Address. Apartado 2957, Managua
Phone. +505 222 5372
Fax. +505 222 5372
E-mail. cst/cor@aflanumeric.com.ni
History and character. The CST was founded immediately following the 1979 revolution, growing out of the workers' insurrectionist committees and their later form, the comités de defense de trabajadores Sandinistas, and rapidly became the dominant labour organization in the country. The CST is closely linked to the FSLN. After Chamorro assumed office the CST led a large number of strikes, particularly in 1991. It was formerly affiliated to the WFTU.
International affiliation. ICFTU

Central de Trabajadores Nicaragüenses (CTN)
Nicaraguan Workers' Centre
Address. Calle 27 de Mayo, Pinolero 25 Varas arriba, 75 Varas Sur, Managua
Phone. +505 2 683 061
Fax. +505 2 2 652 056
E-mail. ctn@nicarao.apc.org.ni
Leadership. Carlos Huembes (secretary general)
History and character. In 1962 the Christian-inspired Nicaraguan Autonomous Trade Union Movement (MOSAN) was formed, recruiting several thousand members principally in rural areas, and in 1972 this became the CTN. Members of the CTN were subjected to periods of detention without charge by the Sandinista government. During the 1980s conflict the WCL and its regional organization CLAT criticized the Sandinista government for infringements of human

and trade union rights, but opposed US aid to the contra rebels. The CTN is identified with the social Christian trend in politics.
International affiliation. WCL

Confederación de Unificación Sindical (CUS)
Confederation of Labour Unification
Address. Apartado 3098, Managua
Phone. +505 2 483 681
Fax. +505 2 223 139
Membership. 21,000
History and character. The CUS was formed as the Nicaraguan Trade Union Council (CSN) under the auspices of ORIT in 1964, absorbing independent and pro-government unions. Following the Sandinista take over of power it declined rapidly as a consequence of its accommodation with the previous regime. Leaders and members of CUS were detained for periods under the Sandinistas. The ICFTU opposed US aid to the contra guerrillas and also the US economic embargo of Nicaragua imposed in 1985, arguing that the USA should maintain relations with Nicaragua linked to the observance of human and trade union rights.
International affiliation. ICFTU

Niger

Capital: Niamey
Population: 11.36 m. (2004 est.)

1 Political and Economic Background

Niger gained independence from France in 1960. A coup in 1974 was followed by 15 years of military rule. In 1988 the National Movement for a Development Society (MNSD) was formed as the sole legal party and a joint military–civilian government was formed. Multi-party elections were held in 1993 under a constitution approved in a referendum in December 1992. There was a military coup in January 1996, however, with a National Salvation Council taking power and its leader, Brig.-Gen. Ibrahim Barre Mainassara, becoming President the following year. A further coup took place in April 1999, when Mainassara was assassinated, and an army-led National Reconciliation Council took power. Following this elections were held in November 1999 resulting in victory for the MNSD and its presidential candidate Mamadou Tandja and a return to civilian government.

Niger is an impoverished country. The formal economy is very small and 90% of the country's workers are engaged in subsistence farming and herding. The main export is uranium but this has been affected by depressed prices in the past decade. Drought, desertification, population expansion and debt are major problems and there is a reliance on international assistance.

GDP (purchasing power parity) $9.06bn. (2004 est.); GDP per capita (purchasing power parity) $800 (2004 est.).

2 Trade Unionism

Niger ratified ILO Convention No. 87 (Freedom of Association and Protection of the Right to Organize, 1948) in 1961 and Convention No. 98 (Right to Organize and Collective Bargaining, 1949) in 1962.

The constitution provides for the right to establish and join trade unions. However, 95% of the workforce is engaged in subsistence agriculture and petty trading and unions represent primarily the small minority employed in formal public sector occupations such as civil servants and teachers or in state enterprises. Most unions are affiliated to the USTN or the CNT centres. Several unions were suspended or closed down by the government in the late 1990s.

Collective bargaining exists in both the public and private sectors. The USTN represents civil servants in bargaining with the government. There is a legal right to strike for all workers (other than the police and armed forces) subject to a notice period and the maintenance of essential services. The main cause of strikes in recent years has been unpaid wages and poor working conditions in the public sector.

3 Trade Union Centres

Confédération Démocratique des Travailleurs du Niger (CDTN)
Democratic Confederation of Workers of Niger
Leadership. Sidibé Issoufou
Membership. 40,000 (est.)
History and character. Founded in 2001 by breakaway members of the USTN.

Confédération Nigérienne du Travail (CNT)
Nigerien Confederation of Labor
Address. Bourse du Travail, BP 10620, Niamey
Phone. +227 73 41 05
Fax. +227 73 75 15
Leadership. Seybou Issou (secretary-general)
Membership. 15,000
History and character. Founded in 1996 and affiliated to the WCL in 1998. The CNT counts 5 constituent unions and emphasizes education, job training and solidarity work.
International affiliation. WCL

Union des Syndicats des Travailleurs du Niger (USTN)
Union of Workers' Trade Unions of Niger
Address. BP 388, Niamey
Phone. +227 73 52 56
Fax. +227 73 52 56
Leadership. Abdou Maigandi (secretary-general)
Membership. 60,000
History and character. The Union Nationale des Travailleurs du Niger (UNTN), was established at independence in 1960. Its name was changed to the Union des Syndicats des Travailleurs du Niger (USTN) in 1978.

The USTN was linked to the MNSD, set up by the military regime in 1988 as the sole legal party. However, its support for the pro-democracy movement (which included mounting a general strike against austerity measures) led to police raids on its premises and the detention of secretary-general Laouali Moutari in 1990. The President told union leaders in October of the same year that their role should not extend beyond defending the workers' interests. A further general strike, this time for five days, was mounted in November in support of calls for a conference on the country's political future. It was a major factor in forcing the regime to concede multi-party democracy.

Following the military coup of January 1996 the USTN faced further pressures because of its demands for democratic reforms. 22 trade union leaders were detained in March 1997 following a strike called by the USTN to protest against civil servants' pay arrears, tax increases and privatisation measures. Four of those detained were convicted of sabotage and received prison sentences, but after international pressure all 22 were released. Since that time the USTN has continued to call numerous strikes over the issue of public sector pay arrears.

The USTN participates in a wide range of national social and economic agencies. In 1998 the USTN established a national training centre for trade unionists and has also set up a cooperative irrigation and agricultural project. There are 38 affiliated unions, in both the public and private sectors, with most members in the public sector.

International affiliation. ICFTU, OATUU

Union Général des Travailleurs Nigériens (UGTN)
General Union of Workers of Niger
History and character. Founded 2002 as a breakaway group from USTN.

Nigeria

Capital: Abuja
Population: 137.25 m. (2004 est.)

1 Political and Economic Background

Nigeria, the most populous country in Africa, became an independent member of the Commonwealth in 1960 and established a Federal Republic in 1963. It has generally been under military rule since that time, but a civilian government (albeit headed by a former military dictator) has been in office since May 1999.

Maj.-Gen. Ibrahim Babangida seized power in 1985. After seven years he conceded legislative assembly elections which resulted in victory for the Social Democratic Party (SDP). But civilian rule was not restored and Babangida refused to acknowledge the results of the June 1993 presidential election won by Chief Mashood Abiola. He eventually resigned when unions staged a general strike, but after a confused interval, the military again seized power under General Sanni Abacha in November 1993. When in June 1994 Abiola declared himself president he was charged with treason and arrested and new disturbances followed. In November 1995, following the execution of the leader of the Movement for the Survival of the Ogoni People, Ken Saro-Wiwa, Nigeria's membership of the Commonwealth was suspended. Abacha died in June 1998 and was succeeded by Gen. Abbubakar, who instituted liberalization leading to elections in February 1999 and the installation of a civilian government headed by President Olusegun Obasanjo in May 1999. Obasanjo is himself a former general, who headed a military government from 1976–79. He was the candidate of the People's Democratic Party, which also won a majority in the legislature. In April 2003 Obasanjo was comfortably re-elected for a second four-year presidential term while in the legislative elections the PDP again won an outright majority.

Nigeria faces continual internal unrest on several fronts, including in the oil-producing Niger delta region, where the activities of militias demanding self-determination for the local Ijaw people, caused temporary suspensions or cutbacks in oil production at times in 2003-04. There is tension between the (mainly Christian) South and the (mainly Muslim) North; hundreds died in clashes in March 2000 over the introduction of Islamic (sharia) law in the northern city of Kaduna.

Nigeria benefited from wealth generated by the oil price boom of the 1970s. However, this wealth was not effectively invested in the national infrastructure, and Nigeria became associated with rampant corruption and collapsed public services and became saddled with huge debts as oil prices slumped in the 1980s. Per capita income is estimated to have fallen an average of 1.5% per annum between the mid-1970s and 2000. Its largely subsistence agricultural sector proved unable to increase output to match population growth while manufacturing output in 1999 was 23% below 1991 levels, representing only 7% of GDP.

Nigeria has of late again benefited from windfall profits from rising oil prices, oil accounting for 95 per cent of export earnings and 65% of budget revenues. In October 2004 the Obasanjo government announced that these windfall gains would allow government spending to be increased by one-quarter in 2005. However, Nigeria's foreign debt is $33bn and the government still only intends to meet half the repayments due in 2005 – Nigeria is excluded from the Highly Indebted Poor Countries (HIPC) initiative because of its oil wealth, but has a long-running campaign to secure debt write-offs. International financial institutions have argued that privatization of inefficient parastatals and better control of public finances are among the pre-conditions needed for write-offs to produce long-term benefits; although the IMF agreed a new assistance package in August 2000, Nigeria pulled out of the programme in 2002 after failing to meet its targets. The government has announced plans to privatize dozens of state-controlled enterprises, but privatization has been fitful and the inefficiency and cost of power, transport and telecommunications are seen as obstacles to investment in the economy generally.

Following World Bank criticism of the slow pace of privatization, in July 2004 the government said it was determined to complete the main part of its privatization programme by the end of the current presidential term in 2007, including power, telecoms and the oil industry.

GDP (purchasing power parity) $114.8bn. (2004 est.); GDP per capita (purchasing power parity) $900 (2004 est.).

2 Trade Unionism

Nigeria ratified ILO Conventions No. 87 (Freedom of Association and Protection of the Right to Organize, 1948) and No. 98 (Right to Organize and Collective Bargaining, 1949) in 1960.

Nigerian trade unionism dates from the turn of the 20th century. By the 1930s a number of unions were well established and during World War II the British colonial authorities began to register them, giving organized labour official recognition for the first time. By the early 1970s there were several hundred unions and four competing trade union centres but in the mid-1970s these centres were dissolved by the military government.

The present Nigeria Labour Congress (NLC) was launched in 1978 by government decree as the sole legal organization with a large subvention of public funds. The several hundred unions and staff associations were rationalized into 42 affiliated industry-based unions. In 1989 a decree made membership of international trade secretariats illegal and under it four transport unions were fined the following year. The government also barred public employees from being members of one or other of the two legal political parties.

In 1993 there was a three-day general strike by the NLC in protest at the failure to restore democracy. The NLC's agreement to call off the strike angered its oil workers' affiliate NUPENG whose members stayed out for ten days. In July 1994 NUPENG, this time joined by another energy union PENGASSAN, began strikes in support of a demand to release Abiola. After six weeks of growing chaos Gen. Abacha dissolved the leadership of both unions and the NLC and put them into administration. They had been guilty, he charged, of "economic sabotage". Other unions failed to join the oil workers on strike. In early September the oil stoppage crumbled and normal working gradually resumed.

A series of decrees in 1996 forced the merger of the 41 NLC unions into 29; banned professional union organizers from holding positions in the NLC; required the inclusion of no strike clauses in collective bargaining agreements; required unions to pay 10 percent of members' dues to the NLC; and banned affiliation to non-African international organizations without government permission. Nigeria refused to accept ILO missions and in 1997 the ILO Committee on Freedom of Association condemned a "persistent deterioration of trade union rights".

Following the death of Gen. Abacha in June 1998, Gen. Abbubakar overturned the 1996 decrees. He removed the administrators running the NLC, which was allowed to form an independent executive. He also released Frank Kokori, NUPENG general secretary, and Milton Dabibi, PENGASSAN general secretary, who had been detained without charge or trial since the 1994 strike.

A new constitution adopted in May 1999 provides for freedom of association, albeit with significant restrictions for certain sectors. Not only are the armed forces, police and firefighters barred from joining unions, but senior staff workers and those employed in a range of services that the authorities maintain are "essential" (including the immigration department and the central bank) are similarly denied rights of freedom of association. Workers in Export Processing Zones may not join a union during the first 10 years of operation of the enterprise. An estimated 10% of the total workforce is unionized, with members mainly in the public sector and larger enterprises in the formal private sector.

At the present time the NLC remains the only recognized national centre, although in April 2004 the government introduced a reform bill amending the 1990 Trade Union Act that would derecognize the NLC (by the end of 2004 this bill had passed the Senate largely unchanged but had yet to be approved by the House of Representatives). The proposed derecognition is ostensibly to allow other national centres to be recognized in future, but it is likely also to have a damaging impact on the most powerful and effective centre for organized labour in Nigeria, the NLC. The NLC is not opposed to recognition of the other union centres, but NLC leaders have questioned why their federation must first be publicly and formally derecognized. There are a number of independent associations, comprising those senior workers who are barred from joining NLC unions, organized within the Trade Union Congress (TUC) with a membership of 600,000. The TUC and its associations have never been officially recognized by the government. In 2003 eight of the TUC's affiliates left to form a new coordinating centre, the Congress of Free Trade Unions (CFTU). The NLC maintains good relations with both TUC and CFTU, and the three occasionally issue joint statements and undertake coordinated action, as in the strikes against fuel prices rises in 2004.

Collective bargaining is practised in many sectors. The right to strike has been restored, although here too the unions face several serious restrictions, including a clause within the Trade Union (Amendment) Decree of 1996 which makes payment of check-off contributions to a union dependent upon the union adopting and observing a no-strike agreement within the collective agreement. In spite of the restrictions on union freedom, numerous strikes and other protests have occurred since 1999. Initially wage arrears and the minimum wage were a primary cause of strikes, although fuel price rises were the focus of a series of bitter national disputes in 2003-04. The fuel disputes saw the NLC, with the support of the TUC, argue that tax increases that took the cost of fuel beyond the reach of ordinary workers were unacceptable in a major oil-producing nation. The unions launched a ten-day nation-wide general strike on June 30, 2003, that shut down much of the economy. As the strike took hold at least 19 protesters were killed in a series of incidents that included police firing on unarmed protesters during the first day of the strike.

3 Trade Union Centre

Nigeria Labour Congress (NLC)
Address. Labour House, Plot 820/821, Central Business District, Abuja
Phone. +234 9 234 6042
Fax. +234 9 234 4342
E-mail. info@nlcng.org
Website. www.nlc.org
Leadership. Adams Oshiomhole (executive president); John Odeh (general secretary); Owei Lakemfa (acting general secretary)
Membership. Reports 4 million in 29 affiliated industrial unions
History and character. Although formed under state sponsorship in 1978, the NLC subsequently exercised considerable autonomy and frequently opposed government policy in the 1980s on issues such as wage agreements, structural adjustment programmes and minimum wage legislation, including by strike action.

In 1988 the government dissolved the NLC executive and put its affairs in the hands of an administrator. The dissolution, presented as a move against factionalism within the NLC, prompted national and international protests. The presence of an IMF team in the country added fuel to the fire and unrest flared. Rallies were banned, universities closed and many unionists arrested. Three committees were set up to consider union grievances but detainees continued to be held, and the government established an anti-strike division, the Labour Intelligence Monitoring Unit, followed by a unit to maintain essential services during strikes. Meanwhile a promised reconstitution of the NLC was repeatedly postponed, and the tenure of the administrator extended until 1990. The administrator drew up a joint slate representative of both factions and it was returned unopposed for all offices under the presidency of Paschal Bafyau of the Nigeria National Union of Railwaymen.

The 1992 quadrennial congress re-elected most of the leadership, including Bafyau, and established a Women's Commission. A Labour Transport Corporation was set up to run buses in Lagos and Abuja, with cheaper fares for union members, and a monthly newspaper was launched. However, the events of 1993 onwards associated with the refusal of the military to accept elected civilian rulers inevitably renewed the tension between the NLC and the state. Although the NLC came under some criticism from affiliates, notably the oil workers, for being over-conciliatory, it was again put into administration in 1994, the government appointing its officers.

Following the death of Gen. Abacha in June 1998, the NLC was allowed to run its own affairs. Its right to affiliate to organizations outside Africa was also restored. In January 1999, in the first major trade union election in Nigeria since 1994, Adams Oshiomhole (formerly deputy to Bafyau, and general secretary of the National Union of Textile and Garment Workers) was elected president of the NLC.

Under its slogan of "A New Beginning", the leadership emphasizes the NLC's role in the consolidation of democracy and its aim is to "challenge the political monopoly of conservative, feudal and neo-colonial forces which continue to deploy looted funds, ethnic and religious caucuses and state power to perpetuate their hegemony". NLC president Oshiomhole (who is also general secretary of the affiliated National Union of Textile, Garment and Tailoring Workers) was briefly detained by the security services in October 2004 amid heightened tension between the government and the NLC over strikes called in protest against fuel price rises. The NLC seeks the formation of a viable nationwide political party representative of workers, but there is no party currently fulfilling this role in Nigeria.
International affiliations. ICFTU; CTUC

Norway

Capital: Oslo
Population: 4.57 m. (2004 est.)

1 Political and Economic Background

Norway is a parliamentary democracy under a constitutional hereditary monarchy. Governments are usually formed by coalitions, and the Labour Party (DNA) has led the government for long periods since World War II, most recently from 1990–97. The latest parliamentary elections, in September 2001, eventually led to the formation of a new centre-right minority coalition government comprising the Christian People's Party (Krf), the Liberal Party (Venstre) and the Conservative Party (Høyre), with the weakened Centre Party (SP) no longer in the coalition. The Labour Party remained the largest single party, winning 43 of the 165 seats in Parliament. The coalition parties now hold 62 seats together in Parliament (Høyre 38, Krf 22, Venstre 2) and Høyre has an absolute majority of ministers, although the Krf still retains the position of Prime Minister. The far right populist Progressive Party (Fremskrittspartiet – Frp) did notably well in the 2001 elections and eventually took 25 seats in the Parliament, thus making it the most important party in the government's parliamentary base even though not part of the government.

Norway has a mixed economy and a high standard of living. Since the 1960s offshore oil and gas have been a major contributor to prosperity and only Saudi Arabia and Russia export more oil. After a downturn in the early 1990s Norway enjoyed good growth rates in the following years, although growth was only 1.0% in 2002 and 0.5% in 2003, reflecting the general sluggishness of the European economy. Unemployment nonetheless remains low and in 2003 was estimated at 3.1%. Norway is a welfare state and public sector expenditure exceeds 50% of GDP, with heavy spending on health and social services and subsidies for vulnerable sectors of the economy such as agriculture and fishing. There are concerns about the impact on the resources available for public spending of the long-term depletion of energy reserves. However, the government has made partial provision by a major programme of diverting oil revenues to overseas investments via a Government Petroleum Fund and, in common with other Nordic countries (and unlike most other developed nations), Norway runs a budget surplus to build margin to absorb the impact of future adverse conditions, including an ageing population. It has a good record in technological adaptation and was ranked sixth of 101 countries in the World Economic Forum survey of global competitiveness for 2004. Some 79% of the workforce are in services, and 14% in manufacturing. Norway has twice, in 1972 and 1994, rejected membership of the European Union in popular referenda despite the DNA government on both occasions urging a vote in favour.

GDP (purchasing power parity) $171.7bn. (2004 est.); GDP per capita (purchasing power parity) $37,800 (2004 est.).

2 Trade Unionism

Norway ratified ILO Convention No. 87 (Freedom of Association and Protection of the Right to Organize, 1948) in 1949 and Convention No. 98 (Right to Organize and Collective Bargaining. 1949) in 1955.

Union density is high in Norway compared to the European average, although below the levels seen in other Scandinavian countries. Density has not greatly altered in the last four decades. In the 1990s it declined fractionally, but the total number of union members increased because of the expansion of the number of jobs. The highest rate of organization is in the public sector, where 83% of employees are unionized, compared with 43% in the private sector. The most heavily organized private sector areas are manufacturing, banking and insurance. In Norway, occupations requiring higher levels of education tend to be more organized than those requiring lower levels.

The oldest trade union centre is the LO, founded in 1899. With 830,000 members (including pensioners and unemployed) the LO is the leading factor in most of the private sector and in many public sector areas also, outside health and education. Its membership has increased by some 60,000 since the early 1990s. LO's dominance of the Norwegian trade union movement has, however, declined since the 1970s with the formation of competing centres, the Confederation of Academic Professional Unions in Norway (AF) and the Confederation of Vocational Unions (YS). The AF was created as a confederation of unions catering for those with college and university qualifications, while the YS, although with a white-collar flavour, tended to compete more directly in LO's core areas. LO's relative position has eroded in the face of changes to the structure of the labour force, with the loss of blue-collar manufacturing jobs (LO's power base) and the rise of service industries (with lower unionization rates) and white-collar public sector jobs. Whereas the LO in 1980 organized 38% of the total workforce and other organizations only 19%, by 1997 the LO organized 30% and the others 27%.

In the late 1990s major realignments of the centres took place. In 1997–98 the AF lost nearly half its members to a new organization, Akademikerne, which capitalized on the feeling that AF was dominated by less-qualified groups such as nurses. Akademikerne was set up to cater only for those with university degrees at master's level and above and to win back positions lost in a general flattening of salary differentials. After the split in AF, when the unions later forming Akademikerne walked out, the AF made an unsuccessful attempt at a merger with the YS. When this failed it eventually led to the dismantling of the AF in 2001. Some of its affiliate unions, eg. Norsk Sykepleierforbund (Norwegian Nurses Union) and Lærerforbundet (Union of Teachers), and some independent unions, such as Norsk Lærerlag (Norwegian Union of Teachers) and Politiets Fellesforbund (General Union of the Police), joined forces to establish the new trade union centre called UHO in December 2001. Norsk Lærerlag merged in January 2002 with the other major teachers' organization, Lærerforbundet, into Utdanningsforbundet (Union of Education).

The ancillary nurses' union (Norsk Helse og Sosial Forbund) left the YS and entered into a "joint venture" (cooperation agreement with an intention to merge) with Norsk Kommuneforbund (Norwegian Municipal Workers' Union), which is affiliated to the LO. In June 2003 these two unions merged under the new name Fagforbundet (literally "The Trade Union" – although it is, in fact, a general union), which retains membership in the LO. Fagforbundet has taken over from the Norwegian Union of Municipal Employees (NKF) the place as the biggest single Norwegian trade union federation, with a membership of approximately 290,000. The merger has caused some resentment among some of the union's traditional blue collar members, e.g. firefighters in Bergen, who have left the union to join a small YS-affiliated union of machinists (formerly naval machinists). Their claim is that Fagforbundet after the merger with the ancillary nurses is dominated by the large group of female hospital workers, to the detriment of the blue-collar workers, and their wage claims.

In December 2003 five trade union federations affiliated to LO and one to YS signed an agreement of intent to merge into a large union for the service and transport sector. According to the agreement the final decisions to merge will be taken in the federations concerned during 2005, with the intention of having the new union federation in operation by 2006. The federations involved are the following: Handel og Kontor i Norge (Union of Employees in Commerce and Offices), Norsk Transportarbeiderforbund (Norwegian Union of Transport Workers), Norsk Post- og Kommunikasjonsforbund (Norwegian Union of Post and Communication), Norsk Jernbaneforbund (Norwegian Union of Railway Workers), Hotell- og Restaurantarbeiderforbundet (Norwegian Union of Hotel and Restaurant Workers, HRAF) and Yrkestrafikkforbundet (YTF), YTF being the only one of these affiliated to YS. Apart from financial distress in some of these federations (e.g. HRAF), and the argument "bigger is stronger", one motivation behind the agreement is connected with privatization of public entities and the drive towards switching from relatively costly public sector collective agreements with extensive occupational pension schemes to private sector collective agreements without such schemes. If successful the new federation will partly bridge the public-private divide in the transport sector (the missing piece in the totality being Fagforbundet, which organizes the employees within the municipally owned public transport entities).

The LO-affiliated Norsk Grafisk Forbund (Norwegian Graphical Union) in 2003 decided to enter into negotiations with the largest federation in the private sector, Fellesforbundet, with the intention of a merger. The merger is contingent upon the establishment of a graphical section within Fellesforbundet. The final decision is due to be taken at NGF's next convention in February 2005.

The relations between LO and YS have continued to improve, as also between their affiliated unions, despite competition over recruitment of members. The competing federations in transport had, for instance, a joint strategy in the central collective bargaining process in 2002. Another significant indication of this development is that LO withdrew its opposition to admitting YS as a member of the European Trade Union Confederation (ETUC), with the result that YS became affiliated at the end of 2002.

Relations between the three major confederations (UHO, LO and YS) are quite good, while Akademikerne remain marginalized in the camp of the employees. This was demonstrated when the government-appointed commission preparing a new labour code delivered its proposal in February 2004. Akademikerne sided with the majority of the commission in all major aspects, while the three other confederations constitute a minority bloc, opposing proposals to liberalize the present strict conditions for the use of fixed term contracts, flexibilization of working time arrangements etc. Just after the commission had had its official press conference, the three confederations had theirs, announcing a joint campaign to combat the majority proposals.

The LO has historically been close to the Labour Party (DNA), which has been in office for long periods. LO leaders have served as Labour ministers and the leaders of the two organizations meet regularly. The other centres have, in contrast, stressed their political independence. The LO's leadership position in the labour movement, and its political ties, have meant that it was often the only voice of labour on government committees, a source of dissatisfaction to the growing rival confederations. In 1999 the government broadened the representative base of a number of advisory committees.

Relations between the LO and AF (before the latter's dissolution) were generally positive in recent years, and these two ICFTU affiliates had a cooperation agreement. Relations between the LO and YS, in contrast, have been strained by their frequent competition to organize the same groups of workers, but have also tended to improve and the idea of a merger of the two organizations has begun to gain currency, although hindered by the LO's links to the Labour Party.

Since 1935 successive Basic Agreements (Hovedavtalen), negotiated between the LO and Confederation of Norwegian Business and Industry (NHO) have provided a detailed framework for the conduct of industrial relations and the settlement of disputes. Employers recognize the right of the unions to speak and act for the workers and their own obligation to deal with the unions, while the unions accept the constraints of submitting to highly formalized negotiating procedures. Such constraints include the "duty of peace", whereby unions will not call strikes or disrupt production while an agreement is in force (although sympathy strikes and political strikes are excluded from this ban). Collective agreements, which typically apply for two years, are submitted to referendums of the membership. Disputes over the interpretation of collective agreements can be referred to the Labour Court.

Where breakdown in negotiation of collective agreements occurs, disputes are referred for conciliation and mediation. More controversially, compulsory arbitration may be imposed by the government with the approval of Parliament. The government maintains that this occurs only where there is a serious risk to life or health or vital interests. The unions maintain that arbitration has been imposed in cases not involving such level of jeopardy. Strikes are banned in the offshore oil industry. Strikes are fairly infrequent, but because they typically take place at the national rather than enterprise level, the impact of individual strikes can be serious. Strikes over pay in several sectors in Spring 2000 were the most extensive since 1986.

3 Trade Union Centres

Akademikerne
Federation of Norwegian Professional Associations
Address. Akersgata 16, 0158 Oslo
Phone. +47 23103410
Fax. +47 23103411
E-mail. akademikerne@akademikerne.no
Website. www.akademikerne.no
Leadership. Christl Kvam
Membership. 128,074 in15 associations
History and character. In October 1997 seven associations within the Confederation of Academic and Professional Unions (AF), representing chartered engineers, business economists, dentists, lawyers, architects, veterinarians and psychologists, announced they were breaking away to join the Norwegian Medical Association in the formation of Akademikerne (literally, "The Academics"). In 1998 they were joined by a further five AF affiliates, most importantly the 36,000-member Civil Engineers.

The creation of Akademikerne reflected the belief that the AF was over-centralized and too influenced by unions of lesser-qualified occupational groups and that those with high qualifications had been left out in a process of flattening differentials. Akademikerne was to admit only those with higher university qualifications, representing five years' study. The majority of members of the associations joining Akademikerne were also in the private sector or self-employed whereas those left within AF were overwhelmingly in the public sector. The declared objective of the new confederation was to seek "differentiated and market-based wage determination, as far as possible through local bargaining at the firm level". So far they have had some success in achieving their objectives in the collective bargaining strategy, notably in the municipal sector in 2002, where they managed to get the groups where they have most of their members exempted from the stipulations regarding remuneration levels in the central collective agreement.

Landsorganisasjonen i Norge (LO)
Norwegian Confederation of Trade Unions
Address. Youngsgata 11, 0181 Oslo
Phone. +47 23 06 10 50
Fax. +47 23 06 17 43
Website. www.lo.no (Norwegian; English section)
Leadership. Gerd-Liv Valla (president)
Membership. 842,485 (of which about three-quarters are in employment)
History and character. The LO (literally the National Organization in Norway) was founded in 1899 and was initially known as the Arbeidernes Faglige Landsorganisasjon i Norge (Workers' Federation of Trade Unions in Norway). Its status was secured during the inter-war years and entrenched in the first of the Basic Agreements in 1935. Following World War II the LO played a leading role in the building of the social state. Agreements between the LO and the Confederation of Norwegian Business and Industry (NHO) have continued to provide the basic structure for industrial relations and incomes policy in the economy as a whole. Historically, the LO has maintained considerable central power over its affiliates and has been much more centralized than the other Norwegian confederations.

The LO remains much the biggest of the Norwegian confederations although its share of the organized workforce has fallen with the rise of rival confederations, based mainly in the white collar sector, since the 1970s. In 1999 it represented 56% of the unionized work force. It dominates in manufacturing industry, where unionization rates are high.

There is a deep historical identification with the Labour Party (DNA) although the former practice whereby trade union branches were given collective memberships in the party ended in the 1990s. The LO and Labour Party have a joint committee where the organizations' leaders (including the Prime Minister when Labour is in office) meet on a weekly basis and the LO's president, and the leaders of its largest affiliates, are on the Labour Party executive committee. The Labour Party has been the leading party of government since the 1930s, and Cabinet ministers have commonly come from the LO ranks. In the 1997 elections the LO provided 2.5m. NOK for direct campaign support for the LO. Some of the LO's affiliates have constitutions declaring them to be politically independent, and there is also a degree of support for other parties within the LO, with some affiliates providing financial support for the Socialist Left party (SV, which did well in the 2001 elections at the expense of the DNA, winning 23 seats). The close identification of the LO with the Labour Party has proved both a strength in securing union influence on government and a weakness in enabling the development of other albeit smaller confederations that emphasize their politically non-partisan position.

During the early 1990s Norway experienced an economic downturn and rising unemployment. The LO, NHO and Labour government entered a social pact, the "solidarity alternative" that provided for wage moderation in return for commitment to job creation. Unemployment dropped steadily from 6% in 1993 to 3% and the 1997 LO congress reaffirmed its commitment to a continuation of the solidarity alternative. Although Labour lost office in elections later in 1997 the incoming minority government retained the main outlines of the pact. Smaller union and employer confederations have been critical of the dominance of centralized bargaining and the development of industrial policy by the LO and NHO and there has been an opening up of tripartite committees to other unions since the change of government in 1997.

The LO has sought to modernize its image to reflect changes in the work place. Its image as a male-dominated blue-collar manufacturing confederation had proved problematic with the increase in services in the private sector and the rise of public sector unions with heavily female memberships. 45% of LO members are now women compared with one-third in the early 1980s. Although its 1997 congress rejected a formal policy of setting a quota for women to sit on its ruling bodies, five of the top eight leaders elected were women. The LO has also promoted active campaigns to recruit younger members and to recruit those with higher qualifications. However, its basic position remains in support of flattening pay differentials (which in Norway in any case tend to be relatively modest) and other confederations have dominated the recruitment of better-paid white-collar and professional employees.

The LO comprises 25 national unions, varying in size from under 1,000 members to the 239,000-member municipal employees' union. Their representatives meet in congress every four years. There are 15,000 local branches at enterprise level and 3,000 local unions. In 1994 the LO established four cartels grouping unions for the development of sectoral policy and bargaining purposes, covering central government (LO State), local government (LO Municipal), private sector industry (LO Industry) and services (LO Services). The objective was to provide better coordination for collective bargaining, but the individual unions still lead the bargaining process. Most blue-collar unions are, in accordance with an LO policy adopted in 1923, based on the industrial union principle (i.e. so that all workers in one plant are members of the same union); however, there are exceptions in the white-collar field.

Both the Labour Party and the LO have been divided over the issue of Norwegian accession to the EU. In 1994, a Labour conference voted two-to-one in favour of joining, but at an extraordinary congress the LO narrowly voted against. In a November 1994 referendum the electorate as a whole voted not to join. The EU dimension is nonetheless seen as important by the LO, which maintains a Brussels office, and it advocates the development of framework industry agreements at the European level. In common with other Scandinavian centres it also has an active international solidarity programme, now working with unions in central and eastern Europe as well as the Third World.

Since the 1960s the LO has adopted a series of so-called Programmes of Action. The programme covering the period 1997–2001, named "Equity", called for work for all, equitable distribution of wealth, protection of the social state, the development of co-determination in industry, national ownership of natural resources and the development of a "strong, cost-conscious and service-minded public sector with a view to counteracting privatization of public services".

The LO operates a workers' educational association (AOF) and there is a People's Correspondence School, owned jointly by the labour movement and the cooperatives. The LO is a co-owner of an insurance company. The trade union movement has also for more than 50 years had its own bank, the Landsbanken NS. The Framfylkingen is a children's organization within the labour movement.

At the beginning of 2000 the LO and affiliated unions sold their shares in the co-owned insurance company and bank (VÅR Gruppen ASA) to a consortium of mutual bank and insurance companies (SpareBank 1 Gruppen AS), and entered into a cooperation agreement with the share buying group. Most federations and the LO have experienced dwindling incomes from membership fees over the last years, and the revenue from the sale was therefore more than welcome, especially in some of the federations. The cooperation agreement secures that the strike/dispute funds can be kept on the same terms as before, and that individual members retain favourable terms regarding postponement of payment of loans/instalments during industrial disputes.

International affiliations. ICFTU; ETUC; NFS; TUAC

Affiliates. The following LO affiliates each have at least 30,000 members:

EL & IT Forbundet
Address. Youngsgata. 11, 0181 Oslo
Phone. +47 23 06 34 00
Fax. +47 23 06 34 01
Website. www.elogit.no (Norwegian only)
Leadership. Hans O. Felix (president)
Membership. 37,516
History and character. Founded in 1999 by merger of the unions of Electricians and Power Station Workers and Data and Telecommunications workers.

Fagforbundet
Norwegian Union of Municipal and General Employees
Address. Postboks 7003 St. Olavs plass, 0130 Oslo
Phone. +47 23 06 25 00
Fax. +47 23 06 25 01
E-mail. post@fagforbundet.no
Website. www.fagforbundet.no (Norwegian only)

Membership. 287.438
Leadership. Jan Davidsen

Fellesforbundet
United Federation of Trade Unions
Address. Lilletorget 1, 0184 Oslo
Phone. +47 23 06 31 00
Fax. +47 23 06 31 01
E-mail. felesforbundet@fellesforbundet.no
Website. www.fellesforbundet.no (Norwegian; English section)
Leadership. Kjell Bjørndalen (president)
Membership. 139,661
History and character. Founded in 1988 by the merger of five unions representing workers in the clothing, building, iron and metal, paper, and forestry and land industries. It is the largest private sector union in Norway and, reflecting the breadth of occupations represented, is affiliated to several global union federations (ITGLWF, IFBWW, IMF, ICEM, IUF, ITF). It is leading initiatives for the coordination of collective bargaining at the Nordic level. Fellesforbundet has staff of about 156 at head office and 18 district offices.

Norsk Arbeidsmandsforbund (NAF)
Norwegian Union of General Workers
Address. Postboks 8704, Youngstorget 0028 Oslo
Phone. +47 23 06 10 50
Leadership. Arnfinn Nilsen (president)
Membership. 32,035

Handel og Kontor I Norge (HK)
Union of Employees in Commerce and Offices
Address. Youngsgt. 11, 0181 Oslo
Phone. +47 815 48 055
Website. www.handelogkontor.no (Norwegian only)
E-mail. Norge@handelogkontor.no
Leadership. Sture Arntzen (president)
Membership. 59,689

Norsk Kjemisk Industriarbeiderforbund (NKIF)
Norwegian Union of Chemical Industry Workers
Address. Youngsgt. 11, 0181 Oslo
Phone. +47 23 06 13 40
E-mail. nkifpost@nkif.no
Website. www.nkif.no (Norwegian only)
Leadership. Olaf Støylen (president)
Membership. 31,777

Norsk Kommuneforbund (NKF)
Norwegian Union of Municipal Employees
Address. Augustsgt. 23, 0164 Oslo
Phone. +47 23 06 25 00
E-mail. post@nkf.no
Website. www.nkf.no (Norwegian only)
Leadership. Jan Davidsen (president)
Membership. 239,952
History and character. This public sector union is the largest LO affiliate.

Norsk Naerings– og Nytelsesmiddelarbeiderforbund (NNN)
Norwegian Union of Food, Beverage and Allied Workers
Address. Postbox 8719 Youngstorget, 0028 Oslo

Phone. +47 22 20 66 75
Fax. +47 22 36 47 84
E-mail. firmapost.nnn@nnn.no
Website. www.nnn.no
Leadership. Torbjørn Dahl
Membership. 32,699

Norsk Post og Kommunikasjonsforbund
Norwegian Post and Communications Union
Address. Møllergata 10, 0179 Oslo
Phone. +47 23 06 22 50
Website. www.postkom.org (Norwegian only)
Leadership. Odd Christian Øverland (president)
History and character. Founded 2000 by the merger of two LO affiliates, the Norwegian Postal Organization and the Norwegian Union of Postmen.

Norsk Tjenestemannslag (NTL)
Norwegian Civil Service Union
Address. Møllergata 10, 0179 Oslo
Phone. +47 23 06 15 99
Fax. +47 23 06 15 55
E-mail. post@ntl.no
Website. www.ntl.no (Norwegian only)
Leadership. Turid Lilleheie (president)
Membership. 46,729

Utdanningsgruppenes Hovedorganisasjon (UHO)
Confederation of Higher Education Unions
Address. Stortingsgaten. 2, 0158 Oslo
Phone. +47 22 70 88 50
Fax. +47 22 70 88 60
E-mail. post@uho.no
Website. www.uho.no
Leadership. Anders Folkestad
History and character. This is Norway's second largest confederation of professional unions. UHO, founded in December 2001, considers itself politically neutral. It has seven member unions, with a total of nearly 230,000 members. Membership groups include police officers, educators, nurses, physiotherapists, occupational therapists and deacons. The confederation is dominated by educational groups below university level.

In 2003 the government decided for the first time to transfer its historical position as collective bargaining agent vis-à-vis the teachers' unions and UHO to the teachers' employers, the municipalities, and their bargaining association (Kommunenes Sentralforbund - KS). The new central collective agreement with the teachers' unions therefore has KS as the new party on the employers' side from May 2004. At the same time the teachers' central collective agreement on working time will be renegotiated. On both scores KS want more flexibility and local diversification.
Affiliates. Principal affiliates include:

Utdanningsforbundet
Union of Education
Address. Postboks 9191 - Grønland, 0134 Oslo
Tel. +47 24 14 20 00
Fax. +47 24 14 21 00
E-mail. post@utdanningsforbundet.no
Website. www.utdanningsforbundet.no (Norwegian only)
Membership. 132.503
Leadership. Helga Hjetland

Norsk Sykepleierforbund
Norwegian Nurses' Association
Address. Tollbugt. 22, Postboks 456, 0104 Oslo
Phone. +47 22 04 33 04
Fax. +47 22 04 32 40
E-mail. post@sykepleierforbundet.no
Membership. 70.000
Leadership. Bente G. H. Slaatten

Yrkesorganisasjonenes Sentralforbund (YS)
Confederation of Vocational Unions
Address. PB 9232, Grønland, 0134 Oslo
Phone. +47 21 01 36 00
Fax. +47 21 01 3720
E-mail. kaus@ys.no (international affairs)
Website. www.ys.no (Norwegian only)
Leadership. Randi Bjørgen (president)
Membership. 201,552
History and character. The YS was founded in 1977 as a politically independent alternative to the LO. Although recruiting especially in growing white-collar areas, it was a more general confederation than the education-based AF and consequently competed more for members with the LO. A large majority of its members are in the public sector and two-thirds are women. Most of those in the private sector are in banking and insurance.

In May 1999 YS leader Randi Bjørgen proposed merger with the AF, which had suffered the defection of half its membership to the newly formed Akademikerne. The June 1999 YS conference approved the merger in principle. Ultimately, however, opposition grew within the YS to what was seen as the increased centralization involved in the planned new organization, and in June 2000 the AF announced it would dissolve. Central coordination has traditionally been much looser in the YS than in the LO. As a result of the collapse of the AF, the YS is now the leading confederation behind the LO.
Affiliates. The YS comprises 17 affiliated unions, the largest of which are:

Kommunalansattes Fellesorganisasjon (KFO, municipal employees)
Address. Brugata 19, 0134 Oslo
Phone. +47 21 01 36 00
Fax. +47 21 01 36 50
E-mail. kfo–post@kfo.no
Website. www.kfo.no (Norwegian only)
Membership. 55,483
Leadership. Alf O Bowitz

Norsk Helse– og Sosialforbund (NHS, Norwegian Association of Health and Social Care Personnel)
Address. Postboks 151, Bryn, 0611 Oslo
Phone. +47 22 07 25 00
Fax. +47 22 07 25 10
E-mail. nhs@nhs.no
Website. www.nhs.no (Norwegian only)

Leadership. Tove Stangnes (president)
Membership. 52,337

Finansforbundet (Finance Sector Union)
Address. PO Box 9234 Grønland, 0134 Oslo
Phone. +47 22 05 63 00
Fax. +47 22 17 06 90
Website. www.finansforbundet.no
Email. post@finansforbunet.no
Leadership. Jorunn Berdal
Membership. 36,000

Oman

Capital: Muscat
Population: 2.90 m. (2004 est.) (including 577,000 non-nationals)

1 Political and Economic Background

The Sultanate of Oman is ruled by decree of the Sultan. There are no political parties and there is no parliament per se, although there is a Consultative or Shura Council. Shura members were appointed until the first direct elections were held in September 2000. The popular vote was open to men and women, who returned two women to the 83-member assembly. Most decisions, however, are still taken by the ruling family, in consultation with other leading citizens. Criticism of the Sultan is forbidden by law.

Oman has a mixed economy with a heavy dependence on oil, reserves of which are modest. The government is trying to encourage private investment and diversification. Agriculture is mainly at a subsistence level, with most food imported.

The Omani labour force was estimated at 920,000 in 2002. Up to 2000, it was estimated that at least 50% of the total work force were foreigners. Most of these workers came from South Asia, and the government sought to reduce their numbers, so as to improve employment prospects for Omani citizens. There are specific quotas in different sectors, ranging from a 60% requirement in transport, storage and communications, to 15% in contracting establishments.

Reports vary about the preponderance of foreign workers: it was earlier believed that foreigners constituted an overwhelming majority in the private sector workforce, although a US Department of Energy survey in 2004 suggested otherwise. The number of Omani workers in the private sector grew by 3.8 per cent to reach 68,378 for the five months ending May 2003. Meanwhile government sources say expatriate employees in the sector totalled 407,000 in 2003. Prospective foreign workers need clearance from the Ministry of Labour; various visas are required for work, under the Omani Alien Residence Law. Educated women especially have made gains in the workplace, achieving maternity leave and equal pay for equal work. An estimated 20% of all civil servants are women.

Alleged mistreatment of foreign labourers remains an ongoing problem and foreign women employed as domestic servants and garment workers have complained that their employers have withheld their salaries.

GDP (purchasing power parity) $36.7bn. (2003 est.); GDP per capita (purchasing power parity) $13,100 (2003 est.).

2 Trade Unionism

Oman joined the ILO in 1993 but has not ratified ILO Convention No. 87 (Freedom of Association and Protection of the Right to Organize, 1948) or Convention No. 98 (Right to Organize and Collective Bargaining, 1949). Trade unions are illegal and do not exist inside Oman. Objections were raised concerning the eligibility of the Omani workers' delegate at the 91st session of the ILO, held in Geneva, in 2003. The WFTU recognizes an exile National Committee of Omani Workers.

There is no provision for collective bargaining and wages and other conditions are set by employers within guidelines from the Minister of Labour and Social Affairs. A law – passed in 1973 pursuant to the Sultan's Decree no.34 – requires the formation of joint labour-management committees in enterprises with more than 50 workers. Similarly, any firm with more than 50 employees must establish a "grievance procedure". But the committees are not authorized to discuss wages, hours, or conditions of employment.

The 1973 law also expressly forbids forced or bonded labour by adults or children. Employers have been known to withhold letters of release from foreign workers, making it difficult for them to switch jobs. The law absolutely prohibits strikes and none have been reported in recent years. Individual or (less commonly) collective grievances may be referred to the Labour Welfare Board, and this is a frequently used mechanism. It is available to both foreign and local workers, and applies to employees of all firms, regardless of size.

Pakistan

Capital: Islamabad
Population: 159.2 m. (2004 est.)

1 Political and Economic Background

Pakistan became an independent state following the partition of the British Indian Empire in 1947. East Pakistan seceded (as Bangladesh) in 1971. Military interventions in politics have been frequent with the military ruling directly or indirectly for much of the period since independence.

In 1977 a military coup brought to power General Zia ul-Haq, who overthrew the Pakistan People's Party (PPP) government of Zulfiquar Ali Bhutto. Bhutto was executed by the military regime in 1979 but in elections in 1988, after Zia's death, the PPP became the largest party and Bhutto's daughter, Benazir Bhutto, Prime Minister. However, following accusations of corruption, she was dismissed in 1990 by the President in a move backed by the military. A new government under Nawaz Sharif lasted less than three years before it too was dismissed on corruption charges. New elections in 1993 brought Bhutto back to office as leader of the largest single party, but without an overall majority. Her government fell in late 1996 and elections in February 1997 delivered a convincing victory to Nawaz Sharif and his Pakistan Muslim League (PML–N). However, on Oct. 12, 1999, Gen. Pervez Musharaff seized power in a bloodless coup, suspended Parliament and declared a state of emergency. Gen. Musharaff, whose coup appeared to have a measure of support within the country, said his objectives were to restore economic stability, root out corruption and build strong civil institutions. Nawaz Sharif was subsequently put on trial in connection with his efforts to stop the coup, convicted of hijacking and terrorism, and sentenced to life imprisonment, but in December 2000 allowed to go into exile.

In July 2001 Musharraf declared himself President for three years and dissolved the National Assembly, the Senate and the provincial assemblies (all of which had been in recess since October 1999). Musharraf held a referendum in April 2002 that secured the extension of his term of office as President by a further five years, until 2007, 97.7% of those voting being in favour of the extension, according to official figures. Elections to a reformed National Assembly were held in October 2002 and resulted, after allocation of seats reserved for women and minorities, in the pro-Musharraf Pakistan Muslim League–Qaid-i-Azam (PML-QA) taking 99 of the 342 seats in the Assembly, the pro-Bhutto Pakistan People's Party – Parliamentarians (PPP-P) taking 78 and an alliance of six conservative Muslim parties, the Mutiha Majlis-i-Amal (MMA), taking 63. In October 2004 Musharraf announced he would remain the head of the army beyond the end of 2004, going back on previous declarations that he would stand down. Benazir Bhutto remains in self-imposed exile.

Pakistan's economy is primarily agricultural, with two-thirds of the population relying directly or indirectly on this sector; rice and cotton are the main agricultural exports. The modern sector of the economy is limited, and there is extensive use of child labour in some small-scale industries such as brick kilns, glass making, and carpets. The most important industries are textile production and manufacture of clothes, which together account for two-thirds of exports. In the 1990s successive governments said they intended to liberalize the economy, attract foreign investment, privatize state enterprises and control Pakistan's perennial problems with public debt and inflation but the weakness of governments was reflected in the indifferent rate of implementation of such goals. After taking power, Gen. Musharraf said he would resume the privatization programme although political factors have proved a continuing deterrent to widespread change and a significant proportion of industry remains in state hands. Since 2001, when it emerged as a key US ally in the "war on terror", particularly in respect of the situation in Afghanistan, Pakistan has benefited substantially from US-led debt reduction and increased international assistance, though foreign direct investment remains very limited. According to government figures the economy grew by 6.4% in the financial year to the end of June 2004, boosted by a recovery in construction and manufacturing, following GDP growth of 5.1% in the previous financial year. However, the agricultural sector actually contracted slightly.

GDP (purchasing power parity) $318bn. (2004 est.); GDP per capita (purchasing power parity) $2,100 (2004 est.).

2 Trade Unionism

In 1949 an All Pakistan Confederation of Labour (APCOL) was founded, with affiliates in East and West Pakistan, and which adhered to the ICFTU. In 1962 dissatisfied affiliates of APCOL, notably the Petroleum Workers' Federation and the Cigarette Labour Union, formed the Pakistan National Federation of Trade Unions (PNFTU), with 59 member unions at that time. A further series of splits in APCOL led to it losing its ICFTU affiliation while the PNFTU gained ICFTU affiliated status in 1964. APCOL's component parts each claimed the name West Pakistan Federation of Trade Unions simultaneously until one faction changed its name to the All-Pakistan Federation of Trade Unions (APFTU) and it too affiliated to the ICFTU. The third contemporary ICFTU affiliate is the All-Pakistan Federation of Labour (APFOL).

Attempts at unity between the various national centres have been made from time to time, without success. As a result Pakistan still has three ICFTU affiliates (APFOL, APFTU, PNFTU), the WCL one (All-Pakistan Trade Union Congress, APTUC) and the WFTU claims to have five. The three ICFTU affiliates joined in an alliance as the Pakistan Workers' Confederation (PWC) in October 1994. They pledged not to compete for members and to extend their cooperation in extending recruitment. Many unions are highly politicized, reflecting divergent political streams. Other unions are not directly involved in politics. Nine national federations now participate in the Pakistan Workers' Confederation.

Although the unions dispute these figures, the government estimates union members make up only about 10% of the industrial labour force and 3% of the total estimated workforce. Large sections of the labour force are in the informal sector and there is widespread use of contract labour. Where employers are opposed, the process of union registration can be extremely protracted and costly and union organizers can be victimized during the registration process.

Trade unions have been subject to periods of repression and government intervention throughout Pakistan's history, and were weakened by the loss of East Pakistan (a stronghold of militancy) as Bangladesh in the early 1970s. Numerous restrictions were placed on trade union activity under martial law from 1977, when strikes and some unions were banned, though these restrictions eased after the ending of martial law in 1985.

New labour legislation was introduced recently in

the form of the Industrial Relations Ordinance (IRO) 2002. Although the stated aim of the 2001 Labour Policy was compliance with ILO conventions it remains the case that many industries are excluded from the ambit of the legislation. Workers in these industries have no rights to register trade unions or to achieve recognition as the Collective Bargaining Agent under the IRO procedures. Although a general right to freedom of association exists under the Constitution (Article 17) in practice this has not proved sufficient to promote and protect freedom of association in industries not covered by the IRO legislation. The excluded sectors include railway workers, agricultural workers, hospital workers, civil servants, supervisory and managerial staff, state banking, workers in export processing zones and those working in state enterprises such as oil and gas production, electricity generation and transmission, the state-owned airline (Pakistan International Airlines), and ports. Where workers may not form unions they can in some cases join associations, but these have limited powers and cannot engage in collective bargaining or strike. In 1997, the Supreme Court overturned a ban in force since 1978 on the right to form trade unions and bargain collectively at the Pakistan Television Corporation and the Civil Aviation Authority, but maintained a ban on strikes. In 2001 the ban in place since 1998 on trade union activity in the Water Power and Development Authority was lifted.

Under the Essential Services Maintenance Act of 1952 (ESMA), the government can declare any service or enterprise a public service utility and limit workers' rights. Striking in an industry or service designated under the ESMA carries a penalty of up to one year's imprisonment. Under the Act, the Government must make a finding, renewable every 6 months, on the limits of union activity.

While the legislation prohibits employers from discriminating against union members, such discrimination occurs. Workers are discouraged from pursuing cases through the labour courts because of the cost, delays and what is perceived as widespread corruption.

Although the 2002 Industrial Relations Ordinance (IRO) provides for collective bargaining by legally constituted unions, the restrictions on forming unions mean that collective bargaining is denied to many sectors of the workforce, including most agricultural workers and many of those employed in the public sector.

In addition, it is not uncommon for employers to maintain their own controlled unions, and in some cases, to refuse to recognize a bargaining agent. The IRO permits the establishment of only one "Certified Bargaining Agent" where bargaining with management is permitted. The formal restrictions on lockouts by employers are as extensive as are those on strikes, but unions claim that practice is less even-handed. Where collective bargaining is prohibited under ESMA, tripartite wage boards decide on pay, with disputes referred to the National Industrial Relations Commission.

The law formally prohibits acts of recrimination by employers against those involved in legal strikes. However, strikes are infrequent, and usually illegal and of short duration. Compulsory conciliation procedures and cooling-off periods constrain the right to strike, and the government may ban strikes that may prejudice the national interest or have continued for 30 days.

Unions are affected by general crackdowns on opposition and dissent. In recent years these shifting conditions have seen unions face bans on demonstrations, strikes or "civil commotions". In spite of the constitutional protection of freedom of association it remains the case that a trade union organizer who does not operate entirely within the restrictive framework of the IRO may be liable to arrest or dismissal and may expect to suffer various forms of harassment. There were several reported arrests and incidents of repression in 2003. The ICFTU reported evidence of collusion between employers and the police in at least one high profile case.

Pakistan ratified ILO Convention No. 87 (Freedom of Association and Protection of the Right to Organize, 1948) in 1951 and Convention No. 98 (Right to Organize and Collective Bargaining, 1949) in 1952. The ILO has, however, frequently criticized Pakistan for violations of these conventions, and others relating to forced and child labour. The United States revoked generalized system of preferences (GSP) trade benefits in 1996 for failure to make progress on worker rights issues. However, the European Commission failed to take similar action despite pressure from the ICFTU and other bodies.

3 Trade Union Centres

All-Pakistan Federation of Labour (APFOL)
Address. Union Plaza, Plot No. 3, Bank Road 62, GPO Box 1709, Rawalpindi
Phone. +92 51 520 137
Fax. +92 51 513 348
Leadership. Zahoor Awan (general secretary)
History and character. APFOL was founded in 1951 by Rahmatullah Khan Durrani ("the father of labourers"), who remained central president until his death in 1985. On his death the presidency was claimed by his son, Auranzeb. This succession was challenged and Auranzeb seceded to found a federation known as APFOL, Durrani Group, which allied with the WFTU.
International affiliations. ICFTU; CTUC

All-Pakistan Federation of Trade Unions (APFTU)
Address. Bakhtiar Labour Hall, 28 Nisbat Road, Lahore
Phone. +92 72 22192
Fax. +92 72 39529
E-mail. apftu@brain.net.pak
Leadership. Khurshid Ahmed (general secretary)
Membership. 602,300
History and character. The West Pakistan Federation of Labour was founded in 1947, following the establishment of Pakistan, and was part of the All-Pakistan Confederation of Labour. The organization was subsequently renamed first as the West Pakistan Federation of Trade Unions and then, following the secession of East Pakistan (Bangladesh), as the All-Pakistan Federation of Trade Unions. The late president, Bashir

Ahmed Bakhtiar, was a co-founder in 1947.

The APFTU describes itself as an independent trade union without political links, and seeks to unify the trade union movement to press the government to formulate labour policy in conformity with ILO Conventions No. 87 and No. 98, including the repeal of the Essential Services Act and the restoration of trade union rights to public sector employees. The APFTU joined the umbrella organization the Pakistan Workers' Confederation (PWC) on its formation in 1994 (see above) and APFTU general secretary Khurshid Ahmed is also general secretary of the PWC.

APFTU established Pakistan's first-ever Institute for Education, Training and Research in Labour Studies, which provides for the training of trade union representatives. It has set up a range of welfare projects.

The Pakistan WAPDA Hydro Electric Central Labour Union, with 140,000 members, is APFTU's largest industrially based affiliate. The union campaigned against the part privatization of WAPDA, and in December 1998 the government suspended the union and handed over the management of WAPDA to the armed forces.
International affiliations. ICFTU; CTUC

All-Pakistan Federation of United Trade Unions (APFUTU)

Address. Union House, Imtiaz Manzil, Qasim Pura, Railway Road,, Gujrat
Phone. +92 433 533 736
Fax. +92 433 52 53 02
Leadership. Salman Riaz Choudhry (president)
Membership. 183,435.
History and character. APFUTU was founded in 1992 and registered in 1993. It affiliated to WFTU in 1993 but now has no international affiliation. Affiliates are diverse and include unions in areas such as brick kilns, textile mills, banks, sugar mills, yellow cabs, jute, and municipal offices, as well as general labour unions and the Pakistan Bonded and Child Labour Liberation Front (PBCLF).
International affiliations. None

All-Pakistan Trade Union Congress (APTUC)

Address. 1st Floor, Delhi Muslim Hotel, Aram Bagh Road, PO Box 1004, Karachi
Phone. +92 21 2626142
Fax. +92 21 7780240
E-mail. shouket@fascom.pk
Leadership. Sarwari Khan (president); Shouket Ali (secretary general)
International affiliation. WCL

All Pakistan Trade Union Federation (APTUF)

Address. 14-N, Gulberg Industrial Area, Gulberg II, Lahore
Phone. +92 42 5755078/9
Fax. +92 42 6665301
E-mail. aptuf@brain.net.pk
Leadership. Rubina Jamil (chair); Gulzar Ahmed Chaudhry (general secretary)
History and character. The All Pakistan Trade Union Federation was founded in 1948 and now affiliates 240 public and private sector trade unions. Affiliated unions are in industries such as transport, chemicals, paper, steel, pharmaceuticals, rubber, shoe and commerce, as well as unions in unorganized sectors like brick kilns, oil tankers, and carpet workers. APTUF is part of the Pakistan Workers' Confederation.

APTUF is active among workers in the informal sector and brick kiln workers. The Pakistan Bhatta Mazdoor federation, which is an industry-wide trade union federation of brick kilns workers, is also part of APTUF. APTUF has a wing for women workers which aims to build a leadership capability among women to struggle for their rights (APTUF has a woman chair).

APTUF describes itself as fighting against privatization; the free market economy; erosion of wages; attacks on workers' rights; retrenchment; unemployment; feudalism and capitalism; oppression of women; child and forced labour; the subcontracting system; anti-worker laws; and gender discrimination.
International affiliations. WFTU; CTUC

Pakistan National Federation of Trade Unions (PNFTU)

Address. 406 Qamar House, M. A. Jinnah Road, Karachi 74000
Phone. +92 21 231 3371
Fax. +92 21 331 0981
E-mail. pnftu@cyber.net.pk
Leadership. Mohammad Sharif (president)
International affiliation. ICFTU; CTUC

Palau

Capital: Koror
Population: 20,000 (2004 est.)

1 Political and Economic Background

Palau (also known in its local form as Belau) comprises 300 islands in the western Pacific and since 1994 has been an independent nation in free association with the United States. There is subsistence agriculture and fishing, with tourism as the principal element of the private sector formal economy; however, the government employs 29% of the workforce and the public budget is heavily dependent on financial assistance from the US. Some three-quarters of the workforce are foreigners, mostly from east and south-east Asia, employed in areas such as domestic service, hospitality and construction.

GDP (purchasing power parity) $174m. (2001 est.); GDP per capita (purchasing power parity) $9,000 (2001 est.).

2 Trade Unionism

The Constitution provides the for the right to free association, though there is no specific legislation concerning trade unions or collective bargaining. In practice there are no functioning trade unions. There is no constitutional right to strike and strikes have not recently been reported. Palau is not a member of the ILO.

Palestinian Entity

Government centre: Ramallah and Gaza City
Population: Gaza 1.32 m.; West Bank 2.31 m. (excluding Israeli settlers) (2004 est.)

1 Political and Economic Background

Under a series of interim agreements made in 1993-95 Israel has transferred limited powers of autonomy in the Gaza Strip and parts of the West Bank (territories occupied as a result of the 1967 six-day war) to a Palestine National Authority (PNA), in which the Palestine Liberation Organization (PLO) has been the leading force. Negotiations on a permanent settlement were stalled under the Netanyahu government from 1996–99, but resumed following the election of a Labour government in Israel in May 1999 before faltering amid renewed violence during 2000. Following the death of PNA President and PLO leader Yasser Arafat in November 2004, presidential elections – the first since 1996 – were held in January 2005.

Living standards are much lower than in Israel and the economy has further deteriorated in the period of renewed intifada from October 2000, with repeated Israeli raids and border closures. The majority of the 120,000 Palestinians from the occupied territories who previously worked legally or illegally in Israel are reported to have lost their jobs because of the security situation. The collapsed economy is propped up by international aid.

Gaza GDP (purchasing power parity) $768m. (2003 est.); GDP per capita (purchasing power parity) $600 (2003 est.).

West Bank GDP (purchasing power parity) $1.7 bn. (2002 est.); GDP per capita (purchasing power parity) $800 (2002 est.).

2 Trade Unionism

Following the 1967 Arab–Israeli war, when Israel occupied the West Bank and Gaza, many Palestinian unions were permanently closed on the West Bank and there was complete suppression in Gaza.

In 1989 the ICFTU Executive Board heard a report from a fact-finding mission to the West Bank and urged Israel to lift restrictions on union activity there. It also called on the West Bank unions to rationalize and exhorted the Histadrut (the Israeli trade union centre) to engage in dialogue with bona fide West Bank and Gaza union leaders. Histadrut responded with a policy shift at its 1990 convention, and in 1991 formed a Committee for Workers from the Occupied Territories under the leadership of its Arab Affairs Department.

In this period the Palestine General Federation of Trade Unions (PGFTU) consolidated its position as the representative centre, and by 1993 claimed 100,000 members. It held its first bilateral meeting with the Histadrut in November 1993. By 2002 the PGFTU claimed 290,000 members in 20 affiliated unions.

The Palestinian authorities have been drafting a Palestinian labour code. Pending its enactment, labour activity has been governed by a mix of former Jordanian law and Israeli military decrees (on the West Bank), and by Palestine Authority decisions in Gaza. Government is the largest provider of formal employment in the territories, but early drafts of the labour code included a ban on public servants joining unions, leading to opposition from the PGFTU. Unions must submit grievances prior to strike action to the Palestine Authority Labour Ministry. If the union strikes following arbitration, this is to be referred to the courts. There is no body of legislation in this area. Since the outbreak of the intifada in 2000 the situation has changed dramatically. The PGFTU's activities are now predominantly poverty-reduction and unemployment relief rather than traditional industrial relations. Unemployment rates have passed 60% and are much higher in certain areas (such as Gaza).

Unions in Jerusalem (regarded by Israel but not internationally as part of Israel proper) are formally prohibited from federating with West Bank unions, although this has not been enforced. In practice some Palestinian workers in Jerusalem belong simultaneously to unions affiliated with West Bank federations and to Histadrut. The estimated 150,000 Palestinians from the West Bank and Gaza who formerly worked in Israel or Jerusalem were not full members of Histadrut, but were required to contribute 1% of their wages to Histadrut. In 1996 it was agreed that half of this levy would be transferred to the PGFTU. However, a lack of action on the part of Histadrut to make the transfer proved a controversial problem for both unions, with the PGFTU claiming that the payment should be worth millions of dollars. By 2004, however, almost no Palestinians were working legally in Israel.

During the intifada PGFTU and its officers reported instances of victimization and even direct attacks by Israeli forces. In February 2002 Israeli fighter aircraft and helicopters carried out an attack in Nablus City which ICFTU reported to have destroyed 40% of the PGFTU headquarters. In March 2004 the house of Shaher Sae'd, general secretary of the PGFTU, was raided by Israeli military forces. According to ICFTU reports, Sae'd was escorted from his home at gun-point and questioned before being released.

3 Trade Union Centre

Palestine General Federation of Trade Unions (PGFTU)
E-mail. pgftu@p-ol.com
Leadership. Shaher Sae'd (general secretary)
Membership. The great majority of unions affiliate to the PGFTU and there has been extensive reorganization and consolidation of unions. An estimated 290,000 workers are in membership of the 12 PGFTU-affiliated unions in the West Bank and the eight PGFTU affiliates in Gaza.
International affiliation. ICFTU (November 2002)

Panama

Capital: Panama City
Population: 3.0 m. (2004 est.)

1 Political and Economic Background

Panama has a history of political instability and military involvement in government. During the 1980s, despite a façade of civilian government, the effective ruler was Gen. Manuel Noriega, the commander of the National Guard. In 1989, however, after Noriega annulled the result of a presidential election, US troops invaded, deposed Noriega, and installed the elected president, Guillermo Endara Gallimany. Three years later Endara faced a massive crisis in the shape of riots against unemployment and official corruption, ruining a brief visit by US President Bush. The following year his administration began to disintegrate ahead of the 1994 elections. These were won by the Democratic Revolutionary Party (PRD), a party formerly identified with Noriega but now under reformed leadership, whose nominee, Ernesto Balladares, took office as president in September 1994. In the May 1999 elections, Mireya Moscoso (widow of former President Arnulfo Arias) was elected president as the candidate of the Union for Panama coalition led by her Arnulfist Party (PA). However, the unicameral legislative assembly was dominated by a coalition of opposition parties, led by the PRD. In the May 2004 elections, the presidential race was won by the PRD candidate, Martín Torrijos, while the PRD also gained an absolute majority in the legislature. Gen. Noriega is currently serving a 40–year sentence in the USA for racketeering and drug trafficking.

The Panamanian economy is dominated by services, with shipping and port services linked to the Panama Canal pivotal. Formal ownership and control of the Canal passed from the USA to Panama on Dec. 31, 1999, also ending 89 years of US military presence in the country. During the 1990s the government sought to liberalize trade, attract foreign investment, privatize state enterprises and reform the labour code. Unemployment stands at 14% of the labour force.

GDP (purchasing power parity) $18.78bn. (2004 est.); GDP per capita (purchasing power parity) $6,300 (2004 est.).

2 Trade Unionism

Trade unions were recognized under the 1946 constitution, and Panama ratified ILO Convention No. 87 (Freedom of Association and Protection of the Right to Organize, 1948) in 1958 and Convention No. 98 (Right to Organize and Collective Bargaining, 1949) in 1966. There have been repeated revisions of the labour code. Historically, the WCL, ICFTU and WFTU have all been represented in Panama and that remains the case. The centres have cooperated with each other in a coordinating organization, CONATO.

Private sector workers are free to join unions and there are understood to be some 130,000 union members in the private sector, organized into ten confederations and 341 unions. Legislation adopted in 1995 made it simpler to register unions but also introduced greater flexibility in the labour market. In 1997 a law was passed to regulate collective bargaining and provide a framework for settling disputes in the export processing zones. Private sector workers are often hired on a series of continually renewed temporary contracts to avoid labour code regulations.

Public employees may not join unions but a 1994 law allows the formation of public employee associations, which may engage in collective bargaining, although multiple associations in the same institution are not allowed. In 1998, the government refused to allow the FENASEP public service federation to affiliate to the trade union centre, Convergencia Sindical. The great majority of public sector workers do not have the right to strike. In the public sector political patronage is commonplace and wholesale dismissals of opponents occur after a change of government.

In 2003 plans to privatize the social security fund were opposed by popular demonstrations led by the trade unions. In September police clashed violently with the protesters, injuring many and arresting 21 union leaders.

3 Trade Union Centres

Central National de Trabajadores de Panama
Address. Calle 6ta Rio – Abajo final, No. 31-A, Apartado 3253, Panama 3
Fax. +507 224 0840
International affiliation. WFTU

Confederación General de Trabajadores de Panamá (CGTP)
General Confederation of Workers of Panama
Address. Av. 3, Casa n° 15, Perejil, Apartado 3370, Zona 4, Panama City
Phone. +507 269 9741
Fax. +507 2 235287
E-mail. cgtpan@cwpanama.net
Leadership. Mariano Mena (secretary general)
International affiliation. WCL

Confederación de Trabajadores de la República de Panamá (CTRP)
Confederation of Workers of the Republic of Panama
Address. Calle 31 No. 3–50, Apartado 8929, Zona 5, Panama City
Phone. +507 225 0259
Fax. +507 221 5985
E-mail. ctrp@sinfo.net
Leadership. Aniano Pinzón Real (secretary-general)
Membership. 35,000 claimed in 13 federations.
History. Founded 1956.
International affiliation. ICFTU

Convergencia Sindical
Address. Ave Perú Final, Casa No. 3936, Apartdao 10536, Zona 4, Panama City
Phone. +507 225 6642
Fax. +507 225 6642

E-mail. conversind@cwpanama.net
International affiliation. ICFTU

Papua New Guinea

Capital: Port Moresby
Population: 5.42 m. (2004 est.)

1 Political and Economic Background

Papua New Guinea is a parliamentary democracy and has been an independent member of the Commonwealth since achieving full independence from Australia in 1975. Party political allegiances are fluid, with numerous small parties represented in the legislature – 24 parties won seats in the 109-member Parliament elected at the most recent elections in 2002. Sir Michael Somare, the leader of the National Alliance (and who had been the country's Prime Minister at independence) became Prime Minister as a result of the 2002 elections. Papua New Guinea comprises 1,000 tribes and the world's greatest diversity of languages (800) and there have been secessionist threats from a number of provinces, especially the island of Bougainville, where the Bougainville Revolutionary Army fought a secessionist war from 1988-97, with a political settlement of the conflict finally being reached in 2001.

Much of the country is remote and rugged with little infrastructure, and 85% of the population live in isolated villages practicing (mainly subsistence) agriculture. The capacity of the state is limited and in practice its impact on local communities away from the main centres is small. Mineral extraction generates three-quarters of export revenues. Real incomes have declined in recent years and there is a dependence on aid from Australia (its largest trading partner and external donor) and international agencies.

GDP (purchasing power parity) $11.48bn. (2004 est.); GDP per capita (purchasing power parity) $2,200 (2004 est.).

2 Trade Unionism

Papua New Guinea ratified ILO Convention No. 98 (Right to Organize and Collective Bargaining, 1949) in 1976 and Convention No. 87 (Freedom of Association and Protection of the Right to Organize, 1948) in 2000.

The majority of the population lives in isolated villages engaged in subsistence and small-scale agriculture, but in the formal economy there is a substantial trade union presence. About half the 250,000 wage earners in the formal economy are organized in about 50 trade unions. There are legal prohibitions on discrimination against union members and organizers. Unions must be registered with the Department of Industrial Relations to enjoy legal protection, but the government has not used the denial of registration to control unions. Most of the private sector unions are in the Papua New Guinea Trade Union Congress (PNGTUC), while one-third of public sector workers are in the Public Employees' Association. Unions are independent of the government and of political parties.

The ICFTU has complained that the Department of Industrial Relations is slow or fails to investigate complaints against employers by workers who are harassed or dismissed for trying to form unions. It says that multinationals operating in areas such as forestry and plantation agriculture have refused to allow the formation of trade unions and that working conditions in these sectors are poor, with little access to health care or reasonably priced food. Provincial labour offices have few resources to investigate complaints.

The right to engage in collective bargaining is protected by the constitution and is practiced. However, the government has discretionary powers to cancel arbitration awards or wage agreements when they are considered contrary to the national interest. The government itself is a major employer but declines to negotiate, preferring to deal with pay adjustments under the minimum wage legislation. In the 1990s the government pursued labour market flexibility by declining to index-link wages under the legislation. There is increasing use by employers of individual contracts rather than registered agreements achieved through collective bargaining.

Disputes are relatively rare and secret ballots are needed to make strikes legal. In 1999 engineers working for the national airline struck; the employer dismissed the workers and selectively re-hired some of them. The courts ruled that both parties had acted illegally. To combat separatist movements, the government adopted the 1993 Internal Security Act, which limits freedom of assembly and gives broad powers of detention without trial. However, while the government has been accused of human rights abuses in its application of the Act, and the PNGTUC has called for its abolition, it does not seem to have been used against trade unions. In recent years there have been sporadic strikes over the issue of privatization.

In November 1998 the government announced that it would cut off budget funding in 1999 to its industrial relations institutions, the Arbitration Commission, the Minimum Wages Board, the Office of the Registrar of Trade Unions and the National Tripartite Consultative Council. The move was seen as effectively abolishing these institutions. However, following a work stoppage organized by the PNGTUC, the government abandoned its action.

3 Trade Union Centre

Papua New Guinea Trade Union Congress (PNGTUC)
Address. PO Box 4279, Boroko, NCD
Phone. +675 311 3055
Fax. +675 311 3055
E-mail. naea@daltron.com.pg
Leadership. John Paska (general secretary)
Membership. 70,000
History and character. The PNGTUC was formed in 1970 after the failure of several previous attempts to establish a trade union centre. In the late 1980s the

ICFTU and its regional arm APRO gave considerable assistance in turning the PNGTUC into a true national centre, and membership increased from 12 affiliates with 17,000 members in 1986 to 30 affiliates with 60,000 members by June 1988. In November 1998 the PNGTUC successfully took industrial action to stop the government from withdrawing funding for industrial relations institutions. The PNGTUC negotiates with the Employers' Federation of Papua New Guinea on labour-related issues. PNGTUC general secretary John Paska launched the Papua New Guinea Labour Party in August 2001 as the latest in a series of labour-linked parties, none of which has had much electoral success; this pattern was repeated in the most recent national elections in 2002 when the party failed to make an impact.

International affiliations. ICFTU; CTUC

Paraguay

Capital: Asunción
Population: 6.19 m. (2004 est.)

1 Political and Economic Background

Gen. Alfredo Stroessner took power in a military coup in 1954 and then ruled Paraguay under a permanent state of siege until 1989, winning successive stage-managed elections as the candidate of the right-wing Colorado party, the major force in Paraguayan politics throughout the 20th century. In 1989 Stroessner was overthrown in a "palace coup" led by Gen. Andrés Rodríguez, who in turn was elected President later that year as the Colorado Party candidate. Subsequent elections resulted in victories in 1993 for Juan Carlos Wasmosy and in 1998 for Raúl Cubas Grau, both of the Colorado Party (ANR-PC). In March 1999, however, Vice President Luis Maria Argaña was assassinated, apparently as part of a power struggle within the government, with Cubas and former General Lino César Oviedo (who had made a coup attempt against Wasmosy in 1996, but been rehabilitated after Cubas came to power) suspected of involvement. After several days of mounting crisis, with workers on strike and an impeachment vote pending in Congress, Cubas fled to Brazil, where he was given political asylum. He was replaced as President by the leader of the Senate, Luis González Macchi, who formed a government of national unity. In April 2003 Oscar Nicanor Duarte Frutos (ANR-PC) was elected President. However, though he has made a good start on reducing the national debt, and Paraguay has continued to benefit from its membership of the regional trade organization Mercosur, poverty has worsened, kidnapping has become a major social problem, and the legacy of the dictatorship has been a very unequal land distribution which has spurred widespread occupations.

The Paraguayan economy is based on agriculture, fisheries and forestry which together account for 48 per cent of the labour force. There is a large informal sector. Consistent economic policy has been undermined by political faction-fighting within the ruling ANR-PC.

GDP (purchasing power parity) $28.03bn. (2003 est.); GDP per capita (purchasing power parity) $4,600 (2003 est.).

2 Trade Unionism

Under Stroessner Paraguay ratified ILO Convention No. 87 (Freedom of Association and Protection of the Right to Organize, 1948) in 1962 and Convention No. 98 (Right to Organize and Collective Bargaining, 1949) in 1966. In practice, however, trade unions faced considerable harassment in the Stroessner period. Many trade union activists were exiled following a 1958 general strike. According to the WFTU, Antonio Maidana, the exiled leader of the teachers' association and First Secretary of the Communist Party of Paraguay, who was a leading figure in the 1958 strike, was abducted from Argentina to Paraguay by the regime in 1980 and disappeared without trace.

Nonetheless independent trade unionism developed significantly in the 1980s and the Inter-Trade Union Movement of Paraguayan Workers (MIT–P) was founded in 1985 to unite opposition to the regime. Trade union activists were frequently detained and there were regular reports of torture at the hands of the police and armed forces; the most brutal harassment occurred in the rural areas, as in most Latin American countries.

The fall of Stroessner in 1989 brought a degree of liberalization. Basic union rights and freedoms were incorporated in the country's new constitution of 1992. Public servants, previously allowed to associate only for social and cultural purposes, were permitted to form unions. Restrictions on strikes were reduced. Under the 1993 labour code trade union leaders were given protection from dismissal for union activities. In practice, however, dismissals and harassment of union organizers have reportedly remained fairly common, and employers have sometimes disregarded court orders to reinstate unionists. Collective bargaining is said to be increasing but only involves a minority of workers. Strikes are a common occurrence.

There are an estimated 121,000 members of 1,600 trade unions. There are three trade union centres (centrals), two of them (the CNT and CPT) affiliated to the WCL and the other (the CUT) to the ICFTU. The CUT is the largest of the three. In February 1998 the three centrals organized a "congress of unity" to discuss the economic, social and political crisis in the country. The same month, the CUT president and Eduardo Ojeda, the general secretary of the CNT, were detained for eight days because of their involvement in a transport workers' demonstration which had closed an avenue in Asuncion.

3 Trade Union Centres

Central Nacional de Trabajadores (CNT)
Address. Piribebuy 1078 entre Hernandarias y Colón, Asunción
Phone. +595 21 44 4084
Fax. +595 21 49 2154

E-mail. cnt@telesurf.com.py
Website. www.clat.org/cnt-paraguay
Leadership. Eduardo Ojeda (secretary-general)
History and character. The National Workers' Central (CNT) originated in 1963 as the Christian Workers' Central (CCT), taking its present name in 1978. It claims to have some 80,000 members.
International affiliation. WCL

Central Unitaria de Trabajadores (CUT)
Address. San Carlos 836, Asunción
Phone. +595 21 44 3936
Fax. +595 21 49 8482
E-mail. cut-paraguay@hotmail.com
Leadership. Alan Flores (president); Jorge Alavarenga (secretary-general)
History and character. The CUT was formed in 1989 and is now reported to be the largest of the Paraguayan centrals. The CUT called an indefinite strike and led demonstrations after the March 1999 assassination of Vice-President Argaña, accusing President Cubas and former General Lino César Oviedo of being behind the killing. The unrest led to Cubas fleeing the country.
International affiliation. ICFTU

Confederación Paraguaya de Trabajadores (CPT)
Address. Yegros 1309-33 y Simón Bolívar, Asunción
Phone. +595 21 44-3184
Fax. +595 21 44 3184
Leadership. Gerónimo López (president); Julio Etcheverry Espinola (secretary-general)
History and character. The CPT was founded in 1951 under the influence of the Colorado Party. Independent elements gained control during the 1950s, however, and led a general strike in 1958. Following this many trade unionists were exiled, forming a CPT in exile (CPT–E), while the organization within the country was brought firmly under government control. The CPT is now functioning again in Paraguay after some years of exile in Mexico and elsewhere. It still associates with the Colorado Party although the ties have loosened. It claims to have 43,000 members.
International affiliation. The CPT was affiliated to the ICFTU/ORIT until 1974, when its affiliation was suspended. It is now affiliated to the WCL.

Peru

Capital: Lima
Population: 27.54 m. (2004 est.)

1 Political and Economic Background

Peru ended 13 years of military rule in 1980, but the administration of the centre-left Peruvian Aprista Party (APRA) struggled from 1985 to deal with the subversive activities of the Maoist guerrilla movement, Sendero Luminoso (Shining Path) and with economic decline. In 1990 APRA's Alan García was succeeded as President by Alberto Keinya Fujimori. However, in the face of growing internal disarray Fujimori staged a coup with military support in 1992. He thereafter ruled in an increasingly authoritarian manner. In 1993 a new constitution was approved by referendum, and the 1995 presidential elections held under its auspices resulted in Fujimori's return to office. In May 2000 Fujimori was re-elected by an apparently wide margin but a widespread belief that the result was fraudulent led to months of unrest and in November 2000 Fujimori was forced from office. The president of Congress took over pending new elections. Presidential elections held in April–June 2001 resulted in victory for Alejandro Toledo of the Peru Possible (PP) party, who defeated Alan García of the APRA in a run-off, while the PP also emerged as the largest party in legislative elections in April 2001, taking 45 of the 120 seats in the National Congress. Although still in existence the Shining Path and Tupac Amarú guerrilla movements were largely destroyed under Fujimori with key leaders arrested; the Shining Path now operate mainly in the High Huallaga valley, where they provide protection to peasants who continue to grow coca in defiance of government eradication programmes.

Minerals and fish products account for about two-thirds of the country's export earnings, and the economy is vulnerable to downturns in the price of minerals and metals on world markets. There was extensive privatization of state-controlled enterprises during the 1990s, including in mining, electricity and telecommunications. The Fujimori government struggled with the problem of economic growth lagging behind the increase in population, but the economy grew 5% in 2002 and 4% in 2003. There is extensive under-employment and widespread poverty.

GDP (purchasing power parity) $146bn. (2004 est.); GDP per capita (purchasing power parity) $5,100 (2004 est.).

2 Trade Unionism

Trade union activities gained strength in the 1920s, assisted by the rise of the populist APRA movement, and a Marxist-influenced General Confederation of Peruvian Workers (CGTP) was established in 1929. However, the trade unions were suppressed in the 1930s, a time of violent labour unrest, and remained generally weak until the 1970s, with intervals of repression.

Peru ratified ILO Convention No. 87 (Freedom of Association and Protection of the Right to Organize, 1948) in 1960 and Convention No. 98 (Right to Organize and Collective Bargaining, 1949) in 1964.

After failing to establish a government of national unity, President Fujimori staged an army-backed presidential coup in April 1992, suspending the constitution and ruling by decree. Legislation introduced by decree in 1992 allowed unions to continue to function but imposed greater restrictions and regulations on their activities. Unions were prohibited from taking part in political activities; workers were prohibited from striking over general economic and social policy issues; names of workers who attended strike meetings had to be given to employers. The law contained a broad definition of "essential" services, including health, electricity, water, gas, energy, sanitation, communications and telecommunications, and public transport, where compulsory arbitration could be imposed.

The 1992 legislation, the new national constitution adopted in December 1993, and other measures such as the 1993 Employment Promotion Act, were intended to increase labour market flexibility. A 1996 measure removed guaranteed rights such as annual paid holidays and bonuses and industrial accident compensation, and made these subject to bargaining. Procedures for laying off workers were made easier, with an increase in the use of temporary contracts.

Only about 5% of the workforce (half of which is in the informal economy) are in unions. Unions are permitted and exist in both the private and public sectors. However, temporary employees may not join unions, and an increasing proportion of the workforce is hired on a temporary basis, although there is a formal (but disregarded) ceiling of 20% on the proportion of employees than can be temporary hires. No effective means exist to oblige employers to reinstate workers who have been dismissed for union activities. The law provides a framework for collective bargaining and the implementation of agreements, although this is reportedly often ignored by employers.

The ICFTU, WCL and WFTU each have an affiliated trade union centre. Many unions were active in the opposition movement that drove Fujimori out of office in the autumn of 2000.

3 Trade Union Centres

Central Autónoma de Trabajadores del Perú (CATP)
Address. Av. Nicolás de Pierola 757, Oficina 300, Apartado 1069, Lima 1
Phone/Fax. +51 1428 7692
Leadership. Alfredo Lazo Peralta (secretary-general)
International affiliation. WCL

Confederación General de Trabajadores del Perú (CGTP)
Address. Plaza 2 de Mayo Puerta 4, Lima 1
Telephone. +51 1 431 4738
Fax. + 51 1 424 2357
Leadership. Juan José Gorritti Valle (secretary-general)
History and character. The CGTP was formed in 1968 under the leadership of the Peruvian Communist Party (PCP), and regards itself as the successor to the CGTP formed in 1929. It resisted the policies of Fujimori, leading a series of strikes against privatization and other policies and being involved in the demonstrations that led to his fall in 2000. CGTP is the largest federation in Peru, and has affiliates based throughout the regions.
International affiliation. WFTU

Confederación de Trabajadores del Perú (CTP)
Address. Jr. Ayacucho 173, Lima 1
Phone/Fax. +51 1 426 6138
Leadership. Douglas Figueroa Silva (general secretary)

Confederación Unitaria de Trabajadores del Perú (CUT)
Address. Jr. Talara 751, Lima 11
Phone. +51 1 423-9008
Fax. +51 1 431-5415
Leadership. Julio César Bazán (secretary-general)
Membership. 300,000
History, and character. Formed in 1992. The CUT was active in the movement that led to President Fujimori's fall from office in 2000.
International affiliation. ICFTU

Philippines

Capital: Manila
Population: 86.24 m. (2004 est.)

1 Political and Economic Background

The Philippines became independent from the United States in 1946. In 1965 Ferdinand Marcos became President, imposing martial law in 1972 and thereafter ruling by decree. In August 1983, Bengino Aquino, the country's foremost opposition figure, was shot dead at Manila airport upon returning from a three-year period of self-imposed exile in the USA. Aquino's death, in which the military was implicated, had the effect of unifying the growing opposition to the rule of Marcos. In 1986, in the face of a massive "people power" movement, Marcos reluctantly conceded elections, and although he claimed victory over Aquino's widow, Corazon Aquino, he was forced to stand down in the face of the defection of his senior military commanders and US pressure. A new constitution was adopted in 1987. As President, Corazon Aquino dismantled the coercive apparatus of the Marcos regime, and the institutions of the republic's American-style democracy were re-established. Her term was punctuated by unsuccessful military uprisings and growing disillusionment on the left. In 1992 she was followed as President by her Defence Secretary and chosen successor, Fidel Ramos. In May 1998 Joseph Estrada, the candidate of the opposition Struggle of the Nationalist Filipino Masses (LAMMP) party was elected President in succession to Ramos (to whom he had been Vice-President), running on a populist platform that emphasized the needs of the poor and opposition to corruption and Philippines "pork barrel" style of politics. Estrada himself became mired in accusations of corruption and was forced from office in January 2001, being replaced as President by Gloria Macapagal-Arroyo. Parties supporting Arroyo, allied as the People Power Coalition (PPC), went on to gain a victory in legislative elections later in 2001. In May 2004 Arroyo secured a fairly narrow victory in presidential elections in which she was backed by a coalition of parties called the Coalition of Truth and Experience for Tomorrow (K-4), while K-4 candidates won almost 70% of the seats in the House of Representatives. Political parties remian highly personalist and fluid with fluctuating coalitions built around individuals.

The Philippines economy comprises a large agricultural sector (employing 45% of the workforce) and (mainly light) industry (including textiles, chemicals, electronics assembly and food processing), with industry employing about 15% of the workforce. The government has pursued policies aimed at deregulation and privatization. The availability of low-cost skilled labour has encouraged substantial inward investment from Japan and elsewhere although the Philippines has not matched the level of economic progress of the leading newly industrialized countries of East Asia. GDP growth has been in the range 3-4 per cent per annum since 2000 but this growth has been considerably discounted by a population growth rate of 2% per annum. The unemployment rate in 2004 was close to 14% and seven million Filipinos, mainly unskilled, work outside the country (especially in the US, Saudi Arabia and Malaysia), their remittances making an estimated $7bn. annual contribution to the domestic economy. The public debt burden of 136% of GDP is one of the highest in Asia and growing, but proposals by the government to introduce extra revenue-generating measures proved politically difficult in Congress in 2004 despite President Arroyo's victory in the May 2004 presidential elections and the ruling coalition having a majority in the legislature.

GDP (purchasing power parity) $390.7bn. (2004 est.); GDP per capita (purchasing power parity) $4,600 (2004 est.).

2 Trade Unionism

Trade unions were first legalized in 1908 (under US rule) and the first labour congress was held in 1913. The Philippines as an independent state ratified ILO Conventions Nos. 87 and 98 in 1957 and 1953 respectively. Following the declaration of martial law by Marcos in 1972 (when many trade union leaders were dismissed), the labour code was revised in 1974 to curb the right to strike. Unions were resurgent before the fall of Marcos in 1986, playing a role in the wave of "people power" protest that drove him from office. Under Corazon Aquino the labour laws were liberalized.

The 1987 constitution offers "full protection to labour, local and overseas, organized and unorganized" and commits the country to "promote full employment and equality of employment opportunities for all." Both private and public sector workers (other than the armed forces and police) may join unions. There is a great proliferation of trade unions. As of 2003 there were 171 registered labour federations and nearly 20,000 private sector trade unions. However their membership of 1.7 million represented only 5% of the workforce. There were 1,242 public sector unions with just under a quarter of a million members. Since the 1990s the number of firms, primarily large employers, that use non-union contract labour has grown, and this was given an extra stimulus by the 1998–99 downturn caused by the Asian financial crisis. The ICFTU reports that while the right to join unions is in theory guaranteed, in practice there are many obstacles to workers joining unions and legislation is not adequately enforced in cases where employers act illegally. Employers frequently dismiss activists prior to union registration or certification elections.

Unions may federate freely but there is no united national trade union centre. The Trade Union Congress of the Philippines (TUCP) was founded under Marcos in 1975 to unify the labour movement, but its official backing ensured that it was suspect with sections of the labour movement. It is the ICFTU's sole affiliate and the largest centre. Also significant is the WCL's affiliate, the Federation of Free Workers (FFW), while the leading left-wing organization is the May First Labour Movement Centre (KMU). Other organizations include the National Association of Trade Unions (NATU) and the Trade Unions of the Philippines and Allied Services (TUPAS). The different organizations tend to be political and enter (fluid) alliances with each other, with frequent splits and a blurring of identity between trade union organizations and political organizations claiming to be based in the labour movement.

The election of Ramos in 1992, in succession to Aquino, polarized the union centres. The FFW and a faction of the Workers' Strength Labour Centre (LMLC) backed him and some of their leaders were appointed to government posts, among them the FFW vice-president Fil Joson, who headed the Overseas Employment Administration. In contrast the TUCP had endorsed the rival bid for the presidency of Ramon Mitra. In 1993 union campaigns were mounted against the increase in energy prices and the power crisis, the emergency powers taken by President Ramos, inflation and wage issues. But these campaigns also divided the union centres with the militant May First Labour Movement Centre (KMU) opposing the government across the policy range while the TUCP, FFW, and some members of the LMLC tended to be loyalist. In 1993 two KMU breakaway centres, the NCL and BMP, signed a Covenant of Unity with the TUCP and on May 1, 1994 formed a Caucus for Labour Unity (CCU) on a platform of industrial peace. The anti-labour policies of Estrada led to the creation in February 2000 of the Labour Solidarity Movement (LSM), supported by the TUCP, FFW and TUPAS, which ultimately called for Estrada's removal from office as part of the broader political movement which ended in Estrada facing impeachment in Congress and standing down in favour of Arroyo. In October 2004, the TUCP, the FFW and TUPAS signed a social accord with the employers and the Arroyo government. Under the accord, which was denounced by the KMU, the unions agreed to show restraint in the use of industrial action while employers agreed to minimize the impact of retrenchments.

The labour code provides for the right to bargain collectively for private sector employees and for employees of government owned or government controlled corporations. However, only some 15 percent of union members are covered by collective bargaining agreements.

Under Marcos there were extensive limitations on strike action but Aquino made radical changes to the country's labour code and established the framework for a more liberal labour relations policy to comply with ratified ILO conventions. It became easier to call a strike in the private sector and employers could no longer recruit strike-breakers or dismiss workers for failing to comply with return-to-work orders. All means of reconciliation must be exhausted before a strike takes place and those leading illegal strikes may be sentenced to prison terms (though this provision has not recently been applied). Public sector workers, although they may form unions, may not strike. In the private sector the Secretary of Labour can intervene to impose compulsory arbitration and order strikers back to work if the strike is in an industry considered to be vital to the national interest. Industrial action can result in violence, sometimes involving the use of hired company security guards – in November 2004 clashes between striking farm and sugar cane workers and the police and military at a ranch belonging to the politically powerful Cojuangco family resulted in 14 deaths. Cases have been reported of employers refusing to re-hire workers dismissed for strike activities when ordered to do so by the Secretary of Labour. Following the fall of Marcos, a National Conciliation and Mediation Board (NCMB) was established in 1987. This settles most unfair labour practice disputes advanced as grounds for strikes before strikes take place. Disputes not settled by the NCMB can be referred to the quasi-judicial National Labour Relations Commission (NLRC). The creation of the NCMB has been one of the factors in the decline of legal strikes from a high of 581 in 1986, immediately before it was established, to 38 in 2003.

The position in the export processing zones (EPZs), and other special economic zones, is similar to that in many other countries. Although the national labour laws nominally apply, in practice unions are systematically excluded or replaced by company unions; activists are dismissed and blacklisted; companies facing labour problems simply threaten to relocate. Local political leaders and officials generally work with employers to keep the zones union free.

Despite legal prohibitions, there is widespread use of child labour, in areas such as banana and sugar plantations, docks, quarries, and mines, and in domestic service. Forms of child bonded labour are reported.

3 Trade Union Centres

Federation of Free Workers (FFW)
Address. FFW Building, 1943 Taft Avenue, Malate 1004, Manila
Phone. +63 2 521 9435
Fax. +63 2 526 3970
Leadership. Ramon Jabar (president)
Membership. Reported as around 400,000
History and character. The FFW was founded in 1950 and developed with the assistance of the Roman Catholic clergy. It is one of the WCL's leading Asian affiliates. The FFW favours a managed, cooperative economy, with profit-sharing and extended social benefits. During the Marcos era it positioned itself as an independent, democratic force, distinct from the government-backed TUCP and left-wing formations such as the KMU. It joined the Labour Solidarity Movement set up in 2000 to oppose President Estrada. In October 2004 it signed the social accord with employers and government, alongside the TUCP.

The FFW is campaigning to eradicate child labour, launching educational and other schemes in association with civic groups.
International affiliation. WCL

Kilusang Mayo Uno (KMU)
May First Labour Movement Centre
Address. No. 63 Narra St. Bgy. Claro, Proj. 3, Quezon City
Phone. +63 2 421 0986
Fax. +63 2 421 0768
E-mail. kmuid@i-manila.com.ph
Leadership. Elmer Labog (chairman)
History and character. Formed on May 1, 1980, the KMU describes itself as the "centre for militant unionism" standing for "freedom, democracy and socialism".

Rolando Olalia, KMU leader and chairman of the Party of the Nation (Partido Ng Bayan – PNB), was found brutally murdered in November 1986, and party leaders attributed his killing to forces within the military. He was succeeded as KMU leader by Crispin Beltran. The Armed Forces had regarded the KMU as a communist front since its formation and the day before Olalia's assassination, the KMU had stated that it would call a general strike in the event of a military coup (which was widely expected at the time) to overthrow the Aquino government. It boycotted the 1986 elections that brought Aquino to power, but subsequently backed her government while calling for fundamental reforms. During the Aquino presidency it appeared to have increased in strength at the expense of the TUCP, which was seen by some workers as a "Marcos union", on the basis of militant activity and organization. However it faced widespread accusations that it was provoking unrest for ideological reasons. Aquino at one point threatened to ban the KMU, which for its part complained to the ILO of violations of union rights. It claims to have lost a number of members, killed by government forces, and was the only major union centre not to sign an Industrial Peace Accord in 1990.

At the March 1993 national council a dissident group defected after protesting against the KMU's 1992 election slogan of "revolution not election". They subsequently formed groups known as the National Confederation of Labour (NCL) and the Solidarity of Filipino Workers (Bukluran ng Manggagawang Pilipino, BMP).

The KMU campaigned for the removal from office of President Estrada, whom it accused of failing to respond to the needs of low wage earners. It opposes the privatization of state industries and the "unholy trinity" of the IMF, World Bank and the WTO and has called for the government to stop debt servicing. The KMU has continued its militant tradition under the Macapagal-Arroyo administration and in October 2004 denounced the social accord signed by the TUCP, FFW and TUPAS. It retains its general identification with the Communist Party of the Philippines (CPP), an essentially unreconstructed if fragmented formation which has a small but active following and a proliferation of associated organizations, including a still active armed wing, the New People's Army. The CPP-linked Bayan Muna party, to which the KMU is close, topped the party-list poll in the 2004 congressional elections (the party-list being a device to secure representation in the legislature for marginal groups). Crispin Beltran, formerly the president of the KMU, is now a Congressman for the Bayan Muna party.

International affiliation. None

Trade Union Congress of the Philippines (TUCP)
Address. TUCP/PGEA Compound, Masaya Street, corner Maharlika Street, 1101 Diliman, Quezon City
Phone. +63 2 924 7551
Fax. +63 2 921 9758
E-mail. secrtucp@tucp.org.ph
Website. www.tucp.org.ph
Leadership. Democrito T. Mendoza (president)
History and character. The TUCP is the largest trade union centre in the Philippines and has previously claimed one million members with 28 federations and 2,544 local unions, though this was probably an overstatement. It describes itself as a "democratic organization composed primarily of trade unions, workers' organizations, and other groups of workers". Its membership is broader than trade unions as it recruits in the informal sector, cooperatives, among the urban poor, peasants, youth and civil society groups. It lists among its goals improving conditions for all working people, not just its own members, building democracy, and "instilling nationalism, solidarity, equity and social responsibility".

The TUCP was originally formed with official backing under Marcos in 1975 in response to the implementation of the 1974 labour code, which emphasized the coordination and unification of the trade union movement. Some sections of organized labour subsequently charged the TUCP with being unduly close to the Marcos government; it did, however, mobilize 7,000 volunteers for the watchdog National Citizens' Movement for Free Elections (NAMFREL) which unofficially supervised the 1986 election that preceded Marcos's downfall.

On May Day 1990 the TUCP co-launched Labour Unity for Democracy and Peace with the FFW and LMLC and later that month was a signatory to the Industrial Peace Accord. In 1993 TUCP was in the forefront of a campaign to raise the minimum wage, review employment law and seat representatives of labour on local government councils; in 1995 it pressurized the government over the continued existence of child labour. It is generally considered the most moderate of the various trade union centres, although in 2000 it joined the Labour Solidarity Movement which called for the removal of the Estrada administration. It was in October 2000 a signatory to the impeachment petition, charging the President with corruption, and then organized demonstrations calling for his removal, all of which contributed to the broad movement that led to Estrada's downfall in 2001. Under the Arroyo administration it has maintained a position of support for the legal government balanced by criticism of specific policies and is hostile to efforts by leftist groups, notably the KMU, to exploit strikes for political goals (communist-aligned groups retaining a small but active presence in the Philippines). It has criticized the personalist character of Philippines politics as entrenching ruling oligarchies and called (without notable impact) for the 2004 elections to be fought on issues of social cohesion, health, housing, employment, education and development.

The TUCP provides a range of services, including legal assistance to affiliate federations; credit and consumer cooperative programmes; free medical and dental services for members; a primary health care programme conducted by TUCP doctors and nurses; research and information dissemination for collective bargaining purposes; education and research seminars and training for trade union leaders and members; mass basic trade unionism seminars for members; and assistance to affiliates in organizing campaigns. It seeks to encourage reorganization of affiliates on industrial lines to increase their effectiveness. Reflecting the legacy of past turbulence in Philippines politics, the TUCP emphasizes that it abhors violence, uses strikes only as a last resort and that "we have no armed group". Political parties specifically identified with the TUCP have had little impact despite the introduction in the late 1990s of the party-list system designed to give representation to sectoral and marginalized groups.

TUCP membership totals fell sharply in the early 1990s and it has since tried to broaden its recruitment, including in the export processing zones, where union activity faces considerable employer and official hostility.

International affiliation. ICFTU

Poland

Capital: Warsaw
Population: 38.63 m. (2004 est.)

1 Political and Economic Background

Poland was overrun by Germany and the Soviet Union in World War II and at the war's end became part of the Soviet bloc. The emergence of the Solidarity trade union, led by Lech Walesa, as a political movement in 1980 provoked a crisis in the regime and although martial law was declared in December 1981 and Solidarity suppressed it remained an underground force. In the late 1980s, as part of the weakening of communist rule throughout Eastern Europe, it re-emerged to win elections in 1989 and form the government. In December 1990, Walesa was elected President.

Post-communist politics were characterized by governmental instability and factionalism, with Solidarity itself fragmenting. Against this background, elections in October 1993 resulted in the formation of a government led by the former communists of the Democratic

Left Alliance (SLD), itself created from the alliance of the Social Democracy of the Republic of Poland (SdRP) political party and the OPZZ trade union, the official union structure set up after Solidarity was dissolved. In presidential elections in 1995 Walesa was narrowly defeated by Aleksander Kwasniewski, who was backed by the SLD. Elections to the legislature (Sejm) in September 1997, however, resulted in the Solidarity Electoral Action (AWS) coalition winning 201 of the 460 seats, while the SLD came second with 164. The AWS government was led by Prime Minister Jerzy Buzek, a veteran Solidarity leader. In the October 2000 presidential elections, President Kwasniewski was re-elected with AWS leader Marian Krzaklewski coming only third, with 15% of the vote, and in September 2001 elections to the Sejm resulted in an alliance of the SLD and the small Union of Labour (UP) taking 219 of the 460 seats – the AWS failing to pass the threshold percentage of the vote needed to achieve parliamentary representation. The government formed under Prime Minister Leszek Miller (the leader of the SLD) faced a series of crises culminating in the defection of part of the SLD in March 2004 to form a new Social Democracy of Poland (SDPL) party. This defection was immediately succeeded by Miller's resignation as Prime Minister, to take effect on May 2 – the day after Poland joined the European Union. Miller was succeeded as Prime Minister by the former Finance Minister, Marek Belka, leading a weak minority government. The AWS has been largely eclipsed on the centre-right by the Citizens' Platform (PO), which won 63 seats in the 2001 Sejm elections and came first in the June 2004 elections to the European Parliament.

In the early 1990s Poland experienced "shock therapy" as it faced the consequences of the dismantling of the state-controlled economy. The immediate results of the 1990 shift to the market were severe but by 1992 Poland had become the first post-communist country to show signs of recovery. By 1994 industrial production was close to the levels preceding the shock therapy of 1990. Poland's adjustment to the market thereafter was considered one of the most successful in Eastern Europe, and by the end of the 1990s foreign direct investment represented 40% of the total into the whole former Soviet bloc, with substantial privatization completed, although with state control remaining in some politically sensitive areas such as coal and steel. The SLD returned to government in 2001 on a broadly social democratic programme, emphasizing the importance of EU accession and favouring market-oriented reforms, but with a "social dimension". However, although Poland has now consolidated its position by achieving entry to the European Union and growth in 2004 was a healthy 5%, recent years have demonstrated persistent economic difficulties that contributed to the fall of Miller in 2004. Unemployment in 2004 stood at 20%; there are increasing disparities of income; measures to combat mounting budget deficits (representing over 5% of GDP in 2004) have lacked parliamentary support; and the privatization programme has largely ground to a halt. Threats of strikes by miners and railway workers in 2003 proved effective in maintaining subsidies for their loss-making industries. The Polish economy, in contrast to that of other of its Central European neighbours, is bogged down by the scale of its agricultural sector; this provides employment for 25% of the labour force but generates only 5% of GDP, is characterized by inefficient small farms and low investment and has been the source of considerable political unrest, providing a base for the anti-EU radical populist Self-Defence party of Andrzej Lepper.

GDP (purchasing power parity) $427.1bn. (2004 est.); GDP per capita (purchasing power parity) $11,100 (2004 est.).

2 Trade Unionism

Poland ratified ILO Conventions No. 87 (Freedom of Association and Protection of the Right to Organize, 1948) and No. 98 (Right to Organize and Collective Bargaining, 1949) in 1957.

Communist rule in Poland was punctuated by massive industrial unrest, often accompanied by attempts to establish independent unions. In 1970–71, 44 people were killed in illegal strikes and disturbances on the Baltic coast. In 1976, after huge strikes against falling real incomes, a group of intellectuals formed Komitet Obrony Robotnikow (KOR – workers' defence committee) to assist the families of those dismissed in strikes. (KOR was subsequently renamed the committee for social self defence – KSS, and joined Solidarity in 1990.) In May 1978 a committee of free trade unions for the Baltic coast was formed under the leadership of Andrzej Gwiazda.

Official trade unionism in Poland was organized by a single body, the Central Council of Trade Unions (CRZZ). In 1980, however, the independent union Solidarity was created and, following massive popular pressure, accorded recognition by the government. At its height Solidarity had 9.5 million members (including agricultural wage earners), while the peasants' organization Rural Solidarity had 2.35 million members and there were 3 million members of branch and autonomous trade unions. For more than a year Solidarity functioned both as a union and as a vehicle for the expression of Polish national, religious and political aspirations, posing an increasingly apparent threat to the role of the ruling Polish United Workers' Party (PUWP) and by implication to the Warsaw Pact alliance. Following repeated rumours in both Poland and the West of the possibility of a Soviet invasion, martial law was declared on Dec. 13, 1981, and Solidarity banned.

The Solidarity organization was formally dissolved by the Trade Union Act of October 1982, which also provided for the creation of a new structure of official trade unions that would take over the property of the dissolved unions. The All-Poland Alliance of Trade Unions (OPZZ) was formed in November 1984 to coordinate the official unions. Amendments to the 1982 Trade Union Act passed by the Sejm in July 1985 confirmed a trade union monopoly by prohibiting the establishment of more than one trade union in any enterprise. Solidarity remained active underground, however, and in the late 1980s re-emerged as a major political force.

Amid mounting political and economic crisis the regime in April 1989 was forced to agree to the re-legalization of Solidarity and to partially free elections. This process culminated in the formation of the first Solidarity-backed government in August 1989. Thereafter Solidarity's position was complicated by the twin identity of Solidarity as a political movement and a trade union, with a history of internal conflict, factionalism and breakaways. After the collapse of communism, the OPZZ positioned itself as opposed to government austerity policies, capitalizing on four consecutive years of falling real wages. OPZZ opposition was joined by some dissident elements within Solidarity and the period was marked by political factionalism. In September 1993 the former communists of the Democratic Left Alliance (SLD, a creation of the Social Democracy (SdRP) party and the OPZZ) came to power and Solidarity returned to opposition. Their roles reversed after the election of a Solidarity-based government in 1997 and then again after the SLD returned to power in 2001.

Solidarity and the OPZZ remain the two main trade union centres, but their relative strengths are disputed. In post-communist Poland, no longer a carrier of national aspirations, Solidarity's membership fell steadily. By 2004 it was variously estimated at between 800,000 and one million. Over the years various small breakaway groups from Solidarity have appeared, including Solidarity '80, the August '80 Free Trade Union (WZZ - August '80) and the Christian Trade Union Solidarity. The OPZZ, in common with former official unions throughout Eastern Europe, claimed membership levels in the post-communist era in excess of real participation in its structures. It now claims 1.3 million members, of whom 870,000 are in employment, but other estimates suggest the figure is significantly less. Whatever the exact size of the memberships of Solidarity and the OPZZ, they have retained a rough equality and this fact, plus the existence of unions outside the two main centres (possibly in total amounting to the equivalent in membership of one of the main centres), has led to a fragmentation of the labour movement. Where enterprises are unionized, there are commonly competing unions linked to either of the main centres or independent of them. In 2002 a third centre, the Trade Unions Forum (FZZ) was established, mainly by unions that had been operating independently. Solidarity, the OPZZ and the FZZ are the three national centres now accorded representative status by the Tripartite Commission for Social and Economic Affairs.

Overall only some 13% of Polish employees are now thought to be in unions. There is little unionization in the emergent private sector economy although unions have retained a position in privatized state firms. As of 2004, only 6% of employees in private sector non-farm businesses worked in firms where there was some form of trade union presence, compared with 60% of state enterprise employees and 40% in enterprises jointly owned by the state and private investors. Surveys suggest that in the privatized state enterprises the unions have input primarily in areas such as social benefits and dismissals of individual workers rather than an involvement in broad issues such as restructuring. In contrast, in the remaining state enterprises, the unions retain considerable influence, even down to the appointment (though workers' councils, strongly associated with the trade unions) of managing directors. The unions have used this position to impose a considerable restraining hand on restructuring.

Reflecting the origins of the OPZZ and Solidarity in the political struggles of the 1980s, unions remain highly politicized. While Solidarity's trade union strength declined after the end of communism, as a political movement (Solidarity Electoral Action, AWS) sharing a common origin with the trade union, it remained significant. The complex AWS coalition which took 201 of the 460 seats in the 1997 Sejm elections included 62 deputies linked to the Solidarity union, but in the 2001 elections AWS slipped beneath the threshold for parliamentary representation. Likewise the OPZZ is a core element of the Democratic Left Alliance (SLD). Hostility between the OPZZ and Solidarity has nonetheless declined with the creation of a pluralist post-communist society, and while there is a legacy of tension in practice they often agree on policy issues. Solidarity is an affiliate of the ICFTU, WCL and ETUC. The OPZZ has no international affiliation, although it has applied to join ETUC.

In July 1991 a new Trade Union Act was adopted, providing the current legal base. Trade unions have the right to bargain collectively and to make agreements and, where there is no agreement, must be consulted. The former distinction between enterprise and other unions was abandoned for the right of any ten people to form a union. Once established, unions may make their own rules subject to certain mandatory inclusions such as the aims of the organization.

The 1991 law provides for disputes to be referred to the labour courts and there are several thousand such referrals each year, while dozens of cases per year go as far as the Supreme Court. In most such cases employees were successful.

Collective bargaining typically takes place at the enterprise level. Within the state-owned enterprises collective bargaining agreements are widespread, but such agreements are much less common in the private sector, and rare in smaller private sector enterprises. Reflecting the parlous state of the Polish economy, with many enterprises facing serious financial difficulties, recent collective agreements have tended to incorporate only minimal standards, often for little more than the minimum wage and basic labour law provisions on such matters as hours and holidays; in addition, agreements are frequently suspended because of enterprises' financial problems. There is a right to strike except in "essential services" and only one-quarter of the workforce must vote in favour to authorize a strike. There are lengthy pre-strike procedures, however, so a majority of strikes are illegal, although meaningful sanctions are not commonly imposed against unions that call such illegal strikes.

Conversely, sanctions imposed against employers who penalize strikers tend to be negligible. Although occasional strikes are reported (mainly in state-owned enterprises or privatized former state enterprises), non-strike forms of protest are more common, and in recent years peasant organizations have been more militant than trade unions. According to official figures there were 966 work-related "protest actions" in 2003, including strikes, warning strikes, demonstrations, marches, pickets, road blocks and occupations; however, of these only 24 were actual strikes, involving a mere 3,000 employees, and the majority of protests were staged by farmers rather than trade unionists. Farm protests were organized by groups such as the populist political party Self-Defence and by the Solidarity peasant wing (NSZZ Solidarnosc RI). Privatization continues as a live issue in some important sectors of the economy and on Dec. 21, 2004, unions in the Polish National Railways (PKP) staged a warning strike over privatization and restructuring. As of the end of 2003 there were still 1,166 state-owned enterprises (although half of these were in liquidation or bankrupt).

The Tripartite Commission for Social and Economic Affairs, founded in 1994, which is chaired by the Minister of Labour, has a role in determining public sector pay, gives opinions on social policy issues, and provides a forum for the resolution of conflict. In the past both Solidarity and OPZZ have withdrawn from it at different times, but both currently participate in its work.

3 Trade Union Centres

NSZZ Solidarnosc
Independent and Self Governing Trade Union Solidarity
Solidarity
Address. ul. Waly Piastowskie 24, 80–855, Gdansk
Phone. +48 58 308 42 32
Fax. +48 58 308 44 82
E-mail. zagr@solidarnosc.org.pl
Website. www.solidarnosc.org.pl (Polish; English section)
Leadership. Janusz Sniadek (chairman)
Membership. 800,000- 1 million (estimated)
History and character. The rise, suppression, and ultimate victory of Solidarity was an historic factor in the process which eventually led to the collapse of the Communist bloc.

The elevation of the Pole Karol Wojtyla as Pope John Paul II and his visit to Poland in June 1979, encouraged the fusion of Catholic religious and nationalist sentiments with economic grievances which proved a catalyst in the rise of Solidarity. A rolling wave of strikes began in July 1980 against price rises with Lech Walesa (a Gdansk shipyard worker) emerging as the most prominent leader of the movement. Workers struck at the Lenin shipyards in Gdansk on Aug. 14, occupying the yards, which became the centre of the unrest. On Aug. 16 the inter-factory strike committee (MKS) was formed in Gdansk to coordinate activity, and as a result of negotiations with the MKS held on Aug. 23–30, the government on Aug. 31 conceded (in the "Gdansk accords") the right of workers to form free unions independent of the monolithic structure organized by the Central Council of Trade Unions (CRZZ), with the right to strike, and ancillary demands such as the broadcasting of Masses, Saturday holidays, and greater civil liberties. Government leadership changed, and on Sept. 15 it established a procedure for the registration of the new trade unions in the Court of the Voivodship of Warsaw, outside the CRZZ register, and applied the Gdansk accords nationally.

On Sept. 22, 1980, delegates from 36 regional independent unions met in Gdansk under the name of Solidarity and Walesa's chairmanship. Solidarity applied for registration with the Warsaw Court on Sept. 24.

In October the Sejm adopted an Act to amend the Trade Union Act of 1949, thereby giving statutory validity to the procedure established by the Council of State on Sept. 15, and the following month the Polish Supreme Court overruled a decision by the Warsaw Court that the charter legalizing Solidarity would be invalid without the inclusion in the union's statutes of recognition of the PUWP as the leading political force in the country (although this recognition was by compromise inserted in the annexes to the statutes). This action averted a general strike.

The CRZZ was dissolved in January 1981, most of the former official trade unions having by this time dissolved or voted to become autonomous. In April 1981 the government agreed to recognize the creation of Rural Solidarity, which had held its first congress on March 9; it was registered on May 12. September–October 1981 brought the first Solidarity delegate conference in Gdansk, revealing splits between a Walesa faction which, fearing Soviet intervention and alarmed by persistent industrial disorders and the collapse of productivity, wished to pursue a policy of greater accommodation towards the government, and militants who wished to press broad political demands. On Oct. 2 Walesa was elected chairman of Solidarity, but congress elected a radical-dominated national commission.

The conflict at the congress presaged a continuing dispute over relations with the communist regime, now led by Prime Minister Jaruzelski. In December 1981, the national leadership, contrary to Walesa's advice, voted to call a national referendum in which the people would be asked if they favoured the establishment of an interim government and the holding of free elections, and whether they wished to continue to provide "military guarantees" to the USSR. The regime responded by establishing a Military Council of National Salvation under Gen. Jaruzelski. Martial law was declared, strikes were banned, Solidarity leaders (including Walesa) arrested and all trade unions suspended; according to government figures, 7,000 persons were interned in detention camps. The representation of the interests of workers was subsequently placed in the hands of social committees set up by the military government in January 1982.

According to the Polish government Solidarity had proceeded beyond the limits of the Gdansk accords and its constitution and under the influence of extremist elements had approached an attempt to seize power; martial law had been necessary to prevent this and end mounting disorder and economic disintegration which posed a threat to Poland and world peace. Particular concern was expressed at Solidarity's appeals to the population of neighbouring countries and its questioning of Poland's international alliances.

The government initially represented the suspension of the newly formed trade unions as a short–term measure. The position and role of the hierarchy of the Church had by this time become ambiguous, the Church supporting the principles of Solidarity but expressing a desire for stability and national unification.

There were no reports of violence or deaths related to the activities of Solidarity in the period from its emergence in the summer of 1980 to its dissolution under martial law, and strikes had been avoided in the health services and some other essential services. Following the imposition of martial law, nine miners died in a confrontation with security forces at the Wujek mine near Katowice (although most protest strikes were ended relatively peacefully), and according to the ICFTU, WCL, and other reports several dozen persons were killed by the security forces in demonstrations, strikes and other incidents in the following months. There were also numerous reports of torture of detainees, dismissals from employment of previous Solidarity activists and the imposition of loyalty oaths requiring disavowal of support for or sympathy with Solidarity. Extensive purges were also carried out of Solidarity supporters in the judiciary, government service, universities and the media. In decisions of May and July 1982 the Supreme Court held that protection against dismissal under the labour code could not be applied while trade union activities were suspended. Lech Walesa was not released until November 1982 and in October 1983 was awarded the Nobel Peace Prize, provoking a formal complaint by the Polish government.

For four years from 1983 Solidarity maintained an underground identity through a temporary coordinating committee (TKK), while Lech Walesa remained chairman. Its strength appeared to decline steadily and calls for strikes and demonstrations against price rises in 1985 and 1986 were poorly supported. Its activists were victimized and imprisoned, and there were several cases of brutal treatment including at least 15 deaths. Proceedings were also briefly brought against Walesa but abandoned. Not until early 1987 were all leading figures released.

In September 1986, Walesa and other leaders formed a public Temporary Council of Solidarity (TRS), to work within the system "to improve the country's social, political and economic conditions", and to "seek to ease the transition to legal and open undertakings." It was announced that Walesa would remain titular chairman, but would not be a member of the TRS. Any decision to disband the underground TKK was apparently dependent on the attitude of the government to the TRS. In response, however, the Polish authorities stated that the TRS was illegal, and the Polish Supreme Court on Nov. 16 rejected an appeal by Baltic shipyard workers to create a union called Solidarity on the grounds that the creation of more than one union in an enterprise was forbidden. By November 1986 temporary councils of Solidarity had sought registration in at least 10 provinces. It was reported that the Solidarity leadership was divided on the question of how far it should seek to cooperate with the authorities. In the autumn of 1986 in a gesture of international support both the ICFTU and WCL affiliated Solidarity.

On Oct. 25, 1987, a national meeting of Solidarity activists announced the creation of a National Executive Commission (KKW), with Lech Walesa as chairman. This was in response to fragmentation of the leadership between the TRS and the TKK leading to complaints that it was losing touch with grass-roots support. An application for official registration of the KKW was rejected by a Gdansk court on Nov. 9, and in late 1987 and early 1988 courts rejected several other attempts to obtain registration for Solidarity branches in individual enterprises.

The failure of the government's referendum on economic reform and limited political liberalization gave Solidarity (which had called for a boycott), its chance. In spite of the lack of majority support the government proceeded with the programme, albeit modified, from Feb. 1, 1988, when retail price rises averaging 27% took effect. Solidarity announced it would support local stoppages by workers demanding wage rises. They started almost immediately, and a major wave of strikes began on April 25 when transport workers in Bydgoszcz won a 63 per cent wage increase after a 12-hour stoppage. This sparked off a strike at the Nowa Huta steelworks near Krakow on the following day, and workers at the Lenin shipyards in Gdansk began a strike on May 2. The authorities reacted by having nine members of the Solidarity KKW arrested, and on May 5 police stormed the Nowa Huta steelworks and arrested the strike coordinators. The strike at the Lenin steelworks was called off on May 10 without any concessions from the authorities. Some of those arrested remained in police custody until May 25, and 19 workers lost their jobs at Nowa Huta.

But now a further wave of strikes began on Aug. 15–18 with the occupation of mines in the Silesian coalfields, and by Aug. 22 the action had spread to enterprises in several cities, including the Lenin shipyard, prompting the declaration of a curfew in the three worst affected provinces. Following mediation by Roman Catholic Church representatives, Walesa held talks with the Interior Minister, Lt.-Gen. Kiszczak, on Aug. 31, and the strikes were called off after Walesa had received guarantees that the government would involve Solidarity in proposed round-table discussions, and was prepared to consider the union's re–authorization. However, these discussions failed to convene following arguments about procedure and participants. Doubts were cast on the sincerity of the government by a leaked PUWP document that declared that the re-legalization of Solidarity was the main danger facing the party and would not be permitted. Furthermore, Solidarity interpreted as a deliberate provocation a government decision announced on Oct. 31 to use special powers of intervention in the management of enterprises, which it had acquired under a temporary law of May 31, to close the Lenin shipyards on Dec. 1.

The final collapse of communist government was attended by further industrial and political action by local Solidarity unions. In January 1989 alone there were 173 pay disputes and 39 strike situations. By this time it was clear that no solution to the crisis could be found without the involvement of Solidarity. On Feb. 6, against a background of increasing economic chaos, the government opened "round table" talks with Solidarity (which was still nominally illegal). After two months of talks with an increasingly impotent government, the seven-year ban on Solidarity was lifted and partly democratic elections were announced for June. Solidarity formally applied for registered status, declaring that the National Executive Commission (KKW) would administer the movement until a congress could be held.

In the elections of June 1989 (when 65% of Sejm seats were still reserved for communist-sponsored deputies) Solidarity swept the board, candidates it supported winning every one of the freely contested seats in the Sejm. A prolonged government crisis which found the leading communist candidate unable to form a coalition led to his displacement at the head of a new coalition by Tadeusz Mazowiecki, a Solidarity nominee, with another well known Solidarity figure, Jacek Kuron, as Minister of Labour.

The formation of this government led to a new stage in the history of Solidarity. Factions appeared such as the "working group" of well-known leaders from 1981 (Andrzej Gwiazda, Jan Rulewski, Seweryn Jaworski) who were opposed to voluntary restrictions on the right to strike, and members of the Polish Socialist Party (Democratic Revolution) who played leading roles in some important localities. Not until April 1990 did Solidarity finally meet in congress at Gdansk, with membership having fallen to 2.2 million and in confusion over its role because of pressure to support the Solidarity-inspired Maziowecki government. Objectors to lending support to the government included many within the union's ranks, including the "Solidarity 80" faction, and the congress heard many speeches in criticism of the Balcerowicz "shock therapy" programme, with its dismantling of the planned economy, reduction of subsidies, price liberalization, pay curbs, and escalating unemployment. The following month there were widespread strikes by Solidarity unions on the railways which disrupted the approach to local elections.

The election of Walesa as President of Poland in December 1990, followed by his resignation as Solidarity chairman, compounded the movement's difficulties. It met in extraordinary congress in February 1991 to review its role in the changed circumstances and elect a new leadership. Walesa's successor as chairman was Marian Krzaklewski, who had campaigned on a platform of staying free from political entanglements. President Walesa adopted a similar view: "the union should not and will not replace political parties".

Solidarity's fourth congress was held in Gdansk in June 1992 and re-elected Krzaklewski as president. Delegates passed a resolution expressing disapproval of the role of President Walesa in the fall of the minority government of Jan Olszewski that month. Solidarity brokered the creation of the successor government of Hanna Suchocka in July 1992 and welcomed a new Enterprise Pact with enthusiasm. Its disillusionment set in as government promises remained unfulfilled and it finally moved a vote of no confidence that brought the government down in May 1993. When at first President Walesa refused to accept Suchocka's resignation, Solidarity threatened a general strike.

The resultant elections in September 1993 were a major setback. The unpopularity of shock therapy economics with the voters, and the internal divisions of the Solidarity coalition, contributed to the return to power of the reformed communists of the Democratic Left Alliance (SLD). However, the new government continued much of the general approach of previous post-communist administrations, and Solidarity entered a period of trade union opposition which gave it a new lease of life as it energetically campaigned to prevent any further falls in the real value of wages. It launched a series of selective strikes designed to force the government away from austerity policies. A nationwide day of action in April 1994 against wage controls combined with disputes in the mines to force the resignation of a minister and concessions out of the government.

In December 1995 Walesa narrowly lost in presidential elections to the SLD's candidate, Aleksander Kwasniewski. In June 1996 the 7th congress initiated the creation of a political coalition, comprising dozens of parties and pressure groups but rooted in mainstream Solidarity, called Solidarity Electoral Action (AWS). This came to power in coalition with the Freedom Union (UW) as a result of elections in September 1997. Dozens of Solidarity activists were elected to Parliament. Jerzy Buzek, an early Solidarity leader, became Prime Minister after Solidarity president Marian Krzaklewski had said he would not take the position.

Again Solidarity faced tensions from its dual identity as a trade union and as the base for a political movement. The identities of the Solidarity trade union and political movement remained blurred, with individuals from the union holding many political positions at national and local level. Solidarity trade union leader Krzaklewski, seen as a conservative, became an AWS member of the Sejm and chairman of the AWS party caucus. Solidarity as a union, however, frequently found itself in opposition to the Buzek government on economic and labour issues, warning of the adverse impact of otherwise beneficial market reforms on the unemployed and the poor, while at the same time distancing itself from the "destabilizing" activities of the OPZZ and peasant groups. One particular source of conflict within Solidarity was the implementation of privatization, with a nationalist–populist wing resistant to further sales to foreign investors and Solidarity members concerned at the impact on jobs and wages. In October 2000 Krzaklewski ran for Polish President as the candidate of the AWS, but came only third, with the SLD's Kwasniewski being re-elected. The poor result led to renewed calls for Krzaklewski to choose between union leadership and political ambitions. Meanwhile Solidarity condemned the OPZZ's withdrawal from the Tripartite Commission in April 1999; it criticized the government for not discussing sufficiently with the social partners but blamed the OPZZ for making constructive dialogue between government and unions more difficult.

By the end of the 1990s the issues facing Solidarity were very different from those a decade earlier. They included the impact of deregulation and privatization, the globalization of the world economy, and the decline of traditional industries; the requirements for reform of the Polish economy and society in pursuit of accession to the EU (which Solidarity supported); and the campaign for improved healthcare, education, social insurance and other social benefits. Solidarity also confronted the problem that while it remained a political force with the voters, as a trade union it had continued to lose members as heavily organized state industries were privatized and new private sector businesses were mainly non-union.

In January 2001 Prime Minister Buzek took over the leadership of the overall AWS from Krzaklewski, whose position had been damaged by his poor showing in the October 2000 presidential elections. However, the AWS bloc suffered from continuing factionalism and in May 2001 the Solidarity trade union formally withdrew from the bloc. The AWS entered the September 2001 parliamentary elections in considerable disarray and won only 5.6% of the vote, excluding it from representation in the Sejm. The new government was led by the SLD, thus leaving Solidarity, both as a trade union and a political force, as essentially an opposition formation. One consequence of the electoral debacle was the voting out of office of Solidarity chairman Krzaklewski by the Solidarity trade union congress in September 2002. Krzaklewski, who had held the post since 1991, was accused of having mired the union in the failed policies of the AWS government and of having ignored the interests of the union membership. He was succeeded as chairman by Janusz Sniadek, a compromise candidate who had previously been Krzaklewski's deputy.

Solidarity rejected the idea of a tripartite social pact proposed by the SLD government in March 2003 to deal with the country's economic difficulties, apparently so as not to give succour to the government. In November 2003 Solidarity organized demonstrations described as "nationwide days of protest against the anti-social policies of the government". At the same time, Solidarity sought to emphasize its political independence as a trade union body and a national congress in May 2004 adopted new statutes that specifically prohibit anyone holding a position of management in the union from sitting as a deputy in the Sejm or as a senator. It has also remained within the Tripartite Commission, not repeating the previous tactic adopted by both Solidarity and the OPZZ of withdrawing from the Commission when in opposition to the government. As has historically been the case, Solidarity has various currents, with radicals favouring direct action tactics on issues like privatization and restructuring in Solidarity strongholds such as mining, while the current Solidarity chairman, Janusz Sniadek, has a more moderate posture.

Solidarity has 14,000 enterprise union locals, associated into 37 regions. There are in addition 15 industrially-based branch secretariats, and one for pensioners.

International affiliations. Since November 1986 Solidarity has been affiliated to both the ICFTU and the WCL, and has argued for the ultimate fusion of the two bodies. It affiliated to ETUC in 1995 and TUAC in 1997. The Solidarity occupational branch unions are affiliated to the various global union federations associated with the ICFTU.

Ogolnopolskie Porozumienie Zwiazkow Zawodowych (OPZZ)
All-Poland Alliance of Trade Unions
Address. ul. Kopernika 36/40, 00–924 Warsaw
Phone. +48 22 826 92 41
E-mail. ilka@opzz.org.pl
Website. www.opzz.org.pl (Polish; English section)
Leadership. Jan Guz (president)
Membership. Estimated at 700,00–800,00
History and character. The OPZZ was founded in November 1984 to coordinate the new official trade unions set up with government support after the suppression of Solidarity. It was formally registered on April 12, 1985, and the authorities subsequently turned over to it funds impounded upon the suspension of Solidarity in December 1981. Membership in the Soviet bloc trade union international, the World Federation of Trade Unions (WFTU), was reactivated in April 1985.

The OPZZ held its second meeting on Nov. 26–30, 1986, this being declared the first congress of the Polish Reborn Trade Unions. Alfred Miodowicz, its founding chairman, was re-elected by 879 votes to 159, but the abstention of a significant minority of the 1,480 delegates was viewed as expressing dissatisfaction with his election to the communist party (PUWP) politburo in July 1986. This was seen as compromising the asserted independence of the trade union movement. The congress called for the creation of an effective system of consultation between workers and government, and adopted a final resolution which criticized government attempts to centralize control over the labour movement. The final resolution also reversed a decision taken earlier by the congress to constitute the OPZZ as the sole representative of unionized workers. This followed protests that such a move would jeopardize the status of the estimated 4,000 non-affiliated trade unions (mostly organized in single factories or enterprises) and would give the OPZZ a public image akin to that of its monolithic pre-Solidarity forebear, the Central Council of Trade Unions (CRZZ).

In August 1987 Miodowicz stated that "the OPZZ considered itself to be the heir to the 1980 Gdansk accords" between the government and Solidarity and had a moral obligation to ensure their realization. However, he also rejected trade union pluralism in enterprises, commenting that "a divided workforce serves those who manipulate". The OPZZ criticized the decision announced at the end of 1985 to reintroduce a six-day working week (the five-day working week, conceded in 1981, having been the last major surviving accomplishment of the Solidarity era), and during 1987–88 it frequently criticized other aspects of government economic policy.

The OPZZ adapted remarkably successfully to the progressive collapse of the communist regime through 1988–89, distancing itself from the regime and seeking to re-position itself as the authentic independent voice of the labour movement even as Solidarity was legalized again in the Spring of 1989. On July 29, 1989, Miodowicz resigned from the politburo of the disintegrating Polish United Workers' Party. In December 1990, the OPZZ withdrew from the work of the WFTU (although all links were not finally severed until 1997). It explained this decision in terms of its modest resources, the pluralistic nature of its own movement, and the diminished coverage of the WFTU itself. Miodowicz was replaced as leader by the former Solidarity activist Ewa Spychalska in December 1991. In the Sejm elections of October 1991 the OPZZ joined forces with the post-communist Social Democracy of the Republic of Poland (SdRP) party (the successor to the former ruling Polish United Workers' Party) to campaign as the Democratic Left Alliance (SLD).

With Solidarity a leading force in government from 1989–93, the OPZZ adopted the position of an opposition trade union organization opposed to the impact of "shock therapy" market economics on jobs, pensioners and public services. Following the 1993 election of a government led by the Democratic Left Alliance (SLD), the reformed former communists, the OPZZ enjoyed far better relations with the government, generally endorsing its programme but with conflicts over some issues, notably the process of implementation of privatization. The OPZZ was strongly represented among SLD deputies in the Sejm. It claimed success on issues such as the distribution of shares to workers in newly privatized industries and the adoption of a new labour code. In July 1995, OPZZ vice-president Maciej Manicki resigned to become vice-minister of labour and social policy, while Ewa Spychalska in September 1996 stood down to become Ambassador to Belarus, being succeeded by Jozef Wiaderny.

After the election of a Solidarity-led government in 1997, the OPZZ again generally opposed government policies, and regularly involved itself in strikes and demonstrations. It focused on issues including unemployment, lack of employee rights in privatized industries, and the condition of the rural economy, allying itself with militant peasant groups in organizing demonstrations. It also joined protests with breakaway Solidarity faction "Solidarity 80". A particular target was Leszek Balcerowicz, the Deputy Prime Minister and Finance Minister and leader of the pro-business Union for Freedom (UW), the junior party in the coalition with Solidarity Electoral Action (AWS) until it left the government in June 2000. Balcerowicz was the main architect of the 1990 shock therapy and an advocate of market deregulation and privatization, issues that create tensions within AWS itself. The OPZZ remained within the Democratic Left Alliance, with 42 deputies in the Sejm, about one-quarter of the Democratic Left Alliance caucus. In April 1999 it withdrew from the Tripartite Commission claiming that the government had abandoned social dialogue. Mirroring Krzaklewski's role in the AWS, Wiaderny chaired the SLD Group of Trade Union Deputies and Senators (42 in the Sejm and four in the Senate).

An issue for the OPZZ remained its international isolation since its withdrawal from the WFTU. The OPZZ says that it is now a social democratic organization akin to the mainstream of Western European trade unionism. It has supported EU membership and integration into the wider European trade union movement and applied to join ETUC in December 1998. However, it recognizes there is still considerable distrust of the role of OPZZ outside Poland, given its emergence after the suppression of Solidarity, and that admission to ETUC is unlikely to be achieved quickly – it was still not in membership by 2004.

The election of the SLD government in September 2001 eased relations between the OPZZ and the government. The OPZZ was represented by 19 deputies in the Sejm and 8 in the Senate in the new parliament. However, the OPZZ has proved a critic of various aspects of government policy, such as labour reform and unemployment. As unemployment continued as a major problem under the SLD government, standing at 20% by 2004, this issue has been a source of particular tension.

International affiliation. None

Trade Unions Forum
Forum Zwiazkow Zawodowych (FZZ)
Address. ul. Fordonska 55, 85-719 Bydgoszcz
Phone. +48 52 371 83 33
Fax. +48 52 342 18 71
E-mail. biuro@fzz.org.pl
Website. www.fzz.org.pl (Polish only)
Leadership. Wieslaw Siewierski (president)
History and character. The FZZ originated in the creation in the late 1990s of the Union Labour Forum by the Union of Labour (Unia Pracy) political party, which won 16 seats in the Sejm in the 2001 elections as a junior partner on the SLD list. A crystallizing factor in formation of the FZZ was changes in the law in 2001 which opened the way for membership on the influential Tripartite Commission for Social and Economic Affairs to national union centres with more than 300,000 members – the OPZZ and Solidarity being at that point the only union organizations represented on the Commission. The first FZZ convention was held in April 2002, when the FZZ embraced 17 unions, and a position was adopted rejecting what were styled the "bilateral, opportunistic" ties between the OPZZ, Solidarity and political parties. The FZZ espoused a broadly centre-left platform, favouring accession to the EU and taking a balanced view on privatization as needing to be framed for the moderniza-

tion of the economy rather than a revenue-raising device. It achieved membership of the Tripartite Commission, in the teeth of opposition by the OPZZ in particular.

Portugal

Capital: Lisbon
Population: 10.52 m. (2004 est.)

1 Political and Economic Background

After the establishment of the quasi-fascist Salazar regime in 1933, Portugal was subject to right-wing authoritarian rule, with clerical and corporatist elements, until the overthrow of Salazar's successor, Marcelo Caetano, by the Armed Forces Movement in April 1974. After an initial period when the communists were a major political force and there was considerable turmoil, Portugal has moved into the European political mainstream. The leading political parties are the Social Democratic Party (PSD) (which despite its name is a centre-right party akin to the German CDU or British Conservatives), and the social democratic Socialist Party (PS).

The PSD held office from 1987–95. The PS then led the government from 1995, strengthening its position in the October 1999 elections when it won exactly half the seats in the Assembly. The government was headed by Prime Minister António Guterres of the PS. After a catastrophic result in the local elections of December 2001, Prime Minister Guterres unexpectedly resigned from his office. New elections took place in March 2002 leading to a relative majority for the PSD under the leadership of Manuel Durao Barroso. Barroso formed a coalition government with the small conservative eurosceptic Democratic Social Centre–People's Party (CDS-PP). The Barroso government introduced a programme of austerity in the public administration, which led to major protests across the country. The main purpose of the austerity measures was to bring the budget deficit of 4.1% of GDP under the ceiling of 3% mandated by the EU's Economic and Monetary Union (EMU) and Growth and Stability Pact. The government also introduced major reforms of labour market legislation in order to achieve more competitiveness in the Portuguese economy. In July 2004 Barroso, after taking over as the new president of the European Commission, was replaced as Prime Minister by Pedro Santana Lopes. In February 2005 the PS returned to power with a sweeping victory in parliamentary elections.

Portugal has been a member of the EU since 1986. Although remaining the poorest country in the EU (with Greece) of the pre-2004 group of 15 member states, Portugal made progress in closing the gap between it and the other EU member states after joining in 1986. Per capita income stood at 56% of the EU average in 1986 and had risen to 71% by 1999; however, it declined thereafter, falling to 68% in 2003. Growth since 2000 has been below the EU average. In 2003, the Portuguese economy had negative growth due to the number of firms closing down or filing bankruptcy and growth was only 1% in 2004. Portugal had low unemployment at 4.1% in 2000, but it has been rising since then due to the fragile position of small and medium sized enterprises and stood at 7.1% in late 2004. Furthermore, inflation has been rising since 2000. While in 2000 it ended the year below 2.8%, since 2001 it has been above 3%. Services are the fastest growing sector of the economy, with a decreasing proportion (now only 10%) of the workforce in agriculture. Portugal joined the single European currency on its creation on Jan. 1, 1999.

GDP (purchasing power parity) $181.8bn. (2004 est.); GDP per capita (purchasing power parity) $18,000 (2004 est.).

2 Trade Unionism

In the early decades of the twentieth century the Portuguese labour movement was dominated by revolutionary trade unionism and anarcho-syndicalism. Following the creation in 1914 of the first national confederation, the União Operária Nacional (National Workers' Union), union activity led to the first revolutionary general strike in 1918. The (renamed) Confederaçao Geral de Trabalhadores (CGT, General Confederation of Workers) was dissolved in 1933 by Salazar and replaced by official trade unions within a fascist corporative structure. A revolutionary general strike in January 1934 led to increased repression and the CGT gradually lost influence among the workforce. After World War II no effective trade union movement, either legal or clandestine, existed in Portugal until the emergence of an informal trade union structure, Intersindical, in 1970. This was politically pluralist, but its best organized element was the communists.

After Salazar's death in 1970, restrictions on trade unions were eased to some degree under Caetano before the armed forces took power in 1974. On April 30, 1975, the Supreme Revolutionary Council accorded recognition to the communist-led Intersindical Nacional (IN) as the sole national trade union centre (to which all unions were obliged to affiliate), despite the opposition of the Socialist Party, which had emerged as the dominant party in elections to a Constituent Assembly held on April 25. In October 1976, however, the socialist government formed in July 1976 revoked the status of the IN as sole legal centre. This led to the formation of the União Geral de Trabalhadores (UGT) as an alternative centre, broadly aligned with the socialists and social democrats. Portugal ratified ILO Convention No. 98 (Right to Organize and Collective Bargaining, 1949) in 1964 and Convention No. 87 (Freedom of Association and Protection of the Right to Organize, 1948) in 1977.

The two main trade union centres are now the Confederaçao Geral dos Trabalhadores Portugueses –Intersindical Nacional (General Confederation of Portuguese Workers–Intersindical, CGTP–IN, or CGTP), which is the renamed IN, and the UGT. These centres (of which the CGTP has been generally the stronger, except in the white–collar sector) have remained ideologically opposed to some degree, but also participate in joint actions where views converge. The CGTP–IN represents a relatively unreconstructed trade union wing that opposes most of the market liberalization process and favours state control. It has a mainstream association with the Portuguese Communist Party (PCP), which won 6.94% of the vote and 12 seats in the March 2002 Assembly of the Republic elections, but it also includes socialists and other left party elements. The UGT is more pragmatic and associated with the Socialist Party (PS), but with a minority stream supporting the (centre-right) Social Democrats (PSD), the other major party, which formed the government from the 2002 elections until its defeat in February 2005. The UGT is affiliated to the ICFTU and ETUC, the CGTP to ETUC. Most recently independent trade unions have created a new trade union confederation called União de Sindicatos Independentes (Union of Independent Trade Unions, USI).

A government survey found that trade union membership peaked at 1.6 million in the 1980s and then fell, standing at an estimated 1.15 million in 1995, giving a density of about 36%. In 2003 it was estimated that 1 million people are unionized, or 30% of the working force. About two-thirds are members of the CGTP and one-third members of the UGT. At the 8th conference of the CGTP in January 2004, it was claimed that it had increased in membership by over 222,675, which would give it a membership of over 800,000. The third sector of independent trade unions became more important in the 1990s, but it is very difficult to make an estimate of its strength. Trade union density is average in overall European terms, but trade unions are numerically strong compared with most southern European countries.

Unions developed under the Trade Union Act of 1975 and trade union rights were guaranteed in general terms by the 1976 Constitution. A decree effective April 1, 1999, formally extended trade union rights to the public administration, not covered by the 1975 Act, although in practice trade unionism had also become firmly established in that sector. New trade unions have been emerging in the security forces sector. Since 2002 police associations can form trade unions. Labour legislation is generally protectionist and employers have called consistently for more flexibility in labour markets. In 2003 a new labour code was approved by the Assembly of the Republic after one year of negotiations and consultations. This is the first time that there is such a codified law for the labour market. The purpose of the law is to make the labour market more flexible and competitive. Trade union confederations protested against the labour law throughout 2002 and 2003. Several other pieces of legislation reformed the unemployment protection system, the law on sickness benefit, early retirement for public servants and public administration services.

Collective bargaining is widely practiced with most agreements being sectoral and nationwide in character: 91% of Portuguese employees are covered by sector-level bargaining. Agreements tend to be focused on pay, though issues such as job descriptions, annual holidays and working time also are covered. The number of collective agreements was over 330 in 2000 and 2001; in 2002 it declined to 291 and in 2003 to 285. Two-thirds are sectoral agreements and one-third company level agreements.

Strikes occur regularly and are used as a negotiating tool, a practice encouraged in the late 1990s by the relatively low level of unemployment. Most strikes are short-lived, however. Strikes affecting whole sectors or called for essentially political reasons are also a feature of the industrial relations landscape. There were 312 strikes in 2002 and 246 in 2003. In 2003, about two-thirds were single-company strikes, a quarter were public administration strikes and about 10% were sectoral strikes. The government has powers to order strikers back to work in essential services.

The Economic and Social Council (CES), in existence since 1992, provides an advisory forum for the social partners. Its Standing Committee for Social Dialogue (CPCS) has a specific role in industrial relations. It is chaired by the Prime Minister and includes three representatives each from the CGTP and UGT. The CPCS has provided the context for the negotiation of a series of incomes agreements and social pacts. While the CGTP has been involved in the negotiation of these pacts it has consistently fail to endorse them. The final evaluation of the Strategic Tripartite Dialogue agreed by most social partners for the period 1996-99 was not very positive. In 2000, the Socialist government decided to change the strategy and move towards a more flexible approach envisaging the conclusion of tripartite sectoral agreements. In 2001, three such agreements on improvement of working conditions and health and safety in the workplace, on employment, the labour market, education and training and some aspects of social security were concluded. In 2003, the Barroso government proposed a social contract for competitiveness and employment at a meeting of the CPCS, with discussions continuing in 2004. It envisages pay moderation, and additional measures to make the Portuguese economy and labour market more competitive.

3 Trade Union Centres

Confederação Geral dos Trabalhadores Portugueses – Intersindical Nacional (CGTP– IN) General Confederation of Portuguese Workers
Address. Rua Victor Cordon, n. 1°–2°, 1249–102 Lisbon
Phone. + 351 21 323 6500
Fax. + 351 21 323 6695
E-mail. cgtp@cgtp.pt
Website. www.cgtp.pt (Portuguese only)
Leadership. Manuel Carvalho da Silva (general secretary)
Membership. 800,000 (CGTP figure)
History and character. The CGTP–IN, commonly referred to as the CGTP, traces its origins to the Intersindical Nacional founded illegally in October 1970. It became the main illegal trade union confederation before the end of the dictatorship which lasted from 1926 to 1974. Following the revolution of 1974, Intersindical, under communist leadership, became the sole national trade union centre authorized by the armed

forces, inheriting the assets of the former government-sponsored syndicates. When the socialists came into government in 1976, its monopoly status was revoked.

The second (1977) congress changed Intersindical's name to its present one. With the waning of the revolutionary mood, the confederation (which had supported nationalization and decolonization) lost support and faced a new rival in the UGT, which was formed in 1978. The CGTP experienced rivalry between socialist and the (majority) communist factions, exacerbated by the reluctance of the hardline Portuguese Communist Party to respond to the changing face of the Soviet bloc in the late 1980s and early 1990s.

During the 1990s the CGTP participated in tripartite negotiation of successive social pacts, while consistently refusing to endorse them, in contrast to the UGT. The CGTP shares the UGT's aspirations and emphasis on issues such as the need for convergence with EU average wages and conditions, the strengthening of the social dimension of the EU, and the call for full employment and good quality jobs. However, the CGTP is significantly more hostile to the process of privatization, retains a traditional belief in state ownership and control, and demands the 35-hour week while the UGT encourages its adoption. At the industrial level, the CGTP tends to be more militant, although the two centres have jointly organized strikes, as in the transport sector and civil service in the Spring of 2000. Despite significant differences in emphasis, and their antagonistic origins, the CGTP and UGT now cooperate on many issues. The CGTP's affiliation to the European Trade Union Confederation (ETUC) was assisted by the UGT, which had formerly opposed it, and the CGTP has abandoned its one-time identification with the WFTU bloc.

The CGTP was extremely opposed to the labour law introduced by the Barroso government. It organized a very successful one-day general strike on Dec. 10, 2002. The confederation's general objection was that the new law would only increase the existing precariousness in the labour market. Moreover, the CGTP supported a one-day general strike of public administration employees in 2004 against the modernization agenda of the Barroso government. According to CGTP figures 85% to 90% of employees took part. Its main slogan has been the demand for quality of employment and against the precariousness of employment.

On Jan. 30-31, 2004, the CGTP organized its tenth confederation conference. The secretary-general Carvalho da Silva was confirmed as leader of the confederation. It was also announced that 222,871 new persons had joined the confederation, contributing to an overall increase in the number of members. The CGTP consisted of 97 trade unions in 2004, which generated about €2.3 million in fees for the confederation. Although communist trade unionists dominate the central decision-making bodies of the CGTP, the number of representatives from other ideological tendencies within the CGTP have been gaining in strength. The overall policy of the CGTP is to become more autonomous from the political parties, in particular the Communist Party (PCP). Due to the declining influence of the PCP from election to election, Carvalho Silva pursues a policy of pluralistic representation within the confederation including socialists, modernizing communists, Catholics and representatives of the new parliamentary party, the Bloc of Left (BE).
International affiliation. ETUC

União Geral de Trabalhadores (UGT)
General Union of Workers
Address. Rua de Buenos Aires 11, 1249–067 Lisbon
Phone. +351 21 393 1200
Fax. +351 21 397 4612
E-mail. ugt@mail.telepac.pt
Website. www.ugt.pt (Portuguese; some information in English)
Leadership. Manuela Teixeira (president); João Proença (general secretary)
Membership. 400,000
History and character. The UGT was founded in October 1978 with the backing of the Socialist and Social Democratic parties, in succession to the Carta Aberta (Open Letter) union grouping which in 1976 had challenged the status of the Intersindical Nacional as sole centre. It held its first congress in 1979.

The UGT is smaller than the CGTP–IN but resembles its rival in that there are political factions within it. The Socialists constitute the leading faction, followed by the Social Democrats (PSD, a centre-right party). In May 1992 the UGT at its sixth national congress elected a communist (José Bras) to its national secretariat for the first time, resulting in a secretariat comprising 28 Socialists, 21 Social Democrats and one communist. The UGT customarily maintains a balance by having a Socialist general secretary (since 1995 João Proença) and a PSD president (currently Manuela Teixeira).

After allegations of misuse (unrelated to trade union activities) of European Social Fund money by the UGT's education, training and development arm, this funding was cut off, creating a financial crisis. In March 1997 the Socialist government guaranteed a PTE 600m. bank loan to the UGT, apparently saving it from bankruptcy. The government said that the loan was intended to safeguard the continuation of democratic trade unionism, but the move attracted intense criticism from opposition parties (which united to pass a vote of protest in the Assembly) and some independent unions.

The 8th UGT congress, held in May 2000, had the theme "towards development and solidarity". The congress called for full employment and the defence of the welfare state and achieving convergence of Portuguese wages and living standards with the EU average.

The UGT comprises 59 unions and two federations. It is putting particular emphasis on strengthening its representation at company level and on securing members in emergent sectors of the economy. At national level it participates with the CGTP, employers and government in the Economic and Social Council (CES) and the Standing Committee for Social Dialogue (CPCS). The UGT under the leadership of João Proença has pursued a policy of unity with the CGTP. Although cooperation with the CGTP has been happening more often in recent years, the difficult financial situation of the UGT diminishes its bargaining power in this relationship. The demands of the

UGT between 2000 and 2003 were related to pay rises, an increase in the minimum wage and improvement of pensions. Moreover, they highlighted aspects of the need to find a more friendly approach towards immigrants and work illegality. The UGT also demanded more fairness in any tax reform and proper implementation of equal opportunity policies, in particular in relation to women and other minorities in the labour market. In 2004, its main focus was on the deteriorating social and economic situation of the country, the new legislation relating to individual contracts in public administration and the implementation of the new labour law. Moreover, during 2004 the UGT presented some concerns on the declining number of collective agreeements.

International affiliations. ICFTU; ETUC; TUAC

União de Sindicatos Independentes (USI)
Union of Independent Trade Unions
Address. Avenida Miguel Bombarda nr. 56,2 Esq.,1069-175 Lisboa
Phone. +351 217 963 583
Fax. +351 217 963 583
E-mail. usi@usi.pt
Website. www.usi.pt
Leadership. Eng. Victor Martins (president), Dr. Borges de Oliveira (vice-president)
History and character. Independent trade unions became more self-confident throughout the 1990s. They did not feel represented by the two main trade union confederations due to their ideological inclinations. In December 2000 the USI was founded to be an alternative to the CGTP and UGT. It had its first conference in September 2001, at which the main bodies of the confederation were elected. The first national meeting of the USI took place on Dec. 12, 2003, and comprised 22 trade unions which were either affiliated or not. The second national meeting of USI took place on May 11, 2004. The USI adopted a compromising attitude towards the modernizing agenda of the centre-right Barroso/Santana Lopes government. It was very supportive of the new labour law, which was regarded as a first systematic attempt to modernize labour law in Portugal by integrating all the relevant European directives. It is supportive of the social contract for competitiveness and employment. The membership of USI consists of nine trade unions from the communications, transport, energy and banking sector. It is dominated by white collar workers.

Qatar

Capital: Doha
Population: 840,000 (2004 est.)

1 Political and Economic Background

Qatar is a monarchy in which the al-Thani family holds power, the present Amir having deposed his father in a palace coup in 1995. Amir Hamad's brother is Prime Minister. The Amir holds absolute power but legislates after consulting with leading citizens in an appointed Advisory Council. There are no political parties or general elections, although municipal council elections were first held on March 8, 1999. In early 2004 a series of reforms were introduced, including a written constitution, which provided modalities for a partly elected *shura* (consultative) council. Elections are evidently scheduled for 2005.

The key sectors of the economy are largely state-controlled. Oil accounts for two-thirds of government revenue and has formed the basis for a high standard of living. Qatar also has the third largest natural gas reserves in the world, which are of increasing importance. Most of the workforce are foreigners and only some 150,000 Qataris are deemed to be actual nationals. The government's "Qatarization" programme aims to increase the participation of citizens in the economy. Freedom House described this policy as one where the state "discriminates based on nationality in… employment, education, housing and health services."

GDP (purchasing power parity) $17.54bn. (2003 est.); GDP per capita (purchasing power parity) $21,500 (2003 est.).

2 Trade Unionism

Qatar joined the International Labour Organization in 1972, but has ratified neither ILO Convention No. 87 (Freedom of Association and Protection of the Right to Organize, 1948) nor No. 98 (Right to Organize and Collective Bargaining, 1949).

For most of Qatar's history, trade unions were illegal and collective bargaining was not permitted. However, in early May 2004 the Amir allowed the formation of professional associations for the first time, and on May 24 he decreed a law allowing workers to form trade unions and go on strike. In addition, the legislation bans employing youths under 16, sets a working day of eight hours, and grants women equal labour rights with men, in addition to a paid 50-day maternity leave. The law was to come into effect six months after it was promulgated. Analysts commented that the law reform was part of a general, gradual reform process which includes deregulation and democratization.

Formerly, strikes were banned in the public sector, though were lawful in the private sector after appeal to the Labour Conciliation Board. However, as the overwhelming majority of private sector workers were and still are foreigners, who depend on their employers for residency rights, strikes rarely occur. Exceptions to this rule, quoted in a report of 2002, were strikes by workers against the Korean-owned Hyundai car factory in Qatar, and several "peaceful demonstrations", including one by workers against the World Trade Organization (WTO). In all instances the government chose not to intervene, leading commentators to suppose that the formal ban on strikes was no longer being strictly enforced.

There has been provision for the formation of labour-management joint committees in enterprises, but these were limited in what they could discuss to issues such as health and safety and training and were not a forum for bargaining over pay.

Romania

Capital: Bucharest
Population: 22.36 m. (2004 est.)

1 Political and Economic Background

Under Nicolae Ceausescu the Romanian communists after World War II pursued a policy of some independence from the Soviet Union combined with a domestic regime of uncompromising severity, much of whose inspiration came from North Korea and China. Although communist rule ended in Romania at the same time as in other eastern European countries, it did so without a long process of increasingly organized dissidence such as occurred in Poland or the Czech Republic. Instead Ceausescu's rule ended suddenly in December 1989 when mass demonstrations were joined by the army. Ceausescu was captured and summarily executed and resistance by his internal security forces was quickly crushed.

The repressiveness of the regime and the rapidity of its collapse meant there had been no real development of alternative political forces. A National Salvation Front (FSN), most of whose leaders were members of the former communist nomenklatura, assumed power after Ceausescu's overthrow. The FSN won elections in May 1990, but miner-led riots against its tentative efforts to introduce a free market precipitated its fall in September 1991. Non-party government followed until September 1992 when further presidential and parliamentary elections brought the Democratic National Salvation Front (FSND – a breakaway from the NSF) of President Ion Iliescu to power. Later renamed the Party of Social Democracy in Romania (PDSR), it continued in power but only by means of a coalition with the former communist Socialist Labour Party and two extreme nationalist parties. Elections in November 1996 resulted in the formation of a more decisively post-communist coalition government led by the Democratic Convention of Romania (CDR), itself a coalition based on the National Peasants' Christian and Democratic Party (PNTCD), the National Liberal Party (PNL) and the National Liberal Party–Democratic Convention (PNL–CD). Further elections in November 2000, however, resulted in the collapse of the centre-right coalition with the PDSR returning to government and also a strong showing by the right-wing nationalist candidates of the Greater Romania Party (PRM). In a run-off presidential election in December 2000 the PDSR's Ion Iliescu defeated the PRM's Corneliu Vadim Tudor.

Continuing the post-communist pattern of swings of the political pendulum, Iliescu's chosen successor as President, Prime Minister Adrian Nastase (the chariman of the Social Democratic Party, PSD, as the PDSR was renamed in 2001), was unexpectedly defeated in run-off presidential elections in December 2004. The victor, Traian Basescu, the leader of the Democratic Party, ran as the candidate of the Justice and Truth alliance. In parliamentary elections held on Nov. 28, however, the PSD had taken first place, ahead of the Justice and Truth alliance. A key priority for both the new President and the PSD is making progress on achieving Romania's goal of joining the EU by 2007.

After the collapse of the Soviet bloc Romania lost trading partners and inherited an obsolete base of heavy industry. In 1990 factories with over 2,000 workers accounted for two-thirds of those employed. The NSF government unsuccessfully sought to partly liberalize markets while retaining central control and the period 1990–92 was one of falling GDP and constant unrest. The centre-right government elected in 1996 struggled to make a successful transition to a market economy and the last years of the century were marked by recession combined with very high inflation, which was 151% in 1997 and still stood at 56% in 1999. The new government privatized more than 4,000 enterprises in 1997–99, but state control remained predominant in the heavy industry sector, with the private sector comprising mainly agriculture (36% of the labour force) and service businesses. The new century has seen an improving situation; the economy grew by 4.8% in 2003 and in late 2004 full-year economic growth was forecast as likely to be close to 8%. Privatization has also continued, with the main goals achieved; by the end of 2003 there were only 65 state-owned enterprises with more than 100 employees. Inflation, though still high at 12% in 2004, is greatly reduced from previous levels. The huge scale of the black economy is a continuing major problem which President Basescu has pledged to tackle. Under the accession agreement preparing its way to joining the EU, Romania must implement reforms including ending subsidies to companies run by political cronies and cracking down on corruption. Despite recent improvements living standards still remain well below EU levels.

GDP (purchasing power parity) $155bn. (2004 est.); GDP per capita (purchasing power parity) $7,000 (2004 est.).

2 Trade Unionism

Romania ratified ILO Convention No. 87 (Freedom of Association and Protection of the Right to Organize, 1948) in 1957 and Convention No. 98 (Right to Organize and Collective Bargaining, 1949) in 1958. It is currently preparing the way for proposed accession to the EU in 2007 and in this context a new Labour Code was adopted in 2003, bringing provisions into line with EU standards in various aspects. In addition a new Trade Unions Law was enacted in 2003, amending the previous Trade Unions Act of 1991.

Before 1989 trade unions existed on the communist model with social responsibilities and a single trade union system organized by the central UGSR. Sporadic efforts to form free trade unions had little impact and organizers were beaten and imprisoned. The UGSR survived Ceausescu by only five days, replaced by a "Provisional Committee for the Formation of Free Trade Unions in Romania" (later the National Confederation of Free Trade Unions of Romania, CNSLR) which inherited its assets and initially supported the new National Salvation Front (NSF) government. At the same time the independent centre Fratia (Fraternity) was formed. The CNSLR remained the country's largest centre in the post-Ceausescu era with a claimed membership of 3.5 million. In March 1990 Fratia (which claimed 800,000 members) mounted a demonstration to challenge CNSLR's right to retain the UGSR assets although this later became a demand that UGSR funds be used for unemployment benefit. Both enjoyed good relations with the ICFTU, however, and animosity gradually declined. In June 1993 the two merged to form CNSLR–Fratia, claiming to have 3.7 million members. By early 2002 trade union density had declined to 44% from its level of 80% in the immediate post-communist period. The surviving strongholds of the trade unions are the old industrial sectors, with unionization rates of 85% in mining, 83% in heavy industry, and 76% in oil, gas and chemicals.

Under the 1991 Law on Trade Unions a confederation could be formed by as few as 60 workers, and this contributed to the fragmentation of the labour movement. There are now an estimated 18 national confederations operating, as well as many independent unions. However, only five confederations are recognized as nationally representative – one of the criteria for such status being that the confederation must represent at least 5% of all the employees in the national economy. There are two ICFTU affiliates, CNSLR–Fratia and the National Trade Union Bloc (BNS), and two WCL affiliates, the National Trade Union Confederation "Cartel Alfa" (CNS Cartel Alfa) and the Democratic Trade Union Confederation of Romania (CSDR). All four are also affiliated to ETUC. The fifth nationally representative confederation is the National Trade Union Confederation "Meridian". Of these five, CNSLR–Fratia is the biggest, with 800,000 members, while Meridian is the smallest, with 170,000 members, the others each having in the 300,000-400,000 range. The confederations have generally cooperated with eachother on matters of common interest and the decline in trade union memberships has put pressure on the confederations to consider merging their resources. In August 2004 it was announced that the BNS and CNSLR–Fratia would merge under the name National Trade Union Bloc–Brotherhood, but a merger congress planned for October 2004 was postponed. On Nov. 12, 2004, it was announced that the merger would be delayed until 2005, officially for technical reasons relating to the merger, although tensions had developed between the two organizations over allegiances in the parliamentary elections to be held later that month.

A tripartite Economic and Social Council (CES) was established in 1997, with a role to advise on social and economic issues including the impact of restructuring and privatization. Nine of its 27 members are from the nationally representative confederations. The CES participated in the drafting of the new Trade Unions Law and gave a favourable opinion on it. A one-year tripartite social stability pact was signed in April 2004 by the PSD government and nine employers' confederations but only CNSLR–Fratia and BNS of the trade union confederations. The pact had provisions on a range of issues including the impact of economic restructuring and incorporation into Romanian law of the EU's acquis communitaire, a prerequisite for EU membership. The CSDR and Cartel Alfa, both with a Christian democratic orientation, criticized the pact as intended to help the social democratic government in the approaching national elections.

The right to join and form trade unions is guaranteed by law, and this was strengthened by the new Trade Unions Law in effect from 2003, which incorporated a range of provisions drawn up with reference to ILO standards. Employees of the Ministries of National Defence, Public Administration and Interior, and Justice, as well as of government security and intelligence agencies, may not join unions. A trade union may be formed by 15 workers and (because of the previous difficulty in organizing the increasingly important smaller firms), these can now be in different enterprises, not just in the same enterprise as previously. Elected trade union representatives may not be dismissed while in office or for two years beyond the end of their term of office. However, trade union organization is by no means always straightforward. Some employers (particularly foreign-owned companies) have sponsored company unions or made non-membership of unions a condition of employment.

Collective bargaining was underwritten by the 1991 Law on Trade Unions. Practice was subsequently shaped by the fact that most major enterprises were in state hands and the fragmentation of the unions. The pattern is now one of enterprise-level agreements although a single national level tripartite agreement provides an outline framework for negotiations. Collective bargaining agreements are mandatory in enterprises with more than 50 employees. In 2003 there were 11,200 collective bargaining agreements.

Even under Ceausescu, strikes were reported at times in the 1970s and 1980s although they were savagely suppressed. In June 1990 the miners from the Jiu Valley marched on Bucharest to support the NSF government against demonstrators calling for the complete removal of communists from power. Six were killed and hundreds injured as the miners acted as the government's shock troops, provoking the suspension of aid by several countries. In September 1991, however, with mounting dissatisfaction at economic conditions, the miners virtually occupied Bucharest, forcing the NSF government of Petre Roman to resign. The collapse of much of the Romanian economy in the early 1990s was reflected in regular strikes and demonstrations as real incomes fell 40% from 1989 to 1993. The government frequently declared strikes illegal, although it appeared to lack the means to enforce its decrees. The decline of gross domestic product and falling living standards for three straight years in 1997–99 produced continuing unrest. In May 1997 unions staged a "month of the yellow card", demanding cuts in the price of food and energy and the abandonment of plans to close down or privatize state companies. In January 1999 coal miners from the Jiu Valley tried to march on Bucharest to oppose mine closures and there were violent clashes when a ban on the march was enforced. On March 24, 1999, up to 400,000 people supported demonstrations called jointly by the four leading centres (Cartel Alfa, the CSDR, CNSLR–Fratia and the BNS) to demand lower taxes, inflation-linked wage increases, and cuts in energy prices.

The number of strikes has declined markedly in recent years, reflecting the considerable improvement in economic conditions – 21% of employees took part in strikes in 1999, but this had fallen to 3.6% by 2002. Most recent significant strikes have been about the consequences of privatization and restructuring. The mining industry, the source of much previous unrest, has dwindled in significance, the number of workers directly employed in mining having fallen from 350,000 in the early 1990s to under 70,000 by the end of 2002, with job losses continuing. Unions also complain that the right to strike is heavily circumscribed, that there are excessive pre-strike procedures and that the courts have tended to rule most strikes illegal. These aspects were not changed by the new Trade Unions Law and Labour Code. Union officers who lead illegal strikes may under the law face fines and imprisonment. A minimum standard of coverage must be maintained during strikes in essential services, which are interpreted to include health care, education, energy, transport, telecommunications and broadcasting, and the supply of staples such as bread, milk and meat.

3 Trade Union Centres

Democratic Trade Union Confederation of Romania
Confédération des Syndicats Démocratiques de Roumanie (CSDR)
Address. 1–3 Place Walter Maracineaunu, 70711 Bucharest
Phone. +40 21 310 2080
Fax. +40 21 310 2080
E-mail. csdrdri@fx.ro
Leadership. Iacob Baciu (president)
Membership. 345,000
History and character. Christian democratic in orientation and founded in 1994 as a result of a split in the CNSLR. Its chairman in 1994-96 was Victor Ciorbea (previously chairman of the CNSLR), a Christian democrat, who in November 1996 became Prime Minister in a centre-right coalition government, holding that position until March 1998.
International affiliations. WCL; ETUC

National Confederation of Free Trade Unions of Romania – Brotherhood
Confederatia Nationala A Sindicatelor Libere Din Romania – Fratia (CNSLR–Fratia)
Address. Str. Cristian Popisteanu nr. 1-3, Sector 1-3, 010024 Bucharest
Phone/Fax. +40 21 312 5292 (international department)
E-mail. international@cnslr-fratia.ro
Website. www.cnslr-fratia.ro (Romanian; English section)

Leadership. Marius Petcu (president); Sorin Stan (secretary-general)
Membership. 800,000
History and character. Founded from the remnants of the official centre UGSR which existed under communism, the CNSLR was able to maintain a large percentage of the original membership and held on to most of the UGSR assets. In June 1993 the CNSLR merged with its former rival, the independent centre Fratia. The CNSLR–Fratia has declined to 800,000 members, but is still much the biggest of the Romanian confederations, operating nationwide and in every significant economic sector except mining. It affiliates 44 professional federations and 41 territorial branches.

In 1990 the CNSLR operated as a close ally of the NSF, but this relationship cooled. In 1992 Fratia, together with Cartel Alfa, formed a political party, the Convention for Social Solidarity (CSS) to contest the September elections. However, it polled only 30,000 votes. The unions in 1994 formed the Party of Social Solidarity, described as social democratic in orientation, chaired by Miron Mitrea, a co-president of the merged CNSLR–Fratia. More recently the CNSLR–Fratia has been seen as closest to the Social Democratic Party (PSD), which held both the presidency and first place in parliament from 2000 to the elections of November–December 2004, when it lost the presidency but retained first place in parliament. Political differences between CNSLR–Fratia and the Blocul National Sindical (BNS) in the run-up to the November–December 2004 elections appear to have delayed plans for a merger of the two confederations.
International affiliations. ICFTU; ETUC

National Trade Union Bloc
Blocul National Sindical (BNS)
Address. Splaiul Independentei 202A, 5th Floor, Sector 6, 77208 Bucharest
Phone. +40 21 411 5184
Fax. +40 21 411 5184
Website. www.bns.ro (Romanian)
Leadership. Dumitru Costin (president); Matei Bratianu (secretary-general)
Membership. 375,000
History and character. The BNS dates its origins back to 1991. It now comprises 39 federations and is second in size to CNSLR–Fratia among the confederations. Its fourth national congress, held in November 2003, called for the setting of a national minimum wage of 60% of the average wage and for the minimum to reach the level of the lowest elsewhere in the EU by the time of Romania's planned accession in 2007. It criticized the government of Adrian Nastase for being ready to reach agreement with the IMF without consulting the social partners. BNS has sought various ways to achieve a greater political impact. In April 2004 it set up a National Democratic Bloc, which in turn in August 2004 (ahead of parliamentary elections scheduled for November) entered an electoral agreement with the hardline nationalist Greater Romania Party (PRM) of Corneliu Vadim. In August 2004 it was announced that the BNS would merge with the other (and larger) ICFTU affiliate, CNSLR–Fratia.

However, the apparent identification of the BNS with the PRM in the run-up to the elections apparently delayed plans for the merger. In the elections, the PRM took 13% of the vote.
International affiliations. ICFTU; ETUC

National Trade Union Confederation "Cartel Alfa"
Confederatia Nationala Sindicala "Cartel Alfa" (CNS Cartel Alfa)
Address. Splaiul Independentei 202 A, Floors 2/3, Sector 6, 77208 Bucharest
Phone. +40 21 212 6638
Fax. +40 21 312 3481
E-mail. alfa@cartel–alfa.ro
Website. www.cartel-alfa.ro
Leadership. Bogdan Hossu (president); Ion Homos (secretary-general)
Membership. 325,000
History and character. Founded June 1990. Affiliated to the WCL in 1990 and ETUC in 1996. It has members including heavy and light industry, mining, agriculture and eductaion, organized in 40 professional federations and 38 county-level unions. It is broadly Christian democratic in orientation but emphasizes its independence of political parties.
International affiliations. WCL; ETUC

National Trade Union Confederation "Meridian"
Leadership. Ion Albu (general secretary)
Membership. 170,000
History and character. This is the smallest of the five nationally representative confederations, and the only one not affiliated to either ETUC or a world centre (ICFTU or WCL). It has members in a range of sectors and half of Romanian counties. In 2003 Meridian entered an alliance with the National Association of Craft Cooperatives (UCECOM) and the National Union of Consumer Cooperatives in Romania (CENTROCOOP).

Russian Federation

Capital: Moscow
Population: 143.8 m. (2004 est.)

1 Political and Economic Background

From the mid-1980s Mikhail Gorbachev sought to reform the Soviet Union through the policies of "glasnost" and "perestroika" while retaining Communist Party rule. This policy culminated, first, in the collapse of Soviet hegemony and communist rule in Eastern Europe in 1989, and then, in December 1991 in the dissolution of the Soviet Union itself. The Russian Federation, established as an independent state on Dec. 25, 1991, was left with half the population and a greater proportion of the economic base of the Soviet Union. Russia lacked a pre-communist democratic tradition and the communists have remained a significant minority force, sometimes in alliance with virulent ultra-nationalists, and the development of soundly based centre-right and centre-left mass parties on the Western European model has not occurred. The President has considerable executive powers, and since succeeding Boris Yeltsin (himself President since June 1991) on Dec. 31, 1999, when Yeltsin resigned, former Federal Security Service head Vladimir Putin has consolidated his position, winning successive presidential elections in March 2000 and (with a bigger margin of victory) in March 2004. Elections to the Duma (lower house) in December 1999 left the opposition Communist Party weakened but still as the largest single party, with the government supported by an anticommunist coalition including, most prominently, the Unity party set up in 1999 and associated with Putin. However, Putin's position was further strengthened by elections to the Duma in December 2003, which resulted in the formation of a pro-presidential United Russia bloc holding 300 of the 450 seats, the Communists having declined to 52 seats from the 113 won in 1999.

Like most former Soviet bloc countries, Russia entered a deep recession in the early 1990s as its planned economy collapsed. However, it subsequently proved less successful than some of its former Eastern European satellites in engineering a transition to free markets. Progress was frustrated by forces including rampant corruption, the scale of obsolescent industries, lack of direction and consensus in government, the inefficiency of the workforce, and the emergence of business oligarchies enmeshed with organized crime. Real GDP probably declined by 50% or more in the period 1991–97. Tentative recovery by 1997 received a further setback with the financial crisis of August 1998, resulting in a massive devaluation of the rouble and a vast emergency IMF bail-out.

There was negative net productive investment throughout the economy in the 1990s. Domestic investment dried up as private capital fled abroad and the state slashed spending to try to control public sector deficits and inflation. Foreign investors likewise largely stayed away, regarding Russia as insecure, while much assistance from international funding agencies was poorly monitored and siphoned off by profiteers and criminals. One objective was to close obsolescent Soviet era heavy industry and stimulate new sectors, but this did not happen; on the contrary, consumer goods production contracted more sharply than the economy as a whole and obsolescent industries survived on subsidies. The investment crisis resulted in collapsing infrastructure, exacerbated by sharp falls in government spending on education and training, which de-skilled the work force. The devaluation of the rouble that followed the August 1998 financial crisis had little beneficial impact on manufacturing exports because of the low quality of Russian products, which made them unsaleable at any price, extractive industries producing the bulk of hard currency exports. Wage arrears were endemic and living standards for most of the population remained significantly below those of the Soviet era. Russia's post-communist era admission to the G-8 group of leading industrial nations was the result of political considerations rather than its economic strength.

Since the deep crisis of 1998, however, confounding many expectations, Russia has experienced a steady continuous recovery, with GDP increasing at an average of 6.5% per annum. This recovery has been greatly assisted by rising energy prices on world markets, Russia now rivalling Saudi Arabia as the world's largest exporter of oil, which has allowed Russia to cut its foreign debt sharply and accumulate foreign exchange reserves. There has been strong growth in capital investment and personal incomes (which have doubled since the end of the 1990s on a purchasing parity basis) and the improving situation has strengthened Putin's hand in his campaign to wrest control of the commanding heights of the economy from the oligarchs. The Putin government nonetheless faces considerable continuing difficulties in attempting to restructure and rebuild Russia's industrial base. Privatization has been incompletely pursued and much inefficient industry still remains in state hands; 80% of Russia's exports are of oil, gas, metals and timber, sectors subject to price volatility, and few of its manufactured products are attractive on world markets. The legitimate private sector has been beset by organized crime, lack of business standards or a legal framework, and lack of affordable credit. And, while Putin has presented his campaign against the oligarchs as a necessary reform, it has caused concerns among foreign investors that their assets might in turn be subject to arbitrary state seizure.

GDP (purchasing power parity) $1.28 trillion (2004 est.); GDP per capita (purchasing power parity) $8,900 (2004 est.).

2 Trade Unionism

The USSR rejoined the International Labour Organization in 1954, having been a member from 1934 to 1940. It ratified ILO Conventions No. 87 (Freedom of Association and Protection of the Right to Organize, 1948) and No. 98 (Right to Organize and Collective Bargaining, 1949) in 1956. This ratification is considered to apply in respect of the Russian Federation.

Trade unions within the Russian Empire developed early in the twentieth century, but were of relatively little importance on the eve of the 1917 revolution. Advocates of union political autonomy had considerable influence at this time but were eliminated when the communists consolidated power. Under Soviet rule, unions were used primarily to mobilize and discipline the workers behind the objectives of the revolution and to secure greater productivity. Subsequently, all were organized within the All-Union Central Council of Trade Unions (AUCCTU). Throughout the Stalinist period of the 1930s and 1940s the unions were of little significance, collective agreements were abolished, and there was no AUCCTU congress between 1932 and 1949.

Expanded rights and obligations were accorded from the late 1950s onwards and these were consolidated, extended and codified in legislation adopted from 1970 to 1974, and also given recognition in the 1977 constitution. The Soviet government argued that its labour legislation did not prohibit the establishment of unions outside the AUCCTU and that unification reflected the workers' wishes. In practice, the AUCCTU shadowed party policy, and there was a close interlocking of party membership and trade union office-holding at all levels. Weaknesses in the operation of the trade unions as a "transmission belt" between the party and the workers arose primarily from inertia, bureaucracy, alienation and indifference, rather than any explicit conflict between the trade unions and the party in respect of this role.

Following the appointment of Mikhail Gorbachev as party General Secretary (Soviet leader) in March 1985, the trade unions were affected by the intensifying campaign against corruption and mismanagement. The AUCCTU entered a phase of "self-criticism" in which (following the party line) it said that it had in the past neglected the interests of the workers in favour of "bureaucratic formalism" and would participate in the reform process. The official unions were not prominent, however, in driving forward the Gorbachev doctrines of glasnost and perestroika.

In the summer of 1989 a strike wave in the USSR directly stimulated the establishment of workers' committees in the north (Vorkuta region), in the Ukraine (Donbass in the Don Valley), and east of the Urals (Kuzbass). Before 1990 the AUCCTU itself seemed immune to change but then massive threats to its national coverage forced internal reform. It announced far-reaching structural reform and reorganized in preparation for an October congress where it was re-launched as the General Confederation of Unions of the USSR (GCTU). Independent unions began to proliferate. With origins in the 1989 strike committees, an independent miners' union (NPG) was formed in 1990.

In August 1991 communist hard-liners attempted a coup, seizing Gorbachev. Boris Yeltsin, the President of the Russian Federation, became the symbol of resistance in the defence of the Parliament (White House) and the coup crumbled. The outcome was the collapse of the Communist Party, Yeltsin's assumption of supreme authority, and the disintegration of the Soviet Union. The leader of the attempted coup, Gennady Yanaev, had been chairman of the AUCCTU until 1990. GCTU leaders attempted to meet him and apparently opposed Yeltsin's call for stoppages of production. The GCTU was accused by the Federation of Independent Trade Unions of Russia (FNPR), which organized the unions at the Russian level, of taking a position towards the coup which was "to say the least ambiguous" although the FNPR itself did little beyond calling on workers to maintain "labour discipline." Each organization, however, claimed the responsibility for the dispatch of gas masks to the defenders of the Russian Parliament during Aug. 19–21 and some FNPR representatives were among those defending the Parliament.

Following the dissolution of the Soviet Union, the FNPR established itself as the dominant trade union organization in Russia. Since 1991, the shape of the Russian trade union movement has remained broadly unchanged. The FNPR in the late 1990s still claimed to represent 80% of Russian workers. Its active membership is a fraction of this and its sporadic efforts to mobilize workers in demonstrations and strikes have only ever produced a patchy response. However, the FNPR has inherited both the assets and many of the functions of the old official unions and it has therefore remained a powerful factor in Russian society. It has also retained many of the former bureaucrats of the old structures. In some respects, Russian social and economic organization has not greatly changed since 1991. The enterprise remains the organizing focus for much of people's lives: it provides not just work and pay, but workers' apartments, health services, holidays, even food and consumer goods. The trade unions, as in Soviet times, play a central role in the administration of the range of enterprise services, and indeed it is considered almost impossible in many cases to disentangle what assets belong to the enterprise and what to the unions. The concepts of "labour" and "management" are weakly defined. Enterprise directors are members of, and commonly lead or heavily influence, FNPR unions. Protest strikes and demonstrations are often directed at pressurizing central government to retain subsidies or tax concessions and are organized collectively by enterprise directors, unions and, sometimes, local officials. The FNPR is in effect a network of competing local and sectoral interest groups, focused more on securing benefits from the centre than on issues such as local bargaining. This phenomenon is reinforced by the lack of opportunities for workers to transfer their labour. Wage arrears are endemic, but enterprises often retain workers they cannot pay rather than lay them off; the workers in this situation continue to receive free or subsidized housing, health and other benefits.

The independent union movement has made little impact after its days of influence in 1989–91. Independent trade unions remain largely confined to a few sectors, such as mining, air traffic controllers, the docks, and locomotive drivers, where they originally appeared. The most important independent union has remained the independent miners' union, NPG, but this is smaller than the coal miners' union linked to the FNPR. The independent unions, unlike the official unions, which were organized on the industrial union principle, have tended to be craft-based, limiting their scale. In wide swathes of the economy they do not exist and total membership may be only 500,000, a fraction of that of the FNPR (reliable membership figures do not exist for Russian unions). Most workers who have left the FNPR have joined no other union at all, while many early leaders of independent unions went on to take up official positions in the new order or to direct privatized enterprises. Organization of independent unions has been frustrated by refusal of employers to deal with them and the monopoly position and control of workers' welfare enjoyed by the FNPR in many enterprises.

Likewise, no alternative confederation has developed. The Federation of Socialist Trade Unions (Sotsprof) was founded by Moscow intellectuals in 1989, and espoused a social democratic programme. It recruited independent unions and aimed to be a confederation with contacts across the USSR. It was given a role out of proportion to its real strength by Yeltsin (whom it actively supported for several years) on the Tripartite Commission for the Regulation of Social and Labour Relations set up in 1992 but failed to develop a mass base to rival the FNPR. This is true also of the Confederation of Labour of Russia (KTR), comprised mainly of transport sector workers, and the All-Russian Confederation of Labour (VKT), set up with backing from the NPG and Sotsprof. In the early 1990s foreign groups, such as the AFL-CIO's Free Trade Union Institute, invested considerable resources in supporting independent unions and encouraging the development of alternatives to the FNPR, but to little avail as no significant confederation has taken root. One result of this is that while the ICFTU was able to affiliate trade union centres in Eastern European countries relatively soon after the fall of communism, it was unable to recognize an affiliate in Russia. In November 2000, however, the ICFTU Executive Board announced the affiliation of the FNPR (which the ICFTU claimed had 28 million members) as well as the VKT and KTR. The FNPR accordingly became the largest ICFTU affiliate, with more than twice the membership of the AFL-CIO, although its status, voluntary and active membership and legitimacy compared with other major ICFTU affiliates such as the AFL-CIO, DGB and TUC is arguable.

In the 1989–91 period the independent unions opposed the regime and after the fall of communism in 1991 mostly enthusiastically backed Yeltsin and his policies. Victor Utkin and Aleksandr Sergeyev, leaders of the NPG, became members of Yeltsin's council of advisers. As late as the autumn of 1993, Kuzbass miners offered to march on Moscow to aid Yeltsin in his confrontation with the Russian Parliament, which had blocked his programme. Years of falling living standards, and the failure of a free market economy either to take root or deliver prosperity, produced division and confusion over aims and goals, however. NPG leaders abandoned pro-Yeltsin positions and in 1997 official and independent unions worked together to shut down the coal districts of Kuzbass and Vorkuta. In the crisis of August 1998, the NPG and VKT joined the FNPR in calling on Yeltsin to resign. Sergeyev was briefly detained and NPG headquarters in Moscow was raided by Interior Ministry agents. The NPG was threatened with de-registration, although this did not happen. Overall, issues such as non-payment of wages and disillusion with the results of post-communist reforms have closed the gap between the FNPR and independent unions.

The catastrophic scale of the decline of the Russian economy in the 1990s is difficult to overstate. The real value of the average wage declined some 78% between 1991–97 and many people survived only by engaging in subsistence cultivation of small plots and because they continued to live in heavily subsidized apartments with cheap utilities. There was a process of economic "primitivization". While local pockets (notably Moscow) remained comparatively buoyant, through much of the country there was widespread privation and even malnutrition. This is reflected in indicators for health and mortality: life expectancy for adult males is now at the same level as in Tsarist times.

Wage arrears (as in many post-communist economies) as well as arrears in pensions became endemic from the mid-1990s. Hyper-inflation in the period 1992–93 was followed by government policies aimed at taking money out of the economy. Those Russians who had cash and could send it abroad did so. Inter-enterprise debt accelerated and many enterprises abandoned the cash economy in favour of bartering. In 1997 the labour code was modified so that non-payment of wages was no longer ground for punitive damages. The problem came to a head in 1998 with the broader financial and banking crisis. From January–August 1998, wage arrears increased 40–50% and by this point over 20 million workers had not been paid for months, while 70% of inter-enterprise debts were being settled by barter, promissory notes or mutual cancellations of debts. The August 1998 devaluation of the rouble allowed the reduction of outstanding wage arrears in the following months, before the backlogs began to increase again in 2000.

Against this background, the scale of unrest in Russia was arguably modest. Work stoppages occurred continually, and other forms of protest included blockading of railroad lines, hunger strikes, occasional hostage taking of enterprise managers or local officials, and pickets of government offices. In some areas, protesters faced physical attack, prosecution and punishment; in others they had the tacit support of the local authorities. Strikes are commonly declared illegal and the courts may order confiscation of union assets in compensation for losses. As a result many strikes are organized by ad hoc strike committees rather than by the unions themselves.

Major demonstrations and work stoppages occurred Russia-wide on Oct. 7, 1998, in the wake of the financial crisis, and the FNPR demanded Yeltsin's resignation. Themes of the protests were opposition to continued privatization, the payment of wage arrears, and an end to plunder by the wealthy taking money abroad. However, there was little sustained and organized support for coherent alternatives and much protest focused on the retention of subsidies or limited sectoral demands. Apathy characterizes much of the workforce and the trade union movement has not developed a clear and coherent unified identity to give it a role in social dialogue. In addition, Russia is geographically vast (by far the largest country in the world) and centres of opposition to the government are commonly immense distances from Moscow, isolated from each other and disregarded by the centre.

Politically, the union movement has not formed the base for a social democratic party on the Western European model. Union leaders have allied with different factions, but no party is seen as being preponderantly the party of labour. The Communists, frequently allied with ultra-nationalists and supported disproportionately by the elderly, remained the largest party in the Duma from 1999 to 2003 and have in some regions shared platforms with the unions, but they are also widely distrusted. The FNPR has worked to distance itself from the Communists. Other parties and coalitions are often personality-driven.

The position of the unions has deteriorated. The official unions have retained members through their role in distributing benefits, but this is declining as these functions gradually shift to the government or simply cease to exist. The unions are commonly excluded in the entrepreneurial private sector, where not joining a union can be effectively a condition of employment. Underlying these trends is the overall impoverishment of the economy. Basic functions such as collective bargaining are of limited relevance when the enterprise has no money and is in effect paying for its continuing operations by withholding wages. In such circumstances, the strike threat is an empty one. Strikes and protests are indeed directed more against the government than in pursuit of demands at the enterprise level. Meanwhile social dialogue is intermittent and often unconstructive.

3 Trade Union Centre

Federatsiia Nezavisimykh Profsoiuzov Rossii (FNPR)
Federation of Independent Trade Unions of Russia (FITUR)
Address. 42 Leninsky Prospect, House of Unions, 119119 Moscow
Phone. +7 095 930 89 84
Fax. +7 095 938 22 93
E-mail. sidorov@fnpr.ru
Website. www.fnpr.ru
Leadership. Mikhail Shmakov (president); Vitaly Budko (vice-president), Andrei Isayev (vice-president), Eugene Sidorov (international secretary)
Membership. Claims 31.5 million (2002)
History and character. This is widely regarded as the successor organization to the former communist-era official unions, although technically the successor organization is the General Confederation of Trade Unions (GCTU), associating union centres from the former Soviet republics, to which FNPR is affiliated. FNPR remains as the dominant Russian trade union centre and claims to represent some 80% of all workers.

The FNPR was established in 1990 in what was then the Russian component of the Soviet Union. With the dissolution of the Soviet Union in December 1991 it became the Russian national trade union centre and was, with the military, virtually the only national institution to survive the Communists' loss of power. It retained a number of key assets from the Soviet period, including control over disbursement of social insurance funds, automatic deduction of dues from employee pay, and rights to veto the dismissal of workers. The FNPR also retained considerable numbers of Soviet era union officials, who retained many of their attitudes and ways of working. At the same time, prominent figures from the 1989–90 reform wave also established themselves. Mikhail Shmakov, FNPR president since 1993, came to prominence as leader of the Moscow Federation of Trade Unions (MFP), where he had brought in many new people, active in opposition during the perestroika period. The current FNPR vice-president and former secretary, Andrei Isayev, had organized some of the first opposition meetings in 1987–88 and revitalized the MFP's publication *Solidarnost*.

In 1992 President Yeltsin set up the Tripartite Commission for the Regulation of Social and Labour Relations, and the FNPR was given 9 of the 14 labour seats. The first general agreement to be monitored by the Commission was signed in April 1992 and outlined measures to create a social market while privatizing state property. It included measures for occupational safety and improvement of labour relations. The FNPR failed to achieve an improvement in the level of the minimum wage and opposed plans to hold back the wages of public sector workers. In autumn 1992 the government designated FNPR as its primary social partner, a step which had the effect of diminishing the status of its independent rivals. During 1992–93, however, as its members faced falling living standards and the government failed to keep commitments on wage indexation, the FNPR called many strikes, although these often had little impact. The FNPR identified with forces intent on blocking free market reform. In May 1992 the lobby of state industrial directors, the Russian Union of Industrialists and Entrepreneurs (RUIE), became co-publisher with the FNPR of the newspaper *Rabochaya Tribuna*. The RUIE warned that the government's policies would lead to the "Kuwaitization" of Russia, meaning that they would destroy Russia's industrial base and reduce the country to the status of an exporter of energy to rich Western nations. FNPR president Igor Klochkov proposed alliance with the Civic Union, an anti-reform movement set up in June 1992 and seen as controlled by directors of the big state enterprises.

Although Russian President Yeltsin had defeated Communist hardliners in the August 1991 attempted coup, he continued to face determined opposition from the Russian Congress of People's Deputies (CPD), elected in 1990 in the communist era. Through 1992–93 it blocked much of his reform programme. On Sept. 21, 1993, Yeltsin dissolved the CPD and announced he would rule by decree. The CPD, led by its chairman Ruslan Khasbulatov and supported by Yeltsin's own Vice-President Aleksandr Rutskoy, refused to accept its dissolution and fortified its base in the parliament building (White House) while supporters tried unsuccessfully to seize the Moscow television facility, the Ostankino tower. On Oct. 4, Yeltsin moved against the White House with tanks, resulting in heavy casualties in hand-to-hand fighting before his forces gained control.

An FNPR plenum of Sept. 28 voted to side with the Parliament against Yeltsin and FNPR's leader Igor Klochkov called on workers to mobilize in defence of the Parliament (a call which got little support). The same day a presidential decree stripped the unions of control over social insurance funds, providing disability, child, holiday and other benefits and the source of considerable patronage. After Yeltsin's victory there were threats to end dues check-off or even dismantle the FNPR altogether. In alarm, the FNPR forced Klochkov out of office on Oct. 11 and he was replaced at an emergency congress by Mikhail Shmakov, the leader of the Moscow Federation of Trade Unions (MFP). Following this the government took no further steps against the FNPR, and although the social insurance fund was put under the nominal control of the Labour Ministry, in practice no real change was made to its administration.

A chastened FNPR did not endorse any list in the ensuing (December 1993) elections. This stance confounded the hopes of opponents of the Yeltsin programme, but the lists nonetheless included a large number of individual union leaders scattered among the 26 groups taking part. Former FNPR chairman Igor Klochkov was a member of the political council of the Civic Union, although the Civic Union itself failed to make an impact in the elections.

Thenceforth, the FNPR steered an ambivalent course in relation to the Yeltsin presidency, saying that it favoured market reforms but calling for state intervention to reduce its undesirable effects on jobs and living standards. At the local level it tended to be allied with enterprise directors and local politicians demanding protectionism and subsidies. This was reflected also in the Tripartite Commission where commonly the employers and the unions combined against the government, with a resultant deadlock. In April 1994 the FNPR endorsed Yeltsin's Pact on Social Accord, which offered a compromise on state budget funding in return for social peace and a promise not to campaign for early elections ahead of their due date in 1996. In July 1996 Yeltsin won a comfortable victory over the Communist candidate Gennady Zyuganov in presidential elections, but he continued to face a legislature in which the Communists were the largest party and his opponents were strongly entrenched.

In response to the August 1998 financial crisis, the FNPR sent an open letter to Yeltsin declaring that his policies had led to economic collapse and calling on him to resign. In April 1999 Shmakov praised Prime Minister Yevgeny Primakov (who took office with Duma backing in September 1998 but was dismissed by Yeltsin in May 1999) as the "man who has really stabilized the situation in the country". Primakov's government included no prominent free market reformers. The Union of Labour, the FNPR's social–political movement, was drawn into support of the Fatherland All-Russia coalition, set up by Primakov and Moscow Mayor Yury Luzhkov.

However, Yeltsin appointed Vladimir Putin his Prime Minister in August 1999 and the pro-Kremlin Unity party was set up to counter the Primakov-Luzhkov alliance. Putin launched full-scale war in Chechnya, and buoyed by his resultant popularity, Unity came a close second to the Communists in elections to the Duma in December 1999, coming well ahead of the Fatherland–All Russia coalition. On Dec. 31, Yeltsin resigned and appointed Putin Acting President, following which Putin went on to win the presidential election in March 2000, with Communist Zyuganov again the main challenger. On Feb. 16, 2000, Putin told the FNPR that he wanted to work with the unions and for them to be a "renewed and progressive force". However, a draft new Labour Code subsequently introduced in the Duma was seen as reducing the powers of the unions, and was opposed by the FNPR. The code remained stalled in the Duma during 2000.

An amended version of the Labour Code was adopted by the Duma in 2001 and came into force in January

2002. The new Labour Code represents a compromise between FNPR and the government and was strongly criticized by the other trade union confederations, VKT and KTR. On the one hand the new code has limited the direct rights of trade unions, for example to decide on the fairness of a trade union member's dismissal. On the other hand, it gives more credibility to Collective Bargaining Agreements signed at an enterprise level.

Citing economic stabilization, measures to fight corruption, general incomes increase, and stabilization in the Caucasus region, the FNPR Council voted to support Putin at the 2004 presidential elections.

The FNPR represents to a considerable degree, notwithstanding the changes in Russia since 1991, a continuation of the old Soviet era trade union structures and functions. It retains a major role through its control of facilities such as summer camps, hotels, palaces of culture, sports facilities, and sanatoria. It owns a vast range of facilities. However, it has been affected by closures and sell-offs of many such facilities.

Enterprise directors and managers, on the Soviet model, are commonly FNPR members and often branch leaders. With many basic industries still in state hands, the union branches tend to ally with the directors in support of the enterprise in lobbying for subsidies. Indeed, many strikes and protests have been organized on that collaborative basis. As many Russian cities are "company towns" the government has maintained subsides to avert social collapse. The FNPR has a complex structure of regional and sectoral unions that often take different positions, and this has been reinforced by the increasing fragmentation of the economy. The FNPR has little presence in the entrepreneurial private sector.

Having realized these weaknesses the FNPR 4th Congress adopted a programme aimed at modernization of its structure and activity in November 2001. Youth and gender policy committees were formed to initiate policy programmes to protect the interests of these groups and to attract more young workers. Priority was also given to development of educational, training and information policies.

The FNPR faced considerable suspicion in Western trade union circles as the successor to the official unions of the Communist era. In the early 1990s the AFL-CIO was active in running programmes in Russia through its Free Trade Union Institute to support independent unions opposed to the FNPR. After 1995, when new leadership took over at the AFL-CIO, these programmes were wound down or became more neutral in approach. In 1997 Shmakov was for the first time invited to attend the AFL-CIO congress. In April 2000, the FNPR had observer status at the ICFTU congress in Durban, South Africa, and ICFTU general secretary Bill Jordan said it was in the process of applying for membership. In November 2000 the ICFTU Executive Board announced that the FNPR had been accepted into affiliation, alongside the smaller independent organizations the VKT and KTR. This gave the ICFTU representation inside Russia for the first time in its history. Since affiliation to the ICFTU, FNPR has played an active role to promote ICFTU policy in the region. It provides facilities for the ICFTU regional office and initiated creation of an ICFTU regional information and consultation committee. FNPR is also one of the leading organizations to support the international campaign for protection of trade union rights in Belarus.
International affiliation. ICFTU; GCTU

4 Other Trade Union Organizations

All-Russian Confederation of Labour (VKT)
Address. Rozhdestvenka Street 5/7, 103031 Moscow
Phone. +7 95 925 3213
Fax. +7 95 923 3655
E-mail. vkt@vkt.org.ru
Website. www.vkt.org.ru (Russian; English section)
Leadership. Aleksandr Bugaev (president)
Membership. Reports 1.27 million.
History and character. The VKT was founded in August 1995 by a coalition of independent unions including the Independent Miners' Union (NPG), regional inter-trade union federations and individual unions. By 1997–98 it was actively involved with the FNPR and KTR in the campaign of protest against unpaid wages and in the 1998 financial crisis joined the demands for Yeltsin's resignation. Its then president, NPG leader Aleksandr Sergeyev, was briefly detained at that time. Since December 1999 it has participated in the Tripartite Commission for the Regulation of Social and Labour Relations. In November 2000 it was admitted into affiliation to the ICFTU along with the FNPR and the KTR. It is currently working with the KTR to prepare the basis for merger of the two organizations.
International affiliation. ICFTU; GCTU

Confederation of Labour of Russia (KTR)
Address. 42 Leninsky Prospect, 117119 Moscow
Phone. +7 95 938 8270
Fax. +7 95 938 8270
Membership. Claims 1.25 million.
History and character. The KTR was founded in April 1995, with support from unions of air traffic controllers, doctors, seamen and railway workers. It was affiliated to the ICFTU in November 2000.
International affiliation. ICFTU

Rwanda

Capital: Kigali
Population: 7.95 m. (2004 est.)

1 Political and Economic Background

Rwanda achieved independence from Belgium in 1962. Following a military coup led by Gen. Juvénal Habyarimana in 1973, the Hutu-dominated regime ran a one-party state through the National Revolutionary Movement for Democracy (MRND) until the adoption of a multi-party constitution in 1991. By then, however, a rebellion had been launched by the predominantly Tutsi Rwandan Patriotic Front (FPR) which by 1992 had made extensive territorial gains in northern Rwanda. A fragile peace process in 1993 collapsed in April 1994 when President Habyarimana was killed when his plane was shot down on the approach to the airport at Kigali. This triggered mass killings of genocidal proportions of Tutsi by Hutu supporters of Habyarimana (who also liquidated non-Tutsi political opponents) and this in turn led to the renewal of the FPR military offensive. In July 1994 the FPR claimed a military victory and a new government of national unity was formed, excluding the MRND, whose militia, the Interahamwe, had been heavily involved in the atrocities. Power passed into the hands of a coalition, dominated by the FPR, which controlled an unelected legislature, the Transitional National Assembly. In April 2000 FPR leader Maj.-Gen. Paul Kagame was elected as President by a joint vote of the Assembly and the Cabinet.

A new constitution approved by national referendum in May 2003 provided for an elected President and a bicameral legislature and also included provisions for a commission to combat genocide. Furthermore, it limited the ability of any single political party to gain power through the manipulation of differences between Hutu and Tutsi. Kagame won a landslide victory in presidential elections held in August 2003. The FPR also won a landslide victory in elections to the Chamber of Deputies (the lower house of the bicameral legislature) held a month later.

Rwanda is a poor rural country with about 90% of the population engaged in (mainly subsistence) agriculture. It is the most densely populated country in Africa and landlocked with few natural resources and minimal industry. Primary foreign exchange earners are coffee and tea. The 1994 genocide decimated Rwanda's fragile economic base, severely impoverished the population, particularly women, and eroded the country's ability to attract private and external investment. However, Rwanda has made substantial progress in stabilizing and rehabilitating its economy to pre-1994 levels.

GDP (purchasing power parity) $10.11bn. (2004 est.); GDP per capita (purchasing power parity) $1,300 (2004 est.).

2 Trade Unionism

Rwanda has been a member of the International Labour Organization since 1962, and ratified ILO Conventions No. 87 (Freedom of Association and Protection of the Right to Organize, 1948) and No. 98 (Right to Organize and Collective Bargaining, 1949) in 1985.

Local branches of Belgian unions existed prior to independence but a single trade union system then came into force, organized by the Centrale Syndicale des Travailleurs du Rwanda (CESTRAR). In the early 1990s, as in much of Africa, moves were made towards political pluralism, and as part of this CESTRAR formally became independent of the government and the formation of other unions was permitted. CESTRAR is now affiliated to the ICFTU, and the WCL also has a multi-industry union directly affiliated.

Workers in both private and public sectors are legally free to join unions. However, the 2002 Labour Code specifically excludes civil servants from organizing. The Code also restricts the right to strike in essential services, as defined by the Minister of Labour. Only a few percent of the workforce are paid wages and salaries in the formal economy, but unionization rates are traditionally quite high in this group, especially in the public sector. The civil war and genocide of the mid-1990s devastated civil society and with it the functioning of labour legislation and unions.

3 Trade Union Centre

Centrale Syndicale des Travailleurs du Rwanda (CESTRAR)
Trade Union Centre of Workers of Rwanda
Address. BP 1645, Kigali.
Phone. +250 58 658
Fax. +250 54 012
E-mail. cestrar@rwandal.com
Website. www.cestrar.org
Leadership. Eric Manzi (general secretary)
History and character. CESTRAR was founded in 1985 under single party rule as the only national centre in Rwanda. In 1991 it declared its independence of all political parties following the proclamation of a multi-party system. Since recovering from the catastrophe that engulfed Rwanda in 1994, CESTRAR has set up branches in every prefecture and has made youth education work a priority.
International affiliation. ICFTU

4 Other Trade Union Organization

Syndicat des Travailleurs des Industries, Garages, Enterprises de Constructions, Mines et Imprimeries (STRIGECOMI)
Union of Workers in Industry, Garages, Construction Firms, Mines and Printers
Address. BP 2214, Kigali
Leadership. Emmanuel Ntegekurora (president), Dominique Bicamumpaka (national executive secretary)
International affiliation. WCL; ITGLWF

St. Christopher and Nevis

Capital: Basseterre
Population: 39,000 (2004 est.)

1 Political and Economic Background

St. Christopher (Kitts) and St. Nevis, a federation of two islands, is an independent member of the Commonwealth. The social democratic St. Kitts-Nevis Labour Party (SKNLP), led by Denzil Douglas, returned to power at elections in 1995, ending 15 years of rule by the centrist People's Action Movement (PAM). The SKNLP won a further five-year term at elections in March 2000, and a third term on Oct. 25, 2004.

The economy was traditionally based on the cultivation and processing of sugar, and has been affected by declining world sugar prices. Tourism, offshore banking and manufacturing for export are now the main sectors. A state corporation owns the sugar industry, which will cease sugar manufacturing at the end of the 2005 crop.

GDP (purchasing power parity) $330m. (2003 est.); GDP per capita (purchasing power parity) $7,922 (2003 est.).

2 Trade Unionism

St. Kitts ratified its first eight ILO conventions in 2000, among them Convention No. 87 (Freedom of Association and Protection of the Right to Organize, 1948) and No. 98 (Right to Organize and Collective Bargaining, 1949). Trade unions were legalized in 1939 and are well established and generally recognized by employers, even though there is no formal legislation requiring them to do so. The police and civil service have associations that act as unions. The St. Kitts-Nevis Trades and Labour Union (TLU) continues to dominate trade unionism on the islands, but there are also unaffiliated unions for teachers and dock workers. Collective bargaining takes place at enterprise level and there is a recognized right to strike.

3 Trade Union Centre

St. Kitts-Nevis Trades and Labour Union (TLU)
Address. PO Box 239, Masses House, Church Street, Basseterre
Phone. +1869 465 2229/2891
Fax. +1869 466 9866
E-mail. sknunion@caribsurf.com
Leadership. Walford Gumbs (president); Batumba L. O. Tak (general secretary)
History and character. The efforts of the St. Kitts Workers' League (founded in 1932 and later renamed as the Labour Party) were instrumental in the legalization of trade unionism in 1939, and the consequent formation of the St. Kitts-Nevis Trades and Labour Union in 1940. The union's orientation is social democratic and the relationship with the Labour party (which won all elections from 1937 to 1975 and was in power until 1980, and has since been again in office from 1995) is close. The opposition People's Action Movement (PAM) has accused the Labour Party of favouring the TLU at the expense of independent unions
International affiliations. ICFTU; CTUC; IUF.

St. Lucia

Capital: Castries
Population: 164,000 (2004 est.)

1 Political and Economic Background

St. Lucia has been an independent member of the Commonwealth since 1979. In elections in May 1997, the centre-left St. Lucia Labour Party (SLP), led by Kenny Anthony, defeated the conservative United Workers' Party, which had held power for the previous 15 years. The SLP retained power at elections in December 2001.

The country's main export earnings come from bananas, which face heavy competition from low-cost Latin American producers and are vulnerable to storm damage. St. Lucia has diversified into tourism, offshore banking services and light manufacturing to reduce the dependence on bananas, with agriculture now employing only 20% of the workforce. However, sluggish growth and high unemployment have been features of the economy in recent years.

GDP (purchasing power parity) $866m. (2002 est.); GDP per capita (purchasing power parity) $5,400 (2002 est.).

2 Trade Unionism

St. Lucia has been a member of the International Labour Organization since 1980, and ratified ILO Conventions No. 87 (Freedom of Association and Protection of the Right to Organize, 1948) and No. 98 (Right to Organize and Collective Bargaining, 1949) in that year. Unions operate freely according to the law and in practice.

There is no trade union centre in St. Lucia. However, there are a number of unions and about 36% of the total workforce is organized, the unions being particularly strong in the public sector, where most employees are in unions. The Registration of Trade Unions and Employer Organizations Act, in force from 2000, is reported to have given a boost to trade union recruitment, including in the export processing zones, where union activities had proved difficult; under the Act an employer must recognize a union if it represents over 50% of the workforce. Collective bargaining is widely practiced. Police and firefighters may not strike and workers in a range of other essential services such as utilities and healthcare must give 30 days' advance notice of strike action.

3 Trade Union Centre

There is no trade union centre in St. Lucia

4 Other Trade Union Organizations

National Workers' Union (NWU)
Address. PO Box 713, 60 Micoud Street, Castries
Phone. +1758 452 3664
Fax. +1758 453 2896
Leadership. Tyrone Maynard (president)
Membership. 3,200
History and character. The NWU was founded in 1973 and is a general union with branches for each occupational sector.
International affiliation. WCL

St. Lucia Civil Service Association
Address. PO Box 244, Castries
Phone. +1758 452 3903
Fax. +1758 453 6061
E-mail. csa@candw.lc
Leadership. Francis Raphael (president); Lilia Auguste (acting general secretary)
International affiliation. CTUC

St. Lucia Seamen, Waterfront and General Workers' Trade Union (SWGWTU)
Address. 68 Micoud St, PO Box 166, Castries
Phone. +1758 452 1669
Fax. +1758 452 5452
E-mail. seamen@candw.lc
Leadership. Cecilia Adolph (acting general secretary)
International affiliations. ICFTU; CTUC

St. Lucia Workers' Union (WU)
Address. PO Box 245, 3 Park Street (Reclamation Grounds), Castries
Phone. +1758 452 2620
History and character. Founded 1939 on the recommendation of a commission (appointed by the British government to investigate labour disturbances throughout the then British West Indies). Linked to the St. Lucia Labour Party, the WU is the oldest union in St. Lucia.
International affiliation. ICFTU

Vieux Fort General and Dock Workers' Union
Address. PO Box 224, Theodore Street, Vieux Fort
Phone. +1758 454 6193
Fax. +1758 454 5128
Leadership. Modeste Downes (general secretary)
International affiliation. CTUC

St. Vincent and the Grenadines

Capital: Kingstown
Population: 117,000 (2004 est.)

1 Political and Economic Background

A former British dependency, St. Vincent and the Grenadines became an independent member of the Commonwealth in 1979. The conservative New Democratic Party (NDP) won four successive general elections in 1984, 1989, 1994 and 1998. However, in the 1998 elections, the social democratic Unity Labour Party (ULP), although winning only seven House of Assembly seats to the NDP's eight, took 55% of the vote. The ULP demanded fresh elections and there was a period of unrest until the government in the Grand Beach Accord of May 2000 agreed to hold elections by the end of March 2001. These elections, held on March 28, 2001, resulted in victory for the ULP.

The economy is traditionally based on the cultivation and processing of bananas, this sector still being by far the biggest employer. However, the banana industry has been badly affected by competition from Latin American producers and, in some recent years, by devastating storm damage; the failure to find an adequate solution to the decline of the banana industry was a factor in the defeat of the NDP government in 2001. Tourism and financial services have been targeted for development and in 2003 St. Vincent was removed from the OECD's Financial Action Task Force list of non-cooperative countries after the government took steps to clean up its previously lax offshore financial services regime. Unemployment continues to be a major problem and unofficial estimates have put it for some years at a rate above 30 per cent.

GDP (purchasing power parity) $340m. (2002 est.); GDP per capita (purchasing power parity) $2,900 (2002 est.).

2 Trade Unionism

St. Vincent and the Grenadines joined the International Labour Organization in 1997 and the following year ratified Convention No. 98 (Right to Organize and Collective Bargaining, 1949). It then ratified Convention No. 87 (Freedom of Association and Protection of the Right to Organize, 1948) in 2001. There is no compulsory recognition of trade unions and virtually no employment legislation at all. In practice however, if there is evidence that more than 30 per cent of employees wish for a union, the authorities intervene with the employer to suggest recognition. Union density is only about 10 per cent. There is a legally protected right to strike although under the Essential Services Act workers in the electricity, water, hospitals and police sectors may not go on strike.

3 Trade Union Centre

There is no national trade union centre.

4 Other Trade Union Organizations

Commercial, Technical and Allied Workers' Union (CTAWU)
Address. Union House, PO Box 245, Kingstown
Phone. +1784 45 61525
Fax. +1784 45 71767
E-mail. ctawu@caribsurf.com
Membership. 2,000
International affiliations. ICFTU

National Workers' Movement (NWM)
Address. Suite 3, Burke's Building, Greenville Street, PO Box 1290, Kingstown
Phone. +1784 457 1950
Fax. +1784 456 2858
E-mail. natwork@caribsurf.com
Leadership. Noel Jackson (general secretary)
International affiliation. WCL

St. Vincent and the Grenadines Public Service Union (PSU)
Address. PO Box 875, McKie's Hill, Kingstown
Phone. +1784 457 1801
Fax. +1784 457 1705
Leadership. Harvey Farrell (general secretary)
International affiliation. CTUC

Samoa

Capital: Apia
Population: 178,000 (2004 est.)

1 Political and Economic Background

Samoa (known until 1997 as Western Samoa) achieved full independence in 1962, having previously been under New Zealand administration. There is universal suffrage but the seats in the legislature are reserved for members of the Matai, the traditional clan leaders. The Human Rights Protection Party has won every election since 1982, although politics are primarily based on personal alliances.

The economy is predominantly based on agriculture and fishing, agriculture engaging two-thirds of the workforce and the small manufacturing sector mainly processing agricultural products. Tourism is growing but there is a dependence on development aid and remittances from workers abroad.

GDP (purchasing power parity) $1bn. (2002 est.); GDP per capita (purchasing power parity) $5,600 (2002 est.).

2 Trade Unionism

Workers may by law form and join unions; the US State Department reports that there are no practical obstacles to union membership and that about 20% of the workforce is organized. The Public Service Association (PSA) is the long-established major local union and represents government employees. The Samoa National Union of Workers/Samoa Trades Union Congress was formed in 1995 and is affiliated to the ICFTU. Collective bargaining is not widely practiced in the private sector, but the PSA engages in collective bargaining on behalf of government workers. There is a right to strike in both the private and public sector, subject to public safety limitations. Arbitration and mediation procedures exist, although labour disputes are not common. Samoa is not a member of the International Labour Organization.

3 Trade Union Centre

Samoa National Union of Workers/Samoa Trades Union Congress
Address. PSA House, Fugalei, PO Box 2260, Apia
Phone/fax. +685 22049
E-mail. snuw@lesamoa.net
Leadership. Tutonu Vaomua (president); Su'a Viliamu Sio (general secretary)
Membership. About 3,000
History and character. Founded in 1995 and comprising unions of bank, transport, rural, forestry, public enterprises and community workers. It is campaigning for modernization of the labour laws and for Samoa to join the ILO.
International affiliation. ICFTU; CTUC

4 Other Trade Union Organization

Samoa Public Service Association (PSA)
Address. PO Box 1515, Apia
Phone. +685 24134
Fax. +685 20014
E-mail. psa@samoa.net
Leadership. Apoiliu Warren (general secretary)
International affiliations. CTUC

San Marino

Capital: San Marino
Population: 28,000 (2004 est.)

1 Political and Economic Background

San Marino is a micro-republic entirely surrounded by Italy. Legislative power is vested in a 60-member, elected Grand and General Council; two Council members are appointed every six months to act as Captains–Regent who, with a Congress of State (government) exercise executive power. Following elections in June 2001 a broad "grand coalition" government was formed by the three largest parties, the Christian Democrats, the Socialist Party and the Party of Democrats (the reformed communists).

Tourism generates more than 50% of GDP, and there is also banking, light manufacturing and agriculture. Living standards are similar to northern Italy.

GDP (purchasing power parity) $940m. (2001 est.); GDP per capita (purchasing power parity) $34,600 (2001 est.).

2 Trade Unionism

San Marino joined the International Labour Organization in 1982 and ratified ILO Conventions No. 87 (Freedom of Association and Protection of the Right to Organize, 1948) and No. 98 (Right to Organize and Collective Bargaining, 1949) in 1986.

All employees, except members of the armed forces, may join trade unions and about half the workforce (which comprises some 10,000 Sammarinese citizens and 4,000 Italians) are organized. There are two long-established confederations. The Confederazione Sammarinese del Lavoro (CSdL), founded in 1943, was the only recognized union until the recognition of trade union pluralism in 1957 and the formation of the Confederazione Democratica dei Lavoratori Sammarinesi (CDLS). During the 1960s these two groups tended to adopt similar policies, and in 1976 they formed the Centrale Sindicale Unitaire (CSU – Central United Union) with the ultimate objective of creating an organic union. This goal has not yet been achieved after three decades although the CSdL and the CDLS are both now (since the CSdL joined in 1997) affiliated to the ICFTU.

Collective bargaining agreements are legally binding. A tripartite conciliation committee exists to resolve disputes and strikes tend to be infrequent and brief. However, there was a general stike in 2002, the first for 15 years.

3 Trade Union Centres

Confederazione Democratica dei Lavoratori Sammarinesi (CDLS)
Democratic Confederation of San Marino Workers
Address. Via Cinque Febbraio, 17 – Loc. Fiorina C-3, 47895 Domagnano, Republic of San Marino
Phone. +378 549 962080
Fax. +378 549 962095
E-mail. info@cdls.sm
Website. www.cdls.sm (Italian; some information in English)
Leadership. Marco Beccari (secretary-general)
History and character. Founded in 1957. General orientation is social Catholic, but it believes in trade union autonomy from political organizations. It comprises four federations for different groups of workers and a pensioners' federation.
International affiliations. ICFTU; ETUC

Confederazione Sammarinese del Lavoro (CSdL)
San Marino Confederation of Labour
Address. C. Square 17, Via Cinque Febbraio, 47895 Domagnano, Republic of San Marino
Phone. +378 549 962060
Fax. +378 549 962075
E-mail. info@csdl.sm
Website. www.csdl.sm (Italian only)
Leadership. Giovanni Ghiotti (secretary–general)
Membership. 2,450 in five affiliated federations.
History and character. Founded in 1943. Joined ETUC in 1991 and the ICFTU in 1997.
International affiliations. ICFTU; ETUC

São Tomé and Príncipe

Capital: São Tomé
Population: 182,000 (2004 est.)

1 Political and Economic Background

São Tomé and Príncipe achieved independence from Portugal in 1975 and was then run as a one-party state by the Marxist Movement for the Liberation of São Tomé and Príncipe (MLSTP) until a new constitution providing for a multi-party system was approved by a 1990 referendum. The most recent legislative elections held in March 2002 were closely contested by the revamped Movement for the Liberation of São Tomé and Príncipe-Social Democratic Party (MLSTP-PSD) and the Democratic Movement Force for Change/Party of Democratic Governance (MDFM/PCD) and both went on to form a coalition government. In a presidential election held in July 2001, the candidate of the Independent Democratic Action (ADI), Fradique de Menezes, defeated the MLSTP-PSD candidate and former President, Manuel Pinto da Costa.

Most of the workforce is engaged in subsistence agriculture. The major cash crop is cocoa, produced in state-run plantations. Cocoa production has substantially declined in recent years because of drought and mismanagement, but strengthening prices helped boost export earnings in 2003. There is heavy reliance on external aid. However, the government is optimistic about the development of petroleum resources in its territorial waters in the oil-rich Gulf of Guinea.

GDP (purchasing power parity) $214m. (2003 est.); GDP per capita (purchasing power parity) $1,200 (2003 est.).

2 Trade Unionism

São Tomé and Príncipe joined the International Labour Organization in 1982 and ratified ILO Convention No. 87 (Freedom of Association and Protection of the Right to Organize, 1948) and Convention No. 98 (Right to Organize and Collective Bargaining, 1949) in 1992.

Trade unionism was severely curbed during Portuguese rule. In the 1980s a single trade union system was set up under the ruling party. At the beginning of the 1990s there was a move towards political pluralism and the 1990 constitution provides for freedom of association. However, the modern formal economy is small and there has been little development of trade unions, with most activity in the public sector. There is constitutional provision for collective bargaining although most negotiations are with the government as the primary formal sector employer. There are ICFTU and WCL affiliates.

3 Trade Union Centres

Organizaçâo Nacional dos Trabalhadores de São Tomé e Príncipe – Central Sindical (ONTSTP-CS)
National Organization of the Workers of São Tomé and Príncipe – Central Union
Address. Rua de Cabo Verde, Caixa Postal 8, São Tomé
Phone. +239 22 24 31
Fax. +239 22 66 03
E-mail. ontstpdis@cstome.net
International affiliation. ICFTU

União Geral dos Trabalhadores de São Tomé e Príncipe (UGT/STP)
General Union of the Workers of São Tomé and Príncipe
Address. Rua de Creche, BP 272, São Tomé
Phone. +239 12 33 443
Fax. +239 12 21 466
Leadership. Manuel da Costa Carlos (secretary-general)
International affiliation. WCL

Saudi Arabia

Capital: Riyadh
Population: 25.8 m. (including 5.6 m. non-nationals) (2004 est.)

1 Political and Economic Background

Saudi Arabia is an absolute monarchy ruled according to a conservative interpretation of the laws and precepts of Islam. King Fahd has been the ruler since 1982. He is also the Prime Minister and his Council of Ministers includes family members in most key posts. The kingdom has no elected parliament and no political parties and freedom of association and expression is strictly limited.

Saudi Arabia has the world's largest proven oil reserves and is the world's leading oil exporter. Oil generates 75% of government revenues. A fall in the price of oil in the late 1990s led to relative austerity and budget cuts, but the government has more recently benefited from oil price rises. In December 2004 the kingdom's oil revenues for 2004 were projected at $106bn, the highest ever in nominal terms, with production running at close to capacity. The government announced surplus revenues of $26bn for 2004 and that it would be able to increase government spending by 40% in 2005 while maintaining a balanced budget. It has also been able to cut the large public debt to 66% of GDP.

Despite its oil wealth Saudi Arabia has immense social tensions arising from its rapidly expanding population (which has increased an average 4% per annum since 1975), the great disparities of wealth, the failure to create a broad non-oil economic base, and dissatisfaction with the ruling elite (the extended royal family comprising 20,000 individuals) which cannot find legitimate expression. To avoid the unbalanced development and profligacy that accompanied the 1970s oil boom, the government has for years officially sought to encourage diversification and private sector investment but with mixed results – the government retains control over many key sectors and only 40% of GDP is generated by the private sector. There is high unemployment among Saudi youth, who are often poorly educated in modern skills, alongside a continuing heavy dependence on foreign workers, both unskilled and technical – there are more than five million foreign workers. Since 1995 the government has promoted a campaign to increase the proportion of Saudis in the workforce, although in the private sector this remains negligible. Women constitute only 4% of the workforce.

GDP (purchasing power parity) $287.8bn. (2004 est.); GDP per capita (purchasing power parity) $11,800 (2004 est.).

2 Trade Unionism

Saudi Arabia has been a member of the International Labour Organization since 1976, but has ratified neither Convention No. 87 (Freedom of Association and Protection of the Right to Organize, 1948) nor No. 98 (Right to Organize and Collective Bargaining, 1949).

Trade unions are illegal and dismissal, imprisonment or (in the case of foreign workers) expulsion follow attempts at organization. Trade unions are considered to violate the principles of Islam. The WFTU recognizes an exiled "Workers' Union of Saudi Arabia" but this can not organize within the country.

Collective bargaining is forbidden under Saudi law. Wages are set directly by employers and vary according to the nationality of the worker. Strikes are illegal, although the ICFTU reported that work stoppages took place in 2001 by workers demanding payment of their wages.

In April 2002 legislation was introduced to permit the establishment of the first Workers' Committees. The Committees have a limited remit to "find dialogue between employees and employers in order to improve the level of work performance and eliminate technical and material obstacles impeding that". Only one Committee may be formed in each enterprise, and then only in workplaces with more than 100 employees. Membership of the Committees is further restricted to Saudis aged over 25 who have worked for two years at that workplace. These limited reforms have attracted international approval as an advance on the blanket ban on worker organization that existed previously.

Domestic servants are not protected by labour laws. Foreign workers, who depend on their employers for residency, are reportedly sometimes victims of non-payment of wages or other abuses, and do not complain to the labour courts for fear of deportation. Employed Saudis work mainly in the public sector and private sector employers are reported to be reluctant to take on Saudis because they are difficult to dismiss if they do not do their job. Women face extensive discrimination at work and may participate in only limited areas of the economy.

Senegal

Capital: Dakar
Population: 10.85 m. (2004 est.)

1 Political and Economic Background

Senegal achieved full independence from France in 1960 and was then led by the Socialist Party of Senegal (PSS) for four decades. Senegal had a de facto one-party system in the period 1964-74. In 1974 the first opposition party was permitted, and after 1976 a greater degree of pluralism was allowed. Abdou Diouf became President in 1981 and then held the office until defeated by Abdoulaye Wade of the Senegalese Democratic Party (PDS) in March 2000. The handover of power from the PSS was orderly and Diouf withdrew from politics. The PDS won a landslide victory in legislative elections held in April 2001.

In recent years Senegal has sought to liberalize its economy, privatizing state enterprises and dismantling price controls and subsidies. Real GDP grew by an average of 5% per annum in the period 1995-2003. About 70% of the workforce are involved in agriculture, much of it at subsistence level, and there is a limited industrial sector. However, Senegal also realized full Internet connectivity in 1996, creating a mini-boom in information technology-based services. As a member of the West African Economic and Monetary Union (WAEMU), Senegal is working toward greater regional integration with a unified external tariff.

GDP (purchasing power parity) $17.09bn. (2004 est.); GDP per capita (purchasing power parity) $1,600 (2004 est.).

2 Trade Unionism

Trade unions first developed prior to independence under French rule. Following independence, Senegal ratified ILO Convention No. 87 (Freedom of Association and Protection of the Right to Organize, 1948) in 1960 and Convention No. 98 (Right to Organize and Collective Bargaining, 1949) in 1961. In 1969 the Confédération Nationale des Travailleurs Sénégalais (CNTS) was established as the sole trade union centre, with affiliation to the only permitted party, the Union Progressiste Sénégalais (UPS, known from 1976 as the PSS). Political and trade union pluralism was re-established after 1976. At different times there have been several rival centres to the CNTS, including groupings of independent unions, but it has remained dominant, retaining its close relationship to the PSS.

Following Wade's victory in the 2000 presidential election, the CNTS's support for the PSS became a source of tension with the new President's supporters. In an attempt to secure union backing for his party, the PDS, President Wade facilitated the split of the CNTS into two separate unions: the CNTS and the Confédération Nationale des Travailleurs Sénégalais - Force du Changement (CNTS-FC). In 2002, CNTS-FC supporters attacked and burnt the CNTS headquarters. One man died, and others were severely burned. The police arrested nine persons, including senior CNTS-FC officials Cheikh Diop, Matar Sèye, Dame Lô and Doudou Fall Niang. Six of the defendants were convicted of unlawfully demonstrating, and three were acquitted. They received sentences of 18 months in prison, which was equivalent to the time they had served in pretrial detention.

The new constitution, adopted in January 2001, appeared to undermine the right to strike by stipulating that strike action must not infringe upon the freedom to work or jeopardise the enterprise. Under the constitution and labour code all workers have the right of association, and there are provisions against anti-union discrimination by employers, although government approval is needed for a union to be registered. The unions are highly organized in the small formal economy and there is also some recruitment in the informal sector. There is collective bargaining and the Ministry of Labour provides mediation.

3 Trade Union Centres

Confédération Nationale des Travailleurs Sénégalais (CNTS)
National Confederation of Senegalese Workers
Address. 7 Avenue du Président Laminé Gueye, BP 937, Dakar
Phone. +221 821 0491
Fax. +221 821 7771
E-mail. cnts@sentoo.sn
Website. www.cnts.sn
Leadership. Madia Diop (secretary-general)
Membership. 60,000
History and character. Founded in 1969, the CNTS has historically been allied to the PSS, which was the governing party from independence until losing the presidency in 2000.
International affiliation. ICFTU

Union Nationale des Syndicats Autonomes du Sénégal (UNSAS)
National Union of Autonomous Trade Unions of Senegal
Address. BP 10841, Dakar
Phone. +221 825 3261
Fax. +221 824 8013
E-mail. unsas@ketissacana.sn
Leadership. Mademba Sock (secretary-general)
History and character. UNSAS is he main rival of the CNTS. It is a federation of strategically important unions: electrical, telecommunication, hospital, railroad and sugar workers, teachers, and hydrology technicians.
International affiliation. ICFTU

4 Other Trade Union Organizations

Union Démocratique des Travailleurs du Sénégal (UDTS)
Democratic Union of Senegalese Workers
Address. Rue 10 (face école 5), no. 1369 Pikine, BP 7124, Medina-DKR, Dakar
Phone. +221 343 897
Fax. +221 834 0595
E-mail. trintern@telecompus.sn
Leadership. Sow Alioune (secretary-general)
International affiliation. WCL

Serbia and Montenegro

Capital: Belgrade
Population: 10.83 m. (2004 est.)

1 Political and Economic Background

The former Socialist Federal Republic of Yugoslavia (SFRY) collapsed in the period 1991–92 when the constituent republics of Slovenia, Croatia, Bosnia-Herzegovina and Macedonia, with more than half the population, declared their independence. This was a consequence both of each republic's own respective national aspirations and the rise of a domineering nationalism among the Serbian population (the largest single group) within Yugoslavia. In April 1992 creation of the Federal Republic of Yugoslavia (FRY) was proclaimed but as this comprised only two of the former republics (Serbia and Montenegro), and was entirely dominated by Serbia, it failed to achieve universal recognition as the legitimate successor to the SFRY. Throughout the 1990s power was held by Slobodan Milosevic, the leader of the Socialist Party of Serbia (SPS, the descendant of the former ruling League of Communists), who was successively President of Serbia and then (from 1997) President of Yugoslavia. Under him from 1991–95 a series of wars was waged against all the former Yugoslav republics other than Macedonia. In 1999 Serbian efforts to crush the rebellious Albanian majority in the Serbian province of Kosovo triggered a massive intervention by NATO, and in June 1999 control of Kosovo passed to the United Nations Interim Administrative Mission in Kosovo (UNMIK). In addition, under President Milo Djukanovic (elected in 1997) Montenegro effectively became detached from Yugoslav federal structures and threatened to break away altogether.

In October 2000 Milosevic initially sought to hang on to the presidency after apparently suffering defeat in elections but was forced to concede to opposition leader Vojislav Kostunica after mass demonstrations throughout the country. In December 2000 opposition parties overwhelmingly defeated Milosevic's SPS in elections in Serbia. In June 2001 the new Yugoslav government handed over Milosevic to the International Criminal Tribunal for the former Yugoslavia at The Hague. Montenegrin pressure for a looser relationship culminated in 2003 in the transformation of the FRY into the State Union of Serbia and Montenegro, with the two republics represented in a joint unicameral legislature. However, within the state union most powers (except defence, foreign affairs, foreign economic relations and human rights) reside in the two constituent republics. Although the UN in June 1999 formallly reaffirmed the sovereignty and territorial integrity of the FRY, Kosovo has since that time been de facto a UN protectorate and no early resolution of its final status seems likely.

The FRY was created against a background of war and economic collapse as the inter-dependent economic structure of the former SFRY fell apart. Under Milosevic the economy was characterized by corruption and cronyism (with key posts in state enterprises held by Milosevic supporters), the lack of a transparent and equitable framework for private investment, and chronic inefficiency and under-employment. These problems were exacerbated by the application of international sanctions. Plummeting output, unemployment, widespread wage arrears, shortages, and anxieties about the forthcoming winter in the face of international sanctions were factors that led to Milosevic's loss of the presidency in October 2000. After the fall of Milosevic Yugoslavia rejoined the IMF and World Bank and benefited from debt rescheduling and write-offs. The economy remains at a low level, however, wth the Serbian and Montenegrin economies separately managed and with a detached Kosovo heavily dependent on international funding.

GDP (purchasing power parity) $23.89bn. (2003 est.); GDP per capita (purchasing power parity) $2,200 (2003 est.).

2 Trade Unionism

Yugoslavia joined the International Labour Organization in 1919, but withdrew from 1949 to 1951. It ratified ILO Conventions No. 87 (Freedom of Association and Protection of the Right to Organize, 1948) and No. 98 (Right to Organize and Collective Bargaining, 1949) in 1958. These ratifications were considered to apply to the FRY. However, following the fall of Milosevic, Yugoslavia re-ratified Conventions 87 and 98 (and other conventions) in November 2000, these therefore applying to the federated Serbia and Montenegro.

The trade unions of the former SFRY were essentially the product of the establishment of communist rule after World War II and the subsequent re-modelling of the economy and political and social relations through the principle of self-management. The unions were organized through the Confederation of Trade Unions of Yugoslavia (Savez Sindikata Jugoslavije, SSJ). Neither the national constitution nor the law formally prohibited the formation of unions outside the structure of the SSJ, although as a named organization it had various rights and responsibilities, but no unions outside it appeared before 1988. In Slovenia and Croatia independent unions developed in 1989 and the official union councils there endorsed the principle of freedom of association. The June 1990 (11th) SSJ congress withdrew from the Socialist Alliance of Working Peoples of Yugoslavia, the coordinating body for all communist institutions in the country, and accepted that it would have to function in a pluralistic environment. Thereafter the former federal structure collapsed with the rise of nationalism in the constituent republics. Much of the panoply of industrial relations institutions and practices, including the self-management system for enterprises, dissolved in the face of war, secession and economic collapse.

SERBIA

In Serbia the trade unions have survived in the state enterprises, where some 60-70% of workers are unionized, but only about 5% of workers in the private sector are in unions. The old official unions are now organized as the Confederation of Autonomous Trade Unions of Serbia (Savez Samostalnih Sindikata Srbije, SSSS or SSS), which retained the assets of the former SSJ and benefited from automatic check-off of union dues in state enterprises. The Savez Samostalnih Sindikata in the 1990s claimed 1.8 million members but now reports 850,000. The other leading centre is Nezavisnost (Independence), formed in 1991, which has about 180,000 members and is a member of the ICFTU. The Association of Free and Independent Trade Unions (ASNS) emerged in the late 1990s as a formation linked to political forces opposed to

Milosevic, its first president becoming Minister of Labour in the Democratic Opposition of Serbia coalition government that took office after Milosevic's fall. These three organizations compete for membership. Most other independent unions operate in individual sectors of the economy but formation of independent unions in the state sector has generally faced opposition from enterprise directors.

Collective bargaining was totally dominated by the SSS under Milosevic, although in practice effective collective bargaining was undermined by widespread unemployment and the inability of enterprises to pay wages. However, under the labour law adopted in December 2001 collective bargaining rights were opened up to unions representing 15% of employees in an enterprise or 20% in local and central government. Despite this, collective bargaining occurs mainly in the state sector. In the private sector there are many unregistered workers and only a small minority of employers are in the Serbian employers' association, making collective bargaining of limited application, while widespread unemployment also weakens the unions' position. In wide areas of the economy strikers are required to maintain a minimum service level. However, strikes and other protests have been recorded in various sectors of the economy in recent years over such issues as wage arrears and privatization. A tripartite Social and Economic Council was established in 2001.

Asocijacija Slobodnih i Nezavisnih Sindikata (ASNS)
Association of Free and Independent Trade Unions (AFITU)
Address. Karadjordjeva 71, 11000 Belgrade
Phone. +381 11 623671
Fax. +381 11 632872
E-mail. asns@asns.org.yu
Website. www.asns.org.yu
Leadership. Bratislav Djuric (president); Ranka Savic (general secretary)
History and character. The ASNS was founded in July 1996 under the leadership of Dragan Milovanovic as an opposition trade union. It formed part of the broad-based Democratic Opposition of Serbia coalition that rallied behind Kostunica in the 2000 elections and participated in the strikes and demonstrations that led to the fall of Milosevic. ASNS leader Milovanovic went on to become Minister of Labour and Employment in the new Democratic Opposition of Serbia government, though the Labour Party of Serbia he led for the December 2003 Serbian elections made no impact. The ASNS held its second congress in October 2002 under the slogan "the strength of Serbia", when it claimed to have 300,000 members in 2,000 union branches – although other indications suggest it is much smaller. At that time it called for "democratization and economic revival" but criticized the government for being too cautious in advancing reform. It accepts that privatization is an inevitable part of the process of change but calls for transparency and for the trade unions to be actively involved to protect the workers' interests. The ASNS continued to support the DOS coalition in the 2003 Serbian elections and current ASNS president Bratislav Djuric sits in the Serbian National Assembly

Ujedinjeni Gradjanski Sindikati "Nezavisnost" (UGS "Nezavisnost")
United Branch Trade Unions "Independence"
Address. Nusiceva 4/V, 11000 Belgrade
Phone. +381 11 323 8226
Fax. +381 11 324 4118
E-mail. nezavisn@eunet.yu
Website. www.nezavisnost.org.yu (Serbian; English)
Leadership. Branislav Canak (president)
Membership. 180,000
History and character. Nezavisnost is a federation of 13 member unions, in all the main sectors of the economy, and says that it is active in over 1,000 companies throughout Serbia. Its oldest affiliates are the Metal Workers' Union and the Independent Media Union (founded 1991) and the Teachers' Union (founded 1992). It has regional offices in 10 provincial cities.

Nezavisnost organizers under Milosevic faced problems including job suspensions or downgrading, barring from workplaces, compulsory leave, disciplinary proceedings and dismissal. Nezavisnost led strikes of teachers and health workers in 1998 but in 1999–2000 focused on political action campaigns. Nezavisnost demanded constitutional and legal protection of human and trade union rights and a genuine multi-party democracy. It accused the official trade unions of the SSS of supporting the Milosevic regime and itself participated in the opposition Yugoslav Action Group (Jugoslovenska Akcija) with other civic groups. It played a role in the fall of Milosevic in October 2000, campaigning for the opposition and a high turn-out in the elections, and subsequently backing strikes when Milosevic at first refused to accept defeat. It now emphasizes its independence of political parties and the government and prior to the December 2003 Serbian elections signed co-operation agreements with most of the main democratic parties. Despite the change of regime in Belgrade, Nezavisnost still complains that it is harassed by officials and enterprise directors and that it is subject to repeated delays in registering its affiliates (registration of unions being obligatory) while its members are subject to pay cuts, demotion and intimidation.
International affiliation. ICFTU; ETUC

Savez Samostalnih Sindikata Srbije (SSSS, or SSS)
Confederation of Autonomous Trade Unions of Serbia (CATUS)
Address. Decanska 14 St, 11000 Belgrade
Phone. +381-11 3233 317 (international dept.)
E-mail. intdep@sindikat.org.yu (international dept)
Website. www.sindikat.org.yu
Leadership. Milenko Smiljanic (president); Zoran Vujovic (secretary)
Membership. Reports 850,000 members (80% of them dues paying)
History and character. This is the successor organization to the Yugoslav era SSJ and claims descent from a

workers' confederation established in the then kingdom of Serbia in 1903. It has benefited from inheriting the assets of the SSJ. The official unions from the early 1990s generally supported Milosevic's mix of strident Serbian nationalism and unreformed socialism and subsidization of inefficient state enterprises, although there was periodic unrest caused by inflation, unemployment and wage arrears. On occasions workers in official unions joined with members of independent unions in protest strikes. In August 1999 the increasingly-imperilled Milosevic government concluded an agreement with the SSS whereby its members would get fuel at subsidized prices in the winter of 1999–2000. Following the fall of Milosevic in October 2000, the confederation leadership changed, with Milenko Smiljanic becoming president, a position to which he was subsequently elected by the SSS conference in April 2002. The confederation comprises 29 professional federations and 106 local organizations. Its structure includes the Autonomous Confederation of Trade Unions of Kosovo and Metochia, representing Serbian workers in Kosovo, whose membership fell from 80,000 to 17,000 by 2003 after Serbian forces left the province, with many Serbs following in their wake. In June 2003 the SSS staged demonstrations in Belgrade against government social and economic policies, leading to criticism from the other centres that it now protested more vigorously than it did in the Milosevic era.

MONTENEGRO

In Montenegro, the Confederation of Independent Trade Unions, affiliated to the ICFTU, is the trade union centre. The main concerns are mass unemployment, wage arrears, and the impact of nationalism on regional stability. A new labour law adopted in 2003 was considered to be helpful in facilitating collective bargaining. However, the unions have little basis in the growing private sector and informal economies. A Social and Economic Council was established with effect from 2002.

Confederation of Independent Trade Unions of Montenegro (CITUM)
Savez Samostalnih Sindikata Crne Gore (SSSCG)
Address. Novaka Miloseva 29/1, 8100 Podgorica
Phone. +381 81 230547
Fax. +381 81 230499
Leadership. Danilo Popovic (president); Mico Radovic (secretary)
Membership. 90,000
E-mail. ssscg@cg.yu
Website. www.ssscg.cg.yu (Serbian only)
History and character. The CITUM was founded in 1991. It split in 1998 between a majority group, led by president Danilo Popovic, broadly supporting the line of then Montenegrin President (and now Prime Minister) Milo Djukanovic in seeking greater autonomy from Serbia, and a pro-Milosevic minority. However, the confederation criticized the Montenegrin government for adopting labour legislation without consulting the unions. It comprises some one thousand branch unions and emphasizes it is based on the principles of voluntary membership, solidarity and independence.
International affiliation. ICFTU

KOSOVO

In Kosovo (Kosova in Albanian) the Confederation of Independent Trade Unions of Kosova (BSPK) was founded among the Albanian workforce (Albanians constituting close to 90% of the province's population) in 1990 but faced severe harassment by the Serbian authorities. Following the 1999 expulsion of Serbian forces and the creation of the de facto UN protectorate it has been the main trade union organization in Kosovo. Although UNMIK regulations provide for the right to form and belong to trade unions, this is widely disregarded in practice in the private sector. With the unions weak and unemployment high, collective bargaining is not widespread. The BSPK, UNMIK and Chamber of Commerce have reached tripartite agreement to deal with labour disputes. Some public sector workers and workers in state enterprises have staged strikes in the UNMIK era. The Confederation of Autonomous Trade Unions of Serbia (SSS) has a branch in Kosovo, representing Serbian workers, but its membership has declined drastically with the exodus of much of the Serbian population. Despite underlying political differences, it has collaborated to some degree with the BSPK on issues such as privatization and unemployment.

Confederation of Independent Trade Unions of Kosova (BSPK)
Leadership. Bahri Shabani (chairman)
History and character. The BSPK was founded in 1990 and developed among the Albanian workforce in opposition to the official unions. It claimed to have organized 250,000 members in 24 unions. In March 1999, however, BSPK president Agim Hajrizi was arrested by the Yugoslav authorities and murdered, and union records were destroyed. Following the establishment of a UN protectorate under UNMIK, BSPK began to reconstruct itself. By 2003 it was reported to have 100,000 members, although half of these were unemployed. Its membership is mainly in the state-owned enterprises and it is represented in the Kosovo Assembly. In addition it has one seat on the eight-member Kosovo Privatization Agency, with the other seats being taken by UNMIK and the Kosovo government; although not opposed to privatization per se it has criticized aspects of the privatization process, calling for a greater share of the assets to be given to the workers in privatized enterprises. In September 2004 it signed a tripartite agreement with the government and the Kosova Chamber of Commerce, covering issues such as worker contracts, health and safety, holidays and seniority payments, the first such tripartite agreement to be reached in the province. It was seen as paving the way for a new labour law.

Seychelles

Capital: Victoria
Population: 81,000 (2004 est.)

1 Political and Economic Background

Seychelles achieved independence from the UK in 1976. France-Albert René came to power in a coup in 1977 and established a one-party state with his left-wing Seychelles People's Progressive Front (SPPF) as the sole permitted party. The reform wave seen throughout much of Africa at the start of the 1990s caused the SPPF to endorse a move to political pluralism in December 1991; in April 1992 the President deposed in the 1977 coup, James Mancham, returned from exile, and in 1993 multi-party elections were held. These resulted in victory for the SPPF, a result repeated in legislative elections held in 1993, 1998 and 2002.

President René was re-elected as sole candidate in polling in 1979, 1984 and 1989 and retained the presidency despite challenges in 1993 and 1998. René called further presidential elections two years ahead of time in 2001, following a constitutional amendment in May 2000 relating to consecutive executive mandates. He was re-elected, but with a significantly reduced share of the vote and there were widespread opposition claims of government cheating. In February 2004 René announced his intention to retire and two months later he handed over the presidency to James Michel, hitherto Vice President and secretary-general of the SPPF.

Seychelles is a relatively prosperous country. Economic growth has been led by the tourist sector, which employs about 30% of the labour force and provides more than 70% of hard currency earnings, and by tuna fishing. In recent years the government has encouraged foreign investment in order to upgrade hotels and other services. At the same time, the government has moved to reduce the dependence on tourism by promoting the development of farming, fishing, and small-scale manufacturing.

GDP (purchasing power parity) $626m. (2002 est.); GDP per capita (purchasing power parity) $7,800 (2002 est.).

2 Trade Unionism

Seychelles has been a member of the International Labour Organization since 1977, and ratified ILO Convention No. 87 (Freedom of Association and Protection of the Right to Organize, 1948) in 1978 and Convention No. 98 (Right to Organize and Collective Bargaining, 1949) in 1999.

Following the coup which brought the SPPF to power, all previously existing trade unions were coordinated in 1978 in the National Workers' Union (Seychelles) (NWUS). According to the constitution of the SPPF the NWUS functioned under the direction of the Front, which had to approve every decision of the union. Following the move to political pluralism in the early 1990s the 1993 Industrial Relations Act ended the monopoly of the NWUS. The SPPF-associated centre is now called the Seychelles Federation of Workers' Unions (SFWU) and there is also an independent Seychelles Workers' Union (SWU). Union density is estimated at 15-20%. All workers may join unions other than police and prison officers, the armed forces and firefighters. Efforts to organize an independent union in the government service have been frustrated by the government.

The Industrial Relations Act provides for collective bargaining but the government is empowered to review and approve all agreements. In the public sector, which accounts for more than half of formal employment, the government sets rates of pay.

3 Trade Union Centre

Seychelles Federation of Workers' Unions (SFWU)
Address. Maison du Peuple, PO Box 154, Victoria
Phone. +248 225 226 18
Fax. +248 2253 51
E-mail. seyworkersunion@yahoo.com
Leadership. B. Adonis (general secretary)
History and character. This is the successor to the National Workers' Union (Seychelles) set up in 1978 by the ruling SPPF. The SFWU no longer has its predecessor's monopoly status but remains the leading trade union organization in Seychelles and close to the SPPF.
International affiliation. ICFTU; CTUC

Sierra Leone

Capital: Freetown
Population: 5.88 m. (2004 est.)

1 Political and Economic Background

Sierra Leone achieved independence from the United Kingdom in 1961, originally as a constitutional monarchy, but from 1971 as a republic. In 1978 the All People's Congress of President Siaka Stevens was declared the sole legal party, and the country remained a one-party state until a 1991 referendum approved the introduction of multi-party politics. In April 1992, however, a military coup took place and all political activity was banned until 1995. In February 1996 elections finally took place, resulting in victory for the Sierra Leone People's Party (SLPP) and its presidential candidate, Ahmad Tejan Kabbah, whose grip on power was tenuous in the face of a continuing rebellion by the Revolutionary United Front (RUF) of Foday Sankoh. A further military coup took place in May 1997, led by Lt.-Col. Johnny Paul Koroma, who gained the backing of the RUF. In March 1998 Koroma was ousted by Nigerian-led forces sent under the auspices of the Economic Community of West African States (ECOWAS), and Kabbah restored as President.

In July 1999 the West brokered an agreement, notwithstanding evidence of atrocities committed by the RUF, that involved the RUF in power-sharing and allowed it to retain effective control over the country's diamond mines. UN forces sent to monitor the agreement subsequently became hostages of the RUF and in May 2000 British troops intervened, supervising an evacuation of foreign nationals and detaining the RUF's leader, Foday Sankoh. A further ceasefire in November 2000 initiated a process of disarmament ending in January 2002, and in May 2002 presidential and legislative elections were held. These resulted in an overwhelming victory for President Kabbah and the SLP – the RUF, converted into the Revolutionary United Front Party (RUFP), failed to win a single seat in the elections. Many refugees from the decade of conflict remain in neighbouring countries.

About two-thirds of the workforce are engaged in subsistence agriculture although there is also mining, notably of diamonds. There is some light manufacturing industry but the formal private sector has been set back by persistent conflict in recent years. The country has a dependence on external assistance.

GDP (purchasing power parity) $3.06bn. (2004 est.); GDP per capita (purchasing power parity) $500 (2004 est.).

2 Trade Unionism

There is a long history of trade unionism in Sierra Leone. In 1919 and 1926 there were strikes by railway workers, which were ruthlessly suppressed. In 1938 a strike by Marbella coal miners resulted in the colonial administration passing labour laws that legitimized the role of unions. Trade unions were well established by the time of independence from the British in 1961. The national trade union centre is the Sierra Leone Labour Congress (SLLC). The SLLC was active in campaigning for political pluralism in the early 1990s and was prominent in opposing the military coups of 1992 and 1997.

Sierra Leone ratified ILO Conventions No. 87 (Freedom of Association and Protection of the Right to Organize, 1948) and No. 98 (Right to Organize and Collective Bargaining, 1949) in 1961. The constitution provides for freedom of association other than for the police and the armed forces. Union members are found in the small manufacturing sector and in white-collar urban professions such as government and teaching. However, the great majority of the workforce are engaged in subsistence agriculture or informal activities and are not in unions. Union membership is also believed to have fallen in recent years because of the dislocation caused by conflict. The once mighty Mineworkers' Union had 80,000 members before all of the mining companies closed. The National Union of Teachers is now the largest union with around 25,000 members. The law provides a framework for collective bargaining and collective bargaining does occur in the formal sector. There is a right to strike but strikers have no protection from dismissal.

3 Trade Union Centre

Sierra Leone Labour Congress (SLLC)
Address. PO Box 1333, Freetown
Phone. +232 2 226 869
Fax. +232 2 224 439
E-mail. sllc@sierratel.sl
Leadership. Uriah O.H. Davies (president); Kandeh B. Yilla (general secretary)
History and character. The SLLC was founded in 1976–77 in succession to a number of earlier centres. In 1981 it came into conflict with the government, rejecting its emphasis on external factors as responsible for the country's economic difficulties. Strikes organized by the SLLC led to looting, the detention of numerous trade union leaders, and a number of deaths. Ibrahim Langley, then SLLC president, was appointed a nominated MP by President Stevens in 1982, shortly after he had announced the dismissal as SLLC general secretary of James Kabia, the main organizer of the 1981 strikes. Sweeping emergency regulations giving the government extensive powers were introduced in 1987 following a series of strikes by public sector workers over salary non-payment. They were extended for 12 months the following year, after which the SLLC played a major part in trying to obtain a smooth transition to pluralist democracy, while guarding its political independence.

In the aftermath of the 1992 military coup, property belonging to the SLLC was taken over by the incoming regime; the passport of its general secretary Kandeh Yilla was confiscated and he was for a time ordered to report daily to the police. Two years later after continuing civil strife, Yilla was reported by the ICFTU to be in fear of his life following death threats.

Following the May 1997 coup that overthrew President Kabbah, the new regime confiscated vehicles and other property belonging to the SLLC and its affiliates. The SLLC called on workers to engage in stay-at-home protests until the elected government was restored. The SLLC has received international trade union support for its work for peace and reconciliation in Sierra Leone, which includes providing training and income generation projects for ex-combatants. After the RUF forces of Foday Sankoh attacked UN peacekeepers in April 2000, the SLLC and civic groups organized thousands of demonstrators to join a peace march on May 8. RUF fighters fired on the demonstrators, killing 22, among them the SLLC's finance officer.

The SLLC plays an important role in providing skills and education on democracy and good governance issues in cooperation with NGOs and international trade unions.
International affiliation. ICFTU; CTUC

4 Other Trade Union Organization

Sierra Leone Confederation of Trade Unions (SLCTU)
Address. PO Box 1333, Freetown
Phone. +232 22-226869
History and character. Founded in 1996. SLCTU president John P.F. Cowray was killed by RUF rebels on Jan. 22, 1999
International affiliation. WCL

Singapore

Capital: Singapore City
Population: 4.35 m. (2004 est.)

1 Political and Economic Background

Singapore achieved internal self-rule from the United Kingdom in 1959, and four years later joined the Federation of Malaysia. On leaving the Federation in 1965, the Republic of Singapore became an independent sovereign state. It has been ruled continuously since that time by the conservative and authoritarian People's Action Party (PAP), which in the most recent elections (for a five-year term) in November 2001 won 82 of the 84 elective seats in parliament, being unopposed in 55 seats and taking over 75% of the vote in the 29 contested seats. There have been only three Prime Ministers since 1959: Lee Kuan Yew (1959-90), Goh Chok Tong (1990-2004) and (since August 2004) Lee Hsien Loong, Lee Kuan Yew's eldest son. The continuity is emphasized by the fact that Lee Kuan Yew still remains "minister mentor". There is tight censorship and opposition leaders have been fined and imprisoned in recent years for the offence of "speaking in public without a permit."

Singapore is a city-state that has developed one of the most dynamic and successful economies in Asia, serving as an international trading centre as well as possessing a substantial modern manufacturing base. It proved able to weather the severe 1997–98 Asian financial crisis far better than most regional economies but was then affected by the world economic downturn at the start of the new century. The economy grew by only 1.1% in 2003 but growth was expected to run as high as 8%-9% in 2004, buoyed by strong global demand in export sectors such as electronics. While Singapore has a free market economy, the government has historically played a driving role in shaping investment and economic development. The government seeks to maintain Singapore's position, in the face of high labour costs, by raising productivity through technology and focusing on high value-added industries. It is also now, in the face of globalization, moving to change the previous model of development to deregulate key sectors such as banking, power and insurance, and reducing protectionism. Unemployment was typically only 2% before the economic difficulties from the late 1990s onwards, which pushed levels up; however by September 2004 unemployment had subsided to only 3.4%, the lowest since 1999.

GDP (purchasing power parity) $109.4bn. (2004 est.); GDP per capita (purchasing power parity) $23,700 (2004 est.).

2 Trade Unionism

Trade unions developed after World War II and became associated with opposition to British colonial rule. A Singapore Trades Union Congress appeared in the 1950s in association with the People's Action Party (PAP, which came to power when Singapore achieved internal self-government in 1959). The early 1960s saw the union movement divided, with strikes and unrest, over issues of post-colonial politics such as the short-lived federation with Malaysia (1963–65). In 1961 the Trades Union Congress split into the National Trades Union Congress (NTUC), allied to the PAP, and a leftist Singapore Association of Trade Unions, but the latter collapsed in 1963. Since then, with heavy guidance from the PAP, the overwhelming emphasis has come to be placed on tripartism and building and retaining a reputation for labour stability and productivity. This has been reinforced by the uninterrupted success of the Singaporean model in delivering year-on-year real growth and wage increases with virtually full employment. The Asian economic crisis of 1997–98 was relatively lightly felt in Singapore and had no real impact on the tripartite consensus in favour of industrial peace; although growth in recent years has been slower than in the last quarter of the twentieth century, the essential stability of the Singaporean model has remained intact. The NTUC remains closely allied with the ruling People's Action Party both ideologically and organizationally.

Singapore has not ratified ILO Convention No. 87 (Freedom of Association and Protection of the Right to Organize, 1948) but domestic legislation provides for the formation of trade unions. In the private sector, workers are generally free to join unions of their own choosing and acts of anti-union discrimination by employers are prohibited. Although the Registrar of Trade Unions has extensive powers to refuse or cancel registration of trade unions, particularly where one already exists for workers in a particular occupation or industry, this power has not been exercised for more than two decades.

In the public sector, in contrast, there is no legal right to form and join trade unions and the unrepealed colonial Trades Union Act includes a general prohibition on government employees joining trade unions. However, exemptions may be granted and the Amalgamated Union of Public Employees (AUPE) is one of the largest trade unions in Singapore, representing some 15,000 workers. Since 1999, all public sector employees other than some senior civil servants have been able to join a union.

According to government figures there were 72 registered unions at the end of 2003. These have around 400,000 members (out of a workforce of about 2.15 million) and only a few thousand union members are in unions outside the NTUC – the airline pilots' union is the main non-affiliate. The near-monopoly position of the NTUC has been allied to the enduring domestic popularity of the PAP, which has won every election since the country achieved self-rule (and has increased its share of the vote in each of the last two elections, in 1997 and 2001), and a political culture that does not favour dissent. The NTUC and its affiliates are also able to provide a wide range of benefits and member services.

Singapore ratified ILO Convention No. 98 (Right to Organize and Collective Bargaining, 1949) in 1965. Collective bargaining is widely practiced. Annual guidelines on pay are issued by the tripartite National

Wages Council (NWC), set up in 1972, and provide a framework for bargaining agreements. To be enforceable, collective agreements have to be certified by the Industrial Arbitration Court, and although certification can be refused on public interest grounds, this has never happened. In theory, collective agreements in newly established enterprises cannot provide more favourable conditions than the legal minimum specified in the Employment Act, but in practice this provision is disregarded. Collective agreements reached by NTUC affiliates are customarily approved by the union leadership without reference to the rank-and-file. This issue caused internal conflict within the Airline Pilots Association–Singapore (ALPA-S), not an NTUC affiliate, in 2003, resulting in the dismissal of the leadership by the rank-and-file after it agreed wage cuts. In response the Singapore parliament in April 2004 approved an amendment to the Trade Unions Act so that union leaderships need no longer refer collective agreements to the rank-and-file.

Strikes are legal, other than in some essential services (including water, gas and electricity) and subject to a vote of 50% of all union members in favour. However, while strikes were frequent in the 1950s and early 1960s, the strike virtually disappeared from the industrial relations landscape from the late 1960s onwards and there has now been no strike recorded since 1986. The Ministry of Manpower actively involves itself in resolving disputes, and if conciliation fails cases are usually referred to the tripartite Industrial Arbitration Court. While the law provides for compulsory arbitration in some circumstances, this has not occurred since 1981.

Non-citizens may not be union officers and union funds may not be paid out to political parties or used for political purposes.

3 Trade Union Centre

National Trades Union Congress (NTUC)
Address. NTUC Centre, No. 1 Marina Boulevard, #B1-01, Singapore 018989
Phone. +65 6213 8000
Fax. +65 6339 6713
E-mail. iad@ntuc.org.sg
Website. www.ntucworld.org.sg
Leadership. John De Payva (president); Lim Boon Heng (secretary-general)
Membership. About 400,000 in 63 trade unions and 4 associations
History and character. The NTUC is the sole trade union centre, and 98.5% of union members in Singapore are in its affiliated unions. The NTUC's membership is the highest on record and increasing, and the NTUC says this was assisted by workers' realization of the value of union membership in the 1998–99 period, when the economy was under stress from the Asian economic crisis. The largest public sector affiliate is the Amalgamated Union of Public Employees while the largest private sector affiliate is the 40,000-member United Workers of Electronic and Electrical Industries.

The NTUC's relationship with the People's Action Party (PAP), which has held power continuously since independence, is often described by both the NTUC and the PAP as "symbiotic". The unions backed the PAP when it was set up in 1954 to spearhead the country's struggle for independence from Britain. When the PAP came to power in 1959 it fulfilled its election pledges to create the conditions under which unions could operate effectively. In 1961 the labour movement split, the pro-PAP majority forming the NTUC and a pro-communist minority seceding to form a Singapore Association of Trade Unions. The latter collapsed in 1963, since when the NTUC has been the only trade union centre.

Relations between the PAP and NTUC have been cemented by office-holding. Ong Teng Cheong was simultaneously NTUC secretary-general and Second Deputy Prime Minister from 1985 until he became the country's first directly elected President (non-executive head of state) from 1993–99. His successor (and current) NTUC secretary-general, Lim Boon Heng, is an MP and Minister without Portfolio in the Prime Minister's Office. PAP Members of Parliament in the early stages of their careers commonly hold positions in the NTUC or its affiliates. NTUC policy prohibits union members who actively support opposition parties from holding office in affiliated unions, although there have been cases of local NTUC officials running as opposition candidates. In December 2002, in accordance with this policy, the NTUC stripped a branch chairman of the United Workers of Electronic and Electrical Industries of both his chair and his union membership after he was elected secretary-general of the opposition Singapore Democratic Alliance.

The highest body of the NTUC is the delegates' conference, which meets every two years. The NTUC central committee, whose 21 members are elected for four years, is responsible for the implementation of conference policy. The secretary-general is the chief executive of the NTUC.

The NTUC works closely with the government and employers to promote industrial peace and justice. Tripartism is practiced extensively and there is cooperation at every level of industrial relations, and although in principle the strike weapon remains as part of the union armoury it has not been used since a dispute in 1986. The NTUC has supported wage flexibility as a means of adjusting to economic conditions, and argues its position on this has been a factor in ensuring Singapore has recovered quickly from its two major economic setbacks since the 1960s, the 1985–86 recession and the 1997–98 Asian financial crisis.

The NTUC emphasizes its role in helping to ensure that Singapore remains competitive and that its workers remain employable for life. It is currently engaged in a variety of initiatives, often in cooperation with employers, to equip its members to deal with the impact of rapid corporate restructuring, outsourcing and technological change. It is putting more emphasis on the needs of contract workers and part-time workers. Recognizing that Singapore can only retain competitive advantage, as a high wage economy, through high productivity, and that workers with few skills will be marginalized in the labour market, it operates a Skills Redevelopment Programme, based on company participation.

Since the 1960s the NTUC has progressively developed a wide range of member services, such as consumer cooperatives, insurance services, workplace child care schemes, health facilities, and discount schemes. It provides a range of social and recreational facilities, running its own holiday resorts and country clubs.

It established the Singapore, now Ong Teng Cheong, Institute of Labour Studies as a labour college in 1990.

International affiliations. ICFTU; CTUC

Slovakia

Capital: Bratislava
Population: 5.42 m. (2004 est.)

1 Political and Economic Background

The communist regime in Czechoslovakia collapsed in the so-called "velvet revolution" of 1989. Following this separatist sentiment developed in the eastern region of Slovakia. In June 1992 general elections resulted in victory for the nationalist Movement for a Democratic Slovakia (HZDS) in Slovakia. Agreement for the dissolution of Czechoslovakia was thereafter reached with rapidity and notable lack of conflict and on Jan. 1, 1993 two separate and independent states, the Czech and Slovak Republics, were established. Under Prime Minister Vladimir Meciar of the HZDS (in power from independence, with one short break, until September 1998), Slovakia increasingly became regarded internationally as authoritarian, anti-reform and corrupt and its standing deteriorated compared with the Czech Republic. Whereas the Czech Republic was in the first round of former communist states to be invited by the EU to begin accession negotiations, Slovakia was excluded from the process. In elections in September 1998 the HZDS remained the largest party by one seat, but a coalition government was formed by opposition parties led by the Slovak Democratic Coalition (SDK) of the new Prime Minister Mikulas Dzurinda. The new government then worked to improve Slovakia's international image. In May 1999 Rudolf Schuster defeated Meciar to become Slovakia's first popularly elected President. In National Council elections in September 2002 the HZDS remained the largest party, but a centre-right coalition was created by the Slovak Democratic and Christian Union (SDKU, a new party of Mikulas Dzurinda who continued as Prime Minister), the Hungarian Coalition Party (SMK), the Christian Democratic Movement (KDH) and New Civic Alliance (ANO). In May 2004 Slovakia joined the EU. In presidential elections in April 2004 Ivan Gasparovic was elected in the second-round vote, defeating Meciar of the HZDS.

The divergence of the Slovak and Czech economies after the end of communist rule encouraged the development of the Slovak independence movement. Slovakia, the location of many traditional industrial sectors and the arms industry, experienced much higher unemployment and attracted far less foreign investment than the Czech lands. Separation, however, merely served to reinforce that divergence. This fact, and the policies of the HZDS under Meciar, influenced the relatively slow development of a free market in Slovakia. Although privatization began following 1989, much of the traditional industrial sector had not been restructured a decade later. Since Dzurinda came to office in late 1998, however, there has been wide-ranging structural reform, with most major privatizations now completed and, encouraged by Slovakia's accession to the EU, a pick-up of foreign investment. Slovakia is well into a process of catch-up with the other economies of central Europe. Slovakia nonetheless suffers from a range of economic problems including relatively high inflation (8.5% in 2003) and high unemployment (stablized at 14-18% during 2000-2003) as a consequence of austerity measures introduced by the Dzurinda government to try to control the current account deficit.

GDP (purchasing power parity) $72.29bn. (2004 est.); GDP per capita (purchasing power parity) $13,300 (2004 est.).

2 Trade Unionism

Slovakia ratified ILO Conventions No. 87 (Freedom of Association and Protection of the Right to Organize, 1948) and No. 98 (Right to Organize and Collective Bargaining, 1949) in 1993.

For four decades until 1989 the trade union movement was organized on the communist model within a unified Czechoslovakia (see country section on the Czech Republic for details of that period). Following the collapse of communist rule, the Confederation of Czechoslovakian Trade Unions (CSKOS) was founded in 1990.

The new structure of trade unionism evolved in step with nationalism and was thus fated not to last. CSKOS rested on two subordinate national bodies. Growing Czech and Slovak nationalism forced a rule change just three months into the life of the new organization (see below) and in May 1991 the Slovak Confederation threatened a general strike against the dismissal of the Slovak prime minister and his replacement by a Christian Democrat. CSKOS doubted the advantages to either nation of splitting into two separate states. A memorandum it submitted to the government in the summer of 1992 forecast economic hardship and an explosion of the black market and disputed the assumption that the Czech part of the country could expect easy expansion once economically separate from Slovakia. The September 1992 general council blamed the impending division of Czechoslovakia on mistakes committed by the old regime. In speeches to the ICFTU and the ETUC on Oct. 9 its president Richard Falbr expressed the determination of CSKOS to stay united. Within a month, however, the Confederation of Trade Unions of the Slovak Republic (KOZ SR) had to be founded in acknowledgment of the new national realities.

As of 2004, less than 30% of the workforce was organized despite the fact all employees may join unions except members of the armed forces. Trade unions experienced a sharp decline in membership during the 1990s. While KOZ SR reported 1.75 milllion members in 1992, by 2003 its membership was only 570,000. Discrimination against union organizers and members is prohibited in law and the courts may order the reinstatement of workers dismissed for union activities. In practice anti-union discrimination does not appear to be a major issue.

Collective bargaining is protected in law as is the right to strike. However, strikers enjoy immunity from dismissal only in the case of official strikes, and a strike is official only where in pursuit of collective bargaining, when it is announced in advance, and when a list of strike participants is provided.

3 Trade Union Centre

Confederation of Trade Unions of the Slovak Republic (KOZ SR)
Address. Odborarske nam. 3, 815 70 Bratislava
Phone. +421 7 502 39111
Fax. +421 2 555 61956
E-mail. internat.dep@kozsr.sk
Website. www.kozsr.sk (Slovak, English)
Leadership. Ivan Saktor (president); four vice-presidents – Eugen Skultety (Trade Union Policy), vacant (Economic Policy and Social Partnership), Juraj Blahak (industrial trade unions), Jan Gasperan (non-industrial trade unions)
Membership. 570,000 (as of 2003) in 37 occupationally-based affiliated unions.
History and character. KOZ SR had its origins in the formation in March 1990 of the Czechoslovak Confederation of Trade Unions (CSKOS) at a national congress whose delegates were chosen at nationwide enterprise elections. It inherited the assets of the former Central Council of Trade Unions (URO). In April 1990 a Confederation of Trade Unions was established for each nation, the Czech-Moravian Chamber (CMK CSKOS) and the Confederation of Trade Unions of the Slovak Republic (KOZ SR), and in June the name of the organization was changed to the Czech and Slovak Confederation of Trade Unions. From this point on, as separatist tendencies grew, the new organization sought to avoid a split along nationalist lines. As late as July 1992 a comprehensive CSKOS memorandum foretold dire economic and political consequences should the separation of the Czech and Slovak lands be carried through; within a few weeks however, trade unionists on both sides were forced to start preparations for the inevitable. CMKOS was formed in the Czech lands and KOZ SR in Slovakia. Some leaders of KOZ (Alojz Englis, Roman Kovac) were connected with HZDS and KOZ had relationships with other parties as well – the Party of the Democratic Left (SDL, the reformed Communists) and the "historical" Social Democratic Party of Slovakia. The unions did not look to support any single political party and/or movement.

KOZ SR seeks to defend trade union and individual human rights within the context of a social market economy. Despite the pressure from HZDS in the 1990s, KOZ SR sought to steer a politically non-partisan course. Following its October 1996 congress, Prime Minister Vladimir Meciar withdrew his support for the unions and accused the Party of the Democratic Left of seeking to exercise political power through the confederation. The SDL counter-charged that Meciar's HZDS intended to set up its own unions if it could not get control of KOZ SR. In the 1998 elections, KOZ SR mildly supported anti-Meciar forces, especially the SDK, which won the elections and was able to form a coalition goverment.

By 1999 KOZ SR was concerned at the impact of austerity measures and rising unemployment under the Dzurinda government. A demonstration in Bratislava called by KOZ SR on Sept. 25, 1999, to protest government policies reportedly drew 40,000 supporters. On Nov. 9, 1999, it organized a series of blockades of road junctions. During 2000-02 the relationship between the Slovak government and KOZ SR was rather schizophrenic – both the bodies continued their negotiations in the the Council of Economic and Social Agreement SR (RHSD SR, a tripartite body), where the KOZ SR was granted the position of sole representative of the trade unions. In 2000 both the partners were able to sign a general agreement; the government, however, proved unable to fulfill most of the obligations stated in it. At the same time, KOZ SR organized numerous protest meetings whose goals were social rather than political.

Having won a second consecutive election victory and emerging with a relatively stable legislative majority in 2002, Prime Minister Dzurinda decided to push for a very radical economic reform that would involve privatization of state-owned (monopoly) enterprises. This was accompanied by a growing tension between the Slovak government and KOZ SR, which opposed Dzurinda's measures as anti-social and unconstitutional and undertaken without sufficient consultation. Nonetheless, the government was able to adopt an amended Labour Code whose aim was to boost flexibility of the labour market.

This led to a growing politicization of KOZ SR in 2003, which turned its focus to unconventional political action (strikes, blockades of the border crossings and highways, protest marches). KOZ SR´s activity climaxed with its raising a petition to call a referendum on the holding of early parliamentary elections. The chairman of KOZ SR, I. Saktor, characterized the role of the unions in a changing environment as that of "being a political opposition". The petition drive received moral and material support from the opposition political parties, notably HZDS and Smer (an opposition party formed in 1999 which was highly critical of the social impact of the policies of the Dzurinda government and had won 25 seats in the 2002 parliamentary elections), and the organizers were able to collect the signatures of 600,000 Slovak citizens. There were big doubts about how binding such a referendum would be (from the constitutional point of view) for the government. Nonetheless, the President of Slovakia, Rudolf Schuster, decided to call the referendum and combine the ballot with presidential elections, scheduled for April 3, 2004 (probably aiming to get the protesters' support for his own candidacy). The referendum eventually failed because of a low turnout (about 35% of eligible voters).

As a reciprocal punishment, and in response to the wide-ranging cooperation between KOZ SR and Smer, Dzurinda decided to modify the extent of institutional cooperation with KOZ SR and submitted a bill that would dissolve the Council of Economic and Social Agreement. Simultaneously, Dzurinda's government proposed an amendment of the relevant law that would codify the role of unions as "being a consultative body of the government" (as a replacement of the RHSD SR) and accord the status of "recognized partners" to those trade unions with a membership of at least 100,000. Parliament adopted the bill but newly elected President Ivan Gasparovic refused to sign it and sent it back to parliament in October 2004. Parliament, however, overruled the presidential veto and the bill became law. Dzurinda and his Deputy Prime Minister Pavol Rusko repeatedly argued that any social partnership was impossible with trade unions being proactive rather than reactive in party politics. The result is that the position of KOZ SR in social dialogue has been somewhat undermined as other unions with a membership of at least 100,000 may enter the consultations. KOZ SR dismissed the newly proposed role as being not in accordance with the EU social model.

International affiliations. ICFTU; ETUC; TUAC (observer status)

4 Other Trade Union Organization

Independent Christian Trade Unions of Slovakia (NKOS)
Address. Jiraskova 39, Trnava
Phone. +421 805 5446837
Fax. +421 805 5446837
E-mail. centrum@nkos.sk
Leadership. Peter Novovesky (president)
Membership. 10,000
History and character. NKOS has a social Christian position. It has three affiliated unions (railways, education and industry). It is limited by Slovak legislation that gives majority trade unions a monopoly in concluding collective agreements. In 2003, the NKOS was denied any further dialogue with KOZ SR because of not supporting its protest actions against the government.
International affiliation. WCL

Slovenia

Capital: Ljubljana
Population: 2.01m. (2004 est.)

1 Political and Economic Background

Slovenia declared its independence from Yugoslavia in June 1991 and quickly consolidated its autonomy after relatively brief and small-scale fighting with Serb-led Yugoslav forces. Its transition was eased by the absence of significant ethnic and religious division, Slovenes having been a distinct population within former Yugoslavia and constituting the vast majority within Slovenia's borders. In the most recent general election, in October 2004, seven political parties passed the 4% of the vote threshold for representation in the 90-member National Assembly. The centre-right Slovenian Democratic Party (SDS) emerged as the strongest party, with 29 seats, enabling it to lead the government, while second place was taken by the centrist Liberal Democracy of Slovenia (LDS), previously the strongest party. Slovenia joined the European Union on May 1, 2004, being the only former Yugoslav republic thus far to have achieved EU membership.

Slovenia was the most prosperous of the former Yugoslav republics, with a diverse range of service and manufacturing industries, and it has succeeded in building on that favourable foundation. The initial impact of independence and loss of markets was recession, but since 1993 the economy has steadily expanded with Slovenia increasingly orienting its market to the EU. Growth averaged in excess of 4% per annum in the period 1994-2003, twice the EU average, despite the country attracting relatively little foreign direct investment – most of its larger companies remain domestically owned, and the state itself has a majority stake in a number of large concerns. The country entered the EU in May 2004 in the strong position of having achieved per capita GDP of 70% of the (pre-2004 15-member) EU average and as the most prosperous of the new Central and Eastern European accession states. Successive governments have followed a cautious path in reducing the public sector. However, although Slovenia has well developed public services and comparatively generous social benefits, the public sector budget deficit remained only 1.6% of GDP in 2004. Unemployment was over 11% in 2003, as measured locally, but 6.7% by international standards.

GDP (purchasing power parity) $36.82bn. (2003 est.); GDP per capita (purchasing power parity) $19,000 (2003 est.).

2 Trade Unionism

In the Yugoslav period the trade unions in Slovenia were organized as a republican branch of the federal Confederation of Trade Unions of Yugoslavia (SSJ), although with a certain degree of autonomy in practice. Following independence, Slovenia ratified ILO Conventions No. 87 (Freedom of Association and Protection of the Right to Organize, 1948) and No. 98 (Right to Organize and Collective Bargaining, 1949) in 1992. The trade unions are by regional standards large and well organized against the background of a labour market characterized as rigid and with many companies emphasizing commitment to all stakeholders and not just shareholders. The enterprise is the basic trade union organization building block.

There is no one trade union centre. There are four confederations represented on the tripartite 15-member Economic and Social Council (ESSS), these being the Confederation of New Trade Unions of Slovenia "Independence" (KNSS "Independence"); the Confederation of Trade Unions of Slovenia Pergam (Pergam); the Confederation of Trade Unions '90 of Slovenia (Konfederacija '90); and the Association of Free Trade Unions of Slovenia (ZSSS). The ZSSS has two representatives on the ESSS, and each of the other three confederations has one. The ZSSS, created from the old Yugoslav-era structures, is accepted to be the largest (and is the only one in membership of the European Trade Union Confederation, ETUC), and all four have existed since the early 1990s, each being accorded nationally representative status under the 1993 Law on Representativeness of Trade Unions. However, there are also unions outside the established confederations, including white-collar unions in public services (where the Education, Science and Culture Union claims to be the largest public sector independent union, with 40,000 members), the police and banking unions, some small regional unions, and unaffiliated unions at enterprise level. Two organizations, Slovenska Zveza Sindikatov Alternativa (Alternativa) (Slovenian Union of Trade Unions – Alternative) and Zveza Delavcev Solidarnost (Union of Workers' Solidarity) were recognized as nationally representative in 1999 and 2001, respectively, though appear to have little presence.

Under the 1993 Law, nationally representative status is open to organizations operating throughout the country and comprising at least two sectoral (occupational) unions having at least 10% of the workforce in their sector or occupation within membership. However, nationally representative status has thus far been accorded on a permanent basis without periodic case-by-case assessment and the only figures for union memberships are those claimed by the unions themselves. There are no reliable figures on contemporary union membership totals or for union density. Despite the fragmentation, the different union organizations often coordinate activities.

The upper house of the Slovenian parliament, the National Council (Drzavni Svet), is a 40-member body, elected for a five-year term but with only limited powers, representing the various social, economic, professional and local interests. It includes four representatives of the trade unions; it was last elected in 2002 with all four union representatives being from the ZSSS.

A new law on on collective bargaining agreements was in preparation in 2004. The current format is for a framework national collective agreement for the entire private sector to be negotiated (with reference to tripartite social and pay policy agreements) and then national sectoral agreements and finally enterprise-level agreements. The unions generally favour strengthening negotiations at the sectoral level. A similar system applies to the public sector, with one national-level agreement first being concluded. Negotiation of national sectoral agreements in 2004 was accompanied by demonstrations and warning strikes by some goups of workers. The right to strike is guaranteed although restricted in some public sector areas; official statistics are lacking but strikes were common in the years of economic difficulty after independence, but have become much less frequent since then.

Social dialogue is actively pursued, with the Economic and Social Council as the main national-level mechanism. Tripartite social agreements have been concluded since 1996. The April 2003 agreement covered the period 2003-05 and included detailed provisions on the direction of social and economic policy, including taxation, wage policy, public finances, restructuring, education and training, social exclusion, pensions and healthcare. It was agreed for wage growth to be restrained to 1% below the growth in productivity and for legislation to be introduced on the minimum wage. The agreement was signed by all four union confederations on the ESSS as well as by several other trade union organizations. Issues surrounding indexation of public sector pay and greater flexibility in private sector pay are to the fore as the government seeks to keep the lid on public spending and inflation, and to enhance competitiveness, as Slovenia prepares for adoption of the euro. In April 2004 the social partners signed a tripartite agreement on private sector pay for 2004-05, one of a series since 1994, laying down specific principles and percentage rates to be taken account of in collective bargaining, including the principle that pay increases should run 1% behind gains in productivity. However, the agreement was signed on the trade union side only by the ZSSS.

3 Trade Union Centres

Konfederacija novih sindikatov Slovenije "Neodvisnost" (KNSS)
Confederation of New Trade Unions of Slovenia "Independence"
Address. Linhartova 13, 61000 Ljubljana
Phone. +386 1 1329 141
Fax. +386 1 302 868
Website. www.mc-ii.si/knss
Leadership. Drago Lombar (president)
History and character. The KNSS held its founding congress in March 1990 and in the 1990s was thought to represent 10% of trade union members.

Konfederacija sindikatov Slovenije Pergam (KSS Pergam)
Confederation of Trade Unions of Slovenia – Pergam
Address. Trg Osvobodilne Fronte 14/IV, 1000 Ljubljana
Phone. +386 1 231 0476
Fax. +386 1 230 2247
E-mail. pergam@siol.net
Website. www.sindikat-pergam.si (Slovenian only)
Leadership. Dusan Rebolj (president); Vida Fras (general secretary)
History and character. The KSS Pergam was created as a breakaway from the ZSSS in 1991 and has its membership concentrated in the paper and printing industries, though also with members in areas such as health and medicine.

Konfederacija sindikatov '90 Slovenije (Konfederacija '90)
Confederation of Trade Unions '90 of Slovenia
Address. Komenskega 7, 1000 Ljubljana
Phone. +386 1 430 7300
Fax. +386 1 430 1742
E-mail. ks90@sindikat-ks90.si
Website. www.sindikat-ks90.si
Leadership. Boris Mazalin (president)
History and character. This is essentially a regional organization, founded in February 1991, and based in the south-west of the country in the area around Koper.

Zveza svobodnih sindikatov Slovenije (ZSSS)
Association of Free Trade Unions of Slovenia
Address. Dalmatinova 4, 1000 Ljubljana
Phone. +386 1 43 41200
Fax. +386 1 231 7298
E-mail. zsss@sindikat-zsss.si
Website. www.sindikat-zsss.si (Slovenian; English section)
Leadership. Dusan Semolic (president); Milan Utrosa (general secretary)
Membership. Reports 300,000 in 20 branch trade unions
History and character. The ZSSS is the largest Slovenian trade union confederation and emerged from the old Yugoslav-era unions, retaining their assets (which it still does). The ZSSS currently holds all four trade union seats in the National Council (the upper house of parliament). The ZSSS is particularly strong in large-scale production industries (with 60% of its total membership in manufacturing) and much less so in some public sector areas such as health and education. In February 2004 seven of the ZSSS's affiliated sectoral unions staged a one-hour general "warning strike" over sectoral collective bargaining negotiations, with 120,000 workers taking part.
International affiliation. ETUC

Solomon Islands

Capital: Honiara
Population: 524,000 (2004 est.)

1 Political and Economic Background

The Solomon Islands, a South Pacific archipelago, became independent from the UK in 1978 and is a member of the Commonwealth. In 1999 conflict between the indigenous inhabitants of Guadalcanal (Isatabu) and immigrants from elsewhere in the country led to a four-month state of emergency and closed the nation's largest palm oil plantation. In June 2000 there was widespread violence in Honiara involving paramilitaries of rival ethnic groups set up in response to the Guadalcanal crisis. A peace agreement between the rival militias was reached under Australian auspices in October 2000, resulting in limited disarmament, and elections held in December 2001 were followed by the formation of a governing coalition between the People's Alliance Party (PAP) and the Association of Independent Members, with Sir Allan Kemakeza of the PAP as Prime Minister. Following further unrest, an Australian-led peacekeeping force of troops and police was sent to the Solomon Islands in July 2003 and the situation has since been stable.

The majority of the population is dependent on agriculture (subsistence and commercial), forestry and fishing for a livelihood. Manufacturing industry is largely restricted to the processing of local primary commodities. The economy was affected by spillover from the 1997–98 Asian economic crisis, and thereafter by ethnic violence – the economy contracting an estimated 14% in 2000 and almost 9% in 2001 as a result of the closure of businesses and damage to infrastructure. The economy began to recover in 2003 as the security situation improved. However, the Central Bank in 2003 estimated that it would take a decade of annual growth of 10% before the economy recovered to the levels of the late 1990s.

GDP (purchasing power parity) $800m. (2002 est.); GDP per capita (purchasing power parity) $1,700 (2002 est.).

2 Trade Unionism

The Solomon Islands joined the International Labour Organization in 1984 but has yet to ratify ILO Conventions No. 87 (Freedom of Association and Protection of the Right to Organize, 1948) or No. 98 (Right to Organize and Collective Bargaining, 1949).

Trade unionism developed rapidly in the 1970s, encouraged by the creation of the Solomon Islands General Workers' Union (subsequently known as the Solomon Islands National Union of Workers – SINUW) in the mid-1970s. The right to organize trade unions and bargain collectively was provided for in the 1981 Trade Disputes Act. Some 85–90% of the workforce is outside the formal economy, but in the formal sector unionization rates are high, being estimated at 90% in the public sector and 50% in the private sector. The government has not sought to prevent the formation of unions and there are legal protections against anti-union discrimination.

Collective bargaining is practiced and unresolved disputes are referred to the tripartite Trades Disputes Panel for resolution, either before or during strikes. Unions are free to engage in political activities.

3 Trade Union Centre

Solomon Islands Council of Trade Unions (SICTU)
Address. PO Box 271, Honiara
Phone. +677 22629
Fax. +677 22516
Leadership. Tony Kagovai (national secretary)
History and character. The Solomon Islands National Union of Workers (SINUW) was formed in the 1970s. In 1986 the name Solomon Islands Council of Trade Unions (SICTU) was adopted, although the older name still remains in use. It is one of the few regional or Commonwealth centres still claimed as an affiliate by the WFTU. The SICTU and all its affiliated unions

endorsed the Australian-led intervention in July 2003 to restore stability, although disputes subsequently arose over the apparent intervention of Australian officials in public sector pay negotiations.
International affiliation. WFTU; CTUC

Somalia

Capital: Mogadishu
Population: 8.3 m. (2004 est.)

1 Political and Economic Background

Somalia was created by the unification of the British Somaliland Protectorate and the UN Trust Territory of Somalia at independence in 1960. In 1969 Mohammed Siyad Barre seized power and under him the Somali Revolutionary Socialist Party held power until his overthrow in a rebellion led by United Somali Congress (USC) guerrillas in January 1991. The USC quickly split into factions with different groups controlling different areas of the country. A UN peacekeeping presence from 1992-95, aimed primarily at protecting relief operations, was unable to restore any degree of order and there has been no effective, Somali-based government since 1991, with Ethiopian and Eritrean forces also becoming embroiled in the conflict and no clan-based faction controlling more than a small part of the country. However, in January 2004 the leaders of Somalia's warring factions signed a peace agreement in Nairobi, the capital of Kenya. Under the terms of the agreement a new 275-member, Nairobi-based transitional legislature was put in place in August 2004. Somalia's four main clans selected 61 members to the new legislature, while one coalition of smaller clans selected the remaining 31 members. In October 2004 the new legislature elected Col. Ahmed Abdullahi Yusuf, the President of the self-proclaimed autonomous region of Puntland, as the new President of Somalia. The President subsequently appointed a new government headed by Prime Minister Ali Muhammad Gedi. In addition to Puntland, there are two other self-declared autonomous regional administrations: the Republic of Somaliland with its capital at Hargeisa and South-western Somalia with its capital in Baidoa.

Somalia is an impoverished country. The ongoing civil disturbances and clan rivalries have interfered with any broad-based economic development and international aid arrangements. It is heavily dependent on the rearing of livestock, which supports up to three-quarters of the predominantly nomadic or semi-nomadic population. Food production falls far short of the country's requirements. There is little industry and much of it is closed because of civil conflict. There is a serious refugee problem and chronic external debt.

GDP (purchasing power parity) $4.361bn. (2004 est.); GDP per capita (purchasing power parity) $500 (2004 est.).

2 Trade Unionism

Somalia has been a member of the International Labour Organization since 1960 but has ratified neither ILO Convention No. 87 (Freedom of Association and Protection of the Right to Organize, 1948) nor No. 98 (Right to Organize and Collective Bargaining, 1949).

Under Siyad Barre a single trade union system prevailed, organized in the General Federation of Somali Trade Union (GFSTU), founded in 1977. Under the amended 1990 constitution, promulgated in Siyad Barre's last year in power as part of the general reform wave affecting one-party states in Africa at that time, the right to form independent unions was proclaimed, though no such unions were formed prior to his fall. Before this strikes were outlawed and organizing them was punishable by death.

During the 1990s, however, civil strife led to a general collapse of all civil institutions in Somalia. The GFSTU ceased to exist as did significant trade union activity. The vast majority of the population (much of which is nomadic) is in any case not engaged in formal employment relationships. However in the self-declared Republic of Somaliland there is the Somaliland Trade Union Organization, which claims to have a membership of 26,000 and has received assistance from the ILO. It claims to be independent.

South Africa

Capital: Pretoria
Population: 42.72 m. (2004 est.)

1 Political and Economic Background

The Union (from 1961, Republic) of South Africa was ruled by the (Afrikaaner-dominated) National Party (NP) from 1948 until May 1994. The NP created the system of apartheid (separate development) which divided the population into whites, coloureds, Indians and Africans. In general terms the system served to maintain white supremacy while providing fewest rights to the black segment of the population. Against this background, South Africa also created 10 bantustans ("homelands") as isolated islands within South Africa where blacks had a higher degree of autonomy.

In the 1980s the apartheid regime faced international isolation and sanctions and mounting unrest, although the internal politics were complex, with conflict among blacks between the African National Congress (ANC) and the (Zulu) Inkatha movement of KwaZulu homeland premier Chief Mangosuthu Buthelezi. As NP leader from 1989 State President F.W. de Klerk moved rapidly to dismantle legislative apartheid, lifting the ban on the (mainly black) ANC and the Pan-African Congress (PAC), and in February 1990 releasing Nelson Mandela, deputy president and leading figure in the ANC, from jail after 26 years' incarceration. Despite further bloodshed the way was cleared for establishment (in 1993) of a new constitution and elections on a single non-racial roll. Sanctions were finally lifted in December. The first non-racial multi-party elections, held in April 1994, resulted in a clear victory for the ANC (with 62.6% of the vote), whose leader Nelson Mandela subsequently became President. In 1999 Mandela was succeeded as President by the ANC's Thabo Mbeki, and in legislative elections, generally conceded as fairly conducted, the ANC increased its majority, taking 66% of the vote. The ANC's dominance was further consolidated in the April 2004 general election when it took nearly 70% of the vote and won 279 of the 400 seats in the National Assembly. It now also leads the government in all nine of the country's provinces.

South Africa under white rule had social and economic stratification on racial lines. The economy was the most dynamic in sub-Saharan Africa, drawing in (black) labour from neighbouring countries to work in its gold and coal mines and industries and providing a Western style of life for the white minority. International sanctions were, however, increasingly onerous. The ANC government since 1994 has sought to achieve greater access to wealth and opportunity for the excluded majority while retaining the confidence of the white business community and international investors. In practice, although declining, considerable economic stratification on racial lines persists. The economy has shown steady growth at an average 3.29% per annum in the period 2001-04. President Mbeki has said there is a need to further liberalize the economy to build investor confidence in the face of unemployment estimated at 30–35%, and there has been some cautious movement towards privatization of state-owned enterprises. However, sections of the ANC are seen as hostile to this policy. Racial tension, though subdued, is persistent and AIDS (which according to government figures affected 5.6 million people by 2003) and rampant crime are major problems.

GDP (purchasing power parity) $456.7bn. (2004 est.); GDP per capita (purchasing power parity) $10,700 (2004 est.).

2 Trade Unionism

Trade unions first developed among white workers in the 1880s, and a white Federation of Trade Unions was recognized in 1911. White workers were represented by the South African Confederation of Labour (SACoL), which favoured employment policies based on racial discrimination.

The Trade Union Council of South Africa (TUCSA) included white, coloured and Asian members and some blacks in dependent organizations. It was formed in 1954 and reached a peak of 500,000 members in 1983, but dissolved itself in 1986 with 120,000 members after 25 member unions had disaffiliated. TUCSA had claimed to be the only truly non-racial federation in South Africa, believing it lost membership because of the rise of politicized unions using industrial conflict as a means to broader political change. It became fully open to all races in 1980, while remaining white-run, but foundered despite the use of closed shop agreements with employers designed to discourage the defection of blacks to other independent unions. It opposed economic sanctions against South Africa and had a system of "parallel unions", under which black workers were recruited into separate subsidiary sections of white unions. These parallel black unions still had 32,000 members in 1984.

The first trade union organizing blacks appeared as early as 1917, followed in two years by the Industrial and Commercial Workers' Union of Africa. During the 1930s some black unions affiliated to the white-dominated South African Trades and Labour Council (SATLC), and after 1941 other black unions joined the Council of Non-European Trade Unions, which claimed 119 unions with 158,000 members in 1945. However, black trade union activity was suppressed after the National Party came to power in 1948, and in 1954 SATLC was disbanded and replaced by TUCSA, which excluded independent black unions from affiliation. 14 former SATLC members founded the South African Congress of Trade Unions (SACTU) the following year and immediately merged with the Council of Non-European Trade Unions. SACTU developed thereafter as the highly politicized trade union arm of the ANC, claiming 53,000 members by 1961. It was then driven underground by state repression and black unionism lost all internal expression until the 1970s.

The Soweto riots of 1976–77 contributed to the development of black trade unionism. Black unionists opposed to TUCSA had formed the non-racial Federation of South African Trade Unions (FOSATU) in 1979; the Council of Unions of South Africa (CUSA), which stressed black leadership, followed in 1980. Several important unions remained outside these federations. Largely regionally based, they, like FOSATU, were non-racial but opposed to registration: among their number were the Cape-based Food and Canning Workers' Union, the Western Province's General Workers' Union, and the South African Allied Workers' Union, organized mainly in East London and Durban.

In the period from 1979 black union activists emphasized the goal of building effective industrial strength, with strike action built around issues specifically concerning trade unions. The unrest of 1984 onwards began predominantly with community and student groups, but soon several hundred thousand black Transvaal workers were mobilized by FOSATU and CUSA as well as student and community leaders in a two-day stoppage against police action in the townships. In 1985 FOSATU joined the newly formed Congress of South African Trade Unions (COSATU), and in 1986 CUSA merged with the small Azanian Confederation of Trade Unions (AZACTU) to form the National Council of Trade Unions (NACTU). In 1986 Chief Buthelezi formed a Zulu-based organization, the United Workers' Union of South Africa (UWUSA), to oppose disinvestment from South Africa by foreign companies and the other black unions.

1.5 million black workers "stayed away" from work on May 1, 1986, to demand an official May Day holiday (the largest strike in South African history). Under the renewed state of emergency of June 1986, "statements calculated to encourage or promote disinvestment or the application of sanctions or foreign action against the Republic" or "calculated to incite any person to take part in any unlawful strike" were defined as subversive. In July 1986, 200 trade union officials were reported as being among 4,500 detained under the state of emergency, while others were in hiding. Among those detained for periods were the COSATU leaders Elijah Barayi and Jay Naidoo, and Phiroshaw Camay, the CUSA general secretary.

Repression of the labour movement escalated in the later 1980s. Seven strikers were shot in 1987 during a railway strike. COSATU headquarters in Johannesburg were raided and many officials arrested; the office was later bombed. Another mass one-day stay-away followed to mark the 11th anniversary of the Soweto riots; it was followed by further repression. Ten miners were killed in clashes with the police and vigilantes in 1987 and that October Moses Mayekiso, general secretary of the recently formed National Union of Metalworkers (NUMSA), was brought to trial for treason under the emergency regulations and detained until 1989.

In 1988, the NP government severely restricted and in some cases banned the activities of COSATU and 17 other organizations; raids and detentions of unionists followed. The draconian powers taken by government under that year's Labour Relations Amendment Bill, drafted to curb "politically-motivated" strikes, were described by the ILO as "probably the most serious attack on the emerging unions since the early 1970s."

Widespread union protests followed, with numerous work stoppages and demonstrations. Opposition united the rival union centres COSATU and the National Council of Trade Unions (NACTU) which in June mobilized 1.3 million in a protest general strike. The unions negotiated expanded recognition agreements with employers to by-pass the new legal restrictions: COSATU and NACTU reached an agreement with the South African Employers' Consultative Committee on Labour Affairs (SACCOLA) which by implication specifically excluded several of the law's provisions. Faced later with interest of some employers in using the new law, the unions broke off talks with SACCOLA: COSATU and NACTU called a summit at the end of 1988 to discuss further action against the new legislation.

The next year the unions entered a tripartite Labour Commission in surrogate fashion via an umbrella organization, the South African Trade Union Coordination Council (SATUCC), but they continued to press for agricultural, public sector and domestic workers to be covered by the new Act. To protest at exclusion of blacks from the 1989 election unions helped launch the Mass Democratic Movement (MDM) which organized a two-day stay-away from work. It was distinguished from the contemporaneous township revolt of the United Democratic Front (UDF) by its greater discipline, and received widespread support.

The struggle between the labour movement and the government continued in other areas. The unions accused the authorities of using "dirty tricks" to discredit them, by sowing divisions between the COSATU and NACTU, and between the leadership and rank and file of individual unions. Alfred Makeleng, a COSATU and UDF official, died in police custody in suspicious circumstances after 26 months' detention under the emergency regulations. A 1989 anti-apartheid conference called by COSATU for September was hamstrung by the arrest and detention of 28 union leaders together with other anti-apartheid activists. Leaders of the Post and Telecommunications Workers' Association were detained, the union's offices burgled and another official died in suspicious circumstances, against the background of negotiations to secure the reinstatement of postal workers dismissed during a 1987 strike. Twenty members of the COSATU affiliate, the Paper, Wood, Printing and Allied Workers' Union (PPWAWU), were detained under the emergency regulations while involved in strikes in the Transvaal. Striking municipal workers in Soweto also entered serious conflict with the police. 31,000 metalworkers went on strike for two weeks in the same month and won improved benefits from employers. The unions also gave tacit support to the boycott of October's municipal elections; they were banned under the emergency regulations from campaigning openly.

The most significant sectoral organization of blacks occurred in mining, where the National Union of Mineworkers (NUM) developed to become the largest black union. In contrast, blacks working on farms, as domestic servants, and as state employees, were almost entirely unorganized. Mass dismissals occurred after industrial action, and many employers were active in attempting to frustrate trade union activities, in some cases hiring their own company security forces to break up meetings. The threat of deportation to the homelands or neighbouring states was a potent weapon to curb strikes. Numerous activists were also detained incommunicado without charge under the Internal Security Act, and a number of trade union officials died in police custody.

As restrictions on union activity lapsed, COSATU thrived, pushing its membership towards one million. In 1990 it joined in a "revolutionary alliance" with the ANC and the South African Communist Party (SACP). NACTU's membership grew at a lower rate, partly because of its emphasis on black exclusivism and partly because of factional fighting between supporters and opponents of the Pan-Africanist Congress.

After the Soweto riots of 1976–77 SACTU (from exile) had urged unions to affiliate to the United Democratic Front (UDF – the principal grouping of community groups opposing the South African government), arguing that the class struggle must progress within a national struggle against apartheid. It also called for the unification of the progressive trade union movement, opposed "collaboration" with TUCSA, and welcomed the 1985 formation of COSATU, calling for a truly democratic centre of organized activity for all workers who are determined to "liberate our country from its existing oppressive and exploitative social system". SACTU added that "as long as the oppressive apartheid regime exists, where the above-ground trade unionists face detention without trial, torture and murder at the hands of the police ... there will always be a need for the SACTU", which would "continue to maintain its underground structures". After 1990, however, SACTU lost its raison d'être, and at a meeting with COSATU it dissolved and advised its members to join COSATU's affiliates.

The collapse of official apartheid stimulated a nationwide wave of celebratory strikes, but COSATU and NACTU called for the maintenance of sanctions. They met the Manpower Minister to discuss changes to employment legislation, and complained of intimidation at the hands of Inkatha and its union wing UWUSA. After the deaths of members of its affiliate the National Union of Mineworkers (NUM), COSATU pressed for freedom of association in Natal which, in its view, would destroy the basis of Inkatha. It also alleged police collusion in Inkatha attacks and called for an independent inquiry: there were later revelations that UWUSA had been funded by the security forces, and that some employers had worked with it to evict COSATU and NACTU affiliated unions, sustaining a campaign of dirty tricks and killings.

In 1991, following three years' negotiations between COSATU, NACTU and SACCOLA, a new Labour Relations Amendment Act repealed the 1988 restrictions, restored the pre-1988 definition of an unfair labour practice and abolished Labour Court powers to ban lawful strikes and lock-outs. It also lifted union responsibility for illegal, unofficial strikes and eased the conciliation process.

The 1991 Act cleared the way for union entry into the National Manpower Commission (NMC). COSATU argued for enhancement and broadening of its powers, compelling the Minister to ratify decisions jointly reached by the unions and the employers. Like NACTU it believed that places should be allocated proportionally to size thus reducing the influence of white right-wing unions. Both pressed for new legislation on collective bargaining rights, extension of the right to strike and recognition of rights for unions at companies. After protracted negotiations expedited by COSATU with a nationwide protest strike, it was finally agreed to transform the NMC into a tripartite forum for negotiations on all employment matters. In 1992 it incorporated ten members each from employers, unions and government.

From 1992 onwards the Ministry, unions and employers worked together to bring South Africa broadly in line with the standards of the ILO. An earlier ILO commission to South Africa (at COSATU's request) had made sweeping recommendations. (South Africa had joined the ILO in 1919 but left in 1966). Freedom of association was promulgated by the 1991 amendment but public sector collective bargaining was still restricted. A 1992 ILO commission encountered a very different atmosphere. A Labour Appeal Court was agreed and promised for 1993, with judges to be appointed by the Chief Justice following NMC consultation. The 1983 Employment Act was then extended to cover both domestic and farm workers, and plans announced to bring them within the 1956 Labour Relations Act and the 1957 Workmen's Compensation Act.

Apart from the NMC the other key tripartite institution of the new South Africa was the tripartite National Economic Forum (NEF). Labour was represented on it by COSATU, NACTU, and the Federation of South African Labour Unions (FEDSAL). COSATU wished to see the NEF given mandatory powers, while business preferred advisory status, but COSATU also advocated that NEF be merged with the NMC. In 1994 it succeeded in persuading the government to establish the National Economic, Development and Labour Council (NEDLAC) to supersede both. This has become the principal vehicle for tripartite social dialogue.

With the end of apartheid in sight, many leading union figures moved into the political sphere, led by the NUM general secretary Cyril Ramaphosa, who became secretary of the ANC. After the 1994 elections prominent COSATU figures occupied positions of power within the new administration. No less than 20 were elected to the new Parliament. Former COSATU general secretary Jay Naidoo became Minister without Portfolio; another COSATU figure Alec Erwin became Minister of Finance, and Sydney Mufamadi, also of COSATU, was appointed Minister of Safety and Security. Many others were appointed to civil service positions. But the election of an ANC government also showed that COSATU could act independently. On assuming power the ANC called for a moratorium on strikes, but COSATU demurred. Its affiliates were in mounting conflict with a number of private firms, notably in the mines where NUMSA was engaging international conglomerates. In 1994 disputes in the metal, paper, mining, oil, and road freight industries, led President Mandela to appeal to the COSATU congress for industrial peace.

By mid-1994 aggregate union membership was estimated at 3.5 million, an increase of over 500,000 from two years earlier. This figure corresponded to 26 per cent of the economically active population. COSATU affiliates accounted for perhaps 1.3 million of this number.

The Zulu-based UWUSA, launched by Chief Butehelezi in 1986 in opposition to COSATU and sanctions, was affected by revelations in July 1991 that it had received funds from the security police for most of its existence, amounting to at least 1.5 million Rand. Operation Omega (as it was known) brought together UWUSA and anti-union employers in a campaign of dirty tricks that in some cases were said to have resulted in the deaths of COSATU and NACTU activists. After the decision of Chief Buthelezi to participate in the 1994 elections UWUSA fell into obscurity.

The Labour Relations Act, implemented in 1996 after being negotiated by employers, unions and government through NEDLAC, provided a detailed framework for industrial relations and gave statutory effect to the provisions in the constitution on freedom of association. All private sector workers and all in the public sector except those involved with national security may join unions, and the Act enforces rights which enable unions to function in practice, such as access to workplaces, the check-off and paid leave for union officials. The Act guarantees the right to strike except for the security services and essential public services, and strikes may be staged in pursuit of broad "socio-economic protest". In practice, since the end of the apartheid area, the government has not interfered in union recruitment or the internal affairs of unions or generally in collective bargaining. The Act also provided for the establishment of workplace forums in larger enterprises, but these have not taken root.

The Labour Relations Act also set up a Commission for Conciliation, Mediation and Arbitration (CCMA), which has been involved in the settlement of many disputes, and a Labour Court, to which disputes can be referred after failure of the CCMA to achieve a resolution. However, somewhat on the British model, the emphasis has been primarily on employers and unions achieving agreement directly between them without quasi-judicial intervention. In 1996 South Africa ratified ILO Conventions No. 87 (Freedom of Association and Protection of the Right to Organize, 1948) and No. 98 (Right to Organize and Collective Bargaining, 1949). The LRA recognises the main trade union rights protected by ILO Conventions 87 and 98. In 1997 the Basic Conditions of Employment Act set a framework, generally in accordance with union wishes, for such areas as working hours, maternity leave and Sunday pay.

In April 1997 the structure of main trade union centres crystallized when the Federation of Unions of South Africa (FEDUSA), a non-political multi-racial (but majority white) organization, was formed by the merger of the Federation of South African Labour Unions (FEDSAL) and other smaller unions. On its formation it claimed 515,000 members in 25 affiliated unions, making it the second most important confederation after COSATU, and ahead of NACTU. All three are now affiliated to the ICFTU, NACTU having been the first to affiliate, in 1994. By 1998, according to official estimates, union membership had declined from about 3.5 million in 1994 to 2.9 million, with 248 registered trade unions and between 30 and 40 unregistered unions. In 2003 the labour scene witnessed the creation of a fourth centre, the Confederation of South African Workers' Unions (CONSAWU), affiliated to (and, according to COSATU's president, "bankrolled" by) the World Confederation of Labour. The ICFTU has expressed concerns over the creation in 2003 of what it describes as "white only" unions, referring to the mining union now known as "Solidarity" which "collaborated" with the government during apartheid.

COSATU's continued alliance with the ANC, though not without tensions, has been a stabilizing factor in the new South Africa. However, in his state-of-the-nation address to Parliament on Feb. 5, 2000, President Mbeki announced that his government would amend the Labour Relations Act and Basic Conditions of Employment Act, which business leaders had criticized as discouraging employment and investment. The initial proposals were unacceptable to the unions but lengthy negotiations which continued into 2001 resulted in a set of amendments to the LRA that were broadly acceptable to the unions. COSATU also came into conflict with government policy over the privatization of key state industries.

Incidents of anti-union violence are not uncommon during strikes and demonstrations. In one case in 2002 two mineworkers were shot and killed by security guards during a strike at Boksburg goldmine near Johannesburgh. Many other miners were injured.

3 Trade Union Centres

Congress of South African Trade Unions (COSATU)
Address. PO Box 1019, Johannesburg 2000
Phone. +27 11 339 4911
Fax. +27 11 339 5080
E-mail. cosatu@wn.apc.org
Website. www.cosatu.org.za
Leadership. Willy Madisha (president); Zwelinzima Vavi (general secretary)
Membership. Reports 2 million, of which 1.8 million are paid-up.
History and character. COSATU was formed in 1985 by 33 mainly black unions with 558,000 members as a federation that would emphasize opposition to apartheid on a non-racial basis. It absorbed the non-racial Federation of South African Trade Unions (FOSATU), which had nine affiliates, and incorporated the 180,000-member National Union of Mineworkers (NUM), which had left the Council of Unions of South Africa (CUSA). Although membership is open to whites, it is overwhelmingly black.

The founding congress made the following demands: (i) the repeal of the pass laws; (ii) the repeal of the state of emergency; (iii) withdrawal of troops and police from the townships; (iv) unconditional release of Nelson Mandela and all political prisoners, and the repeal of all banning orders; (v) the dismantling of the bantustan (homelands) system; and (vi) an end to the migrant labour system. COSATU committed itself to worker control, representation based on paid-up membership, broad-based industrial unionism, and non-racial recruitment, the demand for a national minimum wage, an end to overtime, sexual equality, and support for disinvestment by foreign firms and economic sanctions against South Africa.

COSATU suffered serious harassment from 1987 onwards. Officials were detained, and offices were raided and sabotaged. With other anti-apartheid groups repressed under the State of Emergency, COSATU was impelled further into the political arena. It was prominent in the organization of the 1986 and 1987 May Day strikes and the June 1987 "stay away". In 1987 it adopted the Freedom Charter and reaffirmed its support for international sanctions against South Africa. In response the government proscribed it from engaging in a wide range of specified political activities, as part of a package of still greater restrictions on anti-apartheid organizations introduced early in 1988.

Before 1989 a "workerist" faction argued for a concentration on industrial activities but the leadership, against a background of escalating change in South Africa, retained support for its political focus.

Following the dissolution of SACTU, the ANC's trade union front, in 1990, COSATU replaced it in a tripartite "revolutionary alliance" with the ANC and the South African Communist Party (SACP).

A special congress of September 1993 elected 20 officials to stand on the ANC list in the forthcoming national and regional elections. Nelson Mandela told the Congress: "The ANC will never betray the cause of democracy, and the cause of the workers. You must support the ANC only if it delivers the goods. If it does not, do to it what you have done to the apartheid regime!" Congress also adopted a Platform of Workers' Rights on the basis of which it negotiated to commit the ANC in the elections: the platform included basic organizing rights, collective bargaining, workplace empowerment, human resource development, and national industry-based provident funds.

In a 1994 conference COSATU developed special proposals for the reform of industrial relations structures, which to a considerable degree were reflected in the subsequent creation of NEDLAC.

Great symbolism was attached to the attendance of Nelson Mandela, then President, at the fifth (September 1994) congress, but he brought an unappetizing message. He appealed to delegates to think of the unemployed rather than of pay demands. Little greater encouragement came from Jay Naidoo (former COSATU general secretary) and Alec Erwin (former COSATU education officer), now key economic ministers. The SACP general secretary Charles Nqakula warned that the new government was in danger of representing only the employers.

Despite tensions, the triple alliance of COSATU, ANC and the SACP has nonetheless continued. It is reflected in political affiliations: SACP members hold government posts and former COSATU general secretary Mbhazima Shilowa is premier of the key industrial province of Gauteng, which includes Johannesburg. Likewise, the current COSATU general secretary Zwelinzima Vavi is an SACP member. COSATU claims credit for securing the enactment of measures such as the 1997 Basic Conditions of Employment Act, which covered issues such as working hours (providing for a 45-hour maximum week), maternity leave and child labour and was relevant to many of South Africa's most vulnerable workers.

At the same time, COSATU has found itself opposed to some key government initiatives, including plans to sell off a range of public assets. In alliance with the SACP, COSATU has attacked the government's Growth, Employment and Redistribution strategy (GEAR), which aims to cut the budget deficit by curbing public spending, claiming it has produced poor growth and increased unemployment. On Jan. 31, 2000 COSATU announced a programme of "mass action" in protest at an estimated unemployment rate of 35%. A few days later President Mbeki, in his state-of-the nation address underlined the need for further restructuring (privatization) of state assets and warned that labour laws would be amended. On May 10, 2000 COSATU called a one-day strike against unemployment, with a response described as patchy. Through 2000 COSATU kept up political pressure against government plans to make it easier for employers to lay off workers. COSATU has also sought to make a practical contribution to easing unemployment by establishing a Job Creation Trust and is working with others to develop coherent alternatives to GEAR.

COSATU has 21 affiliates in all main sectors of the economy, ranging in size from the powerful National Union of Mineworkers to the 450 members of the South African Football Players' Union. It is attempting to build membership in areas such as domestic service and temporary and casual work.

International affiliations. ICFTU; CTUC

Affiliates. The following are the major affiliates in order of size:

1. National Union of Mineworkers (NUM)
Address. PO Box 2424, Johannesburg 2001
Phone. +27 11 377 2000
Fax. +27 11 836 6051
E-mail. Tmlabatheki@num.org.za
Website. www.num.org.za
Leadership. Gwede Mantashe (general secretary)
Membership. 299,509
History and character. Founded in 1982, the NUM grew with great rapidity among black mineworkers and won recognition for bargaining purposes from the employers' organization, the Chamber of Mines, in 1983. It campaigned effectively in the 1980s for the end of the job reservation system whereby the best-paid jobs were reserved for whites. It has been the biggest COSATU affiliate since COSATU was formed in 1985 and has members in mining, energy, engineering and construction. In December 1993 it opened the first union-owned training centre in South Africa; in 1996 the Mine Health and Safety Act, which it had backed, became law. It offers a wide range of member services. It is affiliated internationally to the ICEM.

2. National Education, Health and Allied Workers' Union (NEHAWU)
Address. PO Box 10812, Johannesburg 2000
Phone. +27 11 833 2902
Fax. +27 11 834 3416
E-mail. nehawu@wn.apc.org
Website. www.nehawu.org.za
Leadership. Fikile Majola (general secretary)
Membership. 234,607
History and character. NEHAWU was founded in 1987 and is the largest public sector union in South Africa. It provides a range of member services including scholarships, medical assistance, provident funds, and group insurance.

3. South African Democratic Teachers' Union (SADTU)
Address. PO Box 6401, Johannesburg
Phone. +27 11 334 4830
Fax. +27 11 334 4836
E-mail. sadtu@wn.apc.org
Website. www.sadtu.org.za
Leadership. Thulas Nxesi (general secretary)
Membership. 214,865

4. National Union of Metalworkers of South Africa (NUMSA)
Address. PO Box 260483, Excom 2023

Phone. +27 11 689 1700
Fax. +27 11 833 6330
E-mail. dumisa@numsa.org.za
Website. www.numsa.org.za
Leadership. Silumko Nondwangu (general secretary)
Membership. 174,212

5. South African State and Allied Workers' Union (SASAWU)
Address. PO Box 30654, Braamfontein 2017.
Phone. +27 11 339 7012
Fax. +27 11 339 3406
E-mail. Sasawu@wn.apc.org.za
Leadership. Mzohle Gazi (general secretary)
Membership. 144,127

6. Southern African Clothing and Textile Workers' Union (SACTWU)
Address. PO Box 1194, Woodstock 7915
Phone. +27 21 447 4570
Fax. +27 21 447 4593
E-mail. lynnt@sactwu.co.za
Leadership. Ebrahim Patel (general secretary)
Membership. 110,216

7. South African Municipal Workers' Union (SAMWU)
Address. Private Bag X9, Athlone 7760
Phone. +27 21 697 1151
Fax. +27 21 696 9175
E-mail. samwu@wn.apc.org
Leadership. Roger Ronnie (general secretary)
Membership. 114,127

8. Food and Allied Workers' Union (FAWU)
Address. PO Box 1234, Woodstock 7915
Phone. +27 21 637 9040
Fax. +27 21 638 3761
E-mail. fawu@wn.apc.org
Leadership. Derrick Cele (general secretary)
Membership. 85,069

9. South African Commercial, Catering and Allied Workers' Union (SACCAWU)
Address. PO Box 10730, Johannesburg 2000
Phone. +27 11 403 8333
Fax. +27 11 403 0309
E-mail. biskhulu@saccawu.org.za
Leadership. Bones Skulu (general secretary)
Membership. 107,553

10. South African Transport and Allied Workers' Union (SATAWU)
Address. PO Box 9451, Johannesburg 2000
Phone. +27 11 333 6+27
Fax. +27 11 333 8918
E-mail. nana@satawu.org.za
Leadership. Randall Howard (general secretary)
Membership. 74,325

11. Democratic Nurses Organisation of South Africa
Address. PO Box 1280, Pretoria 0001
Phone. +27 12 343 2315
Fax. +27 12 344 0750
E-mail. Info@denosa.org.za
Leadership. N.T.T. Gwagwa (general secretary)
Membership. 72,000

12. Chemical, Energy, Paper, Printing, Wood and Allied Workers' Union (CEPPWAWU)
Address. PO Box 3219, Johannesburg 2000
Phone. +27 11 833 2870
Fax. +27 11 833 2883
E-mail. secretariat@ceppwawu.org.za
Leadership. Willie Nolingo (general secretary)
Membership. 67,162

13. Police and Prisons Civil Rights Union (POPCRU)
Address. PO Box 8657, Johannesburg 2000
Phone. +27 11 403 0406
Fax. +27 11 403 9377
E-mail. gsecretary@icon.co.za
Leadership. Abbey Witbooi (general secretary)
Membership. 75,937

14. SASBO: The Finance Union
Address. Private Bag X84, Bryanston 2021
Phone. +27 11 442 0030
Fax. +27 11 442,0034
E-mail. training@sasbo.org.za
Leadership. Shaun Oelschig (general secretary)
Membership. 58,656

15. Communication Workers' Union (CWU)
Address. PO Box 10248, Johannesburg 2000
Phone. +27 11 838 8188
Fax. +27 11 838 8727
E-mail. cwu@wn.apc.org
Website. www.cwu.org.za
Leadership. Seleboho Kiti
Membership. 35,008

Confederation of South African Workers' Unions (CONSAWU)
Address. PO Box 572, Pretoria
Phone. +27 12 324 1365
Fax. +27 12 324 5233
E-mail. Consawu@mweb.co.za
Leadership. Hendry Hendricks (general secretary)
International affiliation. WCL

Federation of Unions of South Africa (FEDUSA)
Address. PO Box 2096, Northcliff 2115
Phone. +27 11 476 5188
Fax. +27 11 476 5131
E-mail. fedusa@fedusa.org.za
Website. www.fedusa.org.za
Leadership. Mary Malete (president); Chez Milani (general secretary)
Membership. 555,600 paid-up members in 23 affiliated unions.
History and character. FEDUSA was launched on Apr. 1, 1997 and ranks second to COSATU among South Africa's trade union centres, although much smaller and far less influential. Its leading founder was the Federation of South African Labour Unions (FEDSAL). FEDSAL's membership was 80% white-collar

and this meant that, reflecting South African employment patterns, FEDSAL membership was about 70 per cent white. Thus, although both COSATU and FEDUSA are explicitly non-racial in recruitment, FEDUSA differs in its composition from COSATU, which is heavily black.

Also unlike COSATU, FEDUSA has no political alliances. It emphasizes moderation and participates fully in the range of tripartite institutions, such as NEDLAC and the Commission for Conciliation, Mediation and Arbitration set up after the end of apartheid. Its membership dipped initially after formation but rose from 454,719 in January 1998 to 555,600 by July 1999 as a majority of its affiliates increased their numbers, against the general trend in South African trade unionism.

Its affiliates include the South African Typographical Union, founded 1898 and reportedly South Africa's oldest union.

FEDSAL had cordial relations with the WCL, without being affiliated. In 1998, however, FEDUSA was accepted into affiliation by the ICFTU.

International affiliation. ICFTU; CTUC

Affiliates. FEDUSA has 23 affiliates; the following are the largest, with more than 30,000 members each:

1. Hospital Personnel Trade Union of South Africa (HOSPERSA)
Address. 2nd Floor, Glen Galleries, Glen Manor Avenue, Menlyn, Pretoria 0181
Phone. +27 12 365 2021
Fax. +27 12 365 2043
Membership. 50,000

2. Independent Municipal and Allied Trade Union (IMATU)
Address. PO Box 35343, Menlo Park 0102
Phone. +27 12 460 6276
Fax. +27 12 346 2895
E-mail. info@imatu.co.za
Website. www.imatu.co.za
Membership. 73,000

3. Public Servants Association of South Africa (PSA)
Address. PO Box 40404, Arcadia 007
Phone. +27 12 303 6500
Fax. +27 12 303 6652
E-mail. ask@psa.co.za
Website. www.psa.co.za
Membership. 180,000

4. United Association of South Africa (UASA)
Address. PO Box 565, Florida 1709
Phone. +27 11 472 3600
Fax. +27 11 674 4057
E-mail. jplbez@uasa.org.za
Website. www.uasa.org.za

National Council of Trade Unions (NACTU)
Address. PO Box 10928, Johannesburg 2000
Phone. +27 11 833 1040
Fax. +27 11 833 1032
E-mail. info@nactu.org.za
Website. www.nactu.org.za
Leadership. Cunningham Ngcukana (general secretary)
Membership. 397,000
History and character. NACTU was formed in 1986, by the merger of the former Council of Unions of South Africa (CUSA) and Azanian Confederation of Trade Unions (AZACTU).

NACTU's position was that blacks should always hold the leadership positions in unions even if (as was the case with some CUSA unions) they had some non-black members (AZACTU unions admitted only blacks). While AZACTU was affiliated to the Azanian People's Organization, CUSA had sympathies with the Pan-Africanist Congress (PAC). The new federation was weakened by the disaffiliation from CUSA of the National Union of Mineworkers, the major element in CUSA, to become a founding member of COSATU. NACTU faced divisions in its attitude to the ANC, which had established a clear leadership position in the struggle against apartheid.

In 1994 NACTU became the ICFTU's first post-apartheid South African affiliate. However, it is dwarfed in significance by COSATU.

International affiliation. ICFTU; CTUC

Spain

Capital: Madrid
Population: 40.3 m. (2004 est.)

1 Political and Economic Background

Following his victory in the Spanish Civil War of the 1930s, Gen. Franco maintained authoritarian right-wing rule until his death in 1975. There then followed a political transition with the establishment of a constitutional monarchy and democratic political structures. Under the social democratic Spanish Socialist Workers' Party (PSOE), in office from 1982, Spain gained entry to the European Communities in 1986. In 1996 the PSOE lost power to a coalition government led by the conservative Popular Party (PP). In elections in March 2000, the PP under Prime Minister José María Aznar obtained an absolute majority, winning 183 of the 350 seats in the Congress of Deputies, with the PSOE remaining the major opposition party, with 125 seats. At elections in March 2004, however, the PSOE returned to power, taking 164 seats to the PP's 148. There is a decentralized regional government structure with elected local parliaments.

Spain enjoyed economic growth above the EU average in the years running up to it joining the single European currency at its launch on Jan. 1, 1999, though growth has more recently slowed in the face of the general sluggishness of the European economy. The Spanish economy is based on private enterprise and the Aznar government emphasized market deregulation and increased competition, the approach being to sell profitable public companies and use the proceeds to meet the costs of closing loss-making companies. The change of government in 2004 marked a change in emphasis rather than sharp discontinuity with the Aznar government's policies. Although Spain has demonstrated a high rate of job creation over a long period, unemployment has been a consistent problem, and the proportion of the population of working age at work remains below the EU average. There has tended to be a high rate of transient temporary employment.

GDP (purchasing power parity) $885.5bn. (2004 est.); GDP per capita (purchasing power parity) $22,000 (2004 est.).

2 Trade Unionism

Spain has been a member of the ILO since 1956, having earlier been a member from 1919 to 1941. It ratified ILO Conventions No. 87 (Freedom of Association and Protection of the Right to Organize, 1948) and No. 98 (Right to Organize and Collective Bargaining, 1949) in 1977.

The anarchist Confederación Nacional del Trabajo (CNT) and the socialist Unión General de Trabajadores (UGT) were the largest centres before the civil war of 1936–39, although the trade union movement was highly fragmented. Under Franco a corporatist vertical trade union structure was imposed, and employers were incorporated in the membership of the trade unions. The unions predominantly provided social services and strikes were illegal. The UGT, CNT and the Basque union, ELA-STV, maintained some underground activity, with headquarters in exile, and workers' commissions developed at shop-floor level in the 1960s, contributing to the weakening of the official trade union structure in the latter part of Franco's rule. In 1977, following the return to democratic government, the Francoist trade union structure was dissolved and free trade unionism has since developed. The 1985 Law of Trade Union Liberty superseded legislation of 1977. It guarantees full freedom to almost all employees (excluding the armed forces and those in the judicial system) to join and form unions; the self-employed, unemployed and the retired may join established unions but not set up unions of their own. Unions are free to draw up their own rules and may not be dissolved or suspended except through the courts in the event of a serious breach of the law. They may engage in collective bargaining, organize activities both on and off working premises, strike, and put forward candidates for election as workers' delegates in enterprises. Discrimination by employers against trade union members and organizers is prohibited and such cases have priority in the labour courts.

During the 1980s trade union membership declined sharply. This reflected factors such as the loss of jobs in traditional industries, increasing unemployment, growth in temporary employment, and conflict between the unions, which were also slow to adjust to the changing nature of work and society. At the start of the 1990s, total union membership stood at 1.7m. (14.5% of the workforce), a decline of 750,000 compared with 1978, the year following the legalization of free unions. During the 1990s, however, the unions increased their strength, with membership totalling 2.25m. (18.2% of the workforce) by 1997, and continuing to grow thereafter. In part this growth reflected the rate of job creation (the fastest in the EU) but the unions also proved more successful in focusing on bargaining to improve the wages and conditions of their members.

While the strength of the unions is still concentrated in the industrial areas, especially Catalonia (which includes the second largest city, Barcelona), the capital Madrid, and the Basque country, growth has occurred in other traditionally less organized areas, particularly in the public or semi-public services sector. About 30–35% of union members are in the public sector. Some 60% of workers are employed in businesses with fewer than ten employees and the unions are weak in these small enterprises. Involvement of women in unions also still lags behind their participation in the labour force.

During the transition period of the late 1970s the union movement was fragmented, but its organizational structure has since solidified. The two main centres are the UGT and the Workers' Commissions (CCOO), both now affiliated to the ICFTU. They are of similar strength and together account for three-quarters of union members. Since 1978 workplace elections have been held (every two years before 1982, and then every four years) to elect workers' delegates (in companies with more than 50 members these forming works committees), with responsibility for collective bargaining. The elections, in which turnouts of over 70% are normal, also have a broader significance. Only organizations winning 10% of all seats nationwide are considered representative at sectoral or national level, and only the UGT and CCOO qualify on that basis. At regional level, the cut-off is 15%. Two regional unions are also considered representative in the Basque country (Basque Workers' Solidarity, ELA/STV and the Assembly of Basque Workers, LAB), while in Galicia the Confederación Intersindical Galega (CIG) is considered representative. One effect of the system of workplace elections is that it has tended to marginalize smaller unions unable to cross the 10% threshold, and to consolidate the position of the UGT and CCOO. In addition to the main national centres, the civil service union confederation CSI-CSIF is of influence in its sector.

Relations between the UGT and CCOO were formerly combative, reflecting political differences and the fact that they competed in the same workplaces. The two centres have retained a rough parity in workplace elections since democratization. While the CCOO and UGT compete nationwide and in all main sectors there are some regional variations in strength: the CCOO is stronger in Catalonia and Madrid, the UGT in Aragon, Asturias, Galicia, Murcia and Valencia. The UGT is also stronger in much of the public administration.

In its early stages the CCOO was strongly associated with the Communist Party of Spain (PCE) while the socialist UGT up to the 1980s functioned almost as the alter ego of the PSOE. Nicolas Redondo, UGT leader until 1994, was an architect of the PSOE's post-Franco revival and proposed Felipe González as party leader in the 1970s. However the unions' traditional political alignments were disrupted as the UGT came into conflict with the PSOE, in office after 1982, which adopted cautiously free market policies. In effect the UGT swapped partners, embracing the CCOO as an industrial ally to replace the PSOE. The rapprochement began in 1986 and by February 1988 they were able to sign a pact to "work together for a social shift" in the government's policy. The two centres worked together henceforth (with minor hiccups) jointly calling general strikes in 1988, 1992 and 1994.

The CCCO has adopted centrist positions and the two confederations now emphasize their closeness in perspectives, generally working together to create common positions. They have tended to take similar viewpoints, and with a similar weight of emphasis, on issues such as privatization, tax reform, job creation and defending public services. Both have in recent years generally supported the policy of moderation in wage claims in exchange for measures to promote employment. While they have similar agendas, the CCOO during the Aznar period adopted a slightly more moderate line, emphasizing the achievement of goals through negotiation with employers rather than legislation. This has been a point of difference over achievement of the 35-hour week. In the event, the government has emphatically refused to legislate a 35-hour week, and the first examples of its introduction in 2000 (in the Basque public administration and in a provincial sectoral agreement) were achieved through local bargaining. In October 1997 the CCOO signed a sectoral collective bargaining agreement for the construction industry one day before the UGT was due to hold a general strike in the industry over the high rate of industrial accidents. The issue was finally resolved three months later when the UGT signed the agreement with an annexe on health and safety added. Such breakdowns are unusual, however.

Of particular concern to the Spanish unions are the issues of unemployment and temporary employment. During the mid to late nineties Spain created more jobs than any other EU country, but unemployment although declining, remains high, at just over 11%. The problem of unemployment is exacerbated by the fact that, while unemployment benefits are comparable to elsewhere in the EU, half of the unemployed do not qualify for benefits. During the late 1990s associations of the unemployed appeared in many parts of Spain, and these commonly criticized the unions for focusing on their (employed) members. In response, the unions have emphasized their concern for the position of the unemployed. Both the CCOO and UGT were highly critical of the 1999 governmental National Action Plan on jobs (as required by the EU), adopted in May 1999, saying that they had not been consulted on its content. The unions argue for adoption of the 35-hour week, as well as for positive government intervention in depressed areas, as a means to stimulate extra jobs. However, the employers emphasize the need to remove rigidities in the labour market and reduce Spain's traditional job security.

Following deregulation in 1994, aimed at increasing labour market flexibility, there has been a major increase in forms of temporary employment. This accounts for 31% of all employment, the highest rate of transient temporary employment in the EU. Nearly two-thirds of temporary contracts are for a period of less than one month, and in Spain temporary work is associated not just with insecurity but poor working conditions and low wages. The rate of temporary employment is 25% higher among women than among men, affecting particularly areas such as retailing, catering and domestic service. The unions say that the high proportion of workers on temporary contracts is a deterrent to union organizers, as such workers are unlikely to wish to jeopardize their employment prospects. In July 1999 the Law on Temporary Employment Agencies was adopted obliging employers to pay the same rates to workers on contract from such agencies (responsible for about 15% of temporary recruitment) as to their other workers.

The unions also see the issue of temporary employment as linked to Spain's high incidence of industrial accidents. According to government statistics more than half of all such accidents involve temporary workers. Lack of training of temporary workers, and the prevalent lack of a health and safety culture, are blamed by the unions for this situation. In 1996 a Law on the Prevention of Occupational Risks came into force but since then the number of industrial accidents has increased and the unions say the law has not been effectively enforced.

Collective bargaining is widely practiced in both the private and public sectors. Bargaining tends to be decentralized, with much bargaining at provincial sectoral levels, although there has been some increase in company agreements, sometimes achieved without union involvement. Sectoral collective agreements nominally apply to all in that sector, signatories or not, but the dominance of small and medium-seized enterprises, and the high incidence of transient and precarious employment, reduces their real impact. Spain has complex and multi-layered conciliation and arbitration mechanisms with the system processing some 500,000 conciliation cases and 250,000 judicial cases each year. In 1996 these mechanisms were added to when the employers and unions agreed to set up (effective 1998) the Intersectoral Mediation and Arbitration Service (SIMA). Notwithstanding these systems for dispute resolution, strikes remained fairly common. The right to strike has been interpreted by the Constitutional Court to include general strikes called in opposition to government policy.

3 Trade Union Centres

Confederación Sindical de Comisiones Obreras (CCOO)
Trade Union Confederation of Workers' Commissions
Address. Fernández de la Hoz 12, 28010 Madrid
Phone. +34 91 702 80 00
Fax. +34 91 310 48 04
E-mail. ccoo@ccoo.es
Website. www.ccoo.es (Spanish; English and French sections)

Leadership. José Maria Fidalgo (secretary-general)
Membership. 958,000
History and character. The workers' commissions developed in the 1960s as a shop floor movement, mounting frequent (although illegal) strikes and industrial action. In November 1967 the Supreme Court declared the CCOO illegal as an instrument of the (outlawed) Communist Party of Spain (PCE) and hundreds of members were imprisoned.

Following the death of Franco in 1975 there was a gradual liberalization. In 1976 the CCOO was established as a trade union confederation, and it and other trade unions were formally legalized in April 1997. It held its first congress in June 1978, with Marcelino Camacho elected secretary-general. The veteran Camacho made way at the fourth (1987) congress for the 37 year-old Antonio Gutiérrez. His election represented a victory for the *gerardistas*, supporters of the moderate PCE leadership of Gerardo Iglesias, who favoured a broad left alliance, against the candidate of the previously influential hardline *carrillistas* supporting the former PCE leader, Santiago Carrillo, purged in 1985. Camacho became president in 1987, but was not re-elected in 1996 having "joined minority and critical positions". Under Gutiérrez PCE members were sidelined from key positions in the CCOO. In April 2000 José Maria Fidalgo, a bone surgeon seen as a pragmatist able to do business with the Aznar government (which won a substantial victory in elections the previous month), was elected secretary-general in succession to Gutiérrez.

Since legalization in 1977 the CCOO has been of a similar size to the other principal trade union centre, the UGT. The CCOO's close relationship with the PCE, and that of the UGT with the PSOE, contributed to adversarial relations in the post-Franco period, but the two centres progressively developed a more cooperative relationship in response to PSOE policies from the mid-1980s. Its policy positions are close to that of the UGT in most areas and the two centres generally work closely together.

The CCOO supported Spanish accession to the European Communities (which took effect in 1986) and calls for the development of a "social Europe". Domestically its priorities include Spain's high rates of unemployment, temporary employment and industrial accidents, defence of welfare services, extension of unemployment benefits, and achieving the 35-hour week. It sees the Spanish economy as facing problems of lack of social cohesion, fragmented labour relations, unfair competition, and low quality jobs and work, and rejects further deregulation as the solution for these ills. However, Fidalgo has also emphasized the need to engage with younger sections of the population, who are not attracted by old-style industrial trade unionism, and for the unions to recognize that the labour market has changed, and the issue is no longer trying to retain jobs for life, but employability.

Along with the UGT, the CCOO is recognized as representative at the national level and participates in tripartite negotiations with the government and employers. At the international level, the CCOO was finally admitted to the ETUC in 1991, after many years delay. The 1996 congress decided to apply for membership of the ICFTU and this was subsequently granted.
International affiliations. ICFTU; ETUC; TUAC

Unión General de Trabajadores (UGT)
General Union of Workers
Address. Horteleza 88, 28004 Madrid
Phone. +34 91 589 7691
Fax. +34 91 589 7813
E-mail. internacional@cec.ugt.org
Website. www.ugt.es (Spanish only)
Leadership. Cándido Méndez (secretary-general)
Membership. 944,000
History and character. Founded in 1888, the UGT claimed 2 million members on the eve of the Spanish Civil War in 1936. Its leadership was in exile in France during the Franco period. In 1976 the UGT held its 30th congress in Spain, and in 1977 it was legalized.

For many years the UGT was very closely linked to the socialist PSOE and its fortunes mirrored that of the PSOE: the PSOE took power for the first time in 1982, the same year that the UGT came first in workplace elections, having previously trailed the CCOO. However, the 1980s were marked by the gradual disillusionment of the UGT with the PSOE government and its social and economic policies. Early in the decade it was prepared to enter into tripartite pacts, but the last centralized wage round, the social and economic agreement (AES) lapsed in 1986. After the breakdown of negotiations over the renewal of a social pact in 1987, relations between the UGT and PSOE became increasingly acrimonious. Rival factions within the Catalonian metal workers' federation of the UGT attacked each other with bottles and iron bars in March 1988 during a meeting to choose delegates for the union's congress. Antonia Puerta, the leader of the metal workers and a government supporter, even led a breakaway congress though this attracted only a small minority of delegates. The agreement between the UGT and the CCOO in support of a December 1988 general strike over social security reform hardened the rift as the PSOE attempted to mobilize its supporters within the UGT against the leadership of the union.

At its 35th congress, held in Madrid in April 1990 the UGT symbolized its estrangement from PSOE by inviting all groups represented in the Parliament to attend. After being unanimously re-elected secretary-general, Nicolás Redondo reported that the UGT had consolidated its understanding with the CCOO and the Basque Union ELA-STV, leaving behind the "confrontational relationship of previous years". Relations with the PSOE government remained difficult into the 1990s as the government adhered to policies to control public deficits and inflation to harmonize with the leading EU economies. In 1993 the UGT rejected the government's call for a social pact involving below-inflation wages for three years and reform of the labour market, and joined in a 24-hour general strike in January 1994.

In 1993 the UGT finance arm IGS and its property cooperative PSV, went into receivership. The ventures had been launched in 1988 with the aim of delivering cheap housing for the masses, and it was thought that as many as 50,000 investors had participated. In fact, only 1,100 homes of a planned total of 20,000 had been completed. Only the extension of government credits prevented outright bankruptcy.

Even before this Redondo had announced his intention to retire, an announcement which proved a signal for the disgruntled construction, metal worker and transport affiliates to call for a total change of leadership. At a February 1994 meeting the UGT executive moved to defuse discontent by proposing to the April congress the compromise name of Cándido Méndez as Redondo's successor.

From the mid-1990s the UGT had to deal with an increasingly strong conservative PP government. The 38th congress, held in March 1998, saw a relaxation of past tensions with the PSOE and the UGT calling for the creation of a common front of the social and political left. The UGT is one of only two confederations (the other being the CCOO) regarded as representative at national level. It participates in bilateral and tripartite negotiations with the employers' organizations and the government. While it competes for members in the same sectors as the similarly-sized CCOO, relations between the two centres are generally cordial and constructive and there is active coordination in formulating policies. For both key issues are employment security; extending unemployment benefit cover; achieving the 35-hour week; improving regulation of temporary employment; reducing industrial accidents; adoption of a more progressive tax policy; and seeking more public investment in job creation. Both are committed to seeking the development of the social dimension of the European Union. They also organize jointly, as on Dec. 3, 1998, when the two centres joined to call a day of action in opposition to government policy on unemployment benefit cover, working hours and tax reform. Differences have appeared over the 35-hour week. The UGT has called for legislation, on the French model, to impose a 35-hour week, which it says will help create jobs, but on this it differs from both the CCOO and the PSOE, which have argued for achieving shorter hours through collective bargaining.

The UGT operates nationwide and in all sectors, although it is not as strong as the CCOO in Madrid and Catalonia. It leads in much of the public administration. Women are underrepresented, and the 1998 congress adopted a resolution that union management bodies should aim to have 20% women on their management boards. In January 2000 a Union of Professionals and Self-Employed Workers (UPTA) was formed within the UGT. There are an estimated 1.8 million self-employed in Spain. There is also a Union of Small Farmers linked to the UGT.
International affiliations. ICFTU; ETUC; TUAC

4 Other Trade Union Organizations

Confederación General del Trabajo
General Confederation of Labour
Address. Via Layetana, 18 9ª Plta, 08003 - Barcelona
Phone. +93 310 33 62
E-mail. sp-f.internacional@cgt.es

Website. www.cgt.es (Spanish only)
Membership. 100,000

Euzko Langilleen Alkarasuna/Solidaridad de Trabajadores Vascos (ELA/STV)
Basque Workers' Solidarity
Address. Barrainkua 13, E – 48009 Bilbao
Phone. +34 944 03 77 00
Fax. +34 944 03 77 77
E-mail. nazioarte@elasind.org
Website. www.ela-sindikatua.org (Basque, Spanish and English)
Leadership. José Miguel Leunda Etxeberria (president); José Elorrieta Aurrekoetxea (secretary-general)
Membership. 82,000
History and character. The ELA/STV was founded in Bilbao in 1911 and operated underground in the Franco period. It is politically independent but Basque nationalist in orientation and close to the Basque Nationalist Party (PNV), which favours full regional autonomy but opposes the violence of the ETA movement. The ELA/STV and Polish Solidarity are unique in Europe in that they hold dual ICFTU/WCL affiliation.

ELA/STV is the leading union in the Basque country, and has representative status at the regional level based on workplace elections. In the 1990s ELA/STV's principal strength lay in the white-collar sector, where it had considerable success in achieving higher salaries for public sector professionals than their counterparts received in Madrid. In July 2000 it reached agreement with the Basque regional government on introduction of the 35-hour week in the public administration, the first Spanish province to agree this.
International affiliations. ICFTU; WCL; ETUC; TUAC

Unión Sindical Obrera (USO)
Workers' Union
Address. Príncipe de Vergara 13 7°, 29001 Madrid
Phone. +34 91 577 41 13
Fax. +34 91 577 29 59
E-mail. s.general@uso.es
Leadership. Manuel Zaguirre (secretary-general)
Membership. 106,000
History and character. Founded in 1961, the USO is politically independent and pluralist.
International affiliation. WCL

Sri Lanka

Capital: Colombo
Population: 19.91 m. (2004 est.)

1 Political and Economic Background

Sri Lanka (as Ceylon) gained its independence from the United Kingdom in 1948. Over the last two decades the dominant issue facing the country has been the conflict between the majority Sinhalese and minority Tamil populations, with political life conducted under the shadow of regular assassinations and attempted assassinations. Since a formal ceasefire agreement was reached under Norwegian auspices in February 2002 the conflict has significantly subsided, having resulted in some 64,000 deaths since erupting on a large scale in 1983. The two main political parties since independence have been the Sri Lanka Freedom Party (SLFP) and the United National Party (UNP). The SLFP returned to power in 1994, as the dominant force in the left-wing People's Alliance, after 17 years of UNP rule. In December 2001, however, the People's Alliance was defeated in parliamentary elections by an alliance led by the UNP. This resulted in protracted tension between new Prime Minister Ranil Wickremesinghe (UNP) and President Chandrika Bandaranaike Kumaratunga (SLFP), who had herself been re-elected for a second six-year presidential term in December 1999, the political system depending on a form of "co-habitation". Parliamentary elections in June 2004, in which the SLFP allied with the extreme left-wing and ultra-nationalist Sinhalese People's Liberation Front (JVP) as the United People's Freedom Alliance (UPFA), resulted in victory for the UPFA, with the new Prime Minister coming from the SLFP.

Sri Lanka's economy was built on plantation crops, such as tea, rubber and coconuts, but by 2003 plantation crops had declined to only 15% of exports compared with 93% in 1970. A range of industries has been developed, with textiles and garments now contributing 63% of exports and areas such as telecommunications and financial services being opened up. After 1977 the UNP reversed much of the previous SLFP government's policy of state interference in the economy and the SLFP-led People's Alliance government elected in 1994 committed itself to proceed with some privatization while retaining state ownership of a large number of enterprises. Growth averaged 5–6% per annum for most of the 1990s, but there was a recession in 2001, aggravated by the general global downturn. Economic growth resumed thereafter, GDP increasing 4% in 2002 and 5.2% in 2003. Rural underdevelopment remains a problem, with average incomes in Colombo five times those in the countryside. The economy has benefited from the comparative peace since the 2002 ceasefire with the Tamil separatists, but eastern coastal regions suffered devastating damage from the December 2004 tsunami.

GDP (purchasing power parity) $73.7bn. (2004 est.); GDP per capita (purchasing power parity) $3,700 (2004 est.).

2 Trade Unionism

Sri Lanka ratified ILO Convention No. 98 (Right to Organize and Collective Bargaining, 1949) in 1972 and Convention No. 87 (Freedom of Association and Protection of the Right to Organize, 1948) in 1995. Trade unions were given legal recognition under colonial rule in 1935, by which time substantial development had occurred. Since independence, trade union freedoms have been substantial but subject to periodic modification or suspension according to political conditions. The historical stronghold of the labour movement is the plantations, where over 70% of the workforce, which is predominantly "Indian Tamil", are organized. In total there are approximately one million union members in Sri Lanka, a majority of whom are women, reflecting the role of women in the plantations. Outside the plantations, unions are comparatively strong in the public sector and also in the bigger private sector enterprises, but are not well represented in small and medium-sized enterprises. Members of the police force, the judiciary and armed forces may not join unions. Amendments to the Industrial Disputes Act, adopted in December 1999, imposed an obligation on employers to recognize trade unions and prohibited anti-union discrimination. Employers found guilty of such discrimination are required to reinstate workers dismissed for union activities, but have the right to transfer them to different locations. While workers in the export processing zones are under national law free to join unions, in practice union organizers are commonly kept out of the zones by employers; union membership among the 125,000 workers in the zones is reported as about 10%.

Only seven persons are needed to form a union and this factor in combination with ethnic, linguistic and ideological divisions has fragmented the labour movement. In 2002 the Department of Employment and Labour reported a total of 1,689 registered unions. Many of these have only a few dozen members. Many leading unions are affiliated with political parties and are politically active; political divisions are one factor in a situation where several trade unions often compete in the same enterprise. The Department may cancel the registration of any union that does not submit an annual report, although this is the only legal basis for cancellation of registration. There are 19 trade union federations. Federation of public service unions is in theory not allowed but in practice is tolerated and seven such federations currently exist. Public and private sector federations may not federate.

There is no national trade union centre. The ICFTU-affiliated Ceylon Workers' Congress (CWC) has historically been (and remains) the most influential trade union politically, and the largest in membership, but is based primarily among the Indian Tamils in the plantations, a narrow section of the workforce. Both major political parties have trade union wings, as does the extremist JVP. The WCL is represented by the National Workers' Congress (NWC), while the WFTU claims to have five affiliates, the Ceylon Federation of Trade Unions, the Democratic Workers' Congress, the Sri Lanka Mahajana Trade Union Federation, the Sri Lanka Nidakas Sewaka Sangamaya, and the Progressive Workers' Congress. Various unions and federations affiliate to the global union federations.

Collective bargaining is patchily practiced in the private sector, although complicated by the multiplicity of unions in individual enterprises. In 2003 some 50 employers belonging to the Employers' Federation of Ceylon (EFC) had collective agreements with unions in place. Worker councils exist in some non-union enterprises and the export processing zones as a forum for negotiations, but according to the unions these are ineffective. Four of 200 factories in the EPZs are reported to have collective bargaining agreements.

All workers, other than civil servants (who may submit their grievances to the Public Service Commission), police, the armed forces and prison officers, and those engaged in "essential services", have the right to strike and the law prohibits retribution against strikers. Strikes have historically been quite common, especially in the public services, in areas such as the transportation, medical, educational, power generation, and port sectors. Under the conservative UNP administration (1977–94), the government used a broad interpretation of "essential services" to control strikes and made use of emergency powers. Up to 100,000 employees were dismissed after a 1980 general strike supported by the opposition (most of these were later reinstated). The People's Alliance government from 1994, however, generally showed a more liberal approach to strike action while retaining the power to declare industries to be essential services. In 1998 an essential services designation was used to try to end industrial action in the postal service, leading to the arrest of the general secretary and other leaders of the UPTO postal workers' union. However, the dispute was ultimately settled by negotiation with agreement that strikers would not be victimized.

Sri Lanka has some tripartite elements in its industrial relations system, primarily the Wages Boards. These Boards determine minimum terms and conditions of employment. Conciliation and arbitration services are available through the Department of Labour.

3 Trade Union Centre

There is no trade union centre.

4 Other Trade Union Organizations

Ceylon Workers' Congress (CWC)
Address. 72 Ananda Coomarasamy Mawatha, PO Box 1294, Colombo 3
Phone. +94 11 257 4528
Fax. +94 11 230 1355
E-mail. cwcctuc@slt.lk
Leadership. Arumugan Thondaman (president)
Membership. 180,000
History and character. From its foundation the CWC recruited mainly among up-country plantation workers of Indian Tamil descent who had for decades suffered institutionalized discrimination. (The Indian Tamils, representing about 5% of the Sri Lankan population and being mostly wage labourers on the plantations in central parts of the country, are considered a separate ethnic group from the Sri Lankan Tamils of the north and east. They are still officially stateless.) Although the CWC membership includes other groups such as teachers, mercantile and commercial employees, the bulk comes from the tea and rubber plantations and it remains the most important trade union in the plantations – the most highly organized sector of the workforce. It is also simultaneously a political party (with A. Thondaman leading both party and union), though as a political force its base remains largely limited to its own membership as a trade union. As a political party it has held the rural development or similar portfolio in successive governments since 1978.

The Ceylon Indian Congress Labour Union was founded in 1940 as the labour wing of the Ceylon Indian Congress (CIC), itself formed in 1939 by Shri Nehru as the envoy of Mahatma Gandhi. In its early years the principal objective of the CIC was to secure independence from British rule, and following the achievement of this in 1948, the Labour Union was renamed as the Ceylon Workers' Congress. It became a trade union with a separate political wing, rather than vice versa, in 1950. In 1977 the CWC's political wing became a political party (also called the Ceylon Workers' Congress, and in effect indivisible from the union) and the union/party president, Sovumiyamoorthy Thondaman, was returned to parliament, taking office in 1978 for the first time as Minister for Rural Development in the UNP government of Junius Jayewardene. Using this position within the government coalition, the CWC was able to secure constitutional revisions that extended basic rights to so-called "stateless" persons, most of whom were of Indian descent. S. Thondaman, often regarded as the leader of the people of Indian descent in Sri Lanka, retained a Cabinet post after the change of government in 1994 but died in October 1999. His successor as CWC president, Arumugan Thondaman (S. Thondaman's grandson), became Minister for Livestock Development and Estate Infrastructure, surviving a leadership challenge in the party/union. In 2002 the CWC staged a programme of "non-cooperation" in the plantations in pursuit of a pay campaign. The campaign to achive full rights of citizenship for the up-country Tamils continues and in 2003 then Prime Minister Wickremesinghe (UNP) said legislation was in preparation.

The CWC as a political organization has traditionally split into factions supporting the UNP and the SLFP. In the 1994 and 2000 elections the majority faction supported the SLFP-led People's Alliance. In the April 2004 elections, however, in which the SLFP chose to ally with the militant Sinhalese JVP as the United People's Freedom Alliance (UPFA), the CWC ran under the banner of the UNP-led United National Front. The election resulted in the UPFA heading the polls but just falling short of holding a majority in parliament. The CWC initially joined the opposition ranks. At the start of September 2004, however, the eight CWC members of parliament joined the government benches, thereby giving President Kumaratunga a majority of 113 of the 225 members of parliament. The CWC took the position that this was necessary to protect the interests of the up-country Tamil people and also to give the President the support to move forward the peace process with the Tamil separatists.

The CWC opposes all discrimination based on race, creed, caste or religion. It has established a vocational training complex and a construction consortium with the help of the ICFTU, and has launched credit schemes and a project to create a number of small dairy farm cooperatives on plantations.
International affiliations. ICFTU; CTUC

Jathika Sevaka Sangamaya
Address. 416 Kotte Road, Pitakotte
Leadership. Sirinal de Mel (secretary); Palitha Athukorala (chief organizer)
History and character. The is the trade union wing of the UNP political party and grew to significance in the years of UNP government from 1977.

Lanka Jathika Estate Workers' Union (LJEWU)
Address. 60, Bandaranayakepura, Sri Jayawardenepura Mawata, Welikada, Rajagiriya
Phone. +94 1 872790
Fax. + 94 1 862262
E-mail. ctucljeu@sri.lanka.net
Leadership. Rajah Seneviratne (president)
History and character. The LJEWU was founded in 1958 and is the rival to the Ceylon Workers' Congress in the plantations, both as a trade union and political force, though less powerful. It is linked to the UNP. Gamini Dissanayake, who was assassinated in October 1994 while running as UNP candidate for president, was president of the union and also served as Minister of Plantations, while Ranil Wickremesinghe, who became Prime Minister after the UNP-led United National Front won the December 2001 general election, was formerly the union president. It has a collective agreement with the Employers' Federation of Ceylon which represents the privatized plantation companies.
International affiliations. CTUC; IUF

National Workers' Congress (NWC)
Address. 94 1/6 York Building, York Street, Colombo 1
Phone. +94 1 71 33 86
Leadership. Marcelle Rajahmoney (president); Antony Lodwick (general secretary)
History and character. Founded in 1952; politically independent and non-sectarian. Emphasizes worker education and is focusing on trying to organize in the free trade zones.
International affiliation. WCL

Sri Lanka Nidahas Sevaka Sangamaya (SLNSS)
Address. 301 T. B. Jaya Mawatha, Colombo 10
Phone/Fax. + 94 1 69 40 74
E-mail. slnss@diomand.lanka.net
Leadership. Leslie Devendra (general secretary)
History and character. The SLNSS is affiliated to the Sri Lanka Freedom Party. President Kumaratunga was elected president of the union in 2000 at the same time as being elected leader of the party.

Sudan

Capital: Khartoum
Population: 39.15 m. (2004 est.)

1 Political and Economic Background

Since its establishment in 1956, the Republic of Sudan has experienced political instability, division between the Arab, Muslim north, including the capital, Khartoum, and the mainly Christian and animist, African south. President Jaafar al-Nemery came to power in a coup in 1969 and established a one-party state until he was overthrown in a military coup in 1985. The current President, Omar Hassan Ahmad al-Bashir, seized power in a military coup in 1989. Organized political activity, banned after the 1989 coup, resumed in 1998, although the most important opposition parties remained in exile. In December 2000 Bashir was re-elected President with 86.5% of the vote, the runner-up (with 9.6% of the vote) being former President Nemery, who had returned to Khartoum under an amnesty granted in May 2000. In legislative elections also held in December 2000, Bashir's National Congress party won 355 of the seats in the National Assembly, the remaining five going to independents. Voting did not take place in three southern states under rebel control. Despite periodic peace agreements, the 21-year old civil war in the south continued at the end of 2004, while the activities of government-backed militias in the rebellious western region of Darfur had been described by the USA as constituting genocide; the government has been tacitly backed by China, Russia and Islamic governments, however. There is a large refugee population, from Sudan's wars and those of its neighbours. In all some two million people may have died as a result of conflict and resultant famines since 1983.

Sudan has been impoverished by decades of civil war, the burden of military spending, drought and rapid population increase. Some 80% of the workforce are engaged in agriculture and herding, much of it at subsistence level, and there has been little investment in modern industries and services. However, an oil sector is now under development with foreign investment (with a substantial Chinese involvement), boosting growth in the formal economy, which also includes a small manufacturing sector. The country is heavily indebted.

GDP (purchasing power parity) $70.95bn. (2004 est.); GDP per capita (purchasing power parity) $1,900 (2004 est.).

2 Trade Unionism

Sudan ratified ILO Convention No. 98 (Right to Organize and Collective Bargaining, 1949) in 1957, but has not ratified Convention No. 87 (Freedom of Association and Protection of the Right to Organize, 1948).

Trade unions originally developed after World War II. In the late 1980s there were two centres, the blue-collar Sudanese Workers' Trade Union Federation (SWTUF) – which at that point claimed to have 1.5 million members – and the white-collar Sudanese Federation of Employees and Professional Trade Unions (SFEPTU). After Bashir came to power in 1989 he dissolved the trade unions. The SWTUF leaders kept their personal freedom following the coup but their activities were outlawed; most members of the SFEPTU were arrested however. In the summer of 1990, Dr. Ali Fadul of the Sudan Doctors' Union died in prison as the result of torture.

In 1989 General Bashir set up preliminary committees to run union affairs and other steering committees were announced. In 1991 a Trade Union Dialogue Conference was convened in Khartoum, ostensibly intended to secure agreement of trade unionists to new laws conforming to ILO Conventions. From this conference a tripartite committee was chosen which drafted the 1992 Trade Union Law establishing a new system of enterprise unions.

Under the 1992 Act, which still applies, a single trade union system was set up, in which the government dictates the sectors and enterprises in which unions can exist. The reorganized SWTUF according to its rules functions to "mobilize the masses for production and to defend the authenticity of the Islamic state." In 1992, elections to union office were held, prior to which many union activists had been asked for written undertakings that they would not stand for office or work in opposition. Since by this time a number of union members had also been imprisoned and tortured, a number of leading figures withdrew from the country to organize abroad.

The SWTUF continues to exist as a government-sponsored trade union organization. Following a 1996 merger it now mobilizes 13 unions and claims to have 800,000 members. It remains the case that independent trade unions may not be organized in Sudan and there are continuing reports of the arrest and torture of activists who try to organize independently. The SW(L)TUF, which sees itself as the successor to the SWTUF abolished in 1989, operates in exile and to some degree underground in Sudan. Following the adoption of a new constitution in January 1999, which embodied a right of association, the SW(L)TUF said this appeared to allow a small margin of freedom. However, when it attempted to hold a meeting in Khartoum on July 6, 1999, the authorities arrested 14 members of the executive committee, including the president and secretary-general.

There is a nominal right to engage in collective bargaining but in practice the government dominates the process of setting wages in the formal sector. Strikes are banned but took place in 1998–99 over the impact of privatization on jobs and salary arrears.

Suriname

Capital: Paramaribo
Population: 437,000 (2004 est.)

1 Political and Economic Background

Formerly Dutch Guiana, Suriname achieved complete independence from the Netherlands in 1975. In February 1980, the government was overthrown by Sgt.-Maj. Désiré ('Desi') Bouterse. Since then its politics have been characterized by periods of direct or indirect military intervention, with close relationships between military commanders and civilian politicians.

Jules Wijdenbosch became Prime Minister and Vice-President after a coup (sponsored by Bouterse) in 1990, lost power in elections in 1991, and was elected President (by a United People's Conference) in 1996.

As a result, a coalition government was formed that was led by Wijdenbosch's National Democratic Party (NDP), and including parties based in Suriname's Indonesian and Indian communities. The May 2000 elections for the National Assembly resulted in a victory for Ronald Venetiaan's New Front for Democracy (NF), which, taking 32 of the 51 seats, secured a comfortable victory over its closest rival, the Millennium Conmbination (MC), an alliance of the NDP, led by Bouterse, and two smaller parties. President Wijdenbosch's Democratic National Platform 2000 (DNP 2000) came third in these elections, which had been called early to quell street demonstrations demanding his resignation after the economy collapsed and a series of resignations from his Cabinet had left him with a minority in the National Assembly. In August 2000 Venetiaan was sworn in as the new President of the country, after being elected by a two-thirds majority of National Assembly members.

The largest section of the Suriname workforce is employed by the government and by parastatal industries such as the state oil company, sugar estate, rice farm, banana and palm oil plantations and others. The economy is dominated by the mining of bauxite and its processing into alumina and finished aluminium. The country has been associated with gun running, international drug trafficking and money laundering.

GDP (purchasing power parity) $1.75bn. (2004 est.); GDP per capita (purchasing power parity) $4,000 (2004 est.).

2 Trade Unionism

Suriname ratified ILO Convention No. 87 (Freedom of Association and Protection of the Right to Organize, 1948) in 1976 and No. 98 (Right to Organize and Collective Bargaining, 1949) in 1996. The unions are well established with some 60% of the workforce organized. The labour movement is also highly fragmented: there are six federations and the ICFTU has three affiliates in a country of less than half a million people. There is a tradition of active union involvement in politics and the unions have been politically influential.

About 50% of the workforce are covered by collective bargaining agreements. There is a constitutional right to strike in both private and public sectors and strikes are common. It is difficult for employers to dismiss workers and the Ministry of Labour reviews each dismissal individually, with powers to order reinstatement.

3 Trade Union Centre

There is no recognized trade union centre.

4 Other Trade Union Organizations

Algemeen Verbond van Vakverenigingen in Suriname 'De Moederbond' (AVVS or Moederbond)
General Alliance of Labour Unions in Suriname
Address. PO Box 1951, Coppenstraat 134, Paramaribo

Phone. +597 463 501
Fax. +597 465 116
History and character. De Moederbond was founded in 1951. In December 1982 the military declared a state of martial law, destroyed the union's offices and summarily executed its president, Cyrill Daal, and other opponents of the regime. Following this other leaders of De Moederbond went into exile. The ICFTU suspended De Moederbond's affiliation in 1986 but restored it in 1988, when the ICFTU executive board found that it had now been restored to democratic principles.
International affiliation. ICFTU

Centrale van Landsdienaren Organisaties (CLO)
Federation of Civil Service Organizations
Address. Verlengde Gemene Landsweg 74, Paramaribo
Phone. +597 49 98 39
International affiliation. ICFTU

Organisatie van Samenwerkende Autonome Vakbonden (OSAV)
Organization of Cooperating Autonomous Trade Unions
Address. Keizerstraat 218, Paramaribo
Phone. +597 476 921
Fax. +597 474 866
Leadership. Waldo Bijnoe (chairman)
History and character. OSAV was founded in 1985 after a dispute over the leadership of De Moederbond, of which most of its officers were members.
International affiliation. WCL (extraordinary member)

Progressieve Vakcentrale 47 (C-47)
Progressive Labour Federation 47
Address. PO Box 9331, Paramaribo
Phone. +597 401 044
Fax. +597 490 915
International affiliation. ICFTU

Swaziland

Capital: Mbabane
Population: 1.17 m. (2004 est.)

1 Political and Economic Background

The Kingdom of Swaziland achieved full independence from the United Kingdom in 1968. The present King, Mswati III, acceded to the throne in 1986 and enjoys considerable executive powers, ruling through a Cabinet appointed by him. Emergency powers have been in force since 1973 and political activity is banned under the 1978 Constitution although a number of political associations developed in the 1990s. The majority of members of the lower house of Parliament are elected, on a non-party basis, as representatives of the tribal assemblies (Tinkhundla).

In November 2003 the King adopted a new constitution, which has come under massive criticism from Swazi civil society because it places the monarchical system above the law. According to the constitution the government is subject to the control of the Swazi King, who has absolute executive, judicial and legislative authority.

About 80 per cent of the population are supported by (mainly subsistence level) agriculture, and manufacturing is based largely on the processing of agricultural and forestry products. The domestic mining sector has declined but an estimated 20% is added to national income by remittances from Swazi workers employed in the mines of neighbouring South Africa, which is also by far Swaziland's most important trading partner. There is an extremely high incidence of HIV/AIDS, reportedly affecting one-third of the adult population, threatening future prospects.

GDP (purchasing power parity) $5.7bn. (2004 est.); GDP per capita (purchasing power parity) $4,900 (2004 est.).

2 Trade Unionism

Swaziland joined the ILO in 1975 and ratified ILO Convention No. 87 (Freedom of Association and Protection of the Right to Organize, 1948) and Convention No. 98 (Right to Organize and Collective Bargaining, 1949) in 1978.

Unions are relatively well organized in the formal sector and there is a national centre, the Swaziland Federation of Trade Unions (SFTU). The SFTU is affiliated to the ICFTU. Since the mid-1990s it has been in constant conflict with the government over labour legislation and restrictions on political and civil rights.

Industrial relations legislation provides a framework for trade union activities, requiring employers to recognize unions with 50% membership among the workforce and permitting collective bargaining. However, there is also a range of restrictions on unions, including a ban on engaging in political activity and a restriction on the role of federations to the provision of advice and services. Severe penalties may be imposed in case of illegal strikes and strikes in broadly defined essential services, and sympathy strikes and strikes not considered in the national interest are banned. Trade union federations may not lead or incite work stoppages, and their officials can be sentenced to up to five years' imprisonment for violations. Despite this, and regular arrest of its officials, the SFTU has called numerous strikes, demonstrations and other protests as part of a broad campaign for democratization.

In December 2002 the SFTU and the Swaziland Federation of Labour (SFL) co-organized a stay-away to press for democratic reforms. A follow up strike was held in March 2003. In August 2003 the SFTU called a national strike and a series of demonstrations to protest against the governance record of the King and in particular his draft constitution. The protests were violently broken up by security forces. One trade unionist was killed and another was rushed to hospital with a gunshot wound.

In November 2003 Swazi protesters were joined by COSATU organized protesters on the Swazi/South

Africa border to call for democracy and constitutional reform in Swaziland.

3 Trade Union Centre

Swaziland Federation of Trade Unions (SFTU)
Address. PO Box 1158, Manzini
Phone. +268 50 56 575
Fax. +268 50 56 575
E-mail. sftu@africaonline.co.sz
Leadership. Jan Sithole (general secretary)
Membership. 80,000 in 21 affiliates
History and character. Founded in 1973, the SFTU became the central trade union organization in the mid-1980s, with members from both the public and private sectors, and including agricultural workers.

Since 1994, the SFTU has stepped up its campaign, in alliance with civic and opposition groups, for repeal of restrictive labour legislation, for a democratic and pluralist society and the end of emergency powers legislation. It has called regular strikes and demonstrations and this has led to continual harassment. In 1995 general secretary Jan Sithole was threatened with deportation when the authorities challenged his right to Swazi citizenship, and this threat has recurred in subsequent years. In August 1995 Sithole was kidnapped, according to the SFTU by government agents, and abandoned in the boot of a car on the outskirts of Manzini. In February 1997 armed police broke up an SFTU general council meeting after the SFTU called a national stay-away. Council members were reportedly beaten by police and the death of SFTU treasurer, Mxolisi Mbata, in October 1998 was attributed to injuries sustained at that time. Sithole and three other officials were arrested in connection with the stay-away. They subsequently stood trial on charges of intimidating bus operators into not running services during the stay-away, but were acquitted by a judge.

The SFTU called for a boycott of the legislative elections in October 1998 on the ground that they were not democratic. On Nov. 17, Sithole was held for questioning in connection with an explosion, but released the following day, and over the following months other SFTU officials were subject to arrests and police raids on their homes. In November 2000 Sithole was put under house arrest after the SFTU, in alliance with civic and opposition groups, called a two day strike, banned by the government, on a platform demanding the legalization of political parties and trade union and human rights. In June 2002 a Swazi senator and government delegate to the ILO conference publicly threatened Sithole, warning that he must consider his future and that of his children before he criticized the political situation in his country at the conference. The SFTU's campaign is receiving the active support of COSATU in South Africa.
International affiliation. ICFTU

4 Other Trade Union Organization

Swaziland Federation of Labour (SFL)
Leadership. Vincent Ncongwane (general secretary)
Membership. 4,000 in 3 affiliates

Sweden

Capital: Stockholm
Population: 8.99 m. (2004 est.)

1 Political and Economic Background

The Social Democratic Labour Party (SAP) has been in office continuously since 1936, other than for periods in 1976–82 and again in 1991–94. In the most recent elections in September 2002 the SAP remained the largest party, taking 144 of the 349 seats in parliament with 39.8% of the vote (up from 36.4% in the previous election in 1998), and party leader Göran Persson continued as Prime Minister. The minority SAP government also continued to enjoy the support in parliament of the Left Party (VP) and the Green Ecology Party, although there is no coalition. The opposition is led by the Moderate Party (MSP), which itself formed a centre-right coalition government in the period September 1991–September 1994 under Prime Minister Carl Bildt; although the second largest party in the parliament elected in 2002, it won only 55 seats, well down on its previous strength. After a referendum in November 1994, Sweden joined the EU on Jan. 1, 1995. However, a referendum held in September 2003 on joining the euro currency zone resulted in a substantial majority against, despite Prime Minister Persson's call for a vote in favour. Significant sections of the SAP disregarded the position of the party leadership.

Sweden is a prosperous country that combines a welfare state with a strong private sector. Sweden is notable for its international orientation, reflected in the fact that a country with a population of only nine million is home to an array of major international companies. The "Swedish model" of consensus involving a high degree of social organization, centralized bargaining between employers and unions, and generous social provision came under strain in the late 1980s and early 1990s. Manufacturing jobs were lost and Sweden experienced recession for the first time since the 1930s, with GDP falling year-on-year 1991–93. The centre-right Bildt government of 1991–94 was a period of austerity measures and there was a financial crisis in 1992. From the mid-1990s, however, there was strong economic growth led by areas such as pharmaceuticals, computers and telecommunications and a wide range of private-sector services. Unemployment, which reached close to 15% at mid-decade, had fallen to 4% by late 2000, this being achieved with inflation of only 1% in 2000. The global downturn after the turn of the new century affected Sweden to some degree, but the economy has rebounded; the budget presented to parliament in September 2004 forecast growth of 3.5% in 2004 and 3% in 2005, allowing the government to plan higher public spending and modest tax cuts while maintaining a small budget surplus. Unemployment stood at 5.6% in 2004, with a further 2.3% of the workforce engaged on government schemes. Levels of taxation are among the highest in the developed world.

GDP (purchasing power parity) $238.3bn. (2004 est.); GDP per capita (purchasing power parity) $26,800 (2004 est.).

2 Trade Unionism

Sweden ratified ILO Convention No. 87 (Freedom of Association and Protection of the Right to Organize, 1948) in 1949 and Convention No. 98 (Right to Organize and Collective Bargaining, 1949) in 1950.

Numerous socialist-inclined trade unions appeared in the 1880s and in 1889 these were influential in the formation of the Social Democratic Labour Party (SAP), which functioned both as a political party and as a trade union centre. This in turn led to the formation of the Swedish Trade Union Confederation (LO) in 1898. In 1906 the newly formed Swedish Employers' Confederation (SAF) recognized the LO and the right of workers to bargain collectively. In 1938 the two sides concluded their first Basic Agreement.

The structure of the Swedish trade union movement is similar to that in other Scandinavian countries. The trade union centres form a pyramid. At the base is the largest centre, the LO, which represents blue-collar workers and at the end of 2003 had 1,890,000 members, including 250,000 pensioners and students. Its membership is now very slowly declining along with the relative decline of blue-collar industrial jobs. In the middle of the pyramid is the 1,276,000-strong Swedish Confederation of Professional Employees (TCO). This represents the white-collar sector, where unionization began in the 1930s, and some 63% of its members are women. Its membership has of late been stable. At the apex is the Swedish Confederation of Professional Associations (SACO), with 556,000 members at the end of 2003, which represents employees and professionals with graduate qualifications. SACO has been increasing in membership in line with developments in the economy. In general (and again reflecting a pattern seen in other Scandinavian countries) the LO and the TCO have maintained a cooperative relationship, which has been enhanced by the trend to equalization of pay and conditions between the manual and white-collar sectors. The LO and the TCO have demarcation agreements to reduce intrusions on their various areas of recruitment, but there are few such agreements between the TCO and SACO.

Union density in Sweden is the highest achieved voluntarily anywhere in the world, with the great majority of employees in unions. Density declined slightly from the mid-1980s, standing at 81% in 1990, but then recovered to its previous level of 83% by mid-decade before declining to 79% in 2000. Density peaks at 94% for municipal employees but even in the weakest area – white-collar workers in private sector service industries – density is close to 70%. Overall, there is little difference in density as between white-collar and blue-collar employees. The proportion of self-employed in Sweden, 8% of the labour force, is also the lowest in the EU. The LO has considered but not agreed the principle of recruiting among the self-employed, while SACO freely recruits the self-employed into its member associations.

The exceptional organizational success of Swedish trade unions has been variously explained. The persistence of social democratic government for most of the period since the 1930s undoubtedly provided a favourable environment for trade unionism. However, while the LO has been close to the Social Democratic Labour Party (SAP) the TCO and SACO have grown without political allegiance. The closed shop does not exist (other than to some extent in the building trades) and the unions enjoy few exceptional privileges in law: indeed, the whole basis of the industrial relations system is free bargaining between unions and employers, with relatively light state intervention.

The trade unions have benefited to some degree from their role in the administration of unemployment insurance funds. Most workers automatically become members of an unemployment insurance scheme (97% of funding for which comes from the government) by joining a union. On the other hand, union membership is not obligatory to be a member of an unemployment insurance fund, and the number of workers who have joined such funds directly rather than through a union has increased in the 1990s at the same time as union density has risen.

Factors that in other countries have generally been seen as seriously weakening the trade unions seemed to have had no or the opposite effect in Sweden. Thus union density increased in the period 1990–94 notwithstanding there being a centre-right government in office, the worst recession since World War II, and loss of manufacturing jobs. The Swedish economy has experienced the same movement out of blue-collar manufacturing and into services as other developed countries, but the unions have succeeded in increasing their strength in the services sector. The most rapid growth in union membership in the 1990s came in the blue-collar private services sector, an area with a high incidence of low-paid part-time female working; in many countries such workers have proved difficult or impossible to organize, but in Sweden this is not the case. In recent years LO membership has begun to ebb along with blue-collar jobs in tradtional industries, but it has held its position in services and white-collar union memberships have generally been stable or actually increasing.

In Swedish society there is a traditional emphasis on achieving consensus and a general commitment to maintaining a social safety net. The unions have played a role for decades as social partners and adopted positions in which they have considered the broad national interest as well as their members' sectional interests. In that sense, they have been seen as acceptable and even desirable by the broader community and as a force for social stability. Symptomatically, higher-paid managers and professionals are highly organized – SACO, representing graduate employees, is still growing in size. Similarly, the employers have accepted the place of unions and been prepared to accept them as legitimate representatives of the workforce. These features of Swedish society should not be exaggerated, however. Strikes have always been a an element of industrial relations and the conflict between free market deregulators and advocates of the welfare state has continued in Sweden since the 1980s.

Swedish unions have avoided the political and religious polarization seen in many European countries. The LO identifies with the SAP, but the TCO and SACO are politically neutral rather than anti-SAP. They have also generally avoided conflict over recruitment, not least because the three confederations recruit in distinct areas. Where there are potential overlaps the unions have generally worked to ensure strict demarcation. The continued blurring of distinctions between white-collar and blue-collar, the basic division between the LO and TCO, and between rank-and-file white-collar employees and those with graduate qualifications, the dividing line between the TCO and SACO, has produced remarkably little friction. However, it seems possible that this blurring will produce major changes in the medium-term. The TCO has in the past floated the prospect of an eventual merger with SACO, in view of the increasingly graduate nature of the white-collar workforce, but SACO has shown little enthusiasm.

The high degree of organization of Swedish employers has also worked to strengthen the role of the unions. In many countries the absence of representative employer organizations to deal with seriously undermines national level trade unions, which cannot negotiate national or sectoral agreements that are deliverable at the enterprise level. In Sweden most employers are members of employer organizations and adhere to the agreements these organizations reach. This is the case despite the lack of any legislation binding employers to such agreements.

Swedish collective bargaining arrangements famously express a cooperative spirit and have done so since the 1938 Saltsjobaden Agreement of the Swedish Employers' Confederation (SAF) and the LO. In 1952, they signed their first major national collective pay agreement, which was widely observed even though the participants were not legally or constitutionally bound by it. For several decades thereafter the pattern was one in which the LO and SAF negotiated a central agreement which was then translated into detail in sectoral and in some cases company-level agreements. From the 1970s the "Swedish model" came under strain and finally collapsed at the end of the 1980s under the impact of growing white-collar trade unionism, increasing employer unease over legislated rights for employees in the enterprise, and gathering economic difficulty. From 1983 onwards individual LO and SAF affiliates had sought separate agreements with their counterparts rather than the usual umbrella arrangements, but the main framework survived (with some structural changes) until 1989. That year's central agreement proved to be the last.

Since that time the pattern has been one of sectoral bargaining, with the LO and other confederations playing a looser coordinating role. Since 1998 most national sectoral agreements on pay and conditions have been concluded for three-year periods (1998, 2001 and 2004), with about 200 national sectoral agreements being concluded. However, while a return to the old centralized system is no longer even on the LO's agenda there has been movement to introduce more structure to the bargaining process. In the period 1994–99 wage increases were generally ahead of the average in Sweden's major competitors and the government was concerned that wage drift should not damage Sweden's competitiveness. In 1997 the government set up a committee to review the options for changing the bargaining structure. However, the unions showed themselves divided on the issue. While the LO was keen to strengthen centralized bargaining, the TCO and SACO were against imposed pay norms and any form of incomes policy. In the event the social partners could not produce a consensus and the government went ahead with legislation in December 1999 which embraced a number of the committee's recommendations but fell short of creating a rigid system for centralized incomes policy. Under this legislation a new Mediation Authority (Medlingsinstitutet) was established effective June 2000. This was to be responsible for drawing up an annual report on wage determination, expected to bear heavily on the thinking of employers and trade unions in future bargaining rounds. With the consent of the parties the Mediation Authority could also appoint mediators to lead collective bargaining where the partners could not agree their own mechanisms. The unions generally welcomed the creation of the Mediation Authority and are not unresponsive to the government's anxieties about Swedish firms becoming uncompetitive if wage costs soar, or to the risk of increasing unemployment if inflation triggers rises in interest rates. The 2004 bargaining round for the most part proceeded smoothly against a background of a well-performing economy, low inflation and considerable consensus on the shape of settlements. The pattern is for export-oriented private sector industries to set the benchmarks for agreement, followed by other private sector areas, and then the public sector.

The trade union movement is relatively decentralized and is vigorous at the local level. Union branches within companies maintain a bargaining role and there is no parallel system of works councils. Collective agreements are binding on signatories (but not on those employers who are not members of the signatory organization). There are virtually no restrictions on strikes in either the public or private sector, beyond a duty to give notice. There is no provision for compulsory mediation or arbitration and no legislation on strikes in essential services. SAF (which in 2001 merged with another employers' organization to form the Confederation of Swedish Enterprises) has called for a ban on sympathy strikes (which are legal and still occur from time to time) and on strikes directed against small traders and family firms; it has also called for a principle of proportionality to be legislated, whereby unions could not undertake lightly strikes destroying other people's interests. These calls have been ignored by the government, but the new Mediation Authority has been given powers to force the postponement of industrial action, and the notice period has been extended from 7 to 14 days. Strikes have tended, however, to be at a low level in Sweden over the last decade; only 838 working days were lost to strikes in 2002, although this escalated to 620,000 in 2003, the highest level since 1995, largely because of strikes by the LO-affiliated Municipal Workers'

Union (Kommunal). Successive governments have generally avoided intervening in industrial disputes leaving these to be resolved by the parties.

There is no system of statutory works councils in Sweden. However, the Co-determination Act of 1977 requires employers to advise and consult employees before making any significant changes in company operation. Under the Board Representation Act employees have the right to be represented on the boards of all companies with 25 or more employees. The unions appoint the employee representatives on boards. Employee representatives do not participate in discussions relating to issues such as collective bargaining and are in effect excluded from most critical decision-making, but both unions and the majority of employers believe the system is a beneficial one. Other types of informal co-determination, not under the Co-determination Act, are also quite widespread.

Like Swedish institutions generally, the unions have a strong international focus. The LO and the TCO cooperate with the Swedish International Development Authority (SIDA) and distribute SIDA funds to unions in developing countries through the LO/TCO Secretariat for Trade Union Development.

3 Trade Union Centres

Landsorganisationen i Sverige (LO)
Swedish Trade Union Confederation
Address. Barnhusgaten 18, S-105 53 Stockholm
Phone. +46 8 796 25 00
Fax. +46 8 796 28 00
E-mail. info@lo.se
Website. www.lo.se (Swedish; English)
Leadership. Wanja Lundby-Wedin (president)
Membership. 1,892,000 (end 2003)
History and character. The LO is the organization of blue-collar workers in Sweden. Its membership splits 61% private sector and 39% public sector. A small majority (54%) of its membership is male, in contrast to the white-collar TCO, which has a female majority. During the 1990s the LO had notable success in increasing the organization of blue-collar women workers in services, helping to offset losses of blue-collar male jobs. Its membership is declining gradually, however, year-on-year, having stood at just over 2 million in 2000. Between 2002 and 2003 it declined 1.4%, with all of its affiliates losing members other than the Commercial Employees' Union (Handels). The slow decline essentially reflects changes in the composition of the workforce.

The LO sees its role as providing central coordination and national-level policy direction on behalf of its affiliated unions. The individual unions are responsible for sectoral bargaining and for managing unemployment insurance funds.

The LO was created in 1898 by the Social Democratic Labour Party (SAP), and it has remained close to the party. The SAP first came to power in 1932, applying Keynesian policies to counter the depression. In 1938 the LO reached the first Basic Agreement with the employers' confederation SAF and thereafter pursued in conjunction with the SAP (in office for most of the rest of the century) "middle way" policies of social and industrial reform. Despite strains in the 1980s over government austerity policies, the relationship remains close and explicit, with a general convergence over policy positions, and the LO is represented on the SAP executive committee.

From the 1950s to the late 1980s collective bargaining was highly centralized with the LO reaching a series of Basic Agreements providing a detailed framework. This system, which the LO very much favoured, did not survive into the 1990s as the increasing influence of free market economics, the election of a centre-right government in 1990, and the desire of both the SAF and the white-collar union centres for increased decentralization, undermined it. Even the SAP, back in office since 1994, has not supported a return to the old highly centralized system. However, the desire for a more controlled process for wage determination was reflected in the establishment of the new Mediation Institute, with effect from June 2000, a move welcomed by the LO. The LO now accepts that bargaining should take place mainly at the sectoral level but emphasizes that achieving pay awards that do not stoke inflation or damage competitiveness, as the government wishes, demands a degree of national coordination.

Historically the LO used centralized bargaining to promote a policy of "wage solidarity" whereby differentials between different industries, and different occupations in the same industry, were to be leveled out. It still through its coordinating role seeks to encourage this approach, though it has met declining support from individual unions and members in successful areas of the economy.

Most LO affiliates work on the principle of organizing all blue-collar workers in a workplace in the same union regardless of trade. Exceptionally, the building trade unions are craft-based. The majority of LO affiliates organize 80% or more of the workers in their fields (the average is 82%), except in retailing and services. The LO's role includes the resolution of demarcation disputes between its member unions, although the affiliates are independent. The number of affiliates has been reduced from 24 to 16 over the last two decades in a slow process of amalgamation that is still continuing. In 2002 the small 11,000-member Agricultural Workers' Union (SLF) was merged into the Muncicipal Workers' Union (Kommunal), the biggest LO union. In 2004 two of the major affiliates, the Metal Workers' Union and the Industrial Workers' Union, agreed to merge in 2006; the two unions, which had both lost members in recent years, would have a combined membership (at current levels) of some 470,000, second to Kommunal. However, although most LO unions have seen a decline in membership in recent years, the scale of this has not been such as to precipitate wholesale mergers and consolidation, although there have been discussions among other unions.

The LO has generally been unenthusiastic about admitting the self-employed to membership, in contrast to SACO and some TCO unions. A 1998 LO report concluded that "helping members who have been forced into self-employment is a trade union task, while helping those who want to become self-employed is not". The LO unions for builders, painters and transport workers have all decided against admitting the self-employed. The forestry workers' union has taken a different position, however, reflecting industry changes that pushed many former employees into tied forms of self-employment.

The LO allied itself with SAP in saying that introduction of the 35-hour week, while a goal, should be introduced by industry agreement on a case-by-case basis and not legislated for. The normal statutory working time is 40 hours.

Sweden joined the EU in 1995 and building the social dimension of the EU is an increasingly important priority for the LO. Wanja Lundby-Wedin, the LO's first woman president, elected in September 2000, had previously held responsibility for European-level trade union issues. However, the issue of Swedish accession to the euro currency zone, which was the subject of a national referendum in September 2003, proved divisive in the LO, as in the SAP (where despite the government calling for a "yes" vote some Cabinet ministers were openly opposed). Lundby-Wedin joined Prime Minister Persson in calling for a "yes" vote, but a contrary position was taken by some affiliated unions such as the Transport Workers and the Commercial Employees' Union. In the event the electorate decisively rejected the government's position, 56.1% voting "no", and surveys suggested that 65% of LO members were in the "no" camp. The desire to protect national independence and Sweden's social and economic system seemed to be of paramount importance for those voting "no". In June 2004 the LO congress rejected a call by the Transport Workers for a national referendum on the issue of the proposed European constitution.

The LO has a traditionally strong involvement in international trade union development. Its assistance programmes for central and Eastern Europe and developing countries take place through the LO-TCO Secretariat for Trade Union Development and the Olof Palme International Centre.

The LO favours the extension of worker participation and co-determination in the workplace. It is represented on numerous governmental bodies such as the National Labour Market Board, the National Board of Occupational Safety and Health, and the National Social Insurance Board.

Pensions are a major issue in Sweden, which has an aging population. In 1996 the SAF and LO signed a new pension agreement to provide a supplementary pension scheme for blue-collar workers.

Enterprises linked to the LO include the Workers' Educational Association (ABF), the Correspondence School (Brevskolan) and insurance company Folksam.
International affiliations. ICFTU; ETUC; TUAC; NFS
Affiliated unions. There are 16 affiliates, as follows:

1. Building Workers' Union (Byggnads)
Address. Hagagatan 2, S-106 32 Stockholm
Phone. +46 8 728 48 00
Fax. +46 8 34 50 51
E-mail. forbundert@byggnads.se
Website. www.byggnads.se (Swedish only)
Leadership. Hans Tilly (president)
Membership. 133,000
History and character. Established 1949. Absorbed the small Sheet Metal Workers' Union in January 2000.

2. Electricians' Union (SEF)
Address. PO Box 1123, S-111 81 Stockholm
Phone. +46 8 412 82 82
Fax. +46 8 412 82 01
E-mail. postbox.fk@sef.com
Website. www.sef.com
Leadership. Stig Larsson (president)
Membership. 22,993

3. Building Maintenance Workers' Union (Fastighets)
Address. PO Box 70446, S-107 25 Stockholm
Phone. +46 8 696 11 50
Fax. +46 8 24 46 90
E-mail. info@fastighets.se
Website. www.fastighets.se (Swedish; English section)
Leadership. Hans Öhlund (president)
Membership. 40,000

4. Graphic Workers' Union (Grafiska Fackförbundet, GF)
Address. PO Box 1101, S-111 81 Stockholm
Phone. +46 8 791 16 00
Fax. +46 8 411 41 01
E-mail. gf@gf.se
Website. www.gf.se
Website. www.gf.se (Swedish only)
Leadership. Jan Österlind (president)
Membership. 31,278

5. Commercial Employees' Union (Handels)
Address. PO Box 1+46, S-111 81 Stockholm
Phone. +46 8 412 68 00
Fax. +46 8 10 00 62
E-mail. webmaster@handels.se
Website. www.handels.se (Swedish only)
Leadership. Ninel Janson (president)
Membership. 170,000. Represents workers in retail and wholesale trades, clerical workers, etc. 74% of members are women.

6. Hotel and Restaurant Workers' Union (HRF)
Address. PO Box 1143, S-111 81 Stockholm
Phone. +46 771 57 58 59
Fax. +46 8 411 71 18
Website. www.hrf.net (Swedish; English section)
Leadership. Birgitta Kihlberg (president)
Membership. 61,000

7. Industrial Workers' Union (Industrifacket)
Address. PO Box 1114, S-111 81 Stockholm
Phone. +46 8 786 85 00
Fax. +46 8 10 59 68
E-mail. postbox.fk@industrifacket.se
Website. www.industrifacket.se (Swedish; English section)
Leadership. Leif Ohlsson (president)
Membership. 90,000

History and character. Founded in 1993 by merger of the Factory Workers' Union and the Textile, Garment and Leather Workers' Union. This is a general industrial union with members in industries including textiles, clothing, leather, chemicals, rubber, plastics, oil-refining, glass, gas, pharmaceuticals, sugar, concrete, laundry and others, and it organizes 95% of blue-collar workers in the industries it covers. It has an active international trade union development programme. In August 2004 the union congress voted to merge with the LO-affiliated Metal Workers' Union with effect from January 2006.
Affiliated to ICEM and ITGLWF.

8. Municipal Workers' Union (Kommunal)
Address. PO Box 19039, S-104 32 Stockholm
Phone. +46 8 728 28 00
Fax. +46 8 31 87 45
E-mail. kommunalinfo@kommunal.se
Website. www.kommunal.se (Swedish; English section)
Leadership. Ylva Thörn (general secretary)
Membership. 585,000
History and character. Founded in 1910 and the largest union in the LO. It organizes blue-collar employees in local government, members including care workers, workers in parks, street cleaning, schools, leisure facilities, waters and sewage, fire stations and urban transit. 80% of its members are women, 65% are part-time and 10% are unemployed. Kommunal emphasizes skills development and partnered in founding the Municipal University in collaboration with Göteborg and Linköping Universities and Jonköping University College. It plays an active role in helping members find jobs through its Job Points, which act as employment agencies. In 2002 it absorbed the small Agricultural Workers' Union, whose 11,000 members worked in areas such as gardeners. In 2003 Kommunal staged a series of strikes in pursuit of a pay claim, after cancelling the three-year collective agreement reached in 2001, following dissatisfaction with the results of local pay bargaining compared with what professional groups such as doctors and nurses had achieved. It is affiliated to PSI and ITF.

9. Food Workers' Union (LIVS)
Address. PO Box 1156, S-111 81 Stockholm
Phone. +46 8 796 29 00
Fax. +46 8 796 29 03
E-mail. info@livs.se
Website. www.livs.se (Swedish only)
Leadership. Åke Södergren (president)
Membership. 53,095

10. Metal Workers' Union (Metall)
Address. Olof Palmes Gata 11, S-105 52 Stockholm
Phone. +46 8 786 80 00
Fax. +46 8 24 86 74
E-mail. post.fk@metall.se
Website. www.metall.se (Swedish only)
Leadership. Göran Johnsson (president)
Membership. 379,000
History and character. Founded in 1888. Absorbed the small Mineworkers' Union in 1994. It is the second largest LO affiliate and organizes workers in engineering, the auto industry, mining and similar. In September 2004 the union congress voted to meger with the LO-affiliated Industrial Workers' Union as from January 2006.

11. Musicians' Union (Musikerförbundet)
Address. PO Box 49144, S-100 29 Stockholm
Phone. +46 8 587 060 00
Fax. +46 8 16 80 20
E-mail. info@musikerforbundet.se
Website. www.musikforbundet. se (Swedish only)
Leadership. Jan Granvik (president)
Membership. 5,643

12. Painters' Union (Malareforbundet)
Address. PO Box 1113, S-111 81 Stockholm
Phone. +46 8 587 274 00
Fax. +46 8 587 274 99
E-mail. post@malareforbundet.a.se
Website. www.malareforbundet.a.se (Swedish; English section)
Leadership. Lars-Åke Lundin (president)
Membership. 20,000

13. Paper Workers' Union (Pappers)
Address. PO Box 1127, S-111 81 Stockholm
Phone. +46 8 796 61 00
Fax. +46 8 411 41 79
E-mail. info@pappers.se
Website. www.pappers.se (Swedish only)
Leadership. Sune Ekbåge (president)
Membership. 27,985

14. Union for Service and Communications Employees (SEKO)
Address. PO Box 1105, S-111 81 Stockholm
Phone. +46 8 791 41 00
Fax. +46 8 21 89 53
E-mail. internationella@seko.se
Website. www.seko.se (Swedish; English section)
Leadership. Jan Rudén (president)
Membership. 190,000
History and character. In 1995 the Swedish National Union of State Employees (SF) was reorganized as SEKO and it now has more than 50% of its members in the private sector. It absorbed the Seamen's Union in 1996. SEKO organizes public and private sector workers in areas including telecoms and IT, postal services, public administration, transport, energy, the prison service, and defence. It is the third largest LO affiliate.

15. Forest and Wood Workers' Union (Skogstrafacket)
Address. PO Box 1152, S-111 81 Stockholm
Phone. +46 8 701 77 00
Fax. +46 8 20 79 04
E-mail. postbox.fk@skogstrafacket.org
Website. www.skogstrafacket.org (Swedish only)
Leadership. Kjell Dahlström (president)
Membership. 70,000
History and character. Founded in 1998 by merger of the Wood Workers' Union and the Forest Workers' Union.

16. Transport Workers' Union (Transportarbetareförbundet)
Address. PO Box 714, S-101 33 Stockholm
Phone. +46 8 723 77 00
Fax. +46 8 24 03 91
E-mail. transport.fk@transport.se
Website. www.transport.se (Swedish only)

Leadership. Per Winberg (president)
Membership. 93,000. Organizes truck, taxi and bus drivers.

Sveriges Akademikers Centralorganisation (SACO)
Swedish Confederation of Professional Associations
Address. Box 2206, S-10315 Stockholm
Phone. +46 8 613 48 00
Fax. +46 8 24 7701
E-mail. kansli@saco.se
Website. www.saco.se (Swedish; English section)
Leadership. Anna Eckström (president)
Membership. 556,000 (2003) in 26 member associations
History and character. SACO traces its origins back to 1947, and absorbed the National Federation of Civil Servants (SR) in 1975. It has considerably more than doubled its membership since the mid-1980s and is still growing in line with the ever-increasing role of professionals in the Swedish economy. SACO members are holders of university degrees or other higher educational qualifications, an expanding section of the workforce. An estimated 70–80% of Swedish graduates are members. Students comprise 15% of the membership. Its affiliated organizations are characteristically both trade unions, engaging in collective bargaining and defending members' interests as employees, and professional associations.

SACO functions to coordinate the activities of member unions on matters of common concern. 40% of members are in local government, 26% in central government and 31% in the private sector. Some 9% of members are fully or partly self-employed, and the proportion of members who are self-employed is rising.

SACO members include senior managers who negotiate with SACO unions. SACO states that it has "an unspoken but self-evident rule" that such managers do not participate in aspects of SACO activities that have a bearing on such negotiations. Managers in such positions are not covered by collective bargaining agreements but will receive individual support and advice in situations such as redundancy. Negotiations on salaries and other conditions of employment are conducted through two cartels. SACO-S represents members in central government service; the Federation of Salaried Employees in Industry and Services (PTK) negotiates for private sector salaried employees as well as representing the corresponding membership of TCO. There is a mixed pattern of collective and individual negotiation by unions with members employed in municipalities and counties.

SACO has a joint office with the LO and TCO in Brussels.

All SACO members are in the Graduate Employees' Unemployment Benefit Society (AEA), established by SACO in 1970 as a state-supported scheme. It launched a supplementary unemployment insurance scheme in June 2000.
International affiliations. ICFTU; ETUC; TUAC; NFS
Affiliated unions.

1. Agrifack (Swedish Association of Graduates in Agricultural, Horticultural, Forestry, Environmental and Nutrition Sciences)
Address. Box 2062, S-103 12 Stockholm
Phone. +46 8 613 49 00
Fax. +46 8 20 20 81
E-mail. agrifack@saco.se
Website. www.agrifack.org (Swedish only)

2. Akademikerförbundet SSR (Swedish Association of Graduates in Social Science, Personnel and Public Administration, Economics and Social Work)
Address. Box 12 800, S-112 96 Stockholm
Phone. +46 8 617 4400
Fax. +46 8 617 4401
E-mail. kansli@akademssr.se
Website. www.akademikerforbundetssr.se

3. Arkitekter (Architects)
Address. Box 9225, S-102 73 Stockholm
Phone. +46 8 50 55 7700
Fax. +46 8 55 7705
E-mail. kansli@arkitekt.se
Website. www.arkitekt.se (Swedish; English section)

4. Civilekonomerna (Swedish Association of Graduates in Economics and Business Administration)
Address. Box 4720, S-116 92 Stockholm
Phone. +46 8 783 2750
Fax. +46 8 783 2751
E-mail. kontakt@civilekonomerna.se
Website. www.civilekonomerna.se (Swedish only)

5. Civilingenjörsförbundet (CF) (Swedish Association of Graduate Engineers)
Address. Box 1419, S-111 84 Stockholm
Phone. +46 8 613 8000
Fax. +46 8 796 7102
E-mail. info@cf.se
Website. www.cf.se (Swedish only)

6. DIK-förbundet (Swedish Federation of Employees in the Documentation, Information and Cultural Fields)
Address. Box 760, S-131 24 Nacka
Phone. +46 8 466 24 00
Fax. +46 8 466 24 13
E-mail. kansli@dik.se
Website. www.dik.se

7. Förbundet Sveriges Arbetsterapeuter (FSA) (Swedish Association of Occupational Therapists)
Address. Box 760, S-131 24 Nacka
Phone. +46 8 466 24 40
Fax. +46 8 466 24 24
E-mail. fsa@akademikerhuset.se
Website. www.fsa.akademikerhuset.se

8. Ingenjörsförbundet (TLI) (Swedish Society of College Engineers)
Address. Box 1419, S-111 84 Stockholm
Phone. +46 8 619 51 70
Fax. +46 8 656 36 70
E-mail. epost@ing.se
Website. www.ing.se (Swedish only)

9. JUSEK (Swedish Federation of Lawyers, Social Scientists and Economists)
Address. Box 5167, S-102 44 Stockholm
Phone. +46 8 665 29 00
Fax. +46 8 662 79 23
E-mail. vaxel@jusek.se
Website. www.jusek.se (Swedish only)

10. Kyrkans Akademikerförbund (Association of Church Employees)
Address. Box 19609, S-104 32 Stockholm
Phone. +46 8 441 85 60
Fax. +46 8 441 85 77
E-mail. kansli@kyrka.se
Website. www.kyrka.se (Swedish only)

11. Legitimerade Sjukgymnasters Riksförbund (LSR) (Swedish Association of Registered Physiotherapists)
Address. Box 3196, S-103 63 Stockholm
Phone. +46 8 567 06 100
Fax. +46 8 567 06 199
E-mail. kansli@lsr.se
Website. www.lsr.se (Swedish only)

12. Lärarnas Riksförbund (LR) (National Union of Teachers in Sweden)
Address. Box 3529, S-103 69 Stockholm
Phone. ++46 8 613 27 00
Fax. +46 8 21 91 36
E-mail. lr@lr.se
Website. www.lr.se (Swedish only)

13. Officersförbundet (Swedish Association of Military Officers)
Address. Box 5338, S-102 47 Stockholm
Phone. +46 8 440 83 30
Fax. +46 8 440 83 40
E-mail. kansliet@officersforbundet.se
Website. www.officersforbundet.se (Swedish only)

14. SACO – förbundet Trafik och Järnväg, TJ (Transport and Railways)
Address. Munkbron 9, S-111 28 Stockholm
Phone. +46 8 14 29 65
Fax. +46 8 10 80 67
E-mail. kansli@trafikochjarnvag.a.se
Website. www. trafikochjarnvag.a.se (Swedish only)

15. SACO:s Tjänstemannaförbund SRAT (SACO's General Group)
Address. Box 38401, S-100 64 Stockholm
Phone. +46 8 442 44 60
Fax. +46 8 442 44 80
E-mail. kansli@srat.se
Website. www.srat.se (Swedish only)

16. Skogsakademikerna
Address. Box 760, S-131 24 Nacka
Phone. +46 8 466 24 50
Fax. +46 8 10 55 15
E-mail. skogsakademikerna@saco.se
Website. www.skogsakademikerna.saco.se (Swedish only)

17. Skolledarförbund (Swedish Association of Heads and School Principals)
Address. Box 3266, S-103 65 Stockholm
Phone. +46 8 567 06200
Fax. +46 8 567 06299
E-mail. info@skolledarna.se
Website. www.skolledarna.se (Swedish; English section)

18. Sveriges Farmacevtförbund (Swedish Pharmacists' Association)
Address. Box 3215, S-103 64 Stockholm
Phone. +46 8 507 999 00
Fax. +46 8 507 999 99
E-mail. post@farmacevtforbundet.se
Website. www.farmacevtforbundet.se

19. Sveriges Fartygsbefälsförening (Swedish Ships Officers' Association)
Address. Gamla Brogatan 19, 2 tr, S-111 20 Stockholm
Phone. +46 8 10 60 15
Fax. +46 8 10 67 72
E-mail. info@sfbf.a.se
Website. www.sfbf.a.se (Swedish; English section)

20. Sveriges Läkarförbund (Swedish Medical Association)
Address. Box 5610, S-114 86 Stockholm
Phone. +46 8 790 33 00
Fax. +46 8 20 57 18
E-mail. info@slf.se
Website. www.slf.se (Swedish only)

21. Sveriges Naturvetareförbund (Swedish Association of Scientists)
Address. Box 760, S-131 24 Nacka
Phone. +46 8 466 24 80
Fax. +46 8 466 24 79
E-mail. info@naturvetareforbundet.se
Website. www.naturvetareforbundet.se (Swedish; English section)

22. Sveriges Psykologförbund (Swedish Psychological Association)
Address. Box 3287, S-103 65 Stockholm
Phone. +46 8 567 06 400
Fax. +46 8 567 06 499
E-mail. post@psykologforbundet.se
Website. www.psykologforbundet.se (Swedish; English section)

23. Sveriges Reservofficersförbund (SROF) (Swedish Reserve Officers' Association)
Address. Box 5417, S-114 84 Stockholm
Phone. +46 8 661 8641
Fax. +46 8 791 7966
E-mail. kansli@srof.org
Website. www.srof.org

24. Sveriges Tandläkarförbund (STF, Swedish Dental Association)
Address. Box 1217, S-111 82 Stockholm
Phone. +46 8 666 15 00
Fax. +46 8 662 58 42

E-mail. kansli@tandlakarforbundet.se
Website. www.tandlakarforbundet.se (Swedish; English section)

25. Sveriges Universitetslärarförbund (SULF, Swedish Association of University Teachers)
Address. Box 1227, S-111 82 Stockholm
Phone. +46 8 505 836 00
Fax. +46 8 505 836 01
E-mail. kansli@sulf.se
Website. www.sulf.se (Swedish; English section)

26. Sveriges Veterinärförbund (SVF, Swedish Veterinary Association)
Address. Box 12709, S-112 94 Stockholm
Phone. +46 8 545 558 20
Fax. +46 8 545 558 39
E-mail. office@svf.se
Website. www.svf.se

Tjänstemännens Centralorganisation (TCO)
Swedish Confederation of Professional Employees
Address. Linnégatan 14, S–114 94 Stockholm
Phone. +46 8 782 91 00
Fax. +46 8 663 75 20
E-mail. info@tco.se
Website. www.tco.se (Swedish; English)
Leadership. Sture Nordh (president)
Membership. 1.28 million (2003) in 18 member organizations
History and character. The TCO is the principal trade union centre representing white-collar employees in Sweden. Its members include teachers, engineers, police officers, secretaries, bank clerks and nurses as well as white-collar workers throughout industry. Women have constituted a majority of the membership since 1977, and as of 2003 comprised 63% of the membership. Its membership includes 147,000 pensioners and 68,000 students.

Unions of salaried employees did not exist in Sweden before the 1920s. In 1931 a white-collar centre, DACO, was formed in the private sector. This won rights of association and collective bargaining for private sector white-collar employees in 1936, and in 1937 the TCO was created to campaign for such rights in the public sector. The DACO merged with the TCO in 1944, and freedom of association for white-collar workers was won progressively in the public sector from the 1940s to 1966. The membership of the TCO includes members of the police and armed forces, who are not barred from union membership or industrial action.

Some TCO unions are organized on the principle of recruiting all white-collar workers in a given enterprise, while others are occupationally-based.

Unlike the LO, the TCO has never aligned itself politically, and opinion surveys indicate that its membership is broadly representative of the Swedish population as a whole in its political balance. It has a cooperation agreement with the LO and their member unions have avoided conflicts in recruitment. However, as the proportion of graduates in the white-collar workforce continues to rise, there is thought to be scope for conflict with SACO, which organizes only graduates and with which the same degree of cooperation does not exist. There have been suggestions of eventual merger with SACO from within the TCO, although this has met with little apparent enthusiasm from SACO. The TCO has also sought to enforce demarcation among its own member organizations. In 1997 the TCO congress voted, fairly narrowly, to expel its affiliate representing supervisors in the private sector after this changed its name to Ledarna ('Leaders') and announced its intention to recruit managers at all levels across the entire workforce, in opposition to other TCO unions.

The TCO emphasizes the need to achieve professional development and training for its members, a good working environment and job and income security. It seeks the development of a social Europe. The TCO shares SACO's opposition to a return to the centralized bargaining led by the LO that dominated until the late 1980s. It prefers a devolved system such as now exists. It generally welcomed the creation of the new Mediation Institute in 2000, however, given that this body has a role in influencing but not constraining pay negotiation.

TCO's information services include a web-TV service in English.

Affiliated unions. The TCO has 18 affiliates; those with at least 10,000 members are listed below:

1. SIF (Swedish Union of Clerical and Technical Employees)
Address. Olof Palmes Gata 17, S-105 32 Stockholm
Phone. +46 8 50 89 70 00
Fax. +46 8 791 70 01
E-mail. postservice@sif.se
Website. www.sif.se (Swedish; English section)
Leadership. Mari-Ann Krantz (president)
Membership. 370,000
History and character. SIF was founded in 1920 and is the largest TCO affiliate, and therefore the largest white-collar union in Sweden, with members in areas including manufacturing, construction, computing and consulting.

2. Lärarförbundet (Swedish Teachers' Union)
Address. Box 12 229, S-102 26 Stockholm
Phone. +46 8 737 65 00
Fax. +46 8 56 94 15
E-mail. kansli@lararforbundet.se
Website. www.lararforbundet.se (Swedish only)
Membership. 208,903
History and character. This is the largest Swedish teachers' union, with members in all branches of education. Its headquarters, the Teachers' House, has a staff of 145 and there are 12 regional offices. It organizes union training courses for 30,000 teachers per year.

3. Union of Local Government Officers (SKTF)
Address. Box 7825, S-103 97 Stockholm
Phone. +46 8 789 63 00
Fax. +46 8 789 64 79
E-mail. dan.nielsen@sktf.se (international department)
Website. www.sktf.se (Swedish only)
Leadership. Eva Nordmark (president)
Membership. 177,500

4. Tjänstemannaförbundet (HTF, Salaried Employees' Union)

Address. Box 30102, S-104 25
Phone. +46 8 737 80 00
Fax. +46 8 618 77 19
E-mail. htf@htf.se
Website. www.htf.se (Swedish; English section)
Membership. 160,000
History and character. The HTF organizes in commerce, transport and services, with a substantial majority (63%) of women members. It organizes on the vertical principle and members are in a broad range of occupations and salary levels. It has 280 employees and 18 regional offices.

5. Vårdförbundet (Swedish Association of Health Professionals)

Address. Box 3260, S-103 65 Stockholm
Phone. +46 8 14 77 77
Fax. +46 8 411 42 29
E-mail. info@vardforbundet.se
Website. www.vardforbundet.se (Swedish; English section)
Membership. 112,236. Represents 93% of those in its area, including nurses and midwives, the great majority of whom work for county councils and municipalities.

6. Statstjänstemannaförbundet (ST, Union of Civil Servants)

Address. Box 5308, S-102 47 Stockholm
Phone. +46 8 790 51 00
Fax. +46 8 21 32 82
E-mail. st@stmf.se
Website. www.stmf.se (Swedish; English section)
Membership. 97,000. This is the largest trade union for civil servants; 66% of its members are women.

7. Finansförbundet (Bank and Finance Employees' Union)

Address. Box 38151, S-100 64 Stockholm
Phone. +46 8 614 03 00
Fax. +46 8 611 38 98
E-mail. finansforbundet@finansforbundet.se
Website. www.finansforbundet.se (Swedish; English section)
Membership. 33,091

8. Polisförbundet (Police Union)

Address. Box 5583, S-114 85 Stockholm
Phone. +46 8 676 97 00
Fax. +46 8 23 24 10
E-mail. polisforbundet@polisforbundet.se
Website. www.polisforbundet.se (Swedish; English section)
Membership. 17,500 active members

9. Svenska Journalistförbundet (SJF, Swedish Union of Journalists)

Address. Journalisternas Hus, Box 1116, S-111 81 Stockholm
Phone. +46 8 613 75 00
Fax. +46 8 21 26 80
E-mail. kansliet@sjf.se
Website. www.sjf.se (Swedish; English section)
Membership. 19,000

10. Union of Swedish Insurance Employees (FTF)

Address. Kammakargatan 38, S-103 54 Stockholm
Phone. +46 8 791 17 00
Fax. +46 8 20 87 95
E-mail. ftf@ftf.org.se
Website. www.ftf.org.se (Swedish only)
Membership. 12,560

Switzerland

Capital: Bern
Population: 7.45 m. (2004 est.)

1 Political and Economic Background

The Swiss Confederation is a republic comprising 23 cantons. The cantons enjoy considerable autonomy and the style of government that has evolved out of Switzerland's linguistic and religious diversity is one that emphasizes consensus and caution in adopting change. Symptomatically, the four leading political parties (the Social Democratic Party, SPS; the Swiss People's Party, SVP; the Radical Democratic Party, FDP; and the Christian Democratic People's Party, CVP), although representing different political currents, have together formed a governing coalition continuously since 1959. Elections in October 2003 to the National Council (parliament) resulted in the SVP holding 55 seats, the SPS 52, the FDP 36 and the CVP 28. Smaller parties outside the government won only 29. Recent years have nonetheless seen a modest trend to greater polarization of the electorate. While the two most centrist parties in the coalition, the FDP and CVP, have relatively lost ground, the 2003 election gave the Social Democrats their best result since 1979, while the right-wing Swiss People's Party has become the strongest party, having more than doubled its electoral support since 1991. The most controversial issues in Swiss politics are customarily decided by popular referendums.

Switzerland has a tradition of combining internationalism in business, and providing a base for international organizations, with neutrality and isolationism in its domestic and foreign policy. In 1992, however, Swiss voters approved by referendum a proposal backed both by employers and unions to join the IMF and the World Bank, and in 2002 a referendum resulted in a vote narrowly in favour of joining the UN, which Switzerland did later that year. In March 2001, in contrast, a referendum resulted in an overwhelming vote not to begin negotiations to join the EU.

The Swiss economy is prosperous with strong manufacturing and service sectors (notably banking and offshore financial services). Switzerland imports labour and there are nearly one million foreign workers, mainly Italians. Its economy has performed sluggishly in recent years, with no or negligible growth recorded in 2001-03, reflecting in part weak external demand for its services, though a modest upturn was recorded in 2004. Both inflation (almost nil) and unemployment (about 3.9% in 2004) are notably low.

GDP (purchasing power parity) $239.3bn. (2004 est.); GDP per capita (purchasing power parity) $32,700 (2004 est.).

2 Trade Unionism

Switzerland ratified ILO Convention No. 87 (Freedom of Association and Protection of the Right to Organize, 1948) in 1975, but did not ratify Convention No. 98 (Right to Organize and Collective Bargaining, 1949) until 1999.

The trade union movement is long established and all workers may form and join unions of their own choosing. In 2003, some 792,000 of the 3.1 million workers employed half-time or more were unionized, resulting in an overall union density of about 25.5%. Unionization rates are higher in the public than private sectors.

Women were politically enfranchised at the federal level only in 1971 and the trade unions also have a traditional male dominance. In the private sector, 35% of the workforce are women, but women constitute only 15% of union members; in the public sector, the comparable figures are 51% and 31%. Foreign workers may join unions but have a low rate of participation. There are few foreign workers in the more highly unionized white-collar public sector areas.

Article 28 of the new Federal Constitution, which entered into force on Jan. 1, 2000, confers explicit protection on the right of workers to form and join trade unions. It also recognizes the legality of strikes, provided they are related to industrial relations and in line with "requirements to safeguard social peace or to seek conciliation". Article 8(2) states that men and women have equal rights and that the law shall provide for their de jure and de facto equality, particularly in the family, in education, and at the workplace. Article 8 codifies the jurisprudence on equality of the Federal Court, thus reinforcing legal protections from discrimination.

The trade union movement has divisions between blue-collar and white-collar unions and on a political and religious basis. Throughout most of the twentieth century there were two general trade union centres. The leading centre, the Swiss Trade Union Confederation (Schweizerischer Gewerkschaftsbund, SGB/USS), dates back to 1880 and is close to the Social Democratic Party (SPS). It is affiliated to the ICFTU and has the support of about half of Switzerland's trade unionists. The smaller Swiss Confederation of Christian Trade Unions (Christlichnationaler Gewerkschaftsbund der Schweiz, CNG/CSC), was a WCL affiliate and close to the Christian Democratic People's Party (CVP).

At the end of 2002, there were 792,498 union members, of whom 384,691 were in unions affiliated to the SGB. In 2002, the CNG merged with the Federation of White-Collar Employees, the Vereinigung Schweizerischer Angestelltenverbände (VSA), to form a new organization, Travail.Suisse, with a total of nearly 167,000 members. In addition, there are around 30 independent unions, most of them long established, and based particularly in white-collar and public sector occupations. The most important of the independent unions are the Association of Swiss Teachers (LCH), the Swiss Central Federation of State and Community Employees (ZV), the Swiss Association of Nurses (SBK), the Union of Federal Civil Servants (PVB), and the Association of Swiss Policemen (VSPB). The Association of Bank Employees (SBPV), which had been independent, joined the SGB in 2000.

The devolved style of Swiss society is reflected in the lack of strong central control by the trade union centres. They represent their member unions in respect of social and economic policy formulation and debate at national level, but the individual unions are highly autonomous. Until recently, there has been little systematic cooperation between the different centres and they compete for members. A previous Cooperation Agreement in force between the SGB and VSA from 1928 was terminated by the VSA in 1992, reflecting increasing competition in recruiting white-collar workers. In 2002, however, a merger took place between two of the three centres, the VSA and the CNG. In response to the impact of privatization in the public sector, the unions set up a framework for discussion of common problems following the 1995 Ebenrain Conference. In 2003 the Ebenrain Conference included the two union centres and nine independent union organizations, representing 768,097 trade unionists.

The trade unions lost members during the 1990s and have continued to do so into the new century. Between them the three confederations lost 11% of their members from 1992–97. The major losses were in the manufacturing area, reflecting a shake-out of jobs in older industries. This impacted primarily on SGB and CNG affiliates. The independent unions, based mainly in white-collar public sector areas, in contrast lost only 1.5%. In 2002, SGB affiliates together lost more than 7,000 members, with only a handful gaining ground, most notably Unia, a services union. The unions overall have their strength in manufacturing industry and public sector areas and have had little impact in private sector services. Until the formation of Unia in 1996, the SGB had virtually no representation in this area. In 2003, Unia had more than 17,000 members and was still growing. With a young membership, a majority of whom are women, and in sectors thought to be unorganizable, Unia has been the only Swiss union at the national level that is growing instead of losing members.

A merger process between SGB affiliates has accelerated in recent years. At special congresses in September 2002, the Union of Construction and Building Workers (SIB), with 91,000 members, and the Industry, Construction and Service Workers' Union (FTMH), with 90,000 members, formally approved the merger of their unions in principle. In April 2003 Unia, with more than 17,000 members in the services sector, decided to join the new entity, and the Commerce, Transport, and Food Workers' Union (FCTA), with 16,000 members, was expected to follow suit in 2004. The merger of the four unions was expected to be completed in September 2004 and result in the creation of UNIA, the largest trade union in Switzerland. UNIA would have responsibility for some 500 collective agreements and retain an inter-occupational character, representing workers in four separate sectors: industry, construction, crafts, and services.

The emphasis on consensus and conservative values that pervade Swiss society are reflected in industrial relations. The willingness of employers to reach compromise agreements has reflected the involvement of unions in running public affairs – through consultation machinery, through socialist participation in government, and through direct democracy.

To combat the "wage dumping" that might occur following implementation of the accord on the free movement of persons between Switzerland and the EU member states, set for June 1, 2004, legal measures were adopted aimed at facilitating the extension of national collective bargaining agreements (CBAs). Such agreements covered only 50% of all jobs, much lower than the EU average of about 90%. The measures have led to the conclusion of CBAs in the cleaning, road transport, security services and pharmacy sales sectors, and to requests for additional extensions of coverage.

Switzerland's reputation as an almost strike-free economy is often traced back to an historic 1937 agreement between the employers and unions in the watch making and metal trades. It established collectively agreed industrial relations on the basis of mutual good faith, each party undertaking, for the length of the contract, to forgo any industrial action, with provision for disputes to be resolved through an arbitration panel. Most Swiss agreements remain local, however. Only a minority provide for arbitration in the event of a dispute on the model of the 1937 agreement, and most leave differences to be resolved in bargaining. Strikes can take place (though they rarely do) on expiry of an agreement if it is not immediately renewed. On average there have only been ten strikes per year since 1975. The 2000 revised Constitution provides specific protection for the right to strike.

In recent years, the tradition of maintaining harmonious labour relations has come under strain. Employers have increasingly tried to avoid collective bargaining, with some employers disaffiliating from their employer federations in order to avoid the collective agreement for their industry. For example, in 2000, only 37 of the 270 Swiss textile employers adhered to the collective agreement.

The Ordinance respecting employees of the Confederation, which was approved on July 3, 2001, by the Federal Council and entered into force on Jan. 1, 2002, removed a long-standing prohibition on the right to strike by employees of the federal government and state-owned bodies, such as the railways and the postal service. However, it continues to prohibit the right to strike for persons in positions of authority or providing essential services. Moreover, the ordinance only applies to federal workers. In seven cantons, public workers face an absolute prohibition of the right to strike, and obstacles to this right also exist for workers in many Swiss communes.

On Nov. 4, 2002, construction workers carried out a one-day work stoppage at more than 100 building sites across Switzerland. The walkout was the biggest nationwide strike by any union in 55 years and was aimed at reinforcing the workers' demand for a lower, voluntary retirement age. The action was called when employers reneged on a tentative agreement negotiated in March 2002 to guarantee 70% of their pay to workers who elected to retire at 60. Participation in the action was particularly strong in the French- and Italian-speaking regions.

3 Trade Union Centres

Schweizerischer Gewerkschaftsbund (SGB)
Union Syndicale Suisse (USS)
Swiss Trade Union Confederation
Address. Monbijoustrasse 61, 3007 Bern
Phone. +41 31 371 5666
Fax. +41 31 371 0837
E-mail. info@sgb.ch
Website. www.uss.ch (German; French; Italian)
Leadership. P. Rechsteiner (president); Serge Gaillard (secretary)
Membership. 384,691
History and character. The SGB was founded in 1880 and is the largest Swiss trade union centre, with about half of Swiss trade unionists in its affiliated unions.

The SGB is close to the Social Democratic Party (SPS). In 1992 former SGB official Ruth Dreifuss was elected as a cabinet member, only the second woman in Switzerland to become a Federal Councillor. In December 1998 she became Switzerland's first woman President. In October 2000, Christiane Brunner, previously president of SGB's Industry, Construction and Services affiliate (SMUV/FTMH), became party chair.

After being fairly stable in the 1980s, membership declined in the 1990s (from 443,885 in 1990), reflecting primarily the loss of jobs in manufacturing industry and falling below 400,000 for the first time since 1953. Despite some shift in the gender balance, membership remains 80% male. The SGB is seeking to increase its presence in private sector services, an ambition reflected in the creation of Unia to target this area in 1996. There were a number of mergers during the 1990s, notably leading to the creation of the GBI, the largest affiliate, in 1992. The objective of the SGB is to reduce the traditional isolation of individual unions and create a more integrated and influential trade union movement.

Public sector affiliates form the Public Services Federation (Föderativverband des Personals öffentlicher Verwaltungen und Betriebe, FöV), together with some non-SGB unions, but efforts to convert this into a unitary organization for public sector workers have not come to fruition.
International affiliations. ICFTU; TUAC; ETUC
Affiliated unions. Leading SGB affiliates are:

1. Comedia (Swiss Media Union)
Address. Monbijoustrasse 33, 3001 Bern
Phone. +41 31 390 66 11

Fax. +41 31 390 66 91
E-mail. sekretariat@comedia.ch
Website. www.comedia.ch (French; German; Italian)
Membership. 18,000
History and character. Comedia was formed in December 1998 by four unions. The Swiss Association for Mass Media Workers (SSM) with about 3,000 members and the 6,000-member Swiss Association of Journalists (SVJ) stayed outside.

2. Gewerkschaft Bau und Industrie (GBI)/Syndicat Industrie et Bâtiment (SIB)
Union of Construction and Industry
Address. Postfach 915, 8021 Zurich
Phone. +41 1 295 15 15
Fax. +41 1 295 17 99
E-mail. info@gbi.artemis.ch
Website. www.gbi.ch (German; French; Italian)
Membership. 101,526
History and character. The GBI is the largest SGB affiliate. It was formed in 1992 by the merger of the Union of Textile, Chemical and Paper Industry Workers (GTCP) and the Union of Construction and Wood Workers (GBH).

3. Schweizerischer Eisenbahn- und Verkehrspersonal-Verband/Syndicat du personnel des transports (SEV)
Transport Workers' Union
Address. CP 186, 3000 Bern
Phone. +41 31 357 57 57
Fax. +41 31 357 57 58
E-mail. info@sev-online.ch
Website. www.sev-online.ch (German; French; Italian)
Membership. 53,000

4. Gewerkschaft Industrie, Gewerbe, Dienstleitungen (SMUV)/Syndicat de l'industrie, de la construction et des services (FTMH)
Address. Weltpoststrasse 20, 3000 Bern 15
Phone. +41 31 350 2111
Fax. +41 31 350 22 55
E-mail. mail@smuv.ch
Website. www.smuv.ch (French; German)
Leadership. Renzo Ambrosetti (president)

5. Unia
Address. Monbijoustrasse 61, CP3000, Bern 23
Phone. +41 31 376 09 00
Fax. +41 31 376 09 04
E-mail. unia@access.ch
Website. www.uniacontreubs.ch (French; German; English)
History and character. Unia was founded by the GBI and SMUV in 1996 to cater for employees in services, such as sales people, restaurant and hotel staff, and office workers, with a special emphasis on recruiting women members. These were areas previously little catered for in the SGB.

6. Verkauf, Handel, Transport, Lebensmittel (VHTL)/Fédération suisse des travailleurs du commerce, des transports et de l'alimentation (FCTA)
Commerce, Transport and Food Workers
Address. Birmensdörferstrasse 67, 8004 Zurich
Phone. +41 1 299 25 25
Fax. +41 1 299 25 26
E-mail. vhtl.info@vhtl.ch
Website. www.vhtl.ch (French and German)
Membership. 20,000

7. Verband des Personals Öffentlicher Dienste (VPOD)/Syndicat suisse des services publics (SSP)
Public Service Union
Address. Sonnenbergstrasse 83, case postale, 8030 Zurich
Phone. +41 1 266 52 53
Fax. +41 1 266 52 53
E-mail. central@ssp-vpod.ch
Website. www.ssp-vpod.ch(German; French; Italian)

8. Gewerkschaft Kommunikation/Syndicat de la Communication
Communication Workers' Union
Address. Oberdorfstrasse 32, 3072 Ostermundigen
Phone. +41 31 939 52 11
Fax. +41 31 939 52 62
E-mail. zentralsekretariat@syndicom.ch
Membership. 45,000

Travail.Suisse
Address. Hopfenweg 21, Postfach 5775, 3001 Bern
Phone. +41 31 370 21 11
Fax. +41 31 370 21 09
E-mail. info@travailsuisse.ch
Website. www.travailsuisse.ch
Membership. 166,808
History and character. Formed in December 2002 by merger of the Swiss Confederation of Christian Trade Unions (Christlichnationaler Gewerkschaftsbund der Schweiz, CNG/CSC) and the Federation of Swiss White-Collar Employees (Vereinigung Schweizerischer Angestelltenverbände, VSA). The CNG/CSC dated back to 1907, when it was founded by the Catholic trade union movement; in 1982 it absorbed the smaller Swiss Association of Protestant Workers (SVEA). Its orientation was social Christian and it was traditionally close to the Christian Democratic People's Party (CVP). The VSA dated back to 1918.
Affiliated unions:

1. SYNA, die Gewerkschaft/SYNA, syndicat interprofessionnel
Address. Josefstrasse 59, CH-8031 Zurich
Phone. +41 1 279 71 71
Fax. +41 1 279 71 72
E-mail. zue@syna.ch
Website. www.syna.ch (German; French; Italian)
Leadership. Peter Allemann, Hugo Fasel (co-presidents)
Membership. 80,000
History and character. SYNA was formed in 1998 by the merger of the two main CNG private sector unions, the construction workers' federation (FCTC) and the industry and commerce union (FCOM), together with the Swiss Union of Free Trade Unions (LFSA/USSA) and the graphic arts unions (SAG). SYNA's intention was to target particularly areas where the unions are weak, notably private sector services and women workers.

2. Transfair
Address. Hopfengweg 21, Postfach, 2000 Bern 14

Phone. +41 31 370 21 21
Fax. +41 31 370 21 31
E-mail. zentralsecretariat@transfair.ch
Leadership. Peter Bollinger
Membership. 10,500
Website. www.transfair.ch (German; French)
History and character. Transfair was created in the late 1990s to bring together smaller public sector CNG unions.

Syria

Capital: Damascus
Population: 18.02 m. (2004 est.)

1 Political and Economic Background

The Ba'ath Arab Socialist Party took power in a coup in 1963 and has been the ruling party since that time, with a state of emergency almost continually in force. Lt.-Gen. Hafez al-Assad gained control of the party in 1970, and then led the country as President from 1971. Assad was unanimously re-elected as President by the People's Council (Majlis) for a fifth term in January 1999, this being confirmed by 99.9% of the vote in a popular referendum in March. He died in June 2000, however, and his son, Bashar al-Assad, succeeded him as President. Only candidates from the Ba'ath party or its supporters, organized since 1972 within a nominal National Progressive Front (NPF), may stand for election to the Majlis; there is no organized political opposition.

The state still exercises control over large areas of the economy, including much of manufacturing. About 40% of the labour force are engaged in agriculture. Recent efforts to encourage the private sector began with the passage of Private Investment Law No. 10 (May 1991). However, these efforts have been hampered by factors including poor infrastructure, corruption, bureaucracy, political interference by Ba'ath party officials, and lack of skilled labour. Furthermore, remittances from Syrians working in the Gulf states declined with the fall of the price of oil, and restrictive domestic banking practices dissuaded foreign investment.

The economy stagnated in the late 1990s; after four years of actual regression in GDP, economic growth resumed in 2001-03, but at a slower rate than the increase in the population. With a young population – 56% of Syrians are under the age of 16 – the economy needs to generate between 140,000 and 200,000 new jobs each year in order to accommodate new entrants to the labour market, if the government hopes to stem mounting unemployment.

Syria wields considerable political influence over neighbouring Lebanon, and their two economies are closely linked. In particular, Syria takes advantage of Lebanon's commercial ports, and many Syrians live and work in Lebanon.

GDP (purchasing power parity) $58.01bn. (2003 est.); GDP per capita (purchasing power parity) $3,300 (2003 est.).

2 Trade Unionism

Syria ratified ILO Convention No. 87 (Freedom of Association and Protection of the Right to Organize, 1948) in 1960 and Convention No. 98 (Right to Organize and Collective Bargaining, 1949) in 1957.

Under a decree of 1968 a single-trade-union system is in force, organized by the General Federation of Trade Unions, which has powers to dissolve the executive committee of any union and is closely tied to the ruling Ba'ath party. No unions may be formed outside this structure. A decree of 1969 gave the Ministry of Labour extensive powers of supervision over the financial affairs of the unions.

There is some collective bargaining in both the public and private sectors. The Ministry of Labour and Social Affairs can veto any collective agreement on the grounds of national economic interest. Most disputes are settled directly between labour and management representatives, although there is the possibility of resort to binding arbitration.

Strikes are specifically prohibited in the agricultural, military-industrial and public service sectors and are in any case rare. In the case of the military-industrial sector they are classed as treasonable activity and are punishable by death. The last major strike was in 1980, in protest at emergency powers, and resulted in wholesale detention of strikers, some of whom were still believed to be imprisoned more than two decades later.

3 Trade Union Centre

General Federation of Trade Unions (GFTU)
Address. PO Box 2351, Damascus
Leadership. Mohamed Shaaban Azzouz (president)
History and character. Founded in 1948. The GFTU is controlled by the ruling Ba'ath party. No unions may exist outside it. The GFTU advises the government on relevant legislation. Its president, Mohamed Shaaban Azzouz, is a senior member of the Ba'ath Party. He and his deputy may attend cabinet meetings on economic affairs. The GFTU does, however, act as an "informal channel between decision makers and workers", according to recent US State Department Human Rights Practices reports. It also formulates rules for union members; participates in discussions with employers and the labour ministry regarding conditions, hours and minimum wages; and tries to settle disputes "in collaboration with management representatives".

At an annual conference held in April 2003, the GFTU called for the merger of construction companies in Syria, so as to "activate" the sector, and to provide proper wages and health funds for construction workers. Constituent unions also used the occasion to demand better vocational training, tax exemptions and improved internal union legislation.

The GFTU is affiliated to the International Confederation of Arab Trade Unions (ICATU) and the WFTU. At its meeting in Hanoi, Vietnam, in October 2003, the latter organization condemned pending "American threats" (in the form of sanctions) against Syria.

On May 21, 2004, Azzouz penned a resolution con-

cerning peace, based on the 1984 Declaration of Philadelphia, at the ILO meeting in Geneva, even though he was not an officially credited delegate. He has been vocal in international forums on the conditions of Palestinian trade unionists since the Al Aqsa Intifada began in October 2000.
International affiliation. WFTU

Taiwan

Capital: Taipei
Population: 22.75 m. (2004 est.)

1 Political and Economic Background

Following the establishment in 1949 of the People's Republic of China on the Chinese mainland, the Nationalist Kuomintang (KMT) forces relocated to the island of Taiwan, which they called the Republic of China. The Taipei and Beijing governments thenceforth continued to describe China as one country, of which they were respectively the rightful rulers; Taiwan abandoned its claim to the mainland in 1991 although Beijing still asserts its sovereignty over Taiwan. Although Taiwan was expelled from the UN on China's admission in 1971, the Chinese government has de facto accepted the existence of Taiwan provided that it does not declare itself a separate and independent state.

The end of martial law in 1987 brought significant political liberalization with several independent political parties being formed and a greater political role being accorded to the indigenous Taiwanese population as opposed to the Nationalist elite. During the 1990s the KMT's former virtual monopoly on political power steadily eroded. Relations with China also tended to improve (with Taiwan also being a major investor in the Chinese economy). However, the election in March 2000 of Chen Shui-bian of the Democratic Progressive Party (DPP) as Taiwan's first non-KMT President, triggered a spate of hostile rhetoric from Beijing as the DPP had traditionally called for independence. In the December 2001 legislative elections the DPP likewise displaced the KMT as the leading party. In the presidential election held in March 2004 Chen Shui-bian defeated his KMT challenger by only the slightest of margins, while in legislative elections in December 2004, although the DPP remained the largest party, the KMT-led bloc of opposition parties emerged with a narrow majority. While the KMT's partial recovery was seen as welcome to Beijing, the Chen administration had in any case in practice tempered its pro-independence rhetoric in favour of continued business and other cooperation with China, the two economies being increasingly interdependent.

Taiwan's free market economy, based on export-driven manufacturing, achieved an average real growth rate of 8.5% p.a. in the last three decades of the twentieth century, and Taiwan also in that period became a major investor in other economies. China has now become the largest export market. In 2001, largely because of the global slowdown, the economy experienced a recession for the first time since the creation of the state, with a consequent rise in unemployment, which for years had been at very low levels. Recovery began in 2002 and in 2004 growth was close to 6%. Government direction of trade and investment has lessened although the government still retains a stake in some major banks and industrial companies. Taiwan is seeking to develop capital and technology-intensive industries to retain a competitive edge.

GDP (purchasing power parity) $528.6bn. (2004 est.); GDP per capita (purchasing power parity) $23,400 (2004 est.).

2 Trade Unionism

The Chinese Federation of Labour (CFL), which has close links with the KMT, was the sole permitted trade union centre during the period of KMT rule, a situation which only changed when President Chen was elected in 2000.

In 1988, in response to the climate of increasing liberalization, reflected in the formation of the Democratic Progressive Party in 1986 and lifting of martial law in 1987, a number of unions organized into "voluntary associations" in order to challenge the CFL's role as the sole legal labour centre. The two main such associations were the Brotherhood of Unions and the Labour Union Alliance. In 1987 a Labour Party was formed, which looked to the country's workers to become its principal support base. During 1988 the Labour Party worked within individual unions, attempting to weaken traditional KMT control. In some unions, members rejected KMT candidates for leadership posts, voting instead for non-partisan or opposition figures. In 1988 Kang Yi-yi, a Labour Party member, was elected Chairman of the China Petroleum Corporation Union, the first non-KMT member to head a major union. However, independent unions declined in 1990 in concert with the regression in the fortunes of the Labour and Workers' Parties, both of which did poorly in the 1989 legislative elections.

The monopoly position of the CFL was entrenched by the requirement that no administrative district might have competing labor confederations. In 1994, 12 unions in state-run enterprises said they would withdraw from the CFL and establish a national federation of unions in state-run enterprises. However, their attempt to register a new organization was rejected by the government's Council of Labour Affairs (CLA). Overall the demand to create a trade union centre independent of the CFL declined during the 1990s, reflecting good economic conditions and the limited scale of most unions, as well as the hostile legislative and regulatory regime. Since 2000, when the KMT lost control of the state, the government has relaxed restrictions on rival centres to the CFL, with the Taiwan Confederation of Trade Unions being legalized in May 2000 and several new nationwide federations also being recognized by the CLA.

Under the Trade Union Law, employers may not discriminate against workers on the grounds of union membership, although there are no specific penalties for violation and cases of discrimination, especially against members of unions independent of the CFL, were regularly reported in the past. Nonetheless, union density has been relatively high. In the new climate of liberalization from the late 1980s, the unionized proportion of the workforce rose from 26.4% in 1988 to 34.9% by 1992. The absolute number of union members then stabilized at around 3 million, with density declining slightly to about 31% in 1999 and 29% by 2003. Most unions are small and there has been no effective consolidation: there were 3,657 registered unions in 1992 and this figure had actually increased to 3,710 by 1999 and 4,111 by 2003.

Some groups, including teachers, civil servants and defence industry workers, are not permitted to form trade unions. In 2002 the law was amended so that civil sevants could form professional associations and teachers have staged demonstrations calling for the right of free association (although many teachers prefer to retain the status of professional associations). Trade unions may be dissolved if they fail certification requirements or if their activities are held to disturb public order. However, these powers have not been exercised in recent years. Union leaders must be elected by secret ballot, and, with the decline of the authority of the KMT in the 1990s, workers sometimes began to reject KMT- or management-endorsed union slates.

Collective bargaining is governed by the Collective Agreements Law, which provides for voluntary collective bargaining. In practice, collective bargaining occurs only in large firms and only a minority of unions have achieved collective bargaining agreements. Under Martial Law provisions, strikes were forbidden, as were demonstrations, marches or picket lines. After martial law ended in 1987 the law was amended in 1988, so as to allow workers to legally resort to strike action after one round of mediation, but requiring that they return to work if a second arbitration phase was called. During the same period the country's first labour courts were established, under the aegis of the Judicial Yuan, to deal with labour-management disputes. Strikes remained prohibited in four "essential" industries (power, water, gas, and medical services). Strikes in practice remained uncommon, with the CLA reporting only 36 from from the end of martial law in 1987 to 2003, 23 of which involved bus companies.

Taiwan was expelled from the ILO as a consequence of the admission of China to the UN, hence ILO Conventions are not applicable.

3 Trade Union Centres

Chinese Federation of Labour (CFL)
Address. 7F no. 17, section 1, Jin-Shan South Road, Taipei
Phone. +886 2 33225111
Fax. +886 2 33225120
E-mail. cfl@ma10.hinet.net
Leadership. Lin Hui-kuan (president)
Membership. 1 million
History and character. The CFL originated in a Kuomintang labour organization founded in mainland China in 1948 and thereafter remained closely enmeshed with the KMT. It received funding from the ruling party and had the role of administering workers' insurance schemes and social and leisure programmes for workers. Until 2000 it was the only legal confederation. Relations with the government have at times been difficult since the KMT lost power in 2000.
International affiliation. ICFTU

Taiwan Confederation of Trade Unions (TCTU)
Address. 2F No. 168, Nan-Chang Road Section 2, Taipei 100
Phone. +886 2 83693522
Fax. +886 2 23659390
E-mail. twctu@tctu.org.tw
Website. www.tctu.org.tw
Leadership. Lu Tien-lin (president)
History and character. The TCTU held its founding conference in 1997 but was refused legal status by the CLA. It was recognized by the government on May 1, 2000, as the first legal trade union confederation other than the KMT-linked CFL, following President Chen's victory in the March 2000 presidential election (Chen having promised recognition in his election campaign). It reported 18 national unions with 280,000 members when it was legalized, with most of its members in the state-owned sector of the economy. It now includes 21 national unions, in areas including transport, telecommunications, petroleum and banking, and nine local trade union federations. The TCTU seeks to increase trade union membership in Taiwan, end restrictions on trade union membership in sectors such as education, and oppose the government's privatization policies. Many of its leading figures and affiliates are associated with the DPP but the second congress of the TCTU sought to emphasize its political independence by requiring the union president and and vice-president to resign as members of the DPP.

Tajikistan

Capital: Dushanbe
Population: 7.01 m. (2004 est.)

1 Political and Economic Background

Tajikistan declared its independence from the dissolving Soviet Union in 1991. A civil war broke out in 1992 pitching the former communist establishment against Islamic forces, with the conflict complicated by tribal allegiances. Imomali Rakhmonov has been President since 1992, winning elections in 1994 and 1999 that were generally seen as unfair. Constitutional amendments adopted in 1999 extended the presidential term to seven years, while further amendments in 2003 prepared the way for Rakhmonov to stand again for President in 2006. He is identified with the communist old guard but his power is also regionally based and the government does not hold sway over all parts of the country. Russian forces are present as peacekeepers and under a 1997 peace agreement opposition groups have places in government.

Tajikistan is the poorest and most backward of the

former Soviet republics and its economy deteriorated with the loss of the former Soviet market and the impact of civil strife. It has some mineral resources but little industry. Agriculture (which remains partly collectivized), with cotton the main crop, is the dominant means of livelihood, but there is widespread unemployment and underemployment. There are significant informal and black economies.

GDP (purchasing power parity) $6.81bn. (2004 est.); GDP per capita (purchasing power parity) $1,000 (2004 est.).

2 Trade Unionism

Tajikistan ratified ILO Conventions No. 87 (Freedom of Association and Protection of the Right to Organize, 1948) and No. 98 (Right to Organize and Collective Bargaining, 1949) in 1993. Legislation provides for the right to join and form unions. The trade union centre is the Tajikistan Federation of Trade Unions, which is the continuation of the old Soviet official trade union structure. It claims to have 1.5 million members, including virtually all workers in the state sector, in 19 professional trade unions, though many of the enterprises in which its members are located are not operating. It affiliates to the General Confederation of Trade Unions (GCTU) of trade union centres from the former Soviet republics. There is also a Trade Union of Non-State Enterprises, which claims 40,000 members, scattered in 3,000 small and medium-sized enterprises. It is reported to be closely controlled by the government. Both organizations are consulted by the Council of Ministers in the drafting of labour and social welfare legislation. Unions may not affiliate with international bodies.

The right to organize and bargain collectively is codified in law. However, the collapsed state of the economy has made meaningful collective bargaining a rarity. Compulsory arbitration must precede a strike, but both trade union organizations have said that they will not use the strike weapon in view of the social crisis. There have been no union-approved strikes since the end of the civil conflict in 1997.

3 Trade Union Centre

Tajikistan Federation of Trade Unions (TFTU)
Address. 20 Rudaki Ave., 734012 Dushanbe
Phone. +10 992 372 21 35 43
Leadership. Murodali Salikhov (president)
International affiliation. GCTU

Tanzania

Capital: Dodoma
Population: 36.59 m. (2004 est.)

1 Political and Economic Background

The United Republic of Tanzania was established in 1964, when the newly independent states of Tanganyika and Zanzibar merged. The leftist Revolutionary Party of Tanzania (Chama Cha Mapinduzi, CCM) was the sole legal party until 1992. Multi-party elections were held in 1995, resulting in the CCM gaining a substantial majority in the legislature and the election of its presidential candidate. Benjamin Mkapa. Further elections in October 2000 resulted in Mkapa and the CCM retaining power.

Under President Julius Nyerere Tanzania pursued a policy of socialism and self-reliance. Under his successors from 1985, the government has sought to liberalize the economy but Tanzania remains one of the poorest countries in the world with a continuing dependence on external assistance. The economy depends heavily on agriculture, which accounts for about half of GDP, provides 85% of exports, and employs 80% of the work force. Topography and climatic conditions, however, limit cultivated crops to only 4% of the land area. Industry traditionally featured the processing of agricultural products and light consumer goods. By the later 1990s there was substantial foreign investment in gold mining and increasing revenues from tourism.

GDP (purchasing power parity) $21.58bn. (2004 est.); GDP per capita (purchasing power parity) $600 (2004 est.).

2 Trade Unionism

Tanganyika and Zanzibar ratified ILO Convention No. 98 (Right to Organize and Collective Bargaining, 1949) in 1962 and 1964 respectively, and this ratification now applies in respect of Tanzania. Tanzania ratified Convention No. 87 (Freedom of Association and Protection of the Right to Organize, 1948) in 2000. There are some variations in labour legislation as between mainland Tanzania (Tanganyika) and the island of Zanzibar.

Most of the workforce is engaged in subsistence agriculture, but unions represent an estimated 10-15% of the two million wage earners. Workers in both the private and public sectors may lawfully join unions although in practice this is often difficult.

A single-trade-union system applied from independence until 2000. From 1995 the single trade union organization had been known as the Tanzania Federation of Free Trade Unions (TFTU). The 1988 Trade Unions Act came into force on July 1, 2000. Prior to its enactment only one of the 11 member unions of the TFTU formally had legal status and the Act provided a basis for the legal registration of unions as well as repealing the single-trade-union system. It also gave the Registrar of Trade Unions extensive powers to supervise, suspend and de-register unions. Under its terms the TFTU was formally dissolved and put into administration. This action came despite Tanzania's ratification of ILO Convention No. 87, which specifically bars dissolution of unions by the state, earlier in the year. A new centre, the Trade Unions' Congress of Tanzania (TUCTA), was subsequently formed to replace TFTU. A Zanzibar-based centre, the Zanzibar Trade Union Congress (ZATUC), was formed in April 2003. TUCTA and ZATUC are both affiliated to the ICFTU.

Collective bargaining is limited to the private sector. Collective agreements are generally negotiated by TUCTA or ZATUC with the employers and must be submitted for the approval of the Industrial Court, which is required to take account of the needs of the national economy. Strike action is only legal following long drawn-out mediation and conciliation procedures. Generally, there is a hostile official attitude to industrial action.

3 Trade Union Centres

Trade Unions' Congress of Tanzania (TUCTA)
Address. PO Box 15359, Pillu/Ottu Building, Corner Bibi Titi/Sofia Kawawa Streets (Formerly Lindi St.), Dar Es Salaam
Phone. +255 512 6111
Fax. +255 222 130 036
E-mail. tucta.educ@cats-net.co
Leadership. Margaret Sitta (president); Nestory Ngula (secretary-general)
Membership. 320,000
History and character. TUCTA was formed following the dissolution of the Tanzania Federation of Free Trade Unions (TFTU) in July 2000.
International affiliation. ICFTU

Zanzibar Trade Union Congress (ZATUC)
Address. PO Box 667, Zanzibar
Phone. +255 242 236 614
Fax. +255 242 336 614
E-mail. zatuc_congress@yahoo.com
Website. www.zatuc.or.tz
Leadership. Makame Launi Makame (secretary general)
History and character. ZATUC was formed in April 2003 following the dissolution of the Tanzania Federation of Free Trade Unions (TFTU) in July 2000. It joined the ICFTU in December 2003.
International affiliation. ICFTU

Thailand

Capital: Bangkok
Population: 64.87 m. (2004 est.)

1 Political and Economic Background

Thailand is the only southeast Asian country not to have been colonized by a European power. The military has staged 17 coups since absolute monarchy ended in 1932, most recently in 1991. In September 1992 elections resulted in victory for opposition parties, and a new government was formed under the Democrat Party leader Chuan Leekpai, the first Prime Minister since the mid-1970s with no military background. A new constitution adopted in 1997 defined Thailand as a parliamentary democracy with Cabinet government led by a Prime Minister. Elections in January 2001 resulted in victory for the populist Thai Rak Thai ("Thais Love Thais") party of billionaire Thaksin Shinawatra, who became Prime Minister. He and his party won a landslide victory in further elections in February 2005.

Although 41% of the labour force is engaged in agriculture this accounts for only 9% of GDP. Thailand has developed a diverse industrial sector with a significant export component including textiles and electrical and electronics goods. By the late 1980s Thailand had one of the fastest growing economies in the world, and this rapid growth continued into the 1990s, with growth rates of 7–8% per annum. Thailand was severely affected by the late 1990s Asian economic recession, however, the economy contracting 8.5% in 1998, before recovering in 1999–2000. The economy grew by over 6% per annum in both 2003 and 2004. During 2004, in the run-up to parliamentary elections in February 2005, the government adopted a policy of heavily subsidizing diesel prices, reinforcing its popularity based on buoyant economic conditions since it came into office in 2001. Corruption remains a feature of the Thai economy, with companies close to leading politicians benefiting from favourable treatment by state agencies. Thailand was severely affected by the December 2004 Indian Ocean tsunami but Prime Minister Thaksin Shinawatra stated that the country did not need foreign aid and could pay for its own reconstruction.

GDP (purchasing power parity) $477.5bn. (2004 est.); GDP per capita (purchasing power parity) $7,400 (2004 est.).

2 Trade Unionism

Thailand has been a member of the ILO since 1919 but has ratified neither Convention No. 87 (Freedom of Association and Protection of Right to Organize, 1948) nor No. 98 (Right to Organize and Collective Bargaining, 1949).

All unions were dissolved in 1958 and workers were not permitted to associate again until 1972. The Labour Relations Act, providing for the registration of trade unions, was enacted in 1975. However, by 1991 the number of registered union members was only 330,000, in 732 unions. The strongest unions were in the public sector, which accounted for more than half of union membership but only 6% of all employment. A number of small trade union centres had developed, among them the ICFTU-affiliated Labour Congress of Thailand (LCT) and Thai Trade Union Congress (TTUC), and the WCL-affiliated National Congress of Thai Labour (NCTL).

Following a military coup in 1991, the unions again faced extreme adversity. Agricultural workers and civil servants had always been excluded from coverage of the Labour Relations Act but now public sector unions were effectively dissolved by rescinding its coverage of state employees. Little secret was made of the regime's wish for removal of the state sector unions in order for privatization to succeed. State enterprise workers were now placed under an entirely different and separate employment law, the 1991 State Enterprises Labour Relations Act (SELRA), and allowed only to form State Enterprise Employees' Associations (SEEAs) which had no collective bargaining rights. The number of union members was severely reduced by the state enterprise ban and by January 1992 was put at 194,681, all of them in the private sector.

A period of severe repression of the two main centres, the LCT and the TTUC, followed the 1991 coup during which the president of the LCT disappeared, presumed killed. Despite this, unions were prominent in demonstrations that led up to the fall of the military government in June 1992, although some union leaders supported the military coup.

Conditions have eased since the restoration of democracy in 1992. Under the 1975 Labour Relations Act, still in force, in the private sector ten workers may form a union. However, there are few protections for workers who are dismissed when they attempt to form a union, which is reportedly a common consequence, and the trade unions have only a small foothold in the burgeoning private sector. The position of workers in state enterprises changed in 2000 with the coming into force of an amended State Enterprises Labour Relations Act. The previous SELRA legislation allowed state enterprise employee associations, but these had only an advisory role and could not engage in collective bargaining. The civilian Chuan government appointed in 1992 said that it would reform SELRA and allow workers in state enterprises to form unions. This commitment proved sufficient to achieve suspension of petitions then being filed by the AFL-CIO under the General System of Preferences (GSP). In the event the government failed to bring about reform. It was not until February 2000, in the face of the threat of loss of US trade privileges, that the Thai legislature finally adopted legislation to revise SELRA so as to allow the 330,000 workers in state enterprises to change their enterprise associations into functioning trade unions – although under the Act such enterprise unions are required to promote good relations between employees and employers and to protect the interests and effectiveness of the state enterprise. Unions now exist in the majority of the several dozen remaining state enterprises (with only one union permitted per enterprise), which are consequently the most highly unionized sector of the economy, with 50% of the workforce unionized. In contrast, estimates for the economy as a whole suggest that although 11% of industrial workers are in unions, less than 2% of the total workforce are in unions. The majority of the workforce work on the land, in the informal economy or in small service enterprises, sectors in which trade unions have no presence. Civil servants remain barred from union membership.

The 1975 Labour Relations Act requires that every union official must be a full time employee at the workplace where they are elected, making it difficult to have full-time officials. A measure brought in under the military government in 1991 requires the registration and approval of union advisers and this has been used to restrict the support that can be given by federations. The formation of federations is also restricted by complex legal requirements and state enterprise unions may not join federations of private sector unions. Company-controlled unions are common in the private sector and the corruption seen elsewhere in Thai society has also affected some unions.

The right to collective bargaining in the private sector is recognized by the 1975 Act, which also provides for government-assisted conciliation and arbitration. In practice, real collective bargaining exists in only a small number of enterprises. Wage increases for most workers come as a result of increases in the minimum wage, rather than as a result of collective bargaining. Minimum wages are now set through provincial tripartite committees, but it is reported that many of these tripartite committee have brought in company managers to represent labour. The private sector is covered by a labour courts system and disputes may also be referred to a tripartite Labour Relations Committee. A parallel State Enterprises Labour Relations Committee also exists.

In the private sector a proposed strike must be approved by the majority of the union members in a secret ballot, and registered with the Ministry of Labour, to be legal. The government has powers to ban strikes that it considers may "affect national security or cause severe negative repercussions for the population at large", and striking illegally may result in imprisonment.

There are many migrant workers – primarily Burmese, Laotian and Cambodian – and they face particular problems; although formally accorded the same rights as Thai workers, they may not change jobs without the consent of their current employer, on pain of deportation. Child labour is widespread in Thailand, in both rural and urban areas, and although there are formal legal protections these are inadequately enforced. Women and children are victims of bonded labour and this has attracted international condemnation.

The State Enterprise Labour Association of Thailand provides an umbrella for the 41 unions in the state enterprises. There is a slow continuing process of privatization of state enterprises and this has been a source of conflict between unions and government. There were large demonstrations in 2004 over plans to privatize the Electricity Generating Authority of Thailand.

There is no national trade union centre but a number of labour congresses exist, including the Confederation of Thai Labour (CTL), the Labour Congress Center for Labour Union of Thailand, the National Congress of Private Employees of Thailand (NPET), the National Free Labour Union Congress (NFLUC), the National Labour Congress (NLC) and the Thai Council of Industrial Labour (TCIL). The ICFTU has two affiliates, the Labour Congress of Thailand and the Thai Trade Union Congress, and the WCL one, the National Congress of Thai Labour. There are ten industrially-based labour federations covering the major private sector areas of the formal economy.

3 Trade Union Centres

There is no recognized national trade union centre.

4 Other Trade Union Organizations

Labour Congress of Thailand (LCT)
Address. 420/ 393–394 Moo Baan Thippawan 1, Theparak Road, Samrong, Muang, Samutprakarn 10270
Phone/Fax. +66 2 384 6789
E-mail. lct_org@hotmail.com
Leadership. Prathuang Saengsang (president)
History and character. The LCT was created in 1978.

Following the 1991 coup, LCT president Thanong Po-arn, then the most prominent labour leader in Thailand disappeared, feared dead (his exact fate never being subsequently determined). The LCT subsequently lost 65% of its membership as a result of the ban on unions in the public sector.
International affiliation. ICFTU

National Congress of Thai Labour (NCTL)
Address. 1614/876 Samutprakarn Community Housing Project, Sukhumvit Highway KM30, Tai Baan, Muang, Samutprakarn 10270
Phone. +66 2 389 5134
Fax. +66 2 385 8975
Leadership. Panus Thailuan (president)
International affiliation. WCL

Thai Trade Union Congress (TTUC)
Address. 420/ 393–394 Moo Baan Thippawan 1, Theparak Road, Samrong, Muang, Samutprakarn 10270
Phone. +66 2 384 0438
History and character. The TTUC was founded in 1982 by Paisal Thawatchainant, who had earlier founded the Labour Congress of Thailand (LCT). It affiliated to the ICFTU in 1987. The 1991 State Enterprises Labour Relations Act, dissolving public sector unions, cost the TTUC the bulk of its membership, which fell from 123,150 in July 1990 to 42,748 in January 1992.
International affiliation. ICFTU

Togo

Capital: Lomé
Population: 5.56 m. (2004 est.)

1 Political and Economic Background

President Gnassingbé Eyadéma ruled Togo until his death in February 2005 after seizing power in a coup in 1967. For the first 25 years of his rule the sole legal party was the Rassemblement du Peuple Togolais (RPT). In September 1992 a constitution providing for political pluralism was approved in a referendum and the following year President Eyadéma was confirmed in power in an election. He won a further presidential election in 1998. In July 1999 Eyadéma pledged to relinquish power in 2003 under an inter-Togolese accord reached with the help of French mediation. However, in 2002 Eyadéma announced that in the interests of "peace and stability", he was willing to make the "sacrifice" of standing again for President. The legislature duly abolished presidential term limits and in June 2003 Eyadéma was elected for a further term five-year term. In the most recent legislative elections held in October 2002, the RPT won 72 of the 81 National Assembly seats after most opposition parties had boycotted the poll.

Togo's economy is based on agriculture, both subsistence and commercial, which accounts for 65% of the workforce. Cocoa, coffee, and cotton generate about 40% of export earnings, with cotton being the most important cash crop. Togo is the world's fourth-largest producer of phosphate, but production fell an estimated 22% in 2002 due to power shortages and the cost of developing new deposits. There has been some economic liberalization, but many enterprises remain in state hands.

GDP (purchasing power parity) $8.257bn. (2004 est.); GDP per capita (purchasing power parity) $1,500 (2004 est.).

2 Trade Unionism

Togo ratified ILO Convention No. 87 (Freedom of Association and Protection of the Right to Organize, 1948) in 1960 and Convention No. 98 (Right to Organize and Collective Bargaining, 1949) in 1983. Under the constitution all workers except those in the emergency and security services are free to join unions. About two-thirds of workers in the formal waged economy are reported to be in unions.

All previously existing trade unions were dissolved in 1972 and the Confédération Nationale des Travailleurs du Togo (CNTT) was established by the ruling RPT in the following year. Even at the height of the one-party state, there was no formal establishment of a single-trade-union system. But union contributions were deducted automatically from all wages and salaries, and for many years no unions existed outside the structure of the CNTT.

With Togo affected by the democratic wind of change blowing through Africa in the 1990s, pressure grew for independent trade unionism. This was reflected in the creation of new organizations, such as the Union Nationale des Syndicats Indépendants du Togo (UNSIT) and the Confédération Syndicale des Travailleurs du Togo (CSTT), alliances of unions with civic groups, and a reform movement within the CNTT, which took positions critical of the government. There was appreciable labour unrest in the early 1990s. Conditions have become more settled since the mid-1990s, although union leaders have on occasion been detained by the authorities.

The 1974 labour code provides for collective bargaining. In practice, there is one national tripartite agreement that sets wages for the whole formal sector. Collective bargaining is also undermined by the economic situation, with salary and pension arrears for some public officers running into many months. The government itself is the largest employer in the formal sector and the dominant voice in defining agreements. The law provides exemptions from some provisions of the labour code for companies with export processing zone (EPZ) status, notably the regulations on hiring and firing. Employees of EPZ companies do not enjoy the same protection against anti-union discrimination as other workers.

3 Trade Union Centres

Confédération Nationale des Travailleurs du Togo (CNTT)
National Confederation of Togolese Workers
Address. Bourse du Travail, 160 Boulevard-13 Janvier, BP 163, Lomé
Phone. +228 21 4833

Fax. +228 22 0255
Membership. 35,000
History and character. The CNTT was created in January 1973, absorbing the previous Union Nationale des Travailleurs du Togo (UNTT), founded in 1962, and the Confédération Syndicale des Travailleurs du Togo (CSTT), which was founded in 1946 and was affiliated to the WCL. In the period of single party rule by the RPT, the CNTT's role was defined as the defence of the workers' interests "within the context of responsible participation" in the overall development of the country, with representation on the RPT central committee and in the National Assembly.

In the early 1990s the CNTT increasingly allied itself with independent unions calling for democratic reform, calling strikes on the issue in 1992, while not breaking its alliance with the ruling party. Since that time it has remained the confederation considered closest to the government.
International affiliation. ICFTU

Confédération Syndicale des Travailleurs du Togo (CSTT)
Trade Union Confederation of Togolese Workers
Address. BP 3058, Lomé
Phone. +228 22 11 17
Fax. +228 22 44 41
E-mail. cstt@café.tg
Leadership. Adrien Akouété Beliki (secretary-general)
International affiliation. WCL

Union Nationale des Syndicats Indépéndants du Togo (UNSIT)
National Union of Independent Trade Unions of Togo
Address. BP 30082 Tokoin-Wuiti, Lomé
Phone. +228 21 6565
Fax. +228 21 6565
E-mail. unsit@netcom.tg
Leadership. Tétévi Gbikpi-Benissan (secretary-general)
History and character. UNSIT emerged as part of the democratic movement of the early 1990s. Its participation in a November 1992 general strike resulted in its general secretary, Tétévi Gbikpi-Benissan, fleeing the country for a period. The union said the murder in August 1998 of the UNSIT deputy secretary-general could have been the result of his opposition to the privatization of a state-owned pharmaceutical company. The ICFTU asked the government to set up an independent investigation but this did not happen.
International affiliation. ICFTU

Tonga

Capital: Nuku'alofa
Population: 110,000 (2004 est.)

1 Political and Economic Background

Tonga, comprising 169 small islands in the South Pacific, became fully independent from the UK in 1970 and is a monarchy in which the King exercises substantial powers. The 30-member legislature comprises the King and his Privy Council, nine nobles, and nine popularly elected representatives.

Tonga's economy is primarily agricultural, but food production is mostly on a subsistence basis. There is a limited light industrial sector and tourism generates foreign exchange earnings. There is a dependence on external aid and remittances from overseas workers.

GDP (purchasing power parity) $236m (2002 est.); GDP per capita (purchasing power parity) $2,200 (2002 est.).

2 Trade Unionism

A 1963 Trade Union Act formally allowed the formation of trade unions. However, in practice the authorities refused to allow trade unions until the formation of the Friendly Islands Teachers' Association and Tonga Nurses' Association in 1990, these being set up under the Incorporated Societies Act. Collective bargaining is not practiced. Tonga is not a member of the ILO.

3 Trade Union Centre

There is no trade union centre.

4 Other Trade Union Organizations

Friendly Islands Teachers' Association (FITA)
Address. PO Box 859, Nuku'alofa
Phone/Fax. +676 23972
E-mail. fita@candw.to
Leadership. Tokankamea Puleiku (general secretary)
International affiliations. ICFTU; CTUC

Tonga Nurses' Association (TNA)
Address. PO Box 150, Nuku'alofa
Phone. +676 23200
Fax. +676 24291
E-mail. sela@tongatapu.net.to
Leadership. Pisila Sovaleni (general secretary)
International affiliations. ICFTU; CTUC

Trinidad and Tobago

Capital: Port of Spain
Population: 1.10 m. (2004 est.)

1 Political and Economic Background

Trinidad and Tobago achieved independence from the United Kingdom in 1962. The centre-right People's National Movement (PNM) won every election from its formation in 1956 until 1986, when it was defeated by the centre-left National Alliance for Reconstruction (NAR). In 1988 the NAR split, leading to the formation of the United National Congress (UNC) party under Basdeo Panday. The PNM won back power in 1991, but elections in 1995 resulted in the formation of a coalition government, led by Panday and dominated by the UNC.

Panday, the first Trinidadian of Indian extraction to be Prime Minister, had built his career in the trade union movement. In December 2001 elections resulted in a tie, with the UNC and PNM each winning 18 of the 36 seats in the House of Representatives. This led to a serious political impasse, with the UNC refusing to accept the President's decision to appoint PNM leader Patrick Manning as Prime Minister. It was resolved only by a further election, in October 2002, when the PNM won a narrow majority by taking 20 seats.

Trinidad and Tobago's economy is based on oil and natural gas production and downstream activities, and the country has benefited from increases in the last few years in world energy prices. The government is also seeking to diversify the economy and foreign investment has been attracted into other sectors including tourism.

GDP (purchasing power parity) $10.52bn. (2004 est.); GDP per capita (purchasing power parity) $9,500 (2004 est.).

2 Trade Unionism

Trade union activity dates back to the formation of the Working Man's Association in 1919. Following independence, Trinidad and Tobago ratified ILO Conventions No. 87 (Freedom of Association and Protection of the Right to Organize, 1948) and No. 98 (Right to Organize and Collective Bargaining, 1949) in 1963. The Trinidad and Tobago Labour Congress (TTLC) was formed in 1966, and affiliated to the ICFTU. The 1972 Industrial Relations Act (IRA) replaced the Industrial Stabilization Act (1965) and from then on was the principal legislation under which unions operated.

In 1975, Basdeo Panday, the leader of the All Trinidad Sugar and General Workers' Trade Union (ATS/GWTU), the most important union on the islands, formed the United Labour Front (ULF) in opposition to the ruling conservative People's National Movement (PNM). In the 1976 elections the ULF took 10 of the 36 seats in the House of Representatives, campaigning on a programme which included worker participation, nationalization of key enterprises, and land reform. The ULF later joined the moderate socialist National Alliance for Reconstruction (NAR), which won the 1986 general election. In 1988 the NAR split and Panday and other former ULF members in 1989 founded the United National Congress (UNC), which in 1995 achieved power as the dominant party in coalition with the much-weakened NAR, with Panday as Prime Minister. Panday campaigned in 1995 on the issues of unemployment and crime. The ATS/GWTU has remained close to the UNC.

Until 1994 there were two trade union centres, the Trinidad and Tobago Labour Congress (TTLC) and the Council of Progressive Trade Unions (CPTU). The ICFTU-affiliated TTLC was the larger of the two confederations by a ratio of about 2:1 against the WFTU-affiliated CPTU. In June, however, the two centres united to form the National Trade Union Centre of Trinidad and Tobago (NATUC) with a combined membership of some 50,000. The ATS/GWTU remained independent and affiliates to the WCL. Union density is estimated at 15-25%, with 19 active unions in existence.

Under the 1972 Industrial Relations Act all workers may join or form unions of their own choosing and anti-union acts by employers are prohibited. The Act also provides for collective bargaining and all workers except those in essential services have the right to strike. However, in certain circumstances strikes by minority unions or that are perceived to be against the national interest can be prohibited, with the possibility of six months' imprisonment. Where bargaining is deadlocked the issue in dispute is referred to the Ministry of Labour and may progress to a strike or a lock-out only when the Minister himself declares it unresolved. "Essential services" have been defined to include teaching, with the implication that teachers and central bank employees could face 18 months' imprisonment as a penalty for participation in a strike. There is an Industrial Court, which is empowered to penalize employers and reinstate workers in cases of anti-union discrimination.

3 Trade Union Centre

National Trade Union Centre of Trinidad and Tobago (NATUC)
Address. 91 Abercromby Street, Port of Spain
Phone. +1868 625 3023
Fax. +1868 627 7588
E-mail. natuc@carib-link.net
Leadership. Vincent Cabrera (general secretary)
Membership. 80,000
History and character. Formed in June 1994 by merger of the Trinidad and Tobago Labour Congress (TTLC) and the more left-wing but smaller Council of Progressive Trade Unions (CPTU).
International affiliations. ICFTU; CTUC

4 Other Trade Union Organizations

All Trinidad Sugar and General Workers' Trade Union (ATS/GWTU)
Address. Rienzi Complex, Exchange Village, Couva
Phone. +1868 636 2354
Fax. +1868 636 3372
E-mail. atsgwtu@opus.co.tt
Leadership. Rudranath Indarsingh (general secretary)
Membership. 7,700
History and character. Established in 1937 as a Sugar Workers' Union. Constitution changed in 1978 to represent workers in other industries, recruiting in diverse areas such as rum production, contracting, construction, entertainment, air line, transport, food processing, garment manufacturing, and animal food production. In 1981 membership was 18,000 but has declined to less than half that. Basdeo Panday, the former ATS/GWTU president, now leads the United National Congress Party and was Prime Minister from 1995-2001.
International affiliation. WCL

National Union of Government and Federated Workers (NUGFW)
Address. 145–147 Henry Street, Port of Spain
Phone. +1868 623 4591
Fax. +1868 625 7756
E-mail. headoffice@nugfw.org.tt
Leadership. Jacqueline Jack (general secretary)
International affiliation. CTUC

Tunisia

Capital: Tunis
Population: 9.75 m. (2004 est.)

1 Political and Economic Background

Tunisia achieved independence from France in 1956. One party has held power continuously since independence, although it has had different names: the Neo-Destour Party, the Destourian Socialist Party, and the Democratic Constitutional Rally. The current name, the Democratic Constitutional Rally (RCD), was adopted in 1988 and intended to reflect a greater political openness under President Zine El Abidine Ben Ali, who deposed 'President-for-Life' Habib Bourguiba in November 1987. The democratic opening has been limited and opposition parties are weak, while the government is reportedly generally popular. In elections in October 2004, President Ben Ali was re-elected with 94.5% of the vote, while the RCD maintained its total dominance of the legislature. There have reportedly been several thousand victims of torture under Ben Ali (mainly 1990-95), with political prisoners primarily Islamists or supporters of the outlawed Communist Workers' Party.

Tunisia has a relatively developed economic base and a high per capita income by African standards. Petroleum exports and tourism are the main sources of foreign exchange. The government controls significant portions of the economy but its structural adjustment programme, including modest privatization, is considered to have been generally effective and the economy has grown at an average 5% per annum since 1987. Though growth dipped to 1.9% due to poor rains, slow investment and diminished tourism in 2002, it since rose to 6%. Tunisia has agreed to remove tariff barriers with the EU over the next decade, yet trade shortfalls remain a concern.

GDP (purchasing power parity) $68.23bn. (2003 est.); GDP per capita (purchasing power parity) $6,900 (2003 est.).

2 Trade Unionism

Tunisia ratified ILO Conventions No. 87 (Freedom of Association and Protection of the Right to Organize, 1948) and No. 98 (Right to Organize and Collective Bargaining, 1949) in 1957, following independence. The right to form unions is protected by the constitution and the labour code and discrimination against union members is prohibited. However, the unions say that in some sectors, such as textiles and construction, employers employ mainly temporary workers to make union organization more difficult.

Trade unions developed under French rule and were associated with nationalist politics. The ICFTU-affiliated UGTT has been the sole or only significant trade union centre since independence, although this status is not entrenched in law. After 1978, UGTT relations with the government and the ruling party deteriorated and it experienced severe harassment from the state. At the 1989 (Sousse) congress it was re-organized and has recovered its position since that time, with its leadership seen as allied to the government. An estimated 10–15 percent of the work force are in member unions, although the UGTT says that 30% of the economically active are members. According to the UGTT 60% of its members are in the public sector.

Collective bargaining is widely practiced. Some 80% of the private sector workforce is covered by three-year sectoral framework agreements which are negotiated directly by the UGTT member unions and employers' representatives. The government must approve these agreements, which then apply to all employees in the relevant industry. The UGTT also negotiates wages and work conditions of civil servants and employees of state-owned enterprises.

There are tripartite conciliation and arbitration mechanisms. Unions in both the private and public sectors may call strikes, in theory provided they give 10 days' advance notice and have the approval of the UGTT, although in practice this restriction is commonly ignored. Strikes over pay and conditions, usually of brief duration, are relatively frequent.

3 Trade Union Centre

Union Générale Tunisienne du Travail (UGTT)
Tunisian General Labour Union
Address. 29 Place Mohamed Ali, Tunis
Phone. +216 1 332 400
Fax. +216 1 354 114
E-mail. ugtt.tunis@email.ati.tn
Website. www.ugtt.org.tn (French only)
Leadership. Abdesselam Jerad (secretary-general)
Membership. About 300,000
History and character. The UGTT was founded under French rule on Jan. 20, 1946, by Fahrat Hached (assassinated by French agents in 1952) and was involved in the struggle for independence in association with the Neo-Destour Party (renamed the Destour Socialist Party – PSD – in 1964, and the Democratic Constitutional Rally in 1988) of Habib Bourguiba (and now Ben Ali). The UGTT is traditionally the most significant organized grouping in Tunisia outside the ruling party and the armed forces. It currently represents 23 regional unions, 19 federations and 26 regional syndicates.

In January 1978 the UGTT called a general strike during which several dozen people were killed in clashes between strikers, police and troops. Following this, Habib Achour, the UGTT secretary-general and a vice-president of the ICFTU, who had already resigned from the political bureau and central committee of the PSD, was removed from his post at the UGTT. Achour was replaced by Tijani Abid. In October 1978 the State Security Court sentenced Achour and other former UGTT leaders to imprisonment with forced labour following conviction on charges of plotting to overthrow the government and incitement to violence, looting and murder. In 1979 Achour, who had been released into house arrest, was re-elected a vice-president of the ICFTU at the ICFTU's 12th congress, causing the new leadership of the UGTT to suspend relations with the international body.

All other detained members of the former UGTT leadership were released during 1980. The new UGTT leadership to failed to win international recognition or support within the Tunisian labour movement, and when a unity congress of the UGTT was held in 1981 it elected a new 13-member executive bureau which included 11 members of the executive arrested in 1978. One of these, Taieb Baccouche, became secretary-general, leaving Achour the only former UGTT leader still barred from office.

All seats in the 1981 multi-party National Assembly elections were won by a PSD–UGTT alliance, the UGTT share being 27. After this President Bourguiba granted a full pardon to Achour, who was immediately appointed UGTT chairman and a member of the executive bureau. Two years later the UGTT administrative commission dismissed seven of the 14 members of the executive bureau after they had charged Achour with anti-democratic methods, poor financial management and use of UGTT funds for bribery and secret deals. On Feb. 19, 1984, they formed the Union Nationale des Travailleurs Tunisiens (UNTT), with Abdelaziz Bouraoui as secretary-general, while at the end of 1984 the 16th regular congress of the UGTT elected a new executive committee with Achour succeeding Baccouche as secretary-general.

During 1985 relations with the government again deteriorated following a UGTT campaign of strikes for public sector pay increases after a two-year wage freeze. This was a time of acute economic difficulties which caused widespread unrest and bread riots. Trade union meetings were banned, strikers dismissed, the UGT newspaper Ach Chaab suspended, and the check-off system for union dues ended. By November Achour and 100 UGTT activists were in detention, and regional offices had been occupied by so-called provisional committees, assisted by the police. An agreement to end the crisis proved ineffective, and on Dec. 31, Achour was sentenced to one year's imprisonment (later reduced to eight months) on charges of breaking and entering the premises of a fishing cooperative in a case originally dating from 1982. On Jan. 21, 1986, control of the national headquarters of the UGTT in Tunis was handed over by the police to a provisional committee, and on Jan. 29 the UGTT administrative commission, meeting under the supervision of a national coordination bureau at the Tunis headquarters, announced that it had ceased to recognize the executive bureau and endorsed the work of the national coordination bureau towards the reconstruction of the trade union movement.

In April 1986, Achour was sentenced to a further two years' imprisonment for mismanagement of a union-funded insurance company, after which the provisional committees held an extraordinary UGTT congress and elected a new executive bureau with Ismail Lajeri as secretary-general. In September the UGTT absorbed the UNTT. In December a new executive bureau was formed and Lajeri was replaced by Abdelaziz Bouraoui of the now-defunct UNTT; the next month the UGTT held an extraordinary congress from which it addressed a 'message of faithfulness' to President Bourguiba and pledged itself to responsible participation in the tasks of national recovery. This congress, boycotted by most of the bodies elected under Achour but attended by Bourguiba, elected a new executive bureau comprising five representatives of the former provisional committees, four representatives of the former UNTT, and four representatives of the old UGTT leadership who had broken recently with Achour. Bouraoui was confirmed as secretary-general, on the recommendation of President Bourguiba.

After the fall from power of Bourguiba in November 1987 factionalism declined, and Habib Achour, still recognized by the ICFTU as the legitimate secretary-general, was freed from house arrest. However, Achour never returned to effective top office, and died in March 1999.

In May 1988, ICFTU general secretary John Vanderveken visited Tunisia for talks with government officials and trade unionists and reported that normalization of trade unionism was making good progress. A National Trade Union Commission was set up to organize a new UGTT congress and the government undertook that all public sector workers sacked for involvement in the strikes of 1984 and 1985 would be reinstated. In addition, dismissed private sector workers were to be the subject of talks between the government and employers' federation.

Regional elections were held in early 1989 at which those leaders deposed by President Bourguiba ('legitimistes') were mostly returned to office. The UGTT then held a special congress at Sousse in April 1989 at which a unified list of delegates was put forward for election, and Ismail Sahbani, the metalworkers' union leader, was elected secretary-general. Sahbani had been involved in the political conflict of the early 1980s, but was released from prison after the intervention of foreign sympathizers, including the British Labour MP, Denis MacShane.

After the 1989 Sousse congress, the 50 UGTT federations held elections which, like those of the regions, led to the return of those officers deposed earlier in the decade. According to the UGTT leadership the congress marked the 'rehabilitation' of the UGTT, since when it has re-built its influence and has been able to secure a succession of benefits for its members. The UGTT avoided further damaging conflict with the state and in October 1999 secretary-general Sahbani said that a vote for President Ben Ali in the forthcoming national elections would be a 'vote for stability, security and national solidarity'.

The UGTT reportedly receives substantial government subsidies to assist its work. Internal opponents of the leadership have received the hostile attention of the state. Police detained and questioned about 20 UGTT officials and members, including the secretaries-general of affiliates representing bank workers, posts and telecommunications workers, and teachers in higher education, after they had circulated a petition criticizing the leadership in April 1997. The petition charged that the UGTT had lost credibility with the people and created a 'state of indifference and discouragement' among the workers by failing to defend democracy, human rights and social justice, and becoming the tool of a group around the secretary-general.

In May 1999, ten activists were briefly detained after circulating a petition during the UGTT congress that criticized Sahbani and threatened to set up an independent union. According to the government, the activists were detained on suspicion of threatening the public order and violating the Publications Code, which requires prior approval of publications by the state. In September 2000, Sahbani, who had only recently been unanimously re-elected secretary-general, was effectively ousted from his post after allegations of embezzlement were publicised. The following month the ICFTU announced it would send a delegation to Tunisia to investigate the circumstances surrounding the enforced resignation of Sahbani.

The current UGTT secretary-general is Abdesselam Jerad, born in 1937, who was elected to the post on Sept. 21, 2000, and re-elected with a new executive bureau of 13 on Feb. 10, 2002. His career as a senior union official began in 1969 when he became head of the Tunis branch of the Fédération de la Société Nationale du Transport (FSNT, a constituent member of the UGTT); he was elected FSNT secretary general in 1975. Jerad was arrested along with other UGTT members in 1978; he backed Achour's bid to return in 1980; and he first joined the UGTT executive bureau in 1983. In the 1990s he was often put in charge of the internal regulation of the UGTT, which placed him in a good position to assume the top office in 2000.

In office, Jerad has worked closely with government to ensure improved professional standards, national levels of education, health insurance and salaries. From time to time, however, he has expressed a more critical voice. At the UGTT regional conference, held at Sfax on July 14, 2001, Jerad called for greater democracy "involving the entire public in debate", and a freer, less censored public media; he added that while the UGTT often initiates labour legislation, it loses out in its promulgation. Other delegates decried the UGTT's lack of representation as an organization in Tunisia's national parliament. The ICFTU praised Jerad's demand that the Tunisian League for the Defence of Human Rights (LTDH) be allowed to work freely and independently.

Abdesselam Jerad was appointed acting secretary-general of the pan-Maghrebi confederation, Union des syndicats des travailleurs du Maghreb arabe (USTMA), in December 2003. He replaced fellow Tunisian, Habib Besbes, who was blamed for lethargy and ineffectiveness within USTMA. An extraordinary USTMA congress was held on Jan. 22-23, 2004, at Amilcar, near Tunis, Tunisia, to ratify this change, and on Jan. 26 Jerad was unanimously elected as the permanent secretary-general of USTMA at the meeting. Jerad has pressed for European countries to respect the fundamental rights of Maghrebi workers resident in Europe. The UGTT effected major internal structural changes and expanded its executive bureau in June 2004. It agreed to a new initiative to increase representation of women workers in its decision-marking process. That same month the UGTT recommended streamlining national law to achieve fairer and more efficacious resolution of labour conflicts. Additionally, Jerad has publicly appealed for the creation of an unemployment fund.

International affiliations. ICFTU

Turkey

Capital: Ankara
Population: 71.3m. (2004 est.)

1 Political and Economic Background

Modern Turkey was founded from the remnants of the Ottoman Empire in 1923. Civil conflict in the 1970s culminated in a military coup in September 1980 staged with the objective of ending what was seen by the military as a slide into anarchy through terrorist violence of both the right and the left. A new military-backed constitution approved by referendum in November 1982 began a gradual process of return to a democratic system of government. The formation of political parties was re-authorized in 1983 (although extreme left- and right-wing parties remained banned), and elections to a new Grand National Assembly in November 1983 were won by the conservative Motherland Party (ANAP) led by Turgut Ozal.

Since then successive governments have sought to improve Turkey's poor image for human rights and orient the country more to Europe. All the while governments sought to confront a range of ongoing problems: Kurdish insurgency in the south-east of the country, a significant Islamist movement, and extremist political groups of the right and left. An Islamist-oriented party, Refah (Welfare), won elections in 1995 – a first for Turkey – and its leader, Necmettin Erbakan, became prime minister. In June 1996, however, the governing coalition, including Welfare, began breaking down. In February 1997 the Turkish National Security Council intervened to outlaw the party, which they deemed contravened the secular requirements of political parties. In January 1998 the nation's Constitutional Court banned the party altogether.

A new government was formed under Prime Minister Bulent Ecevit following elections in April 1999. Ecevit's Democratic Left Party (DSP) was the largest in the Grand National Assembly, and formed a fractious coalition government with the Nationalist Action Party (MHP) and the Motherland Party (ANAP). Ecevit was first Prime Minister in the 1970s, and was formally banned from political activity for ten years under transitional provisions of the 1982 constitution until this was overturned in a 1987 referendum. The Islamist Virtue Party (FP) – in effect, a more moderate successor to Welfare – became the leading opposition party. It too was banned by the Constitutional Court, in June 2001; yet many of its members gravitated to a new incarnation, the Justice and Development Party (AKP).

Renewed political and economic crises prompted Prime Minister Bulent Ecevit's resignation in late 2002, and on Nov. 3 new elections were held. A recent electoral law amendment ensured that only two parties passed a required 10% threshold of the popular vote: the AKP, with nearly 30% of the national vote, and the centre-left Republican People's Party (CHP) with just over 17%. All other parties, including virtually the entire political class that ruled till then, lost all political representation. Recep Tayyip Erdogan, leader of the victorious AKP, became Turkey's new prime minister in early 2003, after an interim period pending investigation into his eligibility for the post. The new administration reaffirmed the previous government's aspiration to join the EU. Secularist fears of a radical Islamicization of Turkish society have proven unfounded. Instead, the AKP has striven to assure foreign investors with its sober and cautious economic and diplomatic policies.

Turkey's economy combines an industrial sector, with textiles, iron and steel as the main exports, and a large agricultural sector, much of it traditional, which occupies close to half the workforce. The proportion of the workforce in industry was lower at the end of the 1990s than in the early 1980s. There is still substantial state involvement in the economy in areas such as basic industries, banking, transport and communications. Although the incoming Ecevit government promised to accelerate privatization, curb inflation and tackle the public deficit, this policy lacked consistent political support even within the cabinet. Substantial state resources have been used in military expenditures arising from the prolonged conflict with Kurdish PKK rebels.

Lack of market confidence in the Ecevit government's commitment to reform probably inflamed a financial crisis in December 2000; this crisis forced an emergency IMF bail-out. Unemployment was officially 7% in 2000, but there was considerable underemployment and a low (and declining) rate of workforce participation. A new financial crisis struck the country in February 2001 and led to the collapse of the lira. In 2001 inflation reached 60%, while GDP contracted by 8%. The IMF supported Turkey after the crisis; but the quid pro quo was the imposition of demands to limit the number of workers in the public sector. This trend in turn placed new strains on public sector unions. The crisis ultimately prompted the elections of November 2002 which led to a change in government. It also hastened a series of new demands from the IMF, which included modernizing, restructuring and privatizing the banking sector; reforming the agricultural sector; and limiting the number of workers in the public sector.

Turkey aspires to join the EU and entered the EU customs union in 1995. It was formally accepted as a candidate state for EU membership in December 1999, although it remains underdeveloped and poor by Western European standards, with a highly skewed income distribution and a lack of skills in the workforce. As with many other nations in Eurasia and the Middle East, Turkey has experienced a massive influx of mainly unskilled workers (and their dependents) from the rural areas to the larger cities. Turkey has had minimal success in attracting foreign investment (after a brief rush of investment during 1989-92).

There are hopes that Turkey's economic situation may be improving with new political stability. In addition to the IMF demands, the EU has also called for economic reforms, without which Turkey has little hope of joining the Union. Up to 80% of Turks are said to favour joining the EU. The remaining oppositionists come particularly from the extreme-right and extreme-left. To the extent that their views are represented in particular unions, this has caused some turbulence in national trade union centres – both between rival centres, and within centres, often manifested in clashes between union leaders and grassroots members.

GDP (purchasing power parity) $458.2bn. (2003 est.); GDP per capita (purchasing power parity) $6,700 (2003 est.).

2 Trade Unionism

Turkey ratified ILO Convention No. 98 (Right to Organize and Collective Bargaining, 1949) in 1952 but did not ratify ILO Convention No. 87 (Freedom of Association and Protection of the Right to Organize, 1948) until 1993.

There are varying estimates as to the number of trade union members but the proportion of the workforce that is unionized is low. According to one survey, in the period 1980-2002 official trade union membership figures decreased from 2.5m to 1.2m, of whom 600,000 were covered by collective agreements. Unofficially, membership is probably around 700-800,000, and falling. However, Turkey has large informal and farm sectors (46% work on the land) and the proportion of union members in industry is much higher; the majority of workers in member firms of the Turkish Confederation of Employers' Associations (TISK) are in unions.

There are three trade union centres affiliated to the ICFTU. Turk-Is, the Confederation of Trade Unions of Turkey, is the largest and organizes about 73% of all trade unionists. It was founded in 1952. DISK, the Confederation of Progressive Trade Unions of Turkey, originated as a left-wing breakaway from Turk-Is in 1967, while Hak-Is, the Confederation of Real Turkish Trade Unions, was founded in 1976. The ICFTU also affiliates the public sector Confederation of Public Workers' Unions, KESK. All four of these are also affiliated to ETUC. There is no WCL or WFTU affiliate. The small Confederation of Nationalist Trade Unions (MISK) was revived in 1994. In the 1970s there were widespread rumours of links between MISK and extreme right-wing groups and it was suspended from 1980–84 and subsequently went into dissolution. There are also about 27 independent unions.

The 1961 constitution guaranteed the right to form trade unions and to engage in collective bargaining. Trade union activities were severely restricted after the military coup in 1980. The 1961 constitution, partially suspended after the 1980 coup, was superseded by a new constitution in 1982. Under its various provisions and labour legislation adopted in 1983, the right of association was guaranteed subject to considerable restrictions. Unions could be closed by a court order or (in case of emergencies) by the Minister of the Interior, and trade unions could not pursue political ends or cooperate with political parties. In 1986 a military court ordered the dissolution of the leftist Confederation of Progressive Trade Unions of Turkey (DISK), whose activities had been suspended since 1980, and the ban was not lifted until 1991. Civil servants and workers in public services (including banks, schools, electricity, water and petroleum) could not organize. Meanwhile, since 1980 real wages were estimated to have decreased by a half, or even two-thirds.

From 1988 unions were allowed to make political statements while still barred from having links with political parties or other organizations. Restrictions on political activity by unions were finally lifted in 1997. However, a state of emergency in the southeast, where there was an ongoing Kurdish insurrection, led to curbs on trade unions in five provinces, including the closure by the courts in December 1998 of three union branches that had called for a cessation of military action against the Kurds. There were complaints that anti-terrorist measures, brought in to counter Kurdish insurgency, were being used to intimidate and suppress trade unions in the southeast, and that union activists faced arbitrary detention and torture.

Considerable restrictions remain on trade union activity in both law and practice. Legislation restricts the forms trade union organization may take: the first level of organization must be at sectoral level, so enterprise and occupational unions are not permitted. Union officers must have worked for ten years in the industry covered by the union. This latter provision was used to ban the DISK affiliate in the leather industry. Workers must notify a public notary if they wish to join or leave a trade union.

While discrimination against union members and organizers is prohibited in law, the unions claim that it is widespread. According to the Turkish unions, some 40,000 workers in 2,000 workplaces lost their jobs for union activities in the period 1992–98, with no protection from the courts or authorities. Union organizing campaigns and strikes often see violence erupting between union members and hired security guards and police. Many employers are hostile to union organization in their plants. Furthermore, increases in sub-contracted and temporary employment, as well as self-employment, have hampered the work and status of the unions.

Collective bargaining resumed in 1984 but is circumscribed. To be recognized as a bargaining agent a union must not only represent more than 50% of employees in the bargaining unit, but also 10% of all workers in that industrial sector. This provision has been used to deny bargaining rights especially to smaller unions. However, while the ILO has urged Turkey to abolish the 10% requirement, both Turk-Is (by far the largest confederation) and the employers' confederation have favoured its continuation. Although the government told the ILO in 1994 that it would propose abolition of the rule to the social partners, it has so far not changed the law. Collective bargaining does not take place in the public sector.

From 1984 unions were no longer required to seek official permission to start a strike: the first legal strike since 1980 occurred that year in the docks. By the end of the 1980s industrial action had become widespread, as a newly strengthened trade union movement sought pay increases to offset the impact on real incomes of rampant inflation. During the 1991 Gulf Crisis all collective bargaining and strikes were banned by decree for a period, although this was overturned by the Council of State in February 1991. Unions must obtain permission to hold meetings or rallies. There is a constitutional right to strike, but this is subject to significant restrictions. General strikes, political strikes and sympathy strikes are prohibited, as are strikes in the public sector. The government may suspend strikes for 60 days for reasons of national security or public health, and may impose binding arbitration at the end of this period. Sectors in which strikes are not allowed include the production and distribution of water, gas, electricity, coal, and oil, in transport, and in banking. Strikes are banned in the free trade zones for the first ten years, although the workforce in the zones is small. In sectors where strikes are banned binding arbitration is to be employed. However, employers may not dismiss workers who take part in legal strikes or hire strikebreakers to replace them.

Generally the 1990s brought greater liberalization. This was reflected in Turkey's ratification of ILO Convention No. 87, together with a number of other ILO conventions, in 1993. Liberalization also seemed to improve the climate for foreign investment: the number of foreign companies operating in Turkey increased from 78 in 1980 to 3,161 in 1995. During the 1990s unofficial unions developed in the public sector and in 1997 the law was changed in line with amendments to the 1995 constitution to officially allow public sector workers, such as teachers, municipal workers, and nurses, the right to join unions, although not to bargain collectively or strike. However, in the late 1990s the accelerated pace of privatization was accompanied by lay-offs, sub-contracting, and increased shadow and illegal labour. One source estimates that 1.5m workers lost their jobs in 2001.

During 1999 the main confederations combined to wage a campaign, including demonstrations, against government legislation intended to raise Turkey's retirement age closer to international norms (from 43 to 60 for men and from 38 to 58 for women). The legislation was adopted in September 1999. Another pressing legislative issue concerned a draft law on job security, which is a necessary part of the process of adaptation to the EU. Six Turkish national trade union centres bonded together to form a Labour Platform, to persuade parliament to pass the law. However, an employers' seminar militated against the passage of the law; this factor, plus the political uncertainties of recent years, has left the draft law marooned in parliamentary schedules.

President Ahmet Necdet Sezer signed into law on April 8, 2002 a nine-article harmonization package, earlier passed by the Turkish parliament, which aimed to prepare Turkey for meeting EU norms. Inter alia, the package charged authorized state bodies with responsibility for overseeing the organization of meetings and protest marches of legal groups, such as trade unions, associations and political parties.

The EU issue has provoked harmful confrontation between the different centres. Turk-Is, DISK, Hak-Is and KESK are affiliated to the ICFTU and the ETUC. All four initially participated in an ETUC education project, designed to prepare for Turkey's application for EU membership. However, at a late stage, Turk-Is opted out of the project and accused the remaining three centres of treason in acceping money from the EU.

Turkey's change of government in late 2002, to rule by the mildly Islamist party AKP, has apparently brought only minimal improvements to relations between the state and unions. In May 2003 a court of law ruled that the union, Kristal-Is, was entitled to be the bargaining representative for 5,000 glass workers at 13 out of 15 companies in Turkey. Yet the government sided with Turkish glass manufacturing magnates, who have sought to undermine the union; in late 2003, quoting article 33 of the Law on Collective Agreements, the government banned a nationwide strike by Kirstal-Is. In December 2003 the ICFTU condemned this prohibition as "a major affront to the democratic process in Turkey". Similarly, on March 21, 2004, Prime Minister Erdogan enacted a decree which effectively banned a planned protest by Lastik-Is, the national tyre workers' union. Again, ICFTU protested in the strongest terms, regarding Erdogan's action as contravening ILO conventions 87, 98 and 158, all of which the republic has ratified. There were similar protests against a perceived government campaign directed against Egitim Sen (possibly Turkey's largest union) (for more details, see under KESK centre, below).

In July 2004 the opposition Republican People's Party (CHP) filed charges in parliament against the AKP government for violating the constitution and the law, by forcing labourers to change their unions. In particular, the deputy leader of the CHP parliamentary group, Haluk Koc, accused the AKP of trying to "render useless" the Turk-Is centre, and instead bolster unions belonging to Hak-Is. Similarly there were protests from the International Federation of Journalists against changes in the Turkish Penal Code, made in 2004, that were feared might lead to the extinction of autonomous journalists' unions in Turkey. Nonetheless, in certain respects the AKP seemed more willing than previous administrations to heed union demands. For instance, in May 2004 the ICFTU noted favourably that Turkey had recently abolished legislation that had effectively barred industrial action in the country's export-processing zones (EPZs). There was also evidence of more effective bargaining between unions and employers.

A new round of clashes between unions and the government began in early 2005, culminating in the formation of the so-called Emek Platform, which covers all unions in the country – a rare display of unanimity given the schisms of the past decades. The Platform's spokesman is the chairman of the engineers' and architects' union. A major rally was held in Ankara and 80 other cities on Feb. 16 to protest government corruption and "policies that damage social justice". In particular, the Platform condemned the transfer of Social Security Hospitals to the health ministry, and the closure of the Village Services Department. Platform leaders condemned AKP's economic policy over two years as "privatization, capital and thievery", and called for a proper general health insurance policy. They received support from the opposition CHP.

Union centres appeared bolder in making non-economic political statements, too. All four major centres – KESK, Turk-Is, Hak-Is and DISK – were represented at May Day demonstrations in Istanbul in 2003. On that occasion riot police clashed with demonstrators and arrested 30, after the raising of banners supporting banned and controversial political organizations. In late June 2004 the four centres organised a large and rowdy protest called the "Great Istanbul Demonstration Against Occupation, NATO and Bush", which coincided with the US president's visit to Turkey.

Trade unions negotiate on the employers' side with the Turkish Confederation of Employers' Associations (TISK), led by Refik Baydur; the Turkish Confederation of Tradesmen and Craftsmen (TESK), led by Dervis Gunday; and two business associations which often negotiate with unions – the Independent Industrialists' and Businessmen's Association (MUSIAD), led by Omer Bolat; and the Turkish Industrialists' and Businessmen's Association (TUSIAD), led by Omer Sabanci.

3 Trade Union Centres

DISK
Turkiye Devrimci Isci Senikalari Konfederasyonu
Confederation of Progressive Trade Unions of Turkey
Address. Nakiye Elgun Sokak No: 117, Kat: 5-6-7, Sisli, Istanbul
Phone. +90 212 2310 408
Fax. +90 212 234 2075
E-mail. disk-f@tr-net.net.tr
Leadership. Suleyman Celebi (president)
Membership. 327,000
History and character. DISK was formed by leftist unions in 1967 as a breakaway from Turk-Is, and nearly all its founders were linked to the Turkish Workers' Party (TIP). It assumed the character of a militant socialist labour organization with a Marxist wing, and operated primarily in the private sector, where it organized many strikes. Before 1980 it was the second largest centre, claiming to have 800,000 members.

Most of its members work in the private sector, or as municipal workers.

DISK was often a target for right-wing terrorism in the violent 1970s. Its president and founder, Kemal Turkler, was assassinated in July 1980, shortly before the military seized power, and DISK was suspended and many of its leaders detained following the army coup. A mass trial of members was initiated before a military court in 1981, continuing until 1986. At its peak the trial involved close to 3,700 defendants, and resulted in the conviction of 264 leaders and members of DISK for terms of up to 15 years' imprisonment under Article 141 of the Penal Code relating to intending to overthrow the social and economic order of the country. In addition the court ordered the dissolution of DISK and 28 of its 30 affiliated unions and confiscation of their assets. The case attracted international trade union pressure, the ICFTU, WCL and ETUC opposing the increasing normalization of relations between Turkey and Western Europe while trade union rights continued to be infringed. DISK leaders maintained throughout the trial that they adhered to Turkey's 1961 constitution and the principles of free, democratic trade unionism, and rejected violence as a means. The defendants were subsequently allowed out of prison and DISK president Abdullah Basturk and general secretary Fehmi Isiklar won seats in parliament in the 1987 elections.

The ban on DISK was lifted in July 1991. In March 1992 the Constitutional Court ordered that DISK should have its sequestered assets returned; it actually received them following the passage of enabling legislation by Parliament in December 1992. Its international status was secured when, also in December 1992, it was admitted to the ICFTU as a full affiliated member. In May 1993 the authorities permitted it to organize a May Day rally in Istanbul. During the course of 1993 some 11 DISK affiliates received the authority to engage in collective bargaining activities. Ridvan Budak was first elected president in 1994.

DISK in the 1990s moved closer to the European trade union mainstream, being a member of ETUC as well as the ICFTU. Notwithstanding this, and the relative liberalization within Turkey, DISK continued to report widespread harassment of its officials and activists. In March 1999, Suleyman Yeter, an official of the DISK dockworkers' union, died in police custody after interrogation, having previously been arrested and tortured in 1997. From the mid-1990s some DISK supporters began drifting to Islamist unions affiliated with Hak-Is.

In October 2003 DISK joined KESK and other unions in protesting against a parliamentary vote to send send Turkish troops to Iraq. DISK also appears to be linked to Orhan Dogan's new political formation, the Democratic Society Movement, or DTH. Azat Fazla, DISK's Aegean branch representative, played an important role in the fourth DTH meeting, held in February 2005. In January 2005, 164 municipal workers went on hunger strike after being dismissed, allegedly because they belonged to DISK.
International affiliations. ICFTU; ETUC; TUAC

Hak-Is
Turkiye Hak Isci Sendikalari Konfederasyounu
Confederation of Turkish Real Trade Unions
Address. Tunus Cad. No: 37, 06690 Kavaklidere, Ankara
Phone. +90 312 417 1630
Fax. +90 312 425 05 52
E-mail. info@hakis.org.tr
Website. www.hakis.org.tr
Leadership. Salim Uslu (president); Recai Baskan (general secretary)
Membership. 340,000
History and character. Hak-Is was founded in 1976. In its early days it had close relations with the Islamist National Salvation Party (MSP), which was banned under military rule. Its founding charter emphasized 'partnership at the workplace' and opposition to communism, Zionism and fascism.

Hak-Is was suspended briefly after the 1980 military coup but allowed to continue in operation from February 1981. It subsequently gave its support to the Welfare Party (RP), set up in 1983 in succession to the National Salvation Party. In December 1995 elections, Necati Celik, who had been Hak-Is president for 14 years, was elected to the Grand National Assembly on the RP ticket and the RP became the largest party. It formed a coalition government in which RP leader Necmettin Erbakan became Turkey's first Islamist government leader since the end of the Ottoman Empire, defining a position that mixed Turkey's established secularist and Western-leaning state ethos with closer cooperation with Islamic countries. Celik became Minister of Labour in June 1996. He was succeeded as Hak-Is president by Salim Uslu.

Hak-Is now describes itself as politically independent. It applied to join the ICFTU and ETUC in 1993 but this was rejected after opposition from Turk-Is and DISK. In 1995 Hak-Is adopted a revised charter that incorporated a commitment to 'pluralist and liberal democracy'. Affiliation to both ICFTU and ETUC was finally granted in December 1997. In early 2001 Hak-Is joined a campaign against Turkey's IMF-backed economic programme, and particularly criticized the programme's lack of a 'remedy for poverty'.

The election of the mildly Islamist AKP to power in late 2002 brought with it accusations that the new government was unfairly favouring Hak-Is over other union centres, in particular, the established Turk-Is. On July 23, 2004, according to the opposition CHP, firefighters who belonged to Orman-Is, a union affiliated to Turk-Is, were forced to resign and immediately rejoin a Hak-Is one, Tarim-Orman-Is, in the midst of fighting a forest blaze in Antalya province.

That said, Hak-Is has on occasion criticized the AKP government. In June 2003 Salim Uslu said that Turkey's new Labour Law 'ignored' European norms on social justice and equitable distribution of income. In 2004 Uslu welcomed the chance to join the EU as "Turkey's 43-year dream and national policy". Hak-Is was formally affiliated to the oppositionist Emek Platform, although it appeared less intimately involved as of February 2005, possibly due to its affiliation to the AKP, the target of Emek protests.
International affiliations. ICFTU; ETUC

KESK
Kamu Emekcileri Sendikalari Konfederasyonu
Confederation of Public Workers' Unions

Address. Ataturk Bulvari Unlu Is Merkezi, No:23 B Blok Kat 4-5, Unkapani/Istanbul
Phone. +90 212 635 97 59/60
Fax. +90 212 635 97 61
E-mail. kesk@kesk.org.tr
Website. www.kesk.org.tr (Turkish only)
Leadership. Sami Evren (president)
History and character. KESK was founded in December 1995 and organizes in the public sector, the most unionized sector of the workforce. Its policies include opposition to privatization. KESK was admitted to the ICFTU and ETUC in December 1997. While politically independent, some of its constituent unions are known as left-wing. Since 1996 Swedish PSI affiliates for the municipal sector have co-operated on a major membership training project with seven PSI affiliates in Turkey; six of the seven are KESK members.

A new KESK member union, Egitim Sen, was founded in 1995 out of two formerly competing teachers' unions. Sister unions in Sweden, Norway, the Netherlands and Germany assisted Egitim Sen in matters of registration and implementation of Turkey's new labour law for public service unions. Since 1999 Egitim Sen has grown into the country's largest union, with, according to one source, up to 200,000 members. However, successive Turkish governments have accused it of contravening the constitution (particularly article 42 thereof), because its foundation statute supports the right to be educated in one's mother tongue. This stipulation upsets the national policy of not teaching Kurdish Turks in their own language. In 1998, 2002, and again in August 2004, the attorney general of Ankara sued the union. Judges decided in favour of Egitim Sen in the first two instances. The Ankara labour court threatened to close the union down if it did not expunge the language education clause from its statute by Sept. 15, 2004. The ICFTU called the action politically motivated, and suggested that the attorney general was acting under pressure from the still-powerful Turkish Army, which regards itself as the ultimate bastion of the state. A new trial began on Dec. 10, 2004.

The issue of public sector pay has been a contentious one in recent years, with KESK operating in an environment of pressure from external institutions such as the IMF to impose strict limits on public expenditure. In February 2005 it appeared that KESK president Sami Evren was playing a key role in the Emek Platform, a broad front of unionists whose campaign targets the AKP economic and social record since it took power.

International affiliations. ICFTU; ETUC

Turk-Is
Turkiye Isci Sendikalari Konfederasyonu
Confederation of Turkish Trade Unions

Address. Bayindir Sokak 10, Yenisehir, Ankara
Phone. +90 312 433 31 25
Fax. +90 312 433 6809
Website. www.turkis.org.tr (Turkish only)
Leadership. Salih Kilic (president)
Membership. About 1.75 million (union figure, probably much inflated)
History and character. Turk-Is was formed in 1952 during a phase of liberalization in Turkey's social and political conditions, and developed as the general confederation of the labour movement. Some of its membership formed the more left-wing DISK in 1967, but Turk-Is remained the larger centre. In its early days Turk-Is enjoyed close ties with American unions, notably AFL-CIO, which ran an office in Turkey from the 1950s to the 1980s.

Turk-Is adopted a politically centrist character, and was the only trade union centre not suspended following the 1980 military coup. Its general secretary Sadik Side took office as Minister of Social Security, leading to the suspension of Turk-Is by the ICFTU for a period. The centre's position taken during the mass trial of DISK members from 1981–86 was criticized by trade unionists inside and outside Turkey as being one of relative indifference. In 1986, however, its first demonstration since the 1980 coup called for economic reforms and a restoration of trade union freedoms. As the 1980s wore on, relations with the Ozal government came under increasing strain and Turk-Is led a revival of trade union activity. Its head office was wrecked by a bomb in 1990 but the motive for the attack was not established. In January 1991 about 90% of the Turk-Is membership stopped work to demand a democratic system and respect for civil and trade union rights, but the response of the government was to open legal proceedings against union leaders, a number of whom were detained in custody.

In 1996 the trial began of Turk-Is officials accused of violating the law when Turk-Is announced support for banned political parties during the 1995 elections. All the defendants were acquitted in 1999. On Aug. 6, 1999, the Turk-Is general secretary, Semsi Denizer, was assassinated during the congress of the miners' union, of which he was also president. He had first been elected general secretary on a reform ticket at the 1992 congress.

Owing to the criteria for representativeness, whereby a union must represent 10% of the workers in a particular sector, as well as 50% in a work place, to have collective bargaining rights, Turk-Is is by far the major force in collective bargaining in Turkey. It has been described as dominated by a few large conservative unions.

Regarding the question of EU accession, the Turk-Is congress took a decision confirming commitment to membership. Yet the centre's educational material reflects views as sceptical as those of Turkey's traditionally anti-EU National Security Council. Meanwhile extreme left- and right-wing Turk-Is affiliates (like Turk Metal) have campaigned against the EU, and in favour of Eurasian co-operation.

International affiliations. ICFTU; ETUC; TUAC

Turkmenistan

Capital: Ashkhabad
Population: 4.86 m. (2004 est.)

1 Political and Economic Background

Turkmenistan is a former republic of the USSR that declared its independence in October 1991. President Saparmurad Niyazov, the leader of the Democratic Party of Turkmenistan (the reformed Communist Party) has ruled since independence. No election for President has been held since 1992 (when Niyazov was the sole candidate) and in December 1999 the legislature, the Majlis, unanimously voted to remove the limit on his term of office. As of 2004 this ruling was still in force. All the members of the Majlis are members of the President's party or his supporters and no opposition parties are permitted. Human rights abuses are widespread.

Turkmenistan is largely a semi-desert country with nomadic agriculture, but with intensive agriculture (notably cotton) in irrigated areas and extensive oil and gas reserves. Rising energy prices on world markets in recent years have greatly benefited the country. The formal economy remains under substantial state control. Economic estimates are considered highly speculative in the absence of official statistics.

GDP (purchasing power parity) $27.88bn. (2004 est.); GDP per capita (purchasing power parity) $5,800 (2004 est.).

2 Trade Unionism

The former Soviet single-trade-union system survives, with unions organized under the monopoly umbrella National Centre of Trade Unions of Turkmenistan. This claims a membership of 1.3 million. As in the Soviet era, the trade unions play a role in administering health, social, welfare, cultural and sports facilities and services and participate in the achievement of output and other targets by state enterprises. The unions also participate formally in the negotiation of collective agreements for the enterprises. The trade unions remain close to the government: Rejepbai Arazov, former vice-Premier and Minister of Defence, is the chairman of the trade union centre.

Turkmenistan joined the International Labour Organization in 1993 and ratified ILO Conventions No. 87 (Freedom of Association and Protection of the Right to Organize, 1948) and No. 98 (Right to Organize and Collective Bargaining, 1949) in 1997. However, there are no legal guarantees enabling workers to form or join unions of their own choosing and while there is no specific legal bar to the formation of independent trade unions, none exist.

Strikes are neither allowed nor banned by law, but strikes are rare and few or none have occurred in recent years.

Tuvalu

Capital: Funafuti
Population: 11,000 (2004 est.)

1 Political and Economic Background

Tuvalu, formerly the Ellice Islands, became independent from the UK in 1978 and is a "special member" of the Commonwealth. The country comprises nine small but densely populated coral atolls in the south Pacific. It has parliamentary government but informal groups rather than political parties.

Tuvalu is exceptionally dependent upon foreign aid and remittances from workers abroad. Subsistence farming and fishing are the primary economic activities.

GDP (purchasing power parity) $12.2m. (2000 est.); GDP per capita (purchasing power parity) $1,100 (2000 est.).

2 Trade Unionism

Tuvalu is not a member of the International Labour Organization. Workers are free to organize and join unions of their own choosing, but few work in waged employment, and the only registered union is the Tuvalu Overseas Seamen's Union. There are several hundred civil servants, teachers and nurses, who are enrolled in professional associations. Strikes are legal, but none has been recorded.

3 Trade Union Centre

There is no trade union centre.

4 Other Trade Union Organization

Tuvalu Overseas Seamen's Union
Address. GPO Box 99, Vaiaku, Funafuti
Phone. +688 20609
Fax. +688 20610
E-mail. tuvalutus@aol.com
Leadership. Valo Valo (general secretary)
Membership. 600, who work on foreign vessels. The union affiliates to the ITF.
International affiliation. CTUC

Uganda

Capital: Kampala
Population: 26.4 m. (2004 est.)

1 Political and Economic Background

Uganda became an independent state in 1962 after some 70 years of British rule, a republic being instituted in 1967. As an independent state successive governments were overthrown by military coups, but the current President, Yoweri Museveni, has remained in power since 1986, when his National Resistance Movement (NRM) triumphed after a five-year guerrilla war. As in many African states, a degree of political pluralism was introduced in the early 1990s, and political parties are now permitted, although a system of non-party elections and government has been retained. In the most recent elections, Museveni retained the presidency with 69% of the vote in March 2001, while his supporters won a majority in the National Assembly in June of that year. There is continuing rebellion and acts of terrorism in the north and west of the country.

Uganda's economy is based on agriculture (which generates virtually all export earnings and accounts for over 80% of the workforce). The country has substantial natural resources, including fertile soils, regular rainfall, and considerable mineral deposits of copper and cobalt. Coffee accounts for the bulk of export revenues. Since the mid-1980s, the government, with the support of foreign countries and international agencies, has acted to rehabilitate and stabilize the economy by undertaking currency reform, raising producer prices on export crops, increasing prices of petroleum products, and improving civil service wages. It became the first country to receive debt relief under the Initiative for Heavily Indebted Poor Countries (HIPC), after being declared eligible in 1997.

GDP (purchasing power parity) $36.1bn. (2004 est.); GDP per capita (purchasing power parity) $1,400 (2004 est.).

2 Trade Unionism

Uganda ratified ILO Convention No. 98 (Right to Organize and Collective Bargaining, 1949) in 1963, but it has not ratified Convention No. 87 (Freedom of Association and Protection of the Right to Organize, 1948). Trade unions developed after 1940 under British colonial rule and were given legal recognition in 1952. Under the 1976 Trade Union Decree 1,000 members are required to form a union, and 51% of the workforce must be in membership in order for it to be recognized for collective bargaining purposes. In 1993 the National Assembly enacted legislation amending the 1976 decree to permit unionization of the public service (including teaching) and the central bank, the Bank of Uganda, although the police, armed forces, school heads and senior civil servants may not join unions.

The National Organization of Trade Unions (NOTU) is the single centre to which all unions are by law affiliated. However, recently formed trade unions of public servants and teachers have according to the ICFTU not been required to affiliate to NOTU. In October 2003 five unions abandoned the NOTU and formed a rival centre, the Central Organization of Free Trade Unions (COFTU).

Where the majority of the workforce are in a union, it may engage in collective bargaining. The government is the major employer in the formal sector, in the civil service and state-owned enterprises. Uganda has a tripartite framework, which brings together NOTU with the Federation of Ugandan Employers (FUE) and the Minister of Labour. Bargaining has tended to be highly centralized. There is an Industrial Court but the FUE has charged it with bias and appealed decisions to the High Court, where unions have often lost cases because they could not afford the legal costs.

Notice of strike action must be given to the Labour Minister, who generally refers the matter to the Industrial Court. In practice, in the absence of rulings from the Court, strikes have often been declared illegal, although they have still occurred, sometimes being broken up by police action. Under the Trades Dispute (Arbitration and Settlement) Act of 1964, workers in "essential services" may be prevented from terminating their contracts of service and strikes may be prohibited.

Under the electoral system, representatives for special interest groups have reserved places in the National Assembly, and the unions have three seats.

3 Trade Union Centre

National Organization of Trade Unions (NOTU)
Address. PO Box 2150, Plot 94, William Street, Kampala
Phone. +256 41 256295
Fax. +256 41 259833
E-mail. notu@infocom.co.ug
Website. www.notu.co.ug
Leadership. L.O. Ongaba (general secretary); David Nkojjo (chairman general)
History and character. The Uganda Trade Union Congress (UTUC), the first national trade union centre, was formed in 1955 with the assistance of the ICFTU. In 1964, however, a Federation of Uganda Trade Unions (FUTU), affiliated to the WFTU, was formed as a splinter from the UTUC. In 1966 the trade unions reunited in the Uganda Labour Congress (ULC), and this was succeeded in 1974 by NOTU. NOTU comprised 17 unions in both private and public sectors. However, in October 2003 five of the unions abandoned NOTU and formed a rival centre, the Central Organization of Free Trade Unions (COFTU). The rebel unions accused NOTU of not effectively intervening in a recent dispute concerning the Tri-Star Apparel Factory.

NOTU states that it is non-political and seeks to build a strong labour movement in Uganda without interference in the internal affairs of other organizations. It is represented on a number of government bodies such as the Industrial Court, Social Security Fund and the Industrial Training Council.
International affiliation. ICFTU; CTUC

Ukraine

Capital: Kyiv (Kiev)
Population: 48.5 m. (2004 est.)

1 Political and Economic Background

Ukraine achieved independence with the dissolution of the Soviet Union in 1991. The Communist Party was banned in August 1991 but restored by 1993 and has remained largely unreformed. In subsequent parliamentary elections, most recently in March 2002, it has still been the largest single party, but its influence has been gradually decreasing with its electoral support narrowed to the ageing generation of pensioners. The majority of the Ukrainian parliament, the Verkhovna Rada, comprises pro-govermental parties of the "oligarchs" with "national democrats" representing a formidable opposition. The executive President has substantial powers, and nominates the Prime Minister and other members of the government.

Ukraine steered an uncertain course after independence with a lack of a clear mandate for, or commitment to, major political and economic reform. Initial efforts at deregulation of prices and markets met resistance and were stalled. President Leonid Kuchma was first elected in 1994, as the candidate of the Inter-Regional Bloc for Reform, on a platform including a cautious programme of free market reform. However, he was also supported by the Communists, and the continued influence of communists and former apparatchiks throughout the bureaucracy has been reflected in the slow pace of change, notwithstanding a continuing growth in the private sector. Kuchma was re-elected in November 1999 and served a full term to January 2005. Opposition leader Viktor Yuschenko managed to secure his victory as Kuchma's successor as president only after mass street protests, termed the "orange revolution", against election fraud and attempts to impose Kuchma's chosen successor, Prime Minister Viktor Yanukovych (whose support lay mainly in the eastern, Russian-oriented, part of the country). There were widespread hopes that the new government of President Yuschenko would bring swift changes to the economy, eliminate corruption and bring Ukraine into NATO and possibly the EU. However, it was thought that the large unreformed Eastern Ukrainian industrial lobby with links to Russia and with the support of the communists might attempt to slow down reforms.

Ukraine was the breadbasket of the former Soviet Union as well as an industrial stronghold and it has struggled to maintain its economy in the post-Soviet era. Industrial output declined during the 1990s to only 40% of its 1991 level and many industrial enterprises were engaged only in part-time working or were virtually closed, although official unemployment in 1999 was only 4%. Wage arrears were widespread and there was a large informal sector. The economy has shown some recovery since 2000, recording annual growth of 8-15%, largely due to steel, textile, agricultural as well as arms exports. The outgoing government of Prime Minister Yanukovych claimed annual GDP growth of 12% for 2004. Foreign investment, however, has been discouraged by corruption, opaque regulatory and licensing regimes, and arbitrary and onerous taxation, when most enterprises remain controlled by individuals with political links.

GDP (purchasing power parity) $260.4 billion (2004 est.); GDP per capita (purchasing power parity) $5,400 (2004 est.).

2 Trade Unionism

Independent Ukraine has inherited the Soviet era ratification in 1956 of ILO Conventions No. 87 (Freedom of Association and Protection of the Right to Organize, 1948) and No. 98 (Right to Organize and Collective Bargaining, 1949).

Under the law all employees are free to form and join unions of their own choosing. There was no major development of opposition to the regime within the trade unions prior to the collapse of the Soviet Union in 1991, however, and after independence the reorganized official trade unions retained their dominance. The Federation of Trade Unions of Ukraine (FPU), the successor to the Soviet unions, had the great majority of the workforce in membership, and claimed 26 million members in the early 1990s. In contrast, although independent unions existed in a number of sectors, their total membership was variously estimated at only between 100,000 and 300,000. By the year 2000 overall membership of the FPU and a couple of dozen independent unions had fallen to 17.4 million, of which 14.4 million were associated with the FPU. As in the USSR, membership of the official unions is generally passive and linked to their administration of a range of benefits through the social insurance fund. The official unions retained the property and other assets of the Soviet era unions. In practice giving up membership in the official unions is often difficult. Similarly, the official unions include enterprise managers and directors as members and the unions have retained much of their former character of working closely with management. They have come into conflict with the government, however, over the problem of unpaid wages. In 1997 the FPU created a political party, the All-Ukrainian Party of Workers.

The most influential of the independent unions is the Independent Miners' Union of Ukraine, which is affiliated to the ICEM. Mikhail Volynets, the president of the miners' union, also became president of the Confederation of Free Trade Unions of Ukraine, which is now affiliated to the ICFTU. The All-Ukrainian Organization of Solidarity of Working People (VOST) is affiliated to the WCL.

In September 1999 Ukraine adopted a new trade union law that independent unions saw as weakening their position by setting high barriers to achieving 'national status', which confers a range of privileges including participation in national-level bargaining. The legislation also made registration with the Justice Ministry compulsory and provoked fears that the government might refuse to register unions it did not favour. However, the Constitutional Court subsequently ruled the key clauses of the law unconstitutional.

Wage levels are set in the state sector through agreement between the government and the official unions. The independent unions have little access to or involvement in collective bargaining. The value of agreements is often undermined by the widespread problem of wage arrears. Many enterprises retain workers on their books who are effectively redundant. This is preferable for the enterprise as it avoids paying compulsory redundancy of three months' salary, while workers also prefer to retain their jobs in hope of a recovery and to maintain pension and other benefits. The Law on Disputes Resolution, which came into force in March 1998, provided for the creation of national arbitration and mediation services, though these were not in practice immediately set up.

There is a constitutional right to strike but the constitution also says that strikes must not jeopardize national security, public health, or the rights and liberties of others. Public servants, the military and those engaged in the administration of justice, may not strike. Strikes aimed at overturning the constitutional order are banned. The leading cause of strikes and other forms of unrest, such as occurred in the mines and nuclear power plants throughout the 1990s, were wage arrears, mostly caused by inter-enterprise debt. By the end of 1999, unpaid wages in the mining sector alone were the equivalent of $532 million, resulting from the situation that the power generation industry was only able to pay 5% of its obligations in cash, with the rest bartered or unpaid.

The situation has changed since 2000 as Yushchenko's and subsequent governments have managed to pay off wage arrears in the state sector. Privatization of large state-owned enterprises in coal and steel production led to job losses and subsequently new trade union actions. Unlike in Russia, Ukraine preserved small but vociferous independent trade union organizations that opposed mass redundancies. However, lack of judicial independence in Ukraine means that courts could be influenced by power-holders and oligarchs to weaken unions' actions. A regional court banned an Independent Union of steel workers at "Azovstal" in February 2004 on demand of the administration. The union opposed a lay-off of 4,000 workers after "Azovstal" was privatized by the Donetsk oligarch Renat Akhmetov.

Although traditionally the most influential unions in Ukraine were in the mining industry, a number of high profile murders among journalists with alleged involvement of top ranking government officials led to the creation of the first independent media trade union. The Independent Media Trade-Union of Ukraine was set up in 2003 and is associated with IFJ. It provides monitoring of threats, unfair dismissals and attacks against journalists and media organizations in Ukraine. The independent union played an active role in promoting freedom of the press during the presidential elections in 2004 when journalists of the leading TV channels refused to work according to "temnyky" i.e. under censorship especially after the second round of voting.

With the government of Ukraine under President Kuchma favouring the old and "tamed" ex-Soviet trade unions, independent unions inevitably tended to associate with opposition parties. This dual dependence on government and the opposition parties continued until the "orange revolution" at the end of 2004 when the House of the Republican Unions (FPU) on Independence Square became de facto the headquarters of the National Salvation Committee led by the leaders of the opposition. In the conflict over the presidential succession, the official unions (FPU) dismissed Oleksandr Stoyan on Nov. 27, 2004, for supporting Viktor Yanukovych and elected a new leader – Oleksandr Yurkin. This was partly in reaction to the creation of the National Confederation of the Trade-Union Organizations of Ukraine (NKPU) a day earlier. The NKPU united 17 independent unions with a claimed membership of 1.5 million and elected Petro Petrychenko as its secretary general. The new confederation became the second largest all-Ukrainian union organization and immediately proclaimed support for the future reformist government of Viktor Yuschenko.

3 Trade Union Centres

Confederation of Free Trade Unions of Ukraine (KVPU)
Address. 65 Velyka Vasylkivska Street, Kyiv 03150
Phone. +380 44 227 3338
Fax. +380 44 227 7283
E-mail. info@kvpu.org.ua
Website. www.kvpu.org.ua
International affiliation. ICFTU

Federation of Trade Unions of Ukraine (FPU)
Address. Maidan Nezalezhnosti 2, Kyiv 252012
Tel/Fax. +38 044 2288798
History and character. The FPU is the successor to the Soviet-era official unions. It retained a substantial part of the old official unions' membership and benefited from inheriting their considerable assets. Under Kuchma it was generally seen as associated with the government, but the leadership's support for Kuchma's preferred successor, Viktor Yanukovych, in the struggle over the presidential election in late 2004 led to the break away of a substantial section of its membership and the consequent dismissal of FPU leader Oleksandr Stoyan.

National Confederation of the Trade-Union Organizations of Ukraine (NKPU)
Leadership. Petro Petrychenko (secretary general)
Membership. Claims 1.5 million
History and character. The NKPU was created on Nov. 26, 2004, by unions breaking away from the FPU official unions in protest at the FPU's backing for Viktor Yanukovych in the disputed presidential election. It claimed a membership of 1.5 million in 17 unions on its formation.

United Arab Emirates

Capital: Abu Dhabi
Population: 2.52 m. (2004 est.)

1 Political and Economic Background

The UAE is a federation comprising seven sheikhdoms, each of which is governed by an hereditary ruler with absolute power over non-federal matters. The highest federal authority is the Supreme Council of Rulers, comprising the seven hereditary rulers of the sheikhdoms. There are no political parties or democratic institutions. The founder of the UAE, Emir of Abu Dhabi (largest and wealthiest of the sheikhdoms) and head of state of the UAE, Sheikh Zayed bin Sultan Al Nahyan, died on Nov. 2, 2004, aged 86. He was immediately succeeded in both posts by his eldest son, Khalifa.

The economy is based on oil and gas production, which provides a high standard of living for citizens, with plentiful reserves. The UAE is a huge importer of labour. Nationals represent only 20 per cent of the population, and a lesser proportion of the workforce. Unskilled workers come primarily from South Asia.

By December 2004 there were reports that some 300,000 foreign workers had absconded from their sponsoring companies. Dr Ali bin Abdullah Al Kaabi, Minister of Labour, vowed to tackle the problem using legal means; he spoke of protecting the workers themselves, and instead directed his ire at the bogus companies who, he claimed, were running the racket. Dr Al Kaabi's undersecretary, Dr Khalid Al Khazraji, added that the bank guarantee that companies are meant to pay for each worker it recruits (set at 3,000 UAE dirhams), according to a law passed in 2002, was intended to be "the minimum requirement that ensures workers' rights".

GDP (purchasing power parity) $57.7bn. (2003 est.); GDP per capita (purchasing power parity) $23,200 (2003 est.).

2 Trade Unionism

The UAE has been a member of the International Labour Organization since 1972, but has ratified neither Convention No. 87 (Freedom of Association and Protection of the Right to Organize, 1948) nor Convention No. 98 (Right to Organize and Collective Bargaining, 1949). The UAE has not signed the ILO declaration on the Basic Principles and Rights at Work, but sends the ILO an annual report on procedures taken to implement workers' rights.

There is no legal right to form trade unions and they do not exist. About 85–90% of the workforce are migrant workers who could be deported if they formed unions. There is likewise no provision for or practice of collective bargaining or a right to strike.

Conciliation committees organized by the Ministry of Labour and Social Affairs (MLSA), and labour courts, consider grievances on an individual basis, although fear of reprisals and deportation are a deterrent. Labour laws do not currently apply to government employees, agricultural workers and domestic servants.

However, on Jan. 10, 2005, the MLSA reported that a federal draft law to help facilitate the creation of federal worker unions and professional organizations was in its final stage. Evidently the proposed legislation arose out of the work of a government-backed cross-ministerial technical committee, which also included representation from employers and employees.

United Kingdom

Capital: London
Population: 60.3m. (2004 est.)

1 Political and Economic Background

The United Kingdom comprises Great Britain (England, Scotland and Wales) and the province of Northern Ireland. The leading political parties are the Labour Party and the Conservative Party. Since World War II, the Conservatives have more often formed the government, but with periods of Labour government in 1945–51, 1964–70, 1974–79, and again since 1997. New regional assemblies for Scotland, Wales and Northern Ireland opened in 1999.

During the long period of Conservative government from 1979–97 major steps were taken to liberalize the economy, with privatization of state enterprises and measures to encourage the private sector. The process of 'Thatcherism' was seen as parallel to that of 'Reaganism' in the United States. Despite that, the rate of new business formation was much lower than that in the United States and the overall social and economic model remains closer to that of the European mainland than the United States. The Labour Party leadership has since the 1980s largely abandoned socialist doctrine and instead adopted what Prime Minister Tony Blair calls the 'third way', emphasizing free markets tempered by a developed social welfare system. There has been no attempt to re-nationalize privatized industries, although the maintenance of the rail network was brought back under the control of a single not-for-profit company in 2003. The UK is a member of the EU, but opted not to join the single European currency at its launch in 1999.

A deep economic downturn at the beginning of the 1980s accelerated the closure of wide swathes of traditional industry in areas such as coal mining and iron and steel. There has been an accompanying diversification into services but this process has not aligned geographically with the closure of older industries, with a resultant divide between more dynamic service-based areas, especially in the South-East corner, and less prosperous older industrial zones, especially in the North and Wales. The UK experienced a sharp recession in the period 1990–92, but since then has produced steady growth, with falling unemployment and inflation maintained below 4% for 13 successive years. Unemployment at 4.6% in late 2004 compared with the 10.7% level reached in 1993 and is half that in the other leading European economies. According to official figures released in January 2005, the economy grew by 3.1% in 2004, with the three months to December 2004 being the 50th consecutive quarter of economic expansion – the longest period of uninterrupted growth for 200 years. However, this growth has been driven by services; in contrast employment in manufacturing has fallen by one million since Labour came to power in 1997, continuing previous trends, with the number of manufacturing jobs by the end of 2004 reduced to 3.5 million.

Publicly owned industries such as gas, water and electricity have been privatized, leaving only one major enterprise (the Post Office) in state hands. Apart from this, public sector employment is now concentrated in national and local administration, education, welfare and health, and between the mid-1980s and mid-1990s declined from 29% to 22% of the workforce.

Since coming into office in 1997 the Labour government has emphasized partnership in industry, and prioritization of education and training, to foster innovation and meet what it sees as a productivity gap between the UK and its competitors. To enhance these policies and ensure unions play a role in the workplace, a new Union Learning Fund has been established to finance union-based training in basic skills.

GDP (purchasing power parity) $1.666 trillion (2003 est.); GDP per capita (purchasing power parity) $27,700 (2003 est.)

2 Trade Unionism

The UK trade union movement is the oldest in the world and emerged in three phases. First came the mid-19th century emergence of skilled craft unions in industries such as engineering and printing. Then in the 1890s began the formation of major general unions of unskilled or semi-skilled workers. Finally came the early-20th century emergence and consolidation of white-collar and professional organizations, in areas such as public administration, education and health. In 1871 the Trades Union Act permitted collective bargaining and laid the foundation for the UK's system of 'immunities', in which unions had no positive legal right to act but enjoyed legal immunities, for example against claims for damages by employers. The shape and scope of these immunities were developed over the following decades by judicial rulings and Acts of Parliament, with a general tendency for them to be extended through to the 1970s. The UK ratified ILO Convention No. 87 (Freedom of Association and Protection of the Right to Organize, 1948) in 1949 and Convention No. 98 (Right to Organize and Collective Bargaining, 1949) in 1950.

The Trades Union Congress (TUC), founded in 1868, has never had a serious rival as Britain's trade union centre. It has no direct role in bargaining and its powers over affiliated unions are limited, but its longevity and cohesion give it considerable authority as the voice of British trade unions: since 1918 it has rarely represented less than three-quarters of all union members. Occasionally unions have been expelled but they have usually sought to return to the fold.

In the 1970s, and especially during the Labour government of 1974–79, the unions in general and the TUC in particular reached a peak of influence through their involvement in setting pay policy against a background of high inflation. Key leaders such as Jack Jones of the Transport and General Workers' Union, Hugh Scanlon of the Amalgamated Union of Engineering Workers and Lionel (Len) Murray of the TUC, assumed a public prominence comparable to that of senior members of the government. The government consulted the TUC on many issues and it had representatives on economic planning, industrial, training, educational, community, and health bodies. However, as pay policy collapsed the unions became embroiled in a series of pay disputes, especially in the public sector. The 1978–79 'winter of discontent' of industrial action by low-paid refuse, hospital, transport and cemetery workers contributed to disenchantment with the Labour government, opening the road to the election in May 1979 of a Conservative administration under Prime Minister Margaret Thatcher that was pledged to curb union power. The early 1980s brought deep recession and wholesale closures and unemployment in 'smokestack' industries like coal, steel, shipbuilding and the docks. The double impact of job losses in areas of union strength and a series of increasingly restrictive anti-union laws contributed to a rapid decline in the position of the unions. Continuing conflict in some sectors, notably the miners' strike of 1984, provided momentum for a sustained anti-union policy. Through successive Conservative administrations, consultation of the unions virtually ceased and many tripartite bodies were abolished. Trade union membership plummeted from over 13 million at the start of the 1980s to just over 9 million in the early 1990s. The number of unions shrank and the number of TUC affiliates fell from 109 in 1981 to 72 in 1992 as many merged under financial pressure.

The initial reaction of the unions to restrictive legislation, including measures that would later be accepted as reasonable, such as the introduction of secret postal ballots in place of show of hands to elect officials or call industrial action, was unwaveringly hostile. From the later 1980s, however, unions in dispute generally sought to ensure compliance with the law, made greater efforts to win public support, and tried to minimize the cost to their organizations and members. Union-government relations eased somewhat after the 1992 general election (the fourth in succession won by the Conservatives) but it was not until 1997, with the election of the first Labour government since 1979, that the position of the unions changed significantly. The new Labour administration was elected on a manifesto that emphasized there was no question of a return to the 'bad old days' of the 1970s. There would be no return of the closed shop (outlawed by a series of measures in the 1980s) under which some employees had lost their jobs for refusing to join a union. Nor would old-style methods of calling a strike through a 'show of hands', or 'disciplining' members who declined to participate, be allowed to return, while Conservative restrictions on industrial action, such as the ban on secondary 'sympathy' action taken against other workers' employers, would remain in place. While protection for employees was to be improved, a distinction was drawn between protecting the rights of employees as individuals and increasing the rights of the trade unions, which had traditionally seen themselves as the main guarantors of employee terms and conditions.

At the same time, the manifesto also endorsed the right of workers to union representation as 'promoting orderly industrial relations'. Following the election there was a revival of social dialogue and union leaders had renewed access to government. The government repealed harassing 1993 legislation requiring unions to run (costly) workplace ballots every three years for members to renew check off arrangements for paying union dues, on the ground that this regulation was 'unnecessary and burdensome for employers and unions'. In a significant symbolic gesture the government immediately after the election also restored trade union rights, withdrawn in 1984, to staff at the GCHQ intelligence agency. The issue had been the subject of a long-running union campaign and the ILO had upheld a complaint by the TUC that the dismissals had been a violation of Convention No. 87.

The Employment Relations Act of 1999 was the first piece of legislation assisting trade union organization since the 1970s. Under it procedures were put in place (effective from June 2000) to allow the independent Central Arbitration Committee (CAC) to compel employers (with more than 20 employees) to recognize a union (or more than one union acting cooperatively) for collective bargaining purposes where the union can demonstrate that it enjoys the support of the workforce. If the CAC is satisfied that a union represents a majority of workers in a bargaining unit, it can compel recognition without further action. Where union membership is less than 50%, it can compel recognition where the union wins the votes of a majority of those voting, and at least 40% of those entitled to vote, in a recognition ballot. The new procedure, while similar to that in place in the US since the 1930s, represents a new development in terms of British trade unionism, which has been built up on the voluntarist principle that a union would be recognized where the employer chose to recognize it, or where the union was strong enough to be able to force the employer to do so. The 1999 Act, in other provisions, gave the government power to prohibit the compilation of 'blacklists' of union activists, banned employers from discriminating against union members in awarding benefits, and strengthened protections against dismissal in the aftermath of an industrial action.

A major factor in the decline of union membership was the loss of jobs in traditional manufacturing sectors from the early 1980s, and the declining number of union members in firms that survived. At the same time unions have proved comparatively unsuccessful in organizing the expanding private sector service industries that have driven economic growth, and involvement of young people in the unions has dropped particularly fast. As in Germany, the pattern of union organization tends to reflect the employment patterns of a generation ago. While few employers have staged aggressive drives to weed out unions (cases of union de-recognition are not common), the changed style of management has also undermined the unions. Management has increasingly sought to communicate with staff without union involvement, collective bargaining has declined, and unions have come to seem less relevant to the lives of increasing numbers of employees. Union density shows a pronounced geographical bias, in 1997 ranging from 42% in the older industrial areas of Northern England and Wales to only 23% in the economically more dynamic and prosperous, service-oriented economy of London and the South-East. Excluding older manufacturing industries, the main strength of the unions is in the public sector, where white-collar unionism (among groups such as teachers, social workers and civil servants) is high. In 1998 public sector density was 60%. In contrast density in the private sector was only 19%. Both white-collar and blue-collar jobs are weakly organized in most service industries where private sector jobs are increasingly congregated.

In some countries, unions have been particularly undermined by failure to organize women workers, but this is not broadly true in the UK. Some 46% of trade unionists are women, comparable to women's overall participation in the workforce. This, however, to some degree reflects the preponderance of women in highly-unionized public sector areas such as teaching, and low-skilled women in private services are often not unionized. Part-time and temporary workers are less often in unions than full-timers, but (unlike in much of the EU) the proportion of such workers in the labour force has shown little increase. The proportion of jobs defined as permanent fell only 1% from 1984–99 and average length of time spent in any one job also changed little. In 1999 temporary workers constituted only 6% of the workforce, compared with an EU average of 13%, while the growth in part-time work from 1993–99 was only 1%, the least of any EU country. Similarly, the loss of union members cannot be attributed to factors in operation in some other countries, such as increasing self-employment (the number of self-employed grew in the 1980s but actually fell by 400,000 from 1990–99), or increasing employment in smaller enterprises (the proportion of employees in large firms grew in the 1990s).

In June 2000, the TUC reported that official Labour Force Survey figures showed that union membership had grown 100,000 from 1998 to 1999, rising to nearly 7.3 million, while union density had remained steady. The TUC, while warning that 2000 could see a drop of 16,000 in union membership as a result of job losses in manufacturing, hailed the development as a turning point. It predicted that 1 million new members could be added by its affiliates over the next five years, to take total TUC membership to 7.8 million. The improvement (which paralleled that in the USA) was attributed in part to new recruitment campaigns aimed especially at temporary and part-time workers. In the run up to implementation of the trade union recognition provisions of the Employment Relations Act in 2000, there had also been a reported trend for employers to enter voluntarily into recognition agreements rather than wait for this to be compelled. The TUC said 267 such agreements were signed in 1999, compared with between 85 and 104 in each of the previous four years. Since then the pace of deals – both voluntary and through the statutory procedure – has steadily declined. Nevertheless, the 137 voluntary and 29 CAC agreements signed in 2003 are still much higher than the numbers signed prior to 1999. Moreover, the number of workers covered by each deal is, on average, rising. So each deal covered an average of 195 workers in

2002 compared to an average of 471 in 2003.

Patterns of union organization have traditionally varied considerably, largely reflecting bargaining systems. The craft unions have typically had a well-developed local workplace representative (shop steward) system; they tend to give considerable authority to elected lay officials, and often have strong branches or regions. General unions, whose membership turnover is often higher, tend to have larger branches with relatively little negotiating authority but often with substantial funds and a major role in members' welfare. Shop stewards may rely more on the help of professional full-time union officials who have relatively greater authority. White collar unions are usually organized along semi-craft lines, although there is often less emphasis on pay bargaining and the unions have traditionally offered a wider range of membership benefits such as travel, legal advice and insurance, as well as actively developing members' professional interests.

One aspect of declining union strength in the 1980s and 1990s was the weakening role of union shop stewards. By the late 1990s employee work place representation through trade union representatives was largely confined to the public sector, the privatized utilities and manufacturing. Where unions are not established, alternative formal structures for employee representation and consultation are unusual, the UK having no system to parallel that of the works councils found in most other EU countries, and with management tending to discuss with employees on an individual basis or not at all. With companies commonly seeking to by-pass the unions, employees have come to feel that the union has little real influence, and therefore not worth joining.

This inevitably changed with the introduction of the new statutory recognition procedures and the right of unions to enter the workplace and accompany workers at grievance and disciplinary procedures. During the 1990s the TUC and some unions placed emphasis on 'partnership' as a new model for industrial relations. However, many partnership agreements became discredited as employers continued to take major economic and industrial decisions without any reference to the partnership agreement and unions became more sceptical of the whole concept of partnership.

As partnership deals began to dwindle, emphasis was placed more on European developments around European Works Councils and the Information and Consultation Directive. The TUC in particular came to favour such developments as not only providing opportunities for enhanced employee consultation but as providing a starting point for unionization. While in the past unions often looked upon European-style works councils as potentially a way for employers to by-pass unions, in practice formalized consultation structures of that sort rarely exist in the UK other than in unionized environments.

Until the late 1970s, most collective bargaining was typically conducted nationally at industry level: for example, in engineering, chemicals or the health service. Major companies or organizations often bargained independently. On top of these rates local establishments commonly negotiated top-up rates, bonuses, etc. Such two-tier bargaining was prevalent in manufacturing and the private sector; single-tier national agreements were the public sector norm. Collective bargaining covered over three-quarters of all employees: the service sectors and professional occupations were not usually covered. In the voluntarist tradition agreements were not backed by legal sanctions.

During late 1980s and 1990s the scope of private sector industry-wide collective bargaining declined. The major surviving national sectoral agreement, covering 600,000 workers, is the building and engineering agreement. At the same time, company-level agreements also became fewer. In 1970 83% of workers in the UK enjoyed terms and conditions of employment underpinned by collective bargaining. In 2004 less than 36% have that benefit. In addition, the collective bargaining agenda has tended to narrow, primarily to issues of pay, grievance procedures and heath and safety. The new pattern reflects the weakening of unions following the introduction of anti-union legislation introduced under the Conservative governments, the decrease in the manufacturing sector where unions are strong and the increase of service sectors where unions are weak, the reassertion of managerial authority and government hostility to national bargaining with its connotations of an annual pay round.

Some 1.3 million public sector workers, including nurses, teachers, doctors, the armed forces and senior civil servants, are covered by a system of independent pay review boards. These make annual pay recommendations for the government to decide upon, and government decisions can be highly sensitive and politicized in terms of the lead they set for other workers, including nearly 4 million other public sector workers covered by collective bargaining.

The UK has no tradition of state-mandated minimum wages, other than for specific groups of vulnerable workers for whom minima were set by wages councils. In the 1980s the scope of wages councils was reduced before (in 1992) their role was abolished except in respect of agricultural workers. Following the election of the Labour government, however, legislation was enacted (with effect from April 1999) to provide for a national minimum wage and in March 2004 the TUC claimed that in the five years since its introduction, the National Minimum Wage (NMW) had boosted the pay packets of around a million low paid workers, of whom 70 per cent were women, and that its value had risen at a faster rate than either average earnings or inflation.

The Advisory, Conciliation and Arbitration Service (ACAS) had a prominent role in dispute resolution in the 1970s. However, under subsequent Conservative governments it shifted its emphasis from crisis management to more advisory work. Under the 1992 Employment Act its remit altered from a duty to promote collective bargaining (thus necessarily involving unions) to a duty to promote good industrial relations (improving personnel practice but not necessarily involving unions). In October 2003 ACAS reported that it had provided collective conciliation in 1,325 disputes in the last financial year; 51% of cases involved pay and terms and conditions of employment (down from 52% in 2000) while 41% related to union recognition and redundancy (up from 12% in 2000). These figures for collective conciliation compared with 163 individual claims in the same period.

The UK has never had a formal legal 'right to strike', and indeed strikers are considered in breach of contract and may be dismissed. However, historically official and unofficial strikes were a commonplace feature of British industrial relations, with union participation protected by immunities built up by legislation and legal precedent, and employers rarely dismissing individual workers. Union power was in effect the main guarantee of the right to strike. A series of Acts passed by the Conservative government after 1979 were aimed at curbing the sort of industrial action seen in the 'winter of discontent'. Through successive Employment Acts in 1980, 1982, and 1988 secondary action was prohibited, mass picketing curbed, balloting of union members before industrial action introduced, and union legal immunities reduced.

The 1990 Employment Act made unions liable for any form of industrial action (including unofficial action not sanctioned by union ballots and procedures) which had been organized or supported by officers or members, unless the union explicitly repudiated the action. It gave employers the right to selectively dismiss anyone taking part in unofficial action (previously employers had normally been able to dismiss all those taking part in action, or none). The Act was widely seen as a return to the famous 1900 Taff Vale judgement (reversed by the 1906 Trade Disputes Act) which found that a union could be held liable for acts done by any of its members, authorized or not. The 1992 Trade Union Reform and Employment Rights Act increased public rights to seek redress for injury caused by strike action. A further statute, the Trades Union Reform and Employment Rights Act 1993, required that pre-strike ballots (a requirement of an earlier Conservative statute) should be postal. The new employment rights legislation introduced by the 1997 Labour government introduced a limited right to protection against unfair dismissal during the first eight weeks of industrial action, although such action would only be protected if called in accordance with the complex legislation.

Unions are required to ballot their members before taking industrial action. Such ballots are not uncommon and the majority result in votes for action. Nevertheless, the balloting provisions have been condemned by the ILO amongst other international bodies for introducing over-complicated procedures and restrictions to what should be a fundamental right. Partly due to the complicated nature of the balloting provisions and the harsh legal environment facing unions, the incidence of actual strikes has declined since the 1970s, falling in the 1990s to lower levels than at any time since records began in 1891. In 1998 only 282,000 days were lost to strike action, compared with the 29.5 million lost in 1979. In 2002-2003 strike figures increased mainly due to action taken by firefighters, railworkers and postal workers in defence of their jobs and working conditions, but the UK is still seen as a country with a low rate of industrial action, with the number of days lost per employee running at half the EU average.

It is without doubt the case that the cumulative body of Conservative legislation curbed trade union activity and particularly strikes. Traditionally strike-prone industries such as mining, engineering and the docks, once major employers, have declined greatly in significance and many newer service sectors are without any culture of industrial action. Some employers have shown more willingness to dismiss strikers. The election of a Labour government has not led to a union campaign to restore lost immunities, or indeed to any increase in strike action of the sort predicted by the Conservatives. Only relatively minor changes have been made to the law surrounding industrial action. These have included ending the requirement for unions to give employers advance notice of the names of individual employees intending industrial action (although notice must be given of the action itself) and increasing protections against dismissal in the aftermath of industrial action.

In 1999 an EU working time directive setting a limit of an average 48 hours per week came into force in the UK. However, a number of exclusions were included (for junior doctors, transport workers etc) and the UK was the only country that allowed individuals to opt out. This opt-out was due to end in December 2003 but the government and the employers' confederation, the CBI, are trying to maintain the opt-out, despite evidence that working hours in the UK have actually increased since the introduction of the Working Time Regulations. The percentage of British workers working over 60 hours a week has risen from 12% (in 2000) to 16% (in 2003), an increase blamed by many on the use of the opt-out clause. In practice actual working hours are generally longer than those in other European countries, especially for groups such as white-collar middle managers.

Other changes in the law since 1997 include more family-friendly policies – extended maternity leave, the introduction of parental leave and the right to request family-friendly working arrangements. The Employment Act 2002 introduced Trade Union Learning representatives and gave them the right to take time off to carry out their duties. The government also allocated £40 million to the Union Learning Fund. Additional protection was offered to public sector workers transferred to private companies under the 2003 Best Value Code of Practice. Finally, following the review of the Employment Relations Act of 1999, a new Employment Relations Bill is currently going through Parliament. This includes a proposal for an Unfair Labour Practices Clause, better protection for those taking industrial action, proposals to transpose the Information and Consultation Directive and rights for unions to control membership of the union. However, the new Bill has been criticized by unions for not going far enough. Most notably unions want the recognition procedures to be simplified and extended to the 6 million workers in companies with less than 21 workers.

Recent years have seen moves to create merged or 'super' unions, most prominently seen in the 2002 merger of the AEEU and MSF to form Amicus with over one million private sector members. Amicus's continuing expansion was reflected in 2004 in its absorption of the private sector finance union UNIFI and the Graphical, Paper and Media Union.

3 Trade Union Centre

Trades Union Congress (TUC)
Address. Congress House, 23–28 Great Russell Street, London WC1B 3LS
Phone. +44 20 7636 4030
Fax. +44 20 7636 0632
E-mail. info@tuc.org.uk
Website. www.tuc.org.uk
Leadership. Brendan Barber (general secretary)
Membership. 7 million
History and character. The TUC was founded in 1868, since when it has been the sole national trade union centre. More than 90% of British trade unionists are in unions affiliated to the TUC. There is also a Scottish Trades Union Congress (STUC), and unions may affiliate to both the STUC and TUC. Trade unions in Northern Ireland are represented by the Irish Congress of Trade Unions (Northern Ireland Committee), although most organized workers in Northern Ireland are members of British-based unions which are affiliated to the TUC. There is also a Wales TUC within the TUC structure. Regional committees within England help organize education, research and campaigning. At the local level, trades councils are the TUC's local bodies. The TUC works to coordinate the activities of its affiliates and represents the trade union movement to government and internationally. Its member unions are autonomous, however, and the TUC does not instruct them or negotiate on their behalf. The TUC also has a National Education Centre, based in London, and an office in Brussels.

The TUC was one of the leading British institutions for much of the twentieth century. While never a mass political organization in the manner of many continental European centres (the TUC has only once participated in a general strike, in 1926, and that in pursuit of an industrial dispute), the TUC and its affiliates have historically had a political voice through the Labour Party, which the unions were instrumental in founding. TUC leaders were especially prominent in the 1960s and 1970s (under both Conservative and Labour governments) as participants in the tripartite formulation of economic policy. The TUC assumed great power and status and successive general secretaries were household names. By the end of the 1970s its membership had reached over 12 million. Following the 1979 election of a Conservative government under Margaret Thatcher with a radical free-market anti-union agenda, however, it was largely excluded from access to government policy-making. The TUC also seemed to some to compound its problems by refusing in the early years of the Thatcher government, when anti-union legislation was somewhat tentative and the Cabinet divided, to offer any cooperation or accept any sort of reform even in those areas (such as extended balloting of members or curbs on mass secondary picketing) where there was evidence of widespread public support for the government's position. In terms of national political and economic decision-making the TUC became a fringe organization, and its capacity for influence declined as its membership fell year on year and the labour market was progressively deregulated. At the same time, the TUC re-evaluated its own position and by 1993 had moved to a position of 'new unionism' which sought to position the unions as a force for consensus and partnership in society.

In 1997 Labour returned to power for the first time since 1979, leading to an immediate warming of relations between government and unions. However, 'New' Labour, pursuing its 'third way' policies, was anxious not to appear tied to the unions, reflecting the view that the association of Labour with the unions had been a primary cause of its loss of office in the aftermath of the 'winter of discontent' of 1979. A new generation of Labour leaders, in contrast to those at the time of the last Labour government, had far less by way of roots in the trade union movement with some inclined to view it more as another interest group rather than as the bedrock of the party. Financial ties had also lessened as Labour Party membership swelled in the latter days of Conservative rule. In 1996, for the first time in history, union donations accounted for less than half the party's annual income.

Nonetheless there are continuing strong organizational, ideological and emotional linkages between the TUC, individual unions and the Labour Party. The unions have retained a powerful position in the (nominally) sovereign party conference and on the party's national executive committee. Although individual members inevitably have diverse political views, no prominent union leader is a supporter of any other political party and no TUC union is affiliated to any other party. However, in 2003 one of the unions that helped create the Labour Party – the RMT – was expelled from membership of the party after RMT members voted to support non-Labour Party candidates in elections. It was feared that other unions might follow as union members become disillusioned with the pace of change and the failure to secure fairness at work. The sharp decline in membership of the Labour Party from a 1997 peak of 407,000 to only 215,000 by the end of 2003 (in combination with the dampening effect on large individual donations of the new requirement for all donations above £5,000 to be declared) has also served to reinforce the party's dependence on union funding as the most stable income stream.

Britain has a tradition of numerous unions with ill-defined organizational boundaries, and at one time demarcation disputes between unions were common, with the TUC commonly acting as mediator. Provisions in the 1992 Trade Union Reform and Employment Rights Act that prevent unions refusing membership applications deprived the TUC of its traditional role as adjudicator between affiliates in such disputes. As a result the 'Bridlington rules' which once enforced spheres of membership were replaced by a voluntary code.

The TUC has also had a role in brokering mergers of unions, a process encouraged by the difficulties faced by some unions as membership dues declined. In 1993 three TUC affiliates merged to create the public sector union UNISON, which became the TUC's largest affiliate. Despite this, the number of affiliated unions had actually increased to 77 by 2000, compared with 68 in 1994, as a result of new affiliations by white-collar unions in areas such as financial services. Half (38) of the TUC's affiliates had fewer than 10,000 members. In 2002 two major unions, the Amalgamated Engineering and Electrical Union (AEEU) and Manufacturing, Science, Finance (MSF) merged to create the second largest British union, Amicus, with 1,061,000 members and in 2004 Amicus absorbed two further significant unions.

Most of the small unions with fewer than 10,000 members fall into three groups. Firstly, long-established craft unions representing old industrial trades that have dwindled in significance. These unions are based typically in the industrial North or Midlands, often with a very localized membership, and include unions such as the Card Setting Machine Tenters' Society, which has 88 members, all men, or the General Union of Loom Overlookers, with 322 members, also all men. A second group comprises single employer staff associations, mainly in financial services (banks and building societies). Finally, there are associations representing specific white-collar professional groups, such as the Association of Educational Psychologists and the Society of Chiropodists and Podiatrists. A special case is the National Union of Mineworkers (NUM), which in the 1970s era of industrial militancy and high dependence on coal, was arguably the most powerful union in Britain, but now has only 5,000 members.

The TUC has lost more than five million members since the end of the 1970s. While the decline of the unions in the period from 1980 was driven mainly by structural changes in the economy and the new political climate, it was exacerbated by the fall in dues to fund full-time officials, as these carried the burden of recruiting members in non-union work places. Under John Monks (general secretary, 1993-2003) the TUC sought to re-shape its public image and rebuild its base. In December 1993 the TUC stated its intention to become a campaigning organization, abolishing its complex committee structure and setting up a series of task groups focused on specific campaign issues. A 'New Unionism Task Group' was set up in 1996 with the objective of halting the decline in union membership by assisting the unionization of growth sectors in the economy and trying to win over groups with low density, such as young people. As an outcome of this Task Group, the TUC, in concert with member unions, set up an Organizing Academy in 1998. Unions are also trying to free up more of their full-time officers' time for organizational work by providing training for lay workplace representatives in how to represent employees in grievance and disciplinary proceedings, which consume officials' time. Member unions commonly provide a wide range of services, such as specially negotiated insurance and discount schemes. However, these are generally considered to contribute to retaining members rather than in attracting new ones, and the focus in winning new members is on achieving benefits in terms of collective bargaining on wages and conditions and protecting individual employee rights. The TUC welcomed the Employment Relations Act of 1999, which increased trade union organizing rights by providing for a system of workplace recognition ballots, and a network of Union Learning Reps but is aware that legislation without grass roots organizational activity is likely to have only marginal impact.

Since 1999 the TUC has witnessed small increases in union membership after two decades of decline. Under John Monks, the TUC actively promoted its concept of 'partnership' at the work place, advocating this as the way to improve flexibility, training, competitiveness and employment security. He argued that unionized workforces are the most content, the best trained, have the lowest rate of industrial tribunal cases and are more likely to show high productivity growth. He said that flexibility must be shown by employers as well as workers, in areas such as child care provision, flexible working hours that help the employee, skills training, and giving proper rights to part-time workers. Job security is also viewed as an element of partnership. In January 2001 the TUC launched a new Partnership Institute to foster the development of partnership. In May 2003 John Monks left the TUC to take up a new position as general secretary of the European Trade Union Confederation. He was replaced at the TUC by Brendan Barber. As part of that change, the TUC appointed its first women into leading positions. Frances O'Grady became the deputy general secretary and Kay Carberry became assistant general secretary.

The shift in leadership at the head of the TUC has also been reflected in changes in the leadership of individual unions. A younger more militant leadership has emerged since 2001 in unions large and small. Dubbed the "awkward squad" by the media but referred to as the New Left Majority within the labour movement, these new general secretaries are seeking to quicken the pace of reform. They believe fairness at work can be delivered not by partnership agreements but by the Labour government taking a more pro-worker, pro-union approach. To reverse the impact of 20 years of conservative rule, they believe more radical legislation is required, with more emphasis on collective rights than individual rights.

While divisions about the role and structure of the EU remain, the TUC increasingly emphasizes its social dimension and potential for establishing Europe-wide labour standards. While some manufacturing unions support joining the single currency in an attempt to boost jobs, public sector unions, including the TUC's largest affiliate, UNISON, fear that conforming to the convergence criteria for joining the currency could impact on public spending. The September 2003 TUC congress backed the Labour government's line that the UK should adopt the single currency but only at an undefined future date when circumstances are appropriate.

The TUC participates in tripartite bodies including ACAS, the Health and Safety Commission and the

Low Pay Commission. In the 1960s and 1970s the National Economic and Development Council (NEDC) had considerable prominence as a tripartite forum for wide-ranging economic issues, but under the Conservatives from 1979 its role was curtailed and it was finally abolished in 1992. Following the election of a Labour government in 1997 there has been a renewal of tripartism. In October 2000 the Chancellor of the Exchequer (Finance Minister) Gordon Brown asked the TUC and CBI to participate in a series of working parties on six topics identified by the Treasury as contributing to a 'productivity gap' between Britain and other industrialized countries. These were restrictive practices, low skills, under-investment, resistance to innovation, under-use of technology, and poor management. The TUC warmly welcomed the initiative although CBI reaction was cooler.

The Wales TUC (David Jenkins, general secretary. *Address.* 1 Cathedral Road, Cardiff CF11 9SD. *Phone.* +44 29 20 372 345. *Website.* www.wtuc.org.uk.) is an integral part of the TUC and was set up in 1974 to strengthen the role of the TUC in Wales, where there is partially devolved government. It works with and represents union views to, the Welsh Office, the CBI Wales and the Welsh Development Agency and coordinates the trade unions' interface with the elected National Assembly of Wales, set up in 1999.

International affiliations. ICFTU; ETUC; CTUC; TUAC
Affiliates.

Accord
Address. Simmons House, 46 Old Bath Road, Charvil, Reading, Berks RG10 9QR
Phone. +44 118 934 1808
Fax. +44 118 932 0208
E-mail. info@AccordHQ.org
Website. www.accord-myunion.org
Leadership. Ged Nichols (general secretary)
Membership. 23,772
History and character. The Independent Union of Halifax Staff became Accord in May 2002.

Amicus
Address. 35 King Street, Covent Garden, London WC2E 8JG
Phone. +44 20 7420 8900
Fax. +44 20 7240 4723
Website. www.Amicustheunion.org
Membership. 1.2 million
Leadership. Derek Simpson (general secretary)
History and character. Formed by merger of the Amalgamated Engineering and Electrical Union (AEEU) and Manufacturing, Science, Finance (MSF) in 2002. The AEEU was the largest manufacturing sector union in the UK. The MSF had been formed in 1988 by the merger of two white-collar unions, the Technical, Administrative and Supervisory Staffs union (TASS) and the larger Association of Scientific, Technical and Management Staffs (ASTMS). TASS represented mainly technicians and managers in engineering, while ASTMS, itself formed by merger in 1969, had grown rapidly to become the leading force in multi-sector white-collar trade unionism before being forced to make major cutbacks in the 1990s as membership fell.

Amicus is represented in manufacturing, engineering, energy, construction, IT, defence aerospace, motor industry, civil aviation, chemicals and pharmaceuticals, steel and metals, shipbuilding, scientists, technologists, professional and managerial staff, electronics and telecommunications, tobacco, food and drink, textiles, ceramics, paper, professional staff in universities, commercial sales, the voluntary sector, financial services, and the National Health Service.

In October 2004 Amicus absorbed the 150,000-member financial services union UNIFI, which became a section within Amicus; UNIFI's general secretary Ed Sweeney became a joint deputy general secretary within Amicus. In August 2004 it was announced that the membership of the Graphical, Paper and Media Union (GPMU) had also voted overwhelmingly in support of their union executive's decision to merge with Amicus. In February 2005 Amicus said that it had agreed to begin merger discussions with the Transport and General Workers' Union, one of the other "big four" unions (the others being UNISON and the GMB) and that the GMB had also been invited to participate.

Associated Society of Locomotive Engineers and Firemen (ASLEF)
Address. 9 Arkwright Road, London NW3 6AB
Phone. +44 20 7317 8600
Fax. +44 20 7794 6406
Website. www.aslef.org.uk
Leadership. Keith Norman (acting general secretary)
Membership. 16,172
History and character. Founded in 1880. It has members in all British train operating companies. Affiliated to Labour Party. Main trades and industries railways (drivers, operational supervisors and staff).

Association of Teachers and Lecturers (ATL)
Address. 7 Northumberland Street, London WC2N 5DA
Phone. +44 20 7930 6441
Fax. +44 20 7930 1359
E-mail. info@atl.org.uk
Website. www.askatl.org.uk
Leadership. Dr Mary Bousted (general secretary)
Membership. 110,083
History and character. Founded in 1978 as the Assistant Masters and Mistresses Association through the merger of separate men's and women's teachers' unions. It emphasizes professionalism, and won many members from the main teachers' unions when they staged a series of strikes in the mid-1980s. It changed its name to the ATL in 1993 to help recruitment in the further education sector. It affiliated to the TUC for the first time on 1 January 1999.

Association of University Teachers (AUT)
Address. Egmont House, 25–31 Tavistock Place, London NW1H 9UT
Phone. +44 20 7670 9700
Fax. +44 20 7670 9799
E-mail. hq@aut.org.uk
Website. www.aut.org.uk
Leadership. Sally Hunt (general secretary)
Membership. 46,223
History and character. Members include a wide range of

staff in institutions of higher education and research, including administrators, academics, computer staff and librarians.

Bakers, Food and Allied Workers' Union (BFAWU)
Address. Stanborough House, Great North Road, Stanborough, Welwyn Garden City, AL8 7TA
Phone. +44 1707 260150
Fax. +44 1707 261570
E-mail. bfawu@aol.com
Website. www.bfawu.org.uk
Leadership. Joe Marino (general secretary)
Membership. 28,186
History and character. Founded in 1849. Represents mainly manual and technician bakery workers.

Broadcasting, Entertainment, Cinematograph and Theatre Union (BECTU)
Address. 373-377 Clapham Road, London SW9 9BT
Phone. +44 20 7346 0900
E-mail. info@bectu.org.uk
Website. www.bectu.org.uk
Membership. 24,631
Leadership. Roger Bolton (general secretary)
History and character. Main trades and industries: broadcasting, film, video, theatre, cinema and related sectors.

Ceramic and Allied Trades Union (CATU)
Address. Hillcrest House, Garth Street, Hanley, Stoke-on Trent ST1 2AB
Phone. +44 1782 272755
Fax. +44 1782 284902
Leadership. Geoff Bagnall (general secretary)
Membership. 12,497
History and character. Founded in 1827. Represents pottery workers, almost all in Staffordshire.

Chartered Society of Physiotherapy (CSP)
Address. 14 Bedford Row, London WC1R 4ED
Phone. +44 20 7306 6666
Fax. +44 20 7306 6611
Leadership. Richard Griffin (director of employment relations and union services)
Membership. 34,857

Communication Workers' Union (CWU)
Address. 150 The Broadway, London SW19 1RX
Phone. +44 20 8971 7200
Fax. +44 20 8971 7300
Website. www.cwu.org
Leadership. Billy Hayes (general secretary); Andy Kerr (president)
Membership. 266,067
History and character. Formed in 1994 from the merger of the Union of Communication Workers (UCW) and the National Communications Union (NCU). Members work in posts, telecommunications, cable TV and related areas. The CWU is the largest communications union in the UK and the second largest in the EU. It is affiliated to the Labour Party and internationally to UNI.

Community
Address. Swinton House, 324 Gray's Inn Road, London WC1X 8DD
Phone. +44 20 7239 1200
E-mail. info@community-tu.org
Website. www.kfat.org.uk
History and character. Community was formed in 2004 by the merger of the Iron and Steel Trades Confederation (ISTC) and the National Union of Knitwear, Footwear and Apparel Trades (KFAT). The ISTC, with about 50,000 members, represented process, craft, technician, contractors' staff and middle management in metal manufacture and related industries. KFAT had itself been formed by a merger in 1991 between two 19th century footwear and clothing unions and had suffered severely from the decline of the industries in which its members work, being reduced to about 12,000 members.

Connect: The Union for Professionals in Communications
Address. 30 St. George's Road, TW9 4BD
Phone. +44 20 8971 6000
Fax. +44 20 8971 6002
E-mail. union@connectuk.org
Website. www.connectuk.org
Leadership. Adrian Askew (general secretary), Denise McGuire (president)
Membership. 19,363
History and character. Represents managerial and professional staff in telecoms; changed name from Society of Telecom Executives in January 2000.

Educational Institute of Scotland (EIS)
Address. 46 Moray Place, Edinburgh EH3 6BH
Phone. +44 131 225 6244
Fax. +44 131 220 3151
E-mail. enquiries@eis.org.uk
Website. www.eis.org.uk
Leadership. Ronald A. Smith (general secretary)
Membership. 53,424
History and character. Founded in 1847, and possesses a royal charter. Represents teachers, lecturers and associated staff in Scotland.

Equity
Address. Guild House, Upper St. Martins Lane, London WC2H 9EG
Phone. +44 20 7379 6000
Fax. +44 20 7379 7001
E-mail. info@equity.org.uk
Website. www.equity.org.uk
Leadership. Ian McGarry (general secretary), Harry Landis (president)
Membership. 35,410
History and character. Main trades and industries: performance workers in theatre, film television, radio and variety

Fire Brigades Union (FBU)
Address. Bradley House, 68 Coombe Road, Kingston-upon Thames, Surrey KT2 7AE
Phone. +44 20 8541 1765
Fax. +44 20 8546 5187
E-mail. office@fbu.org.uk
Website. www.fbu.org.uk
Leadership. Andy Gilchrist (general secretary), Ruth Winters (president)

Membership. 52,510

History and character. Founded 1918. Represents almost all firefighters and control staff and many managers. In 2004 the FBU disaffiliated from the Labour Party following disillusionment amongst its members over the perceived role played by the government in their long and bitter pay dispute.

First Division Association
Address. 2 Caxton Street, London SW1H 0QH
Phone. +44 20 7343 1111
Fax. +44 20 7343 1105
Email. head-offfice@fda.org.uk
Website. www.fda.org.uk
Membership. 10,883
Leadership. Jonathan Baume (general secretary), Charles Pitt (president)
History and character. Represents senior managers and professionals in public service.

GMB
Address. 22/24 Worple Road, Wimbledon, London SW19 4DD
Phone. +44 20 8947 3131
Fax. +44 20 8944 6552
E-mail. Kevin.Curran@gmb.org.uk
*Website.*www.gmb.org.uk
Leadership. Kevin Curran (general secretary), Mary Turner (president)
Membership. 703,970
History and character. The GMB is a general union that has been shaped by numerous mergers since the formation of the National Union of General and Municipal Workers in 1924. Among the more notable of these in recent times was the absorption of the white-collar Association of Professional, Executive, Clerical and Computer Staff (APEX) in 1989. The initials GMB were adopted as the union's official title in 1989, and were derived from the previous name of General, Municipal, Boilermakers and Allied Trades Union. The GMB has members in public sector areas such as the National Health Service and local government, and the diversity of its private sector membership is reflected in the fact that 34 of the top 50 British companies employ GMB members. Its membership is approximately 60% male.

The GMB has eight sections, covering clothing and textiles; commercial services; construction, furniture, timber and allied; energy and utilities; engineering; food and leisure; process workers; and public services. It has 10 regional offices, 300 full-time regional organizers and 25,000 workplace shop stewards. It was the first British union to set up a permanent office in Brussels.

The GMB is affiliated to the Labour Party and over 80 of the Labour MPs elected at the general election in May 1997 were GMB members. Its leadership has been prominent in recent years in arguing that the pound's strength against European currencies is damaging manufacturing exports and contributing to the continuing loss of manufacturing jobs.

Musicians' Union (MU)
Address. 60-62 Clapham Road, London SW9 0JS
Phone. +44 20 7582 5566
Fax. +44 20 7582 9805
E-mail. info@musiciansunion.org.uk
Website. www.musiciansunion.org.uk
Leadership. John F Smith (general secretary)
Membership. 31,312
History and character. Founded in 1893, this is the second largest musicians' union in the world.

National Association of School Masters/Union of Women Teachers (NASUWT)
Address. 5 King Street, London WC2E 8HN
Phone. +44 20 7420 9670
Fax. +44 20 7420 9679
E-mail. nasuwt@mail.nasuwt.org.uk
Website. www.nasuwt.org.uk
Leadership. Chris Keates (general secretary)
Membership. 265,000
History and character. Formed 1975 by merger of separate teaching unions for men and women. It competes for members with the National Union of Teachers (NUT), and has grown in membership and influence at the expense of the NUT through an approach that combines political moderation with strong campaigning for teacher interests on issues such as work loads and pupil indiscipline and violence. It has no political affiliation.

NATFHE (National Association of Teachers in Further and Higher Education) – The University and College Lecturers Union
Address. 27 Britannia Street, London WCIX 9JP
Phone. +44 20 7837 3636
Fax. +44 20 7837 44403
E-mail. hq@natfhe.org.uk
Website. www.natfhe.org.uk
Leadership. Paul Mackney (general secretary), Sam Allen (president)
Membership. 66,319
History and character. Formed by merger in 1976, this is the largest lecturers' union.

National Union of Journalists (NUJ)
Address. Acorn House, 314-320 Gray's Inn Road, London WCIX 8DP
Phone. +44 20 7278 7916
Fax. +44 20 7837 8143
E-mail. acorn.house@nuj.org.uk
Website. www.gn.apc.org/media/nuj
Leadership. Jeremy Dear (general secretary), George MacIntyre (president)
Membership. 23,342

National Union of Marine, Aviation and Shipping Transport Officers (NUMAST)
Address. Oceanair House, 750–760 High Road, Leytonstone, London E11 3BB
Phone. +44 20 8989 6677
Fax. +44 20 8530 1015
E-mail. info@numast.org
Website. www.numast.org
Leadership. Brian Orrell (general secretary)
Membership. 19,133
History and character. Represents all officer ranks and cadets in the merchant navy and those in related shore-based employment. Numbers employed in the British merchant

fleet have fallen with many more now employed under foreign flags, and NUMAST has been active in securing government initiatives to arrest this decline and support seafarer training. It is also involved in international initiatives to combat piracy. Affiliated to ETF and ITF.

National Union of Rail, Maritime and Transport Workers (RMT)
Address. 39 Chalton Street, London NW1 1JD
Phone. +44 20 7387 4771
Fax. +44 20 7387 4123
E-mail. info@rmt.org.uk
Website. www.rmt.org.uk
Leadership. Bob Crow (general secretary), Tony Donaghy (president)
Membership. 63,084
History and character. Formed in 1990 by merger of seamen's and rail unions, each dating from the late-19th century. In 2004 the RMT was expelled from the Labour Party for allowing individual regions and branches to support alternative political parties in elections.

National Union of Teachers (NUT)
Address. Hamilton House, Mabledon Place, London WC1H 9BD
Phone. +44 20 7388 6191
Fax. +44 20 7387 8458
Website. www.teachers.org.uk
Leadership. Steve Sinnot (general secretary)
Membership. 331,000
History and character. Founded in 1870, affiliated to TUC in 1970. Represents all teachers, although strongest in primary schools. Traditionally the most militant of the teaching unions and previously lost members to less militant rivals AMMA (now ATL) and NASUWT, both of which are stronger in secondary schools. Affiliated to EI.

Nationwide Group Staff Union (NGSU)
Address. Middleton Farmhouse, 37 Main Road, Middleton, Cheney, Banbury, OX17 2QT
Phone. +44 1295 710767
Fax. +44 1295 712580
Website. www.ngsu.co.uk
Leadership. Tim Poil (general secretary)
Membership. 11,633

Prison Officers' Association (POA)
Address. Cronin House, 245 Church Street, Edmonton, London N9 9HW
Phone. +44 20 8803 0255
Fax. +44 20 8803 1761
Leadership. Brian Caton (general secretary)
Membership. 30,401
History and character. Founded 1919. Absorbed the Scottish Prison Officers' Association in April 2000.

Prospect
Address. Prospect House, 75-79 York Road, London SE1 7AQ
Phone. +44 20 7902 6600
Fax. +44 20 7902 6667
E-mail. enquiries@prospect.org.uk
Website. www.prospect.org.uk
Membership. 105,480
Leadership. Paul Noon (general secretary), David Simpson (president)
History and character. Formed in November 2001 by merger of the Engineers' and Managers' Association (EMA) and the Institution of Professionals, Managers and Specialists (IPMS). Main trades and industries: engineering, scientific, managerial & professional staff in agriculture, defence, electricity supply, energy, environment, health & safety, heritage, industry, law and order, shipbuilding, transport.

Public and Commercial Services Union (PCS)
Address. 160 Falcon Road, London SW11 2LN
Phone. +44 20 7924 2727
Fax. +44 20 7924 1847
Website. www.pcs.org.uk
Leadership. Mark Serwotka (general secretary), Janice Godrich (president)
Membership. 285,000
History and character. PCS is the result of mergers of civil service unions and has members mainly in government departments and agencies and other public bodies, but also includes members in private sector IT and other service companies. It represents mainly lower and middle-level staff, and two-thirds of members are women.

Society of Radiographers (SoR)
Address. 207 Providence Square, Mill Street, London SE1 2EW
Phone. +44 20 7740 7200
Fax. +44 20 7740 7204
Membership. 15,971. Most members work in the National Health Service.

Transport and General Workers' Union (TGWU)
Address. 128 Theobald's Road, Holborn, London WC1X 8TN
Phone. +44 20 7611 2500
Fax. +44 20 7611 2555
E-mail. tgwu@tgwu.org
Website. www.tgwu.org.uk
Leadership. Tony Woodley (general secretary)
Membership. 835,351
History and character. Founded in 1922 by merger of three large late-19th century dock, transport and general unions; represents employees in almost every sector and at every level, although predominantly manual workers in manufacturing and public services, transport, construction and agriculture. Historically the TGWU ('T&G') was the single most influential and important union in the British labour movement, but it lost its long-standing position as Britain's largest union when the public sector super-union UNISON was created in 1993. The TGWU lost membership heavily from the early 1980s, and a large financial deficit forced it to shut some 60 offices and merge regional organizations in the early 1990s. However, by end-decade income and expenditure were in balance. The T&G, like other British unions, is run on the basis of membership dues, without subventions from the state or other sources.

The TGWU has four industrial sectors, each headed by a national organizer. (1) *Food and agriculture* includes food retailing and distribution. (2) *Manufacturing* includes vehicle building and automotive trades, power, engineering, textiles, chemicals, oil and rubber. (3) *Services* covers 300,000 workers in public services, such as refuse collectors, librarians and leisure attendants, as well as construction and other sectors. (4) *Transport* covers 200,000 members on buses, in the freight industry, the docks and water transport. There is a strong emphasis on workplace shop steward organization. There is also a sector for women, race and equality. The TGWU has a range of educational programmes for members, including a National Members' School.

The TGWU is affiliated to the Labour Party and traditionally had an important voice in party policy. The TGWU was the most reluctant major union to endorse the revision of Labour Party objectives in 1995. The T&G has a predominantly (81%) male membership. In 1998 it introduced a rule change to reserve six seats on its general executive council for women after attempts to increase women's representation on a voluntary basis failed.

Transport Salaried Staffs' Association (TSSA)
Address. Walkden House, 10 Melton Street, London NW1 2EJ
Phone. +44 20 7387 2101
Fax. +44 20 7383 0656
E-mail. enquiries@tssa.org
Website. www.tssa.org.uk
Leadership. Gerry Doherty (general secretary)
Membership. 32,345 (excludes members in the Republic of Ireland)

Union of Construction, Allied Trades and Technicians (UCATT)
Address. UCATT House, 177 Abbeville Road, London SW4 9RL
Phone. +44 20 7622 2442
Fax. +44 20 7720 4081
E-mail. info@ucatt.org.uk
Website. www.ucatt.org.uk
Leadership. Alan Ritchie (general secretary); John Thompson (president)
Membership. 115,007
History and character. Founded 1971 on merger of several craft building unions each dating from early-19th century. Represents all building workers but mainly semi-skilled and skilled. Affiliated to Labour Party.

Union of Shop, Distributive and Allied Workers (USDAW)
Address. Oakley, 188 Wilmslow Road, Fallowfield, Manchester M14 6LJ
Phone. +44 161 224 2804
Fax. +44 161 257 2566
E-mail. enquiries@usdaw.org.uk
Website. www.usdaw.org.uk
Leadership. John Hannet (general secretary); Marge Carey (president)
Membership. 321,151
History and character. Founded 1947 on merger of two early-20th century unions. Represents shop workers as well as having members in areas including food processing, laundries, catering, home shopping, insurance agents and milk rounds. 60% of members are women, with a high proportion of lower-paid, part-time and ethnic minority members. USDAW is a strong proponent of partnership agreements with employers and reports a growing membership. Affiliated to Labour Party.

UNISON
Address. 1 Mabledon Place, London WC1H 9AJ
Phone. +44 20 7388 2366
Fax. +44 20 7387 6692
E-mail. direct@unison.co.uk
Website. www.unison.org.uk
Leadership. Dave Prentis (general secretary)
Membership. 1,289,000
History and character. This public sector super-union was formed out of the Confederation of Health Service Employees (COHSE), the National Union of Public Employees (NUPE) and the National Association of Local Government Officers (NALGO) in 1993. It is the largest TUC affiliate. Its members are both manual and white-collar workers. Half the membership is in local government, including schools, and UNISON has the largest education membership of any union. One-third is in health, making UNISON the largest health union, with the remainder mainly in the utilities (electricity, gas and water). It includes some private sector employees who work for contractors providing public services and utilities. About two-thirds of members are women, and 44 of the 67 seats on the National Executive Committee are reserved for women.

UNISON has 13 regions, each with its own delegate council, and six 'service groups', covering local government, health care, higher education, energy, water and transport. It also has 'self-organized groups', representing women, black members, disabled members and lesbians and gay men.

Uniquely, UNISON gives members the option of choosing whether to subscribe to its Affiliated Political Fund, which supports the Labour Party, or its General Political Fund, which is politically non-aligned.

It has opposed entry into the single European currency because of what it fears would be the impact on public spending and welfare provision of meeting convergence criteria. Internationally it is affiliated to PSI.

United Road Transport Union (URTU)
Address. 76 High Lane, Chorlton-cum-Hardy, Manchester M21 9EF
Phone. +44 161 882 2706
Fax. +44 161 862 9127
E-mail. info@urtu.com
Website. www.urtu.com
Leadership. Robert Monks (general secretary), Trevor Bray (president)
Membership. 17,462
History and character. Represents road haulage drivers and offers various specialist services including a 24-hour call centre and distance learning for lorry drivers. Re-affiliated to TUC in 2003.

4 Other Trade Union Organizations

General Federation of Trade Unions (GFTU)
Address. Central House, Upper Woburn Place, London WC1H OHY
Phone. +44 20 7387 2578
Fax. +44 20 7383 0820

E-mail. gftuhq@gftu.org.uk
Website. www.gftu.org.uk
Leadership. Mike Bradley (general secretary)
Membership. 275,000 in 36 unions
History and character. The GFTU was founded at a special congress of the TUC in 1899. Its role today is to provide a service to specialized unions, for which it carries out research and provides education and training for union officials. Membership overlaps with that of the TUC. Its 20 full members are mainly (although not exclusively) small unions with only a few thousand members, and its associate members are mainly specialist sections within three major unions, Amicus, GMB and TGWU.

National Association of Head Teachers (NAHT)
Address. 1 Heath Square, Boltro Road, Haywards Heath, West Sussex, RH16 1BL
Phone. +44 +444 472 472
Fax. +44 +444 473 473
E-mail. info@naht.org.uk
Website. www.naht.org.uk
Leadership. David Hart (general secretary)
Membership. 30,000
History and character. Represents heads and deputies; emphasizes professionalism.

Professional Association of Teachers (PAT)
Address. 2 St. James' Court, Friar Gate, Derby, DEI 1BT
Phone. +44 1332 372 337
Fax. +44 1332 290 310
E-mail. hq@pat.org.uk
Website. www.pat.org.uk
Leadership. Kay Driver (general secretary)
Membership. 35,000
History and character. Founded in 1970, PAT has members in all parts of the UK from nursery schools to tertiary institutions, in both the maintained and independent sectors. It is strictly non-political and has a no-strike rule.

Royal College of Nursing of the United Kingdom (RCN)
Address. 20 Cavendish Square, London W1M OAB
Phone. +44 20 7872 0840
Fax. +44 20 7355 1379
Leadership. Beverly Malone (general secretary)
Membership. 359,000
Website. www.rcn.org.uk
History and character. Founded in 1916; became a certified, independent trade union in 1977. Grew rapidly thereafter. In 1995 it voted to drop its 'no strike' rule. It provides professional, labour relations and higher educational services for its members.

Scottish Trades Union Congress (STUC)
Address. 333 Woodlands Rd, Glasgow G3 6NG
Phone. +44 141 337 8100
E-mail. info@stuc.org.uk
Website. www.stuc.org.uk
Leadership. Bill Spiers (general secretary)
Membership. 630,000 in 46 affiliated unions
History and character. The STUC is an independent centre, founded in 1897, separate from but having reciprocal arrangements with the British TUC. It serves to provide a representative voice for the trade union movement at the Scottish level. Most of its affiliates are also affiliated to the British TUC. It traditionally stands on the left of the labour movement. It was active in the movement to establish a Scottish Parliament, which opened in 1999.

UNITED KINGDOM DEPENDENCY

BERMUDA

Capital: Hamilton
Population: 65,000 (2004 est.)

1 Political and Economic Background

Bermuda is a British dependency with a system of internal self-government introduced in 1968. It rejected independence in a referendum in 1995. The two major political parties are the conservative multi-racial United Bermuda Party (UBP), which won every election from 1968 until the late 1990s, and the centre-left Progressive Labour Party (PLP), which has formed the government since 1998. Bermuda has a high standard of living based on financial services and tourism. There is little agriculture and only a small manufacturing sector.

GDP (purchasing power parity) $2.33bn. (2003 est.); GDP per capita (purchasing power parity) $36,000 (2003 est.).

2 Trade Unionism

Unions have existed since World War II. The principal unions are the Bermuda Industrial Union, traditionally the largest on the island, and the Bermuda Public Services Association. In 2000 seven of the island's ten registered trade unions pressed ahead with the formation of the Trade Union Congress (BTUC), which achieved statutory recognition in 2002. The new federation is an umbrella organization that does not have the power to negotiate directly with employers or to call strikes, but it does have consultative status on various government bodies. The largest union on the island, the Bermuda Industrial Union, has not joined the TUC.

Bermuda Industrial Union (BIU)
Address. 49 Union Square, Hamilton HM 123
Phone. + 1441 292 0044
Fax. +1441 295 7992
E-mail. biu@ibl.bm
Leadership. Molly Burgess (general secretary)
Membership. 4,200
History and character. The BIU was founded in 1946. It is a general union and has collective agreements in both the private and public sectors. It generally supports the PLP and expects it to support the union on all social legislation and other political issues. It supported independence in the 1995 referendum in which the majority of the electorate voted to remain a British dependency.
International affiliation. ICFTU; PSI, CTUC

Bermuda Public Services Association (BPSA)
Address. PO Box HM 763, Hamilton HMCX
Phone. +1441 292 6985
Fax. +1441 292 1149
E-mail. beepsa@ibl.bm

Leadership. Edward G. Ball Jr. (general secretary)
History and character. Originated in 1952 as the Bermuda Civil Service Association, adopting the present name in 1971. It is affiliated to the Union Network International (UNI) and Public Services International (PSI).
International affiliation. PSI, CTUC, UNI

Bermuda Trade Union Congress
Address. PO Box 2080, Hamilton HM HX
Phone. +1441 2926515
Fax. +1441 2926697
E-mail. mcharles@ibl.bm
International affiliation. CTUC

United States of America

Capital: Washington DC
Population: 293.0 m. (2004 est.)

1 Political and Economic Background

Two parties, the Democrats and the Republicans, have dominated US politics at all levels since the middle of the nineteenth century. Following 12 years of Republican Presidents (Ronald Reagan, 1981–89; George Bush, 1989–1993) the Democrat Bill Clinton took office in 1993 and was re-elected for a second four-year term in 1996. The November 2000 presidential election resulted in controversy with Republican George W. Bush ultimately emerging as the winner through vote of the Electoral College, although he had gained a lesser share of the popular vote than the Democratic candidate, Vice-President Al Gore. The closeness of the result was also reflected in Congress where the two parties were left evenly balanced in both Houses, the Senate being tied with 50 seats each. President George W. Bush was re-elected for a second term in November 2004 and the simultaneous congressional elections left the Republicans in control of both houses of Congress. Considerable powers are devolved to the 50 states, where there is a mixed pattern of control.

The USA's market-based economy is the largest in the world and in most innovation-based sectors it has a clear and in some cases increasing lead over competitor nations. Productivity growth, the most important determinant of long-term living standards, averaged 2.6% per annnum from 1948 to 1973, but then declined to 1.5% in the period 1974-94, marking an era of comparative economic weakness. In contrast, productivity growth averaged 3.1% in the period 1995-2003 and the World Economic Forum annual review of global competitiveness for 2004, covering 101 countries, ranked the USA in second place behind Finland. After a shallow recession in the early 1990s the USA enjoyed sustained growth led by investment in technology through the rest of the decade, with buoyant stock markets, low inflation, falling government debt, and large-scale creation of new jobs. The stock market decline of 2000 heralded a more difficult period, with the economy stagnating in 2001 before then achieving renewed growth. There are concerns relating to the swelling size of the current account deficit, which now runs at $500 billion per annum (5% of GDP), with opinions divided as to whether this is sustainable in the long-term. The phenomenon, driven by strong demand in the USA and weak demand elsewhere, is reflected in heavy inflow of investment into the USA from other countries. One dimension of the issue is the federal budget deficit. The Bush administration has said it wishes to rein this in, but it has shown little appetite in practice for raising taxes or cutting programmes such as social security and Medicare to a level significantly impacting on the budget, while pork-barrel spending by Congress is considered to be at a record high for recent times. Bush inherited a fiscal surplus of $200bn in 2000 but by 2004 this had turned into a deficit of $415bn, with two-thirds of the difference being attributed to the impact of tax cuts while discretionary federal spending also grew much faster than the economy.

The economy is characterized by a high level of flexibility, low taxes and light regulation, and an emphasis on risk-taking and innovation. New business start-ups run at a far higher level than in Europe. Falling unemployment in the 1990s (reaching a 30-year low of 3.9% by October 2000) was reflected from 1995 in a slight increase in the proportion of regular full-time jobs, previously in decline, from 73.6% in 1995 to 75.1% in 1999. However unemployment rose sharply from 2001 in line with the general downturn, and the subsequent recovery has not been reflected in a major expansion of employment (unemployment standing at 6% in 2003) – George W. Bush being the first President since Herbert Hoover in the 1930s to end his term with fewer Americans in jobs than at the start. Most of the gains in household income in the last three decades have gone to the top 20% of households. There is also a distinct underclass of under-qualified people in low-wage jobs or without jobs, many of them from minorities, who lack many of the social safety nets common in Western Europe.

GDP (purchasing power parity) $10.99 trillion (2003 est.); GDP per capita (purchasing power parity) $37,800 (2003 est.).

2 Trade Unionism

Trade unions which organized on a national scale developed in the middle decades of the nineteenth century, and the American Federation of Labor-Congress of Industrial Organizations (AFL-CIO), today the sole union centre, has a continuous history dating back (through the AFL) to the early 1880s. The strength of trade unionism was consolidated under the New Deal of the 1930s, especially through the National Labor Relations Act (NLRA), or Wagner Act, of 1935. This Act affirmed the right to organize and engage in collective bargaining, prohibited "unfair labour practices", and established the National Labor Relations Board (NLRB) to supervise and protect trade union activities and conduct representation ballots. The NLRA proved an influential factor in assisting the rapid development in the late 1930s of what became the Congress of Industrial Organizations (CIO), which unlike the craft-based AFL, organized on the industrial union principle. The unions further strengthened their position in the boom economy of World War II and although they faced some reverses in the Cold War period, notably the Taft-Hartley Act of 1947, they retained most of the gains made in the 1930s. In 1955 the AFL and CIO united to form the AFL-CIO, and this represents today more than 13 million of the 16 million union members.

The position of trade unions under federal labour legislation has changed little for several decades, although the rights of individuals in the workplace have been greatly affected by a sequence of laws on equality and discrimination. The states have had little role in shaping private sector labour relations and the courts have generally struck down efforts by states to legislate in this area. The 1935 NLRA defined the basic process for union recognition that still applies today. Once a union has achieved a significant level of workplace support (signed union cards), which in practice usually means a substantial majority, it may (assuming the employer denies recognition, which is usual) ask the National Labor Relations Board (NLRB) to conduct a certification election. If the union then wins 50% of the vote the employer must recognize it for collective bargaining purposes. No further election may be held for a year. The Act also prohibits employers from setting up company unions or favouring one union at the expense of another and defines illegal "unfair labour practices".

The 1947 Labor Management Relations Act (LMRA, or Taft-Hartley Act) put some limitations on union rights under the NLRA. It authorized "employer free speech" to campaign against union representation and defined unfair labour practices by unions. It weakened the right to strike by prohibiting secondary actions against employers or others not directly involved in a dispute. It also enabled individual states to enact "right-to-work" laws, prohibiting the use of agency shops (in which non-union employees are required to pay, as a condition of employment, agency fees to the union for its role as bargaining agent). In other states agency shops remain common, although the Supreme Court held in 1988 that fee payers could not be forced to pay for services other than those related directly to the union's role as bargaining agent. Taft-Hartley also set up the Federal Mediation and Conciliation Service (FMCS) to assist in conflict resolution, and most states also have set up mediation and conciliation offices.

The Labor Management Reporting and Disclosure Act (LMRDA, Landrum-Griffin Act) of 1959 enhanced the rights of individual union members by requiring democratic elections of union officers, free from intimidation and fraud, and transparency in union finances and collective agreements. The Act required unions to file annual detailed reports on their financing with the Department of Labor. Unions complain that this latter provision is onerous and costly, although it is also a measure against racketeering.

These three statutes, as interpreted through the courts and by rulings, underpin the position of unions in most of the private sector. However, 230,000 workers in the railroad industry and 590,000 in the airline industry are covered by the separate provisions of the Railway Labor Act (RLA) of 1926, which provided for collective bargaining and was aimed at providing mechanisms for resolving conflict without strike action. These highly unionized industries have their own National Mediation Board. Farm workers are excluded from the provisions of the NLRA and consequently from the right to collective bargaining (although this right is extended in some states, notably California, by state legislation). Ironically, it was the exemption of farm workers from federal labour law that allowed Cesar Chavez's United Farm Workers (UFW) so effectively to mount secondary boycotts of supermarkets selling non-union grapes in the 1960s and 1970s. The UFW is a small, mainly California union, however, and overall, farm workers have the lowest union density of any important sector. Managerial staff have commonly been excluded from union rights and this has become a significant issue with changes in the composition of the workforce. In the public sector trade union rights to represent workers are more circumscribed. Federal employees were only extended the right to join unions in 1962. The position at state level varies. However, much of the public sector is highly organized.

Trade unions were at their peak strength in the two decades after passage of the NLRA, a period which included the rise of industrial unionism and boom conditions and labour scarcity arising from World War II. Union density hit a peak of 35% in 1945–46, and again in 1954, since when it has declined continuously. Only in the 1990s did the decline in density begin to slow, but density at the end of the century was back at the levels of the mid-1930s, before the NLRA and the creation of the CIO.

Total union membership, while lagging behind the growth in the workforce, continued to increase to the late 1970s, rising from 17 million in 1954 to 20.2 million by 1978. It then fell quickly during the early 1980s recession, to 17.7 million by 1983, and thereafter declined more slowly. In 1998, however, union membership increased by 100,000 and in 1999 there was a net gain of 265,000 (the biggest annual increase in 20 years), taking total membership to 16.48 million. Private sector union membership increased by 112,000 in 1999, only the second increase in 20 years. Despite these encouraging trends for the unions, the main driver of expanded union rolls has been the huge increase in number of jobs as the economy has expanded unrelentingly, and density has continued to decline. By 2003 there were 8,756,000 private sector union members, against a total union membership of 16,107,000.

There has been a strikingly different experience in the public and private sectors over the last two decades. Union density in government employment has risen steadily and by 2003 stood at 37.5%. In contrast, non-farm private sector density has slumped from 17% in 1988 to only 9.5% in 2003 (density in agriculture is even lower, at around 2%). The result is that, although the US has overwhelmingly a private sector workforce, 44% of union members (7.3 million) are now in the public sector. Even in traditional private sector union strongholds, such as construction

(17.2%), transportation (23.8%) and manufacturing (14.3%), density is well below that in the public sector, and wide swathes of private sector services are non-union. In finance, insurance and real estate (highly organized areas in some European countries) density is only 1.9%, a similar figure to agriculture where there are no NLRA protections, while density is only 4.4% in retail trades. The changes in the composition of union membership are also reflected in the gender balance: blue-collar trade unionism was heavily male-dominated, but with the shift to white-collar and public service employment women now make up 43% of union membership. Women trade unionists increased from 5.9 million in 1983 to 6.7 million by 2003.

There is also a pronounced geographical variation in density. Average union density is much lower (at just under 8%) in the "right-to-work" states compared with just under 16% in what the unions call the "free" states. The national average is 12.9%. Although the basic federally-guaranteed right to organize and bargain collectively applies in all the states, union organizers tend to face a more hostile political and judicial climate in the right-to-work states: all those states are in the South and West and have predominantly conservative Republican politics. The largest of the right-to-work states, Texas, has a density of only 5.1%. The map of union density correlates closely with the pattern of voting in presidential elections, the low-density states having mainly backed George W. Bush in the 2000 and 2004 elections and the high-density states having backed the Democrat candidates, Al Gore and John Kerry. Two upper Midwestern states with a special tradition of progressive politics, Minnesota and Wisconsin, have high densities, of 17.6% and 15.6% respectively. The highest density states are mainly urban and industrial states like Michigan (21%), New Jersey (19.6%), and New York (25.3%), with a high proportion of traditional manufacturing jobs. In the South and West "sunrise" industries are mostly non-union, and agriculture, the sector with the lowest density of all, is also much more significant. Exceptions exist for specific local reasons: high density in Nevada (15.3%), for example, reflects the strong position of the unions in Las Vegas construction work and in the leisure industry.

Structural changes in the economy have undoubtedly been the main driver of falling union density, and in this respect the US mirrors the record of many other industrialized countries. In addition to the fundamental shift to a private sector service economy, there has been a long-term increase in part-time and non-standard working. Employees in such arrangements are significantly less likely than are full-time permanent employees to belong to unions. At the same time, the unions' problems have been exacerbated, especially since the end of the 1970s, by the implacable hostility of many employers to unionization efforts. Whereas in many (Western) industrialized countries employers, and particularly major employers, have to a greater or lesser degree accepted the role of unions as negotiating partners, there is no such consensus in the United States. This is reflected in an ambivalence in the US, the NLRA notwithstanding, concerning basic trade union rights. The United States has, for example, ratified neither ILO Convention No. 87 (Freedom of Association and Protection of the Right to Organize, 1948) nor Convention No. 98 (Right to Organize and Collective Bargaining, 1949), which have been ratified by every member state of the European Union. The 1999 ICFTU survey of labour violations accused the US of "massive, ongoing and appalling labour rights violations". In the absence of a collective contract, many workers have few protections in areas such as dismissal, so that conceding union recognition is seen by many employers as likely to lead to significant restrictions on their freedom to act.

In an atmosphere where many employers are overtly hostile, winning union recognition is itself difficult, despite the protective framework established by the NLRB. Trade unions can secure representation rights by winning the support of a majority of the workforce in a ballot. However, hostile employers can and do interfere in this process and "union-busting" is a highly professional industry with its own consultants, private detectives and security firms deployed to undermine union organizers. According to the unions, union activists are dismissed in at least one in four organizing campaigns; nine out of ten employers require workers to attend meetings where they receive anti-union propaganda; half threaten to shut down operations if a union is formed; and 78% hire union-busting consultants. Whereas in Europe supervisory staff are often themselves union members, in the US four in five employers require supervisors to attend union-busting training sessions and seek to persuade workers not to join. In 1994 a Commission on the Future of Worker-Management Relations concluded that "the United States is the only major democratic country in which the choice ... to be represented by a union is subject to such a confrontational process".

A significant blow to the unions' efforts to organize undocumented workers came in the Hoffman case in 2002, when the Supreme Court ruled that an undocumented (illegal) immigrant worker who was dismissed for union organizing could not receive compensation (back pay) under the Act, despite the NLRB having ruled in his favour, finding the employer's conduct to be a clear violation of the National Labor Relations Act.

The unions charge that NLRB procedures to protect union organizers from discrimination are ineffective; it takes the NLRB an average of 557 days to resolve a case and the backlog has at times reached 25,000 cases. Even where reinstatement is ordered, only a minority of workers ever return on a permanent basis. Challenges and litigation are also used to delay or prevent implementation of ballots where the union has won. The NLRB cannot itself enforce its decisions and must resort to the courts, and as many employers believe the courts to be less sympathetic to the unions than is the NLRB they commonly ignore NLRB rulings and let matters go into the legal system. In this way recognition may be bogged down for years. As the only sanction against employers for ignoring NLRB rulings is to have the ruling enforced (there is no other penalty) there is little incentive for employers to concede defeat prematurely. Even in cases where unions win recognition (which occurs in about half of cases), determined employers may work hard to bring about de-certification, or fail to negotiate in good faith (so-called "surface bargaining"). In one-third of cases where the union has won a representation election, they have been unable to secure a collective agreement, even though that is the fundamental right secured under the NLRA election process. Furthermore, in a quarter of cases where unions have won a first collective agreement, they have been unable to secure a second agreement. While the law says that the parties must negotiate in good faith, it does not compel them to reach agreement.

As union density declined, and the unions concentrated on defending their core areas, the number of representation elections fell from an average 7,000 per year in the 1960s and 1970s to 3,800 per year by the 1990s. In addition by the 1980s, de-certification elections (to expel a union from the workplace), occurred with increasing frequency as did termination of workers trying to organize a union. Union members were also more likely to cross picket lines. Against this background employers proved more resistant to union demands. The unions also claimed that appointments to the NLRB and the courts under successive Republican presidents had led to anti-union bias.

The NLRA does not apply to public employees, of whom there are some 19.4 million. Some 2 million federal employees fall under the 1978 Federal Labor Relations Act, which prevents meaningful collective bargaining and bans strikes. Only postal workers have bargaining rights at the national level. For federal employees the principal weapon is direct lobbying of Congress. There are considerable variations at the state level. Nearly half of the 14.9 million state and local government employees may not bargain collectively and 14 states do not allow collective bargaining at all for public employees. In the private sector, collective agreements are typically negotiated at the local level, with the national level unions providing coordination, research, support, and legislative activity. Few unions bargain on an industry-wide basis; only rarely do several combine to coordinate their bargaining proposals while nonetheless concluding separate agreements. It is more common for negotiations to be de-centralized, covering a single plant, corporation or area. Most unions' constitutions require approval of agreements by ballot of the members before they can be ratified. Other than for the conciliation services provided by the FMCS and in case of declared emergencies there is no government intervention.

President George W. Bush urged Congress to give him the authority to create new policies on hiring, pay, collective bargaining, performance appraisal, discipline and dispute resolution for 170,000 government employees who had been transferred into the new Homeland Security Department, created after the Sept. 11, 2001 terrorist attacks. The President cited national security concerns. The following year some 60,000 airport screeners were stripped of all collective bargaining rights on these same grounds.

In 2002 the Pacific Maritime Association employers' body locked out International Longshore and Warehouse Union members on the West Coast docks after failing to negotiate a new collective agreement. The Bush administration invoked the 1947 Taft-Hartley Act ordering work to resume on the docks without a collective agreement, citing national security concerns. This was the first use of the Taft-Hartley Act to force an end a labour dispute since 1971.

In the private sector (other than in areas covered by the Railway Labor Act) there are few legal restrictions on strikes, which are seen as essentially a private matter between employers and workers. No vote is required to authorize a strike (although in practice most unions do ballot their members to ensure they have support). The main restrictions are the Taft-Hartley ban on secondary action and the right of the federal government under the LMRA to seek an injunction where a strike threatens a national emergency. This latter provision has been used at different times in respect of disputes in the steel, coal, atomic energy, maritime transport and telecommunications industries. At the same time, there are few protections for strikers. The US Supreme Court has ruled that employers may permanently replace workers engaged in an economic strike, and there is only protection for strikers where a strike is the result of an unfair labour practice. Unions commonly allege that individual strikes are the result of unfair labour practices. However, this can be a hazardous course because if its members are dismissed and replaced and the courts subsequently (and often long after the strike) decide that the strike was not in response to an unfair labour practice, the dismissed employees have no retrospective protection. These are not merely theoretical concerns, as from the 1980s employers increasingly employed non-union strikebreakers to defeat unions in disputes, reviving a once-common tactic little seen in the post-World War II period. Disputes may be settled with only a proportion of the strikers being taken back, to work alongside replacements who had broken the strike. As in other labour relations matters, the individual states have not had an important role in shaping the right to strike as federal law has taken precedence. In 1992 Wisconsin enacted legislation prohibiting the permanent replacement of strikers, but this was struck down in the federal courts. However, state and local administrations and state courts do exert an influence because they have powers in areas such as controlling pickets: both employers and unions complain of bias depending on the political flavour of the local administration and courts.

While individual strikes can be protracted and bitter, overall the US has a low rate of industrial action. Most bargaining results in agreement without conflict, sometimes through use of the Federal Mediation and Conciliation Service (FMCS). Most collective agreements (which typically have a 3–4 year life span) also have a provision in which the union agrees that there will be no strikes for the duration of the agreement. Disputes during that time are normally referred to an independent arbitrator. There is no government arbitration service and arbitrators are private individuals, with lists of qualified personnel maintained by the

FMCS and the American Arbitration Association (AAA).

Unions have long had a somewhat mixed image in public perception. The tradition of business unionism has tended to be one in which broader social issues have had little consideration, while the interests of members have been pursued with single-minded determination. Unlike in many Western European countries, where tripartism is highly developed, the unions have not benefited from a perceived role in social and economic development and in building national consensus. The lack of a labour party has not allowed the unions to participate nationally in the process of government and in so doing consolidate a position as a core component of society. The image of unions in the period from the 1940s was also shaped to a considerable degree by the history of racketeering and intimidation that affected some unions and locals in blue-collar industries such as transport, construction and sanitation and by the unions' involvement in picket-line violence. Symptomatically, the best-known union leader in the US in modern times was Jimmy Hoffa, the Teamsters' leader (and father of the current IBT president) who disappeared, presumed murdered, in the 1970s and was linked to organized crime.

In recent years, however, many unions have put emphasis on improving and softening their public image. To some degree this has been driven by the changing nature of the labour movement itself. As in European countries, trade union membership is increasingly female (women now making up 43% of union membership) and white-collar (density in the areas covered by the AFL-CIO professional employees' department has increased since the department was created in 1977). A related factor is that membership is also increasingly concentrated in the public sector, where industrial relations are without the history of strike-breaking, intimidation, and use of security guards that have scarred some private sector areas. The AFL-CIO now seeks to portray unions as active community-builders that are good for the whole community not just their own members, and encourages local unions to work closely with other civic groups. The unions' agenda has broadened to embrace broad social issues, such as Medicare, social security (pensions), education and child care, which are meaningful to broad sections of the population that are resistant to the conflictual, workplace-based culture of traditional unionism.

Historically the major US political parties have been coalitions, and in the early part of the twentieth century the progressive wing of the Republican Party was the most significant ally of labour. Since the 1930s New Deal, however, the Democrats have come to be seen as the more pro-labour party, with the Republicans identified as a conservative business party. In many Western European countries the unions and the social democratic parties have an organic unity born of common origins and shared values. There is not this depth of relationship between the unions and the Democrats. The AFL-CIO is officially non-partisan and candidates for office tend to be supported on an individual basis. Nonetheless at national level the weight of union support is for the Democratic Party. While Bill Clinton was not seen as a particularly pro-labour nominee for president, he enjoyed the support of the unions once nominated. On taking office Clinton made various pro-union gestures, including withdrawing an order that federal contractors must post notices informing all non-union members that they did not have to join unions and had the right to stop unions collecting money in lieu of union dues for political purposes. He appointed a chairman of the NLRB, Bill Gould, who was criticized by business as pro-union and whose ratification by the Senate took seven months. However, legislation to end the hiring of permanent replacements for strikers was filibustered in the Senate in July 1994 and in November 1994 the Republicans won control of both Houses of Congress. The AFL-CIO again endorsed the Democratic presidential candidates in the 2000 and 2004 elections.

The US has itself ratified only two (the Abolition of Forced Labour Convention, No. 105, in 1991 and the Worst Forms of Child Labour Convention, No. 182 in 1999) of the eight core labour standards of the ILO. In 1995, US Labour Secretary Robert Reich described the failure to ratify ILO Conventions No. 87 and No. 98 as "a source of shame". However, during the Clinton presidency the US sought to some degree to exert a reforming influence on the labour practices of some other countries through denial of tariff concessions under the Generalized System of Preferences.

The unions feared the extension of the North American Free Trade Agreement (NAFTA) to Mexico would lead to loss of US jobs as employers relocated lower-wage plants south of the border. However, President Clinton pushed ahead with the treaty, criticizing the use of "strong-arm" tactics by the unions to try to persuade members of Congress to vote against it. As adopted, the treaty includes a side agreement on workers' rights called the North American Agreement on Labour Co-operation (NAALC). Under the NAALC labour offices are established in each member country, and have the responsibility of receiving and reporting on breaches of employment law. Compliance is not mandatory, however, except in the case of non-observance of the minimum wage, child labour or health and safety law. The unions tested the NAALC when the AFL-CIO filed complaints against General Electric, Honeywell, and Sony for violating the employment rights of Mexican workers; in each case the charge was that the company had disciplined employees for union membership. However, the findings in these cases did not lead to reinstatement of the workers concerned. At the same time the booming state of the US economy tended to minimize union anxieties about the impact of NAFTA. In 2004 unions were concerned about the implications of the similarly structured Free Trade Agreement of the Americas, which looked unlikely to contain even the minimalist labour rights side agreement seen under NAFTA, and which sought to break down trade barriers throughout the entire Western Hemisphere.

From its first days the administration of President George W Bush was happy to confront the labour movement head-on, the President's first legislative act being to repeal workplace ergonomics legislation that had just been approved following a 10-year struggle by union health and safety campaigners. In 2001 the US witnessed the jarring sight of hundreds of New Jersey teachers being arrested and marched off to jail for continuing to strike following a judicial 'back to work' order. In 2004 Education Secretary Rod Paige went on to refer to the National Education Association (a major teachers' trade union) as a 'terrorist organization'. When asked to apologize he failed to offer an outright apology for the bizarre claim, and said that he had been referring not to the unions' members but only to the union leadership.

3 Trade Union Centre

American Federation of Labor – Congress of Industrial Organizations (AFL-CIO)

Address. 815 16th Street, NW, Washington, DC 20006
Phone. +1 202 637 5000
Fax. +1 202 637 5058
E-mail. feedback@aflcio.org
Website. www.aflcio.org
Leadership. John J. Sweeney (president); Richard Trumka (secretary-treasurer); Linda Chavez-Thompson (executive vice-president)
Membership. 13 million

History and character. The origins of the AFL-CIO lie in the formation of the Federation of Organized Trades and Labor Unions of the United States and Canada in 1881; five years later the American Federation of Labor was born. It grew by emphasizing craft-based organization and trade unionism directed towards immediate bargaining over wages and conditions rather than broader political and social objectives. In the mid-1930s, however, under the impact of the Great Depression and the favourable political climate of the New Deal, some AFL unions sought to organize in the mass-production industries on the industrial union principle, forming the Committee for Industrial Organization within the AFL and becoming involved in many strikes. This led to the creation of the separate Congress of Industrial Organizations (CIO) in 1938. The two streams of the trade union movement were reunited in 1955, at the high tide of the organized labour movement. There is no other trade union centre and AFL-CIO affiliates represent about 82% of the unionized workforce.

The AFL-CIO seeks to coordinate the activities of its affiliates, and to represent the union movement to government. It also settles jurisdictional disputes between its affiliates. The AFL-CIO is a loose federation with no power to instruct its affiliates. Policy is made by the quadrennial convention at which the AFL-CIO executive council (comprising the president, secretary-treasurer, executive vice-president and 51 vice-presidents) is elected by the convention every four years. The executive council guides the day-to-day work of the federation. In addition there is a general board, which deals with matters referred to it by the executive council, and this comprises the executive council members, a chief officer from each affiliate and the AFL-CIO trade and industrial departments, and four regional representatives of the state federations. There are AFL-CIO state federations in each of the 50 states and in Puerto Rico, and 580 central labour councils chartered by the AFL-CIO at community level.

Many of the affiliated unions belong to one or more of the AFL-CIO's seven trade and industrial departments, which group them together around specific areas of interest. These departments are: building and construction trades; food and allied services trades; maritime trades; metal trades; professional employees; transportation trades; and the union label and service trades department, which seeks to promote consumer interest in union-made products and union services and discourage purchases of products on the AFL-CIO boycott list. The departments have their own executive bodies and hold their own conventions.

The AFL-CIO's day-to-day work is carried on through 11 programme departments. *Organizing,* supports the affiliates in membership drives and also runs the Organizing Institute to train activists. *Field mobilization,* coordinates the state federations and the central labour councils. *Corporate affairs,* carries out and disseminates research in areas such as collective bargaining and best practice. *Legislative,* promotes the federation's "Working Families Agenda" in Washington. *Political,* includes non-partisan voter registration and provision of information on political candidates' positions. *Public policy,* provides analysis in the areas of social, economic and trade policy. *Public affairs,* is responsible for a range of publications and also carries out public opinion research. *Civil and human rights,* works to ensure full participation in the union movement and economic life of minorities. *International affairs,* includes the Solidarity Center, supporting independent unions around the world. *Safety and health,* works with affiliates on health and safety issues. *General counsel,* whose work includes assisting in the internal dispute resolution procedure for jurisdictional conflicts between affiliates. In 2002 the Education and Working Women departments were axed, ostensibly on the grounds that AFL-CIO needed to consolidate its staff and activities due to economic pressures. Needless to say, these decisions were greeted with criticism from many commentators actively involved in the fields of trade union education and women's rights at work.

"Constituency groups" include the A. Philip Randolph Institute, the Asian Pacific American Labor Alliance, the Coalition of Black Trade Unionists, the Coalition of Labor Union Women, and the Labor Council for Latin American Advancement. The AFL-CIO Working for America Institute works in partnership with employers, government and community groups to foster training, education and job creation.

During the 1980s, under Lane Kirkland, substantial efforts were made to reintegrate unions beneath the AFL-CIO umbrella. At the 1987 biennial convention the decision was taken to readmit the Teamsters to membership (despite some evidence of misgivings arising from the Teamsters' long history of racketeering). Apart from the Teamsters (America's biggest union), other unions rejoining the AFL-CIO in the

1980s included the United Auto Workers (UAW), United Transportation Union, Brotherhood of Locomotive Engineers, the International Longshoremen's and Warehousemen's Union, the Writers' Guild of America-East, and the Union of Mine Workers.

These successes in consolidating the union movement were, however, overshadowed by the unrelenting deterioration in the unions' position overall. The Reagan (1981–89) and Bush (1989–1993) presidencies saw the unions on the defensive politically and rapid structural changes in the economy eroding their strength. Total trade union membership fell from over 20 million at the end of the 1970s to below 16.7 million in 1994, despite a great increase in the workforce. The AFL-CIO reported a loss of 634,000 members between the 1991 and 1993 conventions and the number of workers voting in NLRB certification elections in 1994 was down to only one-quarter of the level of 25 years earlier. The union movement was losing influence not just in the workplace but also politically and the decline was reflected in increasing dissatisfaction with the style of leadership. For four decades from its foundation as a unified movement in 1955, the AFL-CIO had had only two presidents, the founding president George Meany being succeeded by Lane Kirkland in 1979. By the mid-1990s criticism of the national leadership had built up and intensified after a Republican landslide in congressional elections in November 1994 that resulted in Republican majorities in both House and Senate. Discontent focused on declining density, down to levels not seen since the 1930s, and the unrepresentative character of an executive council that contained only two blacks and three women. It culminated in a May 1995 announcement by secretary-treasurer Thomas R. Donahue that he would resign, a move which seemed at first to open the way to a direct challenge to president Kirkland, who had declared his intention to seek a ninth term. However, Donahue's announcement precipitated a statement by Kirkland that he himself would retire in August and endorse Donahue as his successor. Donahue was appointed president by the executive council in August 1995 but then faced a challenge from a reform slate headed by John J. Sweeney, the president of the Service Employees' International Union (SEIU).

The SEIU had greatly increased its membership under Sweeney, and he urged a new focus on grassroots organization, charging that the AFL-CIO had become a "Washington-based institution instead of a worker-based movement". Organized labour was, Sweeney said, "the only voice of American workers and their families and the silence is deafening". Sweeney was elected AFL-CIO president at the October 1995 convention, bringing with him Mine Workers' president Richard Trumka as secretary-treasurer, while Linda Chavez-Thompson, vice-president of the AFSCME, filled the new post of executive vice-president. This leadership continued to head the AFL-CIO in 2004.

Donahue warned in 1995 that militancy would not appeal to the great mass of working people and that the Sweeney programme would "marginalize us and consign us to the fringes of society for generations to come". However, under Sweeney the emphasis has been less on "militancy" than on intensive work to recruit new union members and build the role of unions in their communities (such as through the "Union Cities" programme). The objective has been to emphasize through campaigning in the workplace and on the streets and in community meeting places that union jobs are better paid, more secure, and contribute more to building strong communities. The AFL-CIO argues that 98% of collective bargaining agreements are reached without conflict. It says that union workers have higher productivity and are more likely to be loyal to their employer, 48% of unionized workers having been with the same employer for more than ten years, compared with 22% of non-union workers. In August 1999 the executive council unveiled plans to build a "new alliance" to energize the unions at the local level, on the grounds that "the political, legislative and organizational battlegrounds are sited increasingly at the state and local level". This would involve creating a new tier of area federations in those urban areas with sufficient critical mass to support full-time organizers. Smaller communities would continue to be represented through labour councils but their role and that of the state federations of labour would be revitalized, with the cooperation of the national unions.

Since 1995 AFL-CIO membership has stabilized at a little over 13 million, and the century ended positively. In 1999 total union membership rose 265,000 and a number of unions recorded their most successful years in recent history: the UAW and IBEW recorded 50,000 new members each and the SEIU gained 150,000 members. A renewed confidence and buoyancy was evident among union leaders and Sweeney said that the increases showed "our renewed emphasis on helping working people form unions is having an impact". Reflecting this confidence, in August 2000 the executive council adopted an ambitious target of adding new members at the rate of one million per annum. This ambition was, however, undermined by the sharp downturn in the economy in 2001 and the subsequent phenomenon of economic recovery without adding new jobs, which resulted in fewer Americans being in work in 2004 than in 2000. At the same time, the union movement has not yet found solutions for the erosion in union density that has gone on since the mid-1950s or for how to organize private sector services where most jobs are now created. Indeed, the executive council concluded in May 1999 that although unorganized areas remained the prize long-term, in the short term resources would have to be focused on major industries that already had relatively high density and on the unions' traditional power base in rust-belt states where their political strength was under immediate attack. Many employers are determined not to surrender unilateral management control of their businesses and concepts of "partnership" with employers, with which the unions have sought to consolidate their position in European countries with problems of declining density, are difficult to realize in the United States.

In 1985 an AFL-CIO report urged consolidation of

member unions, 50 of the then 96 affiliates having fewer than 50,000 members. To some degree, this process has occurred and is continuing and there are now only 61 affiliates. However the US, like Britain, has a strong tradition of craft unionism, and there remain many relatively small unions serving discrete occupational communities. For members of such organizations the benefits of representation specifically focused on their particular needs may well seem to outweigh the benefits of absorption into large unions with theoretically more muscle but in practice less interest in or understanding of niche areas. In addition, also like Britain and in contrast (for example) to Germany, demarcation lines between unions are often ill-defined. A notable example is the area of health care, which has been organized only in the last two to three decades. Numerous unions, including many which in their core areas are totally unrelated to health care, now have a presence in this growing sector. The AFL-CIO has sought to police demarcation issues, and in 1999 the executive council ruled that unions should develop organizing strategies that focused on their core industries and occupations. Where individual unions wished to pursue a policy of diversification this had to be with a long-term strategy in view rather than organizing on an ad hoc basis.

The AFL-CIO has no political affiliation. It gives financial support to individual congressional candidates of both parties (reflecting the status of the parties as diverse coalitions), but mostly favours Democrats. In presidential elections it consistently supports the Democratic candidate. Following the election of Bill Clinton in 1992, many AFL-CIO key personnel as well as officers of affiliates found places in the transition team or in the incoming administration, although concrete measures to assist the unions were limited and frustrated by the Republican-dominated Congress. The AFL-CIO has in recent years emphasized voter registration drives to ensure that union members get out to vote. It reported that in the 1998 mid-term elections union households accounted for 17% of the population but 23% of those who went to the polls, and that 71% of union members who voted did so on behalf of union-backed candidates. It believed that (although the Republicans retained control of both Houses of Congress) this effort had reduced the "anti-worker majority" in the House of Representatives. The AFL-CIO has also promoted the idea of union members themselves running for office and in 1998 identified 626 candidates for state, local and national office as union members. It then set a goal of backing 2,000 union members for office in the year 2000. In the nomination process for the 2000 presidential election campaign there was evidence of some minority support in union ranks for John McCain, contender for the Republican nomination. However, the AFL-CIO announced its backing for Democratic candidate Al Gore from the outset, and George W. Bush, seen as no friend of labour, got the Republican nomination. The union movement made considerable efforts to bring out the vote for Gore in the November 2000 election, one of the factors reflected in the large pluralities for Gore in the more heavily unionized states, which resulted in him winning the popular vote nationally while losing the election. In the primary election campaign to choose the Democratic presidential candidate in 2004 a substantial number of unions initially backed Richard Gephardt of Missouri, seen as a pro-labour traditionalist. However, the AFL-CIO quickly rallied behind John Kerry when Gephardt dropped out after making no impact and it became clear Kerry would capture the nomination. The AFL-CIO worked to bring out the union vote, with 65% of union members, according to exit polls, backing Kerry on polling day, compared with the 48% of the overall vote that went to Kerry.

The relationship between the AFL-CIO and the mainstream of Western trade unionism has at times been an uneasy one. The AFL and the CIO both participated in the formation of the ICFTU in 1949, but never fully accepted its heavily socialist and social democratic orientation, and the AFL-CIO withdrew in 1969. (The AFL-CIO remained a member of, and the dominant factor in, the ICFTU's regional organization for the Americas, ORIT, and individual affiliates remained within ICFTU-linked international trade secretariats). Only in 1981 did it return. The active role of the AFL-CIO in supporting anti-communist worker organizations, with US government funding, caused concern in some socialist European circles. Since the 1990s, however, there has been a far greater convergence between European unions and the AFL-CIO. In part this has reflected the end of the Cold War and the fading of left-wing sentiment in European unions; in that respect socialist-influenced unions in Europe and elsewhere have moved closer to the AFL-CIO. But it also reflects a new emphasis from the AFL-CIO under Sweeney. In international affairs the main concerns of the AFL-CIO today are in areas such as universal fair labour standards and the impact of globalization. It organized protests against the World Trade Organization (WTO) and its "heedless rush towards further trade liberalization" at the 1999 Seattle conference, calling for core labour standards to be built into WTO rules, and launched a "Campaign for Global Fairness" to protest unfair labour practices. In this its positions are close to those of unions in other developed countries. The particular target of the US unions is China, and although that reflects the fact that China is the sole surviving significant country with a communist government, and seen as engaging in numerous abuses of labour and human rights, it relates mainly to China's position as a vast producer of cheap goods that the unions see as undermining US jobs and wages. The US administration's support for admitting China to the World Trade Organization was strenuously attacked by the unions, and – now that China has been admitted – poor labour standards in that country have become an urgent campaigning priority for US unions as a perceived threat to US jobs and conditions.

The George Meany Center for Labor Studies is an AFL-CIO attached national training college for trade union activists. It also hosts the George Meany Memorial Archives, preserving the records of the AFL-CIO, and George Meany Memorial Archives Library.

Address. 10000 New Hampshire Avenue, Silver Spring MD 20903
Phone. +1 301 431 6400
Fax. +1 301 434 0371
E-mail. info@georgemeany.org
Affiliates. The following list excludes some smaller unions.

1. Associated Actors and Artists of America ("4 As")
The 4As is an umbrella for seven member unions. These include **(1) Actors' Equity Association, AEA** (www.actorsequity.org), 165 West 46th Street, 15th Floor, New York, NY 10036, phone +1 212 869 8530; (2) **American Federation of Television and Radio Artists, AFTRA** (www.aftra.org); and (3) **Screen Actors' Guild, SAG** (www.sag.org), 5757 Wilshire Blvd, Los Angeles, CA 90036–3600. Phone +1 323 954 1600.

2. Air Line Pilots Association, International (ALPA)
Address. 535 Herndon Parkway, Herndon, VA. 20170
Phone. +1 703 689 2270
Website. www.alpa.org
Leadership. Captain Duane E. Woerty (president)
Membership. Represents 64,000 pilots at 42 US and Canadian airlines

3. Amalgamated Transit Union (ATU)
Address. 5025 Wisconsin Avenue, NW, Washington, DC 20016-4139
Phone. +1 202 537 1645
Fax. +1 202 244 7824
Website. www.atu.org
Leadership. Warren S. George (international president); Michael J. Siano (international executive vice-president); Oliver W. Green (international secretary-treasurer)
Membership. 170,000 in 270 local unions in the US and Canada. The union represents bus, subway, light rail, and school bus workers.

4. American Federation of Government Employees (AFGE)
Address. 80 F Street, NW, Washington, DC 20001
Phone. +1 202 737 8700
Website. www.afge.org
Leadership. John Gage (national president); Jim Davis (national secretary-treasurer)
Membership. 217,500 (active and retired)
History and character. AFGE is the largest union of federal employees. Collective bargaining is limited for federal employees and for this reason a particular emphasis is on political action and lobbying. Half of AFGE members are in agency-wide bargaining units.

5. American Federation of Musicians (AFM)
Address. Suite 600, 1501 Broadway, New York, NY 10036
Phone. +1 212 869 1330
Website. www.afm.org
Leadership. Thomas F. Lee (international president)
Membership. 105,000

6. American Federation of State, County and Municipal Employees (AFSCME)
Address. 1625 L Street, NW, Washington DC 20036-5687
Phone. +1 202 429 1000
Fax. +1 202 429 1293
E-mail. pubaffairs@afscme.org (public affairs department)
Website. www.afscme.org
Leadership. Gerald W. McEntee (international president); William Lucy (international secretary-treasurer)
Membership. 1.3 million
History and character. Founded in 1936, during the New Deal era that saw a major expansion of state and local public employment, the AFSCME has grown steadily to become one of the most powerful players in the US labour movement, with members in the public services and health care. It is the largest public sector AFL-CIO affiliate. AFSCME explains its rapid growth in the 1960s and 1970s as due in large measure to its reputation for fighting for equal treatment for minorities, a significant element of the workforce in the areas in which it organizes.

Current reported membership of 1.3 million compares with 1.2 million in the early 1990s and AFSCME continues to affiliate independent associations and to organize aggressively, claiming to win 80 per cent of representation elections. About 52% of the membership are women. AFSCME seeks a high media profile and has a staff of 30 in its public affairs department producing news releases, broadcasts, video and other communications. AFSCME was heavily committed to a Clinton-Gore victory in the 1992 presidential elections and seven of its officers joined the incoming president's transition team. Vice-President Gore told the 1994 AFSCME convention that the union's role in his and President Clinton's 1992 victory had been 'pivotal', while Labour Secretary Robert Reich called AFSCME 'the best grass-roots organization in the country'. It campaigned strongly for Al Gore in the 2000 presidential race, and both Clinton and Gore addressed the 2000 AFSCME convention. Politically a key focus for AFSCME is opposition to the privatization of public services.

7. American Federation of Teachers (AFT)
Address. 555 New Jersey Avenue, NW, Washington, DC 20001
Phone. +1 202 879 4400
E-mail. iad@aft.org (international affairs)
Website. www.aft.org
Leadership. Sandra Feldman (president)
Membership. Claims one million. Members are teachers, schools support staff, higher education faculty and staff, health care professionals and state and municipal employees.

8. American Postal Workers' Union (APWU)
Address. 1300 L Street, NW, Washington, DC 20005
Phone. +1 202 842 4200
Website. www.apwu.org
Leadership. William Burrus (president); C. J. 'Cliff' Guffey (executive vice-president); Terry R. Stapleton (secretary-treasurer)
Membership. 330,000 in 1600 locals
History and character. The APWU represents employees of the US postal service who are clerks, maintenance employees, motor vehicle operators, and non-mail processing professional employees. It says it is the world's largest postal union. Postal workers first won the right to bargain collectively under the Postal Reorganization Act of 1970 and APWU was founded in 1971 with the merger of five postal unions. It is affiliated internationally to UNI.

9. Asbestos Workers, International Association of Heat and Frost Insulators and Asbestos Workers (AWIU)
Address. 9602 ML King Jnr Hwy, Lanham, MD 20706
Phone. +1 301 731 9001
Fax. +1 301 731 5058
Website. www.insulators.org
Leadership. James A. Grogan (general president); James Bud McCourt (general secretary-treasurer)

10. Association of Flight Attendants (AFA)
Address. 1275 K Street, NW, Suite 500, Washington DC 20005-4090
Phone. +1 202 712 9799
E-mail. afatalk@afanet.ore
Website. www.flightattendant-afa.org
Leadership. Patricia A. Friend (international president); George M. Donahue (international vice-president); Paul G. MacKinnon (international secretary-treasurer)
Membership. 46,000
History and character. AFA says it is the world's largest union of flight attendants and membership has grown from 36,000 in 1995. All its officers are themselves flight attendants and the union has a strong involvement with safety and security issues

11. Bakery, Confectionery, Tobacco Workers and Grain Millers' International Union (BCTGM)
Address. 10401 Connecticut Avenue, Kensington, Maryland 20895
Website. www.bctgm.org
Leadership. Frank Hurt (president); David B. Durkee (secretary-treasurer)
Membership. 117,083 in US and Canada
History and character. Formed January 1999 by merger of the Bakery, Confectionery and Tobacco Workers' International Union and the American Federation of Grain Millers.

12. Brotherhood of Locomotive Engineers (BLE)
Address. Standard Building, 1370 Ontario Street, Mezzanine, Cleveland, Ohio 44113-1702
Phone. +1 216 241 2630
E-mail. pr@ble.org (public relations department)
Website. www.ble.org
Leadership. Freddie N. Simpson (acting president); Perry Geller (acting secretary-treasurer)
Membership. 55,000. Includes 30,000 active members in the US and 8,000 in Canada.
History and character. BLE calls itself the "senior national labour organization in the United States", dating back to 1863. Its members now include other types of railway employees, in addition to locomotive engineers, and it says its membership is growing despite industry consolidation. Also affiliated to the Canadian Labour Congress.

13. Brotherhood of Maintenance of Way Employees (BMWE)
Address. 20300 Civic Center Drive, Southfield, Michigan 4807-4169
Phone. +1 248 948 1010
Fax. +1 248 948 9140
E-mail. kct@bmwe.org (Kent C. Turner, director of communications)
Website. www.bmwe.org
Leadership. Mac A. Fleming (president); William E. LaRue (secretary-treasurer)
Membership. 60,000
History and character. Founded in 1887, this is the union of workers who maintain the tracks, bridges and buildings on US and Canadian railways. At its height it had 360,000 members but factors such as automation, the development of road freight and airlines, and sell-offs of railroad assets have depleted its membership. Also affiliated to the Canadian Labour Congress.

14. Brotherhood of Railroad Signalmen (BRS)
Address. 601 west Golf Road, Mount Prospect, Illinois 60056-4276
Phone. +1 847 439 3732
Fax. +1 847 439 3743
E-mail. signalman@brs.org
Website. www.brs.org
Leadership. W. D. Pickett (president); W. A. Barrows (secretary-treasurer)
Membership. 9,500 in US and Canada

15. California School Employees' Association
Address. 2045 Lundy Avenue, PO Box 340, San Jose, CA 95106
Phone. +1 408 473 1000
Fax. +1 408 954 048
Website. www.csea.com
Leadership. Clyde Rivers (president)
Membership. 220,000 para-educators, bus drivers, secretaries, maintenance staff, librarians and related occupations.

16. Communication Workers of America (CWA)
Address. 501 3rd Street NW, Washington, DC 20001-2797
Phone. +1 202 434 1100
Fax. +1 202 434 1279
Website. www.cwa-union.org
Leadership. Morton Bahr (president); Barbara Easterling (secretary-treasurer); Larry Cohen (executive vice-president)
Membership. 499,557
History and character. The CWA is the largest US communications and media union and now represents workers in a wide swathe of the information industry including broadcast media (e.g. ABC and NBC), telecoms (e.g. AT&T) and information technology companies such as Microsoft and IBM. It also has some members in other areas including airline customer service, health care and education. It has eight regional district headquarters, 50 field offices and 1,200 local unions in the US, Canada and Puerto Rico. The CWA is party to some 2,000 collective agreements and says that in areas such as training and education and child and family care its contracts are considered pacesetters. Its affiliations include the Canadian Labour Congress, and the global union federations UNI, IMF, IFJ, ICEM and ITF.

The CWA has since 1995 incorporated **The Newspaper Guild, TNG** (501 Third Street, NW, Suite 250, Washington DC 20001. *Phone.* +1 202 434 7177. *Fax.* +1 202 434 1472. *E-mail.* guild@cwa-union.org.
Website. www.newsguild.org.
Leadership. Linda K. Foley (president)).

17. Graphic Communications International Union

(GCIU)
Address. 1900 L Street, NW, Washington, DC 20036
Phone. +1 202 462 1400
Fax. +1 202 721 0600
Website. www.gciu.org
Leadership. George Tedeschi (international president); Gerald H. Duneau (international secretary-treasurer)
Membership. 150,000 active and retired members in Canada and the USA; the largest union representing printing and publishing workers in North America. The union is currently in merger talks with the Teamsters.

18. Hotel Employees' and Restaurant Employees' International Union (HERE)
Note: merged with UNITE in 2004 to form UNITE HERE (see entry).

19. Glass, Molders, Pottery, Plastics and Allied Workers' International Union (GMP)
Address. 608 East Baltimore Pike, PO Box 607, Media, Pennsylvania 19063-0607
Phone. +1 610 565 5051
E-mail. gmpiu@ix.netcom.com
Website. www.gmpiu.org
Leadership. Joseph Mitchell, Sr. (international president); John Ryan (international secretary-treasurer)
Membership. 62,000 in US and Canada

20. International Association of Bridge, Structural and Ornamental Iron Workers
Address. 1750 New York Avenue NW, Suite 400, Washington, DC 20006
Phone. +1 202 383 4800
Leadership. Jake West (general president); James Cole (general secretary); Joseph Hunt (general treasurer)

21. International Union of Painters and Allied Trades
Address. 1750 New York Avenue, NW, Washington, DC 2006
Phone. +1 202 637 0700
Leadership. James A Williams (general president); George Galis (general secretary treasurer)
Membership. 140,000 in construction trades

22. International Association of Firefighters (IAFF)
Address. 1750 New York Avenue, NW, Washington DC 20006
Phone. +1 202 737 8484
Fax. +1 202 737 8418
Website. www.iaff.org
E-mail. Jzack@iaff.org
Leadership. Harold Schaiberger (general president)
Membership. 263,000 (including 17,038 retired) in 2,700 locals across the US and Canada. Members are fire fighters and employees in emergency medical or rescue service activities.

23. International Association of Machinists and Aerospace Workers (IAM)
Address. 9000 Machinists Place, Upper Marlboro, Maryland 20772-2687
Phone. +1 301 967 4500
Website www.iamaw.org
Leadership. R. Thomas Buffenbarger (international president); Warren Mart (general secretary-treasurer)
Membership. 730,000

History and character. The IAM dates its origins back to 1888 and has members active in 200 industries. Its members work in many of the major US industrial corporations such as Boeing, United Airlines and General Electric. It absorbed the woodworkers' union in 1994 and has discussed (unrealized) unification plans with the auto and steelworkers to create the largest union in North America. It is affiliated to the global union federations ITF, IMF, and IFBWW, and to the Canadian Labour Congress.
Associated education centre. The William W. Winpisinger Education and Technology Center provides members with education and training in labour history and skills in leadership as shop stewards, local or district officers or grand lodge representatives. (*Address.* 24494 Placid Harbor Way, Hollywood, Maryland, 20636. Phone +1 301 373 3300. *Fax.* +1 301 373 2860)

24. International Association of Operative Plasterers and Cement Masons of the United States and Canada (OPCMIA)
Address. 14405 Laurel Place, Suite 300, Laurel, Maryland, 20707
Phone. +1 301 470 4200
Fax. +1 301 470 2502
Website. www.opcmia.org
Leadership. John J. Dougherty (general president); Patrick D. Finley (general secretary-treasurer)

25. International Brotherhood of Boilermakers, Iron Ship Builders, Blacksmiths, Forgers and Helpers (IBB)
Address. 753 State Avenue, Suite 570, Kansas City, KS 66102
Phone. +1 913 371 2640
Fax. +1 913 281 8101
E-mail. dcaswell@boilermakers.org (Donald Caswell, director, communications dept.)
Website. www.boilermakers.org
Leadership. Norton B. Jones (international president); Jerry Z. Wilburn (international secretary-treasurer)
Membership. 100,000 in 420 lodges in the US and Canada
History and character. The Boilermakers' union was founded in 1893. Its members are in diverse industries including construction, repair, maintenance, manufacturing and professional emergency medical services. In 1994 it absorbed the 5,800 member Stove, Furnace and Allied Appliance Workers' international union and in 1996 the 4,000-member Metal Polishers, Buffers, Platers and Allied Workers' international union.

26. International Brotherhood of Electrical Workers (IBEW)
Address. 1125 15th Street, NW, Washington, DC 20005
Phone. +1 202 833 7000
Fax. +1 202 467 6316
E-mail. research@ibew.org
Website. www.ibew.org
Leadership. Edwin D. Hill (international president); Jerry O'Connor (international secretary-treasurer)

27. International Union of Painters and Allied Trades (IUPAT)
Address. 1750 New York Avenue, NW, Washington, DC 2006
Phone. +1 202 637 0700

Website. www.iupat.org
Leadership. James A. Williams (general president); George Gatis (general secretary-treasurer)
Membership. 102,402
History and character. This is a craft union whose members include painters, paperhangers, glaziers, carpet installers, sign painters, display decorators, paint and brush makers, and related trades. It reports a growing membership. Through its district councils and local unions it offers a range of training programmes in craft skills for its members with the objective of ensuring that employers who sign agreements with the union have access to the most skilled workers. It also has an agreement with Marshall University in West Virginia which gives college credits for union apprenticeship programmes. IBPAT's COMET programme educates union members in leadership and bargaining skills. Also affiliated to the Canadian Labour Congress.

28. International Brotherhood of Teamsters (IBT)

Address. 25 Louisiana Avenue, NW, Washington, DC 20001
Phone. +1 202 624 6800
Website. www.teamster.org
Leadership. James P. Hoffa (general president); Tom Keegel (general secretary-treasurer)
Membership. 1.4 million in US, Canada and Puerto Rico
History and character. The IBT (or Teamsters) was for decades the largest and most powerful single union in the United States. Its position was weakened in the 1980s by the deregulation of the trucking industry which introduced many small non-union companies; by 1986 only about 200,000 truckers worked under the IBT master agreement compared with 400,000 a decade earlier. It sustained its membership by organizing in other sectors, including clerical, service and high technology workers, and in that respect benefited from not being subject to AFL-CIO demarcation restrictions at that time. Its greatest asset historically has been its reputation for winning high wage settlements and it continues to be an aggressive bargainer, backing up its demands with industrial action.

It has divisions for airlines; automobile transportation; bakeries and laundries; breweries and soft drinks; building material and construction trades; dairy; freight; industrial trades; motion pictures and theatrical trades; newspaper, magazine and electronic media workers; parcels and small packages; ports; public employees; tank haul; trade shows and convention centres; and warehouses.

The Teamsters has for decades been seen as the US union most affected by racketeering. The President's Commission on Organized Crime, reporting in March 1986, found IBT leaders had been 'firmly under the influence of organized crime since the 1950s'. These criminal associations, which included the use of the union's multi-billion dollar Central States Pension Fund to finance activity controlled by the Mafia, had led to expulsion from the AFL-CIO in 1957. In 1967 IBT president James R. ('Jimmy') Hoffa was imprisoned for involvement in misuse of pension funds. He was released in 1971 (in exchange for an agreement that he would stand down as president) but disappeared in 1975 and is generally presumed to have been murdered. A later president, Roy L. Williams, was convicted in 1982 of conspiracy to bribe a US senator in return for favourable trucking legislation. Williams stood down in favour of Jackie Presser, who was in turn indicted by a Cleveland grand jury on embezzlement and racketeering charges in May 1986 (but was reelected as IBT president at the national convention five days later). Many local and regional IBT officials also served prison terms in this period.

After 15 years of talks, the Teamsters finally re-affiliated to the AFL-CIO in October 1987, but readmission occurred as the Justice Department was about to present a civil lawsuit aimed at removing the entire executive and placing the union under a trustee appointed by the Court. The IBT's increased respectability as an AFL-CIO affiliate did not thwart legal proceedings: the suit was duly filed in June 1988 under federal racketeering laws with the Department charging that Mafia figures had played a part in the election of Presser and his predecessor. Presser himself died in hospital a few days later.

The AFL-CIO, with some congressional support, responded that the government was interfering with the right of union members to choose their own leaders. A new organization, Americans Against Government Control of Unions, was launched with support from such diverse figures as Jesse Jackson and Alexander Haig. However, in 1989 the case was settled with the IBT's affairs coming under federal government supervision, which still remains in force. Some 200 IBT officials accused of corruption have been forced out of office under federal supervision.

On Presser's death in July 1988, William McCarthy had been elected as president. McCarthy dismissed a number of key union figures associated with the now discredited regime. McCarthy declined to run for re-election. When elections for the general presidency and leading union posts were finally held in December 1991 the victors were a reform slate headed by Ron Carey, principal officer of local 804 in New York City.

Carey pledged that the IBT would say 'good-bye to the Mafia ... corruption ... and give-back contracts.' The February 1992 general executive board established a grievance panel committee, an ethics sub-committee and other reforms. His first executive act was to reduce his own salary by $50,000. 46 people who made 'outrageous salaries' were removed from the payroll, and the union's luxury jets and limousine were sold. A special pension fund for 22 top officials was wound up. The new leadership argued that the old had exceeded its income for many years, covering shortfalls on its general fund by making withdrawals from the strike fund.

The Carey regime itself, however, in turn faced charges of corruption. William Hamilton, the director of the IBT's government affairs department, was indicted on charges of funnelling union funds into Carey's 1996 re-election campaign, when Carey beat James P. Hoffa (Jimmy Hoffa's son) in a disputed contest in which Hoffa pledged to remove organized crime from the union. In a further election in December 1998, Hoffa was elected president. (He was not sworn in until March 22, 1999, after four months of delays amid allegations of voting irregularities). Between then and year's end, five union locals were placed under direct control by the international union on charges of racketeering, typically involving misappropriation of funds and non-enforcement of collective bargaining contracts. In July 1999, Hoffa announced a new internal anti-corruption programme (Project RISE – Respect, Integrity, Strength and Ethics), to be headed by a former US attorney, and linked this to the IBT's quest to bring to an end the decade-long government oversight of the union's affairs. In November 1999 Hamilton was convicted in federal court on embezzlement charges, and Hoffa praised the verdict as "an important step towards closing a dark chapter in Teamster history" while calling on the government to prosecute others involved with Hamilton.

DRIVE (Democratic, Republican, Independent Voter Education) is the Teamsters' politcal action committee. It was launched in 1963 and became the most powerful labour political action fund. It has supported both Democratic and Republican candidates but the IBT was the only union that supported Republican President Ronald Reagan in both his election campaigns (1980, 1984). In an important switch, following a nationwide survey of members' attitudes that revealed 53.35 per cent backing for the Democratic candidate, the IBT endorsed Democrat Bill Clinton in the 1992 campaign. In 1999 there was press speculation that Hoffa might be a running mate with Pat Buchanan, a maverick right-wing Republican aligned with the IBT's views on protecting American jobs from low-cost foreign competitors, but Hoffa stated in September 1999 that he would not be involved "at this time" in presidential politics. The IBT was slow to endorse any presidential candidate for 2000, and Hoffa attended both the Democratic and Republican conventions, being honoured with a reception at the latter, and even held a joint press conference with Ralph Nader of the Green Party. In September 2000, however, after polling its members, the IBT endorsed Democratic candidate Al Gore, Hoffa declaring that the Teamsters "will not stand idly by while the forces of reaction try to roll back the gains achieved over the past century". In 2004 the IBT endorsed Democratic presidential candidate John Kerry.

Politically the Teamsters have strongly opposed trade liberalization under NAFTA and the WTO, and the admission of China to the WTO. Active IBT hostility was a factor in the Clinton administration's decision to maintain controls on US-Mexico cross-border trucking beyond the Jan. 1, 2000 deadline for opening the borders under NAFTA. The administration officially attributed the decision to concerns about the safety standards of Mexican trucking operators.

29. International Federation of Professional and Technical Engineers (IFPTE)
Address. 8630 Fenton Street, Suite 400, Silver Spring, Maryland 20910
Phone. +1 301 565 9016
Fax. +1 301 565 0018
Website. www.ifpte.org
Leadership. Gregory J. Junemman (international president); Dolores A Gorczyca (secretary-treasurer)
Membership. 75,000. Membership covers a diverse range of occupations – accountants, administrative assistants, laboratory staff, public relations personnel, computer programmers, among them – in both the public and private sectors.

30. International Longshoremen's Association (ILA)
Address. 17 Battery Place, Suite 930, New York, NY 10004
Phone. +1 212 425 1200
Fax. +1 212 425 2928
E-mail. jmcnamara@ilaunion.org
Website. www.ilaunion.org
Leadership. John Bowers (international president); Robert E. Gleason (international secretary-treasurer)
History and character. The ILA, which has about 60,000 members, in 1996 entered a five-year master agreement, covering all ILA ports from Maine to Texas (the eastern and southern seaboards). In March 2000 ILA president Bowers and James Hoffa, president of the much larger Teamsters' union, pledged to "respect one another's jurisdiction" in an effort to end "festering differences." ILA is affiliated to the international transport union ITF and to the Canadian Labour Congress.

31. International Longshore and Warehouse Union (ILWU)
Address. 1188 Franklin Street, San Francisco, California 94109
Phone. +1 415 775 0533
Fax. +1 415 775 1302
E-mail. info@ilwu.org
Website. www.ilwu.org
Leadership. Brian McWilliams (president); Joe Ibarra (secretary-treasurer)
Membership. There are 42,000 members in the western seaboard states of California, Washington, Oregon and Alaska, and Hawaii. An additional 3,500 members belong to the Inland Boatmen's Union of the Pacific and 14,000 to the autonomous ILWU Canada.

32. International Union of Bricklayers and Allied Craftworkers (BAC)
Address. 1776 Eye Street, Nw, Washington, DC 20006.
Phone. +1 202 783 3788
Website. www.bacweb.org
Leadership. James Spinosa (president); William E. Adams (secretary-treasurer)
History and character. With its signatory employer contractors, this craft-based union operates the International Masonry Institute (IMI) as a joint labour-management trust; the IMI has a national training centre in craft skills at Fort Ritchie, Maryland.

33. International Union of Electronic, Electrical, Salaried, Machine and Furniture Workers (IUE-CWA)
Address. 1275 K Street, NW, Suite 600, Washington, DC 20005.
Phone. +1 202 785 7200
Fax. +1 202 785 4563
Website. www.iue-cwa.org
Leadership. Michael Brindas (president)
Membership. 150,000, active and retired. Members work in a miscellaneous group of industrial enterprises, including electronics factories, breweries, and furniture manufacturers. IUE describes itself as 'the industrial division' of the CWA.

34. International Union of Elevator Constructors (IUEC)
Address. 7154 Columbia Gateway Drive, Columbia, MD 21046.
Phone. +1 410 953 6150
Fax. +1 410 953 6169
E-mail. info@iuec.org
Website. www.iuec.org
Leadership. Dana A. Brigham (general president); Kevin P. Stringer (general secretary-treasurer)
Membership. 25,000

35. International Union of Operating Engineers (IUOE)
Address. 1125 17th Street, NW, Washington DC 20036
Phone. +1 202 429 9100
Website. www.iuoe.org
Leadership. Frank Hanley (general president); Vincent J. Giblin (general secretary-treasurer)
Membership. 400,000 in 170 locals in the US and Canada
History and character. Members are primarily employed in operating and maintaining heavy equipment and plant such as diesel engines, generators, air conditioning, electric- and steam-powered systems in the construction industry and in locations such as factories, hospitals, utilities, offices, hotels, and shopping malls. The union also has a minority of members in other areas, such as nurses and other health workers. The union offers apprenticeship and skills development programmes jointly sponsored by IUOE local unions and their contract signatory employers.

36. International Union of Police Associations (IUPA)
Address. 1421 Prince Street, Suite 400, Alexandria, Virginia 22314
Website. www.iupa.org
Leadership. Sam A. Cabral (international president); Richard A. Estes (international secretary-treasurer)
Membership. 80,000 in 480 locals (includes 8,000 in Puerto Rico)
History and character. The IUPA was chartered by the AFL-CIO in 1979, giving law enforcement officers an independent voice within organized labour for the first time. It represents federal, state and local law enforcement officers, deputy sheriffs, corrections officers and law enforcement support staff. Membership grew from under 17,000 in 1990 to over 80,000 by the end of the decade.

37. Laborers' International Union of North America (LIUNA)
Address. 905 16th Street, NW, Washington DC 20006
Phone. +1 202 737 8320
Fax. +1 202 737 2754
Leadership. Terence M. O'Sullivan (general president); Armand E. Sabitoni (general secretary-treasurer)
Membership. 800,000 in 500 locals in the US and Canada
History and character. Founded in 1903, LIUNA has a diverse membership including Alaska pipeline workers, airline machinists and mechanics, park rangers, Disneyland maintenance workers, poultry workers, nurses and many construction trade workers. LIUNA's "tri-funds" are "labour-management cooperatives" where union members and contracting employers discuss common concerns.

LIUNA also incorporates as an affiliate the National Federation of Independent Unions (NFIU). This organization was founded in 1963 to give a voice to independent union members, but membership has declined to 10,000. As a division of LIUNA the NFIU maintains an element of independence, and still recruits in its own name, while its members benefit from the AFL-CIO union privilege programme.

38. National Association of Letter Carriers (NALC)
Address. 100 Indiana Avenue, NW, Washington DC 20001-2144
Phone. +1 202 393 4695
Fax. +1 202 737 1540
E-mail. nalcinf@nalc.org
Website. www.nalc.org
Leadership. William H. Young (president); James E. Broendel (secretary-treasurer)
Membership. 301,514 (211,015 active) in 2500 branches.
History and character. Founded 1889 and with 2,800 local branches. Under US law postal employees are prohibited from going on strike and are subject to a system of binding arbitration should bargaining and mediation fail to produce agreement. Affiliated to Union Network International (UNI).

39. National Air Traffic Controllers' Association (NATCA)
Address. 1325 Massachusetts Avenue, NW, Washington DC 20005
Phone. +1 202 628 5451
Website. www.natca.org
Leadership. John Carr (president); Ruth Marlin (executive vice-president)
Membership. 15,000
History and character. NATCA was certified in 1987 as the sole bargaining agent for air traffic controllers employed by the Federal Aviation Administration.

40. Office and Professional Employees' International Union (OPEIU)
Address. 265 West 14th Street, 6th Floor, New York, NY 10011
Phone. +1 800 346 7348
E-mail. opeiu@opeiu.org
Website. www.opeiu.org
Leadership. Michael Goodwin (international president)
Membership. 145,000 in US and Canada
History and character. The union was the first specifically chartered by the AFL to represent white-collar employees, in 1935. The OPEIU has a highly diverse membership in both the public and private sectors in the US and Canada, including computer programmers, engineers, secretaries, nurses, accountants, attorneys, transit supervisors, security guards, bank tellers and others. It embraces a number of specialist associations, the Models' Guild, the American Guild of Appraisers, the Pennsylvania Nurses' Association, the National Union of Chiropractic Physicians and the National Guild of Medical Professionals, the first trade union for doctors, founded in 1996.

41. Paper, Allied-Industrial, Chemical and Energy Workers' International Union (PACE)
Address. PO Box 1475, Nashville, TN 37202
Phone. +1 615 834 8590
Fax. +1 615 834 7741
Website. www.paceunion.org
Leadership. Boyd Young (international president); James Dunn (executive vice-president); James Dunn (secretary-treasurer)
Membership. 320,000 in US and Canada
History and character. PACE was formed in January 1999 by the merger of the United Paperworkers' International Union (UPIU) with the smaller Oil, Chemical and Atomic Workers' International Union (OCAW). In April 2005 Union delegates voted to merge with the United Steelworkers of America.

42. Seafarers' International Union (SIU)
Address. 5201 Auth Way, Camp Springs, Maryland 20746

Phone. +1 301 899 0675
Fax. +1 301 899 7355
Website. www.seafarers.org
Leadership. Michael Sacco (president)
History and character. This is the largest North American union representing merchant mariners. It represents unlicensed mariners on US-flag vessels in the deep sea, Great Lakes and inland waterway sectors, and licensed mariners in the Great Lakes and inland waterway sectors. In March 2000 membership referenda approved the absorption of the National Maritime Union (NMU) by the SIU.

43. Service Employees' International Union (SEIU)
Address. 1313 L Street, NW, Washington, DC 20005
Phone. +1 202 898 3200
E-mail. info@seiu.org
Website. www.seiu.org
Leadership. Andrew L. Stern (president); Anna Burger (secretary-treasurer)
Membership. 1.6 million
History and character. SEIU has increased its diversified membership by more than 150% over the past quarter-century. Its two main areas are federal, state and local government, and health care. It was the first union to organize the health care sector and is now the largest health sector union in North America, with 475,000 members working in hospitals, HMOs, clinics, nursing homes and blood banks. SEIU also has members in other miscellaneous areas including race tracks and ball parks. 185,000 members are in building services, in occupations such as janitors, window cleaners and security guards. A majority (58%) of its members are women and one-third are black, Hispanic or other minorities. SEIU is the largest and fastest growing union in the AFL-CIO. President Andrew L. Stern has promoted an emphasis on rank and file organizing, directing half of SEIU's annual budget to this end. Stern has made his mark as an outspoken leader and has on occasions been highly critical of the AFL-CIO.

44. Sheet Metal Workers' International Association (SMWIA)
Address. 1750 New York Avenue, NW, Washington DC 20006
Phone. +1 202 783 5880
Website. www.smwia.org
Leadership. Michael J. Sullivan (general president); Thomas J. Kelly (general secretary-treasurer)
Membership. 150,000 in the sheet metal industry in the US and Canada.

45. Transportation Communications International Union (TCU)
Address. 3 Research Place, Rockville, MD 20850
Phone. +1 301 948 4910
Fax. +1 301 948 1872
Website. www.tcunion.org
Leadership.. Robert A. Scardelletti (international president)
History and character. Originated in 1899 as the Order of Railroad Clerks of America, adopting present name in 1987. Members work in a wide range of occupations in transportation, including clerks, skycaps, service workers, truck drivers, supervisors, accountants, police officers, grain handlers and reservations agents.

46. Transport Workers' Union of America (TWU)
Address. TWU, 1700 Broadway, 2nd Floor, New York, NY 10019.
Phone. +1 212 873 6000
Fax. +1 212 721 1431
Website. www.twu.com
Leadership. Michael O'Brien (international president); John J. Kerrigan (international secretary-treasurer); James Little (international executive vice-president)
Membership. 110,000 in mass transportation, airlines, railroads, utilities and other areas.

47. UNITE HERE
Address. 275, 7th Avenue, New York, NY 10001-6708
Phone. +1 212 265 7000
Website. www.unitehere.org
Leadership. Bruce Raynor (general president), John W. Wilhelm (president, hospitality industry)
History and character. UNITE HERE was formed by the merger in July 2004 of UNITE (formerly the Union of Needletrades, Industrial and Textile Employees) and HERE (Hotel Employees' and Restaurant Employees' International Union). The new union represents more than 440,000 active members and more than 400,000 retirees throughout North America. Its membership has a high proportion of African-American, Latin and Asian-American workers, and a majority of members are women.

48. United Association of Journeymen and Apprentices of the Plumbing, Pipefitting and Sprinkler Fitting Industry of the United States and Canada (UA)
Address. 901 Massachusetts Avenue, NW, Washington, DC 20001
Phone. +1 202 628 5823
Fax. +1 202 628 5024
Website. www.ua.org
Leadership. Martin J. Maddaloni (general president); Thomas H. Patchell (general secretary-treasurer)
Membership. 326,000 in 321 local unions across North America
History and character. The UA operates more than 360 training centres across the US and Canada, owned by local joint training committees, and it spends more than $1m per week on training, with 17,000 apprentices being trained at any one time.

49. United Automobile, Aerospace and Agricultural Implement Workers of America International Union (UAW)
Address. Solidarity House, 8000 East Jefferson Avenue, Detroit, MI 48214
Phone. +1 313 926 5000
Fax. +1 313 823 6016
E-mail. uaw@uaw.org
Website. www.uaw.org
Leadership. Ron Gettelfinger (president); Elizabeth Bunn (secretary-treasurer)
Membership. 671,853 active and 500,000 retired members
History and character. The UAW was founded in 1935. More than 400,000 of the active membership are production workers, engineers and draftsmen in the big three automobile companies, General Motors, Ford, and DaimlerChrysler. The UAW is also present in automotive parts, aerospace, defence

and a wide range of other manufacturing industries. Its membership includes a growing number of technical, office and professional employees in manufacturing companies, the public sector, health care, schools and universities and telecommunications, including 48,000 state employees in Michigan and Indiana, 5,000 members of the National Writers' Union, and 3,000 members of the Graphic Artists' Guild. It comprises 1,000 local unions and has contracts with 1,000 employers. It is affiliated internationally to the International Metalworkers' Federation (IMF).

50. United Farm Workers of America (UFW)
Address. PO Box 62, Keene, California 93531
Website. www.ufw.org
Leadership. Arturo S. Rodriguez (president)
History and character. The UFW was founded in the early 1960s by Cesar Chavez and built its reputation in the course of campaigns against exploitation of Californian grape workers. In 1970 for the first time, grape growers signed contracts that ended the most brutal period in the vineyards and Chavez became a revered and inspirational figure on the left. He died in 1993 at a time when the union's membership had declined to less than half the 1970 level of 50,000. Many parks, schools, streets and other public facilities have been named after Chavez and he was awarded the Medal of Freedom by President Clinton.

51. United Food and Commercial Workers' International Union (UFCW)
Address. 1775 K Street, NW, Washington DC 20006
Phone. +1 202 223 3111
Fax. +1 202 466 1562
Website. www.ufcw.org
Leadership. Joe Hansen (international president)
Membership. 1.4 million
History and character. The UFCW was the only private sector union to grow during the 1980s, to rival the International Brotherhood of Teamsters as the largest US private sector union. It has one million members in the food sector, including retail food, meat packing, poultry, and other food processing industries. Other members work in health care (where its 100,000 members include nurses, assistants, pharmacists, technicians and caretakers), insurance, department stores, garment manufacturing, chemicals and textiles. More than half its members are women. It has 13,000 collective bargaining agreements. Its services include a Worker Advisory Project that helps workers who are not members of the union when their rights are being violated. It also emphasizes political action and every local union is directed to set up a grass-roots lobbying programme.

The UFCW incorporates (among others):
(i) Retail, Wholesale and Department Store Union (RWDSU)
Address. 30 East 29th Street, New York, NY 10016
Website. www.rwdsu.org
Leadership. Stuart Appelbaum (president)
Membership. 100,000 in US and Canada
History and character. Affiliated to UFCW in 1993
(ii) International Chemical Workers' Union Council (ICWUC)
Address. 1655 West Market Street, Akron, OH 44313
Phone. +1 330 867 2444
Website. www.icwuc.org

Leadership. Frank D. Martino (president); Larry V. Gregoire (secretary-treasurer)
History and character. Affiliated to UFCW in 1996.

52. United Mine Workers of America (UMWA)
Address. 8315 Lee Highway, Fairfax, VA 22031
Phone. +1 703 208 7200
Website. www.umwa.org
Leadership. Cecil Roberts (president); Jerry Jones (vice-president); Carlo Tarley (secretary-treasurer)
Membership. 112,481
History and character. In addition to mineworkers now includes health care workers, truck drivers and school board employees.

53. United Steelworkers of America (USWA)
Address. Five Gateway Center, Pittsburgh, Pa 15222
Phone. +1 412 562 2400
Website. www.uswa.org
Leadership. Leo W. Gerard (international president)
History and character. Founded in 1942 on the basis of intensive organizing in the New Deal period through the Steel Workers' Organizing Committee, but with 19th century origins. It has 1.2 million active and retired members in the USA and Canada. It has absorbed a range of unions over the years, most recently the American Flint Glass Workers' Union in 2003 and the Industrial, Wood and Allied Workers of Canada in 2004.

54. United Union of Roofers, Waterproofers and Allied Workers
Address. 1660 L Street, NW, Suite 800, Washington DC 20036
Website. www.unionroofers.com
Leadership. John C. Martini (international president); Kinsey M. Robinson (international secretary-treasurer)
Membership. 22,000

55. Utility Workers' Union of America (UWUA)
Address. 815 16th Street, NW, Washington, DC 20006
Phone. +1 202 347 8105
Fax. +1 202 347 4872
Website. www.uwua.org
Leadership. Donald E. Wightman (national president); Gary M. Ruffner (national secretary-treasurer)
Membership. 50,000 in the electricity, gas and water industries.

4 Other Trade Union Organizations

The National Alliance of Postal and Federal Employees (NAPFE)
Address. 1628 11th Street, NW, Washington, DC 20001
Phone. +1 202 939 6325
Fax. +1 202 939 6389
E-mail. headquarters@napfe.com
Website. www.napfe.com
Leadership. James McGee (president)
International affiliation. WCL

National Education Association (NEA)
Address. 1201 16th Street NW, Washington, DC 20036-3290
Phone. +1 202 833 4000
Website. www.nea.org

Leadership. Robert Chase (president); Reg Weaver (vice-president); Dennis Van Roekel (secretary-treasurer)
Membership. 2.7 million
History and character. The NEA was founded as a professional body in 1857. It works to advance the cause of quality public education while providing assistance and representation for its members in areas such as employee protection, legal assistance and collective bargaining. The NEA has affiliates in every US state, plus the Federal Education Association and the Associación de Maestros de Puerto Rico. There are 13,000 local affiliates and members include teachers in both schools and colleges as well as educational support personnel. It is affiliated to Education International.

United Transportation Union (UTU)
Address. 14600 Detroit Avenue, Cleveland, Ohio 44107-4250
Phone. +1 216 228 9400
Fax. +1 216 228 5755
Website. www.utu.org
Leadership. Charles L. Little (international president); Paul C. Thompson (general secretary and treasurer)
Membership. 125,000 active and retired railroad, bus and mass transit workers in the US and Canada. It is the largest railroad union with 700 locals; members are mainly from the "operating crafts", such as conductors, brakemen, switchmen and locomotive engineers.

United Brotherhood of Carpenters and Joiners of America (UBC)
Address. 101 Constitution Avenue, NW, Washington DC 20001
Phone. +1 202 546 6206
Website. www.carpenters.org
Leadership. Douglas J. McCarron (general president); Douglas Banes (general vice-president); Andris Silins (secretary-treasurer)
Membership. 520,000 in woodworking and allied building trades

United Electrical, Radio and Machine Workers of America (UE)
Address. One Gateway Center, Suite 1400, Pittsburgh, PA 15222-1416
Phone. +1 412 471 8919
Fax. +1 412 471 8999
E-mail. ue@ranknfile-ue.org
Leadership. John H. Hovis (president); Bruce J. Klipple (secretary-treasurer)
Membership. 35,000
History and character. At the end of World War II, UE was the third largest CIO union with 500,000 members but it withdrew in 1949 and was subsequently expelled by the CIO on the grounds that it was communist dominated. It continues to adopt positions to the left of the mainstream labour movement in the US and emphasizes that it is a rank-and-file union. Members are in a range of sectors but mostly in electrical manufacturing, metalworking and plastics.

PUERTO RICO

Capital: San Juan
Population: 3.90 m. (2000 est.)

1 Political and Economic Background

Puerto Rico is under its constitution a "free state associated with the USA". Its economy includes industries such as textiles, petrochemicals and pharmaceuticals, and there is a tourism sector. It is heavily dependent upon the USA, its main trading partner.

GDP (purchasing power parity) $65.21bn. (2003 est.); GDP per capita (purchasing power parity) $16,800 (2003 est.).

2 Trade Unionism

US unions have branches in Puerto Rico and the AFL-CIO is represented by the Federación del Trabajo de Puerto Rico.

Federación del Trabajo de Puerto Rico AFL-CIO
Address. Apartdao 19689, Fernandez Juncos Station, Santurce 00910-9689
Phone. +1809 722 13 43
Fax. +1809 725 0907
International affiliation. ICFTU

Uruguay

Capital: Montevideo
Population: 3.40 m. (2004 est.)

1 Political and Economic Background

Historically, Uruguayan politics have been dominated by the conflict between the (dominant) liberal Colorado (red) and conservative Blanco (white) parties. In 1971, however, laws drastically curtailing civil liberties were introduced to give the army a free hand in fighting the Tupamaro guerrilla movement, and in 1973 the armed forces took power, initiating 11 years of military government noted for wide-scale repression and "disappearances". Civilian government was restored in 1984, with the Colorado candidate being elected president in 1984, 1994 and 1999, and the Blanco candidate in 1989. President Jorge Batlle Ibáñez (Colorado), in office from March 2000, ruled with a cabinet of both Colorados and Blancos. However left-wing resistance has been rising over the past decade and the October 2004 presidential elections resulted in the victory of Tabaré Vázquez of the Broad Front (FA), his coalition also winning an absolute majority in both chambers of Congress in the legislative elections.

Uruguay has a mixed economy built primarily on commercial agriculture and the processing of farm products. In the 1990s governments sought to pursue free market policies, control spending and combat inflation, which was in excess of 80% at the start of the decade but down to 4% by 1999. The economy was badly affected in 1999 by knock-on from financial difficulties in Argentina and Brazil, its main trading partners, and in a referendum in 2003 a proposal to privatize the energy industry was rejected. The economy has recently been buoyant, with growth expected to be at least 10% in 2004. Uruguay has a relatively even income distribution and its welfare state is considered the most extensive in Latin America.

GDP (purchasing power parity) $42.94bn. (2003 est.); GDP per capita (purchasing power parity) $12,600 (2003 est.).

2 Trade Unionism

Uruguayan trade unionism dates from the 1880s; the first national confederations appeared early in the twentieth century. Trade union activities continued under generally constitutional rule and in notably favourable conditions by Latin American standards until the early 1970s, when civil liberties were undermined by the conflict between the army and the Tupamaro guerrillas. The leftist Convención Nacional de Trabajadores (CNT) was dissolved in 1973 when it staged a general strike, following which independent trade unionism was crushed. The Confederación General de Trabajadores del Uruguay (CGTU, founded in 1951 as the Confederación Sindical del Uruguay), which was an ICFTU affiliate, came firmly under government control and was eventually suspended by and disaffiliated from the ICFTU.

After the restoration of democracy, the PIT-CNT emerged as a unified central supported by all sections of the labour movement. During 1987–88 it organized a series of strikes, in both the public and private sectors, to oppose President Sanguinetti's austerity policies and his programme of restructuring the economy, especially through the development of free trade zones. It continued to stage general strikes at intervals in the 1990s, against privatization and other policies.

The PIT-CNT remains the sole trade union central with 90% of unionized workers in its affiliated unions, although its membership at 120,000 is only half the mid-1980s level. It is unaffiliated to any of the three world organizations. The WCL-affiliated Uruguayan Trade Union Action (ASU) does not rival the PIT-CNT but rather seeks to gain influence within it. Workers in both the private and public sectors, including civil servants, may join unions but only about 13% of the workforce are unionized.

Uruguay ratified ILO Conventions No. 87 (Freedom of Association and Protection of the Right to Organize, 1948) and No. 98 (Right to Organize and Collective Bargaining, 1949) in 1954. Following the restoration of democracy the repressive industrial relations laws of the 1973–84 period were repealed but not replaced.

Although it has a considerable amount of protective legislation, Uruguay lacks a comprehensive labour code; indeed the conduct of industrial relations is almost entirely unregulated. There are few rules governing union or management behaviour in conflict apart from a few general constitutional guidelines. In the present unregulated situation, where there are no legal procedures, many employers recognize unions and accept the principle of collective bargaining, though a minority does challenge the principle that such accords are legally binding. Although there is no law prohibiting anti-union discrimination, a 1993 executive decree established fines for employers engaging in anti-union activities. The ICFTU says, however, that where union organizers are dismissed "the companies concerned are often able to succeed in fabricating explanations which avoid the penalties under the law". In general governments have sought to encourage consensus, with the Ministry of Labour acting a mediator where disputes arise. The right to strike is generally observed, although the government may order workers in essential services back to work. Strikes were frequent in the early 1990s but have had less worker support in more recent years. National labour legislation applies in the free trade zones but the unions have not been able to establish a base in the zones.

3 Trade Union Centre

**Plenario Intersindical de Trabajadores –
Convención Nacional de Trabajadores (PIT-CNT)**
Address. 18 de Julio 2190, Montevideo
Phone. +598 2 409 6680
Fax. + 598 2 40-0416
E-mail. pitcnt@adinet.com.uy
Website. www.chasque.apc.org/icudu
Membership. 120,000
History and character. The communist-influenced CNT was founded in 1964, bringing together all the major unions, but was dissolved under military rule in 1973, following which 18 members of the CNT central council "disappeared". Trade union activities re-emerged in 1983 under the name of the PIT, which was banned in January 1984 when it led a general strike. The fused PIT-CNT was restored to legal status in March 1985 and convened its congress later that year under the slogan "Consolidating Democracy" with attendance by representatives of the ICFTU, WCL and the WFTU.

Since its legalization, the PIT-CNT has led numerous general strikes, especially in the period 1990–92 against the administration of the right-wing (Blanco) President Luis Alberto Lacalle, on issues such as the impact of structural adjustment programmes, proposals to restrict the right to strike, unemployment benefits, wages, and privatization. Frequent as these strikes were they left much of the private sector relatively unscathed. Industrial action subsided after the election of the Colorado Party's President Sanguinetti in 1994. In June 2000 the PIT-CNT called a one-day strike against the policies of the new president, Jorge Batlle, calling for action against 12% unemployment and for more spending on health and education, but the strike call was little observed outside Montevideo. Left-wing leadership persists in the PIT-CNT but by statute it is not affiliated to any political party. Most unions support the Frente Amplio (FA, Broad Front), a disparate coalition including moderate socialists, communists and even some former Tupamaros. The FL's 1999 candidate for president, Tabaré Vázquez, came a close second to Jorge Batlle of the Colorados in a run-off election, and went on to win the October 2004 contest, raising expectations among the unions.

Although the PIT-CNT represents perhaps 90% of union members, its total membership has fallen considerably in recent years, and its influence has declined.
International affiliation. None

4 Other Trade Union Organization

Acción Sindical Uruguaya (ASU)
Uruguayan Trade Union Action
Address. Calle José E. Rodó n° 1836, Casilla de Correo 1466, 11200 Montevideo
Phone. +598 2 400 4235
Fax. +598 2 408 5684
E-mail. inesasu@chasque.apc.org
Leadership. Alberto Melgarejo (secretary-general)
History and character. Supports the PIT-CNT and does not consider itself as a trade union central or as a trade union but as an organization to promote trade union autonomy and industrial peace.
International affiliation. WCL

Uzbekistan

Capital: Tashkent
Population: 26.4 m. (2004 est.)

1 Political and Economic Background

Uzbekistan is a former republic of the USSR that became independent in August 1991. It has a predominantly Muslim population. In December 1991, the chair of the Supreme Soviet, Islam Karimov, was elected President and he continues to hold that office, being re-elected most recently in January 2000, when he was officially credited with taking 91.9% of the vote. The legislature, the Oly Majlis, is comprised solely of the members of Karimov's People's Democratic Party (the reformed Communist Party) and its allies.

Uzbekistan is an arid country with densely populated irrigated areas, with agriculture and agricultural processing the predominant form of livelihood. It is also a major exporter of cotton, produces gold and gas and has heavy industry. Restructuring of the economy has been limited, with state control remaining paramount.

GDP (purchasing power parity) $43.99bn. (2004 est.); GDP per capita (purchasing power parity) $1,700 (2004 est.).

2 Trade Unionism

Uzbekistan ratified ILO Convention No 98 (Right to Organize and Collective Bargaining, 1949) in 1992, but it has not ratified Convention No. 87 (Freedom of Association and Protection of the Right to Organize, 1948). A 1992 trade union law provides that workers have the right to form and join unions of their own choosing, and that unions should be independent of interference by the state. In practice, however, the former Soviet single trade union structure has largely survived, known as the Federation of Trade Unions of Uzbekistan (FTUU, also referred to as the Trade Unions Federation of Uzbekistan, TUFU). The FTUU is formally accorded a consultative role in the preparation of legislation concerned with labour and social issues. The unions have, however, lost their previous role in state planning and in the management of enterprises. Government officials and representatives of the management of state enterprises sit on union executive committees. As in the former Soviet system, the unions play a role in the administration of social, sports, health and welfare facilities. Various unions in Uzbekistan affiliate to global union federations and the FTUU is an affiliate of the General Confederation of Trade Unions, the Moscow-based organization that associates union centres from former Soviet republics.

In the still dominant state sector of the economy wages and conditions are determined administratively by the government, albeit with consultation with the unions. While collective bargaining is allowed for in the private sector, this does not yet appear to have developed to any degree. There is no specific right to strike, and reports of strikes have generally been rare, although in recent years occasional strikes over the issue of unpaid wages have occurred.

3 Trade Union Centre

Federation of Trade Unions of Uzbekistan (FTUU)
Address. 24 Bukhoro St., 700165 Tashkent
Phone. +10 998 71 2 568315
Leadership. Dilbar Djikhangirova (president)
International affiliation. CGTU

Vanuatu

Capital: Port Vila
Population: 203,000 (2004 est.)

1 Political and Economic Background

Vanuatu, the former Anglo-French condominium of the New Hebrides, became an independent republic within the Commonwealth in 1980. Politics tend to be fractious: there have been frequent changes of government in recent years, with a proliferation of small and constantly fragmenting political parties.

Vanuatu is a poor country with the majority of the population engaged in subsistence and small-scale agriculture and fishing. Most formal sector employment (estimated at 25,000) is in government, tourism and offshore financial services, with some light manufacturing.

GDP (purchasing power parity) $563m. (2002 est.); GDP per capita (purchasing power parity) $2,900 (2002 est.).

2 Trade Unionism

The first trade unions were formed in 1984 and soon organized the Vanuatu Council of Trade Unions (VCTU). The law does not require an employer to recognize a union, but acts of anti-union discrimination are prohibited once a union has been recognized. Collective bargaining exists, with arbitration by a tripartite arbitration board as a backstop, although this is not often used.

There was considerable conflict between unions and government in the period 1993-94, with a series of strikes spearheaded by the Vanuatu Public Services Association (VPSA) and backed by the VCTU. Trade union officials were detained, international trade union observers refused access to the country, and hundreds of public servants and teachers were dismissed in 1994 as a result of strike action that the courts declared illegal. In 1995 legislation was enacted requiring unions to give 30 days' notice of intent to strike, with a list of the names of intending strikers. Combined private and public sector membership in unions has reportedly fallen from more than 4,000 to less than 1,000 in the aftermath of the 1994 unrest.

Vanuatu joined the International Labour Organization in 2003 but has yet to ratify any ILO conventions.

3 Trade Union Centre

Vanuatu Council of Trade Unions (VCTU)
Address. PO Box 287, Port Vila
Phone. +678 23679
Fax. +678 26903
Leadership. Obed Masingiow (president); Charles Cab (secretary)
Membership. Less than 1,000
History and character. The VCTU held its first national congress in December 1985. In 1993-94 it came into bitter conflict with the government of Maxime Carlot, backing a series of public sector strikes which were met by wholesale dismissals of strikers and new anti-strike legislation in 1995. All five unions in Vanuatu are in the VCTU but membership has fallen sharply since 1994.
International affiliations. ICFTU; CTUC

Vatican City

1 Political and Economic Background

The state of the Vatican City (the Holy See) which came into being in 1929, is the seat of the central government of the Roman Catholic Church. Employees are engaged in administration and communications.

2 Trade Unionism

The Vatican City has about 3,000 employees, the majority of whom are now members of the Association of Vatican Lay Workers (ADLV), which achieved recognition in 1993. The Vatican City is not a member of the International Labour Organization.

Associazione Dipendenti Laici Vaticani (ADLV)
Association of Vatican Lay Workers
Address. Arco del Belvedere, I-00120 Citta del Vaticano
Phone. +39 6 6988 5343
Fax. +39 6 6988 4400
History and character. The ADLV originated in 1985. According to its president, workers' requests had hitherto been met "with silence" by the Vatican authorities, wages had been seriously eroded by inflation, and there were no internal Vatican labour regulations. The ADLV was set up to secure labour regulations based on international standards that should also reflect "the social doctrine of the Church and serve as an example to the world". The ADLV organized the first ever strike in the Vatican in 1988. In 1992 the union organized a mass resignation, which led to a Vatican commitment to a pension scheme. In December 1993, after achieving its long-standing aim of recognition, the ADLV announced it would extend its membership to those working for institutions dependent on the Vatican.
International affiliation. ICFTU

Venezuela

Capital: Caracas
Population: 25.02 m. (2004 est.)

1 Political and Economic Background

Venezuela achieved independence from Spain in 1830 and has a history of rule by caudillos ("strong men") and army intervention in politics. The dominant political parties from the 1950s until the late 1990s were the Democratic Action (AD) and the Social Christian Party (COPEI). Economic austerity measures introduced by AD's President Carlos Andrés Pérez in 1989 led to unrest put down by the army with the loss of 600 lives. Discontent continued, and in April 1992 Lt.-Col. Hugo Chávez led an unsuccessful attempted military coup against Pérez; Chávez was jailed, but in November 1992 his supporters staged a second abortive coup. The presidential election in 1993 was won by Rafael Caldera (who had broken with COPEI) as an independent. Elections in late 1998 resulted in Chávez achieving power through the ballot box, being elected President on a nationalist-populist so-called "Bolivarian" platform, in which he offered himself as the opponent of the ruling elites, as the candidate of the Patriotic Front movement. He formed a government with a strong military presence. The election results were seen as disastrous for the AD and COPEI. In December 1999 a new constitution was approved which concentrated more power in the hands of the President. Chávez was re-elected in a landslide victory under the new constitution, for a six-year term, in July 2000. In April 2002 Chávez was briefly deposed in a military-civilian coup, the plotters installing as President the head of the leading private sector business association, Fedecámaras. Popular unrest, backed by sections of the army, restored Chávez to power in two days. In August 2004 Chávez won a recall referendum on his presidency held on the initiative of his opponents and retains a considerable following among the poorer sections of the population.

Venezuela's political instability in the 1990s, culminating in the election of Chávez, was exacerbated by the decline in oil prices, petroleum accounting for more than 80% of exports and more than half of government operating revenues. The country has faced persistent problems of fiscal deficits, high interest rates and inflation, and the economy went into recession in 1998, with GDP contracting 7.2% in 1999 and unemployment escalating. Welfare programmes and cuts in the working week included in the 1999 constitution were, on some estimates, likely to cost the equivalent of 10% of GDP. Opposition to Chávez found expression in a two-month business strike based on the state-owned oil company, with some trade union support, from December 2002, further exacerbating the country's economic problems. GDP declined by 8.9% in 2002 and a further 9.2% in 2003 despite the benefits of rising oil prices on world markets.

GDP (purchasing power parity) $117.9bn. (2004 est.); GDP per capita (purchasing power parity) $4,800 (2004 est.).

2 Trade Unionism

The first Venezuelan unions began to make an impact after the death in 1936 of the dictator Gómez: that year saw a 43-day strike in the oil fields. But the development of trade unions was restricted by predominantly military rule until from 1945-48 the founder of Democratic Action (AD), Rómulo Betancourt, headed a revolutionary junta with wide labour support which became organized in the Venezuelan Confederation of Workers (CTV).

The AD government was overthrown and replaced by a military dictatorship under Pérez Jiménez in 1948, and trade unions were dissolved. Pérez Jiménez fell from power in 1958, and AD candidates served as elected presidents form 1959 to 1969. During this period the re-founded CTV consolidated its position as the dominant trade union centre, maintaining a close relationship to the AD, which provided it with financial assistance. It retained that position for many years, affiliating up to 90 per cent of union members, but has lost support following its confrontations with the Chávez government. The CTV has at times in its history been almost indistinguishable from the AD party but from the late 1980s it adopted a more critical stance in the face of economic austerity packages. Social and economic unrest, including strike action called by the CTV, contributed to the atmosphere which led to the abortive 1992 Chávez coup against the AD government.

Since his election at the end of 1998 Chávez, as part of his campaign against entrenched institutions, has targeted the CTV from a populist position, accusing it of corruption and not serving the needs of the people. In August 1999, a draft decree was issued threatening the dissolution of the CTV and its 3,000 affiliated unions, the confiscation of their assets, and a ban on trade union leaders travelling abroad, pending an "audit" of the unions by the government. The ICFTU warned that if this happened, it would complain not just to the ILO but to the IMF and World Bank, as Venezuela's funders. The WCL regional affiliate CLAT (which is based in the Venezuelan capital), in contrast, issued an ambiguous statement in October 1999 saying that caution was required in assessing the situation brought about by the Chávez programme. This programme would, according to CLAT, lead to the appearance of new political, social and trade union actors, and seemed to be a "favourable evolution" though with "a number of uncertainties". The proposal was subsequently dropped but on Dec. 3, 2000, a referendum approved powers to allow the dissolution of existing federations and confederations and replacement of their leaders within 180 days. In the CTV elections that followed in October 2001 CTV's electoral commission declared Carlos Ortega to be the winner. The government did not accept this announcement and has refused to recognise the CTV leadership ever since.

The CTV led demonstrations on April 11, 2002, calling for Chávez to resign. The political atmosphere in Venezuela was extremely tense, and the demonstrations were marred by violence. Several protestors were shot and killed. The following day, April 12, a coup saw Chávez taken into custody by a section of the military and a new government assembled. But by April 14 Chávez's supporters – Venezuela's poor majority – had rallied their own demonstrations and, with the support of loyal army units, Chávez's government was reinstated.

Later in the year CTV was once again leading national strike action, this time working alongside the employers' federation Fedecámaras to shut down oil production with a strike/lock-out, and demanding Chávez's resignation. The protests lasted into 2003, when the government dismissed some 19,000 oil workers on the grounds that they had "abandoned their posts". In February 2003, a judge issued an arrest warrant for Carlos Ortega, further to allegations of political crimes, treason and revolt. Ortega subsequently fled the country, claiming asylum in Costa Rica.

During this time, and encouraged by the government, independent unions began to organize to challenge the CTV, although at first they tried to work within the Confederation to change its leadership. Finally in August 2003 they founded a parallel federation, the UNT (National Union of Workers). The UNT receives government support but many of its constituent unions insist on political independence even while sympathizing with Chávez. Some important unions remain independent of both federations, for example the steelworkers' union SUTISS (although it also tends to be politically sympathetic to the government).

Venezuela was a founding member of the International Labour Organization, but withdrew briefly in 1957-58. It ratified ILO Convention No. 98 (Right to Organize and Collective Bargaining, 1949) in 1968 and Convention No. 87 (Freedom of Association and Protection of the Right to Organize, 1948) in 1982. All workers, except the armed forces, may join unions.

Collective bargaining has a history dating back to the 1930s. Indeed, the country was one of the first in Latin America to allow public employees to bargain collectively. However, collective agreements are largely to be found at the plant level. The ICFTU reported in its 2004 survey that a million public sector CTV members were not covered by collective agreements because the government had refused to negotiate with their union. There is a right to strike but this is restricted in cases involving a serious threat to the population, where the President may order a return to work and compulsory arbitration. Although there is a strong legislative tradition governing employment conditions, largely designed to protect the worker, it applies only to large enterprises; small and medium-sized workplaces operate outside legal constraints in what is a large informal sector.

The mass dismissal of oil workers in 2003 and the ongoing controversy with the CTV sits uneasily with a generally progressive set of reforms that are bringing Venezuelan labour law closer to compliance with ILO standards. The reforms, although not yet adopted into law, include reducing the number of workers required to form a union, reducing the residency requirement for foreign would-be union leaders from ten to five years, and permitting unions to negotiate collective agreements for their members in workplaces where there is no majority union. It was this quiet reform process which ensured that at the 2004 ILO conference, worker delegates (who had been fiercely critical of the government's position towards the CTV federation) specifically asked that Venezuela should not be criticized in the "special paragraph" procedure that highlights countries for serious breach of ILO conventions.

3 Trade Union Centre

Confederación de Trabajadores de Venezuela (CTV)
Venezuelan Confederation of Workers
Address. Av. Andres Eloy Blanco, Edificio José Vargas, Piso 17, Los Caobos, Caracas 1050
Phone. +58 212 576 0022
Fax. +58 212 574 1994
E-mail. cortega@la-ctv.com
Website. www.ctv.org.ve
History and character. Founded in 1936, the CTV was reorganized in 1947 in close association with the ruling Democratic Action (AD) party, though it traces itself back to the CTV that held its first congress in 1936. It was dissolved under the dictatorship of Pérez Jiménez, but reformed in 1959, since when it has been the principal Venezuelan trade union centre. Its relationship with the AD has always been close, but it criticized the AD governments' adoption of austerity measures in the 1980s, the CTV arguing that a disproportionate share of the burden of the debt crisis was being borne by labour.

Its closeness to government received a severe jolt with the popular unrest of 1989 against the retrenchment programme of President Pérez. Nonetheless the centre's reaction to the government privatization programme was muted and tended to take the form of constructive involvement rather than outright criticism. While the CTV's leadership includes members of a number of parties, the majority are supporters of AD.

During 1999 President Chávez attacked the CTV as a corrupt institution and threatened to dissolve it. In the following years the government and CTV became highly polarized, with the CTV calling numerous protests and eventually joining the employers' federation Fedecámaras in an attempt to shut down the oil industry from December 2002 to February 2003. In its 2004 survey, ICFTU described CTV's aims in the strike as "forcing President Chávez to relinquish power". The Chávez government reacted to the strike by dismissing some 19,000 oil workers, while a judge issued a warrant for the arrest of the CTV's leader Carlos Ortega, who fled the country.
International affiliation. ICFTU

4 Other Trade Union Organizations

Movimiento Nacional de Trabajadores Para La Liberación (MONTRAL)
Address. Av. Las Palmas, Edificio Montral, Urbanización Las Palmas, La Florida, Apartado 6681, Caracas 1010
Phone. +58 212 781 3355
Fax. +58 212 794 1231
Leadership. Dagoberto González (president)
History and character. Founded in 1974 and is a coordinating body for Christian-influenced unions.
International affiliations. WCL

Unión Nacional de Trabajadores (UNT)
National Union of Workers
Address. Sede del Incret (Antigua Casa Sindical), Av. Santander con Av. San Martin, El Paraiso, Caracas
Phone. +58 212 714 4591
Fax. +58 212 451 3001
Leadership. Franklin Rondón, Marcela Maspero, Stalín Pérez, Servando Carbone, Orlando Chirino (national coordinators)
History and character. Founded in August 2003 by the fusion of the Fuerza Bolivariana de Trabajadores (Bolivarian Workers' Force, founded the previous year by pro-Chávez unionists) and independent unions. UNT is assisted by the government in opposition to the CTV, but its leaders insist that it is politically independent, although in general it supports Chávez. UNT has won the allegiance of several discontented union leaders who formerly belonged to the CTV, and is actively recruiting unorganized workers.
International affiliations. None at present, but is seeking recognition by the ICFTU.

Vietnam

Capital: Hanoi
Population: 82.69m. (2004 est.)

1 Political and Economic Background

Vietnam, divided from 1954, was reunified in 1975 after the communist forces of the North defeated the US-backed South. Since that time, power has been held by the Communist Party of Vietnam (CPV). Elections to the National Assembly were last held in May 2002; candidates were nominated by a variety of organizations and approved by the Vietnam Fatherland Front, the CPV-controlled body embracing the country's various mass organizations.

Since 1987 there has been movement away from rigid communist economic orthodoxy towards a more reformist line, including recognition of private enterprise as legitimate, and efforts to attract foreign investment. Economic growth has typically been around 6-8% per annum over recent years. A vigorous small business sector has developed and Vietnam's export-oriented textile industry now employs between 1.2 million and two million people; however the state continues to dominate many areas of the economy. A bilateral trade agreement with the USA entered into force in 2001, but Vietnam is wary of opening its key economic sectors to investment and control by China. Some 63% of the labour force is engaged in agriculture and Vietnam remains a poor country.

GDP (purchasing power parity) $203.7bn. (2004 est.); GDP per capita (purchasing power parity) $2,500 (2004 est.).

2 Trade Unionism

In the former Democratic Republic of Vietnam (North Vietnam) unions were organized on the communist model in the Vietnam Confederation of Trade Unions (VCTU). In former South Vietnam unions were affiliated to the anti-communist Confédération Vietnammiene du Travail (CVT), founded in 1949, which in its latter years was affiliated to the WCL.

After the North's military victory and unification of the country the VCTU was established throughout Vietnam, changing its name to the Vietnam General Confederation of Labour (VGCL) in 1988. The former secretary-general of the CVT, Nguyen Van Phong, spent 10 years in a re-education camp following the fall of South Vietnam, and died in 1986. The ICFTU reported at that time that 20 former CVT officials were still detained in re-education camps. While there was some liberalization of the labour laws in the 1990s in parallel with developments in the structure of the economy, Vietnam did not experience a reform movement parallel to that which swept through most Soviet-influenced states in the early 1990s. The CVT maintained a nominal existence in exile in France.

Vietnam has ratified a number of ILO conventions from 1994 onwards, but not No. 87 (Freedom of Association and Protection of the Right to Organize, 1948) or No. 98 (Right to Organize and Collective Bargaining, 1949). Under the 1992 constitution the VGCL must cooperate with state organs, take part in state affairs and supervise the work of state bodies. Unions cannot be set up without approval from the VGCL. The labour law requires provincial trade union organizations to establish unions within 6 months at all new enterprises with more than 10 employees as well as at existing enterprises that operate without trade unions. Company managers are required by law to accept and cooperate with these unions. However, while the law states that all unions must be affiliated to the VGCL, there has been a growth of hundreds of unaffiliated "labour associations" recruiting occupations such as taxi drivers, cooks, and market porters. The VGCL represents most public sector and state enterprise workers and has some presence in the formal private sector; however, the majority of the workforce work on the land or in the informal economy or small businesses and are not in trade unions, with the result that overall density is only about 10%.

Collective bargaining is provided for under the 1995 labour code but in practice is limited. There is a system of labour arbitration councils. Unions have the right to appeal a council decision to the provincial people's court. The 1995 code also provides a right to strike. While strikes had previously been illegal, they did occur and were tolerated, at least in the non-state sector; there were 32 strikes in 1994, mainly in foreign-owned enterprises. Approximately 250 strikes were reported in the period from January 1995–September 1999. Of these, the majority (132) were in enterprises with foreign investment, and most (80) of the rest in private enterprises. Many strikes began as wildcat actions and were technically illegal, having not completed conciliation and arbitration procedures, although the government tolerated the strikes and did not take action against the strikers. While the VGCL or its affiliated unions did not sanction these strikes officially, they were supported unofficially at the local and provincial levels of the VGCL on an informal basis. Strikes have occurred over issues such as non-enforcement of the labour code, unpaid wages, working conditions, unfair dismissals and allegations of repressive management techniques in foreign-owned enterprises. In 1997, the government claimed that most labour disputes took place at small-scale enterprises owned or partly owned by companies from South Korea, Singapore and Taiwan, while statistics issued in 1998 showed that half of all strikes in the previous three years took place at Korean-owned companies. This pattern has persisted in recent years, with fairly frequent strikes, a majority of them against foreign-owned enterprises and fewest in the state enterprises sector.

Strikes are prohibited in a wide range of sectors including public services, defence industries, water, electricity generation, posts and telecommunications, railways, maritime and air transportation, banking, and the oil and gas industry. The government may also order an end to a strike considered detrimental to the national economy or public safety.

3 Trade Union Centre

Vietnam General Confederation of Labour (VGCL)
Address. 82 Tran Hung Dao Street, PO Box 627, Hanoi
Phone. +84 4 942 1181
Leadership. Cu Thi Hau (president)
Membership. 4.3 million in 64 geographical federations and 20 national industrial unions
History and character. The Vietnam Confederation of Trade Unions (VCTU) was established in communist-controlled North Vietnam and then extended to the whole country after the collapse of the South in 1975. It adopted its present name in 1988. No unions may legally exist outside its structure and it is one of the mass organizations of the Vietnam Fatherland Front;

the VGCL president is a member of the Communist Party central committee. The VGCL has sought to achieve a presence in the new private and foreign-owned sectors. A 1992 conference on building and developing organizations in the emergent non-state sector stressed that this was the foremost task ahead of the VGCL. The VGCL now states that it represents 4.3 million of the 10.8 million workers in the public and private sector formal economy. Its strength is greatest, however, in the state enterprises and public sector.

The VGCL emphasizes the need to secure national economic objectives, while ensuring a tripartite approach to problem-solving and appreciation of the value of labour. It participates in areas such as the drafting of labour legislation and setting of health and safety and minimum wage standards. Its unions generally work to avoid industrial unrest, but have retrospectively supported some strikes, especially in foreign-owned enterprises. The VGCL works with the ILO on various programmes in areas such as child labour and occupational health and safety, has participated in AIDS awareness programmes, and manages facilities such as hotels for workers. The VGCL has had a woman president, Cu Thi Hau, since 1998; she was re-elected at the ninth congress in October 2003.

International affiliation. WFTU

Yemen

Capital: Sana'a
Population: 20.03 m. (2004 est.)

1 Political and Economic Background

The Republic of Yemen was established in May 1990 by the unification of the Yemen Arab Republic (North Yemen) and the People's Democratic Republic of Yemen (South Yemen). Lieutenant-General Ali Abdullah Saleh, the former President of North Yemen, has been President of the unified state since its creation and his General People's Congress dominates the legislature. In 1994 his Vice-President, who had been the leader of the ruling party in South Yemen, declared the secession of the South, but this rebellion was quickly crushed by Northern forces.

Yemen is the poorest Arab country, its problems compounded by a high population growth rate. Unemployment is estimated at 40%. Development of Yemen's small private sector is hampered by lack of resources, poor infrastructure, government interference, corruption and political instability.

GDP (purchasing power parity) $15.09bn. (2003 est.); GDP per capita (purchasing power parity) $800 (2003 est.).

2 Trade Unionism

North Yemen ratified ILO Conventions No. 87 (Freedom of Association and Protection of the Right to Organize, 1948) and No. 98 (Right to Organize and Collective Bargaining, 1949) in 1976. South Yemen ratified only Convention No. 98 (in 1969). The unified country is considered to have ratified both Conventions.

Trade unions first appeared in the 1960s in North Yemen but workers' organization there was strictly regulated by the labour code. There was a national confederation but little indication of significant trade union activity. In South Yemen, the ICFTU-affiliated Aden Trades Union Congress participated in the struggle for independence from the UK. After independence in 1967, the South's unions were reorganized into the General Confederation of Workers' Trade Unions, which joined the WFTU. With the unification of North and South in 1990, the two national confederations merged in 1990 to form the Yemeni Confederation of Labour Unions, but differences persisted as the more militant trade unionists of the South saw continued cause for protest, particularly against the extension of Islamic law.

Existing labour laws were intended to apply in their respective areas until the enactment of a new national code, but this had not been addressed by the time civil war erupted again in 1994. At the time of unification there were no collective agreements in force and bargaining did not take place.

A new labour law was enacted in 1995 that brought a degree of liberalization. Workers, other than those in the public sector or agricultural workers, may form and join unions. While this right exists in practice, the government also ensures that loyalists hold responsible positions in the unions. Employers may not dismiss workers for union activities and cases of anti-union discrimination may be taken to the Ministry of Labour or the labour courts, which are reportedly often sympathetic to workers, especially where foreign companies are involved. The ICFTU supports a grassroots campaign for more unionization amongst women, and for better rights for female workers generally. Women constitute just 15.58% of the workforce.

The Yemeni Confederation of Labor Unions (YCLU) is the sole trade union centre, claiming to have 350,000 members in 15 unions. Its legal monopoly was repealed by the 1995 labour law but no alternative organization has been formed. It is headed by Yahya al-Kahlan, and tends to work closely with the government to avoid labour disputes. The YCLU is also affiliated to the World Federation of Trade Unions.

Collective agreements must be reviewed and registered by the Ministry of Labour and may be rejected if considered contrary to the national economic interest. Such agreements may also be invalidated if they "damage the economic interests of the country". Strikes are lawful provided there has been an irreversible breakdown of negotiation and arbitration, and subject to permission being obtained from the YCLU. In recent years there have been strikes particularly by university lecturers and other educational staff, seeking higher pay and improved salary structures; such action took place in 2000, 2001 and most recently in February 2005. Another case arose in May 2002, with the detention of a well known journalist, Abdul-Rahim Mohsin, and the editor, Mohammed Ahmad al-Hadiri. In July 2002 the Yemeni Journalists' Syndicate sought President Saleh's personal intervention to stop his government's "growing campaign on journalists which include[s] repeated summoning to prosecution, trials, oral warnings and illegal detentions". The union's appeal succeeded in getting the president to call a halt to punitive actions against journalists. Port workers protested when foreign firms fired a number of them after terror attacks on tankers in 2003. In August of that year, oil workers threatened to go on strike over corruption in the ministry. "Political strikes" are formally banned.

Zambia

Capital: Lusaka
Population: 10.46m. (2004 est.)

1 Political and Economic Background

Zambia gained its independence from the United Kingdom in 1964, and its President from then until 1991 was Kenneth Kaunda, whose socialist United National Independence Party (UNIP) was declared the sole legal political organization in 1972. Zambia shared in the early 1990s movement to political pluralism and reform that affected much of Africa. In October 1991, elections were held on a multi-party basis, and resulted in victory for the Movement for Multiparty Democracy (MMD) and its presidential candidate Frederick Chiluba, the chairman of the Zambia Congress of Trade Unions. In November 1996 Chiluba was re-elected President (in an election in which Kaunda had been barred from standing), while in simultaneous legislative elections (which the UNIP boycotted in protest at the bar on Kaunda) the MMD retained control of the National Assembly. The third multi-party elections, in December 2001, resulted in a narrow victory in the presidential contest for the MMD candidate, Chiluba's chosen successor, Levy P. Mwanawasa; in the legislative contest the MMD lost its absolute majority but remained the largest party.

Some 85% of the workforce are engaged in agriculture, much of it at subsistence level. Copper mining and processing dominate in the formal economy. Zambia derives around 90% of its export earnings from copper (and most of the balance from other minerals) and was severely affected by the fall in world copper prices which occurred from the late 1970s onwards. Discontent with the economic condition of the country was a major factor in Kaunda's 1991 election defeat. The Chiluba administration then implemented an IMF-backed programme of privatization and deregulation but efforts to privatize the copper mines took seven years to 2000, with output falling to less than half 1970s levels. There is a continuing dependence on international economic assistance.

GDP (purchasing power parity) $8.6bn. (2004 est.); GDP per capita (purchasing power parity) $800 (2004 est.).

2 Trade Unionism

Trade unions first developed under British rule in the copper belt in the 1930s. The Zambia Congress of Trade Unions (ZCTU) is the national trade union centre, although traditionally some unions have operated outside it. The 1993 Industrial and Labour Relations Act is based on the "one industry, one union" principle, and new unions have found it difficult to achieve recognition where an existing union is already established. By African standards, the labour movement is large, independent and influential, and the principle of collective bargaining is well established.

The unions' influence was reflected in the transition to political pluralism. Frederick Chiluba, the chairman of the ZCTU, became the leader of the Movement for Multiparty Democracy, set up in 1990 to oppose Kaunda's UNIP party. In October 1991 Chiluba won 75% of the vote to defeat Kaunda for the presidency in the first elections under a new multi-party constitution. Chiluba also appointed the ZCTU secretary-general, Newstead Zimba, to his Cabinet. In 1996 the Chiluba government ratified ILO Conventions No. 87 (Freedom of Association and Protection of the Right to Organize, 1948) and No. 98 (Right to Organize and Collective Bargaining, 1949).

The Chiluba government sought to involve the unions in the restructuring of the economy on the basis of tripartite consultations. Ahead of privatization the reduction of the copper mines workforce by 10,000 was agreed with the unions in 1994. But despite supporting the MMD, the ZCTU was critical of its economic policies and willingness to implement IMF-inspired structural adjustment programmes.

From 1997 onwards workers were free to join and form trade unions outside of the ZCTU. Splinter unions were formed which later formed a trade union federation known as the Federation of Free Trade Unions of Zambia (FFTUZ). The rise in splinter unions resulted in a reduction in trade union strength, particularly as it coincided with dwindling membership. The number of trade unions increased to 31. Many of the unions that left the ZCTU and joined the FFTUZ eventually returned to the ZCTU, the main exception being the ZUFIAW (Zambian Union of Financial Institutions and Allied Workers). Trade union membership is now split between the two federations with roughly 90% in the ZCTU.

Collective bargaining is well established and tends to be centralized, with employers and unions in each industry negotiating agreements through joint councils without government involvement. Public service employees such as civil servants and teachers negotiate directly with the government. In the event of a breakdown of negotiations, conciliation and arbitration disputes can be referred to the Industrial Court. The Court also provides protection for workers victimized for union activities. All workers other than those in essential services and the police, judicial and security services have the right to strike, but because strike action can be taken only after lengthy procedures, most strikes are in practice illegal.

Many local government workers have been affected by lengthy pay arrears. The Public Order Act, which requires police permission for public meetings and demonstrations, has been used to arrest workers protesting against such arrears.

There was a significant decline in the numbers of people in formal employment in Zambia throughout the late 1980s and the 1990s. Formal sector employment dropped from 543,300 in 1990 to 467,347 in 2000. As a result trade union membership declined. Between 1990 and 1995, ZCTU membership dwindled from 477,000 to 274,000. This can be attributed to the privatization, liquidation and restructuring of public enterprises and public sector reform programmes which led to massive job cuts. At the end of the 1990s the restructuring and then privatization of the mining giant, Zambia Consolidated Copper Mines, led to a big decline in the membership of the Mineworkers' Union of Zambia (MUZ). The MUZ's membership dropped from 38,000 in 1998 to 24,245 in 2002.

Mining and manufacturing are both in decline. Agriculture has also suffered from a combination of poor policies and bad climatic conditions. HIV/AIDS has also reduced the number of people in work. With the decline in mining and manufacturing the public service now forms more than 49% of the total trade union membership. The Civil Servants' and Allied Workers' Union of Zambia (CSAWUZ) is the largest trade union with a membership of about 35,000 in 2002.

3 Trade Union Centre

Zambia Congress of Trade Unions (ZCTU)
Address. National Centre, Solidarity House, PO Box 20652, Kitwe
Phone/Fax. +260 2 228 284
E-mail. zctusap@zamnet.zm
Leadership. Silvester Tembo (secretary-general)
History and character. The ZCTU was formed in 1965 in succession to the United Trades Union Congress (UTUC). It affiliates all but one of the major unions in the country.

During single-party rule under Kenneth Kaunda and UNIP, the ZCTU sought to assert its independence of the government. The ZCTU leaders Frederick Chiluba and Newstead Zimba, and 15 other prominent trade unionists, were expelled from UNIP in 1981 following a wave of strikes that the government linked to a thwarted plot to stage a coup. The expulsions were followed by protest strikes in the copper-belt and other sectors, and after three months the expelled trade unionists were re-admitted to the party. Chiluba, Zimba and others were detained a second time in 1981 after further industrial unrest, when President Kaunda stated that they were instigating illegal strikes with the aim of toppling the UNIP leadership. All detained union leaders were released on the order of the courts by November 1981.

Early in 1985, in response to a wave of wildcat strikes triggered by the imposition of austerity measures required by the IMF, the government banned strikes in various sectors of the economy and ordered employers to end the statutory check-off of union dues for illegal strikers. These measures were revoked in 1986, but the labour movement still complained that it was hamstrung by legal restrictions, censorship and pressure to succumb to the demands of the ruling party. The passports of Chiluba and Zimba were withdrawn in 1987. At the end of that year Chiluba was expelled from his own union, the National Union of Building, Engineering and General Workers (NUBWEGW), amid charges of constitutional irregularities. However the ZCTU alleged that this internal discord was engineered by the government as part of its campaign to disable the labour movement. Chiluba retained his position as ZCTU chairman-general and the courts later ruled that the ZCTU could overrule his expulsion from the NUBWEGW.

In the late 1980s living standards continued to fall and there was growing pressure for political change. In July 1990 Chiluba was prominently involved in the launch of the Movement for Multiparty Democracy (MMD) as a new opposition party. At the end of the year the ZCTU severed all ties with UNIP. In October 1991 multi-party elections Chiluba, as the candidate of the MMD, defeated Kaunda for the presidency. Of seven ZCTU leaders who stood for election, six were successful and all joined the government, including ZCTU secretary-general Zimba.

After Chiluba's election the ZCTU sought to act as an independent force, insisting that, despite the presence of trade unionists within it, the MMD was not a labour party. In May 1993 ZCTU leaders visited IMF headquarters to put their views on the need for leniency in imposition of restructuring programmes on Zambia. Simultaneously they proposed to the government a solidarity pact to work out an equitable distribution of the burden through tripartite bodies.

In October 1994 defeated candidates in ZCTU leadership elections complained of government interference in the elections. This culminated in five of the ZCTU's affiliates, most prominently the Mineworkers' Union, breaking away and setting up a rival federation. With the re-affiliation of the Mineworkers in 1999, however, the Zambia Union of Financial and Allied Workers remained the only one of the country's 19 major national unions outside the ZCTU.

In 1997 the government announced a wage freeze for public sector workers and plans to make tens of thousands of public sector workers redundant. In February 1998 the ZCTU warned it would stage a one-day strike on March 9 unless the government agreed to negotiate, leading former ZCTU secretary-general Zimba to threaten to de-register the ZCTU and any of its affiliates that took such action. Workers in essential services were warned that they could not take part in work stoppages under emergency regulations introduced in October 1997. The strike went ahead nonetheless and the unions were not de-registered.
International affiliations. ICFTU; CTUC

4. Other trade union centres

Federation of Free Trade Unions of Zambia (FFTUZ)
Address. PO Box 31174, Lusaka
Phone. +260 1 222105
Fax. +260 1 231364
Email. fftuz@zamnet.zm
Leadership. Joyce Nonde (president)
International affiliations. CTUC

Zimbabwe

Capital: Harare
Population: 12.67m. (2004 est.)

1 Political and Economic Background

The white minority regime in Rhodesia, which had declared unilateral independence from the United Kingdom in 1965, ended in 1979. In 1980 the country achieved full independence as the Republic of Zimbabwe and has been ruled since then by the Zimbabwe African National Union-Patriotic Front (ZANU-PF) of Robert Mugabe, who was Prime Minister until 1987 and thereafter President. In 1991 Mugabe announced he had abandoned plans to introduce a one-party state structure and the party deleted references to Marxism, Leninism and scientific socialism from its constitution. In elections in 1995 ZANU-PF won all but two of the 120 elective seats (with the President also being able to himself appoint a further 30 MPs), while in 1996 Mugabe was re-elected as President with 93% of the vote after other candidates withdrew. In further parliamentary elections in June 2000, marked by widespread intimidation by ZANU-PF supporters of their opponents, ZANU-PF narrowly retained its majority of elected seats but 58 opposition MPs were elected, 57 of them from the Movement for Democratic Change (MDC) founded in 1999. In March 2002 Mugabe defeated his MDC challenger, Morgan Tsvangirai, in a further presidential election, but the result was widely questioned.

About three-quarters of the population depend on agriculture for a livelihood, with the majority engaged in subsistence cultivation. The economy continued to deteriorate in the 1990s, with rising inflation and unemployment, an escalating budget deficit, and underlying chronic mismanagement and corruption. The highly developed commercial agriculture sector, contributing 10% of GDP, was dominated by a few thousand white farmers, and in 1999–2000 ZANU-PF began a programme of seizures and redistribution of white-owned land saying this should be redistributed to landless black "war veterans". The outcome, with 90% of white commercial farmers now having been displaced, has been a decline in the value of farm production of one-third. Zimbabwe also has mining, manufacturing and service sectors, with the non-farm sector dominated by loss-making state monopolies. Zimbabwe has one of the highest incidences of HIV/AIDS in the world, affecting one-quarter of the adult population and threatening the country's future prospects. Most international financial support has been suspended in view of the government's policies. However, despite five years of cumulative economic decline, the government budget for 2005 presented in November 2004 (ahead of elections scheduled for March 2005) predicted real growth of at least 3.5% and assumed a doubling of public expenditure without an increase in taxes.

GDP (purchasing power parity) $24.03bn. (2004 est.); GDP per capita (purchasing power parity) $1,900 (2004 est.).

2 Trade Unionism

Zimbabwe ratified ILO Convention No. 87 (Freedom of Association and Protection of the Right to Organize, 1948) as recently as 2003 and only ratified Convention No. 98 (Right to Organize and Collective Bargaining, 1949) in 1998. However, in recent years the country has experienced a wave of anti-union repression that has seen Zimbabwe Congress of Trade Unions (ZCTU) leaders arrested, officers and activists kidnapped, union offices looted and in some cases workers denied the right to hold public meetings. Under the 1985 Labour Relations Act, private sector workers (but not managers) are technically free to join and form unions of their own choosing and employers are prohibited from discriminating against union members. The Labour Relations Amendment Act of 2002 extends the right of freedom of association to public service workers (who previously were only permitted to form associations). At the same time unions complain that the 2002 law has made it almost impossible to organize legal industrial action.

After independence, previously competing centres representing European and African workers were merged into the ZCTU. About 25% of the workforce in the formal sector are members of the 31 unions affiliated to the ZCTU. While the government may de-register individual unions the High Court has ruled it may not suspend or de-register the ZCTU. In October 1996 a Zimbabwe Federation of Trade Unions (ZFTU) was launched with the objective of working in collaboration with the government, but it has gathered little support. The ICFTU stated in its 2003 report of violations of trade union rights that the ZFTU was "under the control of ZANU-PF". The ZFTU has been accused of violent take-overs of ZCTU-organized workplaces.

Under the 1992 Labour Relations Amendment Act a framework is provided for collective bargaining. Negotiations generally take place on an industry-wide basis between unions and employer bodies meeting in joint national employment councils. The government does not involve itself in these negotiations but retains the right to veto agreements it considers contrary to the national interest. Typically wage settlements did not keep pace with rapid inflation, but many unions accepted these small increases within the context of the economic crisis. For this reason quarterly pay negotiations came to be used in a number of industries. The 1985 Labour Relations Act also provided for works councils to be set up (in parallel with trade unions) to negotiate with management on various plant-level issues, excluding wages. Under the 1992 Labour Relations Amendment Act the role of works councils was extended and they were given powers to negotiate collective agreements overriding industry-wide agreements, a development opposed by the unions. But despite the increasing powers of the works councils, collective bargaining on wage issues was reserved for unions. Collective agreements have to be submitted to the Registrar for approval, and can be vetoed if viewed as contrary to the national interest.

Strikes are illegal in "essential services" and these have been given a broad definition, including fire and water services, railway engineers, electricians, and transport and communications workers. The Minister of Labour retains a power to re-classify any industry as an essential service and hence to ban strike action in that industry.

Relationships between the ZCTU and the government deteriorated sharply in the late 1990s. Industrial action over declining living standards began to gather pace in 1997 as the economy continued to deteriorate. On Dec. 9, 1997, the ZCTU led the biggest protest strike yet seen in Zimbabwe. The strike was triggered by a 5% levy imposed on workers to finance compensation projects for "war veterans", the imposition of sales taxes and increases in fuel and electricity costs. This was followed by a succession of "stay-aways" and other protests through 1998. In the aftermath of two successive widely supported general strikes in November 1998, on Nov. 27 Mugabe used emergency powers to ban national strikes for six months. Employers were encouraged to dismiss any worker taking part in a banned strike. By this time the ZCTU and the Institute of Directors were united in blaming Mugabe and the mismanagement and corruption of ZANU-PF for the collapse of the economy. However, the government abandoned plans to convert the six-month ban into permanent restrictions in the face of legal and political challenges.

In September 1999, the ZCTU and civic groups formed the Movement for Democratic Change (MDC), with ZCTU secretary-general Morgan Tsvangirai as its leading figure, to oppose ZANU-PF in elections due to be held in 2000. The MDC called for a "people's constitution", with open, accountable government. The MDC's policies included: the withdrawal of Zimbabwean troops from the Democratic Republic of Congo; negotiation on the foreign debt; restrictions on unnecessary imports and incentives for exports; removal of the managers of non-performing state enterprises; the distribution of unused agricultural land to subsistence farmers; and the declaration of a national emergency over AIDS.

The MDC's support base was seen as largely urban, and in escalating conflict in the months preceding the June 2000 elections, Mugabe sought to mobilize his rural support with a campaign of occupations of white-owned commercial farms by ZANU-PF "war veterans". Mugabe claimed the ZCTU and the MDC were being used by white farmers as a front for their own opposition to his land redistribution policy. In the elections, the MDC won 57 of the 120 elected seats in Parliament, emerging as the strongest party in the capital and other urban areas, and enabling it to create a viable parliamentary opposition to ZANU-PF for the first time since independence. Tsvangirai, who had stood down from the ZCTU but was not elected to Parliament, unsuccessfully contested the presidential election in 2002.

From 2002 trade union rights violations escalated; on several occasions dozens of unionists (including ZCTU leaders) were arrested at mass rallies in the capital, while kidnappings, beatings and lootings were increasingly used against union activists. The introduction of the Public Order and Security Act 2002 provided a legal framework for interference with union business by requiring unionists to obtain advance permission for any public meeting and by imposing fines or prison terms for a list of offences centred around public order and peace. According to ICFTU's 2003 report the Act was used regularly "to obstruct trade union activities and to harass trade unionists".

3 Trade Union Centre

Zimbabwe Congress of Trade Unions (ZCTU)
Address. PO Box 3549, Harare
Phone. +263 4 794742
Fax. +263 4 728 484
E-mail. info@zctu.co.zw
Website. www.samara.co.zw/zctu/
Leadership. Wellington Chibebe (secretary-general)
Membership. 400,000 in 31 affiliated unions
History and character. The ZCTU was founded after independence in February 1981. In its early years it adopted the characteristic position of many African trade union centres at that time, associating closely with the ruling party and emphasizing its role in assisting national social and economic development.

From the late 1980s the ZCTU became more outspoken in criticism of the government, and in 1989 secretary-general Morgan Tsvangirai was arrested after condemning the closure of the University of Zimbabwe, under powers inherited from the previous white regime. He was held for two months in defiance of High Court orders to free him and refused to join other ZCTU officials in endorsing Mugabe's 1990 re-election.

In the 1990s the ZCTU continued to be an irritant to the government, and sharply critical of its interference in industrial relations matters. Since 1997 the ZCTU has emerged as a major source of opposition to the Mugabe government, leading a succession of strikes and protests which have had considerable support in the urban areas and provoked government harassment and use of emergency powers legislation. Two days after the protest strike of Dec. 9, 1997 (see above), Tsvangirai was attacked and beaten unconscious by armed men; the ZCTU reportedly provided the police with names of suspects but no action was taken. In January 1999, Isidore Zindoga, the then deputy secretary-general, was beaten unconscious in an attack linked to the police.

In September 1999, the ZCTU was the leading force in the formation of the Movement for Democratic Change (see above), and at its first congress in January 2000 Tsvangirai was elected MDC president and ZCTU president Gibson Sibanda became MDC vice-president.
International affiliation. ICFTU; CTUC; OATUU

INTERNATIONAL AND REGIONAL ORGANIZATIONS

Baltic Sea Trade Union Network (BASTUN)
Website. www.bastun.nu
Phone. +46 8 20 98 80
Leadership. Kristjan Vaigur (secretary)
Membership. 22 organizations with 20 million members in the Baltic Sea countries
History and character. Founded in 1999 to give a regional voice and assist cooperation among the trade union centres of the countries wiith a Baltic seaboard (Denmark, Estonia, Finland, Germany, Latvia, Lithuania, Norway, Poland, Russia and Sweden). It was involved in helping trade unions from the new EU member states to prepare for the accession of their countries to the EU (which Estonia, Latvia, Lithuania and Poland joined in May 2004). A permanent secretariat has been esablished in cooperation with the Council of Nordic Trade Unions (NFS).

Caribbean Congress of Labour (CCL)
Address. NUPW Complex, Dalkeith Road, St. Michael, Barbados
Phone. +246 427 5067
Fax. +246 427 2496
E-mail. cclres@caribsurf.com
Leadership. Lincoln Lewis (president); George De Peana (general secretary)
Membership. 500,000 in 33 affiliates
History and character. Founded in 1960, the CCL now has 33 affiliates in 17 countries in the English and Dutch-speaking Caribbean (including the mainland nations of Belize, Guyana and Surinam).

The CCL provides research, educational and campaigning support to its affiliates and works to encourage the development of trade unionism and national centres in the region. It represents trade union concerns to the Caribbean Community (CARICOM), the Organization of Eastern Caribbean States (OECS) and the Association of Caribbean States (ACS) and works closely with the ICFTU and its regional organization ORIT. During 2003 the CCL experienced serious financial and administrative difficulties and its activities were substantially reduced.

Commonwealth Trade Union Council (CTUC)
*Ceased end 2004
Website. www.commonwealthtuc.org
History and character. The CTUC was established in 1979. Based at the London headquarters of the British Trades Union Congress, it provided a representative voice for trade unions in dealing with the institutions of the Commonwealth and Commonwealth governments, with 30 million members in Commonwealth countries. It also fostered cooperation among member unions and assisted in trade union education, training and solidarity activity. Campaigns in more recent years in the area of human rights and trade union freedoms covered countries such as South Africa, Nigeria, Fiji, Sierra Leone and Zimbabwe. From 2000 CTUC's main donor organizations began a gradual reduction of funding. The shortfall was initially met by the British TUC, but as funding reductions continued a decision was taken to discontinue the work of the CTUC. The CTUC's 2004 annual conference took place in Geneva during the ILO conference. 65 delegates from 30 Commonwealth countries agreed to the proposal to wind up the CTUC at the end of 2004, noting that they did so "reluctantly".
Affiliates. The CTUC had members (usually national trade union centres) in 53 independent states and dependent territories.

Confédération Européene des Syndicats Indépendants (CESI)
European Confederation of Independent Trade Unions
Address. Avenue de la Joyeuse Entrée 1–5, B–1040 Brussels, Belgium
Phone. +32 2 282 1870
Fax. +32 2 282 1871
E-mail. info@cesi.org
Website. www.cesi.org
Membership. 5 million members in independent unions in Europe.
History and character. CESI was founded in 1990 and represents the views of minority, independent unions. Its affiliates are a mix of European umbrella organizations, national multi-sector organizations, and national industry-level unions and professional associations. It has affiliates in Belgium, Denmark, France, Germany, Hungary, Italy, Luxembourg, Poland, Portugal, Romania, Spain and Switzerland. Its more significant affiliates include the CGB and DBB in Germany and CISAL in Italy. The membership is diverse, but with particular strength in public administration, as well as several unions of train drivers. CESI has an education institute, "Academy Europe".

Confédération Internationale des Fonctionnaires (CIF)
International Confederation of Public Servants
Address. 59/63 rue du Rocher, 75008 Paris, France
Phone. +33 1 40 85 08 98
Fax. +33 1 41 21 46 47
Leadership. Pierre Trausch (president)
History and character. The CIF was founded in 1955. It is independent of political and religious organizations. Its membership of affiliated unions overlaps to some degree with that of the European Confederation of Independent Trade Unions (CESI) but is smaller. It has an annual summer academy in association with CESI. All its affiliates are in Western Europe. CIF's website was taken down in 2001 and its affiliation with CESI is no longer recorded in CESI's publicly available membership list. However, CIF remains active and was represented at the 2004 ILO conference.

Council of Nordic Trade Unions
Nordens Fackliga Samorganisation (NFS)
Address. Drottninggatan 75, S-111 60 Stockholm, Sweden

Phone. +46 8 209 880
Fax. +46 8 789 8868
E-mail. eva.carp@nordtuc.se
Website. www.nfs.net
Leadership. Tom Saxén (general secretary)
Membership. 8 million
History and character. The NFS is a coordinating organization for unions in the Nordic countries. Its member organizations consist of blue-collar, white-collar and academic unions in Denmark, Finland, Iceland, Norway and Sweden. Nordic unions have a history of cooperation dating back to the nineteenth century. For a long time this cooperation was informal and irregular, but at the beginning of the 1970s greater formality was introduced leading to the formation of the NFS in 1972. The NFS provides the secretariat for the Baltic Sea Trade Union Network (BASTUN).

European Trade Union Confederation (ETUC)
Confédération Européene des Syndicats (CES)
Address. 5 Boulevard Roi Albert II, B–1210 Brussels, Belgium
Phone. +32 2 224 0411
Fax. +32 2 224 0454
E-mail. etuc@etuc.org
Website. www.etuc.org
Leadership. Cándido Méndez Rodríguez (president); John Monks (general secretary)
Membership. 76 member unions from 34 countries.
History and character. ETUC was formed in 1973 by the merger of the previous European Confederation of Trade Unions in the European Community with the European Free Trade Area Trade Union Committee. In 1974, the member unions of the WCL's former European organization also joined.

Over the last 15 years ETUC's membership has increased significantly in the wake of the general collapse of communism in Europe. In part, this has resulted from the admission of formerly communist-led centres from Western Europe. The Spanish Workers' Commissions (CCOO) joined in 1991, to be followed by the Portuguese CGTP-IN. Finally, in 1999, 25 years after it first applied for membership, the French CGT was admitted, its application approved by all member organizations except the CGT-FO. In addition, there has been a measured process of extending ETUC's membership eastward into the former communist bloc. There are now full ETUC members from across the 25 member states of the EU but also including Norway, Romania, Switzerland, Turkey and a number of other non-EU states. National confederations from Serbia, Croatia and Macedonia have observer status.

In addition to expanding its reach eastwards, ETUC has also increased its role in line with the deepening of social and economic integration among the EU member states. Its position as the representative cross-sectoral European-level trade union voice is reflected in its access to the EU's core institutions and it is an active lobbyist for trade union rights and more broadly for enhancing the social dimension and democratization of the EU. It campaigned for the European Works Council Directive on Information and Consultation rights. The ETUC is regarded as the pan-European voice of the union movement.

It also works with employers at the European level in developing social dialogue and has reached three cross-sectoral framework agreements (on parental leave, part-time work and fixed-term contracts) with the employers' representative pan-European body UNICE and CEEP (the state employers' organization). These agreements are signed by the EU Council of Ministers and have the force of law in the EU.

In the 1990s there was a growth in significance of the ETUC's affiliated industrial committees, which are expected by some observers ultimately to be the cutting edge of European-wide collective bargaining. ETUC works closely with the ICFTU, which does not have a separate regional organization for Europe.

The Council of European Professional and Managerial Staff (EUROCADRES) works under the auspices of ETUC (EUROCADRES: Rue Joseph II 3, B–1000, Brussels, Belgium. *Phone* +32 2 230 7455. *Fax.* +32 2 230 7566. *Website.* www.etuc.org/eurocadres), as does the European Federation of Retired and Elderly Persons (FERPA).

The ETUC's research arm is the European Trade Union Institute (ETUI, 5 Boulevard du Roi Albert II, B–1210 Brussels, Belgium. *Phone* +32 2 224 04 70. *Fax.* +32 2 224 05 02. Director, Reiner Hoffmann).
Affiliated national trade union organizations: 76 national trade union confederations from 34 countries and 10 European industry federations make up a total membership of 60 million.
Affiliated European Industry Federations:

1. European Alliance of Media and Entertainment (EEA)
Address. Rue de l'Hôpital 31, B–1000 Brussels, Belgium
Phone. +32 2 234 5650
Fax. +32 2 235 0861
E-mail. jim.wilson@union-network.org
Leadership. Jim Wilson (secretary-general)

2. European Federation of Food, Agriculture and Tourism Trade Unions (EFFAT)
Address. Rue Fossé-aux-Loups 38, B–1000 Brussels, Belgium
Phone. +32 2 218 7730
Fax. +32 2 218 3018
E-mail. effat@effat.org
Website. www.effat.org
Leadership. Harald Wiedenhofer (general secretary)
History and character. Formed by merger of the IUF regional affiliate and the European Federation of Agricultural Workers' Unions (EFA) in December 2000. It comprises 120 trade unions in 35 countries with 2.6 million members.

3. European Federation of Building and Wood Workers (EFBWW/FETBB)
Address. Rue Royale 45 bte 3, B–1000 Brussels, Belgium
Phone. +32 2 227 1040
Fax. +32 2 219 8228
E-mail. info@efbh.org.be
*Website.*www.efbww.org
Leadership. Harrie Bijen (general secretary)
Membership. 50 affiliates in 17 countries with 2.3 million members.

4. European Federation of Journalists (EFJ/FEJ)
Address. Rue de la Loi 155, B-1040 Brussels, Belgium
Phone. +32 2 235 2200
Fax. +32 2 235 2219
E-mail. efj@ifj.org
Website. www.ifj-europe.org
Leadership. Aidan White (general secretary), Renate Schroeder (director)
Membership. 280,000 in more than 30 countries
History and character. The EFJ is constituted as the regional organization of the International Federation of Journalists (IFJ), with a close working relationship with ETUC.

5. European Mine, Chemical and Energy Workers' Federation (EMCEF)
Address. Av. Emile de Béco 109, B–1050 Brussels, Belgium
Phone. +32 2 626 2180
Fax. +32 2 646 0685
E-mail. info@emcef.org
Website. www.emcef.org
Leadership. Hubertus Schmoldt (president); Reinhard Reibsch (general secretary)
Membership. 2.5 million in 128 unions in 35 countries
History and character. EMCEF relates at the international sectoral level to ICEM but is separate from it.

6. European Metalworkers' Federation (EMF/FEM/EMB)
Address. Rue Royale 45, bte 2, B-1000 Brussels, Belgium
Phone. +32 2 227 1010
Fax. +32 2 277 5963
E-mail. emf@emf-fem.org
Website. www.emf-fem.org
Leadership. Tony Janssen (president); Peter Scherrer (general secretary)
Membership. 6.5 million in 65 unions in 30 countries

7. European Federation of Public Service Unions (EPSU/FSESP)
Address. Rue Royale 45, Box 1, B-1000 Brussels, Belgium
Phone. +32 2 250 1080
Fax. +32 2 250 1099
E-mail. epsu@epsu.org
Website. www.epsu.org
Leadership. Anna Salfi (president); Carola Fischbach-Pyttel (general secretary)
History and character. Represents 8 million public service workers in 216 trade unions in national and local public administration, health and social services and public utilities; this is the largest of the ETUC industry federations and works with PSI at the international level.

8. European Transport Workers' Federation (ETF/FEST)
Address. Rue de Pascale 22, B–1040 Brussels, Belgium
Phone. +32 2 285 4660
Fax. +32 2 280 0817
E-mail. etf@etf.skynet.be
Website. Access via the website of global union federation ITF (www.itf.org)
Leadership. Wilhelm Haberzettl (president); Doro Zinke (general secretary)
History and character. The ETF held its founding congress June 14–15, 1999 in Brussels. It operates both as the European regional organization of the International Transport Workers' Federation (ITF) and as the transport federation of ETUC and replaced the former Federation of Transport Workers' Unions in the European Union (FST).

9. European Trade Union Committee for Education (ETUCE/CSEE)
Address. 5 Boulevard du Roi Albert II, 9th floor, B–1210 Brussels, Belgium
Phone. +32 2 224 0692
Fax. +32 2 224 0694
E-mail. secretariat@csee.etuce.org
Website. Access via the website of global union federation EI (www.ei-ie.org)
Membership. 81 teaching unions in 19 countries

10. Union Network International–Europa
Address. Rue de l'Hôpital 31, B–1000 Brussels, Belgium
Phone. +32 2 234 5656
Fax. +32 2 235 0870
E-mail. uni-europa@union-network.org
Website. www.uni-europa.org
Leadership. Bernadette Ségol (regional secretary)
History and chaacter. This is the regional organization of the global union federation Union Network International (UNI), created in 2000. It has 7 million members.

Federation of International Civil Servants' Associations (FICSA)
Address. Palais des Nations, Office BOC.74, 10 Route de Pregny, CH–1211 Geneva 10, Switzerland
Phone. +41 22 917 3150
Fax. +41 22 917 0660
E-mail. fisca@unog.ch
Website. www.ficsa.org
Leadership. Maria Dweggah (general secretary)
History and character. FICSA was established in 1952 and represents the interests of the staff of the United Nations and its specialized agencies. It has 27 member organizations, eight associate members and 24 organizations in consultative membership.

General Confederation of Trade Unions (GCTU)
Address. 42, Leninsky Prospekt, 119119 Moscow, Russian Federation
Phone. +7 095 938-79-15 / 938-81-28 (International Dept.)
Fax. +7 095 938-21-55
E-mail. inter@vkp.ru; mail@vkp.ru
Website. www.vkp.ru
Membership. Claims 75 million in 48 affiliated organizations
History and character. The GCTU, founded April 16, 1992, is the formal successor organization to the communist-era trade union centre of the Soviet Union. GCTU now operates as a regional union confederation across the member countries of the Commonwealth of Independent States (CIS), and affiliates trade union centres in Armenia, Belarus, Georgia, Kazakhstan, Kyrgyzstan, Moldova, Russia, Tajikistan, Ukraine and Uzbekistan. The Russian centre FNPR is GCTU's largest affiliate. The GCTU also affiliates a wide range

of industrial trade union internationals.
Leadership. Vladimir Scherbakov (president)

International Confederation of Arab Trade Unions (ICATU)
Address. Al-Tahrir Square, PO Box 3225, Damascus, Syria
E-mail. icatu@icatu.org
Website. www.icatu.org (in Arabic with English sections)
Leadership. Hacène Djemam (general secretary)
History and character. ICATU was founded in 1956, and based in Egypt until it moved in 1978 in protest against the international policies of President Sadat. Its role and international status is limited by the low level of development of trade unions in much of the Arab world and the close government control under which most of them operate. It tended to have close ties in the past with WFTU. Its 10th congress, held in Damascus Nov.29–Dec. 2, 1999, aimed to strengthen relations with WCL, ICFTU, ETUC and OATUU, and also to restore historical links with unions in Eastern Europe. The 11th congress, held in Syria in December 2004, was attended by representatives of trade unions in 15 countries. It participates in the Arab Labour Organization and the ILO.

International Confederation of Free Trade Unions (ICFTU)
Confédération Internationale des Syndicats Libres (CISL)
Confederación Internacional de Organizaciones Syndicales Libres (CIOSL)
International Bund Freier Gewerkschaften (IBFG)
Address. 5 Boulevard Roi Albert II, B–1210 Brussels, Belgium
Phone. +32 2 224 0211
Fax. +32 2 201 5815
E-mail. internetpo@icftu.org
Website. www.icftu.org
Leadership. Guy Ryder (general secretary); Sharan Burrow (president)
Membership. 145 million members in 233 organizations in 154 countries
History and character. The ICFTU is a worldwide confederation of national trade union centres. It is one of three such confederations, but is of immensely more importance than the other two (World Confederation of Labour, WCL, and World Federation of Trade Unions, WFTU). The ICFTU today represents nearly all the leading national centres worldwide that operate independently of governments. While overwhelmingly a confederation of national centres, it does permit some individual union affiliations where no such centres exist or for other historical reasons. Affiliates must be free of the control of any other (outside) body, although in practice a few of them operate in countries where social organizations are effectively controlled by a single party. They must also derive their authority only from their members, have a freely and democratically elected leadership, and voluntarily accept the aims and constitution of the ICFTU.

The ICFTU provides leadership and a representative voice for its affiliates at international level. It participates in the work of the International Labour Organization (ILO) and has consultative status with the various specialized agencies of the UN system. Increasingly, it is seeking to build an interface with the International Monetary Fund (IMF), World Bank and World Trade Organization (WTO). It sends regular missions to investigate violations of trade union freedoms in individual countries and makes representations on behalf of its members to international agencies and governments.

The ICFTU originated in the early days of the Cold War when in 1949 unions in Western countries broke away from the WFTU. The principal founding organizations were the AFL and the CIO from the United States, the British TUC and the Dutch NVV, which in a manifesto stated that the WFTU was 'completely dominated by communist organizations, which are themselves controlled by the Kremlin and the Cominform'. For four decades thereafter the ICFTU represented most of the leading Western trade union centres, most of the centres in the newly industrializing countries of Asia, and competed with the WFTU, and to a lesser extent the WCL, for the allegiance of unions in Africa and Latin America.

The general collapse of communism and disintegration of the Soviet Union in the period 1989–91 gave the ICFTU an opportunity to transcend the divisions of the Cold War. It gained the affiliation of new independent confederations, or reformed former official trade union centres, through much of Eastern Europe, where the national centres had previously affiliated to the WFTU. This process, slowed by the uncertain development of authentic independent unions in some parts of the region, is not yet complete, but reached a climax in 2000 with the affiliation of the Russian FNPR. The early 1990s also saw a parallel process in Africa, where much of sub-Saharan Africa, previously dominated by one-party states, saw a movement (in some cases not long sustained) towards political pluralism. Many African centres, previously affiliated only to the Organization of African Trade Union Unity (OATUU) or in some instances also to the WFTU, moved into the ICFTU camp. The ICFTU also recorded important gains with the end of apartheid in South Africa, which brought the affiliation of COSATU, and added the three national centres in Brazil. As a result of this process the ICFTU by the end of 2000 claimed 150 million members, compared with 87 million in 1988. This numerical gain had come about entirely through affiliation of new organizations, and a broadening of the number of countries represented, because most of its established affiliates in the developed world had experienced little growth, and in most cases membership losses, during the same period.

From the 1940s to the 1980s the stronghold of the ICFTU was clearly Western Europe. It was founded in London, had its headquarters in Brussels, and the majority of its most influential and biggest members were European. While never monolithic, its predominant values were those of democratic socialism, and its leading European affiliates were closely allied with the democratic socialist parties in their own countries, such as the DGB in West Germany, the TUC in Britain and the LO in Sweden. In this the ICFTU stood in antithesis to the Prague-based WFTU, which was dominated by communist party-controlled official unions in the Soviet bloc, with a tail of independent leftist unions and unions linked to national liberation movements or one-party states in the developing world. The Western European democratic socialist identification also created tension at times with ICFTU affiliates, more conservative in focus or working within authoritarian political structures, in other parts of the world, especially Asia and Latin America. The ICFTU's regional organization for the Americas, ORIT, for long reflected this tension with the ICFTU centre. From 1969–81 the United States AFL-CIO withdrew from participation in the work of the ICFTU because of its socialist orientation, but continued to participate in and dominate ORIT. There was persistent unhappiness among some European unions at the emphasis of the AFL-CIO, with financial support from the US government, on supporting anti-communist unions even in situations where those unions might seem compromised in their relationships with right-wing regimes. Only in the 1990s, with the end of the Cold War, did the AFL-CIO move from the sidelines to a position closer to the centre ground of the ICFTU.

Despite the fall in union density in much of the region since the early 1980s, Western Europe remains the leading single base for free and developed trade unionism, with its well-organized unions having an established and significant role in industrial relations and more broadly as social partners. However, the huge increase in ICFTU membership outside Western Europe in the last 15 years has influenced, and is likely increasingly to influence, the organization's development. The largest affiliate, nominally at least, is now the Russian FNPR. However, its origins in (only partly reformed) official Soviet era trade unionism, the uncertain identification of much of its membership with the FNPR and its goals, and the intensely difficult economic and political environment in which it works, clearly present issues and challenges not faced by the Western European centres. Into the 1980s a high proportion of ICFTU affiliates were in countries in which basic rights of association and trade union freedoms were broadly accepted and established. In contrast, most of the affiliates added since 1990 – whether in Eastern Europe and Russia, Africa, or Latin America – are in countries where only a decade-and-a-half or so ago free trade unionism was met with repression, imprisonment, or even murder and "disappearances". For these new affiliates, the building of sound trade union structures, and working to guarantee their survival in political circumstances that are still not yet entirely secure and settled, have been great challenges. While, at one level, as reflected in the swelling number of ICFTU members, the position of free trade unionism has never been stronger, it is also the case that the proportion of ICFTU members facing very real threats to the free exercise of trade union rights is greater than ever before. The ICFTU's *Annual Survey of Trade Union Rights* covers two-thirds of the countries in the world, and whereas the infringements of rights described in some countries may seem relatively marginal, in many other cases trade unions affiliated to the ICFTU face serious attack. The ICFTU's commitment to, and involvement in, international solidarity work in support of its more hard-pressed affiliates is a major part of its work, and an area that seems likely only to increase.

The globalization of the ICFTU's membership has also marched in step with the increasing globalization of the world economy. Economic globalization has had two consequences. On the one hand, it is opening up the labour practices of unseen corners of the world to scrutiny in ways that were previously unknown. The casual ratification of core ILO conventions by one-party states that entirely ignored them in practice, and the unchallenged participation of such countries in the ILO, served only to undermine the ILO's credibility. At the same time, the onward rush of globalization, beginning with the structural adjustment programmes introduced by many countries at the behest of the IMF from the 1980s, and gaining pace with the creation of the World Trade Organization in the 1990s, has pushed forward social and economic models in which the claims of the free market, and not those of organized labour, have been paramount. Accepting that globalization is inevitable, the ICFTU is pressing for the values embodied in ILO conventions (but often ignored by autonomous, insulated states in practice) to be given vitality through integration into the agenda of the Bretton Woods institutions (the IMF and World Bank) and the WTO. While the ICFTU continues to emphasize its belief in the importance of the ILO, with its mandate to create conditions of dignity and equality for workers, in practice the focus is increasingly on the campaign for ILO values to be incorporated in the programmes and rulings of the now much more powerful IMF, World Bank and WTO. These bodies have real powers over governments because they control the purse strings, whereas the ILO is in this respect essentially toothless. In this, and alongside the WCL and the global union federations (international trade secretariats), the ICFTU has put its emphasis on achieving adoption of the so-called ILO "core labour standards", covering trade union rights of association and collective bargaining, equality of opportunity, and abolition of child and forced labour.

While to some extent these standards may be seen as providing only a minimum safety net, securing their implementation remains a massive uphill struggle. Neither of the world's two biggest economies, the USA and China, have ratified the basic ILO conventions covering trade union freedoms, No. 87 (Freedom of Association and Protection of the Right to Organize, 1948) and No. 98 (Right to Organize and Collective Bargaining, 1949). Furthermore, in many countries, whether or not they have ratified the conventions on paper, neither the spirit nor the letter of the conventions is properly observed. In developing countries, cheap and "flexible" labour is seen as a critical element in competitive advantage and the development of strong unions as an impediment to national progress. Even in middle-income countries, especially in Asia, the view is often taken that unions are not beneficial unless they play a role in ensuring labour discipline and productivity. ICFTU affiliates in these countries inescapably work within a different set of assumptions and rules than do those in Europe.

Supreme authority in the ICFTU is vested in the congress, held every four years (most recently in Miyazaki, Japan in December 2004), composed of delegates from the member federations in proportion to the size of their membership. The congress elects an executive board, which directs activities between congresses. Day-to-day authority is exercised by the Brussels-based secretariat, under the direction of the general secretary. The ICFTU is financed solely by its member organizations. In 1988 it was resolved that a Women's World Conference should meet every four years between congresses; it most recently convened in Melbourne, Australia in 2003.

During 2004 the long-running closed-door discussions between the ICFTU and WCL concerning closer cooperation of the two confederations apparently reached agreement on a proposal for what has been described as either the preparatory stage for a merger, or the creation of a new trade union international. Little information was publicly available at the time of writing concerning this proposal.

ICFTU offices. The ICFTU has offices in a number of countries to provide support at a more localized level or liaise with international agencies. Among the most important are the offices in Geneva (the site of the ILO), New York (United Nations) and Washington (IMF and World Bank).

Geneva Office
Address. Avenue Blanc 46, CH–1202, Geneva, Switzerland
Phone. +41 22 738 4202
Fax. +41 22 738 1082
E-mail. icftu.ge@geneva.icftu.org

UN Office
Address. 211 East 43rd Street, Suite 710, New York, NY 10017, USA
Phone. +1 212 370 0180
Fax. +1 212 370 0188
E-mail. icftuny@igc.org

Washington Office
Address. 1925 K Street, NW, Suite 425, Washington DC 20006, USA
Phone. +1 202 463 8573
Fax. +1 202 463 8564
E-mail. pbakvis@earthlink.net

Regional Organizations of the ICFTU. The ICFTU has regional organizations for Asia-Pacific (APRO), Americas (ORIT), and Africa (AFRO). It has no European regional organization, but has close relations with the European Trade Union Confederation (ETUC), which also affiliates the ICFTU's member national centres.

1. ICFTU Asian and Pacific Regional Organization (ICFTU–APRO)
Address. One Marina Boulevard, NTUC Centre, 9th Floor, Singapore 018989
Phone. +65 6327 3590
Fax. + 65 6327 3576
E-mail. gs@icftu-apro.org
Website. www.icftu-apro.org
Leadership. Noriyuki Suzuki (general secretary)
Membership. 30 million in 40 affiliates in 28 countries.

2. Inter-American Regional Organization of Workers (ORIT)
Address. Avda. Andrés Eloy Blanco (Este 2), Edificio José Vargas, Piso 15, Los Caobos, Caracas, Venezuela
Phone. +58 2 578 3538
Fax. +58 2 578 1702
E-mail. vbaez@cioslorit.org
Website. www.cioslorit.org
Leadership. Víctor Báez Mosqueira (general secretary)

3. ICFTU African Regional Organization (AFRO)
Address. Kenya Re Towers - 4th Floor, Upper Hill, Off Ragati Road, P.O. Box 67273, Nairobi
Phone. +254 20 244336
Fax. +254 20 215072
E-mail. info@icftuafro.org
Website. www.icftuafro.org
Leadership. Andrew Kailembo (general secretary)

National affiliates. The ICFTU records affiliates in the following countries and territories (see country sections for details): Albania; Algeria; Angola; Antigua; Argentina; Australia; Austria; Azerbaijan; Bahamas; Bangladesh; Barbados; Belgium; Belize; Benin; Bermuda; Bosnia-Herzegovina; Botswana; Brazil; Bulgaria; Burkina Faso; Burundi; Cameroon; Canada; Cape Verde; Central African Republic; Chad; Chile; China (Hong Kong); Colombia; Congo, Democratic Republic of; Congo, Republic of; Cook Islands; Costa Rica; Côte d'Ivoire; Croatia; Cyprus; Czech Republic; Denmark; Djibouti; Dominica; Dominican Republic; Ecuador; El Salvador; Eritrea; Estonia; Fiji; Finland; France; French Polynesia; Gabon; Gambia; Georgia; Germany; Ghana; Greece; Grenada; Guatemala; Guinea; Guinea-Bissau; Guyana; Honduras; Hungary; Iceland; India; Indonesia; Ireland; Israel; Italy; Jamaica; Japan; Jordan; Kenya; Kiribati; South Korea; Latvia; Lebanon; Liberia; Lithuania; Luxembourg; Madagascar; Malawi; Malaysia; Mali; Malta; Mauritania; Mauritius; Mexico; Moldova; Mongolia; Morocco; Mozambique; Namibia; Nepal; Netherlands; New Caledonia; New Zealand; Nicaragua; Niger; Nigeria; Norway; Pakistan; Palestine; Panama; Papua New Guinea; Paraguay; Peru; Philippines; Poland; Portugal; Romania; Russia; Rwanda; St. Helena; St. Kitts-Nevis; St. Lucia; St. Vincent; Samoa; San Marino; Sao Tome and Principe; Senegal; Seychelles; Sierra Leone; Singapore; Slovakia; South Africa; Spain; Sri Lanka; Suriname; Swaziland; Sweden; Switzerland; Taiwan; Tanzania; Thailand; Togo; Tonga; Trinidad and Tobago; Tunisia; Turkey; Uganda; Ukraine; United Kingdom; United States; Vanuatu; Vatican City; Venezuela; Zambia; Zimbabwe.

Publications. The ICFTU has a wide range of publications, variously available in hard copy or on its website, including the *Annual Survey of Trade Union Rights*. ICFTU's monthly journal *Trade Union World* ceased publication in 2002 (but fact files continue to be published in electronic form under the *Trade Union World* logo). Its press and publications department can be contacted by e-mail at: press@icftu.org

Global Union Federations

There are ten global union federations (GUFs, formerly known as international trade secretariats) providing a global voice for unions on a sectoral basis by industry. These all originated in Western Europe, and all still have their headquarters in European countries (including four each in Belgium and Switzerland), although all now act globally and (like the ICFTU) have increased their world-wide representation over the last decade-and-a-half. The GUFs are fully autonomous and in most cases have a history pre-dating the formation of the ICFTU, but are associated with the ICFTU and in general work closely with it in coordinating campaigns. ICFTU, the ten global union federations and TUAC are collectively grouped under the 'Global Unions' banner which operates as a loose forum, coordinating the work of the 12 organizations. Global Unions has its own website (www.global-unions.org) but does not have a secretariat.

The GUFs (see separate entries for each) are: Education International (EI); International Federation of Building and Wood Workers (IFBWW); International Federation of Chemical, Energy, Mine and General Workers' Unions (ICEM); International Federation of Journalists (IFJ); International Metalworkers' Federation (IMF); International Textile, Garment and Leather Workers' Federation (ITGLWF); International Transport Workers' Federation (ITF); International Union of Food, Agricultural, Hotel, Restaurant, Catering, Tobacco and Allied Workers' Associations (IUF); Public Services International (PSI); and Union Network International (UNI).

1. Education International (EI)

Address. 5 boulevard du Roi Albert II (8th), B–1210 Brussels, Belgium
Phone. +32 2 224 0611
Fax. +32 2 224 0606
E-mail. educint@ei-ie.org
Website. www.ei-ie.org
Leadership. Thulas Nxesi (president); Fred van Leeuwen (general secretary)
Membership. 26 million teachers and workers in education in 343 unions in more than 150 countries.
History and character. EI is a global union federation. It was created in 1993 by the merger of the International Federation of Free Teacher Unions (IFFTU), one of the international trade secretariats associated with the ICFTU, and the World Conference of Organizations of the Teaching Profession (WCOTP).

EI is in formal associate relations with UNESCO and the ILO and works closely with the ICFTU. It is represented on the board of the European Trade Union Committee for Education (ETUCE). In 2004 the WCL-affiliated World Confederation of Teachers was in discussions with EI over a draft merger agreement.

2. International Federation of Building and Wood Workers (IFBWW)

Address. 54 route des Acacias, PO Box 1412, CH–1227 Carouge GE, Switzerland
Phone. +41 22 827 37 77
Fax. +41 22 827 37 70
E-mail. info@ifbww.org
Website. www.ifbww.org
Leadership. Roel de Vries (president); Anita Normack (general secretary)
Membership. 10 million members in 287 unions in 124 countries
History and character. The IFBWW is a global union federation. It was established in 1934 by the merger of the Building Workers' International and the Wood Workers' International. Its membership is in the building, wood, forestry and allied trades.

The IFBWW has regional offices for Latin America, Africa and Asia–Pacific. At the European level it cooperates with the ETUC-affiliated European Federation of Building and Wood Workers (EFBWW), as well as the Nordic Federation of Building and Wood Workers. It runs project offices in several regions.

IFBWW members commonly work in hazardous occupations and health and safety is a prominent issue. It is campaigning for ratification of ILO Conventions 167 (safety in construction) and 162 (asbestos). It is also campaigning for sustainable development in forestry and has recently campaigned on migration issues.

3. International Federation of Chemical, Energy, Mine and General Workers' Unions (ICEM)

Address. Avenue Emile de Béco 109, B–1050 Brussels, Belgium
Phone. +32 2 626 2020
Fax. +32 2 648 4316
Website. www.icem.org
Leadership. John Maitland (president); Fred Higgs (general secretary)
Membership. 20 million in 399 unions in 108 countries
History and character. The ICEM is a global union federation and was founded in 1995 by the merger of the International Federation of Chemical, Energy and General Workers' Unions (ICEF) and the Miners' International Federation (MIF). Members are blue- and white-collar workers in energy (including electricity, oil and gas), all types of mining, plastics, petrochemicals, chemicals, pharmaceuticals, pulp and paper, rubber, glass, ceramics, cement, environmental services such as waste disposal, and miscellaneous other industries not covered by other GUFs. On Nov. 1, 2000, the ICEM also absorbed the Universal Alliance of Diamond Workers (UADW).

The ICEM's activities include support for union-building in countries where unions are weak or non-existent; solidarity work on behalf of member unions; information and services for member unions in areas such as collective bargaining and health and safety; and trade union skills training. It is developing networks of trade unions to coordinate their activities in negotiating with transnational corporations.

The ICEM believes it is necessary to engage with bodies such as the International Monetary Fund, World

Bank and World Trade Organization which are now more influential in shaping the position of workers than traditional UN agencies like the ILO. It has called for these bodies to be made democratically accountable.

The ICEM has a Global Health and Safety Initiative focused on the mining industry. This aims to win changes in national health and safety legislation, ratification by ILO Member States of ILO Convention No. 176 (1995) on safety and health in mines, and inclusion of health and safety in collective agreements. It supports the campaign of the IUF to protect workers from misuse of pesticides. The ICEM says that fear of job losses in the sectors it represents has often kept workers quiet over environmental issues, but that it is necessary for unions to engage with environmental organizations and industry in solving problems "or suffer from someone else's solutions later that take no account of workers or their communities."

4. International Federation of Journalists (IFJ)

Address. Rue de la Loi 155, B-1040 Brussels
Phone. +32 2 223 2200
Fax. +32 2 219 2219
E-mail. ifj@ifj.org
Website. www.ifj.org
Leadership. Chris Warren (president); Aidan White (general secretary)
Membership. 500,000 journalists in more than 100 countries
History and character. The IFJ is a global union federation.. It originated in 1926. It speaks for journalists within the UN system and cooperates with other GUFs and the ICFTU. It has consultative status with UNESCO, the ILO, World Intellectual Property Organization (WIPO) and the UN Centre for Human Rights.

Issues for the IFJ include women's rights in the media, concentration of ownership, authors' rights, and attacks on press freedom. It has an International Safety Fund to support journalists in need.

5. International Metalworkers' Federation (IMF)

Address. 54bis, route des Acacias, Case Postale 1516, CH–1227 Geneva, Switzerland
Phone. +41 22 308 5050
Fax. +41 22 308 5055
E-mail. info@imfmetal.org
Website. www.imfmetal.org
Leadership. Jürgen Peters (president); Marcello Malentacchi (general secretary)
Membership. Nearly 25 million in 200 unions in 100 countries
History and character. Founded in Zurich in 1893; membership collapsed to only 190,00 on eve of World War II; re-built in post-War period. Membership increased from 12.7 million in 1989 to 18 million in 1993 as a result of affiliation of unions in Eastern Europe.

The IMF has regional offices worldwide. Its structure includes the IMF World Auto Council, with company councils for major manufacturers.

6. International Textile, Garment and Leather Workers' Federation (ITGLWF)

Address. 8 rue Joseph Stevens, B–1000 Brussels, Belgium
Phone. +32 2 512 2606
Fax. +32 2 511 0904
E-mail. office@itglwf.org
Website. www.itglwf.org
Leadership. Peter Booth (president); Neil Kearney (general secretary)
Membership. 216 unions in 106 countries with over 10 million members
History and character. The ITGLWF is a global union federation. It works to represent unions in its sector in international organizations, provide solidarity support for member unions, and carry out education and development work to build unions in countries where they are weak or do not exist. It has regional organizations for the Americas, Europe, Asia and Africa. The ITGLWF has particular concerns about the impact of globalization because it represents workers in industries which "because they are labour intensive...are among the easiest to relocate, making it easy for companies to shift production as soon as national governments impose restraints on their operations, or as soon as workers organize for better wages and working conditions".

7. International Transport Workers' Federation (ITF)

Address. ITF House, 49–60 Borough Road, London SE1 1DS, United Kingdom
Phone. +44 20 7403 2733
Fax. +44 20 7357 7871
E-mail. mail@itf.org.uk
Website. www.itf.org.uk
Leadership. David Cockroft (general secretary)
Membership. Over 5 million in 600 unions in 140 countries
History and character. The ITF was founded in 1896 in London by European seafarers' and dockers' leaders. It subsequently expanded to embrace railways, road transport and civil aviation. The ITF represents the interests of its affiliates to transport-specific bodies such as the International Maritime Organization and the International Civil Aviation Organization as well as to the ILO. It has regional offices for Africa, Asia-Pacific, North America and Latin America. In Europe it works closely with the Brussels-based European Transport Workers' Federation (ETF), which is made up primarily of ITF affiliated unions.

At international level key issues for the ITF include the use of flags of convenience in the maritime sector; working hours in road transport; and the impact of globalization, which it sees as undercutting national laws, regulations and collective agreements.

The ITF has nine industrial sections, each of which has its own committees and conferences, as follows: road transport, urban transport, railways, seafarers, civil aviation, docks, fisheries, tourism, inland navigation.

8. International Union of Food, Agricultural, Hotel, Restaurant, Catering, Tobacco and Allied Workers' Associations (IUF)

Address. Rampe du Pont-Rouge 8, CH-1213 Petit-Lancy, Switzerland

Phone. +41 22 793 2233
Fax. +41 22 793 2238
E-mail. info@iuf.org
Website. www.iuf.org
Leadership. Paul Andela (president); Ron Oswald (general secretary)
Membership. 12 million members in 326 unions in 120 countries
History and character. The IUF traces its origins back to 1920, when it was initially known as the International Union of Food and Drink Workers. The current name was adopted as the outcome of a series of mergers with the International Federation of Tobacco Workers (1958), the International Union of Hotel, Restaurant and Bar Workers (1961), and the International Federation of Plantation, Agricultural and Allied Workers (1994).

The IUF operates in sectors where trade union organization is often difficult. In the agricultural sector (where the IUF represents 3 million waged workers) unions are weak or banned or actively persecuted in many countries. Leading issues for IUF include agricultural child labour and the exposure of farm workers to dangerous pesticides, which the World Health Organization says leads to 40,000 deaths per annum. In 1998 the IUF launched a Global Pesticides Project to provide education and training on pesticide safety issues for activists, and it is calling for an ILO convention specifically on health and safety in agriculture. At the international level it seeks to intervene directly with transnational corporations on behalf of its national member unions.

The IUF structure includes regional secretariats for Africa, Asia-Pacific, the Caribbean, Latin America and North America. In Europe it works through the ETUC-affiliated European Federation of Food, Agriculture and Tourism Trade Unions (EFFAT). It also has a number of local offices worldwide, including Moscow. Three IUF sectors (agricultural workers; hotel, restaurant and catering workers; and tobacco workers) hold their own conferences in addition to the IUF congress held every four years.

9. Public Services International (PSI)
Address. 45 Avenue Voltaire, BP 9, Ferney-Voltaire Cedex, 01211 France
Phone. +33 4 50 40 64 64
Fax. +33 4 50 40 73 20
E-mail. psi@world-psi.org
Website. www.world-psi.org
Leadership. Hans Engelberts (general secretary)
Membership. 20 million in 528 affiliated unions in 144 countries
History and character. PSI is a global union federation that works in association with other GUFs and with the ICFTU. It dates its origins back to 1907. Its membership is in all public sector areas, including administration, utilities, public works, health and social services, police, the law, leisure and taxation, with the principal exception of teaching, which is covered by Education International (EI).

PSI is an officially recognized non-governmental organization for the public sector within the ILO and has consultative status with ECOSOC and observer status with other UN bodies such as UNCTAD and UNESCO. Its has regionally based committees with executive powers for the Inter-Americas, Asia-Pacific, and Africa and Arab Countries and Europe. In Europe it works closely with the European Federation of Public Service Unions (EPSU), which is affiliated to ETUC.

The key issues for PSI include "the new challenges of globalization, the threats from ideological privatization, commercialization and contracting out of public services... attacks on services through structural adjustment polices and the intrusion of transnational corporations into public services". It runs an education programme to train trade union activists.

10. Union Network International (UNI)
Address. Avenue Reverdil 8-10, CH-1260 Nyon 2, Switzerland
Phone. +41 22 365 2100
Fax. +41 22 365 2121
E-mail. contact@union-network.org
Website. www.union-network.org
Leadership. Joe Hansen (president); Philip Jennings (general secretary); Philip Bowyer (deputy general secretary)
Membership. 15.5 million in 900 unions in 140 countries
History and character. UNI is a global union federation. It was formed on Jan. 1, 2000 as "a new international for a new millennium". The founding partners were:

International Federation of Commercial, Clerical, Professional and Technical Employees (FIET), dating back to 1904 and with 10 million members in 435 affiliated unions in 136 countries;

Communications International (CI), itself formerly known as Postal, Telegraph and Telephone International (PTTI) and with origins in 1911, with 4.5 million members in posts and telecommunications, broadcasting and electricity, in 281 unions in 127 countries;

International Graphical Federation (IGF), with 1 million members in 103 unions in 76 countries;

Media and Entertainment International (MEI), with 200,000 members in 130 unions in 65 countries. MEI was the smallest of the international trade secretariats and was itself founded only in 1993 by merger of the International Secretariat for Arts, Mass Media and Entertainment Trade Unions (ISETU) and the International Federation of Audiovisual Workers (FISTAV).

The general secretary of UNI, Philip Jennings, was formerly general secretary of FIET, and his deputy, Philip Bowyer, was general secretary of Communications International. Jennings stated as a reason for the formation of UNI that "workers across the service, communications and entertainment sector increasingly face the same employers and the same issues and are increasingly lobbying the same international organizations." Bowyer stated that "communications companies like Sprint, MCI-WorldCom, Cable and Wireless and UPS strenuously oppose union organization. We are bringing unions together everywhere such companies operate in the world to force them to listen to their workers and to allow them to organize."

UNI is organized into the following sectors: Casino Employees; Commerce; Electricity; Finance; Graphical; Hair and Beauty; IBITS (white collar, professional and IT staff); Media, Entertainment and Arts; Postal; Property Services; Social Insurance and Private Health Care; Telecommunications; and Tourism. There are also three cross-sectoral groups, for Women, Youth, and Professional and Managerial Staff.

UNI has four regional organizations, for Africa, Americas, Asia-Pacific, and Europe (UNI-Europa also being the sectoral federation of ETUC).

Organization of African Trade Union Unity (OATUU)
Organisation de l'Unité Syndicale Africaine (OUSA)
Address. PO Box M 386, Aviation Road, Accra, Ghana
Phone. +233 21 508 851/55
Fax. +233 21 508 851/53
E-mail. oatuu@ighmail.com
Leadership. Hassan Adebayo Sunmonu (secretary-general)
Membership. 73 affiliates in Africa
History and character. The OATUU provides a collective voice for African trade union centres. It is independent of other international trade union confederations.

The first pan-African trade union organization was the All-African Trade Union Federation (AATUF), founded in Casablanca in May 1961. In an attempt to exclude the influence of the ICFTU and the Christian unions, which were seen as dampening militancy and 'revolutionary zeal', the AATUF insisted on the principle of disaffiliation of all its member national centres from any non-African union organizations. National centres which maintained affiliation to the ICFTU or the International Federation of Christian Trade Unions (IFCTU, the forerunner of the World Confederation of Labour), or which were unwilling to accept this policy, formed the African Trade Union Confederation (ATUC) in January 1962. In 1973 these two rival federations, and a third smaller grouping known as the Pan-African Workers' Congress, were merged into the Organization of African Trade Union Unity (OATUU), under the auspices of the Organization of African Unity (OAU, now the African Union). The OATUU suffered a split in 1986 in which different countries backed opposing camps. This ended in a reconciliation in which Hassan Sunmonu, a former president of the Nigeria Labour Congress, became secretary-general in October 1986, a position he continues to hold.

The OATUU long advocated the position that African trade unions should not affiliate to global trade union centres. In part this reflected a wish to avoid damaging conflict between African unions arising from competition between the ICFTU, WFTU and WCL, although some African governments were also actively hostile to their national unions having non-African alliances. In practice, however, many national centres did form such affiliations. With the end of the Cold War and the movement to greater pluralism in many African countries in the early 1990s, many OATUU affiliates are now also affiliated to the ICFTU.

OATUU's activities include representing the interests of its affiliates before African governments and in international organizations, and it has consultative status with the ILO, the UN Economic and Social Council (ECOSOC), UNESCO and FAO. It has engaged in campaigns on issues such as strengthening the African Economic Community, promoting the African Alternative Framework to Structural Adjustment Programmes, and calling for debt cancellation. It believes that globalization and the policies of the IMF, World Bank and WTO are undermining the ability of African nations to protect domestic industries and develop fair labour standards and opposes the growing influence of these agencies. It supports the strengthening of African political, social and economic integration through the African Union.

OATUU runs worker education programmes on trade union and broader social and economic issues. It also has a health, safety and environment programme. However, it has generally suffered from lack of funding and is not financially self-sufficient.

OATUU's regional organizations are: the Organization of Trade Unions of West Africa (OTUWA); Organization of Trade Unions of Central Africa (OTUCA); Southern Africa Trade Union Coordinating Council (SATUCC); and the Organization of Trade Unions of Arab Maghreb (OTUAM). In addition it has a series of specialized agencies for each industrial sector.

Trade Union Advisory Committee to the OECD (TUAC)
Address. 26 avenue de la Grande Armée, 75017 Paris, France
Phone. +33 1 5537 37 37
Fax. +33 1 47 5498
E-mail. tuac@tuac.org
Website. www.tuac.org
Leadership. John Sweeney (president); John Evans (general secretary)
Membership. 56 trade union organizations in OECD countries
History and character. TUAC originated as a trade union advisory committee to the Organization for European Economic Cooperation (OEEC), set up in 1948 to implement the post-War European Recovery Programme (the Marshall Plan). It brought together most of the non-communist union national centres in Western Europe. Under a convention in force from September 1961, the OEEC became the Organization for Economic Cooperation and Development (OECD), with a broad role in promoting sound economic development, and adding the USA and Canada as full members alongside the European membership.

TUAC has consultative status with the OECD and regularly meets the OECD secretariat and specialist committees as well as member governments. It also coordinates trade union input to the G-7 economic summits and works closely with the ICFTU, WCL,

ETUC and global union federations. Its membership has expanded with the OECD and now comprises 56 organizations in the 30 OECD countries.

Plenary sessions, involving representatives of all the affiliates and the international organizations, are held twice yearly and make policy decisions and approve the budget. An administrative committee oversees administration and draws up the budget; it currently comprises representatives of the following organizations: DGB, Germany; CLC, Canada; TUC, United Kingdom; AFL-CIO, United States; FO and CFDT, France; CISL, Italy; RENGO, Japan; ÖGB, Austria; TCO, Sweden; and CSC, Belgium together with the president, vice-presidents and general secretary. There are also various working groups. Decision-making is generally by consensus. There is a small secretariat based in Paris.

Affiliated unions. (See under country sections for detailed entries). Australia, ACTU; Austria, ÖGB; Belgium, CGSLB, CSC, FGTB; Canada, CLC, CSN; Czech Republic, CMKOS; Denmark, AC, FTF, LO; Finland, AKAVA, SAK, STTK; France, CFDT, CFTC, CGC, CGT, CGT-FO, UNSA; Germany, DGB; Greece, GGCL; Hungary, LIGA, MSZOSZ; Iceland, ASI, BSRB; Ireland, ICTU; Italy, CGIL, CISL, UIL; Japan, Rengo; South Korea, FKTU, KCTU; Luxembourg, CGT-LG, LCGB; Mexico, CTM, FESEEBES; Netherlands, CNV, FNV; New Zealand, NZCTU; Norway, LO, YS; Poland, NSZZ Solidarnosc; Portugal, UGT-P; Slovak Republic, KOZ SR; Spain, CC.OO, ELA-STV, UGT; Sweden, LO, SACO, TCO; Switzerland, Travail Suisse, USS; Turkey, Turk-Is; United Kingdom, TUC; United States of America, AFL-CIO.

World Confederation of Labour (WCL)
Confederación Mundial del Trabajo (CMT)
Confédération Mondiale du Travail (CMT)

Address. Rue de Trèves 33, B-1040 Brussels, Belgium
Phone. +32 2 285 47 00
Fax. +32 2 230 87 22
E-mail. info@cmt-wcl.org
Website. www.cmt-wcl.org
Leadership. Basile Mahan Gahe (president); Willy Thys (secretary-general)
Membership. The WCL reports that its affiliates have 26 million members, in 116 countries
History and character. The WCL was founded in 1920 as the International Federation of Christian Trade Unions (IFCTU), with a mainly European membership. Following World War II it lost ground as the European trade union movement became polarized between the WFTU, representing the trade union centres of the communist countries, and the ICFTU, representing most of the centres in Western Europe. To counter these losses the IFCTU began in the 1950s to establish contacts with unions in the Third World. The interchanges with unions sharing similar values, although not coming from the same (European) Christian tradition, contributed to overstepping the borders of narrow denominationalism and laid the basis of a more ecumenical approach. In 1968 the IFCTU changed its name to the World Confederation of Labour, ending the explicit association with the Christian Church. The changing geographical composition of its membership may be gauged by the way a total of only three non-European delegates at the 1952 congress had increased to 82, predominantly from the Third World, by the 1977 congress. Its core European and Latin American membership remains mainly Christian, however, whereas that of its affiliates elsewhere is more diverse.

The WCL represents an alternative and distinctive voice to the ICFTU for free trade unions, but operates on a much smaller scale. Overall the WCL claims to have some 26 million members in its affiliated organizations, although reliable membership figures for many of its affiliates are not available and some of them have a tenuous or marginal position. In some countries its affiliates are small organizations focused mainly on training, education and solidarity work rather than fully developed trade union centres.

It has minimal presence in the major countries of the developed world. In the G-7 group of leading industrialized countries (USA, Japan, Germany, UK, France, Italy, and Canada) there is a WCL affiliated national-level confederation only in France and Italy, and in both cases these are minor organizations. In Europe the WCL-affiliated centres of most significance are the CSC/ACV in Belgium and the CNV in Netherlands. With 1.5 million members, the Belgian Confederation of Christian Unions (CSC/ACV) is the only case in the member states of the European Union of the WCL affiliate being larger than the ICFTU affiliate.

In contrast, the WCL has more presence in the developing world, especially (but not exclusively) in countries with a Christian tradition. It is influential in South and Central America although this is usually from a minority position, with the big trade union centres in the major economies such as Argentina, Brazil, Chile and Mexico all affiliated to the ICFTU. It is represented on a more fragmentary basis in Africa and Asia and made few gains when many trade union centres joined the ICFTU in the early 1990s as part of a widespread move to greater pluralism in sub-Saharan Africa. A notable new affiliate in recent years has been the SBSI, which grew to prominence in the late 1990s in (mainly Muslim) Indonesia.

The WCL (jointly with the ICFTU) affiliated Polish Solidarity (which had a heavy Catholic influence) in 1986, when it was a banned organization. However, the WCL's efforts to build its position in the former communist countries of Eastern Europe since then have not overall had much success, although it has assisted in trade union development and training. To the degree that trade unionism has not just collapsed, or remained dominated by communist-era structures, the more significant organizations in Eastern Europe have preferred to join the world trade union mainstream by seeking affiliation to the ICFTU. In some cases the WCL complained that national laws in post-communist countries effectively encouraged a single-trade-union system, or limited trade union pluralism, for example by confining collective bargaining rights to most-representative national unions, thereby assisting

ICFTU affiliates at the expense of its own smaller member organizations. The WCL has also confronted the difficulty of validating the authenticity and independence of new union structures in countries with no tradition of independent trade unionism.

The WCL historically adopted a non-aligned position in global power politics, and emphasized the right to national self-determination of the countries of the Third World. The WCL believes that human fulfilment must have a spiritual as well as a material dimension, and that workers possess individual human rights in addition to their collective rights. This individualistic and spiritual dimension has meant that in Europe its affiliates have often been seen as standing to the political right of the socialist-led union mainstream, whereas in authoritarian regimes in developing countries its affiliates have often had a radical campaigning edge. The WCL favours the development of forms of worker participation in the management of enterprises. Like the ICFTU it currently emphasizes issues arising from globalization, calling in particular for adoption and enforcement of fair labour standards worldwide and a globalization of social justice to match that of the globalization of capital and trade. The WCL's "Norm" programme is aimed at promoting the universal observance of international human rights instruments and especially the ILO's core minimum labour standards (Conventions 87 and 98 on freedom of association, 100 and 111 on equality of opportunity and treatment, 29 and 105 on the abolition of forced labour, and 138 on the minimum age of employment).

The WCL's work with other trade union bodies is coordinated by the International Solidarity Foundation. The Foundation provides resources, funds campaigns and backs projects intended to promote independent trade unionism. The WCL enjoys consultative status with the ILO, the Economic and Social Council of the United Nations, and the other agencies of the UN system, and with the OECD. It has permanent representatives in Geneva, Rome, Paris, Vienna and Washington.

The congress is the ruling body, comprising delegates from national centres, regional organizations and the associated international trade federations. The congress, which meets every four years, sets overall policy and elects the confederal board. The confederal board, consisting of 48 members (representing the national confederations, the continents and the trade sections) and elected for four-year terms, meets annually and is the ruling body between congresses. The nine-member executive committee, composed of the president, the secretary-general, the six vice-presidents, and the treasurer, is responsible for the concrete implementation of policies laid down by the congress and the confederal board and meets at least twice a year. The secretariat in Brussels (led by the secretary-general and assisted by three confederal and two executive secretaries) is responsible for day-to-day affairs.

The WCL is based upon affiliations of national centres or confederations or other broad-based organizations. Exceptionally it accepts direct affiliations of individual unions, as was the case in Africa before the democratization wave of the mid-1990s.

During 2004 the long-running closed-door discussions between ICFTU and WCL concerning closer cooperation of the two confederations apparently reached agreement on a proposal for what has been described as either the preparatory stage for a merger, or the creation of a new trade union international. Little information was publicly available at the time of writing concerning this proposal.

Regional organizations. The WCL has had no regional organization for Europe since 1973. Instead its main European affiliates are members of the European Trade Union Confederation (ETUC). The WCL has little presence in North America, where it is represented in the USA by a small union (the National Alliance of Postal and Federal Employees) and in Canada by the Christian Labour Association of Canada and the Centrale des Syndicats Démocratiques (CSD), a minority union based on the province of Quebec.

1 Central Latinoamericana de Trabajadores (CLAT)
Address. Apartado 6681, 1010A Caracas, Venezuela
Phone. +58 32 72 07 94
Fax. +58 32 72 04 63
E-mail. clat@telcel.net.ve
Website. www.clat.org
Leadership. Eduardo García (secretary general)
History and character. CLAT is the WCL's regional organization for Latin America and the Caribbean, a region in which the WCL is traditionally relatively strong. Historically it has been the most important regional component of the WCL. It was founded in 1954. Much of its success lay in the establishment of new independent unions, sometimes in collaboration with the worker-priest movement. Many of its affiliates have faced severe difficulties arising from the prevalence of military rule and death squad activities in various parts of the continent over several decades, although the 1990s brought an amelioration of conditions in many countries. It campaigns for trade union organization, for the defence of human and civil rights, against dictatorship, and for the political, social and economic integration of the countries of the continent (it favours the creation of a Latin American Community of Nations). CLAT has sub-regional organizations for the Southern Cone (CTCS), Central America (CCT), Caribbean (CTC) and Andes (CSTA), and it also maintains the Workers' University of Latin America (UTAL), based in Caracas.

2. Brotherhood of Asian Trade Unionists (BATU)
Address. Foundation, Inc., Block 73, Lot 11, Phase 8, North Fairview 1121, Quezon City, Philippines
Phone. + 63 2 930 7181
Fax. + 63 2 938 6789
E-mail. batu_org@hotmail.com
Leadership. Juan Tan (president)
History and character. Asian sub-regional structures include liaison offices in Tokyo and Singapore, a project development office in Manila, and the Rerum Novarum Labour Centre in Taiwan.

3. Democratic Organization of African Workers' Trade Unions (DOAWTU/ODSTA)
Address. Route Internationale d'Atakpamé, Lomé-Agoenyive, Togo

Phone. +228 25 07 10
Fax. +228 25 61 13
E-mail. odsta@cafe.tg
Website. www.odsta.org
Leadership. Toolsyraj Benedyn (president); Akouete B. Adrien (general secretary)
History and character. DOAWTU claims 32 member unions in 24 countries and eight 'pan-African federations' in the following sectors: building and wood workers, education, food and agriculture, industry, public service, salaried staff, textiles and transport. It also has three sub-regional offices.

International Trade Federations. The WCL's structure includes a number of international trade federations, the more important of which are listed below. These lack the scale or autonomous significance of the global union federations associated with the ICFTU. There are also regional-level trade groups affiliated at industry level to the international trade federations and at regional level to WCL's regional organizations such as CLAT.

1. International Federation of Employees in Public Service (INFEDOP)
Address. rue Montoyer 39, B-1040 Brussels, Belgium
Phone. +32 2 230 38 65
Fax. +32 2 231 14 72
E-mail. info@infedop-eurofedop.com
Leadership. Fritz Neugebauer (president); Bert Van Caelenberg (secretary-general)

2. International Federation Textile-Clothing (IFTC/FITH)
Address. Koning Albertlaan 27, B-9000 Gent, Belgium
Phone. +32 9 222 57 01
Fax. +32 9 220 45 59
E-mail. acv.csc.textura@acv-csc.be
Leadership. Dirk Uyttenhove (president); Jaap Jongejan (secretary-general)

3. International Federation of Trade Unions of Transport Workers (FIOST)
Address. Rue de Trèves 31-33, B-1040 Brussels, Belgium
Phone. +32 2 285 47 35
Fax. +32 2 230 87 22
E-mail. olga.nicolae@cmt-wcl.org
Leadership. Michel Bovy (president); Jaap van der Kamp (secretary-general)

4. World Confederation of Teachers (WCT/CSME)
Address. Rue de Trèves 45, B-1040 Brussels, Belgium
Phone. +32 2 285 47 35
Fax. +32 2 230 87 22
E-mail. wct@cmt-wcl.org
Website. www.wctcsme.org
Leadership. Claudio Corries (president); Gaston de la Haye (secretary-general)

5. World Federation of Agriculture, Food, Hotel and Allied Workers (FEMTAA/WFAFW)
Address. Rue de Trèves 31-33, B-1040 Brussels, Belgium
Phone. +32 2 285 47 35
Fax. +32 2 230 87 22

E-mail. olga.nicolae@cmt-wcl.org
Leadership. Carlas Ancizar (president); Timothee Boko (secretary-general)

6. World Federation of Building and Woodworkers' Unions (WFBW/FMCB)
Address. Rue de Trèves 31-33, B-1040 Brussels, Belgium
Phone. +32 2 285 0211
Fax. +32 2 230 74 43
E-mail. piet.nelissen@cmt-wcl.org
Website. www.wfbw-fmcb.org
Leadership. Jacky Jackers (president); Bert van der Spek (secretary-general)

7. World Federation of Clerical Workers (WFCW/FME)
Address. Rue de Trèves 31-33, B-1040 Brussels, Belgium
Phone. +32 2 285 47 35
Fax. +32 2 230 87 22
E-mail. olga.nicolae@cmt-wcl.org
Leadership. Roel Rotshuizen (president); Mogens Stig Nielsen (secretary general)

8. World Federation of Industry Workers (WFIW/FMTI)
Address. Rue de Trèves 31-33, B-1040 Brussels, Belgium
Phone. +32 2 285 47 33
Fax. +32 2 230 87 22
E-mail. piet.nelissen@cmt-wcl.org
Leadership. Bart Bruggeman (president); Italo Rodomonti (secretary-general)

National affiliates. The WCL reports that it has affiliates in the following countries or territories (details of most are included under individual country entries): Antigua; Argentina; Aruba; Austria; Bangladesh; Belgium; Belize; Benin; Bolivia; Brazil; Bulgaria; Burkina Faso; Cameroon; Canada; Central African Republic; Chad; Chile; China (Hong Kong); Colombia; Congo, Democratic Republic of; Congo, Republic of; Costa Rica; Côte d'Ivoire; Cuba; Cyprus; Czech Republic; Dominica; Dominican Republic; Ecuador; El Salvador; France; French Guiana; Gabon; Gambia; Ghana; Guadeloupe; Guatemala; Guinea; Guyana; Haiti; Honduras; Hungary; India; Indonesia; Iran; Italy; Kazakhstan; Liberia; Liechtenstein; Lithuania; Luxembourg; Macedonia; Madagascar; Malawi; Malaysia; Malta; Mauritania; Mauritius; Morocco; Namibia; Netherlands; Netherlands Antilles; Nicaragua; Niger; Pakistan; Panama; Paraguay; Peru; Philippines; Poland; Portugal; Puerto Rico; Romania; Rwanda; St. Lucia; St. Vincent; Sao Tome and Principe; Senegal; Serbia and Montenegro; Sierra Leone; Slovak Republic; South Africa; Spain; Sri Lanka; Switzerland; Suriname; Taiwan; Thailand; Togo; Trinidad; United States; Ukraine; Uruguay; Venezuela; Vietnam; Zambia; Zimbabwe.

World Federation of Trade Unions (WFTU)
Fédération Syndicale Mondiale (FSM)
Address. Branicka 112, Branik, 14701 Prague 4, Czech Republic
Phone. +42 2 4446 2140

Fax. +42 2 4446 1378
E-mail. wftu@login.cz
Website. www.wftu.cz
Leadership. K.L.Mahendra (president); Alexander Zharikov (secretary-general)
Membership. In 2004 WFTU claimed a membership of 129 million in more than 130 countries. This represented a considerable fall from the membership of 208 million which WFTU reported at its 12th Congress in 1990.
History and character. The WFTU was formed in 1945, as a reflection of the unity of purpose among the trade union centres in the countries of the anti-fascist coalition during World War II. It fractured in the Cold War period, most of the major Western trade union centres leaving to create the ICFTU in 1949. Those that remained in the WFTU after the split included the CGT (France), CGIL (Italy), AUCCTU (Soviet Union), CTC (Cuba), AITUC (India), and a number of centres in newly independent states of Asia, Africa, and Latin America as well as the communist states of Eastern Europe.

There have been major changes in the WFTU's composition over the decades. In the 1970s the Italian CGIL (along with the French CGT its most important Western affiliate), reflecting the shift of the Italian Communist Party (PCI) to Eurocommunism, downgraded its relationship with the WFTU and then left altogether in 1978. However, the basic Cold War polarization between the ICFTU and WFTU remained in place through to the beginning of the 1990s, when the situation was transformed by the collapse of communism in Eastern Europe and the dissolution of the Soviet Union. This led to the dissolution or breakaway of WFTU affiliates in much of the former Soviet bloc and the creation of new centres, mostly affiliating to the ICFTU. The French CGT, the main remaining bastion of the WFTU in the West, disaffiliated, while the movement of many one-party states in Africa to more pluralist forms of government also led to numerous affiliations to the ICFTU of centres which had previously been either unaffiliated at a global level or linked to the WFTU.

Since the early 1990s the WFTU has lost all significant influence in Europe, although a number of industrial federations are affiliated with the WFTU's associated trade union internationals (TUIs). It has no presence in North America (other than Mexico, where it has an industrial federation for the oil and energy sectors) and in Latin America, Africa and most of the Asia-Pacific region it has been eclipsed by the ICFTU. The Chinese ACFTU, the world's largest trade union centre, has not participated as an affiliate of the WFTU since the 1960s, although it has since 1994 attended the WFTU's 13th and 14th congresses as an observer. At the global level the WFTU remains divorced from the mainstream of trade unionism now clearly represented by the Global Unions group and by the growing level of cooperation between ICFTU and WCL. Although the WCL attended the WFTU's 14th congress (New Delhi, March 2000) as an observer, the ICFTU was not represented.

The 12th (Moscow, 1990), 13th (Damascus, 1994) and 2000 world congresses made changes in strategy, policy and structure to take account of the changing context in which the WFTU found itself. Past excessive centralization was heavily criticized and greater emphasis was placed on regional activity and the specific needs of industrial and service sectors. The 13th congress resolved that the WFTU was to become a "flexible, light and operational structure".

The reports presented at the 2000 congress attacked the impact of globalization, liberalization and privatization. Support was reiterated for the commitments and programme of action adopted by the World Summit for Social Development held in Copenhagen in 1995, including the commitment to take positive action to promote full employment. The report said that this programme had been nullified by the policies imposed by the IMF, World Bank and WTO. The WFTU called for the implementation of the UN Declaration for a New International Economic Order which was adopted by the UN General Assembly in 1974, upholding international economic cooperation based on equality of rights of all countries and an end to unequal trade and economic exchanges. The WFTU declared that the drive for neo-liberal globalization undermined the national sovereignty and economic independence of individual states while it introduced elements of neo-colonialism. Monopoly control of the information media, particularly the electronic media, was strongly criticised as transforming the emerging "information society" into a virtual "misinformation" society.

The detailed resolutions of the 14th congress, while reflecting shared concerns of the ICFTU and WCL with the impact of globalization and the general triumph of free markets, were perhaps most notable for the similarity with congresses prior to the collapse of communism. The "anti-capitalist" and "anti-imperialist" rhetoric and endorsement of states such as North Korea, Iraq and Yugoslavia in their "struggles", demonstrated the degree to which the WFTU remains ideologically unreconstructed and fundamentally hostile to the framework of beliefs espoused by the ICFTU and WCL. With the defection of former centres in the developed world, the WFTU has been left primarily as a representative of the monopoly trade union systems of one-party states and of mostly marginal left-wing centres elsewhere. Its roster of vice-presidents includes leaders of the trade unions of such countries as Cuba, Vietnam, North Korea, Libya and Syria. The WFTU accepts a contradiction between its own freedom of action and that of many of its affiliates. According to principles adopted at the 1994 congress, the WFTU's position is that: "as an international organization, and notwithstanding the relations established at national level by member organizations, the WFTU maintains its independence from governments, political parties and employers".

The ruling body is the congress, which last met in March 2000 after a six-year gap, and this elects the general council. The 15th congress has been scheduled for late 2005 to mark the 60th anniversary of the foundation of the WFTU. The general council is made up of representatives of the affiliated national centres and trade union internationals, and this meets between congresses, establishes plans of work, decides on the composition of the presidential council, and elects the general secretary, vice-presidents and secretaries as well as the auditing commission. The presidential council elects the president from among its members annually. The secretariat is composed of the secretary-general and deputy secretaries-general elected by the general council. The WFTU's trades union internationals (TUIs), covering specific industrial sectors, have been restructured in recent years and consolidated into six organizations.

Geneva office
Address. 10 rue Fendt, Geneva, Switzerland
Fax. +41 22 733 9435
Email. fsmgin@bluewin.ch
Leadership. Ramon Cardona Nuevo (deputy general secretary)
Regional offices. The WFTU has the following regional offices:

Asia
Address. 4 Windsor Place, New Delhi 110 001, India
Phone. +91 11 23311 829
Fax. +91 11 2311849
E-mail. wftuasiapacific@vsnl.net
Leadership. H. Mahadevan (deputy general secretary)

Africa
Address. Union des Travailleurs du Sénégal (UTS), Icotaf No. 2212, B.P. 7017, Pikine, Dakar, Senegal
Fax. +221 837 88 91
Email. uts@sunumail.sn
Leadership. Ibrahim Sylla (vice-president)

Americas
Address. Calle 190 No. 1306 entre 13 y 15, Siboney – Municipio Playa, C. De la Habana, Cuba
Phone. +53 7 294531
Fax. +53 7 335921
E-mail. secamfsm@ceniai.inf.cu
Leadership. Jose Ortiz (deputy general secretary)

Europe
Address. 28 Em. Benaki Str, 10678 Athens, Greece
Fax. +30 210 3302652
E-mail. info@eurof-wftu.gr
Leadership. George Mavrikos (vice president)

Middle East
Address. PO Box 30383, Damascus, Syria
Phone. +963 11 452513
Fax. +963 11 231 4212
E-mail. nassib-rezek@maktoob.com
Leadership. Nassib Rezek (director)

Trade union internationals. The WFTU has the following associated trades union internationals (TUIs):

1.TUI of Energy, Metal, Chemical, Oil and Allied Industries
Address. Antonio Caso No.45, Colonia Tabacalera, CP 06470 Mexico, D.F., Mexico
E-mail. uis-temqpia@sme.org.mx
Website. www.uis-ui.org
Leadership. Rosendo Flores (general secretary)

2. TUI of Agriculture, Food, Commerce, Textile and Allied Industries
Address. Case 428, 93514 Montreuil Cedex, France
Fax. +33 1 48 51 57 49
Leadership. Freddy Huck (president)

3. TUI of Workers in the Building, Wood and Building Materials Industries
Address. PO Box 281, 00101 Helsinki, Finland
Fax. +358 9 6931020
Leadership. J. Dinis (general secretary)
E-mail. info@uitbb.org

4. TUI of Public and Allied Employees
Address. 10A, Shankharitola Street, Calcutta 700014, India
Fax. +91 33 246 9593
E-mail. aisgef@cal2.vsnl.net.in
Website. www.tradeunionindia.org
Leadership. Sukomal Sen (general secretary)

5. World Federation of Teachers' Unions (FISE)
Address. 6/6 K. C. Ghose Road, Calcutta 700050, India
Fax. +91 33 557 1293
Email. fise1@vsnl.net
Leadership. Mrinmoy Bhattacharyya (general secretary)

6. TUI of Transport Workers
Address. PO Box B. 2361, Damascus, Syria
Phone. +963 11 339 900
Fax. +963 11 332 0743
Leadership. Nasser Zarif Mouhrez (president)

National affiliates. The following list shows affiliates reported by the WFTU in 2004. The list should not be regarded as in all respects reliable. In some instances these affiliates have little or no current organizational identity.
Angola: União Nacional dos Trabalhadores Angolanos (UNTA)
Argentina: Coordinadora Nacional de Agropaceres Agustin Tosco (CONAT); Movimiento Politico Sindical "Liberación" (MPSL)
Austria: Fraktion des Gewerkschaftlichen Linksblocks im ÖG B
Bahrain: Bahrain Workers' Union
Bangladesh: Bangladesh Trade Union Kendra (BTUK); Jatio Sramik Jote; Jatio Sramik League; Ganotantrik Sramik Federation; Jato Sramik Federation; Jatyo Sramik Jote Bangladesh; Socialist Labour Front
Belarus: Federation of Trade Unions of Belarus
Bolivia: Central Obrera Boliviana
Brazil: Central Geral dos Trabalhadores (CGT)
Bulgaria: National Council of Independent Trade Unions "EDINSTVO"
Burkina Faso: Union Syndicale des Travailleurs du Burkina
Cambodia: Cambodia Federation of Trade Unions
Colombia: Federación Nacional Sindical Unitaria Agropecuaria; Federación Nacional de Trabajadores de la Alimentacion, Bebidas, Afines y Sim.; Sindicato Unitario de

Trabajadores de la Industria de Materiales de Construccion
Congo, Democratic Republic of: Confédération Générale du Travail
Costa Rica: Confederación Unitaria de Trabajadores (CUT); Confederación de Trabajadores de Costa Rica; Asociacion de Servicios de Promocion Laboral; Sindicato de Trabajadores de la Universidad Nacional (SITUN); Union Nacional de Empleados de la Caja y la Seguridad Social (UNDECA)
Cuba: Central de Trabajadores de Cuba (CTC)
Cyprus: Pancyprian Federation of Labour
Czech Republic: Trade Union Association of Bohemia, Moravia and Silesia
Djibouti: Union Générale des Travailleurs de Djibouti
Dominican Republic: Corriente Unitaria de Trabajadores
Ecuador: Confederación de Trabajadores del Ecuador (CTE)
El Salvador: Federacion Unitaria Sindical de El Salvador; Sindicato Trabajadores del Instituto Salvadorean del Seguro Social (STISS)
Eritrea: General Union of Eritrean Workers
Ethiopia: Confederation of Ethiopian Trade Unions
French Guiana: Union des Travailleurs Guyanais
Greece: All Workers' Militant Front
Guadeloupe: Confédération Générale du Travail de la Guadeloupe
Guinea-Bissau: União Nacional dos Trabalhadores da Guiné-Bissau (UNTG)
Guyana: Guyana Agricultural and General Workers Union (GAWU)
Haiti: Centrale Générale des Travailleurs Haïtiens
Honduras: Federación Unitaria de Trabajadores de Honduras (FUTH)
India: All-India Trade Union Congress (AITUC); United Trade Union Centre (Lenin Sarani); United Trade Union Congress
Iran: Commission de Liaison des Syndicats Iraniens
Iraq: General Federation of Trade Unions of Iraq
Jamaica: Independent Trade Unions Action Council (ITAC); University and Allied Workers Union
Japan: WFTU Japanese affiliates council
North Korea: General Federation of Trade Unions of Korea
Kuwait: Kuwait Trade Union Federation
Laos: Fédération des Syndicats du Laos
Lebanon: Fédération Nationale des Syndicats des Ouvriers et des Employés du Liban (FENASOL)
Libya: General Federation of Producers in the Great Jamahiriya
Madagascar: Fédération des Syndicats des Travailleurs de Madagascar (FISEMA)
Martinique: General Workers' Federation
Mauritius: General Workers' Federation (GWF)
Mexico: Central Independiente de Obreros Agricolas y Campesinos; Union General de Obreros y Campesinos de Mexico "Jasinto Lopez"; Sindicato Mexicana de Electricistas; Sindicato Unico de Trabajadores de la Industria Nuclear; Union General Obrera y Campesina de Mexico
Nepal: Nepal Trade Union Federation
New Caledonia: Confédération Syndicale de Nouvelle Calédonie, Maison des Syndicats; Union des Syndicats des Travailleurs Kanaks et Exploités
Oman: National Committee of Omani Workers
Pakistan: All-Pakistan Federation of Labour (Durrani Group); All-Pakistan Trade Union Organization; Pakistan Trade Union Federation (PTUF); All-Pakistan Trade Union Federation (APTUF); Pakistan National Federation of Trade Unions (Malik Group); Pakistan National Federation of Trade Unions; All Pakistan Federation of United Trade Unions
Palestine: Palestine Trade Union Federation
Panama: Central Nacional de Trabajadores de Panama (CNTP)
Peru: Confederación General de Trabajadores del Péru (CGTP)
Philippines: National Association of Trade Unions (NATU); Trade Unions of Philippines and Allied Services (TUPAS); National Congress of Workers (KATIPUNAN); National Congress of Workers (Kalookan)
Poland: Federacja Spoldzielczch Zwiaskow Zawodowych
Puerto Rico: Union General de Trabajadores
Réunion: Confédération Générale du Travail de la Réunion
Russia: Central Committee of the Trade Unions of Workers in Agro-Industrial Complexes
St. Vincent and the Grenadines: Progressive Trade Union Centre
Saudi Arabia: Workers' Union of Saudi Arabia
Senegal: Union des Travailleurs du Sénégal (UTLS)
Solomon Islands: Solomon Islands National Union of Workers (SINUW)
Sri Lanka: Ceylon Federation of Trade Unions; Sri Lanka Mahajana Trade Union Federation; Sri Lanka Nidakas Sewaka Sangamaya; Central Council of Ceylon Trade Unions (CCTU)
Sudan: Federation of Sudanese Professionals and Technicians Trade Union; Trade Union Front of Sudan; Sudan Workers' Trade Union Federation
Syria: General Federation of Trade Unions
Togo: Union Générale des Syndicats Libres
Trinidad and Tobago: Council of Progressive Trade Unions
Uruguay: Sindicatos UIS-FSM
Venezuela: Central Unitaria de Trabajadores de Venezuela (CUTV)
Vietnam: Vietnam General Confederation of Labour
Western Sahara: UGTSARIO

INDEX OF TRADE UNIONS

Index page references are to the main heading in directory listings

Accord (UK) 366
ACFTU (China) 69
ACLVB (Belgium) 31
Action Sociale (France) 121
Actors' Equity Association (USA) 380
ACTU (Australia) 12
ACV (Belgium) 31
ADEDY (Greece) 139
ADLV (Vatican City) 391
Administration Générale de l'Etat (France) 121
AEU (Australia) 13
AFA (USA) 381
AFGE (USA) 380
AFITU (Serbia-Montenegro) 297
AFL-CIO (USA) 377
AFM (USA) 380
AFRO (International) 405
AFSCME (USA) 380
AFT (USA) 380
AFTRA (USA) 380
Agrifack (Sweden) 331
AIMPE (Australia) 14
Air Botswana Employees' Union 43
Air Line Pilots Association, International (USA) 380
AITUC (India) 154
Akademikerförbundet SSR (Sweden) 331
Akademikerne (Norway) 252
Akademikernes Centralorganisation (Denmark) 90
AKAVA (Finland) 110
AKT (Finland) 111
ALAEA (Australia) 14
Alberta Federation of Labour 59
Algemeen Belgisch Vakverbond (Belgium) 33
Algemeen Christelijk Vakverbond (Belgium) 31
Algemeen Verbond van Vakverenigingen in Suriname 'De Moederbond' 323
Algemene Centrale der Liberale Vakbonden (Belgium) 31
Algemene Onderwijsbond (Netherlands) 238
All Japan Federation of Transport Workers' Unions 182
All Japan Postal Labour Union 182
All Nepal Federation of Trade Unions 234
All Trinidad Sugar and General Workers' Trade Union 346
All-China Federation of Trade Unions 69
All-India Trade Union Congress 154
All-Japan Prefectural and Municipal Workers' Union 181
All-Pakistan Federation of Labour 258
All-Pakistan Federation of Trade Unions 258
All-Pakistan Federation of United Trade Unions 258
All-Pakistan Trade Union Congress 259

All-Pakistan Trade Union Federation 259
All-Poland Alliance of Trade Unions 274
All-Russian Confederation of Labour 288
ALPA (USA) 380
Althydusamband Íslands (Iceland) 151
Amalgamated Transit Union (USA) 380
Amalgamated Transport and General Workers' Union (Ireland) 163
Amalgamated Workers Union (Northern) (New Zealand) 242
Amalgamated Workers Union (Southern) (New Zealand) 245
AMEA (New Zealand) 245
American Federation of Government Employees 380
American Federation of Labor - Congress of Industrial Organizations (USA) 377
American Federation of Musicians (USA) 380
American Federation of State, County and Municipal Employees (USA) 380
American Federation of Teachers (USA) 380
American Federation of Television and Radio Artists (USA) 380
American Postal Workers' Union (USA) 380
Amicus (Ireland) 165
Amicus (UK) 366
AMIEU (Australia) 13
AMOU (Australia) 14
AMWU (Australia) 14
ANF (Australia) 14
ANG (Austria) 20
Antigua and Barbuda Public Service Association 8
Antigua Trades and Labour Union 8
Antigua Workers' Union 8
AOB (Netherlands) 238
APESMA (Australia) 13
APFOL (Pakistan) 258
APFTU (Pakistan) 258
APFUTU (Pakistan) 258
APTUC (Pakistan) 259
APTUF (Pakistan) 259
APWU (USA) 380
Arkitekter (Sweden) 331
Aruban Workers' Federation 239
Asbestos Workers (USA) 381
ASÍ (Iceland) 151
ASLEF (UK) 366
ASMOF (Australia) 14
ASMS (New Zealand) 242
ASNS (Serbia-Montenegro) 297
Asocijacija Slobodnih i Nezavisnih Sindikata (Serbia-Montenegro) 297
Associated Actors and Artists of America (USA) 380
Associated Society of Locomotive Engineers and Firemen (UK) 366
Association of Croatian Public Sector Unions 83

Association of Danish Lawyers and Economists 91
Association of Flight Attendants (USA) 381
Association of Free and Independent Trade Unions (Serbia-Montenegro) 297
Association of Free Trade Unions of Slovenia 307
Association of Professional Engineers, Scientists and Managers, Australia 13
Association of Salaried Medical Specialists (New Zealand) 242
Association of Secondary Teachers, Ireland 165
Association of Staff in Tertiary Education (New Zealand) 242
Association of Teachers and Lecturers (UK) 366
Association of University Staff of New Zealand Inc 243
Association of University Teachers (UK) 366
Association of Vatican Lay Workers 391
Associazione Dipendenti Laici Vaticani 391
ASTE - Te Hau Takitini O Aotearoa (New Zealand) 242
ASU (Australia) 14
ASU (Uruguay) 390
ASzSz (Hungary) 149
ATL (UK) 366
ATLU (Antigua) 8
ATS/GWTU (Trinidad and Tobago) 346
ATU (USA) 380
ATUC (Azerbaijan) 21
AUS (New Zealand) 243
Australasian Meat Industry Employees' Union 13
Australian Council of Trade Unions 12
Australian Education Union 13
Australian Institute of Marine and Power Engineers 14
Australian Licensed Aircraft Engineers' Association 14
Australian Manufacturing Workers' Union 14
Australian Maritime Officers' Union 14
Australian Nursing Federation 14
Australian Professional Footballers' Association 14
Australian Salaried Medical Officers' Federation 14
Australian Services Union 14
Australian Workers' Union 14
Australian Writers Guild 14
Austrian Federation of Trade Unions 19
AUT (UK) 366
Autonóm Szakszervezetek Szövetsége (Hungary) 149
Autonomous Trade Union Confederation (Hungary) 149
Autonomous Trade Unions Centre (Benin) 35

INDEX

Aviation & Marine Engineers Association (New Zealand) 245
AVVS (Suriname) 323
AWG (Australia) 14
AWIU (USA) 381
AWU (Antigua) 8
AWU (Australia) 14
AWUNZ Northern (New Zealand) 242
AWUNZ Southern (New Zealand) 245
Azerbaijan Trade Unions Confederation 21

BAC (USA) 384
Bahrain Workers' Union 23
Bakers, Food and Allied Workers' Union (UK) 367
Bakers' & Pastrycooks' Union (New Zealand) 245
Bakery, Confectionery, Tobacco Workers and Grain Millers' International Union (USA) 381
Baltic Sea Trade Union Network 400
Bandalag Starfsmanna Rikis og Baeja (Iceland) 151
Bangladesh Free Trade Union Congress 25
Bangladesh Ganotantrik Sramik Federation 25
Bangladesh Jatio Sramik League 26
Bangladesh Jatyatabadi Sramik Dal 26
Bangladesh Jatyo Sramik Jote 26
Bangladesh Labour Federation 26
Bangladesh Mukto Sramik Federation 26
Bangladesh Sanjunkta Sramic Federation 26
Bangladesh Trade Union Kendra 26
Bank and Finance Employees' Union (Sweden) 334
Banking and Insurance Union (Netherlands) 239
Barbados Workers' Union 27
Basque Workers' Solidarity (Spain) 319
BASTUN (International) 400
Bâtiment et Industrie (Belgium) 32
Bâtiment-Travaux Publics, Bois, Céramique, Papier Carton -Matériaux de Construction (France) 121
BATU (International) 411
BBEIUW (WA)) (Australia) 15
BBV (Netherlands) 239
BCTGM (USA) 381
BECTU (UK) 367
Belarus Free Trade Union 29
Belarusian Congress of Democratic Trade Unions 29
Bermuda Industrial Union 371
Bermuda Public Services Association 371
Bermuda Trade Union Congress 372
Beroepsorganisatie Banken en Verzekeringen (Netherlands) 239
BFAWU (UK) 367
BFTU (Botswana) 41
BFTUC (Bangladesh) 25
Bharatiya Mazdoor Sangh (India) 155
BIU (Bermuda) 371
BJSL (Bangladesh) 26
BLE (USA) 381

Blind Workers' Union of Victoria 15
Blocul National Sindical (Romania) 282
BMS (India) 155
BMWE (USA) 381
BNS (Romania) 282
Bolivian Workers' Central 38
Bonaire Federation of Labour (Netherlands Antilles) 239
Botswana Agricultural Marketing Board Workers' Union 42
Botswana Bank Employees' Union 42
Botswana Beverages & Allied Workers' Union 42
Botswana Commercial & General Workers' Union 42
Botswana Construction Wood Workers' Union 42
Botswana Diamond Sorters & Valuators' Union 42
Botswana Federation of Trade Unions 41
Botswana Hotel Travel & Tourism Workers' Union 43
Botswana Housing Corporation Staff Union 42
Botswana Manufacturing & Packaging Workers' Union 42
Botswana Meat Industry Workers' Union 42
Botswana Mining Workers' Union 42
Botswana Postal Services Workers' Union 42
Botswana Power Corporation Workers' Union 42
Botswana Private Medical & Health Services Workers' Union 42
Botswana Railways Amalgamated Workers' Union 42
Botswana Saving Bank Employees' Union 43
Botswana Telecommunication Employees' Union 42
Botswana Vaccine Institute Staff Union 42
Botswana Wholesale, Furniture & Retail Workers' Union 42
BPSA (Bermuda) 371
Breweries and Bottleyards Employees' Industrial Union of Workers WA 15
British Columbia Federation of Labour 59
Broadcasting, Entertainment, Cinematograph and Theatre Union (UK) 367
Brotherhood of Asian Trade Unionists 411
Brotherhood of Locomotive Engineers (USA) 381
Brotherhood of Maintenance of Way Employees (USA) 381
Brotherhood of Railroad Signalmen (USA) 381
BRS (USA) 381
BSPK (Serbia - Kosovo) 298
BSPSh (Albania) 2
BSRB (Iceland) 151
BSSF (Bangladesh) 26
BTU (New Zealand) 243
Building and Allied Trades Union (Ireland) 163

Building Maintenance Workers' Union (Sweden) 329
Building Workers' Union (Sweden) 329
BUPL (Denmark) 91
Bustamante Industrial Trade Union (Jamaica) 176
BWU (Australia) 15
BWU (Barbados) 27
Byggnads (Sweden) 329

C-47 (Suriname) 324
California School Employees' Association (USA) 381
Canadian Auto Workers 58
Canadian Federation of Nurses' Unions 58
Canadian Labour Congress 57
Canadian Teachers' Federation 60
Canadian Union of Postal Workers 58
Canadian Union of Public Employees 58
CANZ (New Zealand) 243
CAOOAA (Australia) 15
Caribbean Congress of Labour 400
CASC (Dominican Republic) 96
CAT (Brazil) 46
CAT (Chile) 66
CATC (Congo, Republic of) 77
CATP (Peru) 265
CATS (El Salvador) 103
CATU (UK) 367
CATUS (Serbia-Montenegro) 297
CAW (Canada) 58
CBTC (Brazil) 46
CBTUC (Bahamas) 22
CCAS (Argentina) 10
CCAS (Belgium) 32
CCL (International) 400
CCMECC-CSC (Belgium) 32
CCOO (Spain) 317
CCPET-CSC (Belgium) 33
CCSL (Cape Verde) 61
CCTU (Cameroon) 54
CDLS (San Marino) 293
CDT (Congo, Democratic Republic) 76
CDT (Morocco) 224
CDTN (Niger) 247
CEDOC (Ecuador) 99
CEMNL (Belgium) 33
Central Autónoma de Trabajadores (Chile) 66
Central Autónoma de Trabajadores del Peru 265
Central Autónoma de Trabajadores Salvadoreños 103
Central Autónoma de Trabalhadores (Brazil) 46
Central Bank Union (Botswana) 42
Central de Trabajadores Argentinos 10
Central de Trabajadores de Costa Rica 79
Central de Trabajadores de Cuba 84
Central de Trabajadores Democráticos (El Salvador) 103
Central de Trabajadores Nicaragüenses 246
Central del Movimiento de Trabajadores Costarricenses 79

418

INDEX

Central des Syndicats Autonomes du Bénin 35
Central Ecuatoriana de Organizaciones Clasistas 99
Central General de Trabajadores (Dominican Republic) 96
Central General de Trabajadores (Honduras) 147
Central General de Trabajadores de Guatemala 142
Central General di Trahadonan di Corsow (Netherlands Antilles) 239
Central Geral de Sindicatos Independentes e Livres de Angola 7
Central Latinoamericana de Trabajadores 411
Central Nacional de Trabajadores (Paraguay) 263
Central National de Trabajadores de Panama 261
Central Obrera Boliviana 38
Central Organization of Finnish Trade Unions 111
Central Organization of Trade Unions (Kenya) 188
Central Sandinista de Trabajadores (Nicaragua) 246
Central Única dos Trabalhadores (Brazil) 45
Central Union of Workers (Colombia) 74
Central Unitaria de Trabajadores (Chile) 66
Central Unitaria de Trabajadores (Colombia) 74
Central Unitaria de Trabajadores (Paraguay) 264
Centrale Chrétienne de l'Alimentation et des Services (Belgium) 32
Centrale Chrétienne des Communications et de la Culture (Belgium) 32
Centrale Chrétienne des Mines, de l'Energie, de la Chimie et du Cuir (Belgium) 32
Centrale Chrétienne des Professeurs de l'Enseignement moyen et normal libre (Belgium) 33
Centrale Chrétienne des Services Publics (Belgium) 32
Centrale Chrétienne du personnel de l'Enseignement technique (Belgium) 33
Centrale de l'Alimentation-Horeca-Services (Belgium) 34
Centrale des Syndicats Démocratiques 60
Centrale des syndicats du Québec 60
Centrale des Syndicats Libres de Côte d'Ivoire 81
Centrale du Métal (Belgium) 33
Centrale du Textile, Vêtement, Diamant (Belgium) 34
Centrale Générale (Belgium) 33
Centrale Générale des Services Publics (Belgium) 34
Centrale Générale des Syndicats Libéraux de Belgique 31
Centrale Nationale des Employés et Cadres (Belgium) 32
Centrale Syndicale des Travailleurs du Rwanda 289
Centrale van Landsdienaren Organisaties (Suriname) 324
Centrale van Middelbare en Hogere Functionarissen (Netherlands) 239
Centre of Indian Trade Unions 155
CEOSL (Ecuador) 99
CEP (Canada) 58
CEPPWAWU (South Africa) 314
CEPU (Australia) 15
Ceramic and Allied Trades Union (UK) 367
CES (International) 401
CESI (International) 400
CESTRAR (Rwanda) 289
CETU (Ethiopia) 107
Ceylon Workers' Congress (Sri Lanka) 321
CF (Sweden) 331
CFDT (France) 116
CFDT cadres (France) 118
CFE-CGC (France) 118
CFL (Taiwan) 340
CFMEU (Australia) 15
CFNU (Canada) 58
CFTC (France) 118
CFTUI (India) 156
CFTUK (Kazakhstan) 186
CGB (Germany) 134
CGIL (Italy) 172
CGSI (Guinea-Bissau) 144
CGSILA (Angola) 7
CGSL (Gabon) 124
CGSLB (Belgium) 31
CGT (Argentina) 9
CGT (Brazil) 45
CGT (Dominican Republic) 96
CGT (France) 119
CGT (Honduras) 147
CGTB (Benin) 36
CGTC (Netherlands Antilles) 239
CGTD (Colombia) 74
CGT-FO (France) 120
CGTG (Guatemala) 142
CGTL (Lebanon) 197
CGT-L (Luxembourg) 204
CGTLC (Cameroon) 54
CGTM (Mauritania) 215
CGT-Moyano 10
CGTP (Panama) 261
CGTP (Peru) 265
CGTP- IN (Portugal) 277
Chartered Society of Physiotherapy (UK) 367
Chemical Workers' Union (Finland) 112
Chemical Workers' Union (New Zealand) 245
Chemical, Energy, Paper, Printing, Wood and Allied Workers' Union (South Africa) 314
Cheminots (France) 121
Chinese Federation of Labour (Taiwan) 340
Christelijk Nationaal Vakverbond (Netherlands) 236
Christelijk Onderwijzers Verbond (Belgium) 33
Christelijke Onderwijs Centrale (Belgium) 33
Christian Confederation of Malagasy Trade Unions (Madagascar) 207
Christian Labour Association of Canada 60
Christian Labour Confederation (Czech Republic) 89
Christian Workers' Union (Belize) 35
Christlicher Gewerkschaftsbund Deutschlands (Germany) 134
CIF (International) 400
CIOSL (International) 403
CISAL (Italy) 175
CISL (International) 403
CISL (Italy) 173
CITU (India) 155
CITUB (Bulgaria) 49
CITUM (Serbia-Montenegro) 298
Civil Air Operations Officers Association of Australia 15
Civil and Public Service Union (Ireland) 163
Civil Servants' Confederation (Greece) 139
Civilekonomerna (Sweden) 331
Civilingenjörsförbundet (Sweden) 331
CLAC (Canada) 60
CLAT (International) 411
CLAW (New Zealand) 243
CLC (Canada) 57
CLK (Kazakhstan) 186
CLO (Suriname) 324
Clothing, Laundry and Allied Workers Union of Aotearoa (New Zealand) 243
CLTM (Mauritania) 216
CLTT (Chad) 64
Club Managers' Association Australia 15
CMAA (Australia) 15
CMHF (Netherlands) 239
CMKOS (Czech Republic) 88
CMT (International) 410
CMTC (Costa Rica) 79
CMTU (Malta) 213
CMTU (Mongolia) 223
CNE (Belgium) 32
CNS Cartel Alfa (Romania) 283
CNSLR-Fratia (Romania) 282
CNT (Niger) 247
CNT (Paraguay) 263
CNTB (Burkina) 51
CNTC (Central African Republic) 63
CNTD (Dominican Republic) 96
CNTG (Guinea) 143
CNTS (Senegal) 295
CNTT (Togo) 344
CNV (Netherlands) 236
CNV Bedrijvenbond (Netherlands) 237
CNV Publieke Zaak (Netherlands) 236
COB (Bolivia) 38
Cobas (Italy) 174
COC (Belgium) 33
Coiffure, Esthetique et Parfumier (France) 121

INDEX

COIWRP 22
COLETU (Lesotho) 199
COMATU (Malawi) 208
Comedia (Swiss Media Union) 336
Commerce, Transport and Food Workers (Switzerland) 337
Commercial Employees' Union (Sweden) 329
Commercial, Technical and Allied Workers' Union (St Vincent) 291
Committee for Oil Industry Workers' Rights Protection 22
Commonwealth of the Bahamas Trade Union Congress 22
Commonwealth Trade Union Council 400
Communication Workers of America 381
Communication Workers' Union (Ireland) 164
Communication Workers' Union (South Africa) 314
Communication Workers' Union (Switzerland) 337
Communication Workers' Union (UK) 367
Communications, Electrical and Plumbing Union of Australia 15
Communications, Energy and Paperworkers' Union of Canada 58
Community (UK) 367
Community and Public Sector Union (Australia) 15
Confederação Brasileira de Trabalhadores Cristâos (Brazil) 46
Confederação Geral dos Sindicatos Independentes 144
Confederação Geral dos Trabalhadores (Brazil) 45
Confederação Geral dos Trabalhadores Portugueses - Intersindical Nacional 277
Confederaçãodos Sindicatos Independentes e Livres de Moçambique 228
Confederación Autónoma Sindical Clasista (Dominican Republic) 96
Confederación Costarricense de Trabajadores (Rerum Novarum) 80
Confederación de Trabajadores de Colombia 74
Confederación de Trabajadores de Costa Rica 80
Confederación de Trabajadores de Honduras 148
Confederación de Trabajadores de la República de Panamá 261
Confederación de Trabajadores de México 219
Confederación de Trabajadores de Venezuela 393
Confederación de Trabajadores del Ecuador 99
Confederación de Trabajadores Unitaria (Dominican Republic) 97
Confederación de Trahajadores del Perú 265
Confederación de Unidad Sindical de Guatemala 141
Confederación de Unificación Sindical (Nicaragua) 247
Confederación Ecuatoriana de Organizaciones Sindicales Libres 99
Confederación General de Trabajadores de Panamá 261
Confederación General de Trabajadores del Peru 265
Confederación General de Trabajadores Democráticos (Colombia) 74
Confederación General del Trabajo (Spain) 319
Confederación General del Trabajo de la República Argentina 9
Confederación General del Trabajo-Moyano 10
Confederación Internacional de Organizaciones Sindicales Libres 403
Confederación Mundial del Trabajo 410
Confederación Nacional de Trabajadores Dominicanos 96
Confederación Paraguaya de Trabajadores 264
Confederación Revolucionaria de Obreros y Campesinos (Mexico) 220
Confederación Sindical de Comisiones Obreras (Spain) 317
Confederación Sindical de los Trabajores Campesinos de Bolivia 38
Confederación Unitaria de Trabajadores (Costa Rica) 80
Confederación Unitaria de Trabajadores de Honduras 148
Confederación Unitaria de Trabajadores del Perú 265
Confederatia Nationala A Sindicatelor Libere Din Romania - Fratia 282
Confederatia Nationala Sindicala "Cartel Alfa" (Romania) 283
Confederatia Sindicatelor din Republica Moldova 221
Confédération Africaine des Travailleurs Croyants (Congo, Republic of) 77
Confédération Démocratique des Travailleurs du Niger 247
Confédération Démocratique du Travail (Congo, Democratic Republic) 76
Confédération Démocratique du Travail (Morocco) 224
Confédération des Syndicats Chrétiens (Belgium) 31
Confédération des Syndicats Démocratiques de Roumanie 282
Confédération des Syndicats du Burundi 52
Confédération des Syndicats Libres (France) 122
Confédération des Syndicats Libres Autonomes du Congo 78
Confédération des Syndicats Nationaux (Canada) 60
Confédération Européene des Syndicats 401
Confédération Européene des Syndicats Indépendants 400
Confederation Française de L'Encadrement CGC 118
Confédération Française Démocratique du Travail 116
Confédération Française des Travailleurs Chrétiens 118
Confédération Gabonaise des Syndicats Libres Gabonese 124
Confédération Générale des Travaillaurs du Bénin 36
Confédération Générale des Travailleurs de Mauritanie 215
Confédération Générale des Travailleurs du Liban (Lebanon) 197
Confederation Générale du Travail - Force Ouvrière (France) 120
Confédération Générale du Travail (France) 119
Confédération Générale du Travail du Congo 76
Confédération Générale du Travail du Luxembourg 204
Confédération Internationale des Fonctionnaires 400
Confédération Internationale des Syndicats Libres 403
Confédération Libre des Travailleurs de Mauritanie 216
Confédération Libre des Travailleurs du Tchad 64
Confédération Mondiale du Travail 410
Confédération Nationale des Travailleurs de Centrafrique 63
Confédération Nationale des Travailleurs de Guinée 143
Confédération Nationale des Travailleurs du Burkina 51
Confédération Nationale des Travailleurs du Togo 344
Confédération Nationale des Travailleurs Sénégalais 295
Confédération Nigérienne du Travail (Niger) 247
Confédération Syndicale des Travailleurs du Mali 212
Confederation of All Indonesian Workers' Union 159
Confederation of Autonomous Trade Unions of Serbia 297
Confederation of Burundi Unions 52
Confederation of Cameroon Trade Unions 54
Confederation of Christian Trade Unions (Belgium) 31
Confederation of Electric Power Related Industry Workers' Unions of Japan 182
Confederation of Estonian Trade Unions 105
Confederation of Ethiopian Trade Unions 107
Confederation of Free and Independent Unions of Mozambique 228
Confederation of Free Trade Unions (France) 122

INDEX

Confederation of Free Trade Unions of India 156
Confederation of Free Trade Unions of Kazakhstan 186
Confederation of Free Trade Unions of Ukraine 358
Confederation of Higher Education Unions (Norway) 255
Confederation of Independent Trade Unions of Bosnia and Herzegovina 39
Confederation of Independent Trade Unions of Bulgaria 49
Confederation of Independent Trade Unions of Kosova 298
Confederation of Independent Trade Unions of Montenegro 298
Confederation of Indonesia Prosperous Labour Union 158
Confederation of Japan Automobile Workers' Unions 181
Confederation of Labour "Podkrepa" (Bulgaria) 49
Confederation of Labour of Kazakhstan 186
Confederation of Labour of Russia 288
Confederation of Labour Unification (Nicaragua) 247
Confederation of Malagasy Workers (Madagascar) 206
Confederation of Malta Trade Unions 213
Confederation of Mexican Workers 219
Confederation of Mongolian Trade Unions 223
Confederation of New Trade Unions of Slovenia "Independence" 306
Confederation of Progressive Trade Unions of Turkey 352
Confederation of Public Workers' Unions (Turkey) 354
Confederation of South African Workers' Unions 314
Confederation of State and Municipal Employees of Iceland 151
Confederation of Trade Unions (Albania) 3
Confederation of Trade Unions '90 of Slovenia 307
Confederation of Trade Unions of Armenia 10
Confederation of Trade Unions of Slovenia - Pergam 306
Confederation of Trade Unions of the Republic of Moldova 221
Confederation of Trade Unions of the Republika Srpska 40
Confederation of Trade Unions of the Slovak Republic 304
Confederation of Turkish Real Trade Unions 353
Confederation of Turkish Trade Unions 354
Confederation of Unions for Academic Professionals in Finland 110
Confederation of Vocational Unions (Norway) 255

Confederation of Workers of Colombia 74
Confederation of Workers of the Republic of Panama 261
Confédération Syndical des Travailleurs du Cameroun 54
Confédération Syndicale Burkinabe 51
Confédération Syndicale Congolaise (Congo, Republic of) 77
Confédération Syndicale des Travailleurs de Centrafrique 63
Confédération Syndicale des Travailleurs du Congo (Congo, Republic of) 78
Confédération Syndicale des Travailleurs du Togo 345
Confédération Syndicale du Congo 76
Confédération Syndicale Gabonaise 124
Confederazione del Comitati di Base (Italy) 174
Confederazione Democratica dei Lavoratori Sammarinesi (San Marino) 293
Confederazione Generale Italiana del Lavoro 172
Confederazione Italiana Sindacati Autonomi Lavoratori 175
Confederazione Italiana Sindacati Lavoratori 173
Confederazione Sammarinese del Lavoro (San Marino) 293
Conferência Cabo-Verdiana de Sindicatos Livres 61
Congolese Trade Union Confederation (Congo, Republic of) 77
Congrès du Travail du Canada 57
Congress of Lesotho Trade Unions 199
Congress of Malawi Trade Unions 208
Congress of South African Trade Unions 312
Congress of Unions of Employees in the Public and Civil Services (Malaysia) 211
Connect: The Union for Professionals in Communications (UK) 367
CONSAWU (South Africa) 314
Consejo Coordinador Argentino Sindical 10
CONSILMO (Mozambique) 228
Construction Trade Union (Finland) 111
Construction, Forestry, Mining and Engineering Union (Australia) 15
Convergencia Sindical (Panama) 261
Coordination Syndical Haitien 147
Corrections Association of New Zealand 243
Corriente de Renovación Independiente y Solidaridad Laboral (Bolivia) 38
Corriente Unitaria de Trabajadores (Dominican Republic) 97
COSATU (South Africa) 312
Costa Rican Confederation of Workers 80
COSYBU (Burundi) 52
COSYGA (Gabon) 124
COSYLAC (Congo, Republic of) 78
COTU (Kenya) 188
Council of Free Labour Unions (Cape Verde) 61
Council of Nordic Trade Unions 400
COV (Belgium) 33

CPSU (Australia) 15
CPT (Paraguay) 264
CRISOL (Bolivia) 38
Croatian Association of Trade Unions 83
CSA (Benin) 35
CSB (Burkina) 51
CSC (Belgium) 31
CSC (Congo, Democratic Republic) 76
CSC (Congo, Republic of) 77
CSC Textura 32
CSC-CCSP (Belgium) 32
CSD (Canada) 60
CSdL (San Marino) 293
CSDR (Romania) 282
CSEE (International) 402
CSL (France) 122
CSME (International) 412
CSN (Canada) 60
CSP (UK) 367
CSQ (Canada) 60
CSRM (Moldova) 221
CST (Nicaragua) 246
CSTC (Cameroon) 54
CSTC (Central African Republic) 63
CSTC (Congo, Republic of) 78
CSTM (Mali) 212
CSTT (Togo) 345
CTAWU (St Vincent) 291
CTC (Canada) 57
CTC (Colombia) 74
CTC (Cuba) 84
CTD (El Salvador) 103
CTE (Ecuador) 99
CTF (Canada) 60
CTH (Honduras) 148
CTM (Mexico) 219
CTN (Nicaragua) 246
CTP (Peru) 265
CTRN (Costa Rica) 80
CTRP (Panama) 261
CTU (Dominican Republic) 97
CTUC (International) 400
CTV (Venezuela) 393
Cuban Workers' Solidarity 84
CUEPACS (Malaysia) 211
Cuirs, Textiles-Habillement (France) 121
CUPE (Canada) 58
CUPW (Canada) 58
CUS (Nicaragua) 247
CUSG (Guatemala) 141
CUT (Brazil) 45
CUT (Chile) 66
CUT (Colombia) 74
CUT (Paraguay) 264
CUT (Peru) 265
CUTH (Honduras) 148
CWA (USA) 381
CWC (Sri Lanka) 321
CWU (Belize) 35
CWU (South Africa) 314
CWU (UK) 367
Cyprus Turkish Trade Unions Federation 86
Cyprus Union of Bank Employees 86

INDEX

Czech - Moravian Confederation of Trade Unions 88

Dairy Workers' Union (New Zealand) 243
Danish Association of Masters and PhDs 91
Danish Confederation of Professional Associations 90
Danish Confederation of Trade Unions 91
Danish Financial Services Union 91
Danish Food and Allied Workers' Union 93
Danish Medical Association 91
Danish Nurses' Union 91
Danish Pre-School Teachers' Union 91
Danish Timber Industry and Construction Workers' Union 93
Danish Union of Metalworkers 93
Danish Union of Professional Technicians 93
Danish Union of Public Employees 93
Danish Union of Teachers 91
Dansk Metalarbejderforbund (Denmark) 93
DAWU (Dominica) 95
DBB (Germany) 135
DECONT (Nepal) 233
Défense, Industries de l'Armament et Secteurs Assimilés (France) 122
Democratic Confederation of Labour (Morocco) 224
Democratic Confederation of Nepalese Trade Unions 233
Democratic Confederation of San Marino Workers 293
Democratic Confederation of Workers of Niger 247
Democratic Federation of Labour (Morocco) 225
Democratic Labour Federation of Cyprus 85
Democratic Nurses Organisation of South Africa 314
Democratic Organization of African Workers' Trade Unions 411
Democratic Trade Union Confederation of Romania 282
Democratic Union of Senegalese Workers 295
Demokratiki Ergatiki Omospondia Kyprou 85
Denki Rengo (Japan) 181
Denryoku Soren (Japan) 182
DEOK (Cyprus) 85
Deutscher Beamtenbund 135
Deutscher Gewerkschaftsbund 131
DEV-IS (Cyprus) 86
DGB (Germany) 131
Dienstenbond CNV (Netherlands) 237
Dignité (Côte d'Ivoire) 81
DIK-förbundet (Sweden) 331
DISK (Turkey) 352
DLF (Denmark) 91
DOAWTU (International) 411
Dominica Amalgamated Workers' Union 95
Dominica Public Service Union 95
Dominica Trade Union 95
DSR (Denmark) 91

DTU (Dominica) 95
DUP (Austria) 20
Dutch Airline Pilots' Association 239

EAKL (Estonia) 105
East Timor Trade Union Confederation 97
Ecuador Confederation of Free Trade Union Organizations 99
Education International 406
Educational Institute of Scotland (UK) 367
EEA (International) 401
EFBWW (International) 401
EFFAT (International) 401
EFJ (International) 402
Egyptian Trade Union Federation 101
EI (International) 406
EIS (UK) 367
EL & IT Forbundet (Norway) 254
ELA/STV (Spain) 319
Electricians' Union (Sweden) 329
EMB (International) 402
EMCEF (International) 402
EMF (International) 402
Employés et Cadres (France) 121
Energie, Electrique et Gaz (France) 122
Engineering, Printing and Manufacturing Union (New Zealand) 243
Enseignement, Culture et Formation Professionelle (France) 121
EPMU (New Zealand) 243
EPSU (International) 402
Equipement des transports et des services (France) 122
Equity (UK) 367
Estonian Employees' Unions' Confederation 106
ETA (Ethiopia) 107
ETF (International) 402
Ethiopian Teachers' Association 107
ETUC (International) 401
ETUCE (International) 402
ETUF (Egypt) 101
ETYK (Cyprus) 86
European Alliance of Media and Entertainment 401
European Confederation of Independent Trade Unions 400
European Federation of Building and Wood Workers 401
European Federation of Food, Agriculture and Tourism Trade Unions 401
European Federation of Journalists 402
European Federation of Public Service Unions 402
European Metalworkers' Federation 402
European Mine, Chemical and Energy Workers' Federation 402
European Trade Union Committee for Education 402
European Trade Union Confederation 401
European Transport Workers' Federation 402
Euzko Langilleen Alkarasuna/Solidaridad de Trabajadores Vascos (Spain) 319

F&AI (Australia) 15
FAAA (Australia) 15
Fagforbundet (Norway) 254
Fagligt Faelles Forbund 93
FARSA (New Zealand) 243
Fastighets (Sweden) 329
FAWU (South Africa) 314
FBU (UK) 367
FCE (France) 117
FCSU (Mauritius) 218
FCTA (Switzerland) 337
FDT (Morocco) 225
FEAE (France) 117
Fédéchimie CGTFO (France) 122
FEDEDBON (Netherlands Antilles) 239
Federación Boneriana di Trabao (Netherlands Antilles) 239
Federación de Trabajadores Arubanos (Netherlands – Aruba) 239
Federación del Trabajo de Puerto Rico AFL-CIO 388
Federación Nacional Sindical de Trabajadores Salvadoreños 103
Federacion Unitaria de Trabajadores de Honduras 148
Federatie Nederlandse Vakbeweging (Netherlands) 237
Fédération chimie énergie (France) 117
Fédération communication et culture (France) 117
Fédération de l'habillement, du cuir et textile (France) 117
Fédération Démocratique du Travail (Morocco) 225
Fédération des banques et sociétés financières (France) 117
Fédération des établissements et arsenaux de l'état (France) 117
Fédération des finances et affaires économiques (France) 117
Fédération des Instituteurs Chrétiens (Belgium) 33
Fédération des services (France) 118
Fédération des services de santé et services sociaux (France) 118
Fédération des syndicats généraux de l'éducation nationale (France) 118
Fédération formation et enseignement privés (France) 117
Fédération générale agroalimentaire (France) 117
Fédération générale de la métallurgie et des mines (France) 117
Fédération générale des transports-équipements (France) 117
Fédération Générale du Travail de Belgique (Belgium) 33
Fédération nationale construction bois (France) 117
Fédération nationale INTERCO (France) 118
Federation of Autonomous Trade Unions of Côte d'Ivoire 81
Federation of Bhutanese Trade Unions 36

422

Federation of Civil Service Organizations (Suriname) 324
Federation of Civil Service Unions (Mauritius) 218
Federation of Free Trade Unions of Zambia 397
Federation of Free Workers (Philippines) 267
Federation of Independent Trade Unions of Russia 286
Federation of International Civil Servants' Associations 402
Federation of Korean Trade Unions (S. Korea) 192
Federation of Managerial and Professional Staff Unions (Netherlands) 238
Federation of Municipal Officers (Finland) 112
Federation of Non-Life Insurance workers' Union of Japan 182
Federation of Norwegian Professional Associations 252
Federation of Organizations Affiliated to ODSTA/WCL (Liberia) 200
Federation of Progressive Unions (Mauritius) 217
Federation of Trade Unions of Belarus 29
Federation of Trade Unions of Burma 229
Federation of Trade Unions of Macedonia 205
Federation of Trade Unions of the Republic of Kazakhstan 187
Federation of Trade Unions of Ukraine 358
Federation of Trade Unions of Uzbekistan 390
Federation of Unions of South Africa 314
Federation of Workers' Councils and Unions in Iraq - Union of the Unemployed 162
Fédération protection sociale, travail, emploi (France) 118
Fédération suisse des travailleurs du commerce, des transports et de l'alimentation (Switzerland) 337
Fédération Syndicale Mondiale 412
Fédération Syndicale Unitaire (France) 123
Fédération unifiée des postes et des telecoms (France) 118
Federatsiia Nezavisimykh Profsoiuzov Rossii (Russia) 286
FEDUSA (South Africa) 314
FEJ (International) 402
Fellesforbundet (Norway) 254
FEM (International) 402
FEMTAA (International) 412
FENASTRAS (El Salvador) 103
FEP (France) 117
FESACI (Côte d'Ivoire) 81
FEST (International) 402
FETBB (International) 401
FFTUZ (Zambia) 397
FFW (Philippines) 267
FGA (France) 117
FGMM (France) 117
FGTA Agriculture, Alimentation et Tabacs (France) 121
FGTB (Belgium) 33
FGTE (France) 117
FICSA (International) 402
FICTU (Fiji) 109
Fiji Islands Council of Trade Unions 109
Fiji Trades Union Congress 108
Finance Sector Union (Norway) 256
Finance Sector Union of Australia 15
Finances (France) 122
Financial Sector Union (Finland) 112
Finansforbundet (Denmark) 91
Finansforbundet (Norway) 256
Finansförbundet (Sweden) 334
Finnish Association of Graduate Engineers 110
Finnish Association of Graduates in Economics and Business Administration 111
Finnish Confederation of Salaried Employees 112
Finnish Electrical Workers' Union 112
Finnish Foodstuff Workers' Union 111
Finnish Transport Workers' Union 111
Finnish Union of Practical Nurses (Finland) 112
FinSec (New Zealand) 243
FIOST (International) 412
Fire Brigades Union (UK) 367
First Division Association (UK) 368
FISE (International) 414
FITA (Tonga) 345
FITH (International) 412
FITUR (Russia) 286
Fivondronamben'ny Mpiasa Malagasy (Madagascar) 206
FKTU (S. Korea) 192
Flight Attendants and Related Services Association (New Zealand) 243
Flight Attendants' Association of Australia (Australia) 15
FMCB (International) 412
FME (International) 412
FMM (Madagascar) 206
FMTI (International) 412
FNPR (Russia) 286
FNV (Netherlands) 237
FNV Bondgenoten (Netherlands) 238
FNV Bouw (Netherlands) 238
FNV KIEM (Netherlands) 238
FOBTU (Bhutan) 36
Fonctionnaires (France) 122
Food and Allied Workers' Union (South Africa) 314
Food Rengo (Japan) 182
Food Workers' Union (Sweden) 330
Forbundet af Offentligt Ansatte (Denmark) 93
Förbundet Sveriges Arbetsterapeuter (Sweden) 331
Forbundet Trae - Industri-Byg I Danmark 93
Força Sindical (Brazil) 45
Forest and Wood Workers' Union (Sweden) 330
Forum for the Cooperation of Trade Unions (Hungary) 150
Forum Zwiazkow Zawodowych (Poland) 275
FPB (Belarus) 29
FPRK (Kazakhstan) 187
FPU (Mauritius) 217
FPU (Ukraine) 358
Free Confederation of Chadian Workers 64
Free Confederation of Mauritanian Workers 216
Free Trade Union Confederation of Latvia 196
Free Trade Union of Workers of the Kingdom of Cambodia 53
French Confederation of Christian Workers 118
French Confederation of Professional and Managerial Staff 118
French Democratic Confederation of Labour 116
Friendly Islands Teachers Association (Tonga) 345
FS (Brazil) 45
FSA (Sweden) 331
FSCC (Mauritius) 218
FSESP (International) 402
FSM (International) 412
FSU (Australia) 15
FSU (France) 123
FSzDL (Hungary) 149
FTA (Netherlands - Aruba) 239
FTF (Denmark) 91
FTF (Sweden) 334
FTILAC (France) 117
FTMH (Switzerland) 337
FTUB (Belarus) 29
FTUB (Myanmar) 229
FTUC (Fiji) 108
FTUK (Kazakhstan) 187
FTUU (Uzbekistan) 390
FTUWKC (Cambodia) 53
Független Szakszervezetek Demokratikus Ligája (Hungary) 149
Funeral and Allied Industries Union of New South Wales 15
Funktionærernes og Tjenestemændenes Fællesråd (Denmark) 91
FUPT (France) 118
Furniture, Manufacturing & Associated Workers Union (New Zealand) 243
FUTH (Honduras) 148
FWCUI-UUI (Iraq) 162
FZZ (Poland) 275

G10 Solidaires (France) 123
Gabonese Confederation of Free Trade Unions 124
Gabonese Trade Union Confederation 124
Gambia Workers' Union 125
Gambian Workers' Confederation 125
GAWU (Guyana) 146
GBI (Switzerland) 337
GCIU (USA) 381

INDEX

GCTU (International) 402
GDE (Austria) 20
GDG (Austria) 20
GdP (Germany) 134
GEFONT (Nepal) 233
General Alliance of Labour Unions in Suriname 323
General Centre of Independent and Free Unions of Angola 7
General Confederation of Democratic Workers (Colombia) 74
General Confederation of Free Workers of Cameroon 54
General Confederation of Greek Labour 139
General Confederation of Independent Unions (Guinea-Bissau) 144
General Confederation of Labour - Workers' Strength (France) 120
General Confederation of Labour (Argentina) 9
General Confederation of Labour (France) 119
General Confederation of Labour (Spain) 319
General Confederation of Lebanese Workers 197
General Confederation of Liberal Trade Unions of Belgium 31
General Confederation of Mauritanian Workers 216
General Confederation of Portuguese Workers 277
General Confederation of the Workers of Benin 36
General Confederation of Trade Unions (International) 402
General Confederation of Workers (Brazil) 45
General Confederation of Workers of Panama 261
General Federation of Belgian Labour 33
General Federation of Jordanian Trade Unions 185
General Federation of Labour in Israel 166
General Federation of Nepalese Trade Unions 233
General Federation of Private Railway and Bus Workers' Unions of Japan 182
General Federation of Trade Unions (Syria) 338
General Federation of Trade Unions (UK) 370
General Federation of Trade Unions of Iraq 161
General Federation of Trade Unions of Korea (N. Korea) 189
General Federation of Workers Trade Unions in Bahrain 23
General Labour Union (Italy) 175
General Union of Algerian Workers 4
General Union of Djibouti Workers 94
General Union of Moroccan Workers 225
General Union of the Workers of Guinea 143
General Union of the Workers of São Tomé and Príncipe 293
General Union of Workers (Portugal) 278
General Union of Workers (Spain) 318
General Union of Workers of Niger 248
General Workers' Federation (Mauritius) 217
General Workers' Union (Malta) 214
Georgian Trade Union Amalgamation 126
German Christian Workers' Federation 134
German Civil Servants' Federation 135
German Trade Union Federation 131
GEW (Germany) 133
Gewerkschaft Agrar, Nahrung, Genuss (Austria) 20
Gewerkschaft Bau und Industrie (Switzerland) 337
Gewerkschaft Bau-Holz (Austria) 20
Gewerkschaft der Chemiearbeiter (Austria) 20
Gewerkschaft der Eisenbahner (Austria) 20
Gewerkschaft der Gemeindebediensteten (Austria) 20
Gewerkschaft der Polizei (Germany) 134
Gewerkschaft der Post und Fernmeldebediensteten (Austria) 21
Gewerkschaft der Privatangestellten (Austria) 21
Gewerkschaft Druck und Papier (Austria) 20
Gewerkschaft Erziehung und Wissenschaft (Germany) 133
Gewerkschaft Handel, Transport, Verkehr (Austria) 20
Gewerkschaft Hotel, Gastgewerbe, Personlicher Dienst (Austria) 20
Gewerkschaft Industrie, Gewerbe, Dienstleitungen (Switzerland) 337
Gewerkschaft Kommunikation (Switzerland) 337
Gewerkschaft Kunst, Medien, Freie Berufe (Austria) 20
Gewerkschaft Metall-Textil (Austria) 20
Gewerkschaft Nahrung-Genuss-Gaststätten (Germany) 134
Gewerkschaft Öffentlicher Dienst (Austria) 21
GF (Sweden) 329
GFJTU (Jordan) 185
GFL (Ghana) 136
GFTU (Iraq) 161
GFTU (Syria) 338
GFTU (UK) 370
GFTUK (N. Korea) 189
GFWTUB (Bahrain) 23
Ghana Federation of Labour 136
Glass, Molders, Pottery, Plastics and Allied Workers' International Union (USA) 382
GMB (UK) 368
GMP (USA) 382
GÖD (Austria) 21
GPA (Austria) 21
Grafiska Fackförbundet (Sweden) 329
Graphic Communications International Union (USA) 381
Graphic Workers' Union (Sweden) 329
Graphical, Paper and Media Union (Ireland) 164
Grenada Trades Union Council 140
GSEE (Greece) 139
GTUA (Georgia) 126
GTUC (Grenada) 140
GTUC (Guyana) 145
Guyana Agricultural and General Workers' Union 146
Guyana Trades Union Congress 145
GWC (Gambia) 125
GWF (Mauritius) 217
GWU (Gambia) 125
GWU (Malta) 214

HACUITEX (France) 117
Haitian Trade Union Coordination 147
Hak-Is (Turkey) 353
Handel og Kontor I Norge (Norway) 254
Handels (Sweden) 329
Handels- og Kontorfunktionaerernes Forbund i Danmark (Denmark) 93
Health Services Union (Australia) 15
HERE (USA) 382
HGPD (Austria) 20
Hind Mazdoor Sabha (India) 155
Histadrut (Israel) 166
Histadrut Haovdim Haleumit (Israel) 166
HK (Denmark) 93
HK (Norway) 254
HKCTU (China - Hong Kong) 72
HKFTU (China - Hong Kong) 72
HKTUC (China - Hong Kong) 72
HMS (India) 155
Honduras Workers' Confederation 148
Hong Kong and Kowloon Trades Union Council 72
Hong Kong Confederation of Trade Unions 72
Hong Kong Federation of Trade Unions 72
HOSPERSA (South Africa) 315
Hospital Personnel Trade Union of South Africa 315
Hotel and Restaurant Workers' Union (Sweden) 329
Hotel Employees' and Restaurant Employees' International Union (USA) 382
Hout- en Bouwbond CNV (Netherlands) 237
HRF (Sweden) 329
Hrvatska Udruga Sindikata 83
HSU (Australia) 15
HTF (Sweden) 334
HTV (Austria) 20
HUS (Croatia) 83
IAFF (USA) 382
IAM (USA) 382
IAMAW (Canada) 59
IBB (USA) 382
IBEW (USA) 382
IBFG (International) 403
IBT (USA) 383
ICATU (International) 403
Icelandic Federation of Labour 151
ICEM (International) 406

INDEX

ICFTU (International) 403
ICFTU African Regional Organization 405
ICFTU Asian and Pacific Regional Organization 405
ICFTU-APRO 405
ICTU (Ireland) 163
ICWUC (USA) 387
IEU (Australia) 15
IFBWW (International) 406
IFJ (International) 407
IFPTE (USA) 384
IFTC (International) 412
IFTU (Iraq) 161
IG Bauen-Agrar-Umwelt 133
IG Metall (Germany) 133
IGBAU (Germany) 133
IGBCE (Germany) 133
IGM (Germany) 133
ILA (USA) 384
ILWU (USA) 384
IMATU (South Africa) 315
IMF (International) 407
IMF-JC (Japan) 182
IMPACT (Ireland) 164
Independent and Self Governing Trade Union Solidarity (Poland) 271
Independent Christian Trade Unions of Slovakia 304
Independent Education Union of Australia 15
Independent Municipal and Allied Trade Union (South Africa) 315
Independent Schools Teachers Association (New Zealand) 243
Independent Trade Unions of Croatia 83
Independent Union of Maritime and Related Workers (Angola) 7
Indian Labour Organization 155
Indian National Trade Union Congress 156
Indonesian Teachers' Unity 159
Indonesian Trade Union Confederation 159
Industrial Workers' Union (Sweden) 329
Industrial, Wood and Allied Workers of Canada 59
Industriegewerkschaft Bergbau, Chemie, Energie (Germany) 133
Industrifacket (Sweden) 329
INFEDOP (International) 412
Ingenjörsförbundet (Sweden) 331
Institute of Development Management Workers' Union (Botswana) 42
Inter-American Regional Organization of Workers 405
International Association of Bridge, Structural and Ornamental Iron Workers (USA) 382
International Association of Firefighters (USA) 382
International Association of Machinists and Aerospace Workers (USA) 382
International Association of Machinists and Aerospace Workers (Canada) 59
International Association of Operative Plasterers' and Cement Masons of the United States and Canada 382
International Brotherhood of Boilermakers, Iron Ship Builders, Blacksmiths, Forgers and Helpers (USA) 382
International Brotherhood of Electrical Workers (USA) 382
International Brotherhood of Teamsters (USA) 383
International Bund Freier Gewerkschaften 403
International Chemical Workers' Union Council (USA) 387
International Confederation of Arab Trade Unions 403
International Confederation of Free Trade Unions 403
International Confederation of Public Servants 400
International Federation of Building and Wood Workers 406
International Federation of Chemical, Energy, Mine and General Workers' Unions 406
International Federation of Employees in Public Service 412
International Federation of Journalists 407
International Federation of Professional and Technical Engineers (USA) 384
International Federation of Trade Unions of Transport Workers 412
International Federation Textile-Clothing 412
International Longshore and Warehouse Union (USA) 384
International Longshoremen's Association (USA) 384
International Metalworkers' Federation 407
International Textile, Garment and Leather Workers' Federation 407
International Transport Workers' Federation 407
International Union of Bricklayers and Allied Craftworkers (USA) 384
International Union of Electronic, Electrical, Salaried, Machine and Furniture Workers (USA) 384
International Union of Elevator Constructors (USA) 384
International Union of Food, Agricultural, Hotel, Restaurant, Catering, Tobacco and Allied Workers' Associations 407
International Union of Operating Engineers (USA) 385
International Union of Painters and Allied Trades (USA) 382
International Union of Police Associations (USA) 385
Intersyndicale Premier Mai - Batay Ouvriye (Haiti) 147
INTUC (India) 156
Iraq Federation of Trade Unions 161
Irish Bank Officials' Association 164
Irish Congress of Trade Unions 163
Irish Medical Organisation 164
Irish Municipal, Public and Civil Trade Union 164
Irish National Teachers' Organisation 164
Irish Nurses' Organisation 164
ISTANZ (New Zealand) 243
Italian Confederation of Free Workers' Unions 175
Italian Confederation of Workers' Trade Unions 173
Italian General Confederation of Labour 172
Italian Labour Union 174
ITF (International) 407
ITF New Zealand Inspectorate 244
ITGLWF (International) 407
IUEC (USA) 384
IUE-CWA (USA) 384
IUF (International) 407
IUOE (USA) 385
IUPA (USA) 385
IUPAT (USA) 382
IWA (Canada) 59

JAM (Japan) 181
Jamaica Confederation of Trade Unions 176
Japan Association of Metal, Machinery and Manufacturing Workers 181
Japan Confederation of Railway Workers' Unions 182
Japan Council of Metalworkers' Unions 182
Japan Federation of Basic Industry Workers' Unions 182
Japan Federation of Food and Tobacco Workers' Unions 182
Japan Federation of Service and Distributive Workers' Unions 182
Japan Federation of Telecommunications, Electronic Information and Allied Workers 182
Japan Federation of Transport Workers' Unions 182
Japan Postal Workers' Union 182
Japan Public Sector Union 182
Japan Railway Trade Unions Confederation 182
Japan Teachers' Union 181
Japanese Electrical, Electronic and Information Union 181
Japanese Federation of Energy and Chemistry Workers' Unions 182
Japanese Federation of Textile, Garment, Chemical, Mercantile, Food and Allied Industries Workers' Unions 181
Japanese Trade Union Confederation 179
Jathika Sevaka Sangamaya (Sri Lanka) 322
Jatio Sramik Federation (Bangladesh) 26
Jatyo Sramik League (Bangladesh) 26
JAW (Japan) 181
JCTU (Jamaica) 176
JEC Rengo (Japan) 182
Jichiro (Japan) 181
Jidosha Soren (Japan) 181
Joint Organization of Unions - Hong Kong 72
JR-Rengo (Japan) 182
JR-Soren (Japan) 182

INDEX

JUSEK (Sweden) 332
Jyoho Roren (Japan) 182

Kamu Emekcileri Sendikalari
Konfederasyonu (Turkey) 354
KCTU (S. Korea) 193
KEMIA (Finland) 112
Finnish National Union of State
Employees and Special Services 112
KESK (Turkey) 354
KFO (Norway) 255
KFTU 195
Kikan Roren (Japan) 182
Kilusang Mayo Uno (Philippines) 267
Kiribati Trade Union Congress 189
KMFB (Austria) 20
KMU (Philippines) 267
KNSB (Bulgaria) 49
KNSS (Slovenia) 306
KOK (Czech Republic) 89
Kokku Rengo (Japan) 182
Kommunal (Sweden) 330
Kommunalansattes Fellesorganisasjon
(Norway) 255
Konfederacija '90 (Slovenia) 307
Konfederacija novih sindikatov Slovenije
"Neodvisnost" (Slovenia) 306
Konfederacija sindikatov '90 Slovenije
(Slovenia) 307
Konfederacija sindikatov Slovenije
Pergam (Slovenia) 306
Konfederasaun Sindicatu Timor Lorosa'e
(East Timor) 97
Konfederasi Serikat Buruh Sejahtera
Indonesia 158
Konfederasi Serikat Pekerja Indonesia 159
Konfederasi Serikat Pekerja Seluruh
Indonesia 159
Korean Confederation of Trade Unions (S.
Korea) 193
Kotsu Roren (Japan) 182
KOZ SR (Slovakia)
Krestanska Odborova Koalice 89
KSBSI (Indonesia) 158
KSPI (Indonesia) 159
KSPK (Kazakhstan) 186
KSPSI (Indonesia) 159
KSS Pergam (Slovenia) 306
KSSh (Albania) 3
KSTL (East Timor) 97
KTR (Russia) 288
KTUC (Kiribati) 189
KTUF (Kuwait) 194
KTV (Finland) 111
Kuwait Trade Union Federation 194
KVL (Finland) 112
KVPU (Ukraine) 358
Kyrgyzstan Federation of Trade Unions 195
Kyrkans Akademikerförbund (Sweden) 332

Laborers' International Union of North
America (USA) 385
Labour Congress of Thailand 343
Landelijke Bedienden Centrale-Nationaal

Verbond Kaderpersonneel (Belgium) 32
Landsorganisasjonen i Norge (Norway) 253
Landsorganisationen i Danmark 91
Landsorganisationen i Sverige (Sweden) 328
Lanka Jathika Estate Workers' Union (Sri
Lanka) 322
LANV (Liechtenstein) 202
Lao Federation of Trade Unions 195
Lärarförbundet (Sweden) 333
Lärarnas Riksförbund (Sweden) 332
LBAS (Latvia) 196
LBC (Belgium) 32
LCGB (Luxembourg) 204
LCT (Thailand) 343
LDF (Lithuania) 203
LECODU (Lesotho) 199
Legitimerade Sjukgymnasters Riksförbund
(Sweden) 332
Lesotho Congress of Democratic Unions 199
Lesotho Trade Union Congress 199
Lëtzeburger Chrëschtleche Gewerkschafts-
Bond (Luxembourg) 204
LFLU (Liberia) 200
LFTU (Laos) 195
LHMU (Australia) 16
Liberian Federation of Labour Unions 200
Liechtenstein Employees' Association 202
Liechtensteiner Arbeitnehmerverband 202
Lietuvos Darbo Federacija (Lithuania) 203
Lietuvos Profesine Sajunga
"Solidarumas"203
Lietuvos Profesiniu Sajungu
Konfederacija (Lithuania) 203
LIGA (Hungary) 149
LIGA Democratic Confederation of Free
Trade Unions 149
Liquor, Hospitality and Miscellaneous
Workers' Union (Australia) 16
Lithuanian Federation of Labour 203
Lithuanian Trade Union - Solidarity 203
Lithuanian Trade Union Confederation 203
LIUNA (USA) 385
Livre (France) 122
LIVS (Sweden) 330
LJEWU (Sri Lanka) 322
LO (Denmark) 91
LO (Norway) 253
LO (Sweden) 328
LPSK (Lithuania) 203
LR (Sweden) 332
LSR (Sweden) 332
LTUC (Lesotho) 199
Luxembourg Confederation of Christian
Trade Unions 204
Luxembourg Confederation of Independent
Trade Unions 205
Luxembourg General Confederation of
Labour 204

Magyar Szakszervezetek Országos
Szövetsége 150
Majlis Kebangsaan Kesatuan Pekerja -
Pekerja Kakitangan Rendah, Kerajaan
Malaysia 211

Malareforbundet (Sweden) 330
Malawi Congress of Trade Unions 208
Malaysian Trades Union Congress 210
Malta Workers' Union 214
MANDATE (Ireland) 164
Manitoba Federation of Labour 59
Manufacturing and Construction Workers'
Union (New Zealand) 245
Maritime Union of Australia 16
Matica Nezavisnih Sindikata Javnih
Djelatnika 83
Mauritius Labour Congress 217
Mauritius Trade Union Congress 217
May 1st - Workers' Fight Federation
(Haiti) 147
May First Labour Movement Centre
(Philippines) 268
MCTU (Malawi) 208
MEAA (Australia) 16
Meat and Related Trades Workers Union
of Aotearoa (New Zealand) 243
Media, Entertainment and Arts Alliance
(Australia) 16
Medical Scientists' Association of
Victoria 16
Metal Workers' Union (Sweden) 330
Métal-CSC (Belgium) 32
Metall (Sweden) 330
Metalli (Finland) 111
Metalworkers' Union (Finland) 111
Métaux (France) 122
MHP (Netherlands) 238
Miabanutiun Trade Union 11
Mineurs, Miniers et Similaires (France) 122
Minju Nochong (S. Korea) 193
MKTR (Malaysia) 211
MLC (Mauritius) 217
Moederbond (Suriname) 323
MONTRAL (Venezuela) 393
Moroccan Workers' Union 225
MOSz (Hungary) 150
Movimiento Nacional de Trabajadores
Para La Liberación (Venezuela) 393
Mozambique Workers' Organization 228
MSAV (Australia) 16
MszOSz (Hungary) 150
MTUC (Malaysia) 210
MTUC (Mauritius) 217
MU (UK) 368
MUA (Australia) 16
Municipal Workers' Union (Finland) 111
Municipal Workers' Union (Sweden) 330
Munkástanácsok Országos Szövetsége
(Hungary) 150
Musicians' Union (Sweden) 330
Musicians' Union (UK) 368
Musikerförbundet (Sweden) 330

NACTU (South Africa) 315
Naerings-og Nydelsesmiddelarbejder
Forbundet (Denmark) 93
NAF (Norway) 254
NAHT (UK) 371
NALC (USA) 385

INDEX

NAPFE (USA) 387
NASUWT (UK) 368
NATCA (USA) 385
NATFHE (UK) 368
National Air Traffic Controllers' Association (USA) 385
National Alliance of Postal and Federal Employees (USA) 387
National Amalgamated Local and Central Government & Parastatal Manual Workers' Union (Botswana) 41
National Association of Head Teachers (UK) 371
National Association of Letter Carriers (USA) 385
National Association of School Masters / Union of Women Teachers (UK) 368
National Association of Teachers in Further and Higher Education (UK) 368
National Confederation of Central African Workers 63
National Confederation of Eritrean Workers 104
National Confederation of Free Trade Unions of Romania - Brotherhood 282
National Confederation of Guinean Workers 143
National Confederation of Hungarian Trade Unions 150
National Confederation of Senegalese Workers 295
National Confederation of the Trade-Union Organizations of Ukraine 358
National Confederation of Togolese Workers 344
National Confederation of Trade Unions (Japan) 182
National Confederation of Workers of Burkina 51
National Congress of Thai Labour 344
National Congress of Trade Unions (Bahamas) 22
National Council of Trade Unions (South Africa) 315
National Council of Unions of the Industrial and Lower Income Group of Government Workers (Malaysia) 211
National Development Bank Staff Union (Botswana) 42
National Distribution Union (New Zealand) 243
National Distribution Union (New Zealand) 245
National Education Association (USA) 387
National Education, Health and Allied Workers' Union (South Africa) 313
National Federation of Christian Trade Unions (Netherlands) 236
National Federation of Construction Workers' Unions (Japan) 182
National Federation of Independent Unions (France) 123
National Federation of Life Insurance Workers' Unions (Japan) 181

National Federation of Workers' Councils (Hungary) 150
National Labour Federation in Eretz-Israel 166
National Labour Union of Morocco 226
National Organisations of Free Trade Unions (Burkina) 51
National Organization of Free Unions of Guinea 143
National Organization of the Workers of São Tomé and Príncipe - Central Union 293
National Organization of Trade Unions (Uganda) 356
National Tertiary Education Union (Australia) 16
National Trade Union "Promyana" (Bulgaria) 50
National Trade Union Bloc (Romania) 282
National Trade Union Centre of Trinidad and Tobago 346
National Trade Union Confederation "Cartel Alfa" (Romania) 283
National Trade Union Confederation "Meridian" (Romania) 283
National Trade Union Congress of Belize 34
National Trade Union Council (Japan) 182
National Trade Unions Confederation (Mauritius) 217
National Trades Union Congress (Singapore) 302
National Union of Angolan Workers 7
National Union of Autonomous Trade Unions of Senegal 295
National Union of Commercial and Clerical Employees (Denmark) 93
National Union of Congolese Workers (Congo, Democratic Republic) 76
National Union of Government and Federated Workers (Trinidad and Tobago) 347
National Union of Independent Trade Unions of Togo 345
National Union of Journalists (UK) 368
National Union of Marine, Aviation and Shipping Transport Officers (UK) 368
National Union of Metalworkers of South Africa 313
National Union of Mineworkers (South Africa) 313
National Union of Namibian Workers 231
National Union of Public and General Employees (Canada) 59
National Union of Public Employees (New Zealand) 245
National Union of Public Workers (Barbados) 27
National Union of Rail, Maritime and Transport Workers (UK) 369
National Union of Teachers (UK) 369
National Union of the Unions of the Workers of Benin 36
National Union of Workers (Australia) 16
National Union of Workers (Mexico) 220
National Union of Workers (Venezuela) 393
National Union of Workers of Guinea-Bissau 144

National Workers' Union of Jamaica 176
National Workers' Congress (Sri Lanka) 322
National Workers' Movement (St Vincent) 291
National Workers' Union (Dominica) 95
National Workers' Union (Guyana) 146
National Workers' Union (St Lucia) 290
National Workers' Union of Mali 212
Nationwide Group Staff Union (UK) 369
NATUC (Trinidad and Tobago) 346
NCEW (Eritrea) 104
NCTL (Thailand) 344
NEA (USA) 387
NEHAWU (South Africa) 313
Nepal Trade Union Congress 233
Nepal Trade Union Federation 234
Netherlands Trade Union Confederation 237
New Brunswick Federation of Labour 60
New South Wales Nurses' Association 16
New Zealand Airline Pilots' Association 245
New Zealand Building Trades Union 243
New Zealand Council of Trade Unions 241
New Zealand Meatworkers & Related Trades Union, Inc. 243
New Zealand Merchant Service Guild 244
New Zealand Nurses' Organization 244
New Zealand Postal Workers' Union 244
New Zealand Professional Fire Fighters Union 244
New Zealand Seafarers' Union 244
New Zealand Trade Union Federation 244
New Zealand Tramways and Public Passenger Transport Union 245
New Zealand Writers' Guild 244
Newfoundland and Labrador Federation of Labour 60
Newspaper Guild (USA) 381
Nezavisni Hrvatski Sindikati (Croatia) 83
Nezavisnost (Serbia-Montenegro) 297
NFS (International) 400
NFWC (Hungary) 150
NGG (Germany) 134
NGSU (UK) 369
NHS (Croatia) 83
NHS (Norway) 255
Nicaraguan Workers' Centre 246
Nigeria Labour Congress 250
Nigerien Confederation of Labor 247
Nikkyoso (Japan) 181
NKF (Norway) 254
NKIF (Norway) 254
NKOS (Slovakia) 304
NKPU (Ukraine) 358
NLC (Nigeria) 250
NLF (Israel) 166
NNF (Denmark) 93
NNN (Norway) 254
Nochong (S. Korea) 192
Nordens Fackliga Samorganisation 400
Norsk Arbeidsmandsforbund (Norway) 254
Norsk Helse- og Sosialforbund (Norway) 255
Norsk Kjemisk Industriarbeiderforbund

427

INDEX

(Norway) 254
Norsk Kommuneforbund (Norway) 254
Norsk Naerings- og
Nytelsesmiddelarbeiderforbund
(Norway) 254
Norsk Post og Kommunikasjonsforbund
(Norway) 255
Norsk Sykepleierforbund (Norway) 255
Norsk Tjenestemannslag (Norway) 255
Norwegian Association of Health and
Social Care Personnel (Norway) 255
Norwegian Civil Service Union 255
Norwegian Confederation of Trade
Unions 253
Norwegian Nurses' Association 255
Norwegian Post and Communications
Union 255
Norwegian Union of Chemical Industry
Workers 254
Norwegian Union of Food, Beverage and
Allied Workers 254
Norwegian Union of General Workers 254
Norwegian Union of Municipal and General
Employees 254
Norwegian Union of Municipal
Employees 254
NOTU (Uganda) 356
NSWNA (Australia) 16
NSZZ Solidarnosc (Poland) 271
NTEU (Australia) 16
NTL (Norway) 255
NTUC (Mauritius) 217
NTUC (Nepal) 233
NTUC (Singapore) 302
NTUCB (Belize) 34
NTUF (Nepal) 234
NUGFW (Trinidad and Tobago) 347
NUJ (UK) 368
NUM (South Africa)
NUMAST (UK) 368
NUMSA (South Africa) 313
NUNW (Namibia) 231
NUPE (New Zealand) 245
NUPGE (Canada) 59
NUPW (Barbados) 27
NUT (UK) 369
NUW (Australia) 16
NVK (Belgium) 32
NWC (Sri Lanka) 322
NWM (St Vincent) 291
NWU (Guyana) 146
NWU (St Lucia) 290
NZ Educational Institute 243
NZBTU (New Zealand) 245
NZCTU (New Zealand) 241
NZEI Te Riu Roa (New Zealand) 243
NZTUF (New Zealand) 244
NZWG (New Zealand) 244

OATUU (International) 409
OAU (Mauritius) 218
ODSTA (International) 411
Office and Professional Employees'
International Union (USA) 385

Officersförbundet (Sweden) 332
ÖGB (Austria) 19
OGB-L (Luxembourg) 205
Ogolnopolskie Porozumienie Zwiazkow
Zawodowych (Poland) 274
Onderwijsbond CNV (Netherlands) 237
Onofhängege Gewerkschaftsbond
Lëtzebuerg (Luxembourg) 205
ONSL (Burkina) 51
ONSLG (Guinea) 143
Ontario Federation of Labour 60
ONTSTP-CS (São Tomé) 293
OPCMIA (USA) 382
OPEIU (USA) 385
Operative Plasterers and Allied Trades
Society of Ireland 164
OPZZ (Poland) 274
Organisatie van Samenwerkende
Autonome Vakbonden (Suriname) 324
Organisation de l'Unité Syndicale
Africaine 409
Organisation Nationale des Syndicats
Libres 51
Organisation Nationale des Syndicats
Libres de Guinée 143
Organização dos Trabalhadores de
Moçambique 228
Organização Nacional dos Trabalhadores
de São Tomé e Príncipe - Central
Sindical 293
Organization of African Trade Union
Unity 409
Organization of Artisans' Unity
(Mauritius) 218
Organization of Cooperating Autonomous
Trade Unions (Suriname) 324
ORIT (International) 405
OSAV (Suriname) 324
Österreichischer Gewerkschaftsbund
(Austria) 19
OTM (Mozambique) 228
OUSA (International) 409

PACE (USA) 385
Painters' Union (Sweden) 330
Pakistan National Federation of Trade
Unions 259
Palestine General Federation of Trade
Unions 260
PAM (Finland) 111
Pancyprian Federation of Labour 86
Pancyprian Public Servants' Trade Union 86
Pankypria Ergatiki Omospondia 86
Paper Workers' Union (Sweden) 330
Paper, Allied-Industrial, Chemical and
Energy Workers' International Union
(USA) 385
Paperworkers' Union (Finland) 111
Pappers (Sweden) 330
Papua New Guinea Trade Union
Congress 262
Pardia - Confederation of State
Employees´ Unions (Finland) 112
PASYDY (Cyprus) 86

PAT (UK) 371
PCS (UK) 369
PEO (Cyprus) 86
Personnel des Services des Départements
et des Régions (France) 122
Persutuan Guru Republik Indonesia 159
PFA (Australia) 14
PFA (Australia) 16
PGFTU (Palestine) 260
PGRI (Indonesia) 159
Pharmacie (France) 122
PIT-CNT (Uruguay) 389
Plenario Intersindical de Trabajadores-
Convención Nacional de Trabajadores
(Uruguay) 389
PNFTU (Pakistan) 259
PNGTUC (Papua New Guinea) 262
POA (UK) 369
Podkrepa (Bulgaria) 49
Police (France) 122
Police and Prisons Civil Rights Union
(South Africa) 314
Police Federation of Australia 16
Police Union (Sweden) 334
Polisförbundet (Sweden) 334
POPCRU (South Africa) 314
Post Primary Teachers' Association (New
Zealand) 244
Postal Workers' Association (Auckland)
Inc 244
Prison Officers' Association (UK) 369
Professional Association of Teachers
(UK) 371
Progressieve Vakcentrale 47 (Suriname) 324
Progressive Labour Federation 47
(Suriname) 324
Promyana (Bulgaria) 50
Prospect (UK) 369
PSA (New Zealand) 244
PSA (Samoa) 292
PSA (South Africa) 315
PSAC (Canada) 59
PSI (International) 408
PSTE (France) 118
PSU (St Vincent) 291
PTT (France) 122
Public and Commercial Services Union
(UK) 369
Public Servants Association of South
Africa 315
Public Service Alliance of Canada 59
Public Service Association (New
Zealand) 244
Public Service Executive Union
(Ireland) 164
Public Service Union (Switzerland) 337
Public Services International 408
PUU (Finland) 111
PWA (New Zealand) 244
Quebec Federation of Labour 60

Rail and Maritime Transport Union Inc.
(New Zealand) 244
Rail, Tram and Bus Union (Australia) 16

RCN (UK) 371
Rengo (Japan) 179
Retail, Wholesale and Department Store Union (USA) 387
Revolutionary Confederation of Workers and Peasants (Mexico) 220
Revolutionary Trade Unions Federation (Cyprus) 86
RLPA (Australia) 16
RMT (UK) 369
RMTU (New Zealand) 244
Royal College of Nursing of the United Kingdom (UK) 371
RTBU (Australia) 16
Rugby League Professionals Association (Australia) 16
RWDSU (USA) 387

SACCAWU (South Africa) 314
SACO - förbundet Trafik och Järnväg (Sweden) 332
SACO (Sweden) 331
SACO:s Tjänstemannaförbund SRAT (Sweden) 332
SACTWU (South Africa) 314
SADTU (South Africa) 313
SAG (USA) 380
SAK (Finland) 111
Salaried Employees' and Civil Servants' Confederation (Denmark) 91
Salaried Employees' Union (Sweden) 334
Salaried Pharmacists' Association of Western Australia 16
Samoa National Union of Workers/Samoa Trades Union Congress 292
Samoa Public Service Association 292
SAMWU (South Africa) 314
San Marino Confederation of Labour 293
Sandinista Workers' Centre (Nicaragua) 246
Sario Federation of Labour (Morocco - W. Sahara) 227
SASAWU (South Africa) 314
SASBO: The Finance Union (South Africa) 314
Saskatchewan Federation of Labour 60
SATAWU (South Africa) 314
Savez Samostalnih Sindikata Bosne i Hercegovine 39
Savez Samostalnih Sindikata Crne Gore (Serbia-Montenegro) 298
Savez Samostalnih Sindikata Hrvatske 83
Savez Samostalnih Sindikata Srbije (Serbia-Montenegro) 297
Savez Sindikata Republike Srpske 40
SCCC (Belgium) 32
Schweizerischer Eisenbahn- und Verkehrspersonal-Verband (Switzerland) 337
Schweizerischer Gewerkschaftsbund (Switzerland) 336
Scottish Trades Union Congress (UK) 371
Screen Actors' Guild (USA) 380
SDA (Australia) 16
Seafarers' International Union (USA) 385
Seafarers' Union of Burma 230

SEF (Sweden) 329
Seiho Roren (Japan) 181
SEIU (Canada) 59
SEIU (USA) 386
SEK (Cyprus) 86
SEKO (Sweden) 330
SEKRIMA (Madagascar) 207
SEL (Finland) 111
Sendika Kristianina Malagasy (Madagascar) 207
Sentral di Sindikatonan di Korsou (Netherlands Antilles) 239
Service Employees' International Union (Canada) 59
Service Employees' International Union (USA) 386
Service Ryutsu Rengo (Japan) 182
Service Unions United (Finland) 111
Service Workers and Food Union of Aotearoa (New Zealand) 244
Services Industrial Professional Technical Union (Ireland) 164
Services Publics et de Santé (France) 122
SETCa (Belgium) 34
SEV (Switzerland) 337
Seychelles Federation of Workers' Unions 299
SFL (Swaziland) 325
SFTU (Swaziland) 325
SFWU (Seychelles) 299
SGB (Switzerland) 336
SGEN (France) 118
Sheet Metal Workers' International Association (USA) 386
Shitetsu Soren (Japan) 182
Shop, Distributive and Allied Employees' Association (Australia) 16
SIB (Switzerland) 337
SICTU (Solomon Islands) 307
Sierra Leone Confederation of Trade Unions 300
Sierra Leone Labour Congress 300
SIF (Sweden) 333
SIMA (Angola) 7
Sindicato Independente dos Marítimos de Angola 7
SIU (USA) 385
SJF (Sweden) 334
Skogsakademikerna (Sweden) 332
Skogstrafacket (Sweden) 330
Skolledarförbund (Sweden) 332
SKTF (Sweden) 333
SLCTU (Sierra Leone) 300
SLLC (Sierra Leone) 300
SLNSS (Sri Lanka) 322
SMUV (Switzerland) 337
SMWIA (USA) 386
Socialist Labour Front (Bangladesh) 26
Society of Radiographers (UK) 369
Solidaridad de Trabajadores Cubanos 84
Solidarity 271
Solidarity G10 Trade Union (France) 123
Solidarumas (Lithuania) 203
Solomon Islands Council of Trade

Unions 307
Sonpo Roren (Japan) 182
SoR (UK) 369
South African Commercial, Catering and Allied Workers' Union 314
South African Democratic Teachers' Union 313
South African Municipal Workers' Union 314
South African State and Allied Workers' Union 314
South African Transport and Allied Workers' Union 314
Southern African Clothing and Textile Workers' Union (South Africa) 314
Southern Local Government Officers' Union (New Zealand) 245
SPA of WA (Australia) 16
SPB (Belarus) 29
Spectacle-Presse-Audiovisuel (France) 122
Sports (Sporta-as) (Belgium) 32
Sri Lanka Nidahas Sevaka Sangamaya 322
SROF (Sweden) 332
SSK (Netherlands Antilles) 239
SSM (Macedonia) 205
SSP (Switzerland) 337
SSRS (Bosnia) 40
SSS (Serbia-Montenegro) 297
SSSBiH (Bosnia) 39
SSSCG (Serbia-Montenegro) 298
SSSH (Croatia) 83
ST (Sweden) 334
St. Kitts-Nevis Trades and Labour Union 290
St. Lucia Civil Service Association 290
St. Lucia Seamen, Waterfront and General Workers' Trade Union 291
St. Lucia Workers' Union 291
St. Vincent and the Grenadines Public Service Union 291
Statstjänstemannaförbundet (Sweden) 334
STC (Cuba) 84
STF (Sweden) 332
STRIGECOMI (Rwanda) 289
STTK (Finland) 112
STUC (UK) 371
SUB (Myanmar) 230
SULF (Sweden) 333
Suomen Ammattiliittojen Keskusjärjestö 111
SUORA (Finland) 112
SuPer (Finland) 112
Svenska Journalistförbundet (Sweden) 334
Sveriges Akademikers Centralorganisation (Sweden) 331
Sveriges Farmacevtförbund (Sweden) 332
Sveriges Fartygsbefälsförening (Sweden) 332
Sveriges Läkarförbund (Sweden) 332
Sveriges Naturvetareförbund (Sweden) 332
Sveriges Psykologförbund (Sweden) 332
Sveriges Reservofficersförbund (Sweden) 332
Sveriges Tandläkarförbund (Sweden) 332
Sveriges Universitetslärarförbund (Sweden) 333

INDEX

Sveriges Veterinärförbund (Sweden) 333
SVF (Sweden) 333
Swaziland Federation of Labour 325
Swaziland Federation of Trade Unions 325
Swedish Association of Health Professionals 334
Swedish Confederation of Professional Associations 331
Swedish Confederation of Professional Employees 333
Swedish Teachers' Union 333
Swedish Trade Union Confederation 328
Swedish Union of Clerical and Technical Employees 333
Swedish Union of Journalists 334
SWGWTU (St Lucia) 291
Swiss Trade Union Confederation 336
SYNA, die Gewerkschaft (Switzerland) 337
SYNA, syndicat interprofessionnel (Switzerland) 337
Syndicat de l'industrie, de la construction et des services (Switzerland) 337
Syndicat de la Communication (Switzerland) 337
Syndicat des Employés, Techniciens et Cadres de Belgique 34
Syndicat des Travailleurs des Industries, Garages, Enterprises de Constructions, Mines et Imprimeries (Rwanda) 289
Syndicat du personnel des transports (Switzerland) 337
Syndicat Industrie et Bâtiment (Switzerland) 337
Syndicat suisse des services publics (Switzerland) 337
Synomospondia Ergaton Kyprou 86
Szakszervezetek Együttműködési Fóruma (Hungary) 150
SzEF (Hungary) 150

Taiwan Confederation of Trade Unions 340
Tajikistan Federation of Trade Unions 341
TALO (Estonia) 106
TCFUA (Australia) 16
TCO (Sweden) 333
TCTU (Taiwan) 340
TCU (USA) 386
Teachers' Union of Ireland 164
Teamsters Canada 59
Technical, Engineering and Electrical Union (Ireland) 164
TEHY (Finland) 112
Teknisk Landsforbund (Denmark) 93
Telekommunikationsforbundet (Denmark) 93
Tertiary Institutes Allied Staff Association (New Zealand) 244
Textile, Clothing and Footwear Union of Australia 16
TFTU (Tajikistan) 341
TGWU (UK) 369
Thai Trade Union Congress 344
TIASA (New Zealand) 244
TID (Denmark) 93

Timor Lorosae Trade Union Confederation (East Timor) 97
Tjänstemannaförbundet (Sweden) 334
Tjänstemännens Centralorganisation (Sweden) 333
TLI (Sweden) 331
TLTUC (East Timor) 97
TLU (St Kitts) 290
TNA (Tonga) 345
TNG (USA) 381
Tonga Nurses' Association 345
Trade Union Advisory Committee to the OECD 409
Trade Union Centre of Curaçao (Netherlands Antilles) 239
Trade Union Centre of Workers of Rwanda 289
Trade Union Confederation of Burkina 51
Trade Union Confederation of Togolese Workers 345
Trade Union Confederation of Workers' Commissions (Spain) 317
Trade Union Congress of Namibia 231
Trade Union Congress of the Philippines 268
Trade Union International of Agriculture, Food, Commerce, Textile and Allied Industries 414
Trade Union International of Energy, Metal, Chemical, Oil and Allied Industries 414
Trade Union International of Public and Allied Employees 414
Trade Union International of Transport Workers 414
Trade Union International of Workers in the Building, Wood and Building Materials Industries 414
Trade Union of Education in Finland 110
Trade Unions Forum (Poland) 275
Trade Unions of Cape Verde Unity Centre 62
Trade Unions' Congress of Tanzania 342
Trades Union Congress (Jamaica) 176
Trades Union Congress (UK) 364
Trades Union Congress of Ghana 136
Transfair (Switzerland) 337
TRANSNET Gewerkschaft GdED (Germany) 134
Transport and General Workers' Union (UK) 369
Transport Salaried Staffs' Association (UK) 370
Transport Workers' Union (Sweden) 330
Transport Workers' Union (Switzerland) 337
Transport Workers' Union of America (USA) 386
Transport Workers' Union of Australia 17
Transportarbetareförbundet (Sweden) 330
Transportation Communications International Union (USA) 386
Transports (France) 122
Travail.Suisse (Switzerland) 337
TSSA (UK) 370
TTUC (Thailand) 344
TU (Finland) 112

TUAC (International) 409
TUC (Ghana) 136
TUC (UK) 364
TUCNA (Namibia) 231
TUCP (Philippines) 268
TUCTA (Tanzania) 342
Tunisian General Labour Union 347
Turk-Is (Turkey) 354
Turkiye Devrimci Isci Senikalari Konfederasyonu (Turkey) 352
Turkiye Hak Isci Sendikalari Konfederasyounu (Turkey) 353
Turkiye Isci Sendikalari Konfederasyonu (Turkey) 354
TURK-SEN (Cyprus) 86
Tuvalu Overseas Seamen's Union 355
TWU (Australia) 17
TWU (USA) 386

UA (USA) 386
UASA (South Africa) 315
UATUC (Croatia) 83
UAW (USA) 386
UBC (USA) 388
UBOT (Belgium) 34
UCATT (UK) 370
UCEO-CSC (Belgium) 33
UCIW (Australia) 17
UCR (France) 118
Udruga Radnickih Sindikata Hrvatske 83
UDT (Djibouti) 94
UDTS (Senegal) 295
UE (USA) 388
UFCW (Canada) 59
UFCW (USA) 387
UFFA (France) 118
UFU of A (Australia) 17
UFW (USA) 387
UGL (Italy) 175
UGT (Portugal) 278
UGT (Spain) 318
UGT/STP (São Tomé) 293
UGTA (Algeria) 4
UGTCI (Côte d'Ivoire) 81
UGTD (Djibouti) 94
UGTG (Guinea) 143
UGTM (Morocco) 225
UGTN (Niger) 248
UGTSARIO (Morocco - W. Sahara) 227
UGTT (Tunisia) 347
UHM (Malta) 214
UHO (Norway) 255
UI. Zensen (Japan) 181
UIL (Italy) 174
Ujedinjeni Gradjanski Sindikati "Nezavisnost" (Serbia-Montenegro) 297
UMT (Morocco) 225
UMWA (USA) 387
UNI (International) 408
Unia (Switzerland) 337
União de Sindicatos Independentes (Portugal) 279
União Geral de Trabalhadores (Portugal) 278
União Geral dos Trabalhadores de São

INDEX

Tomé e Príncipe 293
União Nacional de Trabalhadores Angolanos 7
União Nacional dos Trabalhadores da Guiné 144
Uniao Nacional dos Trabalhadores de Cabo verde-Central Sindical 62
Unie Van Onafhankelijke Vakorganisaties (Netherlands) 239
Unified Workers' Centre (Chile) 66
Union Belge des Ouvriers du Transport 34
Union Chrétienne des membres du Personnel de l'Enseignement officiel (Belgium) 33
Union confédérale des retraités (France) 118
Union Démocratique des Travailleurs du Sénégal 295
Union des cadres et Ingénieurs (France) 122
Union des fédérations des fonctions publiques et assimilés (France) 118
Union des Syndicats Autonomes de Madagascar 207
Union des Syndicats des Travailleurs du Niger 247
Union des Syndicats du Tchad 64
Union des Syndicats Libres du Cameroun 55
Union des Travailleurs de Mauritanie 216
Union Djiboutienne du Travail 94
Union for Service and Communications Employees (Sweden) 330
Unión General de Trabajadores (Spain) 318
Union Général des Travailleurs Nigériens 248
Union Générale des Travailleurs Algériens 4
Union Générale des Travailleurs de Côte d'Ivoire 81
Union Générale des Travailleurs de Djibouti 94
Union Générale des Travailleurs de Guinée 143
Union Générale des Travailleurs du Maroc (Morocco) 225
Union Générale Tunisienne du Travail 347
Union Haddiema Maghqudin (Malta) 214
Union Marocaine du Travail (Morocco) 225
Union Nacional de Trabajadores (Mexico) 220
Unión Nacional de Trabajadores (Venezuela) 393
Union Nationale des Syndicats Autonomes (France) 123
Union Nationale des Syndicats Autonomes du Sénégal 295
Union Nationale des Syndicats des Travailleurs du Bénin 36
Union Nationale des Syndicats Indepéndants du Togo 345
Union Nationale des Travailleurs du Congo 76
Union Nationale des Travailleurs du Mali 212
Union Nationale Marocaine du Travail 226
Union Network International 408
Union Network International-Europa 402

Union of Autonomous Trade Unions of Croatia 83
Union of Central African Workers 63
Union of Christmas Island Workers 17
Union of Civil Servants (Sweden) 334
Union of Construction and Industry (Switzerland) 337
Union of Construction, Allied Trades and Technicians (Ireland) 164
Union of Construction, Allied Trades and Technicians (UK) 370
Union of Djibouti Workers 94
Union of Education (Norway) 255
Union of Employees in Commerce and Offices (Norway) 254
Union of Free Trade Unions of Cameroon 55
Union of Health and Social Care Services 112
Union of Independent Trade Unions (Portugal) 279
Union of Local Government Officers (Sweden) 333
Union of Mauritanian Workers 216
Union of Professional Engineers in Finland 111
Union of Salaried Employees (Finland) 112
Union of Shop, Distributive and Allied Workers (UK) 370
Union of Swedish Insurance Employees 334
Union of Trade Unions of Chad 64
Union of Workers in Industry, Garages, Construction Firms, Mines and Printers (Rwanda) 289
Union of Workers' Trade Unions of Niger 247
Unión Sindical de Trabajadores de Guatemala 142
Unión Sindical Obrera (Spain) 319
Union Syndicale - G10 Solidaires (France) 123
Union Syndicale des Travailleurs de Centrafrique 63
Union Syndicale des Travailleurs de Guinée 143
Union Syndicale Suisse (Switzerland) 336
Unione Generale del Lavoro (Italy) 175
Unione Italiana del Lavoro 174
UNISON (UK) 370
Unitary Workers' Centre (Brazil) 45
UNITE HERE (USA) 386
United Association of Journeymen and Apprentices of the Plumbing, Pipefitting and Sprinkler Fitting Industry of the United States and Canada 386
United Association of South Africa 315
United Automobile, Aerospace and Agricultural Implement Workers of America International Union 386
United Autonomous Unions of Madagascar 207
United Branch Trade Unions "Independence"(Serbia-Montenegro) 297
United Brotherhood of Carpenters and

Joiners of America (USA) 388
United Electrical, Radio and Machine Workers of America 388
United Farm Workers of America (USA) 387
United Federation of Trade Unions (Norway) 254
United Firefighters' Union of Australia 17
United Food and Commercial Workers International Union (Canada) 59
United Food and Commercial Workers' International Union (USA) 387
United Independent Albanian Trade Unions 2
United Mine Workers' of America (USA) 387
United Road Transport Union (UK) 370
United Seamen Ports and General Workers' Union of Liberia 201
United Steelworkers of America 387
United Trade Union of Guinean Workers 143
United Transportation Union (USA) 388
United Union Federation (France) 123
United Union of Roofers, Waterproofers and Allied Workers (USA) 387
University of Botswana Non-Academic Staff Union 42
UNMT (Morocco) 226
UNSA (France) 123
UNSAS (Senegal) 295
UNSIT (Togo) 345
UNSITRAGUA (Guatemala) 142
UNSTB (Benin) 36
UNT (Mexico) 220
UNT (Venezuela) 393
UNTA (Angola) 7
UNTC (Congo, Democratic Republic) 76
UNTC-CS (Cape Verde) 62
UNTG (Guinea-Bissau) 144
UNTM (Mali) 212
Unyu Roren (Japan) 182
UOV (Netherlands) 239
URSH (Croatia) 83
URTU (UK) 370
Uruguayan Trade Union Action 390
USAM (Madagascar) 207
USDAW (UK) 370
USI (Portugal) 279
USLC (Cameroon) 55
USO (Spain) 319
USPOGUL (Liberia) 201
USS (Switzerland) 336
UST (Chad) 64
USTC (Central African Republic) 63
USTG (Guinea) 143
USTN (Niger) 247
USWA (USA) 387
Utdanningsforbundet (Norway) 255
Utdanningsgruppenes Hovedorganisasjon (Norway) 255
Utility Workers' Union of America 387
UTM (Mauritania) 216
UTU (USA) 388

INDEX

UWUA (USA) 387
Vakcentrale Voor Middengroepen en Hoger Personeel (Netherlands) 238
VAL (Finland) 112
Vanuatu Council of Trade Unions 391
Vårdförbundet (Sweden) 334
VCTU (Vanuatu) 391
Venezuelan Confederation of Workers 393
ver.di (Germany) 134
Verband des Personals Öffentlicher Dienste (Switzerland) 337
Vereinte Dienstleistungsgewerkschaft e. V. (Germany) 134
Vereniging van Nederlandse Verkeersvliegers (Netherlands) 239
Verkauf, Handel, Transport, Lebensmittel (Switzerland) 337
VGCL (Vietnam) 394
VHTL (Switzerland) 337
Victorian Psychologists Association 17
Vietnam General Confederation of Labour 394
Vieux Fort General and Dock Workers' Union (St Lucia) 291
VKT (Russia) 288
VNV (Netherlands) 239
Voyageurs-Représentants-Placiers (France) 122
VPA (Australia) 17
VPOD (Switzerland) 337

Wales TUC 366
WAPOUW (Australia) 17
Waterfront and Allied Workers' Union (Dominica) 95
WAWU (Dominica) 95
WCL (International) 410
WCT (International) 412
Western Australian Prison Officers' Union of Workers 17
WFAFW (International) 412
WFBW (International) 412
WFCW (International) 412
WFIW (International) 412
WFTU (International) 412
WIFOL (Netherlands Antilles) 239
Windward Islands Federation of Labour (Netherlands Antilles) 239
Wood and Allied Workers' Union (Finland) 111
Woolclassers' Association of Australia 17
Workers' Trade Union Association of Croatia 83
Workers' Central Union of Cuba 84
Workers' Trade Union Confederation of Mali 212
Workers' Union (Spain) 319
World Confederation of Labour 410
World Confederation of Teachers 412
World Federation of Agriculture, Food, Hotel and Allied Workers 412
World Federation of Building and Woodworkers' Unions 412
World Federation of Clerical Workers 412
World Federation of Industry Workers 412
World Federation of Teachers' Unions 414
World Federation of Trade Unions 412
WTUAC (Croatia) 83

Yrkesorganisasjonenes Sentralforbund (Norway) 255
YS (Norway) 255

Zambia Congress of Trade Unions 397
Zanzibar Trade Union Congress (Tanzania) 342
ZATUC (Tanzania) 342
ZCTU (Zambia) 397
ZCTU (Zimbabwe) 399
Zen Yusei (Japan) 182
Zenken Soren (Japan) 182
Zenrokyo (Japan) 182
Zenroren (Japan) 182
Zentei (Japan) 182
Zimbabwe Congress of Trade Unions 399
ZSSS (Slovenia) 307
Zveza svobodnih sindikatov Slovenije (Slovenia) 307